Dearest Michael

Happy Bir...

my love,

Erica.

fruit
&nuts

A comprehensive
guide to the
cultivation, uses
and health benefits of
over 300 food-producing
plants

Susanna Lyle

Timber Press

Copyright © Susanna Lyle, 2006
Copyright © David Bateman Ltd, 2006

Published in North America in 2006 by
Timber Press Inc.
The Haseltine Building
133 S.W. Second Avenue, Suite 450
Portland, Oregon 97204-3527, U.S.A.
www.timberpress.com

ISBN-13: 978-0-88192-759-7
ISBN-10: 0-88192-759-7

A catlog record for this book is available from the Library of Congress

Cover Jag Graphics, Auckland, New Zealand
Design Jag Graphics, Auckland, New Zealand
Printed in China through Colorcraft Ltd., Hong Kong

CONTENTS

Inspiration for this book came from exploration of the wide diversity of fruit and nut plants that can be grown in temperate and subtropical regions. The hundreds of species described are naturally found in a wide range of environments and climates around the world. Many are already popular garden ornamentals but are little utilised or valued for their edible crops. Others are relatively unknown species that may have potential as future commercial crops. Though many fruit and nut species are probably not suitable for large-scale commercial production, perhaps because of harvesting problems, yields or storage times, they make exotic and interesting projects for the home garden.

Each main plant species is explored, with information about its origins and history, where and how to grow it, its suitability for different soils and climates, the best methods of propagation and pruning, its nutritional and medicinal qualities, plus ideas for its culinary use. This book is a comprehensive reference source. It is hoped you will find it inspirational in looking at fruits and nuts in a new way, and helpful in gaining an appreciation for the amazing health benefits many of these species can provide.

The following introductory section outlines the biology and anatomy of fruit and nut plants, how this determines the way they obtain moisture and grow in different conditions, and how floral arrangement determines the shape and structure of the resulting fruits. There are notes on the establishment and maintenance of plants, the theory behind pruning and propagation, and an outline of nutritional terminology.

In the main section, commencing on page 46, the plants are arranged alphabetically according to their botanical name. Their common names are listed on page 7 and an index including botanical names is on page 478. Many of these species are derived from relatively few plant families. A list of plants with the family in which they belong is found on page 9. A plant checklist, which suggests species for different environmental situations, e.g. acid soils, waterlogged soils, exposed locations, is provided at the back of the book.

Happy reading.

ACKNOWLEDGEMENTS

I would like to thank the following people in New Zealand for generously providing many of the images: thanks to Incredible Edibles (who supply a wide range of wholesale unusual fruit and nut plants: www.edible.co.nz), and to Bernard King (a plantsman in Auckland, who grows and explores many unusual fruit and nut plants), who, apart from supplying some of the images, also gave me lots of advice and information including alerting me to the wondrous medicinal value of the goji berry (benking@smallminingtown. com). Thanks also to Roy Hart, from Motueka in the South Island, for supplying several of the images.

I would also like to acknowledge, in particular, the following as sources of information for many of the species described herein: Julia Morton's wonderful, informative book titled *Fruits of warm climates*, and to the excellent web sites of the Californian Rare Fruit Growers (www.crfg.org), the Natural Food Hub site (www.naturalhub.com) and to Plants for a Future (www.pfaf.org).

Thank-you to the following for providing several of the images. To those from www.davesgarden.com and www. toptropicals.com, Todd Boland (Newfoundland, Canada), FarmerDill (USA), Susan Gammons (Piedmont, USA), Ken Harris (Victoria, Australia), Trois Helvy (Texas, USA), Scott G. Shepherd (Salt Lake City, USA), Max W'berg (USA), Hazel Topoleski (Texas, USA). Also thanks to Dave Thompson of Dave's Travel Corner (www.davestravel.com), Forest and Kim Starr (www.hear.org/starr/hiplants/images) and to New Zealand Hops Limited.

During the collection of images, the following generously gave up their time and provided much useful information: Exotic Nurseries (Northland, NZ), with their wonderful collection of plants; to Nam and Fraser Head for showing me around their nut farm in Kaikohe (NZ), to Colin Bradshaw of the Auckland Domain Gardens; to Mark Rehbein at Rockhampton Gardens, Queensland, who showed me around the large and impressive collection of fruit trees at the gardens, and to John Ford (Northland, NZ), for showing me around his collection of unusual fruits and nuts. Also thanks for advice from dumNatives, a nursery that specialises in indigenous New Zealand plant species (dumNatives@kol. co.nz).

Also to friends Janet Clark (who shared her garden knowledge with me) and to Christine Wilson (in the UK, who looked through some of the text and supplied the wonderful image of tea). Thanks also to my husband Jim Lyle, for his support throughout this project.

I am also very grateful for the tremendous effort, diligence and editing support from Andrea Hassall and to Tracey Borgfeldt for believing in this book (both of David Bateman Ltd).

INDEX OF COMMON NAMES

PLANT FAMILIES

The majority of fruiting species are members of only a few plant families. Below, the main species described in this book are listed according to the family they belong to. As you read through the individual species descriptions, the similarity between members of the same family is often quite apparent.

FAMILY	SPECIES	PLANT NAME
Aceraceae	Acer saccharum	Sugar maple
Actinidiaceae	Actinidia spp.	Kiwifruit
Agavaceae	Yucca spp.	Yucca
Aizoaceae	Carpobrotus edulis	Hottentot fig, ice plant
Anacardiaceae	Anacardium occidentale	Cashew
	Harpephyllum caffrum	Kaffir plum, wild plum
	Mangifera indica	Mango
	Pistacia vera	Pistachio
	Pleiogynium timorense	Burdekin plum
	Rhus spp.	Sumach
	Sclerocarya caffra	Marula
	Spondias dulcis	Ambarella
Annonaceae	Annona cherimola	Cherimoya
	Annona spp.	Atemoya, mountain soursop
	Asimina triloba	Asimoya, American pawpaw
Apocynaceae	Carissa congesta	Karanda
	Carissa macrocarpa	Carrisa, Natal plum
Araceae	Monstera deliciosa	Ceriman, Swiss-cheese plant
Araucariaceae	Araucaria araucana	Monkey-puzzle tree
	Araucaria bidwilli	Bunya-bunya pine
Asteraceae	Helianthus annuus	Sunflower seeds
	Stevia rebaudiana	Stevia
Berberidaceae	Berberis spp.	Barberry
	Berberis spp.	Berberis
	Mahonia aquifolium	Oregon grape
Betulaceae	Betula spp.	Birch
Boraginaceae	Cordia spp.	Cordia
Bromeliaceae	Ananas comosus	Pineapple
Cactaceae	Hylocereus, Selenicereus and Cereus spp.	Pitaya
	Opuntia spp.	Prickly pear
Cannabidaceae	Humulus lupulus	Hops
Caprifoliaceae	Lonicera spp.	Honeysuckle
	Sambucus spp.	Elderberry
	Viburnum spp.	Viburnum berries

FAMILY	SPECIES	PLANT NAME
Caricaceae	Carica heilbornii var. pentagona	Babaco
	Carica papaya	Papaya
	Carica pubescens	Mountain pawpaw (papaya)
Chenopodiaceae	Chenopodium foliosum	Strawberry sticks
Clusiaceae	Garcinia livingstonei	Imbe
Combretaceae	Terminalia catappa	Sea almond
	Terminalia ferdinandiana	Kakadu plum
Cornaceae	Cornus mas	Cornelian cherry
Corylaceae	Corylus spp.	Hazelnut
Cucurbitaceae	Citrullus spp.	Watermelons
	Cucumis spp.	Melons
	Cucurbita pepo	Pumpkin seeds
	Telfairia pedata	Oyster nut
Cyperaceae	Cyperus esculentus	Tigernut, chufa
Davidsoniaceae	Davidsonia spp.	Davidson's plum
Ebenaceae	Diospyros digyna	Black sapote
	Diospyros kaki	Persimmon
Elaeagnaceae	Elaeagnus spp.	Elaeagnus
	Hippophae rhamnoides	Sea buckthorn
	Shepherdia spp.	Buffalo berry, soapberry
Ericaceae	Arbutus unedo	Strawberry tree
	Empetrum nigrum	Crowberry
	Gaultheria spp.	Wintergreen, snow-berry, checkerberry
	Gaylussacia and Vaccinium spp	Huckleberries
	Vaccinium macrocarpon	Cranberry
	Vaccinium spp.	Bilberry
	Vaccinium spp.	Blueberry
	Vaccinium vitis-idaea	Lingonberry
	Arctostaphylos spp.	Manzanita
Euphorbiaceae	Flueggea virosa	Chinese water-berry
	Phyllanthus emblica	Amla, Indian gooseberry
	Ricinodendron rautanenii	Manketti nut

9

FAMILY	SPECIES	PLANT NAME
Fabaceae	Arachis hypogaea	Peanut
	Ceratonia siliqua	Carob
	Geoffroea decorticans	Chilean palo verde
	Inga edulis	Inga bean
	Prosopis spp.	Mesquite
	Tamarindus indica	Tamarind
	Glycyrrhiza glabra	Licorice
	Gleditsia triacanthos	Honey locust
Fagaceae	Castanea spp.	Chestnut
	Chrysolepis and Castanopsis spp.	Chinquapin
	Fagus spp.	Beech nut
	Quercus spp.	Acorns
Flacourtiaceae	Dovyalis spp.	Kei apple, dovyalis
	Flacourtia indica	Governor's plum
	Oncoba spinosa	Oncoba
Ginkgoaceae	Ginkgo biloba	Ginkgo
Grossulariaceae	Ribes spp.	Currant
	Ribes spp.	Gooseberry
Juglandaceae	Carya illinoinensis	Pecan
	Juglans spp.	Walnut
Lardizabalaceae	Akebia quinata, Holboellia spp.	Akebia; holboellia
	Lardizabala biternata	Zabala fruit
Lauraceae	Persea spp.	Avocado
Liliaceae	Smilacina racemosa	False spikenard
Malpighiaceae	Malpighia punicifolia	Acerola
Malvaceae	Pachira aquatica	Malabar chestnut
	Quararibea cordata	Chupa-chupa
	Hibiscus spp.	Roselle and other hibiscus spp.
Moraceae	Artocarpus heterophyllus	Jackfruit
	Broussonetia papyrifera	Paper mulberry
	Cudrania tricuspidata	Che
	Ficus carica	Fig
	Morus spp.	Mulberry
Musaceae	Musa spp.	Banana

FAMILY	SPECIES	PLANT NAME
Myrtaceae	Austromyrtus dulcis	Midgen berry
	Eucalyptus gunii	Cider gum
	Eugenia aggregata	Cherry of the Rio Grande
	Eugenia uniflora	Pitanga, Brazilian/ Surinam cherry
	Feijoa sellowiana	Feijoa
	Kunzea pomifera	Muntries
	Myrciaria cauliflora	Jaboticaba
	Myrciaria dubia	Camu-camu
	Psidium cattleianum	Cattleya guava, strawberry guava
	Psidium guajava	Tropical guava
	Rhodomyrtus tomentosa	Ceylon hill gooseberry
	Syzygium spp.	Rose apple; water berry
	Syzygium spp.	Lillypilly
	Ugni molinae; Myrtus communis	Chilean guava; myrtle berry
Nelumbonaceae	Nelumbo nucifera	Lotus
Oleaceae	Ligustrum lucidum	Glossy privet fruit
	Olea europaea	Olive
Onagraceae	Fuchsia spp.	Fuchsia
Oxalidaceae	Averrhoa carambola	Carambola
Palmae	Brahea edulis	Guadalupe palm
	Butia capitata	Jelly palm
	Jubaea chilensis	Chilean wine palm
	Parajubaea cocoides	Quito palm
	Syagrus romanzoffianum	Queen palm
	Washingtonia filifera	California fan palm
Pandanaceae	Pandanus spiralis	Pandanus
Passifloraceae	Passiflora spp.	Passion fruits
Philesiaceae	Lapageria rosea	Chilean bellflower
Pinaceae	Pinus spp.	Pinenut
Pittosporaceae	Billardiera scandens	Apple-berry
Poaceae	Saccharum officinarum	Sugar cane
Podocarpaceae	Podocarpus totara	Totara
Polygonaceae	Coccoloba uvifera	Sea grape
	Rheum spp.	Rhubarb
Proteaceae	Gevuina avellana	Gevuina
	Macadamia spp.	Macadamia
Punicaceae	Punica granatum	Pomegranate

FAMILY	SPECIES	PLANT NAME
Rhamnaceae	*Hovenia dulcis*	Raisin tree
	Reynosia septentrionalis	Darling plum
	Zizyphus jujuba	Jujube, Chinese red date
Rosaceae	*Amelanchier alnifolia*	Saskatoon, amelanchier, juneberry
	Aronia spp.	Aronia, chokeberry
	Crataegus spp.	Mayhaw
	Crataegus spp.	Hawthorn
	Cydonia oblonga	Quince
	Eriobotrya japonica	Loquat
	Fragaria x *Ananassa*	Strawberry
	Malus spp.	Apple; crabapple
	Mespilus germanica	Medlar
	Prunus armeniaca	Apricot
	Prunus dulcis	Almond
	Prunus pensylvanica	Pincherry
	Prunus persica	Peach, nectarine
	Prunus salicifolia	Capulin cherry
	Prunus spp.	Damson, greengage, sloe
	Prunus spp.	Plum cherry
	Prunus spp.	Cherry
	Prunus spp.	Plum and prune
	Pyrus spp.	Pear—Asian and European
	Rosa rugosa	Rosehips
	Rubus chamaemorus	Cloudberry
	Rubus parviflorus	Thimbleberry
	Rubus phoenicolasius	Wineberry
	Rubus spp.	Dewberry
	Rubus spp.	Raspberry
	Rubus spp.	Blackberry
	Sorbus spp.	Rowan, mountain ash
Rubiaceae	*Coffea* spp.	Coffee
	Mitchella repens	Mitchella

FAMILY	SPECIES	PLANT NAME
Rutaceae	*Aegle marmelos*	Bael fruit
	Casimiroa edulis	Casimiroa, white sapote
	Citrus spp.	Lemon
	Citrus medica	Citron
	Citrus reticulata	Tangerine, mandarin and tangelo
	Citrus spp.	Australian native citrus spp.
	Citrus spp.	Grapefruit
	Citrus spp.	Lime
	Citrus spp.	Orange
	Clausena lansium	Wampee
	Fortunella spp.	Kumquat
	x *Citrofortunella mitis*	Calamondin
Santalaceae	*Santalum acuminatum*	Quandong
Sapindaceae	*Dimocarpus longan*	Longan
	Litchi chinensis	Lychee
	Staphylea spp.	Bladdernut
Sapotaceae	*Manilkara zapota*	Sapodilla
	Pouteria australis	Black apple
	Pouteria obovata	Lucuma, lucmo
	Synsepalum dulcificum	Miracle fruit
Scrophulariaceae	*Halleria lucida*	Tree fuchsia
Solanaceae	*Cyphomandra betacea*	Tamarillo
	Lycium barbarum	Wolfberry
	Lycium barbarum var. *goji*	Goji berry
	Physalis spp.	Tomatillo
	Physalis peruviana	Cape gooseberry
	Solanum muricatum	Pepino dulce
	Solanum quitoense	Naranjilla
	Solanum sessiliflorum	Cocona
	Solanum spp.	Huckleberry
Sterculiaceae	*Firmiana simplex*	Chinese parasol tree
	Sterculia quadrifida	Peanut tree
Taxaceae	*Torreya nucifera*	Torreya
Theaceae	*Camellia sinensis*	Tea
Tiliaceae	*Grewia asiatica*	Phalsa
Ulmaceae	*Celtis laevigata*	Sugarberry
Vitaceae	*Ampelopsis brevipedunculata*	Porcelain berry
	Vitis spp.	Muscadine, scuppernong
	Vitis spp.	Grapes

PART I: INTRODUCTION TO FRUITS AND NUTS

This book describes a wide range of fruit and nut species that grow from the coldest regions on Earth to the subtropics, and in a diversity of habitats. This first section introduces aspects of plant classification, flower and fruit structure, methods of cultivation, and plant usage. In addition, the health benefits of the main nutrients found within fruits and nuts are described. These sections can be referred to for further information while accessing the various individual species, e.g. for pruning methods. The main text lists and describes hundreds of fruit and nut species, and is followed by a checklist that contains several environmental situations, with plants suited to these.

PURCHASING PLANTS

Many of the plants listed here are available at garden centres and nurseries. Many of the more unusual species can be raised from seed, and many sites exist online that sell a wide range of species. However, because biosecurity is increasingly becoming an issue, if importing seeds, please check the legality of bringing these into your locality or country. The cultivation of many species is restricted or is illegal due to the invasive characteristics of the plant or because they are a potential host for a disease of a common crop plant.

Fig. 1. Simple classification of plant groups, family, genus and species

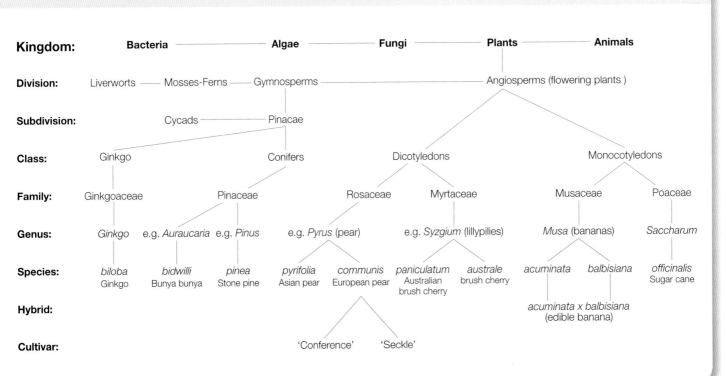

In addition, ensure the seed is as fresh as possible. There is also plenty of information available online, from societies, research establishments and specialist groups concerning the finer details of cultivation, plus many different opinions concerning their usage and benefits.

PLANT GROUPS: THEIR EVOLUTION AND CLASSIFICATION

The taxonomic classification of organisms is ordered into hierarchies, with animals and plants being two of the main groups. Below these are various subdivisions (see Fig. 1). Plants are classified into several taxonomic groups depending on the arrangement of their floral structures. Each individual plant has its own Latin name consisting of its **genus** and **species**, and each genus contains several to many species. For example, the fig has the Latin name *Ficus carica*, where *Ficus* is the genus and *carica* the species. Traditionally, these Latin names are printed in italics. From the list of families and species (see p. 9), you can see that *Ficus* belongs to the Moraceae **family**. You can also see that a few families tend to contain a large majority of the fruit and nut species, e.g. Rosaceae, Myrtaceae. These names are often derived from descriptions of the flower parts, but may also refer to other distinguishing characteristics of that genus or species.

In addition, species are often further divided into **varieties** (**var.**) or **cultivars** (**cv.**), which may have either formed naturally in the wild or have been selected by horticulturalists. Varieties (or cultivars) can fertilise each other and become genetically mixed, i.e. they will form fertile offspring. In contrast, the definition of a species is that they are genetically isolated: two different species cannot usually pollinate each other, and if they do, their offspring are not fertile.

One of the older, more 'primitive' groups is the **gymnosperms**. This group includes the conifers, ginkgo and cycads, of which a few conifer species and ginkgo are included in this book. This group has the following main characteristics:

- The 'flower' is simple and, usually, the pollen is dispersed by wind.
- The seed is 'naked', i.e. it does not have a seedcoat. It is usually borne inside a cone or scale, or in a few species, within fleshy tissue known as an aril, e.g. totara.
- If there is a cone, this usually remains on the tree for several years from the time it is first formed to when it is pollinated and finally produces seeds.
- Gymnosperms' reproduction is almost exclusively by seeds; vegetative reproduction, e.g. by runners, is rare.
- As conifers mature, their root systems develop from a taproot to one where lower thick 'branch' roots are formed.
- They are almost all evergreen species.
- The conducting and strengthening tissues within the stem are simpler and arranged in a less ordered way compared with angiosperms (see below). Because of the diffuse arrangement of the tissues in the stem, this group can be seldom propagated by grafting.

- Most conifers have both male and female 'flowers' on the same plant, although they are very different structures. Ginkgoes have separate male and female plants.

The next, and main group of plants to evolve after the gymnosperms was the **angiosperms**. This includes the majority of plants we see around us and, at the present geological time, is a hugely successful group. Both gymnosperms and angiosperms have conducting tissues that transport water and nutrients from the roots, and other vessels that transport sugars from the leaves. In angiosperms, **xylem** vessels carry water from the roots to the leaves and this then passes out of the leaf through the **stomata**. Xylem is largely dead tissue and gives a plant its rigidity and strength: it is what the majority of the stem or trunk consists of. **Phloem** vessels carry sugars, produced in the leaves from photosynthesis, to other parts of the plant. In many angiosperms this occurs outside the xylem layer. Outside this is the outer cortex and bark.

The angiosperms are further divided into two groups: the **dicotyledons** (or **dicots**) and the **monocotyledons** (or **monocots**). Both produce true flowers and seeds with some sort of covering, many of which have complex designs and structures. The dicot group includes most broad-leaved plants, and most fruit and nut species. The monocot group, which is generally thought to have evolved more recently, includes the grasses and palms. A few monocots are listed in this book, such as some of the sugar cane palm species, and banana.

Fig. 2. Simple cross-section of a dicot and monocot stem

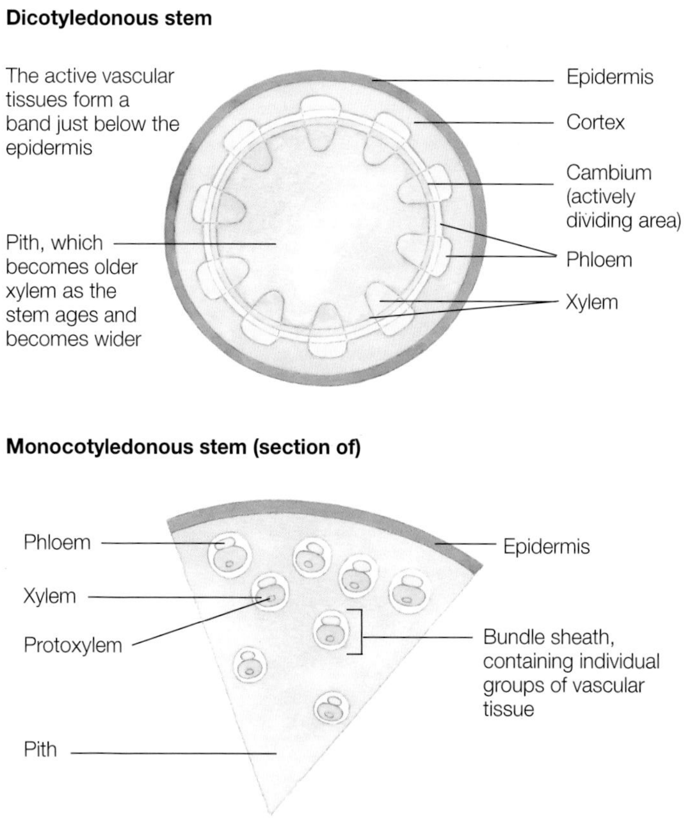

Dicotyledonous stem

The active vascular tissues form a band just below the epidermis

Pith, which becomes older xylem as the stem ages and becomes wider

Epidermis
Cortex
Cambium (actively dividing area)
Phloem
Xylem

Monocotyledonous stem (section of)

Phloem
Xylem
Protoxylem
Pith

Epidermis
Bundle sheath, containing individual groups of vascular tissue

The main features that distinguish the monocots and dicots from each other are:

- Monocotyledons have a single leaf that first emerges from the seed; dicotyledons have two first leaves, hence their names, with 'cotyledon' meaning 'first leaf'.
- The arrangement of the conducting vessels within the leaves, stems and roots varies (Fig. 2): it is relatively easy to graft a dicot, but not a monocot. Dicots usually have a central region of older, water-conducting xylem vessels, surrounded by a thin layer of current xylem vessels. This is intimately bordered by a **cambium** layer and an outer phloem layer. The thin cambium layer is an active region of cell division that produces new xylem cells to the inside and new phloem cells to the outside. This 'active' band of tissue resides just below the bark surface. If this is extensively damaged, it kills the tree. Monocots do not have this structure. Instead, they have scattered groups of conducting tissue throughout the stem, with each group containing xylem, cambium and phloem. Monocots do not have a woody centre of older xylem tissue, or a continuous layer of cambium towards the outside of the stem. Propagation, by grafting two separate plants together, places the two active cell-dividing regions of cambium in close proximity so that the tissues become fused together to form a single plant: this is not possible with monocot stems.
- Dicots have secondary thickening formed from old xylem vessels, which gives them strength and forms the mass of the trunk. Because of the bands of tissue in dicots, branches and leaves can grow out from the central trunk. Monocots cannot form secondary thickening; the leaf bases form the trunk and new leaves grow up through the centre of the plant. They do not usually form side branches.
- Many dicots use insect pollination, particularly 'modern' species, which include most fruit species (although many nut species are wind-pollinated). In contrast, many monocots are wind-pollinated.
- In monocots, petals on flowers usually occur in multiple of threes; in dicots they are usually in multiples of fours and fives.
- Some monocots have evolved a system called **C4 photosynthesis** (compared to the **C3** system of most other plants), which, through biochemical and structural adaptations to their leaves, enables them to achieve much higher photosynthetic rates and to use carbon dioxide more efficiently. (See also p. 20.)

PLANTS AND SEX

In animals, the norm is that male and female sex cells (**gametes**) are produced in different individuals. In plants, in many species, the male and female gametes are produced on the same plant. Some of these species have flowers that contain both male and female gametes (**bisexual**); other species produce separate male and female flowers on the same plant (**monoecious**). Other species have either only male or female flowers on a particular plant, and these are known as **dioecious,** where more than one plant is needed for fertilisation and to produce fruits. In addition,

a few species can actually change the sex of their flowers during their life cycle. Whether a species is monoecious or dioecious can be an important consideration when choosing and growing fruits and nuts. Will you need more than one plant to produce a crop? If you need several plants, have you got the space for these?

Because dioecious plants, which have male and female flowers on separate trees, need pollen transferred between individuals, their genes become mixed, which increases the genetic diversity of the offspring. Some monoecious species, which have both flower sexes on the same plant, are **self-fertile** and can pollinate themselves, which can be a good thing if you are growing in isolation, but diversity is also reduced. The offspring produced by self-fertilisation are similar to the 'parent'. Other monoecious species have evolved mechanisms to avoid this and, even though both male and flowers are produced, they need to be **cross pollinated** with another plant.

There are a range of methods that species use to avoid self-pollination. One of the main methods is for male and female flowers, on the same plant, to open at different times; the male pollen is then carried, by insect or wind, to another plant where there are receptive female flowers. Another method, used by some species, is that even if pollen reaches a receptive female flower on the same tree, it is chemically unable to fertilise the female ovary. As a consequence, from a gardening perspective, it needs to be borne in mind that not all monoecious species will fruit properly if just planted individually; some need at least one companion to achieve good pollination, and most then produce more fruits, which are often of better quality.

In horticulture, if species are planted that need cross pollination, i.e. they are either dioecious or monoecious species that need cross fertilisation, it may not be enough to just plant more than one of the same species. Why is this? In the wild, there will be natural cross pollination between neighbouring trees, and the resulting seedlings will be unique; in cultivation, young plants may have been propagated either by seed or vegetatively. If they are produced from seed, then there will be **genetic variation**, and the offspring produced will be able to cross pollinate each other satisfactorily. If the young plants are vegetatively propagated by either cuttings or grafts, however, then they will be clones of their 'parent' and cross pollination won't be effective. In these cases, it is recommended that a variety of cultivars are planted to overcome this. Planting a mix of cultivars often results in increased resistance to pests and diseases, also better and more consistent fruit yields. Often the result is also increased variability of fruit quality. This sometimes yields surprisingly good-quality new fruit cultivars. If these are 'discovered', then save some seeds for further propagation!

Another quirk that occurs in a few species described in this book is that, although a plant may be self-infertile and need another plant to pollinate it, if grown alone, it may be still able to produce some fruits. In these species, the flowers are not pollinated, but the flowers still go on to produce fruits that are seedless (**parthenocarpy**). A well-known example of this is the edible banana, which is always a seedless fruit, formed without pollination. Many species that produce parthenocarpically often form fruits that are smaller, though may be of as good quality as pollinated fruits.

Nucellar embryony is yet another method of producing fruits, with the resulting seedlings being identical clones of the parent. Although pollination is needed to trigger nucellar ovule development, here the ovules do not undergo any exchange of genetic material; instead, embryos are formed from tissue that surrounds the ovary, the nucellus, rather than from the tissue within the embryo itself. (Normally, the nucellus, or **integument** goes on to form the seedcoat.) Nucellar embryos are produced vegetatively; there has been no genetic exchange and the seedlings are therefore exact genetic copies of the parent tree. Within the same flower, nucellar embryos begin development as soon as pollination occurs, whereas embryos that have undergone normal genetic exchange take ~2–4 weeks to develop. Nucellar embryos are therefore able to 'crowd out' genetic embryos. Nucellar embryos form young fruits sooner than other embryos. In addition, these seeds are often **polyembryonic**: instead of producing a single seedling, they can produce several. Polyembryonic seedlings, from one seed, can be a mix of nucellar and 'normal'. This process occurs in a number of fruiting species, and is particularly common amongst the citrus species and in mango. Nucellar seedlings are identical to the parent, but there is no advantageous diversity to the species in the longer term.

EVOLUTION OF POLLINATION

In the dicotyledons, there is a huge diversity of seed and flower structures, with much of this coming about through symbiotic relationships between pollinating insects, fruit-eating birds and animals. Many insects and birds have become wholly dependent upon the pollen or fruit from particular species. Plants, in return, although requiring some metabolic energy, are pollinated or have their seeds dispersed through the guts of birds or animals. In fact, some metabolic energy is saved by insect pollination because far less pollen needs to be produced compared to wind-pollinated species, who have to ensure abundant production for their haphazard distribution to a receptive flower. These steps in evolution have resulted in most fruit species needing insect pollination, and also in the development of many tasty, tempting fruits that can be eaten, often along with their seeds, which can then be dispersed far and wide.

Flowers and fruits have evolved scents and bright colouring to attract pollinators to them. Interestingly, the chemicals involved in the coloration of fruits (**anthocyanins**) are now the object of increasing research for their wide-ranging nutritional and health benefits. However, many seedcoats and stones around kernels contain toxins which, if eaten in quantity, can lead to serious illness or death, but over hundreds of thousands of years of usage and experimentation, people have learnt that, in smaller doses, many of these seeds have medicinal benefits, e.g. tannins.

ARRANGEMENT AND STRUCTURE OF FLOWERS

The arrangement, structure and number of flowers and fruits varies widely between species; however, a general description of their development and organisation is given below. How different floral structures are arranged and which tissues develop after pollination, determines the shape and form of the fruit or nut.

Flowers can be borne singly or, more commonly, in groups towards the tips of stems from leaf axils. In some species, they occur on short stubby lateral branches called **spurs**. In addition, a few species produce flowers and fruits directly from the main stems and trunk (**cauliflorous**).

In the centre of the flower, inside the petals, is a central structure(s), called the **carpel**(s), which holds the female gametes or sex cells (known as ovules). Each ovule can potentially form a single seed or kernel. Each carpel can contain a single or several ovules. A flower may have a single carpel (e.g. cherry), many individual carpels (e.g. raspberry) or many carpels within a single structure, which is then known as an ovary (e.g. tamarillo, orange), with the carpels often becoming fused as segments within the ovary. The main structure containing or holding the carpels, ovary and other floral structures is known as the **receptacle**.

The carpels (or ovary) are connected to the outside world via a 'tube', which is topped by a **stigma** (usually a closed, sticky pore). The pollen travels down the **style** to the ovule(s). If the flower contains both male and female gametes then there will also be numerous **stamens**, consisting of an **anther** and **filament**, which produce the pollen (see Fig. 3).

In fruits and nuts, the fusion of the carpels can be achieved in many ways, depending on the species. It is believed that the more complex the fusion of carpels, the more recently the species evolved: ancient angiosperms had simple carpels. A situation where many carpels are fused together and contain many ovules is typical of what occurs in many fruits. Nuts tend to have simpler structures and often only consist of one or two simple carpels containing single ovules, where only one ovule fully ripens and develops (e.g. hazel). Carpels can be fused in a simple straight line to form

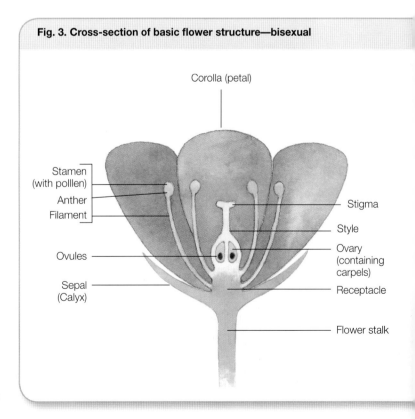

Fig. 3. Cross-section of basic flower structure—bisexual

Corolla (petal)

Stamen (with pollen)
Anther
Filament

Ovules

Sepal (Calyx)

Stigma

Style

Ovary (containing carpels)

Receptacle

Flower stalk

the familiar pea structure, or they may fuse so that the ovules project into the centre in rows, as with the gooseberry. Alternatively, the carpels may not fully fuse, but be linked and each contain numerous ovules, as in some of the Solanaceae family, e.g. tamarillo, Cape gooseberry, pepino.

Angiosperm means 'seed in a vessel', with the vessel being originally formed by the folding or fusion of primitive 'leaves' that are no longer visible, but act to protect the kernel (carpel, ovary). The kernels are attached to the edges of these ancestral leaves and, depending on how the leaf was folded, the seeds can end up attached to either the inside (most fruits, e.g. seeds in centre of tamarillo or tomato) or on the outer edge of the ovary pointing inwards (e.g. gooseberry).

INFERIOR OR SUPERIOR?

Another variation in flower structure that affects how the resulting 'fruit' is formed is the position of the carpels. If this reproductive structure is positioned above the other whorls of sepals, petals and stamens (if there are any), then the flower is termed as being **superior** (**hypogynous**), e.g. the tomato, persimmon, and the **calyx** (several green leaves that are a remnant of the sepals) are often present at the base of the fruit. If the carpels are situated at the base of the flower below these whorls, then the flower is termed as **inferior** (**epigynous**), e.g. apple, guava, and the remnants of the calyx are positioned at the apex of the fruit. In the *Malus* genus (which contains the apple), the carpels are actually embedded within the receptacle, which then develops into the fleshy apple, with the core being the carpels. The calyx is then seen at the apex of the fruit, with the bulging receptacle below it. There is also an **intermediate** (**perigynous**) form between these two, where the sepals, petals and stamens are formed around the sides of the often cup-shaped receptacle and form a ring around the carpels (ovary), e.g. the cherry. The position of these structures in relationship to each other determines how and what form the fruit takes (see Fig. 4).

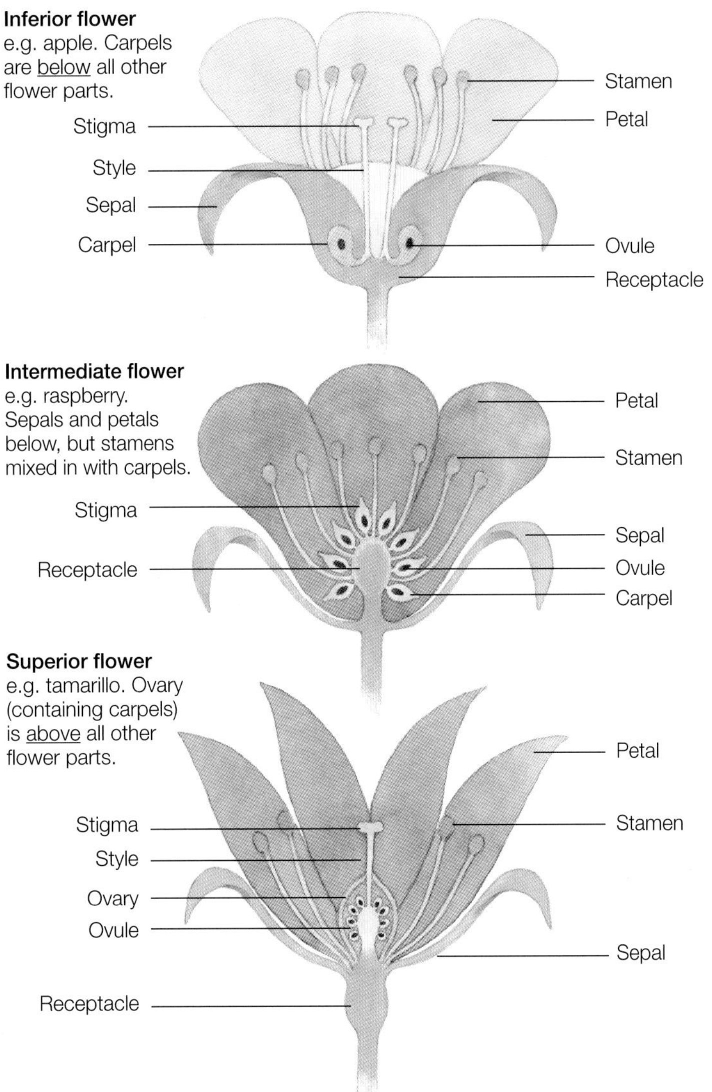

POLLINATION AND BEYOND

Pollination is necessary for the formation of most fruits and nuts. Flowers are mostly pollinated by bees and other insects, though some species, often with long, decorative stamens, produce lots of nectar to attract bats or birds, and still other species need wind to disperse their pollen. A few flowers can be pollinated without a pollinator, i.e. by parthenocarpy, e.g. banana, but this is unusual in the plant world. The transfer of genetic material to form seeds is the usual rule. Some flowers just open at night, are often white in colour, but are usually wonderfully fragrant to attract moths. A few species, e.g. fig, yucca, have become so specialised that only a specific insect, e.g. wasp or moth, can pollinate their flowers. Good pollination leads to good fruit production. However, a number of problems can occur to prevent this. Cold or wet weather can deter bees and insects, as can a shortage of the pollinating species. In addition, many plant species have evolved various physiological traits to avoid cross pollination, e.g. male and female flowers becoming receptive at different times.

Sadly, and perhaps even catastrophically for us in the future, bee populations around the world are declining, possibly due to disease or indiscriminate use of insecticides, etc. Recent research has suggested that populations of non-social bees can be introduced as additional pollinators, and these may be less susceptible to disease. The mason or blue-orchard bee (*Osmia lignaria*) lives on its own in holes in the ground or in trees, and not in hives; these bees are also not aggressive. They do not make honey, but are excellent pollinators. Consider encouraging or introducing some to your garden if experiencing pollination problems. Apparently, they do particularly well on land that has a range of different fruiting species.

Pollination

Female animals are born with their full complement of eggs for reproduction. In contrast, plants produce new 'eggs' each time they flower. Within a carpel (ovary) there can be from one to many ovules that can be fertilised. After arrival by wind, insect, bird or human hand, the male **pollen grain**

Fig. 4. Inferior, intermediate and superior flowers

Inferior flower
e.g. apple. Carpels are below all other flower parts.

Stamen
Petal
Stigma
Style
Sepal
Carpel
Ovule
Receptacle

Intermediate flower
e.g. raspberry. Sepals and petals below, but stamens mixed in with carpels.

Petal
Stamen
Stigma
Sepal
Receptacle
Ovule
Carpel

Superior flower
e.g. tamarillo. Ovary (containing carpels) is above all other flower parts.

Petal
Stigma
Stamen
Style
Ovary
Ovule
Sepal
Receptacle

germinates on the stigma on the tip of the carpel. The pollen grain then forms a tube, the style, down which two male gametes travel, towards the ovule(s), where fertilisation takes place. They travel downwards in response to a lower oxygen level within the carpel. Several pollen grains can land on a stigma, and each can send down a pollen tube. If there is more than one ovule within the carpel, then each pollen grain can fertilise an ovule to form a group of fertilised seeds. If there is only one ovule, the first pollen tube to reach the ovule becomes the successful pollinator.

Unlike animal sex cells, in the pollen grain there are two gametes, not just one: one fertilises the ovule, the other fuses with a central nucleus to form a nutritive layer called the **endosperm**. After fertilisation, cell division occurs in the ovule until an **embryo** plant is formed. The endosperm becomes the food supply for the developing embryo before it forms an adequate root system for independent growth. The first leaves to be formed are the cotyledons; these are a different shape from future leaves. As cell division continues, the embryo expands and, in some species, can crush the outer wall of the embryo (the **testa**). In other species, this tissue remains and develops into nutritive tissue. Species that use up all their endosperm are termed **non-endospermic**, e.g. apple seed, beans, peas. When the endosperm is not all used, these are termed **endospermic**, e.g. avocado stone, hazel, wheat and many nuts, which often results in an oily kernel (Fig. 5).

During development, the outer wall of the carpel develops differently in different species, and may form the tissue of fruits and nuts; it can become woody (many nuts) or fleshy (e.g. grapes and berries). The modified carpel wall (the **pericarp**) and the fertilised ovules within it become 'a fruit'. Adaptations to produce fleshy, juicy, colourful fruits are relatively recent, evolutionarily, and probably developed alongside animal- and bird-eating species as a method to encourage seed dispersal. The seed itself is usually sealed in a tough, hard-to-digest coat that passes through the animal. In addition, many fleshy fruits have seeds that contain powerful often toxic compounds to deter being eaten, e.g. the cyanogenic compounds within the Rosaceae family, which include cherry, apple, peach and almond.

TYPES OF FRUIT AND NUTS

The term fruits encompasses many structures that are formed to surround and protect the kernel. They are often commonly subdivided into dry or fleshy fruits. The dry fruits include, e.g. grains, legumes and nuts, with the latter described below. The fleshy fruits are also divided into several groups, with the main categories of drupe, pome and berry described below.

WHAT IS A NUT?

True 'nuts', although produced by many different species, are grouped together because the fruit is usually a semi-hard **kernel** without a fleshy outer layer. The kernel usually has a hardened exterior carpel wall (the **pericarp**) that surrounds, usually, a single kernel. The hard outer pericarp layer protects the kernel from being eaten or damaged. Examples of nuts include hazelnut, acorn, beechnut. The term 'nut' is often used incorrectly, botanically, to describe foods such as peanut, macadamia or oyster nut, which are not formed with just a hardened pericarp; instead these examples are more correctly termed a legume, a drupe and a seed, respectively.

Many 'true' nuts form a cup-shaped structure (an **involucre**), which is derived from the calyx (sepals) of the flowers. The involucre may be leafy or tubular (such as in the filberts and hazelnuts), spiny (as in beech and chestnuts), or may be composed of fused scales as in the oak, where the nut and involucre together form the familiar acorn. Many 'true' nuts are formed from a superior flower structure, where the whorls (including the involucre) are below the carpel (or nut). Many nut species are also wind-pollinated, which, evolutionarily, tends to be a more primitive pollination mechanism amongst dicotyledons. Horticulturally, the gardener wants fertilised nut 'fruits'; if they form without being pollinated then the kernel has little flesh and is of low quality.

Nuts, unlike fruits, do not 'advertise' their edibility to wildlife. Instead, they are generally designed to fall in the area around the tree, and for the outer pericarp to slowly soften and allow germination of the seed. However, animals such as squirrels and rats do tend to carry them off for winter storage, aiding their spread.

Kernels, which include seeds and nuts, because they are embryos, are packed with oils and protein, with the latter in the form of enzymes, DNA and RNA, for future differentiation and growth. Most kernels contain high levels of 'healthy' monounsaturated fats (see later), including omega-3 oils, and are often high in vitamin E. They commonly contain good levels of the B-vitamins: thiamine, riboflavin and niacin.

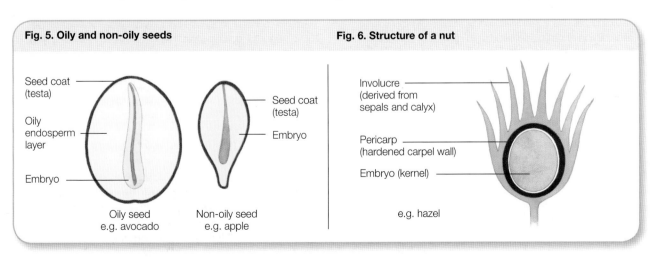

Fig. 5. Oily and non-oily seeds

Seed coat (testa)
Oily endosperm layer
Embryo
Oily seed e.g. avocado

Seed coat (testa)
Embryo
Non-oily seed e.g. apple

Fig. 6. Structure of a nut

Involucre (derived from sepals and calyx)
Pericarp (hardened carpel wall)
Embryo (kernel)
e.g. hazel

However, because they are an embryo, they generally contain much less vitamin A and C than fleshy fruits.

A relatively small serving of nuts can provide a good amount of a person's daily energy requirements. Nuts can be termed as being 'low glycaemic'. This means they burn slowly and do not cause a surge in insulin levels, which results in rapid decreases in blood-sugar levels. This is of particular interest in these times of increasing diabetes disease. Research has shown that, when the whole kernel is eaten, the oil component of the nut enters the bloodstream more slowly than if just eating the expressed oil (e.g. walnut oil), so contributing to this slow-burn effect.

WHAT IS A DRUPE?

Fruits, known as **drupes**, have a hard, inner layer that contains the embryo (or kernel) plus two hard or fleshy outer layers. These three layers are collectively known as the **pericarp**. The outer layer of the pericarp is known as the **epicarp**, which usually forms the outer skin, the middle layer is the **mesocarp**, which is often fleshy, and the inner layer is the **endocarp**, which is usually hard and surrounds the kernel. The inner carpel usually occurs singly (e.g. cherry, plum) or in threes, which become fused. They are derived from a flower with a superior, simple ovary. In many ways they are similar to 'true' nuts, except that the pericarp is divided into three layers.

As mentioned earlier, drupes can be termed 'dry' (e.g. almond, macadamia) or 'fleshy' (e.g. many of the Rosaceae family: peach, plum, cherry, but also avocados, mango and coconut). The fleshy epicarp is what is eaten in peaches, cherries or mango. These types of drupes are often also known as **stone fruit**.

The almond, an example of a dry drupe, is a kernel within a hard endocarp (the shell), surrounded by a tough, non-fleshy mesocarp, with a tough, greenish skin of epicarp. Technically, almonds are not 'true' nuts because, in true nuts, the hard outer wall constitutes the entire pericarp: there would be no layer of green tough meso- and epicarp, for the pericarp would be fused as one. Similarly, the walnut is a kernel within an endocarp. It is formed from two fused carpels, which in this genus are two pre-cotyledonous storage leaves, and these form the familiar convoluted walnut kernel. The coconut is another example of a dry drupe, with a thin, green outer layer (the exocarp), a thick, fibrous middle layer (the mesocarp) and a very hard inner layer surrounding the large seed or endocarp, with the embryo being a small structure near the base embedded within the endocarp.

Blackberries and raspberries, although confusingly called 'berries', are botanically classified as drupes or, more correctly, as **aggregates of drupes** (or **drupelets**). Each, of many ovules within a single flower, forms an individual fruit consisting of a small, hard endocarp surrounding a central kernel, around which is the juicy mesocarp surrounded by its skin. The fruits are formed by the fusion of these many individual drupes, which are attached around the top of the flower's receptacle.

Drupes display colourful fruits to advertise their edibility to birds and other wildlife, but also have a hard endocarp to deter the kernel being digested. The flesh tends to only remain sweet and edible for a short time before deteriorating.

The stones of many drupes can pass through the guts of animals without germinating, or the fruits with the stone may be carried away from the parent tree. Often, the hard stone (endocarp) contains toxic compounds to deter being eaten, e.g. the cyanogenic compounds within the Rosaceae stone fruits such as peach, almond and cherry. However, the kernel itself is often quite edible, e.g. macadamia, almond.

Many drupaceous fruits are native to warm-temperate climates, needing only a brief period of winter cold to initiate leaf and flower production in spring. They also tend to blossom earlier in spring, which is a disadvantage in areas prone to late spring frosts, but is fine for more Mediterranean-type climates, ensuring a long growing season.

WHAT IS A POME?

Pomes (or **pip fruit**) include the apple, pear and quince. Although familiar commercially, there are not many pome fruit species. When fertilised, the ovary forms the inner part of the apple, while the surrounding receptacle becomes modified to form the fleshy, juicy, outer covering. The flower has five fused carpels. These go on to form the area within the core, which is surrounded by remnants of the pericarp. The flower is inferior, and the remnants of the sepals (calyx) can be seen at the apex of the fruit. One of the main factors that has made these pomes so popular commercially, apart from their tasty fruits, is the long periods of time they can be stored for compared to many other fruits.

Pomes often have brightly coloured skins to attract birds and wildlife. The seeds (pips) are small and will tend to pass through the gut intact and the seedcoat also often contains toxic, bitter compounds to make it inedible. Many pome species are native to northern temperate regions, tolerating cold winters. They tend to blossom later in spring, so missing late frosts, and all need a longer period of chilling to come into leaf and produce flowers in spring.

WHAT IS A BERRY?

In **berries**, the whole of the pericarp becomes fleshy and does not form a woody inner endocarp as in drupes, which is the opposite of nuts, where the whole of the pericarp is hard. Tamarillo, blueberry, grape, orange and Cape gooseberry are berries; the pericarp forms a thick juicy covering around the fertilised ovules (seeds) within. The kernel is surrounded by a fairly hard, often bitter, seedcoat. In bananas, the female flowers form a berry from three fused carpels, with the tiny, unfertilised seeds just visible running up the centre of the fruit. Around this is the fleshy-banana endocarp, surrounded by a thin layer of white mesocarp, which is encased within the outer protective banana skin, the epicarp, its outer ridges reflecting the inner form of the fruit.

Citrus are also classified as berries. They consist of six or more fused carpels (or segments), which, together, are known as an ovary. The pericarp consists of the outer epicarp skin, which is rich in fragrant oil glands, the white pithy mesocarp layer, and the membranous endocarp within the fruit, which has many outgrowths that contain the juicy pulp. The Cape gooseberry is formed by the simple fusion of two carpels, like the tomato, with the endocarp reduced to an inner region around the central seeds within their pulp, and the outer, juicy flesh being the mesocarp surrounded by the skin (epicarp).

Berries usually contain several or many seeds within their flesh, though the date fruit is an exception, being a single-seeded berry. In addition, berries can be divided into 'false' and 'true' berries because of the placement of their ovary in the flower, and its subsequent effect on the fruit.

True berries have a superior ovary, and so their fruits often have the remnants of the calyx at the base, e.g. tamarillo, persimmon, citrus.

Fruits are classified as false berries if the flowers have an inferior ovary and, therefore, the calyx or sepals occur at the apex of the fruit. These berries are also often formed partly from receptacle tissue. False berries include blueberry, banana, feijoa, guava and many more.

PLANT STRUCTURE

A BIT ABOUT LEAVES

By understanding the physiology of leaves, a greater understanding can be gained of how to choose and care for plants. Leaves are the main structures that catch the sun's light waves, and convert it via a series of complex, delicate, biochemical reactions into a form of energy that can be stored in high-energy molecules. The energy is trapped by green molecules called **chlorophyll** that reside within structures called **chloroplasts** inside the leaf cells. The process of trapping the sun's energy is known as **photosynthesis**. This energy can then be used to build up carbohydrate molecules, using carbon dioxide that enters the leaf via pores called **stomata**. No other life form can achieve this amazing feat. Without this ability to trap the sun's energy, it is highly unlikely any higher life could exist on Earth.

The stomata are usually positioned on the undersides of dicotyledonous leaves (broad-leaved species), though they are more equally divided between the upper and lower surfaces in moncotyledonous species (grasses, etc.), where the leaves tend to be held more vertically. In most species, these pores open during the day when the plant is photosynthesising, and then close at night. However, a problem with this system is the loss of water through these same pores. At first this seems like poor design, but the removal of water also helps to maintain the 'suction' of water from the roots. Water has to travel a long way from the roots to the top of a kauri or giant redwood tree, and huge forces are needed to achieve this. Water is partly drawn into roots from the soil by the difference between the (relatively) salty interior of the roots and the water outside, a process called **osmosis**. However, the main force is the dynamic stream of water that travels from the roots, through the vessels of the trunk, along branches and into the leaves, and then out through the stomata. This occurs because of strongly negative pressures that develop within the system: from the moist soil, to the low humidity of the atmosphere outside the leaf. In effect, water is drawn up through the plant by an ingenious vacuum system. The difference in pressures between the different environments drives this system and can transport huge amounts of water from the soil to the air every day. Additional to this, water's tendency to rise up the fine xylem tubes (capillary action) aids this process. This 'suction' would be much more difficult to achieve with wider vessels.

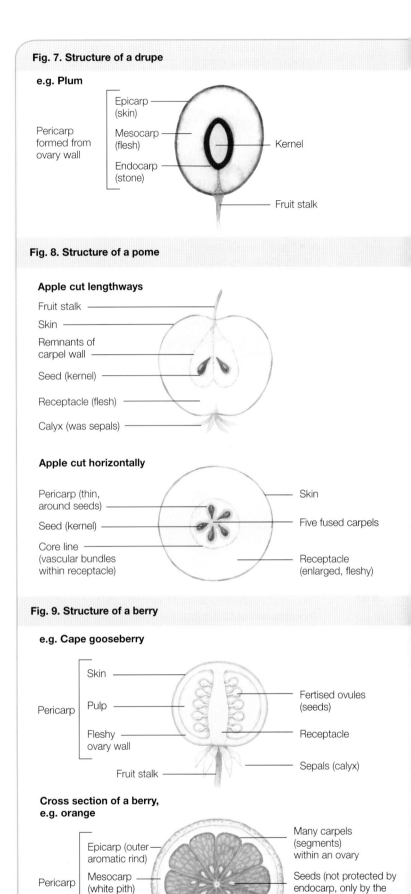

Fig. 7. Structure of a drupe

e.g. Plum

Pericarp formed from ovary wall

Epicarp (skin)
Mesocarp (flesh)
Endocarp (stone)
Kernel
Fruit stalk

Fig. 8. Structure of a pome

Apple cut lengthways

Fruit stalk
Skin
Remnants of carpel wall
Seed (kernel)
Receptacle (flesh)
Calyx (was sepals)

Apple cut horizontally

Pericarp (thin, around seeds)
Seed (kernel)
Core line (vascular bundles within receptacle)
Skin
Five fused carpels
Receptacle (enlarged, fleshy)

Fig. 9. Structure of a berry

e.g. Cape gooseberry

Skin
Pericarp
Pulp
Fleshy ovary wall
Fruit stalk
Fertised ovules (seeds)
Receptacle
Sepals (calyx)

Cross section of a berry, e.g. orange

Pericarp
Epicarp (outer aromatic rind)
Mesocarp (white pith)
Endocarp (membranes within fruit)
Many carpels (segments) within an ovary
Seeds (not protected by endocarp, only by the seedcoat: testa)
Fleshy juice sacs, derived from endocarp, and containing juice

How do water relations affect different species? Plants with small leaves and thick cuticles lose less water, particularly if they are grey, reflecting the sun's radiation, or have fine hairs. Plants with large, thin leaves lose water more rapidly, particularly in heat and wind, and can easily lose more water than they are able to take up from the roots. These types of plants usually grow better in partial shade, with shelter from wind and a moist soil. Plants grown in shade at lower light levels naturally form larger, greener leaves with longer stems. Care needs to be taken if these plants are moved to a location in full sun; this should be done gradually or plants can be stressed to a point where irreversible damage occurs.

Many species that have evolved to tolerate hotter, drier conditions are able to close their stomata if there is a water shortage through the day; plants that have evolved in wetter conditions often have much poorer stomatal control. Many monocots (including maize) have a modified leaf structure as well as a more efficient photosynthetic mechanism. They are able to use carbon dioxide much more efficiently and to still photosynthesise during the day when their stomata are almost closed: this mechanism is know as **C4 photosynthesis**. These plants are often able to grow more vigorously under adverse conditions compared to the majority of plants, which are known as C3 plants. Their stomata can be almost closed on a hot day, and yet they can still efficiently photosynthesise, whereas the growth of C3 plants almost ceases during heat stress. Still other plants, including many cacti, have evolved **Crassulacean metabolism**, whereby the stomata are closed all day to avoid moisture use during the heat, although the plant is still able to trap the sun's energy. At night, the stomata open to take in carbon dioxide and use this to produce sugars from the stored energy.

ROOTING ABOUT

As well as leaf structure and dynamics, the ability of a plant to conserve water is also determined by the type and extent of root growth. Often overlooked, the health and growth of roots can be one of the most important aspects in the vigour of a plant.

In general, plants that form deep roots are able to bring nutrients and water up from depth to the growing plant. Then as leaves are dropped and recycled, they are added to the upper-soil layers. Shallow-rooted plants can only harvest nutrients from a shallower depth of soil and hence their overall effect on soil fertility and structure is less. Deeper rooting plants, in general, are more beneficial to soil structure and to the plants that grow around them.

The type and depth of roots of a species can make a big difference as to where and how the plant grows. Roots come in two main types: **tap** and **fibrous**. Taproots are deep, main roots, equivalent to a plant having a dominant, main stem. Lateral roots branch off these deep roots. They are able to access water and nutrients at depth, but are susceptible to damage during transplanting. In some species, the taproot can divide and become fleshy. In others, the taproot becomes diminished as the plant matures, and mostly fibrous roots are formed. Deep taproots often mean that the plant is more drought tolerant, as it can reach water at depth. Such plants also may be more tolerant to wind. However, they may be more susceptible to waterlogging as

well, for deep roots tend to sit in water for longer. In addition, taproots often do not have as many small, fine roots for nutrient uptake, although they can obtain nutrients from deeper layers that other plants cannot reach.

Fibrous roots generally occur nearer the surface and, as their name suggests, they have a large surface area for the uptake of water and nutrients. They are formed after taproots, and may become the main root type. Being nearer the surface, though, they are often susceptible to drought as the surface soil becomes dry, particularly in sandy soils. In addition, plants may not have the same strength in windy conditions as plants with deep roots. Shallow-rooted species will, generally, need regular applications of water, particularly at final fruit development, and particularly with stone fruits. However, they are less affected by wetter soils, as water drains from the surface more rapidly. The ideal is a mix of the two root types, with deep roots to enable the plant to survive drought periods, but also a system of finer, surface roots to obtain surface moisture and nutrients. Several fruiting species have these hardy characteristics, e.g. pistachio, carob, olives, *Elaeagnus* spp., sea grape, ginkgo.

In addition, roots form fine **root hairs**, which are specialised cells that extend outwards to squeeze in between soil particles. These cells are able to absorb water and nutrients much more efficiently than the main corky roots, though root hairs are delicate and can be easily damaged during transplanting, with seedlings being particularly susceptible. They are mostly formed near root tips. The number of root hairs produced varies considerably between species. Plants from acidic soils tend to produce few and, instead, rely more on mycorrhizal relationships (see below). Avocado and gevuina also have very few, and are both notoriously difficult to establish. Tougher, drought-resistant species often have many root hairs.

When irrigating, short periods of watering only moisten the upper soil layers and encourage surface roots; longer, deeper watering sessions are better. Deeper watering can also be achieved by inserting a half-metre-long plastic tube vertically into the soil near the rooting area when planting a tree. This tube can then deliver water directly below the soil surface.

Many plants form **symbiotic relationships** with bacteria and fungi in the soil to fix nitrogen or to obtain additional nutrients (see below). These relationships take time to develop and need the right conditions, including the minimisation of chemicals in the root vicinity, and the inclusion of organic matter, such as leaf mould, to encourage their formation. Changes in pH, adding excess fertiliser or transplanting the trees can also affect these relationships.

When choosing plants from a garden centre or nursery, check the plants are not root bound and that they have a large enough pot for the size of the plant. It is better to buy a well-rooted plant with a smaller shoot than viceversa, although the latter is initially often more appealing.

PLANT TYPES

TEMPERATE PLANTS

Temperate plants can be divided into cold- and warm-temperate types. **Cold-temperate** species can tolerate long, cold winters with temperatures below −10°C, with many species tolerating temperatures down to –30°C and colder. They usually cannot tolerate intense heat. **Warm-temperate** plants can withstand cold winter temperatures, but not excessively so. They may be damaged by temperatures below –8°C. They can tolerate frosts, but not for extended periods.

Most temperate plants actually need a period of **winter chilling** to initiate flowering and leaf growth in spring: if it is not cold enough for long enough, flower buds may open unevenly or not at all (see p. 22). In contrast, if the plant species comes into blossom too early, then there is a risk of frost damage. Cold-temperate species usually need long periods of winter chill, and do not grow well in warmer areas for this reason. Warm-temperate species are more adaptable, needing less winter chill, and can grow in a wide band around the middle latitudes, though are often more susceptible to late winter frosts. In regions with long, cold winters, it is wise to plant late-flowering cultivars. Typically, the earliest common fruit tree to come into blossom is the almond, followed by Japanese plum and apricot, peach, sweet cherry, pear, European plum, sour cherry and, one of the last, the apple.

In temperate areas it is possible to grow more frost-tender species as long as they are given extra protection and a sunny location. Avoid hollows that may become frost pockets in winter. Cold air sinks, and there is often a striking difference between the bottom of a valley and the ridge above it in degrees of frost. Growing plants in containers and moving these into a glasshouse or conservatory in winter can be another way to avoid cold temperatures.

In general, blossom and leaves are the most vulnerable to cold damage, followed by younger stems. If these are damaged, many species will grow back from older wood, so give time in spring for this to happen before discarding any frost-damaged trees.

Within the temperate classification are areas where winters are only somewhat cold, with just an occasional light frost and no snow. In these regions, there is a balance between selecting species that can tolerate some winter frost but will also receive sufficient winter chill to blossom in spring. In these warm-temperate regions, it may be possible to grow some subtropical species of *Citrus*, as well as peaches, low-chill stonefruit, figs, loquats, feijoa, kiwifruit and casimiroa, with tamarillo, avocado, banana (and others) in protected locations.

SUBTROPICAL PLANTS

A subtropical climate is generally classified as having cooler winters, but no or only light frosts. Temperatures below ~–4°C usually cause some damage to the plant. It is only moderately or barely cold in winter, and the summers may be humid or dry. In these regions, it is also sometimes possible to grow a number of tropical species, though obtaining a sufficiently long growing season often determines if a species can produce a mature crop.

In warmer climates, a lack of winter chill limits the growth of some temperate species. However, there are many exciting warm-temperate and subtropical plants to explore instead. There is overlap between the subtropical and tropical species, but tropical species cannot tolerate

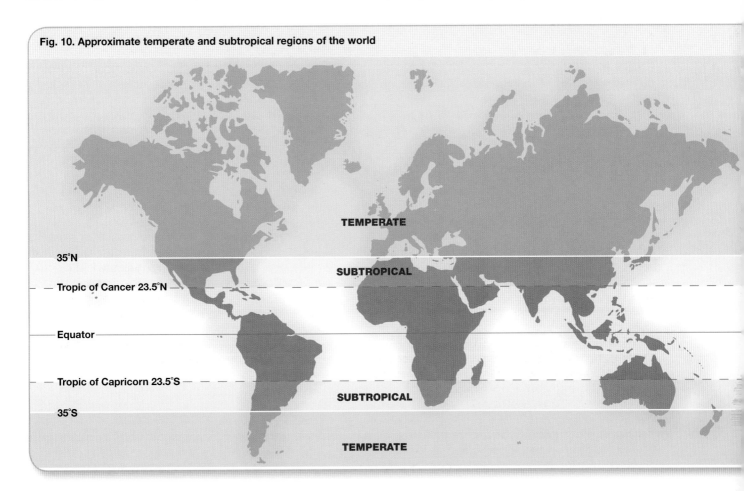

Fig. 10. Approximate temperate and subtropical regions of the world

TEMPERATE

SUBTROPICAL

35°N

Tropic of Cancer 23.5°N

Equator

Tropic of Capricorn 23.5°S

SUBTROPICAL

35°S

TEMPERATE

temperatures near freezing, seldom grow well and almost never flower or fruit in warm-temperate regions.

CULTIVATION

LOCATION

Sun and shade: Most fruit and nut plants grow best when placed in a sunny position that is sheltered from strong winds. Sun is needed by many species to fully ripen the fruits and develop the best flavours. Many species have also evolved to grow best in open sites, though some prefer the forest edge and a little shade. These latter species often have larger, greener leaves with longer stems as the plant tries to catch what light energy is available and stretch itself towards the light. Many climbing species are tolerant of partial shade, as they grow up through the host tree to reach the light. Leaves on shade trees can be easily scorched by sun that is too bright.

Wind: In windy sites, strongly rooted species are needed that have tough leaves with thick cuticles to avoid desiccation. Sparse, thin, small leaves withstand wind better. Trees with densely leaved crowns are more vulnerable, particularly if they are evergreen. Strong winds can ruin delicate blossoms and fruit-set, break branches and stunt trees. Walls and fences are great for trapping heat and giving protection, as long as they do not shade too much. In exposed locations it is often beneficial to plant windbreaks. Thinner windbreaks allow some wind through; dense, thick windbreaks allow no wind through, but also cause turbulence on the lee side. The height of a windbreak will give protection for a horizontal distance of up to ten times its height on the lee side. Another factor to consider is that strong eddies can develop at the ends of windbreaks, and crops planted too near to these regions can be damaged. Possible windbreak species to choose include nitrogen-fixing species, such as *Acacia*. Other good windbreak species are pinenuts, sea grape and hawthorn. Planting these species as hedging or windbreaks doubles their usefulness and potential. Try and choose species that are not too vigorous or nutrient-robbing of the soil around them.

Topography: The bottoms of valleys can trap colder air in winter, resulting in more frosts. Sun-facing slopes are ideal for some species, but can be too fierce for shade-loving plants. The tops of ridges are often exposed and may benefit from a windbreak. Very steep slopes are best planted with tougher, wide-rooting, drought-resistant plants. Water can stream off slopes and be quickly lost and the soils are usually thin. In contrast, hollows can fill with water in winter and quickly kill many species. Large open areas will benefit from windbreaks.

Maritime: A wide range of fruit and nut species can be grown in sheltered maritime locations. Exposed locations, where salt-laden spray can lash the vegetation, are a particular problem; however, there are a few species that can even tolerate these conditions, e.g. palms, hottentot fig, sea grape, sea buckthorn, beach plum. Silvery, down-covered leaves are often a signature of maritime locations, where the light can be brighter and the salt from spray can easily burn leaves. Plants that are more tolerant of alkaline soils are often able to grow in maritime locations. A few fruit and nut species can tolerate regions where the groundwater has become contaminated with salt to form brackish water, e.g. pandanus.

TEMPERATURE

Low, freezing temperatures are probably one of the main limiting factors for many species. Topography can make a big difference to susceptibility: cold will roll down hills, so try not to plant frost-sensitive species in dips and valleys. In addition, if plants have some shade in the morning after a frost, they are less likely to experience such serious damage as plants that are rapidly thawed and heated after being frozen. Although some of the plants described in this book are frost susceptible, many can be successfully grown in containers and therefore moved to protected areas if freezing conditions seem likely. Otherwise, if planted outside in cooler areas, try to site them where they can obtain additional heat and protection from buildings and structures. This is of particular importance for young plants; most plants become more frost hardy as they grow older. In winter, vulnerable plants can be covered with cloth or plastic sheeting to give added protection. Trunks can be wrapped and thick mulches applied around the roots to protect them, though take care that coverings and mulch too near to the trunk do not encourage excessive moisture. This can increase the risk of fungal root- and stem-rot infections.

Chilling requirements: Most temperate, deciduous fruit trees, including stone fruits, require exposure to cool temperatures during winter to allow leaf growth and flower production the following spring. If there is not enough chill, then the blossom and leaves do not open properly. The length of time needed varies for each cultivar. The chilling requirement is measured in terms of the total hours needed during a winter period for the temperature to be below 5–7°C, although temperatures between 7–13°C also have considerable benefit and 'count' towards chilling time.

Chilling is mainly needed by deciduous species; evergreen species seldom require it. In general, plants that can grow in colder areas need longer chilling times. For example, citrus need none, strawberries only need a short chilling period of 200–300 hours, peaches need 600–1000 hours, apples need 250–1700 hours and raspberries need a longer chilling time of 800–1700 hours to break dormancy in spring. If there are lots of warm and cold temperature changes during winter, the plant may need a longer chilling period than if it had experienced continual cold temperatures. By spring, as it gets warmer, and the plants' chilling needs have been fulfilled, they lose their winter hardiness and the leaf and flower buds become active. However, some species, e.g. stone fruits, often tend to bloom very soon after the chilling requirement is satisfied, but this can often be before the spring frosts have ended. It is best therefore to locate these trees in protected areas if possible.

Strangely, plants from very cold regions often actually need less winter chilling, as if they naturally come into leaf and flower in late winter to make the best of the short season, e.g. crowberry. The young leaves and flowers of these species are tolerant of temperatures well below freezing. In contrast, temperate plants, such as apples and cherries, to reduce damage by late spring frosts, need a longer period of chilling before they satisfactorily come into leaf and produce blossom. Species from warm-temperate regions need less chilling, e.g. peaches, as late frosts are not as likely, with species such as citrus needing no chill time at all to complete their annual cycle.

WATER

Waterlogging: A few trees, such as cranberry, lotus, pear, figs, black sapote and pecan, can tolerate heavy, wet clay soils, but most plants, including raspberry, chestnut and walnut, cannot tolerate any waterlogging. It is not so much the water, but the lack of oxygen to the roots that causes the problems. Roots can rapidly build up metabolic toxins, which some species are very sensitive to, and just a day of flooding may kill them. Other species are more tolerant of these toxins or have developed alternative ways of obtaining oxygen and can tolerate extended periods of waterlogging. If waterlogging occurs around deciduous trees in winter, then the damage is usually much less than if plants are waterlogged while they are actively growing.

Clay soils can easily become waterlogged because they hold water so readily. Sandy soils drain the best. If a clay soil is all you have, then there are a few options. The addition of gypsum can break up the clay, as can the addition of coarse organic matter and sand. When establishing plants, try to ensure that there is somewhere for excess water to run off so that they aren't left sitting in clay bowls of water. If necessary, they can be planted partially above the ground surface, but a good organic mulch will be needed. Alternatively, large containers can be used for cultivation.

The other problem that can occur with soils that are wet for extended periods is that many heavy metals become more 'available', and can, in some locations, reach toxic levels and poison the plant.

Drought: In contrast to the above, too little water can be a problem for many species. Those with large, thin leaves and shallow root systems are particularly susceptible. Adequate moisture is often of particular importance during flowering and fruit-set. Dry conditions during this period can result in only a few, poorly formed fruit, and often lead to premature fruit drop. Free-draining sandy soils benefit from a mulch and the incorporation of organic matter into the soil. It could also be worth considering installing an irrigation system, as watering by hand can take a long time and much effort.

SOILS AND NUTRIENTS

Most of the species described in this book will grow and produce best at slightly acid to neutral pH values (5.5–7.0, see below) in organic-rich, deep, moist but freely draining loam soils. However, unless you are lucky enough to live somewhere with such wonderful, fertile soil, then either the soil needs to be modified or plants need to be selected that tolerate adverse conditions. Some of the species described in this book will actually grow in poor, wet soils, very alkaline soils, dry arid soils, or even very acid soils. There is an Appendix listing different environmental and soil conditions with the species that are suited to them.

The following are the main soil types suited to fruit and nut cultivation. If your soil falls into none of these categories and is truly terrible, then grow dwarf species in large containers. (See container culture on p. 26.)

Sand: Sandy soils are wonderful for deep-rooted plants. They have no waterlogging problems, but do dry out easily, with plants becoming more rapidly susceptible to drought. In addition, these soils are often poor in nutrients, which may need to be added in greater amounts than usual. They also tend to harbour more nematodes than other soil types.

Clay: These soils are usually fairly high in most nutrients, though can be deficient in a particular element, depending on what rocks they are derived from. Waterlogging is the main problem with clay soils, coupled with problems of root penetration. Gypsum can be added to help break up and flocculate the clay, but can be quite hard work! Organic matter can also help this process. With these soils, it is important to position plants on slopes or ensure that water can run off from the root area. It is also best to avoid cultivation when these soils are wet, or they can turn into a quagmire of structureless mud. Clay soils that become waterlogged at depth often have a grey colour. This means that the iron in the soil, which normally appears yellow and red, has lost oxygen and has become reduced and **anaerobic** (without air). It also means that several other elements have become much more soluble, and can be toxic to the plant. Roots hate these conditions, and can die alarmingly quickly. Roots need oxygen; without it there is no root growth and no, or very little, nutrient uptake.

Limestone/chalk soils: These are often well-drained, but frequently thin and stony. The main other problem is the high pH and the consequent nutrient availability (see Fig. 11 on p. 24) or, more often, the unavailability, e.g. a lack of iron, which causes yellow leaves and a disorder known as iron chlorosis. However, micronutrients can be supplied to overcome this. In addition, alkaline soils can be partially modified by adding an acidic compost such as peat or pine needles, and acidic matter can be incorporated directly into areas to be planted with species requiring less limey conditions. The addition of organic matter to improve the soil's moisture retention is also likely to be beneficial. Alkaline lovers include acerola, olive, elaeagnus, persimmon, roselle.

Silt: Silty soils are usually high in nutrients. They allow efficient root penetration and enable good plant growth, but have a poor structure. Therefore, it is important not to compact or disturb these soils too much, particularly when they are wet, or they lose all of their air spaces and become very dense.

MULCHES

The addition of a rich **organic mulch** to the soil reduces water loss in lighter soils, helps drainage in heavier soils, builds up soil fertility, and improves the growth and health of the plant. It also improves soil structure and suppresses weed growth. A lack of water is one of the main factors that reduces fruit yield; therefore, organic mulches can be invaluable in drier regions. It is a good idea to remove weeds before placing mulch around the tree. Avoid stacking it against the trunk, as this can encourage fungal and other diseases. The mulch could be straw, grass clippings, leaves, hay, wood chips, sawdust, newspaper or a similar material. Note though that mulches with a high carbon-to-nitrogen ratio, such as straw, bark and newspaper, often cause nitrogen deficiencies because soil microbes use up any other local sources of nitrogen as they break down the mulch. These organic materials therefore may need supplemental nitrogen and other nutrients added to balance this loss.

Fig. 11. Nutrient availability at different pH

Relationship between soil pH and plant-nutrient availability, with the wider the bar, the greater the availability

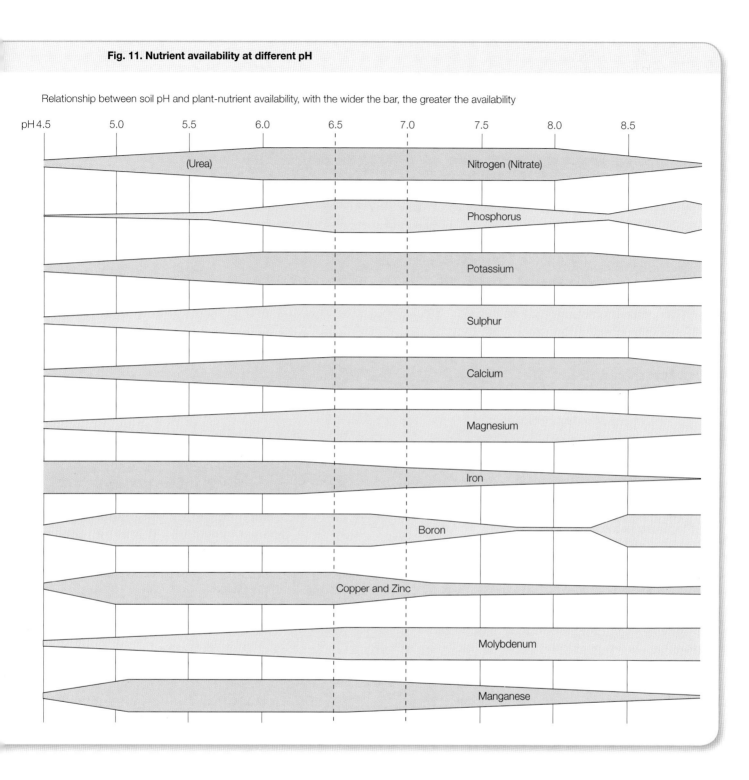

pH

What does pH mean to nutrient availability in the soil? By studying something about pH and soil types, a good understanding can be gained of how and what nutrients need to be applied. pH is a logarithmic scale of acidity and alkalinity between 1–14, with neutral being 7. pH actually measures the amount of 'free' hydrogen **ions**. The more free hydrogen ions there are, the more acid the soil, i.e. the lower the number below 7. For alkalinity, the converse is true: the less hydrogen ions, the more alkaline (or basic) the soil, the greater the pH is above 7.

As discussed above, the majority of fruit and nut plants prefer a pH that ranges from~5.5–7.0, slightly acid to neutral. Plants have adapted to differing pH conditions, not because of the concentration of hydrogen ions, but because of the effect of the other elements, some of which are nutrients and others **heavy metals**, with the latter reaching toxic concentrations at certain pH levels. For example, aluminium and iron become much more soluble and available at more

Artificial mulches, such as plastic sheet or weed mat, can be used, and are effective in reducing weed growth, but do not have many of the benefits of an organic mulch. If mulches aren't used, then any cultivation around plants to remove weeds should be as shallow as possible to avoid root injury.

acid pH levels. Although plants take up and use iron as a nutrient, they do not need aluminium: too much aluminium is toxic to plants and can kill them. In addition, many metals become more available at acid pH, e.g. manganese, copper, zinc.

Figure 11 shows the availability of the main nutrients at different pH values. It can be seen that, at more acidic pH values, most nutrients, such as potassium, phosphate, nitrogen and molybdenum become less available to the plant. This does not mean that they are not in the soil, but that they are chemically locked up and unavailable. Also note that bacteria do not like acid soil. At more alkaline or higher pH values, nutrients, such as phosphate, iron, manganese and zinc become unavailable.

In alkaline soils **iron deficiency** is common. This causes iron chlorosis, with leaves becoming yellowish (due to lack of chlorophyll) because iron is necessary in the pathway that produces sugars during photosynthesis (as is magnesium). The application, to the leaves, of a liquid containing the various micronutrients can overcome this, as can the addition of acidic organic matter, such as peat, to the soil. At acid pH values, plants can also suffer various nutrient deficiencies, but these can be simply remedied by the addition of lime to raise the pH, rather than the addition of more nutrients, which can result in more problems than it cures.

NUTRIENTS

Below are brief descriptions of the different nutrients. (Also see Deficiency symptoms, p. 38.)

Nitrogen (N) Nitrogen is a somewhat different nutrient from most others because of its dependence on bacteria. It is essential for plant and animal growth, and is needed for protein and enzyme formation, as well as for the formation of DNA and RNA. It is also related to the uptake of other nutrients by the plant: a deficiency of nitrogen can result in a poorer uptake of other nutrients. It is a mobile nutrient within plants, and deficiencies first show up in older leaves. All the nitrogen in our bodies is derived from plants, albeit that some may be secondhand through meat and dairy products. However, plants cannot get hold of nitrogen very easily either. Although nitrogen gas constitutes >70% of the air around us, it takes tremendous energy to convert this into a form useful to plants or humans. Plants are not able to do this. They get virtually all of their nitrogen, either directly or indirectly, from bacteria. Without these bacteria, life on Earth could not exist.

Most plants uptake nitrogen in the form of **nitrates** (e.g. NO_3); these forms of nitrogen are much more available in neutral to alkaline soils. Nitrates are mostly formed by free-living bacteria, but a few plant species also form a **symbiotic relationship** with bacteria in their roots. In this relationship, the plant supplies the bacteria with sugars and a protective environment; in return, the plant receives a supply of nitrogen, even in poor soils. We are all familiar with one of the main families that carries this out: the legumes (clover, peas, beans, peanuts, *Acacia*). If you look carefully at legume roots, you can easily spot the nodules that contain the bacteria. However, these bacteria do not like to be waterlogged or to be in very acid soils, so this needs to be considered when planting leguminous species.

Some species of plants have evolved to grow in more acid soils, and are often from colder climates where peat-like soils are prevalent. In acid conditions, nitrate is not available and, instead, plants use **ammonia** (NH_4, or urea) as their nitrogen source. Although needing less chemical energy to be formed, it is still obtained indirectly from plants via organic breakdown products. Also, like nitrates, it is easily leached and lost from the soil.

Nitrogen increases leaf area and growth, and gives foliage a rich green colour. However, too much nitrogen also results in lush, thin-leaved foliage which is more susceptible to pathogen attack, to droughts and to frost. Addition of some nitrogen is generally beneficial, but not too much, and it is best added when the plant is actively growing or it tends to be simply leached away. A deficiency of nitrogen results in pale green leaves with poor growth.

Apart from fertiliser, fish meal, well-rotted manure, and blood and bone are all good sources of nitrogen. As nitrates are very easily leached from soil, if they are added in the last two forms, they are released more slowly. Excess nitrate is rapidly transported down to the groundwater and into rivers and lakes to cause environmental problems (eutrophication).

Potassium (K) This is a mobile nutrient within the plant: it is needed for transport, is important in fruit formation and in photosynthesis. It is involved in cell permeability and increases disease resistance. Levels of potassium in soils are often quite high, but it is often locked up within the soil minerals. Available potassium is fairly easily leached from the soil and so deficiencies can be fairly common, particularly in sandy, lighter soils. Wood ash can be a source of potassium, as can well-rotted manure, etc.

Phosphate (P) In the plant, this nutrient is part of the cell nucleus and is needed for producing biochemical energy and cell division and is particularly necessary at root and shoot tips where active growth is occurring. It is also involved in opening of the stomata. It is not very mobile within the plant, so deficiencies show up in newer leaves, but can be difficult to detect. A dull, mauve grey-green colour is often an indicator. Deficiencies affect fruit production and lead to poor root growth.

In the soil, this nutrient is also not very mobile and can form a range of complex molecules, which can be easily locked away from plants at either high or low pH values. Because phosphate is also not easily leached, deficiencies are usually a result of an unsuitable pH rather than a shortage within the soil.

Calcium (Ca) Plants need calcium for actively-dividing tissues, such as the growing tips of plants and roots, but also in cell walls. Generally, fruit and nut plants do not need large amounts of calcium. It can be in short supply in some soils, though can be easily supplied as limestone or dolomite (with magnesium).

Magnesium (Mg) This is needed by chlorophyll molecules, which trap light energy in photosynthesis. A shortage results in pale leaves. It is also involved with phosphate use and often accumulates in plants that have seeds rich in oil. Magnesium can be in short supply in certain soils, and is often not as available as calcium. It can be added as dolomite and is included in many general fertilisers.

Sulphur (S) Needed for protein and enzyme formation by the plant, and involved in photosynthesis, sulphur is also a component of certain vitamins. This nutrient is fairly mobile in the soil and can be leached, but does not generally become deficient. In many countries there is no shortage of soil sulphur because of emissions from cars and industry; deficiencies are also unlikely near coastal or volcanic regions. If needed, it can be easily added as gypsum.

Micronutrients: Needed by plants, but only in small amounts. They may be included with the main nutrients in fertilisers or are often added as a **foliar application** of chelates, being effectively absorbed through the leaves. They should only be sprayed at low concentration initially as certain species are susceptible to burning on their leaves.

Boron (B) A deficiency can result in poor water uptake by the plant. Boron may be deficient in some soils, but, because plants only need a little, toxicities can also easily occur, so care needs to be taken when applying it.

Chlorine (Cl) This nutrient is needed in small amounts, and its role is not fully known. Too much is toxic. Shortages are unlikely near the coast.

Cobalt (Co) Required for fixing nitrogen, cobalt is therefore particularly needed by leguminous species.

Copper (Cu) This is needed in respiration and for the usage of iron within the plant.

Iron (Fe) There is lots of iron in the soil; it just needs to be available to the plant at the 'right' pH. For example, if *Citrus* species are planted in more alkaline soils they are likely to suffer from pale chlorotic leaves. These plants are unable to take up enough available iron, and because iron is needed indirectly for photosynthesis, the leaves become pale and stunted. Foliar applications remedy this problem; if iron is added to the soil, it is likely to become unavailable again.

Manganese (Mn) Needed in certain enzyme reactions.

Molybdenum (Mb) Only needed in small amounts, though can be deficient in some soils. *Citrus* species can be susceptible to deficiencies. However, excess applications are a risk. Can be given through foliar applications but it is not as readily transported around the plant as iron.

Sodium (Na) This may help some plants develop greater drought tolerance.

Zinc (Zn) Needed by certain enzymes and growth hormones within the plant.

Fungal symbiosis: A few plants form symbiotic relationships with nitrogen-fixing bacteria; many others form them with fungi. These fungi, called **mycorrhiza**, spread their mycelium ('roots') extensively through the soil, and are able to take-up and contribute substantially more available nutrients (in particular phosphates) to the plant. In return, the fungi receives sugars from the plant. These relationships are of great importance to the survival of certain species, particularly those from colder regions with acidic soils, but do take time to develop. The addition of soil from around the roots of established plants can help to establish seedlings (e.g. macadamia, gevuina), as can the addition of organic matter (such as leaf mould) to adult plants.

Mixed plantings: It can be worth planting a mix of species together for a number of reasons. Deeper rooted plants can take up nutrients from deeper in the soil layer, particularly potassium, and recycle these to the surface layers through leaf fall. In addition, groupings of different species reduces pest problems (see later). Short-lived fruiting species can be planted amongst longer-lived trees as these develop, so making optimum use of space.

CONTAINER CULTURE

Many trees can be successfully grown in containers. If your garden is small, or even if there is just a deck or balcony, this cultivation method offers a way to create a small fruit and nut garden. Containers can be arranged in groups to give a satisfying display, or moved around to give different effects; you can create colour, scent, interest and food right outside the window. Potted plants have the big advantage of being easily protected from frost, wind or other adverse conditions. It may be the best way to grow subtropical species in colder areas.

A great variety of fruit and nut plants, including many climbers, can be grown in containers, e.g. strawberries, avocado, banana, blueberry, calamondin, Cape gooseberry, cherry, citrus, coffee, dwarf apples and pears, figs, grapes, guava, imbe, jaboticaba, kumquat, lemon, lillypillies, lime, miracle fruit, monstera, naranjilla, papaya, passion fruits, pineapple, pomegranate, tamarillo. In areas with particularly poor soils, large containers or raised beds could be a solution. Many factors, such as irrigation, weed control and pests, can be more easily controlled. Many of the species described in this book are suitable for growth in restricted areas.

CULTIVATION TIPS

Container size and colour: Pick as large a pot as is feasible for the size of the plant. (You can transplant into larger pots later, but this can often be quite an effort.) Large containers in light colours will help to keep the roots cooler: roots that get too hot in containers are a commonly overlooked problem. Black pots really heat up in the sun and metal pots can quickly roast. Think creatively; containers can come from many sources and be of many materials, e.g. wood or concrete, and a whole range of discarded objects can be used, e.g. old electrical appliances can be adapted and painted. Just ensure that there are adequate drainage holes at the bottom.

Pot filling: Place gravel and stones at the base of the pot to provide drainage. Fill with a good compost adjusted to the nutrient and pH conditions required by your plant. A mixture of one-part sand to one-part peat and one part bark, perlite or vermiculite can be used, or just select a good organic compost. It is much easier to modify the soil at this stage than later.

Planting and watering: When planting, make sure any grafts are not buried. If they are, this can rapidly cause disease problems. Covering the soil surface with a fibrous mulch helps retain moisture, which is one of the biggest problems with pot culture, and also stops the soil hardening. When watering and feeding, it is often difficult to ensure that the soil is evenly and thoroughly moist: mulch aids this. The soil surface can also be covered with ornamental materials such as bark, shells, small pebbles or gravel. Many container-grown plants suffer as much from over-watering as from under-watering. The frequency of watering will depend on the type of species, the season, humidity and temperature. Generally, for most species, the soil surface can be allowed to become dry before watering.

Plant health: As the plants develop, keep a check on their growth and foliage: pot-grown plants tend to need more regular applications of nutrients. Re-pot every couple of years depending on growth rate. Although adequate nutrients are important, excessive application can lead to salt build-up in the soil; for this reason, water-soluble fertilisers are a good idea. In general, if the leaves are a deep green colour, then the plants are OK. Fertilisers should be balanced and also contain micronutrients.

Pot location: Many fruit crops grow best in full sunlight, though some species are adapted to growth in partial shade (e.g. coffee, miracle fruit, naranjilla, currants, ceriman). Try to acclimatise plants to shade if taking them from a sunny location, and viceversa, and position plants away from cold draughts. For subtropical species, give protection if temperatures drop suddenly. This also applies to roots, which can be damaged by cold, particularly when grown in pots where there is a reduced mass of soil to buffer them. Acclimatisation to temperature is often more important than the temperature itself, with a sudden change in temperature often causing more damage.

Pruning: Generally, container-grown fruit trees need minimal pruning, just to control their size. Plants grown under low light conditions may become leggy and need cutting back to encourage bushiness. After a time, the top may outgrow the root volume and some leaf shed and twig dieback can occur. Fairly severe pruning can alleviate this problem. Some species (e.g. fig) can tolerate root pruning, which, consequently, reduces the size of the crown, and may mean that naturally larger plants can be grown for longer in containers. These species also often fruit more as a consequence.

Other points: Many fruit crops will produce fruits in containers, given time, good care and adequate size and age, but large fruit trees do need a large container to bear good crops as the amount of fruit produced is often proportional to the plant's size. Many fruit species need to be quite large before they fruit at all, and this can limit their utilisation as potential container species. Some consideration also needs to be given to access for pollinating insects. Hand-pollination is also an option.

PLANTING OUT AND ESTABLISHMENT

The health of a plant's roots is as important as that of the above-ground stem and leaves, perhaps even more so. When purchasing a pot-grown plant, check the roots are not bursting out of the bottom, or have been trimmed off at the base. Also, check for potential problems of disease or pests. Keep the roots of bare-rooted plants moist till they are placed in their permanent position. Bare-rooted, deciduous plants should only be planted when they are dormant. Evergreens, in general, should not be bare rooted; their rates of survival are often poor.

When planting out, don't space plants too close together. This is very tempting to do when planting-up an area with small, young plants. Overcrowding leads to competition for nutrients and water, and an increased likelihood of disease, particularly fungal attacks. It can also result in shading from nearby plants, which can further inhibit branching and leads to lopsided growth. This, as well as being aesthetically displeasing, can also make the plant more susceptible to wind damage. It can also make the fruiting wood difficult to access.

Rather than leaving large gaps between young trees, consider infilling with temporary annuals, biennials or short-lived perennials such as raspberry, most Solanaceae species, peanuts or melons. A leguminous species, such as licorice, will fix nitrogen; other species may encourage natural predators or pollinators.

Pot-grown plants can be planted out year round, but will need regular watering if planted in the drier months. Ideally, planting out should be done in late autumn, late winter or early spring. If the site is prone to waterlogging, wind damage or frost, then it is best to leave planting till early spring. Bare-rooted plants should definitely only be planted out when dormant, otherwise the stress involved in a plant trying to form a root system, as well as losing water through its actively growing leaves, will be too much. In addition, soak the roots for a few hours before planting.

When planting out, prepare a hole with the soil broken up below and to the sides to allow for root penetration. Generally, but not always (see notes on individual plant species), it is beneficial to dig in a small amount of slow-release granular fertiliser or well-rotted manure, below the root zone. Plants also benefit from organic compost being mixed with the soil. Keep roots moist during planting. It is useful to water the hole before planting, as well as after, to ensure the soil is moist at depth. Position the plant in the hole so that any grafts are not covered by soil. When filling the hole, ensure the soil has intimate contact with the roots, but is not compacted. Some plants, particularly many dormant, deciduous species, benefit from the roots being spread out; however, many others hate root disturbance, e.g. many evergreen species, gevuina, macadamia, avocado, which should have no root disturbance whatsoever. (See notes on individual species.)

If planting a tree, position a stake while filling the hole. Press firmly down on the soil once the hole is filled to remove air pockets. Attach the tree to the stake with a tie that will not cut into the bark and that can be easily removed later as the tree matures. Water plants well after planting. For the first year or two, all plants need regular watering during dry periods. Good deep soakings are more beneficial than shallow moistening of the soil, with the latter encouraging surface rooting, which makes plants more susceptible to water shortages as well as encouraging weed-seed germination. Getting water to deeper rooting regions results in much better overall growth.

The regular addition of nutrients is beneficial to some species (e.g. citrus and walnuts), particularly in sandy soils, but it is possible to add too much. Excess of any nutrient, particularly nitrogen, can result in lush vegetative growth, which can attract fungal and bacterial disease, and this is often at the expense of flower and fruit production. As a survival mechanism to reproduce, some species actually produce more flowers and fruits when somewhat nutrient hungry.

Once your trees are established and of a reasonable height, rather than using herbicides, consider allowing sheep, geese and chickens to cut the grass and reduce the number of insect pests. They are also less noisy, less work, and are more interesting to talk to (though, sheep will eat *anything* in reach, and, from personal experience, can strip a young citrus tree of all its leaves in less than 5 minutes). Geese can also double up as house guards.

PROPAGATION

Propagation is the process of increasing plant numbers. Below is an outline of the methods that can be used. (For more detailed examples and descriptions, the reader is referred to the Bibliography.)

PLANTS FROM SEED

This is often the easiest method to 'create' new plants, particularly in large numbers, but the main drawback is that such plants take considerably longer to produce their first crop, and the progeny are much more variable and unpredictable than those produced by vegetative methods. However, seeds can often be the only material to propagate from. Germination conditions vary with seed species, but the following information should be considered.

Freshness: In general, seeds are best sown when fresh, soon after their removal from fully ripened fruits. Germination inhibitors are often present in the surrounding flesh, and this should be thoroughly removed. It can be tricky to separate small seed from pulp (e.g. passion fruits, tamarillo), though a short period (2–3 days) of fermentation of the pulp with warmth can make this easier. A few species of seeds actually germinate better after storage, but this is unusual. Usually, stored seeds tend to lose their viability and take longer to germinate. If seeds have to be stored, they are best kept slightly moist, cool (~5°C), in the dark and in a sealed container.

Storage: Stored seeds often need some prior treatment before they will germinate. Some species simply need soaking in warm water for a short period (~24 hours) before sowing. Do not soak seeds for too long, or they can become denatured. Seeds from plants derived from colder climates usually need a period of **cold stratification**, to mimic winter, before they will germinate. The period of time and temperature required varies with species, but is usually 2–3 months at ~4–6°C. Temperatures should not be colder than this. The seeds also need to be kept moist during this period. They can be kept in a refrigerator, but not the freezer. Another problem during germination is a hard seedcoat or stone (endocarp or pericarp), which has evolved to allow seeds to pass through the gut of an animal without being digested, or to resist being bitten or pecked open. In some larger seeds, it is beneficial to carefully crack or cut open the hard outer covering to expose the inner kernel. In smaller seeds this is not practical, and seeds can be **scarified**, which means chipping or scoring the seedcoat to allow moisture and oxygen to reach the kernel. Some seeds need a mix of all these treatments, plus a period of warmth

(~15–20°C for ~1–2 months) before cold stratification. The requirements of different species are in the main text.

Seedcoat softening: Apart from being scarified (see above), seeds can be soaked and softened in weak acid or bleach for ~20 minutes. They should be thoroughly washed afterwards to remove any residues before sowing in compost. Household bleach diluted to 10% can be used, with caution. This also sterilises the seed and kills any fungal disease. You can also soak seeds in grain alcohol, e.g. vodka, which partially dissolves hard waxes in the seedcoat.

Hormones: The use of plant 'hormones' such as ethylene, gibberelin and cytokinin can break the dormancy of many seeds and initiate the start of biochemical reactions. They are often more effective if used together. (See Plant hormones section below.)

Depth: The depth that seeds should be buried is, in general, proportional to seed size, i.e. smaller seeds are sown closer to the soil surface. However, large stones, e.g. avocado, mango, often need to be only partially buried to germinate well. Seed sown too deep may not have the reserves for its first photosynthesising leaves to reach the soil surface.

Temperature: Seeds generally have an optimum temperature for germination, with many subtropical species needing warm temperatures of ~25°C to germinate. All seeds need some warmth to germinate.

Willow washings: The bark or stems of the willow, if crushed and soaked in water, produce a liquid that acts in a similar way to various plant hormones. Seeds soaked in this extract for ~24 hours may germinate quicker and at a higher rate.

SEEDLINGS

Once seeds have germinated, they should not be given too much moisture as they can be killed by **damping off**, a fungal disease that leads to the stem of the seedling rotting through. Once they are large enough, seedlings can be gently pricked out into individual pots to grow on until of suitable size to plant out. The time this takes varies with species. Select a soil type suitable for the species, e.g. peaty soil for acid-loving plants, sandy, gritty soil for succulents. Young seedlings appreciate some shade, and acclimatisation to sun or cold prior to planting out improves their survival chances.

PLANT HORMONES

Plant hormones are not true hormones in an animal sense, e.g. adrenaline, but are a group of chemicals that have varying mobility around the plant and can powerfully induce effects such as increasing growth, flowering and fruit production, preventing and inducing senescence, and ripening. They are often used horticulturally to control various aspects of plant growth, and are briefly listed and described below.

There are a number of other hormones and much work is being done in this area to determine how plants respond to their environment. This is still a relatively unexplored field, but is full of interesting theories such as the response of plants to stress, e.g. predation, and how they are able to communicate with each other, which scientifically, many have been proven to do.

Auxin (IAA [indole acetic acid]): One of the best-known plant hormones, auxin's main mode of action is to retain apical dominance and ensure that the main leader or stem grows taller and preferentially to lateral branches. (See the Pruning section on p. 32.) It also initiates the production of roots, as well as stimulating cell enlargement in regions undergoing active cell division (stem and root tips), but also inhibits growth in other regions (lateral buds), depending on its concentration.

Gibberelin: This hormone can increase internode length, and, therefore, makes plants taller. It is particularly active in plants kept in shaded locations, where they become spindly and tall in an effort to reach any light. Horticulturally, it is used to increase the height of plants, but, more importantly, it also initiates flowering, and can also reduce the time until trees start producing fruits, which can be a long time for some species, i.e. more than 10 years. It also initiates enzymatic reactions within seeds to break their dormancy. Seeds can be soaked in gibberelin at 100–1000 ppm for ~24 hours. Gibberelin can travel freely around the plant, unlike most other hormones.

Cytokinin: This hormone can stimulate cell division, bud and flower formation, as well as germination. It is often used on pineapples to stimulate flowering. It can also 'break' apical dominance. It is not very mobile within plants. Horticulturally, cytokinin is difficult to purchase. If used, it needs to be kept cool to prevent its rapid deterioration.

Ethylene: This gas occurs naturally in the leaves and fruits of many plants and initiates senescence of leaves and ripening of fruits. It is often referred to as a way to ripen fruits that have been harvested when they are under-ripe. Certain ripe fruits produce lots of ethylene gas, which affects the fruits around them and hastens their ripening; e.g. ripe bananas increase ripening of other fruits around them. Ethylene also stimulates seed germination.

Abscisic acid: As its name suggests, this compound initiates the abscission of leaves, but also helps to induce and retain dormancy. It is probably involved in the chilling response that enables plants to retain dormancy during winter. It is also involved in stomatal closure during times of stress.

VEGETATIVE PROPAGATION

The main methods of vegetative propagation are described below. Vegetative propagation has the advantages of giving predictable offspring and plants fruit sooner. Fruit quality is also predictable. However, there are no new beneficial characteristics added to plants, and the risk of disease (e.g. viral, bacterial, fungal) is much greater when these methods are used.

Cuttings: This is often a quick, easy and inexpensive method to obtain new plants. Many species can be easily propagated by cuttings, which can be taken from stems, roots, rhizomes, leaves or buds. They should be removed with a clean knife or secateurs. Dipping the base of the cutting in **rooting hormone** can be beneficial. Rooting hormone usually contains IAA (see Auxin above). Cuttings can also be dipped in a liquid in which crushed willow-stems have been soaked for ~24 hours, and this works in similar way. (See p. 28.) Cuttings can also be watered with this liquid.

Most succulent species root better if the stem/leaf cutting is allowed to callus over for a few days before inserting in well-drained compost. If the cutting is inserted while the cut surface is still moist, rooting is slower and reduced. Cuttings root best when placed in compost that is a mix of coarse particles and a moisture-retentive component, such as organic matter or vermiculite, so that it is moist, but well drained. The grittiness of the medium initiates greater rooting. Cuttings establish better if given some shade initially, some warmth and, if possible, mist to reduce transpirational loss through leaves while they are rooting. For the same reason, cuttings root better if most of their leaves are removed, except for a few that are young and actively growing. This prevents the cutting from struggling to uptake adequate water to supply the leaves.

Once cuttings have rooted, they can be transplanted into individual pots and grown on in moist, warm (but not too hot), semi-shaded locations until well established. The types of cuttings that can be taken include:

Bud and eye cuttings: A cutting is taken from semi-ripe wood (this season's), and includes a leaf and a bud (Fig. 12). The cutting is laid into compost with the bud just above soil level. This method is commonly used for ornamental species. Eye cuttings can also be taken from vines, by removing a length of stem, with a bud, during winter. The bark is peeled off from the opposite side of the bud, and the cutting is placed on its side in gritty compost with the bud above soil level. Keep the soil warm and moist.

Leaf cuttings: Used mostly for houseplants and more delicate ornamentals. A leaf is pinned onto compost to encourage roots to grow from the leaf axil, or cuts are made across the leaf veins to encourage rooting from these. The leaf needs to be kept in high humidity and warmth.

Root cuttings: These are taken in the dormant season. Pieces of fleshy root, rhizome or stolons are removed by cutting off lengths from the root with the cut nearer the stem being right angled and the outer end at a slant. Select material that has several healthy buds, which will later form shoots. Rooting material without buds is generally unlikely to grow. The root cutting is planted with the angled cut facing downwards, and the right-angled cut buried just below the soil surface. These cuttings do not need heat and should have rooted by the following spring.

Softwood cuttings: These cuttings are taken from young fresh growth in spring and early summer, and are cut to just below a node. The lower leaves are removed and the cuttings are placed in coarse growth media with warmth and high humidity. Place either under mist or they can be covered with polythene. The young growth easily desiccates so moisture is important, but check regularly for fungal infections.

Semi-ripe cuttings: These are taken in mid–late summer from lateral shoots from the present season's growth (Fig. 12). They are best cut just below a node or, alternatively, some species root better if a heel of tissue from the node is included. Either way, the tissue around the node will have more active cells to produce new roots and shoots. Remove the lower leaves and place in gritty compost in semi-shade. Many species can be propagated by this method.

Hardwood cuttings: Taken at the end of the season, i.e. in late autumn, from that season's stem growth, just below a node. Remove lower leaves and place outside in a sheltered, cool location till spring. Hardwood cuttings do not need heat or extra water; in fact they need some cold to root and grow. Although some moisture is helpful during winter, care needs to be taken that disease, particularly fungal, does not develop because of the soil being too wet. Horticulturists often prepare a trench containing some coarse sand for the cuttings. The following year, after they have some new growth, they may be moved to their final position. Many trees and soft-fruit bushes are propagated by this method.

Suckers: A sucker is a type of root cutting made from stolons or rhizomes which have produced stems. These can be removed in early spring or in autumn, with some root if possible, planted and supplied with regular moisture until established. It can be desirable to reduce the height of the shoot to allow preferential root development. These often take well. Several fruiting species sucker freely. Any root disturbance tends to encourage more suckers. In addition, young shoots that have formed at the base of trunks at, or below, ground level can be removed and generally root easily.

Division: This method involves dividing up the plant itself in the dormant season. It is used widely for herbaceous, deciduous plants and some of the fruit species described in this book, e.g. raspberries, rhubarb. The plant to be divided needs to be established and is usually 3–4 years old, probably no older or the roots will be unsuitable. Carefully divide plants into sections, each of which should have some roots, and establish these plantlets in well-drained compost before planting out, though some species can be planted directly into their final positions. It is often advisable to reduce stem length by half, while retaining several healthy buds, to preferentially encourage root growth during the first season. Do not allow these plants to flower or fruit in their first year, to conserve metabolic energy.

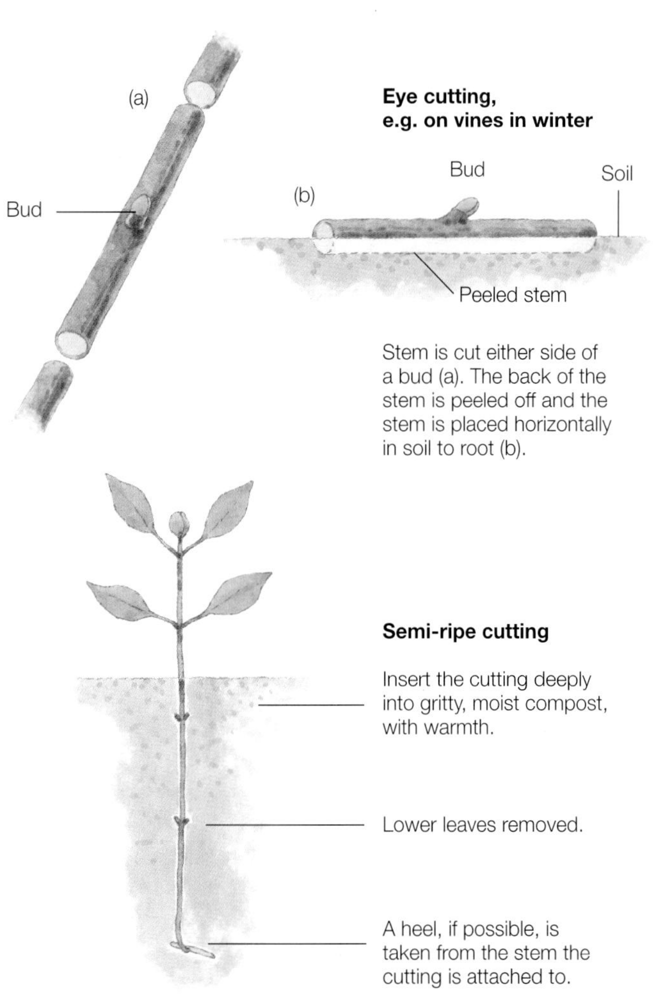

LAYERING

Some plants naturally form roots from stems that touch the ground, e.g. strawberries, blackberries. This **ground layering** process can be encouraged by pinning shoots or burying tips in the ground (Fig. 13). In addition, rooting can be further encouraged by lightly wounding small areas of the stem. These areas are then pegged onto the soil, and respond by producing roots. Autumn is often a good time to do this. The time taken to root depends on species, though new plantlets often take 12–18 months before they can be removed and grown on elsewhere.

Air layering (or marcotting) is another method often practised by horticulturists, and frequently used on fruit crops. It can be used if a branch is too far above the ground, or too stiff, for ground layering and is best done in spring, as active growth commences. Make a cut upwards to partially split a stem from just below a node or leaf stalk and treat the cut with rooting hormone. Keep the cut open with a twist of moss or pack further wet moss around the cut. Wrap the area in polythene and seal above and below with tape. The area treated should form roots in ~2–3 months. The new plantlet can then be cut from the parent and the polythene removed. Establish it in moist compost.

Another air-layering method is to constrict the cambium layer of a branch by girdling or lightly cutting around its circumference (but not completely). The cut is allowed to callus or heal over for 1–2 days, and is then packed with moss and soil, wrapped in plastic or foil, though allowing the exchange of air, and is tightly secured above and below. Once sufficient roots are formed, the new plantlet can be detached from the parent, and is further established in moist compost. It is best to select branches that are ~1.75 cm wide, and that receive lots of sunlight. A disadvantage of air-layering is that resultant plants often have weaker root systems.

GRAFTING

Grafting and budding techniques tend to be trickier and more specialised than other methods. There are many detailed texts on specific techniques for different species and only the concept is outlined here, with possible methods listed in the main text. Grafting is the method of creating a union between a **rootstock** and a **scion**. The rootstock has to be compatible with the plant it is to support. This means that, usually, it has to be in the same genera. The rootstock is usually disease resistant, has vigorous growth and is often the wild type or species. It is often selected for its ability to withstand drought, waterlogging, cold, disease, etc. It

---

Fig. 12. Types of cuttings

(a)

Bud

Eye cutting, e.g. on vines in winter

(b)

Bud

Soil

Peeled stem

Stem is cut either side of a bud (a). The back of the stem is peeled off and the stem is placed horizontally in soil to root (b).

Semi-ripe cutting

Insert the cutting deeply into gritty, moist compost, with warmth.

Lower leaves removed.

A heel, if possible, is taken from the stem the cutting is attached to.

provides the root structure, base and stem of the plant. A healthy strong root base can improve the overall quality of the plant. The scion is a piece of stem (~10 cm long) or bud from the previous season's growth, from a plant that will give the fruit qualities required. It is usually taken from a selected cultivar whose particular characteristics can be preserved and enhanced by growing onto a tougher rootstock. Usually, in most grafting methods, the scions are cut from healthy material during the winter. The cut stems are planted in a cool, protected area till used for grafting in the spring.

Many fruit and nut species take many years to start producing fruits; grafting can reduce this waiting time significantly. It is commonly used on a number of fruit and nut species, e.g. apples.

The grafting process can be described as follows. The physiology of a plant stem determines how and if grafting can 'work' to bind two regions of actively dividing cells together as one. In dicots (not conifers or monocots), the stem of the plant usually consists of a central region of older, inactive **xylem** vessels, surrounded by a thin layer of current xylem vessels that carry water and nutrients up from the roots. This is bordered by a thin cambium layer and an outer phloem layer. (See the dicot stem in Fig. 2 on p. 13.) The **phloem** is a thin layer of conducting tissue that carries sugars made in the leaves to other parts of the plant; it occurs just below the protective layer of outer cortex and bark. Between the xylem and phloem is a thin **cambium** layer. This active area of cell division produces new xylem cells to the inside and new phloem cells on the outside. Because it is an area of actively dividing cells, grafting works by connecting and binding these tissues from different plants together to fuse as one.

There are many grafting methods, and a few of these are briefly described below.

Budding: A sliver of bark, with a well-developed bud, is taken from the chosen species and grafted onto a rootstock (Fig. 14a). Trees to be budded are cut back during the dormant season, leaving several of the branches intact to insure good growth until the new buds are established. It is best carried out from early to mid summer when there is active growth. The bud is inserted into a T-shaped incision made in the bark of the rootstock and is bound on firmly with raffia. The position where it is inserted will depend on what shape and form the grower wants the final tree or shrub to be. Although there may be a union within four weeks, it is best to wait till the following spring by which time the bud should have sprouted, and the stem of the rootstock above can then be removed.

Cleft and crown grafting: These methods are used mostly to rejuvenate older trees. Late winter is often the best time of year for this type of graft. For **cleft grafts**, a fairly large limb is cut on the older tree and a split is made down into the stem where two scions are inserted, one on either side of the split and in contact with the cambium, where they will form two new shoots. They are bound in place with raffia, the slit is filled with clay and the whole is sealed with grafting wax or wrapped in plastic. **Crown grafts** are similar, but several scions with cut slanting ends are inserted down under the bark ensuring they are touching the cambium (Fig. 14a). The scions give the impression of a crown. The wounds are bound and waxed. In spring there may be numerous shoots

Fig. 13. Diagram showing layering methods

Stem layering

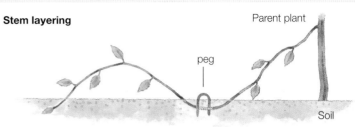

Tips can be simply buried to root, e.g. blackberry.

Small areas of stem can be lightly scored or injured; and then these areas are lightly buried and pegged down to root.

Air layering

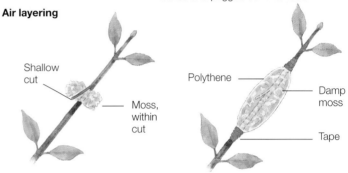

A section of stem, still on the plant, is stripped of leaves and a cut is made lightly up the stem. This is packed with damp moss. The whole is then bound in damp moss and wrapped within polythene, sealed, and allowed to form roots.

Fig. 14a. Types of budding and grafting

T-Budding (Shield)

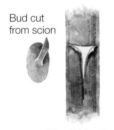

'T' cut into stem of root stock

Bud inserted into 'T' cut

Stem bound with raffia until the bud has sprouted

Whip-and-tounge grafting

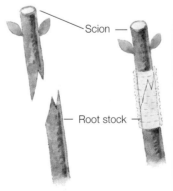

Scions and rootstocks need to be of similar diameter. Long matching cuts are made in each, with the two then 'slotted' together and bound in raffia, until a union is formed.

Crown grafting

Used with thin-diameter scions and thicker rootstocks.

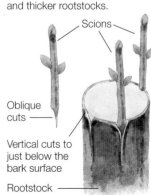

Scions are inserted into the rootstock. The whole is covered with grafting wax.

growing from the rootstock and these need to be removed, leaving only the scions. Most trees should be well developed by autumn.

Framework grafting: There are various methods of grafting where scions can be inserted into various parts of a plant to add a different branch type; this is generally used more for ornamental plants and isn't discussed further here.

Inarching or approach grafting: This method uses intact rootstock and scion plants (Fig. 14b). The two are grown in pots and placed next to each other. A sliver of bark is removed from the stem of each plant at the same height in spring. The exposed tissue is then bound together with raffia so that the cambium layers are touching. The union is covered with grafting wax to keep the tissues moist and deter the entry of disease. After a couple of months, a union should be formed, and the top of the rootstock can be removed along with the base of the scion to leave the grafted plant. This type of grafting is often practised on vines.

Whip-and-tongue grafting: This is a fairly simple graft where two equal-sized stems are joined together (Fig. 14a). A very common method for grafting fruit trees. The rootstock is cut from just below ground to ~20 cm above ground level, and a scion of similar width is also prepared. Slanting cuts are made on each, with an inner cut on each that forms the tongue. These can then be slotted together, bound with raffia and waxed.

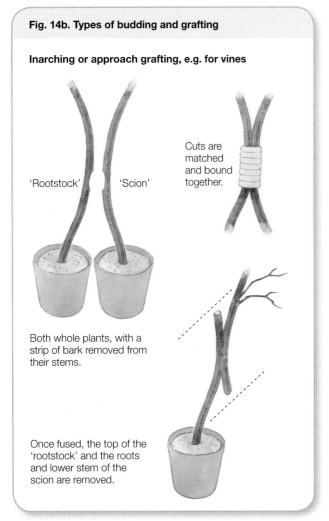

Fig. 14b. Types of budding and grafting

Inarching or approach grafting, e.g. for vines

'Rootstock'   'Scion'

Cuts are matched and bound together.

Both whole plants, with a strip of bark removed from their stems.

Once fused, the top of the 'rootstock' and the roots and lower stem of the scion are removed.

VARIATIONS IN YIELD: BIENNIAL (ALTERNATE) BEARING

This can be common in many fruit and nut species, e.g. pistachio, beech and citrus. The plant produces a bumper crop one year, but then meagre crops for at least the following year or more. The reasons for this are probably a combination of factors to do with nutrient and water availability, growth rate, fruit yield and genetics. Because the plant produces lots of flowers and fruit one year, it is thought that 'hormones' produced from the developing fruits/nuts diffuse back into the stems and inhibit flower-bud formation the following year. Alternatively, because the plant's carbohydrate and nutrient resources are used up in a bumper year, it needs to 'rest' and put its efforts into vegetative growth rather than fruit production until it has recovered. It is likely that the reason is a mix of these.

The main solution is to remove or **thin** some of the young fruit just after they have formed in bumper years to even out yields; this usually seems to work and also increases the size of the fruits left to mature and improves the overall quality of the crop. Pruning at the end of the season after a bumper year can have the opposite effect: it can increase vegetative growth even further the following year, and set the plant back further. Therefore, if pruning has to be carried out, it is better done either after a light crop or before an expected heavy crop to balance out the carbohydrate balance of the tree.

Large crops of small fruits are fine if a large crop of not perfect-quality fruits is required, e.g. table grapes; alternatively, a crop of fewer fruits, but of higher quality, may be sought, e.g. grapes for wine.

Many larger forest trees (e.g. beech, oak, chestnut, bunya-bunya) often tend to have a cycle of seed production, bearing a moderate or small crop for several years, but then, every 2–5 years, producing a bumper crop (mast crop). Pruning or fruit thinning of these species is only partially helpful or practical, and the erratic cropping cycle needs to be just accepted as a feature of the species.

PRUNING AND TRAINING

Why prune? The main objectives of pruning are as follows:
To develop the shape and form of young trees, to ensure there is enough, but not too much, branching, and that branches are strong enough to support a heavy harvest. Many growers recommend that trees should be pruned when first planted; this is particularly important if they are planted bare-rooted. These plants usually have damaged root systems and need a lesser shoot-to-root ratio in order for the roots to recover and establish. The main stem can be cut back by about a third to a healthy bud, as can the lateral branches. This helps the tree get off to a better start. It is preferable to direct tree growth with training when young than to have to correct it later with pruning. Pruning is less necessary with container-grown plants.
To encourage the growth of new fruiting wood. The removal of stem tips initiates the growth of lateral fruiting branches, as well as reducing the length of long stems, which can become susceptible to breakage from the weight of fruits; the fruits are also kept within practical reach (see Heading cut, below).

To allow light and air to enter the centre of the tree by removal of dense or crossing branches. Light is important for flower-bud development, fruit-set and fruit ripening. Air circulation reduces the risk of many diseases, particularly fungal infections.

To reduce the spread of disease to other parts of the tree by the removal of diseased branches. Pruned material should be burnt and destroyed rather than left near the tree. Diseases are often spread by wind or moisture, and thrive in humid weather. Many systemic fungal and bacterial diseases kill the wood within stems, and cut branches often display a range of unhealthy colours within the heart wood and outer vascular system. Pruning should ensure that wood is removed beyond this discoloration.

To control the tree's height and spread. To obtain optimum fruit production it is often beneficial to prune to reduce vegetative growth, while encouraging the growth of fruiting wood. This also makes fruit harvesting easier.

To thin out the fruit. Removal of very young fruits, just after fruit-set is beneficial, in seasons that have bumper crops. This evens out the yields in following years, as the tree would normally 'rest' after producing a huge crop. Removal of excess fruits also increases the size of those fruits remaining and improves their quality. Some fruit species are much more susceptible to overbearing than others.

Moderate annual pruning is far better for the tree than irregular severe pruning. It is also worth noting that pruning is not beneficial to all species, particularly some evergreens, and can even reduce yield and productivity. (See the notes on individual species.)

HOW TO PRUNE

Make sure secateurs are sharp and clean. Make cuts just above each bud, and try to make the cuts slope away from the bud for water run-off and to encourage the wood to heal quickly. A stub or an uneven cut will delay wound healing and increase the probability of infection. When removing dead or diseased wood, always cut through healthy tissue below the diseased section and, if possible, make cuts flush with the limbs to which the unwanted branches are attached. Paint large wounds with a sealing compound to protect against disease, otherwise let the wound heal naturally. Peach trees are an exception to making clean cuts; with these, if a ridge of bark is left at the base of the cut, then the wood from larger limbs heals more rapidly.

TYPES OF CUT

Heading cut: This takes off only the end of young shoots, to remove the **apical dominance** of the main shoot (**leader**), and promote the growth of side (**lateral**) branches below, as well as strengthening the branch. The plant hormone auxin promotes the growth of the main shoot and enhances apical dominance, while inhibiting the growth of laterals. If the stem tip is taken off, this hormonal action is removed, and the growth of dormant lateral buds, with more fruiting buds, immediately below the cut stem is initiated. Some species (e.g. poplar, maple, birch, bunya-bunya) have stronger apical dominance than others (e.g. olive, feijoa, citrus, tropical guava), with the latter developing a crown with many branches and no main stem. Removal of the shoot tips of species with weak apical dominance does not

greatly affect the shape of the future plant, but does result in a more densely branched one. Removal of shoot tips from species with strong apical dominance does greatly affect the future shape and form of the tree, so needs to be considered aesthetically for more ornamental species. If a longer length of stem, which includes wood older than 1 year old, is removed, then the release of apical dominance is less and has a lesser effect on lateral-stem initiation.

Thinning cut: This removes an entire shoot back to a side shoot, and does not encourage the growth of side shoots as a heading cut does. It is more useful for removing vegetative growth. This cut can remove vigorous, upright shoots and results in opening up the centre of a tree and encourages the remaining branches to grow outwards to allow more light into the centre. However, this cut removes more wood and should be done with care. Increased vegetative growth, in response to pruning, is greatest when the largest limbs are removed. Such pruning may lead to a reduction in yield the first year, and then a slow yield recovery in subsequent years, although this varies with health and age of the tree. It encourages longer growth of the remaining terminals and can result in a larger, more open tree.

WHEN TO PRUNE

Trees respond very differently to winter and summer pruning. One of the first factors to consider is if pruning is needed to restrict vegetative and root growth, or to encourage it.

Spring/summer: Pruning in summer removes the active energy or food-producing parts of the tree and so does not encourage new growth. It is particularly useful for cordons and espaliers. Summer pruning, therefore, is most beneficial when very little vegetative growth is wanted. It can be carried out in spring or, more usually, in early summer. It is done to reduce vigorous growth and unwanted side shoots, but,

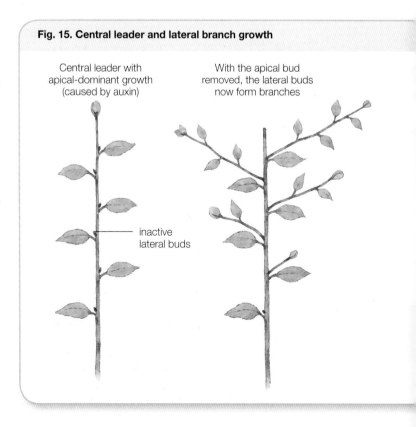

Fig. 15. Central leader and lateral branch growth

Central leader with apical-dominant growth (caused by auxin)

With the apical bud removed, the lateral buds now form branches

inactive lateral buds

because it removes the energy-producing leaves, it will also result in reduced root growth, and can affect fruit production. In addition, removal of large branches can increase the risk of disease, particularly in certain species, such as peach and nectarine, due to the entry of fungal and bacterial disease. The other main factor is that developing fruits are also likely to be removed.

Late summer: Pruning at this time has little or no effect on stimulating new vegetative growth, but it is not as dwarfing as early-summer pruning. In addition, because it reduces vegetative growth, it can make more sugars available to the developing fruits (resulting in improved flavour), although fruit size may be reduced. The root system is only slightly affected. In warmer areas, it can be done to reduce the height and width of trees.

Winter: This is the season when most main pruning is done, when trees are dormant; however, it does encourage new growth the following spring. This is because, in temperate, deciduous plants, the energy from the last year's growth is stored within the stems and roots for spring growth. If heavy pruning is done during winter, the tree's energy reserve is unchanged. In spring, because there is now more storage for the reduced volume of tree, there is vigorous new growth, often as side shoots and suckers, which can be at the expense of flower and fruit production. This is usually undesirable for fruit and ornamental trees. In addition, in colder areas, any pruning should be carried out in late winter or early spring to avoid frost damage to newly cut branches. Younger trees are more susceptible to frost damage, so prune last, just before spring. Winter pruning is done to remove dead, diseased and damaged wood, upright growing shoots and to control the length of lateral branches. Note that stone fruits, such as cherries and plums, can 'bleed' a lot if pruned during winter–spring, and these are better pruned when in leaf, when their cuts heal quickly.

AGE OF FRUITING WOOD

Deciduous trees can produce their flower buds on the current year's wood, on the previous summer's wood (this is common, e.g. peaches), on 1- and 2-year-old wood, or even older wood, e.g. almond. In addition, many fruiting species, e.g. the *Malus* genus, produce fruits for 2–4 years on **fruiting spurs**. These are short, stubby, lateral branches, and species tend to either produce fruits on stem tips or be spur-producing. The positioning of future flower buds needs to be considered when pruning to avoid cutting off next year's potential crop. For fruits produced on young wood, removal of leader tips produces more lateral growth and, consequently, more fruits, but these trees also need to be thinned from time to time to remove excess branching. A balance needs to be achieved between the two. For fruits produced on older wood, most wood older that 4 years is removed to encourage new growth.

Limbs and spurs: Pears and cherries produce most of their fruits on stubby spurs; different apple cultivars produce fruits on either spurs or tips. Spur-type trees produce less limb growth and so require less pruning, though older spurs need to be thinned periodically, and this is best done in autumn. A spur will produce fruits for 2–4 years, after which it should be removed to encourage new, more vigorous

spurs. If a tree forms spurs, laterals can be removed in early spring to encourage development of the flowers and fruit on its spurs.

BRANCH ANGLE

The angle of the lateral branches is of considerable importance in fruiting trees. Different plant species have their own natural branching angles: this gives them their own natural silhouette shape and form. Some plants have very set angles of branching, and little selection is needed (e.g. ginkgo), others (e.g. apple) form a range of branching angles.

Narrow-angled branches (<35°) often have more vigorous growth, but tend to be weak at the point of attachment and often break under a heavy fruit load. Narrow angles are often further weakened by water, ice and fungal pathogens, so it is usually better to remove these branches. Ideally, the fruiting branches should form a 60–70° angle between main stem (leader) and the side shoot. These tend to have a slower growth rate, increased flowering and form more side shoots than vertical shoots, possibly because of a change in the distribution of growth substances and carbohydrates. Therefore, for fruit and nut production, horizontal branches give better results. However, branches that are nearer to 90° may flower and fruit more, but are at more risk of breakage, particularly when loaded with fruits.

To achieve horizontal branches in species that tend to grow naturally upright, e.g. plums, some growers tie on weights or peg down branches temporarily. Alternatively, the natural weight of a crop can help to pull branches downwards and has a similar effect.

STYLES OF TRAINING

Trees can be trained and pruned in many ways, and the method chosen depends on the tree species, the size available for it, harvestability, ornamental considerations, shade, etc.

Central leader: Trees that bear large crops of heavy fruit should be pruned to form a central leader. This encourages the growth of strong side branches from one main trunk: the leader. In the first year, three or four branches are selected that are uniformly spaced around the trunk and not directly across from one another. Above this first whorl, leave an area of between 0.5 and 1 m (depending on species) without branches to allow light and air into the centre of the tree. This area is followed by another whorl of three to four branches. This alternates up the trunk. During this time, other competing central leaders are removed. The central leader can be removed once the desired maximum height of the tree has been reached; this then also stimulates the growth of side shoots. Secondary branches that grow from lateral branches may also need to be thinned. The tree takes on a pyramid shape with one central leader and tiers of fruiting branches. In order to maintain this shape as the tree gets older, lateral branches need to be cut back into 2-year-old wood to a side-growing shoot. If possible, cut back to a side shoot that is nearly the same diameter as the lateral being cut.

Mature trees that have been regularly and properly trained will need little pruning as they get older: just the removal of dead, diseased, crossing and damaged wood, and shoots that are either too upright or those below the horizontal.

Unpruned or neglected trees often have sprawling crowns that can shade out lower branches. These upper branches do need to be removed to get good fruiting, but not more that 30% should be removed at any one time or there will be too much vegetative growth with little fruit development.

Cordons: A cordon is a single, supported straight stem with short fruiting spurs that is trained to receive most of the plant's vigour and light. They are often apple or pear trees. For the first 3 years, until fruiting begins, the tree is shaped by forming a central stem and shortening new laterals to three leaves beyond their basal cluster of leaves. Any shoots that grow from these laterals should be cut back to one leaf. Once the leader has reached the required height, its new annual growth is pruned to ~3 cm long and the laterals are pruned as before. These trees are best pruned in summer, except when spurs age and become crowded, at which point they should be thinned out during winter.

Espalier and fans: These are pruned in the same way as cordons, but each branch is treated as a separate cordon. This is a less common method, is more labour intensive and needs regular maintenance, but is becoming more popular for smaller gardens. It is a great method for growing trees near warm, sun-facing walls and structures. The trees are compact and produce good crops. Some people also find the style decorative. The tree is trained with either horizontal branches (e.g. apples and pears) or into a fan shape (stonefruit) on wires or fences. For fan-trained trees, in spring, pinch out buds that point either towards or away from the wall, leaving just those that grow outwards. Pinch these side shoots out in summer to ~15 cm long and then shorten them to three leaves after harvest.

Modified leader: This pruning style begins in the same way as the central leader method, with one main stem. However, in the first and second year, several other competing leaders, rather than being removed, should be left and maintained in the same way as a single leader. This modified leader style is often easier to prune because most fruit trees tend to grow in this way naturally. It is ideal for varieties, such as pear, that are susceptible to fireblight and, if one leader becomes infected, it can be removed but will still leave other main branches.

Open centre or vase shape: A traditional system that has four to five leaders growing from an open centre where the main leader has been modified. This method allows lots of light into the tree and is suited to many high-vigour fruiting species, such as plums, cherries, peaches, and for other fruiting species that naturally have weak apical dominance and form a bushy crown. However, the side branches produced can be weaker and this method is not suited to such species as apples and pears. It is done by selecting four to five uniformly spaced branches around the tree, with wide branch angles and not directly across from another lateral branch. These branches are known as **scaffolds**. The scaffold branches should be pruned to outward-growing buds during the dormant season for the first 3 years to promote lateral branching and to stiffen and strengthen the main branches. All other leaders should be removed, particularly those growing from the central area because they shade and inhibit the growth of fruiting laterals growing from the scaffold branches. It is advisable to encourage fruiting laterals nearer to the central stem; the weight of laterals that

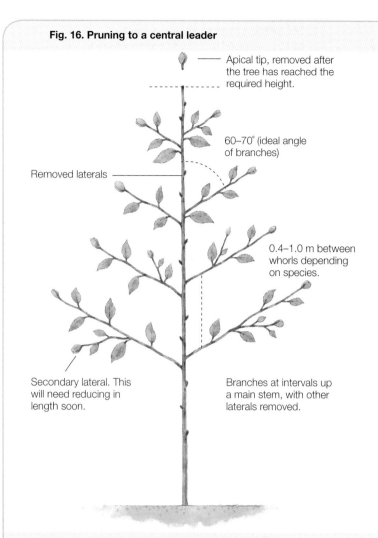

Fig. 16. Pruning to a central leader

Apical tip, removed after the tree has reached the required height.

60–70° (ideal angle of branches)

Removed laterals

0.4–1.0 m between whorls depending on species.

Secondary lateral. This will need reducing in length soon.

Branches at intervals up a main stem, with other laterals removed.

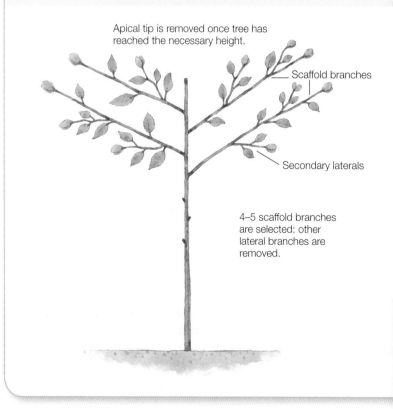

Fig. 17. Pruning to a modified leader

Apical tip is removed once tree has reached the necessary height.

Scaffold branches

Secondary laterals

4–5 scaffold branches are selected: other lateral branches are removed.

form towards the ends of scaffold branches can over-stress the scaffolds.

Girdling: This is a technique mostly used on peaches and nectarines. It can seriously weaken, damage or even kill many other fruiting species, and needs to be undertaken with caution. The bark of larger stems is cut through to the tissue below, often without removing any bark, or a stem is constricted with an inelastic band. This practice enhances yields and fruit size, concentrates the harvesting period and encourages fruits to ripen earlier. This method has been practised worldwide for centuries. Girdling of peach trees does not seem to have a detrimental, though they should be at least 3–4 years old. Any girdling needs to be done with care. The theory behind this method is that the stressed branch reacts by producing earlier and better quality flowers and fruits as a defensive system.

Girdling is carried out about a week after any fruit thinning, or soon after fruit-set, and affects subsequent fruit development. Ensure that the branch is not completely ringed, or this will kill it. Leave a region uncut to ensure nutrients can still reach the branches. Cuts should not be more than 0.3 cm deep.

DEALING WITH PESTS AND DISEASES

It is not intended here to give detailed information about different pest and disease problems or how to chemically treat them. Although some problems are inevitable, their risk and spread can often be reduced by improved cultivation techniques and by adjusting spacing between plants. A healthy, not over-fertilised plant is much less likely to succumb. In addition, a mix of species can diffuse any potential difficulties more than a large monoculture, where any problem can rapidly reach epidemic proportions.

Healthy living: Picking healthy plants from the nursery is an obvious first priority, making sure the roots are not confined and that the leaves look green and are not diseased. Prepare the planting area carefully to ensure the plant has a good start. Try and match the pH of the soil with the plant's needs. Bear in mind that most fruit and nut species do not last long in waterlogged soil: wet soils and humid environments invite many fungal and bacterial problems, including some serious root rots. A weak or struggling plant is much more likely to succumb to other disease problems. Try and match the type of location with the plant; a tree that thrives in full sun will struggle in a shaded site. Remove any diseased branches and burn them if possible. Prune with clean tools and make clean cuts that shed water easily.

Healthy spacing: When planting a small seedling, the area of its eventual spread is often difficult to grasp. Overcrowding means competition between plants, less air circulation, less nutrients and less sun, and all these factors can induce disease. In addition, many species do not grow properly if their branches touch, and they develop lopsided structures. Either try to resist spacing plants too close together or, for slow-growing species, plant trees closer and then thin out some as they get larger. Alternatively interplant them with shorter-lived species.

Healthy nutrients: The addition of extra nutrients, either as fertiliser or as natural organic supplements, increases fruit yield and gives better plant growth. However, excess fertiliser for many species can result in greater susceptibility to certain diseases. Too much nitrogen, in particular, can result in lush, vigorous, thin-leaved growth that is more vulnerable to attack by insects (e.g. aphids), bacteria and fungi. A few species actually fruit better with minimal nutrients. Most plants benefit from a mulch of organic material, which reduces weed competition, conserves moisture, adds nutrients and encourages the proliferation of soil organisms such as worms, which help to recycle and circulate nutrients, and improve soil structure.

Chemical and biological control: There are various organic–biological herbicides and pesticides on the market, and although many are less harmful to the environment than chemical solutions, many are also very unspecific in what they kill, e.g. pyrethrum, which can kill both friends and foes alike. A balance of methods is probably the most prudent approach, along with the practice of 'prevention rather than cure'.

The main problems that can occur are listed in the main text, though the majority of these are unlikely to be too serious in smaller gardens. Below is a brief description of the main groups of pests and diseases. The reader is advised to seek out more local literature to establish specific risks in their area.

PESTS

Aphids (greenflies, blackflies): Common, and attack a wide range of plants. Their numbers can rapidly build up. Relishing young, lush growth and some fruits, aphids suck the sap from the phloem layer and leave a sticky exudate that attracts sooty moulds and other fungus. They are also a carrier of several viruses. Because they attack new growth and become so numerous, they can do extensive damage. Most of the aphids you see are females and reproduce without the need of a male, with the young being produced as small adults, which is very unusual in the insect world. At a certain point in the season, aphids start producing males as well as females, take off to mate and then usually overwinter on a different plant species. There are numerous insecticides available to combat aphids, or a spray with soapy water can sometimes give some control.

Beetles: Many beetles are allies and do a good job of pest control; only a few species are a serious problem to fruit and nut species. The raspberry beetle can eat the flower buds of several *Rubus* species and the larvae can badly damage the fruits. Check for these at appropriate times.

Birds: Birds can be a pest and may devour all ripening crops. They find some fruits particularly attractive, e.g. soft fruits, which benefit from being temporarily netted as they ripen. In addition, many finches and tits damage flower buds, e.g. *Prunus* species. The erection of bird scarers with fluttering, glittery appendages can work well, though birds do build up familiarity with these, so they are more effective if only erected during vulnerable periods.

Capsid bugs: Several of these attack fruit and nut species, and do damage by sucking leaf sap and fruit flesh. Much of the damage they cause is a result of wounds they make in fruits, which often become brown and unsightly. They do not cluster in colonies like aphids, and are much larger. The common green capsid bug has nymphs that feed on the leaves of many Rosaceae species in spring and early summer, causing small holes, before metamorphosing into bugs and travelling to other host species.

Caterpillars: The young of many species of butterflies and moths cause considerable damage to the leaves, roots, fruits, seeds and bark of many species. Attacks usually occur in spring and summer before the caterpillars form an over-wintering chrysalis. The codling moth attacks the fruits of apples, burying into the flesh. Other pests are the winter moth, the swift moth, tortrix moth. Many are difficult to control. The adults seldom do any damage.

Fruit flies: Can cause serious damage to many species of ripening fruits in warmer climates. Their populations can rapidly increase, and the small flies feed off the ripe flesh, rapidly reducing its quality. They are strongly attracted to the smell of ripe fruits. Insect-eating birds can be good allies.

Mealybugs: Related to scale insects, these bugs are usually only a problem in glasshouses in cooler-temperate climates, but can be a problem outside on a wide range of species in warmer climates, where they feed year round. They are usually pink or yellow, though their bodies are normally covered with a distinctive white wax. They suck the sap of leaves, stems, fruits or roots, and leave a black sooty deposit where they have been.

Mites: Related to spiders, these tiny creatures are usually not visible. They can rapidly build up in numbers, particularly in hot climates, and attack a wide range of plants. As mites are of a different order to insects, most insecticides have little effect in controlling them. The big-bud mite lives in and feeds on young leaf and flower buds during winter, and causes swelling of the buds. It can be found on a wide range of *Ribes* species. They also carry a few viral diseases, such as reversion disease. A spray of lime sulphur can help control them, though some plant species can be sensitive to applications (e.g. black currants). The mites also do not like moisture, and keeping plants well watered and spraying the leaves with water can reduce this pest. There are several types of red-spider mite, and these attack a wide range of fruit and nut species (e.g. *Malus* spp., *Ribes* spp., Solanaceae spp.). In large numbers they can cause premature leaf fall and stunt growth. The two-spotted mite causes a lot of damage on fruit and nut trees, and their damage is often seen as bronzing of the leaves, with a fine webbing on the undersides.

Nematodes (eelworms): These tiny worm-like creatures, invisible to the naked eye, can attack roots badly and kill plants. Their numbers can rapidly increase to several million within a single plant. Infected plants usually die and need to be destroyed. Avoid planting similar species in known infected areas. It is often difficult to accurately diagnose nematode damage as it happens underground. Symptoms are often similar to those of a number of viral diseases or even nutrient disorders. On infected plants the root-knot eelworm forms small nodules, which contain many young eelworms. Nematodes can be a serious problem in sandy soils, though are less of a problem in heavier or alkaline soils.

Sawflies: These are the larvae of small insects and can cause extensive damage. Apple-sawfly larvae bore into fruits such as apples, and leave trails of their passage across young fruits. They also create an unpleasant smell on damaged fruits. Gooseberry, pear and cherry sawflies attack leaves and can seriously stunt a plant's growth.

Scale insects: These are small, sap-sucking insects which, as their name suggests, have a hard scaly skeleton. They form stationary small hard scales on plants and can suck so much sap that leaves and young stems wilt. Some also secrete a sticky exudate, which further attracts sooty mould fungus. They can attack fruits, bark and leaves. Small infections can be easily scraped off, though an insecticide may be necessary for larger infestations.

Slugs and snails: These are classified as gastropods, and slugs, in particular, can extensively destroy many species, though damage is usually worst on young, low-lying plants. A few species eat roots, others eat low-lying fruits such as strawberries. There are various controls, including the use of slug pellets, though these can also poison birds who eat the poisoned slugs. Slugs do not like lime or soot, and either of these can be sprinkled around young plants. They also dislike rough sharp surfaces. Some place a saucer of beer, which the slugs are said to drink until they burst!

Thrips: These are tiny, long insects that puncture and damage the young leaves and flowers of many species, with the leaves then becoming silvery. They can also transmit several diseases.

Wasps: Several species of wasps seek out ripe fruits and either bite an entry or enlarge any existing small holes to reach the sweet fruit flesh. This damage, in turn, can attract fungal disease and other problems. Wasps can be a considerable pest problem around orchards during fruit ripening.

Weevils: These are small beetles with distinctive pointed snouts. Both adults and larvae can damage flowers, fruits and leaves. The cream-coloured grub-like larvae of apple-blossom weevils can seriously damage young flowers. The adults then climb down the tree in summer, and may be trapped at this stage. Clay-coloured weevils are also a problem on fruit crops, and are nocturnal so are difficult to spot. Leaf-eating weevils may attack several species.

Whiteflies: Both the small adult moths and their larvae can become a problem in warmer climates, or in greenhouses, where they feed on the underside of young leaves and the nymphs leave a sticky exudate that can become infected by sooty mould. A plant's growth can be seriously stunted as the whiteflies' population numbers can rapidly increase.

DISEASES

Bacterial: Microscopic, simple, single-celled organisms can cause serious damage within the tissues of many species. These do need moisture though, and tend to remain in fallen leaves and plant material around trees. Therefore, clearing up pruned cuttings and cultivating plants under drier conditions can minimise infection. Disease is worst in wet soils, and bacteria readily enter plants through any wounds, such as pruning cuts. This is one of the reasons why cuts should be clean and not ragged, and why pruning is best done at times when the tree can quickly heal. The more serious diseases are bacterial canker, crown gall and fireblight. These diseases are difficult to treat, and prevention is better than cure.

Bacterial canker shows up as brown marks on leaves and, later, as dark staining of the heartwood. Shoots and branches can die back, and it may kill plants.

Crown gall affects many fruiting species, including many members of the Rosaceae family. They typically attack at ground level in wetter soils and cause the production of 'tumours', which sometimes, though not always, kill the plants.

Fireblight is a very serious disease in many *Prunus* species, and often rapidly kills the plant. It enters through injuries and causes an orange-red stain throughout the vascular system. Its risk can be reduced by minimising pruning and fertiliser use.

Fungal: There are several classes of fungal disease. Most are more prevalent in humid conditions. Several can be prevented and controlled with lime sulphur, a natural product, which is usually applied just before infections are likely to occur. Spacing plants to allow good ventilation is also a good preventative method, as is pruning to allow air to freely circulate.

Anthracnose is a general term for several fungal diseases that attack many deciduous and evergreen trees and shrubs. It is much more virulent in damp conditions. Often called leaf, shoot or twig blight, it tends to attack young tissue, and severe infections can lead to the loss of many leaves, and even to the death of smaller branches.

Blight can affect several *Ribes* spp., causing leaves to wilt.

Botrytis (grey mould) attacks flowers, fruits and leaves, and causes a light grey fluff on infected tissue. Is more common at higher humidity. Some forms of this disease can be more serious and can badly damage gooseberries, peaches, raspberries, strawberries.

Brown rot affects flowers, fruits and stems of many fruit species, including many Rosaceae spp. It forms brown lesions, through which other pathogens can enter. Can seriously damage fruit crops.

Canker Serious on many fruit trees, especially apples, cankers form sunken areas on bark or on young stems, and can spread around the diameter to cut off the vascular system and so stunt and sometimes kill the branch. Causes discoloration of the wood. Any diseased wood should be removed and destroyed.

Damping-off Caused by *Pythium* fungi, this occurs on young seedlings, usually if they are over-watered, and causes collapse of the young stems. Once seeds have germinated, seedlings need good ventilation and only moderate moisture. *Pythium* can also attack the roots of mature plants, though needs a damp environment.

Leaf-curl is a problem on peaches, almonds and similar species. Symptoms include characteristic reddening and curling up of leaves, with blisters that turn white as they mature. If trees become badly infected it can stunt growth and seriously reduce fruit yields. Remove fallen, infected leaves.

Leaf spot Round discoloured spots occur on leaves and stems. Good ventilation reduces the risk. Can be serious on many *Ribes* spp. and strawberries.

Mildew occurs in two types: downy and powdery. **Downy fungus** penetrates deeper within the plant tissues, and can be serious on young plants. **Powdery mildew** causes a white powdery covering on leaves and stems, and their hyphae penetrate to take up plant sap; infections may weaken plants. Often occurs on fruits such as apples, where it can seriously deplete crops, and also on *Ribes* spp. and strawberries.

Root rots These fungi mostly attack roots that are sitting in wetter soils or have nutrient disorders. Unfortunately, the symptoms cannot usually be detected until the disease has progressed too far. The roots become thick and the hyphae block the vascular system, so preventing water and nutrients reaching the shoot. The most damaging of these is the **honey fungus** (*Armillaria mellea*), which can kill large, mature trees. The fungus produces characteristic black threads under the soil, and any diseased plants, along with any black threads, need to be destroyed to avoid it spreading to neighbouring plants. The fungus also produces large honey-smelling fruiting bodies.

Rust disease There are many serious rust diseases, but these are usually of more concern on cereals. They form orange-reddish-coloured lesions on stems and leaves, and have many stages to their life cycle, with spores travelling to other species to over-winter. The disease is generally not too serious on fruit and nut trees, though it can occur on several *Ribes* spp. and plums, and other species can act as the over-wintering host.

Scab This is a general term for the damage caused by various fungal species, which cause scab-like damage on certain fruits. It generally only disfigures rather than seriously damages fruits.

Silver-leaf can be serious. The fungi causes silvering of stems and leaves, but also the wood becomes stained dark brown. Branches and even trees can die. Prune out any stained wood and destroy infected material as spores are easily transferred to healthy plants. Can affect many Rosaceae species. The fungi are least active in early summer, and any pruning of diseased wood is best carried out during this period.

Viruses: These minute particles live in the sap of plants. Often their symptoms are minor, and some are actually used to create ornamental variegation within plants. Others can cause more serious diseases, such as mosaic disease, which can damage the leaves of a number of *Ribes* spp. Viruses are easily spread by aphids and other sap-sucking pests, and can be transferred via infected pruning tools and through vegetative propagation, but do not usually cause serious damage to fruit and nut species. Seeds do not carry viruses.

NUTRIENT-DEFICIENCY SYMPTOMS IN PLANTS

Nitrogen: Older leaves affected first. Plants are usually much smaller than normal and leaves turn light green. Lower leaves turn yellow and foilage senesces more rapidly.

Phosphorus: Older leaves affected first. Plants are decreased in size. Young leaves sometimes develop red/purple colours; older leaves turn yellow.

Potassium: Older leaves affected first. Irregular marginal or interveinal chlorosis appear on leaves, turning to pale brown-black patches; leaves become cupped.

Magnesium: Older leaves affected first. Interveinal chlorosis, with persistent green leaf margins, also forms yellow patches and brown necrotic areas. Brilliant orange, red or purple tints appear.

Molybdenum: Older leaves affected first. Bright yellow-green interveinal chlorotic mottling visible before leaf margins curl and whither. Symptoms are more intense when nitrate is applied. Citrus develop yellow spots on older leaves.

Calcium: Younger leaves affected first. Terminal buds die, young leaves show distortion and necrosis. Die-back in tips and margins. Root tips soft, pulpy and swollen.

Sulphur: Younger leaves affected first. Smaller leaf size, pale green-yellow leaves, shortened internodes. Leaf veins become chlorotic.

Boron: Younger leaves affected first. Young leaves light green-yellow at base, die-back of terminal bud, older leaves misshapen, thick, brittle and small. Cracks and splits occur in petioles and stems. Root tips enlarged.

Copper: Younger leaves affected first. Young leaves are permanently wilted without chlorosis. Leaves rolled or curled. Emerging leaves often trapped in subtending leaves. Pollen often sterile.

Iron: Younger leaves affected first. Uniform chlorosis of younger leaves, veins remain darker green.

Manganese: Younger leaves affected first. Chlorosis often interveinal and produces a bold pattern of dark green major veins. Unlike iron, necrotic spotting or lesions appear on affected leaves; these may be brown or black.

Zinc: Younger leaves affected first. Leaf malformation, irregular mottling with yellow-ivory interveinal areas and extreme rosetting of terminal and lateral shoots in woody species. In some cases, necrotic spots appear on affected leaves.

HEALTH BENEFITS FROM FRUITS AND NUTS

Modern research is increasingly indicating that it is much more beneficial to eat a wide variety of fruits, nuts and vegetables rather than rely on specific, isolated vitamin or nutrient supplements. The synergistic relationship between compounds is increasingly being more fully appreciated. Compounds in isolation are increasingly being found to have a lesser, or quite different, physiological effect than when they are eaten in combination with other compounds. For example, the greatly increased benefit of taking vitamin C with certain polyphenolics (see below) has now been proven and, indeed, some of these compounds, when studied in isolation, have the opposite effect when taken on their own than when taken with other compounds. The consumption of a variety of fruits, nuts and vegetables provides a wider range of antioxidants, oils, soluble fibre, minerals, amino acids and vitamins.

Antioxidants: The colour of fruits and vegetables seems to reflect their nutritional value and content. Strongly coloured foods seem to be more packed with goodies, from dark purple and bright red berries, to large orange and yellow tropical fruits, to deep green leafy vegetables. In general, it seems that fruit species tolerant of cold winters tend to form small berries that are often dark red-purple in colour, and have high levels of many types of polyphenolics (see p. 42), whereas plants from warmer subtropical and tropical regions have much larger fruits, and these are often yellow or orange in colour when ripe.

Antioxidant nutrients include vitamins C, E and A (beta carotene, alpha tocpheral), coenzyme Q-10, glutathione, superoxide dismutase, many polyphenolics (e.g. flavonoids), as well as the micronutrient selenium. When antioxidants are taken in combination, their effects are often much more impressive than if used individually. Antioxidants work by reacting with destructive substances called **free radicals** (charged oxygen molecules) and **reactive metal cations** (positive ions) to render them harmless before they are able to harm DNA, thereby preventing mutations and tumour growth.

The **free-radical theory of ageing** (and disease promotion) is that there is a gradual accumulation of damage to our cell membranes, DNA, tissue structures and enzyme systems as we age or come into contact with toxins, and this predisposes us to many diseases. Although the body produces its own enzymes that act as antioxidants (e.g. glutathione peroxidase, catalase, superoxide dismutase), it is now thought that additional antioxidants within the diet can give extra protection against this damage and the ageing of tissues.

When plants first evolved, there was little free oxygen in the atmosphere. As oxygen levels increased, which was a direct result of plant metabolism (plants take in carbon dioxide and give off oxygen as a by-product), their environment became increasingly 'polluted' with oxygen. Over time, plants acquired antioxidant compounds, which gave them protection from this highly reactive oxygen. In addition, plants also evolved many compounds in defence of attack by insects, fungi, bacteria, animals, as well as by ultraviolet radiation, and many of these compounds have now been found, often in small amounts, to have startling medicinal and dietary properties. Animals have evolved to produce many of the nutrients they need from other foods. However, they still need to take some nutrients, including many vitamins and all polyphenolics, directly from plant sources, and this, of course, applies to humans as well.

Antioxidants seem to have many beneficial properties, including protecting the genetic material from damage, strengthening and increasing the suppleness of smooth muscles, reversing some of the signs of ageing, helping to prevent and also sometimes reduce cancers, reduce heart disease, enhance the immune system and improve visual acuity.

FOOD GROUPS

Below are described the main food groups found in fruits and nuts: sugars, fats and proteins. This is followed by descriptions of the main vitamins found in fruits and nuts: vitamins A, B, C and E. The final section outlines the large and diverse group of polyphenols, which give many fruits such wondrous health benefits.

Sugars

Sugars are simple carbohydrate molecules that are readily broken down when digested. Apart from concerns about obesity, it is thought that because refined foods such as sugar and refined carbohydrates are released so rapidly into the body, this leads to hormonal imbalances connected with glucose control. Glycaemic indices are now increasingly referred to, and give an indication of how long it takes for carbohydrates to be broken down and used by the body. The foods that are broken down more slowly, to give energy over a period of time, have benefits over quick-energy foods such as sugar, unless a fast burst of energy is needed.

The glycaemic index (GI) gives a numerical value to the speed at which carbohydrates and sugars are able to increase a person's blood glucose level. Basically, the higher the food's number, the faster it is broken down during digestion to increase blood glucose level. Foods with lower scores are generally higher in dietary fibre, and have benefits, particularly for diabetics. Surprisingly, although fruits are often high in sugars, they also have fairly low glycaemic numbers because of their other constituents, with apple, banana and plum having lower numbers than some foods high in bran. Banana has a GI of ~60, apricot is ~44 and peanuts are ~20, compared to white bread at ~100, and a baked potato at ~130. Also, surprisingly, sugar has a lower value than many refined foods, such as white bread. The addition of protein and fats slows down the absorption of carbohydrates, hence nuts have low GI numbers and are considered a good food source that can provide nutrients and energy over a long time period.

Fruits contain several types of sugars, including glucose, fructose (levulose) and sucrose, with the proportions of these varying between species. Apple, for example, has more fructose, grape is high in glucose and fructose. Fructose has a lower GI and is often recommended to diabetics rather than eating sucrose; it takes longer and is more difficult to digest.

Carbohydrates: These consist of many sugar molecules linked to form long chains, such as starch. They are broken down during digestion into their sugar components. In plants, they are produced within leaves, and are then mostly shunted to storage organs within plants, such as tubers and rhizomes.

Fibre is a complex carbohydrate that is not broken down, or only partially, by digestion. Its benefits are now widely realised: it prevents constipation, minimises intestinal disorders, may aid weight loss, lowers cholesterol blood levels and triglycerides levels. Many fruit are high in fibre, e.g. apples, blueberry, date, guava, olive, oranges, raspberry.

Pectin is a type of soluble fibre found in apples, the rind of citrus fruits (particularly in grapefruit) and many other fruits. It forms the middle layer of plant cell walls. It has received much attention lately because of its scientifically proven ability to lower blood cholesterol levels and to reduce the incidence of thrombosis. It may also help prevent colorectal cancer, and has been used to treat constipation and diarrhoea.

Fats

Not all fats are bad. In fact, fats are important in the diet and are a source of the essential vitamins A, D, E and K, with nuts being an excellent source of many unsaturated fats. About 95% of body fat is in the form of triglycerides, which are classified as simple fats. Triglycerides can be either saturated fatty acids, where all the sites are filled with hydrogen ions (it is saturated with hydrogen) or unsaturated fatty acids, where only some of the sites are filled by hydrogen, and these are liquid at room temperature. The types of simple fats are as follows:

Unsaturated fats are found primarily in fruits and seeds and they come in three main types; *superunsaturated*, *polyunsaturated* and *monounsaturated*. They differ in the ease with which they are broken down inside the body. All three types are classified as triglycerides.

Superunsaturated fats, e.g. omega-3 essential fatty acids (e.g. alpha-linolenic acid), are easily broken down in the body and are used in many metabolic processes. These are 'essential fatty acids' because they cannot be manufactured by mammals, and need to be obtained through the diet. A lot of interest and research indicates that omega-3 fatty acids can reduce the risk of arterial disease. They seem to be able to decrease the levels of 'bad' cholesterol (low-density lipids [LDL]; see below), and decrease the tendency of blood platelets to clot together. They also discourage narrowing of the arteries, and increase the production of an anti-clotting agent. The main sources of omega-3 fatty acids are flax, nuts, seeds, green vegetables, fish and soybeans.

Polyunsaturated fats, e.g. omega 6 essential fatty acids, are missing two or more hydrogen pairs, or have two or more double bonds in their chemical structure. They are easily broken down and used throughout the body. They are liquid at room temperature, and are found mainly in vegetable oils, except saturated tropical oils (coconut, palm oils). They are thought to lower both high-density lipids (HDL) ('good') and LDL ('bad') cholesterol. Polyunsaturated fats include linoleic acid, which is an essential fatty acid, that cannot be made by mammals, and needs to be included within the diet. It is found in corn, sunflowers, sesame, walnut, pumpkin seeds, etc. Consuming nuts, which are rich in linoleic acid, has been shown, in trials in the USA, to lower total cholesterol and to reduce low-density lipids ('bad' cholesterol; LDL) and triglycerides, by 2–10% in 16 weeks compared with a control group. Other polyunsaturated fats are gamma-linolenic acid, which is found in a few foods, such as black currants. Both linolenic and linoleic acids are important in the diet. Linoleic acid in converted to arachidonic acid, which is a crucial component in the production of a number of hormones that have many functions within cells of the body as well as in the functioning of blood platelets.

Monounsaturated fats, e.g. oleic acid, omega-9 fatty acids, are easily broken down. Good sources are found in olive, almond, avocado, peanut, pecan, cashew, filbert and macadamia oils. Monounsaturated fatty acids are missing a hydrogen pair to give them one double bond in their chemical structure. They are liquid at room temperature and may help lower total blood cholesterol level as well as lowering LDL ('bad') cholesterol levels. It is thought that most fat should be sourced from monounsaturated fatty acids, such as oleic acid in olive oil. People in Mediterranean areas consume large amounts of oleic acid and have very low rates of heart disease and cancer.

Saturated fats, usually solid at room temperature, are found in many animal and dairy products, as well as tropical oils such as coconut. Saturated fatty acids have no double bonds and are saturated with hydrogen ions, making these fats very stable. In the diet, they cause total blood cholesterol level to rise. The saturated fats, palmitic acid, myristic acid and lauric acid, all raise serum cholesterol levels, although stearic acid does not. High levels of these fats are also implicated in the occurrence of cancer.

Trans fats do not occur naturally, but are produced artificially and are chemically altered. They are often labelled as 'hydrogenated' or partially hydrogenated. They are bad news for health. They raise LDL cholesterol and may also lower HDLs (see below). They are intermediate in consistency between unsaturated and saturated fats. They are popular in the food-processing industry because they prolong the life of fatty foods, as these can quickly become rancid with age. They are used in a wide range of processed foods, such as cakes, biscuits, pizzas, crisps, dips, margarine, salad dressings and many more. There is increasing evidence that these fats are as, or more, harmful than saturated fats. High levels have also been implicated in the occurrence of cancer.

Cholesterol is not a true fat, but is a lipid-like, waxy substance. It is needed by the body for many metabolic processes, including being a major component of cell membranes, and is needed for the synthesis of steroids and bile salts. Although some cholesterol is obtained through the dietary intake of dairy products, meat, eggs and fish, much is also produced by the liver, and the amount produced is determined by the type of fat that is eaten. Interestingly, because dietary cholesterol is derived from the cell membranes of animals, plants do not contain cholesterol. It is the amount of cholesterol that the body produces that can cause problems. And, saturated fats, which are at high levels within dairy products and fatty meats, can encourage the production of excess cholesterol. Most nuts contain larger ratios of unsaturated fats, which do not have this effect. As saturated fats are broken down in the liver, some of the breakdown products are used to produce cholesterol. Cholesterol needs to be attached to a protein to enable it to travel around the body; it thus forms three main types of lipoprotein: low density lipoproteins (LDL), high density lipoproteins (HDL) and very low-density lipids (VLDL). All are needed and are essential to maintain good health; however, there is a lot of misinformation surrounding them, mostly about the relationship between the types.

- LDL contains 60–70% cholesterol. It enables the transport of cholesterol from the liver to cells throughout the body, including smooth muscle, which is what arteries are composed of. This cholesterol, in excess, can initiate the formation of deposits in arteries and, as a consequence, can result in an increased risk of heart disease.
- HDL contains 20–30% cholesterol. It transports cholesterol away from the tissues and back to the liver where it is recycled or eliminated. Greater levels of HDL will lower the levels of cholesterol in the body and lead to a reduced risk of heart disease.
- VLDL only contains 15–20% cholesterol, though is high in fat. It is also involved in the development of arteriosclerosis problems, but its mode of action is still being researched.

Although high levels of blood cholesterol need to be monitored, of more importance is the ratio between LDL/HDL, with a ratio of <1 being very low and excellent, with a very low risk of heart disease, but ratios >3.5 should be treated with some concern for an increased risk of heart disease. In addition, LDL levels should be less than 160 mg/dL and HDL levels should be more than 40 mg/dL.

Proteins

One of the main ways that proteins differ from fats or carbohydrates is by the inclusion of nitrogen. They can form very large molecules within the body. They are built up from ~20 different smaller units, collectively known as **amino acids**. Proteins are multi-functional within the body and are needed for everything from their inclusion within enzymes, to the formation of many types of blood cells, to forming structural materials such as collagen. About half of these amino acids can be synthesised within the body from other foods, but nine need to be taken with the diet: these are known as essential amino acids (e.g. tryptophan, leucine, phenylalanine, arginine [for children]). Different foods contain different types and ratios of different amino acids, and these foods also vary in their digestibility. Many proteins are found in meats and dairy products, but nuts and seeds are also a good source of amino acids, with many of the nuts described in these pages containing ~30% protein, although they are often low in amino acids that contain sulphur.

THE VITAMINS

Vitamin A (carotenoids) An antioxidant. Men need ~5000 IU (1000 mg) and women ~4000 IU (800 mg) of vitamin A per day. Vitamin A is fat soluble, can be stored in the body for a long period, but needs bile salts and fat to be absorbed from the gut. Its storage is so effective that the body can last without additional vitamin A for a couple of years without suffering deficiency. Carotenoids are a group of compounds that have pigments that give fruits and vegetables their vibrant orange, yellow and green colours. Beta-carotene, lycopene, lutein and zeaxanthin are all different varieties of carotenoids. Not all carotenoids (e.g. lycopene, lutein) are converted to vitamin A, though some are (e.g. beta-carotene), but all tend to be classified together. They all act as antioxidants with strong cancer-fighting properties. Studies have suggested that carotenoids may help prevent skin, breast, lung and prostate cancer. They are involved in cell division and cell differentiation. They are also well-known for improving vision as they are involved with the formation of rhodopsin, which is needed for light-sensitive rods in the eye. A lack of this vitamin leads to night blindness, many digestive, urinary and respiratory infections, as well as nervous disorders and skin infections. Vitamin A is also important for the proper formation of bones and teeth. It maintains membranes, and so helps prevent infections, and is involved with the immune system.

The best sources of vitamin A are obtained through fruits and vegetables because the body converts natural carotenoids to vitamin A in the amount it needs, whereas vitamin A within supplements, given in doses of just four to five times the recommended daily allowance (RDA), can be toxic. The body is unable to rid itself of excess vitamin A and stores it in the liver for a long period. Toxicity from vitamin A can cause dry, peeling skin and, in severe cases, osteoporosis; it can initiate birth defects and even liver failure.

In general, the more colourful the food on your plate, the more likely you are to have an abundance of carotenoids and other healthy nutrients. Beta-carotenes are found abundantly in apricots, cantaloupe and peaches.

Lycopene, not converted to vitamin A, is found in apricots, guava, pink grapefruit, mango, oranges, peaches, papaya, tomatoes and watermelon. Recent research has shown excellent health benefits from lycopene, which gives food its red colour. In addition, unlike most other vitamins and antioxidants, its values actually increase with cooking and processing. Similar compounds are lutein and zeaxanthin, with these being particularly linked to preventing cataracts and macular degeneration. These two antioxidants are mostly found in eggs and green vegetables, but are also found within many yellow fruits, such as oranges and kiwifruits.

Vitamin B The B vitamins are not antioxidants, but are essential nutrients needed for health. They are water-soluble vitamins. Good quantities are found in many nuts and seeds, as well as beans, yeast, meats and eggs. Being water soluble, they are not stored for long in the body, and need to be eaten regularly. Heat destroys many of them. They are each briefly described below.

B1 (thiamine): Needed in many metabolic pathways, and is essential for neuronal and muscular transmission. Destroyed by heat.

B2 (riboflavin): Needed in many metabolic pathways, and involved in carbohydrate and protein metabolism.

Niacin (nicotinamide): Is derived from an amino acid (tryptophan: an essential amino acid). Needed in many metabolic pathways that are involved with producing energy and lipid metabolism. It inhibits the production of cholesterol, as well as helping to break it down.

B6 (pyridoxine): Needed for amino-acid metabolism, involved in the production of antibodies, as well as in fat metabolism and neuronal action.

B12: The only vitamin not found in fruits or vegetables.

Pantothenic acid: Needed in many metabolic pathways, and necessary for the synthesis of cholesterol.

Folic acid: An important part of the production of DNA and RNA, and needed for red and white blood cells.

Biotin: Needed in many metabolic pathways.

Vitamin C (ascorbic acid) An antioxidant. A recommended dosage of vitamin C a day is 250–500 mg, though some authorities only recommend ~60 mg, with the latter value being the minimum needed to stave off scurvy. This disease, caused by a lack of vitamin C, results in the weakening of bones and connective tissues. Vitamin C is best known these days for its ability to reduce the effects of colds and flu. In addition, recent research has confirmed its benefits in helping fight cancer due to its powerful antioxidant properties, which help to eradicate cancer-causing free radicals. It also protects against heart disease and stress, is involved with energy production within cells, as well as the production of collagen, a protein widely needed for cartilage, joints, skin, and blood-vessel formation and maintenance. In addition, vitamin C helps boost the immune system, binds with certain poisons to render them harmless, works with antibodies, helps to increase the absorption of nutrients (e.g. iron) in the gut, thins the blood, and is essential for sperm production.

Vitamin C is water-soluble and thus protects against free radicals within the watery areas of the body, such as blood and inside cells. It helps to recycle vitamin E, also an antioxidant. It also works much better if combined with various polyphenols (see below). It cannot be stored and, unlike fat-soluble vitamins (e.g. vitamin E, carotenoids), it needs to be consumed on a daily basis. Vitamin C is easily destroyed by heat when cooked or processed, and also degrades rapidly with storage or with commercial freezing (as foods are blanched beforehand). Strangely, apart from guinea pigs, the Indian fruit bat and a few other species, humans are one of the few animals that cannot make vitamin C within the body. We are missing the enzyme necessary to produce it from glucose and, therefore, have to include it within our diet.

Vitamin C is found in many fruits and vegetables, and some of the species included in this book are bursting with it, with the fruits historically having been used for thousands of years for their healing and medicinal properties. The amounts of vitamin C within fruits varies with ripeness, cultivar, the length of time it has been stored, etc., but the levels are often highest in slightly under-ripe fruits (an exception is jujube where vitamin C content rises with increased ripeness). Fruits that have 6–15 mg of vitamin C are regarded as a 'good' source; fruits with 15–30 mg are considered a 'very good' source; fruits with >30 mg are considered 'excellent'. Many fruits listed here are way above the upper scale. Fruits with lots of vitamin C often have a sharp, tangy taste. Fruits from warmer climates often have high levels of vitamin C, possibly because the high temperature and light intensities they encounter promote stress, which, in turn, produces more free radicals. Plants are thought to produce more vitamin C to counteract this.

Vitamin E (alpha-tocopherol) An antioxidant. A recommended dosage a day is 100–400 IU per day, or 8 mg/day for women and 10 mg/day for men, and it is most beneficial when taken with vitamin C. Vitamin E is an antioxidant and helps to fight tumour formation. It is an oil-based vitamin. Levels of vitamin E in sunflower seeds are just about the best, though many nuts also have wonderfully high levels, e.g. almonds, hazelnuts, peanut, but also avocado, kiwifruit and mango. It is a fast-acting vitamin that helps maintain the integrity of cell membranes, is involved with the formation of DNA and RNA, and is also needed to form red-blood cells. It promotes wound healing, helps the normal functioning of the nervous system, greatly helps skin healing and reduces scarring (good to take extra after surgery), is involved with vision (it may reduce the incidence of eye cataracts), and is beneficial to the liver as it neutralises certain toxins. Vitamin E seems to enhance immune function. It is protective against arthritis, heart disease, diabetes, bowel, lung and renal disease, and cancer (prostate, colon, bladder, breast and lung). Recent research indicates that vitamin E helps prevent or delay coronary heart disease by limiting the effectiveness of LDL to form clots in arteries. A study of ~90,000 nurses showed that the incidence of heart disease was 30–40% lower in those who had a higher intake of vitamin E either through their diet or via supplements. Other studies, but not all, have confirmed these findings. Vitamin E, like vitamin C, is derived from plants, but is found mostly in plant oils. Although it can be stored in the body for longer than vitamin C, it does need to be regularly 'topped up', unlike the long storage times of vitamin A. Humans can only last 2–6 weeks without an intake of vitamin E before health starts to deteriorate.

POLYPHENOLICS

The term 'polyphenolic' is given to a large group of compounds, which includes tannin, but also many related compounds and derivatives of tannin that are increasingly being found to have startling health-promoting benefits. They are exclusively found within the plant world. Surprisingly, although the benefits and necessity of vitamins has been known for many years, e.g. vitamin C, many other compounds within fruits, nuts and vegetables are only just being discovered, along with the realisation that many of these molecules work together in a more synergistic manner than when taken on their own. The mix of these with vitamin C, E and A has now been shown to give protection against cardiovascular disease and helps reduce the activity of LDL ('bad') cholesterol.

Polyphenols are antioxidants. They are a group of negatively-charged compounds (–OH) that protect plants from disease and ultraviolet light, help prevent damage to seeds until they germinate, and deter invasions from pests. At least 5000 naturally occurring polyphenolics have been identified, though many remain unidentified, for example there may be 10,000 chemicals in the tomato, and only a small fraction of these have been researched for their benefits to human health. They range from simple molecules, such as phenolic acid, to large highly polymerised compounds, such as tannins. The most common polyphenols are those formed from various sugar molecules, organic acids and lipids (fats), and are linked together to form a phenolic ring structure. The differences in their chemical structures gives them their different modes of action and health properties.

An excess of certain reactive elements in the body, which are often positively charged metals (cations), can promote too many free radicals, so leading to possible oxidative damage of cell membranes and cellular DNA. Polyphenols can form complexes with these reactive metals, such as iron, zinc and copper, thus reducing their activity. Polyphenols are also able to neutralise other types of free radicals before they can cause any damage. In addition, they protect and help regenerate other dietary antioxidants, such as vitamins C and E. Flavonoids (see below) may also increase the levels of glutathione, a powerful antioxidant.

Polyphenols' antioxidant properties have been shown to reduce the incidence of various forms of cancer, prevent cardiovascular disease, improve certain brain diseases, help fight infections, stimulate immune function and prevent chronic disease. No significant adverse effects have been noted from the regular consumption of most polyphenols; however, high intakes of tannin can lead to adverse medical scenarios (see text below). This large polyphenol group can be subdivided into several groups, of which the most important is tannin and its subgroups.

Tannins

Tannins are polyphenolic secondary metabolites of higher plants. They are usually divided into two groups: **hydrolysable tannins** and **condensed tannins** (proanthocyanidins). The hydrolysable tannins can be broken apart by weak acids or alkalis (hence 'lyse'). These tannins are partly made up of phenolic groups such as gallic acid, i.e. gallotannins, or ellagic acid, i.e. ellagitannins (see below), which are released when they are lysed (along with carbohydrate). Condensed tannins are a large group of different polymers (compounds) that are collectively known as **flavonoids**. These compounds are not as easily lysed or broken apart by hydrolysis.

Tannins are common throughout the plant world and are often found within roots, bark, leaves and unripe fruits. Tannins are astringent, bitter-tasting polyphenols that bind and precipitate protein. The name 'tannin' is derived from the Celtic word for the oak tree, which yields high levels of tannin and was widely (and still is) used for tanning leather. It also yields strong brown dyes. In plants, tannins may partially act as a waste product, but are also produced as a defensive compound against predation. They have been used by humans for thousands of years. Their astringent and antimicrobial properties mean that, medicinally, they are effective at controlling diarrhoea, slowing internal bleeding, treating scalds, burns and skin infections. However, in larger quantities, and if taken regularly they may be carcinogenic (though may also help reduce certain cancers) and may reduce the absorption of proteins and iron from the gut, through precipitation.

This group of powerful compounds, in small amounts, is very beneficial but, in excess, can lead to possible imbalances and toxicities.

Hydrolysable tannins (phenolic acids): This group includes the main groups of ellagic acid and gallic acid, but also ferulic, chlorogenic, neochlorogenic, caffeic, benzoic and cinnamic acids. Of these, ellagic acid is of particular importance within fruits.

Ellagic acid Contained in *Rubus* spp., Saxifragaceae spp., *Amelanchier* spp. and many members of the Rosaceae family, ellagic acid is found at particularly high concentrations in raspberries, but also strawberries, blueberries, pomegranates and walnuts. It seems to have an effect against a wide range of cancers in several tissues; it has been shown to significantly inhibit cancers of the breast, pancreas, oesophagus, skin, colon, prostate, liver, lung and tongue in rats and mice. It has been clinically proven to rapidly bind to, or cause the death of, cancer cells and to inhibit their further division. If that is not enough, it may also protect normal cells from the effects of chemotherapy and radiation. Ellagic acid also has antibacterial and antiviral properties, and can reduce populations of *Helicobacter pylori*, a bacteria that has recently been associated with the formation of stomach ulcers. It may also reverse some toxicities within the liver and may control internal haemorrhage.

Ellagic acid does not actually occur within fruits, but is converted to this compound in the body from ellagitannins, which are molecules that occur in large quantities within raspberries. It also seems to retain its potency after heating, freezing and other processing. Small amounts of ellagitannins from natural dietary sources may be more effective than large doses of purified ellagic acid. The highest quantities are found in leaves, but also in fruits and nuts. Within the plant, it may act to regulate plant growth and seed germination, and to protect plants from insect and microbial attack.

Condensed tannins: Flavonoids (syn. vitamin P, bioflavonoids) This group, which contains >2000 compounds, contains some of the most potent plant antioxidants. They cannot be produced by the body and need to be eaten in the diet; an estimated intake of at least 150–300 mg per day is advised. Water soluble, they are often divided into several groups of pigments. They consist of carbon aromatic molecules and are found in all green plants, occurring as coloured pigments in flowers, fruits, bark and roots. Flavonoids function as astringent parasite deterrents, help to heal wounds by lignification, protect against UV radiation, and their colours attract flower pollinators as well as advertising their edibility (and hence the scattering of indigestible seeds). Their presence in the plant is often increased after injury.

Flavonoids' effects are much increased if taken with vitamin C, and viceversa. Their efficacy is greatly reduced by cooking. These powerful antioxidants seem to boost the immune system and reduce inflammation. In some cases, they can directly disrupt the function of certain viruses or bacteria, and are being studied to help treat the HIV and *Herpes simplex* viruses. Some studies have shown that mortality from coronary heart disease is inversely related to the intake of flavonoids, and they may help prevent strokes. Flavonoids may work, with other compounds, to reduce the risk of cancer, and have been linked to many other benefits, including helping relieve varicose veins, arthritis, haemorrhage, phlebitis, general inflammation, bleeding gums, blood clots, oedema and hypertension. A lack of flavonoids may manifest itself as poor resistance to infection, bruising easily and swelling after injury.

Antioxidant-rich food can be classified into an ORAC scale (oxygen-radical-absorption capacity), with high-scoring values being the best. High-scoring fruits are blueberries, blackberries, black raspberries, black currants, wolfberries and gooseberries. Many wild selections have considerably higher antioxidant levels than common commercial varieties. These antioxidant values correlate well with total phenolic and total anthocyanin contents. The table to the right shows a range of ORAC values from different fruits. Note that only eating a few blueberries is equivalent to eating a much larger volume of melon to get the same results.

The flavonoids are divided into many groups, including the following: **anthocyanins** (these are found in brightly coloured fruits and vegetables, and are encountered frequently within this book); **catechins** (tea, grapes, wine); **coumarin** (mostly found in leaves); **flavanones**; **flavones**; **flavonols**; **isoflavones** (e.g. genistein/daidzein; found in soybeans); **lignans** (found in nuts, whole-grain cereals); **myricetin**; **naringenin** (hesperidin; found in citrus fruits); **proanthocyanins** (including pycnogenol; found in grapes, pine bark); **quercetin** (found in grapes, wine, onions); **resveratrol** (found in grape skins); **rutin** (very similar, chemically, to quercetin); **tannins** (tea, nuts); **theaflavins** (derived from catechins); **xanthone** (a yellow pigment, often found in petals). A few of these are described more fully below.

Anthocyanins (anthocyanidins) An important group of flavonoids that are responsible for the rich, dark purple-red colours of many fruits, e.g. blackberries, black currants, black grapes, plums, *Berberis* spp., wolfberry, black cherries, etc., and are also the pigment responsible for the beautiful purples and reds of autumn leaves. Fruits with high levels of anthocyanins (e.g. bilberry) have been long recognised to treat circulatory disorders, reduce heart disease and improve vision. They may also have anti-inflammatory, antiviral and antimicrobial properties, and may be beneficial for treating diabetes and ulcers. Recent studies in the USA have found

that anthocyanins are able to boost insulin production by up to 50%. They are chemically related to quercetin. Subgroups of anthocyanins include cyanidin, delphinidin, pelargonidin, peonidin, petunidin, malvidin, procyanidin, prodelphinidin, propelargonidin. Interestingly, these compounds can act as pH indicators, changing colour with acidity or alkalinity.

Catechins Found in green tea and red wine. These, like quercetin, may inhibit the activity of an enzyme that normally breaks down the hormone norepinephrine, thus raising its levels. Raised levels seem to result in weight loss and in the relief of allergies and asthma. Thus, these compounds may aid weight loss, as well as helping to relieve allergic and asthmatic reactions. Other similar catechins are epicatechins and taxifolin.

Proanthocyanidins (see 'tannin' above) is a precursor of anthocyanin and quercetin. The proanthocyanidins (also known as oligomeric proanthocyanidins, or OPC) are very powerful antioxidants and free-radical scavengers. Technically, OPCs are flavonols rather than flavonoids. Flavonols (and OPC) are colourless, water soluble and are always formed from a compound called flavan-3-ol; whereas flavonoids are yellow, relatively insoluble and formed from many different compounds. Both, though, generally occur together in plants. Proanthocyanidins greatly enhance the activity of vitamin C in the body. They have up to 50

Fruit	ORAC value
Wolfberry	7228
Prunes	5770
Raisins	2830
Blueberries	2400
Blackberries	2036
Strawberries	1540
Raspberries	1220
Plums	949
Oranges	750
Red grapes	739
Cherries	670
Kiwifruit	610
Pink grapefruit	495
White grapes	460
Cantaloupe	250
Banana	210
Apple	207
Apricot	175
Peach	170
Pear	110
Watermelon	100
Honeydew melon	97

times stronger antioxidant activity than vitamins A and E, or selenium, and 20 times greater activity than vitamin C. They are readily and quickly metabolised. They help promote tissue elasticity, help heal injuries, reduce swelling, promote the production of collagen and improve peripheral circulation, prevent bruising, strengthen and increase the suppleness of weak peripheral blood vessels, protect against atherosclerosis and inhibit enzymes that induce histamine formation. They remove and prevent lipofuscin formation in the brain and heart. Lipofuscin is a pigmented granule that occurs within neurones and is thought to partially initiate the ageing process. Pycnogenol (found in *Pinus* spp. and grapes), quercetin and resveratrol are examples of other forms of proanthocyanidin.

Quercetin (quercitin, quercetrin) is chemically related to the proanthocyanins. It is a powerful antioxidant and may have an ability to fight certain cancers as well as acting as an anti-inflammatory. It seems to inhibit the activity of an enzyme that normally breaks down norepinephrine, thus raising its levels. Raised levels seem to result in weight loss and in the relief of allergies and asthma, and so may act as an antihistamine. It acts as a powerful vasodilator. It is found at high levels in e.g. green tea, red wine and raspberries.

Resveratrol Found within the skins of red grapes, blueberries, *Pinus* spp. and peanuts, resveratrol seems to inhibit the formation of tumours by preventing DNA damage and also slowing the carcinogenic process. It seems to work by neutralising a toxic compound, piceatannol, which only occurs in cancer cells. It is still experimental, but may be included within cancer drugs of the future. It also has anti-inflammatory, antifungal and possibly antiviral properties, and there are claims for it being an anti-ageing compound. It reduces the death of beneficial cells. It has become well known through the French paradox (how the French live longer and have less heart disease while consuming a high-fat diet), which has been suggested to be partly (or largely) due to the red wines drunk in France. It has been shown to reduce the development of cardiac fibrosis. (See also 'Nutrition' in entry the for *Vitis vinifera*.)

Rutin and *hesperidin* These compounds, e.g. limonoids, are described together because they are closely associated with each other, and need to be taken together, and with vitamin C, to receive their optimum effects. Together, they maintain healthy capillaries by promoting the production of collagen, help wound healing and promote a healthy immune system. They also may have anti-cancer properties, as well as being antiviral, anti-inflammatory and are able to lower cholesterol levels. They are found at good levels in the outer rind of the citrus species, grapes, cherries, plums, peaches, apricots, apples, berries and green tea. ■

PART II: PLANT SPECIES

Acer saccharum
Sugar maple
ACERACEAE

Silver maple (*A. saccharinum*), black maple (*A. nigrum*), red maple (*A. rubrum*)

Attractive, deciduous tree species from the maple family that are native to southern Canada down into the eastern states of the US. Of these maple syrup-producing species, the sugar maple is often the best known. Maple syrup has been made from the sugar maple's sap for hundreds of years. The native Indians collected and boiled the sap in hollowed-out trunks, and their skills have been passed on to the present time. It was their main sweetener (with honey) and they made sweets, beverages and beer, as well as adding it to a variety of food dishes. The sap is tapped in early spring by drilling a shallow, small hole into the trunk and inserting a tube that transports the sap out into a bucket below. It is then boiled, usually for a long period, until it is syrupy. This delicious syrup can then be added to pancakes, various confectioneries and sweets. But, it does need 35 litres of sap to make only 1 litre of syrup!

DESCRIPTION

Forms a fairly densely branched, spreading tree with a rounded crown, ~20–30 m height, 20–25 m spread. It has grey, smooth bark that becomes darker with age and develops rough, vertical grooves. Its young stems are shiny and reddish-brown. It is a hardy, fairly slow-growing, long-lived (~400–500 years) tree.

Leaves: Deciduous, has five distinct lobes and has the typical *Acer* shape. Is medium green above, paler green beneath, 5–24 cm long, depending on its location on the tree. Has spectacular clear yellow or golden-reddish autumn colour.

Flowers: Greeny-yellow, in drooping clusters, from the ends of stems, in spring. *Pollination*: By wind and insects. Although flowers look as though they are combined male and female, they are only one sex or the other (monoecious), but both occur on the same tree, often on different branches.

Fruits: Paired seeds, consisting of almost parallel, veiny wings. Seeds ripen in autumn and the wings aid dispersion. Seed production is usually moderate, with peak years at 2–5-year intervals. Trees can take up to 10 years to produce the first seeds.

Roots: Relatively deep rooted. Forms mycorrhizal (fungal) associations, which enable it to obtain more nutrients from the soil, particularly phosphates.

Harvest: Trees should not be tapped until the trunks have grown to ~25 cm wide for a single tap, and 40 cm for two taps, which may take 15–20 years. If done when the tree is too young, its growth resources can be seriously depleted, which will affect future development of the tree. Can be tapped in late winter–early spring. There are optimum 'windows' of time to tap the trees, and this varies with local conditions. There is a balance between tapping late enough in winter so that the sap has started to fully rise up the tree, and not too late, when the physiology of the tree has changed into leaf production. A few sunny days at the end of winter–early spring is the optimum time to start, and the season can last several weeks. It is getting too late once the leaf buds have started opening: the quality and flow of sap is then reduced. The flow of sap is best on warm, sunny days after a frost. Tapping is done by drilling a hole, ~0.5–0.75 cm depth, into the tree at ~1 m height, on the sunny side of the tree (the phloem layer is not far below the surface). Insert a tube and hang a bucket just below, which you may want to cover to prevent contamination. A good tree, with one tap can produce ~80 litres of sap/season. Collect the drained sap regularly. The sap is then boiled down, usually in an outhouse or outside, until it reaches a syrupy consistency. This will take several hours. The sap should be put into an evaporator pan with heated water below. Ensure the water does not boil dry and that the syrup does not become too smokey. Skim off any foam from the surface. After several hours, the sap suddenly changes consistency and thickens. It needs to be checked regularly at this time and, when the temperature reaches 104°C and/or the sap coats the back of a spoon, then it is finished. Strain the sap, reheat it to 70°C and pack it into sterilised containers. The syrup should then keep for years.

CULTIVATION

In most situations, it is an easy-to-grow, trouble-free tree.

Location: Should not be planted in maritime locations and is not very pollution tolerant. But is fairly wind hardy, though summer gales can damage the leaves. Can tolerate some shade when young, but mature trees prefer full sun.

Temperature: They are very frost hardy, and sap yields are of much better quality in colder areas.

Chilling: For good sugar production, trees need several weeks of sub-zero temperatures.

Soil: Can grow in soils that are surprisingly acid as well as more neutral pH soils (3–7). They prefer soils that are fertile, moist, yet well-drained. However, they will grow in poorer, rocky soil, but do not like compacted soil. Healthy trees can withstand waterlogging for fairly long periods, particularly in winter. Addition of organic matter or a general fertiliser will improve growth in poorer soils, and they like a mulch of pine needles.

Planting: Space trees ~8 m apart: they like room to spread.

Propagation: *Seed*: This is the usual method. Germination is best from non-dried seed, but as germination is in spring, seeds can be stored in a polythene bag in the fridge over winter. If the seed dries, it develops germination inhibitors, which can delay germination by 2 years. Will then need 3–4 months of cold stratification, plus being soaked in warm water for 2–3 days before sowing. *Cuttings*: Not easy from cuttings. *Layering*: Is possible. *Suckers*: Younger trees produce lots of sprouts from the base of the tree, which can be easily removed and rooted.

Pruning: Not usually needed, except to remove diseased or damaged wood. Prune only in late summer or autumn, and not when the tree is dormant to avoid large sap flows.

Pests and diseases: Can get leaf scorch in dry conditions. *Verticillium* wilt can be a problem.

OTHER SPECIES

Other *Acer* species that can produce sweet sap are *A. barbatum* (Florida maple), *A. grandidentatum* (Canadian maple), *A. macrophyllum* (big leaf maple), *A. negundo* (box elder). ■

Food
The syrup is a very desirable, alternative sweetener. It has a rich, delicious flavour. Unfortunately, many maple syrups sold are made from other sweeteners and flavourings. The 'real thing' is wonderful on pancakes and can be used in many desserts, confectionery and as a general sweetener. Wine, beer and liquors can be made from the sap, either as it comes from the tree, or when partially reduced.

Nutrition/medicinal
The sap contains nutrients from the roots that will be transported to the opening leaf buds. The sap itself contains only ~2% sugar. However when it is reduced, it can contain ~85% carbohydrate, of which ~75% is sugar, and although it can cause insulin and adrenaline reactions, like sugar does, its reactions are not as intense. It contains virtually no fat and only a trace of protein. The syrup contains good levels of phosphates and calcium, which are good for bones. It has been used to treat tuberculosis in children.

Other uses
It has good-quality, hard, closely-grained, heavy timber that is used to make furniture, veneer, carving and flooring. The wood, when smoked, imparts a unique taste to foods, e.g. ham.

Ornamental
It forms an attractive, hardy, specimen tree that has glorious, varied autumn colour.

Actinidia deliciosa
Kiwifruit (yang tao, Chinese gooseberry, souris vegetale)
ACTINIDIACEAE
Similar species: Arctic beauty kiwi *(A. kolomikta)*, hardy kiwi *(A. arguta)*, silver vine *(A. polygama)*, golden kiwi *(A. chinensis)*, velvet vine *(A. eriantha)*

The genus *Actinidia* contains many species (>400), most of which are originally native to eastern Asia, particularly China. The Chinese have collected the fruit from the wild for thousands of years, but never domesticated the plant, and it is New Zealanders who have been largely responsible for growing and developing various kiwifruits. The different species vary considerably in the shape and colour of the flowers and fruits. The fruits can vary in colour from orange, red, green, purple, brown, to white, and their flesh from orange, red, purple, green, lime green to yellow. There are many good fruiting species, and these vary in their cold hardiness as well as other traits. The main cultivated kiwifruit was known as *Actinidia chinensis* var. *hispida* until the mid 1980s, after which it was split into two separate species: a smaller-fruited *A. chinensis* species and the larger, hairy

common kiwifruit, *A. deliciosa*. Interestingly, the first *A. chinensis* fruits in New Zealand were derived from a few seeds from a single fruit brought from China, in about 1903, by Miss Isabel Fraser, after a visit there to her sister. Therefore, it is possible that most of the commercial kiwifruits grown around the world originate from this single fruit, but this also means that the genetic base of this species is very limited. By ~1940, kiwifruits were rapidly becoming a commercial crop in New Zealand. Today, most commercial kiwifruits are of the 'Hayward' cultivar, after Hayward Wright who, in the 1920s, selected this cultivar; however, golden kiwifruits are now also gaining commercial importance. One of the factors that has made them so popular commercially, particularly in New Zealand, is that the fruits store so well, 4–6 months at 0°C, which means that shipping is much easier and they can be readily transported around the world. In addition to New Zealand, kiwifruits are also grown in California, Italy, Japan, France, Chile, China, Spain, Greece and Israel.

Below is a description of the cultivation of kiwifruits in general and for *A. deliciosa* in particular. Notes on other edible *Actinidia* species follow.

DESCRIPTION

Kiwifruits form extremely vigorous and long-lived vines, and can grow 6–8 m wide by 3–4 m tall. Trunks can become very woody and measure >20 cm in diameter when mature. Vines produce two types of shoots: terminating and non-terminating. Terminating shoots are shorter, with only 3–6 leaves, and these usually form flower buds the following year. Non-terminating shoots can grow ~3–5 m long in a single season, have smaller leaves and their stem tips coil around the structures they come into contact with (although, botanically, they are not classified as 'true' tendrils).

Leaves: Attractive, large (16–25 cm diameter), deep green, coarsely hairy, dense, oval–circular. Young leaves and shoots are coated with eye-catching bristly, maroon hairs. As they mature, they become hairless and dark green on their upper surface, and develop a white downy surface with distinctive, light-coloured veins beneath.

Flowers: Large (2.5–5 cm diameter), white–cream, often fragrant, borne singly or in small clusters, of 2–3, from leaf axils of the last season's growth, through late spring–early summer. Plants are usually dioecious, so need more than one plant to set fruit. Female flowers have many creamy-coloured styles growing from a swollen, superior ovary. Male flowers are usually smaller and have a pronounced whorl of many stamens, which are longer than the flowers. Very occasionally, these flowers can set fruit from vestigial female organs, but the quality of these is usually poor. *Pollination:* Bees are the usual pollinators, but, unfortunately, they aren't very attracted to the flowers and so the presence of a nearby hive or hand pollination can increase fruit-set and fruit size. Fruit size is proportional to the number of pollinated embryos, and thus the number of seeds: it needs more than 1000 embryos to be pollinated to get a good-sized fruit. The male and female plants can be of different species, as long as their flowers open at the same time.

Fruit: A berry, the shape and size of a large hen's egg, covered with distinctive, thin, brown fuzzy skin. Inside, are many, very small, black, edible seeds that are embedded in vibrant emerald-green flesh that has fine lines that radiate outwards, to form an attractive pattern when the fruits are cut in half horizontally. Unusually, for a fruit, the ripe fruits are green because of their chlorophyll content, which does not degrade as they ripen, as with almost all other fruits. The flesh is firm, until fully ripe, and is usually enjoyed when still tangy, sub-acid and zingy, before becoming fully soft and sweet. Fruits ripen in late autumn to early winter, usually just after the leaves have dropped. Fruits develop on wood formed the previous year.

Yield/harvest/storage: A mature vine can produce 150–200 fruit. A maximum yield from a plant can be ~80 kg, but most vines are more likely to produce ~20 kg of fruits. Plants start to produce good crops of fruits when ~4 years old, reaching full potential at 9–10 years, but can then continue producing fruits for a further >40 years old. Fruits can be harvested when under-ripe and will ripen if kept at room temperature for a few days, or this can be speeded up if the fruits are stored in a polythene bag with other fruits that produce ethylene gas. The vines do nut suffer from premature fruit drop, as many other fruit species do, and fruits that set after pollination will mature. Fruits are picked from the vines when they are about egg size, but can be still hard. Vines can be over-productive and may need some fruit thinning to avoid biennial bearing and to even out yields. Once picked, fruits can be stored in a refrigerator for >4 weeks, or can be stored at 0°C for 3–5 months in a polythene bag.

Roots: They form large, spreading root systems: some grow near the surface, whereas others can grow down very deeply (~15 m), unless the soil is compacted or is poorly drained.

CULTIVATION

Are quite demanding plants as far as soil quality, nutrients and moisture are concerned.

Location: They are not wind hardy, which can break their stems and damage leaves and fruits. The use of windbreaks is advisable in exposed locations. The vines can be grown in full sun or semi-shade. They are not tolerant of high salt and are not suitable for exposed maritime locations.

Food

Delicious fresh, when still firm and just under-ripe, still tangy and not over sweet. Eaten on their own or added fresh to many desserts and savoury dishes as a garnish. They are very rarely cooked. Also made into juice, wine, jam and other products. Kiwifruits go well with avocado, salads, prawns and fish dishes, chicken and anywhere a tangy, but not sour fruit is needed, but not with yoghurt, as an enzyme within the kiwifruit conflicts with those in yoghurt. Slightly under-ripe fruits are best for processing. The peeled, whole fruits can be pickled with vinegar, brown sugar and spices. Strangely, the Chinese have never been very keen on the fruits, although demand is now apparently growing.

Nutrition

Kiwifruit have a higher concentration of vitamins and minerals than most other fruits. The fruits are very high in antioxidants (~8th in the fruit charts) and are also a good source of fibre. The fruits are one of the best sources of vitamin C: 100 mg/100 g of flesh, incredibly high, with the gold varieties (see below) containing even more: ~120 mg/100 g. They also contain lots of potassium (340 mg per large fruit) and folic acid (rare for a fruit). Unusually for a fleshy fruit, they also have good levels of vitamin E, possibly because of all the tiny seeds they contain. They also have good levels of chromium, which seems to be involved with controlling heartbeat and Carbohydrate use, and have quite good levels of calcium (for a fruit). In addition, kiwifruits also contain very good levels of lutein and zeaxanthin (types of vitamin A), which are proven to help reduce the incidence of cataracts and macular degeneration. Fruits contain high quantities of a proteolytic enzyme called actinidin (similar to papain in papaya), and this is effective in tenderising meat. The young leaves of many of these species can be lightly cooked and added to other vegetables or soups.

Medicinal

Actinidin is said to aid digestion. Polygamol, which is obtained from the fruits, is used as a heart tonic. The branches and leaves are boiled in water and the liquid is used to treat mange in dogs.

Other uses

The vine contains a fibre that has been used to make rope, and paper has been made from the leaves and bark.

Ornamental

Although vigorous and fairly demanding in soil conditions and moisture, it can make a very decorative vine for covering pergolas and similar structures. It has large tropical-looking leaves and eye-catching young, red stems, as well as attractive flowers and delicious fruits into early winter.

Temperatures: Primarily, this species prefers a warm temperate to subtropical climate, although is fairly frost tolerant and can survive brief temperatures ~–8 to –12°C, but not for extended periods. Below –12°C, young vines can be killed. Early spring frosts (<–1°C) can kill young shoots. The most cold-hardy species are *A. arguta* and *A. kolomikta*, which can tolerate temperatures down to <–25°C (see below). Vines can acclimatise to cold, but need protecting (e.g. by wrapping the trunks) from sudden drops in temperature in late autumn, particularly when young.

Chilling: Kiwifruits need a period of winter chill to initiate leaf- and flower-bud opening in spring. The 'Hayward' kiwifruit needs ~600–800 chilling hours at <7°C.

Soil/water/nutrients: Vines grow best in deep, fertile, friable loam. They can grow at a fairly wide pH range, from pH 5.5–7.2, but this also depends on the soil type, and they may suffer deficiency problems in some soils. They do not like much salt in the soil and are not tolerant of waterlogging. They need good drainage, but also need regular moisture during their growing season, particularly during fruit formation. They are not drought tolerant and need more moisture than many other fruit species. More kiwifruit plants probably die from water-related problems than for any other reason. Kiwifruits are fairly nutrient hungry and need nutrients spread widely around the plant because of their spreading root systems. They particularly use nitrogen during the beginning of their growing season. Later nitrogen applications can enhance fruit size, but also leads to poor fruit storage. In more alkaline soils, a citrus-type fertiliser is recommended. Additions of micronutrients are also beneficial. Alternatively, the addition of slow-release blood and bone is beneficial, and mulching with organic matter (but not directly next to the stem) can help conserve moisture, suppress weed growth and add nutrients. Possible deficiencies are potassium, magnesium, nitrogen, manganese and zinc, but plants can also suffer from toxicities of boron, sodium or manganese. Potassium deficiency shows as poor bud growth and the margins of older leaves roll upwards, making the leaves look scorched and dead. Magnesium deficiency causes interveinal chlorosis on older leaves. Nitrogen deficiency affects older leaves first, making them pale. Manganese deficiency causes chlorosis of younger leaves, while at toxic levels, often in acidic soils, it causes small black spots along the veins of older leaves. Boron toxicity usually occurs in alkaline soils.

Pot culture: Kiwifruit vines can be successfully grown in large containers, and can then be given extra protection in colder areas.

Planting: Space plants at 4.5–6 m apart. Need a ratio of 4–8 females to one male plant to ensure good cross pollination and fruit-set. A substantial fence, trellis or patio frame needs to be in place before establishing the vines. The vine can grow large and the structure that it grows up needs to be strong. Young stems, although naturally coiling around wires, benefit from also being tied onto their support as they become heavy and far reaching. The stems coil vertically up wires, but cannot coil horizontally very well, so need tying onto these. They look good grown over a patio, along wires, perhaps with a grape vine or hop.

Pruning: The vines produce a lot of vigorous, vegetative growth and do need frequent pruning to reduce this and encourage fruiting. Fruits are formed on last year's wood, so this needs to be considered when pruning. The object is to reduce leaf growth and encourage the formation of fruiting stems. Vines are best pruned and trained so that the flowers and fruits hang outside the leaves; this results in much better flowering, fruit quality and yields. Some leaves are often removed in late summer so that sunlight can increase bud formation for the following year. The main stem is usually the only permanent wood (similar to grapes). Pruning in winter and summer controls vegetative growth and suppresses shoot growth. Winter pruning is usually carried out to remove older wood, whereas summer pruning removes stems that are too vigorous. The flowering shoots from male plants are often pruned back to 5–7 buds during their first summer, and should then produce more pollen the following spring, although some argue for leaving the stem entire. After flowering, the male flowering stems are often immediately pruned out so that they don't compete with female plants.

Normally kiwifruit vines are trained to a single trunk, and all suckers are removed to reduce competition with the grafted top. From thereon, once the main stem has grown to the top wire, two canes are encouraged to grow in opposite directions along the wires of the trellis, to form a T shape. It is from these that all future fruiting canes originate. Each year the cordons are pruned to ~40–50 cm further out from the last season's pruning, to encourage lateral growth from each bud on the stem. Most new stems produce 4–6 fruits at their base and then form flower buds during the summer along the rest of the cane. From there, there are two main methods of pruning: (1) the fruiting branches are left for 2 or more years, and more fruiting laterals are encouraged off these, or (2) the fruiting arms are pruned off each year, so that fruit is always produced on new shoots.

Propagation: *Seed:* Can plant seeds derived from store-bought fruits in spring, and these usually germinate quite well, though the progeny will be variable and the sex of the plant won't be known. Best sown in well-drained, but moist compost with warmth; they should germinate in 28–35 days. *Cuttings:* This method can be successful and gives predictable progeny and predictable sex. Semi-ripe cuttings are taken in summer–autumn and inserted in well-drained, gritty compost with mist, if possible, and you may get better rooting if they are dipped in rooting hormone. Leaves can be cut in half to reduce transpiration. They may not root as well as grafted plants and can suffer from more crown-gall disease. Rooting takes place in 2–4 weeks. *Grafting:* This is the main commercial method. They are usually grafted onto 'Hayward' or 'Bruno' rootstocks in late autumn, using cleft or whip grafts.

Pests and diseases: Kiwifruit plants are fairly healthy though may suffer from various problems particularly if the soil is too wet. Possible fungal and bacterial diseases include crown gall (*Agrobacterium tumefaciens*), *Botrytis* and *Phytophthora* root rot. Also, *Armillaria mellea* (honey fungus)

can kill vines. Other possible problems include scale, leaf-roller caterpillars, passion-vine hoppers, thrips, leaf spot, scale insects and root-knot nematodes. A further, bizarre problem is that stems have a catnip-like aroma, which cats love to rub against, and so may damage new shoots; however, if you happen to have a lion or tiger around, apparently, this compound can also be used to tame them.

CULTIVARS

Need to ensure that male and female plants are chosen that flower at the same time or, for the smaller garden, it is possible to get male and female plants grafted onto the same plant. The main pollinating female cultivars are 'Hayward' and 'Zespri Gold', a cultivar from *A. chinensis* (see below). Two main male cultivars are 'Matua' (meaning 'father' in Maori), which is a mid season cultivar and coincides with 'Hayward' flowers, and 'Tomuri' (meaning 'late blooming' in Maori), which extends the male pollen season for 'Hayward'.

'Allison': From New Zealand. Fruit: oblong, medium size, densely fuzzy, brownish. Flesh: light green, of good flavour. Good storage. Vine: very vigorous, prolific, mid season bloom, fruits ripen late autumn.

'Bruno': From New Zealand. Flowers: early season. Fruit: large, elongated oval, dark brown skin, with dense, bristly fuzz. Flesh: light green, good flavour. Ripens in late autumn. Vine: vigorous, productive. Does not store very well. 'Matua' is a suitable pollinator.

'Hayward': A chance seedling discovered in New Zealand. Late flowering. Fruit: very large, broadly-oval; skin: browny-tan, with a dense, fine fuzz. Flesh: lime green, very good flavour. Fruits keep well. Ripens in late autumn–early winter. Vine: moderately vigorous, blooms very late and needs a late-blooming male. A leading cultivar.

'Monty': From New Zealand. Late flowering. Fruit: oblong, medium size, skin is brownish with dense fuzz. Flesh: light green. Ripens in late autumn. Vine: highly vigorous, prolific yields, so may need thinning. 'Tomuri' is a suitable pollinator.

SIMILAR SPECIES

Arctic beauty kiwi, *Actinidia kolomikta*. Arctic beauty is a native of Japan as well as western China. It has blueish, oblong fruits of sweet flavour. It has the most vitamin C of any *Actinidia*, >5 times that of black currants per unit weight. It is often grown as an ornamental vine, for its pink and white variegated younger leaves. It can be confused with the closely related *A. polygama*, but Arctic beauty has heart-shaped leaves (cf. tapered of *A. polygama*).

Description: Less vigorous than many kiwifruit vines, to ~10 m, and can be trained on a fence. *Leaves:* Deciduous. After ~4 years, some leaves can develop an attractive natural purple–cream variegation, particularly on male plants, though shade reduces this. *Flower:* Early summer, scented, dioecious. *Fruit:* Smooth, ~2 cm diameter, can be eaten whole (with the skin). Stores for ~3 months.

Cultivation: Can be grown in light shade, but full sun gives the best fruit production and leaf colouring. Is very cold resistant, and dormant plants are reported to be hardy to ~–30°C, though new growth can be damaged by late frosts. *Soil:* Prefers a loamy neutral soil, though may become more variegated when grown in more alkaline soils. *Cultivars:* Most breeding has been done in Russia.

Uses: As for *A. deliciosa*. Fruit are eaten fresh, cooked or can be dried for later use. Fruits are sweet and tasty. Young leaves can be lightly cooked and added to soups, etc.

Golden kiwi, *Actinidia chinensis*. The yellow-fleshed kiwifruit needs warmer temperatures than the green-fleshed species, and prefers a warmer temperate or subtropical climate as it is not very frost hardy. It is a very vigorous vine, to 8 m and more, and needs a lot of space. Flowers are scented and mostly dioecious, and so is not self-fertile and needs a male pollinator of the same species. Recently, 'Zespri Gold' has been patented in New Zealand, and is replacing some *A. deliciosa* orchards. They have less fuzz than *A. deliciosa* as well as a yellower skin and yellow flesh. They are also more elongated in shape. The flesh is similar in taste to *A. deliciosa*, but is less sharp and acidic. It also has fewer seeds. There are many other similar cultivars available, which are mainly imported from China or have been developed by amateur gardeners.

Uses: The fruit are delicious fresh and can be used in similar ways to *A. deliciosa*. Extremely high in vitamin C (120 mg/100 g of flesh). *Medicinal:* The fruits, stems and roots are used as a diuretic and as a sedative. They are also used to treat kidney stones, rheumatoid arthralgia, and cancers of the liver and oesophagus. The plant may also have insecticidal properties. *Other uses:* A paper can be made from the bark.

Hardy kiwi (tara berry, bowerberry), *Actinidia arguta*. The hardy kiwi is native to northern China, Korea, Siberia and possibly Japan. It is even more vigorous than *A. deliciosa*, and can grow several metres up structures (20–25 m). It has been in cultivation in the USA since the early 1900s for its fruits, and has been grown in orchards in a similar way to *A. deliciosa*. There are some named cultivars.

Description: *Leaves:* Delicate, smaller (5–12 cm wide) and less fuzzy than *A. deliciosa*; it also has good autumn colour. *Flowers:* Fragrant, white, in spring, ~3.5 cm diameter. Some varieties are self-fertile, others need a pollinator, but fruits of self-pollinating species are larger if a pollinator is located nearby. *Fruit:* Skin is greenish-yellow or greenish-red, oval, fuzzless, ~2.5 cm long. Flesh is green, often sweeter than *A. deliciosa*, tasty, recommended. Because it has no fuzz, it can be eaten whole, with its skin. Looks much like *A. deliciosa* when cut open. Has good yields, and the fruits store well. Fruits are harvested in late autumn, and almost drop from

the vine when fully ripe, though are usually picked when still firm, and then ripened after.

Cultivation: As for *A. deliciosa*. Can grow in full sun or semi shade, though fruits are of better quality when grown in full sun. It is a very cold-hardy plant, tolerating temperatures down to –30°C (or even –50°C when dormant, according to some reports), although young spring growth is susceptible to frost damage, and plants need a warm spring and summer to flower and fruit successfully. Not wind tolerant. Most plants are dioecious, though the cultivar 'Issai' is self-fertile. Because of its size, it needs a strong supporting trellis system.

Cultivars: 'Ananasnaja': Grown as a female; large fruit, ripening in early autumn.
'Issai': Self-fertile, precocious, sets even more fruit if pollinated. Is smaller and less hardy than other cultivars. 'Red Princess' (*A. arguta* x *Actinidia* spp.): Delicate looking, highly ornamental, with large (5–7.5 cm long) green fruit, and green flesh with a reddish tinge. Slower coming into bearing than most, and not as productive.

Other females cultivars include 'Cordifolia', 'Dumbarton Oaks', 'Geneva', 'Ken's Red', 'Michigan State', '119-40B' (claimed self-fruitful). *A. deliciosa* and male cultivars of *A. arguta* can pollinate this species.

Uses: Valued ornamentally and ideal over a pergola or similar. Fruits can be used as for *A. deliciosa*.

Silver vine, *Actinidia polygama*. A native of Japan and western China. Is often confused with *A. kolomikta*. These have tapered leaves, cf. heart-shaped. Grows to ~6 m. *Flowers:* In early summer, scented, usually dioecious. *Fruit:* Yellow, ~4 cm long, bitter.

Cultivation: Are hardy to ~–30°C when dormant, but young growth in spring can be cut back by late frosts. *Cultivars:* '418-77' is very vigorous, may be self-fertile.

Uses: Often grown ornamentally for the silvery colour of new leaves on male plants. The fruits are somewhat bitter and are often eaten when salted, although a few cultivars have better-flavoured fruits. *Medicinal:* The leaves are used as a hallucinogenic and as a sedative.

Velvet vine, *Actinidia eriantha*. A fairly vigorous, frost-sensitive vine, climbing to ~10 m. It has red, dioecious flowers, and needs a pollinating plant close by. The fruits are ~3.5 cm long and have a white fuzz on their skin. The flesh contains good levels of vitamin C.

Other similar species are *A. latifolia*, *Actinidia* x *fairchildii*, *A. melanandra* and *A. coriacea* (which is relatively frost hardy). ∎

Aegle marmelos
(syn. *Feronia pellucida, Crataeva marmelos*)
Bael fruit (matoom, Indian quince, golden apple, holy fruit, stone apple, elephant apple)
RUTACEAE

A relative of the citrus species, bael trees grow wild in dry forests on the hills and plains of central and southern India, Burma, Pakistan and Bangladesh. They have been mentioned in writings dating back to ~800 BC. They are cultivated throughout India, mainly in temple gardens, because of their status as a sacred tree. The species is also grown in Indo-China and Southeast Asia, particularly Thailand and northern Malaysia. In Thailand, it is commonly found growing in many Buddhist temples, where the dried, sliced fruits are boiled with water and are a popular drink with the monks. In Hindu culture, the trees are considered sacred and the leaves are offered to Lord Shiva, who is believed to live beneath a bael tree. For this reason, the trees are not allowed to be uprooted. The fruit forms a hard skin when ripe, within which the flesh is tangy and marmalade-like.

DESCRIPTION
A handsome, slow-growing, small–medium-sized (8–14 m) tree, with a short trunk, and spreading, sometimes drooping branches. Its bark is smooth, thick, soft, flaking, greyish-brown. The older branches are covered with straight, sharp spines, as are young suckers that can develop around the tree. Wounds exude a clear gum, resembling gum arabic, which hangs down in long strands as it dries and becomes solid. If eaten, it is sweet at first, but then becomes irritating to the throat.

Leaves: Deciduous, alternate, ovate–lanceolate, trifoliate, with a larger terminal leaflet, ~4–5.5 cm long, ~2–3 cm wide, and a long stalk. It has shallowly toothed margins. New leaves are glossy, pinkish-bronze in colour, maturing to pale–mid green. Mature leaves are fragrant when crushed.

Flowers: Sweetly fragrant, in clusters of 4–10, from leaf axils along young stems. They have four recurved, fleshy petals, green outside, yellowish inside, and many greenish-yellow stamens. Flowers are bisexual and self-fertile, so only need one tree to set fruits, though more than one can increase fruit-set. Flowers are borne in spring, soon after the new leaves open. *Pollination:* By bees and insects.

Fruit: A round–pyriform berry, 5–20 cm in diameter, weighing ~70 g. The rind can be thin, hard and woody, or may be softer. Fruits are grey-green, ripening to a greeny-yellow colour, and are dotted with aromatic, minute oil glands. The skin hardens as the fruit ripens and turns a tan colour. Inside, there is a hard central core and 8–20 faintly defined triangular segments, with thin, dark orange walls, filled with aromatic, pale orange, somewhat viscous, sweet, resinous, more or less astringent pulp. Embedded in the pulp are 10–15 flattened, oblong seeds, ~1 cm long, bearing white woolly hairs. Fruits take 10–11 months to mature after fruit-set.

Yield/harvest: An average tree can yield 150–200 fruits (~70 kg), with better cultivars producing up to 400 fruits. Seedlings begin to bear in 6–7 years, vegetatively propagated trees in ~5 years. Full production is reached in 15 years. Fruits ripen in the dry season, in winter, just before trees come into flower for the next season's fruit. They need to be picked carefully as they easily crack, and can be damaged if they fall from the tree. They are picked when almost ripe and are yellowish-green, and are then kept at room temperature for ~8 days until the fruits have lost any green tinge and the stem can be easily removed. Fruit can be stored for ~2 weeks at 30°C, or for 4 months at ~10°C.

CULTIVATION
The tree is not fussy about growing conditions and does well in poorer soils.

Location: Can grow in full sun or in semi-shade. Trees are moderately wind tolerant.

Temperature: The bael tree is a subtropical species, but has been reported to survive down to –6.5°C. Young trees are probably more sensitive to cold temperatures and need extra protection.

Soil/water/nutrients: Does best on rich, well-drained soil, but can grow on thin alkaline soils, in wet areas and stony soils. It can grow at pH ranges from 5–8. In India it has the reputation of thriving where other fruit trees cannot. Needs minimal nutrient additions, though additional iron and magnesium, particularly in alkaline soils, can be beneficial. Needs little or no irrigation: is drought tolerant once established. Indeed, apparently it will only fruit if it experiences a long, dry season.

Planting: Space plants at 6–9 m between trees.

Propagation: *Seed:* Commonly grown from seed, which germinates in 7–21 days at 30°C. Best to sow seeds when they are fresh, and to remove any pulp from around them. Seedlings are slow growing and produce very variable progeny and quality of fruits, with their taste varying from sharp and unpleasant to pleasant; therefore, it is best to use vegetatively-grown plants from a good-quality stock plant. *Cuttings:* Root cuttings can be taken and may be successful. *Layering:* Trees are sometimes air-layered. *Grafting:* Up to ~90% success can be achieved by budding 1-month-old shoots onto 2-year-old seedling

bael rootstocks in early summer.
   Pests and diseases: Is relatively free from pests and diseases. Protect young plants from slugs and snails.

CULTIVARS
'Kaghzi': A highly rated, large cultivar with a thin rind and few seeds.
'Mitzapuri': Rated well, with a very thin rind, fine texture pulp, free of gum, excellent flavour, contains few seeds. ■

uses

Food
The pulp of the better fruits is sweet and pleasantly aromatic, their quality good, though the flesh of over-ripe fruits turns brown and loses its flavour, so fruits are best eaten before this stage. Another factor is the removal of the external shell, which sometimes needs some force if it is woody. They are usually opened by cutting them in half with a sharp knife. The pulp is often used to make a refreshing drink, often with sugar, or sometimes milk or tamarind is added. Mature, but unripe fruits are made into jam, with the addition of citric acid, or into marmalade and jellies, or they are pickled. The young leaves and shoots are eaten as a vegetable in Thailand and are used to season food in Indonesia. They are said to reduce appetite. An infusion of the flowers makes a cooling drink.

Nutrition
The pulp contains 8% total sugars, 0.2% tannins, 2.5% pectin, which is quite high. A fairly good source of vitamin C at 10–60 mg/100 g of pulp. This fruit is a good source of protein at 5%, and has fairly good levels of phosphorus, potassium, calcium and magnesium. The bark contains umbelliferone and other coumarins. The leaves contain 0.6% essential oil, mostly d-limonene.

Medicinal
Widely used in Asia and India for its medicinal benefits. The fruit, roots and leaves have antibiotic qualities. The unripe fruits are often eaten by those convalescing from diarrhoea and dysentery. They have also been widely used as an aphrodisiac, as well as a general tonic. However, large doses of the fruits are also reported to lower the rate of respiration, depress heart action and cause sleepiness. The bitter,

pungent leaf juice, mixed with honey, is given to allay asthma, catarrh and fever. A tea made from the flowers is used as an eye lotion. Decoctions of the root are taken to relieve heart palpitations, indigestion, bowel inflammations and to stop vomiting. ***Warning:*** There is as much as 9% tannin in the pulp of wild fruits, although less in cultivated types. The rind contains up to 20% tannin and the leaves also contain high levels. This is probably why the bark is used as a fish poison in the Celebes. Tannin ingested frequently and in quantity over a long period of time reduces the absorption of proteins and can act as a carcinogen.

Other uses
The essential oil from the skin is used in perfumes and cosmetics. The wood is strongly aromatic when freshly cut, and is hard, grey-white, but is not durable and is prone to warping. It is mostly used for small-scale turnery and carving and takes a fine polish. The fruit pulp has a detergent action and has been used to wash clothes. The gum enveloping the seeds of unripe wild fruits has been used as a glue, is mixed with lime plaster for waterproofing and is added to cement when building walls. It has been added to artists' watercolours, and it may be applied as a protective coating on paintings. The limonene-rich oil has been used in scenting hair oil. The shells of hard fruits are sometimes painted and used as small containers. The rind also yields a yellow fabric dye and can be used for tanning leather.

Ornamental
Has a similar ornamental value as other citrus species, and the tree's flowers attract bees. It can be planted as a barrier hedge.

Akebia quinata
(syn. *Rajania quinata*)
Akebia (five-leaf akebia, chocolate vine, mu tong fruit)
LARDIZABALACEAE

Similar species: Three-leaf akebia (*Akebia trifoliata, Akebia x pentaphylla*),
Holboellia (sausage vine), *Holboellia latifolia, H. coriacea*

The Lardizabalaceae family has only a few genera, but these are found
separated around the world, making their origins and spread to these
isolated regions a puzzle. Five genera occur in eastern Asia and the
Himalayas, whereas a further two are found only in central Chile. The genus
Akebia consists of hardy, semi-evergreen, climbing plants. They are native
to central China, Korea and Japan, and are often found in thickets, woods
and growing in hilly regions. They have been used for hundreds, if not
thousands, of years in China for their edible fruits, but also for the plant's
medicinal value, particularly to treat infertility. The fruits are often harvested
from the wild. Many of these species are very ornamental, with abundant,
pretty, fragrant flowers in spring, and have attractive foliage. The related *Holboellia* are also attractive climbing species
native to the Himalayas and China. Often grown as ornamentals, they are semi-hardy, with fragrant flowers and oblong
fruits containing white pulp.

DESCRIPTION
The akebia is a vigorous, densely-leaved, twining vine,
growing to ~12 m. It climbs readily if placed near a support,
but will also form a groundcover plant. Young stems are
rounded, mauvish, turning brown as they mature, and will
twine around the supports. Fast growing, and can be invasive
in some locations, growing several metres in a season.

Leaves: Semi-evergreen, or evergreen in warmer climates.
Leaves are borne alternately along the stem and are
composed of five leathery, palmate, notched, leaflets, mostly
equal in size. The leaflets have an attractive, rounded–oval
shape, 3.5–7.5 cm long. Young leaves have a mauvish tinge,
becoming an attractive blue-green colour above, as they
mature, and are grey-green beneath.

Flowers: Monoecious. The female flower is an unusual,
attractive, chocolate-purple colour, hence this plant's name.
It is ~2–3 cm in diameter and has three petal-like sepals,
with ~5–6 small sterile stamens. The male flower is pink,
has three sepals, with six larger stamens that produce white
pollen and surround small, central, non-functional pistils.
The flowers appear in late spring, but sometimes become
hidden behind the new leaves. They occur on last season's
wood, in racemes, with the fewer female flowers positioned
below the male flowers. They have a strong, vanilla- or
allspice-like fragrance that is particularly noticeable at dusk.
Pollination: By moths, bees and insects. Plants are probably
self-sterile as male flowers do not open at the same time as
the stigma is receptive; therefore, it is advisable to plant 2–3
different cultivars to ensure fruit-set. In addition, hand cross
pollination improves fruit yields.

Fruit: Unusual, sausage-shaped berries, 5–15 cm long,
which often remain pale green when ripe, though some
cultivars have purple ripe fruits. They are borne in eye-
catching clusters of 2–4. The fruit has a fairly hard skin,
even when ripe in autumn, at which time it splits open
lengthways. Inside, there is layer of soft, sticky, white edible
pulp, which has a sweet taste, said to resemble that of
tapioca pudding, though it can be somewhat bland. Within
this is a dense, long cluster of many central tiny black
seeds, which are easily removed.

Yield/harvest: Yields can be disappointing, mostly due to
poor pollination. Fruits are harvested when fully ripe and are
beginning to open, in late autumn. Light green fruits do not
change colour as they ripen. The fruit stalk needs to be cut
to remove fruits from the vine.

Roots: Like most climbers, akebia grows better if the
roots are kept cool. They are also sensitive to disturbance,
so avoid both mechanical cultivation and transplanting.

CULTIVATION
Easy to grow, though can grow quickly and may be invasive
in some situations.

Location: Grows in sun, but often performs better with
some shade. Is reported to tolerate quite dense shade.

Temperature: Frost and cold tolerant, surviving
temperatures down to ~–20°C, though young plants need
extra protection during cold weather. Akebia needs a mild
spring to bear flowers and a long, hot summer to produce
fruit, also some cooler weather in winter to initiate flowering.

Soil/water/nutrients: Grows best in moist loams. Can
grow in sandy soils, but not soils with a high clay content.
Needs regular moisture during the growing season to grow
and fruit well. Does not tolerate waterlogging.

Planting: Space plants ~2–4 m apart, with a trellis, fence
or pergola to grow up. Roots can be easily damaged, so
plant with care.

Pruning: In mild climates, the vines can become too vigorous and may need to be restricted by pruning. Long shoots can be trimmed back, and the plant as a whole can be thinned if needed. Prune after harvesting the fruits or in early spring.

Propagation: *Seeds:* Can be sown fresh as soon as the fruits are ripe. Wash off any pulp from around the seeds before sowing in a moist, sandy, well-drained compost. Takes 4–12 weeks to germinate at ~15°C. Stored seed needs to be cold stratified for 4–8 weeks, then briefly soaked (~12 hours) in warm water before sowing in spring. Avoid needing to re-pot seedlings, which should be planted out before they become too large, to avoid root damage. *Cuttings:* Semi-ripe cuttings can be taken during summer and inserted in gritty, moist compost to root. They may be slow to root. *Layering:* Stems can be easily layered by either burying stem tips or sections of stem just below the soil surface until they root. This is best done in late winter or early spring, and the stems should root during the following summer.

Pests and diseases: Has few pest or disease problems, though rust can sometimes infect leaves.

CULTIVARS
'Leucantha': White-flowers and white fruits.
'Purple Bouquet': A more compact cultivar. Has purple flowers.
'Shirobana' ('Alba', 'White-Flowered Chocolate Vine'): Vigorous, semi-evergreen vine. White, fragrant, showy flowers in early spring, with white fruits. More frost sensitive. A Japanese cultivar.

SIMILAR SPECIES

Akebia x pentaphylla. A natural hybrid between *Akebia quinata* and *A. trifoliata*, this is native to eastern Asia, China, Japan and Korea. It forms a vigorous vine that grows to ~10 m. It may need controlling in the same way as other akebias. It is fairly cold hardy, down to at least ~–15°C, and more deciduous than evergreen. Leaves form in threes or fives, and when young they have a bronze-red tint. Racemes of purple flowers appear in spring, with larger female flowers below the smaller male ones. Is probably self-sterile, and it is therefore best to plant more than one vine. Hand pollination increases fruit-set. The sausage-shaped, purplish fruits ripen in autumn. Cultivation, propagation, etc. are as for other *Akebia* species. The fruits are sweet, and can be eaten fresh.

Holboellia (syn. sausage vine), *Holboellia latifolia*, *H. coriacea*. These are ornamental, evergreen, climbing species with *H. latifolia* being native to the Himalayas and *H. coriacea* native to China. Fairly fast-growing climbers, twining up to ~6 m tall, with *H. coriacea* often becoming larger. *Leaves:* Attractive, glossy, evergreen, trifoliate or palmate. *Flowers:* Waxy, trumpet-shaped, wonderfully fragrant; borne in early spring. Can be susceptible to late frosts in some regions. Plants are monoecious, but seem to be self-infertile, so need more than one plant to set fruit. Hand pollination improves fruit-set considerably. Male flowers are small, mauvish-white or greenish-white, and are borne in clusters on last season's growth; female flowers are darker mauve, larger and are borne

on the current season's growth. *Fruit:* Oval, sausage-shaped, 5–8 cm long, and are mauve when ripe in late summer. Inside it has white, juicy, though not very flavoursome, flesh in which are embedded numerous, black seeds.

Cultivation: *Location:* Grows best in a protected area and readily climbs a fence or wall. The roots appreciate being kept in cool and shade. The stems can be grown in sun or shade, though may fruit better if grown in sun. *Temperature:* Of the two, *H. latifolia* tends to be more cold sensitive, and can only tolerate brief frosts, though established plants are said to tolerate temperatures down to ~–12°C. This proably varies with degree of acclimatisation. *Soils/water:* Grow better in somewhat acidic, organic-matter-rich, moist soils, though like good drainage. Are not tolerant of waterlogging or of drought. *Pot culture*: Can be grown in a container and then taken inside during cold winters or given extra protection. *Propagation:* Seeds can be sown fresh with

uses

Food
The fruits can be eaten fresh and have a sweet, delicate flavour, though some consider them bland. Some fruits are almost all seed with very little flesh. The seeds should be discarded as they may cause an upset stomach, although the Chinese use them medicinally. Akebia can be mixed with more tangy fruits to improve their flavour. Some people fry and eat the somewhat tough skin. The young shoots can be used in salads, can be pickled, or used as a tea substitute.

Medicinal
The plants have a long history of medicinal use in China and have been used widely to treat infertility. The stems have antibacterial and antifungal properties and have been used to treat pain, stomach problems, urinary tract infections and lack of menstruation, to improve lactation, as a diuretic, also to relieve fevers and act as a stimulant. The fruits are also used to treat rheumatic disease, as a diuretic, for stomach problems, and as a general tonic and blood cleanser. The Chinese have also used the plant as a popular remedy to treat cancer, particularly gastro-intestinal cancers. **Warning:** Recently, Canadian research has warned about the use of plants that contain aristolochic acid, of which akebia is one. This is probably found predominantly within the leaves and stems. This toxin may cause cancer, mutations in human cells and end-stage kidney failure. Others promote the use of this plant to treat cancer! The fruit is probably safe to eat though.

Other uses
The stems have been used in basket-making.

Ornamental
Good for growing over hedges, low trees, bushes, arbours and pergolas.

all pulp removed. Sow in moist, warm compost in semi-shade. Can be propagated from green cuttings taken in spring and inserted in moist, gritty, warm compost to root in semi-shade. Semi-ripe cuttings can also be taken during summer. Layering can also be practised on healthy stems. These readily root from the tips, or along their length if lightly scored.

Uses: The fruits can be eaten fresh, but do not have a very distinctive flavour. Holboellia is often grown as an attractive, but not invasive, climbing plant rather than for its fruits.

Three-leaf akebia, *Akebia trifoliata*. A native of eastern Asia, from China, Korea and Japan, where it is grown for its edible fruits, medicinal properties and ornamental value. It forms a vigorous, evergreen, woody vine, growing to ~10 m and becoming deciduous in colder regions. Each leaf is divided into three leaflets, and the young foliage is bronze-red. There are racemes of purple flowers in spring, followed by cylindrical, oval, purplish fruits in late autumn. It is probably not self-fertile, and more than one cultivar should increase fruit-set; hand pollination will also increase fruit production. This species is quite cold hardy, down to at least ~–10°C. It can grow in full sun, though grows better with some shade. Like *A. quinata* (above), it dislikes root disturbance, and grows best in a moist soil. It is a vigorous vine, and may need to be controlled. Propagation as for *A. quinata*, and fruits can be used similarly, having the same medicinal properties (and warnings). ■

Amelanchier alnifolia
Saskatoon (amelanchier, juneberry, serviceberry)
ROSACEAE

Similar species: apple serviceberry (*A. lamarkii*), Quebec berry (*A. stolonifera*), shad bush, juneberry (*A. canadensis* syn. *A. laevis*), swamp sugar pea (*A. oblongifolia*), *A. asiatica*
Relatives: apples, pears, cherry

Members of the Rosaceae, along with various other fruits, many species of *Amelanchier* are popular for their abundant spring blossom and good autumn colour. They are sought after ornamental plants, are fully hardy, easy to control and suit smaller gardens. The saskatoon and other *Amelanchier* species frequently form natural hybrids, and often are difficult to specifically identify, but most species produce attractive, tasty summer berries that wildlife and people enjoy. Saskatoon is also known by several other common names (see above). It forms a shrub that is native to the Canadian prairies, the northern plains and southwestern states of the USA. It has been used as a food source by the native Indians for many hundreds of years. They mixed the fruit with meat and fats, then dried the mixture to create pemmican, which was a staple food for the winter. Early northern pioneers also survived the winter by eating the dried berries. However, until ~20 years ago, the fruits were only harvested from the wild or picked from small cultivated plots, but there is now increasing interest in the commercial production of this species for its fruit. The word 'saskatoon' is derived from the Cree word 'misaskwatomin', meaning 'tree of much wood'.

DESCRIPTION

An upright, suckering shrub or small tree, 1–5 m tall, 1–3 m spread, with moderate growth. Spreads by underground stems. Its bark is silvery–reddish.

Leaves: Thin, egg-shaped to a tapering oval shape, deciduous, toothed, non-lobed, dark green leaves (~2.5–6 cm long). Has spectacular yellow–bronze–red autumn colour. Young leaves often have a reddish tinge and fine pubescence, which disappears as they mature.

Flowers: Attractive, creamy-white, five-petalled, star-shaped flowers in clusters of 3–20, which form 5–10-cm-long pendulous racemes in spring. They are borne on the previous year's growth from leaf axils, with a few also occurring on older wood. They are extremely profuse and showy, but only last for 4–7 days.
Pollination: Saskatoons are self-fertile, but seem to produce more fruits when planted in groups.

Fruit: Juicy, good-quality, sweet and tasty: like blueberries, but sweeter, and are often used as a substitute in colder regions. They are borne in clusters. The berries are small (~0.5–1.25 cm diameter) and round, and turn from pink to blue-black as they ripen, and develop a whitish bloom. They have 4–10 small, central seeds per fruit. They ripen in early–mid summer. Young, vigorous branches usually yield the best-quality fruit.

Yield/harvest: Trees usually give good yields. Begin to bear fruits when 2–4 years old, with peak production occurring in a further 2–3 years. Plants can be productive for many years; a mature plant can produce ~2+ kg of fruit/year. The whole fruit cluster often ripens together, so the complete crop can often be harvested at the same time, leading to little wastage due to picking over- or under-ripe fruits. They do not store well, so should be frozen or dried soon after harvesting if they are wanted for longer-term use.

Roots: Has shallow, spreading, suckering roots, so avoid deep cultivation. Minimise weed competition and supply a mulch to reduce moisture loss.

CULTIVATION

Extremely adaptable, hardy and easy to grow, and will thrive under a wide range of environmental conditions. All *Amelanchier* species are hardy.

Location: Can be grown in sun or part-shade. Likes a fairly sheltered location: is not very wind tolerant.

Temperature: Extremely cold tolerant: flower buds have not been injured at temperature of ~–60°C! Although adapted to colder climates, they can also grow and (usually) fruit in hotter climates.

Chilling: Will need a period of chilling, possibly similar to that of apples and pears (>500 hours), though does seem to fruit in warmer areas, so chilling may not be as important for these species. Longer days may give better fruit production.

Soil/water/nutrients: Will grow in many soil types, but grows better in sandy rather than clay loams. Can tolerate somewhat alkaline soils, up to pH ~7.5, but prefers more acidic soils. Plants prefer a drier soil, and are more drought tolerant than many fruit species, though can grow in humid regions. Regular, but not excessive, moisture maximises growth and fruit yield, though plants are not tolerant of waterlogging. Can benefit from applications of a general fertiliser in spring and summer, when the plant is actively growing. Applications in autumn, as the plant becomes dormant, can reduce the plant's winter-hardiness.

Planting: Space plants at 2–3 m apart.

Pruning: Should be done in early spring, after the danger of severe frost has passed and before the plants start to grow. Pruning can significantly extend the plant's life and improve health and yields. Remove all weak, diseased and damaged wood, and thin out the centre to allow air and light to penetrate the canopy. Bushes are often commercially pruned to a height of ~2 m. Once plants are >6–7 years old, prune out some older branches to encourage new, vigorous shoot growth. Older shrubs can be rejuvenated by cutting them back to ground level, and then allowing new sprouts to grow.

Propagation: *Seeds:* Flesh should be washed from the harvested seeds. These can either be stored chilled in a fridge at ~4°C, in a sealed container, for at least 3 months, or can be sown while fresh in autumn, but need to be left in a cool place until the following spring. Germination may be slow, but should be fairly good by both methods. Seedlings do have varying characteristics though. *Cuttings:* Ripe to semi-ripe stem cuttings in spring–summer. Rooting powder or willow washings may improve root growth. Grow on for the first year before planting out. Root cuttings can also be taken when plants are dormant, from young roots, as close to the plant as possible. Make a horizontal cut nearest to the plant and an angled cut at the distal end. Bury the cutting with the horizontal cut nearest the soil surface. *Suckers:* Easy. Remove rooted suckers with as many fine roots as possible, cut back tops to 5 cm; plant and keep well-watered till established. *Layering:* Can layer low-spreading stems in spring: take ~18 months to root.

Pests and diseases: As for most members of the Rosaceae family, problems may include rusts, fireblight, powdery mildews and leafminers, also borers, mites, scales and sawflies, but these tend to be less common. Birds and other wildlife seek out the fruits: may need to use netting as fruits begin to ripen.

CULTIVARS

'Honeywood': A vigorous shrub. Late flowering, with large, pleasant-tasting fruit with few seeds. Produces good crops within 3–4 years.

'Northline': Very productive. Produces sweet fruits within 3 years; suckers freely.

'Pembina': Height: ~3 m. Fruits are large and sweet.

'Regent': A good ornamental, height: ~2 m, few suckers. Fruits are sweet and seedless, but allegedly less tasty than other cultivars.

'Smokey': Height: 2.5–3 m. Lots of suckers. Very productive. Fruits are fleshy, medium-sized, good quality, sweet. Susceptible to rust. Very popular cultivar in Canada.

'Thiessen': Height: ~4.5 m. Good yields. Fruits are large, good flavour, but uneven ripening.

SIMILAR SPECIES

The above general description applies to these species unless stated otherwise.

Apple serviceberry, *Amelanchier lamarkii*. A shrub, native to North America, height ~6 m. Flowers in spring, fruits ripen in summer. Can grow in heavier clay soils. Does not produce suckers. Very good quality, sweet, succulent fruit (~1 cm diameter): can be eaten fresh, cooked or dried. Has a good apple flavour.

Korean juneberry, *Amelanchier asiatica*. Native to Japan and Korea, often forms a larger tree, up to ~10 m, but ornamental, with slender branches. It has small, but good-quality dark-coloured berries. Has long, oval, slender leaves and white flowers. Good autumn colour.

Mountain juneberry, *Amelanchier alnifolia*. A native of western North America, it forms a shrub ~2 m tall. Has white flowers in spring and sweet, juicy, dark purple berries in late summer.

Quebec berry, *Amelanchier stolonifera*. A native of eastern North America. It forms a smaller shrub: height ~1.5 m tall. Flowers in spring; fruits ripen in summer. Good-quality fruits, with an apple taste, and shrubs give good yields. Suckers can start fruiting in their second year. Suckers freely, and can form thickets. Can grow in heavier clay soils. Dislikes alkaline soils. Relatively drought tolerant.

Food

Fruits are of good quality and taste somewhat like blueberries, but often sweeter. Can be eaten fresh or can be added to sauces, pies, juices, confectionery and desserts, or can be canned, frozen or made into wine, or eaten with cheese. They are best when fully ripe. The leaves make a reasonable-tasting tea.

Nutrition/medicinal

The berries contain higher levels of protein, fat and fibre than most other fruit. They have good levels of vitamin C, magnesium, iron and copper. They also contain some calcium, phosphorous, zinc, manganese and vitamin A. Studies have shown that the more intense the purple colour of the fruits, the higher their antioxidant content, and these fruits have a similar antioxidant activity to blueberries, which is very high. They are beneficial in reducing low-density-lipid levels and in protecting against heart disease. They also contain ~20% sucrose and ~10% reducing sugars: sugar levels rise markedly before ripening. The predominant organic acid is malic acid.

Other uses

The wood is hard, straight grained and tough. It is used for tool handles, etc. If the wood is heated, it becomes even harder and can be easily moulded whilst still hot.

Ornamental

Is an excellent ornamental plant with its abundant blossom and autumn colour. Good for small gardens. In general, the flowers and autumn colour show best against dark backgrounds. They are useful shrubs to plant for erosion control.

Shad bush, juneberry, *Amelanchier canadensis* (syn. *A. laevis*). Woolly, young shoots. Height ~6–8 m, spread ~3+ m. Yellow autumn colour. White flowers are abundant in spring, followed by purple–red, round, sweet fruits (~1 cm diameter) that ripen in mid–late summer. Fruit yields are better if grown in a sunny position. Has good autumn colour. More tolerant of waterlogging than many other *Amelanchier* species, and can even grow in heavy clays. Fairly wind tolerant. Food uses as *A. alnifolia*. Has an apple and almond flavour. Can be grown as a windbreak/hedge. Cultivar: 'Prince William' Largish (~3 m height, 2 m spread), multi-stemmed shrub. Crops heavily, good quality fruit (~1 cm diameter).

Snowy mespilus (European juneberry), *Amelanchier ovalis*. Native to central and southern Europe, it forms a small tree or large shrub to ~3 m tall. Has large flowers, ~3 cm diameter, and then small berries that turn from bright red to a deep dark red, almost black, which are covered with a bloom. They are tart, and are usually added to jams or wines, and not eaten fresh.

Swamp sugar pea, *Amelanchier oblongifolia*. A native of southeastern North America. The shrubs are stoloniferous. Can grow in heavy clay soils. Fairly drought resistant and can grow in hotter areas. Good-quality sweet fruit (~1.2 cm diameter). Has good yields and starts cropping when young. Popular with early colonists of the USA. ∎

Ampelopsis brevipedunculata (syn. *A. heterophylla* var. *amurensis*, *Cissus revipedunculata*)
Porcelain berry (blueberry climber, pepper vine)
VITACEAE

Ampelopsis is a genus from the same family as grapes. The name *Ampelopsis* comes from the Greek 'ampelos', meaning 'vine', and 'opsis', meaning 'likeness to'. The porcelain berry is a climber that is a native of eastern Asia: China, Japan, Korea and eastern Russia. It forms a vigorous, attractive vine that has multi-coloured, edible berries in autumn, and also edible leaves and stems. Its spread is fairly easy to control; however, it has become a problem weed on the northeastern coast of the USA.

uses

DESCRIPTION

An ornamental, vigorous, plant that climbs by two-pronged tendrils and also sticky pads on its shoots that adhere to rough surfaces. It grows to ~3–6 m height, ~3–5 m spread. Mature vines can form a thick trunk. Young stems are finely downy.

Leaves: Deciduous, alternate, ~10 cm wide, heart-shaped, wavy surface, have 3–5 deep lobes, coarsely serrated, finely hairy beneath, dark green.

Flower: Small, greenish-white, borne in mid–late summer. Are pollinated by bees, and are also popular with butterflies.

Fruit: Often grown ornamentally for its fruit, but they need a warm summer and mild autumn to develop. They are 0.6–0.8 mm in diameter, and are borne in grape-like bunches. Colours range from wonderful shades of green, pale yellow, lilac, turquoise to porcelain blue, depending on their stage of development, and a single cluster of berries can have many shades at a given time, though this also means that fruits within a cluster ripen at differing times.

CULTIVATION

Easy-to-grow vigorous vine that does need good hot summers to fully ripen its fruits.

Location: Prefers a sunny location, but can also grow in semi-shade. Is not wind tolerant, and is best sited in a sheltered spot.

Temperature: Is hardy and will survive frosts, but not prolonged cold winters, although the subspecies *A. brevipedunculata maximowiczii* (syn. *A. heterophylla*) is very hardy. Needs summer light and warmth for the berries to develop fully.

Soil/water/nutrients: Grows best in a deep, fertile loam and prefers pH values of 6–6.5, but can grow in soils either side of that range. It will also grow in poor-quality soils. In fact, high fertility results in vigorous leaf growth, often at the expense of flower and fruit production. As is the case for many climbers, they seem to flower and fruit better on poorer soils. Similarly, if the roots are restricted or pruned, vines tend to fruit more because this stresses the plant into seed-survival mode. Porcelain-berry vines only need a little water in winter, but prefer moisture from spring–autumn. Will not tolerate wet or waterlogged soils, but is somewhat drought tolerant once established.

Pot culture: Can be grown in pots with a wire frame, particularly the more frost-sensitive cultivar, 'Elegans', and can then be moved inside in colder weather. In addition, by confining the roots in a smaller space, the plant responds by producing more flowers and fruits. However, like most climbers, they grow better if their roots are kept in the shade and cool, and over-heating of roots within containers is a common, often overlooked, problem. A top mulch on the soil and planting in a lighter-coloured container may help to reduce root heat stress, as will siting plants in semi-shade.

Planting: Best sited against a trellis, wall or fence in sun or semi-shade. It will twine around a wire structure, but may need some additional tying-in as the plant becomes larger and heavier.

Food

The fruits are usually cooked, but cannot be highly recommended for their flavour. The leaf buds, young leaves and stems can be also lightly cooked as a vegetable.

Medicinal

The plant has been used to treat fevers, as a blood cleanser and to dissolve clots.

Ornamental

Is an attractive ornamental vine with showy, colourful berries, although may need keeping in check. Can be grown as a bonsai species. Birds are attracted to the ripe berries.

uses

Propagation: *Seed:* Germinates easily from fresh seed. Sow when fresh in autumn and over-winter in a cool place to germinate in spring. Stored seeds benefit from a period of cold stratification, i.e. 2–4 months at 5°C, before sowing in spring in warm, moist compost in semi-shade. *Cuttings:* Take semi-ripe cuttings, ~8 cm long, in summer, or hardwood cuttings in autumn or winter. Insert in gritty but moist compost, in semi-shade, to root. *Layering:* Gently score areas of a trailing stem, and bury these sections shallowly in soil, from early–late summer. In the following spring, partially cut through the stem connecting it to the mother plant, and then remove the rooted plantlets in autumn.

Pruning: Only needs pruning to control its growth and spread: this is better carried out in winter or early spring. Roots can be pruned back in winter to encourage more fruiting.

Pests and diseases: Can get problems with scale, mildew and black rot. The leaves are very susceptible to insect damage; unfortunately, they can also be easily damaged by pesticide sprays. Trailing branches often die back in the winter, however, the plant regrows from its crown.

CULTIVARS

'Elegans': Attractive plant. Young leaves are variegated white and green, and it has pinkish stems. More frost sensitive than other cultivars. ■

Anacardium occidentale
Cashew (cashew apple)
ANACARDIACEAE
Relatives: mango, pistachio, sumac, poison ivy, smoke tree

The cashew is native to northeast Brazil. The cashew tree and its nuts and fruits have been used for centuries by the indigenous tribes of the rainforests, and it is a commonly cultivated plant in South America. In the 16th century, Portuguese traders introduced it to Mozambique and coastal India, but only to prevent soil erosion at the coast. It flourished and ran wild and formed extensive forests in these locations and on nearby islands, and eventually became dispersed in East Africa and throughout the tropical lowlands of northern South America, Central America and the West Indies. Trade in cashew nuts started at the beginning of the 20th century and grew particularly fast in the 1930s, being dominated mainly by India. In the 1960s, the cashew completed a full circle by coming back to its land of origin, Brazil, where large commercial plantations were set up together with processing factories. India is now the dominant producer (~50% of market), with Brazil the next largest producer. West Africa, Indonesia and Vietnam also have many plantations. Worldwide ~60% of cashews are consumed as salted snacks, mostly by Americans, but also by the English. Cashew trees are very tough and can grow with little maintenance in a variety of conditions; in addition, their nuts, fruits and other plant parts are used for a multitude of purposes.

DESCRIPTION
A fairly large, spreading, fast-growing tree, 9–14 m tall, 6–10 m wide. Lower limbs often bend to touch the ground.

Leaves: Evergreen, simple, oval with rounded tips, which are sometimes notched. They occur mainly in terminal clusters, large, oval, leathery, 10–20 cm long, 5–14 cm wide.

Flowers: Aromatic, yellowish-pink, small, five-petalled, in 15–25-cm wide terminal panicles. Flowers can be male, female or bisexual on the same panicle. Trees can flower for ~2–3 months, usually from spring onwards. *Pollination:* Mostly by bees, but also other insects.

Fruit: It has unusual, bizarre, colourful, two-piece fruits. The nut is kidney-shaped, the size of a large bean, thick-shelled, and is borne externally and beneath a yellow/orange fleshy receptacle or pseudo-fruit, more commonly called a 'cashew apple'. The kernel is covered in two shells, between which is a thick, caustic, toxic oil that contains cardol and anacardic acid, which must be removed. Unprocessed nuts should be handled with gloves because of this oil. The nut develops first and, when full-grown, but not yet ripe, the cashew apple becomes plump, fragrant, fleshy, pear-shaped, 5–11 cm in length, with a waxy, yellow, red, or red-and-yellow skin with spongy, fibrous, very juicy, astringent, acid to sub-acid, yellow pulp. The flavour of the 'apples' varies from tree to tree, but is usually slightly astringent, though refreshing. Yellow fruits are usually sweeter. Flowers and fruits in various degrees of development are often present in same panicle.

Yield/harvest/storage: Seedling trees take ~3–5 years to start producing fruits; vegetatively-produced trees take 2–3 years to start fruiting. Trees are at full production by their 8–10th year, and then continue to bear until they are ~30–40 years old. Under good conditions, a tree can produce ~50 kg of apples, of which ~3 kg are kernels. Fruits take ~2–3 months to form after fruit-set. The apple and nut fall together when both are ripe. They should be handled using gloves because of the toxic cardol oil, which has to be removed before the kernels can be accessed (see Uses below). Commercially, the apples are often not utilised, which is a great shame because they have several uses and are quite tasty. However, they only have a short storage time before they start to deteriorate and ferment, so need to be processed soon after harvesting. Kernels, once removed from their shells, and dried to ~12% moisture to reduce the risk of aflotoxin infection, can be kept in sealed containers in the cool and dark for extended periods. They rapidly deteriorate in humid environments.

Roots: In order to survive poor soils, the trees form long taproots with extensive lateral roots so that they can make the most of soil nutrients and moisture. Avoid transplanting.

CULTIVATION
Once established, cashew trees need little care.

Location: They grow best in full sun. It is reported by some that they are wind tolerant; others say that they are not.

Temperature: Can grow in warm-temperate moist climates, tropical climates and also dry arid locations. They prefer annual temperatures of 21–28°C. They are frost sensitive, with leaves being damaged at 0°C, and serious damage can occur at –4°C. However, although older trees can be damaged by cold temperatures, they usually recover.

Soil/water/nutrients: Can be grown on poor, sterile, very shallow, dry, impervious soils where few other trees or crops will grow. They are also tolerant of saline soils and are drought tolerant once established. Best growth is at somewhat acidic pH 4.3–6.5, but can also grow in soils up to pH 8.7. Trees may also tolerate brief periods of flooding.

They grow best with some moisture, particularly during nut development, but trees also benefit from a 3–4 month dry season. Although not nutrient hungry, one or two annual applications of a balanced general fertiliser can increase growth and yields.

Planting: Space plants at ~10 m apart, thinning to ~20 m between trees as the trees become larger. Plant carefully to avoid damaging the taproot.

Pruning: For the first 3 years, the lower branches and suckers should be removed. Otherwise there is minimal pruning, just to remove any crossing or crowded branches, or any damaged or diseased wood.

Propagation: *Seed:* Generally propagated by seed, but it germinates slowly and often poorly. Plant seedlings in deep

Preparation
The whole nuts should be roasted at 180–200ºC to remove the caustic oil, but the oil released during heating can damage skin and eyes, so they need to be contained. After roasting, the whole nuts are washed in water and detergent to remove any residual oil, and then the nuts are cracked open, and the thin pellicle removed from around the kernel. Commercially, cashews are heated in a perforated, rotating drum to release the caustic oil, and then sprayed with water to cool them. Once the oil and shells are removed, the kernels can be roasted or boiled to remove any remaining toxins.

Food (nut)
Apart from the problems of actually removing the kernel, the cashew is one of the most delicious nuts after being roasted. Kernels can be eaten raw, roasted and salted, or mixed in chocolates. They can be used in stuffing, confectionery and other dishes where nuts are used. The kernel can yield about 45% of a pale yellow, edible oil that resembles almond oil.

Food ('apple')
In Goa, the apples are still trampled by foot to extract the juice for the locally famous distilled liquor, feni. They are also popular in South America. In Brazil the apples are sold in local markets. A juice or wine can be made from them. They can also be eaten fresh, or preserved as jam, chutney, or added to desserts. Yellow apples are said to be sweeter than red apples. However, unfortunately, the apples are often just discarded as a waste product because they deteriorate so quickly.

Nutrition
Of the 45% oil within the kernel, at least 25% of this is monounsaturated, though ~50% of this is saturated. The nuts also contain ~30% carbohydrate and ~15% protein. They make an excellent, nutritious, sustaining energy food. They are also high in magnesium, phosphates, copper and manganese. The apple is very high in vitamin C (>150 mg/100 g of pulp), and also contains calcium, phosphorous and iron.

Medicinal
The plant has been reported to have antibacterial, anti-diarrhoea, antimicrobial, antiseptic, anti-inflammatory, cough-soothing, aphrodisiac, astringent, diuretic, parasite-ridding, hypoglycaemic, calming, soothing, intestinal-easing and tonic properties. One of the plant's main active compounds is anacardic acid, with greater quantities found in the nut shells. This compound has proven antibiotic activity against many Gram+ (*Escherichia coli* and *Pseudomonas aeruginosa*) and Gram-negative bacterium (e.g. *Helicobacter pylori*, now known to cause stomach ulcers); a recent study showed it to be effective against 13 of 15 micro-organisms tested. It also inhibits tyrosinase activity (i.e. inhibits the darkening effect of skin ageing) and is toxic to certain cancer cells. Also, there is some evidence it has a protective effect on diabetes by stabilising blood-glucose levels. People in South America still use the fruit juice against influenza, and the leaves, fruit and bark for diarrhoea. A bark tea is used for colic, as a vaginal douche and as an astringent after a tooth extraction. The toxic seed oil is used for warts. The leaves have been used to treat syphilis, skin infections, as an aphrodisiac and a mouthwash; the bark has been used to treat urinary disorders, asthma, muscular and skin problems, and bronchitis. Both the bark and leaves are a rich source of tannins and have anti-inflammatory and astringent properties, and are used to treat diarrhoea. Frederick Rosengarten reports that in the West Indies the oil's drastic properties have been used in an alarming way by women as a beauty treatment. They applied the oil to the face, and the resulting blistering was so severe that the surface skin peeled off, to leave a new complexion underneath: probably not to be recommended! *Warning:* Skin contact with various parts of the fresh plant (leaves, bark, fruit, oil) may cause dermatitis and react as an allergen, though roasting or heating should deactivate most allergens. A very few people are allergic to the kernel itself: it may cross-react with pistachio nuts.

Other uses
The caustic cardol oil is commercially extracted and used as a preservative, a lubricant, a waterproofing agent and in a wide range of industrial processes. It is also used to termite-proof timber. The wood is used to make furniture and for boatbuilding. The high tannin content of the bark makes it suitable for tanning. The stems exude a clear gum, cashawa gum, which is used in pharmaceuticals and as substitute for gum arabic. It is used as a varnish for books and woodwork, and protects against insects and ants. Extracts from the tree can kill molluscs. The sap turns black on exposure to air and provides an indelible ink. The apples, because of their high vitamin C and other compounds, are used in cosmetic preparations for premature ageing of the skin and to re-mineralise skin. It is also used as a hair and scalp conditioner and is included in shampoos and creams. The flowers attract bees.

Ornamental
Trees can be planted as a shelter belt, windbreak and to stabilise sand dunes.

biodegradable pots to reduce stress when transplanting. Seedlings do not transplant well. *Layering:* Air-layering during the growing season can be practised successfully. *Grafting:* Trees are sometimes grafted onto seedlings to obtain reliable characteristics and get earlier harvests.

Pests and diseases: Cashew trees have few serious diseases or pests, although thrips can be a problem. The 'apples' can attract fruit flies. ∎

Ananas comosus
Pineapple (ananas, pina)
BROMELIACEAE
Similar species: heart of flame (*Bromelia balancia*), red pineapple (*Ananas bracteatus*)

The pineapple is the main edible member of the family Bromeliaceae, which includes ~60 genera and ~1800 species, most of which are epiphytes and are often strikingly ornamental. Many of these species are native to the southern US regions down to the Caribbean. This family includes many tremendously well-adapted species that can grow in extreme environments. Many are able to grow at very low moisture levels, and include 'air plants', which grow from the branches of trees relying on atmospheric moisture alone and scavenging nutrients from organic remains within the canopy, and have no roots that penetrate soil. Other species are able to grow in arid, desert-like environments, and many can grow in very salty soils. In addition, many species have edible fruits. The pineapple is a native of southern Brazil and Paraguay, and its fruits have been used for many hundreds of years. It was probably domesticated by the native populations and was then taken to Central America, Mexico and the West Indies, long before the arrival of the Spanish or Portuguese. It was first 'discovered' by Europeans (Christopher Columbus) on the island of Guadeloupe in 1493, and from there was taken, cultivated and transported around the world on sailing ships as a protection against scurvy. Caribbean Indians placed pineapples outside the entrances of their homes as a symbol of friendship and hospitality. Europeans adopted this symbolism and the fruit was represented by carvings placed over doorways in Spain, England and, later, New England. The pineapple reached England in 1660, and was grown in greenhouses, often of large stately homes, for its fruit during Victorian times. It was named pineapple because of the fruit's resemblance to a pinecone. The plant is now naturalised in most Central American countries, but wild fruits are of very poor quality. Commercially, selected varieties have now become one of the main fruit crops of the tropics.

DESCRIPTION
A small, herbaceous, perennial, with long, rough, sword-like leaves, arranged in a spiral around a short stem. Up to 1 m tall.

Leaves: Long, 50–150 cm, sword-like, tough, fibrous, arranged in a tight spiral around a short stem. Its edges have very fine teeth, or are smooth with a fine silver band. Leaves can be light–dark grey-green, but some cultivars have coloured leaves that can be mixes of red, yellow, purple, crimson or silver. The leaves are adapted to low water levels and bright light. The rosette shape the leaves form ensures that any rain is funnelled down into the centre of the plant. Both sides of the leaves are covered in a fine silvery hair, which bounces bright sunlight away. The leaves also have a thick cuticle to prevent moisture loss. In addition, plants carry out Crassulacean photosynthesis, which means that they trap light energy during the day, but do not open their stomata at this time, like most other species. Instead they only open their stomata at night to allow the entry of carbon dioxide, which then biochemically combines with the stored sunlight's energy to produce sugars. By only opening at night, much less moisture is lost from the leaf. In all, the pineapple is superbly adapted to deal with hot, dry conditions.

Flowers: Initially, the short flower stem elongates and enlarges. Clustered around it are numerous small purple–red flowers, each with a single red, yellow or green bract. The stem then continues to grow and forms a crown of stiff, short leaves above the flower cluster. Plants usually bear only one flower stalk at a time, though occasionally there can be 2–3 heads. The oldest flowers are formed at the base of inflorescence. The time of flowering for pineapples is often unpredictable and, commercially, plant hormones (e.g. ethylene) are often used to induce flowering and subsequent fruiting. Flowering may be initiated by a drop in temperature of ~10°C during the colder months. *Pollination:* Flowers are bisexual and are self-fertile. However, commercial pineapples are seedless, and the fruits are formed without pollination (like bananas; parthenocarpy). If the flowers are pollinated, they produce small, hard seeds. In the wild, hummingbirds are attracted to the abundant nectar these flowers produce, and fertilise the flowers.

Fruit: The 'fruit' consists of a whole cluster of fruitlets. As the individual flowers mature, their ovaries become fleshy, and the many ovaries fuse to form a single pineapple, with hexagonal-shaped cells on the fruit's surface indicating the individual 'true' fruits. The somewhat fibrous stem runs through the fruit and continues out beyond the top of the fruit to form a leafy bract (crown). Pineapples measure ~30 cm in length. The outer covering is tough and waxy, and is actually the modified sepals and bracts of the individual flowers. Fruits are green when young, ripening to yellow, orange or reddish when ripe. The flesh ranges in colour from nearly white to yellow. After the fruits have ripened, the plant develops new shoots from axillary buds on the stem, and these can go on to produce further fruits.

Yield: Plants are 18–24 months old before they start to produce fruits. They can then produce fruits for 3–5 years before needing to be replaced. In warmer climates, fruits can be produced for much of the year. Fruits take ~150–275 days from flowering until maturity in warmer climates. They should only be picked when fully ripe and have developed full flavour and sweetness. This is usually during summer, with fruit taking several weeks to fully ripen. However, over-ripe fruits start to lose their tangy flavour and deteriorate quickly. Ripeness can be assessed by tapping the fruit: ripe fruits have a dull, solid sound, unripe fruits have a hollow sound.

Roots: Pineapples form two main types of roots. They have short, shallow, adventitious feeder roots that form at the base of the stem; in addition, there are longer main roots that grow deeper. Cultivation around plants should be minimised. Plants will benefit from an organic mulch to suppress weeds and conserve moisture.

CULTIVATION

Location: Plants can grow in full sun or light shade. In cooler areas they should be planted in the sunniest spot, but because they are small plants they can be easily covered to protect them from the cold.

Temperatures: Plants grow best in warmer climates, ideally >22°C: they stop growing at temperatures below ~13°C. Temperatures that are too high can cause sunburn and split the fruit. They are not frost tolerant: leaves are damaged at −2°C and plants are killed at lower temperatures. Even prolonged temperatures of 5°C result in tissue deterioration and acidic fruit. They like even temperatures throughout the year.

Soil/water/nutrients: They grow best in a well-drained, friable, loam, but can grow in a number of soil types including pure sand, clay loam and gravelly soils. They like a rooting depth of at least 60 cm. Organic matter adds nutrients and helps the soil to hold more moisture. They can grow at a fairly wide pH range: 4.5–7, from quite acidic to fairly alkaline soils. They are able to grow in both humid (semi-tropical/tropical) and dry climates. They cannot tolerate waterlogging, but can tolerate drought once established, though fruit quality is likely to be compromised if it is too dry for too long. Pineapples are moderately nutrient hungry,

particularly when they are actively growing. They benefit from fertilisers that contain more nitrogen, but less potassium. Nitrogen is needed for fruit size and yield; this can be achieved using urea sprays. Phosphorus is only needed in deficient soils. Pineapples also need adequate iron, which will be of more importance in alkaline soils where this becomes unavailable at pH >6.5. This can be supplied by a foliar spray of ferrous sulphate. Commercially, tar-paper or black plastic is often used as a mulch. A mulch is used to conserve moisture, heat up the soil and to suppress weeds. An organic mulch can also be used.

Pot culture: Because of their small size, they are ideal for growth in containers in colder regions. They can then be moved inside to a conservatory or similar for winter protection. Plant in well-drained soils. Variegated forms are particularly attractive.

Planting: Crowns are planted at ~5 cm depth; suckers at 10 cm depth. Planting is best done in late spring or early summer. Space plants 30–45 cm apart. Because they are short lived, they can be planted between longer-term crops. Planting in a raised bed can ensure good drainage.

Propagation: Cuttings: This is the main method of propagation. Cuttings can be taken from 'crowns', which grow from the top of fruits, 'slips', which grow out from the stalk below the fruit, 'suckers', which grow out from the axils of leaves and 'ratoons', which grow out from underground stems. Crowns are the most readily available method when starting out, as these can be removed from shop-bought fruit. The crowns can be cut off the mother plant, the bottom leaves removed, the crown is then left to dry for ~2+ days and is then planted or stood in water to start forming roots. Slips and suckers often produce better plants and are preferable if you have established plants already. Remove these, or ratoon suckers, from the base of the mother plant, allow the wound to callus over for about a week, and then plant these in well-drained compost to establish.

Pests and diseases: The most likely problems are mealybugs and nematodes. Nematodes can destroy roots and seriously stunt plants. These problems can be reduced by rotating plants in new soil areas and by not growing plants in soils with a high sand content. Controlling ants should help control mealybugs. If the weather is cool and damp, then fungal rots can be a problem: both top and root rots. Planting in raised beds can reduce this risk.

CULTIVARS

Most commercial pineapples are cultivars of *A. comosus*. There are many cultivars and a few of these are listed below.
'Abacaxi': Plant is spiny and disease-resistant. Leaves: bluish-green with red-purple tinge. Has numerous suckers. Fruit: 1–5 kg, can sunburn, is very fragrant. Flesh: white–pale yellow, rich, sweet, succulent and juicy. Highly rated by many.
'Kona Sugarloaf': Fruit: 2.5–3 kg, flesh is white, inner stem is non-woody. Cylindrical in shape, has a high sugar content, but no acid. Delicious fruit.
'Queen' or 'Table Queen': Fruits 0.9–1.3 kg, flesh is rich yellow, mild in flavour, crisp, juicy, fragrant, low acid, a good fresh fruit. A dwarf plant, compact. Fruits mature early, but plants sucker freely and yields are low. Stores well, but is susceptible to *Phytophthora*, chilling and internal browning.

Food

The rind is usually peeled from the fruit and the flesh diced or sliced. In tougher cultivars the inner core may be removed. Pineapple is tangy, yet sweet, and is delicious when fully ripe. Excellent eaten fresh, or can be added to desserts, pies, made into conserves, added to meat, chicken or fish dishes, added to curries, salads, cakes, cereals or made into sauces. In the Philippines, the fermented pulp is made into a popular sweetmeat called *nata de pina*. The juice can be fermented to make an alcoholic drink. The flesh does not freeze well. In Africa, the young, tender shoots are eaten in salads. The terminal bud and young flowers can be eaten raw or cooked.

Nutrition/medicinal

Fruits have reasonable levels of vitamin C (15–55 mg/100 g of flesh), and a very high antioxidant capacity: 1–4 times greater than pure vitamin E. Fruits contain some B6, thiamine and folate. They are high in manganese, and have reasonable levels of fibre. Pineapples produce bromelain, a mix of several protease enzymes. Commercially this is used as a meat tenderiser, in manufacturing pre-cooked cereals and in certain cosmetics. Bromelain is also used as a digestive, for its strong anti-inflammatory properties and to reduce swellings. It is also a nematicidal. It has been shown to interfere with the growth of malignant cells, to inhibit platelet aggregation and for skin debridement. It also seems to reduce the number of white blood cells. It is possible that it works by interfering with the synthesis of inflammatory substances in the body, such as prostaglandins (see also Warning note). The ripe fruits also act as a diuretic, but, in large doses, may cause uterine contractions. Juice from the leaves is consumed as a vermifuge and as a purgative. Steroid compounds from the lower leaves possess oestrogenic activity. The fruit, peel or juice is used on corns, tumours and warts. *Warning:* The juice from unripe fruits can act as a violent purgative and cause abortion. At high doses, bromelain may cause nausea, vomiting, diarrhoea, skin rash and menorrhagia.

Other uses

Pineapple leaf fibre is considered to be more delicate, yet stronger in texture, than any other plant fibre. It is white and creamy, shiny like silk and easily takes and retains dyes. It makes a very high-quality, smooth, thin paper and, in the Philippines, it is made into a fine-quality cloth. In some areas, pineapples are just grown for fibre production.

Ornamental

It makes an interesting, attractive houseplant, or border plant in warmer climates.

'Ripley' or 'Ripley Queen': Grown in Queensland, is a dwarf, compact plant, with crimson tinge on leaves; is an irregular bearer. Fruit: 1.3-2.7 kg; yellow-brown skin, pale yellow flesh, is non-fibrous, very sweet and rich.

OTHER SPECIES

Heart of flame, *Bromelia balancia*. Closely related to pineapple, this species is native to Argentina, Bolivia and Brazil. The plant is ~1 m tall and, in general, is similar in appearance to the pineapple, with spiny leaves. These are long, 0.5–1.5 m, bluey-grey-green in colour, coarse and fibrous. Their upward-facing spines can be painful, and so the plant is best not sited near to thoroughfares. Typical of many bromeliads, this species has very colourful inner leaves, which inspired its common name. They turn a vivid red-violet colour during flowering, becoming more noticeable than the flowers. Similar to those of the pineapple, these flowers are violet in colour, small (~2 cm long), and occur along an erect flower spike (~20 cm long), but are borne in looser clusters than those of pineapple. The fruit is composed of many fruitlets, in the same way as pineapple, but these are not closely fused. Its flesh is yellow and juicy. The fruits can remain on the plant for quite long periods before deteriorating, encouraging the wildlife to eat the flesh and scatter the inner seeds.

Cultivation: This species can be grown in tropical and subtropical regions, but will also grow and fruit in warm-temperate regions. They are relatively cold hardy, though benefit from extra protection in cold weather. They are best planted in a warm, protected site in cooler areas. They grow better in more acidic soils, and do not tolerate alkaline conditions very well. Plants tend to spread readily in the right location by underground stolons, and removal of suckers is an easy method of propagation. This species can be also grown from seed, though will take longer to start producing fruits. Cleaned seeds have a good rate of germination and should germinate within a few days in warm, moist, but well-drained, compost.

Uses: Reports on the edibility of its fruits vary from being acidic and unpalatable to being sweet and quite tasty. It is likely that fruit quality varies from plant to plant, and the conditions they are grown under. The expressed juice can be used in drinks. The fruits may contain quite high levels of calcium oxalate (like spinach), and so probably should not be eaten in quantity. The fruits contain several compounds that are similar to papain (as found in papaya), which can be used to tenderise meat, but are also being investigated for their ability to solidify milk. The plants are attractive, and make a fine ornamental, exotic specimen for borders in full sun or semi-shade, and can be grown beneath trees.

Red pineapple, *Ananas bracteatus*. Tropical in appearance, but surprisingly hardy, this species has been known to fruit in temperate–warm temperate regions. The fruits are sweet and juicy; flesh is pinky-yellow, weighs ~1 kg. A well-tended plant with lots of suckers can produce up to six fruits in 3 years. Plant in a sunny location in well-drained soil. ■

Annona cherimola
Cherimoya (custard apple)
ANNONACEAE

Similar species: llama, *Annona diversifolia*

Relatives: soursop, sugar apple, atemoya

Many of the *Annona* genus produce edible fruits, and these are composed of numerous embryos more or less fused together to form a fleshy receptacle. Cherimoya is the best known fruit of this genus and is sometimes misnamed 'custard apple'. In Australia, it is sometimes also known as atemoya (a cherimoya-sugar apple hybrid). Cherimoya has been cultivated for centuries in the highlands of Peru and Ecuador, and was highly prized by the Incas. In 1757, it was carried to Spain where it was grown locally as a garden tree until the 1940s, after which it gained importance as a replacement for the many orange trees that succumbed to disease and had to be removed. It is a very popular tree in Central and South America. It is also grown, to a limited extent, in Portugal, New Zealand and Australia, where a range of cultivars are being evaluated for various climatic and environmental conditions. A growing commercial interest exists for this tasty, large fruit.

DESCRIPTION

A fairly dense, fast-growing tree, to ~10 m height. It forms a thickly-leaved spreading crown. Grows throughout most of the year in warmer regions. The wood is fairly brittle and liable to wind damage.

Leaves: Attractive, single, slightly scented, alternate, 5–20 cm long, ~10 cm wide, dark green on top, velvety green below, with prominent veins. New growth is curved. Almost evergreen: it may lose its leaves briefly after harvest or during adverse conditions, but new leaves often appear before all the old leaves are lost.

Flowers: Fragrant, with three fleshy, greenish-brown, oblong, downy outer petals and three smaller, pinkish inner petals. They are borne singly or in clusters of 2–3 on short, hairy stalks along the branches. They appear with new growth flushes on the current season's wood and on older wood from spring until mid summer. They are bisexual, and are only open for ~2 days. They open in two stages, with the female being receptive first for ~36 hours and then later once the male stamens have released pollen, so individual flowers are often self-sterile. *Pollination:* By small insects. Pollination can be tricky because of the timing of receptivity, but may be better in humid weather, and hand pollination helps considerably. Pollen can be collected in the late afternoon and either applied to any receptive female flowers at that time or can be stored overnight in a refrigerator, and then applied to female-stage flowers in the morning. Trees are fairly large, and this can be a tricky task. Because of the long flowering period, it will need to be repeated several times.

Fruit: An irregularly shaped, knobbly, pale green, large fruit that tends to often be heart shaped. It is actually a compound fruit made up from many fused embryos, and has the same botanical form as a raspberry, though is very different! It is an aggregate of drupelets. It can be 10–20 cm long, 10 cm wide and weigh ~0.5 kg. The skin can be thin or thick, is often smooth and has fingerprint-like indentations or protuberances. The flesh is white, sweet, succulent, juicy, melting, sub-acid and fragrant. Because it is made of many fused segments, each segment contains a single hard, black, bean-like seed, which should be discarded (see later). Fruit size is generally proportional to the number of seeds within it and, hence, pollination. Fruits take a long time to mature after fruit-set, and grow through the winter and spring, to ripen a year or more later.

Yield/harvest: A grafted tree can start fruiting within 2–3 years of planting, but can take longer depending on cultivar; seedlings take 5–8 years to begin. Yield then steadily increases from years 5–10, when yields of ~25 fruits/tree are likely. The fruits turn a pale green or creamy-yellow when ripe. They are usually cut from the tree when still firm and allowed to soften at room temperature for ~4 days. Ripe fruits become slightly soft; over-ripe fruits are dark brown. Fruits left on the tree too long usually split and begin to decay. Fruits can be stored at ~10°C for a few days; temperatures much below this can be damaging.

Roots: Start as a taproot, but it is slow growing and rather weak, particularly when young: may need staking. Benefits from an organic mulch to retain moisture and add nutrients.

CULTIVATION

Location: Best in sheltered locations because wind can damage branches and can interfere with pollination and fruit-set. Prefers a sunny location, with cool nights. It is fairly tolerant of salty air.

Temperature: Cherimoyas are subtropical or mild-temperate climate plants. Young trees are fairly frost sensitive and need extra protection for the first few years. Young growing tips can be killed at –2°C and mature trees can be severely injured at –4°C, although some cultivars are more cold tolerant. Because fruits remain on the tree over winter,

Food

Has a succulent, custard-like consistency and a sweet, sub-acid flavour somewhat like banana/papaya/pineapple mix. It is one of the best fruit of the genus, though the seeds need to be removed (see below) and this can be somewhat fiddly. Good eaten fresh after the fruits have been sliced in half. Fruits can be also juiced or added to sorbets and milkshakes, or they can be pureed and used in sweet sauces. They can be added to various fresh fruit desserts, and the juice makes a delicious wine. Ripe cherimoyas can be frozen and eaten like icecream.

Nutrition/medicinal

Sugar content is high, acids are low. It is high in fibre. Has good levels of potassium and has moderate amounts of manganese, copper and magnesium. It is a good source of vitamin B6 in particular, but also thiamine, riboflavin (B2) and folate. Has good levels of vitamin C: ~36 mg/100 g of flesh. The fruits have significant antimicrobial properties. In addition, research by the National Cancer Institute in the USA, on a close relative to cherimoya, has shown that the leaves and stem contain compounds (acetogenins) that are actively toxic against many types of cancer cells without harming healthy cells, and are effective at doses of only 1 part per million. Acetogenins, only found in the Annonaceae family, seem to inhibit enzyme processes that are only found in the membranes of cancerous tumour cells. They are also being studied at an anti-AIDS screening programme at Purdue University, USA.

Warning: The seeds contain several alkaloids that, if ingested in quantity, can cause dilated pupils, intense photophobia, vomiting, dryness of the mouth, burning in the throat, flatulence and other symptoms similar to those of atropine. This plant may also stimulate uterine activity and, therefore, should not be used during pregnancy. It may also have hypotensive, vasodilator and cardiodepressant activities and is best not eaten in excess by people with low blood pressure.

Other uses

The seeds, like those of other *Annona* species, can be crushed and used as an insecticide.

they and the outer leaves can be damaged by cold. In cooler areas, plant trees next to a warm wall or building to give them extra protection. They suffer more cold damage than avocados, oranges or lemons.

Chilling: Conversely, cherimoyas need 50–100 hours of chilling or they become dormant and do not produce spring leaves or flowers.

Soil/water/nutrients: They can grow in a wide range of soil types from sandy to clay, but do best on well-drained loams of moderate fertility. They grow best at neutral pH values: 6.0–7.0, but can also grow in high-calcium soils, where they can produce abundant, good-quality fruits. They are not tolerant of waterlogging, and wet soils often result in increased fungal and bacterial root rots. They produce their best fruits with regular moisture during flowering and just before fruit harvest, but only need minimal water during autumn–winter. During drought, stressed trees can drop their leaves, and fruit can be sunburnt; however, conversely, water stress just before flowering can increase flower (and hence fruit) production. They are moderately nutrient hungry, and benefit from regular applications of a nitrogen-rich fertiliser, particularly during the growing season. They appreciate additions of well-rotted organic matter or manure. Note that yellow leaves may mean that the soil is too dry or the weather too cold rather than that the trees are nutrient deficient.

Planting: Space plants at 7–9 m apart, and dig in organic matter when planting. Young trees benefit from staking because they have weak roots. Plant carefully to avoid damaging the taproot.

Pruning: Young trees tend to form a natural espalier shape, and can be trained against a wall or fence, or trees can be pruned to form a regular vase shape. Trees regrow easily from severe pruning and produce lush new growth. Prune during the dormant period or early spring to develop strong branches that can support the heavy fruit, and thin out crossing or damaged branches. One method of pruning suggests initially training the tree to two, strong 60- to 90-degree angled branches per 60 cm of trunk, and prune these to 60 cm length. In the following years, remove two-thirds of the previous year's growth, leaving six or seven good buds.

Propagation: Seeds: Easy. Seeds remain viable for 2–3 years if kept dry. With warmth, they will germinate in ~21–40 days. Seedlings should be grown on in deep containers to promote development of a deep taproot. *Cuttings*: Cuttings of mature, healthy wood should root in sand, with bottom heat, in 28 days. *Grafting*: Trees can be grafted, and the scion is grafted onto seedlings already growing in their final positions. Grafting is most successfully done from late winter through spring. During this period no scion preparation is required other than removal of leaves. All normal grafting techniques seem to be successful. Grafted plants should bear fruits in 2–3 years. Can be grafted onto the custard apple; this can give 90% success.

Pests and diseases: Mealybugs and snails are the main pests. Keep ducks and chickens, or apply copper strips to the trunks to control the snails. Mealybugs, especially at the base of the fruit, can be flushed off. Is resistant to nematodes, but susceptible to *Armillaria* and *Verticillium*. Do not plant in old vegetable gardens, or near tomatoes, eggplant or asters. Crown rot can kill trees damaged by frost or growing in saturated soil.

CULTIVARS

'Big Sister': Fruit: large, very smooth, good flavour. Often self-fruitful.

'Booth': Among the hardiest of cherimoyas. Tree 6–10 m tall. Fruit: conical, medium size, rather seedy, flavour is papaya-like.

'Bronceada': Better for cooler locations. Delicious fruit. Good ability to self-pollinate.

'Burton's Favourite': Good ability to self-pollinate. Delicious fruit.

'El Bumpo': Fruit: conical, medium size. Skin soft, almost edible. Flavour among the best.

'Honeyhart': Fruit: medium sized, skin smooth, yellowish-green. Pulp: smooth, excellent flavour, very juicy. Ripens in summer.

'Nata': Ecuadorian. Tree: vigorous, bears quickly, flowers profuse, tendency to self-pollinate. Fruits: smooth, light green, conical, 0.5–1.25 kg. Skin thin, tender. Flavour has good sweet–acid balance.

'Sabor': Fruit varies in size. Among the best in flavour.

SIMILAR SPECIES

Ilama, *Annona diversifolia*. Similar to the cherimoya, but tends to grow in warmer regions. The fruits and its seeds are larger than those of cherimoya, though the seeds are easier to remove. The fruits vary in colour from pale green, where the flesh is sweet, to pale pink, where the flesh is more acidic. ■

Annona squamosa x *A. cherimola*
Atemoya
ANNONACEAE
Relatives: mountain soursop (guanabana), *Annona montana*

The atemoya is a hybrid of the sugar apple (*Annona squamosa*) and cherimoya (*A. cherimola*). It is native to South America and has been used and cultivated by the indigenous peoples since pre-Inca times. It was, for many years, often mistakenly called custard apple or cherimoya in Australia. The first cross of this hybrid was made in 1908. The fruits are generally considered to be superior in quality to the sugar apple and the tree was given the name 'atemoya' as a combination of 'ate', an old Mexican name for sugar apple, and 'moya' from cherimoya. This is a fruit that is being researched for possible commercial production, and it is grown commercially, on a small scale in Florida, California and South America.

DESCRIPTION
A small–medium-sized tree that closely resembles cherimoya. It is fast growing, to ~4–8 m tall, with about the same spread. It has an open, spreading canopy with branches that are typically drooping, with the lowest often touching the ground, and often forms a multi-stemmed tree.

Leaves: Elliptic, ovate or lanceolate, though often of variable shape on the same tree. Length 10–20 cm, width 4–8 cm. Deciduous, with the duration of leaflessness dependent on climatic conditions. Leathery, and less hairy than those of cherimoya.

Flowers: Produced, along with new growth, in spring, with a few also occurring in summer. They have a triangular shape, ~2–4 cm long, with three fleshy, pale, yellowish-green petals, which are borne singly or in small clusters of 2–3 from the leaf axils on last season's growth or on new shoots. They have long flower stalks. *Pollination:* It is self-fertile, but individual flowers are not usually self-pollinated because stigmas are not receptive at the same time as the pollen is shed. The flowers are unusual in that they function first as a female and then as a male. Because of this, as well as problems encountered by the pollinators due to the flower's anatomy, pollination can sometimes be poor, or incomplete, resulting in misshapen fruit. Pollination can be improved by planting more than one tree, is better in warm, humid weather, and hand pollination can considerably improve fruit-set. The female part of the flower is receptive from mid-afternoon until about midday of the following day, after which, by mid-afternoon of the second day, the male stamens start to produce pollen. To hand fertilise, pollen is collected, with a light brush, during the male stage, when the petals are fully open and the stamens have become brownish. This pollen is then transferred to younger flowers where the petals have just opened and the female structure is receptive.

Fruit: An aggregate, often heart-shaped fruit, with many fertile individual drupelets (berries) becoming fused into a conical or heart-shaped, irregular (though sometimes smooth), large fruit, ~10 cm long, with some fruits weighing ~2 kg. Each individual drupelet forms a slight rounded shape on the skin. When ripe, the fruit colour subtly lightens to a pale bluish-green or yellowy-green. The skin is moderately thick (~0.3 cm), firm yet leathery. The flesh is fragrant, white, fine textured, almost solid, with barely discernible drupelets. It has a sweet, smooth, juicy, sub-acid flavour, similar to that of cherimoya. There are ~40 drupelets, each with a cylindrical, ~2-cm-long, dark brown, hard seed embedded within the flesh.

Yield/harvest: Seedling trees grow vigorously and begin to fruit at 3–5 years of age, but are variable in form and fruit quality; grafted trees begin to bear in 3–4 years and are more predictable. Trees may only produce poor yields of

Food

The atemoya, preferably chilled, is a delicious fruit eaten fresh and on its own. It can be simply eaten from its 'shell', with the seeds discarded as you go. The flesh is sweet, juicy, yet firm, and has a somewhat nutty flavour. The flesh can also be added to other fresh desserts. Some people blend the pulp with orange juice, lime juice and cream, and freeze this as icecream.

Nutrition

The fruits are high in fruit sugars, but are also a good source of antioxidants and have quite good levels of vitamin C. They also have useful levels of riboflavin (B2), and about 5% RDA of niacin (B3). Also contains good levels of iron, phosphates and calcium, as well as dietary fibre. **Warning:** The seeds, like those of all *Annona* species, are toxic and should be carefully discarded. See cherimoya, p. 65.

fruits, mostly due to poor pollination. A 5-year-old tree can bear ~50 fruits annually. Fruits take ~5 months to mature after fruit-set, and tend to ripen in late autumn, though this varies somewhat with climate. Fruits are best tree ripened; however, fruits that develop from summer blossom may struggle to ripen sufficiently before the weather cools. These late fruits may need picking when still under-ripe and to be artificially ripened, though their flavour is often not as good. Fruits are best picked when ripe but still firm. Over-ripe fruits may split if left too long on the tree and the seeds can start to prematurely germinate. Mature, harvested fruits should not be stored in a refrigerator, but at 13°C or above: lower temperatures may cause chilling injury. Fruits can be kept for a few days at room temperature.

Roots: Has a shallow, spreading root system. Avoid mechanical cultivation and a mulch will help conserve moisture, reduce weed competition and supply some nutrients, though do not stack mulch against the stem. Roots are vulnerable to damage and being handled. Only re-pot when necessary.

CULTIVATION

Location: Prefers to grow in full sun. Has some salt tolerance, but is not very wind tolerant. Can be grown in sheltered coastal areas.

Temperature: Young trees can be injured at temperatures below −1°C. Older trees are more cold hardy, and can tolerate temperatures of −3°C without serious damage. They grow best in semi-tropical and warm temperate regions, and grow well in areas with warm winters with fairly high rainfall and humidity. They are often considered to be not as cold hardy as cherimoyas. However, they also do not grow well in very hot climates.

Soil/water/nutrients: Best growth and fruit production occur in deep, loamy soils, rich in organic matter and a moderate amount of moisture, though trees will grow in various soil types, including sandy loams, basalt-type soils and even heavy clays. They grow best at pH values around neutral, though there are reports that they can tolerate quite alkaline soils. Trees do need good drainage though: waterlogging is fatal. Trees like regular moisture during their growing season, particularly during fruit-set and development, though too much rain during fruit ripening can cause fruits to split. Trees need less moisture during the winter months. Atemoyas need little additional nutrients once established. An application of a general, complete fertiliser, with a larger ratio of phosphate, can be given in spring before flowering, with a further application during summer, if needed.

Planting: Plant trees when dormant at ~9 m apart, and cut these trees back to ~0.7 m height to encourage root development. Trees dislike being transplanted.

Pot culture: Can be grown and will fruit successfully in large containers: it makes a good specimen container plant. It can then be grown in regions with colder winters and either taken inside or given extra protection when temperatures drop.

Propagation: *Seed:* The atemoya is a hybrid, so seeds won't come true to type. (However, the seeds of its parents germinate readily and well, particularly if soaked in warm water for ~24 hours before sowing.) *Cuttings*: Cuttings of mature, healthy wood should root in sand, with bottom heat, in 28 days. *Grafting:* Is done in early spring, usually by a whip-and-tongue-graft. Older trees can be top-worked by cleft- or crown-grafting. Scion wood is best taken from selected cultivars after the leaves have fallen, and then inserted in damp compost in the cool until spring. Can also use chip-budding. Can bud or graft atemoya onto sugar apple (*A. squamosa*), to produce a smaller, more compact, less vigorous tree, custard apple (*A. reticulata*), which gives less variability, or pond apple (*A. glabra*), which can grow in wetter soils, though graft incompatibility can sometimes occur. However, many of these species have poor cold tolerance.

Pruning: During the first 2–3 years, the trees are pruned in early spring to establish an open-centre with a few main scaffold branches, and any long shoots are shortened. Once established, only light pruning is needed. Fruit is produced on both the previous season's wood and on new shoots. Trees can split at the crotch of branches under the weight of fruit and if exposed to wind, so select and promote scaffold branches and sub-laterals that do not grow at too narrow an angle to the main trunk. Atemoyas can be easily espaliered.

Pests and diseases: The major problems are seed borers, scale and *Anthracnose*. Mealybugs produce a sticky exudate, often on the fruits, on which sooty mould may develop. Atemoyas are also prone to collar rot (*Phytophthora* spp.), particularly in wetter, colder soils, with the first sign being an exudation of gum near the base of the trunk and on surface roots. A condition called 'littleleaf' is not actually a disease, but is caused by zinc deficiency.

CULTIVARS

'African Pride' ('Kaller'): From South Africa. Trees can start bearing in their third year after planting, and often have good yields, though hand pollination can improve fruit-set. Tends to be more seedy than some cultivars.

'Gefner': Good-quality fruits without needing to hand pollinate.
'Pinks Mammoth': A vigorous tree with large fruit, though doesn't start bearing until ~fifth year.

SIMILAR SPECIES

Mountain soursop (guanabana), *Annona montana.* A native of the West Indies and South America, where it is now cultivated to a limited extent, as well as in the Philippines, mountain soursop is larger than atemoya and hardier, withstanding temperatures several degrees below freezing. However, the fruits are not of as good quality.
   Description: A medium-sized tree, up to ~7 m, closely resembling atemoya. *Leaves:* Evergreen (though becoming more deciduous in cooler regions), large, leathery, glossy

green, emitting a strong odour when crushed. *Fruit:* Nearly spherical, becoming yellowish when ripe, with the skin sparsely covered in short, fleshy spines. The flesh is orange-yellow, aromatic, somewhat fibrous and varies in flavour from tree to tree; it is sometimes sub-acid–sweet, but more often it is sour and bitter. Trees produce fruits after just 2–3 years. Fruits become very soft and fall when ripe.
   Cultivation: Is quite cold hardy, tolerating temperatures below freezing once established, though can be seriously damaged below –5°C. Can grow in full sun or light shade. *Soils:* Tolerates a variety of soils including sandy or clay. Needs regular water, though some reports say it is fairly drought hardy once established. *Propagation:* Mostly by seed. Also by budding
   Uses: *Food*: Eaten fresh, better quality fruits are used much like atemoyas. *Medicinal*: An infusion of leaves has been used to alleviate pain during pregnancy. ■

Arachis hypogaea
Peanut
FABACEAE (Leguminosae, Pappilionideae)
Relatives: honey locust, carob, licorice

All species within the genus *Arachis* originate from South America. Remains of peanuts have been found in Peru, and have been dated at 3500 and 6000 BC. They are known to have been cultivated by the Incas, and were used as currency, medicine and food. In around 1500, the Spanish took the peanut back to Spain, and the Portuguese and Spanish took it to the Philippines, from where it spread across Asia. In the USA, peanuts were first grown commercially around the time of the Civil War, and were known as 'goober peas'; since then, their popularity has kept increasing. By 1900, large areas of peanuts were being grown and, partly because of overproduction, many peanut-based products were devised, which included their addition to plastics, wallboard, soaps, coffee, shaving cream and massage oils. At present, the most important peanut-growing countries are India, China and America; others include Indonesia, Senegal, Brazil and Nigeria. Peanut oil is the world's second largest source of vegetable oil.

DESCRIPTION
They form small, annual, attractive plants, growing only to ~30–60 cm tall. They can be upright or sprawling.
   Leaves: Alternate, small, typically Leguminosae-like, usually in groups of four, oval and tapering at the base. Attractively delicate, light green or grey-green, the leaves close together at night or if conditions become too dry, to reduce moisture loss.
   Flowers: Small, yellow, 1–2 cm long, typically pea-like, borne from the leaf axils. They only last for about half a day; they open at sunrise and have started to wither by the afternoon. Flowers are bisexual, and are self-fertile: a single plant can be grown and produce nuts. *Pollination:* Are bee and insect pollinated. The pollen is released at sunrise, and pollination occurs soon after.

Fruit: This species has an odd way of fruiting. About 4 days after pollination, a stem (also called a peg) grows out from the flower's centre and down towards the soil. The end of the stem develops a hard point that then 'drills' itself into the soil for several centimetres, which is unique in nature. Once buried, after ~6 days, a seedpod begins to develop at the stem tip. It takes ~3–4 months to mature into a pod with seeds. The pod (~3–5 cm long) is straw-coloured, dry, brittle, but fairly soft, and has prominent veins running along its length. It is indented between the seeds. Usually, there are two (or more) nuts (or kernels) within each pod, each with a thin, papery, reddish-brown skin. The kernel has no endosperm but, instead, consists of two large pre-cotyledons.
   Yield/harvest/storage: Can get 25–50 kernels per plant.

Food

The nuts are eaten fresh, or are often roasted and salted as a snack. To roast peanuts, sauté with a light oil for ~3 min, drain and sprinkle with salt or cayenne pepper. To make peanut butter, dry-roast the nuts in an oven, grind them up and add salt and a small amount of peanut oil. The nuts are also added to Asian sauces, curries, confectionery, cookies and are added to many types of commercial products as a general nut flavouring. The roasted nuts can be used as a coffee substitute. The peanuts are also ground up and added to cakes, bread, etc. to improve their taste and protein levels. Peanut oil is used for frying, dressings, spreads and roasting. The oil can be extracted by placing peanuts in a press or by grinding them up, covering the pulp with boiling water, and leaving them over night. In the morning, the oil has floated to the surface and can be skimmed off. It is commercially used in cooking oils, margarine and salad oils, etc. The oilseed cake, left after extracting the oil, is said to be a good source of arginine and glutamic acid, which are used to treat mental disorders. The young pods and young leaves can be lightly cooked and eaten as a vegetable. The germinating seed sprouts can also be eaten.

Nutrition/medicinal

Often undervalued, possibly because they can contain high amounts of saturated fats, peanuts nevertheless are a valuable nutritional food. The nuts contain ~25% protein, higher than fish, dairy products and many meats, but are deficient in sulphur-containing amino acids. They also contain many B vitamins: and are particularly rich in thiamine, folate and niacin, but also B6, riboflavin and pantothenic acid. Also have very high levels of potassium and manganese, and are rich in calcium, phosphates, iron, zinc, copper and magnesium. They have no cholesterol. They also contain lots of fibre. The kernels are high in oils (up to 50%), which are non-drying: of the total oil content ~25–40% is monounsaturated, 20–30% is polyunsaturated and ~30–50% is saturated. They also contain reasonable levels of vitamin E. Nuts in general, and peanuts in particular, have good levels of the flavonoid resveratrol, as found in red wine. Levels of this can be as high as those found in grapes. Resveratrol can inhibit tumour formation by stopping DNA damage, slow or halt cell transformation from normal to cancerous, and also slow tumour growth. (It may be particularly useful in preventing colon cancer.) It is also thought to help prevent the formation of arterial plaques and has anti-inflammatory properties. Studies have indicated that eating a small amount of peanuts can reduce low-density lipids by 14%. **Warning:** A few people are allergic to peanuts, even in very small quantities.

Other uses

Poorer quality oil is used to make soap, lubricants and wood oils. Pods can be used in compost and have been added to biofuels.

Ornamental

A small, pretty plant that can be easily squeezed into a border, and is an interesting plant to observe as it develops. In addition, the plants fix nitrogen, and so are ideal for poorer soils.

Peanuts are harvested when the leaves start to yellow. Veins within the pod change to a darker colour when the kernels are ripe, with those pods nearer the plant ripening before those further away. The soil needs to be dry when harvesting the pods so that they can be easily dug up and separated cleanly from the soil. For storage, the pods and nuts should be air- or sun-dried to reduce moisture content to ~8%: the time this takes will vary with heat and humidity. If not sufficiently dry (<12% moisture), the peanuts can develop a carcinogenic fungi called aflotoxin (peanuts are more susceptible to this than most nuts). Also, if not properly dried, the oil within the nuts can become rancid. Dried kernels can then be stored in a fridge, freezer or in sealed bags.

Roots: They have a fairly deep taproot, and seedlings should be planted out with care. Plants also form many lateral roots.

CULTIVATION

Easy to grow.

Location: They like to be grown in full sun, and are somewhat wind tolerant because of their small size.

Temperature: Need a growing period of 4–5 months with fairly high temperatures (25–30°C). They are not frost tolerant, but they are an annual and grow quickly, so care just needs to be taken that plants are planted out after any risk of cold weather has passed. The plants will grow in colder areas, but the peanut kernels form best between latitudes 40°S and 45°N.

Soil/water/nutrients: They grow best in a well-drained, sandy loam. If the soil is too heavy, the stems have difficulty in penetrating the soil, the pods are difficult to harvest and there is a greater risk of rot diseases. They like a moist, but well-drained soil, though can tolerate periods of drought. Can also tolerate short periods of flooding, but not during the latter stages of seedpod formation. They grow best at a pH range of 6–6.5, but can grow in fairly acid soils, and are reported to be able to grow at pH levels of 4.3–8.7, but at the limits of these, nutrient deficiency or toxicities are likely. Weed control is very important as weeds can inhibit nut development by competing for light, nutrients and water. Peanuts are good to use in crop rotation practices because of their ability to fix nitrogen. Their nutrient requirements are fairly moderate, needing just a little fish or seaweed fertiliser now and then. The addition of calcium, though, does help seed set. If peanuts are grown for several years in the same soils, they tend to deplete the soil of calcium and potassium, and so it is best to rotate this crop.

Pot culture: Because they are an annual, are small in size and have an unusual way of fruiting, they make an interesting plant for a patio or for educational purposes: plus there's a harvest. Just make sure they are grown in pots with enough soil area around them for the stems to arch out and still touch soil around the mother plant. Place the pots in a warm spot in colder regions, or in a conservatory or glasshouse to encourage nut production.

Propagation: *Seed:* Unless treated or processed, ordinary peanuts, if relatively fresh, will form seedlings. Soak seed for a few hours before planting at ~5 cm depth in compost, and then just give warmth and moisture. Seeds germinate in ~14 days. Prick out seedlings and grow on in pots in good compost, and plant out when the weather becomes warm. Makes a good school project.

Planting: Plant out once all risk of frost has passed. Space plants 10–15 cm apart, with ~50 cm between rows Make sure the soil is loose to enable the stems to penetrate easily.

Pests and diseases: Possible problems include leaf spot, white mould, caterpillars, thrips, leaf hoppers, aphids and mites.

CULTIVARS

'Early Spanish': Nuts: 2–3 in pod, small, sweet, fine quality and flavour. Tends to have a higher oil and protein content, though somewhat smaller yields. Plant is a compact, erect bush. Easy to grow and early maturing. As it only needs a short growing season, it can be planted in colder areas, e.g. Canada.

'Spanish': Nuts: 2–3 in pod, small, round, full, sweet, rich taste, mostly used for roasting, suitable for peanut butter or to eat as is. Tends to have a higher oil (~50%) and protein content, though somewhat smaller yields. Forms a compact, erect shape: ~45 cm tall. Usually roasted with skins on. Only needs a short growing season.

'Runner' ('Peruvian', 'Jumbo', 'Florunner'): Has large yields and is mainly used for peanut butter. Very popular commercially. Grows as a prostrate plant. Needs a longer growing season.

'Valencia': Suitable for peanut butter or to eat as is. Often incorporated into chocolate bars. Usually 2–4, sweet, medium-sized nuts in a pod. Has reddish stems and larger leaves. Can grow up to ~1.3 m and has a bushy, erect shape. Tends to have a higher oil (~50%) and protein content, though somewhat smaller yields. Only needs a short growing season, though probably grows better in warmer regions.

'Virginia': This cultivar is eaten with or without salt. Nuts are large, oblong and are often sold in-shell. Has a more 'nutty' flavour. Usually two nuts to a pod. Has high yields. Oil content is only ~35%. Forms a sprawling shape, ~45 cm tall. Grows better in warmer regions and needs a longer growing season. ■

Araucaria araucana
(syn. *A. chilensis, A. dombeyi, A. imbricata*)
Monkey-puzzle tree (Chilean pine)
ARAUCARIACEAE

Similar species: *Araucaria brasiliensis* (syn. *A. brasiliana*)

Relatives: bunya-bunya tree, Norfolk Island pine

The monkey-puzzle tree is one of 18 species from the *Araucaria* genus. These trees are coniferous, evergreen and are all natives of the Southern Hemisphere. The monkey-puzzle tree is a native of Chile and Argentina, and although logging of this species was banned in 1990, natural stands are still disappearing due to forest fires, etc. It is a conifer, with a bizarre, spectacular shape, and natural stands are found closer to the South Pole than any other conifer. From fossils, this species is estimated to be ~60 million years old. The origins of its name, 'monkey-puzzle tree', are somewhat disappointing. Apparently it is derived from the comments made by an Englishman during Victorian times, who, in the 1800s, said he thought it would be a puzzle for a monkey to climb. He was referring to the tree's distinctive branching pattern and its scaly, difficult-to-climb branches. It is claimed that the tree was originally, almost accidentally, taken to England from Chile by a Mr Menzies who, when dining out one evening in Chile, was given some monkey-puzzle nuts during the meal. Intrigued as to what they were, he took a few with him to England. During the voyage home some sprouted, so he arrived in the UK with several small seedling trees. From these trees the popularity of the monkey-puzzle tree rapidly spread throughout Victorian England, and many fine specimens can now be seen around the country in the gardens

of stately homes and in churchyards. These trees are now fully mature and make a distinctive, unmistakable silhouette in the landscape, and a striking contrast to native English trees. The unusual shape and character of these trees have made them popular ornamental specimens around the world, and many love to see them, although some find them too bizarre and unusual. However, this tree, and similar species (e.g. the bunya-bunya pine), produces huge cones that contain many edible seeds. These have been valued by the native peoples of South America for hundreds to thousands of years. In its native area, the seeds have been used as a staple food, and are sold in local Chilean markets. Spiritually important, the tree is used as a centrepiece on the altar during harvest and fertility ceremonies of the Pehuenche/Mapuche peoples of Chile. In 1990, the Ministerio de Agricultura declared *Araucaria araucana* a Chilean national monument. The cooked nuts are described as 'rich and delicious'. The tree, hardy and easy to grow, has potential to be more widely cultivated for its large, tasty kernels, as it produces good yields which can be easily accessed once the heavy cones have dropped.

DESCRIPTION

A slow-growing, large, bizarre-looking, evergreen tree, 20–35 m tall, 10–12 m spread, though the tallest specimens can be >50 m. It can take 10 years to reach ~1.3 m. Female trees are usually taller (~30 m), whereas male trees usually only attain ~15 m. The trunk can become 1–1.5 m in width. It has a regular, geometric shape of whorls of branches, with a new whorl formed every 18–24 months, or sometimes annually, to form a regularly spaced pattern up the main stem. It forms an open pyramidal shape when young, changing to a more dense, rounded shape as it gets older, although sometimes branches of older trees sweep down to the ground. The branches are horizontal, in whorls of five. They are strong and quite tolerant of wind. The bark is grey-brown, resinous, smooth, and is marked by annual rings formed from old branch scars. Trees probably live for more than 2000 years.

Leaves: Evergreen, scale-like and reptilian in appearance, leathery, dark green, broadly triangular with sharp pointed tips, 3–5 cm long, stiff and densely arranged on branches that sweep upwards. They also occur on younger parts of the trunk, or down to the base in younger trees. They persist on the tree for 10–15 years, and leave conspicuous leaf scars when they fall. They are shiny green, have stomata on both surfaces, and are marked with longitudinal lines. They differ from bunya-bunya in that the monkey-puzzle leaves thickly overlap, whereas the bunya-bunya leaves are arranged in two rows.

Flowers: Usually dioecious, but sometimes monoecious. So, for seeds you will need to plant at least one male and one female tree to get fruit-set. Unfortunately there is no way of telling the sex of trees until they flower, unless they are vegetatively propagated (see below). Male flowers are solitary or occur in small clusters at the ends of branches, and are ~8–15 cm long, yellow-brown, tapering, with ~20 whorled pointed scales: they produce pollen in early summer. Female cones are solitary and are borne on the upper sides of stems. *Pollination:* By wind.

Fruit: The female cone is green, ripening to dark brown, globular, ~10–25 cm long, 8–20 cm width, and consists of many small scales. It takes 2–3 years to mature after being pollinated. It breaks open on the tree or as it falls to release large edible kernels, ~2.5–4 cm long. Each cone contains ~100–200 kernels. These are brown-orange, triangular, with a long inner narrow kernel, ~3 cm long by 1 cm wide.

Yield/harvest: Has reliable good crops, with many cones per tree, but the main disadvantage is that it takes 40 years to first produce! Because the cones tend to open while still on the tree, it can be problematic to gather the widely scattered kernels. Try to pick cones (if possible!) just before they shed their seeds, otherwise you will need to have fairly regular searches around the base of the tree for the triangular kernels, which are, fortunately, quite large. Cones usually ripen in autumn. If stored in a cool, dry place, the kernels can be kept for several months.

Roots: Does have surface roots that can lift concrete and interfere with mowing, so best not to plant trees too near buildings or paths.

uses

Food
The nuts can be boiled, or are usually roasted. They are rich in carbohydrate and fat. They have a soft texture and have a mild, tasty, nutty flavour, similar to pinenuts. They can be eaten in quantity, and could (and do) form a staple food. The native South Americans used to make a liquor from them.

Medicinal
The resin from the trunk has been used to treat ulcers and wounds.

Other uses
Has yellowish wood that is very fine grained and is used in interior woodworking. It has also been used in aeroplane construction.

Ornamental
It is a popular ornamental, specimen tree in temperate regions, and is often used for its distinctive shape in larger gardens, parks and avenues. It also makes an excellent windbreak for a coastal situation. Do not site these trees where people are likely to sit or walk as their hard, sharp leaves drop throughout the year.

CULTIVATION

Temperature: Hardy to frosts and can tolerate down to at least −12°C: it is the hardiest of the genus. Does not grow well in hot climates.

Location: Grows best in a sunny location or semi-shade. It is very tolerant of maritime exposure and salt-laden winds, and thrives in cool, mild climates. Dislikes atmospheric pollution. Are very wind tolerant.

Soil/water: Is surprisingly tolerant of many soil types, and tolerates clay remarkably well, as well as growing well in loam and sandy soils. It can also grow at a wide pH range from acidic to alkaline. Prefers well-drained, but moist soils, though is moderately drought tolerant.

Pot culture: The Victorians used to grow this as a pot plant because of its slow growth and its unusual shape, and it could be easily started off in container for a few years before being planted out into its final site.

Pruning: Needs little or no pruning, just to develop a strong structure when young. Is breakage resistant. Unlike most conifers, the monkey-puzzle can be coppiced.

Propagation: *Seed:* Fresh seeds will germinate easily. Stored seeds lose viability quickly, and are best stored in a plastic bag in a fridge till spring. Do not let them become too dry before sowing. Take ~8 weeks to germinate at ~15°C. Just place seed partly in the soil to germinate: do not cover the seed completely with soil. Seedlings are variable, and won't reveal their sex for many years. *Cuttings:* Can take cuttings using small adventitious growths that sometimes protrude from the trunk, thereby obtaining plants of known sex. It is also likely that these cuttings will fruit more quickly than seedlings. Can also take stem-tip cuttings from vertical shoots in summer, and insert in well-drained compost in a cool location. Cuttings from these stems may, however, develop into sprawling shrubs.

Pests and diseases: No pests or diseases of major concern. Possible minor problems with scales, sooty mould or leaf spot.

CULTIVARS

Several selections have been named, mostly for their ornamental properties. Some are dwarf, some have yellowish foliage and some have fewer branches with a more open shape.

SIMILAR SPECIES

Araucaria brasiliensis (syn. *A. brasiliana*). A similar species to the monkey-puzzle tree. A native of Brazil, it grows to ~30 m tall. Evergreen, with branches in whorls. Old trees shed lower branches. The kernels have been eaten by the indigenous peoples for many hundreds of years. The kernels are large, and need to be boiled for some hours, then the outer shells can be peeled off. The nut meat is edible, sweet, nutritious and tastes a little like sweet potato. ■

Araucaria bidwillii
Bunya-bunya pine
ARAUCARIACEAE
Relatives: monkey-puzzle tree, Norfolk pine

From a genus of about 18 species that are mostly native to Australia and South America, the bunya-bunya pine originated in the wetter forests of southeastern Queensland, Australia, and is a physically impressive and culturally significant tree. Despite its name, it is not closely related to pine trees. It is a very ancient tree, historically, and has a primitive, appealing appearance. It has been the source of a popular, sought after food for many thousands of years The Aboriginal word for bunya pine is actually 'bon-yi', and bon-yi feasts were an eagerly anticipated occasion. When the cones were ready to harvest, indigenous Aborigines used to travel long distances to gather them for tribal ceremonies, hunting, feasting and corroborees, with each tribe having its own set of trees. They scarred the trunks of big pines to climb them, and these scars are still evident on many giant trees. Cones were then knocked to the ground, where the soft young nuts were eaten raw and the mature nuts were roasted. After cracking the outer shells of mature nuts over the fire, kernels were pounded into meal and roasted into a kind of cake that would keep for several weeks. Bunya pines are still grown as a plantation tree for use as timber. No other tree in this genus produces larger cones than the bunya-bunya pine.

Food

The nuts can be eaten fresh, usually when young, but are often boiled (for ~30 minutes) or roasted and sprinkled with butter and salt, and then eaten like chestnuts. They can be added to dishes where other nuts would be used. They have been used in soups, casseroles, pies, pastas, with vegetables, in desserts, cakes and biscuits, pastry and in porridge. Dried and ground, they have been mixed with flour in cakes, bread, etc.

Other uses

The cream-coloured wood has an attractive grain and is used for veneers, plywood and boxes.

Ornamental

Bunya-bunyas are a popular, distinctive specimen tree, but are best planted in larger gardens. The sharp leaves are uncomfortable to walk upon.

DESCRIPTION

The bunya-bunya is a type of conifer. It forms a large, tall tree, sometimes growing to 40 m high, with a rounded, dome-like crown, and distinctive whorls of branches which give it a very recognisable silhouette. The trunk, in mature specimens, can reach 1–1.2 m wide. As it grows, it sometimes loses its lower branches, leaving a tall branch-free trunk; other specimens retain most of their lower branches. Trees are usually single stemmed, though can be grown/pruned to form multi-stemmed trees, which can be easier to access and more manageable. The branches are long, somewhat drooping, and form in distinctive whorls of 10–15 spaced at regular intervals up the tree. The bark is grey-brown, thick, roughish, and partially peels into thin scales. Trees are long lived, probably living for >600 years.

Leaves: They have two types of evergreen leaves. Juvenile leaves are stiff, shiny, narrow, light yellow-green, 2.5–5 cm long, often incurved, with a sharp point, ~0.5 cm long. They are borne in two rows along young stems. Trees also have mature leaves, which are more oval, smaller, ~1.2 cm long, and scale-like. They are arranged in a dense, overlapping, spiral pattern around older branches. These are also sharp, hard and leathery, but are darker green and not quite as painful to tread on as the young leaves. They lack a central mid rib. Both types of leaves tend to drop year round, and take a long time to decompose.

Flowers: Male and female flowers occur on separate trees: they are dioecious. Female 'flowers' are fairly large, pale green, rounded, and are located at the tips of stems of higher branches. They are composed of numerous leaf-like scales, each of which can potentially form a seed. The male flowers are borne in clusters of 15–20, and measure ~1.2 cm wide. They occur on higher branches, on short branchlets. They form upright, catkin-like flowers that turn from light green to yellow-brown as the stamens start shedding copious pollen. *Pollination:* By wind.

Fruit: Females produce very large cones on branches high from the ground. These cones are erect, often globular in shape, and are a waxy, shiny green colour. They can measure ~30 cm long by ~25 cm wide, and weigh 5–8 kg: very heavy—this is not a tree to stand beneath when they are falling! The cones consist of many scales, each with a recurved spine. Within the scales are rounded seeds, with rudimentary wings, 4–7 cm long, ~2.5 cm wide. There are ~50–150 seeds per cone. Within the seed is a tan-coloured kernel that is firm, waxy, and is tasty when eaten young and fresh; older seeds are tasty once stored for a period, or are roasted or boiled. A fine brown fuzz sometimes covers the kernel, but this is quite edible. Trees may not flower and fruit every year, though some specimens do. Cones take 2–3 years to ripen and fall from the tree.

Yield/harvest: Trees do not produce cones until they are ~15–20 years of age. The ripe cones fall from late summer till early autumn, and because of their weight and size, are often broken apart as they hit the ground. As the cones age, the separate kernels are easily broken apart. The kernels, in their shells, can be stored in a refrigerator in a sealed container for several months; they then develop a much sweeter taste, while remaining of good quality, even though the shells start to look old.

CULTIVATION

An interesting tree to grow, but does take a long time to start producing cones, and you must have more than one of these large trees to set seed, so need a large garden, or a neighbour who is willing to plant one too!

Location: Trees can grow in full sun or in semi-shade. They are quite wind tolerant, despite their height, and are fairly tolerant of salt spray.

Temperature: Fairly hardy. Can grow in temperatures from below freezing to 30°C, but the tree grows best in warm temperate to subtropical climates. It is not as hardy as the monkey-puzzle or Norfolk pine.

Soil/water/nutrients: Bunya-bunya prefer a humid atmosphere and moist, but not waterlogged, loamy soil. They naturally grow in wet forests. They benefit from additions of organic matter or an organic mulch, particularly when young. They can grow in sandy or clay soils, but if the soil is too dry, then lower branches may die and the trees lose their vigour. Trees are not very nutrient hungry, but a sprinkling of a balanced, complete fertiliser 2–3 times during the growing season will keep them healthy and vigorous.

Pot culture: Strangely, these trees can be easily grown in a container and taken inside in colder regions. They can be grown within the home for periods of time, as long as not sited in heavy shade. They form an interestingly-shaped pot plant. Give plants a mix of loam, organic matter and sand and keep this moist, but not waterlogged. Trees do not need much root space, and can be grown for several years in a largish container before needing to be planted outside. Keeping the roots confined reduces the growth of the rest of the plant. Annual additions of fresh compost to the soil surface will help keep your bunya-bunya healthy.

Propagation: *Seeds:* Can be sown in pots of sandy soil indoors. These germinate easily and grow well, but you won't know the sex of the progeny for many years. *Cuttings:* Can be taken from new growth from trees that have been cut back in spring. These can be inserted in a sandy, gritty compost, indoors, to root, though the rate of success can be low. They will sometimes form roots if inserted in sandy soil outside. ■

Arbutus unedo, Arbutus x *andrachnoides*
Strawberry tree (arbutus, cane apple, Killarney strawberry)
ERICACEAE
Relatives: blueberry, huckleberry, cranberry

A much larger, warmer-climate member of the Ericaceae family, the strawberry tree is also adapted to grow in different soil types from that preferred by its relatives the blueberry and cranberry. The strawberry tree is a native of western Britain, southern Europe and eastern Mediterranean regions, where it grows in rocky, well-drained soils. It is a very popular ornamental because of its attractive leaves, and because it produces pink-red flowers and red fruits in late autumn–early winter, when many other plants have become dormant. Older specimens are especially attractive with their shredding grey-brown bark and twisted, gnarled trunks.

DESCRIPTION
Beautiful, slow-growing, smaller, evergreen tree or shrub, height to 5–8 m, spread 3–7 m. Some varieties of this are only 1–2 m tall. Has a spreading, attractive form. Its bark is grey-brown and peels off in older trees to reveal new, reddish bark beneath. Older specimens develop attractive twisted and gnarled trunks and branches.

Leaves: Evergreen, elliptic, lanceolate, on short pinkish stalks (~0.5 cm), toothed, glossy dark green above, though paler beneath, 5–10 cm long.

Flowers: Racemes (~8 cm long) of pretty, drooping, urn-shaped, waxy, white–pink flowers, often tinged with green, in late autumn–early winter. Are sweetly fragrant, with recurved lobes, ~1 cm long, and often occur at the same time as last season's berries. Plants begin flowering when young. *Pollination:* By bees and insects, and flowers are self-fertile.

Fruit: Take 12 months to ripen, so the tree often carries berries and flowers at the same time, and is particularly attractive during this period. The round berries, ~1.5–2.5 cm diameter, ripen from yellow to scarlet–ruby red, and contain several small, edible seeds. Although called a strawberry tree, the fruit do not taste or look like strawberries, but are sweet and pleasant, though lack a distinctive flavour.

Yield/harvest/storage: Yields are quite good and regular. Berries ripen over a period of several weeks, from late autumn–early winter. Are best picked when they are deep red in colour and soft to the touch. They can also be picked when still a little under-ripe, i.e. when deep red in colour, but are still firm, and can then be stored for a few days. If picked when fully ripe, they need to be eaten within 24 hours or they deteriorate.

Roots: Because they dislike root disturbance, it is best to only repot seedlings when necessary and to plant them out in their final position as soon as possible. They may, therefore, need additional protection during cold winters till established in these locations.

CULTIVATION
A very easy and trouble-free plant to grow.

Location: Can be planted in sun or semi-shade. Prefers a fairly sheltered location away from cold winds, especially when young. It can, however, tolerate some exposure as long as the wind is not too cold. Can be grown in maritime locations and is fairly tolerant of salt. It is also fairly pollution tolerant.

Temperature: Fairly hardy, should survive temperatures down to –20°C without injury, though young plants need to be protected. However, it does best in Mediterranean-type climates: cool, wet winters and hot, dry summers. Does not do as well in climates with humid summers.

Soil/water/nutrients: Grows best in a nutrient-rich,

uses

Food
Although the skin can be somewhat tough, most people consider the fruit to be delicately sweet with a good, juicy flavour; although some do not rate them highly. They can be eaten fresh or used in conserves, sauces, preserves or made into a jelly. On the Mediterranean islands of Sardinia and Corsica, and in Portugal, the fruits are used to make wines, liqueurs and a strong spirit (medronho).

Nutrition/medicinal
Fruit are high in vitamin C. Contain ~20% sugar. The leaves are an astringent and a diuretic and they can be used to treat urinary infections. They contain fairly high levels of tannin.

Other uses
The bark is used to tan leather (contains ~50% tannin).

Ornamental
Makes a good specimen tree for its winter interest, and it also produces tasty fruits. Cultivars are differing sizes, so pick one to suit your garden's size. Grows well on the edge of a woodland garden, in shrub borders or in a container. The birds like the berries.

moisture-retentive soil, but can also grow well in heavy, clay soils and in very dry soils. Prefers a somewhat acid to neutral pH, but can also be grown in quite alkaline soils, including chalk, unlike most other members of this family. Can be very drought tolerant once established, and will grow in dry, arid regions, only needing water during autumn and winter. Needs only little, if any, additional nutrients.

Propagation: *Seed:* Good results from fresh seed, which can be sown in late winter–early spring in moist compost. Stored seeds need to be soaked in warm water for 5–6 days before sowing. May take 3–4 months to germinate. The seedlings are slow growing and are prone to damping off, so, although the compost needs to be moist, it should not be too wet, and seedlings need good ventilation in a semi-shaded position. Grow on seedlings for the first couple of years. *Cuttings:* Semi-ripe cuttings, taken with a heel, in summer, can give good results: bottom heat can encourage rooting. They may take a while to form roots, and watering with willow extract may help. *Layering:* Is possible from lower branches, but can take 2 years to root.

Pruning: Minimal, just to enhance shape, and perhaps remove lower branches to expose the attractive twisting branches.

Pests and diseases: Fairly problem free, though may have problems with aphids, scale, leaf spot and sooty mould.

CULTIVARS

Most cultivars of this species have been developed for their ornamental attributes, and often form smaller trees.
'Compacta': A slow-growing, dwarf shrub, height ~2 m. Usually fruits well, even when small. An attractive, useful plant for small gardens and for growing in containers.
'Croomei': Small tree, to ~4 m tall, ~4-m spread, flowers are reddish. Good crops of fruit.
'Elfin King': A slow-growing shrub, height may be only 1 m. Flowers last a long time in winter; has good-sized sweet, flavoursome fruits, ~2.5 cm diameter. Young trees produce good crops. Good for containers.
'Rubra': Slow-growing, small tree or shrub, ~3–4 m tall, ~3–4 m spread. Flowers are tinged with red. Young trees flower and fruit well.

OTHER SPECIES

Arbutus x andrachnoides. A natural hybrid. Is native to eastern Mediterranean regions. Forms a small–medium-sized tree, ~10 m tall. Flowers from late autumn into winter. Can be grown in more alkaline soils. Frost hardy down to ~10°C, but seems to need a good hot summer/autumn to fruit well. Does not like to be transplanted. ■

Arctostaphylos spp.
Manzanita
ERICACEAE

Alpine manzanita (*Arctostaphylos alpinus*), bigberry manzanita (*A. glauca*), Columbia manzanita (*A. columbiana*), downy manzanita (*A. tomentosum*), greenleaf manzanita (*A. patula*), kinnikinick (*A. uva-ursi*), manzanita (*A. manzanita*), pine-mat manzanita (*A. navadensis*)

Relatives: blueberry, cranberry, strawberry tree

A genus of small, deciduous or evergreen trees and shrubs that thrive in acidic soils. Many are native to the warmer regions of the USA and Mexico, though a few species originate from colder regions such as Canada or the UK. They are often grown as ornamentals for their attractive red stems and pretty flowers, and some species make good groundcover plants. Many of these species are indigenous and thrive in the Californian climate, and were used extensively, historically, by the native populations as a food source and as a medicine.

DESCRIPTION

Either small trees or sometimes sprawling, groundcover species. Plants often have attractive reddish stems.
Leaves: Small, shiny, dark green, oval and leathery.
Flowers: Typically heather-like, with small, waxy, urn-shaped, pinkish-white flowers, in clusters. *Pollination:* By bees and other insects.
Fruit: Small, ~1 cm diameter, rounded berries that may be dark red or bright red when ripe, depending on species. Often have a sub-acid, good, cranberry-like taste, though some species have fruits that are rather dry and mealy. Some species probably should only be consumed in

moderation as they may be difficult to digest.
Yield/harvest/storage: Yields vary, and can sometimes be poor as pollination seems to vary. Fruits are best picked when fully coloured and ripe. Berries last for a few days in the fridge, or can be dried for later use.
Roots: Has many surface roots, and mechanical cultivation should be avoided in the root vicinity. Forms a mycorrhizal fungal relationship that enables the plant to obtain extra nutrients, particularly phosphates. The addition of organic matter, such as leaf mould, encourages this. Also benefits from a thick organic mulch to conserve moisture and suppress weeds.

CULTIVATION

Location: Can grow in full sun or semi-shade, though produces better-quality fruits in direct sun. Many species are quite wind tolerant, but do not like maritime conditions.

Temperature: Most species prefer warmer-temperate climates, though a few can grow in cold-temperate regions.

Soil/water/nutrients: Manzanitas need a peaty, moist acidic soil to grow in and are not tolerant of alkaline conditions. Grow best with regular moisture and are not drought tolerant. A moderate annual application of an acidic fertiliser, with nitrogen added as urea rather than nitrate, benefits growth. Too much fertiliser can reduce the mycorrhizal fungal association as well as leading to excess leaf growth at the expense of fruiting.

Planting: Spacing depends on species. Organic matter improves growth. Plants do not transplant well, and should be planted with care to avoid root disturbance.

Propagation: *Seed:* Fresh seeds can be sown just below the surface of compost and over-wintered outside to germinate in spring. Stored seed needs a period of ~3 months of cold stratification before sowing, with warmth, in spring. *Cuttings:* Semi-ripe cuttings taken in summer can be inserted in peaty, gritty, moist compost to root. *Suckers:* These can be dug up, with some root, and are easily established; try to avoid disturbing the rest of the root system. *Layering:* Young stems can be either tip or stem layered: this is usually done in spring.

Pruning: Little to none required. More spreading species may just need some pruning to control their size.

Pests and diseases: Very few problems.

THE SPECIES

Alpine manzanita, *Arctostaphylos alpinus*. A deciduous species which, as its name suggests, can grow in colder-temperate regions and is very cold hardy. Grows in cool, damp sites and forms a creeping, low shrub, only growing to ~10 cm tall, by ~30 cm width. Has small, oval, finely toothed, glossy green leaves. Flowers are borne in late spring in small clusters and are pinkish-white. These develop into small (~0.6 cm), purple-black berries that have a reasonable flavour, though can sometimes be bitter.

Bigberry manzanita, *Arctostaphylos glauca*. As its name suggests, this species produces berries larger than most others. Is native to the warmer areas of California and only tolerates temperatures down to ~–10°C. Forms a small tree ~3 m tall, and grows best in full sun. Has many pinkish-white flowers in late spring, which develop into dark red berries ~1.5 cm long. The fruits are of reasonable quality and are used in jams, desserts, etc., and make a tasty alcoholic drink that is said to resemble cider. The leaves are often used medicinally as an astringent antiseptic to treat urinary problems. However, the leaves also contain arbutin, which can be converted into toxic hydroquinone.

Columbia manzanita, *Arctostaphylos columbiana*. A native of western North America, and is hardy enough to grow as far north as British Columbia. It forms an irregular shrub growing to ~1–1.5 m tall. Young stems are covered with a red fuzz. Has many white flowers in spring, which develop into small, bright red berries in late summer–autumn.

Downy manzanita, *Arctostaphylos tomentosum*. Native to the warmer western states of the USA, e.g. California, and only tolerates temperatures down to ~–5°C. An evergreen shrub, growing to ~1.5 m tall. The pinkish-white flowers are borne in spring and the red berries ripen in autumn. The berries are sweet but dry. They were widely used by the indigenous populations and were often dried for later use. They make a refreshing drink, and are sometimes used as a tangy fruit if eaten when just under-ripe. The leaves were used medicinally as an astringent antiseptic to treat urinary problems. However, the leaves contain arbutin, which can be converted into toxic hydroquinone. Has good-quality wood, though is of small dimensions.

Greenleaf manzanita, *Arctostaphylos patula*. Native to the warmer western states of the USA. Forms an ornamental, evergreen, spreading shrub ~2 m tall. Can tolerate temperatures down to ~–10°C. Has pinkish-white flowers in spring, and red berries, ~1 cm diameter, in autumn. These have quite a good flavour, and may be eaten fresh or added to jams, desserts, etc. They are also made into a cider-like drink.

Kinnikinick (bearberry), *Arctostaphylos uva-ursi*. Grows naturally in the colder regions of the Northern Hemisphere. Has been used by North American Indians, the Chinese and Europeans for a variety of purposes. Is an evergreen, sprawling, groundcover plant, growing to ~1.5 m tall, with the same spread. Spreads by suckering from rhizomatous roots. Has small, shiny leaves, ~1 cm long, that often turn reddish in autumn. Its flowers are small, pink, in racemes, at shoot tips in spring. Fruits are rounded, red and shiny. It grows best in a moist soil with partial shade.

Uses: The fruits are sweet but fairly bland, though can be used for preserves. North American Indians used the leaves as a tobacco. The leaves contain arbutin, a substance that is very effective as a diuretic and produces an antiseptic effect on the urinary system, though, apparently, is more effective if taken with sodium bicarbonate. Is widely used for many urinary problems from bedwetting to kidney stones, and even to treat gonorrhoea. Women use an infusion of the leaves as a bath or douche after childbirth to aid healing and prevent infections, though tea should not be drunk during pregnancy as it may stimulate the uterus to contract. A tea from the leaves and fruits has also been drunk to control weight and cystitis. The fruits also contain catechins.

Food
The berries can be eaten fresh, but are generally too tart; instead, they are often combined with other fruits in pies, desserts, jam, preserves, etc. Several species can make a refreshing, cider-like beverage.

Manzanita, *Arctostaphylos manzanita*. A common native of California, it forms a shrub or small tree to ~2 m tall. Has attractive, peeling, reddish bark. The leaves are leathery and grey-green in colour. The pinkish-white flowers are borne in early spring, and are followed by small berries that become dark red when ripe. These may be better harvested when just under-ripe as ripe fruits are reported to be mealy. Pollination is sometimes poor, and planting more than one individual may improve this. Propagation is tricky as it does not grow easily from seed or cuttings. Soaking seeds in hot water before sowing may help.

Pine-mat manzanita, *Arctostaphylos navadensis*. A native of California and Oregon, it forms an evergreen, low, (~20 cm), spreading (~2–3 m) shrub. Has a rhizomatous, suckering habit. Leaves are small and oval. Has pinky-white flowers in spring, in compact panicles. Fruits are rounded, bright red when ripe in autumn. ∎

Aronia melanocarpa
Aronia (black chokeberry)
ROSACEAE

Red chokeberry: *Aronia arbutifolia* (syn. *Pyrus arbutifolia*)
Purple chokeberry: *Aronia prunifolia*

Relatives: pincherry, chokeberry, plum, peach, almond

Aronia species include a number of plants commonly known as chokeberries. The name 'chokeberry' comes from a tendency of some *Aronia* species to possibly choke birds, which may be an unfair name as they also attract song- and game-birds. They are related to, but are a different genus from, the *Prunus virginiana* chokeberry. The black chokeberry, *A. melanocarpa*, is considered by some to be the most pleasant to eat. The *Aronia* species are indigenous to northeastern North America, from Nova Scotia to Michigan to northern Florida. However, aronia have not been widely commercially cultivated in the USA, and any selection or cultivation has been mostly for ornamental purposes. *A. melanocarpa*, today, is much more popular in eastern Europe and Russia (especially Siberia) than in its native land. The fruit was designated as a 'healing plant' in the former Soviet Union. Experimental plantings of cultivars have been established in the Czech Republic, Scandinavia and Germany.

DESCRIPTION
Aronia is a deciduous, spreading, rounded shrub, 1.2–3.0 m tall, 0.3–2 m spread, and often wider than it is tall at maturity. Plants produce suckers that can form thickets. Though it does have very vigorous growth, *A. melancoarpa* is not as invasive as some of its cousins.

Leaves: Smooth, dark, oval, mostly on the tips of stems, leaving lower areas almost leafless. In most varieties, the leaves turn a rich, flame colour in autumn, which contrasts with the dark berries.

Flowers: Small, pinkish-white, in clusters, are borne in late spring. *Pollination:* Usually insect-pollinated, though will sometimes set fruits without pollination (parthenocarpic). Needs cross pollination for the production of viable seeds.

Fruit: Berries, black–dark purple, ~0.75–1.25 cm diameter, in clusters of ~10, which hang from leaf axils and can be easily harvested. Ripe fruits can be left to 'store' for several weeks into winter, and become sweeter after a frost.

Yields/harvest: Can get up to 16 kg per plant, with 10 kg per plant reported as an average in eastern Europe. Shrubs start producing some fruits after just 1 year of being planted. Fruits are best picked when fully ripe and when fully sweetened.

CULTIVATION
Easy-to-grow plants with no special needs.

Location: Generally not choosy about where it will grow. Widely adapted to sun or shade, will tolerate some wind and some salt.

Temperature: Very cold tolerant, and can be grown in regions with long, cold winters. Probably not suited to areas that have little or no winter chill temperatures.

Soil/water/nutrients: Plants grow best in loamy, well-drained soils, though will grow in most soil types, including peaty soils. They prefer moist, more acidic or neutral soils. Grow best with regular moisture, and can tolerate some waterlogging, though, once established, are reported to be able to grow in drier environments.

Propagation: *Seed:* Best sown when fresh. Pulp should be thoroughly cleaned from the seed before it is planted shallowly in a sand-peat mix, in a cold frame. Stored seed needs a period of 2–3 months of cold stratification, then soaking for ~18 hours before sowing in well-drained compost in spring. Germination can take 1–3 months at 15°C. *Cuttings:* Semi-ripe cuttings taken in summer can be inserted in moist, gritty compost to root. *Suckers:* These can be divided during autumn–spring and placed in moist compost to root before being planted out. *Layering:* Young, vigorous stems can be layered from spring–autumn.

Pests and diseases: Few pest problems. Rust can sometimes occur on the fruits.

SIMILAR SPECIES

Red chokeberry, *Aronia arbutifolia (syn. Pyrus arbutifolia).* A native of the warmer areas of eastern North America, from Texas to Florida, *A. arbutifolia* forms a shrub, ~3 m tall, and is found growing in acidic wet areas, often where pine trees have grown. Frequently forms suckers around its base. Flowers are borne in late spring, and fruits ripen in early winter. It is cold hardy, tolerating temperatures down to –25°C. Also tolerant of air pollution. *Soil:* More acid-tolerant than some species, and also probably more tolerant of wet soils. Not tolerant of alkalinity.

Uses: The fruits, ~0.7 cm diameter, vary in quality from plant to plant, but are often pleasant, particularly when fully ripe or when picked after a frost when they have fully sweetened. The fruits are also good when dried. Fruits, when ripe, can be left for several weeks on the plant in 'storage'.

Purple chokeberry, *Aronia prunifolia.* A native of eastern North America, it forms a shrub ~3 m tall. The flowers are not borne until mid–late summer, and the fruits do not ripen until winter. This shrub is fully cold hardy, and can tolerate temperatures below –25°C. Grows best in moist, acidic soils. The fruits are ~0.8 cm diameter, and can be used as suggested above, but are often dried for later use. ■

Food
The fruits are used in fruit juices, blended or diluted with other fruits to reduce their tartness. They are high in pectin, and are excellent in jam, jelly, conserves, etc. They are generally too sour to be eaten fresh. The fruits can be dried for later use.

Medicinal
The fruits contain high levels of antioxidants that may strengthen the cardiovascular system as well as provide many other benefits. It has 5–10 times the levels of anthocyanins and polyphenols as cranberry (and cranberries have high levels). It is up there with black currants and other dark-coloured fruits in its health benefits and its antioxidant properties. The fruits may also help in urinary problems, in the same way as cranberries. The full benefits of these fruits have not been fully explored as yet, but the levels of phenols, leuco-anthocyanins, catachines, flavonoles and flavones within black chokeberries merit further investigation. In addition, their high levels of pectin may help with many digestive problems.

Ornamental
Can be grown as an ornamental shrub for its flowers, autumn colour and colourful fruits.

uses

Artocarpus heterophyllus
Jackfruit (jakfruit)
MORACEAE

Similar species: Kwai muk (*Artocarpus hypargyraeus*), Lakoocha (*A. lakoocha*), Marang (*A. odoritissima*)

Relatives: breadfruit, fig, mulberry

The jackfruit is native to the rainforests of India, and from there it spread to many regions of Asia. Its huge fruits have been valued for thousands of years, and it is now grown in many tropical and subtropical regions of the world, including Africa, South America, the warmer parts of the USA and Australia. In South India, the jackfruit is a very popular fruit and the government has promoted planting jackfruit trees along highways and elsewhere as a food supply. The trees, although strictly a more tropical species, can be grown in warm temperate regions with care, such as Sydney and northern New Zealand, and is much more tolerant of colder weather than its close relative, the breadfruit. It is an interesting and handsome tree to grow, and has fruits that are one of the largest in the world. They are huge, semi-prickly and hang directly from the main trunk and branches. The fruit flesh can vary, but is generally sweet and tasty, though ripe fruits have an off-putting smell. The fruits also contain edible seeds and the trees themselves are valued medicinally and for their timber.

Food

The flesh is very mucilaginous, and it can be a very messy business to prepare them unless you coat the knife and hands with a little oil. However, the flesh has a crisp sweet texture. Once the fruit is sliced open, the flesh around the numerous seeds is separated from its fibrous segments. The core is also discarded. The seeds are also generally removed. The flesh varies in taste, with the flesh from better fruits enjoyed fresh on its own. It can be combined with other fruits in a range of desserts, juice, etc., or the ripe flesh can be readily fermented to make an alcoholic drink. It can be frozen for later use. Otherwise, under-ripe flesh, with its seeds intact, can be lightly boiled in water or coconut milk, or fried, pickled or added to curries. This is a popular method of preparing this fruit as some find the smell from the ripe fruits difficult to deal with. However, the fruit do produce a lot of gummy latex when cooked, which can be a nuisance to remove. The seeds can be boiled or roasted, and then salted and eaten as a snack, or can be added to many savoury dishes. The seeds can also be roasted and ground up to make a flour. The young leaves and flowers are sometimes lightly cooked and eaten as vegetables.

Nutrition

The flesh contains good levels of potassium, manganese, copper and magnesium as well as vitamin A (~500 IU) and C (~11 mg/100 g flesh). The fruits also contain riboflavin and B6. The seeds are high in carbohydrate and are similar to chestnuts. They are a good source of vitamins B1 and B2.

Medicinal

The flesh and seeds have been used by the Chinese as a tonic and as a hangover cure. The seeds are used to relieve biliousness and are also though to act as an aphrodisiac. An extract of the root is taken for fever and diarrhoea. The latex from the tree has antibacterial properties and has been used to treat abscesses and glandular swellings. **Warning:** The ripe fruit can act as a laxative. Raw jackfruit seeds contain a powerful protein (trypsin) inhibitor, but this is destroyed by heat.

Other uses

The latex has been used as a glue and as a sealant. It contains ~84% resin. A yellow dye is derived from the wood, which is used to dye silk as well as Buddhist robes. Its timber is of excellent quality. It is hard, dense, orange-yellow-red-brown in colour, and is resistant to many fungi, bacteria as well as termites. It is considered superior to teak for making furniture and a wide range of other items. Roots from old trees are valued for carving and for making picture frames.

Ornamental

A handsome, specimen, shade tree that gives a tropical feel, as well as producing enormous fruits.

DESCRIPTION

The jackfruit tree can become large (>20 m tall) in tropical regions, though elsewhere is usually much smaller. It has a dense, oval–round, spreading canopy and forms a handsome, fast-growing tree. All parts, when injured, produce a sticky, white latex. Trees may live for ~100 years.

Leaves: Evergreen, dark green, waxy, shiny, large, with most trees having simple entire leaves; only the leaves of young seedlings are lobed. They are oval to elliptic in shape, 10–20 cm long.

Flowers: Trees are monoecious, with male and female flowers borne in separate clusters on the same tree. Male flowers are borne in clusters on the new season's growth, often above female flowers on the same branch. The male flowers are oval, large (~2.5–10 cm long), with the main part being greenish in colour. Their stamens are covered with yellow pollen for a short period. The female flowers are larger, and are borne in small clusters directly from the main stems and branches, or even sometimes from the base of the trunk. They are similar in appearance to the male flower, but do not produce pollen. *Pollination:* Are wind and insect pollinated, though planting more than one tree (even though they are monoecious) or hand pollination will increase fruit-set.

Fruit: This tree produces one of the largest fruit in the world. Because of their huge weight and size, they are borne directly from the main stems and trunk, and, in older individuals, can even grow from the roots. These large, oval–rounded fruits can become up to 1 m in length. The skin of the fruit is greeny-yellow when ripe, and consists of many knobbly, semi-sharp prickles. Inside, it is not dissimilar to a pineapple, and consists of many segments around a central stem or core. Each fused segment is a fertilised fruit and contains a single, but large, oval (~1.5–3 cm long, ~1–2 cm wide), tan-coloured, edible seed. The flesh within the white fibrous segments is yellowish, and can be quite soft and sweet but mucilaginous, or can be crisper, tangy but less sweet in flavour, depending on cultivar, with the latter type being more popular commercially. Fruit quality also varies from tree to tree. In general, the flesh has a banana–pineapple flavour. There are between 100–500 segments per fruit. Its main disadvantage is that the skin of ripe fruits has a strong, unpleasant smell, although the flesh inside has a less strong odour. This fruit definitely tastes better than it smells.

Yield/harvest/storage: Trees vary considerably in how long they take to start producing fruits; some may start before 5 years of age, others can take >10 years. However, when they do start, mature trees can produce >100 fruits, which is quite impressive when you consider the size of the fruit, although they often produce fewer. Older trees tend to produce fewer fruits. Most fruits mature in summer, and the time from fruit-set to maturity varies between 5–7 months. The large fruits are often cut from the tree using gloves to avoid being covered with the difficult-to-remove latex. They are often harvested when fully ripe, give slightly when pressed and have a hollow sound when tapped. However, some pick them when they are under-ripe (1–3 months old) and use them like a vegetable. Somewhat under-ripe fruits will continue to ripen once picked. Unfortunately, for the size of the fruit, and thus the amount that needs to be consumed, the fruit do not store well, and deteriorate within a few days unless they are processed in some way.

Roots: Trees develop taproots as well as wide ranging, spreading roots and grow best if given a large soil area to grow in. They benefit from an organic mulch to help retain moisture and add nutrients.

CULTIVATION
Generally trouble free and need little maintenance once established.

Location: Trees are quite wind hardy in warmer areas.

Temperature: Grow best in humid tropical or subtropical climates. Freezing temperatures can damage leaves and branches, but they can tolerate temperatures down to freezing, unlike many tropical species. They can be grown in subtropical and even warm temperate areas if grown in a warm, protected area. Young trees will need extra protection in cold weather.

Soil/water/nutrients: Trees grow best in fertile, organic-matter rich, deep, loose soil. Trees need regular moisture, though need less during colder weather. Established trees can tolerate short periods of drought. Although they like moisture, they need the soil to be free-draining: trees succumb rapidly to any waterlogging. Although trees can grow in poorer soils, they grow best with a good nutrient supply, and regular applications of a balanced, complete fertiliser will be appreciated.

Pot culture: Unfortunately, the tree becomes too large to make a good container plant.

Planting: Space young trees at 4.5–7 m apart. Because of their spreading roots they are best not planted too near to buildings. The more moisture and care that can be given when trees are young, the better their later growth and fruit production will be. Take care when planting out that the taproot is not damaged. Young trees that are pot-bound do not subsequently grow well.

Pruning: Generally, these trees need little or no pruning other than to prune out any damaged or diseased wood, and to remove branches that prevent light penetrating into where the fruits are ripening. Prune to enhance the development of horizontal rather than upright branches. After harvesting, the removal of old fruiting stems induces next season's flowers to form.

Propagation: *Seed:* This is the usual method. Seeds need to be sown when just removed from the fruits as their viability rapidly diminishes, some reports say within 4 days. Soaking in a 10% solution of gibberellic acid is said to result in 100% germination. Sow seeds in moist (but well drained), warm, shaded compost. Germination takes 3–8 weeks. Young seedlings should be grown-on in deep pots to encourage the development of deep taproots. *Cuttings:* Semi-ripe cuttings taken during the summer may be successful. Insert cuttings into moist but gritty compost. *Layering:* Trees can be air-layered successfully. *Grafting:* This is also practised, using chip-budding or side veneer, cleft or approach grafting.

Pests and diseases: In the tropics, there are a number of possible problems, but elsewhere, problems should be few. Young fruits may need protecting from attacks by pests and diseases.

SIMILAR SPECIES

Kwai muk, *Artocarpus hypargyraeus*. Native to China, it forms an ornamental, slow-growing, slender tree that has long, slender leaves. The trees are not very cold hardy though, and can be damaged at ~–1°C. This could be a good species to grow in a container and could then be moved inside or given extra protection in colder weather. Its round fruits are much smaller than those of jackfruit, ~5–7 cm diameter, have a thin, velvety, orange-brown skin, but the orange-red, soft, sub-acid flesh has a good flavour. Fruits may be seedless or contain a few small, edible seeds. It is good eaten fresh or can be dried for later use. They are best eaten when fully ripe.

Lakoocha (monkey jak), *Artocarpus lakoocha*. Native to northern India, this tree is valued for its fruits, but also for its hard timber and, therefore, is becoming more uncommon in the wild. It is also grown in the Far East and other parts of India. It grow best in warm, humid climates, though can tolerate temperatures down to freezing once established. It forms a small tree, 6–9 m tall, and has large, attractive, leathery, evergreen leaves. It is monoecious, with orange male flowers and reddish female flowers. The trees are self-fertile, though will produce more fruits if grown with other trees nearby. *Fruit:* The compound, round fruits have a structure similar to jackfruit, but are much smaller, being only 5–15 cm in diameter. The dull yellow-pinkish skin is covered with a fine pubescence. The fruits contain 20–30 seeds that are fleshy, with a thin seedcoat. They can be propagated from seeds, though viability rapidly diminishes once they are removed from the fruit (~7 days). In addition, the progeny are very variable. Cuttings are seldom successful. Seedling trees start to produce after ~5 years, and yields per tree can be ~80 kg once the tree is established.

Uses: *Food:* The fruits are of fairly good quality, have a sub-acid-sweet taste and can be eaten fresh, though they, with the male flowers, are often used in chutneys and pickles. *Medicinal:* The fresh fruits are eaten as a tonic for the liver. The bark is high in tannin (~8%) and is used to treat skin infections. *Other uses:* The hard wood is highly valued, being similar to teak. It is very durable and has many uses including outside construction, furniture and boats. The wood and roots also yield a good-quality dye. *Ornamental:* This large-leaved, attractive tree makes a good ornamental species, and is also used as a shade tree.

Marang, *Artocarpus odoritissima*. Native to the Philippine Islands, it is now grown in several regions of the world, including parts of the USA. It has oval fruits, ~15 cm long, which have a thick skin covered with knobbly, semi-sharp spines. It has a similar inner structure to jackfruit, although the flesh is translucent, white, sweet, aromatic and juicy. ■

Asimina triloba
Asimoya (American pawpaw, asimina, Indiana banana, poor man's banana)
ANNONACEAE
Relatives: cherimoya, atemoya, custard apple

Asimoya is the only temperate member of the tropical Annonaceae family. Related to cherimoya and atemoya, asimoya is in a different genus. Asimoya is native to temperate North America and has long been cultivated by native Americans. Asimoya can be found growing wild in 25 states of eastern USA, and are often found in deep, fertile soils near rivers as understorey trees or as trees in thickets. It is an under-utilised tree that has potential as a landscape tree, a fruit crop and as a source of medicinal products. The trees have a lush, tropical appearance, as well as autumn colour and delicious fruit. There are some commercial fruit plantings of asimoyas in North America, Asia, Australia and Europe.

DESCRIPTION

A small, relatively slow-growing deciduous tree, 5–10 m tall. In sunny locations, trees typically assume a pyramidal habit with a single straight trunk. If given optimum light, moisture and heat they can be induced to grow faster.

Leaves: Long, drooping, elliptical, giving a tropical feel. They are lush, dark green, and turn gold and brown during autumn. Have a heavy, unpleasant odour when crushed.

Flowers: Emerge before leaves in mid spring. Velvety, dark brown flower buds develop in the leaf axils of the previous year's shoots. These open into maroon, bell-shaped flowers, ~5 cm diameter. Trees flower for ~6 weeks. Each flower contains several ovaries (3–7), and so a single flower can produce many fruits. *Pollination:* By flies and beetles, which is consistent with the dark red, meat-coloured petals and the flowers' foetid smell. Can be highly productive if the right pollinating insects are present; if not, then hand pollination can increase fruit-set. Although the flowers are bisexual, and have both male and female structures, they are also strongly protogynous, meaning that the stigma is receptive before pollen is shed. This results in flowers not being self-fertile and some cross pollination is needed, although a few trees can be self-compatible. Hand pollination can be done with a soft, fine brush, with pollen taken from older, fully opened flowers, usually in the afternoon, and this is then applied to the stigma of younger flowers that have just opened their petals.

Fruit: Long, oblong, cylindrical berries, ~7.5–12.5 cm long, 3–10 cm wide, which can weigh 200–400 g each. They may be borne singly or in small clusters, which resemble the 'hands' of a banana plant, although they actually originate from a single bloom. The fruit ripens through late summer–autumn from green to yellow-green, and finally to black. The flesh is highly aromatic, orange or white in colour, with a creamy texture when ripe. It has a flavour that is a mix of banana, mango, pineapple and cherimoya, though this does vary from tree to tree. The best fruits have a tasty, tropical, sweet flavour. Some regard the more orange-fleshed cultivars as having a richer flavour than white-fleshed fruits, with the latter also often maturing later. Within the flesh are two rows of large, brown, bean-shaped seeds (2–3 cm long), which should be discarded.

Yield/harvest/storage: Fruits take 4–5 months to mature after fruit-set. Trees in optimum conditions can produce good yields of 50–100 fruits per tree. Trees take ~4–6 years to first flower and fruit. Fruits can be harvested from late summer into autumn, depending on cultivar, etc. They are picked when just beginning to soften, although some wait until the fruits have fully coloured and have become even softer. They can only be kept for 2–3 days at room temperature because of their thin skins, though may be kept for up to 3 weeks with refrigeration.

Roots: Has a deep taproot, so needs to be grown in a deep pot and planted carefully. Trees are difficult to move or transplant because of this. They also have extensive root systems. However, the roots tend to be brittle, have few root hairs and are susceptible to damage. They may form beneficial fungal mycorrhizal associations, which enable them to obtain more nutrients, particularly phosphates; thus incorporating well-rotted organic matter, particularly leaves, is beneficial. Plants also form stolons (underground stems), which often form suckers at intervals along their length, particularly if the plant is multi-stemmed.

CULTIVATION

Location: Young plants can be damaged in full sunlight and benefit from some shade for the first year or two. After this, they can be grown in full sun. They are not wind hardy; and grow better in sheltered locations.

Temperature: Trees are very cold hardy, tolerating temperatures down to ~–30°C once established, though they also need a growing season of at least 6–8 months, and grow best with warm–hot summers.

Chilling: Trees do need a minimum of 400 hours of winter chilling to trigger flowering and subsequent fruiting.

Soil/water/nutrients: The best growth and fruits are produced when trees are grown in soils that are deep and rich in organic matter, though can also grow in clay or sandy loams. The soil should be kept moist, particularly when trees are young, and during flowering and fruit development, but avoid waterlogging. They grow well in regions with higher humidity. They grow best at pH values of 5.5–7. Trees are not very nutrient hungry, though benefit from the application of a general, complete fertiliser at the beginning of the growing season and also from a mulch of organic matter to conserve moisture.

Pot culture: Can be grown as a container specimen, although this is not often practised.

Planting: Space trees at ~3–5 m apart, and plant while they are dormant. Young trees may need some shade and additional protection until established. They also need regular moisture and minimal weed competition. Growth is slow for the first couple of years.

Pruning: Ordinarily, little pruning is required, except to remove dead, damaged or crossing branches. However, periodic pruning stimulates new growth on older trees, which then produces flowers and fruits the following season.

Propagation: Seeds: Difficult to germinate. Fresh seed from ripe fruits needs to be thoroughly cleaned of flesh to remove any inhibitors and to avoid fungal infection. The seeds are then kept moist but not wet, in polythene bags, and are cold stratified at ~5°C for ~3 months. Seeds can be stored for longer in this way, if required, with little loss in viability. In spring, soak seeds for ~24 hours before sowing at ~3-cm depth in deep, biodegradable pots, with warmth, to encourage taproot growth. These seeds will grow a taproot and lateral roots before forming a shoot ~9 weeks later. Seedlings benefit from regular moisture and liquid feeds that include trace elements. If the seedlings run out of soil depth they stop root and shoot growth. Therefore, deep pots are important, and seedlings need to be planted out before they have outgrown their pots. *Cuttings:* Difficult. Semi-ripe cuttings taken in summer, with intermittent mist, bottom heat (~25°C) and supplemental lighting of 14 hours a day may lead to rooted cuttings. Hardwood cuttings do not seem to root, nor do root cuttings. *Suckers:* It could be worth trying to establish suckers during the growing season, with moist and warmth. *Grafting:* Easily propagated by whip-and-tongue, cleft, bark inlay and chip-budding carried out in spring. Chip-budding is best done on wider-stemmed seedling rootstocks. Any scion budwood should have received adequate winter chilling. Whip grafting can be successfully done on seedling rootstocks with thinner stems, provided the scion is of a similar diameter.

Pests and diseases: Asimoya trees are virtually disease free, though check for scale and leafroller. The plants have a biocidal resistance to most problems, with this being concentrated mainly in the stems, unripe fruits, seeds, root and bark, with smaller stems being particularly toxic to pests. The fruits may be eaten by birds and other wildlife.

CULTIVARS

'Davis': Fruit: small. Flesh: yellow; skin: green. Seeds are large. Flavour excellent. Productive.

'Mitchell': Fruit: medium. Flesh: golden; skin: yellowish. Flavour excellent.

'Overleese': Fruit: large. Few seeds, but are larger. Flesh:

Food
Delicious eaten fresh on its own or added to other fresh desserts. It has a taste of papaya/pineapple/banana/mango mixed, with the best fruits being very sweet, with a rich tropical flavour like no other. However, other fruits can have a poorer flavour. The flesh is also very aromatic, and has been added to processed foods. Fruit can be puréed and frozen. They are used as a banana substitute in many recipes.

Nutrition
An excellent fruit: it exceeds apple and grape in most vitamins, minerals and food energy value. It has an unusually high protein content for a fruit, and is an excellent source of vitamin A and a good source of vitamin C: (~14 mg/100 g of flesh).

Medicinal
The fruits are used as a laxative and as a diuretic. The leaves are applied externally to boils, ulcers and abscesses. The seeds contain the alkaline asiminine, which is emetic and narcotic. They have been powdered and applied to hair to kill lice. The bark is bitter and high in the alkaline analobine, which is used medicinally. Twigs, leaf and bark are the source of annonaceous acetogenins, which are being used in the development of anti-tumour drugs (acetogenins) and pesticides (asimicin). The high level of natural defence compounds in the tree makes it highly resistant to insect/disease infestation. A trial of 40 varieties of asimoya is under way at Purdue University. **Warning:** Seeds contain alkaloids in the endosperm that are emetic. If chewed, the seed may impair digestion, but if swallowed whole, seeds may pass through the digestive tract intact. Handling the fruit may cause allergic reactions in sensitive individuals.

Other uses
The aromas are used commercially in cosmetics and skin products. A fibre from the inner bark is used to make strong rope and string. A yellow dye is made from the ripe flesh of the fruit. *Ornamental:* The large leaves create a semi-tropical effect in the landscape.

yellow, flavour excellent. Late ripening.
'Prolific': Fruit: large. Flesh: yellow, flavour excellent.
'Sunflower': Good flavour and size, partly self-fertile. Fruit: medium–large. Flesh: golden; skin: yellowish; Few seeds. Late blooming, late ripening.
'Taylor': Fruit: small. Flesh: yellow; skin: green. Flavour is mild and excellent.
'Taytoo': Fruit: medium. Flesh: yellow; skin: light green. Flavour excellent. Prolific bearer.
'Well's Delight': Fruit: very large, excellent flavour. Flesh: orange; skin: green. ■

Austromyrtus dulcis
Midgen berry (sand berry)
MYRTACEAE
Relatives: myrtle, jaboticaba, pitomba

Austromyrtus comes from the Latin, 'australis', meaning southern; *myrtus* is Greek for myrtle; and *dulcis* is Latin for sweet. There are at least 11 species of *Austromyrtus* native to Australia, with most occuring on the east coast from central New South Wales to northern Queensland. They are small trees or shrubs, and can be found in woodlands, heaths or rainforest fringes. The midgen berry (or sand berry) is a spreading plant whose berries have been used by the Aborigines for many hundreds of years. It often grows in sandy soils or open forests. It forms an-easy-to-manage, small, ornamental shrub and is considered by many to produce one of the best edible Australian native fruits.

DESCRIPTION
Low spreading, highly ornamental shrub, up to 2 m tall, though often shorter, and spread can be as large as, or more than, its height. Fairly slow growing.

Leaves: Evergreen, glossy, dark green, lanceolate, opposite, small, 1–3 cm long, 0.3–1 cm wide, in two rows, with numerous conspicuous oil glands. They have a downy covering on their undersides, making them appear pale grey-green. Young leaves are coppery-pink in colour, and are densely coated in white, fine silky hair. In cold weather, older leaves also often become reddish, to form a range of colours throughout the shrub.

Flowers: White, pretty, delicate, borne singly or in clusters of 2–5 flowers from leaf axils. They are small, 0.6–1 cm in diameter, and are borne in spring–summer in warm regions, but from summer–mid autumn in cooler locations. A simple shape with five petals and with numerous fluffy stamens in the centre.

Fruit: Currant-like fruits, ~1–2.5 cm in diameter, attractive, pale lilac to almost white in colour, with darker purple flecks when ripe. Has a soft, thin skin and several (3–9) small, pale brown seeds that are edible and barely noticeable. The flesh is soft, aromatic and has a sweet, delicious flavour. The whole fruit can be enjoyed. Bushes usually have very good yields.

Harvest: Pick berries when they are fully coloured and just turning soft. They are harvested from summer to late autumn.

Roots: Plants seem to exude a substance from their roots or leaves that deters the growth of many weed species around them.

CULTIVATION
Needs little maintenance once established.

Location: If grown in full sun, it forms a dense, spreading shrub (~40 cm tall, ~1.5 m spread); if grown in semi-shade, it becomes less dense. Can grow in maritime locations, but does not like exposed locations.

Temperature: Tolerates some frost, but not prolonged or very cold temperatures, and is best grown in a sheltered spot. Prefers warmer climates.

Soil/water: Can grow in fairly dry sandy soils, as well as various other soil types, but does need regular moisture year round. Can grow in medium–fairly alkaline soils. Plants only need moderate amounts of fertiliser: one or two applications of a complete fertiliser (or similar) annually, or less in better-quality soils.

Pot culture: In colder areas, they can be grown as a container plant as their size is easy to control, and they only have a moderate growth rate. Plants can then be moved inside or more easily protected in regions that have colder winters.

Pruning: Only necessary if wanting to obtain a particular shape, e.g. a low hedge.

Propagation: Relatively easy species to propagate. *Seed:* Easy to grow from seed. Sow fresh cleaned seed in well-drained compost: germinates in 21–28 days; unwashed fruits take about 7 days longer to germinate. Although it has a hard seedcoat, this does not need treatment to soften it. Stored seed may take considerably longer to germinate,

uses

Food
The small berries are sweet, but slightly sub-acid, and are very tasty. They are often described as being one of the most delicious Australian bush foods. Their flavour also combines an interesting mildly aromatic, perfume-like flavour. They can be eaten fresh, or can be added to desserts, pies, jams, icecream, yoghurt, etc. They can also be dried for later use.

Ornamental
Makes an attractive groundcover plant, for either full sun or semi-shaded locations. Attracts the birdlife. It can be grown as an informal hedge.

and soaking or scarification before sowing can improve germination. *Cuttings:* Semi-ripe wood can be taken in summer and inserted into gritty, moist, warm compost.

These should root easily.

Pests and diseases: Relatively free from pests and diseases. ∎

Averrhoa carambola
Carambola (starfruit)
OXALIDACEAE

The carambola probably originated in Sri Lanka and the surrounding regions, but has been cultivated in southeastern Asia and Malaysia for many centuries. It is a popular tree in the Philippines, many South Pacific islands and in Queensland. It can also be grown in the northern areas of New Zealand and many areas of California. In many regions, it is grown more as an ornamental than for its fruits.

DESCRIPTION
A slow-growing, short-trunked tree that forms a much-branched, bushy canopy. The crown often becomes broad and rounded, reaching 6–9 m in height and spread in warmer regions, though is often much less in warm-temperate areas.

Leaves: Mostly evergreen, though becoming deciduous in colder regions or under adverse conditions. They are pinnate and consist of 6–10 pairs of leaflets with a terminal leaflet. Each leaflet is 5–12 cm long, often long and thin, ovate-oblong. They are soft, medium-green, and smooth on their upper surfaces, and finely hairy and whitish beneath. The leaves are sensitive and tend to close together at night or when the tree is exposed to strong winds.

Flowers: Fragrant, white-pinkish-mauve, ~0.5 cm in diameter, and are borne in clusters from the leaf axils of either young or older branches, in early summer. The flowers are bisexual, with both male and female structures within the same flower. In warm/hot climates, trees can flower and fruit year round; in subtropical or warm-temperate areas, most fruits are produced during the cooler season. *Pollination:* By bees and other insects. Although plants are bisexual, planting more than one cultivar will improve yields. Flowers vary, by cultivar, in whether they have short or long female structures (styles), and it is thought that the best fruit yields are obtained from a mix of short- and long-styled cultivars. Heavy rains during flowering can reduce pollination.

Fruit: Have two main cropping periods in tropical regions and a single period in cooler regions. Do need warmth year-round for plants to set fruits. Although trees can grow well in warm-temperate regions, they seldom set fruits. The fruits are very ornamental and attractive, being a distinctive star shape when seen in cross-section. The star consists of 5–6 points, and the fruits are generally 7–12 cm long. Their thin, waxy skin becomes orange-yellow when ripe. There are two main types of fruits: one has smaller, tasty, but sourer fruits with a high content of oxalic acid; the other type has larger, sweeter, but less tasty fruits that contain less oxalic acid. In the centre are several (up to 12) flat, thin, brown seeds, or some fruits are seedless. It takes 60–80 days from fruit-set to maturity, depending on temperature, cultivar, etc.

Yield/harvest: Seedlings take ~5 years to start producing fruits; grafted trees can start producing fruits as soon as a year after planting. In warm, sheltered locations trees can produce many fruits. Can get yields of 5–15 kg from young trees, which increases to ~55 kg within a few further years, to ~130 kg when fully mature at ~10 years. Fruits are best harvested when fully coloured and ripe, which occurs mostly through autumn. Ripe fruits tend to fall and should be gathered soon after. Slightly under-ripe fruits will continue to ripen once picked. Fruits can be easily damaged and should be handled gently. Under-ripe fruits can be stored for ~4 weeks at 10°C; ripe fruits can only be kept for a few days.

CULTIVATION
Location: Trees love full sun. They are tolerant of some wind exposure, though protected trees are often more vigorous and productive. They are not very tolerant of high salt conditions, though can be grown near the coast in sheltered locations.

Temperature: Trees are classified as subtropical/tropical, but mature trees can tolerate temperatures down to ~–2.5°C for short periods with little damage. Young trees are much more sensitive to cold though, and need to be protected for the first few years if frosts threaten.

Soil/water/nutrients: Trees grow best in deep, loamy soils, though can also grow on light or heavy soils. They grow best in moderately acid to moderately alkaline soils (pH 5.5–7). Alkaline soils can induce nutrient deficiencies, such as iron chlorosis, and plants then need additions of chelated micronutrients. However, some reports suggest that flowering and fruiting can be improved in more alkaline soils. Carambolas grow best with regular moisture and do not tolerate dry conditions for extended periods, even in winter. They may be able to tolerate flooded soils for short periods, but will grow better in freely draining soils. Trees are only moderately nutrient hungry and only need one or

Food

They are often cut into star-shaped cross-sections, and are used fresh as a garnish on many sweet and savoury dishes (particularly seafoods). The fruit can be eaten fresh by itself but is often combined with other fruits or is added to salads. Some add raisins to give them more character. They are mildly sweet and lack a strong flavour. They are more often used for their ornamental value. They can also be added to cooked desserts, tarts, stews and curries. In Malaya, they are often stewed with sugar and cloves, alone or combined with apples. The Chinese cook carambolas with fish. Slightly under-ripe fruits are salted, pickled or made into jam or other preserves. In Queensland, the sweeter fruits are cooked green as a vegetable. A relish can be made from the unripe fruits, combined with horseradish, celery, vinegar, seasonings and spices. Carambola juice makes a refreshing drink, and Filipinos sometimes use the juice as a seasoning. The flowers are tart and are added to salads in Indonesia, or are made into preserves in India. The leaves have been eaten as a substitute for sorrel.

Nutrition

Fruits are a good source of potassium and copper, and have good vitamin C (~45 mg/100 g of flesh) and vitamin A (100–1000 IU, variable) levels. They also contain good amounts of fibre, as well as folate and pantothenic acid.

Medicinal

The fruits and other parts of the plant are often used medicinally. The ripe fruits have been used to reduce haemorrhages, to treat fevers, to reduce biliousness and diarrhoea, as a diuretic, and as a cure for alcoholic hangovers. A salve, made from the fruit, has been used to treat eye problems and eczema. Leaves placed on the temples have been used to soothe headaches. The flowers have been used to expel internal parasites. The crushed seeds have been used to increase milk production, but are also mildly intoxicating. **Warning:** Under-ripe fruits often contain quite high levels of oxalic acid. Levels can also be quite high in sharper-tasting ripe fruits. In moderation, oxalic acid is not a problem (i.e. there's lots in spinach and rhubarb), but in larger amounts it can cause health problems.

Other uses

Acid-type carambolas have been used to clean and polish metal, especially brass, as they dissolve tarnish and rust. The juice can also remove rust stains from white cloth. Unripe fruits can be used instead of a conventional mordant in dyeing. *Wood*: White, becoming reddish with age; close-grained, medium-hard and used for construction and furniture.

Ornamental

In a sheltered, warm spot it can make an attractive ornamental. The foliage is mid-green and attractive, the flowers are fragrant and its fruits are eye-catching.

two applications of a complete, balanced fertiliser annually in moderate-quality soils. This may need to be increased in poor-nutrient soils.

Pot culture: Make good plants for containers as their growth is fairly slow and they are manageable. They can also be protected from frosts in colder areas. They make an attractive ornamental, interesting pot plant, though may not fruit. They can be pruned to be kept manageable.

Planting: Space trees at least 6 m apart in warmer areas. In warm-temperate areas, trees never become very large and can be planted closer together.

Pruning: Trees need little to no pruning except for the occasional removal of damaged or dense crossing branches. The height of taller stems can be reduced to keep the fruits within reach. They can be trained to an espalier against a wall, or can be pruned to retain a smaller size for container growth.

Propagation: *Seeds*: Often grown from seed. Viability may be reduced within a few days after removal from the fruit, although other reports claim the seeds germinate fine after storage. If possible, select the plumpest seeds and insert these in damp, warm compost. Germination rates are quite good, and takes 7–21 days. Grow-on seedlings in a well-drained sandy loam until they are large enough to withstand the local conditions. However, seedlings are highly variable. *Layering:* Air-layering can be practised, but the results are variable. Roots take a time to develop, and the resulting plants can be smaller and weaker. *Grafting*: This method gives good predictable results. The main methods used are cleft-grafting on green wood or side-whip-and-tongue grafting of mature wood onto seedlings. Top-working is also practised on older trees. The scion wood is best taken from mature twigs where the buds are just beginning to grow.

Pests and diseases: No serious diseases are known, but fruit may be attacked by fruit fly, fruit moths and fruit-spotting bugs in areas that have these infestations. Birds and other wildlife may eat the fruits.

CULTIVARS

'Arkin': Larger fruited, mildly sweet fruits, 10–15 cm long. Bright yellow when ripe. Juicy, firm flesh with few seeds. Keeps well. Fairly self-fertile. Bears in winter, and can be grown in warm-temperate regions. Not very wind tolerant. The leading commercial cultivar.

'Fwang Tung': Larger fruited, mildly sweet fruits, 10–20 cm long. Pale yellow skin and flesh when ripe. Juicy, firm, with few seeds. Attractive star shape. Not very wind tolerant.

'Golden Star': Larger fruited, mildly sweet, but also sub-acid fruits, deeply winged and attractive. Skin is bright golden yellow and waxy when ripe. Flesh is juicy and crisp. Trees are more self-fertile than most cultivars. High in vitamins A and C. Can be grown in more alkaline soils. Is fairly wind tolerant.

'Hoku': Larger fruited, mildly sweet fruits, 15–20 cm long. Are bright yellow when ripe; juicy and firm, few seeds. Attractive star shape.

'Kary': A heavy cropper. Fruits are quite sweet, good flavour. Has more cold tolerance than other cultivars. Few seeds.

'Kembagen': Fruits are bright yellow-orange when ripe, and fairly sweet. Are somewhat elongated and pointed. Flesh is juicy and firm, few seeds. ■

Berberis spp.
Barberry (chitra)
BERBERIDACEAE

Common barberry (*Berberis vulgaris*), Indian barberry (*B. aristata*), Allegheny barberry (*B. canadensis*), barberry (*B. georgii*), Darwin's barberry (*B. darwinii*), Magellan barberry (*B. buxifolia*)

Relatives: berberis, Oregon grape

A genus of ~450 species of deciduous and evergreen, usually spiny, shrubs, the majority of which are hardy and are very easy to cultivate, needing minimum maintenance. They are often grown as ornamental plants for their attractively coloured leaves, flowers and brightly coloured berries, also for the autumn colour of the deciduous species. The name 'berberis' is Arabic and means a 'shell', which may be derived from its glossy leaves that have been likened to the inside of an oyster-shell. Barberry is a common name for a few of these species, which are generally distributed over most of Europe, Northern Africa and temperate Asia. They are fairly common ornamentals in gardens, but are also known and grown for their somewhat acidic, but edible fruits.

DESCRIPTION
Common barberry, *Berberis vulgaris*. An attractive ornamental shrub, growing ~2.5–3.5 m, and forming an upright, multi-stemmed shape. The stems are smooth, have a white pith and are covered with light silvery-grey bark. They are somewhat brittle.

Leaves: Deciduous, often darker green above, pale green beneath, shiny, and have good autumn colour. Leaves are alternate, 2.5–5 cm long, or in small clusters, on short leaf stalks. Leaves are simple, oval, often tapering at the base, with finely serrated margins, with each small tooth terminating in a small bristly spine. As stems age, they become more spiny, with older regions of stems forming clusters of three-forked spines; these are ~1.5 cm long, and are actually modified leaves, with secondary leaves forming from the axils of these spines.

Flowers: Small, ~0.6 cm in diameter, shades of yellow, in pendulous clusters, produced from the axils of younger leaves in late spring–early summer. They have six petals, six sepals and six stamens with a central stigma. They are scented, though this is not pleasant to all. *Pollination:* Popular with bees and insects, as they produce abundant nectar. As bees or insects (or people) touch the stamens, these spring from a protective position lying between the petals to strike inwards against the stigma and, thus, the pollen is scattered in the close vicinity of the female stigma. Because insects mostly visit flowers in drier weather, this is also the ideal time for the stamens to be 'sprung' and pollinate. Flowers are bisexual and self-fertile.

Fruit: The berries turn a rich red colour when ripe, and are ~1.25 cm long, oval, shiny and pleasantly sub-acid. They are borne in clusters and often have a light bloom on their skin. The juicy, red flesh contains 2–3 small seeds. After ripening, in autumn, the fruits can persist on the bush for quite a long period, though they tend to drop in heavy rain.

Yield/harvest: The fruits are best picked when fully ripe. Shrubs often produce very good yields. To harvest the bark from the stem and roots, scrape off and gently dry, the inner yellow bark can then be peeled off and used medicinally (see below).

Roots: Tends to form a spreading, surface root system, but also has deeper roots. These species also usually have rhizomatous roots near the soil surface, which often produce suckers, particularly if damaged by mechanical cultivation. In addition, the shallow roots can be damaged by freezing temperatures and benefit from an organic mulch, which also helps to conserve moisture.

CULTIVATION
An easy-to-grow, low-maintenance plant.

Location: Shrubs can grow in either semi-shade or full sun. Not very tolerant of salt spray.

Temperature: Are fully cold hardy, and can survive severe winters. These are temperate species.

Soil/water/nutrients: They grow best in warm, moist, loamy soils, though are adaptable and can grow in poorer-quality soil with few nutrients, and either sand or heavy clay. They can even tolerate temporarily waterlogged soils. They can grow in a range of pH soils from moderately acidic to moderately alkaline. Once established, they can tolerate some drought, but grow and fruit better with regular moisture during the growing season. They are not very nutrient hungry, and need only an occasional application of a complete fertiliser, with micronutrients, particularly in poorer soils.

Pot culture: These species are sometimes grown in containers and can be pruned to be kept smaller and manageable. They can even be trained to form a bonsai. They are popular for their autumn colour, flowers and eye-catching fruits. Pots benefit from being mulched or protected in winter to reduce any frost damage to the roots.

Planting: Space plants at 1.5–2 m apart, or wider for larger species. Plant deciduous species in late autumn or early spring. For hedges, plants are spaced at 30–45 cm apart, and the tips of shoots are removed to encourage the formation of lateral branches.

Propagation: *Seed*: Best sown when fresh in a cold frame; this should germinate in late winter or early spring. Seeds from over-ripe fruit will take longer to germinate. Stored seed may require cold stratification for 2–3 months before sowing in early spring. Grow-on seedlings in separate pots for a year or so before planting out. Seedlings are vulnerable to damping off, so should not be over-watered and need good ventilation. *Cuttings:* Semi-ripe cuttings, taken with a heel, in summer, can be inserted in a peat-sand mix, though rooting is often poor. *Division:* Any suckers can be dug up and placed in a moist peat-sand mix, in pots, to establish. However, although this is an easy method to use, plants grown from suckers produce more suckers than plants grown from layers. *Layering:* Young, vigorous stems can be pegged down to the soil surface to form roots from regions that have been lightly scored. This is best done in autumn, and stems take ~12 months to root and become established, before being removed from the parent plant.

Pruning: Generally need very little, just to tidy up any straggly growth or old, unproductive stems. Fruits are formed on older wood, so you need to bear this in mind when pruning. Deciduous species are best pruned in late winter; evergreen species are pruned after they have fruited in late autumn. Plants can be pruned to form a hedge. They can also be pruned severely and will grow back from the base.

Pests and diseases: Has few problems with pests or diseases, though is susceptible to honey fungus, and has occasional problems with *Anthracnose*, powdery mildew, aphids and scale insects. The cultivation of some barberry species is banned in some countries because they can be a host for black rust, which then goes on to attack wheat. The fruits are often sought by birds.

uses

Food
The fruits are fairly acidic, but are tasty, and are often used in jellies, preserves, desserts, pickles or used to garnish dishes. They are, generally, too acidic to be eaten in quantity when fresh. The delicious *confitures d'epine vinette*, for which Rouen (in France) is famous, is made using these fruits. The leaves are also acid, and have been used in similar ways as the fruit. The leaves can be used as a salad vegetable.

Nutrition
The fruits contain citric and malic acids, and contain a small amount of vitamin C: ~4.5 mg/100 g of flesh.

Medicinal
These species contain berberine within their rhizomes, which has recently been shown to have a marked antibacterial action. It has been found to be therapeutically effective against several Gram-positive and negative bacteria, and an Indian study has shown it to be effective in treating cholera. It is a bitter alkaloid that, unusually, occurs in several plants from different natural orders. It is not readily absorbed through the skin and is often ingested to treat various gastrointestinal disorders, as well as showing some anti-tumour activity. The bark from the stem and roots has also been used to treat constipation, diarrhoea, to relieve heavy menstruation, to aid digestive problems, inflammation, biliousness, to induce sweating, as a tonic and to treat eye problems and skin diseases. It also makes a good gargle for a sore mouth. It should not be taken with liquorice as this nullifies its effects.

Other uses
The roots yield a yellow dye, which has been used to dye wool, linen and leather. The dye is described as one of the best tannin dyes available in India.

Ornamental
Popular, easy-care, ornamental shrubs, suitable for borders or they can be pruned to form a good barrier hedge. They grow readily in most sites.

THE SPECIES

Allegheny barberry, *Berberis canadensis*. A shrub native to North America, growing from Alberta down to Georgia. It grows to ~1.8 m tall and flowers in late spring. Fruits ripen in early autumn. The fruits are ~0.9 cm diameter. It is quite cold hardy, surviving frost quite well. It can grow in sun or semi-shade, and is able to grow in almost any soil, from thin dry soils to clay, but is not tolerant of waterlogging. It is an alternate host for black-stem rust, which infects cereals. Its fruits are quite acidic, and are usually used in preserves or in cooked desserts. A few leaves can be eaten fresh or added to salads. Its medicinal properties are as for the common barberry.

Barberry, *Berberis georgii*. The origin of this species is not known, and it is probably a natural hybrid, possibly with *B. vulgaris*. A shrub, ~3 m tall, it flowers in late spring, and its fruits ripen in late autumn. These are ~1 cm long, quite acidic and are usually added to preserves, pies, desserts, etc., though a few can be tasty eaten fresh. A refreshing tangy drink can be made from the fruits. It often produces very good crops of fruits. It has the same uses as other *Berberis* species. Plants are very cold hardy, surviving temperatures of −35°C. It may be an alternate host for black-stem rust of wheat.

Darwin's barberry, *Berberis darwinii*. A native of South America, from Chile and Argentina. It forms an ornamental, evergreen, spreading shrub, ~3 m tall, ~3.5 m wide. Is not as cold hardy as some *Berberis* species, but can tolerate temperatures of ~−15°C. It is quite wind hardy and can grow in maritime locations. Like other *Berberis*, it can tolerate most soil types, including more alkaline soils, though prefers acidic conditions. It flowers in spring, and fruits ripen in late summer. Bees love the flowers, and birds flock to eat the fruits, so shrubs may need netting to protect fruits while they ripen. The fruits are ~0.7 cm in diameter. They are sub-acid and have a very pleasant taste, which becomes sweeter when they are fully ripe. They can be eaten fresh, in porridge or muesli, etc., or added to various desserts, preserves, etc. Unfortunately they also have lots of seeds.

Indian barberry (chitra, tree turmeric, Nepal barberry), *Berberis aristata* (syn. *B*. *chitria*. *B*. *coriaria*). A native of eastern Asia, from the Himalayan regions, Indian barberry forms an evergreen, spiny, erect shrub, to ~2–3 m tall, which can twine around branches of trees and other structures. It is a very cold hardy plant, tolerating temperatures of less than –30°C, though young growth can be damaged by frost. It can grow in full sun or semi-shade, though fruits better in full sun. Is not very wind tolerant. Propagation by cuttings is difficult for this species. *Flowers:* Yellow, in clusters ~2.5 cm long, in late spring. Several cultivars of this species may be dioecious, so will need a male and female plant to set fruits. *Fruits:* Are ~0.7–1 cm long, ripen in late autumn. Plants can have very good yields, producing ~650 g of fruits per season.
Uses: *Food:* The fruits have a sub-acid, yet sweet, good flavour and can be eaten fresh or added to preserves, desserts, sauces, etc. The seeds can give a bitter overtone. The fruits are dried and used like raisins in India. The flower buds can be eaten, and are added to sauces. *Medicinal:* It is an important medicinal plant with every part having some medicinal value, and it is widely used in India in Ayurvedic medicine. Infusions from the roots have been used to treat malaria, eye complaints, as an antiseptic, for skin diseases, menorrhagia, diarrhoea and to treat liver problems, such as jaundice. It is also applied to aid wound healing. It is used as a safe sedative, and also to possibly reduce incidence of tumours. Has the beneficial uses of common barberry. *Other uses:* This species is an important source of dyes obtained from the roots.

Magellan barberry, *Berberis buxifolia*. A native of South America, from Chile and Argentina. Often found growing on the edges of forests, and moister regions near the coast. It forms an evergreen shrub, growing to ~2.5 m tall. It can grow well in full sun, and most soil types. Plants are cold hardy, tolerating temperatures down to ~–15°C, but can become deciduous in cold winters. There are dwarf cultivars available. It flowers in spring, and flowers are probably self-fertile, though there are reports to the contrary. The black fruits, ~0.8 cm diameter, ripen by late summer, and plants usually yield good crops. They have a very good flavour that is sub-acid but pleasant. They can be eaten fresh or used in conserves, desserts, sauces, etc. The unripe fruits can be used like gooseberries. ■

Berberis spp.
Berberis aggregata, B. angulosa, B. asiatica, B. wilsoniae
BERBERIDACEAE
Relatives: Oregon grape, barberry

A genus of ~450 species of deciduous and evergreen, usually spiny, shrubs, the majority of which are hardy and are very easy to cultivate, needing minimum maintenance. The name 'berberis' is Arabic and means a 'shell', which may be derived from its glossy leaves that have been likened to the inside of an oyster-shell. Native to Northern Africa and Asia, they later spread to much of Europe and in the past they were often cultivated for their fruits. Nowadays they are usually grown as ornamental plants for their attractively coloured leaves, their abundant, yellow flowers, brightly coloured berries and for the autumn colour of deciduous species. However, their cultivation is prohibited in some regions as many of these species are carriers of a rust that goes on to infect wheat. Below is a general description of the species, followed by individual examples.

GENERAL DESCRIPTION
They form shrubs, 1.5–2 m tall, sometimes larger, often with the same spread. They frequently hybridise, and the exact species is sometimes difficult to accurately identify. The bark is brown on the surface and mustard-yellow beneath, due to the presence of berberine.
Leaves: Can be evergreen or deciduous, with deciduous species often having brilliant red and orange autumn colours. Leaves are usually fairly small, ~1–2 cm long, often obovate, with tips at the apices and narrow tapering bases, and are often spiny. Often in attractive whorls.
Flowers: Globular or cup-shaped, drooping, mostly found in small clusters, ~2.5 cm long, though sometimes occur singly, usually yellow in colour, borne in spring to early

Food

Although these shrubs are widely grown in gardens, few people are aware of the edibility of the fruits, which are acidic but tasty, and are usually cooked and used in preserves, desserts, pickles, etc.

Nutrition

The fruits contain ~2% protein, 12% sugars, 0.6% tannin, 0.4% pectin. They have a small amount of vitamin C: ~4.5 mg/100 g of flesh.

Medicinal

These species contain berberine within their rhizomes, which has recently been shown to have a marked antibacterial action. It has been found to be therapeutically effective against several Gram-positive and negative bacteria and an Indian study has shown it to be effective in treating cholera. It is a bitter alkaloid that, unusually, occurs in several plants from different natural orders. It is not readily absorbed through the skin and is more usually ingested to treat various gastrointestinal disorders. Berberine has also shown anti-tumour activity. The bark from the stem and roots has also been used to treat constipation, diarrhoea, to relieve heavy menstruation, to aid digestive problems, biliousness, to induce sweating, as a tonic, and to treat eye problems and skin diseases. It should not be taken with liquorice as this nullifies its effects.

Other uses

A yellow dye can be obtained form the roots.

Ornamental

Very popular, easy-care, ornamental shrubs, suitable for borders or can be pruned to form a good barrier hedge. There are many ornamental cultivars that have been selected for leaf colour, autumn colour, flowers and berry colour. They grow readily in most sites.

summer. Most species are monoecious and self-fertile, so only need one plant to set fruits, though a few are dioecious. *Pollination:* By bees and insects.

Fruits: The berries are usually rounded, and vary in colour from bright red to deep red or dark purple when ripe. Are ~1 cm in diameter, with juicy, sub-acid, often good-flavoured flesh, within which are several, small, edible seeds, that can sometimes be slightly bitter. Most fruits can be dried for later use. They are formed on last season's wood, and also on spurs from older wood.

Yield/harvest: Many species produce large crops of fruits, which should be harvested when fully coloured and ripe. They often make a dazzling display. To harvest the bark from the stem and roots, scrape this off and dry it gently. The inner yellow bark can then be peeled off and used medicinally (see Uses).

Roots: Tend to form a spreading, surface root system, but also have deeper roots. They also usually form rhizomatous roots near the soil surface, which often produce suckers. Avoid deep mechanical cultivation, which can damage roots, but will also increase suckering. An organic mulch can help conserve moisture.

CULTIVATION

An easy-to-grow, low-maintenance plant.

Location: Can be grown in full sun or semi-shade, though fruit better in full sun, where the leaf colour of deciduous species is also improved. Evergreen species are more tolerant of shade. Are usually fairly wind tolerant, and are moderately tolerant of maritime exposure.

Temperature: The majority of *Berberis* species are fully cold hardy, tolerating cold, frosty winters.

Soil/water/nutrients: They grow best in well-drained, loamy soil, but can grow in almost all soil types, including shallow, stony soils or clay soils. However, they are not tolerant of waterlogging. They can grow in moderately acidic to moderately alkaline soils. Once established they can tolerate some drought, but grow and fruit better with regular moisture during the growing season. They are not very nutrient hungry, and only need an occasional application of a complete fertiliser, with micronutrients, particularly in poorer soils.

Pot culture: These species are sometimes grown in containers and can be pruned to be kept smaller and manageable. They can even be trained to form a bonsai. They are popular for their autumn colour, flowers and eye-catching fruits. Pots benefit from being mulched or protected in winter to avoid cold damage to roots.

Planting: Space plants at 1.5–2 m apart, or wider for larger species. Plant deciduous species in late autumn or early spring. For hedges, plants are spaced at 30–45 cm apart, and the tips of shoots are removed to encourage the formation of lateral branches.

Propagation: *Seed:* Often does not come true from seed because of hybridisation. However, fresh seed germinates easily. Sow, when ripe, in damp, well-drained compost and it germinates over winter or in spring. Stored seed needs 2–3 months of cold stratification before sowing. Seedlings are vulnerable to damping-off, so should not be over-watered and need good ventilation. Seedlings are variable in appearance and fruit quality. *Cuttings:* Semi-ripe cuttings, taken with a heel, in summer, can be inserted in a peat-sand mix. These should root and become established by the following spring. Grow these on for a further 1–2 years before planting out. Can also take cuttings of mature wood, with a heel, in late autumn–early winter, and insert these in gritty soil in a cold frame. *Division:* Any suckers can be dug up and placed in a moist peat-sand mix, in pots, to establish.

Pruning: Generally need very little, just to tidy up any straggly growth or old, unproductive stems. Fruits are formed on older wood, so you need to bear this in mind when pruning. Deciduous species are best pruned in late winter; evergreen species are pruned after they have fruited in late autumn. Plants can be pruned to form a hedge; they can also be pruned severely and will grow back from the base.

Pests and diseases: Has few problems with pests or

diseases, though are susceptible to honey fungus, and occasional problems with *Anthracnose*, powdery mildew, aphids and scale insects. The fruits are often sought by birds.

THE SPECIES

Berberis aggregata. A native of western China. *Cultivation:* As general notes. Plants can grow in sun or light shade. It forms a bushy shrub, ~1.5 m tall, with a similar spread. *Leaves:* Deciduous, oval–lanceolate, and have very good red–orange autumn colour. In summer they are mid green. *Flowers:* Has clusters of ~2.5-cm-long, yellow flowers in summer. *Fruits:* Abundant, bright red, waxy, round, ~0.6 cm in diameter, ripening in autumn–early winter and can remain on the plant for some time after they have become ripe. The fruits are pleasant to eat and have a lemony taste. They can be eaten fresh or added to preserves, desserts, sauces, etc. Other uses as for general notes.

Berberis angulosa. A native of eastern Asia, from around the Himalayas. It forms a smaller, evergreen shrub, only growing to ~1 m tall. It is fairly cold hardy, and can grow in full sun or semi-shade. *Flowers:* Yellow, in clusters ~2 cm long, in late spring. Fruits ripen in late autumn and are ~1.2 cm in diameter, larger than most barberries; can be eaten fresh, and they are tasty and recommended.

Berberis asiatica, (syn. *B. chitria*, *B. glaucocarpa*). A native of eastern Asia, from around the Himalayas. It forms a tall, evergreen, semi-climbing shrub, growing to ~3.5 m tall. It can grow in sun, but also in quite dense shade. Cold hardy, but severe frost can damage plants, though they usually resprout from older wood. The fruits are ~0.8 cm long, and are produced in abundance during autumn. They are sub-acid, fairly juicy and have a good flavour, though are quite seedy. In India, they are popular when dried, and are used like other dried fruits. Infusions of the root are used to treat ulcers, urinal infections, eye problems, jaundice and fevers.

Berberis wilsoniae. A native of eastern Asia, from western China. It forms an ornamental, evergreen shrub, ~1 m tall. It flowers in early summer, and fruits ripen in late autumn. Plants are fairly cold hardy, though cannot tolerate extended freezing periods, and do prefer somewhat warmer climates. Grows in most soil types. The fruits are ~0.6 cm long and can be eaten fresh, but they are very acidic, like lemons, and are usually included in preserves, desserts, pies, chutney, etc. Uses, etc. as for general notes. ■

Betula lenta
Sweet birch
BETULACEAE

Similar species: Silver birch (*B. pendula*), paper birch (*B. papyrifera*), white birch (*B. alba* syn. *B. pubescens*), yellow birch (*B. alleghaniensis*)
Relatives: hazel

The name 'birch' is very ancient, and may be derived from the Sanskrit '*bhurga*', meaning 'a tree whose bark is used for writing upon'. The many species of birch trees are native to Europe, Asia and North America, and all are very hardy. The species *B. lenta* described here is the main species utilised for its sap and its wintergreen-like oils. Sweet birch is native to eastern North America, from Quebec down to Georgia, where it often occurs in mixed woodland. Its cultivation has increased in recent times, and it is being commercially grown in many northern regions, including Alaska, for its sap, which can be tapped in a similar way to that of maples.

DESCRIPTION

It forms a medium-sized tree, 15–20 m tall; mature individuals have trunks 0.75–1.0 m in diameter. Its bark is reddish-brown, almost black, dull and broken into large, irregular, but not papery, areas. It has a smell and taste of wintergreen. Young stems are shiny, brown, very aromatic, and are covered with attractive, wide, white lenticels (wide 'breathing' pores). The lenticels of birch (and other species, e.g. many *Prunus* spp.) are formed by a persistent cork-cambium layer (unlike most other tree species, which produce a succession of cork cambium layers), and this results in 'stretching' the lenticels wider around the tree trunk as it expands. The tree's buds are distinctively pointed. Birch trees are moderately long lived, probably up to ~200 years. They have a moderate growth rate.

Leaves: Ovate–oblong, 5–10 cm long, often in pairs, on short spur-like growths. They are finely serrated, with pointed tips and rounded or heart-shaped bases. They are dark green above, paler yellowish-green with finely pubescent veins beneath, and smell of wintergreen when crushed.

Flowers: Monoecious. Male catkins are usually borne in hanging clusters of 3–4 from the ends of branches. They are formed in summer, and produce pollen the following spring. Female catkins or 'cones' are small, erect, globular, yellow-green in colour and are covered in small leaf-like scales. These become receptive in spring. *Pollination:* Are wind-pollinated. Although bees and other insects often visit catkins to obtain pollen for food, they are not known to visit female flowers. Tend to need more than one tree to set seed.

Fruits: Seeds develop within the female cones and are wind-dispersed throughout autumn and winter. Seeds can germinate the following spring, or may become dormant for long periods. Trees produce copious numbers of seeds.

CULTIVATION

An easy tree to grow, needing minimum maintenance once established.

Location: Can grow in full sun or in fairly dense shade. This species is not very wind tolerant.

Temperature: They naturally grow in cold climates, and are extremely cold hardy.

Soil/water/nutrients: Trees prefer a moist, rich, well-drained soil, but can also grow in stony, rocky, poor soils, as well as soils that are sandy or contain some clay. They grow best in fairly acid to neutral soils and are not very tolerant of alkaline conditions. Can grow on disturbed sites, including abandoned mine spoils. They grow better with regular moisture during the growing season, but once established

uses

Tapping

The main product from this species is its sap, which is collected in spring, before the leaves have opened. The process is similar to that used for maples, but a smaller diameter 'pipe' is used for birch. The sap-collecting season is shorter for birch. In addition, the collection of too much sap, and too often, can reduce the life of the tree and make it susceptible to heart rots. A hole is made, just as the sap begins to rise. This can be tested by drilling a small hole to see if sap flows out. If it does, insert a tube just a short distance into the trunk and the sap should then flow for ~7–14 days before the leaves begin to open. The sap flows best on sunny days, after a frost. Once the leaves open, root pressure is reduced and, hence, so is the sap. In addition, towards the end, the sap becomes milky and bitter, so this needs to be checked and tapping should be stopped at this point. About 65 litres of sap can be obtained from a single, large tree, with this volume representing only 10–15% of the total sap production of the tree. It is best to only have one tap per tree to avoid over-stressing it. The sap can be reduced to a syrup by heating on a very low heat. Birch sap can very easily burn at higher temperatures. The use of a double boiler to reduce moisture content can often give more control. It takes ~100 litres of sap to produce ~1 litre of syrup.

Food

The sap of various species of birch is fairly sweet, but not as sweet as maple; it often has a slight wintergreen flavour. The fresh sap can be used to make beer, wine, spirits and vinegar, with ingredients such as honey, cloves or lemon peel added for extra flavour. It is then fermented with yeast to make a pleasant-tasting birch wine, or, for beer, the sap is placed in a jug with a small quantity of a sweetener added to promote fermentation. Birch syrup is used as a sweetener, on desserts, pancakes, in breads, candies, marinades, salad dressing, on popcorn and to coat nuts. The inner bark can be cooked or dried, ground into a powder and added to soups, flour, etc. It has a sweet and spicy flavour.

Nutrition

Its sugar is mainly fructose, compared to being mainly sucrose in maple syrup. Birch sap contains many acids

(e.g. malic, phosphoric, succinic, citric) and minerals (e.g. potassium, calcium, manganese). It also contains thiamine. The leaves contain many compounds including betuloresinic acid, an essential oil, ether, betuloside, methyl salicylate and ascorbic acid.

Medicinal

In Russia, the sap is valued as a medicine and tonic, and is bottled and sold commercially. It is said to cure most skin problems, such as acne, etc. It is effective in treating rheumatic diseases, gout and bladder obstructions. The outer bark contains methyl salicylate (an aspirin-like compound), ~16% tannin and 10–15% betulin (betula camphor). The twigs and bark are cut and distilled for the production of birch oil. This is thick, bituminous, pungently balsamic and smells almost identical to wintergreen oil. It is used as a flavouring in pharmaceuticals. In the past, many American tribes used bark extracts to stop diarrhoea, as a cold remedy, to relieve gastrointestinal problems, reduce fever and as a stimulant. Many of these benefits may be traced to its high concentration of methyl salicylate, known to be an analgesic. The sap and a tea, made from the leaves, have been used to treat rheumatism, headaches and as a diuretic to dissolve kidney stones, as well as a mouthwash. **Warning:** Some people may be allergic to the pollen from birch trees.

Other uses

Excellent wood, used in the manufacture of furniture, plywood, cotton spools. The bark of many species naturally peels off in sheets and has been used as a paper or parchment. The twigs make great toothbrushes, and are often used to stimulate blood flow and for their aroma in Russian saunas. A brown dye can be obtained from the bark, and the tar can be used to treat leather. The oil can be dissolved in turpentine.

Ornamental

Trees can be used to stabilise soil and are useful in stony soils and as a reclamation plant. They are beautiful, graceful trees that are not imposing or dominant. They are often planted in groups. Many species have good autumn colour.

are fairly drought tolerant. Do not survive waterlogging very well. Are not nutrient hungry and need little or no additional fertiliser, although a little around young trees can help their establishment in poorer soils.

Planting: Space plants at ~4 m apart. They are usually planted in autumn or early spring.

Pruning: Need very little if any pruning, just to improve their shape or remove any diseased or damaged branches. Older birch trees do not respond well to pruning, so any pruning done should be carried out while trees are young. Pruning, even of young trees, should not be done in early spring because the tree will 'bleed' lots of sap; any pruning is best done in summer, when the sap has finished rising.

Propagation: *Seeds:* These can be sown in autumn or spring in light, sandy soil and placed in a frame. *Grafting:* Varieties that don't come true from seed can be grafted onto rootstocks of a similar species.

SIMILAR SPECIES

Paper birch, *Betula papyrifera*. A native of northern North America, up to Greenland. Paper birch trees have a thin bark that separates into sheets, almost like paper. Can grow 20–25 m high. It flowers in spring, and seeds ripen in autumn. The tree is extremely cold tolerant, but not very wind tolerant. Its bark is smooth, thin, chalky-to-creamy-white, peeling in horizontal papery strips, with brown horizontal lines of raised pores or lenticels. Has orange inner bark. *Leaves:* Dull green, oval–round and sharp-pointed. Has slender, dull red-brown younger stems that lack the wintergreen smell when cut. Terminal bud absent, lateral buds are gummy, chestnut brown in colour.

Uses: This species is also used for sap collection, and has food and medicinal uses similar to sweet birch, though the sap contains less sugar. However, recent research has found that the white, shedding bark may have anti-cancer and anti-HIV properties, as it is high in betulinic acid. It also contains methyl salicylate (see above). *Other uses:* The outer bark can be easily removed without damaging the tree, and can be used as a weather-proofing layer, and was widely used by the peoples of the far Northern Hemisphere. It is durable, tough and resinous. It is usually removed in late spring–early summer. It can also be used as a paper or parchment. An infusion of the leaves has been used as a hair shampoo, and is effective against dandruff. It has good quality, light, strong, hard, dense wood, but is not very durable. Often used for turnery, veneers, etc. *Ornamental:* It is a good pioneer species in colder areas, and readily re-vegetates open clearings. It has an extensive and tough root system, and is often planted to control soil erosion.

Silver birch, *Betula pendula*. An attractive, fast-growing, popular, ornamental, medium-sized tree, growing to 15–20 m tall, and mostly native to Britain. It flowers in spring, and seeds are produced in autumn. Can grow in many soil types, including sand and clay, preferring more acidic soils; it does not grow well in alkaline conditions. Is fairly wind tolerant. Its bark is silvery-white, and its crown is upright and lightly leaved. It is a fairly short-lived tree, and prefers to grow in full sun; it does not grow well in shade.

Uses: The inner bark and sap can be used as sweet birch (above). The sap has a good, sweet flavour. The young leaves can be eaten fresh in salads or lightly cooked as a vegetable. *Medicinal:* As for sweet birch. The bark acts as a diuretic and laxative. The oil from the bark is effective against various problems such as eczema and psoriasis. The inner bark is used to treat fevers. The leaves have similar properties to sweet birch, and are also an effective germicide. A tea made from the leaves has been used to treat gout, rheumatism and to dissolve kidney stones. *Other uses:* Similar to sweet birch. In addition, its outer bark can be easily removed without damaging the tree, and this can be used as a waterproofing agent for many surfaces, as well as being used as a paper or parchment. The tar obtained from the bark has fungicidal properties and can be used as an insect repellent. It also makes a good shoe polish. It produces a good quality wintergreen-type oil from the inner bark, which is used medicinally. A brown dye can be obtained from the inner bark, and a glue can be made from the sap. Has good quality, light, durable wood that is used for furniture, toys and carving. The young stems are flexible and are used to make thatching, baskets, etc. A high-quality charcoal obtained from the bark is used by artists. *Ornamental:* Attractive trees, often planted in small groups, with silver bark displayed throughout the year, and fine, light foliage. It is a good pioneer species.

White birch, *Betula alba* (syn. *B. pubescens*). A native of Britain and Europe, from Sicily to Iceland, and is also found in northern Asia. Coleridge speaks of it as the 'Lady of the Woods'. The tree has a lightness and grace, as well as elegance, and after rain it has a wintergreen aroma. It grows 15–20 m high. It flowers in spring, and the seeds ripen in autumn. It is able to grow in wetter soils and is fairly wind tolerant. Young branches are reddish-brown or orange-brown, whereas the trunks are usually white. The outer layer of bark can be separated into thin layers, which can be used as a substitute for oiled paper. It yields birch tar oil, popular for processing Russian leather, and also stopping fungal disease. The production of this birch tar oil is an important Russian industry. It is also distilled in Holland and Germany, but these oils are said not to be as good as the Russian oil. The oil can deter insect attacks and acts as an insect repellent when applied to the skin. It is also employed in photography. It makes a good tree for colonising new areas, and grows rapidly, but is fairly short lived. It is an excellent tree for attracting wildlife, and is associated with the life cycles of >200 insect species. Its inner bark and sap can be obtained and used as for sweet birch. Its leaves, bark and medicinal properties are similar to those of sweet birch.

Yellow birch, *Betula alleghaniensis*. A medium-sized, slow-growing tree, ~10 m tall, a native of northeastern North America. It flowers in late spring, and seeds ripen in late autumn. This tree is fully shade tolerant, and will also grow in clay soils. Its sap can be collected and used as for sweet birch, as can the inner bark. It also has a strong wintergreen-like aroma, particularly from its bark. It produces a good-quality wood that can be used for floors, furniture, boxes, etc. ■

Billardiera scandens
(*B. longiflora, B. cymosa*)
Apple-berry (dumplings, garrawang)
PITTOSPORACEAE

A small genus of about 25 species, native to most states of Australia. Its natural habitat is by mountain streams or scrub country in forests, by coasts and on tablelands. The fruits of these species have been long used by the Aborigines, who often baked them, or dried them for later use. *Billardiera scandens*, along with other species, including *B. cymosa* and *B. longiflora*, are attracting interest as potential 'bush-food' species. They are also very ornamental climbing plants, with pretty bright flowers and fruits, and, although they can grow as a vine, they are not invasive. They deserve to be more popularly grown as both an ornamental and for their edible fruits. The name 'scandens' means 'to climb'.

DESCRIPTION

A sprawling groundcover or climber, with wiry, red to brown-grey woody stems up to 2–3 m long. In open positions it tends to form a more shrubby plant, growing to ~1.5 m tall, and can be grown as a groundcover plant. Its shoot tips are very hairy, with a fine white fringe. In semi-shade it becomes a twining and/or scrambling plant, though is not too vigorous, and so does not smother out other plants in the way that many climbing species do.

Leaves: Evergreen, hairy, are narrowly oval, lance-shaped, mid green, smallish, ~5 cm long, ~0.5 cm wide. The leaves have a wavy, sometimes recurved margin. The underside of the leaf is pale green and silky. The leaves of *B. longiflora* are a shiny green, without hairs.

Flower: Pendulous, bell-shaped, ~2–2.5 cm long, develop on the end of stems or on short lateral branches. They frequently have a long flowering season. They are usually borne singly, or occasionally in small clusters of 2–3. Each flower has five creamy-yellow petals that may become tinged purple as the flower ages. The flowers of *B. cymosa* are white-pink-mauve, those of *B. longiflora* are a creamy-green colour. Flowers may persist on the plant as the first fruits develop. Peak blooming occurs in spring, though they may not flower until summer. Flowers are bisexual, with both male and female organs occurring in the same flower. Plants are self-fertile. *Pollination:* By butterflies, and are also popular with nectar-feeding birds. Bees and insects may also help with pollination.

Fruit: An oblong, cylindrical, fleshy green, sometimes purple, berry, 2.5 cm long, ~1 cm wide, which ripens through late summer into autumn. The skin is hairy, and the sweet astringent flesh has a kiwifruit-like flavour. Has many small, black, edible seeds within the central pulp. Those of *B. longiflora* turn a wonderful blue-purple colour, and do not ripen until late autumn–early winter. The fruits seem to vary in quality, with some reporting them as having dry, poor-tasting flesh, whereas others report the fruits to be aromatic and pleasant. The fruits of *B. cymosa* are smaller, only ~1.5 cm long, but are reported to have a tasty, aniseed-like flavour.

Harvest: Pick fruits when they are ripe and fully coloured. If they become over-ripe they lose their juiciness and tangy flavour. They also tend to fall when they are ripe and need to be gathered before the wildlife finds them.

Roots: As with many climbers, they prefer their roots to remain cool and in shade, and benefit from a deep organic mulch to retain moisture, add nutrients, protect them from frost damage in winter and to suppress weed growth. The vine forms mycorrhizal associations with fungus in the soil, which enable it to obtain additional nutrients, especially phosphates. The roots improve soil structure.

CULTIVATION

Plants are tolerant of a range of conditions.

Location: Can grow in semi-shade as a climber, or in full sun where it becomes more bushy and compact. Seems to grow best in semi-shade up a support, where its flowers and fruits can be fully appreciated. May be fairly wind tolerant (for a climber), though grows best in a sheltered spot.

Temperature: Plants are fairly cold hardy, tolerating temperatures down to ~–7°C, and can be grown in warm temperate regions, or in more cool temperate regions if given extra protection during extended cold periods. If damaged by frost, they often resprout from the base. They do flower and fruit better with warm summer temperatures.

Soils/water/nutrients: Grow best in moist, well-drained, humus-rich soil. However, they can grow in a range of soil types, including sandy loams, though not clay soils. They prefer a somewhat acid to neutral pH, and do not tolerate alkaline soils. They are not tolerant of waterlogging, though prefer regular moisture during their growing season. However, when established, they are quite drought tolerant, though do not grow or fruit as well. Plants benefit from light applications of blood and bone or a slow-release fertiliser. Only need minimum nutrient applications.

Pot culture: A good plant for pot culture or for hanging baskets. They can be sited in semi-shade, and grown in moist, rich compost. Their size can be easily managed. In colder areas they can be moved inside during colder weather.

Planting: Space plants at 0.5–0.8 cm apart.

Propagation: *Seed:* Are best sown when fresh, with the pulp removed. Sow in moist, warm compost, just below the soil surface. Seeds take 8–10 weeks to germinate. Sow stored seed in early spring, with warmth. Germination of fresh seed is usually good, but stored seed can take a year to germinate. Treatments, such as washing dried seeds in alcohol or briefly fermenting the seeds in warm water, may improve germination. Grow on seedlings in a protected area for at least their first winter. *Cuttings:* Semi-ripe cuttings can be taken, 10–12 cm long, with a heel, in summer. Insert these in a gritty–peaty, moist, warm soil to root. Should get a good percentage take. *Layering:* Stems tips or sections of young stems can be buried, and these should form roots.

Pruning: Can just be pruned to tidy up long straggly stems or remove any old or dead wood. This helps to rejuvenate the plant and initiate young growth. This is best done after the fruits have been harvested, in autumn, or left until early spring.

Pests and diseases: Do not have any specific pest or disease problems. Leaves can develop fungal problems in very humid regions. If humidity is commonly high, try to ensure good ventilation around and through the vine.

CULTIVARS

A subspecies, *B. longiflora fructo alba* has white fruits. ∎

Food

The fruits vary in quality and taste, with some being tangy, yet sweet when eaten fresh, whereas others are reported to be of poor quality. The fruits can be roasted and spiced and eaten like mushrooms, if picked when under-ripe. Ripe fruits have a pleasant sub-acid flavour that is said to be like dried apples/kiwifruits, often with aniseed over-tones. Experience will indicate the best time to harvest these fruits, and they are best enjoyed when not over-ripe. The fruits can also be dried for later use. **Warning:** The leaves of *B. longiflora* may contain saponins, which are toxic, although tend to pass through the body without being digested as well as being destroyed by heat.

Ornamental

Very ornamental, delicate climbing plants, with bright flowers and fruits; they look their best when trained up a trellis in semi-shade. Can also be grown as a shrub in borders in sunny locations. It can be even planted under *Eucalyptus* species, where many plants struggle to survive. The flowers attract nectar-eating birds and butterflies.

Broussonetia papyrifera
Paper mulberry
MORACEAE
Similar species: jackfruit, fig, che, mulberry

Paper mulberry is distantly related to mulberry. It is a native of northeastern Asia, and particularly China, and is found occasionally as a naturalised tree in southeastern Europe. The tree has been used for ~1500 years for its fibre and fruits. It is widely grown in areas of eastern China for the fibre within its bark. There are many named varieties of paper mulberry, which have been mostly selected for their fibre and ornamental qualities. In China, the trees are coppiced annually to remove the bark. In colder regions, the tree is only coppiced once every 2–3 years.

DESCRIPTION

An attractive, moderately fast-growing, small–medium-sized, spreading tree, height ~9–12 m, spread ~9–14 m. Branches become gnarled and twisted with age (if not coppiced). Bark: grey–brown, lightly furrowed on older trees; stems are reddish-brown, often covered with a pale fuzz and have a milky sap. They form a rounded, dense crown. The tree readily suckers and, left to itself, it naturally forms thickets.

Leaves: Attractive, alternate (sometimes opposite), rough, mid green, with white velvet beneath. Leaf shape is very variable, even on the same branch, but often five lobed or heart shaped, 7.5–16 cm long. The tree is deciduous.

Flowers: Dioecious. The male flower is a green–russet-coloured catkin; 4–7 cm long, borne in clusters, in mid spring. Female flowers are unusual and form small (~1.25-cm diameter), round, greeny-brown spiky balls, in mid spring. *Pollination:* By wind. Needs more than one tree to set fruit.

Fruit: Red, ~2 cm diameter, consisting of many small fruits that have become fused together, and each small fruit has been formed from an individual flower. This is similar to the raspberry fruit, but in raspberries, the drupes are derived from many embryos within a single flower, rather than from many flowers. The individual fruits each develop a succulent, juicy covering around the seed.

Yield/harvest: Can produce good crops of fruits. Fruits

are harvested in autumn and are picked when they have reached full colour and have become softer.

CULTIVATION

A tough, versatile tree that can grow in many environments. Easy to cultivate.

Location: Likes a warm, sunny location: they do not grow well in shade. Will tolerate some atmospheric pollution. They also tolerate heat and wind.

Temperature: Somewhat cold hardy, and can tolerate temperatures down to ~–10°C. It can be grown in tropical climates, but also in temperate zones.

Soil/water/nutrients: Grows best in deep, fertile soil, but will grow in a wide range of soil types, including sandy or gravelly soils. It is drought resistant once established. Can grow at a wide pH range, including fairly alkaline soils.

Propagation: *Seed:* Good results from seed. Seed can be sown fresh or in spring, and needs no pre-treatment. Takes 1–3 months at ~15°C to germinate. Self-sown seedlings are common around groups of trees, and these can be dug up and established in pots. *Cuttings:* Take half-ripe cuttings, with a heel, in summer, and insert in light sandy soil. There should be a good percentage take. Hardwood cuttings can be taken from the current season's growth in late autumn and over-wintered in a cool frame. Can also take root cuttings in winter. *Layering:* Is possible in spring. *Suckers:* Trees also freely produce suckers, and these can be easily dug up and established in pots.

Pruning: If trees are not grown for their fibre, but for their fruit, then only minimal pruning is needed. It is best done in late autumn or early spring, and only removal of diseased, crowded branches or damaged or straggly wood is necessary. Competing suckers may need removing, to avoid a thicket developing around the tree. ■

uses

Food

The fruits are reported to be sweet and tasty, though their quality may vary from tree to tree. They can be eaten fresh or added to desserts, conserves, etc. The leaves can be lightly cooked.

Medicinal

The leaves are used to induce sweating and for diarrhoea and as a poultice on skin disorders, bites, stings, etc. The sap is used as a mild laxative in Hawaii. The Chinese use the leaves and fruit as a tonic for the liver and kidneys. They are also thought to clear the vision and nourish the eyes and are used for weakness of joints and muscles. The fruit has been used as a diuretic, as a stimulant and for stomach problems. Parts of the tree are reported to have high antioxidant levels, and may also have antifungal and antibacterial properties. Extracts are also being researched for their de-pigmentation effects, i.e. for their use to remove freckles or moles, etc.

Other uses

The fibre from the bark is used to make fine-quality paper, cloth, rope and many other products. There is still an active industry in China that harvests and processes the fibre. The fibre can be made into cloth by beating strips of bark with a wooden mallet and the more it is beaten, the finer the cloth produced. To make the cloth wider, more than one strip of bark can be beaten together. The Polynesians use the inner bark to make tapa cloth. When used for making paper, the branches are harvested in autumn. These are then steamed, the fibres are stripped off and are then steeped in lye for ~2 hours. The inner and outer layers of fibre can be used separately or together to make different shades of paper. The fibre is also used to make fans, umbrellas and many other items. The wood is coarse grained, soft and easily worked, but is not very durable. It is used for cups, bowls, etc.

Ornamental

Attractive and hardy, the paper mulberry makes a good shade tree. Its tolerance to air pollution makes it a good choice for a town site.

Camellia sinensis (syn. *Thea sinensis*)
Tea
THEACEAE
Relatives: camellia, azalea

Tea is obviously not a fruit or a nut plant, but I have included it because it is easy to grow in many regions and because of its health-giving attributes. Tea is the second most commonly drunk liquid on Earth, after water. A member of the same genus as many popular ornamental species that have attractive, evergreen leaves and showy, colourful, spring flowers, the tea plant probably originates from the Asia–China region, and most likely first grew in hilly, forested regions. It has been used by the Chinese for at least 3000 years. It is now grown commercially in many semi-tropical and tropical regions of the world, and many varieties have evolved over the years, with the type of tea often named after the province it originated in or the colour of the liquid. For example, Chinese teas may be described as green, red, yellow or white. Green, oolong and black teas are all made from *Camellia sinensis*; it is the 'fermentation' process (meaning an oxidation process and not actual fermentation, as no micro-organisms are involved) that gives them their different colours and tastes. Green tea is made by wilting the leaves in hot air and then rapidly heating the leaves to stop the 'fermentation' or oxidation processes that occur. Oolong tea leaves are wilted, then bruised and allowed to partially 'ferment' until reddening of the leaf edges occurs. Black teas' leaves are produced by 'fermenting' them in cool, humid rooms until the entire leaf has darkened.

Tea was first introduced into Britain in 1664, and since then Britons have become some of the greatest tea drinkers in the world, at ~4.5 kg of tea leaves per person a year. The average annual per capita consumption in the world is 0.75 kg. Most tea (~90%) is grown in India and Asia, with Africa growing most of the remainder. In the USA, taxes on tea levied by British became increasingly unpopular to the early American settlers. They began buying cheaper 'illegal' tea smuggled in by the Dutch. The British were not keen on losing this tax revenue, and when envoys sent by King George III tried to force the colonists to only purchase tea through them, it ended in the infamous Boston Tea Party of 1773, which began the birth of the USA.

DESCRIPTION

Small, evergreen tree that can grow to 5–10 m, but is pruned back to form a 'bush' for commercial cultivation. It forms a rounded–oval shape, and is naturally multi-branched with no dominant central leader. Tea bushes are long lived, and can be harvested for 40–50 years, or sometimes longer. There are reports of bushes being >150 years old that are still flowering, though the shoots are not suitable for tea.

Leaves: Evergreen, oval, tapering to a point, alternate, ~5–20 cm long (sometimes longer), ~2–6 cm wide (sometimes wider), pubescent or hairless, often with wavy margins, can be serrated.

Flowers: Fragrant, white, sometimes pinkish or reddish, ~2–4 cm in diameter. Are borne singly from the leaf axils. Flowers have 5–7 sepals and petals, with many central stamens. Flowers are borne in autumn. Flowers are bisexual and not very self-fertile, and will only set a few seeds if grown individually: seed set is better when planted in groups. *Pollination:* Very attractive to bees, moths and insects.

Yield/harvest/preparation: Only the leaves of the tea bush are used to make tea. A well-tended tea bush should never produce flowers; this is seen as a sign of stress. Plants take 3–4 years to start producing enough leaves for cultivation. At 2–3 years of age, the bush is shaped – flattened on top – to form the initial 'plucking table'. Normally, 'two leaves and a bud', the small unopened leaf bud and the first two opened leaves, are hand-picked from each shoot. Care needs to be taken that stems are not damaged during picking. In Assam, yields range from 1200–2250 kg/ha, and clonal tea yields in Sri Lanka have attained 6700 kg/ha. Ten kilos of green shoots produces 2–2.5 kg of dried tea. Commercially, bushes are plucked every 7–14 days, during the summer, depending on shoot development. Leaves that are slower to develop make a better quality tea. The 'second flush' – tea made from the second plucking of the season – usually makes the best quality tea. For black tea, freshly picked leaves are spread thinly on trays and placed in the sun until wilted (~12 hours). They are then rolled into a ball, allowed to 'ferment' (oxidation, not true fermentation, no microbes are involved) in

a damp place for 3–6 hours, by which time the ball has turned a rich coppery or yellowish-brown colour, and has developed a fruity, pleasant aroma. If this stage is taken too far, toxic fungi can develop and the leaves become sour, poor tasting and need to be discarded. After fermentation, the ball is broken up and the leaves spread out on trays to dry until they are brittle. Tea is then stored in air-tight boxes or cans. For green tea, the leaves are steamed or heated to dry the natural sap and prevent fermentation. They are still soft and pliable after the initial treatment; the leaves are then rolled and dried further before being stored. Differences in taste of teas depend as much on the region they are grown in and the processing methods used, as the cultivar of the tea bush. Tea yields are greatest in tropical and subtropical regions, but finer teas can be grown in cooler regions from plants with slower growth.

Roots: Has a strong taproot and a surface mat of feeder roots that form mycorrhizal association with soil fungi, so helping them gain more nutrients, particularly phosphate. The surface roots are fine and are susceptible to drying out; they benefit from an organic mulch to conserve moisture and add nutrients. Avoid surface soil cultivation.

CULTIVATION

An easy-to-grow plant that flourishes in a range of climates.

Location: Can grow in full sun, though often prefers light shade, particularly when young. Bushes are best protected from cold winds. They are not very tolerant of salty maritime conditions.

Temperature: Prefers warmer climates, though can grow in wet tropical sites or on dry hillsides. Grows best at temperatures between 14–28°C. Plants are not very frost tolerant, though can withstand brief frosts if acclimatised, surviving temperatures down to ~–5°C without damage. Is more cold hardy than many other warm-temperate species, though young plants need extra protection. Could be grown in warm-temperate climates in a sunny, sheltered spot. Grows better with a little cold during winter, and likes a wet, warm summer. Some Chinese varieties are reported to be more cold tolerant.

Soil/water/nutrients: Like other familiar ornamental members of this genus, tea grows best on deep, well-drained, organic, somewhat acid soils, with a pH of 4.5–6.5. The addition of organic matter is beneficial. Tea plants generally prefer light–medium soils, though can tolerate heavier clay soils if given adequate drainage. Prefers regular moisture during the spring and summer; its surface roots are susceptible to drying out. Plants are moderately nutrient hungry, and grow best with fairly regular additions of a complete, balanced fertiliser, with some extra nitrogen when plants are younger. This should be added in an acid form as urea (not nitrate). Probably best not to add too much fertiliser though, particularly phosphate, as this can affect the beneficial mycorrhizal relationships within the roots.

Planting: Young plants are best planted in semi-shade or with some protection for the first year or so. Space plants at 1–1.4 m apart for a dense bushy stand, but at ~2–3 m apart for specimens.

Pruning: Commercially, the aim is to keep the bush at a height that permits easy plucking: ~1 m tall. In Assam, the bushes are allowed to grow for 3 years before being topped at ~0.5 m height, and are then encouraged to form a bushy shape from this height. Picking the young shoots encourages lots of lateral branches and a very bushy form, which naturally controls the height and growth of the plant, though the 'plucking table' does rise slightly with every plucking round. Every few years (~36 months), the bush must be aggressively pruned back to maintain a convenient plucking table and to ensure the most tender shoots are made into tea.

Propagation: *Seed:* This is best sown when ripe, with warmth and moisture. Stored seeds need to be pre-soaked for ~24 hours in warm water, as well as the hard seedcoat being scarified with a file or similar. Germination can be quite slow: 1–3 months at 23°C. Grow on seedlings for 1–2 years before planting out. *Cuttings:* Take semi-ripe cuttings, with a

uses

Green tea is made from leaves that are steamed and dried, whereas black tea leaves are withered, rolled, fermented and dried. Steam distillation of black tea yields an essential oil (theol), which is used to flavour alcoholic beverages, perfume, frozen desserts, baked goods, puddings, etc. Dried fruits can be soaked in tea before use, and it can also be added to various dishes as a flavouring. The oil within the leaves is of good quality, and could be used instead of rapeseed or olive oils. It is non-drying and undergoes little oxidation.

Nutrition
The leaves contain carotene, riboflavin, nicotinic acid, pantothenic acid and some vitamin C (though this is destroyed in hot tea). High polyphenol/tannin content: catechins (theaflavin formed from catechins) and quercetin. The catechins (and theaflavins) are very potent therapeutic compounds that have antiseptic properties and can readily form complexes with reactive oxidative molecules, thereby rendering them harmless. Catechins make up ~12% of dried green-tea leaves, and ~90% of the active ingredients. There are several catechins present, of which the most powerful is epigallocatechin gallate (EGCG), which is 25–100 times more powerful than vitamins C and E as an antioxidant. A cup of green tea can provide more antioxidant activity than a serving of broccoli or strawberries. Tannin gives tea its characteristic colour and aroma. Tea also contains a caffeine-like compound, theine (2–5%). Green tea contains more antioxidants, vitamins and minerals than other teas.

Medicinal
Tea, as a drink, has recently been rediscovered medicinally. The Chinese consider it to be one of the 50 fundamental herbs, and have long used it as a cure for cancer, as a blood cleanser, a diuretic, to relieve phlegm, as a stimulant, for digestive problems and to treat certain heart diseases. Tea has antibacterial, antiseptic and detoxifying properties. It has been used to protect teeth from decay possibly because it contains high levels of fluorine. In addition, toothpaste made from tea has been shown to decrease plaque, and to prevent bacteria from adhering to teeth as well as reducing bacterial exudates. Tea is said to give a feeling of comfort and exhilaration. It is being studied for its ability to possibly prevent, and even reduce, some cancers (e.g. leukaemia, prostate, breast, urinary, stomach), due to its catechin content. Recent research in Arizona has shown that drinking a lot of tea can reduce the risk of skin cancer by 40%. It is also said to improve the immune system. As little as 3–4 cups of tea a day can lead to significant proven benefits. Externally, tea, as a poultice, can be used to treat cuts, burns, bruises, insect bites, etc. It has also been used as a nerve sedative and to relieve tension headaches. Teabags can be laid on tired eyes, placed on foreheads for headaches or used to soothe sunburn. Green tea is said to have more pronounced effects in the search for the above medicinal benefits. In addition, the catechins in tea may reduce cholesterol and triglycerides levels and tea may promote weight loss by initiating an increase in the use of calories, by promoting greater heat loss. A possible theory for this is that green tea increases levels of norepinephrine, a form of adrenaline, and so prepares the body to burn fat for the 'fight or flight' response. Raised norepinephrine may also be linked to the relief of allergies and asthma. All from drinking a cup of tea! **Warning:** Tea has high levels of tannin (15%); in high doses, taken regularly, it has been associated with oesophageal cancer, though tea has also been shown to reduce the size of oral pre-cancerous lesions. Excessive use may lead to dizziness, constipation, indigestion, palpitations and insomnia. Tea, in large quantities, may reduce the body's ability to absorb iron.

Other uses
A grey dye can be obtained from the pink petals. The wood is moderately hard, dense and close grained, though is of small dimensions. *Ornamental:* Makes a good herbaceous, ornamental plant with attractive evergreen leaves, and it is fun to just go outside to pluck your own tea!

heel, during summer and insert, at an angle, in gritty, acidic, moist compost in semi-shade. They take fairly well, but are slow. Hardwood cuttings from the present season's growth can be taken in early winter and inserted in a cold frame. Leaf-bud cuttings can also be taken in summer.

Pests and diseases: Numerous fungi can attack the tea plants.

CULTIVARS
Camellia sinensis is divided into two main subspecies: *assamica*, which is tall, tree-like, with large leaves, and is found in China and Assam; or *sinensis*, which is smaller and more bushy with smaller leaves, and is found in the east and southeast of China. Most Japanese green tea is derived from *sinensis*. There are also many named varieties. ■

Carica x *heilbornii* var. *pentagona*
Babaco (tree papaya)
CARICACEAE
Similar species: Toronchi (*Carica crysopetela*)
Relatives: papaya, chamburro, pawpaw

Babaco is not known in the wild and it may be a hybrid between two 'mountain' or 'highland' papaya species, *Carica pubescens* and *C. stipulata*. It is found growing in Ecuador at higher elevations, and has been cultivated in Ecuador since before the arrival of Europeans. In more recent times, it has been introduced into other parts of the world, such as Israel, the Middle East and New Zealand, and is grown to a small extent as a new crop. It produces seedless fruits that have a good, sweet–sub-acid taste. Because there are only female plants, babaco cannot be improved using conventional breeding techniques, but it also does not need pollination. Can grow and fruit well in warmer temperate or subtropical regions.

DESCRIPTION
Ornamental, small, herbaceous tree/shrub, erect, with a soft trunk lined with old leaf scars. It rarely branches, but shoots often appear around the base. The thickness of the trunk is proportional to the vigour of the plant. It can grow to ~3–4 m tall, and gives a tropical effect. Precocious in cultivation, and can be coppiced to regrow. The tree is eye-catching when packed with the large green and yellow fruits.

Leaves: Semi-evergreen, they are moderately large, attractive, palmate, with prominent ribs and veins on long hollow leaf stalks that radiate out in a spiral arrangement from a single stem. Average life of a leaf is 4–6 months. During the cold winter months, the leaves degenerate and are gradually shed. The stems exude a white latex when injured.

Flowers: Waxy, inconspicuous, five-petalled, fleshy, covered with fine hairs, are greeny-yellow in colour and are fragrant at night. They are usually solitary and are borne in leaf axils from the main stem from late spring into summer. Are borne on the newly developing trunk, with thicker trunks often producing more flowers. *Pollination:* Flowers are all female. Fruits set parthenocarpically, and so there are no seeds present in the fruits and no need for a pollinator.

Fruit: Classified as a berry. Usually seedless, or with only a few seeds at most. Is often extremely productive, producing large fruits that can weigh ~2 kg each. They are green, torpedo-shaped and hang in clusters around the trunk. They exude a white latex when under-ripe. Multi-stemmed plants bear smaller fruit. Young fruits set and grow immediately after flowering, reaching a maximum size during autumn. 'Smaller' fruits are about the size of tropical papaya (~6–12 cm long), but babacos can be ~30 cm long, by ~20 cm wide. They are distinctly five-sided, rounded at the stem end and pointed at the apex. Take ~2 months to ripen.

Yield/harvest: Trees can have enormous yields, better than those of a good papaya plantation (have exceeded 100 ton/ha), and often within 1–2 years of planting. Fruits are harvested when they lose their green tinge and become yellow all over. Fruits ripen progressively from the lower stem upwards, with lower, first fruits often being the largest. Fruit picked at first signs of yellowing will ripen fully off the plant, though not if they are picked when too green. Ripe fruits can damage easily and need careful handling. Pick before they become soft and over-ripe. Fruits can be stored for ~3–5 weeks at ~6°C, though damaged fruits will deteriorate more rapidly. However, even damaged, bruised areas of tissue do not usually affect nearby healthy tissue, as often happens with many other fruits.

CULTIVATION
Location: Can grow in coastal areas, but not if they are too exposed to wind. Will grow and fruit in shady locations, but prefers a sunny spot.

Temperature: Thrives in either cool, humid, subtropical or warm temperate climates, with little or no frost. It is much more tolerant of cool, damp winters than the papaya. Will withstand temperatures down to ~–2°C, although it may lose most of its leaves. However, it is more susceptible to root rot. Because of their form and non-invasive roots they are a good candidate to grow near buildings so that they get additional frost protection.

Soil/water/nutrients: Will grow on many types of soil, including clay, but prefers a light, fertile, well-drained soil with a pH of 6–6.5. They benefit from additional organic matter in the soil. Adequate moisture is needed during the growing season, but they are relatively drought tolerant. Do not grow well with too much moisture during the cooler months. During the growing season, babaco grows well with an application or two of fertiliser with additional phosphates or, even better, rotted down chicken manure placed around the tree. As with many crops, too much nitrogen can result in excess foliage growth at the expense of fruit production, and also softer fruit.

Pot culture: Is ideally suited to container culture and also the compactness and productivity of babaco plants makes them great for greenhouse production. They can be taken inside or given extra protection in cooler areas. Make an attractive, tropical, easy-to-control plant for a patio, deck or conservatory.

Propagation: *Seed:* No viable seed produced. *Cuttings:* Important to choose disease-free plants. Cuttings are taken by removing an entire stem at ~30 cm from the ground and cutting the stem into ~30-cm-long sections. Use clean, angular cuts to reduce the entry of disease. This is best done soon after fruiting. Cuttings can be dipped in a fungicide and a rooting hormone. The cut end should then be allowed to dry out for a few days before being inserted vertically in a low-moisture medium, such as sand or sandy loam, to form calluses.When rooted, and top growth has commenced, they can be inserted into their final position. Plants from

cuttings can begin producing fruits in ~18 months. They root better if not soaked in water before planting.

Pruning: Although trees can become multi-stemmed, the size and quality of fruits is better if only one or two stems are allowed to grow at any time, with other stems being removed at the base. However, once these have fruited, a second or third shoot can be allowed to develop in the following spring. Each stem is often only allowed to fruit for a year or two before being removed to allow younger stems to develop in their place. Stems should be cut back on an angle to reduce the risk of water entering the cut and initiating fungal disease. This type of pruning/coppicing also produces wood for propagation.

Pests and diseases: During moist, cold spells fungal diseases readily affect the leaves and roots.

CULTIVARS

There are no recognised babaco cultivars at this time. Hybrids with *Carica pubescens* produce edible fruit, but they are not as good as those of babaco.

SIMILAR SPECIES

Toronchi, *Carica crysopetela*. A natural hybrid that originates from the villages of southern Ecuador.

Description: A vigorous plant that can grow to 5 m, although most selected types are smaller, reaching only 2.5 m. Fast growing, these plants bear within 12 months. *Pollination:* Although the plant functions as a sterile hybrid, pollination seems to increase production, and the fruits often contain viable seeds. *Fruit:* There is much variation, but all specimens produce attractive, good quality, aromatic fruits. Mature fruits are five-sided, ~10–15 cm long, green to lemon-yellow in colour, and weigh up to 0.5 kg. The flesh is juicy with a soft, creamy-white pulp. Smooth skinned, it can be eaten without peeling, and has a medium papain content. Picked ripe, the fresh, raw fruits are superior in flavour to most other highland papayas. However, they need to be handled more carefully than babaco, even when moderately ripe.

Cultivation: It is only slightly frost-resistant, tolerating temperatures down to ~1°C. Prefers warmer climates.

Uses: Has fairly good levels of vitamin C: 21–32 mg/100 g of flesh. The very refreshing fruits are lemony, fragrant, sub-acid, very soft, juicy and sweet, but only become sweeter after mid summer with sufficient heat. The fruits are usually eaten fresh, are delicious and are made into a tasty, healthy juice. They are also used in preserves, sauces, jams, pie fillings and pickles, as well being added to cheesecakes, icecream and yoghurts. ■

uses

Food
The fruits are aromatic, sub-acid, refreshing, melon-like, with juicy cream-to-white flesh, and are described as having overtones of strawberry, pineapple and papaya. Fruits are best eaten fresh when fully ripe. Being seedless, the whole fruit can be eaten, including the smooth, thin skin. A little sugar can enhance its flavour. Pieces of the fruit can also be added to fruit salads. Babaco fruits make a quick and interesting drink when processed in a blender with a little honey or added sugar; or, with the addition of icecream or frozen yoghurt, it becomes a tasty milkshake. The fruits also make an excellent preserve, and can be added, with other fruits, to pies. They can also be added to soups and stews, to which it gives a rich, fruity flavour. Prepared fruit keeps well and does not turn brown (oxidise) over time. Contains papain, a protein-dissolving enzyme, so can be used for tenderising in the same way as papaya.

Ornamental
Plants look good in many planting schemes; with their broad green leaves and yellow fruit, they add an exotic touch.

Carica papaya
Papaya (tropical papaya, pawpaw, mamao, tree melon)
(not to be confused with *Asimina triloba* or mountain pawpaw)
CARICACEAE
Relatives: babaco

The papaya is probably native to southern Mexico and Central America. It was spread south by the native populations, and throughout the Caribbean by the Spanish. The Spanish also carried it to Europe and various Pacific islands. It is now often cultivated as a garden tree, for its attractive leaves, its manageable size, as well as its fruits, in most tropical and subtropical countries. If the climate is right, it grows rapidly and performs well. It is adapted to a wide range of soils and climates and can produce large, delicious fruit from its first year.

DESCRIPTION

Papayas grow into small (3–5 m tall), non-spreading trees, with an exotic form and can be very productive. They usually have a single, straight unbranched stem (~8–30 cm in diameter), and only usually branch when injured. The trunk has a hollow centre, and is often green or dark mauve in colour with prominent leaf scars towards the top of the stem. The trees are fast growing, but short lived (~4–6 years).

Leaves: Attractive, exotic, evergreen: they live for 4–6 months and are lost and replenished throughout the year. They are spirally arranged around the trunk, and have long leaf stalks (0.3–1 m) with attractive, deeply lobed (5–9 segments), large (30–60 cm diameter), waxy, smooth, yellowy-green leaves, with prominent yellowish ribs and veins. Both the stem and leaves exude a white latex if wounded.

Flowers: Waxy, five-petalled, fleshy, creamy-white and slightly fragrant. They are borne from leaf axils, but the leaf may no longer be there, so they look as though they have formed directly on the trunk. They are borne for most of the year in warmer climates, but usually only in late spring–early summer in cooler regions. Trees have three sexual variations of flower formation. (1) Trees are usually dioecious. Female flowers are larger, have no stamens, are short-stalked and usually do not set fruit if grown on their own. However, a few do set parthenocarpic fruits and, therefore, lack seeds. Male flowers are smaller, thinner, contain stamens, a small vestigial ovary and are borne on long (~1.5 m long) drooping panicles, and do not set fruit. There are also two types of monoecious trees. (2) Some monoecious trees produce just bisexual flowers (each flower is both male and female), and these are borne on short stalks. Bisexual flowers are intermediate in size, have stamens with pollen and a plump ovary. These flowers are usually self-fertile. (3) Other monoecious trees are only partly bisexual. At certain times the tree produces short-stalked male flowers, at other times it produces bisexual flowers. Sex changes are brought about by high temperatures in mid summer, with heat suppressing the formation of the ovary and so just male flowers are produced and, therefore, no fruit are set. In addition, these trees can even change completely to just producing female flowers if their top shoots and leaves are removed.

The ratios of seedlings produced as determined by parental type is the following:

male x female = 1 male + 1 female
female x bisexual = 1 female + 1 bisexual
bisexual x bisexual = 1 female + 2 bisexual
bisexual x male = 1 female + 1 male + 1 bisexual.

Therefore, a bisexual and female cross gives the best combination to produce fruiting trees. In addition, certain cultivars tend to form certain types of flowers. Therefore, it is best to err on the safe side and establish at least 3–4 trees close together to ensure fruit-set. *Pollination:* By wind or insects, though hand pollination can greatly assist fruit-set.

Fruit: Fruits are formed singly or in small groups from leaf axils on the main stem (but are not truly cauliflorous), on the current season's growth. Fruits come in two main types: Hawaiian and Mexican. Hawaiian cultivars are the main commercial type, and form smaller trees (<2 m). Fruits are pear-shaped, have a thick, waxy skin that turns yellow when ripe, and weigh ~0.5 kg. The flesh is a rich orange–pink colour, is melting, sweet, luscious and very tasty. It has many, hundreds of small, black, rounded seeds in a central cavity. The seeds are edible and have a peppery taste like watercress or nasturtium seeds. Mexican papayas are taller (~3 m) and their fruits are larger (~40 cm long and ~4–5 kg each). The flesh can be yellow–orange–pink. They are not quite as flavourful as Hawaiian papayas, but are slightly easier to grow.

Yield/harvest/storage: Fruits take ~60–120 days (depending on climate) to mature after fruit-set. They need a long, warm summer to fully ripen. A healthy tree can produce ~30 kg of fruit a season. Fruits can ripen year-round if the climate is warm enough; in cooler regions fruits usually ripen in late autumn–early winter. Trees can begin producing fruit when less than a year old, but in colder regions, fruit may not form till the second or third year. Unfortunately, trees only fruit for 3–4 years before yields start to decline, though can produce a few fruits for a few years longer. Fruits are picked when they have lost most of their green colouring. They ripen fairly well at room temperature if picked when not quite ripe, and are at their best when they have gone slightly soft. Store fruits stalk downwards to extend their life. Very unripe fruits do not ripen well once picked. Do not store fruits in a fridge, as temperatures <10°C cause flesh damage; they are best just kept in a cool place. They do not store well (3–7 days) before they become over-ripe and succumb to fungal disorders.

Roots: Fairly shallow, and benefit from an organic mulch to help retain moisture and suppress weed growth. Avoid mechanical cultivation. Their roots are non-invasive and they can be planted near to buildings. They also have a taproot that can be easily damaged when planting out.

CULTIVATION
If plants are given a warm climate, a long summer and adequate moisture, they should produce many delicious fruits. In tropical areas they can be grown as an annual.

Location: Grow best in full sun and, ideally, are best grown against a sunny wall. Although they can grow in shade, fruits do not develop their full sweetness. They are not wind tolerant and the leaves are easily damaged. They are not tolerant of salty maritime conditions.

Temperature: They do need warmth throughout the year and are more cold sensitive than the mountain pawpaw: in cool weather, growth is reduced, flowers can drop and fruit

Below: *Carica papaya.*

<table><tr><td>

u s e s

</td><td>

Food
Sweet, rich, musky, delicious when fresh: just cut in half, remove the seeds and scoop out the flesh, perhaps with a squeeze of fresh lime juice. Yellow-fleshed fruits often have an almost turpentine-like background taste. Red or salmon-flesh coloured fruits are usually sweeter and much better flavoured. You often do not know the flesh colour until the fruit is cut open but, in general, bisexual plants give the best quality fruits. The fruit can be added to many desserts, icecream or savoury dishes. It can be processed into chutney or conserves. Unripe fruits can be eaten, but should be cooked before use because of their latex content; they can then be used as a vegetable and added to soups. The seeds are edible and have a watercress-like, spicy flavour. To tenderise meat, green papaya can be rubbed into it, cooked with it or crushed leaves can be wrapped around it.

Nutrition
Has very good levels of vitamin C (~60 mg/100 g of flesh). Also, good levels of vitamins A (~1750 IU), with some as lutein and zeaxanthin, which help reduce the incidence of cataracts and macular degeneration. They also contain some folate, and the minerals calcium, phosphate, have high levels of magnesium, and have more iron than most fruits or nuts, or even meat, as well as having high levels of copper, and as much potassium as bananas. They are very low in sodium, fat and calories. Papaya latex contains four proteolytic enzymes (papain, chymopapain A and B, and papaya peptidase A), which are extensively used to tenderise meat and clarify beer. They also contain good levels of fibre.

Medicinal
The proteolytic enzyme, papain, is chemically similar to pepsin, can be taken instead of anti-acid digestive tablets, and seems to reduce stomach acid secretions. Papain

</td><td>

retains its proteolytic activity over a wide pH range, unlike other proteases, and is used during surgical procedures to dissolve ruptured spinal discs; it is called 'nature's scalpel' because it preferentially degrades dead tissue. The inner bark has been used to relieve toothache. The latex and seeds are used in Central America to kill *Entamoeba histolytica*, which causes dysentery and liver abscesses. It is also used to treat ulcers, swelling, fever and to expel wind. Fresh latex can be smeared on boils, warts or freckles to remove them. Research has shown that extracts of ripe and unripe papaya fruits and seeds have an active ingredient against Gram-+ bacteria, and are also probably fungicidal. The bruised leaves, as a poultice, can be applied to rheumatic areas. **Warning:** The milky latex from the stems and unripe fruit may cause dermatitis. The unripe fruit may induce abortion. Some individuals are allergic to papain. Young leaves can be eaten like spinach, but they must be cooked to destroy the alkaloids (carpaine and pseudocarpaine) which, otherwise, act on the heart and respiration like digitalis. The seeds have been shown to affect sperm fertility in rats.

Other uses
The green fruits are commercially tapped by making incisions on the fruit and catching the latex in a container hanging beneath for 3–4 days. The latex is then dried, ground up and sold worldwide: ~1000 fruits produce 0.5 kg of papain. Because of the fruit's proteolytic enzymes, the fruit pulp is used in facial creams, salves and shampoos. They are also used in photography, to make leather, process wool and to make rayon. Papaya leaves have been used instead of soap to wash delicate fabrics. The seeds are said to inhibit the reproduction of marsupials, and, therefore, could be a deterrent in New Zealand where introduced possums have become a problem.

</td></tr></table>

quality is poor. They are very frost sensitive and are badly damaged at –2°C, although Mexican cultivars are somewhat more cold hardy than Hawaiian. Cold, wet soil is likely to kill them. Consider giving young plants extra protection to speed up their establishment.

Soils/water/nutrients: Papayas grow best in a light, well-drained, fertile loam. They prefer a pH range of 5.5–6.5, and do not grow well if the pH is far out of this range. They cannot tolerate waterlogged soils, and can be rapidly killed. However, they do need regular moisture in hot weather, but not in winter, when the soil should be kept drier. They benefit from regular applications of a balanced all-purpose fertiliser or well-rotted manure. Although they grow best with a good nutrient supply, too much nitrogen can lead to excessive vegetative growth. Phosphorus deficiency causes dark green leaves with a reddish-purple discoloration of leaf veins and stalks.

Pot culture: In cooler regions, consider growing these plants in containers, which can be moved inside in cold weather, or in a conservatory. They take up little room, have attractive, exotic-looking leaves and, if planted in a group, given warmth and regular moisture, they should do well. Apparently, *Carica papaya* have fruited in the Soviet Union when grown in a conservatory.

Planting: Space plants at ~2 m apart. Take care when planting as their taproot can be easily damaged. If the soil is likely to have drainage problems, plant them on a mound or in a container. A plastic mulch during winter can help keep the soil warmer and dry, but needs to be removed in spring. Plant at least three or four plants to improve pollination and fruit-set. Trees are often replaced after 4–6 years.

Pruning: Papayas do not need pruning. However, seedlings and established plants can be cut back to encourage the growth of several stems, though these can be weaker and are easily broken.

Propagation: *Seed:* This is the main method of propagation and, unlike many species, papaya seeds can retain viability for up to 3 years. Because they are warm-climate plants, the time of year when the seed is sown affects when they flower and fruit, and this can be important in cooler regions. It is best to sow seeds as early as possible, and to give the seedlings extra warmth and protection if necessary. Germination takes 12–28 days, and needs temperatures >22°C. The seeds should be washed, then soaked in warm water for ~3–4 hours to remove tannic acid, which inhibits germination, before sowing in well-drained compost. Germination rates are very good. Seedlings can then be grown on in tall, biodegradable pots before planting out. Do not over-water seedlings as they easily succumb to damping off. It can help to know the parentage of the seeds to enable prediction of the sex ratio of seedlings. (See Flowers notes.) *Cuttings:* These should be taken in summer and allowed to harden off for a few days before inserting in compost: they should root within a few weeks. These often grow well and produce fruits the following year.

Pests and diseases: Trees can be attacked by mildew, *Anthracnose*, root rot and various viral diseases. Wet, cold conditions will greatly increase the risk of many of these problems. The occurrence of papaya ringspot virus can be particularly devastating. Thrips, white flies, red spider mites and fruit spotting bugs are also potential problems in some areas. Nematodes can attack the roots. Papayas are best not planted repeatedly in the same soil to decrease the risk of *Pythium* and *Phytophthora* infections.

CULTIVARS

'Solo': Popular cultivar. Only produces bisexual and female plants. Has shallowly furrowed, pear-shaped, yellow fruits, 0.5–1 kg each. Their flesh is firm, reddish-orange, very sweet, excellent quality. At least two-thirds of seedlings will produce fruiting trees. It is resistant to papaya ringspot virus.

'Higgins': Fruit are of high quality, pear-shaped, with orange-yellow skin, deep yellow flesh, weight ~0.5 kg, if kept well watered, but are smaller in dry soils.

'Hybrid No. 5': Fruit: smooth, yellow, rounded–oval, ~1.3 kg. Flesh: excellent flavour, popular commercial variety. Has good yields.

'Mexican Red': Fruit: medium–very large: can be ~40 cm long. Has pinky-red flesh. More hardy than many other cultivars. Very productive, and starts flowering when only 0.6 m high. It is not as sweet as Hawaiian types though.

'Waimanolo Solo', 'Waimanolo': Fruit: yellow, roundish, ~0.5–1 kg, glossy, cavity is star-shaped. Starts bearing very early, i.e. when only ~1 m tall. Flesh: orange-yellow, thick, sweet, keeps well. Fruits of female plants have a rough skin. ■

Carica pubescens (syn. *C. candamarcencis*)
Mountain pawpaw (papaya, mountain papaya, chamburro)
(not to be confused with *Carica papaya*)
CARICACEAE
Similar species: Chamburro (*C. stipulata*), *C. goudotiana*, *C. parviflora*, *C. quercifolia*

The mountain pawpaw is native to South America and is cultivated from Panama to Bolivia, Chile and Argentina at elevations above 1000 m. It is commonly found growing around mountain villages and is sold in local markets. The trees, flowers and fruits are less affected by cool weather, wind and other environmental factors than those of the more tropical papaya (*Carica papaya*): it is adapted to the cold, cloud forests of the Andes. It is probable that this species was selected from the forests and grown in gardens as a decorative plant and for its fruit. The flesh of the fruit is similar to the tropical papaya, but is not as sweet and is usually cooked. There are several species of 'mountain pawpaw', but *C. pubescens* is the most widely grown in the USA and Australasia.

DESCRIPTION

The trees have a single or multiple straight, relatively unbranched trunks, with large, lobed leaves that are pubescent beneath. They form a small tree (2–4 m tall) that looks similar to papaya. It is distinguished from tropical papaya by the coating of hairs on the underside of its leaves. They are fairly slow growing, and produce leaves year round in warmer climates. They are fairly short lived (5–7 years).

Leaves: Evergreen, attractive, with a tropical look, large (20–25 cm long, 35–40 cm wide) and have deep lobes, one main lobe with 3–5 side lobes; they are variable in shape. There are fine hairs on the underside of the leaf. They have long petioles, 16–34 cm. The stems exude a white latex when injured.

Flowers: Waxy, inconspicuous, five-petalled, fleshy, covered with fine hairs, are greeny-yellow in colour and are fragrant at night. They are borne in leaf axils from the main stem, below the leaves. They exude a white latex when under-ripe. Most plants are dioecious, and have separate sexes on different plants; a few are monoecious and bisexual, and have both sexes within the same flower. They are borne for much of the year in warmer climates, but from early spring–late summer in cooler climates. Like the papaya, plants can change the sex of their flowers during the year, probably as a result of temperature change. The formation of male and female flowers is not affected by temperature changes whereas bisexual flowers, which can change from female to male to hermaphrodite, do so in response to seasonal temperatures. For sex information see *Carica papaya* on p. 101.

Fruit: Is formed on the current season's growth. Fruits are small compared with tropical papaya (8–20 cm length), are five sided and are yellow-orange when ripe. They are borne from leaf axils, directly off the main stem, from spring through to autumn in cooler areas, though can be year-round in warmer regions. The flesh is juicy, yellow and sharp in taste, even when fully ripe. They take 3–4 months to ripen in cooler regions, and then develop a lovely fruity aroma. It has many hundreds of small, black, rounded seeds within the central cavity, which are embedded in sweet, aromatic pulp, and this part is often eaten, though it is difficult to remove the seeds.

Yield/harvest: A healthy tree can produce 50–60 fruits in a season, but often less. Harvest fruits when they turn yellow and have slightly softened, between mid summer–late autumn. Plants can start to produce fruits after 10–12 months, or 1–2 years in cooler regions; they then fruit for about 5–7 years.

Roots: See notes for *Carica papaya* on p. 102.

CULTIVATION

Location: They are fairly wind hardy and can grow in full sun or semi-shade. They grow best in more humid climates.

Temperature: Plants grow best in warm temperate to semi-tropical climates, with a mean temperature range of 12–18°C year round. However, they are more frost tolerant than the tropical papaya, and can tolerate temperatures down to ~–3°C without serious injury once established. Young trees need extra protection. Although it may lose its leaves in winter, these will regrow as long as frost has not damaged the stem.

Soil/water/nutrients: It grows best in a deep, fertile,

Food

The flesh can be eaten fresh, though usually it is boiled or baked. It can then be added to desserts, pies, marmalade and icecream, or to savoury dishes, such as soups or stews, or stuffed with fruits or vegetables, or it can be preserved. The pulp around the seeds is sweeter than the outer flesh, which generally needs to be stewed before eating. Its flesh remains firm when cooked. It is pleasantly flavoured, but is not as sweet or tasty as tropical papaya. It can also be rubbed onto meat as a tenderiser. The numerous seeds can be eaten, with the pulp, and have a hot peppery taste. See the Warning for *C. papaya*.

Nutrition

Has good levels of vitamin A, including lutein and zeaxanthin, which can help reduce the incidence of cataracts and macular degeneration. They also contain some folate, and the minerals calcium, phosphate, magnesium and iron. It also contains proteolytic enzymes (e.g. papain), which give it its tenderising properties. Fruits also contain good levels of fibre and some vitamin C.

Medicinal

The fruit is used to treat arterial sclerosis in South America. It is also used in liver disease. The latex from the stems and fruits is used to treat warts and veruccae.

Ornamental

Is a good, ornamental small tree in a subtropical border with its exotic leaves and yellow, aromatic, edible fruits. Can be grown in cooler regions than the papaya.

well-drained soil, but can grow in poorer soils as long as they are not waterlogged. Once established, it is fairly drought tolerant, although prefers a moist soil. Grows best with fairly regular additions of nutrients, e.g. well-rotted manure or compost, particularly in spring and summer.

Pot culture: See notes for *Carica papaya* on p. 103.

Planting: Space plants at ~3 m apart. A plastic mulch during winter can help keep the soil warm and dry, but needs to be removed in spring. Plant at least three or four plants to ensure good pollination. Plants are often replaced after 4–6 years.

Pruning: They do not need pruning except to allow a low side shoot to grow out as the new main shoot. Last season's main stem is removed after it has fruited: this rejuvenates the plant and prevents it from becoming too tall.

Propagation: *Seed:* Trees are often grown from seed, and there are no widely recognised selections. Wash seeds from the pulp, and soak for ~3–4 hours in warm water to remove the germination inhibitor on the outside of the seed. Sow seeds in well-drained compost and they should germinate in ~30 days, with ~60% germination rate. The seedlings can be pricked out and grown on in tall, biodegradable pots, to encourage the growth of the taproot, before planting out. *Cuttings:* See notes for *Carica papaya* on page 103.

Pests and diseases: It has fewer problems than tropical papaya, and is fairly tolerant of nematodes and is perhaps resistant to papaya ring-spot virus, the most devastating disease of the common papaya. However, it is still susceptible to root rots and similar diseases if the soil becomes too wet and cold.

Above: Mountain pawpaw, *Carica pubescens*.

with sugar or syrup, and can be tasty prepared this way. Chamburro has attractive leaves.

Carica goudotiana. A very tropical, single-stemmed, handsome tree with purplish-red-veined leaves, ~5-m tall, and orange-yellow, fragrant fruit similar to *C. pubescens*, but the fruit are drier, with little sweetness or flavour, and are better when cooked. They are grown more as an ornamental, though plants are difficult to source.

Carica parviflora. A much smaller plant, ~50 cm tall, with tiny bright orange fruit, stunning purple flowers, but the fruits have very little edible flesh.

Oak-leaved pawpaw (baby pawpaw), Carica quercifolia. Native to South America. A handsome, tall, spreading tree, being much more spreading and larger than papaya. Has attractive, large leaves. Fruits are orange, ~3–4 cm long, very sweet, musky, have a zesty perfume. The skin is very thin and tender and can be eaten with the flesh. Takes 2–3 years to fruit. Needs well-drained soil. More frost hardy than papaya and is cold hardy to -5°C. Grows well in subtropical and warm temperate climates. Is dioecious and needs both female and male plants. Can produce hundreds of small fruits. ∎

SIMILAR MOUNTAIN PAWPAW SPECIES

Chamburro, Carica stipulata. An Andean mountain species, this is rarely found outside South America. It is similar to *C. pubescens*, but its trunk is covered in short, stout spines, the flowers are deep yellow, the fruits are ~10 cm long, have no ridges and a fairly soft skin. Their flavour is not very sweet, and the flesh has a very high papain content, which means it cannot be eaten fresh. It is best cooked

Carissa congesta (syn. *C. carandas*)
Karanda (naam daeng, kerenda, Bengal currant, caramba)
APOCYNACEAE
Similar species: Egyptian carissa (*Carissa edulis*)

Originally, karanda was known as *Carissa carandas*, but has recently been changed to *C. congesta*. It was originallly thought there were two distinct varieties of karanda, but it is now thought there is just the single form of this species. The tree is a native of India, Sri Lanka, most countries in the Far East, and is often grown locally as a security hedge, as well as for its fruit, which are often sold in local markets. The karanda has also been cultivated to a limited extent in Florida, California and the Caribbean for its fruits.

DESCRIPTION

A sprawling, semi-shrubby vine or small tree, growing to ~3–5 m tall, though sometimes growing to the tops of trees. The stems contain a white latex. The branches are numerous, dense and spreading; they have sharp, long spines in ones or twos, from the leaf axils. Plants are slow growing when young, but then become moderately vigorous as they mature, and can, if grown in the right soil and climate, become somewhat invasive.

Leaves: Evergreen, small, elongated oval (3–6 cm long), dark green, shiny, opposite, glossy green on their upper surface, lighter dull-green beneath. If the leaves or stems are injured, a white milky latex is excreted, which is a characteristic of *Carissa* species.

Flowers: Small, fragrant, particularly at night, tubular (composed of five fused petals), 3–5 cm diameter, white–pinkish, in clusters (2–12) from leaf axils at the ends of stems, and are borne between early spring–late autumn, and occasionally at other times in warmer climates. Plants are usually dioecious. Male flowers tend to be larger with long stamens, although often also have a vestigial style. In functional female flowers, the stamens are the same length as the style and do not have pollen. There is often not a clear division between whether the flower is self-fertile or not. It is best to plant more than one plant to ensure better fruit-set. Flowers have a superior ovary. *Pollination:* By insects and moths, although pollination can be poor, and some hand pollination can increase fruit yields.

Fruit: In clusters of 3–10, small (1–2.5 cm long), rounded–oval true berries, which ripen from late spring through to autumn, and at other times of year in warmer climates. The fruits have a green basal calyx, which remains on the tree when the fruits are picked. Young fruits are pinkish-white, becoming red–dark purple when mature, with a few (2–8) small, flat, brown, edible seeds. The skin is thin, fairly tough, smooth and shiny. The flesh is red–pink in colour, juicy and varies from very acid to fairly sweet. It may also contain some latex, which can make the taste somewhat bitter.

Harvest/storage: Fruits are best picked when fully ripe and are fully coloured, although unripe fruits can be picked in spring for processing for chutney, etc. When picked, the wound created by the removal of the calyx exudes some latex onto the fruit. The fruits do not store very well, and only last for 3–4 days before beginning to shrivel.

Roots: Are non-invasive. Mostly forms deeper roots.

CULTIVATION

Once established, they need very little maintenance or watering.

Location: Grow best in full sun, though are tolerant of light shade and will still produce fruit. Are very tolerant of salt within the soil and of salt spray, thus can be grown in maritime locations.

Temperature: Plants are quite cold hardy, and can tolerate temperatures down to about ~–4°C without serious damage, but cannot tolerate prolonged colder weather.

Soil/water/nutrients: Plants can grow in a wide range of soil types, including poor sand, rocky or limestone soils, but need well-drained conditions. However, the best-quality fruits are produced on plants that are grown in deep, fertile, well-drained soils. Prefer a neutral soil or can also grow in fairly alkaline soils. Once established, plants need very little irrigation, and are quite drought tolerant. They do not grow well in wet soils and cannot tolerate waterlogging. Regions with high rainfall tend to encourage excess leaf growth at the expense of flower and fruit production. They are moderately nutrient hungry, and grow better with 2–4 light applications a year of a balanced fertiliser (or blood and bone, or similar), with micronutrients.

Planting: Space plants at ~3 m apart. If growing plants up fences, pergolas, etc., remember that their spines are sharp and so vines are best not planted too close to thoroughfares.

Propagation: *Seed:* Can be propagated from seed, although the progeny are variable, as is their fruit quality, yield, etc. *Cuttings:* Can be grown by this method, though there are varying reports of how successful this is. Semi-ripe cuttings do not seem to root well, and hardwood cuttings, taken in late autumn or early winter are more likely to root if dipped in rooting hormone before inserting in well-drained, gritty compost. *Layering:* Air-layering is also practised, using wide-diameter stems where possible. *Grafting:* This is also reported to be possible, grafted onto self-seedlings.

Pruning: Karanda have a variable growth form that can be a mix of shrub- and tree-like, but can also develop like a scrambling vine. They can be pruned to retain a shrub form, but often grow better if allowed to sprawl and grow like bougainvillaea, and can climb to the tops of trees. May need tying into structures initially. Removal of stem tips will

uses

Food

Many fruits are of very good quality, and are said to taste like blueberries, with a sub-acid flavour. A few fruits are more sour or even bitter, and these are better if cooked with sugar. The skins are sometimes a little tough. Fruits can be eaten fresh or used in jellies, jam, in sauces, or added to various desserts. When cooked, the fruits exude a latex, but this then clears to leave a deep red juice. In India and Thailand, they are used in pickles, curries and chutney. They are also used in beverages. The juice has been used in soda drinks in Florida.

Nutrition/medicinal

The fruits have been used as an astringent, as a source of vitamin C and to relieve vomiting. A leaf decoction is used to treat fever, diarrhoea and earache. The roots have been used to treat digestive problems, to expel internal parasites and as an insect repellent. They also contain salicylic acid (which is also in aspirin) and cardiac glycosides, which causes a slight decrease in blood pressure.

Other uses

The wood is hard and dense, and is used to make small utensils.

Ornamental

Makes an attractive, good security hedge or barrier because of its spines, particularly if it can be grown up a fence for support.

promote the growth of flowering and fruiting laterals.

Pests and diseases: Have very few problems. Occasional fungal leaf diseases have been recorded, as well as twig dieback, caused by *Diplodia natalensis*, and stem canker, induced by *Dithiorella* sp. Birds are attracted to the ripening fruits.

Egyptian carissa, *Carissa edulis*. This plant's fruits are a little smaller and rounder than those of Karanda, but they taste similar, and many people prefer them. ■

Carissa macrocarpa (syn. *C. grandiflora*)
Carissa (Natal plum)
APOCYNACEAE

Carissa is a native of coastal South Africa, and is cultivated far inland in the Transvaal. It is valued mainly as a protective hedge because of its spines and the fruits are often a by-product. However, carissa makes an attractive shrub with ornamental leaves, fragrant pretty flowers for much of the year, plus tasty fruits.

DESCRIPTION
Attractive, vigorous, spreading, woody shrub with abundant white, gummy sap, may reach 4.5–6 m height and breadth, but is often smaller. Branches have sharp, stout, double-pronged thorns 3–5 cm long.

Leaves: Handsome, evergreen, opposite, broad-ovate, 2.5–7 cm long, dark green, glossy, leathery.

Flowers: Sweetly fragrant, especially at night; white, waxy, five-petalled, tubular, to 5 cm broad. They are borne singly or in small clusters at the tips of stems for most of the year in warmer regions, though mostly in spring. Although flowers have both male and female structures, these are often only functionally male or female on different plants. Therefore, plants tend to be classed as dioecious. Male flowers are larger and have stamens that are much longer than the style. Female flowers have stamens the same length as the style and smaller anthers without pollen. *Pollination:* In its homeland, the carissa is pollinated by small beetles, hawk-moths and other night-flying insects. Elsewhere, poor fruit yield may be a result of poor pollination, though some plants are naturally light croppers. To increase fruit crops, it is best to grow more than one plant, cross pollinate by hand and/or site plants near a beehive.

Fruit: A round–oval–oblong berry, ~6 cm long, ~4 cm wide, smooth, a rich green, coated in latex when unripe. As the fruits ripen, the skin turns cerise-red and develops a thin, whitish bloom, and finally develops streaks of darker crimson red. The flesh is tender, very juicy, rose-coloured, with a sweet cranberry flavour, though some fruits can be more astringent, with flecks of milky sap. In the centre are many (6–14) small, thin, flat, brown, edible seeds.

Yield/harvest: Seedlings can begin to produce fruits in 2 years; trees grown from grafts can produce even sooner. In warmer climates, trees can fruit all year, but the main harvesting period is through summer. Fruits need to be fully dark red, and slightly soft to the touch when picked. Unripe fruits are astringent. The five-pointed calyx remains attached to the plant when the fruit is picked.

Roots: Not invasive. Mostly forms deeper roots.

CULTIVATION
Once established, these shrubs are tough and adaptable to many sites and conditions, requiring a minimum of maintenance.

Location: Can grow in full sun or semi-shade, and tolerates a wide range of lighting conditions. Trees are

Food
Fruits are good to eat whole and fresh, including their skins and seeds, though some remove the seeds before eating. The tasty cranberry-like fruits can also be added to fresh desserts, icecream, yoghurt, pies, cakes and sauces. If cooked, the latex tends to adhere to the sides of cooking utensils, which should not be aluminium. Fruits can also be preserved whole, or made into jam, jellies, chutney, etc. Some under-ripe fruits can be included to sharpen the flavour and enhance colour. Fruits can be frozen, dried or bottled for later use.

Nutrition
Has very good levels of vitamin C: ~50–60 mg/100 g of flesh. Also has good levels of iron, copper, magnesium and potassium. It also contains some riboflavin and thiamine. **Warning:** All other parts of carissa may be poisonous except for the ripe fruits.

Ornamental
Grows well as an indoor bonsai. It has attractive leaves, fragrant flowers and fruit. It makes a good barrier hedge because of its thorns, and can be used for foundation plantings. It is often grown as a seaside hedge in the USA. Because of its non-invasive root system, it can be grown near buildings.

uses

tolerant of salt spray and are resistant to wind damage, so can be grown in fairly exposed maritime locations.

Temperature: Prefers warm temperate, subtropical or near-tropical climates, though can withstand temperatures as low as ~–4°C when well established. Young plants need extra protection at temperatures below –1.5°C.

Soil/water/nutrients: Can grow in dry, rocky terrains, in clay or sandy soils, or in alkaline soils, though the latter can induce deficiencies of micronutrients such as manganese or iron, causing leaf chlorosis. This can be remedied by applications of chelated trace elements. Shrubs have good drought tolerance and are very resistant to soil salinity and salt spray, though cannot tolerate waterlogging. They are not very nutrient hungry, but benefit from occasional additions of a complete, well-balanced fertiliser. Plants are slow growing and should not be overfed.

Pot culture: Make good container plants, as they are slow growing, tough and can be grown in shade, though they do have vicious thorns and shouldn't be placed too near thoroughfares. Growing in containers can extend their possible climate range as they can be moved inside or given extra protection in colder winters.

Pruning: Is very tolerant of pruning, and will still produce fruit even when trimmed. Dwarf cultivars need to be regularly trimmed or they often revert to the ordinary form. Fruits are formed at the tips of stems, so plants are best pruned just after fruiting and not once growth has commenced in spring.

Propagation: *Seeds:* Should germinate in ~14 days, but seedlings grow very slowly at first and are highly variable. Seeds are best sown fresh, with all pulp thoroughly washed from them. *Cuttings:* These root poorly unless the tips of young branches are cut half-way through and left attached to the plant for ~8 weeks. After removal and planting in sand, they should root in ~30 days. These stem-tip cuttings are best taken in spring or autumn. Select light green, fresh growth. *Layering:* Air-layering, or ordinary layering of stems then pegged down onto soil, can be successfully carried out during the growing season. *Grafting:* Shield-budding is practised.

Pests and diseases: Few pests or diseases affect this plant. Spider mites, thrips, whiteflies and occasional scale insects can attack young plants, especially in nurseries or in shade. There can be possible problems with fungal diseases, particularly in wetter soils.

CULTIVARS

'Fancy': From California. An erect plant, with many large fruits with few seeds.

'Frank': Produces fewer fruits, though does have a good supply of pollen.

'Gifford': From Florida. Produces very good yields.

'Torrey Pines': Produces good crops of fruit and pollen. ■

Carpobrotus edulis (*Mesembryanthemum edulis,* syn. *Dorotheanthus* spp.)
Hottentot fig (ice plant, fig marigold)
AIZOACEAE
Similar species: *C. asinaciforme, C. chilensis*

This plant was a member of the *Mesembryanthemum* genus, along with ~1000 other species, and does closely resemble them. However, this species, with others, was recently assigned to a new genera, *Carpobrotus*. The hottentot fig is a fleshy succulent with eye-catching, attractive flowers that originates from South Africa, but is now widely grown as an ornamental groundcover plant. It is thought that it was introduced into Europe, possibly inadvertently, in the 1500s. It is a remarkably tough plant and can grow in sand dunes, very thin soils, steep hillsides, exposed rocky ledges and places where few other plants will grow, and is very valuable for soil stabilisation. However, in some areas it has become too successful, and has become naturalised and spread to smother native species. It is now commonly found in California, Mexico, Australia, southern UK, southern Europe and many other areas. Apart from its bright, attractive flowers, it also produces tasty, edible fruits. Similar species are *C. asinaciforme,* which is ~14 cm tall and has purple flowers, and *C. chilensis,* which is very similar to *C. edulis.*

DESCRIPTION

A perennial, succulent, low, sprawling plant, 15–25 cm tall, with stems trailing to ~3 m from the plant. It has succulent stems and leaves, which root as they sprawl across the soil. It is fast growing.

Leaves: Evergreen, succulent, blue-green, waxy, smooth, entire, slightly curved, 6–10 cm long, 1–2 cm wide, usually opposite, with a triangular cross-section, sometimes with fine teeth near the tip. These plants have Crassulacean photosynthesis, whereby they trap sunlight during the day, but only open their stomata at night to allow the entry of carbon dioxide, which then biochemically reacts with the trapped sunlight to produce sugars and starch. The main advantage of this is that plants do not lose valuable moisture by opening their stomata during the hot day, and this enables them to grow in very dry locations and survive on a minimum of water. The leaves are also filled with juicy, watery, mucilaginous flesh, which acts as a water store, a further aid to drought survival.

Flowers: Lemon yellow or pinky-purple. Very attractive, bright, typical daisy-shaped flower, 6–8 cm diameter, with numerous, very narrow petals (more correctly called ligules), which are borne in mid spring until late summer, on a short flower stalk. A very closely related species, the sea fig (*C. chilensis*), has no leaf stalks, though the two freely hybridise and can be difficult to tell apart. The flowers are monoecious and bisexual, having both male and female structures within the same flower, so only need a single plant to set fruit. They have many hundreds of tiny, yellow stamens, with 8–10 central styles and an inferior ovary. *Pollination:* By bees and other insects.

Fruit: Fleshy purple-greeny fruit, fig-like in appearance, ripening to brown. When fully ripe and ready to harvest, they begin to shrivel. The flesh is divided into several sections and is tasty and sweet–sub-acid, though rather mucilaginous. The fruits ripen from late summer– late autumn.

Harvest: Harvest fruits when fully ripe and beginning to shrivel; under-ripe fruits are very astringent.

CULTIVATION

Readily grows where little else will, and needs very little maintenance, but can become invasive in some locations and crowd out native species. It has become wild on many steep, inaccessible cliffs and hillsides.

Location: Grows best in full sun. Is tolerant of salt, and because it is so low growing it can tolerate very exposed maritime locations.

Temperature: Can grow in hot climates in direct sun. Grows best in a warmer temperate–subtropical climate. This species is quite frost sensitive and can be damaged by temperatures much below freezing, though can tolerate brief frosts, and longer cold periods may set back these plant's growth, but they usually recover from the roots the following year.

Soil/water/nutrients: Prefers to grow in sandy, well-drained soils. Once established, plants are very drought tolerant, though regular moisture will give better growth. Best to not water until the soil is quite dry. They do not tolerate waterlogging. Needs very few nutrients and will grow in poor soils. Nutrients are likely to increase leaf production and reduce flower and fruit production. They grow well in neutral to very alkaline soils. These plants are able to accumulate salts around their roots, often making the soil very alkaline, which makes it difficult for other plants to establish in their vicinity.

Pot culture: Ideal for pot culture, to contain its spread, but also to provide bright, cheerful colour near to the house, with

Food

The fruits are somewhat mucilaginous, but are sweet and sub-acid. They need to be fully ripe or they are too astringent. The fruits are often eaten when fresh, but can also be added to preserves, jellies and jam, or can be dried for later use. The leaves can also be eaten, used in salads or as a substitute for cucumber, but they are mucilaginous and do contain high levels of tannin, so should only be eaten in moderation.

Medicinal

The stems have long been used to treat diarrhoea and as an antiseptic mouthwash. Various flavonoids from this species have been shown to have strong antibacterial properties. Another study has shown that extracts can increase the efficiency of drugs given to treat cancers. They also increase the efficiency of certain white blood cells (macrophages) ability to kill *Staphylococcus aureus* and also increase cellular immune functions.

Ornamental

Great when controlled and grown on the tops of walls, in rockeries, and anywhere dry where most other plants won't grow. Gives leaf cover year round, a long flowering season and fruits.

edible fruits in autumn, while needing the absolute minimum of maintenance.

Planting: Space plants at ~1–1.5 m apart.

Propagation: *Seed:* Grows very easily from seed. Take seeds from fully ripened fruits and thoroughly wash away any pulp. Just sprinkle on compost and they should germinate in 7–10 days at ~22°C. *Cuttings:* Leaf and stem cuttings can be easily removed through spring–summer. Leave them to callus over for a day or two and then they should root when inserted in well-drained, gritty compost.

Pests and diseases: Generally very few problems, though, if the soil becomes too wet, fungal root rots can develop. ∎

Carya illinoinensis (syn. *C. pecan*, *Hicoria pecan*)
Pecan, hickory nuts
JUGLANDACEAE

Similar species: shellbark (*C. lacinosa*), mockernut (*C. tomentosa*), pignut hickories (*C. glabra*, *C. ovalis*), bitternut (*C. cordiformis*)
Relatives: walnuts

There about 20 species of *Carya* and these are native to the eastern USA and Mexico. They used to also grow widely in Europe, but most were killed by the

last Ice Age. Pecan is the main commercial species of this genera. The term 'hickory' is used as a general name for all *Carya* species. Hickories tend to have harder, rougher shells and are usually smaller than pecans. Most hickories, although they have tasty nuts, often have problems setting fruits, have fairly low yields, are difficult to transplant, have thick shells and are slow growing compared to pecans. Some can hybridise with pecan, and many are more cold tolerant than pecan. The southeastern Native American tribes believed the pecan tree was a manifestation of the Great Spirit, and have used the nuts for at least 8000 years. The Crows may have cultivated them and selected good trees with tasty nuts and thin shells to propagate from, so improving their quality. The term 'Pecan' comes from the American Indian word *pacane*, meaning 'nut so hard as to require a stone to crack'. The pecan tree is an important commercial crop in North America, and the kernels are widely used in confectionery and desserts. Modern commercial orchards were first started in Louisiana in the mid-1800s. There was a pecan-type 'gold rush' for establishing pecan orchards in the early 1900s, with expectations of large financial rewards. Unfortunately, the market became swamped with too many nuts, and not enough attention was paid to the long wait needed (10–12 years), without an income, until the first harvests: many people went bankrupt. Other hickory species include *C. aquatica*, *C. carolinae-septenrionalis*, *C. cordiformis*, *C. glabra*, *C. myristiciformis*, *C. ovalis*, *C. pallida*, *C. texana* and *C. tomentosa*. However, the nuts of several of these are astringent, small and have very hard shells. Asian species of *Carya* that produce edible nuts include *Carya cathayensis* and *C. tonkinensis*.

DESCRIPTION

The tallest and fastest-growing hickory, *Carya illinoinensis* forms a beautiful, large tree: height and spread can be ~25–30 m. It has a vase-shaped crown, and a stout trunk that can be >2 m in diameter. The bark is smoother and thinner than that of other hickories. Branches are not very strong, and break easily, even in non-exposed locations. The pecan is a very long-lived tree, i.e. some trees in Mississippi are thought to be ~1000 years old, and are still producing nuts!

Leaves: Pinnate, with 7–17 leaflets, lanceolate to oval, and often lopsided, with half of the leaf smaller than the other. They have finely toothed margins. The leaves form good shade.

Flowers: As catkins, in late spring, and so are usually after late frosts. Trees are monoecious, but often the female is not receptive at the time the male pollen is shed: sometimes the male flower produces pollen before the female becomes receptive, and viceversa. This can vary from year to year, and between cultivars. Therefore, good pollination can only occur if more than one tree of more than one cultivar is planted. Male flowers occur in pendulous catkins, borne from the leaf axils of 1- and 2-year-old wood; female flowers are yellow-green and form smaller spikes of flowers, borne terminally on the current season's growth. *Pollination:* By wind, so pollination is reduced if the weather is humid.

Fruit: The nuts are borne in clusters of 2–10, in late autumn. They have a green, fleshy outer husk (composed partly of ovarian tissue: both exo- and mesocarp), which surrounds the nut until maturity. When ripe, the husk dehisces into four segments and the nut is released. The nut is egg-shaped, 2.5–4 cm long and contains a large kernel (embryo), consisting of two pre-cotyledons (first leaves, like walnuts). There is a thin, papery partition between the cotyledons. Trees tend to bear alternately, with a bumper crop one year and a meagre crop the next. This can be remedied by thinning the fruit, but also by ensuring maximum leaf growth occurs in bumper years, to build up 'food' reserves for next year's flowers and nuts. Therefore, do not prune trees during the summers of bumper crops, try to control leaf-eating pests and keep the soil around trees moist in late summer when the second leaf flush occurs, or leaves can drop prematurely.

Yield/harvest/storage: Trees take a long time to start producing nuts: 7–10 years, and maximum yields are not obtained until the tree is >10 years old (this depends on cultivar). A good tree can produce 30–50 kg of nuts per year (a weight of 400 kg was reported for one tree!). Tends to bear biennially. Some nuts fall from the tree, others may need to be picked, or the tree shaken. The nuts ripen in late autumn–early winter, and are mature when the outer shuck splits. Picking from the tree reduces losses to squirrels, etc. For storage, nuts are best partially dried to ~5–10% moisture to reduce the risk of fungal infection, including the carcinogenic aflotoxin fungus. They can then be stored for several weeks or longer if they are left within their shells and stored in polyethylene bags in a fridge or freezer.

Roots: Because of their very deep taproots, they are difficult to transplant except as very young trees. The taproot can penetrate down to >10 m, although it also has many lateral roots at 1–2-m depth. Lateral roots can also be wide spreading: they can span twice the width of the crown. These lateral roots only start to fully grow and develop once the taproot is established.

CULTIVATION

Location: Trees are not tolerant of maritime conditions. They like a sunny location. They are not wind tolerant and branches easily break.

Temperature: The nuts need a long, warm–hot summer to mature fully. They grow best with hot, dry days and warm nights, but also need some winter chill, and can put up with snow. They do not like temperatures to drop too quickly. However, acclimatised, dormant trees can tolerate temperatures down to –32°C, and young trees are tolerant of temperatures down to ~–20°C; unfortunately, young leaves are frost tender, but, luckily, are very late into leaf in spring.

Chilling: Trees usually need a period of winter chill to come into leaf and form flowers. They need ~500 hours (but this can range from 300–1000 hours) below ~7°C. In some places pecans come into leaf without any chilling (Mexico, Israel).

Soil/water/nutrients: Trees prefer a fertile, deep, non-compacted, well-drained loam, with a pH range of 5.5–6.5, but can grow in a range of soil types, though sandy soils can be too free-draining; they also won't grow in saline soils. They can grow in fairly heavy clay, and in soils that are fairly alkaline (pH 8), though zinc deficiency can occur, causing stunted, bronze growth, misshapen nuts and twigs and even branches to die back. The soil does need to be deep, with a water table below the root zone during the growing season. They naturally grow in floodplains and river bottoms, and like adequate moisture. Pecans bear best in warm, moist regions, and regular irrigation increases yields, even in humid regions. Trees benefit from an application, in spring, of a general fertiliser with trace elements, but also with additional zinc, particularly when trees are young. As the trees mature, the ratio of nitrogen can be reduced. The main likely deficiency is zinc or magnesium, with the latter often occurring in sandy soils. It causes yellowing of leaves with interveinal chlorosis and necrosis. Manganese deficiency may occur in acidic soils, resulting in deformed leaves, but can be easily remedied by applying manganese or by raising the soil pH by adding lime.

Planting: Space plants at 10–20 m apart because of their large size. Dig a deep hole, and take care when planting because of the long taproot. Do not fertilise at planting time, and do not let young trees dry out, or they will die. Also, keep weeds to a minimum during the first couple of years. Because of this wide spacing, filler trees can be planted in between, e.g. peaches, that have a quick life cycle and will have finished being productive by the time the pecan trees have started producing nuts. If planting in a group, plant pollinators at a ratio of ~1:10 fruiting trees. If possible, and space allows, plant an early and a late pollinator. Can give young trees frost protection by wrapping the trunks with foil or cardboard.

Propagation: *Seed:* Nuts should be planted when fresh as they lose their viability quickly, particularly if stored in the warmth. If keeping seeds till spring, store them at 0°C, and soak them for a couple of days before planting. Can test for viability by floating them in water; choose only those that sink. Grow on seedlings in deep, biodegradable pots. Seedlings do take longer to start fruiting and are more variable. *Cuttings:* Take semi-ripe cuttings in late summer–autumn. They root fairly easily under mist. Rooting hormones can also help. Roots develop in 4–6 weeks. However, during winter many can rot, so do not over-water during this period. *Grafting:* Is the most popular method, but can be tricky. Rootstocks (from pecan seedlings) are often whip-and-tongue grafted in early spring, using 1-year-old scions. They can also be patch-budded, usually in late summer, using buds from the current season's wood.

Pruning: Pecan trees sometimes form a lot of vegetative growth, and pruning is then important. Try to prune so that the tree's energy goes into a main trunk. During the first 3 years, trees are trained to a central leader with scaffold branches at 30–45-cm intervals up the main stem. After this, very little pruning is needed because trees form a natural vase shape by repeat forking at the ends of branches. Mature trees just need dead, diseased or damaged branches removed. If the centre of the tree becomes dense, some branches can be removed to allow sunlight to enter and prevent overcrowding.

In addition, pecans can have sudden summer limb drop, where a branch suddenly breaks in the middle, often on a hot, summer day with no wind. Therefore, longer branches may need reducing in length (and therefore weight) to reduce this risk. In general the branches break off for no apparent reason.

Pests and diseases: They are relatively free of problems, but high humidity and rainfall during early nut development can lead to pecan scab, a serious disease that can cause extensive crop loss. Try and select a scab-resistant cultivar. Other possible problems are powdery mildew, silver leaf, various galls, mealybug. Can get insect attacks from bronze beetles, scales, hickory-bark beetles (which can be serious and kill branches), grass grubs, aphids and green vegetable bugs, although most do not usually cause serious damage. Regular watering will minimise stress and reduce disease.

uses

Food
This tasty nut is eaten as a snack or can be used in pralines, pecan pie, cakes, desserts, and can be added to many types of dishes. Pecan-nut oil can be used as a cooking oil. *Nutrition:* The nuts are a good source of zinc, thiamine; they are relatively high in vitamin A and linolenic acid (an omega-3 fatty acid). They have quite a high vitamin E content, and a very high oil content (67%), of which ~33% is monounsaturated, and most of the remainder is polyunsaturated. Their protein content is relatively low (7 g protein/100 g of nut). Its oil is said to lower the level of low-density lipids in the blood. The nuts also contain some phosphorus, magnesium, copper, zinc and lots of manganese. They are rich in thiamine, with some B6, niacin, pantothenic acid and riboflavin. Leaves and fruits contain juglone and linalool, which are allelopathic and fungitoxic, similar to walnuts.

Medicinal
The kernels have been used as an astringent for blood ailments, dyspepsia, fever, flu and stomachache. ***Warning:*** Pecan nuts (and all other nuts) stored for long periods may develop a fungal disease that produces aflotoxin, which is a dangerous poison: dry nuts well for storage and do not eat mouldy nuts. Pecan pollen is a common allergen.

Other uses
Pecan oil is used in drugs, essential oils and cosmetics. The shells can be added to compost, are used for paths and driveways, as a mulch and soil conditioner, as charcoal and are added to abrasives, paints and polishes. The tree can be coppiced, and regrows fast. The smaller branches are used for posts, handles and for hosting Shitake mushroom cultivation. The wood is not as good as that of hickory (see below).

Ornamental
This large tree can be grown as a specimen tree, for shade and as a windbreak.

CULTIVARS

'Cado': Tolerant of high humidity. Early crop. Tolerant of scab, lovely foliage, moderately precocious, a good nut. Pollen in mid season, female receptivity late.

'Curtis': Tree bears early, is moderately resistant to scab and is somewhat dwarf. Nut: small–medium, thin shell, cracks easily. Kernel: plump, high quality, excellent flavour, large.

'Elliott': Tree: vigorous, large, rounded crown. Resistant to scab. Prolific and consistent bearer. Nut: small, plump, medium–thick shell, easy to crack. Has good flavour and quality, large kernel.

'Hican': Are crosses between pecan and hickory species. They are mostly hybrids of shagbark and bitternut x pecan: there are ~12 named selections. Generally, they are of low quality, with small kernels and fairly low yields.

'Moore': Tree bears at an early age and is prolific: is medium sized. Susceptible to scab. Nut: small–medium, good quality, early to harvest. Shell: medium thickness, cracks easily. Kernel: fairly plump, of good quality and flavour.

'Schley': Outstanding variety, but very susceptible to scab. Tree is vigorous with thick foliage, round-topped. Admired for its ornamental appearance. Begins to bear fairly early and is moderately prolific, also a regular bearer. Nuts: medium–large, with very thin shell, cracks easily. Kernel: plump, rich in oil, excellent quality and flavour.

'Stuart': Trees are upright, fairly tall, productive, but not precocious. Tolerant of scab disease. Does poorly in arid areas. Fairly late to start bearing, but then bears consistently. Nut: medium–large, attractive, medium-thick shell, cracks easily. Kernel: good-sized, plump, good flavour.

A FEW HICKORY SPECIES

Bitternut, *Carya cordiformis*. Thin-shelled nuts, but very astringent flavour. Very hardy.

Mockernut, *Carya tomentosa*. More upland range than other hickories, which usually grow in floodplains. Grows to ~30 m tall. *Nuts:* Very hard, thick shells that are often smashed when trying to open them: even the squirrels can't open them! They have a small but sweet nut.

Pignut hickories, *Carya glabra* and *C. ovalis*. Native to southern USA. Height 20–25 m. Small kernels that can be bitter. Smooth bark. Of very little importance.

Shagbark hickory, *Carya ovata*. A native of eastern North America, from southern Canada to northern Mexico. Native Americans cultivated small plantations of shagbark hickories. Naturally, they grow on higher country. There are more named cultivars of this hardy species than any other hickory.

Description: Height ~16–30 m tall, spread 8–15 m. Has a very long lifespan and slow growth, particularly for the first few years. Shaggy, rough-barked trees. Trunk diameter up to ~55 cm. *Leaves:* compound, with five leaflets, 15–22 cm long. *Flowers:* Monoecious. Green catkins. *Fruit:* Shells are very hard: soaking in hot water for 20 minutes may help when cracking them open. *Nuts:* Small, but are highly rated, 3.2–4.5 cm long, kernels are rounded and furrowed. Has a late spring bloom and late harvest. Nuts are storable for ~3 months. Trees can take 40 years before bearing in commercial quantities, but 300-year-old trees can still bear small crops.

Cultivation: Adapts well to disturbed areas, such as strip mines: appears to tolerate high soil levels of lead and zinc. Very cold hardy. *Soil:* Does not like waterlogged soil or partial shade. Can grow on poor soils, and is said to be able to store more aluminium in its leaves than any other known plant. They are also good at taking up heavy metals. *Pruning:* Only needed early in life, to establish a good structure. *Pests and diseases:* Aphids, leaf spot.

Uses: *Food:* The nuts are good fresh or cooked. The native Indians used the nuts extensively for food and also fermented them to make a potent liquor called 'pawcockhickoria', and hence the name hickory. *Other uses:* The wood of this and other hickory species is rated one of the best hardwoods in the USA, behind black walnut and black cherry. It is used for furniture, tool handles, skis, gymnastic bars, flooring, piano construction, interior trim, dowels, ladder rungs. It is famous for smoking meats and cheeses. The shells can be used for driveways, for mulch around plants and for fuel. *Ornamental:* Sometimes grown as an ornamental, for shade and as a windbreak. Excellent planted in problem soils.

Shellbark, *Carya lacinosa*. Similar to shagbark, but the nuts are larger with thicker shells. A sweet nut. Leaves are compound, with seven leaflets, 15–22 cm long. Trees tend to naturally occur near watercourses. ■

Casimiroa edulis
Casimiroa (white sapote, icecream fruit, matasano)
RUTACEAE

Relatives: citrus spp., bael fruit, wampi, rue

The genus *Casimiroa* includes a few tree and shrub species, of which *C. edulis* produces the best quality fruit. Casimiroa or white sapote is a native of the central Mexican highlands, parts of Central America and is occasionally found growing wild in California. It has been used by indigenous peoples for many hundreds, if not thousands, of years for its edible fruits, but also for its seeds, which have been eaten for their hypnotic properties. Although called sapote, it is not related to the other sapotes and is, instead, related to the aromatic rue plant and to citrus species. It is often cultivated, sometimes commercially, in Mexico and Central America and occasionally in northern South America, California, the West Indies, in parts of the Mediterranean around Spain, India, the East Indies, South Africa and in New Zealand, in warmer areas. It is also sometimes grown as an ornamental. The casimiroa is a rewarding tree to plant and could be potentially grown more widely in warmer climates and enjoyed for its very undervalued, delicious, creamy-fleshed fruits as well as for its appearance.

DESCRIPTION

A medium-sized tree, 4.5–18 m tall, depending on climate and soil conditions. Trees often develop long, drooping branches as they mature. Branches can sometimes be weak and easily broken. Growth is rapid, and trees have two main spurts of growth a year, in spring and in early autumn. Young trees tend to form a single-stemmed tree that has pronounced apical dominance for the first few years; as a consequence, young trees often need staking. Their bark is light grey, thick, warty.

Leaves: Can be evergreen, but often becomes deciduous in cooler climates or in extremes of heat, though then re-leaf once the adverse conditions have passed. Leaves are large, alternate, usually in groups of five, bronze when young, becoming dark green with age, pale grey-green beneath. The crown casts a dense shade.

Flowers: Small, greenish-yellow, 4- or 5-petalled, borne along the main branches in panicles. They are bisexual, and are usually self-fertile, although a few flowers are just male because of aborted embryos. They usually flower in spring, and may flower again in autumn in warmer areas, particularly the cultivar 'Suebelle'. Trees can drop a high percentage of their leaves during and after flowering. *Pollination:* Flowers are very popular with bees, hoverflies and ants. There is great variation in the amount of pollen produced. Some flowers bear virtually no pollen, others have an abundance. Sterile pollen or lack of cross pollination causes seeds to abort and heavy shedding of immature fruits. Planting more than one tree increases fruit-set and fruit quality.

Fruit: Pollinated fruits, classified as berries, grow larger and have 1–6 large seeds. Unpollinated fruits can form, but are seedless and are usually much smaller. Fruits are often ~12 cm long and 6–12 cm wide, round–oval, symmetrical or irregular, and are more or less five-lobed. Yellowy-green-skinned cultivars have white flesh; yellowy-gold-skinned cultivars have yellow flesh. Their skin is usually covered in a fine bloom and is not usually eaten. The flesh has a smooth consistency, with many tiny, yellow oil glands; it is somewhat similar to avocado flesh but not as oily, though it is creamy. Fertilised seeds are white, plump, oval, hard, 2.5–5 cm long, 1.25–2.5 cm thick; unfertilised seeds are usually much smaller and very thin. The seeds should not be eaten as they are bitter and have narcotic properties. (See warning below.)

Yield/harvest/storage: Seedlings produce fruits within 7–10 years; trees grown from grafts fruit within 3–8 years. In general, trees start producing good crops from about 10 years of age. Casimiroas produce very good yields of fruits compared to many other fruit and nut species, and a healthy tree can produce 1000 fruits! However, some cultivars also tend towards alternate bearing and benefit from having some fruits removed in bumper years to even out yields and avoid a meagre crop the following year. Trees can produce fruits for >100 years. Fruits ripen 6–9 months after fruit-set. In warmer areas most fruits ripen in autumn, with some in spring from autumn flowers. In cooler regions, most fruits ripen from late autumn into winter. Fruit should be picked when they are just beginning to soften and change colour from green to yellow. If picked too soon they are too astringent. Once picked, the fruits fully soften in 2–5 days, and are then at their most delicious, although a few cultivars have flesh that is edible while still firm. Fruits taste best when they are tree-ripened, but they usually tend to fall first and are then smashed and badly bruised. Fruits are best clipped from the branches, leaving a short piece of stem attached, which later falls off as the fruits soften. They should be handled carefully as they bruise easily and then become bitter. Ripe fruits can be kept in good condition in a refrigerator for ~2 weeks or longer, but rapidly ferment if kept at room temperature.

Roots: Has a large taproot and other more surface, fibrous roots that are spreading and nutrient hungry. They can be disruptive if trees are planted too close to buildings and paths.

CULTIVATION

Casimiroa needs similar cultivation conditions to oranges.

Location: Fairly tough trees, but branches can be damaged in wind. Can grow in shade, but grow and fruit better in full sun. Can be grown near the coast, but in more sheltered locations. Has vigorous growth and should not be planted too near to buildings.

Temperature: Young trees can be damaged at –1°C. Can withstand more frost than avocado, but needs extra protection while young. Mature trees can tolerate ~–5°C without injury, though trees prefer warmer temperate or subtropical climates. Can grow where citrus can. May not fruit as well in the tropics if trees do not receive a brief cool season, which induces flowering and fruiting.

Soils/water/nutrients: Trees will grow in almost any soil type as long as it is well-drained, even in clay, although they grow best in deep, lighter soils that have added organic matter. They prefer a pH range of 5.5–7.5 Trees are tolerant of cold and even wet soils, as well as being fairly drought tolerant, but produce the best fruits when trees receive regular, deep watering as summer droughts induce premature fruit drop. Deep watering also keeps root growth deeper rather than forming many shallow roots. They are often most productive after wet winters. They are quite nutrient hungry and should be fertilised as citrus trees to achieve optimum growth and yields. However, too much nutrients, particularly nitrogen, can lead to excessive leaf growth at the expense of fruit production. Trees can suffer from magnesium deficiency.

Pot culture: Grafted trees are suitable for containers for

Food

What an undervalued fruit! Perhaps this is because the skin is simply a coarse green colour when ripe and the flesh just cream-coloured. However, whatever it lacks in appearance, it certainly makes up for in taste. The flesh has an unusual creamy, custard-like texture and a rich, sweet delicious flavour reminiscent of peach/banana/papaya/pear/butterscotch and vanilla icecream. Some cultivars are slightly bitter just beneath the skin, but others are very sweet. They are delicious just eaten fresh on their own, or can be added to fruit salads or other fresh desserts. They can be added to icecream or milkshakes, or some make a marmalade. Good infant food. De-seeded fruits freeze well and make an excellent smoothee, with the fruit even developing flavour through freezing. The skin is better removed as it is sometimes bitter.

Nutrition

Very high in sugars (~20–25%) and low in fats and acids. Has good levels of vitamin C: 30 mg/100 g of flesh. Also contains calcium, potassium, iron, as well as vitamin A and the B vitamins, thiamine, riboflavin and niacin.

Medicinal

The fruit has a relaxing effect on the central nervous system and is said to relieve the pains of arthritis and rheumatism. The bark, leaves and seeds contain a compound that is being researched for its ability to reduce anxiety, as an antidepressant and as a relaxant. It also induces a hypnotic effect. It may also act to reduce seizures and is being investigated for its possible use as an anti-epileptic. In Costa Rica, the leaves are taken for diabetes and in China it is used to lower blood pressure. *Warning:* A few reports say the seeds can be fatally toxic if eaten raw, but, more likely, it acts as a narcotic. Recent studies have shown that the seeds act as a vasodilator and increase cardiac output, which may be of concern to some, if they eat the seeds.

Other uses

The wood is yellow, fine-grained, fairly dense, heavy, non-shrinking and needs almost no seasoning before use, but is not very durable.

Ornamental

Casimiroas are popular specimen ornamentals in warmer regions, often with a semi-weeping form and attractive leaves, though should not be planted too near buildings.

a few years; seedling trees grow too fast. However, cultivars such as 'Fernie' may be possible to grow because of their smaller size, and can then be grown in colder regions and moved inside or given extra protection from cold weather.

Planting: Space trees at 6–12 m apart, depending on climate, and wider apart in warmer regions. Take care when planting that the deep taproot is not damaged. Young trees, because of their tall whippy growth, benefit from staking.

Pruning: Young trees tend to have strong apical dominance and form few lateral branches: therefore, after planting, pinch out terminal buds to encourage the production of lateral branches, which will spread out rather than upwards, and these should also fruit sooner. In later years, branches that are angled too near to the vertical or horizontal should be pruned out as these are more susceptible to wind breakage. Trees only need moderate pruning, just to encourage a strong structure; too much pruning can encourage excessive, weak growth and less fruiting wood. Casimiroas can be trained to an espalier or cordon shape. Pruning is best carried out after fruiting, or after any danger of frost has passed.

Propagation: Seeds: Seedlings are variable, as are their fruits, but this can be a satisfactory method. Seeds are best sown when fresh and all pulp has been thoroughly removed. Seeds germinate easily and seedlings transplant well. Are best grown in deep pots to enable good taproot development. *Cuttings:* Are very difficult to root. *Layering:* Trees can be successfully air-layered in spring–summer. *Grafting:* Usually grafted onto seedlings that have been grown *in situ* for ~3 years. Simple grafts (e.g. shield-budding, side-grafting) are easy and successful, and are best done in spring. Keep grafted trees cool and wrap a plastic bag around the graft until healed. Scions are best girdled for 1 to 2 months before use. Cleft, splice or approach grafts are successful on larger rootstocks. Grafted plants tend to be slower growing than seedlings. Seedlings of 'Pike' are a popular rootstock.

Pests and diseases: Trees are seldom bothered by pests or diseases, but some fruits can be attacked by fruit flies. Mealybugs are sometimes found around fruit stems, and aphids can infest new growth. Casimiroa are resistant to *Armillaria* and *Phytophthora*. Although they may be attacked by borers, these seldom seem to cause serious damage. Slugs and snails love new growth, and birds and other animals seek out the fruits.

CULTIVARS

Best not to choose the woolly-leafed sapote (*C. tetrameria*) as its flesh is often bitter and unpleasant. It has larger, thicker leaves than *C. edulis*; these are also velvety-white beneath. It is also less cold hardy than casimiroa.

'Cuccio': From California. Very quick to come into bearing. Fruit: green when ripe, tastes excellent, keeps well.

'Fernie': Tree: naturally small, ~3 m in 10 years. Fruit: good flavoured, oval, small–medium sized, but are larger when pollinated or if the fruits are thinned. Has ~1 small seed. If soil volume is limited, this limits tree size.

'Henriksen': A good fruiting cultivar that does not need a pollinator tree.

'Lemon Gold': From California. Tree: less vigorous, moderate crops. Fruit: keeps well, can be picked immature and ripens well off the tree, attractive appearance. Flesh: yellow, excellent flavour, with lemony overtones.

'Parroquia': From California. Fruit: oval, yellow-green, smooth. Flesh: ivory, very good flavour. Fairly prolific bearer.

'Pike': Tree: small, almost weeping form, compact, is a heavy, regular cropper, mid season. Fruits: large, oval, green, skin bitter, very fragile. Flesh: white–yellow, rich.

'Suebelle': From California. Fruit: round, small–medium,

yellowish-green. Flesh: excellent flavour, sweet. Tree is medium-sized, precocious: can bloom and fruit all year. The best known cultivar and is common in nurseries. Pick fruits when soft.

'Wilson': From California. Tree: productive. Fruit: round–oval, poor keeper, medium–large, smooth. Flesh: high quality and excellent flavour. Most fruits ripen in autumn and winter. ■

Castanea spp.
Chestnut
FAGACEAE

European chestnut *(Castanea sativa)*, Japanese chestnut *(C. crenata)*, Chinese chestnut *(C. mollissima)*, American chestnut *(C. dentata)*

Relatives: oak *(Quercus)*, beech *(Fagus)*

The genus *Castanea* has been around for a long time. Fossils from trees have been found in Europe that date back ~75–100 million years ago. In the Mediterranean region, chestnuts have been cultivated for at least 3000 years. The ancient Greeks are thought to have been among the first to cultivate the chestnut, introducing the European chestnut *(Castanea sativa)* from Asia Minor, via Turkey, into southern Europe and North Africa. The Romans later extended the cultivation of *C. sativa* into northwest and central Europe and they also named chestnuts '*Castanea*', possibly after the name of the town where chestnuts were once very common. In Asia, the Japanese chestnut *(C. crenata)* has been cultivated since at least the 11th century and the Chinese chestnut *(C. mollissima)* has been grown for possibly 2000–6000 years. In the USA, the American chestnut *(C. dentata)* was once a major species of the temperate indigenous forests and then, at the beginning of the 20th century, a terrible fungal epidemic *(Endothia parasitica*, chestnut blight fungus) swept through the population, killing most of these magnificent trees. European chestnuts can also sometimes be attacked. China is now the leading producer of chestnuts.

DESCRIPTION

Long-lived, deciduous trees. Usually single-stemmed, unless coppiced, trees are large, handsome and strong, with angular irregular branches that form a pyramidal–oval crown. The bark is brown-grey, often with a strong, spiral pattern.

Leaves: Deciduous, large, ~15 cm long by ~5 cm wide, shiny, stiff, oval and lanceolate, with saw-toothed margins. They are dark green above and lighter below, sometimes with pubescence on the underside. Have marked parallel veining, with each vein ending in the point of a sawtooth. Have good orange-brown autumn colour.

Flowers: Monoecious, borne in late spring, so are seldom damaged by late frosts. Musky, fragrant male flowers have numerous pollen-bearing stamens that are borne along catkins, which are located on the current year's growth. These release most of their pollen in late spring. Immediately below the male flowers, on the same flowering stem, are female flowers that are small, spiky and insignificant. Each female flower usually contains 1–3 free ovaries, each of which can develop into nuts; hence, 1–3 nuts are found within each spiny husk (involucre). Often the male pollen is not dispersed until after the female flowers have finished being receptive, so planting more than one tree will improve nut production. *Pollination:* Mostly by wind, though insects

also play a role. Although partially self-fertile, will produce more nuts if trees are planted in groups. It is best to plant at least two different varieties so that there is overlap with pollen production and receptivity of female flowers. Some trees set fruits without being fertilised, and these fruits have no nuts. Well-pollinated trees produce 2–3 nuts per burr; if not cross pollinated, they only produce flattened empty shells with no or only poorly formed kernels. They hybridise freely with other chestnut species.

Fruit: Produced inside a painfully prickly, green husk, in autumn. The inner surface of the husk is white, soft and velvety. When ripe, the husk splits into 2–4 valves allowing the chestnuts to be released either on the tree or once the husks have fallen to the ground. The nut is fairly large and hard, shiny, brown, with a large, pale basal scar, and a pointed (often quite hairy in American chestnuts) tip. Inside the seedcoat are 1–3 plump brown kernels.

Yield/harvest: Seedling trees start producing fruits after 4–10 years or longer (depending on species), and the best yields are not obtained for 8–15 years; grafted trees may produce their first crops after ~3 years. A tree may produce ~35–70 kg nuts a year once mature, and sometimes considerably more: yields of >500 kg of nuts per tree have been recorded. The nuts fall to the ground in late autumn and within ~7 days of becoming ripe. Many nuts need to be extracted from their prickly husks, which can be time consuming and needs thick gloves. The nuts can be also

Food
Flavour, texture and sweetness varies from tasteless and bland to very sweet and flavoursome, depending on variety. Chestnuts are best either boiled or roasted. To prepare them, boil whole in their shells for ~30 minutes, then cut in half. The soft kernel can then be scooped out. Alternatively, they can be roasted in-shell in an oven, in an open fire or in the microwave, but you *must* pierce the shell beforehand to prevent them from exploding when they cook! To eat, remove the outer shell and inner bitter-tasting skin. Specialised hand-held chestnut peelers remove the shell and inner skin before cooking, making preparation easier. Chestnuts can then be used in soups, stuffing (particularly for turkey) and desserts, or they can be dried, ground and made into a good-quality flour for bread, biscuits, gravies, etc. Sometimes peanut-butter manufacturers add chestnut to their product. In Italy, the chestnut flour is used in confectionery and to make polenta.

Nutrition
The nuts have reasonable levels of vitamin C (~12 mg/100 g of kernel), good levels of copper, manganese and potassium, but are low in protein (~5%); however, the protein is of good quality and is easily absorbed during digestion. They also contain good levels of folate, thiamine and B6. They contain more water and much less oil (~1%) than other nuts. Can be a good food source, and can be used as a dietary staple. Contain a lot more complex carbohydrates than most other nuts. Are very low in sodium and are free of cholesterol.

Medicinal
The leaves and bark can be used as an anti-inflammatory, an astringent, to expel phlegm and as a tonic, and have often been used to treat convulsive coughs and other respiratory problems. The plant is also used in Bach flower remedies for 'extreme mental anguish', 'hopelessness' and 'despair'.

Other uses
The wood is multi-purpose and also resists rot, though tends to crack with age. The trees coppice readily and are used to produce fences and posts. The bark and leaves have a high tannin content, and have been used to tan leather. A hair shampoo can be made from the leaves and the skins of the fruits, and gives a golden gleam to the hair.

Ornamental
The trees make an attractive specimen or group planting. They can be used as shade trees and as a windbreak. They have golden autumn colour.

quickly eaten by wildlife or become mouldy if not harvested at frequent intervals. The nuts ripen over a period of time and several harvests are needed, particularly if the weather is damp. Chestnuts can be stored fresh, but because they contain more water and less oil than most nuts, they do not keep well unless they are stored at cold temperatures. When storing nuts for eating, the kernel should be dried for a few days until they develop a spongy texture, which also increases their sweetness. However, over-drying makes them hard and they lose their taste. Nuts should be stored with good ventilation and, if dried to ~50% moisture content, they can be stored for >8 weeks at ~0°C.

Roots: Trees have long taproots; therefore care is needed when transplanting.

CULTIVATION
Once established, chestnuts need very little care.

Location: Are quite wind tolerant, but grow and produce much better with shelter, particularly when young. Also like a sunny location to promote female flower production, but not too hot. They do not fruit well in subtropical climates because of a lack of winter chill. Can grow in maritime locations, though may not develop as well.

Temperature: Trees can withstand –20°C after acclimation; however, young leaves can be killed at –6°C. They are tolerant of high summer temperatures, and need temperatures of ~24–30°C to satisfactorily ripen the nuts.

Chilling: Need only a fairly short chilling time, ~450–650 hours, though if they do not receive this then flower production is poor.

Soil/water/nutrients: The best crops are produced if the tree is grown in well-drained, deep, loamy soil, with an acidic pH of ~5–6.5. They can be planted with acid-loving pines. Heavier, wet soils increase the likelihood of root-rot problems, and trees usually do not live as long. They do not like limestone, but can tolerate nutrient-poor soils. They need adequate moisture to achieve optimum growth and yields, particularly during summer and autumn, though can be quite drought tolerant once established. Trees are only moderately nutrient hungry, but will respond to applications of a complete, balanced fertiliser, with nitrogen, potassium and magnesium in particular. Apply twice: in early spring and in mid summer. Chestnuts are not as nutrient hungry as walnuts. Too much fertiliser can result in root burn. They probably have a good fungal mycorrhizal population, which reduces the need for extra nutrients.

Planting: They are large trees so need to be spaced at least ~6 m apart, and these are then thinned to a 12–16-m spacing as they mature. They do not transplant well because of their deep taproots.

Propagation: *Seed:* Collect seeds in autumn and store over winter in a moist environment at ~0°C. Seeds germinate well when planted in spring. Sow seedlings in deep pots to allow good taproot growth and plant out with care. *Grafting:* Whip-and-tongue grafting, or T-budding when the leaves are just emerging in spring, or by chip-budding. Grafting can be problematic because cut stems often bleed profusely.

Pruning: Trees are usually pruned to form a central leader shape to ensure a strong structure. Remove any crowded or crossing branches for the first few years. After this, little pruning is needed.

Pests and diseases: Possible problems with chestnut are blossom-end rot, two-spotted mite, *Verticillium* wilt, with chestnut blight (*Endothia parasitica*) being the most serious, having killed most chestnut trees in the USA. In Japan, chestnuts are highly susceptible to *Phytophthora* trunk cankers, and European chestnuts are even more susceptible to this disease. Need to avoid cold wet soils. A root-rot caused by *Phytophthora cinnamomi* may also kill trees at any age and, similarly, is more prevalent on heavier, wetter soils. Nuts can be also infected by fungal diseases, e.g. *Phomopsis, Botrytis*, and can seriously damage crops. Various wildlife are also attracted to the ripening nuts.

MAIN CHESTNUT SPECIES

American chestnut, *Castanea dentata*. The largest (~30 m) and straightest stemmed of all the chestnut species. Was once a prized timber tree in the USA before most were killed by chestnut blight, which girdles and kills trees. The nuts are usually very small, but are sweet and tasty, with easy-to-remove inner skins.

Chinese chestnut, *Castanea mollissima*. A medium-sized tree (~15 m), often multi-stemmed and wide spreading. Usually have easy-to-remove inner skins. Kernels range in size, though are often smaller than Japanese chestnuts. The nut is sweet, tasty and recommended by many. It is the most

tolerant species to chestnut blight. Trees have fairly good yields and can bear fruits in 2–4 years after planting. This is the smallest tree of the chestnut family. Will grow well with little care. Some nuts are produced on solitary trees, but more nuts are produced with cross pollination.

European chestnut (sweet chestnut, Spanish chestnut), *Castanea sativa*. A tall (~30 m), wide-spreading tree, originating from Turkey and the Black Sea region. The nuts are variable, but the best are large, sweet and easy to remove from their seedcoats. They have good yields. Somewhat susceptible to chestnut blight. Better for timber than other chestnuts.

Japanese chestnut, *Castanea crenata*. A small- to medium-sized tree (~10 m), typically multi-stemmed and wide spreading. Some varieties have very large nuts, nearly the size of small potatoes, but are starchy and astringent because of tannin. Inner skins are difficult to remove. Well adapted to wet and humid weather conditions and hot summers (~30°C). Very resistant to chestnut blight.

HYBRIDS
Chestnuts hybridise easily and many different hybrids exist, amongst which are hybrid crosses between European and Japanese species. These often have rapid growth when young and are early bearing, with nuts harvested from 4–5-year-old trees. However, their inner skin is difficult to remove. ∎

Celtis laevigata
Sugarberry (sugar hackberry, hackberry, nettle tree)
ULMACEAE
Similar species: southern hackberry or lotus berry (*C. australis*), common hackberry (*C. occidentalis*)
Relatives: elms

The name *Celtis* is Greek for 'a tree that bears sweet fruit', and *laevigata* means 'smooth', referring to the smooth leaves. There are several similar *Celtis* species that are native and common in the southeastern states of the USA. The fruits of these species were used as a food by the indigenous populations and by the early settlers. The sugarberry is now a popular tree in urban environments because of its tolerance of air pollution.

DESCRIPTION
A moderately-fast-growing, handsome, medium-sized tree, height ~16–25 m, width 20–24 m. It has a broad crown with spreading, pendulous, angular branches that become more symmetrical as the tree ages. The wood is brittle and can be broken by strong wind, snow or ice. It has grey–light brown, smooth bark with distinctive corky, 'warty' patches with smooth areas in between. Its young stems are slender, reddish-brown and angular. Can live up to ~150 years.
Leaves: Deciduous, almost triangular, long, pointed, with typical elm-like lopsided bases, with one lobe larger than the

other, and three prominent veins. They are alternate, with toothed or entire leaf margins, simple, 5–12.5 cm long, 2.5–5 cm wide. Have yellow-green autumn colour.
Flower: Very small (~0.25 cm), inconspicuous, greenish-white, produced on stalks, appearing in spring. *Pollination:* Trees are monoecious and either bisexual flowers or separate male and female flowers, but on the same tree. Are wind-pollinated, so although monoecious, probably have better fruit yields if planted in small groups.
Fruit: Fleshy, sweet, cherry like, round-oval, small (0.5–1.0 cm), orange-red drupe, turning purple-black when

Food
The fruits, though small, are sweet and can be eaten raw or used in desserts, sauces, jams or jellies, as well as making a reasonable wine.

Other uses
Its timber is not very strong and does not weather well.

Ornamental
Makes an excellent town tree as it tolerates a wide range of conditions, except for very exposed sites. Makes a good shade tree and a good street tree in urban areas. Very tough and hardy. Excellent source of food for wildlife, particularly birds.

the growing season), but not prolonged. Will even tolerate periodic saltwater flooding. Can develop chlorosis on soils with very high pH. Is fairly drought tolerant.

Propagation: *Seeds:* Germinate best with cold stratification at 5°C for 2–3 months before sowing in moist, but well-drained compost in early spring. Do not over-water seedlings. *Cuttings:* Can be propagated easily by semi-hardwood cuttings taken in summer and inserted into gritty, well-drained compost to root.

Pests and diseases: Resistant to witches-broom, which is common on related species, and to *Verticillium* wilt and Dutch elm disease. Potential problems are trunk and root rots. Lace bugs and scales can cause minor problems. Also sometimes gets galls on the leaves, which do no serious harm to the tree, but can make it look unattractive.

SIMILAR SPECIES

Common hackberry, *Celtis occidentalis*. Native to North America. A large, fast-growing tree (~20+ m tall, spread ~16 m), forming a rounded crown. Flowers and leaves are similar to the sugarberry. Drupes are usually purple-black when ripe, though sometimes orange-red. They can be eaten fresh or cooked. It only has a liitle flesh, and this can be fairly dry, but has a sweet and pleasant flavour. Can be used in desserts, sauces and preserves, but fruits are small and fiddly to harvest. The fruit and seed have been dried, ground up together and used as a flavouring. Likes a sunny location, and although it prefers better soil, like the sugarberry, it will grow on poor soils, at varied pH and is tolerant of pollution, drought, some waterlogging and compacted soil, and is fairly wind tolerant. Is very cold hardy. Does not like being transplanted. Propagation by seed, cuttings or grafted. Good grown as a shade tree. Wildlife love the berries.

Southern hackberry (lotus berry), *Celtis australis*. A native of southern Europe, north Africa and Asia minor. Has round cherry-like fruits (~1 cm) that are red to begin with, turning brown as they mature. The flesh has a sweet, pleasant, but fairly neutral taste. Can be eaten raw or cooked. ∎

ripe. The drupes have a thin skin and sweet yellowish flesh surrounding a central stone. Maturing in autumn. Good seed crops are produced most years, some individuals produce good crops every year. Berries can persist on the tree into winter if not eaten by the wildlife before.

Yield: First produces fruit at ~15 years; best bearing years are between 30–70 years. Trees often produce very good yields of fruits. Berries are best harvested when fully ripe.

Roots: Has some deep roots, but mostly relatively shallow ones. Benefits from a mulch when young to retain moisture and add nutrients. Its roots are not invasive.

CULTIVATION
Location: Prefers partial shade to full sun. Not very wind resistant. Can be grown in a sheltered location near the coast.

Temperature: Best growth at average summer temperatures of ~26°C. Frost hardy down to –29°C.

Soil: Can grow in a wide range of soil pH, 4–8, and is happy in most soil types, including heavy clay and sandy soils. Tolerates soils poor in nutrients and compacted soils. Can withstand short periods of waterlogging (i.e. ~10% of

Ceratonia siliqua
Carob (St John's bread)
FABACEAE (Leguminosae)
Relatives: licorice, inga bean, tamarind, peanut

Carob pods are known as St John's bread because they are thought to be the 'locusts' that, according to the Bible, sustained St John the Baptist in the desert. The word 'locust' was originally applied to the carob tree and only later to the insect. The tree probably originates from the Middle East and has been cultivated there since ancient times. It was used by the Greeks, who took it to Italy, and by the Arabs, who took it to Morocco and Spain. In the Mediterranean, peasants have used it as a famine food, but the pods on the trees are also used to feed livestock. Imported pods used to be regularly sold by street vendors in the Italian section of lower New York City for chewing. Today, its seeds are mainly used as a chocolate substitute. It is a very tough tree, growing in very poor, dry soils and can be planted as a soil improver and stabiliser, as well as providing an interesting crop.

DESCRIPTION

A largish tree, reaching ~15 m in ~20 years, with a trunk of ~80 cm width. They are long-lived trees.

Leaves: Evergreen, pinnate, with 6–10 opposite leaflets, oval, rounded at the apex, dark green, leathery, 2.5–6 cm long.

Flowers: Tiny, red, in short, slender racemes, borne along the branches. The tree is unusual in that flowers and pods often arise directly from the limbs and branches of trees (cauliflorous). They are borne on wood that is at least 3 years old. *Pollination:* By bees and other insects. Trees are dioecious, so need more than one tree to set fruit. It is possible to graft a male branch onto a female tree to save space in smaller gardens.

Fruit: A typical leguminous pod, light to dark brown when ripe, oblong, flattened, straight or slightly curved, with a thickened margin, 10–30 cm long, 1–2.5 cm wide. It is glossy, tough and fibrous and is filled with soft, semi-translucent, pale brown, sweet pulp, which can be scant or plentiful. Within the pulp are embedded 10–14 hard, flattened seeds, which rattle when the pod is fully ripe and dry. The unripe pod is green, moist and very astringent; the ripe pod is sweet when chewed (avoiding the seeds).

Yield/harvest: Grafted trees begin to bear fruits in their 6th year from planting, and can yield ~2 kg of pods. At 12 years, they can produce ~45 kg of pods, and productivity keeps increasing up to 25–30 years, when yields can average 90 kg. Some ancient trees in the Mediterranean region have been reported to bear 1360 kg in a season! A carob tree may remain productive for 80–100 years. The pods are easy to harvest, but should not be exposed to rain or heavy dew after they have turned brown and developed a high sugar content. Wet pods ferment quickly. They are shaken down or knocked off with a pole. They are then sun-dried for 1–2 days or gently, artificially dried until the moisture content is reduced to ~8%. They can then be crushed and the seed is separated from the pod.

Roots: Has deep, long roots that help draw nutrients from depth. They form a symbiotic relationship with nitrogen-fixing bacteria. Because of its deep taproot it is susceptible to being transplanted.

CULTIVATION

Easy to cultivate once established. It grows slowly during the first year: some growers use the plant-hormone giberellin to increase stem growth.

Location: They are susceptible to wind damage: windbreaks can protect young trees and reduce damage to flowers and young pods in older trees. They prefer a site in full sun. They are fairly tolerant of salt spray.

Temperature: Carob is slightly cold hardier than orange, though young trees can suffer frost damage. Mature trees can tolerate temperatures down to –7°C, although frost

Food

Carob is a delicious low-fat food usually known as a chocolate substitute due to its similarities to cocoa in taste and texture. The pods can be chewed as a snack (though not the seeds), or gently roasted and ground to make a brown-coloured flour. This can be added to cold or heated milk to make a beverage; mixed in with cakes, pancakes, muffins, etc. or combined with breakfast cereals and confections. A carob syrup can be made by coarsely grinding the pods and boiling them in water to give a thick, sweet liquid. The seeds contain a tragacanth-like gum (manogalactan), called Tragasol commercially, which is used as a stabiliser and thickener in many food products, both sweet and savoury, e.g. icecream, cheese, canned meats, mustard, etc. The seed residue, after gum extraction, can be made into a starch- and sugar-free flour that contains 60% protein. In Europe, the roasted seeds have been used as a coffee substitute. The pod pulp can be fermented into an alcoholic beverage.

Nutrition

Sugars in the pod are sucrose, glucose, fructose and maltose in a ratio 5:1:1:7. Sugar content may be as high as 72%. It does not contain caffeine. It is fairly high in calcium, iron, copper, potassium and manganese. It also contains good levels of riboflavin, B6 and has very good levels of dietary fibre and protein. The odour of the broken pod is faintly like cheese because of its 1.3% isobutyric acid content. *Warning:* The pods contain ~1% tannins and, in excess, it can be toxic.

Other uses

Animals love the pods, but they are fairly high in tannin, so should only be fed in moderation. They should not be fed to chickens. The gum from the seeds is used in cosmetics, pharmaceuticals, detergents, paint, ink, adhesives, photographic paper, insecticides and match heads. It is also used for bonding paper pulp and thickening silkscreen pastes and has many other applications. The heartwood is hard and close-grained and is used for turnery and for furniture. It yields a light brown textile dye.

Ornamental

The trees make a good choice for stabilising and improving poor soils in dry areas where little else will grow. They also fix nitrogen.

during flowering can reduce or prevent fruit-set. The tree does best in a Mediterranean-type climate with cool, not cold, winters, mild to warm springs, and warm to hot summers with little or no rain.

Soil/water/nutrients: Can grow well in many types of soil, from rocky hillsides to deep sand or heavy loam, but must have good drainage. It is not tolerant of acid or wet soils. Trees prefer lower rainfall and are extremely drought tolerant. However, water should be provided in very dry seasons if the tree is grown for its fruits. Trees are not at all nutrient hungry and do not need any additional fertilisers.

Planting: One-year-old seedlings can be planted into deep, well-prepared holes. Because of the long taproot, large trees cannot be successfully transplanted. A good spacing is ~9 m apart. Should include one male for every 25–30 female trees, or plant a grafted male/female tree.

Pruning: Prune to open up the tree and allow air and light to penetrate. Flowers form on wood that is at least 3 years old so space is required in the canopy. Newer wood can be safely removed without affecting yields. Remove crossing or dense branches and any damaged or diseased wood.

Propagation: *Seed:* Fresh seeds germinate quickly. Dried, hard seeds need to be scarified or chipped and then soaked in water or dilute acid until they swell (and then thoroughly rinsed), then placed in sand and kept damp for 6 weeks or more, periodically removing those that have swollen to three times their normal size. These can then be sown in moist, well-drained compost, but germination may then only be ~25%. When 30 cm tall, they can be transplanted into pots. Because they have long taproots, make sure the pots are deep and, if possible, biodegradable. The sex of plants won't be known though until they flower and progeny are variable. *Grafting*: This gives more guaranteed results and a known sex. Top grafting can be done when the plants are growing strongly. Feeding the seedling tree with nitrogen ~3 weeks prior to grafting will stimulate its growth and sap flow, and improve grafting success. Budding can also be done when the stem is at least 1 cm thick. Shield-budding can be used, or a blend of budding and grafting in spring and early summer.

Pests and diseases: Few pest and disease problems. The larvae of a midge, *Asphondylia gennadii*, causes stunting of the pods, though some cultivars are resistant to this pest. Can be subject to several scale insects.

CULTIVARS

'Amele': From Italy. Female. Pod: are light brown, straight or slightly curved, ~15 cm long, 54% sugar, good flavour. Ripens in autumn.

'Casuda': From Spain. Female. Pod: brown, mostly straight, 12 cm long, 53% sugar, fair flavour. Ripens in autumn.

'Clifford': A bisexual. Pod is light brown, slightly curved, 13 cm long, 53% sugar, fair flavour. Ripens in autumn. Tree: bears regularly and heavily.

'Santa Fe': From California. Bisexual and self-fertile. Pod: light brown, slightly curved, often twisted, ~20 cm long, 48% sugar, flavour excellent. Ripens in autumn. Tree: bears regular, good crops. Good for coastal foothills.

'Sfax': From Tunisia. Female. Pod: red-brown, straight or slightly curved, 15 cm long, 50% sugar, flavour excellent. Ripens late summer–autumn. Tree: a regular, medium–heavy bearer.

'Tantillo': From Sicily. Bisexual. Pod: dark brown, mostly straight, 14 cm long, fair flavour. Ripens in autumn. Tree: bears heavily and regularly.

'Tylliria': From Cyprus. Female. Pod: dark brown, slightly curved, 15 cm long, 49% sugar, flavour good. Ripens in summer–autumn. Adapted to coastal foothills. ■

Chenopodium foliosum (syn. *Blitum capitatum*)
Strawberry sticks (strawberry-fruited fat-hen)
CHENOPODIACEAE

The Chenopodiaceae family is large, and contains numerous species, many of which, in the past, were valued and widely used for their nutritious leaves, though are less so now. Many of these species are now more familiarly known as small, common, garden weeds, particularly in the UK and Europe, e.g. fat-hen, which grows rapidly in rich, garden soils. Another species, which is gaining in popularity because of its tasty, highly nutritious seeds, is quinoa. A further species, strawberry sticks, is similarly undergoing a revival of popularity as an easy-to-grow annual that produces brightly coloured fruits. It is probably native to the mountainous regions of south and central Europe, as well as western Asia. This plant has also become a minor weed in wasteland and gardens in many states of the USA, as well as northern Africa, but is easily controlled. It used to be widely grown as a leaf vegetable in medieval times and its seeds have been found in many areas of northern Europe; some of these have been dated back to the 11–12th centuries in the Ukraine. This species was also popularly grown in England during Victorian times as a vegetable. Apart from its edible leaves, it also produces attractive, bright red, edible berries. These annuals are easy to grow, take up little space and can be grown in cooler regions. A very similar species is *C. capitatum*, both in appearance and usage.

DESCRIPTION

An annual, growing to 30–50 cm height. Often multi-stemmed. Forms an erect or semi-sprawling plant.

Leaves: Irregularly lobed, roughly triangular in shape, with a pointed apex, ~7–10 cm long. Dark green above, paler green beneath, similar in shape to other members of this family.

Flowers: Small, ~0.4 cm wide, in clusters from the main stem, from late spring through summer. Are insignificant, almost leaf-like and are greeny-yellow in colour. Are bisexual, so only need one plant to set fruits, though more than one plant will probably increase fruit yields. *Pollination:* By wind, so benefit from being planted in groups.

Fruits: Berry-like, consisting of many drupelets in a tight cluster, resembling a loganberry, but with a bright scarlet-red colour, 1–1.5 cm long. Fruits can be juicy, though some are dry. Each drupelet contains a single, small seed. Fruits ripen from late summer to late autumn. They are borne singly or in twos from the leaf axils, directly off the main stem. Fruits lower down the stem mature first.

CULTIVATION

Easy to grow.

Location: Prefers a site in full sun: does not grow well in shade. Is moderately tolerant of salty air, but not strong winds.

Temperature: This species is not tolerant of winter frosts, but is usually grown as an annual anyway, so just ensure that seedlings are not planted out till all risk of frost has passed.

Soil/water/nutrients: Plants grow best in a fertile, loamy, garden soil that is moist during the summer, but not waterlogged. Young plants, in particular, benefit from regular moisture; however, established plants can be quite drought tolerant, though will not grow or fruit as well. They prefer soils with good amounts of organic matter added.

Pot culture: Makes a great, low-maintenance, quick-growing plant for pots or small borders. Its brightly coloured fruits are eye-catching, and are edible.

Propagation: *Seed:* Mostly, if not always, grown from seed. Sow seeds in early spring, inside in colder regions. Simply scatter the seeds in moist compost and cover them lightly. Give some warmth and keep them moist (but not wet). There should be good germination within 7–14 days. Prick out seedlings and grow on these in pots till they are a reasonable size to plant out. Seeds can also be sown outside *in situ* in warmer regions, though there is a risk they may be eaten or damaged before becoming established.

Planting: Space plants at ~30–50 cm apart. Plants that sprawl may need staking.

Pests and diseases: Has few problems. ■

uses

Food

The berries are juicy, but their flavour is disappointing, being bland and tasting of little, though some say they have a chestnut-like flavour. However, they make an attractive, eye-catching garnish or decoration on various dishes, both sweet and savoury. The leaves can be eaten, and are usually lightly boiled and eaten as greens; they have a reasonable taste. **Warning:** Some species within this family have leaves that contain fairly high amounts of saponins. However, these tend to pass through the digestive system without being digested and their properties are largely nullified by cooking, so should not be a problem.

Ornamental

Mostly grown as an ornamental for its bright, red fruits and contrasting dark green foliage, as a small filler species or an eye-catching specimen in a pot or in a border near the house.

Chrysolepis spp.

Chinquapin (giant chinquapin, bush or dwarf chinquapin, golden chinquapin, goldenleaf chestnut)

FAGACEAE

Similar species: *Castanopsis cuspidatus*

Relatives: sweet chestnut, beech nut

Chrysolepis is a genus of about 100 species of evergreen trees and shrubs, most of which are native to tropical and subtropical areas of the world, especially southeastern Asia, southern USA and India. The genus *Castanopsis*, which is native to Asia, is often listed with *Chrysolepis* as a single genus. The main difference between these two is that the nuts of *Castanopsis* need one year to mature, whereas the nuts of *Chrysolepis* need two. Many of the species are known for their timber, and for their nuts that can be eaten raw, roasted or boiled. Their flowers and fruits are similar to those of sweet chestnut, and the name 'Castanopsis' means 'resembling *Castanea*', the chestnut. These species have several growth forms and are found in a variety of habitats. The chinquapins are mostly native to the USA. *Chrysolepis chrysophylla*, the giant chinquapin, is a native of southwestern USA. The name '*chrysophylla*' means 'golden leaf', and refers to the golden-yellow scales on the underside of its leaves. Bush chinquapin (*C. sempervirens*) is a smaller species from the east and south of the USA. Other chinquapins include the Ozark chinquapin (*C. ozarkensis*), which is a small tree with long, deeply toothed leaves, and the Allegheny chinquapin (*C. pumila*), a tall shrubby tree with lightly serrated leaves. Chinquapin nuts are small, but sweet, with each kernel encased in a fairly hard shell within a prickly, round husk. They have been used as a food by indigenous tribes for many hundreds, if not thousands, of years. They are very attractive trees with evergreen leaves and young golden shoots, leaves and fruits, and are often planted ornamentally.

DESCRIPTION

Giant chinquapins (*C. chrysophylla*) grow vigorously and can develop faster than conifer seedlings when young, though their growth rate slows as they mature. Mature trees tend to have straight trunks that can be >1 m wide, and form upright, narrow crowns. They can grow as tall as >32 m, and are long-lived, living to >400 years. Young stems are yellowish. The bark on young trees is smooth and reddish or greyish-brown, becoming mottled white, furrowed and ridged in older trees. Bush chinquapins tend to have an upright form in more exposed sites and are more spreading in shaded sites. They are usually multi-stemmed, 2–6 m in height, and their trunks are smooth.

Leaves: Attractive, evergreen, simple, alternate, lanceolate (though variable), 5–15 cm long, leathery, smooth with entire margins. They are yellow-green above, and are velvety or scaly and golden beneath.

Flowers: Abundant, attractive, creamy-white, fragrant erect catkins are borne in late spring on the current year's growth. Plants are monoecious, and are partially self-fertile, though planting them in small groups will increase fruit-set and fruit quality. The abundant male flowers, 2.5–7.5 cm long, are yellow-brown in colour, fragrant and are borne in clusters of three from leaf axils. Female flowers are much smaller and are clustered at the base of the male flowers or in short separate catkins: they are purple-red in colour. They flower over a long period, from early summer–midwinter. *Pollination:* By wind, but bees also visit the fragrant flowers and may help pollination, though the pollen they collect gives honey a poor taste.

Fruits: Giant chinquapins have tight clusters of spiny, tan-coloured husks, within which are 1–3 kernels, each kernel being 1.5–2.5 cm long. The nuts of this species do not mature until autumn of their second year. Dwarf chinquapins only usually produce one nut per bur, which then opens into two halves as the husk dries out. The kernels of all species are sweet and tasty.

Yield/harvest/storage: Trees take 3–6 years to start fruiting. Vigorous giant chinquapins produce some kernels every year with a bumper (or mast) year occurring at 2- to 5-year intervals, though some specimens may only give poor yields. Yields from dwarf chinquapins can also be poor, varying from nothing up to ~1 kg per year. In addition, the husks do not naturally drop from the trees when ripe, but can remain on the tree through winter; however, the husk usually dries to release its kernels before then, but these are rapidly sought by birds, etc. Nuts are best picked from the tree in late summer–early autumn when they are ripe, but just before the husk has fully opened. The other problem is that, unfortunately, not all nuts ripen at the same time, and several pickings/gatherings are usually needed. Gathered husks that still contain nuts can be gently dried to allow them to open naturally. Another potential problem is that kernels from these species naturally germinate in autumn, and often begin to do this while still on the tree. However, kernels are fairly easy to remove from their shells.

CULTIVATION

These are tough tree species, tolerating many adverse soil conditions and needing minimum maintenance.

Location: Can be grown in sun or semi-shade, or sometimes even deeper shade.

Temperature: Hardy to frost and fairly cold winters, though prefer a warmer climate. Once acclimatised, they tolerate cold better, but can be seriously damaged by rapid drops in temperature.

Soils: Trees can grow on a wide range of soils, from dry, poor soils, serpentine soils (high in magnesium) or stony soils to deep, well-drained loams, where they do best. They prefer a pH range of somewhat acidic to neutral, and do not like alkaline conditions. They are not nutrient hungry and, indeed, often grow better in nutrient-poor soils. They are quite

uses

Food
Kernels are tasty when roasted and can be served with butter and salt. Taste somewhat like hazelnuts.

Medicinal
Historically, the roots of dwarf chinquapins have been used as an astringent, a tonic and to expel internal parasites.

Other uses
The wood is light, fairly hard, strong and is used for panelling, cabinets, furniture and turnery, but does tend to warp while it is curing.

Ornamental
The attractive, golden, evergreen leaves make it a good ornamental tree, but its adaptability also makes it good for planting for soil stabilisation and re-establishment of degraded areas.

drought tolerant once established, though grow better with regular moisture. They are not very tolerant of waterlogged soils. Dwarf chinquapins can grow in drier sites than giant chinquapins, and are often used as reclamation plants.

Planting: Space larger trees at 8–10 m apart, though can be planted closer for groupings. They need a fair amount of space. Dwarf chinquapins can be planted closer together.

Propagation: *Seed:* Stored in sealed containers at ~6°C, seeds can remain viable for ~2 years. Easy to germinate and do not need any pre-treatment. Sow seeds in moist, well-drained soil in shade, in autumn or spring. Germination takes 2–4 weeks, with ~30% germination rate. *Suckers:* These can be removed, with some root if possible, and should root and establish well. *Layering:* Layering of drooping stems in autumn is possible. *Grafting:* Can be grafted or budded.

Pruning: Giant chinquapins produce numerous, vigorous suckers and sprouts when cut or injured, so these need to be removed. Other pruning needs to be done with care so that developing nuts are not accidentally removed.

Pests and diseases: Few diseases or insect pests. Can be susceptible to heart-rot fungi. Giant chinquapin is resistant to chestnut blight, though dwarf chinquapins is not.

SIMILAR SPECIES

Castanopsis cuspidatus. A native of China and Korea, where it is also often grown as an ornamental, it forms a large tree with elegant drooping branches. It produces clusters of edible smallish nuts that can be boiled or roasted. ∎

x *Citrofortunella mitis, Citrus mitis*
Calamondin
RUTACEAE
Relatives: kumquat, orange, lemon, lime

Prized for its ornamental value more than for its fruit, the calamondin was formerly identified as *Citrus mitis,* but has now been given the hybrid name x *Citrofortunella mitis*, a hybrid of citrus and kumquat. The calamondin is believed to be native to China and is thought to have been taken in early times to Indonesia and the Philippines. It became the most important citrus-juice source in the Philippine Islands and is widely grown in India and throughout southern Asia and Malaysia.

DESCRIPTION
A tree, ranging widely in height from 2–7.5 m high, depending on climate, soil, etc. It forms an erect, slender, often quite cylindrical tree, which is frequently densely branched, with these forming close to the ground. It is slightly thorny.

Leaves: Evergreen, alternate, aromatic, broadly oval, dark green, glossy on the upper surface, yellowish-green beneath, 4–7 cm long, faintly toothed at the apex, with short, narrowly-winged petioles. Aromatic when crushed.

Flowers: Rich and sweetly fragrant, with five oval, pure-white petals, ~2.5 cm wide. The flowers are borne singly or in small clusters (2–3) from leaf axils towards the ends of stems. They have a persistent green calyx. The flower has numerous prominent stamens, with bright yellow anthers. It has a superior ovary. Flowers can be borne from spring through summer. *Pollination:* By bees and other insects. Trees are self-fertile and require no cross pollination: only need one tree to set fruit. Calamondins produce a high percentage of nucellar seedlings, which are clones of their parents. The embryo is formed from non-genetically exchanged tissue that surrounds the ovary, and the seeds produced are identical to the tree from which they came. (See p. 15 for more details.) In addition, some flowers are not pollinated, yet still go on to produce seedless fruits (parthenocarpy).

Fruit: Showy, round–oblate berries, ~4 cm diameter, with very aromatic, orange-red peel, glossy, and dotted with numerous small oil glands. The skin is tender, thin, easily removed, sweet and edible. The pulp, in 6–10 segments, is orange, very juicy, highly acid, sometimes seedless, sometimes with 1–5 small, greenish, pointed oval seeds. The fruit is somewhat intermediate between a kumquat and a tangerine: the skin peels from the flesh like a tangerine, but its edibility and appearance are more like a kumquat.

Yield/harvest: Fruits take a while to mature: 8–12 months from fruit-set to fruit maturity. A well-cared for calamondin will grow at a rate of ~30 cm a year, should produce many fruits at the age of 2 years, and can continue to bear fruits year-round in warmer locations. Fruits are best picked when fully ripe, as unripe fruits ripen poorly after they are picked. Fruits can be kept in good condition for ~14 days at ~10ºC (not in a fridge), in a humid environment.

Roots: Trees develop a very long, deep taproot, so care is needed when repotting, planting or moving them. The roots are non-invasive.

CULTIVATION
Calamondins are ornamental compact trees that look good planted near the house. They are easy to grow.

Location: They grow best in full sun, but can also grow in

Food

Fruit pieces can be served with iced tea, seafood and meats, or can be squeezed for their acidic juice, which has been used as a substitute for lime. The sliced fruits can be cooked with cranberries to make a tart sauce, or they may be preserved whole in sugar syrup, or made into sweet pickles, or into a good-quality marmalade, particularly when mixed with kumquats. Whole fruits, fried in coconut oil with various seasonings, are eaten with curry. The preserved peel is added as flavouring to other fruits that have been stewed or preserved.

Nutrition

Has good vitamin C levels and contains flavonoids in its essential oils, mostly within the skin. These can protect cells from becoming cancerous and also help fight existing cancers, by inhibiting certain enzymes that activate carcinogens. The fruit flesh is also high in these flavonoids. The fruits may also lower cholesterol levels and aid in the digestion of fatty foods.

Medicinal

The fruits, when eaten, are a cough remedy, help expel phlegm and act as a mild laxative. The distilled oil from the leaves (~1%) acts as a heart tonic. **Warning:** As with all citrus species, those who peel many fruits may experience a dermatitis rash or blisters on their hands, and sucking calamondins can cause irritation around the mouth. These symptoms can be exacerbated if juice on skin is exposed to sunlight. Sensitive individuals may have respiratory reactions to the essential oil released from the peel.

Other uses

The fruit's juice can be applied to the scalp after shampooing to eliminate itching and promote hair growth though it may also have a bleaching effect. Rubbing calamondin juice on insect bites can reduce itching and irritation. It can also be used to bleach freckles and clear up acne. The juice can bleach ink stains from fabrics. It also serves as a body deodorant.

Ornamental

Often grown as an ornamental in a similar way to other citrus species.

semi-shade. They are not very wind tolerant but reasonably tolerant of salty, maritime conditions.

Temperature: Relatively hardy for a citrus: are as cold hardy as satsumas. Trees can survive temperatures of ~–5°C, although fruits can be damaged at ~–2° C. Young trees can be killed by brief frosts, and need extra protection. Cold may be more injurious if preceded by drought and if trees are not acclimatised.

Soil/water/nutrients: Trees tolerate a wide range of soils, from clay loams to limestone, or sand. Calamondins, however, do need adequate moisture for good fruit yields and growth. Drought and wind can lead to considerable leaf damage, although, during colder periods, trees are fairly drought tolerant. The deeper the soil, the better the root system, and the greater the ability to withstand drought. Trees are moderately nutrient hungry, and a complete fertiliser with a 1:1 nitrogen to potassium ratio gives the best growth when given twice a year. Applications of micronutrients are also beneficial.

Pot culture: They make an attractive pot plant. Ensure sufficient nutrients and organic matter are mixed in with the soil. A surface mulch will help prevent the soil drying out. The plants need little maintenance and provide attractive, fragrant leaves year round, fragrant flowers and eye-catching fruits. Container growth is ideal in colder areas, where they can be moved inside in winter. Feeds of liquid nutrients are beneficial.

Planting: Space at 3–6 m apart. Keep young plants well watered and weed-free for the first few years.

Propagation: *Seed:* Can be easily grown from seeds, which are often polyembryonic, with 3–5 embryos each. They are also nucellar (see above), so can get predictable progeny. Seedlings should be established in deep, ideally biodegradable, pots to allow the taproot to develop and ensure minimal disturbance when planting. Seedlings are often more disease resistant, more vigorous and often more productive, but may take a little longer to start producing fruit. Sow washed seeds, when fresh, in early spring and, given warmth, they should germinate in ~21 days. *Cuttings:* These generally root easily. Semi-ripe cuttings can be taken in summer and inserted in well-drained compost, under mist if possible. Leaf cuttings should also readily root. Plants grown from cuttings can even fruit during their rooting period and can grow 45–60 cm tall in ~12 months. *Budding:* Selected cultivar scions can be budded onto calamondin seedlings.

Pruning: Calamondin trees form a neat shape and need very little pruning. Prune out any diseased, densely crossing or damaged wood. In general, because the tree is evergreen, much of its resources for flowering and fruiting are stored in the leaves. Heavy pruning will remove these resources and can, consequently, reduce flowering and fruiting.

Pests and diseases: In general, they have few problems, but are a prime host for Mediterranean and Caribbean fruit flies. They may also be attacked by other pests and diseases that affect lemon and lime, including the viruses crinkly leaf, exocortis, psorosis, xyloporosis and tristeza, but trees are immune to canker and scab. ■

Citrullus vulgaris, C. lanatus
Watermelons
CUCURBITACEAE

Similar species: egusi (*C. colocynthis*)

Relatives: pumpkins, melons, oyster nut

A family of plants comprising about 120 genera and 760 species, most of which are natives of Asia and the hot, dry regions of Africa, although some have New World origins. Archaeological evidence has determined that some Cucurbitaceae species were used by the peoples of Peru as long ago as 12,000 BC. They have been widely used around the world since ancient times, and can be found growing in a great variety of habitats, from tropical, to arid deserts, to temperate locations. The watermelon has been cultivated for thousands of years in the Middle East and the Far East, and was known in these regions and in southern Europe long before the Christian era. They are very popular in eastern Europe and the Middle East, and are commonly sold at roadside stalls. They are also grown around the world in many warmer climates. The plants are often grown for their juicy pulp, but are also used for their seeds, leaves, shoots, roots and flowers. In addition, the fruit will store naturally in its rind for a fairly long period.

DESCRIPTION

Watermelons are quick-growing, herbaceous annuals, with somewhat prickly, juicy stems. They have a creeping form, and rapidly sprawl across the ground. They have tendrils, which are borne from the bases of leaf stalks.

Leaves: Coarse, often lightly lobed, large (~15–25 cm length), roughly hairy, particularly beneath. Usually have five main veins.

Flowers: Pretty, yellow or pale lemon, five sepals, five petals, five stamens (variously fused together), an inferior ovary, usually with three fused carpels. Male and female flowers can be on separate plants or on the same plant, so it is better to grow more than one plant to get good fruit-set. *Pollination:* By bees and insects, but hand pollination, with a soft, small brush, can increase fruit-set. For the best fruits, flowers should be pinched out until the plants are thoroughly established.

Fruits: Everyone is familiar with these huge fruits: ~12 kg is common, and they can be up to 45 kg. Correctly termed as berries(!), they have an inferior ovary, with the remnants of the calyx visible at the apex. They are often oblong in shape (~40 cm long), otherwise rounded, with dark green–lime green-mottled stripy skin, and deep pink or yellow, extremely juicy flesh. A few cultivars have white-, orange- or apricot-coloured flesh. The rind is smooth and harder than that of other melons, and has a thick inner rind. The seeds, unlike those of other melons, are interspersed amongst the flesh, and are often larger. They are usually black or reddish when ripe, but can also be white or yellow, and are fairly easily removed when eating the flesh. They have a thin shell surrounding an oily kernel. In northwest China, the cultivation of watermelons with edible seeds is an important crop; these watermelons tend to be smaller (2.5–3.5 kg) and have a high ratio of seed to flesh. The seeds are usually roasted before eating. Seedless watermelon cultivars have also been developed, but tend to be susceptible to physiological problems.

Yield/harvest/storage: Each plant usually produces 4–6 fruits. Smaller cultivars take ~10–12 weeks to fully mature after fruit-set, and up to 14–16 weeks for larger-fruited cultivars. Fruits are produced from late spring right up until the first frost or early winter (whichever comes first). They are picked when fully coloured. The ends do not soften like those of other melons, but fruits can be tapped, and a deep, dull thump indicates ripeness, as does a shrivelling stem. They store for longer than other melon types, and are not as susceptible to fungal disease.

Roots: Melons have shallow roots, so mechanical cultivation needs to be minimal and weed growth kept to a minimum. An organic mulch helps conserve moisture and add nutrients.

CULTIVATION

Location: Watermelons naturally grow in very hot, very arid locations, and are highly valued in these areas for their refreshing, precious juice. They are not very wind tolerant, though are tolerant of fairly salty soils, so could be grown in sheltered, maritime locations.

Temperature: They need a hotter climate than other melon species to grow well. However, they are annuals, and if the seedlings are given an early start and are sited in a hot, sheltered spot, they can be grown in warm-temperate regions. Frost will kill them.

Soil/water/nutrients: Grow best in well-drained, sandy loams with extra organic matter added. Can grow at a wide pH range from 5.5–7.5. They do not grow well in very acid or poorly drained soils. Although drought tolerant, they grow best with moisture throughout summer, and respond to regular additions of nutrients during the summer, e.g. as foliar feeds with fish or seaweed extracts. Extra nitrogen is beneficial until flower formation; after which, extra phosphorous and potassium are of more use. Too much nitrogen during fruit formation can reduce the storage time of fruits.

Planting: Incorporate some well-rotted manure (or similar) before planting the seedlings, after all danger of frost has passed, in a warm, sheltered location. Space at 2.5–3 m apart: they are best planted on mounds if the soil is prone to

Food

A chilled slice of watermelon on a hot day is difficult to beat for its refreshing properties. It is full of watery juice, with almost crunchy flesh, but generally this does not have much flavour. The flesh can be diced and mixed with other fruits, it can be used in many desserts, including icecream and yoghurt, though does not cook well. It can also accompany savoury foods, such as cheese or ham. Fruit can be hung from a support, in warmth, with a hole cut at the top where sugar (and rum if you like) is inserted. A few days later, a small hole is also cut at the base for the resulting alcoholic liquid to flow out from. The inner rind of the melons can be cooked like a vegetable and served with butter and pepper, or can be added to jams and pickles. The seeds can be eaten raw or are often roasted and salted. To aid seedcoat removal, leave the seeds to ferment in their own juice for a couple of days before processing. The kernels can also be added to soups, stews, bread and cakes.

Nutrition

Watermelons have fairly good levels of vitamin C, 10 mg/100 g of flesh, and vitamin A. They also contain some lycopene, as well as a high proportion of water. The fruits contain good pectin levels, and can be added, with other fruits, to jam, to help them set. Seeds contain 20–45% oils, ~35% protein. The seed oil is of good quality and can be used in cooking and as a salad dressing.

Medicinal

In Egypt, the fruits are used to treat fevers and as a diuretic. The seeds have been used to treat urinary infections and may have diuretic properties, and have been used as a tonic, to expel internal parasites and may decrease blood pressure.

waterlogging. A mulch of black polythene also makes the soil warmer and speeds up their growth.

Pruning: Watermelon shoots are not pinched out like those of other melon types, and plants are allowed to sprawl on the ground because of the weight of their fruits.

Propagation: *Seed:* Readily and easily grown from seed: this is the main method of propagation. They are sown at ~1.25 cm depth, and lengthways. They need warmth and moisture to germinate, and in cooler regions they are best sown in a glasshouse or similar. They should germinate in ~6–14 days. Prick out and grow on seedlings in pots before planting out when they have about five main leaves. Seeds collected in autumn should be washed free of pulp and stored in a cool, dry place until spring. Be careful that stored seeds do not go mouldy. Pick the largest seeds from the healthiest plants to save for next year's crop. Soaking stored seeds (~24 hours) before sowing should improve germination rate and time.

Pests and diseases: Plants are susceptible to powdery mildew. Growing plants in drier conditions and not too close together can reduce this risk. Applications of foliar fish extract is said to help prevent mildew. Plants can also develop various viral diseases: the removal of weeds and non-crowding of plants reduces this risk. In addition, many insects are vectors of viruses, so try to minimise their numbers around plants (although this is not always easily done!). Chickens can be a useful ally in clearing up insect pests, once the plants are established. Cucumber beetles can be a serious pest in some areas.

CULTIVARS

Cultivars will readily cross fertilise, within species, to form plants that can be quite different from their parents. There are many commercial cultivars.

SIMILAR SPECIES

Egusi, *Citrullus colocynthis*. A relative of watermelon, egusi is a native of tropical Africa and is highly drought tolerant. Productivity is greater during dry, sunny periods, and is reduced during wet weather and high humidity. It is suitable for production in marginal arid areas. The fruits are very bitter, but the seeds can be roasted and eaten. They are rich in oils. ■

Citrus spp.
Australian native citrus species
RUTACEAE

Australian finger lime (*Citrus australasica*), Australian round lime (*C. australis*), Russell River lime (*C. inodora*), Mount White lime (*C. garrowayi*), Australian desert lime (*C. glauca*)

Relatives: orange, lemon, lime, grapefruit, kumquat

Aborigines and then early Australian colonists have used these fruits as a food, with the latter making refreshing drinks and good-quality marmalades. There has been recent increased interest and research in investigating

the potential of these six indigenous citrus fruiting species of Australia. They were previously classified into two other genera, *Eremocitrus* and *Microcitrus,* but are now included in the same genus as lemons, oranges, etc., and are able to hybridise with these fruits. Indeed, trials by CSIRO have been and are under way to graft these indigenous species onto more traditional citrus species, as well as viceversa. These native Australian species are often very drought tolerant, salt tolerant and are not as susceptible to the same pest and disease problems as commercial citrus species. They are now being cultivated to a limited extent, as well as their fruits being harvested from the wild. The fruits are added to preserves, sauces, etc., and are in demand in many restaurants that specialise in more unusual dishes and bush foods. The fruits usually have dryish flesh and are not as juicy as many other citrus, but they do have a strong, sharp, tangy flavour. More commercial plantings are being developed to ensure supply and quality, also to prevent wild fruits being over-harvested. These species can be propagated from seed or cuttings.

DESCRIPTION

Australian finger lime, *Citrus australasica* **(syn.** *Microcitrus australasica***).** One of the best known Australian citrus species, its growth and usage is becoming more widely popular. It is a very slow-growing shrub or tree from the rainforests of southern Queensland and northern New South Wales. It is now, unfortunately, becoming rare in the wild. Grows to ~3–5 m tall (sometimes taller) and has sharp 2-cm-long spines.

Leaves: Sparse, ovate, ~3 cm long.

Flowers: It can take many years (5–17 years) before it starts to flower and fruit, though may do sooner if placed under stress or if grafted onto a more vigorous rootstock. Flowers are creamy-white, fragrant, and are produced singly from leaf axils in spring and summer, or at other times in warmer climates.

Fruit: It produces an unusually shaped cylindrical, finger-shaped fruit (berries), up to 10 cm long, with a thin, green-yellow skin. However, some varieties can have skin colours that range from crimson, blood red, purple, black, to yellow and green. They are borne on the previous season's growth. The flesh is divided into 5–7 segments, and is yellow-green on maturity. It has unusual, individual compressed vesicles that burst open to release their juice when the skin is cut. The flesh is pleasant, but very acid, and often has a lingering turpentine-like aftertaste. Individual plants and their fruits vary considerably, with some producing good-quality fruits for much of the year, though yields tend to be fairly small: ~0.8 kg per tree. Fruit vary in weight from 7–40 g.

CULTIVATION

Location: Can be grown in sun or semi-shade.

Temperature: Needs a warm, frost-free climate.

Soil: Can grow in a range of soil types, but prefers a moist, though well-drained, soil.

Propagation: *Seed:* Can be grown from seed, but takes a long time to produce fruit. Germination is erratic, slow, and seedlings can be slow to establish. Often doesn't bear true to type. *Cuttings*: Slow to root (up to 6 months with warmth and moisture) and may only give ~50% take. *Grafting:* Shortens the time to fruiting and trees produce considerably

more fruit for more of the year. Budding can be done, but is tricky due to the small size of buds. Grafted or budded trees may have increased vigour and greater disease resistance.

CULTIVARS

CSIRO have developed a number of cultivars, amongst which are the following:

'Australian Sunrise lime': A hybrid between *C. australasica* and calamondin (itself a hybrid between mandarin and kumquat). It forms an upright shrub/small tree, 2–3 m tall, 1.5–2.5 m wide. The oval-shaped leaves are dark, glossy-green, ~4 cm long, 2.5 cm wide. Short spines are borne from the leaf axils. Its flowers are creamy-white and are borne in spring–early summer. Its pear-shaped fruits, 3–4.5 cm long, ripen in winter to a golden colour. Second crops sometimes occur, and these fruits often have a greener colour. It has small, plump seeds. The juice has a refreshing acid–sweet, clean taste and a light 'floral' aroma. The fruit may be eaten whole like a kumquat, with the skin having a sweeter taste.

'Rainforest Pearl': Has ornamental qualities and an open form. Trees are 4–6 m tall, thorny and fairly slow growing. The fruits have pink flesh and are harvested in late summer–autumn.

'Australian Blood lime': A hybrid between *C. australasica*

Food

Used in chutneys, jams, marmalades, savoury sauces and refreshing drinks. Becoming a popular fruit for culinary use. The bursting juice vesicles make an attractive garnish. Also used in salad dressings, beverages, desserts, jellies and pastries. Fruit can be frozen for later use without any deterioration.

Nutrition

Contains good levels of vitamin C: ~80 mg/100 g of flesh.

var. *sanguinea* and Rangpur lime (*Citrus* x *limonia*), or mandarin. The tree forms a dense, upright shrub/small tree, 2–3 m tall, ~2 m wide. It often forms long, sweeping branches. Its oval leaves are ~3 cm long, dark, glossy green, with reddish-bronze new growth. They have slightly serrated margins. Short, stiff, slender spines occur in the leaf axils, and can make harvesting painful. Flowers are borne on last season's growth, often within the canopy. These ornamental trees produce fruits in winter, which are oval and 3–5 cm long. Their most striking feature is their colour, which can be a rich blood-red or gold with red flecking. The flesh is often tinged red, with depth of colour dependent on climate. It does not have the individual pulp vesicles like the finger lime. It has small, plump seeds. The juice has a sharp, crisp, clean flavour. Pruning may make the fruit more accessible. Fruits ripen in winter and can remain 'stored' on the tree until spring. They may be susceptible to rots, and often do not store well once harvested. Fruits are used in cordials, preserves, marmalades, sauces, etc.

OTHER SPECIES

Australian round lime (dooja, native lime, gympie lime), *Citrus australis* (syn. *Microcitrus australis*). A prickly shrub or tall, upright tree, ~5 m tall (though sometimes much taller, up to 18 m), found naturally on drier rainforest margins or in the open in southeastern Queensland. It tends to form a more compact, multi-stemmed shape when growing in the open. Is the most vigorous of the native citrus species. Can grow in full sun or shade. Responds to applications of nutrients. Leaves are elliptical, dark green, ~5 cm long, with young leaves being much smaller. Flowers are creamy-white, fragrant, ~2 cm diameter, and are borne in spring. It produces round, lime-like fruit, ~6 cm diameter, with a thick (~0.7 cm), rough, green–lemon skin and pale green flesh, but does not have juicy pulp vesicles. The flesh can be eaten when still green, though it ripens to a more lemon colour. It has an acidic flavour, and is used in cordials, sauces, marmalades and as a lime flavouring. The thick skin could also be potentially used for candied peel. There is also a hybrid between *C. australasica* and *C. australis*, known as the 'Sydney hybrid', which has more vigorous growth than any other known citrus species. It is extremely drought tolerant and much tougher than commercial citrus species.

Russell River lime (large-leaf Australian wild lime), *Citrus inodora* (syn. *Microcitrus inodora*). Now a rare tree in the wild, this is native to the rainforest areas of northern Queensland, and grows best with high rainfall. It forms a shrub or small tree, ~4 m tall, with large, shiny leaves. It also has pairs of small spines from the leaf axils, unlike other similar species. Its flowers are creamy-white and do not have a perfume, hence its name. The fruits are lemon-shaped, ~6.5 cm long, and greeny-yellow when ripe. These are not sold commercially. A further species, Maiden's Australian wild lime (*C. maideniana*, syn. *Microcitrus maideniana*), is very similar in appearance and is found in the same region.

Mount White lime, *Citrus garrowayi* (syn. *Microcitrus garrowayi*). This is native to, but now uncommon in, the rainforest regions of northern Queensland. It generally forms a small shrubby plant, though some individuals grow to 15 m. It is similar to the finger lime, but has small, thick, broader leaves. The flowers are borne singly. Its fruits are cylindrical and finger shaped, and are similar to those of *C. australasica*, though shorter and thicker, with a pale lemon skin, light green pulp and fewer pulpy vesicles. The skin is thick and contains numerous essential-oil glands. Borne through the winter in northern Australia, the fruits are not sold commercially, but are used in the same way as commercial limes.

Australian desert lime (desert lemon, native kumquat, limebush), *Citrus glauca* (syn. *Eremocitrus glauca*). Native to Queensland and New South Wales, and has some amazingly tough and hardy characteristics, making it a potentially very useful species as a rootstock. In addition, this species has been used as a scion on commercial citrus species to gain a faster growth rate. It can tolerate extreme drought, much more than any other citrus species. It manages this by developing a large, extensive root system before making shoot growth. In addition, under extreme drought, the leaves can be shed and then the green, leafless twigs carry on photosynthesis. This species also tolerates high temperatures (up to 45°C), but also extreme cold (–24°C or lower) when dormant. It also has roots that can tolerate high salt concentrations. The period from fruit-set to fruit maturity is only ~8–10 weeks, making it the citrus species with the shortest fruiting season. It is thought that the desert lime may have evolved this toughness as it slowly moved westward across Australia over a long period of time. Trees vary from being short shrubs, 2–3 m tall, which often form thickets, to tall upright trees, up to 12 m tall. Generally, they are very slow growing. They tend to have numerous spines and few leaves, and the leaves are thick and blue-green in colour. The trees sucker freely if disturbed, and propagation by removal and establishment of these is easy. The fruits are small, rounded, ~1.5–3 cm diameter, thin-skinned, yellow-green and lime-shaped. The skin contains numerous, large essential-oil glands. The flesh is juicy, acidic and often seedless. They are used whole or sliced, and can be frozen or made into marmalades, sauces, dressings and seasonings. Trees tend to flower in spring and fruit mature in summer, though often have poor yields.

Cultivars: CSIRO have developed a hybrid from this species called the 'Australian outback lime', which has larger, better-flavoured fruit, high yields, no thorns, and fruits that ripen at the same time. It forms an open, upright shrub or small tree, 2–4 m tall, 1.5–2 m wide. The leaves are ~8 cm long, ~1.5 cm wide, grey-green, with slightly serrated edges and rounded ends. Mature trees have no thorns, though young trees may have some. Flowers are small, white, and are borne on last season's growth, towards the outside of the canopy. Fruits are rounded, ~2 cm diameter, with a thin skin that ripens to greeny-yellow in early summer. The fruits can be eaten whole, though are often dry and can also be oily, but have a tangy, refreshing flavour. ■

Citrus spp.
Grapefruit
RUTACEAE

Common grapefruit (*Citrus* x *paradisi*), pummelo (*Citrus maxima*), wheeney (*Citrus maxima* x *C. reticulata*)

Grapefruit is a general name for several hybrids that have bitter-tasting flesh and are larger in size than oranges.

Common grapefruit (smaller shaddock, toronja), *Citrus* x *paradisi*.
C. paradisi is the main species cultivated as grapefruit. It is a relatively new citrus species, and is probably a natural hybrid between pummelo and orange, hence its botanical name. It is sometimes confused with the pummelo. This grapefruit is probably a native of the West Indies and was originally known as smaller shaddock or as the 'forbidden fruit'. When it reached Europe, it became known as grapefruit, which is strange because it does not look or taste like a grape. Then American horticulturists wanted to change the name to pomelo, but this was never widely accepted (being too similar to pummelo) and so it retained its name of grapefruit. It is widely cultivated in California, Florida, Mexico, Israel, Argentina, Brazil, Morocco, India and Cuba, and is known and eaten around the world, often traditionally as a breakfast fruit, though it has many other food and medicinal uses.

DESCRIPTION

A medium-sized tree, to 4.5–6 m, or sometimes larger. It forms a rounded crown with spreading branches. The trunks of older trees can become massive. It has thin, angular stems that bear short, supple thorns.

Leaves: Evergreen, glossy, waxy, oval, with pointed tips, 7–15 cm long, 4–7 cm wide. They are dark green above, lighter beneath, with tiny teeth on the margins. They are covered with many tiny oil glands. The leaf stalk is flattened.

Flowers: Creamy-white, slightly fragrant, ~5 cm diameter, borne singly or in clusters (6–20) from leaf axils. They are four-petalled, monoecious and are usually bisexual (i.e. both male and female structures within the same flower). Flowers have numerous prominent stamens with bright yellow anthers. It has a superior ovary, and the fruit is classified as a true berry. Flowers can be borne from spring through summer. *Pollination:* Pollinated by bees and other insects. They are self-fertile and have good fruit-set, so only need a single tree to set fruit. As well as a few ordinarily pollinated seeds, which give variable offspring, this species mostly produces nucellar seeds, where the seedlings produced are genetically identical to the parent. The embryo has been pollinated but there has been no genetic exchange and so is a 'clone' of the tree from which it came (see p. 15). In addition, some flowers are not pollinated, yet go on to produce fruits that are seedless (parthenocarpy).

Fruit: Nearly round–globose, 10–15 cm. Some cultivars develop huge fruits. It has a pale yellow, waxy, smooth peel (~1 cm thick) that contains numerous aromatic oil glands. The inner layer of the peel is white, spongy and has no oil glands. The pulp (endocarp) is pale yellow, and consists of loosely packed, membranous juice sacs enclosed in 11–14 wedge-shaped compartments. The pulp is very juicy, acid or sweet-acid when fully ripe. Some fruits are almost seedless, whereas others may have numerous whitish, elliptical seeds, ~1 cm in length. There can be several fruits in a cluster.

CULTIVATION

Location: Trees grow best in full sun. They are not very tolerant of strong winds or of salt spray.

Temperature: Grapefruit need a warmer climate than many citrus species, and need a subtropical climate, unless given extra winter protection. The fruits are more acidic in cooler areas. Trees will only tolerate very light frosts.

Chilling: Citrus trees need no winter chilling to produce flowers and fruits.

Soil/water/nutrients: Grapefruits can grow in a range of soil types, but prefer a deep, fertile lighter soil, though can grow in clays. Can grow in somewhat acid to fairly alkaline soils. Much of the tree's tolerance to varying soil types and conditions is due to the species of the rootstock. Trees are poorly tolerant of saline soils. In wetter regions, the peel is thinner; in drier regions, the peel is thicker and the pulp is less juicy. Trees need less water in autumn to avoid the production of tender new leaves that might be damaged in winter, but need adequate moisture in spring. The deeper the soil, the better the root system and the greater the ability to withstand drought. Nutritionally, trees need regular additions of a complete fertiliser containing, in particular, phosphorous, potassium, sulphur and calcium. Too much nitrogen results in fruits with a coarser texture and less juice. Because they are evergreen and form fruit during the winter months, two or three applications of a citrus-type fertiliser throughout the year are beneficial.

Yield/harvest/storage: Commonly, although many flowers are formed, only a few go on to produce fruit. Fruits take ~6–8 months to mature after fruit-set. A healthy tree can produce ~100 fruits a season. Grafted trees begin bearing in 2–3 years; seedlings can take 3–5 years. Pick when fully coloured: grapefruits do not ripen well if picked too early. The fruits can be left on the tree for ~3 months after they first ripen to 'store' for later use. However, leaving fruits on the tree very late can result in lesser yields the following year, although picking some of the largest fruits before can partially counteract this effect. When picked, they will store for ~3 months at ~10° C, and up to 5 months at ~3°C. As they age, they tend to lose moisture and become dry.

Roots: Grapefruits have some surface roots, but most are deeper, so care is needed when transplanting that roots are not damaged. Their deep roots make them more susceptible to waterlogging.

Pot culture: They make an attractive pot plant. Ensure they have sufficient nutrients and organic matter mixed in with the soil. A surface mulch will help prevent the soil drying out. Grapefruit plants need little maintenance, and provide evergreen leaves year round, as well as fruits. Container culture is ideal for colder areas, where they can be moved inside in winter. Feeds of liquid nutrients are beneficial.

Planting: Space at 6–8 m apart. Keep young plants well watered and weed free for the first few years.

Propagation: *Seed:* There are benefits and disadvantages of growing from seed. Grapefruits form mostly nucellar seeds, which are often polyembryonic, and seedlings will be clones of the parent and, therefore, the progeny are predictable. Seedlings are also often more disease resistant, more vigorous and often more productive, but take longer to start producing fruit (~3–5 years). Sow seeds fresh in early spring and, given warmth, they should germinate in

~21 days. *Cuttings:* Take semi-ripe cuttings in summer and insert in well-drained compost to root. *Grafting:* The main method is by budding onto 1- or 2-year-old seedlings of the same or a related species. Often shield-budding is used. The main rootstocks used are sweet orange, 'Swingle Citrumelo' (resistant to root-rot and citrus nematode, and has heavy crops), 'Troyer' citrange and sour orange.

Pruning: Grapefruit trees form a neat shape and need very little pruning. It is advisable to remove suckers that sometimes form from the base of the tree. Prune out any diseased or damaged wood. In general, because the tree is evergreen, much of the tree's resources for flowering and fruiting are stored in its leaves. Heavy pruning will remove these resources and can, consequently, reduce flowering and fruiting.

Pests and diseases: Grapefruits may be affected by fruit flies, citrus rust mites, several scale insects, mealybugs, whitefly, citrus blackfly and aphids. Grapefruits can be attacked by citrus canker and a number of viral diseases, which are often transmitted via grafting or pruning tools.

CULTIVARS
'Duncan': Fruit: round–globose, large, 9–12.5 cm diameter. Peel: light yellow–whitish, with large oil glands, medium-thick, highly aromatic. Pulp: Very juicy, of good flavour. Seeds: medium–large, numerous (30–50). Early to mid season. Tree: very cold hardy.

uses

Food
Has long been an item on diet menus. It is traditionally often eaten for breakfast, cut in half and sprinkled with sugar, honey or cinnamon. The fruit sections are often used in fruit salads and various desserts, often to balance the sweetness of the other ingredients. They can be added to various preserves, including marmalade, or made into jelly, or a juice. They can be lightly grilled and served as a savoury with bacon, fish or vegetables. Try grapefruit broiled with maple syrup and cinnamon. It can make a good-quality vinegar or even a wine. The peel can be candied, and the oil from its skin is used commercially as a flavouring. The seed oil, mostly unsaturated, has a dark colour, but is very bitter.

Nutrition
The pulp is a good source of vitamin C: 34–40 mg/100 g of pulp, and of potassium. The fruits have good levels of pectin. The outer peel oil contains nookatone, which is used as a flavour enhancer in fruit juices. Naringin is extracted from the inner peel and is used as a bitter in various foods. Pink and red varieties are high in vitamin A.

Medicinal
Grapefruits contain some unusual flavonoids, e.g. naringin, which may reduce the risk of cancerous tumours. Much of the vitamin A content of pink grapefruits occurs as lycopene and beta-carotene. Lycopene has been shown to reduce prostate and mammary cancer risk. The flowers are taken to reduce insomnia, for digestive problems and as a cardiac tonic. The pulp has been used to treat various

urinary disorders. Leaf extracts have some antibiotic activity. The oil has many medicinal properties, and acts as an antibacterial, antidepressant, antiseptic, antitoxic, aperitif, astringent, a blood cleanser, disinfectant, diuretic, stimulant, general nerve tonic and aids digestion. It is said to stimulate fat digestion and act as a liver tonic. The seeds are widely used medicinally. They are a good source of folate, iron and calcium, and contain flavonoids. They are known for their antibacterial and antifungal properties and may be able to kill many pathogenic species, and have been used as an antibiotic, antifungal, anti-protozoan, antiviral, antiseptic and a disinfectant. The main active compounds are hesperidin, apigenin and campherol. **Warning:** This grapefruit (and possibly other types) have recently been found to have potentially dangerous interactions with certain medications. If grapefruit is mixed with benzodiazepines, caffeine, calcium antagonists, cisapride, clomipramine, cyclosporin, ethinyloestadiol, HMG CoA reductase inhibitors, non-sedating anti-histamines, perhexiline, quinidine or tacrolimus it can result in increasing the activity of these drugs several fold. If you are taking these medications, it may be best to avoid eating grapefruit. However, the positive aspect is that further trials may prove that people can take less of these pharmaceutical drugs to get the same effect, if they are taken with grapefruit.

Other uses
The sapwood is pale yellow and the heartwood is tan coloured: it is hard, fine-grained and is used for various woodworking projects.

'Marsh' ('Marsh Seedless'): Fruit: round–globose, medium sized, 9–12 cm diameter. Peel: light yellow, smooth, mildly aromatic. Flesh: Extremely juicy and rich in flavour. Seeds absent or very few, medium-sized. Medium–late season; fruits hold well on the tree. Keep tree well-watered after harvesting.

'Oroblanco': A triploid form, a grapefruit x pummelo cross. Peel: pale and thick. Pulp: Has a larger hollow in the centre; easily sectioned and peeled, tender, juicy, non-bitter, seedless. Early season. Tree: vigorous, large, hardy down to –2°C. Has medium–heavy crops, can tend to alternate bearing.

'Star Ruby': An orange–pummelo hybrid, but can be grown in cooler climates. Fruit has a low seed number. Fruit: medium–large. Peel: Yellow with a red blush; flesh is richly red, juicy, smooth and firm.

'Thompson': Pink-fleshed, seedless juicy fruits. Fruit: round–globose, medium sized, 7–10 cm diameter. Peel: light yellow, smooth, faintly aromatic.

'White Marsh': Common in the USA. Can be stored on the tree, with fruit becoming sweeter. Fruit are large, only a few seeds.

SIMILAR SPECIES

Pummelo (pamplemousse, shaddock), *Citrus maxima* (syn. *C. grandis*). Thought to originate from Southeast Asia. By 300 BC, *C. maxima* was being grown commercially in China. It is important in Chinese medicine and trees are also grown for their beauty and fragrance. From China, its cultivation spread to India, North Africa and Spain. It is named after Captain Shaddock, who first took the plant to Barbados. Varieties differ in their fruit sweetness, size, shape, colour, seediness, and amount and kinds of essential oils. It forms a large, ornamental tree with a rounded crown, fuzzy twigs when young and large oval leaves. Its flowers are scented and white, and it has very large, globose fruits, which are the largest of any citrus. It has a fairly thick skin. Inside, it is divided into 11–14 sections, within which the pale yellow or pink flesh is fairly coarse, with large juice sacs. Seedlings often flower when only 1 year old, but then do not again until several years later; grafted plants start to fruit after 3–4 years. May well be able to tolerate brackish water.

Wheeney (gold fruit), *Citrus maxima* x C. reticulata. Often called the New Zealand grapefruit, where it is widely cultivated. It is a cross between pummelo and probably mandarin, or between orange, grapefruit and mandarin, depending on the literature source. The fruits are slightly bitter in flavour, and can withstand colder temperatures than pummelo or *C. paradisi*.

Description: Height: 4.5–6 m, or >12 m with age. Its cold tolerance is equivalent to the sweet orange. It has a round, dense crown, and has vigorous growth. The buds are triangular and hairless. The young stems bear short, supple thorns. *Leaves:* Larger than the orange, smaller than the pummelo, oval and not pointed, 7–15 cm long. Can be crinkled, which is not a disease problem, but natural. *Fruits:* Larger than orange, but smaller than most

pummelos. Round–globose, 10–15 cm wide, smooth, pale lemon, sometimes blushed pink, aromatic. Thick-skinned and juicy, ripen during spring–summer. Its centre may be solid or semi-hollow. The flesh is pale yellow–pink–deep red, in 11–14 segments, with somewhat bitter walls, although the pulp is juicy, and is acid to sweet-acid when fully ripe. Many segments can be seedless. Most seeds are nucellar. Fruits are more coloured, sweeter and more aromatic in warmer, humid areas.

Cultivation: Can survive –4°C for brief periods. Is hardy, vigorous, but tends to bear fruits biennially. Prefers a semi-tropical or warm temperate climate. Cooler weather results in a longer period between flowering and fruit maturity. Humid weather gives thinner skinned, juicier fruits. *Soil:* See notes above.

Cultivars: 'Cutlers Red': A deep red skin. Good bearer. Highly ornamental. Flesh is sweet–sharp. Harvested in late winter, though fruits can be 'stored' on the tree till spring. 'Golden special': Important cultivar in New Zealand. A good cropper. Ripens in spring, but can be 'stored' on the tree till summer. Is sweeter when grown in full sun. Tree is vigorous, large. Yellow fruit, medium-large with tangy flesh. Free of seeds if grown alone, though is often seedy if grown near other grapefruits. Good for breakfasts, drinks and marmalade. 'Melogold': A grapefruit x pummelo cross that has more pummelo characteristics. Fruit are large and have a distinctive taste with a high sugar content: less acidic than other grapefruits. Peel is thick. ■

Below: Citrus paradisi.

Citrus spp.
Lemon
RUTACEAE

Common lemon (probably a hybrid of *C. limon*, Indian lime and pummelo)

Similar species: Volkamer lemon (*C. volkameriana*), rough lemon (*C. jambhiri*), Rangpur lime (*C. limonia*), I chang (*C. ichangensis*)

Relatives: lime, orange, grapefruit, mandarin

There are many species/cultivars of lemons, though all are actually hybrids between different citrus species: there is no one 'wild' original lemon species. Often the parentage of these hybrids is not fully known. The common lemon was first cultivated in Pakistan and India. The 'Meyer' lemon, another popular hybrid, is an orange or mandarin crossed with a lemon hybrid, and comes from China. There are many other hybrid lemons, including the rough lemon (*C. jambhiri*) and the sweet lemon (*C. limetta*). Initially discovered in northern India, it was then taken to Persia, and then to the regions between the Tigris and Euphrates rivers. Although lemons were appreciated in Rome at the time of the Roman Empire, their cultivation did not spread to the rest of Italy. It was the Arabs, at the beginning of the 8th century, who took lemons to northern Africa and to Sicily (where many lemons are still produced). They only reached France and Spain by Medieval times. Columbus then took them to the Americas, and it was during these long voyages that their curative properties were discovered, for dealing with one of the most easily prevented diseases, scurvy. They became commonly cultivated in California by the mid 1700s. They are now grown throughout the world and are highly valued for their juice, which is used widely in many sweet and savoury dishes, as well as medicinally, cosmetically and within many other products.

DESCRIPTION FOR THE COMMON LEMON

The tree reaches 3–6 m in height, and usually has sharp thorns on its stems. It often forms a dense, rounded crown of evergreen leaves.

Leaves: Evergreen, alternate, reddish when young, become dark green above, light green below; are oblong–elliptical, with pointed tips, 6–11 cm long, finely toothed, with slender wings on the leaf stalks. Are often citrus-fragrant when crushed.

Flowers: Fragrant, may be solitary or in small clusters, from leaf axils. Flower buds are reddish. Flowers are monoecious and bisexual (i.e. usually both male and female). The flower has five concave, pointed sepals that form a green calyx, and five white petals. There are numerous (20–40) prominent stamens with bright yellow anthers. It has a superior ovary. Flowers are often borne year round, but mainly in spring through summer. *Pollination:* Lemons are pollinated by bees and other insects. They are self-fertile and have good fruit-set, so only need a single tree to get fruit. However, as well as ordinarily pollinated seed, which gives variable offspring, some seeds can be nucellar. These produce seedlings that are genetically identical to the parent because there has been no genetic exchange to form the embryo (see p. xx). In addition, depending on the species, some flowers are not pollinated, yet still go on to produce seedless fruits (parthenocarpy).

Fruit: Oval, with a nipple-like protuberance at the apex; 7–12 cm long. The peel (epicarp) is usually light yellow (though some lemons are variegated), wonderfully aromatic when fresh, dotted with oil glands; 0.6–1 cm thick. The inner rind (mesocarp) is white, spongy, bitter and non-aromatic. The pulp (endocarp) is pale yellow, and consists of tightly packed membranous juice sacs enclosed in 8–10 wedge-shaped compartments, which are not readily separated. They are juicy and acid. Some fruits are seedless (parthenocarpy), most have a few oval, white seeds.

Yield/harvest/storage: Yields vary considerably between cultivars and with environmental factors. When mature, lemon trees can yield just a few dozen lemons up to >2000 fruits a year. A 9-year-old tree in India is reported to have produced a total of 3173 fruits in one year. Grafted trees begin bearing in 2–3 years; seedlings trees may take 3–5 years to fruit. Fruits can be picked fully ripe, or before, and can be kept indoors to ripen slowly. They can be harvested almost year round, depending on cultivar, and there is usually at least one ripe lemon on the tree to pick at any time. *Storage:* The fruits can be left on the tree for some time after they ripen to 'store' for later use. Green fruits can be stored in the cool for ~4 months or more. Ripe lemons can be kept for a few weeks in a fridge.

Roots: Lemons have some surface roots, but most are deeper, so care is needed when transplanting that the roots are not damaged. The deep roots make them more susceptible to waterlogging.

CULTIVATION

Forms a compact tree that is ornamental and looks good planted near the house. They are fairly easy to grow.

Location: They grow best in full sun, but can also grow in semi-shade. Grow better in maritime locations than oranges.

Are not very wind tolerant, and leaves are easily blown off and fruit damaged in high winds. Can be grown in both dry and humid areas.

Temperature: More sensitive to cold than oranges and less able to recover from cold injury. Leaves can be killed at ~–5°C, and temperatures below ~–6.5°C can kill wood, unless the tree is well acclimatised. Flowers and young fruits can be killed at ~–1.5ºC. However, summers do not need to be as hot as for oranges, to fully ripen the fruit. They are best grown in warm-temperate to subtropical climates, though can be grown in cooler temperate regions if given winter warmth or protection.

Chilling: Citrus trees need no winter chilling to produce flowers and fruits.

Soil/water/nutrients: Trees prefer a fertile, well-drained loam, but can grow in may other soil types. They can grow in quite nutrient-poor soils, in sandy soil and in clay soils. They cannot tolerate extended waterlogging, but seem to survive periodically wet soils, though may not grow very well. They prefer a pH range of 5.5–6.5, and do not grow well in alkaline soils. They need moisture during dry periods, and are not very drought tolerant, although too much moisture can increase disease. Need less moisture in winter. Nutritionally, trees need regular additions (~3 times a year) of a complete citrus fertiliser containing, in particular, nitrogen, phosphorous, potassium, sulphur and calcium.

Pot culture: They make an attractive pot plant. Ensure there are sufficient nutrients and organic matter mixed in with the soil. A surface mulch will help prevent the soil drying out. The plants need little maintenance, and provide shiny, fragrant leaves year round, attractive flowers and useful fruits. Container growth is ideal in colder areas, where they can be moved inside in winter. Feeds of liquid nutrients are beneficial.

Planting: Space plants at 5–8 m apart. Keep young trees watered and free of weeds. They appreciate an organic mulch to retain moisture, suppress weed growth and add nutrients.

Propagation: *Seed:* The rough lemon is widely grown from seed. There are benefits and disadvantages of growing from seed. Cross pollinated seeds will give variable progeny; however, nucellar seeds, produced by some lemon types, are often polyembryonic and most offspring are not formed by a genetic mixing. They are, therefore, clones of their parent. Seedlings are often more disease resistant, more vigorous and often more productive, but take longer to start producing fruit. Sow seeds fresh in early spring and, given warmth, they should germinate in ~21 days. *Cuttings:* The 'Meyer' lemon is easily reproduced by cuttings. Plants grown from cuttings should fruit 2–3 years sooner than budded trees, the trees have a longer life and produce fruits for at least 30 years. Semi-ripe cuttings can be taken in summer and inserted into well-drained, warm compost to root. *Grafting:* Grafting can introduce specific traits onto an otherwise tough, but not very interesting rootstock, and the trees are usually less thorny and give predictable progeny. The main method is by budding onto 1- or 2-year old seedlings of the same or a related species. Often shield-budding is used. The main rootstocks used are sweet orange, 'Cleopatra' mandarin, 'Volkamer' lemon (*C. limon*), *C. macrophylla* or trifoliate orange, *Poncirus trifoliata* (used in colder areas).

Pruning: Lemon trees form a neat shape and need very little pruning. Prune out any diseased or damaged wood, and any basal suckers. In general, because the tree is evergreen, much of the tree's resources for flowering and fruiting are stored in the leaves. Heavy pruning will remove these resources and can, consequently, reduce flowering and fruiting.

Pests and diseases: The lemon is less susceptible to disease than many other citrus. The main diseases are scab, *Anthracnose*, greasy spot, gummosis, mal secco (*Deuterophoma tracheiphila*) and stem-end rot. Red algae can infest lemon trees and causes dieback. Common micronutrient deficiencies are zinc, which causes stunting of twigs, reduces flowering, causes premature fruit drop and yellow banding along leaf veins, and also manganese, which causes interveinal chlorosis and shedding of leaves, flowers and young fruit.

CULTIVARS

'Eureka': From an Italian lemon. Fruit: elliptical, with a moderately protruding nipple at the apex. Peel: yellow, slightly ridged, many sunken oil glands, medium-thick, tightly clinging. Flesh: greenish-yellow, ~10 segments, tender, very juicy, very acid. Borne in large clusters outside the leaf canopy. Bears all year. Tree: medium-sized, almost thornless, early-bearing, prolific, cold-sensitive, not insect-resistant; relatively short lived, productive.

'Femminello Ovale': An old Italian variety. Fruit: round–elliptic, low, blunt nipple; slightly necked or rounded at base, medium size. Peel: yellow, medium-thick, tightly clinging. Pulp: ~10 segments, tender, juicy, very acid, excellent quality, with only a few, mostly undeveloped, seeds. Fruits all year, but mainly in late winter and spring. Fruit stores well. Tree: almost thornless, fairly vigorous.

'Lisbon': Fruit: similar to 'Eureka'; elliptical, prominent nipple at apex. Peel: yellow, sometimes slightly ribbed, medium-thick, tightly clinging. Pulp: greenish-yellow, ~10 segments, tender, juicy, very acid, few or no seeds. Has two main crops: in late winter and in late summer. Fruit is borne inside the canopy. Tree: large, ~8 m tall, dense foliage, vigorous, many long thorns, prolific, resistant to cold, heat and wind.

'Meyer': A hybrid, possibly lemon x mandarin. From Beijing. Fruit: rounded–elliptical, round at the base, occasionally faintly necked, short nipple, ~6–9 cm long. Peel: light orange with many small oil glands, 3–6 mm thick. Pulp: pale orange-yellow, ~10 segments, juicy, sweeter than most lemons, seeds are small, 8–12. Fruits year round. Tree: small, few thorns, prolific, cold-resistant, only moderately susceptible to greasy spot and oil spotting. Is easily and commonly grown from cuttings. Its peel is of poor quality though, and is deficient in a 'true' lemon flavour. A good cooler-climate lemon, frost hardy to –2°C.

'Perrine': A Mexican lime x 'Genoa' lemon hybrid. More lemon- than lime-like. Fruit: lemon-shaped, with small nipple at apex, medium size. Peel: pale lemon-yellow, smooth, thin, tough. Pulp: greenish-yellow, 10–12 segments, tender, very juicy, with slight lime flavour, but acidity more like lemon, 4–6 seeds. Everbearing. Tree: cold-sensitive, but less so than lime. Resistant to withertip and scab, but prone to gummosis and other bark diseases.

SIMILAR SPECIES

Ponderosa lime, *Citrus limon*. A type of lemon with huge, somewhat bumpy fruits. May be a cross between pummelo and citron. The fruits have a thick peel, excellent for making marmalade, etc. and some central flesh, which is edible though tart. Has a high quantity of essential oils. It also has large flowers. The tree grows from 3–6 m tall, though is possibly somewhat more sensitive to cold than some citrus species. Benefits from regular applications of fertiliser during its growing season, while its fruits keep getting larger and larger. Makes a good container plant or can be grown inside for part of the year in colder regions. Is very eye-catching with its huge fruits. Can be grown from seeds or cuttings, though is often also grafted onto various citrus rootstocks. Seeds are often nucellar-like, coming true to the parent plant.

Volkamer lemon, *Citrus volkameriana*. Probably a hybrid between the lemon and possibly the sour orange (or mandarin lime). Tree: a little smaller than the average lemon tree has few if any spines. Flowers: slightly fragrant. Fruits: borne profusely, are lemon-shaped, ~6 cm long, rough, reddish-orange. Pulp: yellow-orange, 7–11 segments, very juicy, acid, faintly bitter, good aroma and flavour, few seeds. Fairly resistant to rot and mal secco.

Rough lemon, *Citrus jambhiri*. May be a lemon x citron cross. Fruit: large, round–oval, with an almost sunken nipple, ~6 cm long. Peel: lemon-yellow to orange-yellow, irregular, large oil glands, often ribbed; 5–10 mm thick. Pulp: lemon-yellow, ~10 segments, medium-juicy, medium-acid, moderate lemon odour and flavour; seeds are small, 10–15. Grows true from seeds (nearly all are nucellar). Tree: large, with lots of small thorns; new leaves are tinged red. Often used as a rootstock. Imparts drought tolerance, high vigour and yield, but the tree itself is of low vigour and susceptible to young tree decline. Intolerant of *Phytophthora* and nematodes. Is cold hardy and grows well in clay soils. Used for grapefruit, oranges and lemons where yield and not quality is important.

Rangpur lime, *Citrus limonia*. Often used as a rootstock. Actually not a lime but is probably descended from rough lemon and sour orange parentage. Very similar to rough lemon in many characteristics, but generally better fruit quality and more tolerant of high pH and salt.

I chang (ichang papeda), *Citrus ichangensis*. A native of southwest China, this is a strange, very cold hardy citrus. The fruit is oblong, otherwise much like a lemon, with rough, pale orange rind and dryish flesh with many seeds. ∎

uses

Food
Slices of lemon are served as a garnish with all types of dishes, are added to iced or hot tea, and other drinks. Chilled water and lemon juice is a very refreshing drink. The juice can be enjoyed fresh, concentrated and frozen. Lemons are used in pies, tarts, cakes, cookies, chocolates, etc., they can be added to jams, chutneys, preserves and are used in pharmaceutical products. A few drops of lemon juice added to cream before whipping gives it stability. Added to meat, it acts as a tenderiser. If added to fruits or vegetables that oxidise, it prevents them turning brown. Lemons provide lemon oil, pectin and citric acid. The outer peel is also used in all types of dishes (sweet and savoury). Preserved lemons, in salt, are delicious added to many savoury dishes.

Nutrition/medicinal
Good levels of vitamin C: 46 mg/100 g of flesh. Contains a lot of citric acid. Lemons have 'monoterpenes' in their skin that act as powerful antioxidants, which protect against cells becoming cancerous and help fight existing cancers. Lemon juice has been widely used medicinally as a diuretic, as an astringent, to treat inflammations and infections of the mouth, as a laxative and to prevent the common cold. It is also good for skin problems such as acne, boils, insect bites, warts and cold sores. The lemon is highly recommended for acute rheumatism. Limonene, in the peel, is thought to reduce the risk of breast cancer, and may be able to reduce high blood pressure, varicose veins and help stop bleeding. Recent research in Arizona has found that lemon peel in a tea can reduce the risk of skin cancer by 70%. The oil, taken internally, stimulates the circulation, may promote white blood-cell formation, dissolve cellulite and promote a sense of well being. It works as an antiseptic and an antibacterial. It also stimulates the digestive system. It can also serve as an insect repellent and can be applied to sunburn. **Warning:** Large, daily doses can erode the enamel of the teeth and make them more susceptible to caries. Also, the oils within the peel can be an irritant and can cause dermatitis in some people. If lemon juice, on human skin, is exposed to sunlight it can cause blistering in some individuals. Sucking lemons can also cause irritation around the mouth.

Other uses
Lemon juice removes stains and cleans through grease. Rinsed on the hair, and then exposed to sunlight, it acts as a bleach. Also used to bleach freckles. Used in many pharmaceutical products. The oil from the outer peel is pale yellow and has a wonderful aroma, but it takes >1200 lemons to produce 0.5 kg of oil. The oil is used in furniture polishes, detergents and soaps, in many cosmetics, e.g. perfume, and is widely used in aromatherapy. Apparently, if added with water to potted plants, it keeps their flowers fresh for longer, but must not be used on chrysanthemums, as it turns their leaves brown. Lemon-tree wood is fine-grained, compact and easy to work. It is used for finer, smaller articles.

Ornamental
Lemon trees make good and very useful specimen trees, with their glossy, fragrant evergreen foliage, fragrant blossoms and leaves, and an almost year-round supply of fruits.

Citrus spp.

Lime

RUTACEAE

Mexican lime (*Citrus aurantifolia*), Tahitian lime (*Citrus latifolia*), sweet lime (*Citrus limettioides*), mandarin lime (*Citrus* x *limonia*), Mexican lime x kumquat hybrids

Mexican lime (West Indian lime, key lime), *Citrus aurantifolia* (syn. *Citrus acida, C. lima, C. medica* var. *acida, Limonia aurantifolia*). The name 'lime' is derived from the Persian or Arabic name for lemon, 'limun', because limes and lemons were often confused. There are two main acid–sour limes grown commercially. The most popular, highest rated and longest known is the widely cultivated Mexican lime (or West Indian or key lime). The other main commercial lime is the Tahiti or Persian lime. The Mexican lime is native to southeast Asia (and not Mexico or the West Indies). It was unknown in Europe before the Crusades and is assumed to have been carried to North Africa and the Near East by the Arabs, and then taken by the Crusaders from Palestine to Mediterranean Europe. In the mid-13th century, it was cultivated and was well-known in Italy and probably also in France. It was almost certainly introduced into the Caribbean and Mexico by the Spaniards. Production of Mexican limes, for their juice, has been the major industry on the Caribbean island of Dominica for many generations. Several factories express the juice and export it worldwide for use in lime-juice cordials and other drinks. They also export distilled lime oil, which is often used in the cosmetics industry. Persian limes are similar, but are not as acidic as Mexican limes. In many ways they are commercially easier to grow and have fewer problems than the Mexican lime and, consequently, have often replaced Mexican lime trees, though many believe the Mexican lime fruit to be superior in aroma and flavour.

DESCRIPTION

Small (~5 cm long), oval, with a thin yellow–green rind, the fruit are wonderfully aromatic, very juicy and have a more complex flavour, and are more acidic than Persian limes. The tree is very vigorous, and varies in height from 2–4 m tall. It has many slender, spreading branches and, usually, many sharp spines (~1 cm long) originating from the stems.

Leaves: Evergreen, shiny, mid green, leathery, alternate and are pleasantly aromatic when crushed. They are elliptical in shape, rounded at the base, with a pointed tip, 5–7.5 cm long. Young leaves are mauvish, maturing to dark green above, paler beneath. Have tiny rounded teeth on their margins and flattened leaf stems. They form a dense crown

Flowers: Faintly fragrant or scentless, formed from leaf axils, ~5 cm diameter, solitary or in small clusters (2–7). Flowers have five pointed sepals that form a green calyx, and five white petals, which are mauvish when young. They have numerous prominent yellow-tipped stamens. It has a superior ovary. They are both monoecious and bisexual, and have both male and female structures within the same flower. *Pollination:* By bees and insects. Plants are mostly self-fertile, though most fruits are set without fertilisation. Only need one plant to set fruit, though a mix of varieties can result in better fruit-set. In addition, as well as producing ordinary seed, which gives variable offspring, some lime seeds are nucellar and produce progeny that are genetically identical to the parent (see p. 15).

Fruit: Borne singly or in small clusters, at the ends of stems. They are elliptical–rounded, sometimes with a slight indentation at the apex, ~3.5–6 cm in diameter. The skin is yellow-green when immature, pale yellow and shiny when ripe, and is usually fairly smooth, thin (1.5–3 mm) and contains numerous essential-oil glands within its upper layer. Beneath the outer skin is a thin layer of white, non-aromatic tissue. Within the fruit are numerous tightly packed membranous juice sacs enclosed in 6–15 wedge-shaped compartments, which do not readily separate. The juice is greenish-yellow, aromatic, juicy, very acid, tangy and full of flavour, with few or many small green-white seeds in each section. Both Mexican and Persian limes have a higher sugar and citric acid content than lemons. Trees can produce too many fruits in some years, leading to biennial bearing, with meagre crops in the following year(s). This can be remedied by thinning very young fruits if there are too many, to even out yields.

Yield/harvest/storage: Commonly, although many flowers are formed, only ~5% actually go on to produce fruit. Fruits take ~5–6 months to mature after fruit-set. Seedlings begin to fruit after 3–6 years and reach full production after 8–10 years; trees grown from air-layers or cuttings can fruit in the first year after planting, or in years 2–3. Lime trees can give good yields and often ripen irregularly throughout the year, though tend to have two main harvests, in mid summer, and another in mid winter. They store as well as lemons and can be left on the tree for some time after they ripen, to 'store' for later use. They are best picked when the skin has turned a lemony-green colour, and the fruit feels slightly soft to the touch. They will store for ~3 months at ~10°C, but can be cold damaged if stored in a fridge at <5°C. As they age, they tend to lose moisture and become dry.

Roots: Limes have some deeper roots, and care is needed when transplanting that these are not damaged.

Food

Limes are acidic, but are thought by many to be more aromatic and interesting in flavour then lemons. Lime juice can be used instead of lemon, and adds a marvellous, aromatic flavour. It is wonderful squeezed on fruits and desserts, but also as a juice on fish and meats. It is exceptionally refreshing, and is added to many drinks and cocktails. Limes can also be used in syrup, sauces, pies, flans, cakes, jam, jelly or marmalade. It makes a great marinade (with other spices) for raw fish. The lime softens and tenderises the fish, which can then be mixed with coconut cream and salad vegetables. To preserve limes, incisions can be made through the skin with a knife, the fruits are then covered with salt, and thereafter kept in vinegar to preserve. Before serving, the pickled fruits can be fried in oil and sugar, and then eaten as an appetiser. Limes can also have chilli peppers, turmeric, ginger and other spices pickled with them. In the Middle East, ripe limes are boiled in salt water and dried until their flesh darkens in colour. The resulting spice, called loomi, gives a distinct citrus, tangy flavour to legumes, meats, rice and other dishes. The limes are either crushed or pierced before adding them to slowly-cooked dishes. The leaves can be minced and are used in certain Javanese dishes. In the Philippines, the chopped peel is made into a sweetmeat with milk and coconut.

Nutrition

The juice contains 30 mg vitamin C/100 g of flesh, which is quite good (but not as high as lemons). It also contains good levels of potassium. The skin contains ~7% essential oil. Lime is a good source of limonene, which possesses anti-coagulatory and anti-inflammatory properties. It may inhibit some chemically-induced cancers. (See Lemon).

Medicinal

Lime juice helps calm the irritation and swelling of mosquito bites. It is also used as a tonic, as an astringent, as a diuretic, as a digestive stimulant, as a remedy for intestinal haemorrhage and haemorrhoids, for heart palpitations, headache, convulsive cough, rheumatism, arthritis, hair loss, bad breath, as an antiseptic for all kinds of ulcers, as a gargle for sore throats, and to relieve stomach ailments. Mixed with oil, it is given as a vermifuge. Lime juice can also relieve the effects of stinging corals and jellyfish. **Warning:** The oil from the skin can cause dermatitis in some sensitive individuals, which can then blister if exposed to the sun.

Other uses

The juice has been used to dye leather. The essential oil is used in many cosmetics, e.g. perfumes, skin conditioners. Lime juice is often added to shampoo and, if applied to wet hair after shampooing, and the hair is then exposed to sunlight, it can act as a bleach.

Ornamental

Lime trees make attractive and useful small specimen trees, with their glossy evergreen foliage and blossom, and ornamental as well as edible fruits.

Above: Lime fruit on bush.

These deep roots make them more drought tolerant, but also more susceptible to waterlogging. They also have many surface roots, which readily sucker if damaged. Trees benefit from an organic mulch to conserve moisture, suppress weed growth and add nutrients.

CULTIVATION

Location: They grow best in full sun, in a sheltered location. They are not very tolerant of salt spray or of strong winds.

Temperature: More sensitive to cold than the lemon, and can only be grown in protected locations. It grows best in semi-tropical and warm-temperate climates.

Soil/water/nutrients: The tree grows reasonably well in a variety of soils. It can grow in limestone, sandy loams or gravelly, well-drained soils. It prefers a medium–alkaline pH range. It does not grow well in heavy clays, and is not tolerant of waterlogging. On poor soils, the fruits form thicker skins and have less juice. They like regular moisture and warmth year round, but do tolerate drought better than most other citrus fruit. If it is too humid, trees are more susceptible to fungal diseases. Trees are relatively nutrient hungry, but do not need too much nitrogen, which increases leaf growth at the expense of fruiting. Traditionally, well-rotted seaweed has been used, which supplies good levels of potassium: this reduces leaf growth, but increases fruiting. Apply a well-balanced citrus fertiliser, with micronutrients, about 2–3 times a year.

Propagation: *Seed:* The Mexican lime is usually propagated by seed because most seeds are nucellar (and polyembryonic) and so the progeny are predictable. *Cuttings:* Cuttings from mature wood can be used, but the resulting plants often do not develop strong root systems. *Suckers:* The root sprouts and suckers from mature trees can be dug up and planted in compost to establish. Any damage to the roots around the parent plant will readily form suckers. *Layering:* The tree is often air-layered, and this method gives good success, particularly with the use of rooting hormones. *Grafting:* Selected cultivars can be budded onto rough lemon or sour orange (very wind hardy) or pummelo.

Pot culture: Ensure there are sufficient nutrients and organic matter mixed in with the soil. A surface mulch will help prevent the soil drying out. The plants need little maintenance, and provide attractive, fragrant leaves year round, and flowers and fruits for much of the year. Container growth is ideal in colder areas, where the plants can be moved inside in winter. Feeds of liquid nutrients are beneficial.

Planting: Space plants at ~7 m apart.

Pruning: Lime trees form a neat shape and require very little pruning. It is advisable to remove suckers that sometimes form from the base of the tree. Prune out any diseased or damaged wood, and larger wounds should be sealed with pruning compound. In general, because the tree is evergreen, much of its resources for flowering and fruiting are stored in the leaves. Heavy pruning will remove these resources and can, consequently, reduce flowering and fruiting. Fruit thinning may also need to be done to even out yields and avoid biennial bearing.

Pests and diseases: Potential problems can be scale insects, lime *Anthracnose* and, if the weather is too humid, scab caused by the fungus, *Elsinoe fawcetti,* or a collar rot caused by *Phytophthora* spp. Other possible citrus pests include citrus rust mites, mealybugs, whitefly, citrus blackfly, aphids and fruit flies.

CULTIVARS

'Everglade': Needs to be pollinated by flowers of grapefruit or pummelo, though the fruits show no characteristics of these. Fruit: lime-like, 4–5 cm diameter, light yellow when ripe, smooth, borne in large clusters. Pulp: light green, 8–10 segments, aromatic, very juicy, sprightly-acid, of excellent quality and texture. Seeds: 2–10 per fruit.

'Palmetto': Fruit: elliptical–round, small, 3.5–4 cm diameter; peel is pale yellow when ripe, smooth, very thin. Pulp: light greenish-yellow, 8–10 segments, tender, very juicy, fine quality, aromatic, with acid flavour; 3–6 seeds/fruit.

OTHER LIME SPECIES AND HYBRIDS

In general, the description and notes for the Mexican lime apply to the different lime species described below, unless stated otherwise.

Mandarin lime (Rangpur lime, kusiae lime, Canton lemon), *Citrus x limonia*. A hybrid between mandarin (*C. reticulata*) and lime (*C. aurantifolia*). Thought to have originated in southeastern Asia, it had spread to China and India by 1000 AD. This name includes three similar fruits that resemble a mandarin orange. Sometimes grown in the USA and Australia.

Description: Fast-growing, bushy–spreading, ~4.5–6 m tall; has a few short thorns. Leaves are pale green when young. Tends to sucker badly, so can be grafted onto sour orange or a similar non-suckering citrus rootstock to avoid this. *Flower:* Buds and petals have a mauve tinge. *Fruits:* Round–oval, with a slight neck; 4–6 cm long. Skin is deep yellow–orange, thin, easily removed, with large oil glands. *Pulp:* Lime-like aroma, yellow–orange, 8–10 segments that separate readily from each other, very juicy; flavour is sour, but not as sharp as Mexican lime. There may be 6–18 small seeds. *Harvest:* Fruits ripen through winter, and will 'store' on the tree for several weeks. Trees begin fruiting in 2–3 years, and produce regular, reliable crops. In Hawaii, mature trees have produced ~2000 fruits (~90 kg) per tree.

Cultivation: More cold tolerant than the Mexican lime. Withstands short frosts; susceptible to scab and root rot.

Uses: Uses as for Mexican lime. Makes very good marmalade; some say better than that from sour oranges. It is often grown as an ornamental tree as well as for its fruits.

Mexican lime x kumquat hybrids. A vigorous, evergreen, nearly spineless tree with winged leaf stalks and prolific flowers, more cold-tolerant than the Mexican lime, but not as hardy as kumquat. Fruit are much like the Mexican lime. Resistant to withertip. There are three named cultivars: 'Eustis', 'Lakeland' and 'Tavares'. Fruits are roundish–oval, 3–7 cm diameter. Peel is yellow, shiny, with prominent oil glands, thin, edible. Pulp: Light green, 5–9 segments, tender, juicy, tangy or can be very acid, several small seeds. Regular bearing. Fruit ripens in autumn–winter.

Otaheite, *Citrus taitensis*. Now thought to be a non-acid form of mandarin lime. It is popular in France for its fruits and in the USA, where it is often grown as an ornamental Christmas 'orange'. *Fruit:* Fairly spherical, 4–5 cm wide. *Peel:* Orange with small oil glands, thin. *Pulp:* Orange, 7–10 segments, juicy, slightly lime-like, but not as aromatic and tangy as Mexican lime, not very acidic, usually seedless. *Trees:* Often dwarfing, spreading, thornless; new leaves are purple. *Flowers:* Fragrant, purple outside. *Propagation:* Cuttings or air-layers.

Sweet lime, *Citrus limettioides* (syn. *C. lumia*). The sweet lime is often confused with the sweet lemon (*C. limetta*) in the literature. It is probably a hybrid between a Mexican lime and sweet lemon or sweet citron. It may be native to India. It is mostly grown in India, the Middle East, tropical America and northern Vietnam. It is widely utilised as a rootstock for the sweet orange and other *Citrus* species, but is susceptible to a number of viruses.

Description: Its leaves, shape and size are similar to the Tahitian lime, but the leaves are serrated and the leaf stalks almost round. Fruit are greeny-orange-yellow when ripe. The fruit is often very juicy, non-acid, but faintly bitter. Trees are quite hardy. Flowers are self-fertile and produce many fruits. Cross pollination with sweet orange or grapefruit gives increased fruit size, but also increased seed number. *Propagation:* Usually from air-layering or cuttings.

Uses: Uses as for Mexican lime. Some enjoy to simply eat the fruit fresh. It can also be cooked and preserved. It is used medicinally in India to treat fever and jaundice.

Tahitian lime (Persian lime, Bears' lime), *Citrus latifolia*. Mexican limes are more sensitive to cold weather than Tahitian limes. The latter are easier to grow, their fruits easier to pick, have no or very few thorns and are somewhat cold hardier (because they have a thicker skin), but, to many, their flavour is considered inferior to the Mexican lime. The origin of the Tahitian lime is unknown, but is presumed to be a hybrid between the Mexican lime and the citron or possibly the lemon. It is believed that the Tahitian lime was introduced into the Mediterranean region via Iran, from where it was probably taken to Brazil by the Portuguese. From there, it was, apparently, taken to Australia in about 1820.

Description: More vigorous and spreading, with drooping branches, but less thorny than the Mexican lime. A medium–large tree, ~4.5–6 m tall. *Leaves:* Broad, flat-winged leaf stalks; young leaves are mauvish. *Flowers:* Fragrant, occur during the year, but mostly in mid winter; are slightly purple-tinged. *Fruit:* Oval–short and elliptical, occasionally has a short neck; apex is rounded; 5–7.5 cm long. Peel: Vivid green until ripe, then becomes pale yellow; smooth, thin, tightly clinging. Pulp: Light greenish-yellow when ripe, ~10 segments, tender, acid, but with less aroma than Mexican lime; usually seedless (or, rarely, 1–2), especially if planted among other citrus species. It produces no viable pollen. Most fruit are formed parthenocarpically (without fertilisation). Fruits are simply picked as they ripen throughout the year, but most mature from early–late summer. An average yield varies from 28–40 kg of fruit per tree. Fruit can be 'stored' on the tree for a while when ripe, and for 6–8 weeks in a fridge.

Cultivation: *Temperature:* Is hardier than the Mexican lime, and can tolerate more frost. *Soil:* As Mexican lime.

Needs moderate fertiliser applications, with less amounts given throughout the year seeming to work better. A ratio of less nitrogen with more potassium can give better growth and fruit yield. *Planting:* Trees can be planted closer, at ~4–6 m apart. *Pests and diseases:* The citrus red mite and the broad mite can infest Tahitian lime leaves and fruits. Moderately susceptible to scab and greasy spot, and also to several viruses. *Propagation: Seeds:* The few seeds it has are monoembryonic (genetically mixed, compared to nucellar) and result in seedlings with variable characteristics. *Grafting:* Often budded onto rough lemon or *C. macrophylla*. *Layering:* Air-layering is the main method used (see orange propagation notes). Although air-layered trees begin to bear a year before budded trees, they often do not yield as well.

Uses: As for Mexican lime. ■

Citrus medica
Citron (citrus apple)
RUTACEA

Relatives: orange, lemon, grapefruit

Citron is considered to be one of the oldest species and was being grown for its fruits ~8000 years ago. It is probably a native of India or the fertile area between the Tigris and Euphrates rivers, in what is now Iraq. Its cultivation then spread to the Near East and China, and it was probably the first citrus species to be taken to the Mediterranean regions. Alexander the Great may have carried the citron to these regions in ~300 BC. It was known in Greece and was a popular fruit in Rome by AD 300. Unfortunately, most trees were destroyed by barbarians in the 4th century AD but those in Naples, Sardinia and Sicily survived, and for centuries these areas supplied citrons to the Jews in Italy, France and Germany for their Feast of the Tabernacles ceremony. The Palestinian Greeks called the fruit a *kedromelon* (cedar apple), and this evolved into *citrus,* and subsequently changed to citron. For many years, most *Citrus* species were identified as botanical varieties of *Citrus medica.* Today, citron is not grown commercially, but many trees exist in gardens around the Mediterranean. It is now mostly known as a source of candied peel, but also for its bizarrely-shaped fruits that make excellent marmalade.

DESCRIPTION
A slow-growing shrub or small tree reaching 2.5–4.5 m tall with stiff branches and twigs, with short or long spines from leaf axils. It is a fairly short-lived tree.

Leaves: Evergreen, ovate-lanceolate or elliptic, large (7–18 cm long), with prominent oil glands, which are filled with very aromatic, citrus essential oils.

Flowers: Large buds, which open to fragrant flowers, ~4 cm wide, with 4–5 petals, and are white outside, pinkish-purplish inside, with numerous stamens. They are borne in short clusters, are mostly bisexual, though some are just male. They can bloom for most of the year, but mostly occur in spring. *Pollination:* By bees and other insects.

Fruit: Very aromatic, mostly oval, occasionally pear-shaped, but highly variable. Large, varying from 8–20 cm, to even >25 cm long. They can be smooth or bumpy, often with many oddly-shaped fruits on the same branch. Some cultivars have fruits that are deeply divided into sections to form bizarre shapes like many protruding fingers. Fruit is

dark green when young, taking ~3 months to ripen to pale yellow. Peel is mostly very thick, tightly clinging. The pulp is pale yellow to greenish, and is divided into 12–15 segments. It is firm, not very juicy and can be acid or sweet. It contains many oval, non-nucellar seeds.

Yield/harvest: Begins to bear when ~3 years old and reaches peak production in 15 years. Trees live for ~25 years. A precocious bearer, a citron tree can yield as many as 2000 fruits a year.

Roots: Citron has some surface roots, but most are deeper, so care is needed when transplanting that the roots are not damaged. The deep roots make them more susceptible to waterlogging.

CULTIVATION
Location: Best grown in sun in cooler regions, but with some shade in hotter areas. Is not very wind tolerant. Is best grown in regions with no extremes of temperature.

Temperature: The tree is highly sensitive to frost and

Food

Mostly used for its peel. Commercially, the fruits are halved, de-pulped, immersed in salt water to ferment for ~40 days, with the brine changed every 2 weeks. It is then rinsed, and placed into denser brine in wooden barrels for storage and for export. After partial de-salting and boiling to soften the peel, it is candied in a strong sucrose/glucose solution. The candied peel is sun-dried or placed in jars for future use and as an ingredient in cakes, desserts and confectionery. The peel is eaten raw in Indonesia with rice. The peel and flesh make an excellent marmalade. The juice can be used for drinks and desserts. A product called 'citron water' is made in Barbados and shipped to France for flavouring wine and vermouth.

Medicinal

Historically, 'Etrog' was used as a remedy for seasickness, pulmonary troubles and intestinal ailments. Citron juice with wine was considered an effective purgative to rid the system of poison. In India, the peel is a remedy for dysentery and is eaten to overcome halitosis. The distilled juice is given as a sedative. The candied peel is sold in China for stomach ailments, as a stimulant, to expel phlegm and as a tonic. The essential oil of the peel is regarded as an antibiotic. In Thailand, the skin is used as an anti-flatulent. The juice is used to cure coughing. **Warning:** Citron contains coumarins that, when placed on skin and exposed to sunlight, can cause blisters and dermatitis in some people.

Other uses

Chinese and Japanese people prize the citron for its fragrance, and in central and northern China it was common to carry a ripe fruit in the hand or place the fruit in a room to perfume the air. The dried fruits are stored with clothing to repel moths. In southern China, the juice is used to wash fine linen. An essential oil has been distilled from the peel and flowers for use in perfumery. The wood is white, hard and dense.

does not enter winter dormancy as early as other citrus species, so is sensitive to early winter frosts. Leaves and fruits are also easily damaged by intense heat and drought.

Chilling: Does not need a period of winter chilling.

Soil/water/nutrients: Can grow on a range of soils, but require good aeration. Can grow in sands or non-waterlogged clays, though dislike wet, poorly drained soils. They grow best at a pH range of fairly acid to neutral, and do not grow well in alkaline soils where iron deficiency causes chlorosis. Trees need less water in autumn to avoid the production of tender new leaves that might be damaged in winter, but need adequate moisture in spring. The deeper the soil, the better the root system and the greater the ability to withstand drought. Nutritionally, trees need regular additions of a complete fertiliser containing, in particular, nitrogen, phosphorous, potassium, sulphur and calcium. Because they are evergreen and form fruit during the winter months, two or three applications of a citrus-type fertiliser throughout the year are beneficial.

Planting: Space trees at 5–7 m apart. Keep young plants well watered and weed free for the first few years.

Propagation: *Seed:* Can be grown from seed. Sow seed fresh in early spring and, given warmth, it should germinate in ~21 days. Progeny will be variable though. *Cuttings:* Easily grown from cuttings, taken from 2–4-year-old branches, which are inserted deeply into soil without defoliation. *Layering:* Can succeed well. In the initial years, it grows profusely. *Grafting:* For quicker growth, it can be budded onto rough lemon, grapefruit, sour orange or sweet orange, but the fruits do not attain the size of those produced from cuttings, and the citron tends to overgrow the rootstock.

Pruning: Needed to remove water sprouts and low drooping branches. Italian producers keep the tree low and stake the branches. Prune out any diseased or damaged wood. In general, because the tree is evergreen, much of its resources for flowering and fruiting are stored in the leaves. Heavy pruning will remove these resources and can consequently reduce flowering and fruiting.

Pests and diseases: Subject to most problems of other *Citrus* species. In particular, the citrus bud mite (*Eriophyes sheldoni*), citrus rust mite (*Phyllocoptruta oleivora*) and snow scale (*Unaspis citri*) may cause problems.

CULTIVARS

Citron cultivars are mainly of two types: acid citrons with pinkish new growth, purple flower buds and acid pulp; and sweet citrons with no pink or purple tint on their new growth or flowers, and with non-acid pulp. Some better-known cultivars are listed below.

'Etrog' or 'Citron of the Jews': An acid citron. A variety cultured in Israel, and is the official citron used in the Feast of the Tabernacles. It has rounded leaves, purplish flowers and spindle-shaped or lemon-like fruit, with a prominent apical stalk. It has thick, fleshy peel, pale yellowish when ripe. Flesh is dry, acid. If not picked, it remains on the tree and continues to enlarge for years until the branch can no longer support it! Tree is small, not vigorous.

'Liscia Diamante' (syn. 'Italian', 'Calabrese'): An acid citron. Fruit are large (~20 cm long), bottle shaped, furrowed at base, lemon-yellow when ripe, smooth or faintly ribbed. Peel is very thick (thicker than any other citrus: 60–70% peel), smooth, intensely fragrant. It provides essential oils, liqueurs and the world's most sought-after candied peel. Flesh is crisp, non-juicy, acid and seedy. Trees are small and spreading, with few thorns, leathery leaves, purplish buds.

'Buddha's Hand': Semi-acid citron. It is a strange shaped fruit, hence its name, which resembles fingers. It is cultivated in Japan and Indochina for decorative and religious purposes. A highly fragrant, large fruit, with thick peel.

'Corsican': Sweet citron. The buds do not have a purplish tint. Fruit: ellipsoid with thick, leathery peel. Pulp: Sweet, dry, no juice, with a central void, seedy, not of good quality. Tree: small, spreading, moderately thorny. ■

Citrus spp.

Orange

RUTACEAE

Sweet orange, (*Citrus sinensis*), sour orange (*Citrus aurantium*), bergamot (*C. aurantium*, var. *bergamia*), trifoliate orange (*Poncirus trifoliata*), myrtle-leaved orange (*C. aurantium*, var. *myrtifolia*), citrange (x *Citroncirus Webberi*), orangelo, tangelo, tangor

Relatives: lime, lemon, grapefruit, citron

There are 13 genera of *Citrus*, and many commercial hybrid crosses between these. Orange is a hybrid between pummelo (*C. grandis*) and mandarin (*C. reticulata*). The orange is unknown in the wild, and was probably selected in China or northeastern India. It is mentioned in Chinese literature from 2400 BC, and later in Sanskrit writings (800 BC). The name 'orange' is derived from the Arabic 'narang', which may date back to the Sanskrit word 'nagarañja', meaning the 'favourite fruit of elephants'. The orange had spread to the Mediterranean region by the 1400s. From the mid 1600s onwards, the Spanish took the orange to South America and Mexico, and the French probably took it to Louisiana. The navel orange cultivar originated in Brazil in the 1800s. However, it was not until the seafaring voyages of Columbus that the vitamin C benefits of citrus fruits were discovered, and it was then included within the ship's stores to stave off scurvy, which was otherwise endemic on long ocean voyages. In Europe, the orange was valued for its medicinal properties, but also as a status symbol, and was grown by the wealthy in private conservatories, called orangeries. Ponce de Leon carried them to Florida in 1513, and required his sailors to plant 100 seeds each wherever they landed and, thus, the great Florida citrus industry began. Nowadays, the orange is the most commonly grown fruit tree in the world. It is an important crop in the Far East, South Africa, Australasia, the Mediterranean regions, parts of South America and the Caribbean, but the USA leads world production, with Florida producing >200 million boxes of oranges a year.

DESCRIPTION

Trees reach ~7.5 m in height, or even up to ~15 m. They have a dense, rounded crown. They have thin, twisted, angled stems, with slender, bluntish spines borne from the leaf axils.

Leaves: Oval, with pointed tips, 6.5–15 cm long, 2.5–10 cm wide, waxy, smooth, mid–dark green. They are evergreen, alternate, usually not toothed, or only slightly, and are wonderfully aromatic when crushed.

Flowers: Borne singly or in clusters (2–6) of sweetly fragrant, white flowers, ~2.5–4 cm diameter. Flowers are monoecious and bisexual (i.e. usually both male and female). The flower has five concave, pointed sepals that form a green calyx, and five white petals. There are numerous prominent, bright yellow-tipped stamens. It has a superior ovary. Flowers can be borne from spring through summer. *Pollination:* Oranges are pollinated by bees and other insects. They are self-fertile and have good fruit-set, so only need a single tree to set fruit. However, as well as ordinarily pollinated seed, which gives variable offspring, they also produce seedlings that are genetically identical to the parent by nucellar embryony. There has been no genetic exchange and they are 'clones' of the tree from which they came (see p. 15 for more details). In addition, depending on the species, some flowers are not pollinated, yet still go on to produce seedless fruits (parthenocarpy).

Fruit: Rounded to globe shaped, 6.5–9.5 cm diameter, with a thick, waxy, outer orange rind (epicarp) containing many tiny essential oil glands. The inner rind (mesocarp) is white, spongy and non-aromatic. The pulp (endocarp) is yellow-orange, and consists of tightly packed membranous juice sacs enclosed in 10–14 wedge-shaped compartments, which can be readily separated into individual segments. Each segment has 2–4 whitish, central seeds (though some can be seedless). The sweet orange has a solid centre.

Yield/harvest/storage: Commonly, although many flowers are formed, only 1–5% actually go on to produce fruits. Fruits take ~6–8 months to mature after fruit-set. A healthy tree should produce ~100 fruits a season. It is claimed that very old, large orange trees in the Mediterranean bear >3000 oranges each year. Grafted orange trees begin bearing in 2–3 years; seedlings may take 3–5 years. Pick when ripe and fully orange in colour: oranges do not ripen well if picked too early. Oranges become more orange in cooler climates: in the tropics, oranges do not turn fully orange even though the fruits are ripe, so these need to opened to test for ripeness. The fruit can be left on the tree for several weeks after they are ripe, to store for later use. If picked, they will store for ~3 months at ~10° C, and up to 5 months at ~3ºC. As they age, they tend to lose moisture and become dry.

Roots: Oranges have some surface roots, but most are deeper, so care is needed when transplanting that these roots are not damaged. The deeper the soil, the better the root system and the greater the ability to withstand drought. However, their deep roots make them more susceptible to waterlogging. Their roots are non-invasive.

CULTIVATION

It forms a compact tree that is ornamental and looks good planted near the house. Fairly easy to grow.

Location: They grow best in full sun, but can also grow in semi-shade. They are not very wind tolerant. Are reasonably tolerant of salty, maritime conditions, but not exposed locations.

Temperature: The orange is a subtropical species, not tropical. It does not like too much heat. Ideal winter temperatures are 1.5–10ºC. However, mature, dormant trees can survive brief temperatures of ~–4ºC. Fruit is damaged at ~–2º C. Young trees can be killed by brief frosts, and need extra protection. Hardiness varies with cultivar and rootstock, with seedlings often being more cold hardy than grafted or budded trees. Cold is more injurious if preceded by drought.

Chilling: Citrus trees do not need any winter chilling to produce flowers and fruits.

Soil/water/nutrients: Oranges grow best in well-drained, deep, fertile loams. But they can also grow in a range of soil types, including clay soils, although they do not grow as well. They dislike wet, poorly drained soils, although sometimes tolerate wetter soils once established. They grow at a pH range of fairly acid to neutral, and do not grow well in alkaline soils, where iron deficiency causes chlorosis. However, different rootstocks are adapted to different conditions. Trees need less water in autumn to avoid the production of tender new leaves that might be damaged in winter, but need adequate moisture in spring. They are moderately drought tolerant, and too much moisture can lead to less sweet, less orange fruits. Nutritionally, trees are quite hungry and need regular applications of a complete fertiliser containing, in particular, nitrogen, phosphorous, potassium, sulphur and calcium. Because they are evergreen and form fruit during the winter months, two or three applications of a citrus-type fertiliser throughout the year are beneficial.

Pot culture: They make an attractive pot plant. Ensure there are given sufficient nutrients and organic matter is mixed in with the soil. A surface mulch will help prevent the soil drying out. The plants need little maintenance, and provide attractive, fragrant leaves year round, fragrant flowers and eye-catching fruits. Container growth is ideal in colder areas, where they can be moved inside in winter. Feeds of liquid nutrients are beneficial.

Planting: Space at 5–7 m apart. Keep young plants well watered and weed free for the first few years.

Propagation: Seed: There are benefits and disadvantages of growing from seed. Cross pollinated seeds will give variable progeny; however, nucellar seeds are often polyembryonic and the offspring are genetically identical to their parent. Oranges produce many nucellar seeds. These can sometimes be told apart from 'ordinary' seeds by the speed at which they germinate, with nucellar seeds germinating much quicker. Seedlings are often more disease resistant, more vigorous and often more productive, but do take longer to start producing fruit (~10–15 years). Sow seed fresh in early spring and, given warmth, it should germinate in ~21 days. *Cuttings:* Take semi-ripe cuttings in summer and insert in well-drained, gritty compost to root. *Grafting:* Grafting can introduce specific traits onto an otherwise tough, but not very interesting rootstock, and grafted trees are usually less

thorny and give predictable progeny. The main method is by budding onto 1- or 2-year-old seedlings of the same or a related species. Often shield-budding is used. The main rootstocks used are sour orange (*C. aurantium*), for areas with good-quality soils; 'Rough' lemon or 'Volkamer' lemon (*C. limon*), used in warm areas with sandy soils; and trifoliate orange (*Poncirus trifoliata*), which is used in colder areas. However, these rootstocks do have various disease susceptibilities.

Pruning: Orange trees form a neat shape and need very little pruning. It is advisable to remove suckers that sometimes form from the base of the tree. Prune out any diseased or damaged wood, and larger wounds should be sealed to prevent the entry of pathogens. In general, because the tree is evergreen, much of its resources for flowering and fruiting are stored in the leaves. Heavy pruning removes these resources and can, consequently, reduce flowering and fruiting. In Israel, the practice of girdling has been revived, but is probably not recommended for citrus if you want the tree to have a long life. (See the Introduction, p. 36 for details.) It is said that, if done in winter, more flower buds are produced in spring; if done in summer, then fruit size is increased.

Pests and diseases: Oranges may be affected by citrus rust mites, several scale insects, mealybugs, whitefly, citrus blackfly, aphids, thrips and fruit flies. Many of these can now be combatted with biological controls. Possible diseases include collar rot, citrus canker, greasy spot, sooty mould; the fungus *Diaporthe citri* affects stems and various *Phytophthora* spp. can cause root rot. In addition, there are a number of viral diseases, which are often transmitted via grafting or pruning tools. Blight, or young tree decline (YTD), is the leading cause of death of orange trees in Florida.

CULTIVARS

Blood oranges: Common in Mediterranean areas. Among the well-known cultivars are 'Egyptian', 'Maltese', 'Ruby' and 'St Michael'.

'Navel': Good cultivars for home growing, and can be easily raised from seed. (Often are nucellar, see notes above.) They do not produce large crops, but the fruit are often juicy and sweet. Cultivars of 'Navel' include 'Washington' (see below) and 'Cara Cara', which has red flesh. The fruit mature in autumn till mid-winter.

'Pineapple': Is pineapple scented, smooth, highly coloured, especially after cold spells, with a rich, good flavour, medium-seedy. Has a tendency to pre-harvest drop. If the crop is allowed to remain too long on the tree, it may induce biennial bearing. Does fairly well in hot climates, and is more cold sensitive.

'Valencia': Medium–large, juicy, sweet fruit. Trees are large and upright. Bears heavily and tends to biennial bearing. Fruits may be greenish when ripe, but are still sweet and juicy. A late maturing variety. Thin rind, nearly seedless. Needs a warm climate. It can bear two crops a year, overlapping, giving it a late and long season lasting until mid summer.

'Washington Navel' (syn. 'Bahia'): Fruit: large, with a thick but easily removed rind, not very juicy, of excellent flavour, nearly seedless. A very popular commercial orange for eating fresh. Does not like a tropical climate.

Food

Enjoyed on its own or in fruit salads, desserts, as a garnish, as juice, in preserves. It makes an interesting wine, and a brandy. Orange slices and peel are often candied, and the peel is delicious in dark chocolate. Its essential oil is commercially used in many foods. The white pith contains pectin. The honey from orange trees is delicious and light-coloured.

Nutrition/medicinal

One orange will meet ~20% of an adult's daily folate needs. It also has very good vitamin C levels: 53 mg/100 g of fruit; unfortunately, most is concentrated in the peel and the white pithy layer beneath. Also contain lots of flavonoids in their skins (comprising ~90% of the essential oils); these can protect cells from becoming cancerous and also help fight existing cancers. Of these, limonene is thought to reduce the risk of breast cancer; and hesperedin has been found to be effective in reducing the risk of various other forms of cancer. The fruit flesh is also high in flavonoids, and rates as fifth in effectiveness against damaging oxidative processes in cells. They inhibit certain enzymes that can activate, e.g. cigarette smoke or pesticides, in the body to become carcinogens. They may lower cholesterol levels and aid in the digestion of fatty foods. In addition, these fruit contain good levels of lutein and zeaxanthin (types of vitamin A), which can help reduce the incidence of cataracts and macular degeneration. The roasted pulp is prepared as a poultice for skin diseases. The fresh peel is rubbed on acne. A decoction of the dried leaves and flowers is given in Italy as an antispasmodic, cardiac sedative, antiemetic, digestive and remedy for flatulence. The inner bark, macerated and infused in wine, is taken as a tonic and carminative. They also contain inositol, have high levels of potassium and, surprisingly, also have one of the highest fibre levels of fruits. **Warning:** Some who peel quantities of oranges may suffer a dermatitis rash or blisters on their hands, and sucking oranges can cause irritation around the mouth. Sensitive individuals can have respiratory reactions to the essential oil in the peel.

Other uses

The essential oil from the peel, flowers and leaves is used in perfumes and soaps (see bergamot below). Because of its 90–95% limonene content, it has a lethal effect on houseflies, fleas and fireants: its potential as an insecticide is under investigation. It is used in engine cleaners and household cleaners. Oil obtained from citrus seeds is used as a cooking oil and in soap and plastics. Terpenes, extracted from the outer peel, are important in resins and for paints for ships. The wood is yellowish, close-grained and hard, and is used for cabinetwork, turnery and fine, hard woodwork.

Ornamental

Orange trees make beautiful and useful specimen trees. With their glossy evergreen foliage, fragrant blossoms and leaves, and ornamental as well as edible fruits, an orange tree is hard to beat. Its non-invasive growth means that it can be planted near to buildings.

OTHER ORANGES

Descriptions are as above, unless otherwise stated.

Bergamot, *Citrus aurantium* var. *bergamia* (syn. *C. bergamia*). The bergamot orange yields neroli oil from its flowers, which is used in perfumery (e.g. in Eau de Cologne), and added to Earl Grey tea to give this its distinctive taste and smell. It has been grown in the Mediterranean since the 16th century, mostly in Italy. It is most successfully grown in the province of Reggio Calabria, Italy.

Description: It is a small tree, only ~3–4 m tall. It has irregular branches, like other orange species, and richly scented leaves. Its flowers are small and sweetly fragrant, and are borne in spring. The fruits are round–pear-shaped, have strongly aromatic peel, acid pulp. They mature from late autumn through winter, and are harvested when yellow in colour. They weigh 80–200 g. They are often budded onto sour orange when ~4 years old, but then take a further 3 years before starting to produce fruits.

Cultivation: They grow best when planted in full sun, but need protection from sudden changes in temperature and moisture variation: they do not like very wet or very dry soils. Today, most fruits are grown for their oil: it takes ~200 kg of fruit to produce 1 kg of oil. The oil's fragrance is fresh, pleasant and delicate, and is the base of almost all perfumes.

Uses: All parts of the bergamot orange are very aromatic. The flowers are widely used by the perfume industry. Petitgrain oil is distilled from the leaves, twigs and immature fruits. These oils are also used in cosmetics, soaps, confectionery and liqueurs. The oil has also been used to treat wounds, as an analgesic, as a vermifuge, as a balsamic and as a bactericide in respiratory illnesses. The essential oil is used in suntan lotions (as it contains substances that stimulate melanogenesis) and as a flavouring in pipe tobacco and candied fruit. In the pharmaceutical industry it is used as an anti-diarrhoeal, to help blood clot around wounds, as an antidote to metal poisoning and as a retarder in antibiotics. The wood is used to make fragrant boxes.

Myrtle-leaved orange, *Citrus aurantium* var. *myrtifolia*. A compact small tree, with small leaves and no thorns. Only propagated and grown on the French and Italian Riviera for its small fruits, which are preserved in brine and exported for candying.

Sour orange (Seville orange, naranja), *Citrus aurantium*. The sour orange is a much older species and is much hardier than the sweet orange. It is native to southeastern Asia. Peoples of the Pacific Islands believe the tree to have been brought to their shores in prehistoric times. It was reported to be growing in Sicily in 1002 AD, and was cultivated around Seville, Spain, at the end of the 12th century. For 500 years, it was the only orange in Europe and was the first orange to reach the New World. Spaniards introduced the sour orange into Florida. It was quickly adopted by the early settlers and local Indians and, by 1763, sour oranges were being exported to England. One of its main uses now is for its famous marmalade.

Description: A smaller tree: 3–9 m tall, it is more erect and compact than that of the sweet orange. It has smooth, brown bark, with angular, flexible young stems, and long, though not very sharp, thorns, ~2.5–8 cm long. It is long lived: some trees in Spain are reported to be >600 years old. *Leaves:* Has longer leaf stalks than sweet orange, 6.5–14 cm. Leaves are minutely toothed, dark green above, pale beneath, dotted with tiny oil glands. *Flowers:* Highly fragrant, ~3.75 cm wide. 5–12% of flowers are male. *Fruit:* Rough-surfaced, thickish aromatic bitter peel, becoming bright reddish-orange at maturity, 7–8 cm diameter. Has 10–12 segments containing acidic pulp with several–many seeds. The centre becomes hollow when mature.

Cultivation: Generally, it tolerates many adverse conditions and needs less attention than the sweet orange. *Temperature:* Grows best in warmer climates, but can tolerate several degrees of frost for short periods. *Soil:* It can grow in wetter soils, as well many other soil types. *Propagation:* Grows readily from seed. Used widely as a rootstock for other citrus species. *Pests and diseases:* Less susceptible to most problems than sweet orange, but can succumb to a disease called tristeza and to the viruses that causes crinkly leaf, gummy bark, psorosis and xyloporosis. *Cultivars:* There are many cultivars and hybrids around the world, with the most well-known being Bergamot.

Uses: *Food:* Because of their sourness, they are not usually eaten fresh; however, the Mexicans cut them in half, salt them and coat them with a hot chilli pepper paste, and then eat them! Their most popular use is in marmalade. The juice is also used in fish and meat dishes. In Egypt it has been fermented to make wine. The essential oil expressed from the peel is used in many commercial food products. The oil from the cultivars 'Jacmel', from Jamaica, and the very aromatic 'Curacao orange' give a rich, distinctive flavour to certain liqueurs. *Nutrition/medicinal:* The fresh young leaves contain an amazing 300 mg of ascorbic acid/100 g of leaf. Sour orange juice is an antiseptic and is taken to settle biliousness. Africans apply the juice to the skin in areas affected by rheumatism. In Italy, Mexico and Latin America, a tea from the leaves is taken as an antispasmodic, a stimulant, a tonic and for stomach problems. The flowers, prepared as a syrup, are said to act as a sedative in nervous disorders and induce sleep. An infusion of the bitter bark is taken as a tonic, a stimulant, to produce sweating and to eliminate internal parasites. *Other uses:* Throughout the Pacific, the crushed fruit and macerated leaves, both of which make a lather in water, are used as soap for washing clothes and as a hair shampoo. All parts of the sour orange are more aromatic than those of the sweet orange and are used for their fragrant oils, particularly that from bergamot. Wood: as the sweet orange.

Trifoliate orange, *Poncirus trifoliata* (syn. *C. trifoliata*). Has been grown for thousands of years in central and northern China, and from at least the 8th century in Japan. It is a small, fast-growing, very cold hardy (down to ~–20°C), deciduous tree, and is by far the most cold hardy citrus. It has palmate leaves, usually with three leaflets (rarely 4 or 5, hence its name); has long thorns. Its flowers are showy, white, 5-petalled. Its fruits are round–pear-shaped, 3–5 cm wide; the peel is fragrant, dull-yellow, minutely downy, rough, with numerous oil glands, thick. The pulp is scant, sour, and seeds are plump and numerous. Immature fruits and dried mature fruits are used medicinally in China. The peel can be candied and used as a spice, and is a source of pectin. The plant is much grown as an ornamental in cool areas of Europe, Asia and North America. It can be grown as a hedge. It is a popular rootstock for other citrus species.

HYBRIDS

There are many orange hybrids and a few are listed below. The reader is advised to consult more specialist literature for details of the cultivars available.

Citrange (x *Citroncirus webberi*): A trifoliate orange x sweet orange hybrid. The tree is evergreen or semi-deciduous, usually trifoliate, not as cold-resistant as the trifoliate orange. Good vigour, fruit quality and yields. Susceptible to blight, poor tolerance of salt and high pH. Fruits are fairly aromatic, look like an orange, 5–7.5 cm wide; peel is thin, yellow-orange, may be hairy or non-hairy, wrinkled, ribbed or smooth. The pulp is often very juicy and tender, richly flavoured, highly acid, slightly bitter; seedless, or with a few, mostly nucellar seeds. Used in pies, jams and marmalade.

Citrangequat (*Fortunella* sp. x citrange): see p. 213.

Orangelo: An orange x grapefruit hybrid, not very well known or successful. Tree: ~6 m tall. Leaves smell and look like those of grapefruit, except are often deformed. Young shoots may have prominent thorns. Usually flowers in spring, and then fruits ~7 months later, but can flower and fruit throughout the year. Fruit is round–pear-shaped, grapefruit in size; peel is yellow, easy to remove. The pulp is yellow-orange, 9–13 segments, juicy, with a mild flavour that is partly orange, partly grapefruit, not too acid or bitter. Have 7–15 seeds/fruit, but sometimes less. A 7-year-old tree can produce ~200 fruits a year. Fruits picked a little under-ripe store for longer than ripe fruits. Uses somewhere between that of orange and grapefruit!

Tangelo: A hybrid of mandarin orange (*C. reticulata*) and grapefruit or pummelo (*C. grandis*). The trees are large, more cold-tolerant than the grapefruit, but not quite as hardy as the mandarin. Most trees are self-fertile and often come true from seed. They also produce many seedless fruits. Fruit size is mid way between orange–grapefruit, but has an inverted-pear shape. The peel is fairly loose and easy to remove. The pulp can be colourful, sub-acid, very juicy with a good flavour.

Tangor: A hybrid of mandarin (*C. reticulata*) and sweet orange (*C. sinensis*). A larger tree, with large, sweet, orange fruit. Thick skin, easy to peel. Flesh is deep orange. Fruit ripen in late winter–spring. Cultivars include 'Dweet' and 'Ugli', with the latter cultivar forming a strange, wrinkled, irregular spherical shape. ∎

Citrus reticulata, C. deliciosa
Tangerine (naartjie), mandarin (satsuma) and tangelo (hybrid)
RUTACEAE
Relatives: orange, grapefruit, lemon, lime

The names tangerine and mandarin are often used interchangeably for a group of small orange-like fruits that have an easy-to-peel rind. The satsuma is a group of cultivars derived from these and is common in Japan: these fruits are usually seedless, and may also be called mandarins. The name 'tangerine' is sometimes used for types with a red-orange skin. These species have been known in China since 500 BC; by 300 BC they were being grown commercially in central China, and by 400 AD, grafting methods were being used to grow selected varieties on which the Chinese encouraged the cultivation of aggressive, tree-nesting taylor ants that protected the fruits from pests. The tangerine has and still is the most important citrus species in China, both commercially and in people's gardens. It has been grown in Japan for >400 years, and is also a favourite citrus species. It was here that the satsuma cultivar was developed, and there are now >100 cultivars. The tangerine has been also widely grown in tropical southeastern Asia. However, despite its popularity in Asia, it was only in the 1800s that it became established in Europe, North Africa, the West Indies, the Americas and Australasia.

DESCRIPTION
The trees are small, sometimes spiny, with slender, angular branches. They form a dense, rounded crown. When mature, they can be ~7 m tall, but are more usually ~3–4 m tall, with 3–4 m spread.

Leaves: Evergreen, oval–elliptical, with pointed tips, shiny, waxy, deep green in colour. They are smooth and non-serrated. They have a fragrant citrus smell when crushed. Leaf stems are flattened.

Flowers: White–creamy, ~2.5 cm diameter, in late summer–autumn, are wonderfully fragrant. Borne singly or in small clusters (2–6) in leaf axils. Flowers are monoecious and bisexual (i.e. both male and female parts within the same flower). The flower has five concave sepals that form a green calyx, with five white petals. There are numerous prominent stamens with bright yellow anthers. It has a superior ovary.
Pollination: Very popular with bees and other insects. They are self-fertile and have good fruit-set, so you only need a single tree to get fruit. However, as well as ordinary seeds, which produce variable offspring, some seeds are nucellar. The seedlings produced from these are clones of the parent as the embryo is formed without any genetic exchange; the seedlings are, therefore, totally predictable (see p. 15 for more details). In addition, some flowers are not pollinated, yet still go on to produce seedless fruits (parthenocarpy).

Fruit: Orange in colour, 5–10 cm in diameter, usually smaller than oranges. Most are juicy and sweet, with a waxy, loose rind that is easy to peel. The rind (epicarp) contains many tiny glands that contain essential oil. The inner rind (mesocarp) is white, spongy and non-aromatic. The pulp (endocarp) is yellow-orange, and consists of loosely packed juice sacs enclosed in ~8–12 wedge-shaped compartments, which can be easily separated. Each segment has 1–2 greeny-white, small seeds, though many segments (and fruits) can be seedless. The pulp is succulent and sweet.

Many tangerines need a cool period to initiate flowering and to produce good-flavoured fruits. Trees have a tendency to overproduce, which leads to biennial bearing, and fruit are best thinned as early as possible to avoid this. Fruits of most varieties mature during winter.

Yield/harvest/storage: Yields can vary due to biennial bearing, but, in general, trees crop well. Grafted trees start bearing 2–4 years after planting; seedlings may take 4–6 years. Citrus fruits do not continue to ripen after they have been picked, so leave them on the tree until needed. However, note the species reviewed here cannot be 'stored' on the tree as long as many other citrus species as they tend to dry out. Tangerines can store for 4–5 weeks at ~6°C and at a humidity of ~85%.

Roots: Have some surface roots, but most are deeper, so care is needed when transplanting that these are not damaged. Their deep roots make them more susceptible to waterlogging, but more tolerant of drought. Their roots are non-invasive and trees can be safely planted near walls and buildings.

CULTIVATION
Easy to grow and need little maintenance; can be grown in a wide range of soils and conditions.

Location: Can be grown in full sun or partial shade. They are not very wind tolerant. Are reasonably tolerant of salty, maritime conditions, but not if they are exposed.

Temperature: Grow best in semi-tropical or warm-temperate climates. Some cultivars are quite cold hardy and can tolerate temperatures as low as ~−10°C, or lower if they have been cold-acclimatised. Most cultivars can tolerate light frosts, but not prolonged freezing. Sudden drops in temperature cause more damage than the actual temperature it reaches. Freeze-damaged trees may lose some leaves, but usually recover. Young trees are more sensitive to cold and should be given extra protection.

Soil/water/nutrients: Grow best in deep, well-drained, fertile loam, though will grow in other soil types, such as sandy soils or even heavy clay. Can grow at a pH range of fairly acid to neutral, but do not grow as well in alkaline soils, where iron deficiency causes chlorosis. However, different rootstocks are adapted to different conditions. Do not grow well in cold, wet soils. Young trees need regular moisture till established, but mature trees are quite drought tolerant, more so than oranges. However, fruit quality is reduced if trees do not receive enough moisture during fruit development. Nutritionally, trees need regular additions of a complete fertiliser containing, in particular, nitrogen, phosphorous, potassium, sulphur and calcium. Because they are evergreen and form fruits during the winter months, two or three applications of a citrus-type fertiliser throughout the year are beneficial.

Pot culture: They are an ideal plant for containers because of their smaller size, compact growth, their evergreen, attractive leaves, fragrant flowers and bright fruits. A surface mulch helps retain moisture and adds nutrients. They can be moved indoors during colder weather.

Planting: Space at 3–5 m apart. Keep young plants well watered and weed free for the first few years.

Propagation: Seed: Many fruits are almost seedless. Seeds may produce variable progeny if they have been pollinated ordinarily, or be nucellar and produce clones of the parent. Seedlings are often more disease resistant, more vigorous and often more productive, but take somewhat longer to start producing fruits. Sow seeds when fresh, in early spring, and give them warmth: should germinate in ~21 days. *Cuttings:* Take semi-ripe cuttings in summer and insert in well-drained, gritty compost to root. *Grafting:* Usually grafted onto the same or a closely related species, e.g. the trifoliate orange (*Poncirus trifoliata*) or 'Cleopatra' mandarin seedlings.

Pruning: Tangerine trees form a neat shape and need very little pruning. Prune out any diseased or damaged wood. In general, because the tree is evergreen, much of its resources for flowering and fruiting are stored in the leaves; heavy pruning will remove these resources and can, consequently, reduce flowering and fruiting.

Pests and diseases: In small plantings and if kept healthy, they tend to have few problems. However, trees can be attacked by the guava moth, which can burrow into fruit causing damage, and also citrus-rust mites, several scale insects, mealybugs, whitefly, citrus blackfly, aphids and fruit flies. Many of these can now be combatted with biological controls. Possible diseases include greasy spot, stems affected by the fungus *Diaporthe citri* and root rot caused by various *Phytophthora* spp. In addition, there are a number of viral diseases, which are often transmitted via grafting or pruning tools.

CULTIVARS/HYBRIDS

There are various hybrids derived from crosses of tangerines and other citrus species. Many cultivars of these fruits exist, and a few are listed below.

'Clementine': Tree is of medium size, almost thornless, small yields. Fruit: medium size, 5–6 cm wide, deep orange-red. Skin: thick, loose. Flesh: deep orange, 8–12 segments; juicy, and of fine quality and flavour; 3–6 seeds, non-nucellar. Harvesting starts early, and then extends into summer.

'Cleopatra': Tree is very ornamental and is much used as a rootstock in Japan and Florida. Fruit: roundish, small, remain on the tree until next crop matures. Skin: dark orange-red; pulp is of good quality, but seedy.

'Dancy': Tree: vigorous, cold-tolerant, bears abundantly. Tends toward alternate bearing. Is disease resistant, but susceptible to chaff scale. From China. Fruit: roundish–pear-shaped; medium-sized, 6–8 cm diameter. Skin: deep orange-red, glossy at first, lumpy and fluted later, thin, leathery, tough. Flesh is dark orange with 10–14 segments, fine quality, richly flavoured, several small seeds. Harvested in late autumn–winter.

'Ponkan': Tree: Small, upright; can be maintained as a dwarf tree. Fruit: large, 7–8 cm diameter. Skin: orange, medium thick; flesh is salmon-orange, with 9–12 segments, very juicy, aromatic, sweet, of very fine quality and with few seeds. Not as cold hardy as 'Dancy'.

Tangelo: A cross between a mandarin and (usually) a grapefruit or (sometimes) a pummelo. They look and grow like a cross between orange and grapefruit. They fruit better when there is a mandarin (not another tangelo) nearby to pollinate them. Tree is medium–large in size, with very good yields. The flesh is juicy, but fairly acid and has several seeds, with a taste more like grapefruits than mandarins. They peel fairly well. Fruits are bright orange-red, 7–12 cm in diameter

uses

Food
Fruits are usually enjoyed fresh and unprepared, though can be added to desserts such as flans, fruit salads, cakes, etc. The essential oil from the peel is used commercially to flavour candies, icecream and liqueurs. Petitgrain mandarin oil, distilled from the leaves, twigs and unripe fruits, is used in the same way.

Nutrition
The 'Dancy' cultivar contains more synephrine (a decongestant) than any other citrus fruit. Fruits contain good levels of vitamin C: 32 mg/100 g of flesh. In addition, tangerines are a good source of vitamin A (920 IU/100 g), particularly of lutein and zeaxanthin, which have been shown to reduce the incidence of cataracts and macular degeneration.

Medicinal
The skins contain monoterpenes (tangeretin and nobiletin), which can protect cells from becoming cancerous and help fight existing cancers. They may actually increase the benefit of Tamoxifen (an anti-oestrogenic medicine used in the treatment of metastatic cancer). It is unknown if these compounds survive cooking.

Other uses
The essential oils from these fruits are used in perfumes and colognes.

Ornamental
Make excellent, smaller, specimen trees that can be planted close to buildings. Give year-round interest.

and are very ornamental. Harvested in late winter/spring, they do not 'store' for long on the tree.

'Willow-leaf': Tree: small–medium, slender branches, almost thornless. Reproduces true from seed. Often grown as an ornamental and for breeding. Fruit: medium-sized, 5–6 cm diameter. Skin: orange, glossy, thin; pulp is orange, 10–12 segments; very juicy, sweet, rich flavour, several seeds. Early harvest.

SATSUMA CULTIVARS

Satsumas tend to be highly cold-resistant, and are more resistant to canker, gummosis, psorosis and melanose. Usually budded onto *Poncirus trifoliata* or sweet orange.

'Kara': Tree is vigorous, thornless, large leaves. Fruit: medium-sized, 5–7 cm diameter. Skin: deep orange to orange-yellow, thin to medium, fairly tough; pulp: yellow-orange, ~12 segments, tender, very juicy, aromatic, rich flavour, acid until fully ripe, then sweet; usually 12–20 large seeds, but can be nearly seedless. Late harvest.

'Owari': Tree: small, almost thornless, large-leaved. Fruit: medium-sized, 4–6 cm diameter. Skin: orange, slightly rough, thin, tough; pulp: orange, a rich, sub-acid flavour; nearly seedless. Early but short harvesting season. Peel may stay green at maturity.

'Wase': Tree: dwarfing, slow-growing, heavy-bearing, but susceptible to pests and diseases. Fruit: large, ~6 cm diameter. Skin: orange, thin, smooth; pulp: pinky-orange, melting, sweet, with ~10 segments. Very early harvest. ■

Clausena lansium (syn. *C. wampi, C. punctata, Cookia wampi, Quinaria lansium*)

Wampee (wampi, mafai-jean)

RUTACEAE

Relatives: *Citrus*

Is a native and a popular fruit and ornamental garden tree in many parts of southern China and is also grown in the Far East, including Thailand, southern Malaysia and Singapore. It is grown commercially for its fruits, on a small scale, in China. Although related, its appearance is quite different to citrus species.

DESCRIPTION

An attractive, evergreen, slender tree, growing to ~7 m, with long, vertical-slanting, flexible branches. Fairly fast-growing or rather slow, depending on its situation. It has grey-brown, rough bark.

Leaves: Dark green, evergreen, oval, wavy, resinous, pinnate, in 10–30-cm-long groups of 7–15 alternate leaflets that are often spirally arranged. The leaflets have finely serrated margins. The upper leaf veins have a fine fuzz of hair, while the underside has a yellow, prominent midrib. Attractive autumn colours. The petiole is warty and hairy.

Flowers: Fragrant, whitish-yellow-green, five petals, ~2 cm diameter, borne in long clusters on slender panicles (10–50 cm long) in late autumn. Are bisexual and are probably self-fertile, though benefit from being planted in groups. *Pollination:* By bees and other insects.

Fruit: Aromatic, round–oblong, pale yellow berries (~2.0 cm long), forming grape-like bunches of showy strands (10–60 a bunch). The berry is divided into five sections, each marked with a pale ridge that extends a short distance down from the apex. The yellow–pale brown skin is thin, pliable, but can be tough and is covered with tiny, raised, brown oil glands. The flesh is very juicy, refreshing, clean, sweet–tangy-tasting with colourless–yellow-cream glutinous flesh. In some varieties, the flesh taste is more sub-acid. There are usually 1–2 oval, bright green seeds per fruit, ~1.4 cm long.

Yield: The fruits develop during winter and spring to ripen in spring or summer in warmer areas, or sometimes later in cooler regions. Fruits should be picked when fully coloured and ripe. Trees can first produce fruits after 3–6 years, but sometimes longer. Mature trees can yield 45–50 kg of fruits per tree a season. When harvesting, retaining the stalks on the fruits extends their storage time.

Roots: Do not form massive roots, so can be planted near to buildings.

CULTIVATION

A species for warmer, protected areas and should be treated as *Citrus* species.

Location: Likes full sun and protection in winter. Can be grown in sheltered maritime locations.

Temperature: The wampee prefers a subtropical–tropical climate, but young and mature trees can survive frosts and temperatures down to −2.2ºC, though temperatures of −6.6ºC and lower can kill trees. Can be grown outside in warm-temperate regions, with care.

Soil/water/nutrients: Relatively tolerant of a range of soils, but prefers neutral to acid conditions. On more alkaline soils, iron chlorosis can be a problem, although applications of nutrients that include iron, manganese and zinc may help. Prefers a well-drained, loam-sandy soil, and appreciates some moisture year round. Does not tolerate waterlogging,

Food

The fruits are best eaten fresh. When fully ripe, the sweeter varieties have a sweet refreshing flesh: the rind and seeds are discarded. The flesh can be added to fruit desserts, pies, chutney, curries, drinks and jam. The Chinese serve the de-seeded fruits with meat dishes and also preserve it in many forms. A Chinese recipe says to soak the wampees in brine (0.3 kg of salt:10 kg of water) for 6 hours, remove the seeds, then mix the flesh with sugar and leave for at least 2 hours. The mixture is then sun dried, turning occasionally. When dried thus, wampee flesh can then be kept for several years. In southeast Asia, a bottled, carbonated beverage resembling champagne is made by fermenting the fruits with sugar.

Nutrition/medicinal

Good levels of vitamin C (~30 mg/100 g of fruit). The fruits are said to help stomach disorders, increase appetite and act as a vermifuge. The dried immature fruits and/or dried roots are used in the Far East for bronchitis.

Other uses

The juice from the leaves is used as a hair wash to remove dandruff and 'preserve the colour of hair'.

Ornamental

An attractive medium-sized tree that makes a good shade tree as well as having attractive flowers and fragrant fruits. Wildlife and birds love the fruit.

---

or grow well in dry soils. Appreciates the addition of organic matter to the soil or a mulch. In general, the tree has the same requirements as citrus species and benefits from regular applications of a citrus-type fertilser.

Propagation: *Seed:* Good germination in a few days from fresh seed. Wash all pulp from the seed before sowing in warm, moist compost. *Cuttings:* Grows well from softwood cuttings taken from young growth. *Layering:* This species can be air-layered successfully. *Grafting:* Can be whip-and-tongue-grafted onto its own seedlings.

Pruning: The crop is produced at the tips of the branches so pruning needs to be done with care to avoid removing the fruiting wood. Larger branches can be removed to enable it to fit into smaller gardens.

Pests and diseases: Few disease problems are reported apart from citrus canker and occasional aphids.

CULTIVARS

'Guy Sahm': From Australia. Has excellent brown fruits with a sweet, tangy, aromatic flavour.

'Yeem Pay': From Australia. Fruits are larger, oval, yellow-skinned with a very sweet flavour. Good cropper. ■

Coccoloba uvifera
Sea grape
POLYGONACEAE
Relatives: Darling plum

The Polygonaceae form a large and diverse family of herbs, shrubs and trees that are often adapted to maritime locations. The sea grape is an exotic, attractive, medium-sized tree that is native to the coastal grassland and dune regions of the tropics and subtropics of the Americas. Its growth is reduced in colder areas. It has ornamental leaves, fragrant flowers and produces an abundance of grape-like fruits.

DESCRIPTION

A medium-sized, moderately fast-growing, sprawling tree, reaching heights ~8–12 m, and 6–10 m spread. It forms a variety of shapes, depending on its location. Naturally, it tends to be multi-stemmed and sprawling, and forms a vase shape or, as the tree ages, its branches become somewhat more drooping. It can, however, be pruned to form a tree with a single trunk. Its bark is thin and forms beautiful, irregularly-coloured patches that range from blue-grey to

yellow-grey. This can be easily damaged.

Leaves: Trees have unusual, large (~20–30 cm), evergreen, simple, shiny, waxy, leathery, alternate leaves, roundish, with a heart-shaped base, similar to many within the Polygonaceae family. Young leaves, in spring, have an attractive reddish colour, which matures to dark green. Leaves have striking, prominent, red veins.

Flowers: Numerous, small, creamy-white, fragrant, five-petalled. Are borne in clusters in racemes, 15–25 cm long,

Food

The fruits are acid and musky, yet sweet and tasty. They can be eaten fresh, or can be added to desserts and sauces, made into jam, and are particularly recommended for jelly, or can be made into a wine.

Medicinal

The bark is used to treat sore throats.

Other uses

The timber is used for cabinet work. The resin from the bark is used for tanning and yields a red dye.

Ornamental

Given space, it can form an attractive tropical-looking specimen that gives year-round interest because of its leaves, its multi-stemmed shape, fragrant flowers and its fruits. It makes a good shade tree. Occasionally they are planted closer together and are pruned to form a larger screen/hedge. However, it does need careful hand pruning to avoid cutting up the large attractive leaves. Can be planted in sandy soils to stabilise them. Is a common, urban-landscaping tree in Florida. Birds are attracted to the fruits.

in late spring–early summer. *Pollination:* Dioecious, so need both male and female trees to set fruit.

Fruit: Round berries, 1.5–2 cm in diameter, borne in grape-shaped clusters of ~40, occurring on female trees. Young fruits are green, turning red–deep purple as they ripen in late summer, or sometimes not till autumn. The skin is tougher than that of grapes. The flesh is juicy when fully ripe, and has a sub-acid, musky yet sweet flavour. A large, single, pointed seed is embedded within the flesh.

Yield/harvest: Yields can be plentiful, a single large plant producing several thousand fruits per season. Trees grown from seedlings first start producing fruits after ~5+ years; trees grown vegetatively can start producing fruits in their second year. Pick clusters when the fruits have softened and fully changed colour: they need to be ripe to be fully enjoyed. Unfortunately, fruits do not all ripen at the same time within the clusters, which means that there is either some wastage or that plants need picking more frequently.

Roots: Has a fibrous, spreading root system that helps to stabilise sandy soils. There are no reports that it should not be planted near to buildings.

CULTIVATION

They are a tough species and need little maintenance.

Location: Can be grown in semi-shade or full sun. It is fairly wind tolerant with relatively strong branches and tough leaves that can survive and desiccating and damaging winds. It is often grown as an urban tree in Florida, and seems to be surprisingly tolerant of air pollution, compacted soil and poor drainage.

Temperature: Plants are frost sensitive and prefer warmer climates, although several reports say that they can survive some frost (−4°C). As with all plants, younger trees will be more susceptible to frosts, and need extra protection in colder areas.

Soil/water/nutrients: Can be grown in a range of soils: i.e. clay or loam, but are particularly adapted to sand. They can grow in sand dunes and other coastal environments. Has excellent salt tolerance, and is a very good tree for maritime location. Can grow at a range of pH values from acidic to alkaline. Prefers a well-drained soil. Is very drought tolerant, though young plants should be kept well-watered till established. Trees grow better and give better yields if they are given supplementary nutrients in poor soils. These are best applied while the tree is actively growing. On alkaline soils, deficiencies of iron, manganese and magnesium can occur, and should be remedied with an application of trace-elements or bonemeal.

Planting: Space young trees several metres apart to give them adequate room for growth.

Pruning: Prune trees well before any risk of frost. Generally only give minimum pruning if a multi-stemmed tree is wanted. In exposed locations, the trees may need branches tidying up and broken branches removed. Look out for weak, narrow-angled notches between branches, which may be more susceptible to breakage. If a single-stemmed tree is required, trees need extra pruning for the first few years to achieve this. It is better to remove competing trunks soon after they have formed rather than later when they are larger: this reduces the effect on the overall shape of the tree and decreases the risk of disease.

Propagation: *Seed:* Usually by seed. There is good germination. But, whether a seedling is male or female cannot be ascertained for ~5+ years until they first flower. *Cuttings:* Semi-ripe cuttings in summer. These have the advantage of being vegetatively grown, but are more difficult (though reports vary on this). *Grafting:* Whip-and-tongue grafting is possible. *Layering:* By either ground- or air-layering: take can be variable, but the progeny are more predictable.

Pests and diseases: Generally trouble free. May get occasional gall damage to the upper leaf surface.

CULTIVARS

Although there are a few cultivars available, these have been mostly selected for their ornamental properties, e.g. a variegated cultivar has been produced. In the future, perhaps cultivars will also be selected for their fruiting qualities. ∎

Coffea spp.
Coffee
RUBIACEAE

Coffea arabica, C. robusta, C. liberica, C. dewevrei

Relatives: gardenia

Coffee trees are native to Ethiopia, from a region called Kaffa. From there they spread to Yemen, Arabia and Egypt, where the drink made from coffee beans became widely used in everyday life. Coffee has been popular as a beverage, at every level of society, since at least 800 BC. It was also used as a medicine, and its stimulating properties have long been known. Initially, coffee was met by hostility from devoted Muslims. Then, too, in Italy, Pope Clemente VII was urged by fellow churchmen to forbid the faithful to drink the 'devil's beverage'. He is reported to have said after tasting this new black, fragrant beverage, 'This beverage is so delicious that it would be a sin to let only misbelievers drink it! Let's defeat Satan by blessing this beverage, which contains nothing objectionable to a Christian!' By the late 1500s, the first traders were selling coffee in Europe, and coffee entered into Western life and custom. The increasing needs of a growing market improved botanical knowledge of the coffee plant, and high taxes imposed at the ports of shipment led dealers and scientists to grow coffee in other countries. The Dutch grew it in Batavia and Java, the French grew it in Martinique and the Antilles, and the English, Spanish and Portuguese introduced it into the tropical areas of Asia and America. In 1727, coffee growing began in Brazil. Coffee is big business and is one of the main commodities in world markets. Although coffee is usually grown in warmer regions of the world, it can be grown in semi-tropical and warm temperate areas. Given winter warmth and protection, it could even be grown as a container species in colder regions.

DESCRIPTION

In the wild, trees can be 10–12 m tall, but, in cultivation, they are usually kept to 2–5 m to make harvesting and cultivation easier and more economic. There are several species and many cultivars of coffee. However, the two main commercial species are *Coffea arabica* and *C. robusta* (see below). Most instant and canned coffees are produced from *C. liberica* and *C. robusta* beans. Gourmet coffees are almost always made from those of *C. arabica*.

Leaves: Evergreen, glossy, lanceolate, up to 20 cm long, dark green above, lighter beneath.

Flowers: White, delicate, with five petals and a jasmine-like fragrance, are borne in clusters in spring, from the leaf axils. The flowers only last ~2–3 days. *Pollination:* By bees and other insects. Flowers are bisexual, so only need one plant to set fruits, though cross fertilisation increases yields and bean quality.

Fruit: Green, rounded, cherry-like, a drupe, ~1.5 cm in diameter. As it ripens, the skin turns a bright cherry-red colour, and finally to brown when fully ripe in late summer. They have a soft, sweet, inner red pulp. Within the pulp are two coffee 'beans', the kernels of the coffee fruit. These are semi-oval, furrowed along one side, and are bluish-green or a brown-bronze, depending on species. *C. arabica* beans are flatter and oval, with a crooked furrow; *C. robusta* beans are convex, rounder and have a straight centre furrow.

Yield/harvest: Seedlings begin producing fruits when 2–4 years old; cuttings can start producing fruits after 18 months. Good yields are obtained after 5–6 years. Yields are ~0.4 kg of beans per tree from *C. arabica* (from ~2 kg of fruit), and ~0.6 kg of *C. robusta* beans per plant (from ~2 kg of fruit). Trees should produce for at least ~30 years, and they can live for ~80 years. The fruits take a long time to ripen, and are left unpicked until ~6–9 months after fruit-set. The trees often carry both fruits and flowers at the same time, as well as their intermediate stages. Crops need to be picked from trees several times, just selecting ripe fruits, so this is fairly time-consuming. Harvested fruits are ideally left to dry in the sun and the bean is then separated from the skin and pulp before the pulp starts to ferment.

Commercially, there are two main methods of coffee bean preparation: dry and wet. The 'dry' method is mostly used in Brazil and Western Africa. The beans are dried in the sun for 15–20 days (or are artificially dried at 45–60°C for 2–3 days). They are then mechanically cleaned of their pulp and skins. These beans usually age better. In the 'wet' process, the beans are soaked and washed to remove the outer pulp of the fruit. The beans produced are called 'washed' or 'mild'. This method is mostly done in Central America, Mexico, Colombia, Kenya and Tanzania. Whichever initial stage is used, all beans are then soaked in water to initiate a fermentation process, which enhances the coffee's aromatic and flavour qualities, as well as its colour. They are then dried and placed in sacks for storage and shipment.

Roots: Plants are shallow rooted; therefore, care is required with mechanical cultivation. The roots need good aeration, so it is important that the soil structure is loose. Trees benefit from an organic mulch to retain moisture, add nutrients and maintain good soil structure.

CULTIVATION

They are quite fussy about growth conditions and temperature.

Location: Trees prefer some shade, and do not like direct sun, which can lower the rate of photosynthesis. They are not wind tolerant. Are best planted in a sheltered, shady, warm location.

Temperature: Prefer warm/hot humid climates with temperatures of 15–25°C for *C. arabica* and slightly warmer for *C. robusta*. They are not frost hardy, tolerating ~–2°C at most, though can withstand some cold nights. However, trees can be grown outside in warm temperate locations, with care and protection during colder spells.

Soil/water/nutrients: Trees need well-aerated soils: clay soils lack aeration. However, although sandy soils have good aeration, they usually lack water-holding capacity, and so you need to add organic matter to overcome this. They prefer a slightly acid soil, and like lots of nitrogen. The best soils are often on slopes with deep volcanic soil and plentiful organic matter. Trees like plenty of moisture, and are not at all drought tolerant. They also like lots of nutrients, and need regular applications of a complete fertiliser throughout the year. Additions of well-rotted manure or blood-and-bone fertilisers are beneficial.

Pot culture: A good species for container culture: they are shallow rooting and like some shade. They can be moved to a warmer position in winter, but do need to ensure they receive sufficient moisture and nutrients. A good plant for a shaded conservatory.

Planting: If pruning to restrict size, space plants at 2–4 m apart, though should be wider apart for specimen plantings. Plant carefully, and try not to disturb the roots too much.

uses

A very popular beverage. Coffee has ~900 volatile aromas. Once cleaned, fermented and dried (see above), the beans are roasted. This is a critical phase and gives coffee about 70% of its unique aroma, taste and colour. As the temperature rises, the beans lose 20% of their moisture, but also expand in size by ~60%. Temperatures should not exceed 230°C. The longer the roast and the higher the final temperature, the stronger and more intensive the final flavour, and the darker the beans. Roasting times vary between 6–11 minutes. As they are heated, the beans make a popping sound, and aromatic oil and volatile aromas are released. However, beyond a certain point, darker roasted coffee will lose its character. The characteristics of the various roasts are as follows:

Light–medium roasts

Are less developed in body and flavour. The lighter roasts are referred to as 'institutional' or 'American' roasts, with the latter having more body. They tend to be more acidic.

Medium–dark roasts

'Full city' and 'Viennese' are medium roasts, are darker in colour and have a richer flavour. They have little acidity. 'Continental' roast is a darker coffee. 'French' and 'Italian' are even darker roasts with a subtle smoky flavour: they are full-bodied and have a sweeter taste.

Dark–espresso roasts

Espresso is the darkest roast of all, with a smoky, almost burnt taste that overrides other coffee flavours. It is usually used to make extremely strong coffee, but can be used in cappuccino, cafè latte and café au lait for a milder taste.

Medicinal

Coffee beans, apart from their caffeine, contain high levels of polyphenolics, which can act as excellent antioxidants. However, roasting can destroy some of these and milder roasted blends will contain more antioxidants. The high caffeine levels within coffee beans can also help clear congestion, help prevent asthma attacks and boost athletic performance, but too much caffeine causes the 'jitters', insomnia and can bring on migraines. A recent article by Etherton and Kochar, entitled *Coffee facts and controversies* published in the *Archives of Family Medicine*, reported that 'coffee appears to pose no particular threat in most people if consumed in moderation'. The caffeine content in a cup of instant is ~60 mg of caffeine, a cup of percolated coffee contains ~100 mg, and a 2.5-ounce espresso coffee also contains ~100 mg. Because caffeine opens the bronchial tubes and relieves congestion, it is included within many cold formulas, and it also helps to counteract the sedative effects of the antihistamines these drugs contain. Caffeine is also being increasingly used in party drugs and pick-me-ups. Caffeine within tablets may have different enhancing factors than when taken within a substance such as coffee. Several studies show that a combination of aspirin and caffeine relieves pain significantly better than aspirin alone. Caffeine can improve stamina, and can help weight loss by boosting the number of calories you burn per hour by ~4%. Coffee may relieve the effects of jet lag and help shift the body's rhythms back to normal.

Warning: Coffee is addictive: regular users develop a tolerance and require more coffee to obtain the desired effect. If deprived of caffeine, withdrawal symptoms can include nausea and headaches. It can also cause insomnia, increase anxiety, irritability and nervousness, and can aggravate panic attacks. It remains in the body for 8–12 hours. It can also cause stomach upset because it increases the secretion of stomach acids. People with ulcers or gastrointestinal conditions should drink little if any. Coffee raises blood pressure in people who aren't accustomed to it; however, once a caffeine tolerance is developed, normal consumption no longer affects blood pressure. Some studies have linked high levels of coffee consumption to increased risk of heart attack, so those at risk should drink less than four cups of coffee a day.

Ornamental

Coffee trees can be grown indoors as an attractive specimen plant, or outdoors as a feature plant in a tropical garden, or as a container plant on a patio or deck. Its rich dark green leaves and its requirement for shade make it ideal for an exotic, interesting inclusion in a planting scheme.

Propagation: *Seeds:* Sow seeds when fresh if possible. The fruits can be placed in water, and those that float rejected. The pulp needs to be thoroughly washed from the seeds, and then the seeds can be soaked for ~24 hours in warm water before sowing at ~2 cm depth. Keep seeds moist, warm and in shade. *Cuttings:* Ripe cuttings can be taken in spring and early summer, and should root within 45 days. These are then grown on in pots before planting out. Keep in the warmth and protect till plants are ~0.5 m tall before planting out. *Grafting:* Is used for some varieties.

Pruning: There are many methods of commercial pruning, but the coffee plant is usually pruned to a few vertical central leaders with several horizontal branches. Older verticals are then removed after about the fourth year, and a few new verticals are selected for development, with other newer competing verticals removed. They can be pruned to control size and shape, and coppiced about every 4 years. Pruning is usually done in late winter or early spring.

Pests and diseases: In most areas they have few problems. Commercially, they can be attacked by coffee-berry borer, which can destroy the crop. The larvae of the coffee-leaf moth can feed on the leaves and sometimes the flowers and fruits, and coffee rust (a fungus) can result in die-back.

MAIN COFFEE SPECIES

Coffea arabica. This species has been grown and selected for several centuries, and represents 75% of total world production. As the name suggests, it comes from Arabia. Its leaves are thin, have a wavy leaf margin and are light green. It thrives in soils that are rich in nutrients. Its better-known sub-varieties are *Moka*, *Maragogipe*, *San Ramon*, *Columnaris* and *Bourbon*. It makes a full-bodied, good-quality coffee that is sharp in taste, and has a lower caffeine content than other species. While still generally regarded as the finest coffee species, *C. arabica* now has a great many cultivars, some of which are actually inferior to the best *C. robusta* hybrids. The tree of *C. arabica* is more fragile and has lower yields than that of *C. robusta*.

Coffea robusta. A larger tree, it can grow to >12 m high. Fast growing and more hardy and resistant to parasites than *C. arabica*, the tree has characteristic umbrella-shaped growth, and thin leaves with wavy margins. Discovered in the Congo in ~1900, this species is now widely grown in Africa, Asia and Indonesia. It represents ~25% of total world production. It has about double the caffeine content of *C. arabica*. The coffee is stronger and tends to have a harsher flavour, and is often used in speciality blends. About 5% is usually added to espresso blends. Improper processing can result in cheap and bitter-tasting coffee.

Coffea liberica. Originates from West Africa. Hardy and requires less maintenance than *C. arabica*, but beans tend to be harsher in flavour. Has the largest fruits, and these are borne singly or in small clusters. Its leaves are thicker and longer. It is tolerant of drought and can grow in a wide range of soils. The caffeine content can be 50% higher than that of *C. arabica*. Likes forest environments and produces high yields. Only 1% of world supply.

Coffea dewevrei (Excelsa coffee). Only 1% of world supply. It has wider, thicker leaves that have smooth edges. Young leaves are often shiny, with a bronze-violet colour, and the fruits are often larger that those of *C. arabica*. ∎

Cordia spp.
Cordia
BORAGINACEAE (Ehretiaceae)

Wild olive (*Cordia boissieri*), *Cordia monoica*, *Cordia subcordata*, cordia (*C. dodecandra*), geiger tree (*C. sebestena*), large sebesten (*C. obliqua*), lasura (*C. myxa*), septee saucer-berry (*C. caffra*), sebesten plum (*C. dichotoma*)

Relatives: borage, echium, comfrey

Cordia is a genus of ~300 mostly ornamental trees and shrubs that grow worldwide in warmer regions of tropical America, India, Africa and the Middle East. Many of them have fragrant, many petalled, attractive flowers and edible fruit, and are popularly grown in gardens. They vary in their hardiness. Most have hairy leaves, and some are used as herbs. They all have typical terminal flowers that sometimes coil at their tips. Many of the species have wood that is valued commercially.

DESCRIPTION

Wild olive (anacahuita), *Cordia boissieri*. A native of North America, it forms a small tree, ~5–7 m in height, 3–5 m spread. It has a rounded canopy and a slow-to-moderate growth rate. It has thin bark. It is one of the more cold tolerant species of this genus.

Leaves: Are yellow-green above, silvery-green beneath, large, 5–10 cm long, 5–8 cm wide, oblong to ovate, velvety, thick, alternate, simple with entire leaf margins. Evergreen, though may be deciduous in colder regions.

Flowers: Very showy, trumpet-shaped, white, ~7 cm wide, with yellow throats, with a terminal flower and others clustered below it down the stem. They can be borne for most of the year if enough moisture is available and if it is warm enough; if not, then they flower from late spring to early summer. *Pollination:* Bees and insects are attracted to the sweetly scented flowers.

Fruits: A drupe, olive-like, 1.5–2.5 cm long, white or yellow-green, turning brown with age, popular with wildlife, particularly birds. They have a single hard stone, which contains two seeds. The pulp is fleshy.

Roots: Has many surface roots that benefit from an organic mulch to retain moisture and add nutrients. Also has deep taproots, but the root system is not invasive.

CULTIVATION

Location: Likes full sun or partial shade. It is not very tolerant of coastal conditions or of exposed locations.

Temperature: Although hardy to ~–7°C, trees may lose their leaves in a severe frost.

Soil/water/nutrients: Can grow in clay, loam or sandy soils, but likes well-drained conditions. Grows best at slightly acidic to neutral pH: 5.5–6.5. They can grow in more alkaline soils, but may suffer nutrient-deficiency problems, such as iron chlorosis, which need to be remedied by applications of micronutrients. Plants grow best in drier soils, and can tolerate drought, though need regular watering to produce flowers and fruits year round. Plants are not nutrient hungry, and only need one or two applications of a general, balanced fertiliser (or similar) during the growing season, particularly with potassium.

Pot culture: A good species for container culture for its flowers and attractive evergreen leaves. It can be kept looking good for several years, if carefully maintained.

Planting: Seedlings grow slowly to begin with, but speed up growth in their second and third years. They often grow better with a little shade, plus warmth and moisture.

Pruning: Can be trained as a standard tree, with several trunks or with just one. Only needs pruning to form an aesthetically pleasing shape and to encourage a strong structure. Prune to remove crowded or crossing branches and to allow light and air to penetrate into the crown.

Propagation: *Seeds:* Germination is better if sown when fresh, otherwise, they may need warm stratification at ~20°C for ~30 days, followed by cold stratification at ~4°C for a further ~30 days. However, seeds from most of these species do remain viable for a year or so. Seeds are difficult to extract from the hard stone without damaging them, so are usually sown within the stone, and this can be lightly scarified to speed up germination. They are best sown at a depth of ~2 cm. Germination takes 3–6 weeks, or sometimes longer. If more than one seedling emerges from a stone, these need to be gently separated. *Cuttings:* Softwood or semi-ripe stem cuttings can be taken in summer, treated with a rooting hormone, and placed under mist. *Layering:* Air layering is successful.

Pests and diseases: No serious problems.

OTHER CORDIA SPECIES

The foregoing notes apply to the species below, unless specifically mentioned.

***Cordia monoica* (syn. *Cordia ovalis*).** Is grown in India and many parts of Africa, and is common along watercourses in rocky areas and in clay soils. It is a spreading, densely branched bush, shrub or tree, normally 3–5 m tall. The bark is yellow-grey, smooth and flaking. *Flowers:* Cream-coloured. *Fruits:* Round, yellow-orange, up to 2 cm diameter. *Propagation:* By seed, sown directly and without pre-treatment.

Uses: Fruits are very sweet and can be eaten fresh. The fruit is usually peeled, and the seed discarded. *Other uses:* Can be grown as a live fence. The wood is good for carving.

***Cordia subcordata*.** Often a coastal plant found in tropical or subtropical areas. A moderately fast-growing, small tree (~8 m tall) with a broad, dense crown. It can grow in many soil types from sands to clays. It can tolerate brackish water and droughts. It often forms suckers from its shallow root system. The plants are not cold tolerant. *Leaves:* Evergreen. *Flowers:* Showy, in panicles, deep orange, and are mostly borne in spring. Trees usually fruit within 3–5 years. The fruit, a drupe, is globose, ~2.5 cm long, and contains 1–4 white seeds, ~1 cm long. It becomes brown and hard when ripe.

Uses: The kernel and mucilaginous pulp are both eaten. The kernel tastes a bit like a filbert nut. In India, the flowers and young fruits are eaten as vegetables. The flowers are also pickled. *Other uses:* Its wood is light with an attractive grain: soft and easily worked. *Ornamental:* Often planted as an ornamental and shade tree in warmer regions.

Cordia, *Cordia dodecandra*. A native of Mexico and through Central America, often grown for its good-quality

uses

Food
The fruits can be eaten fresh or cooked, and are used to make jelly, jam or are added to desserts. However, some reports recommend that not too many are eaten as they may cause dizziness and intoxication.

Medicinal
Fruits used in Mexico as a cold and cough medicine.

Ornamental
Good for general landscaping or as a specimen tree. If watered well they can flower year round.

fruits. It can grow in arid and hot, dry areas, and has been introduced into dry tropical forests elsewhere in the world. It also grows well in maritime locations. A deciduous tree, growing to ~30 m in ideal conditions, but often much smaller in cooler areas, it has a straight, short trunk, with a rounded or pyramidal dense crown, made up of rising branches. Sometimes has a multi-stemmed shape. *Leaves:* Elliptic–ovate, simple, 5–15 cm long, 5–10 cm wide. They are tough and rough. *Flowers:* Very showy. Deep, vivid orange, in panicles, borne mostly in spring–summer. *Fruits:* Round to pear-shaped. Fairly hard, 3–4 cm long, greeny-yellow when ripe with a fleshy, sweet or bittersweet, fragrant pale yellow pulp. Inside are 1–2 seeds. They ripen in mid–late summer.

Cultivation: Trees can grow in dry, alkaline soils as well as sandy soils. They are not cold tolerant and need year-round warmth. *Propagation:* Seeds benefit from scarification. Germination varies from good and within 14–21 days, to poor and taking much longer.

Uses: The fruits are sweet and are used to make preserves and jams. *Medicinal:* The bark, flowers and fruits are used to treat coughs, diarrhoea and dysentery. *Other uses:* The wood is highly valued and is dark-coloured, hard, resistant and also very oily. It is often used on ships, to make furniture, handicrafts, veneer, etc. *Ornamental:* Often planted as an ornamental shade tree.

Geiger tree (scarlet cordia, lolu), *Cordia sebestena*. A native of the Caribbean and the southern states of the USA, it forms a dense, rounded, evergreen, small tree to ~7.5 m tall, ~7 m spread. It is one of the most popular ornamental *Cordia* species. It can form a single or multi-stemmed tree and has thin bark. This species, for some unknown reason, was named after John Geiger, a 19th-century pilot and ship-wrecker from Key West. It is fairly slow growing. *Leaves:* Evergreen or can be deciduous in drier regions, large, ~15–25 cm long, 10–15 cm wide, stiff, dark green, very rough and hairy. *Flowers:* Very showy, tubular, dark orange, ~3–5 cm diameter, in large clusters through spring and summer, though in good conditions can be borne almost all year round. *Fruit:* Oval–pear shaped, 2.5–4 cm long, greenish-white when ripe, in clusters. They have a poor flavour.

Cultivation: Trees are not at all cold hardy, but could be grown in containers and given extra protection in colder weather. Much more frost tender than many other *Cordias*, resistant to only 0°C. Likes full sun. Is drought tolerant, but does better with regular watering, and is reported to be even quite tolerant of waterlogging, salt spray and brackish water. Is more tolerant of wind then some *Cordia* species, so is ideal for coastal locations. Is fairly tolerant of air pollution. *Soil:* Can grow in a range of soil types. *Pot culture:* Can be grown in containers, particularly in colder regions. *Propagation:* Seeds, cuttings, layering (see general notes). *Pruning:* Trees can be pruned to form a single or multi-trunk form. *Pests and diseases:* Mites, scales and caterpillars can attack this species, but it is generally trouble free.

Uses: The fruits are not very tasty, and may be best cooked and combined with other fruits in desserts, jam, etc. *Medicinal:* All part of this plant are used medicinally to treat catarrh, oedema, malaria, urinary incontinence, venereal disease. *Other uses:* The wood is hard and dense, and is sometimes used to make furniture.

Large sebesten, *Cordia obliqua* (syn. *C. wallichii, C. latifolia*). A vigorous medium-sized tree, native to the lower slopes of the mid Himalayas. Grows to ~10.5 m tall, with a trunk girth of ~0.7 m. Wood, light brown, moderately hard. *Leaves:* Deciduous, alternate, entire to slightly dentate, oval, ~10.0 cm long, 5.5 cm wide. Young leaves are hairy beneath; mature leaves become almost smooth. *Flowers:* White, small, ~ 6 mm wide, smooth, on short stalks, held in clusters of ~15 flowers at the ends of stems and laterally. Borne in spring. Are bisexual, and only need one plant to achieve fruit-set. *Fruit:* A drupe, ~1.75 cm diameter, light yellow-greenish, with a light red tinge at full maturity; skin is thick; pulp is mucilaginous. Stone is hard, ~0.8 cm long, 0.7 cm wide and contains two seeds. The seeds are somewhat sweet. *Yield/harvest:* It can have good yields of ~30 kg per tree. Fruits are harvested when fully ripe from mid–end summer. *Pests and diseases:* Can get serious losses of fruits due to the maggots of fruit flies.

Uses: *Food:* Mature fruits are highly mucilaginous and sweet, and are not very good eaten fresh. A very good pickle can be made from the slightly under-ripe fruits. *Nutrition:* Fresh fruits contain good levels of protein (for a fruit), and also contain phosphorus, potassium, calcium and magnesium. *Medicinal:* The fruits are often used to clear phlegm and are effective in treating lung infections, coughs and chronic fever. They are said to lessen thirst, stop pain from burning urine, remove joint pain, relieve a sore throat and treat diseases of the spleen. *Other uses:* The mucilaginous substance from the fruit can be used as a gum for pasting paper or cardboard.

Lasura (sebesten, Sudan teak), *Cordia myxa* (syn. *C. domestica*). A medium-sized (10–15 m tall), broad-leaved, deciduous tree that is indigenous to China but is now grown in warmer regions of the world: India, southern Asia, Africa, northern Australia and around the Mediterranean. When mature, the girth of its trunk can be 1–1.5 m wide. Its crown spreads widely in all directions, though it can be trained to form a beautiful inverted dome shape, like an umbrella. It is a fairly fast-growing tree. In cooler regions, it forms a smaller tree or a large shrub. Its bark is greyish-brown and has many distinctive longitudinal and vertical fissures. *Leaves:* Broad, oval, with pointed tips, alternate and tend to be smooth above and finely pubescent beneath, especially when young. *Flowers:* Creamy-white, in terminal clusters, with individual flowers being ~0.5 cm in diameter. Borne in spring, though in good conditions it can flower year round. Flowers can be somewhat hairy. Flowers are bisexual, and trees are fairly self-fertile, though benefit from cross pollination. *Fruits:* Ripen in mid–late summer (but also at other times), and turn pale orange-pinkish-brown when ripe, though some become dark brown. The flesh is mucilaginous, sticky and translucent. When fully ripe, the pulp is sweet and pleasant.

Cultivation: It prefers a warmer–tropical or subtropical climate, and is not tolerant of cold. *Soil:* It grows best in deep loamy soils, either sand or clay based, but can be grown in poor, stony soils. This species is quite drought tolerant once established, though prefers regular moisture for best growth and flower and fruit production.

Uses: The fruits can be eaten fresh or used as a vegetable and pickled. The half-ripe fruits can make a tasty broth. The leaves can be lightly boiled and mixed with salt and chilli.

The kernel can also be eaten. *Medicinal:* It has been recently shown to have anti-inflammatory properties and the fruits are sometimes eaten to relieve indigestion. The ripe fruits are also used for hair loss. The bark and roots are used as a remedy for coughs, colds and various indigestion and throat problems. *Other uses:* The pulp from half-ripe fruits can be used as an alternative to paper glue. The wood is of high quality, is moderately hard and takes a good polish. Often used for ornamental furniture, planks, agricultural implements, combs, toys, bowls, kitchen utensils. *Ornamental:* Often planted as an ornamental and for shade.

Sebesten plum (bird-lime tree, glue-berry), *Cordia dichotoma*. A native of southern Asia and northern Australia, it forms a handsome, evergreen tree, ~9–18 m tall, with a broadly spreading crown. *Leaves:* Broad, shiny, to 20 cm long. *Flowers:* Has both male and bisexual white–orange flowers. *Fruit:* Pinkish or yellowish, 2.5-cm long, with very sticky, slimy, mucilaginous flesh.

Cultivation: Likes steady, warm temperatures and moist, well-drained soil. *Propagation:* From seed or semi-ripe cuttings. Is not cold hardy.

Uses: In India, ripe fruits are eaten raw. The green fruits can be eaten as a vegetable, in curry and pickled. Leaves can be eaten as a vegetable. *Medicinal:* The fruits are sometimes used to treat coughs.

Septee saucer-berry, *Cordia caffra*. An attractive native of southern Africa, it forms a smaller tree with smooth, light brown, flaking bark. Relatively frost hardy; young trees need extra protection. It grows equally well in sun or shade; fairly fast growing. *Leaves:* Deciduous, thin, oval, pointed, shiny deep green above, paler beneath, ~6–12 cm long, alternate. *Flowers:* Creamy-white, scented, bell-shaped, borne in clusters at the end of the stems in spring–early summer. *Fruit:* Globose, an attractive deep orange colour when ripe, and are borne in small clusters. Fleshy pulp. They have a large cup-like calyx around their base.

Uses: Fruits can be eaten fresh or can be used in jams, preserves, desserts, etc. Their flavour is not particularly good, but birds love them. *Medicinal:* Parts of this tree have been used to treat sore eyes, fever and wounds. *Other uses:* The durable, easy-to-work, pinkish heartwood makes attractive furniture that takes a good polish. ∎

Cornus mas
Cornelian cherry (cornet plum, cornel)
CORNACEAE

Similar species: Bentham's cornel (*C. capitata*), creeping dogwood (*C. canadensis*), dwarf Cornelian cherry (*C. suecica*), Japanese cornel (*C. officinalis*), Japanese dogwood (*C. kousa*)

Native to central and southern Europe, and to western Asia, the cornelian cherry is not a true cherry, but a member of the dogwood family. The term 'dogwood' is derived from the word 'dog', which meant 'skewer' in the Middle Ages, and refers to a product in common usage at that time. The name 'mas' means male, probably because the plant tends to produce mostly male flowers for a few years, with more female flowers produced as the tree matures. The cornelian cherry has been cultivated since ancient times for its fruit, particularly in the Balkans. Monasteries grew it throughout the Middle Ages, as did Turks, not only for food, but also for the dye in the bark. The fruits from this plant were appreciated and used much more than they are now. Plants vary in fruit quality, and it is best to select good-fruiting specimens to propagate from.

DESCRIPTION

Often multi-stemmed, low-branching, round to oval, deciduous shrubs or small trees, which typically grow 2.5–6 m tall, with 2–5 m spread. It forms many twiggy branches and attractive greyish-brown bark that peels off older limbs. The new season's stem growth is green. This changes to red-brown/purplish at the stem tips but remains light green beneath; this coloration remains until the following spring, when it turns brown-grey. These are long-lived species, and are fairly slow-growing when young. They then grow faster once established, up to a certain size, after which their growth slows again.

Leaves: Bright–dark green, deciduous, somewhat shiny, ~7.5 cm long, opposite, broad and elliptic, with pointed tips. The major leaf veins are parallel to the undulating, curving leaf margins. Has good red–purple autumn colour.

Flowers: Small, 1.25–2.5 cm diameter, star-shaped, golden yellow, abundant, in flattened clusters, giving a mist-like effect. They are borne in late winter–early spring on leafless 1-year-old branches, and last for ~3 weeks. These very early flowers make it a popular ornamental in temperate regions as an early welcoming sign of spring. *Pollination:* By bees and other insects (but see creeping dogwood below). Most *Cornus* species have bisexual flowers, and only need one plant to set fruit, though you may get better fruit-set and fruit quality if more than one plant is established.

Fruit: Scarlet, olive-shaped berries, ~1.5 cm long, elliptic, semi-translucent, often inconspicuous because hidden by the foliage. Ripen mid–late summer. The skin is fairly tough. It has one to several small, edible seeds, with some fruits being rather seedy.

Yield/harvest: The cornelian cherry only produces male flowers up until ~12 years of age, after which it also starts to produce female flowers, so takes a long time to produce fruits from seed-raised plants. Vegetatively produced plants fruit much sooner: after 4–6 years. Can get good yields of 15–35 kg per plant. Fruits are harvested when uniformly dark red and fully ripe. Under-ripe fruits can be fairly astringent. Once picked, fruits are best kept for a few days to fully ripen.

CULTIVATION
An easy-to-grow and tough plant.

Location: Can be grown in either full sun or light shade. Is moderately wind hardy and fairly tolerant of maritime locations.

Temperature: Very cold hardy, tolerating winter frosts and cold winters, though hard frosts can damage early spring flowers. Plants can also tolerate heat. They are best suited to both cold and warm temperate climates.

Chilling: Plants need a short period of winter chilling to flower and leaf well in spring.

Soil/water/nutrients: Prefers a moist, well-drained loam, but can also grow in poor, dry soils at a range of pH values, though does not grow well in very alkaline soils. Can grow in heavy clay. Likes regular moisture during the growing season, though can tolerate some drought. Grows best if its roots are shaded.

Planting: Space plants ~30 cm apart for a hedge, and at 2–4 m apart for individuals. Fairly easy to transplant, but can be slow to re-establish.

Propagation: *Seed:* Wash fresh seed thoroughly of pulp, as the pulp inhibits germination. Sow seeds in well-drained compost in a cold frame. Seeds can take ~18 months to germinate. Stored seeds benefit from being stratified for 3–4 months at ~4°C, and then soaked for a few hours in warm water before sowing in spring. Seedlings are potted up and grown on for 2–3 years before planting out. However, trees often take ~12 years to start producing fruits. *Cuttings:* Take semi-ripe ~8–10-cm-long cuttings, with a heel if possible, in summer. Insert in a moist sand-and-peat mix with warmth. Can also take mature cuttings of the current year's growth, with a heel if possible, in autumn, and place these in a cold frame. High percentage take. Cuttings need to be grown-on for 2–3 years before planting out. These will fruit much sooner than seedlings. *Suckers:* Any suckers can be dug up and should readily establish in pots before planting out. *Layering:* Lightly wound small areas of young, long stems and peg these to the soil in late summer or autumn. Rooting can take 9 months, or sometimes up to 18–24 months, before they can be removed from the parent plant.

Pruning: In general, needs little or no pruning. Can be trained as a small tree by removal of suckers and lower branches to show off the attractive bark. Remove any root suckers to control spread.

Food
The fruits have a sharp but pleasant taste, somewhat like plums, and, historically, have been a popular food crop in many European areas. They are now undergoing a revival of interest as a culinary plant. The fruits can be used in preserves, jam, desserts, syrup, etc. Can be used as a glaze for meat, or added to sauces. The unripe fruits have been pickled in brine like olives since ancient times; they can also be preserved in sugar or honey. Makes a good wine. The fruits can be dried for later use. The seeds can be roasted, ground and used as a coffee substitute.

Nutrition
The fruits are very high in vitamin C.

Medicinal
The bark and under-ripe fruits are used as an astringent and as a tonic, with the fruits being eaten for bowel problems. The flowers have been used to treat diarrhoea.

Other uses
Extremely hard wood. The bark yields a good red dye.

Ornamental
Valued for its very early spring flowers and attractive stems. Can be grown as a hedge or screening plant, or can be used as a foundation plant in shrub–herbaceous borders, or can be planted as a specimen. May also be trained as a small tree. It is low maintenance and non-invasive.

Pests and diseases: Virtually no disease or pest problems apart from birds, which are attracted to the fruit.

CULTIVARS
The species *C. mas* has some of the best fruit, although a few other species of *Cornus* also produce reasonable fruits (see below). Most *Cornus* cultivars have been selected for their ornamental properties. A few *C. mas* cultivars with reasonable fruit quality are 'Elegant', 'Pioneer' and 'Redstone', which all give good yields. 'Flava' has yellow fruits that ripen earlier than most other cultivars. 'Golden Glory' has an upright form, to ~5 m tall, with abundant yellow flowers, and good red autumn leaf colour. The fruits from this cultivar are ~2 cm long, and when fully ripe and soft, have a good, fresh taste. Needs more than one plant to produce fruits and may not be as hardy as other cultivars.

SIMILAR SPECIES
The species below all have edible fruits. Most other species of *Cornus* also have edible fruits, but a few have ambivalent

reports concerning their edibility, e.g. *C. florida* and possibly *C. sanguinea*, so these may be best avoided.

Bentham's cornel, *Cornus capitata*. A native of eastern Asia, from China to the Himalayas, it forms a spreading shrub or small tree, 4–10 m tall, with 4–8 m spread and evergreen, dull green, narrow, lanceolate leaves. *Flowers:* Small, surrounded by 4–6 yellow-creamy-coloured bracts. They are borne in mid summer. *Fruits:* Can produce good yields of red fruits, ~2.5 cm diameter, from autumn–early winter, and these ripen best in warmer autumns. Fruits vary in quality from plant to plant, and so it is best to vegetatively propagate from plants known to produce good-quality fruits.

Cultivation: Is an easy-to-grow plant, if somewhat more cold tender than other *Cornus* species, though tolerates temperatures down to ~–8°C without damage. Can be grown in full sun or shade, though often grows better with some shade. Is tolerant of maritime exposure. *Soil:* As above, but can also tolerate somewhat more alkaline soils. *Propagation, pruning, etc:* As for *C. mas* above.

Uses: The fruits can be eaten fresh or can be used in jams, preserves, desserts, etc. They are reported to have a bitter-sweet flavour, or to taste like over-ripe banana. The pulp is fleshy, is fairly seedy and it has a rather tough skin. *Other uses:* It has very hard wood.

Creeping dogwood (bunch berry), *Cornus canadensis*. A native of North America, with a wide climatic range from Newfoundland and Alaska, south to California and Virginia. They are small, low-lying, spreading, ornamental shrubs 0.1–0.3 m tall, spreading to 1 m or more. Their stems creep along the ground and often root where they touch the soil. These rooted cuttings can be removed and grown on to form new plants. *Leaves:* Mid-green, crowded, small, often in tight clusters at stem tips. Young leaves can be damaged by late spring frosts. *Flowers:* Tiny, greeny-purple with several white bracts. They are borne in flattened clusters in late spring–early summer. There is sometimes a second bloom later in the season. This species is unusual in its method of dispersing pollen. The flowers are synchronised to 'explode' to release their pollen. They have sensitive antenna-like structures on the petals that act like coiled springs and these, with stamens that are also coiled under tension, simultaneously spring open to catapult pollen from the anthers upwards, which then falls onto neighbouring flowers. This type of mechanism in plants is rare. *Fruits:* Small, red, round, ~0.5–1 cm diameter with 1–2 seeds. Can be covered with minute white hairs. They form in dense bunches at the ends of stems and ripen in autumn.

Cultivation: Plants are very cold tolerant. They can be grown in sun or shade. *Soil:* They can grow in sandy soils or clay, but prefer moist and more acidic conditions: they do not grow well in limestone-based soils. They grow well with other acid-loving plants such as heather, blueberry, etc. *Propagation*, etc., as for *C. mas*, but plants can also be divided in spring.

Uses: The fruits can be eaten fresh or used in preserves, jam, desserts, etc. Fruits are high in pectin. They are pleasant, though do not have much flavour. Not very juicy; can be easily dried. *Medicinal:* A tea made from the leaves has been used to treat aches and pains, kidney and lung

ailments, coughs, fevers and as an eye wash. Other potential uses of the plant are as an anti-inflammatory and analgesic. *Ornamental:* Makes a good groundcover plant.

Dwarf cornelian cherry, *Cornus suecica*. A native of northern Europe, this naturally grows in sub-Arctic conditions. As its name suggests, it only grows to ~15 cm high and has a sprawling form with many rhizomes sending up suckers. Grows best in moist, acidic soils. Mostly propagated by division. Has small dark-coloured flowers in summer, followed by tiny red berries, which are fiddly to pick, but tangy and tasty. An ideal plant for tricky sites.

Japanese cornel, *Cornus officinalis*. A native of eastern Asia, through China and Korea. It forms an attractive, fairly cold hardy, moderately-sized, spreading shrub or small tree, ~4–6 m tall by 4–6 m wide. *Flowers:* Are borne very early. *Fruits:* Do not turn fully red and ripen until autumn. They are ~1–1.5 cm in diameter.

Cultivation: An easy plant that can grow in fairly alkaline soils as well as clays, in sun or semi-shade. (See other notes for *C. mas* above.)

Uses: They can be eaten when fully ripe and are sweet and pleasant; under-ripe fruits can be astringent. Fruits can be dried for later use. *Medicinal:* This species has more medicinal uses recorded than other *Cornus* species, and has been used in Chinese medicine for more than 2000 years. Extracts from the fruits have recently been shown to kill and suppress several food-borne pathogens. It is more effective at killing Gram-positive than Gram-negative bacteria. In China, recent studies have shown that extracts from this species increase blood flow to the kidney and spleen, and the motility of human sperm. The fruits are antibacterial, antifungal, hypotensive, anti-tumour, astringent, diuretic, hepatic and a tonic. The fruit, without the seed, is used to treat arthritis, fever, is said to control sperm ejaculation and excessive perspiration, and has been used to treat cystitis and other ailments. The fruits are also said to help relieve tinnitus, poor hearing, dizziness and extreme shock. The stem bark has been used as an astringent, against malaria and as a tonic.

Japanese dogwood, *Cornus kousa*. A native of Japan and Korea, it forms a spreading shrub or small tree ~3–4 m tall, 3–4 m wide. There are several ornamental cultivars. *Leaves:* Narrow, mid–dark green. Have good autumn colour. *Flowers:* Attractive, purple-green, and are borne in flattened clusters. The individual flowers also have four showy white outer bracts, ~2.5–4 cm diameter. Flowers open in late spring–early summer. *Fruits:* Showy, red, ~2 cm diameter, strawberry-like, semi-translucent, ripen in autumn.

Cultivation: An easy-to-grow plant. It is fully cold hardy, surviving temperatures down to ~–20°C. *Soil, propagation, pruning, etc:* As noted for *C. mas* above.

Uses: The fruits can be eaten fresh or can be used in preserves, desserts, etc. Having a high pectin content, they are good for preserves. Fruits are sweet, pleasant and juicy, though very seedy. The skin can be rather tough and somewhat bitter, but the flesh is highly regarded by some as one of the best late-summer fruits. The young leaves can be lightly cooked. *Other uses:* As above. ∎

Corylus avellana, C. maxima, C. americana, C. colurna, C. cornuta
Hazelnut (cobnut, filbert)
CORYLACEAE (Betulaceae)
Relatives: birch, hornbeam

The name *Corylus* originates from 'korys', which means helmet or hood, after the husk of the nut. The term 'filbert' may be derived from 'full beard', describing its long, leafy husk or, alternatively, from St Philibert's Day, which is celebrated about the time that filbert nuts ripen. The name hazelnut is often used as a general term for nine species of *Corylus*, but these species can also be known as cobnuts or filberts. Historically, a 'filbert' is a species where the husk is longer than the nut, a 'cob' is a species where the husk is the same length as the nut, and 'hazel' is a species where the husk is shorter than the nut. However, the distinctions between the different species is often blurred. Here, the name hazelnut is used as a general name to describe all these species. The two main species are *C. avellana* (European hazelnut), which is found wild across western Europe and the UK, and *C. maxima* (European filbert), which is native to southeastern Europe and western Asia. However, so many hybrids have occurred between these two species that they are often difficult to tell apart, and are often generally known as hazels. These two species, and their hybrids, are widely cultivated for their nuts. Another popular species is the Turkish hazel (*C. colurna*), which is native to Turkey, where it can grow to ~25 m, and its large nuts are valued commercially (see notes below). Other *Corylus* species are native to North America, Canada, China and Japan, and though the nuts from these species are often smaller, they have been an important food source through history. *C. americana* (American hazelnut) is native to North America and produces long, but small, hard-shelled nuts.

The trees prefer mild, moist winters and cool summers and, for this reason, most cultivation occurs along a temperate latitudinal band that stretches from the Black Sea to France, with Turkey being a major exporter; they are also cultivated in China, Oregon and New Zealand. In China, they are considered to be one of the five sacred nourishments bestowed by God on humans. Pollen studies have shown that hazel trees covered large parts of Europe between 7500–5500 BC, but have since been largely replaced by other species. Humans from temperate zones have had a very long association with this nutritious food resource. The Greeks were very keen on hazelnuts, and enjoyed eating them as well as using them medicinally. The hazel tree also has many mystical and occult rites associated with it, particularly from Celtic times. The Romans burnt hazel torches during weddings to ensure fertility and a happy marriage. In England, it has been long believed that if you court your sweetheart beneath a hazel tree, you are assured of happiness. Forked hazel rods were used by witches for various rituals. The nuts were burned by priests to enhance clairvoyance, and dowsers still use the hazel twig to find water underground.

DESCRIPTION
Shrubs or small trees that vary is size from 0.6–9 m tall, with a similar spread, usually with an untidy form. They are moderately fast-growing trees and live for ~70–80 years, although coppiced rootstocks can live for hundreds of years. The plants form many, thin stems that have prominent lenticels. Their bark is smooth, grey–brown. Trees tend to sucker a lot, resulting in thickets around the trunks.

Leaves: Leaves are deciduous, 2.5–8 cm long, rounded, with a heart-shaped base, double-toothed, ragged margins and a short pointed apex. They are borne singly on short stalks. They are darkish green, fairly coarse and somewhat wrinkly. They turn yellowish in autumn.

Flowers: Catkins. Plants are monoecious, but they are often not self-fertile so are best planted with other cultivars to get good pollination. Male catkins are formed the previous autumn and open in very early spring into yellow–tan-coloured tassel-like catkins, which are locally known as 'lambs tails' and are a sign that spring is not far away. They

produce yellow pollen for a short period, which can travel ~20 m. Female flowers are tiny and easy to miss; they are also formed during the previous autumn. They are borne at or near the ends of stems and consist of tiny, green, bud-like flowers with tufts of tiny, bright red stigmas protruding from them; they remain open for several weeks. The shoots will only produce flowers if they receive adequate light. Pollinated female flowers slowly develop during the summer to form the nut. *Pollination:* By wind, and trees benefit from being planted in groups to increase fruit-set.

Fruit: In clusters (1–10), with each nut encased within its own green, leafy husk (an involucre), which releases the nut once it has dried and opened. The nuts are smooth and brown when ripe, and have a fairly hard, but brittle shell (pericarp). There is a single, brown kernel. The nuts vary in shape, depending on species, from round–oval–oblong.

Yield/harvest/storage: Trees begin bearing when 4–6 years old, with optimum yields >10 years, and can then bear for 40–50 years. On average, trees produce 6–12 kg of nuts per year, depending on cultivation techniques, climate, etc. Trees tend towards uneven bearing, with one good crop every 2–3 years. Uneven bearing can be reduced by thinning young fruits and pruning off some of the fruiting stems. In addition, any nuts that remain on the tree after autumn tend to inhibit the formation of next season's female flowers, so these should be removed. Harvesting involves simply picking the nuts off the ground, in autumn, when they have turned brown and the husk starts to split and dry out. Species with short husks (hazels and cobs) tend to naturally fall from the tree; species with long husks (filberts) often need the husk to be removed after harvesting. Kernels that are going to be stored should be dried to ~12% moisture content to reduce any risk of toxic fungal aflotoxin developing (a risk with all nuts). Kernels in their shells can be stored for ~5 months if kept dry and cool. Shelled kernels can be stored in a refrigerator for ~1 year and remain in good condition, and for ~2 years in a freezer.

uses

Food
Tasty and used in many ways in desserts and savoury dishes. Hazelnuts can be eaten fresh, but are often roasted and eaten as a snack, or used in spreads, cereals and all types of preparations where nuts are used. They can be ground to a make flour and added to bread, which adds a delicious flavour.

Nutrition
A nutritious kernel. Very high in vitamin E and fat, ~60%, of which ~55% is monounsaturated (oleic), ~15% polyunsaturated (linoleic, omega 6), 25% other polyunsaturated fats and ~5% saturated fats. Few foods are so high in oleic acid: hazels have even more than olives. A study was conducted on the oils within hazels and it was found that consumption of 25 g of hazelnuts a day, for 16 weeks, resulted in reductions of 2–10% lower cholesterol and reduced LDL cholesterol in subjects, who ranged from children to the elderly, compared with a control group who did not eat the nuts. Hazels are also high in calcium (200 mg/100 g of nut, higher than most other nuts, except almonds) and are relatively high in magnesium, potassium, thiamine, and have excellent folate levels. Also high in iron, copper and manganese. They are high in protein (~13%).

Other uses
They have strong, flexible branches and have been planted, cultivated and coppiced for hundreds of years in England, with the wood being used for fences, baskets, for wattle and daub walls, stakes, hoops and for many other purposes. The oil is used in aromatherapy and massage.

Ornamental
There are cultivars with coloured leaves and contorted branches, but some of these do not produce many fruits. Can be used as a screen.

Roots: Tend to be mostly shallow, so grows best in soils that have a good water-holding capacity. Benefit from mulching to add nutrients and retain moisture. Avoid mechanical cultivation. The roots readily form suckers from runners that extend 1–2 m out from the plant, particularly if the roots are injured.

CULTIVATION
Is a very low maintenance plant, and could be suited to smaller gardens.

Location: They grow best in full sun, and light needs to reach the stems for good flower initiation, although can be grown with light shade. Naturally, they often form an understorey species. They can grow in humid or dry climates. Are not very wind tolerant. Not tolerant to exposed maritime locations.

Chilling: Plants need considerable winter chilling of 800–1600 hours.

Temperatures: The plants are very cold hardy when dormant. Their very early flowers make them susceptible to spring frosts where temperatures drop below ~–8°C, although their flowers are more cold hardy than those of many species. Once pollinated, cold temperatures have very little effect on the future nut crop. They do not grow well in areas that have hot summers.

Soil/water/nutrients: Plants prefer a moist, well-drained loam. They grow well in soils with a high clay content, but not sandy soils. They grow best in slightly acid soils: pH 5.5–6.0; they suffer micronutrient deficiencies in alkaline soils, such as iron chlorosis or manganese deficiency. They grow and fruit much better with regular moisture during the growing season and do not tolerate drought. An organic mulch is beneficial. Plants generally have low nutrient needs; just an annual application of a balanced, general fertiliser. Check for nitrogen, potassium and boron deficiencies; boron, in particular, may be needed for fruit-set.

Planting: Space plants at 3–6 m apart, depending on species and their final size. Plant in groups for good fruit-set, with a mix of cultivars. Because pollen only travels ~20 m, try and position the different cultivars within this range. Provide moisture until the plant is established.

Pruning: Filberts readily sucker and form shrubs if not pruned. They can be grown as a shrub, but are more difficult to harvest. If pruned as a tree, they are usually pruned to an open centre. There seems to be little difference between yields of shrubs and trees, although allowing light into the canopy increases flower production. Trees start to lose vigour after ~5 years and can be severely pruned to stimulate new productive fruiting stems. Hard pruning will reduce the following year's yield, but yields thereafter are good. Alternatively, trees can be lightly pruned in the years when they have abundant crops to even out yields. Pruning should be done in late winter or after the male flowers have finished, but try to avoid pruning out the female flowers/fruits. Autumn pruning can remove next season's flowers. They can be grown as a nut hedge, but yields are not as good.

Propagation: Seed: Needs cold stratification before sowing. The progeny are variable. Cuttings: Best taken in spring. Can be treated with rooting hormone for better results. Not very successful. Suckers: Removal of suckers from around the base of the tree is easy and successful, but they sometimes do not grow as well as layered plants. *Rhizomes:* Plants produce runners from the main plant (which later sucker); these can be cut into lengths and produce good quality plants. Select runner sections with 2–4 healthy buds. *Layering:* This is easy and simple by securing a metal ring (or similar) around a stem to girdle it, which will then produce roots around this constriction, but it is a slower method. *Grafting:* By whip-and-tongue in winter, but the success rate is not high. They are usually grafted onto their own rootstocks.

Pests and diseases: Generally fairly healthy. Lemon-tree borer is a problem in some regions (e.g. New Zealand). Big-bud mite can also be a problem, as can aphids. Filbert-blight is an increasing problem on many *Corylus* spp., except *C. cornuta*. If possible, plant blight-tolerant cultivars.

CULTIVARS

'Aveline Blanche': A filbert. Mid season harvest. Nut: smallish, long, very good flavour. Long female-flowering season. Good cropper. Not vigorous.

'Barcelona': A popular filbert, but very susceptible to blight and brown stain. Produces some blank nuts. Good in mild–average climates. Does not sucker too much. Medium-sized, high-quality nut, moderate yield. Early–medium season. Vigorous tree.

'Cosford': Very hardy. Reliable, high yields. Nuts: medium-sized, good quality, thin shell, mid season. Vigorous tree.

'Kentish Cob': Main cultivar in UK. Late season. Cold tolerant. Good yields, large nut, good flavour, nut drops with its husk. Kernels may shrivel in drier soils. Used as a pollinator.

'Merveille de Bowiller' (syn. 'Hallesche Riessen'): Late harvest. Good for severe climates. Vigorous with large nuts, good quality. A pollinator.

'Rode Zeller': Ornamental. Has dark red–bronze leaves, nuts and catkins.

'Tonda de Giffoni': Excellent flavour and blight resistant. Early, vigorous. Top producer.

OTHER SPECIES

Turkish filbert, Turkish hazelnut, *Corylus colurna*. This species is more rugged and tough than many of the *Corylus* species. It is tolerant of air pollution, it grows large enough (~10 m tall, 8 m spread) to form a shade tree, can tolerate heat and drought, is very frost tolerant, can tolerate compacted and wet soils. Trees tend to form a central trunk rather than a shrubby form, and they do not sucker. They also suffer few pest or disease problems. Makes an attractive ornamental tree and produces tasty, large nuts, though not every year. All these features have made it an often-used rootstock. ■

Crataegus spp.
Hawthorn
ROSACEAE

English hawthorn (*Crataegus laevigata*), azarole (*C. azarolus*), *Crataegus schraderiana*, tansy-leaved thorn (*C. tanacetifolia*)

Relatives: maythorn, pear, apple, rose

The *Crataegus* genera includes ~280 species, which are closely related to apple and pear. They have been used as dwarfing rootstocks for both. They are native to northern America, Asia and Europe. They readily cross fertilise to form new species, and their classification is complex. One of the main groups within the *Crataegus* genus is the hawthorns, loosely comprising European and Asian species, and these interlink with the north American *Crataegus* species, the mayhaws (maythorns), which are described on p. 162. The hawthorns are tough, and can adapt to many soil types and environmental conditions. They come into leaf early, and produce abundant, white blossom in spring, with red haws (or fruits) ripening in autumn. The fruits are edible, though not very tasty; and are of more importance for their medicinal properties. Remains of the fruits from *C. laevigata* and *C. monogyna* have been found at archaeological sites in Europe dating back to Neolithic times. The native American Indians and Chinese have used this genus for many hundreds of years for its fruit as a food, but also for its medicinal ability to treat cardiac problems, arteriosclerosis and angina pectoris. Throughout the Middle Ages in England, the fruits were mostly eaten as a food and made into wine. In the West, the medicinal values of hawthorn have only fairly recently been 'discovered', and its ability to treat heart disease only became fully recognised in the 1850s. Its use in modern times has become of increasing importance as the incidence of heart disease has grown in modern societies. Today, hawthorn preparations are used extensively in France, England, Germany, Russia and China, especially for the treatment of heart and cardiovascular ailments. Its generic name, *Crataegus,* is derived from a Greek word 'kratus', meaning strength, and refers to the hardness of the wood.

DESCRIPTION

A large, hardy shrub or small, rounded tree, 6–10 m tall, spread 4–8 m, with attractive leaves, abundant white blossom and brightly coloured fruits. It often has many stout, but slender, solitary spines on its branches. The bark is dark brown and flaking. Trees are fairly long-lived: >100 years, and often take on a dense, tangled form as they age.

Leaves: Deciduous, oblong and thin, simple, tapering towards the petiole, 2–7 cm long. Are shiny, waxy and mid–dark green in colour. May be finely serrate, with shallow–deeply-lobed margins. In clusters of 3–5. Younger leaves are larger and more lobed. Autumn leaves often have yellow–russet–reddish colour.

Flowers: Abundant, pretty, from early–late spring, often scented, though not always pleasantly so. They are borne singly or in round-topped clusters (4–8 flowers) on 1-year-old wood and on short spurs, often before the leaves open. The plant has bisexual flowers (both male and female structures within the same flower), with five petals, often pink, turning white, and an inferior ovary. They bloom for quite a long period. *Pollination:* Mostly by insects, particularly midges and flies. Are bisexual and only need one plant to produce fruit, though more than one will improve pollination rates.

Fruit: Are 1–2.5 cm in diameter, rounded–oval, ripening in early–late autumn. They are classified as a pome. They are usually scarlet or deep red, but can be yellow, orange, or dark blue-purple in some species. The flesh varies considerably within and between species. Some have rather dry, mealy flesh, others are tasty, sweet–sour, juicy and are highly recommended. They form in small clusters, on spurs, at the ends of branches, so are not difficult to pick, despite the thorns. They have a thin skin, and a distinctive, small, green calyx that persists at the apex of the haw (fruit). Have 2–5 brown, oval, hard, central seeds, which are usually clustered together in a group, making them easy to remove.

Yield/harvest: Fruits can ripen rapidly, and may only take ~30–60 days to mature after fruit-set. Can get 30–60 kg of fruit per tree per season. Seedling trees take 5–8 years to

uses

Food

The fruits of some species are too sour and dry to be eaten fresh, whereas the fruits from other plants can be juicy and quite sweet: flavour does vary. If not eaten fresh, they can be cooked and added to other fruits. They are often used in preserves and jellies. The fruits can be dried for later use. The seeds can be boiled or roasted, and used as a coffee substitute. The young leaves can also be eaten, and are tasty when added to a salad.

Nutrition

Fruits are fairly high in iron, magnesium, potassium and calcium, and have good levels of vitamins A and C. The species *C. laevigata*, *C. monogyna* and, to a lesser extent, *C. pentagyna* have particularly high levels of flavonoids (~30 different types). Fruits also contain catechin polymers (condensed tannins), which give the fruit their astringency, and are partly responsible for the plant's effect on cardiac muscles. These compounds, and others, when taken together, have a beneficial effect on the cardiovascular system; however, no single compound is responsible for this effect. Their benefits are greater when used together than when used individually.

Medicinal

Fruit and leaf extracts are prescribed for the treatment of the early stages of congestive heart failure, for angina pectoris and for recovery from heart attacks. They are also used to reduce any stress around the heart, to help age-related heart problems that do not require digitalis and for mild forms of arrhythmias. Studies have shown that they increase cardiac

efficiency by improving blood supply to the heart muscle and by strengthening its contractions. The heart is then able to pump more blood to the rest of the body, while also helping to dilate blood vessels at the same time. It can also improve circulation to the extremities by helping reduce resistance in the arteries. In Italy, hawthorn preparations are used for mild anxiety and other nervous disturbances. In >100 years of clinical use, there have been no reported cases of toxicity with hawthorn preparations. Prolonged use is necessary for it to be efficacious. It is normally taken as a tea or a tincture. The leaves, flowers and fruits of these species are used in preparations. Other species used are *C. azarolus* and *C. nigra*. The indigenous peoples have used unripe *C. tomentosa* fruits for bladder ailments. Hawthorn fruits are also used to lower serum cholesterol levels, for the prevention and treatment of arteriosclerosis and to ease menopause symptoms. The use of hawthorn medicinally was recorded in a Chinese herbal dating to 659 AD where it was used to ease digestion and as a mild laxative. *C. laevigata* leaves have been used as a tobacco substitute, and act as a mild stimulant.

Other uses

The wood is very hard and strong; ideal for smaller items.

Ornamental

The hawthorn species are widely planted as hedging in many temperate regions. Their thorns prevent livestock from escaping, but the berries are also important in attracting wildlife. Their toughness and wind-hardiness makes them ideal in difficult areas as a barrier and a windbreak. There are many ornamental cultivars.

start bearing fruit; grafted trees may produce fruit by their third year. Fruits are best harvested when fully coloured and ripe.

CULTIVATION
Have very few problems and need almost no maintenance.

Location: Can be grown in exposed positions, and are wind tolerant. Also tolerate atmospheric pollution, and will grow well in towns, roadsides, etc. Prefer to grow in full sun, but can be grown in semi-shade, though fruit yields and quality may be reduced. They can usually tolerate maritime locations, even if exposed.

Temperature: They are very cold hardy, and can survive ~–30°C without damage when dormant; however, young leaves and flowers can be frost sensitive.

Chilling: They need winter chilling: 500–1000 hours.

Soil/water/nutrients: They grow best in well-drained sandy loam, but can grow in many soil types, including heavy clay. They can tolerate drought, but also wet soils, and even waterlogged soils for short periods of time. Although they grow best at a pH range of 6–7, they tolerate both acidic and chalky soils. This species is particularly tolerant of waterlogged or marshy sites.

Planting: Space plants at 4.5–6 m apart. Mulching the plants when young will reduce weed competition, help retain soil moisture and add nutrients until they are established.

Pruning: If wanting fruit production, they are best trained to a single trunk, with the first branches occurring at ~0.5–1 m height, for ease of maintenance, harvest, etc. Because they form a dense crown, annual pruning to remove crossing and crowded branches helps to keep the centre of the tree open and allows air and light to enter. Once established, they need minimal pruning, just to remove diseased or damaged branches. Hawthorns can be drastically pruned if needed, and can also be cut back to old wood, and will still regenerate. However, this type of pruning will reduce fruit crops.

Propagation: Seed: The seedcoat contains strong germination inhibitors, and needs various treatments before it will germinate: even then they take 6–18 months. They are best sown fresh in autumn, in a cold frame. Some seeds may germinate in spring, but some will need a further winter before germinating. It is possible to sow the seed when still 'green', and before the seedcoat has hardened: this may germinate in spring. Stored seed is more difficult: it needs to be warm stratified for ~3 months at 15°C, and then cold stratified for a further 3 months at 4°C. It may then take another 18 months to germinate. In addition, the seeds can be scarified before stratifying to enable moisture to reach the kernel, i.e. by scratching the seedcoat in some way, or by fermenting the seed for a few days in its own pulp. Seedlings should not be allowed to grow for >2 years in a nursery bed as they become difficult to transplant. Although tricky to germinate, many seeds are nucellar in origin, and grow into seedlings that are clones of the parent plant, so predictability of offspring is assured. *Cuttings:* Semi-ripe cuttings in summer can be dipped in rooting hormone, then inserted in well-drained compost to root. The use of mist can increase percentage take. Hardwood and root cuttings are also possible. *Grafting:* Can be easily grafted during late winter by whip-and-tongue or simple whip grafts. Cleft grafting can be used on larger trees. They can be grafted onto other *Crataegus* species, with mayhaw seedling rootstocks being best in wetter soils.

Pests and diseases: Relatively disease resistant. They can be susceptible to many of the insects and diseases that attack other Rosaceae fruits, such as plum curculio, hawthorn lace bug, flower thrips, white-fringed beetle, leafminers, scales and mealybugs. Quince rust can also be a problem. Fireblight, although uncommon, is a serious disease, and can kill plants.

CULTIVARS
They hybridise freely with other members of the genus.

OTHER HAWTHORN SPECIES

Below are listed a few of the common hawthorns that have edible fruits. Unless stated otherwise, the general description above applies to these.

Azarole, *Crataegus azarolus*. Widespread in the Mediterranean, where it is often found growing wild and is locally cultivated for its fruit. It is also grown elsewhere in Europe and the UK. It forms a small tree/shrub, 4–7 m tall. Young stems are silvery and downy. Leaves are deeply lobed. *Flowers:* Fragrant, white, in late spring–early summer. Pollinated by midges. *Fruit:* Small, ~1.25 cm diameter, red, in clusters (but can be orange, yellow or white). Fruits are fragrant, tasty, sweet–sharp, a bit like apple.

Cultivation: As the general description, but is not very tolerant of maritime locations. Tolerant of a wide range of soil types and pH values, and is drought tolerant and tolerant of wet soils. The cultivar, 'Fruto Blanco' has large, white fruits and the cultivar 'Julieta' has small red fruits: both ripen from early to mid autumn and have a pleasant aromatic flavour.

Uses: Fruits are sweeter in warmer regions, and then have a good sweet–sour flavour. In cooler areas, the fruits are more sour and are best cooked or used in preserves, jams, cooked desserts, pies, etc., or they can be dried for later use. It makes a fine liquor. The wood is heavy, hard and close-grained.

Chinese hawberry, *Crataegus pinnatifida major*. A native of northern China, it forms a small tree growing to ~7 m. Has few, or sometimes no thorns. Produces white flowers in late spring, which develop into 2–3-cm-diameter deep red-coloured fruits with tiny white dots. The fruits were very popular in China and were often candied.

***Crataegus schraderiana*.** A native of southern Europe and Greece, it forms a medium-sized tree, ~7 m tall. They are very easy to grow and maintenance is minimal. Trees produce regular, good yields. Fruits ripen in early autumn and can be 'stored' on the tree for a few weeks longer.

Cultivation: As the general notes. It is cold hardy and can be grown in cooler, temperate climates. Can grow in a range of soil types and pH values, and can tolerate very wet soils, as well as drought.

Uses: As the general notes. Highly recommended fruits, which have been described as one of the most delicious, temperate fruits. These are 1.25–2.0 cm in diameter, are soft, juicy and have an extremely pleasant flavour. Trees are also very ornamental.

English hawthorn, *Crataegus laevigata* (syn. *C. oxyacantha*). A native of Europe and Britain. It forms a small tree, 4–6 m tall, 4–6 m spread, with a dense, many branched crown. Has clusters of 3–5 shallowly-lobed leaves. *Flowers:* White, in clusters, 5–7.5 cm diameter, sweetly scented, with a purplish tint, borne in spring. *Fruits:* Crimson red, ripening in autumn. This species is particularly valued medicinally, although other *Crataegus* species have similar properties.

Cultivation: As the general description above. Tolerant of a wide range of soil types and pH values, as well as being drought tolerant and tolerant of wet soils.

Tansy-leaved thorn, *Crataegus tanacetifolia*. A native of western Asia, and forms a larger tree, ~10 m tall, ~8 m spread. Flowers are borne in late spring–early summer. The fruit are ~2.5 cm in diameter. It produces regular and good yields of fruits, though is best picked when fully ripe. It is closely related to *C. laciniata*.

Cultivation: As the general notes. Needs virtually no maintenance and is very easy to grow. Can grow in a range of soil types and pH values, and can tolerate very wet soils, as well as drought. Plants are fully cold hardy.

Uses: As the general notes. Fruits are juicy and can be firm (or soft), with a distinct apple-like flavour. Has tough, hard wood. Makes a good ornamental species in an informal planting or as a specimen tree. ■

Crataegus spp.
Mayhaw species (maythorn, applehaw, azarole, hawthorn)
ROSACEAE

Mayhaw (*Crataegus aestivalis*), Arnold hawthorn (*C. arnoldiana*), *C. caesa*, *C. ellwangeriana*, *C. festiva*, Scarlet haw (*C. pedicellata*), *C. pensylvanica*, *C. submollis*, *C. succulenta*

Relatives: hawthorn, pear, apple

The *Crataegus* genera includes ~280 species, which are closely related to apple and pear. They have been used as dwarfing rootstocks for both. They are native to northern America, Asia and Europe. They readily cross fertilise to form new species, and their classification is complex. A group within *Crataegus* is the north American mayhaws, although they interlink with other *Crataegus* species in other parts of the world (see hawthorn p. 159). Many mayhaws occur naturally in low, wet areas and in acid soils around rivers, streams and swamps. They produce edible, tasty fruits, and are a fairly under-utilised species within the USA and elsewhere. They are also important medicinally for their cardiac properties. Historically, indigenous peoples used plants from this genus to treat stomach problems, female ailments and kidney and bladder ailments. They were also used as a general tonic. These species are tough, and can adapt to many soil types and environmental conditions. In the Northern Hemisphere mayhaws often flower early, and produce their fruits early in the season, i.e. by late spring (May). However, included below are also some northern *Crataegus* species that flower in spring, but their fruit do not ripen till autumn.

DESCRIPTION
Mayhaw, *Crataegus aestivalis* (syn. *C. opaca*). Native to the southeastern states of the USA, it forms a medium-sized, fairly slow-growing tree ~9 m tall. It flowers earlier than many *Crataegus* species, in early spring. It is a very popular species in the southern states of the USA and is often grown for its fruits. A few fruiting cultivars have been developed. A large shrub or small, rounded tree (6–10 m tall, spread 4–8 m), with attractive leaves, abundant white blossom and brightly coloured fruits, although it is often very thorny. Trees are fairly long-lived (>50 years), and take on a dense, tangled form as they age.

Leaves: Deciduous, oblong and thin, tapering towards the petiole, 2–7 cm long. Are shiny, waxy and mid green in colour. Attractive. In clusters of 3–5. Autumn leaves often have yellow–russet–reddish colour.

Flowers: Abundant, and in early spring, white–pink, borne on 1-year-old wood and on short spurs. It has the same floral structure as other Rosaceae: five petals, but with an inferior ovary. They bloom for quite a long period. *Pollination:* Bee and insect pollinated. Most are probably monoecious and bisexual, so are able to produce fruit from one plant, though more than one tree will improve fruit-set.

Fruit: Are 1–2.5 cm in diameter, and ripen very early in the summer (in May in the USA, hence their name). They are rounded in shape, have the remnants of the calyx at their apex, and are classified as a pome. Their colour varies from yellow–pinkish–scarlet, and the flesh is fragrant, acid and juicy. Borne in small clusters from short spurs in autumn. Has 2–5 central seeds, often clustered together in a group, making them easy to remove.

Yield/harvest: Fruit take ~30 days to mature from fruit-set to ripening. Can get 30–60 kg of fruits per tree per season. Seedling trees take 5–8 years to start bearing fruits; grafted trees may produce fruits by their third year. Harvest fruits when fully coloured and ripe.

CULTIVATION
They are, generally, very easy plants to grow.

Location: Can be grown in exposed positions, and are wind tolerant. Also tolerate atmospheric pollution. Prefer to grow in full sun, but can be grown in semi-shade, though fruit yields and quality may not be as good.

Temperature: Even though they are native to the

warmer southern states of the USA, they are very cold hardy, and may even fruit at temperatures as low as –25°C. Can survive ~–30°C without damage when dormant; however, flowers may be somewhat frost sensitive.

Chilling: On average, mayhaw needs 250–500 hours of chilling. Some cultivars need less, and bloom earlier; others need longer, and may not bloom till late spring.

Soil/water/nutrients: They grow best in well-drained sandy loam, but can grow in many soil types, including heavy clay. They can tolerate occasional flooding or drought. Although they grow best in a pH range of 6–7, they tolerate both acid and chalky soils. This species is particularly tolerant of waterlogged or marshy sites.

Planting: Space plants at 4.5–6 m apart.

Pruning: Mayhaws are often best trained to a single trunk at the base, with the first branches allowed to develop at ~0.5–1 m height for ease of maintenance, harvesting, etc. Because they form a dense crown, annual pruning to remove crossing and crowded branches helps to keep the centre of the tree open and allow air and light to enter. They are often pruned like apples, to either a central-leader system or a vase shape, with a few main scaffold branches around the stem.

Propagation: *Seed*: The seedcoat contains tenacious germination inhibitors, and needs various treatments before it will germinate: even then they take 6–18 months. They are best sown fresh in autumn, in a cold frame. Some seeds may germinate in spring, but some will need a further winter before germinating. It is possible to sow the seed when still 'green', and before the seedcoat has hardened: this may germinate in spring. Stored seed is more difficult: it needs to be warm stratified for ~3 months at 15°C, and then cold stratified for a further 3 months at 4°C. It may then take another 18 months to germinate. In addition, the seeds can be scarified before stratifying to enable moisture to reach the kernel, i.e. by scratching the seedcoat in some way, or by fermenting the seed for a few days in its own pulp. Seedlings should not be allowed to grow for >2 years in a nursery bed as they become difficult to transplant. Although tricky to germinate, many seeds are nucellar in origin, and grow into seedlings that are clones of the parent plant, so predictability of offspring is assured. The embryo was formed from nucellar tissue around the ovary, and not from within it; no sexual exchange of genes has taken place. *Cuttings:* Semi-ripe cuttings in summer can be dipped in rooting hormone, then inserted in well-drained compost to root. The use of mist can increase percentage take. Hardwood and root cuttings may also be possible. *Grafting:* Can be easily grafted during late winter by whip-and-tongue or simple whip grafts. Cleft grafting can be used on larger trees. They can be grafted onto other *Crataegus* species, though mayhaw seedling rootstocks are best in wetter soils.

Pests and diseases: Relatively disease resistant, but can be susceptible to many of the insects and diseases that attack other Rosaceae fruits, such as plum curculio, hawthorn lace bug, flower thrips, white-fringed beetle, leafminers, scales and mealybugs. Quince rust can also be a problem.

Food
The fruit are juicy and acid, but have a pleasant flavour. They are not usually eaten fresh because of their sour taste, but are good when cooked and added to other fruits. The fruits are popular in the southern states of the USA, where plants are often cultivated as well as the fruits being gathered from the wild. They are popularly used in preserves and jellies. They can be also used in marmalades, condiments, syrups, wines, desserts and juices. The fruits can be dried for later use. The seeds can be boiled or roasted, and used as a coffee substitute.

Nutrition
Fruits are fairly high in iron, magnesium, potassium and calcium, and have good levels of vitamins A and C. The fruit, leaves and flowers contain several compounds (e.g. sterols, flavonoids, catechins, proanthocyanins and others), all of which, when used together, have a beneficial effect on the cardiovascular system. However, no single compound is responsible for this effect: the whole is greater than its parts.

Medicinal
Members of this genus, e.g. hawthorn, and probably to a certain extent the mayhaw species, have fruit and leaf extracts that can treat the early stages of congestive heart failure, angina pectoris and are given for recovery after heart attacks. They are used to reduce any stress around the heart, to help age-related heart problems that do not require digitalis, as well as mild forms of arrhythmias. Studies have shown that they increase cardiac efficiency by improving the blood supply to the heart muscle itself and by strengthening its contractions. The heart is then able to pump more blood to the rest of the body, while also helping to dilate blood vessels at the same time. It can also improve circulation to the extremities by helping to reduce resistance in the arteries. No side effects or contraindications have been reported for these species. Prolonged use is necessary for it to be efficacious. It is normally taken as a tea or a tincture. The indigenous peoples have used unripe *C. tomentosa* fruits for bladder ailments.

CULTIVARS
They hybridise freely with other members of the genus.
'Royalty': Late blooming and has pretty white flowers, ~2.5 cm diameter.
'Super Spur': Very large yields of fruit.
'Texas Star': Has bright red berries. Is a late blooming variety.

OTHER SPECIES

Below are listed a few other North American *Crataegus* species. Much of the information on *C. aestivalis* applies to these species, and only variations are described.

Arnold hawthorn, *Crataegus arnoldiana*. A native of northeast North America. Has excellent potential as a fruit crop in cooler temperate areas, and is very tough and adaptable to many conditions. It is very easy to grow.

Description: A small tree, to ~3–6 m, 1.5–4 m wide, but it is very spiny. White flowers are borne from late spring. Red fruits, ~2 cm diameter. Fruits ripen in autumn, and trees produce very good yields.

Cultivation: Fully cold and wind tolerant. *Soil:* Adaptable to many soil types and pH values. Is fairly drought tolerant. *Pests and diseases:* Very few problems.

Uses: Uses as *C. aestivalis.* Fruits are of very good quality; soft, juicy, sweet–sour, are said to have a delicious flavour and are highly rated, although some may be somewhat mealy. May be better eaten fresh than *C. aestivalis.* Makes a good ornamental plant with its flowers and fruits.

***Crataegus caesa*.** A native of eastern North America, forming a small tree, ~3 m tall, ~3 m spread. A very easy plant to grow. Similar in cultivation, propagation, uses, etc. to *C. aestivalis.* Fruit are ~2 cm in diameter and ripen in autumn, though can hang on the tree for several weeks longer: the first frosts can further sweeten the fruit.

Cultivation: Can be grown in many soil types and pH values; is drought tolerant.

Uses: The fruits can be eaten fresh or cooked, and used as *C. aestivalis*. Have a somewhat mealy texture, but are fairly juicy, sweet and pleasant to eat. Has a reasonable flesh to seed ratio.

***Crataegus ellwangeriana*.** From eastern North America, and is probably of hybrid origin. A medium-sized, spreading tree, ~6 m tall, ~6 m spread. Flowers are borne in late spring. Fruit are ~1.5–2.5 cm in diameter and ripen in autumn.

Cultivation: As for *C. aestivalis.* Can grow in a wide range of soils and pH values; is drought tolerant.

Uses: The fruits can be eaten fresh or cooked. They are juicy, tasty and have a sweet–acid flavour, but can be somewhat mealy in texture. Is a good dessert fruit. Uses as for *C. aestivalis.* Makes a very ornamental subject for informal plantings or as a specimen tree.

***Crataegus festiva*.** A native of eastern North America, it forms a small easy-to-grow tree, ~3 m tall. It has good crops of fruit in autumn. Fruit are ~1.5 cm diameter.

Cultivation: As for *C. aestivalis.* Can grow in a wide range of soil types and pH values; it can tolerate very wet soils, as well as drought.

Uses: Fruits can be eaten fresh or cooked. They are juicy, have a good sweet flavour, though are slightly mealy. A good dessert fruit. Uses as for *C. aestivalis.*

***Crataegus pensylvanica*.** Native to eastern North America, it forms a medium-sized tree, ~6 m tall, ~5 m spread.

It flowers in late spring–early summer. Fruit ripen in late autumn. It produces regular, good crops of fruits. Fruit's are ~2.5 cm diameter, and are semi-sweet and delicious when ripe, or even when just under-ripe.

Cultivation: As for *C. aestivalis.* Needs virtually no maintenance and is very easy to grow. Can grow in a range of soil types and pH values, and can tolerate very wet soils, as well as drought. Plants are fully cold hardy and can be grown in cooler temperate areas.

Uses: Fruits can be eaten fresh or cooked and are sweet, with a good semi-sweet flavour even when semi-ripe. Makes a good dessert. Uses as for *C. aestivalis.*

***Crataegus submollis*.** A native of northeastern North America, it forms a medium-sized tree, to ~8 m. Flowers in late spring–early summer. Fruits ripen in autumn, and are ~2 cm in diameter. May be confused with *C. mollis* and *C. coccinea*, but has 10 stamens (compared to 20 in *C. mollis*).

Cultivation: As for *C. aestivalis.* Needs virtually no maintenance and is very easy to grow. Can grow in a range of soil types and pH values, and can tolerate very wet soils, as well as drought. Plants are fully cold hardy and can be grown in cooler temperate areas.

Uses: Fruits can be eaten fresh or cooked and may be sweet and juicy, with a thick flesh and a good flavour, but some fruits can be somewhat acid and mealy. Makes a reasonable dessert fruit. Uses as for *C. aestivalis.*

***Crataegus succulenta* (syn. *C. coloradensis*).** A native of eastern North America, it forms a medium-sized tree, ~7 m tall. Flowers are borne in late spring. Fruits are some of the largest in this genus, up to ~2–3.5 cm in diameter, and ripen in autumn. It is closely related to *C. tomentosa.*

Cultivation: As for *C. aestivalis.* Needs virtually no maintenance and is very easy to grow. Can grow in a range of soil types and pH values, and can tolerate very wet soils, as well as drought. They can also grow in poor, rocky, dry soils. Plants are fully cold hardy and can be grown in cooler temperate areas.

Uses: The fruits are sweet, juicy and have a pulpy flesh that is good fresh or for making jams, jellies, etc.

Mississippi hawberry, *Crataegus coccinioides*. A native of the southeastern states of the USA, it forms a small tree growing to ~6 m. Has attractive clusters of white flowers, with red stamens, in early summer. The globose fruits, ~1 cm diameter, are bright red when ripe and are juicy.

Scarlet haw, *Crataegus pedicellata*. A native of northeastern North America, it forms a medium-sized tree, ~7 m tall. It is very easy to grow. Fruits are pear shaped and ~1–2 cm long. The subspecies *C. pedicellata gloriosa* has larger fruits. They are best harvested when fully ripe, in late autumn, and are fairly bitter if eaten when under-ripe.

Cultivation: As for *C. aestivalis.* Can grow in a wide range of soil types and pH values, and can tolerate very wet soils, as well as drought. Plants are hardy down to at least –18°C.

Uses: Fruits can be eaten fresh or cooked. They are sweet, but are also dry and mealy. A reasonable dessert fruit. Uses as for *C. aestivalis.* Its wood is strong and hard. ∎

Cucumis spp.

Melons

CUCURBITACEAE

Rock melon, musk melon, honeydew melon, canary melon, sweet melon, casaba melon (*Cucumis melo*)
Similar species: Cantaloupe melon, *Cucumis cantalupensis*, kiwano (*C. metuliferus*), dudaim melon (*C. dudaim*), serpent melon (*C. flexuosum*)

Melons come from a family of plants comprising about 120 genera and 750 species, most of which are natives of Asia and the hot dry regions of Africa, although some have New World origins. Archaeological evidence has shown that some of the Cucurbitaceae species were used by people in Peru as long ago as 12,000 BC; they have been widely utilised around the world since ancient times. Members of this family can be found growing in a wide variety of habitats: from tropical, to arid deserts, to temperate climates. Melons have been used as a food source since at least 2800 BC, and were taken to India in early times. They have been cultivated in southern Europe since before Christian times, and were taken to China by the 12th century. They are now grown around the world in many climates, and can be grown in cooler temperate regions, if given some protection and help to extend their season. In some parts of the world, the fruits are grown primarily for their sweet flesh; in Africa and China, however, the seeds of some species are also valued and are eaten like nuts. In addition, depending upon the species, the leaves, shoots, roots and flowers can also be used.

Above: Cantaloupe

Below: Kiwano

There are ~25 species of *Cucumis*, and most are native to Africa. *C. melo* includes many cultivars of mostly sweet, juicy melons that have innumerable common names, many of which are used interchangeably.

DESCRIPTION

Melons are quick-growing, herbaceous annuals, with somewhat prickly, juicy stems. They have a creeping–climbing form, with tendrils that are borne from the base of leaf stalks, and can rapidly climb up structures such as trees or fences.

Leaves: Coarse, often lightly lobed, large (~12–20 cm length), roughly hairy, particularly beneath. Usually have five main veins.

Flowers: Pretty, yellow or pale lemon, five sepals, five petals, five stamens (variously fused together), an inferior ovary, usually with three fused carpels. Male and female flowers can be on separate plants or on the same plant, so it is better to grow more than one plant to get good fruit-set. *Pollination:* By bees and insects, but hand pollination, with a soft, small brush can increase fruit-set. For the best fruits, flowers should be pinched out until the plants are thoroughly established.

Fruits: They are classified as false berries, with remnants of the calyx visible at the apex. Sweet melons are usually smaller in size than watermelons (see p. 125), are often rugby-ball shaped, and lemon-yellow–golden in colour (e.g. honeydew melon), or they can be green. Their size and colour varies considerably with species and cultivar. Fruit size is usually ~15–20 cm long, but some cultivars have small ~6-cm-sized fruits. They have a waxy rind that is often lightly ribbed. The flesh can be yellow-green (honeydew), white, yellow or pink, and is succulent, sweet and juicy when fully ripe. In the centre are many small (usually ~1-cm-long), thin seeds that are easy to remove. They range in colour from black–brown–yellow–white. They have a thin shell surrounding an oily kernel. Ripened melons are juicy, sweet, succulent and refreshing to eat, and have a rich spicy aroma. Some of the wild species have a more bitter flavour.

Yield/harvest/storage: A plant can produce 6–10 fruits over a season, from mid till late summer. However, they are often difficult to fully ripen, although are best picked when they are ripe, fully coloured and when the apex (not the stalk end) of the fruit can be slightly depressed with thumb pressure. If picked too green, they do not develop their full sweetness and richness of flavour. They can be stored for a few days (or longer) if kept cool; if kept longer they tend to succumb to fungal disease. If not quite ripe when picked, they can be placed in a polythene bag with other fruits that produce ethylene, such as banana, to speed this up.

Roots: Melons have shallow roots, so mechanical cultivation and weed growth should be kept to a minimum. Plants benefit from an organic mulch, which helps conserve moisture and add nutrients.

Food

The flesh is sweet, juicy, refreshing, sometimes almost spicy. Delicious just eaten fresh from the rind. Good when topped with brown sugar or a little ginger. Melons can be used in many desserts, including icecream and yoghurt, and can be added to jams, preserves, chutney, etc. Can also accompany savoury foods such as cheese or ham. They make a pleasant light-tasting wine. The oil from the seeds (15–50%) is sweet, and can be used for cooking and salad dressings. Although fiddly, after the seedcoat has been removed, the kernels can be eaten raw or roasted. To help seedcoat removal, leave them to ferment in their own juice for a couple of days. The kernels can also be added to soups and stews, or to bread and cakes.

Nutrition/medicinal

Melons have good levels of vitamin C: cantaloupe has 42 mg/100 g of flesh; honeydew has 25 mg/100 g of flesh. They contain good levels of vitamin A, some of it as lutein and zeaxanthin, which have been shown to help reduce the incidence of cataracts and macular degeneration. They also have quite good levels of B6 and folate, as well as high levels of potassium. The levels of these are often higher in honeydew melons than other types, with honeydew melons, in particular, having about 50% more potassium than bananas. Seeds contain oils and ~35% protein. The roots can act as a strong laxative.

CULTIVATION

Location: Melons grow best in warm–hot, dry sunny sites. They are not wind- or very salt tolerant.

Temperature: Because they are annuals they can be grown in temperate regions as long as seedlings are given an early start inside, and the plants are sited in a warm/hot sheltered spot. Frost will kill them.

Soil/water/nutrients: Grow best in well-drained, sandy loams, with extra organic matter added. Melons prefer mid-range pH values of 6–7. They do not grow well in acid or poorly drained soils, although like lots of humidity and moisture when young and during fruit development. Plants benefit from regular feeds of liquid manure (or similar) as the fruits are forming, but this should be discontinued when they are ripening. Although they benefit from the addition of some nitrogen (with other nutrients), too much nitrogen reduces the storage time of fruit.

Planting/pruning: Dig in some well-rotted manure (or similar) before planting the seedlings in a warm, sheltered location. They can be encouraged to grow up frames or fences, and this reduces damage to the fruit. Either insert canes and wires, or plant them near a fence. Space plants at ~1 m apart. Once the plant has grown to ~1 m tall, pinch out the top to encourage lateral branches to develop. (Plants may initially need tying into their support, until established.)

Once lateral branches have formed ~5 leaves, these should also have their tips pinched out to encourage the development of secondary laterals. Flowers then develop on these secondary laterals. Hand pollination will greatly increase fruit-set: use a soft, small brush. Female flowers can be distinguished from male flowers by a small swelling below the flower, which will later form the fruit. It is best to not allow more than 4–6 fruits to develop on each plant to optimise fruit quality and size. The fruits may need supporting in nets as they get larger.

Propagation: *Seed:* Readily and easily grown from seed. It is the main method of propagation. They are sown at ~1.25 cm depth, and lengthways. They need warmth and moisture to germinate and, in cooler regions, they are best sown in a glasshouse or similar. They should germinate in ~6–8 days. Prick out and grow on seedlings in pots before planting out when they have about five main leaves. Seeds collected in autumn should be washed free of pulp and stored in a cool, dry place until spring. Be careful that stored seed does not go mouldy during storage. Pick out the biggest seeds from healthy plants to save for next year's crop.

Pests and diseases: Plants are susceptible to powdery mildew: growing the plants in drier conditions and not too close together will reduce this risk. Applications of foliar fish extract are said to help prevent mildew. Plants can also develop various viral diseases, such as cucumber mosaic virus (the leaves and fruits become mottled). The removal of weeds and non-crowding of plants can reduce this risk. In addition, many insects are vectors of viruses, so try to minimise their numbers around plants (although this is not always easily done!). Can be also attacked by *Verticillium* wilt (the leaves become yellow and wilt).

CULTIVARS

Cultivars will readily cross, within species, to form plants that can be quite different from their parents. There are many commercial cultivars and types, and some have a dwarfing form more suited to those with limited space. Some of the more common ones are:

'Casaba': Oval, larger, pale yellow when ripe, with green, finely ridged skins and white, sweet flesh. Does not have an aroma.

'Crenshaw': Fairly large fruit with yellowish skin and pinky flesh. Is sweet, but spicy in flavour. A cross between casaba and Persian melons.

'Persian': Similar to cantaloupe (see below), but larger. Has netting marks on the skin.

'Honeydew': Has round, creamy-yellow-coloured fruit, ~20 cm long. Flesh is thick, juicy and yellow-green in colour, very sweet. Very popular.

'Santa Claus': Similar to watermelon in looks and taste, with green and gold stripes, but is ~30 cm long.

'Sharlyn': Fruits have a netted pattern, green-orange rind, with white flesh. Flesh tastes like cantaloupe/honeydew and is wonderfully sweet.

SIMILAR SPECIES

The notes above apply to the species described below unless specifically stated otherwise.

Cantaloupe melons, *Cucumis cantalupensis* syn. *C. melo*. Well known and appreciated and is also known as the 'White Antibes'. It has its origins in the Middle East, but has long been cultivated and valued in regions around France as well as Italy. Its name, cantaloupe, is derived from a town near Rome where it has been cultivated since the 1600s.

Description: Fruit often has a distinctive white netted pattern on its mottled green, slightly bumpy skin, which is sometimes slightly ribbed. It has very sweet, juicy, firm, orange flesh (some cultivars have green or red flesh) when fully ripe, with many small straw-coloured central seeds. Contains more vitamin A than other melons.

Kiwano or African horned melon, *Cucumis metuliferus*. Is native to the fringes of the Kalahari Desert in Africa and is a popular food with local populations. It has been introduced into various countries, including New Zealand, and has been evaluated for commercial production. It has interestingly-shaped, attractive orange, spiny fruit, with bright green flesh. The fruit has many seeds, a subtle flavour, and stores well for a long period in a dry atmosphere, although rapidly deteriorates in humid atmospheres. At present, it is marketed as a speciality crop, and is sometimes sold in Israel, Europe and the USA.

Description: The plant is an annual. *Flowers:* It is monoecious, so only needs one plant to set fruit, though male flowers tend to open several days before the female flowers are receptive, so hand pollination should help fruit-set. *Fruit:* It can have good yields of fruits, although fruit size varies and fruit-set can be poor. Fruits are ripe when they have a bright orange rind, with a dark green, juicy interior. They are shaped like a short, stout cucumber, and have many blunt thorns on their rind. The flesh does not have much taste. They like a hot summer to ripen well.

Propagation: Germination rates are very good if seeds are kept warm (but not too hot), and should take 8–16 days. Once established, plants can grow very rapidly and start to flower and set fruits in 6–8 weeks; it then takes a further ~7 weeks before fruit maturity. They are best harvested when ripe and fully orange in colour. *Pests and diseases:* Are susceptible to *Fusarium* wilt.

Dudaim melon (Queen Anne's pocket melon), *Cucumis dudaim*. The Dudaim melon is a native of Persia. It produces a fruit that has a green and orange spotted skin. When fully ripe, it becomes yellow and then whitish. It has a very fragrant, vinous, musky smell, but the pulp is whitish, flaccid and insipid.

Serpent melon (snake cucumber), *Cucumis flexuosum*. The serpent melon is common in both Arabia and Egypt. It is a long fruit (hence its name) and can be eaten fresh or pickled. It has a sweet, cool taste similar to that of watermelon. ■

Cucurbita pepo
Pumpkin seeds (pepitas)
CUCURBITACEAE
Relatives: melons, watermelons, oyster nut

The Cucurbitaceae family is a large group of plants (120 genera, 760 species) that are generally natives of warmer climates. Many species have been and still are used as an important food source by many peoples around the world. The *Cucurbita* genus, apart from melons (see p.165), also includes pumpkins, gourds and squashes. While they are mostly used as vegetables, these also contain many seeds. There is a great deal of interchangeability between their common names. Here, the focus is on pumpkins, which, although they have tasty flesh, also have nutritious, delicious seeds. The pumpkin plant is a native of Central America and southwestern USA, and used to be a common wild plant. Pumpkin remains have been found in settlements used by the indigenous populations of Central America that date back to 7000 BC. They have been cultivated for many hundreds of years, and have been used medicinally for wound healing, as well as for their food value. The flesh, seeds and flowers are all edible, and their biggest bonus is their ability to be stored for long periods. Even the hard rind was and still is used as a container, and for holding candles on Halloween. The pumpkin has been widely grown and used in Europe since the 16th century, and is also a popular vegetable in Asia and China. More recently, although the pumpkin is used widely for its flesh, the seeds have become increasingly popular in the West and are used in many food preparations.

DESCRIPTION
Depending on cultivar, they usually form trailing plants, though a few cultivars are bushy. Creeping cultivars can spread several metres in all directions. Most cultivars are fast-growing annuals. (A few gourd varieties are perennials and can live for 30 years.) The stems are rough, tough and somewhat prickly.

Leaves: Large (~15–25 cm width), rough and hairy, particularly beneath, pale–mid green, heart-shaped, often concave in shape, usually with five main veins, sometimes lobed.

Flowers: Quite large (~5–8 cm diameter), pretty, trumpet shaped and have five fused yellow-orange petals. They are borne singly from upper leaf axils in summer. They have an inferior ovary (so the seeds are formed within the receptacle), which usually consists of three fused carpels (or sections). *Pollination:* Flowers are either male or female, and can occur both on the same or on different plants. It is, therefore, best to grow more than one plant. They are insect pollinated, but hand pollination with a soft brush increases fruit-set. Female flowers can be distinguished by their bulbous base (the ovary). It is best to remove the first flowers formed until the plant is established: larger, more established plants will produce larger, better fruit.

Fruits: Botanically classed as a 'false' berry, with the remnants of the calyx still discernible at the apex. Magnificent, one of the largest fruit: they can be green, yellow or orange. The fruits lie on the ground, next to and beneath the leaves. They have a thick rind, usually pale yellow–orange, which surrounds the orange flesh inside, which is delicious when baked or roasted. It is used in many savoury soups and dishes. In the centre are many seeds. These are white, ripening to yellow–green. They are pointed, flattish, ~2.5 cm long by 1.25 cm wide.

Yield/harvest/storage: Competitions are held by growers to produce the largest pumpkin, and truly awesome specimens have been produced. The record, at present, is ~657 kg for a single pumpkin (more than half a tonne!), and the record weight of pumpkins grown on a single plant is 1235 kg. Normally, they assume a more modest size (~35 cm in width) and weight (~3–4 kg). There are usually between 2–6 pumpkins per plant. Pumpkins can yield ~100 g of seeds per fruit. The pumpkins can be harvested when the outer case has become fully swollen and has turned yellow (or the colour of the cultivar). The seeds can be easily scooped out from the centre of the fruit and the pulp is then washed off. Pumpkins take 100–120 days to mature after pollination. Pumpkins can be stored at ~8°C for ~4+ months. However, after extended periods, the flesh becomes dry and the seeds are at risk of becoming mouldy, or of geminating while still in the fruit. If harvesting pumpkins for their seeds, it is probably prudent to collect these soon after the fruits are picked, removing the pulp and then drying the seeds before storage or processing.

Roots: Pumpkins have shallow roots, so mechanical cultivation needs to be minimal, as does weed growth. They benefit from an organic mulch to help retain mositure and add nutrients.

uses

Food

The pumpkin is widely used for its orange flesh to make such dishes as pumpkin soup and pies. It is also delicious roasted. Recently, the use of nutritious pumpkin seeds has increased in the West, and they are now used in many dishes, salads, breads, cakes and are included in trail mixes. The extracted oils are also used in different food products. The seeds can be eaten like nuts, either raw, roasted or fried. The raw seeds can simply be dipped in salt and eaten. When toasted, the seeds develop a nutty, spicy aroma and taste. In Mexico, the seeds are roasted and eaten as a snack, and are also used as a thickener in sauces, etc. In South America, the roasted seeds are mixed with syrup to make a sweet. The seeds can also be ground to make a flour that can be added to breakfast cereals and confectionery. The extracted pumpkin oil is dark green in colour and has a strong, distinctive taste, not unlike sesame oil. It is more usually added to dressings or where a strong flavour is required. A tasty salad dressing can be made by mixing the oil with vinegar, salt and garlic. The oil can also be added to a salad made from beans, potatoes, onions, garlic and tomatoes. It can be also used to flavour breads, or can be added to stews or soups to give them a pumpkin flavour. The oil is not very suitable for cooking or heating. Most pumpkin oil is produced in Austria and other eastern European countries. It is extracted from the crushed seeds using heat (~60°C); cold-pressed oil has little flavour.

Nutrition

The seeds are a good food source and have high levels of several minerals: they contain good levels of manganese, magnesium, zinc, iron, phosphorus, copper, calcium and selenium, plus some vitamin A, and good levels of the B vitamins B6, niacin, folic acid, riboflavin and thiamine. They also have good levels of vitamin K, some vitamin C and antioxidants, as well as good levels of fibre. The seeds also contain ~50% oil (mostly unsaturated linoleic and oleic acid) and 30% protein (although not the sulphur amino acids). The oil contains carotenoids (they give the oil its green colour), lutein and chlorophylls, all of which act as stains and colourings.

Medicinal

The native American populations used pumpkins for a variety of medical purposes. The seeds were emulsified and applied to wounds and were eaten to treat kidney and urine problems. The seed oil has been used to treat burns and wounds; these properties may be due to their high zinc level. The seeds' high zinc and magnesium levels are said to help men with prostate problems. (Men in many eastern European countries, who have always eaten the seeds, have virtually no prostate problems.) In addition, in Germany, it was discovered that the raw seeds contain minerals that stimulate sex-hormone production, so eating a few raw seeds a day may also help prevent impotence. They are eaten widely throughout eastern Europe for this reason. Medicinally, they have been used by the Chinese and are a symbol of prosperity and fruitfulness. They are also good for improving vision, probably because of their vitamin A content. In addition, they help reduce vomiting and seasickness. The kernels, in South America, have been used to eradicate internal parasites. This historical usage has now been found to probably arise from the powerful isoprenoids they contain, which are non-toxic to humans, but are toxic to parasites, and which are also being investigated for their ability to reduce certain cancers, e.g. prostate.

CULTIVATION

Location: Grow best when planted in full sun.

Temperature: Are relatively cold tolerant, but autumn frosts usually finish them off in temperate climates. They can be grown in tropical and semi-tropical areas. Plants grow best in regions with long, warm, dry summers.

Soil/water/nutrients: Pumpkins prefer mid-range pH values of 6–7, and grow best in fertile, well-drained loams. They do not grow well in acid or poorly drained soils. Are drought tolerant, but grow better with regular moisture during hot summers. Plants benefit from additions of nutrients and organic matter, and/or foliar feeds of fish or seaweed extract. Although some additional nitrogen is beneficial (with other nutrients), too much reduces the time that pumpkins can be stored for.

Planting: Trailing cultivars should be spaced at 2.5–3 m apart; bush-type cultivars are usually planted on mounds at ~1.5 m apart. Plant once all risk of frost has passed. It is best to plant pumpkins in a different area of the garden each year to reduce the risk of soil-borne disease. Young plants grow well in drier soils. In addition, if conditions are humid, slugs are more likely to be a problem: these can rapidly demolish young plants if not controlled.

Pruning: Pinching out the tips of runners once the plants are established encourages the formation of laterals: these tend to form female flowers, rather than male flowers.

Propagation: Seed: Grows readily and easily from seed. Ii is the main method of propagation. Can be just sown *in situ*, but there is a risk of them being eaten by birds, mice, etc. Alternatively, they can be sown in warmth in moist compost, where they germinate within ~6–8 days. Prick out and grow on seedlings in pots before planting out. Seeds collected in autumn should be washed free of pulp and stored in a cool, dry place until spring. Be careful that stored seeds do not go mouldy. Select the largest seeds from healthy plants to save for next year's crop.

Pests and diseases: Plants are susceptible to powdery mildew; growing the plants in drier conditions and not too close together will reduce this risk. An application of foliar fish extract is said to help prevent mildew. Plants may also develop various viral diseases. The removal of weeds around plants and non-crowding of plants can reduce this risk. In addition, many insects are vectors of viruses, so try to minimise their numbers around plants, although this is not always easily done! Chickens can be a useful ally in clearing up insect pests, once the plants are established. Insect pests include wireworm, cutworm, spider mite and aphids.

CULTIVARS

There are many pumpkin cultivars, most of which have been selected for their fruit quality and size. A few cultivars have been selected for their seed quality and production, and these include some European and US cultivars that have no shells around the kernels. 'Lady Godiva' is a well-known US cultivar. It has large, dark green seeds, with no seedcoat, and these seeds are plump and good to eat. ■

Cudrania tricuspidata
Che (storehouse bush, silkworm thorn, Chinese mulberry)
MORACEAE
Relatives: mulberry, breadfruit, jackfruit, fig

The che is a native of eastern Asia, from China to Nepal, and became naturalised in Japan many years ago. In China, the leaves are an alternative food for silkworms when mulberry leaves are scarce. Similar to the mulberry, they have rich red, aggregate, juicy fruits. The tree was introduced into England and other parts of Europe around 1870, and is very cold hardy and can grow in many soil types. It is also very ornamental in shape and leaf, and produces abundant crops of fruit.

DESCRIPTION

A smallish tree with a rounded crown, growing to ~8 m, though can form a large, spreading bush or small tree if not pruned when young. Young trees have thorns, but lose these as they mature. Female trees tend to be larger and stronger than male trees. They are fast growing, but fairly short lived, living only ~30 years.

Leaves: Deciduous, alternate, like those of the mulberry, but smaller and thinner. Entire or sometimes with two rounded lobes, dark glossy green above, paler and slightly pubescent beneath, especially on veins. Leaves may have pointed or rounded tips. As the plant grows, there is a tendency towards larger and entire leaves, with indistinct or irregular lobes; younger leaves are often two-lobed.

Flowers: Dioecious. Both male and female flowers are ~1 cm across, yellowish-green, and are borne in late spring. Male flowers turn yellow as the pollen ripens, whereas female flowers have numerous small stigmas. *Pollination:* By wind. Need at least one male- and some female-flowering trees to get good fruit yields, though there are some reports that female trees may produce fruits parthenocarpically without males around, and that male plants occasionally have a few female flowers that will set fruit.

Fruit: Che fruit are an aggregate of several embryos fused together, and look somewhat like a round mulberry, 2.5–5 cm in diameter. Ripe fruits are an attractive red or maroon-red colour with juicy, rich red flesh, with each drupelet containing a small brown, edible seed. There are between 3–6 drupelets

uses

Food
Fruits can be eaten fresh or cooked, or can be mixed with other fruits to improve their flavour. Makes a wonderful juice, though you do need to strain out the seeds. The seeds can be a nuisance; however, there is a seedless female cultivar. Sugar and acidity content are fairly low, and the fruits are often enjoyed more when mixed with other fresh fruits.

Medicinal
An infusion of the wood is used to treat sore or weak eyes. The inner bark and the wood are used in the treatment of malaria, debility and to reduce heavy menstruation. The root is said to increase milk flow during lactation and is used to treat an absence of menstruation.

Other uses
A yellow dye is obtained from the wood. The wood is fine grained and is used for making utensils.

per fruit. The flavour, when firm, is almost tasteless, being neither very sweet nor very sour. It has been said to be watermelon-like in its flavour. Hot summers are best to ripen the fruit.

Yield/harvest: Seedling trees can take up to 10 years to start producing fruits, though grafted trees should start producing in 3–4 years. Mature trees can produce as much as 200 kg of fruit. The fruits ripen in late autumn. Ripe fruits need to be individually picked and it is important that fruit be thoroughly ripe to be at their best and have become a deep, dark red colour. The fruit will keep for several days in a refrigerator.

CULTIVATION
A very hardy plant. Needs minimal care.

Location: Needs a warm, sunny location: they do not grow well in shade. They are quite wind-resistant.

Temperature: Very cold hardy, withstanding temperatures down below –25°C.

Soil/water/nutrients: Has tolerance of drought and poor soils, but performs best in a deep, warm, well-drained loam. While established trees are somewhat drought-resistant, they also appreciate moisture during hot, dry seasons. If the roots become too dry, trees may lose their leaves and unripe fruits are likely to drop. An annual application of a balanced fertiliser in late spring benefits growth and fruiting.

Planting: One method is to plant a male and female trees close together, ~30 cm apart, to a ratio of ~25% male and ~75% female.

Pruning: Need regular pruning to control their shape and spread. All branches formed the previous season should be pruned to half their length, and male trees may need an additional summer pruning to encourage more growth of flowering lateral branches. To reduce its bushy habit and spread, encourage the growth of some upright branches.

Propagation: *Seed:* Good germination from seed, though trees can take up to 10 years to start producing fruits. Seeds can either be extracted from the pulp, washed and sown when fresh, or can be stored and sown in early spring. Grow on seedlings for at least the first year. Plant out in spring or early summer. However, you won't know the sex of trees until they start flowering. *Cuttings:* The progeny are known. Semi-ripe cuttings can be taken during mid summer and treated with rooting hormone. Mature-wood cuttings in late autumn can be placed outside in sandy soil in a frame. *Grafting:* Che is often grafted onto osage orange (*Maclura pomifera*) rootstocks, by either a cleft or whip-and-tongue graft. These trees tend to be stronger and grow more upright.

Pests and diseases: Few pest or disease problems, though the birds like the ripe fruits. ∎

Cydonia oblonga (syn. *Pyrus cydonia, Cydonia vulgaris*)
Quince (common quince, mu gua)
ROSACEAE

Similar species: flowering quince (*Chaenomeles speciosa, C. cathayensis*), Japanese quince (Maule's quince) (*C. japonica*), Tibetan quince (*C. thibetica*), Chinese quince (*Pseudocydonia sinensis*)

Relatives: apple, pear, medlar

The quinces are pome fruits, and are members of the Rosaceae family. The pome fruits are derived from a flower with an inferior, compound ovary. The seeds develop within the receptacle and the receptacle becomes the fleshy fruit. Quinces are similar in morphology to the *Malus* and *Pyrus* genera of Rosaceae, i.e. the apples and pears, but are different to many Rosaceae genera, e.g. strawberries and brambles, where fruits are formed from flowers with superior

ovaries. There has been much taxonomic confusion concerning the *Chaenomeles* genus, with quince (*Cydonia oblonga*) often being grouped with them. Now it is widely accepted that the *Chaenomeles* species are separate from the quince species. However, they are similar in many ways, and the fruits of both genera are edible (though that of *Cydonia oblonga* is of better quality). Some of the ornamental *Chaenomeles* species are described below. In addition, Chinese quince (*Pseudocydonia sinensis*) is also described, because although this is also sometimes listed as a *Chaenomeles* species, it is in fact more like common quince.

Apple, pear and quince may all originate from the Middle and Near East, and have the same progenitor species, though this is now probably extinct. Quince is mainly cultivated in Mediterranean areas. Historically, the fruits were highly valued by the Greeks and Romans. It was the 'golden apple' that Paris awarded to Aphrodite as a symbol of love, marriage and fertility, and was commonly and symbolically used in marriage ceremonies, in spite of its sourness. It was grown for its fragrant fruits and attractive pink flowers. The original Greek name for the fruit was 'Cydonian apple', with the name 'quince' derived from 'Cydonia' (or Chania), which is the name of a port in Crete from which the fruits were exported. The fruits are still grown in these regions of the island. These days, quince is more important as a rootstock than as a fruit producer, and it is often used as a rootstock for pears. However, the tree is still found in many older gardens and is still appreciated for its aromatic, musky, long-lasting fruits, which make excellent jelly, chutneys and preserves.

DESCRIPTION

A slow-growing, ornamental tree, ~3–7 m height, 3–6 m spread, that takes on a gnarled form as it ages. Forms a multi-stemmed tree, with tangled branches that are usually spiny. Young stems are covered with a pale grey fuzz. It has a tendency to sucker. Trees live ~50 years.

Leaves: Deciduous, though lasting till late autumn or into winter before falling. They are elliptical, with a pointed tip and entire margins (not serrated like ornamental quinces), 5–10 cm long, 4–6 cm wide, often larger than those of apple or pear, shiny and dark green above, with a pale dense woolly fuzz beneath (especially when young). Have large, noticeable, rounded stipules (~2.5 cm) at the base of the leaves. New leaves are reddish-bronze, maturing to dark green. They develop a rich yellow colour before they fall.

Flowers: Abundant, pretty, pink–white, flowers (~3–5 cm diameter) in late spring (after pears have blossomed, and much later than *Chaenomeles* species). They are usually borne singly, but sometimes in clusters of 2–4 on the ends of short shoots from the present season's growth. The flowers open after the leaves, and the flowers are not as showy as those of the ornamental quince (see below). *Pollination:* Are self-fertile and pollination is good in both cool and hot climates, but get more fruits with more than one tree. They are bee and insect pollinated.

Fruit: Formed on short shoots of the current season's wood, so needs care when pruning. They are a pome, with their flesh being derived from the receptacle. Within this are five sections, and each section may contain many ovules (seeds). It has more seeds than apples or pears: i.e. 20 in each section compared with two seeds in an apple section. The fruits are often wonderfully fragrant when ripe, yellow, ~10 cm long. They are either pear shaped, with dry, gritty flesh, or are more rounded, with these fruits being tastier and maturing earlier. The fruits are not eaten fresh, but are cooked in desserts or made into preserves, jam, jelly, etc. Fruits ripen in mid–late autumn, or early winter.

Yield/harvest/storage: Trees can produce ~15 kg of fruit when 5–8 years old, and individual fruits can weigh up to 0.5 kg. The fruits should be only harvested when they are fully ripe; when they have turned from green to deep yellow, but before the first frosts. It is best to cut the fruit stalk when harvesting rather than pulling it, as the fruit stalk does not break easily and can damage the stem. The fruits also bruise easily, so handle them carefully and store them in a single layer, without touching each other. If kept in a cool, dry place, they should last for 2–3 months. Other fruits stored close to them will pick up a quince flavour.

Roots: Is shallow rooting, so take care with mechanical cultivation. A mulch will help retain soil moisture and reduce weed competition.

CULTIVATION

An easy-to-grow, adaptable tree.

Location: They can be grown in a sunny or semi-shaded, sheltered location. They prefer dry rather than humid climates.

Temperature: Quince can be grown in many climates, including hot, dry areas, but prefer a continental or temperate climate with a warm autumn to ripen the fruit. They are quite frost hardy and can tolerate temperatures down to ~–20°C, though flower-bud injury is possible in very cold winters.

Chilling: The quince needs less chilling than apples or pears, i.e. between 100–400 hours.

Soil/water/nutrients: They can grow in a wide range of soil types, but prefer a deep, fertile loam, with a pH range of 6–7. If grown in alkaline soils, chlorosis, caused by iron deficiency, is common and peat or a foliar feed will need to be applied. They are fairly drought tolerant, though grow and fruit better with regular moisture. However, they do not like wet soils and rapidly succumb to disease. In general, they benefit from an annual application of a general fertiliser or some organic matter, particularly in poorer soils.

uses

Food
Most cultivars have fruit that cannot be eaten raw, but are cooked to make preserves, jellies and are added to sauces (is good mixed with apple) and desserts. Quince jelly is historically very popular. When cooked, the juice and pulp have an attractive pink–red colour; used in Mediterranean dishes, e.g. stews, roasts. The peel is often bitter and is usually discarded. Fruits tend to be softer and juicier in warmer regions. A reasonable quality wine and a cider can be made from the fruits. In Medieval times, a popular quince dish was made from the fruit. After being peeled, sliced and boiled in red wine, it was then strained and boiled again in honey and spiced wine. Having cooled and set firm, it was served as a dessert. A liquor of quinces infused in brandy is called ratafia.

Nutrition
Fruits have fairly good levels of vitamin C. Has very high levels of pectin, so is good for jam, etc.

Medicinal
Quinces have been used to treat a sore throat and diarrhoea, to promote blood circulation, to treat and soothe inflammation of the mucous membranes, intestines and stomach, and for arthritic and rheumatic conditions. In ancient Chinese medicine, the bark was used as an astringent for ulcers. The pectin fibre probably contributes to some of these benefits.
Warning: Like all the Rosaceae, the seeds, bark and leaves contain cyanogenic compounds, which are toxic if eaten in quantity: the flesh is perfectly safe.

Other uses
Quinces used to be very popular for their scent.

Ornamental
Some cultivars have attractive flowers. They can be grown as a wild hedge.

Planting: Space young trees at 4–6 m apart. They may need staking for a few years.

Pruning: They can be trained as a fan or an espalier form, and can then be tied into wires or onto a sun-facing wall. They are usually pruned to form a single trunk, though can be grown with multiple stems. Just after planting, the main leaders of young trees can be pruned back by a third, in late autumn or early spring, to encourage root development. Prune stems back to an outward-facing bud to encourage the branches to grow outwards. After this, because fruits are borne on spurs and on the tips of the previous summer's growth, take care not to remove young stems. Established trees need very little pruning, only the removal of any damaged or diseased wood, and to keep the centre of the tree open to allow air and sunlight to enter. Many trees

(unless grafted) sucker freely, and these may need removing.

Propagation: *Seed:* Can be sown fresh in autumn and allowed to overwinter, or stored seed will need ~2–4 weeks of gentle warmth, followed by ~4 months of cold stratification before sowing in moist, warm compost. Germination can be slow. *Cuttings:* Ripe and semi-ripe cuttings taken in late spring–early summer should root well, particularly if dusted with a rooting hormone or watered with willow washings (see p. 28). Semi-hardwood cuttings can be also taken in mid–late summer, and also hardwood cuttings in winter. Root cuttings can also be taken by digging up suckers and then potting them on till they are established. *Layering:* This is also a good method. In spring or autumn, lower branches are laid on the soil surface and a small region of the branch is lightly scored with a knife, and then pegged down to root; this can take up to 12 months. *Grafting:* Can be T- or chip-budded onto a variety of quince or pear rootstocks.

Pests and diseases: Is quite a tough species, and is not generally affected by problems. However, in humid, wet conditions trees are susceptible to leaf-spot diseases and rust, which can also spread to the fruits. Tidying up autumn leaves can reduce the risk of disease. Fireblight is another potential problem, but the risk can be reduced by minimising pruning and fertiliser use. Apple scab can be an occasional problem, as can scales, mites, various moth larvae and aphids. Note, that insecticides may severely damage the leaves.

CULTIVARS
'Aromatnaya': Fruits have a pineapple flavour. This is one of the few quince cultivars that has fruit which can be eaten fresh, when fully ripe.
'Champion': Trees are vigorous. Good yields of large, greenish-yellow fruits with a delicate flavour. Flesh is tender, only slightly astringent. Fruits at a young age.
'Dwarf Orange': Low, bushy tree growing 3–4.5 m tall. Fruit: large, golden-yellow. Early ripening.
'Gamboa': From Portugal. Small, dense tree. Fruit: bright yellow. Flesh: yellowish-white; flavour is sweeter than most.
'Meeches Prolific': US selection. Fruit: golden-yellow, good flavour, early ripening. Fruits at an early age (3 years). Good heavy cropper, slow–medium growth. Fruits store well.
'Orange': Fruit: large, bright yellow skin, orange tender flesh, good flavour. Good for areas with cool summers.
'Smyrna': From Turkey. Fruit: very large, yellow, tender, rich flavour and fragrance. Early maturing. Good yields. Fruits store very well. Moderately vigorous tree with unusually large leaves.
'Vrajna' (syn. 'Bereczcki'): From Serbia. Fruit: very large, very fragrant, golden-yellow, soft flesh, good flavour. Fruits borne at an early age (4–6 years). Good cropper. Can be fan trained. Has very vigorous, erect growth.

CHAENOMELES SPECIES: FLOWERING OR ORNAMENTAL QUINCES

Chaenomeles species are known as the ornamental quinces. They are usually grown for their very early, colourful flowers that appear in late winter and can last till spring, even in cold areas. Fruits are used to make jams, jelly and also juiced.

GENERAL DESCRIPTION

These flowering quinces have a medium growth rate.

Leaves: All are deciduous, simple, alternate, serrated, dark green, with large stipules on new growth. Most species have rounded, thorny leaves, borne after the plant has flowered.

Flowers: A very attractive and welcome sight in dark, grey winters. Their flowers have five petals, and can be white, orange, pink, scarlet or deep red. Occur as 1–6 flowers in clusters on 2-year-old or older branches. They usually form during the previous late summer and autumn. Can sometimes be bisexual (have both male and female organs), though others are sometimes self-infertile, so is best to plant more than one plant to set fruits. *Pollination:* By bees.

Fruits: Smaller than those of common quince, and are more fibrous; a lovely fragrance, they can be juicy and produce good yields. Used to make a sharp-tasting jelly. New cultivars are being developed that have larger, tastier fruit. Have many seeds within each fruit (80–120). The fruits are apple or pear shaped. They ripen in autumn or early winter; the fruits become yellow-green, sometimes with a reddish tint, and the seeds turn brown, but the fruits do not soften.

CULTIVATION

Location: Grow in full sun or semi-shade, though fruits ripen best in full sun. Can tolerate atmospheric pollution.

Temperature: These species are cold hardy and can tolerate temperatures down to ~–25°C.

Soil/water: Adaptable to many soil types (sand, loam, heavy clay), and does well in dry situations. Can become chlorotic in alkaline soils (iron deficient), and prefers more acidic soils. Needs good drainage. Benefits from an annual addition of a balanced fertiliser.

Propagation: Easy to propagate. *Seed:* Has 95–100% germination, but do not let seeds dry out before sowing. Benefit from 4 weeks of stratification at ~3°C in moist conditions. Plants take 3–5 years before they are large enough to plant out. *Cuttings:* Easy. See notes for quince. Semi-ripe, ripe, hardwood and root cuttings are all possible. Larger cuttings (>20 cm) root more rapidly, produce more roots and survive colder temperatures than shorter cuttings. Rooting hormone increases percentage take. *Layering:* Is good. See notes for quince. *Suckers:* Easy to transplant.

Pruning: Prune to open up the centre to allow light and air to enter. Thin and shape while the plant is in bud and flower. New growth bears next year's flowers. Prune to remove older branches. May need to prune back suckers around plants.

Pests and diseases: Generally there are few problems. Can get leaf spots, grey mould and *Botrytis*. The fruits can be attacked by fungi. Plants are very resistant to honey fungus.

THE SPECIES

Flowering quince, Chaenomeles cathayensis. Native to China. Grows taller than most other members of this genus and forms a tree ~6 m tall. Has narrow leaves and long thorns. Has very large fruits: ~12 cm long weighing >200 g each. Prefers a warmer climate to fully ripen the fruit.

Flowering quince, Chaenomeles speciosa. Native to China. Forms a large shrub, 2–5 m tall, with flowers ~3–5 cm diameter, in small clusters, in various shades of red. Fruits vary in shape and are ~4–7 cm long. Formed on older wood. Prefers a warmer climate to fully ripen the fruit. A popular ornamental. Fruits can remain on the plant for a long time.

Japanese quince, Chaenomeles japonica. Native to Japan. An ornamental, dwarf shrub (0.6–1.2 m tall) with orange-red blossom (~3 cm diameter) in late spring. Has many, small, fragrant fruits that become sticky when ripe; often the first species to ripen.

Tibetan quince, Chaenomeles thibetica. Native to China. A 1.5–3 m tall shrub. Pear-shaped fruits, ~6–10 cm long.

CULTIVARS

There are many named cultivars, mostly selected for their ornamental properties. Ask around for species in your area that produce better-quality fruits.

USES

Food: The fresh fruits are very hard and acid, and are usually cooked and used to make juice, wine, purée, jam, or mixed with apple sauce. In Latvia and Lithuania, syrup, liqueur, soft drinks, marmalades and candies have been made from them. The aromatic juice, with sugar, has been used to flavour icecream and yoghurt. *Nutrition:* Fruit have a high content of vitamin C, phenolic compounds (antioxidants) and dietary fibre, but levels of these vary between species. The fruits do not oxidise and go brown during preparation. *Medicinal:* The Chinese have used these species for a long time for various medicinal purposes. Have been used to relieve muscle spasms and leg cramps, to increase the production of digestive fluids and to treat rheumatism, rheumatic arthritis, vomiting, diarrhoea and dyspepsia. **Warning:** Like all Rosaceae, the seeds are poisonous if eaten in excess. *Other uses:* Fruits have a lovely aroma. *Ornamental:* These species are popular for their very early, brightly coloured flowers, attractive for cutting in winter. The shrubs' spines make these plants useful for a barrier hedge. They are also good for attracting wildlife.

PSEUDOCYDONIA SPECIES

Chinese quince, Pseudocydonia sinensis (syn. Chaenomeles sinensis, Cydonia sinensis, Malus sinensis). This species is a native of China, and is sometimes cultivated there for its fruit. A close relative of the common quince (*Cydonia oblonga*), it has fragrant, often oblong, large yellow fruit that can weigh up to 1 kg each.

Description: It forms an upright, slow to moderately fast-growing shrub or small tree (~3–7 m tall, 1.5–5 m spread), which can form many stems, though is better restricted to three or four. Has attractive green–grey–orange mottled, flaking bark and twiggy branches. It does not sucker like common quince. *Leaves:* Semi-evergreen or deciduous, dark, glossy green, 12.5–22 cm long, alternate, simple. New leaves, in spring, are pinky-bronze in colour. Also has good orange–red autumn colour. *Flowers:* Reports vary: some say it is not self-fertile, so will need more than one tree to get fruit; other reports say it is self-fertile (probably best to get two plants anyway to increase pollination, even if it is self-fertile). Has attractive, five-petalled, pink, waxy blossom. Flowers are borne in clusters of 2–6 in early spring on bare branches of last season's growth; some also occur throughout the summer. Pollinated by bees and insects. *Fruit:* Shiny, smooth, large (~25cm long; 0.25–1 kg in weight), yellow skin, wonderful fragrance when ripe in mid to late autumn. Has a good, strong flavour and is used in a similar way to common quince.

Cultivation: *Location:* Likes full sun or a little shade; does not grow well in heavy shade. *Temperature:* Is fairly hardy, and grows best in warm-temperate or continental climates that have long hot summers. If grown in colder areas, it's best in a warm, sunny, protected location. *Soil:* Will grow in fairly poor soils, including clay, and in a range of pH conditions, from fairly acid to fairly alkaline. Needs moist to wet soil, but not waterlogged. *Pot culture:* Its slow–moderate growth, early flowers and large fruits make it a good choice for growing in a container. In colder regions, it can then also be protected from heavy frosts. *Pruning:* Its twiggy growth may need tidying up. Remove diseased or damaged wood.

Propagation: Seed: Best sown when ripe in autumn in a cold area: needs some stratification (~3 months) to get good germination. Grow on seedlings for at least a year before planting out. *Cuttings and layering:* See notes for common quince. *Pests and diseases:* Is less susceptible to fireblight and rust than other quince species. See notes for quince.

Cultivars: 'Dragon Eye': Hard, yellow medium-sized fruit, suitable for pickling. Ripens in mid–late autumn. 'Chino': Large fragrant fruit with few seeds. Ripens in mid–late autumn.

Uses: *Food:* The fruits need to be cooked. They go a darker colour than common quince. Can be candied, preserved in syrup or made into a liqueur. The juice can be mixed with ginger and made into a beverage. *Other uses:* The fruits, when stood in a room, add a wonderful fragrance. The wood is hard and dark red and is used for picture frames. This plant is attractive to bees, butterflies and birds. It can be grown as a bonsai. **Warning:** As with other Rosaceae species, the seeds are toxic if eaten in quantity. ■

Cyperus esculentus
Tigernut (yellownut sedge, bush nut, chufa, earth almond, coquillo)
CYPERACEAE

The sedge family contains about 550 attractive water-loving species, and includes the historic papyrus. The tigernut is smaller, attractive and is found growing wild in northern Africa and southern Europe, where it is often harvested for its 'nuts' and the oil they contain, which can be used in cooking. They have been cultivated and eaten since ancient times and remains have been found in Egyptian tombs dating from 2400 BC. It is also grown in Spain and America, as well as Asia, where it is quite popular. Although called a nut, it is the underground tubers that are eaten. They have a sweet nutty flavour.

DESCRIPTION
A perennial fast-growing sedge, to ~1 m in height. Produces sweet, aromatic underground tubers.

Leaves: Long, glossy, yellow-green, hairless in threes, grass-like in appearance, though they are angular, with a triangular cross-sectional form, sharply pointed.

Flowers: Are borne on graceful stems that are framed by distinctive long, arching green leaves with the flowers themselves being insignificant, yellowish and occurring in small clusters, from mid to late summer. These turn to green and then brown as the seeds ripen. They are monoecious, but because they are wind-pollinated, will benefit from having more than one plant if the seed is needed.

Roots/tubers: Forms a fibrous, spreading root system with tubers. These are, round, swollen storage stems that develop during the growing season. They occur individually attached either to the roots or rhizomes. They will be at their plumpest in autumn and can be ~3 cm wide. They are wrinkled, have a tough skin, and change from a white colour to dark brown through the season. Like potatoes, they also form plantlets from eyes within the tuber. The spread of tubers is greatest in heavier soils and they can spread a metre from the plant. The plant also has rhizomes, which are similar to the tubers, but not as thick, and tend to grow at a deeper level. These can also produce plantlets.

Harvest: The tubers are usually harvested in autumn. Dig up and use them fresh or they can be stored. Leave some tubers to form the next year's plants.

CULTIVATION
Is easy to grow and naturally loves to grow in water margins, so it is one of the few species described in this book that actually thrives in wet conditions. However, the tigernut has become a serious weed in some parts of the world, particularly the USA, especially in cultivated soils, and is difficult to eradicate with chemical herbicides. But, because of the many uses for its tasty tubers, for humans and livestock, and because of its other potential byproducts, some research suggests that it could be used as an ally rather than be seen as an enemy.

Location: Prefers a sunny location.

Temperature: Although originating from warmer regions of the world, growing in the subtropics and tropics, it has now been found to be much hardier than was once thought and can survive frosts down to ~−15°C.

Soil: Grows best in moist loam, but will also grow in moist sand or even heavy clay. Prefers neutral to slightly acid pH. A good organic soil and plenty of moisture will produce much plumper, better-tasting tubers.

Pot culture: The sedges are amenable to being grown in pots as long as the soil has adequate nutrients and is kept moist. Containers can be arranged around ponds and other water features, and given protection in winter if hard frosts are expected. Their spread can then also be controlled.

Propagation: *Seed:* Best sown in spring in moist compost in a warm location. Takes 2–6 weeks to germinate. Prick out the seedling and grow on till large enough to plant out. *Division:* Easy. Divide older plants from spring to early autumn and replant tubers at ~10-cm depth. Some sources suggest storing the tubers over winter and then replanting in spring, but subsequent growth is reported to be slow initially. It is probably better to keep tubers either in moist soil or in their original planting site and give supplementary protection if needed from frost. Once established, most wetland species will grow readily and quickly in spring; however, the initial conditions during establishment can significantly affect the size and performance of the later plant, e.g. plants grown in dry soils will produce smaller plants with thinner tubers and vasculature, even if subsequently watered.

Pests and diseases: Very few problems. ■

Food
The tubers are sweet, aromatic, tasty, nutty. They can be eaten raw, but are usually roasted, added to sweet and savoury dishes, or soups, or can be dried, ground up and used in beverages. The skin is often removed because it can be tough. They have been used as a coffee and almond substitute. A popular drink is made from the crushed tuber in Mexico and California, mixed with spices, sugar, vanilla and ice, and is called 'horchata de chufas'. The tubers are also ground up to make a chocolate-like paste. The crushed tubers produce a good quality yellow oil that has a pleasant smell like burnt sugar, and is said to be of similar quality to olive oil. In addition, it does not set or go rancid with storage.

Nutrition/medicinal
Tubers contain ~30% oil, 40% carbohydrate. The tubers are said to be an aphrodisiac and a stimulant. When chewed, they are believed to improve the breath.

Other uses
The oil is used to make soap. The leaves can be used as fibre for hats, etc. Because plants can grow in waterlogged, nutrient-rich areas there are trials under way for their use to mop up excess nutrients (around sewerage systems) or excess toxic heavy metals (around old mines, etc.).

Cyphomandra betacea (syn. *C. hartwegi, Solanum betaceum*)
Tamarillo (tree tomato, arbol de tomate)
SOLANACEAE

Similar species: casana (*Cyphomandra casana*), *C. fragrans*, *C. sibundoiensis*
Relatives: tomato, Cape gooseberry, pepino, naranjilla

The tamarillo originated in South America, probably from the Andes region, as well as Chile, Ecuador and Bolivia. It is now cultivated and naturalised in other countries of South America and is grown commercially in New Zealand. The natural forms of the fruit are often small, and larger, better-flavoured cultivars are now more common. They come in two main colours: a sharper tasting red fruit and a sweeter yellow fruit (with intermediate forms). They are members of the Solanaceae family, and their cultivation is similar in some ways to that of other fruits and vegetables in this family.

DESCRIPTION
A relatively short-lived (5–12 years), attractive, half-woody, small tree or shrub, ~2–5 m, with large leaves. It tends to have brittle branches and is easily damaged. It is also shallow rooted and prefers a warmer climate, though can be grown in temperate areas with protection.

Leaves: Evergreen or partially deciduous, depending on climate, alternate, heart-shaped, with a musky unpleasant smell when crushed, relatively large (10–35 cm long, 4–10 cm wide), thin, softly hairy, with conspicuous veins beneath.

Can be easily damaged by wind and other factors.

Flowers: Fragrant, 1–2 cm wide, five, pink–mauve, pointed petals with bright yellow stamens and a green–purple calyx. They form in small clusters near the tips of young branches from late spring through summer, depending on location. *Pollination:* Flowers are usually bisexual and are mostly self-pollinating, though fruit-set is greater if planted in groups. They can be pollinated by bees or wind: fruit-set may be reduced if there is not much wind during the pollination period.

Fruit: Formed singly or in small clusters on longish stalks. Are attractively egg-shaped (5–10 cm long, 3.5–6 cm wide) and are formed of two halves. They have a smooth, waxy, shiny, tough skin. Skin colour varies with variety, but ranges from purple, deep ruby red, orange to yellow, and may have hazy dark longitudinal markings. The skin is not usually eaten. Beneath the skin is a layer of juicy, succulent flesh, inside which is a central pulpy region containing many small, edible, seeds. All this flesh is edible. The red-skinned cultivars have a strong sweet–sub-acid, tangy taste. The yellow cultivars are less acid and sweeter, but may be less tasty, whereas the orange cultivars are the sweetest and usually also have a good flavour. The red cultivars need to be very ripe or they can be too acidic. Flesh colour also varies with variety, but can be dark purple, a rich red or yellow.

Harvest/yield/storage: Fruits mature during late autumn and into winter, i.e. it takes ~8 months from pollination to maturity. They are ready to pick when just becoming soft and have turned the colour characteristic of their cultivar. Leave the stem attached when harvesting the fruit. Trees take ~18 months–2 years to first bear fruits and are then productive for 5–7 years. If well nourished and protected they can live and produce for 11–12 years. Yield varies, but can get 10–30 kg of fruit per tree per year. On average, trees need to be replaced every 10 years. Fresh fruits store well and can be kept at room temperature for 1–3 weeks or in a refrigerator for ~12 weeks.

Roots: They have relatively shallow roots and so are susceptible to drought and to being damaged by strong winds.

CULTIVATION

Are fairly particular about the soil and conditions that they grow in, but do not need much maintenance.

Location: Trees need to be grown in a sheltered location; their branches are easily broken, the leaves can be damaged by strong winds and their roots are shallow. However, their modest size makes them suitable for small gardens. They grow best in a sunny spot or just a little shade, and where waterlogging is not a risk.

Temperature: The tamarillo is a subtropical plant and does best where the temperature remains above freezing; however, acclimatised plants can tolerate short frosts. Although some leaves may be damaged, the tree usually recovers. Young plants need extra protection from cold until established.

Soil/water/nutrients: Grow best in a light soil, rich in organic matter. They prefer a pH of ~6, but can grow in somewhat more acid soils. They are very susceptible to waterlogging, so plant on a slope if there's a risk. Trees also do not like prolonged periods of drought. They grow much better without weed competition, and the addition of an organic mulch protects the roots, keeps the soil moist and reduces weed growth. Because trees have shallow roots, avoid deep cultivation. They are fast-growing plants and grow best with regular applications of nutrients. Add a regular NPK fertiliser or bone/fishmeal in spring, and as the fruits are developing. Look out for deficiency symptoms and add extra as needed.

Pot culture: Because it has a fairly small root system, it can be easily grown in a container. Good nutrient-rich soil and adequate moisture should result in a healthy plant. Plants can be moved if there's a risk of frost or a bad storm.

Planting: Plant young trees at ~1 m apart with a wider gap between rows. Young trees may need staking.

Pruning: Young trees should be initially pruned to a height of 1 m to encourage branching. Remove the central growing tip once the tree has reached ~1.5 m tall to encourage

Food

Tamarillos are a versatile and largely undervalued fruit. They can be eaten as a fruit or a vegetable, and used in sauces, soups, chutney, stews, chilli dishes, etc. or grilled or roasted with a little garlic on top. They can also be made into jams, juices and jellies, or added to fruit desserts. The pectin within the fruit helps the setting properties. They can be eaten fresh by simply slicing lengthways and scooping out the flesh. The flesh can be sliced and used like tomatoes in sandwiches, salads and other dishes. They can be added to dried fruit, breadcrumbs and other ingredients to make a stuffing for meat dishes. In Peru, a sauce is made by grilling the tamarillo to remove its skin and then mixing the flesh with chopped green peppers, salt and pepper. This dish is used as an appetiser. The fruit processes well and can be preserved in storage jars or the flesh can be pureed and then frozen. Stored fruits tend to oxidise and turn brownish in colour, though are still fine to eat. The tough somewhat bitter skin is usually removed: this can be easily done by pouring boiling water over the fruit and letting them stand for ~4 minutes after which the skin easily peels off.

Nutrition

Fruits contains high levels of vitamins A, B6, C and E; the red fruits have particularly high levels of vitamin C (but most will be lost if cooked). They also have good levels of iron and potassium, are low in calories and high in dietary fibre. **Warning:** Like all members of the Solanaceae family, many parts of this plant may contain toxic alkaloids, except for its fruits.

Ornamental

Its large exotic leaves, small size and attractive fruits make it a good choice as an ornamental tree in small gardens, perhaps mixing yellow-, golden- and red-fruiting types in a group.

side branching and strong growth. Repeat the process with the laterals when they are >~50 cm in length, but do not encourage fruits to form at the ends of the branches, as these easily break. Remove old or frost- or wind-damaged wood. Growth may need to be pruned to reduce overcrowded or straggly branches. Fruits are formed on new spring growth, therefore prune in late winter/early spring. In the first years, trees often sucker vigorously from the base and it is better to remove these as they take away vigour from the main tree and may break off with the weight of their fruit. The earlier these are removed the better, so that growth resources are not wasted.

Propagation: *Seeds:* Germination is better and faster if seed is washed, dried and then given a quick burst of cold stratification, i.e. 24 hours in a fridge, before sowing. Germination rate is usually very good and occurs in ~5 days. Plants grown from seed tend to form erect trees with high branches. Seedlings will vary from the parent plant. *Cuttings:* Trees grown from cuttings tend to form shorter, bushier trees with lower branches. Long cuttings (~30–50 cm) are best taken from 1–2-year-old wood, cut off just below a node, and then the most lower leaves removed. Cuttings give a good rate of success and form predictable plants, though there is a greater risk of the transfer of viral infections. *Grafting:* Although grafting is relatively easy amongst the Solanaceae family, care needs to be exercised as members of this family contain powerful alkaloids which could be passed onto the grafted tamarillo fruit.

Pests and diseases: Occasionally attacked by white fly, aphids, powdery mildew, nematodes, viruses and caterpillars. Dieback can occur and the green vegetable bug can disfigure fruits. Plants grown under cover should be checked for houseplant pests, e.g. mealybugs, cotton scale, white flies. Hard areas of flesh or 'stone cells' can form around the centre of fruits; this can be an indicator of the plant not receiving enough moisture or needing additional nutrients. Tamarillos are resistant to tobacco virus, but are susceptible to many other viruses; unfortunately these cannot be cured, but removal of possible vectors, e.g. chickweed, nightshade, aphids, should reduce the risk of infection.

CULTIVARS

'Ecuadorian Orange': Skin and pulp are orange coloured. The flesh is less acid than red cultivars. Good quality, fresh or cooked.

'Goldmine': A new cultivar from New Zealand. Has large, golden-yellow skin and flesh. It is sweet and tasty, good quality and not too acidic.

'Oratia Red': Large red fruits, good-quality when fresh or for jams, chutneys, cooking. Sweeter than many red cultivars: best when fully ripe.

'Rothamer': Tree is vigorous with very large, bright red fruits that have golden-yellow, sweet, tasty flesh. Seeds are dark red. Good eaten fresh. Good yields.

'Ruby Red': Large, red-skinned fruits, with dark red flesh, full of flavour, though can be sharp if eaten fresh. Good for culinary uses. Ripening them for an extra 2–3 weeks after harvesting makes them less acid.

'Solid Gold': Large golden-orange fruit, pulp is soft and sweet. Very good for eating fresh and fairly good to cook.

Casana, *Cyphomandra casana* (syn. *Casana cajanu-mensis*). A native of the Andes, with a similar range and appearance as its close relative, the tamarillo, except with hairier leaves and fruits some say are not as tasty. This plant is still an unimproved wild fruit and is not long-lived.

Description: Umbrella-shaped plant with a single stem and a small canopy. Forms a fast-growing tree, 2–3 m tall that has an exotic appearance when growing well. *Leaves:* Evergreen, very large, deep green, heart-shaped, up to ~2.5 m long. Pungent smell when crushed. Are stiffer than those of tamarillo and covered in fine hair. *Flowers:* Purple-black, scented, bisexual, and are self-fertile, though fruit-set is improved with more than one plant. Pollination is by bees and insects. *Fruit:* Egg-shaped, ~8 cm long, green, turning golden-yellow when ripe, often with fine purple stripes, in small clusters along the branches. Fruits vary in quality from plant to plant: some are seedy, fairly dry, with a poor flavour; others are sweet, delicately flavoured, aromatic with juicy pulp and are good to eat fresh. The skin is leathery and is usually discarded. *Yield/harvest:* Large yields, but plants only live ~7 years. Plants fruit in their second year and peak in 3–4 years. Fruits ripen from late autumn into winter. *Roots:* Has shallow, spreading roots. Avoid surface cultivation. Benefits from a good mulch.

Cultivation: *Temperature:* Is frost tender, and can be damaged at temperatures of ~–1.5°C. Does not respond well to extremes of hot and cold, and fruits best with cooler summer temperatures. *Location:* Grows best in semi-shaded, misty, rainy locations. Prone to wind damage. Not as adaptable as tamarillo. *Soil/water/nutrients:* Can grow in light, medium and heavy soils, including heavy clay soils. Likes organic matter and moisture, but needs very good drainage. Incorporate blood and bone at planting and apply a low-nitrogen fertiliser twice during the growing season. *Pot culture:* Because of their small size, short time till fruiting and frost sensitivity, these can be easily grown as short-term container plants, which can placed in a greenhouse or be given extra protection during winter. *Propagation: Seed:* Mostly by seed, but plants are variable. Seeds usually germinate within 4 weeks at 15°C, or within 2 weeks at 25°C. Grow on seedlings in pots for the first year, then plant out in late spring–early summer. *Cuttings:* Semi-ripe cuttings taken in spring–summer can be inserted in gritty, well-drained compost to root. *Pruning:* To encourage strong growth and branching, remove the central growing tip when 1.5 m tall. Repeat the process when laterals have reached 60 cm. Prune to remove old, dead and crowded wood to promote growth and maintain shape. *Pests and diseases:* Birds like the fruit, even when unripe. Subject to attacks by red-spider mites.

Uses: Fruits can be eaten fresh or prepared as tamarillos. Sweet and juicy, the flavour is said to be a blend of peach and tomato. Unripe fruit may be slightly toxic.

***Cyphomandra fragrans*.** Not as tasty as tamarillo. It has small yellow fruit and glossy green leaves.

***Cyphomandra sibundoiensis*.** A tall, shade-loving tamarillo relative from Colombia. It has large fruit with whitish flesh and purple seeds. ∎

Davidsonia pruriens, D. jerseyana
Davidson's plum (munumba, ooray)
DAVIDSONIACEAE

The name *pruriens* is Latin and means 'an itching sensation'; it refers to the hairs on the surface of this plum's leaves and stems that are irritating to some. It is a reasonably well-known, popular plant in Australia, to which it is native. Its English name, Davidson's plum, comes from a sugar grower in Queensland who, in the 1860s, was the first to 'officially' collect and record the fruits. The early European settlers widely used these plums to make jam. However, the Aborigines had been using these plums for hundreds and probably thousands of years, and regard them as a popular bush food. Davidson's plums have been described as one of the best of the native fruits. There are two main species of these plums. *D. jerseyana* is native to New South Wales and *D. pruriens* is native to northern Queensland. Both are now fairly uncommon in the wild, but are widely grown as ornamental garden species. More recently, a further *Davidsonia* species has been classified (*D. johnsonii*). This Davidson's plum is even rarer in the wild, and does not produce viable seed, so can only be propagated from cuttings. Today these species are becoming popular again for their fruits as well as for their ornamental attributes. Commercial fruit plantings are increasing in New South Wales and Queensland, with the fruits being used to make jam and other products, as well as becoming a popular addition to the menus of many restaurants. It is also cultivated, to a limited extent, in the eastern states of the USA.

DESCRIPTION
Attractive, slender, small–medium trees. *D. jerseyana* resembles a cross between a small palm and a tree fern, height to 4–5 m. *D. pruriens* is similar, but slightly larger, and can reach >10 m under ideal conditions.

Leaves: Attractive, long (up to 80 cm–1 m), drooping, and covered with fine brown hairs that can be irritating. The leaves are compound, and consist of crinkly groups of leaflets, resembling a cross between a palm and a tree fern. The margins are finely serrated. Leaves are different shades of velvety pink/red when young, and mature to deep green.

Flowers: Individual, small, self-fertile, pink-brown flowers appear in pendulous clusters, ~20 cm long, in late winter to early spring. Occur, unusually for a tree, directly on the trunks (cauliflorous). Only need one tree to produce fruits, though more than one tree should increase fruit-set and fruit quality. *Pollination:* By bees and other insects.

Fruit: Eye-catching, drooping bunches of deep, dark purple, plum-shaped fruit, ~3–6 cm diameter, ~3–6 cm length. Ripe fruit are covered in a blue bloom, like grapes or damsons, or some have brown, fine, irritating hairs, which need to be washed off before the fruit is eaten. Has soft, juicy, vibrant deep red/purple flesh, which contains two small, flattened seeds with a fibrous coating. The flesh is tart, but tasty.

Yield/harvest: Can set between 10–18 fruits a cluster, so is quite productive. Trees, if growing in good conditions, can give good yields of fruits, though yields vary from year to year. The fruits generally ripen from spring to summer, depending on climate.

CULTIVATION
A fairly easy plant to grow.

Location: Likes a sheltered location, protected from strong cold or hot winds. Can grow in semi-shade or full sun, and can be grown beneath other trees. Probably best planted with shade in hotter regions.

Temperature: Do not like extremes of frost or heat, with *D. pruriens* being more susceptible to frost and cold damage. They are best suited to warm temperate and subtropical climates.

Soil/water/nutrients: Grow best in fertile, loamy, well-drained soils, and prefer a pH range of slightly acidic to neutral. Do not tolerate waterlogged soils, though do grow better with moisture throughout the year, particularly during fruit-set, which improves fruit yield and quality. Regular applications of a complete fertiliser are beneficial, as is a regularly replenished organic mulch.

Food
Strongly flavoured, tangy, but delicious, acidic flesh. They can be eaten fresh, though their tangy taste is too strong for some, and they are commonly made into an excellent jam, or are added to tarts, sauces (both sweet and savoury), various desserts, or just stewed with sugar. Can be made into a rich, full-bodied wine.

Medicinal
The fruits have been eaten to treat diarrhoea. No parts of the plant are poisonous.

Ornamental
A popular, ornamental plant, striking for its leaves and unusual clusters of fruit, borne from its trunk, as well as for its overall shape. Can fit smaller gardens.

Pot culture: Can be grown in containers in cooler regions and given extra protection or moved inside in colder weather. Both species are highly decorative and make great plants for indoors as they can tolerate low light intensities for fairly long periods of time.

Propagation: *Seed:* Usually propagated from fresh seed. Wash all pulp from the seed before sowing. *Cuttings:* Semi-ripe cuttings can be taken during summer and inserted in moist, well-drained gritty compost. ■

Dimocarpus longan (syn. *Euphoria longan, E. longana, Nephelium longana*)

Longan (lungan, dragon's eye)
SAPINDACEAE.
Relatives: lychee, rambutan, akee, Spanish lime, soapberry

The longan is a member of the soapberry family, the Sapindaceae. Closely allied to the lychee, the longan tree is tougher and less demanding with respect to soil conditions, and it fruits in cooler areas. The word 'longan' is Chinese, and literally means 'dragon-eye' and describes the black, shining central seed, with a circular white spot at its base, sitting within white, succulent flesh, giving it the appearance of an eye. The longan is native to southern China, and grows naturally on well-drained hillsides.

DESCRIPTION
The longan tree is fairly large, handsome, spreading, to 9–20 m in height, ~7–14 m in width. Its branches are thick and long, somewhat brittle and often slightly drooping, with a dense covering of leaves. The trunk has rough corky bark that splits and peels.

Leaves: Evergreen, alternate, pinnate, with 4–10 opposite leaflets. The leaflets are elliptic–oblong and can have pointed or blunt tips, 10–20 cm long, 3.5–5 cm wide. They are leathery, wavy, glossy-green on their upper surface, felty grey-green beneath. Usually has attractive, showy bronze-red new growth.

Flowers: Pale yellow, on hairy stalks, they are small, though larger than those of lychee. They have 5–6 sepals and petals, which are brownish-yellow or greenish-yellow in colour. They are borne in upright, terminal panicles, 10–45 cm long, which can carry a few to ~350 flowers. They are borne from the leaf axils during late winter–early spring on growth produced during the previous summer–autumn. *Pollination:* They are particularly attractive to butterflies. Excessive rainfall during flowering can result in flower drop. In addition, pollination can be tricky. Although both male and female flowers occur on the same tree (monoecious), there are three flower types: two male types (i.e. M1 and M2) and one female type (~30% of the total). In general, M1 flowers open first, female flowers open second and M2 flowers (with more pollen than M1 flowers) open last. Many of the male flowers do not produce very effective pollen. Therefore, planting more than one tree may increase fruit-set.

Fruit: In drooping clusters, rounded, 1.25–2.5 cm diameter, with thin, brittle, yellow-brown to light reddish-brown rind, more or less rough, with less prominent protuberances than those of lychee fruits. The flesh is slightly mucilaginous, translucent–creamy-white, somewhat musky, tangy, sweet. The single seed is round, dark brown, shiny, with a circular white spot at its base (hilum), and is easy to remove from the flesh. Fruits ripen in mid–late summer.

Yield/harvest/storage: A lighter yield per tree is 20–45 kg of fruits, and a heavy yield can be ~180–225 kg. Larger trees produce larger crops, but also become difficult to harvest. Seedlings take ~6 years to start bearing fruit; air-layered trees can start bearing fruits 2–3 years after planting. Trees often have variable yields, and tend towards biennial bearing, with often only one good year every 2–3 years. This can be evened out by thinning the fruit when they are very young and/or removal of some of the fruiting laterals. Fruits take a long time to form and ripen 140–190 days after fruit-set. Cloudy weather during fruit ripening can result in premature fruit drop. Fruits need to be harvested when fully ripe and the rind is fully red-brown, which can be tricky to accurately judge. The main indicator is the sweetness of the fruit. Once picked, the fruits do not continue ripening. It is easiest to cut off entire clusters rather than picking individual fruits. In addition, leaving the stalks with the fruits extends their storage time considerably; and they can then be kept at room temperature for several days. Longan's rind is firmer than that of lychee and this gives it a longer storage life. The fruit can also be successfully frozen and remain entire when defrosted.

Roots: Trees have many fairly shallow roots, therefore mechanical cultivation is not advisable, and an organic mulch will help retain moisture and add nutrients. However, their roots are, in general, deeper than those of lychee.

CULTIVATION
Location: They can tolerate more wind than lychees. Even young trees can be established in fairly exposed

Food

Some say the fruit is of lesser quality than lychee and others say the taste is less aromatic, but has greater depth of flavour, and although often smaller, they are often sweeter than lychees. They are wonderful and juicy eaten fresh, but can be cooked or dried and used in a variety of sweet and savoury dishes. The Chinese completely dry the extracted flesh over a slow fire until black, leathery and smoky in flavour. It is then often used to prepare a refreshing drink. Fruits can also be successfully frozen. A liqueur can be made by macerating the longan flesh in alcohol.

Nutrition

A good source of vitamin C (~60 mg/100 g of flesh) and potassium.

Medicinal

The flesh is used to aid digestive problems, taken as a tonic and for the treatment of insomnia and neurosis. The seeds have been used to counteract heavy sweating and to reduce heavy bleeding, as well as being ground up to treat skin diseases.

Other uses

The seeds, because of their saponin content, can be used like soapberries as a hair shampoo. The wood is durable and of high quality. It is used for posts, agricultural implements, furniture and construction. The heartwood is red, hard and takes a fine polish.

Ornamental

Valued for its shade and attractive foliage, racemes of flowers and clusters of fruits. A good specimen tree.

ocations and smaller mature trees are reported to be able to withstand hurricane-force winds, although windy weather during flowering reduces fruit-set. The longan is not tolerant of saline soil or maritime locations. Can grow in full sun or shade, though grows better with some shade in hot regions.

Temperature: Longans are best grown in subtropical to warm-temperate regions and, although frost sensitive, also need a period of winter chill. They prefer a dry, cool period between autumn–winter, a warm, wetter spring (~22°C+) and a hot summer. Young trees are very susceptible to freezing temperatures and can be severely damaged at –0.5°C, and killed at ~–3°C. Older trees are more cold tolerant, but branches can be injured at ~–4°C, with severe damage below this temperature. Dry, cool weather during flowering reduces fruit-set.

Chilling: A few weeks of cool weather, with no frost, induces the tree to bloom well. Warm winters produce poor flower formation.

Soil/water/nutrients: Trees grow best in a rich, sandy loam, but can also grow in limestone soils or even moderately acid soils. They do not like saline soils. Longan can survive droughts, but adequate water is required for good production. From flowering and through fruit development, trees should be well watered and drought stress avoided. A warmer, wetter autumn–early winter initiates more leaf growth, but not flower production. Trees can tolerate brief flooding, but not prolonged waterlogging. Trees grow best in relatively fertile soils, and benefit from regular applications of a balanced fertiliser, with magnesium, plus additional essential micronutrients (manganese, zinc, boron, molybdenum), 2–3 times throughout the year. There are some reports that excess nutrients reduces flowering and fruit production, probably by encouraging more leaf growth. However, trees are also susceptible to various nutrient deficiencies, so a balance needs to be achieved. Trees greatly benefit from regular applications of a good, deep organic mulch to help retain moisture and reduce weed growth.

Planting: Space plants at ~12 m apart. They are fairly fast-growing, large trees and are best not planted too near to buildings, etc.

Pruning: Trees need little pruning, although a specimen can tolerate fairly severe pruning to enable it to fit into smaller gardens, and it usually still produces fruits. More fruiting laterals can be formed by removing stem tips, though often the problem is the converse, and trees need to be pruned to remove these fruiting laterals and the fruiting clusters thinned to prevent biennial bearing. Prune to remove crowded and diseased branches, and to take out branches with narrow crotch angles, which reduces the risk of breakage in gales.

Propagation: *Seed:* Trees are often grown from seed. Seed is best sown fresh as it loses its viability quickly. Wash all pulp thoroughly from the seed and plant at ~2 cm depth in well-drained, warm compost. Germination should take 7–10 days. Seedlings are grown on in pots for 2–3 years before planting out. However, progeny are variable and trees take longer to start producing fruits. *Cuttings:* Cuttings can be taken from semi-ripe wood in summer and inserted in gritty compost, with heat, and mist if possible. *Layering:* (marcotting) is a very popular method, particularly in China, where it has been practised for ~800 years. It is done between spring and late summer, and roots should form within 10–12 weeks. It has a very good success rate. (See lychee propagation notes.) *Grafting:* Not often practised, but side veneer or cleft grafting are reported to be successful. Trees can also be top-worked.

Pests and diseases: Trees are relatively free of pests and diseases. Leaf-curl can occur, also lychee webworm, mites, stinkbugs (can cause serious damage), scale and aphids. Birds are attracted to the fruits, and trees may need netting temporarily (if feasible).

CULTIVARS

'Fukien Lungan' and **'Lungan Late'** are good varieties. **'Kohala':** Fruit: large, small seed. Flesh: aromatic, sweet, spicy. Tree produces fairly good crops in mid summer. **'Wu Yuan'** (**'Black ball'**): Fruits: small, sour, often used for canning. Tree: vigorous. Seedlings are valued as rootstocks. **'Kao Yuan'** may be a slightly better, but similar, cultivar. ■

Diospyros digyna (syn. *D. ebenaster*), *Diospyros obtusifolia*
Black sapote (chocolate-pudding tree, black persimmon)
EBENACEAE
Relatives: persimmon, ebony

The black sapote is not, as might be assumed, related to either the sapote *(Pouteria sapota)* or the white sapote *(Casimiroa edulis)*. Instead, it is closely related to the persimmon. For many years it has also been widely misidentified as *Diospyros ebenaster*. It is native to Mexico and the forested lowlands of Central America, and is often cultivated there. It was carried by the Spaniards to other areas of the world, including the Philippines in about 1750. It also reached Malacca, Mauritius, Hawaii, Brazil, Cuba, Puerto Rico and the Dominican Republic. Outside of Mexico, the fruit has not become widely known and cultivated, although the attractiveness of the tree and the novel colour and consistency of its fruits make it an interesting addition to a fruit garden.

DESCRIPTION
A handsome tree, with a broad crown, slow-growing, furrowed trunk and black bark. Can reach a height of 25 m, but is often much shorter in cooler regions: 5–8 m in height.

Leaves: Evergreen, dark green, leathery, glossy, alternate, tapered at both ends, or rounded at the base and bluntly acute at the apex, 10–30 cm long.

Flowers: Borne singly or in small clusters of 3–7, from leaf axils. Trees can produce some flowers year-round in warmer areas, though most flowers are usually borne in autumn. They are tubular, lobed, white, 1–1.5 cm in diameter. Flower has a superior ovary. Trees are generally self-fertile, and often have bisexual flowers, with both male and female organs; these flowers also have a large calyx and are faintly fragrant. Other flowers can be just male, with a pronounced gardenia-like scent and a few black specks in the throat of the flower. In addition, many fruits can be set without fertilisation, and these are seedless. *Pollination:* By bees and insects.

Fruit: Classified as berries. In some regions, these berries can be large, ~12 cm diameter, and weigh ~0.8 kg, but are often much smaller (5–10 cm), possibly due to poor pollination. Fruits are rounded, and have a large, prominent, persistent, four-lobed, rounded, green calyx clasping their base. Fruits change from a shiny, bright green to olive-green to a deep dark green when fully ripe. The skin is smooth, waxy and thin, but is not normally eaten. The flesh is soft when fully ripe, similar to that of ripe persimmon or plum, and has an almost jelly-like consistency. Its main feature is its unusual colour, a dark chocolate colour, which has also been likened to the consistency of chocolate pudding. The flesh is sweet, with a mild flavour. Within the central region of flesh are 1–10 flat, smooth, brown seeds, ~2 cm long, which are discarded, although some fruits are seedless.

Yield/harvest/storage: In warmer regions, fruits ripen virtually all year; in cooler climates most fruits mature in late winter–early spring. Trees can bear well. Most begin to bear in 3–6 years, though sometimes longer. Assessing ripeness

uses

Food
When fully ripe the flesh becomes black and mushy. It is then quite sweet with virtually no acidity. On its own it is almost bland, but the pulp, without its large seeds, is usually eaten fresh, and can be mixed with milk, orange, lemon or lime juice, depending on the taste required, with the latter sharp fruits giving more depth of flavour to the whole. The pulp is also used in juices, cakes, fruit salads, pies and other desserts. It can be just cut in half and eaten covered in passion fruit juice and it can also be added to icecream. In Mexico, the pulp is mashed with orange juice or brandy, and simply served with cream, or it can be mixed with wine, cinnamon and sugar. The fruits are also fermented to make a brandy-like liqueur. The pulp can be frozen for storage.

Nutrition
Has good levels of vitamin C: ~30–60 mg/100 g of flesh, and fairly good levels of vitamin A (~400 IU), as well as potassium, calcium and phosphates. **Warning:** A rare, wild relative, *D. revoluta*, has also occasionally been named as *D. ebenaster*. It has smaller, thicker leaves, smaller fruits and the calyx is square. The fruits are poisonous and, with the bark, are used as a fish poison.

Other uses
The wood is often a deep yellow colour with black markings, and is dense and hard. It could be used to make fine furniture.

Ornamental
Makes a handsome specimen tree, with flowers and fruits during winter.

can be tricky as any colour change is subtle, although under-ripe fruits will continue to ripen once picked. They can be picked when green and still ripen satisfactorily. Fruit need to be harvested carefully as they bruise easily. They do become very soft when fully ripe. Fruits are best eaten when fully ripe; under-ripe fruits are unpleasantly very astringent. Ripe fruits can be stored at room temperature for 3–5 days or a little longer in a refrigerator, but do become progressively softer.

CULTIVATION

Once established, trees are naturally vigorous and need little maintenance.

Location: Trees grow best in full sun. They are only moderately wind tolerant.

Temperature: With protection or in the right location trees can produce fruits in warmer temperate climates, though are happier in subtropical climates. Young plants are very frost sensitive and need extra protection. Mature trees can withstand temperatures down to ~–2°C, but cannot tolerate long, cold winters. Black sapotes flower and fruit during the colder months, which makes them more susceptible to cold weather, and trees only flower and set fruit with warmer temperatures.

Soil/water/nutrients: Black sapotes can grow in a very wide range of soil types, including dry soils, clayey soils, wet soils that are prone to flooding, moist sandy soils or even thin, limestone soils. They are fairly drought tolerant, but also fairly tolerant of temporary waterlogging. They can also grow at a range of pH values, from somewhat acid to alkaline. Trees grow and fruit best with moderate applications of an all-purpose fertiliser, with micronutrients, given once or twice a year.

Pot culture: Given a large pot, these plants can make a handsome, unusual patio plant, and may produce flowers and fruits after ~3 years. In colder areas, they can be moved inside or given extra protection during winter.

Propagation: *Seed:* Usually grown from seed, which remains viable for several months in dry storage and germinates ~30 days after sowing. Transplant seedlings into pots and plant these out when 1–2 years old (~30–60 cm height). *Layering:* Young, healthy stems can be air-layered. *Grafting:* Trees can be shield-budded using mature scions.

Planting: Space plants at ~6–8 m apart, or further apart in warmer climates. ■

Diospyros kaki
Persimmon (Oriental persimmon, Japanese persimmon)
EBENACEAE
Similar species: American persimmon (*D. virginiana*), date plum (*D. lotus*), Texas persimmon (*D. texana*)
Relatives: black sapote, ebony

The genus name *diospyros* translates as 'food of the gods'. Persimmons are originally native to China, where they have been cultivated for centuries, and more than 2000 different cultivars now exist. Early in the 1300s, Marco Polo recorded that the Chinese were trading persimmons. It is now cultivated most extensively in Japan, where they rank as the fifth most important tree fruit. The plant was introduced into California in the mid 1800s. It is now cultivated commercially, as well as being a popular garden tree, in northern New Zealand and Australia, plus many other warm-temperate and subtropical regions of the world.

DESCRIPTION

The persimmon is a multi- or single-stemmed deciduous tree, ranging from 4.5–18 m tall, ~4.5–6 m spread. It is fairly long-lived (60–80 years) and typically has a round-topped form; it is fairly open, and the branches tend to be fairly erect. It is a handsome ornamental, with attractive dark green, largish leaves. The bark is a smooth, light grey, but the branches are somewhat brittle and can be damaged in high wind or if they are carrying a large harvest. Persimmons belong to the ebony family, and have the hard wood one expects of this family.

Leaves: Alternate, deciduous, simple, entire, oval, with pointed tips, ~15 cm long, 9 cm wide. They are yellowish-green when young, turning a dark, glossy green as they mature. In autumn, they turn a rich golden-yellow colour.

Flowers: Inconspicuous, ~2.5 cm diameter, with five waxy green outer sepals and five yellow inner petals. Flowers are borne in early summer in the leaf axils of 1-year-old wood. Their sexuality is varied. Some cultivars can have both male and female flowers on the same tree (monoecious), but most cultivars have either male or female flowers (dioecious). Female flowers are borne singly and are cream-coloured; male flowers are pink-tinged and are usually borne in threes. Many non-astringent varieties have only female flowers and set seedless fruits (they are not pollinated, i.e. parthenocarpic). If these flowers cross pollinate with a tree close by, the fruit may be more abundant, larger, but will also have seeds. Some male-flowering plants can produce bisexual flowers at the same time. Rain or very hot, dry weather during flowering can reduce fruit-set. *Pollination:*

By bees and other insects. Trees are classified as pollination constant (do not need pollinating) or pollination variant (do need pollinating). In addition, persimmon fruit are also classified according to fruit quality: there are those that bear astringent fruit, which are inedible until fully ripe, and those that have non-astringent fruits, which can be eaten and enjoyed when still crisp. These two classifications are related.

– Trees that are pollination-variant, and also non-astringent, produce fruits that can only be eaten firm if they have been pollinated. A tree with this mix that has not been pollinated produces inedible fruit until they ripen and become soft.

– Trees that are pollination-constant, and also non-astringent, always produce fruits that are edible when still firm.

– Trees that are pollination-variant, but are also astringent and have been pollinated, bear fruit with dark flesh that is non-astringent even when hard; therefore these perform like a non-astringent type, and are sometimes classified as such.

– Trees that are pollination-constant, but also astringent, will not be pollinated and their fruits will remain astringent, and their flesh colour remains clear orange.

Generally, astringent cultivars are better than non-astringent cultivars at forming and ripening seedless fruit. Commercially, non-astringent orchards need good pollination to produce early ripe fruit and to prevent early fruit drop. However, the pollination of lots of seeds stresses and weakens the tree, more than producing unpollinated fruits, and this also leads to alternate bearing. Generally, in non-astringent orchards, a pollinator tree ratio of 1:~12–40 trees is practised. An ideal ratio is one that ensures that sufficient fruits are pollinated for a good crop, but not all of the fruits, so that the trees are not overly stressed.

Fruit: They are a 'true' berry. Their skin is bright golden-orange or dark orange-red when fully ripe, and the fruits have a distinctive green, persistent large calyx at their base. Fruits are 5–7.5 cm in diameter, size varying with cultivar, and ripen from late autumn–early winter. They need sunshine to fully ripen; regions with rainy autumns should choose early-ripening varieties. Alternate bearing is common, and can be partly overcome by thinning some of the fruits, though many immature fruits often drop anyway in late summer. The flesh colour varies from yellow through to dark brown and, when ripe, flesh is gelatinous and juicy. Pollinated fruits have 4–8 flat, oblong, brown seeds, ~2 cm long. Fruits are borne towards the ends of stems. The entire fruit is edible except for the seeds and calyx. (Unpollinated seeds are hardly noticed.)

Yield/harvest/storage: Annual yields from a young tree can be 20–40 kg and for a mature tree, 150–250 kg. Trees usually crop well, and in bumper years can yield 300–500 fruits, which is too many, and should be thinned to ~200 to avoid a meagre yield in the following year. Most flowers develop at the ends of stems, so pruning out some of the less vigorous stems within the centre of the tree will also reduce fruit formation. Trees start to produce fruit after ~3–5 years, but take ~10 years to reach full cropping. Astringent cultivars should only be picked when fully ripe and have just begun to soften (but see storage below), usually in early winter. However, if they become over-ripe they become mushy and lose their flavour. Non-astringent cultivars can be picked when they are fully orange in colour, but are still crisp. Fruits are picked with their calyx. Fruits bruise fairly easily.

Late fruits can be sweetened further if they remain on the tree through the first frost. Hard persimmons store well and can be kept in a fridge for ~28 days, and can then complete ripening if left at room temperature for a few days. They can also be frozen for 6–8 months. Softer fruits can only be stored for a short time at room temperature.

Roots: They form a deep taproot with few lateral roots. Care needs to be taken with seedlings and when planting out.

CULTIVATION

Location: Young trees do not like direct, hot sun, whereas older trees do. Trees will grow in regions that are semi-arid or have high humidity. They are not tolerant of windy locations.

Temperature: Trees need a long, warm summer to fully ripen the fruit. Astringent varieties are better suited to cooler climates. They are fairly cold sensitive and, although they can tolerate temperatures down to ~–16°C when fully dormant, young leaves can be killed at ~–2°C; however, leaves open fairly late in spring (after apples and blueberries).

Chilling: Only need a short period of winter chilling: ~100–200 hours. The danger with this is that they may break dormancy during an early warm spell, only to be damaged by later spring frosts.

Soil/water/nutrients: Can survive in a wide range of soil types as long as the soil is not overly salty, but do best in deep, well-drained loam. Can grow in clay soils if they are well drained and in sandy soils if well irrigated. A pH range of 6.0–6.5 is best, but possibly up to 7.5. They can withstand short periods of drought, but the fruits will be larger and of higher quality with regular watering, particularly in spring and early summer. Extreme drought will cause the leaves and fruit to drop prematurely. Because trees are susceptible to root rots, they are best not grown in soils that are wet for long periods. Trees are moderately nutrient hungry, and an organic fertiliser or mulch can supply most of their needs. Too much nitrogen leads to excessive vegetative growth and to fruit drop. Only apply fertiliser if the tree looks like it needs it, and only in spring. Applications in autumn can cause the bark to split. Look out for magnesium and manganese deficiencies; note too that excess manganese can be a problem in acid soils, showing up as green marks on the apices of fruits.

Planting: Space plants at ~5–7 m apart. Dig a deep hole for the long taproot. Keep watered and staked till established. Young trees may need some shade as they are susceptible to sunburn.

Pruning: Trees require little pruning, but can be pruned to an open centre or modified central leader. Young trees are initially pruned back to ~80 cm. New shoots are then thinned and pruned to form a well-shaped tree with wide-angled branches. If branches become long and straggly, then these may need reducing in length for manageability and to prevent them breaking with the weight of fruit. If trees start to overbear or become very straggly, they can be drastically cut back to give them a fresh start. They can also be pruned to form a hedge or an espalier.

Propagation: *Seed:* Wash the flesh from the seed and either sow when fresh at ~7 cm depth, or store seeds in a plastic bag in a fridge until early spring. Germination at >15°C takes from 2–6 weeks. Transplant seedlings into deep, biodegradable pots to establish. *Cuttings:* Can take

uses

Food

Persimmons can be eaten fresh, or they can be frozen, cured, or they can be peeled, cut into slices and dried. Dried astringent fruits lose all their astringency and develop a sweet, date-like consistency. They can be stewed and then dried. Other methods to get rid of astringency are: (a) place persimmons in a bag with other ripening fruit that produce ethylene, e.g. banana; (b) place fruits in a freezer for 24 hours (works well); or (c) convert the astringent tannin into sweeter compounds with alcohol vapour (the Japanese sometimes store persimmons in sake barrels). The skin is often removed, particularly if it is a thicker-skinned cultivar. When eaten fresh, the fruits are often chilled and can be eaten with lime juice and honey. The fruits can be used in a wide variety of dishes: pies, salads, icecream, confectionery, cakes, desserts, sauces, etc. The pureed pulp can be added to cream cheese, orange juice, honey and a pinch of salt to make an unusual dressing. The fruits can also be made into cider, beer or wine. A tea can be made from the fresh or dried leaves.

Nutrition

Persimmons are high in vitamin A and have very good levels of vitamin C (~40–60 mg/100 g of fruit), with American persimmons having more than Japanese varieties. The red-skinned persimmons also probably contain good levels of lycopene, mostly in the skin. Their astringency is due to tannin. They also contain good levels of fibre.

Other uses

The tannin from unripe fruits has been used to brew sake, as a dye and as a wood preservative. The astringent juice can be used as an insect- and moisture-repellent. It is a relative of ebony, and its wood is fairly hard, dense and heavy: it is black with streaks of orange-yellow-pink-grey. It takes a good finish and is used in Japan for fine, decorative work, but it does have a strange odour.

Ornamental

It is an attractive ornamental tree with tropical-looking leaves and many bright eye-catching fruits, sometimes after the leaves have dropped. It can be grown as a specimen tree. It also has wonderful rich red and golden autumn colours. Makes an attractive specimen or street tree with its interesting shape and ornamental bark (only on older trees), attractive leaves and bright fruits. Because trees generally have such good yields it is possible to share a few with the local birdlife, which for some reason seems to find them irresistible. The tree becomes, for a few weeks, a mass of bright orange fruits and many, small excited birds.

half-ripe cuttings in summer. *Layering:* Can be done in spring. *Grafting:* Grafting is mostly done onto *D. virginiana*, *D. kaki*, *D. lotus*. See notes on these species below. *D. kaki* is a good rootstock for warmer areas; it has a long taproot with few fibrous lateral roots. Whip-grafting is used on young trees; cleft-grafting is preferred for older trees. Budding can also be done in early spring, and trees can be top-worked.

Pests and diseases: Trees are fairly disease resistant, but can be susceptible to crown gall, *Phytophthora* (which cause root and collar rot), *Anthracnose*, mealybugs, thrips, mites, fruit flies, leaf-roller caterpillars, two-spotted mite. The fruit are also very appealing to many kinds of birds.

CULTIVARS

The flesh of the different cultivars varies considerably. (See list below.) The main pollinating species are the astringent cultivars 'Nishumura Wase' and 'Komasoskie'. Also 'Gailey' is a good, reliable pollinator.

'Eureka': USA variety. Astringent. Small tree, vigorous, drought and frost resistant, precocious and heavy-bearing. Medium–large fruit, bright orange-red. Flesh is of good quality, ripens late. Pollination-variant fruit.

'Fuyu': Japan and Florida's most important non-astringent variety. Low tannin variety, needs warmth, fruit very good when tree-ripened. Deep orange colour. Matures in early winter. Heavier crop if cross pollinated. Medium-large fruit. Flesh: light orange, sweet and mild. Firm when ripe; non-astringent even when unripe; very few seeds. Keeps well. Tree is vigorous, spreading, productive. Fruit thinning is usually necessary.

'Gailey': Astringent. A standard male-flowering pollinating cultivar. Has small–medium, dull maroon fruit. Is a pollination variant. Flesh: dark, firm, juicy, of fair flavour. Tree: small–medium. Has attractive autumn foliage and ornamental value.

'Hachiya': Large, glossy, deep orange-red, conical fruit. Flesh: astringent till fully ripe and soft. Is dark yellow, sweet, juicy, rich and of high quality. Good for drying. Ripens mid–late season. Tree vigorous, upright and spreading.

'Honan Red': Small, roundish fruit, with thin skin. Skin and flesh ripen to an orange-red. Very sweet and rich. Good eaten fresh or can be dried. Ripens mid–late season. Tall, upright, moderately vigorous tree. Bears good crops.

'Hyakume': Large, round fruit, deep orange skin, orange-brown flesh with juicy, firm texture. Spicy, very good flavour with little to no astringency, even when the fruit is hard. Fruits store well. Vigorous tree, but bears modestly. Needs to be cross pollinated. Is a pollination variant. Ripens mid season.

'Jiro': Important cultivar in Japan and California. Fairly small tree. Good fruit colour. Fruit: low tannin, very large, good quality, yellow flesh, never astringent whether seedless or not. Matures fairly early, so good for regions with short summers. Good yields.

'Saijo': Very hardy, down to ~–25°C. Good yields of very sweet, small fruits, excellent quality. Skin dull yellow when mature. Mature fruits are attractive when dried. Tree is vigorous and of medium height. Fruits ripen early–mid season, have a long conical shape, with translucent orange flesh.

'Tanenashi': Medium-sized, conical, orange-red fruits. Flesh: astringent until soft, then yellow, sweet, somewhat dry when ripe. Ripens early. Tree vigorous, rounded, prolific. Tends to biennial bearing. Matures heavy crops without pollination and will seldom set seed even if pollinated. Fruit may need thinning. Harvesting from autumn–early winter. Much used for drying. Popular in southeastern USA.

Below: Diospyros kaki.

SIMILAR PERSIMMON SPECIES

Unless stated otherwise, the descriptions above are applicable to those listed below.

American persimmon, *Diospyros virginiana*. Native to North America. The native Algonquins dried the fruits for winter use, and the name 'persimmon' is of Algonquin origin.

Description: Forms a small–medium-sized tree, 15–20 m tall, spread 6–15 m, with an irregular crown. Is usually single-stemmed. Its bark is grey-black and blocky, with orange showing between the blocks. Has attractive leaves with good autumn colours of yellow–red. *Flowers:* In summer. *Pollination:* Generally needs a pollinator species. However, the female tree can produce seedless fruits in the absence of a pollinator, but these are more astringent than fertilised fruits. *Fruit:* Smaller than those of oriental persimmon (~3–4.5 cm diameter), orange, fleshy and succulent. Their flavour has been compared to butterscotch. Harvested in early winter. Has a deep, strong taproot (so needs to be planted carefully), and shallow, very wide-spreading roots (~20 m), which readily sucker if injured.

Cultivation: Is more shade-tolerant than Asian varieties, and is more cold resistant and tolerant of wet soils than most persimmon species. It is also larger, more vigorous and yet bears consistently good crops, but, is prone to sunburn, though can tolerate drought once established. Is fairly pollution tolerant. Needs ~300 chill hours. Very adaptable to a range of soil types, including alkaline soil. Young plants are somewhat tender, but dormant, mature trees tolerate temperatures down to ~–35°C. *Propagation:* By cuttings or suckers. Also see grafting notes above.

Uses: *Food:* As above. The fruits have a very good rich flavour when fully ripe to almost over-ripe, but are

very astringent before then. Need a warm/hot summer to ripen fully. Early autumn frosts help to sweeten the fruit. Fruits can be bletted: fruits are kept in a cool place and only eaten when they are very soft and almost at the point of going rotten. Native Americans used the seeds in bread. *Medicinal:* A tea made from the inner bark is highly astringent and has been used for sore throats, and externally as a wash for warts or cancer. *Nutrition/Other uses:* As above. It is a popular rootstock for other cultivated persimmons. *Ornamental:* It makes an attractive specimen tree and is suitable for urban planting or reclamation use.

Date plum, *Diospyros lotus*. A native of eastern Asia (China, Japan, Himalayas) and is sometimes cultivated for its edible fruits in these countries, as well as Italy. Forms a fairly short-lived tree, growing to ~6–8 m tall, spread ~6 m. *Flowers:* Borne in mid summer. Female-flowering trees can produce seedless fruits in the absence of a pollinator, but unfertilised fruits are more astringent than fertilised ones. *Fruit:* Small (1–2 cm), and turn from yellow to blue-black when fully ripe. They are very astringent till absolutely ripe, but can also be bletted (see above). Do not produce very good yields.

Cultivation: Fully cold hardy, it can grow in full sun or semi-shade, but likes a sheltered position. Does not tolerate acidic soils, but can grow in wetter soils than most other persimmon species. Needs a good warm–hot summer to fully ripen the fruit, although frosts can sweeten under-ripe fruit. This species is more susceptible to crown gall.

Uses: *Food:* As above. The fruits have a good, rich flavour when fully ripe, but are very astringent before then. The fruit are good dried. *Medicinal:* The fruit have been used to treat fevers, to promote secretions and, in China, the seed is used as sedative. *Other uses:* It is sometimes used as a rootstock for oriental persimmon species. The wood is durable, pliable and rot resistant: is used in general carpentry, etc.

Texas persimmon, *Diospyros texana*. A slow-growing, native North American tree. It is fully hardy. Its bark is particularly attractive, consisting of smooth peeling layers of white-grey-pink bark. Branches have an attractive, twisted form, unlike most other persimmon trees.

Description: Is slow-growing and tends to produce multiple stems, which form a vase-shaped crown, height 6–12 m, spread 5–8 m. It may have thorns. *Leaves:* Shorter than those of many persimmons (~5 cm long, ~4 cm wide), leathery, simple. They do not have autumn colour, but can remain on the tree year-round in warmer areas. *Fruit:* Small, dark purple-green, round, ~1.25–2.5 cm diameter, fleshy, contain many hard seeds.

Cultivation: Withstands drought, pollution and neglect very well. Best grown in full sun. It does not tolerate waterlogging, but can grow on a range of soil types (sand and clay), and at a wide range of pH values, from quite acidic to alkaline soils. Needs very little maintenance or additional nutrients (just occasionally if it looks like it needs it). *Propagation:* As notes above. *Pests and diseases:* Very few problems, and none are normally serious.

Uses: *Food/Nutrition:* As above. May also have fairly good levels of lycopene, particularly in the skin. *Other uses:* In Mexico, the fruits are used to make a black dye. ∎

Dovyalis caffra
(syn. *Aberia caffra*)
Kei apple (umkokolo)
FLACOURTIACEAE

Similar species: tropical apricot, dovyalis or ketembilla (*Dovyalis abyssinica* x *D. hebecarpa*), kitembilla or Ceylon gooseberry (*D. hebecarpa*)

Relatives: Governor's plum, Ceylon gooseberry

Left: Dovyalis hebecarpa
Below: Dovyalis caffra

The kei apple is native to the Kei River area of southwest Africa and grows abundantly in these regions. It is cultivated for its fruit in the Transvaal. In 1838, it was introduced into England and from there was distributed to Egypt, Algeria, southern France and Italy, the Philippines, northwest Australia, Jamaica, southern California and Florida. The kei apple forms a very drought and salt tolerant shrub or small tree that produces many plum-sized fruits. It is being trialled for its commercial viability in Israel.

DESCRIPTION
A vigorous, attractive, spreading shrub or small tree, growing to ~3–5+ m tall, ~4 m spread. Has grey, smooth bark, flaking into rectangular shapes as the tree matures. It usually has many sharp spines, either singly or in small clusters (2–3), which can be ~2.5–6 cm long and are quite vicious, though plants can become almost spineless if not trimmed. It is moderately fast growing.

Leaves: Rich green in colour, glossy, often clustered on short spurs, are oblong–obovate, 2.5–7.5 cm long, with short leaf stems. They have an entire margin, which is sometimes rolled under.

Flowers: Greeny-yellow, small, with no petals, and are clustered in leaf axils. They are usually borne in spring. Trees are usually dioecious. Male flowers are very small (3 mm long) and are in dense clusters of 5–10 flowers. Female flowers occur in clusters of ~3 and are 0.4–1 cm long. Usually need more than one plant to set fruit, although some female trees have been known to produce many good-quality fruits in the absence of a male pollinator, presumably without seeds (parthenocarpically).

Fruit: Deep yellow, small, plum-shaped or round, aromatic, 2.5–6 cm long. The yellow skin is thin, finely downy and somewhat tough. The pulp is acid, fleshy with an apricot-like texture, juicy. The flesh contains several (5–15) flat, pointed, aromatic-flavoured seeds that are surrounded by small hairy fibres and are arranged in two rings around the centre. The fruits mature, on female bushes, in late summer–autumn. Trees can produce many fruits, and are very eye-catching when covered with these bright yellow globes.

Yield/harvest: Trees can produce very good yields. Trees begin to produce fruits in 4–5 years. Fruits should be fully coloured and ripe when harvested: unripe fruits can be very sour. The long thorns make harvesting difficult, though fruits can also be gathered from the ground as they fall.

Roots: Forms deep taproots that reach down to the water-table deep in the ground. Also has some spreading surface roots that catch any moisture and take up nutrients. Take care when planting them out that the taproot is not damaged. In addition, the roots excrete chemicals that act as a natural herbicide, and prevent other plants germinating or growing in their vicinity.

CULTIVATION
Location: Grows best in full sun. Can be grown in maritime locations.

Temperature: The kei apple prefers a warm-temperate or

uses

Food
The fruits are too sour for most people to eat fresh, even when fully ripe, and they are more usually peeled, cut into pieces, the seeds discarded, sprinkled with sugar and allowed to stand for a few hours before serving as a dessert or mixed with other fruits. If cooked, the fruits rapidly become mushy, but can be used in a sauce. They are sometimes used in jams and jelly, or, if under-ripe, they can be added to pickles.

Nutrition
Very good levels of vitamin C: 83 mg/100 g of flesh.

Medicinal
Studies in Egypt have shown that the roots, stem and fruits contain compounds that have antibiotic properties.

Ornamental
Because of its drought tolerance and tolerance to salt it is often grown in dry, coastal areas as an ornamental species. Because of their spines, plants make an excellent security barrier or hedge. They are probably best not planted near paths, or where children play as any spiny stems that drop take a long time to rot down. Can also be cultivated as a bonsai specimen.

subtropical climate. It can survive short drops in temperature to ~–6°C, but prolonged periods of cold can do serious damage, and temperatures below ~–9°C can be lethal. Likes a warm–hot summer.

Soil/water/nutrients: The kei apple can grow in many soil types as long as they are free-draining and do not have a high water table. They cannot tolerate waterlogging. Trees are extremely drought resistant and can tolerate saline soils and salt spray. They are not very nutrient hungry and only need minimal additions of nutrients unless grown in very poor soils.

Planting: Space plants at not less than 3.5–4.5 m apart, although they can be planted as a hedge, at 1–1.5 m apart. Plant trees at a ratio of one male per every 20–30 females trees, although some female trees can produce fruits without a male pollinator.

Propagation: *Seed:* Usually propagated by seed. Sow seeds when fresh, if possible, as they lose viability quite rapidly. Clean all flesh from the seeds before planting in gritty, well-drained compost. Place seeds just below the soil surface. *Cuttings:* Hardwood cuttings can be taken in late autumn and treated with rooting hormone before inserting in well-drained compost. *Layering:* This can be successfully done during the growing season.

Pruning: If not pruned, the trees develop fewer spines, but can then become sprawling and difficult to manage. If pruning for fruit, remove tips of branches to encourage the formation of fruiting laterals. Shrubs/trees are very resistant to pruning and will grow back even if severely cut back to ground level. When grown as a hedge, it is usually trimmed twice a year.

Pests and diseases: Generally, has very few problems, but look out for fruit flies as the fruits ripen.

SIMILAR SPECIES

Tropical apricot (dovyalis, ketembilla), *Dovyalis abyssinica* x *D. hebecarpa*. The tropical apricot is a popular sweeter variety of *Dovyalis* and is a natural hybrid between *D. abyssinica* and *D. hebecarpa*, originating from Florida. It is similar to Ceylon gooseberry (*D. hebecarpa*), but has better-quality, sweeter fruits, much fewer thorns and is self-fertile. The Ceylon gooseberry, as its name suggests, is native to Sri Lanka. The tropical apricot is easy to grow and needs very little maintenance. It is often grown in Florida for its fruits as well as in other warm-temperate regions.

Description: Large, spreading shrub/small tree, height to ~6 m, ~6 m width. Often has long, drooping branches and generally only has a few, if any, thorns. Can grow very quickly under ideal conditions: ~1–1.3 m a year. *Leaves:* Deep green, densely grouped, 7.5–10-cm-long. *Flowers:* Greeny-yellow, distinctive, small, with no petals, and are clustered in leaf axils. Male flowers have numerous long, yellow pollen-tipped stamens. Usually borne in spring. Trees are monoecious, which is a big advantage over most other *Dovyalis* species, as only one tree is needed to set fruit. *Fruits:* Cherry-shaped, ~3.0 cm diameter, velvety or smooth and an attractive pinky-brown colour when fully ripe, sometimes with tiny white spots. The flesh is yellow-orange to deep red, sweet–sub-acid, very soft with a distinctive apricot flavour.

Fruiting occurs mostly from summer–autumn, depending on location, but can fruit at other times of the year in warmer areas. *Yield/harvest:* Trees are often prolific producers. Come into fruiting rapidly: plants from layers can fruit in the same year; cuttings take ~1 year to fruit. Fruits are best harvested when fully coloured and are beginning to soften. Fruits do not store very well, and only last for a few days before they become over soft and mushy. *Roots:* Non-invasive, so can be planted near buildings, etc.

Cultivation: *Location:* Grows best in full sun. Can be grown in maritime locations. *Temperature:* Relatively hardy, but can be badly damaged at ~–3°C; however, if cut back to undamaged wood they can recover quickly. *Soil/water/ nutrients:* Can tolerate many soil conditions, from light to heavy soils, and those with a relatively acid pH, but can develop nutrient deficiencies on highly alkaline soil, where you may need to give additional minor elements to prevent e.g. iron chlorosis. Do not need a lot of moisture, though benefit from an organic mulch that keeps the roots moist during dry periods. Can tolerate wet soil, and needs adequate moisture for proper fruit development. Benefits from regular 2–3-month applications of a complete fertiliser during the growing season. *Planting:* Space plants at ~4–5 m apart. If there is room, more than one tree may increase fruit-set and yields. *Propagation: Seed:* Cannot be grown true from seed as it is a hybrid. Seedlings will be very variable, and may revert to producing sour fruits. If seed is being tried, sow this when fresh, if possible, as they lose viability quite rapidly. Clean all flesh from the seeds before planting in gritty, well-drained compost. Place seeds just below the soil surface. *Cuttings:* Hardwood cuttings can be taken in late autumn and treated with rooting hormone before inserting in well-drained compost. *Cuttings:* Gives predictable progeny that fruit in a short time and can also predict the sex of the tree. *Layering:* Air-layering is successful and has the same advantages as cuttings. *Pruning:* Can be trimmed to shape if stems become long or straggly. Remove any crossing or dense branches to allow light and air to reach the fruits. *Pests and diseases:* Few pests bother *Dovyalis* species. Aphids can sometimes be found on fresh growth, but are seldom too serious. Birds may try the fruit, but usually only take a few.

Uses: *Food:* Fruits can be eaten fresh, as they are usually sweet–sub-acid, though some may be more acidic, and can then be used in jellies, jams, pies and drinks with other sweeter fruit. Makes a wonderful wine. *Nutrition:* Very high in vitamin C. Has a good pectin content. *Ornamental:* Can be grown as a useful ornamental shrub or pruned to form a specimen tree.

Ketembilla (Ceylon gooseberry), *Dovyalis hebecarpa*. A native of Sri Lanka and India, as its other common name suggests. This species forms a large shrub/small spiny tree that is one of the parents of tropical apricot. It is now commercially grown within the southern USA and the Caribbean, and

is an easy plant to grow. Plants are dioecious, so need both a male and female plant to set fruits. The fruits are abundant, dark purple when ripe, ~2.5 cm diameter, and are juicy, tart yet sweet, and often have a good taste, though are too sour for some. They are not usually eaten fresh, but are popular for jams, jellies, juices and many other uses. The fruits are best used for these purposes when they are slightly unripe, as they then contain more pectin. They have a gooseberry-like taste. The fruits are high in vitamin C: ~100 mg/100 g of flesh. The fruits also contain some calcium, iron and phosphates. ■

Elaeagnus spp.
Elaeagnus
ELAEAGNACEAE

Autumn olive (*Elaeagnus umbellata*), *Elaeagnus* x *ebbingei*, *Elaeagnus macrophylla*, *Elaeagnus pungens*, goumi (*E. multiflora*), lingaro (*E. philippensis*), oleaster (*E. angustifolia*), trebizond date (*E. orientalis*)

The *Elaeagnus* genus contains ~40 species found widely in the temperate regions of the Northern Hemisphere. They can be deciduous or evergreen shrubs or trees, and are often grown for their ornamental properties and as a hedge or a screen. Many species make excellent windbreaks, particularly for exposed maritime locations. The flowers are small, fragrant and fuchsia-like. Some produce edible fruits and research is being conducted in the USA to find hybrids that produce good fruit. In addition, recent research indicates that the fruits also have many health and medicinal benefits. Several of the *Elaeagnus* species have quite large, edible seeds, which have a mild flavour, can be eaten raw or cooked, and are a rich source of protein and fats. All the species have a symbiotic relationship with nitrogen-fixing bacteria, which means that they are good colonisers of poorer soil and can fix nitrogen for themselves and for plants around them. When grown in orchards, for example, they can increase the yields of fruit trees by up to 10%. (This is especially the case with nuts, which respond more to nitrogenous fertilisers.)

DESCRIPTION

Flowers: Bell-shaped, small (1.5–2 cm diameter), sweetly fragrant, drooping, borne in inconspicuous clusters from the current season's leaf axils.

Fruit: Round–olive shaped, ~1.5–2.5 cm long, dark orange with small white spots or red when ripe. Become softer and sweeter as they ripen. The fruit contain a largish seed, which is edible, though does have an inedible fibrous coat that is best discarded. Yields are usually good, though can tend towards biennial bearing in some species. There is also variability between plants, and it is best to propagate from plants that are known to fruit well.

Roots: Most species have wide-spreading, fairly shallow roots, so avoid deep cultivation. A mulch will help retain moisture. They also have deeper roots that enable them to be quite drought tolerant.

CULTIVATION

These species are tough, can tolerate a wide range of soil conditions and are very easy to grow, needing minimal maintenance. Usually tolerant of maritime conditions and some wind. In fact, they are often grown as windbreaks in exposed maritime locations. Evergreen species usually like some shade, whereas deciduous species prefer a location in full sun. *Elaeagnus* species vary in their cold hardiness, with some requiring warmer temperate climates and being only moderately frost hardy, whereas others grow and fruit well in cold temperate regions.

Soil: Most species will grow in most soils, including shallow sandy or alkaline ones, or even fairly saline soils. They can also grow in clay, as long as it does not become waterlogged. They can usually tolerate considerable drought. Strangely, the best fruit seem to be produced on poorer soil and when the plant is stressed.

Planting: Space plants at ~2–3 m apart, or ~0.8–1.2 m apart for a hedge.

Propagation: Seed: Can be slow to germinate. Seeds are best stratified by placing in a polythene bag and giving them an initial period of ~4 weeks warmth, and then placing them in a fridge for ~3 months before sowing in spring. *Cuttings:* Semi-ripe cuttings can be taken in summer and inserted in well-drained, gritty compost to root in semi-shade with moisture. Can also take longer cuttings, with a heel, in autumn from riper wood. They take 3–8 weeks to root, and should be potted into individual pots as soon as possible. *Layering:* Can be done in autumn or spring and is fairly successful. Takes ~12 months to root.

Pruning: Generally needs little if any pruning, though they are often trimmed to form a hedge or screen. Fruit and flowers form on the current season's growth, so only prune ust after harvesting the fruit to avoid removing next season's flower buds.

Pests and diseases: Very few problems.

SOME EDIBLE SPECIES

Autumn olive, *Elaeagnus umbellata*. Autumn olive is a native of China, Korea and Japan. It is also commonly grown in India, especially on dry and exposed hillsides. It is an attractive plant with its silvery foliage and fragrant flowers. It was widely planted in the USA to revegetate damaged land, even on mine spoil, but concerns about its invasiveness have reduced this practice. The autumn olive is definitely a plant with a future for its fruit, with new cultivars being currently developed.

Description: A deciduous, thorny shrub, up to ~3 m tall. The thorns are ~2.5 cm long. Young stems are covered with attractive white-silvery scales, which, unfortunately, disappear as the season progresses. The bark tends to peel off in long thin strips, to expose white younger wood beneath. *Leaves:* Oval, with pointed tips, simple, alternate, variable in size, but ~2.5 cm long, ~1.2 cm wide. The margins are entire, although may be somewhat wavy. The underside of the leaf is covered with fine silvery scales, which give it a striking attractive appearance from a distance. The top of the leaf is slightly hairy when young, but becomes smooth as it matures. *Flowers:* Abundant, small (~0.8–1 cm long), fragrant, white–pale yellow, opening shortly after the leaves in spring. They are borne in clusters from lateral leaf axils. Flowers are bisexual, so only need one plant to set fruit, though cross pollination will probably increase yields and fruit quality. *Pollination:* Produces lots of pollen; is popular with bees. *Fruits:* Abundant, small (0.4–1 cm diameter), round, juicy, and dotted with silver or brown scales. Skin is thin, turning from green through yellow to red to dark purplish-red when fully ripe in autumn. The flesh is juicy and pulpy, and contains a single, tan-coloured stone, ~0.7 cm long. The fruits yield a good amount of juice considering the size of their seed. *Yield/harvest/storage:* Should get ~0.7–5 kg of fruit per bush within a season. Begin to flower and fruit after 3 years, and sometimes only after 2 years. Produce very good, regular yields of fruits. Fruits are picked when fully coloured and ripe. They take ~4 months to mature after fruit-set. Watch out for thorns when harvesting. Fruit stores well, and can be stored at room temperature for ~15 days.

Cultivation: A very hardy plant, grows easily, sometimes almost too easily. Burned, mown or cut plants can resprout vigorously. See general notes above on temperature, etc. Being deciduous, it is better planted in full sun. *Soil:* Can grow in acid to alkaline soils, pH 4–8. Can grow in poor quality soil. It is a non-leguminous, nitrogen-fixing woody shrub, so good for improving soil. Can grow well in dry conditions, and is quite drought hardy, though regular moisture during fruit formation improves fruit quality. *Pests and diseases:* Birds and other wildlife love the fruits.

Uses: *Food:* The fruit is sweet–acidic and is good to eat fresh, along with its seeds. It can also be cooked, and makes good juices, jams or jelly, or it can be added to sauces. Best to extract juice by pressing rather than heating, which affects its colour. Luckily, lycopene (see below) is not affected

Food
The fruits have a sweet–sharp taste and are often eaten fresh, or can be used in pies, jams sauces and other desserts.

Medicinal
The fruits of these species are rich in vitamins (especially vitamins A and E), minerals, flavonoids and other bioactive compounds. They are also a good source of essential fatty acids, which is fairly unusual for a fruit. Current research indicates that consumption of these compounds greatly reduces the incidence of cancer in humans, and they may also slow or even reverse the growth of cancers that are already present (see below).

Ornamental
Many species are used widely as ornamental plants, and for growing as windbreaks or screens. Often the leaves are variegated, e.g. bright green and yellow. The fruits are popular with birds and other wildlife. Because of their hardiness, they are often planted to re-establish and reclaim poor soils.

by heat, in fact it can be increased, so a preserve made from this fruit has particularly healthy properties. *Nutrition:* Fruit contains ~8% sugars, 4.5% protein and has a modest vitamin C content of ~12 mg/100 g of flesh. It has good levels of vitamins A and E, flavonoids and other bioactive compounds. It is also a fairly good source of essential fatty acids. The fruits are particularly important nutritionally for their very high concentrations of lycopene: 15–54 mg/100 g of flesh, compared to 3 mg/100 g in fresh tomatoes. For this reason alone, the berries could have considerable commercial possibilities. Lycopene is a powerful antioxidant and may help treat and prevent cancers. Fruits also contain beta-carotene, lutein, phytofluene and phytoene. *Medicinal:* Apart from these fruits being used to reduce the incidence of cancer, and to perhaps halt or reverse the growth of cancers, they also may help prevent heart disease. The seeds and flowers have been used to treat coughs and the oil from the seeds is used for pulmonary infections. The flowers are also used as an astringent and for cardiac problems. *Ornamental:* Because of its thorns it makes a good protective hedge around fields and homes. It is useful for revegetating areas and for improving poor soils.

***Elaeagnus* x *ebbingei*.** This hybrid species is the result of a cross between *E. macrophylla* and *E. pungens* and is commonly grown as a garden ornamental. It forms a wide-spreading shrub growing to ~3–5 m tall, ~3–5 m spread. When planted under trees it adopts a semi-climbing habit and can reach its way up into the lower branches. Moderate growth of ~75 cm/year. *Leaves:* Evergreen, silver-grey, leathery. *Flowers:* Small, silvery, inconspicuous, but very fragrant, borne in autumn. Self-fertile. *Fruits*: Small, ~2 cm long, egg-shaped, red or orange with silvery flecks, borne in early spring (they over-winter on the plant). The fruits can be astringent till fully ripe, so pick when fully coloured. When ripe, they are sweet and delicious. The seed also has a mild but pleasant flavour. *Roots:* Do not like disturbance, so avoid transplanting.

Cultivation: Very easy to grow. Very tolerant of a wide range of conditions and can grow in full sun to fairly dense shade. Is very tolerant of exposed maritime locations. Tolerant of moderate frosts, but heavy frosts can knock the plants back and may cause fruiting to be poor. *Soil:* Can grow in many soil types, including nutrient-poor soils, but does not like waterlogging. Very drought resistant. *Pruning:* Can be cut hard back to control its shape and size. Prune after it has finished fruiting in spring. Most fruit is produced on new wood, so autumn pruning will remove the next season's flower buds. *Propagation:* Cannot be propagated from seed as it is a hybrid. Best from cuttings from plants that are known to produce good crops (some do not).

Elaeagnus macrophylla. A moderately fast-growing, evergreen shrub, ~3 m tall, which is a native of eastern Asia, from Japan and Korea. It is closely related to *E. pungens* (see below) and *E. glabra*. It can grow in full sun or semi-shade. This species is very tolerant of wind and maritime exposure. It is moderately cold hardy, surviving temperatures to ~–15°C. It can grow in the same soil conditions as described above. Yields vary from plant to plant, and vegetative propagation is best from plants known to fruit well. *Leaves:* Leathery, silvery-grey when young, maturing to a deep shiny green. *Flowers:* Yellow-silver, aromatic. Borne in winter. *Fruit:* Bright red, oval, large, ~3 cm in diameter. Ripen very early. Has good potential as a commercial fruit crop. The fruits have a good flavour when fully ripened, but are fairly sour when under-ripe; fruits can be eaten fresh or cooked. They have a fairly large, but edible seed, which can also be eaten fresh or cooked, and can be eaten in quantity, though is somewhat fibrous. The plants can be readily trimmed to form a hedge. If pruned back hard, they regrow well.

Elaeagnus pungens. A vigorous, spreading, evergreen shrub, growing to ~3 m, with ~3 m spread, this is a native of eastern Asia, often found in Japan. It is sometimes spiny. Can grow in a range of soil types, as described above, including clays, and is very drought tolerant. It is also happy growing in fairly dense shade, though can also grow in sun. Tolerates maritime exposure. Shrubs are fairly cold tolerant, surviving temperatures down to ~–15°C. *Leaves:* Leathery, glossy, mid-green, grey-green beneath. *Flowers:* Yellowy-silver, scented, borne in early winter. *Fruits:* Red-orange, oval, small (~1 cm diameter), and ripen early, when few other fresh fruits are available. Has a single edible seed that can be eaten fresh or cooked, though is somewhat fibrous. It contains ~40% protein and 20% fat. The flesh is sub-acid but pleasant when fully ripe, though is sour before then. This plant has potential to be grown more for its fruits, although most cultivars are ornamental and are variegated, so grow slower than other *Elaeagnus* species.

Goumi (gumi, cherry elaeagnus), *Elaeagnus multiflora*. A native of China, and is cultivated in Japan for its fruits, as an ornamental and as a bonsai. Is also grown ornamentally in Europe, the UK and the USA, and did undergo some preliminary trials as a commercial species in the USA. It forms an attractive, rounded, spreading shrub, ~2 m tall, ~2 m spread. *Leaves:* Deciduous, dark green above, silvery beneath. *Flowers:* Yellow-white, drooping, fragrant, in spring. Bisexual, and is probably self-fertile, though planting more than one plant can improve fruit-set. *Fruit:* Abundant, scarlet with silver specks, ~1.25 cm diameter, in loose clusters in autumn. Bushes produce ~4–8 kg of fruits a season.

Cultivation: A tough, fairly fast and easy-to-grow shrub. Is best grown in full sun, but can grow in light shade. Is very tolerant of poor, dry soil, polluted air and windy locations. Is one of the most cold hardy *Elaeagnus* species, tolerating temperatures down to ~–20°C, with roots being tolerant of ~–30°C. *Propagation:* Easier to propagate by cuttings than seed.

Uses: As above. Under-ripe fruits are very sour. The fruits are best eaten when fully ripe, and are then sweet–sub-acid, but are usually processed or made into a good-quality wine. Has similar health properties as described above.

Lingaro, *Elaeagnus philippensis*. A shrubby evergreen, which can form a semi-vine. It is native to the Philippines. *Leaves:* very attractive, light green on the upper surface and thickly dotted with small, reddish-brown scales beneath. *Flowers:* Abundant, fragrant. *Fruit:* Attractive, ~1.5–2 cm long, ripening during late summer–autumn.

Cultivation: Is very salt tolerant. Is not very cold hardy and can be damaged by temperatures of ~–3°C. *Soil:* Can grow well in a range of soil types, and does well on alkaline soils. *Propagation, disease, etc:* See the general notes above.

Uses: Fruits can be eaten fresh or, more usually, are made into good quality jams and jellies. It can be grown as a clipped hedge or can be left to grow as a climber. If left untrimmed, it forms a large shrubby bush.

Oleaster (winter olive, Russian olive), *Elaeagnus angustifolia*. Oleaster forms a wide-spreading, large shrub–small tree, ~4–6 m tall, ~3–5 m spread. Young stems are attractively silver, with older branches becoming drooping. It is fast growing initially, slowing as it matures. Has an attractive winter shape. Is often spiny, though this varies from plant to plant. Often fairly short lived. *Leaves:* Deciduous, silver-grey green. *Flowers:* White-silvery, fragrant, in spring. *Fruit:* Oval–round, ~1.25 cm diameter, yellowy-silver. Persist on the tree till winter. The fruits tend to be dry and somewhat mealy.

Cultivation: Prefers to grow in full sun. Can grow in many soil types, including stony, fairly saline, alkaline or poor soils or clays, and is drought tolerant. Fixes nitrogen. Is a tough plant. Moderately cold hardy. *Pruning:* Benefits from some shaping and training to develop a well-formed tree.

Uses: *Food:* As above. *Ornamental:* Looks good planted in larger gardens and contrasts well with dark green, evergreen species or purple-leaved plants. Makes a good reclamation plant.

Trebizond date, *Elaeagnus orientalis*. Native to the eastern Mediterranean, this plant has good quality fruits and wonderfully fragrant flowers. The 'date' was a popular fruit around Turkey, and was often sold in markets. Unfortunately, it is now seldom encountered. ∎

Empetrum nigrum, E. hermaphroditum
Crowberry (black crowberry)
ERICACEAE
Relatives: blueberry, cranberry

A small genus of about six species of evergreen, extremely cold hardy, prostrate shrubs that are native to the colder regions of Earth, including northern Eurasia, Iceland, northern North America and southern South America. They often grow where little else survives, in exposed, acid, peaty soils, in thin rocky soils or on maritime cliffs. Crowberry is found growing in boreal forests and on Arctic islands. It is valued for its fruits that are found in places and at times where little else survives. It is popular with Laplanders. There are two very similar species, often difficult to tell apart: *Empetrum nigrum* and *E. hermaphroditum*, and these are described generally below.

DESCRIPTION
Forms a creeping, rhizomatous, perennial shrub, only growing to ~15 cm tall, though spreading ~0.5–1 m. Has reddish stems and small leaves.

Leaves: Small, ~0.5 cm long, evergreen, needle-like, overlapping, with a deep central groove. Its margins roll inwards to protect itself from wind and salt-spray damage. The leaf litter is high in phenolic compounds and only slowly breaks down. It also effectively inhibits the growth of competing plants or seeds around it.

Flowers: Small, inconspicuous, mauvish-purple, singly, from leaf axils near stem tips in late spring–early summer. Flowers can be bisexual (and tetraploid) or have separate male and female flowers (which are diploid) on the same plant. Are quite self-fertile, though benefit from being planted in groups to increase fruit-set. *Pollination:* Seems to be mostly by wind due to the lack of insect pollinators.

Fruit: Small, juicy, dark purple-black berries that ripen in autumn into winter. Are borne in small clusters. Fruits contain 6–9 small, edible seeds. Can have a fairly tart flavour, or be tasty and sweet–sub-acid. Others may lack flavour. Can have turpentine-like overtones.

Yield/harvest/storage: The berries are small and fiddly to harvest. Yields are often only moderate. But, it can grow in locations where little else will, and will produce fruits. These are best picked when fully coloured and ripe, and after a frost to develop their full sweetness. Can be stored for several days in a fridge. Can also be 'stored' on the plant into winter, though wildlife are likely to seek them out.

Roots: Has may rhizomatous roots as well as many surface roots, though also has a large biomass of fine roots at depths greater than 50 cm. Most of the plant's biomass is as root rather than shoots. The roots resent being disturbed, and plants are best not moved once established. They form important mycorrhizal fungal relationships that enable the plant to obtain extra nutrients, in particular phosphates. These fungal links are easily broken.

CULTIVATION
Location: Can grow in sun or semi-shade. Is wind hardy because of its low size. Is tolerant of salt and can be grown on exposed, maritime cliffs. Is also tremendously tolerant of pollution and heavy metals such as copper and nickel. Is one of the few species that can grow around factories producing high levels of heavy metals.

Temperature: Extremely cold hardy. Probably won't grow well in warmer climates.

Soil/water/nutrients: Grows best in moist, acidic, peaty soils. Does not tolerate alkaline soils. Likes organic matter incorporated into the soil. Once established, is tolerant of drought, but grows better with regular moisture. It is likely that

uses

Food
The small berries are often tasty and can be eaten fresh or added to desserts, jams, juice, etc. Sometimes used as a blueberry substitute. Their juice adds a rich colour to jams, etc. A tea is made from the young leaves.

Nutrition
The berries contain good levels of vitamin C: ~30 mg/100 g of flesh. They also have high levels of flavonoids, particularly anthocyanins.

Medicinal
The berries have been long used medicinally to treat various eye problems, and for respiratory infections and kidney problems.

Other uses
The fruits yield a strong, deep purple dye.

Ornamental
Make excellent groundcover plants for colder regions with poor soils. Grow well beneath acidic plants, such as pines. Also makes a good rockery plant. The fruits are popular with birds.

this species can tolerate periods of water saturation, but not prolonged periods of waterlogging. Also, grows better with a modest application of an acidic fertiliser at the commencement of the growing season, though too much fertiliser can inhibit the beneficial mycorrhizal fungal association.

Pot culture: Suitable for growing in a pot, particularly in areas with more alkaline soils. Its slow growth, tolerance of cold and some shade make it suitable for tricky areas.

Planting: Space plants at ~0.3 m apart. Plants dislike being handled and transplanted. Appreciate organic matter being incorporated into the soil.

Propagation: *Seed:* Can be propagated from seed, though germination can be poor and irregular. Wash all pulp from the seed before sowing in well-drained, moist compost and leave to over-winter. Stored seed needs a period of ~4 months of warm treatment followed by 2–3 months of cold stratification before they will germinate. *Cuttings:* Semi-ripe cuttings can be taken during summer and inserted in gritty, moist compost, in shade, to root in ~3 weeks. Usually root well. Hardwood cuttings can also be taken in autumn, with a heel, and root quite well. Often propagated by removal of suckers, with some roots. These are established in moist, peaty soil, in shade, before planting out. Avoid root disturbance.

Pruning: Only to reduce their spread, if needed; otherwise not necessary. ■

Eriobotrya japonica
Loquat (Japanese medlar, nispero, Japanese plum)
ROSACEAE (Pomoideae subfamily)
Relatives: apples, medlar, pears

The loquat is a native of southeast China, but was introduced into Japan and became naturalised there in ancient times. It has been cultivated in Japan for >1000 years and has also became widely known throughout southeastern Asia. However, its spread to other areas was slow, and it was not until ~1690 that a Western botanist took the plant back to Europe. By the early 1800s, good-quality fruits were being grown in hot-houses in England (where it was sometimes called a Japanese medlar), and its cultivation also spread to India, the East Indies, Australia, New Zealand, South Africa and southern USA. It is also cultivated in regions around the Mediterranean and the fruits are used commercially in jams and jellies. It is very easy to grow and forms an exotic, evergreen, small–medium-sized tree that readily forms numerous small, round–pear-shaped yellow-orange fruits. It is one of the few subtropical fruit species within the Rosaceae family, and its appearance is not at all similar to other related species. Its popularity is not as great as one would expect for a tree of its versatility, attractiveness, minimum maintenance requirements and abundant fruits.

DESCRIPTION

Easy-to-grow, evergreen, small tree/large shrub with an erect or rounded crown, a short trunk and white-woolly new twigs. Often tends to not have very strong apical dominance and develops a bushy form, with many divided branches. Depending on cultivar, some trees are dense, vigorous and can grow to 5–6 m; others (some of the Japanese varieties) only grow to ~1.5 m tall. They grow quite rapidly, but can also live and produce fruits for ~25 years. The bark is smooth, and dark grey.

Leaves: Evergreen, attractive, dark rich green, elegant, long and oval, with pointed leaf tips and a rounded base, 12–30 cm long and 7.5–10 cm wide. They are thick, stiff, waxy and shiny above, and white- or rust-coloured and felty beneath. They have conspicuous oblique leaf veins, and these terminate on the margins in a short, prickly point. Young leaves are pale greeny-grey and velvety all over.

Flowers: Flower buds are covered with a white–rust-coloured felty texture. Opening to small, pale yellow–white flowers, 1.5–2 cm diameter, borne in terminal clusters of 30–100 flowers, in late autumn and winter. They emit a strong, musky, vanilla-like fragrance. They have the Rosaceae form of five white petals with many central stamens and a central ovary. They also have a prominent brown, felty calyx, and an inferior ovary. *Pollination:* Normally by bees. Flowers are monoecious and bisexual, and some cultivars are self-fertile; however, others are self-infertile and others are only partially self-fertile. It is, therefore, beneficial to plant more than one tree to get good fruit-set. One of the problems with poor pollination is that early and late flowers often have abnormal stamens and, therefore, very little viable pollen.

Fruit: In clusters, from leaf axils. They are oval–rounded–pear-shaped, and variable in size, from ~2.5–4 cm diameter. They are classified as pomes, and remnants of the calyx are visible at the fruit's apex, like apples. They have a fairly thin, smooth or downy, yellow–orange skin. The flesh varies from being very sweet to quite acid, but is usually juicy, succulent and tangy, and varies in colour from white–yellow–orange.

The flesh is usually firm, and has an apricot/plum flavour in many Chinese and Japanese types, and is sprightly and more lychee-like in flavour in fruits with cream–white-coloured flesh. Each fruit contains 2–8 largish, central, brown seeds, which sit is a central cavity and are easy to remove. Trees tend to overbear and produce many small fruits, and also tend towards biennial bearing: thinning flowers and young fruits will increase the size and quality of the fruit overall, and even out yields.

Yield/harvest/storage: A mature tree can produce 32–50 kg of fruits a year. Grafted trees begin to bear fruit in 2–3 years, and can give reasonable yields at 5 years; seedlings start producing fruit after 4–6 years from seed. Yields then keep increasing until trees are 25 years or more in age. Fruits take ~90 days to mature after fruit-set. Loquats normally ripen in late winter–early spring; often very early when few other fresh fruits are available. Harvest fruits when they are fully ripe and coloured yellow-orange, and when the flesh is still firm, but sweet. Tree-ripened loquats develop their full sweetness and flavour. Pick fruits with their stalks attached to avoid tearing the skin: often harvested using clippers. Fruits can be easily bruised. *Storage:* At room temperature, loquats should keep for ~10 days, or for ~60 days in cool storage.

Roots: They form a fairly shallow root system, so care needs to be taken with mechanical cultivation, and a mulch will help reduce moisture loss, as well as supplying additional nutrients. Roots are not invasive, and trees can be safely planted near buildings.

CULTIVATION

The loquat is an easily-grown, minimum maintenance, good-yielding tree.

Location: Grows best in full sun or partial shade. If grown in semi-shade, the leaves become larger and deeper green in colour. They are relatively wind tolerant and are fairly salt tolerant, so can be grown in maritime locations, though their shallow roots make them somewhat susceptible to being knocked over.

Temperature: Trees prefer a subtropical to warm temperate climate, but are fairly frost hardy. They can tolerate temperatures down to ~–10°C, but flower buds and young fruits can be killed at ~–4°C, which can be a risk as they flower and fruit during late autumn–winter. Young trees need extra protection from frost for the first couple of years. Fruit production is reduced by too much cold, but also by too much warmth year round.

Soil/water/nutrients: Loquats can grow in a variety of soils of moderate fertility, from light sandy loam to heavy clay, and even limestone soils, where serious iron chlorosis seems to be rare. Although it prefers good drainage, it can even tolerate moderately wet soils. Grafting onto quince rootstocks increases this tolerance of wet soils, although quince rootstocks are notorious for producing many suckers. Loquats can survive periodic droughts, but will have better fruit quality with regular, deep watering during flowering and fruit formation. Trees are only moderately nutrient hungry, and over-fertilising can increase the tree's sensitivity to fireblight, and too much nitrogen can reduce flowering at the expense of leaf growth. However, extra potassium, especially in spring, can improve fruit production. Once established,

Food
The fruit is juicy, sweet and mild, and is delicious eaten fresh, though can be fairly sharp. The seeds are removed, as can be the skin, but this is not necessary unless the skin is tough; it also contains five times more vitamin A than the flesh. The fruits are tasty mixed with other fruits such as banana, pineapple and coconut. They are delicious stewed with a little sugar. They have good levels of pectin and are useful in jams, preserves, chutney, etc. The fruits can be used in desserts, or as a pie filling, or in sauces. Spiced loquats can be prepared, with cloves, cinnamon, lemon and vinegar. Loquats also make a fine-tasting wine.

Nutrition
Fruits are high in vitamin A (but poor in vitamin C) and have a good level of potassium. They contain laevulose, sucrose and malic acid. The leaves are high in triterpenes and tannin. Young leaves contain saponins.

Medicinal
The fruit has been used as a sedative and is eaten to halt vomiting. An infusion of the leaves has been used to relieve diarrhoea and depression, and to counteract intoxication from consumption of too much alcohol. Leaf poultices are applied on swellings. *Warning:* Like all Rosaceae species, the seeds contain hydrocyanic acids, which are toxic if eaten in quantity, but, because these seeds are fairly large, they are unlikely to be accidentally eaten.

Other uses
The wood is pink, hard, close-grained, medium-heavy and has been used to make drawing instruments. In France, the flowers were investigated for their essential oils for perfumes but, although the oil was of good quality, the yields were small.

Ornamental
Their foliage adds a tropical look to the garden and contrasts well with other plants, or makes a good small-sized specimen tree. The flowers attract many bees.

trees generally only need a maximum of one feed a year of a good balanced fertiliser, probably in late summer before flowering and fruiting.

Pot culture: Because of their small size and easy manageability, they can be readily grown in a large container for many years in colder areas. They have attractive foliage year round, and give a good tropical effect. They also easily flower and produce small, tasty, juicy orange fruits. The plant benefits from a good organic mulch to retain moisture. It is worthwhile selecting dwarf cultivars.

Planting: Space plants at 5–8 m apart.

Pruning: Need minimal pruning, just to open up the

centre to allow light and air to enter. Trees are best pruned just after harvesting, before summer growth, or the tree's vigour is wasted in producing growth that will be removed. Trees may need reducing in height to make harvesting easier. Because these trees readily produce many lateral branches, it is best to remove older fruiting laterals to leave newer vigorous shoots to form next season's fruit. This will increase the size of fruit and reduce biennial bearing, though not as many fruits will be produced. In addition, fruits may also need to be thinned if they are too numerous. Trees can be pruned to an attractive espalier.

Propagation: *Seed:* Easy from seed, just need warmth and moisture. Good germination rate. Often grown as a rootstock or as an ornamental. Seeds are best sown when fresh, but can remain viable for ~6 months if stored at ~5°C in humidity. Seeds should be washed clean of flesh before sowing in well-drained compost. *Cuttings:* Not easy to root. *Layering:* Air-layering can be a successful method of propagation. *Grafting:* Trees can be top-worked, but can also be grafted using shield-budding, side-whip-and-tongue grafting or cleft-grafting. Loquat rootstocks tend to give taller trees, whereas quince forms smaller, but more suckering trees, though fruit size is unaffected.

Pests and diseases: There are few pests that bother loquats. May get occasional infestations of black scale, fruit flies, leaf-roller caterpillar and aphids. Diseases include crown rot, caused by *Phytophthora* spp., cankers caused by *Pseudomonas* (this can be serious), and blackspot (more likely in humid climates). Because the loquat belongs to the Rosaceae family, fireblight can also be a risk. One of the main problems is birds getting to the fruits before they are harvested; however, fruits are best harvested when fully ripe, so covering the tree, temporarily, with a net or enclosing the best clusters of fruits may be the best option.

CULTIVARS

'Advance': Japanese. Tree is a natural dwarf, ~1.6 m tall. Fruit: medium–large, pear-shaped–round, in large compact clusters. Skin downy, thick and tough. Flesh: whitish, translucent, melting, very juicy, sub-acid, very pleasant, quality good. Ripens mid season. Seeds: 4–5. Highly resistant to fireblight. Self-infertile, a good pollinator for other cultivars.

'Big Jim': From California. Tree vigorous, upright, highly productive. Fruit: large, round, ~3 cm diameter. Skin: pale orange-yellow, medium-thick, easy to peel. Flesh: orange-yellow, very sweet but with some acidity, excellent flavour. Ripens mid season.

'Champagne': Japanese. Tree: prolific, fruits in large clusters, is self-infertile. Fruit: pear-shaped, small–large; skin: pale–deep yellow, thick, tough, astringent; flesh, white or yellow, soft, melting, very juicy, mild–sub-acid–sweet, excellent flavour. Seeds: 3–5. Mid season–late harvest. Does not store well, though good for preserving.

'Tanaka': Japanese. Tree: medium-sized, ~3 m, precocious, vigorous, bears regularly; mostly self-fertile. Highly cold-tolerant. Fruit: oval–round, medium–large; orange-yellow skin. Flesh: brownish-orange, medium thick, coarse, firm, juicy, sweet or sub-acid, excellent taste. Ripens late. Fruit stores well.

'Victory': From west Australia. Fruit: large, oval; skin: yellow–orange. Flesh: white–cream, juicy, sweet. Ripens early–mid season.

'Wolfe': From Florida. Tree: ~7 m tall, bears well, regularly. Fruit: oval–pyriform, ~5 cm long. Yellow, fairly thick skin. Flesh: pale yellow, thick, firm, juicy, excellent flavour, sweet–acid. Seeds: 1–3. Harvest: winter–early spring. Suitable for all purposes, including cooking. ■

Eucalyptus gunii (syn. *E. divaricata*)
Cider gum
MYRTACEAE

The *Eucalyptus* genus is huge, containing ~650 species and subspecies. They vary widely from magnificent giant trees to small shrubs. The largest broad-leaved tree in the world is a eucalypt, *E. regnans,* reaching heights of ~120 m. Eucalypts can be found growing in cold alpine regions, baking-hot deserts and tropical rainforests. Characteristically, they have distinctive sparse branches and silvery blue-grey, resinous, leathery tough leaves, often with attractive shedding bark, and most are tough and hardy. Most *Eucalyptus* species are native to Australia, and the cider gum grows naturally in Tasmania. This well-known eucalypt is popular in gardens of many temperate regions of the world and is a fast-growing, hardy, attractive tree that contrasts well with dark green- or purple-leaved trees, and fits well into mixed architectural plantings. It is also well-known as a forestry species in Australia and China, and is much cold hardier than many other eucalypt species. Recently, there has been interest in Australia and New Zealand in its cultivation for syrup production from tapping the sap.

E

DESCRIPTION

A small- to medium-sized tree, but can grow to 40 m tall in the right conditions, with a trunk diameter of 2.5 m. It has sparse, large spreading branches. Attractive smooth, pale green bark that, in autumn, peels off to show yellow-green young bark below. Young stems are greeny-pink in colour. It only castes light shade. Trees keep growing year round in warmer climates, and do not form resting buds like most plant species. It is fast growing, and can measure ~6 m in 3 years.

Leaves: Evergreen, thick, leathery, attractive and occur in two forms: juvenile and mature. Younger branches have attractive, round juvenile leaves, ~5–8 cm diameter, silvery-white, and occur in whirls around the stems. These live for ~2 years. Mature leaves are more olive-green in colour, long, thin, lanceolate, and are quite different from juvenile leaves. A tree can change from one form to the other over a period of a year or so. If cut to the ground, new shoots produce juvenile leaves again. The leaves are 'designed' to retain moisture and have thick cuticles, are coloured to reflect bright light and are often on long petioles that wave easily in any breeze to cool them. Leaves are pleasantly aromatic when crushed.

Flowers: Flower buds are formed in leaf axils the year before they open. They form oval green capsules with a round, lighter green cap, which is derived from the calyx, and is where its name *Eucalyptus* is derived. These open into small, flat clusters of three powder-puff-like flowers consisting of tufts of attractive stamens, with no true petals or sepals. Flowers are creamy-white in colour, ~1.25–2.5 cm in diameter, and have a sweet fragrance. Trees start flowering and producing seeds after 4–6 years Flowers are borne from late spring through to early summer. *Pollination:* Produces abundant nectar; popular with bees and nectar-feeding birds.

Fruits: Hard, woody seed capsules are formed soon after the tree has flowered, but the seeds inside them do not mature for a further 12 months. The capsule contains many tiny, hard, black seeds.

Harvest: The trees should not be tapped until the trunks have grown to ~25 cm width for a single tap, and wider for two taps. If done when the tree is too young, its growth resources can be depleted, which will affect its future development. Is usually tapped from late spring until mid summer. The flow of sap is best on warm sunny days. Tapping is done by drilling a hole ~0.5–0.75 depth into the tree at ~1 m height on the sunny side of the tree (the phloem layer is not far below the surface). Insert a tube and hang a bucket just below, which you may want to cover to prevent contamination. Collect the drained sap regularly. The sap can then be boiled down until it reaches a syrupy consistency. This can take several hours. The sap can be placed in an evaporator pan with heated water inside. Ensure the water does not boil dry and that the syrup doesn't become too smokey. Skim off any foam from the surface. After several hours, the sap suddenly changes consistency and thickens. It needs to be checked regularly at this time until the sap can coat the back of a spoon: it is then finished. Strain the sap, reheat it to 70°C and pack it into sterilised containers. The syrup should then keep for several months or longer.

Roots: Many *Eucalyptus* species are tough because of their root systems, which can be very deep, reaching down to groundwater in the soil; they also have many surface roots that obtain any moisture and nutrients near the surface. Many of their roots are tuber-like. They also form associations with mycorrhizal fungi that enable them to obtain extra nutrients, particularly phosphates.

Food
Aborigines used to tap this tree for its sap and then ferment it. The syrup is said to taste like Cointreau, very sweet with a fruity orange flavour. Sap is collected in about mid summer, when it can flow at rates of 15 litres a day. (See notes on harvesting above.) The sap is golden-yellow in colour and as the liquid ferments it and is said to become almost apple-like in flavour, and is quite sweet. The sap can also just be drunk straight from the tree.

Medicinal
The leaves contain essential oils that have strong antifungal properties and act as an antiseptic. Its oils are often used for bronchial and pulmonary infections, for chest rubs and as a gargle for sore throats. The oil can also be used as a rub to ease muscle or tension pains. Many species of *Eucalyptus* are harvested for their essential oils, in particular *E. globulus*. **Warning:** The essential oil, like most other essential oils, should not be consumed in any quantity as it can result in severe illness and intestinal disturbances.

Other uses
The leaves and seed capsules are sought-after for their use in floral arrangements. Cattle and sheep can eat the leaves.

Ornamental
An excellent, attractive tree as a specimen or planted with species with contrasting foliage. However, it needs a fair amount of space, and its leaves and bark produce chemicals that inhibit the germination and growth of other species around it.

CULTIVATION
An easy tree to grow, being very hardy and adaptable.

Location: Somewhat wind tolerant once established, though does not like to be sited in areas exposed to cold, strong winds. Grows best in full sun. Can tolerate salty locations.

Temperature: Is very cold hardy, tolerating temperatures down to ~−15°C, though young trees need extra protection from cold till fully established. In addition, because trees do not become dormant, they are more affected by sudden drops in temperature if they have not had the chance to acclimatise.

Soil/water/nutrients: Can grow in a variety of soils, including fairly nutrient-poor, dry soils, but can also grow near peat bogs, although not very happily. They are sometimes grown in

195

boggy areas to dry out the soils, and so reduce the breeding areas for mosquitoes. They prefer neutral to slightly acidic pH soils; some reports say they can grow in moderately alkaline soils. Once trees are established, they are quite drought hardy. Trees are not very nutrient hungry, but can benefit from annual additions of a slow-release fertiliser when younger, particularly in sandy, nutrient-poor soils. Trees can also benefit from an organic mulch to help retain moisture, add nutrients and to protect roots from sudden drops in temperature.

Planting: Space plants at ~3–4 m apart, or specimen trees further apart. Trees are sensitive to root disturbance and are best planted out when they are still small. Keep young trees well watered till established. Because of their rapid growth, young trees benefit from staking for the first few years.

Propagation: *Seed:* This is the main method of propagation. Because progeny are variable, try to obtain seed from trees growing in a similar locality to your own, as there is considerable variation between trees in cold hardiness, etc. Pick last season's hard seed capsules at about the time the tree comes into flower. Dry the capsules at room temperature until the seeds are released. Sow seeds just below the soil surface, and keep them warm and moist: they should germinate in 2–3 weeks. Transplant young seedlings carefully as their roots are easily damaged. Grow on in individual pots till they are large enough to plant out. Keep them moist and give them some shade initially. Seeds remain viable for a long time.

Pruning: Needs little, but can regenerate strongly from any branch damage to produce a more vigorous tree. Can be burnt or cut to the ground and usually regenerates, often more strongly than before. These species have strong apical dominance and tend to just form a single shoot or only 2–3. If the tops of trees are damaged they form a more branched shape that may need pruning to prevent it from becoming top heavy. For sap collection, little or no pruning is needed.

Pests and diseases: They are generally quite healthy, although in some regions are more susceptible to various eucalypt problems. In general, can get some problems with the blue gum psyllid, which damages young leaves. Young trees can be susceptible to damping-off or *Botrytis*. ■

Eugenia aggregata
Cherry of the Rio Grande
MYRTACEAE

Similar species: Pitomba, *E. luschnathiana*
Relatives: grumichama, Surinam cherry

The cherry of the Rio Grande is member of the *Eugenia* genus, along with many other fruiting and ornamental species. It is a native of Brazil, and is still cultivated locally for its fruit. It forms a beautiful, small tree with showy flowers and tasty, colourful fruit.

DESCRIPTION
A beautiful small tree, 5–10 m in height. As the tree gets older its bark peels off, resulting in a smooth, attractive trunk. It is fairly slow growing: 30–60 cm per year.

Leaves: Evergreen, smallish, dark green, glossy, waxy, aromatic when crushed.

Flowers: White, quite showy, borne in early spring and extending over several months. *Pollination:* By bees and insects. Usually bisexual and is self-fertile, so only needs one tree to set fruit.

Fruit: Plum shaped, rich dark red–purple when ripe, ~2.5 cm long. Produced only 4–8 weeks after flowering. The juicy flesh has a good, sub-acid flavour and contains 1–2 white, rounded seeds that are not eaten.

Yield/harvest: Seedlings usually take 4–5 years to start producing fruits (or ~third year after planting) under favourable conditions, but may take longer. Fruits are harvested when fully coloured and ripe.

Roots: The cherry of the Rio Grande has a shallow root system and benefits from an organic mulch to reduce moisture loss, suppress weed growth and to add nutrients. Avoid mechanical cultivation.

CULTIVATION
Easy to grow, requiring relatively little maintenance to produce healthy, productive plants. Fruit size and quality depend to a large extent on proper nourishment and an adequate water supply at the time of fruit development.

Location: Is not very tolerant of salt spray, but has good wind resistance and can grow in relatively exposed locations. Likes a sunny spot.

Temperature: Can tolerate temperatures down to –6°C with only twig damage, but is adapted to warmer growing conditions. Small trees are more frost sensitive, and should be protected from temperatures below –1°C.

Soil/water/nutrients: Can grow in most soil types, provided they are well drained. Trees do best in slightly acid soils that are low in salts. On alkaline soils, they may develop micronutrient deficiencies such as iron chlorosis. Although they are fairly drought tolerant once established, they benefit from a good moisture supply at all times, particularly at flowering and fruit development to give optimum fruit yields and quality. However, too much water can create problems in the root system. When first planted, trees need a complete fertiliser that contains magnesium. Apply regularly when

Food

The fruit is good eaten fresh or can be added to jellies, jams, juices, icecream. It makes a good wine. The fruits can be picked at maturity and frozen for later use; they can also be dried. The seeds should be removed. Chilling the fruit, perhaps with a little sugar or honey, is said to remove any resinous taste.

Nutrition

Fruits contain good levels of vitamins C (40 mg/100 mg of flesh) and vitamin A. They also contain thiamine, riboflavin and niacin. **Warning:** The seeds should not be eaten as they can cause diarrhoea.

Other uses

The leaves yield an aromatic essential oil containing many compounds, including citronella and geranyl. The leaves can be also used as a pot pourri, and the smell from the crushed leaves is said to repel flies. The bark contains ~25% tannin and is used to tan leather.

Ornamental

Makes a very attractive specimen large shrub or small tree, depending on how it is trained, particularly when covered with fruit. It is a great choice for small gardens. Can also be used as a screening hedge.

actively growing to achieve optimum growth and yields. Nutritional sprays to supply other minor elements can also be applied. After the tree has matured, a fertiliser with more nitrogen, potassium and magnesium may be beneficial.

Pot culture: Makes a good, large container specimen because of its slowish growth. It can be kept to shrub or small tree size and still produce fruits.

Pruning: Requires very little pruning to make an attractive tree, but it can be pruned to form a hedge or shrub.

Propagation: *Seed:* Usually propagated by seed. Germinates in ~21–28 days, though seedlings may take 4–5 years to begin producing fruit. Although there can be a lot of variation in the size of seedling fruits, there is not a lot of difference in quality. *Grafting:* Good varieties with especially large fruit can be whip-and-tongue-grafted onto seedling rootstocks.

Pests and diseases: No serious pest or disease problems. Die-back can be a problem, which can occur any time, but often shows up when plants are approaching maturity. It is not known what causes this; however, usually only smaller branches are affected and these can be pruned out and the plant will continue growing normally. Fruit may attract fruit flies. Birds also like the fruit.

SIMILAR SPECIES

Pitomba, *Eugenia luschnathiana*. The pitomba is also a native of Brazil, and is cultivated locally for its fruit. It forms a medium-sized tree with attractive flowers and tasty, colourful fruit.

Description: Fairly slow-growing, upright tree, with a compact growth habit and dense foliage. It is quite attractive, especially when in fruit. It is medium-sized, ~6–8 m tall, ~5 m spread. The trunk is mottled brown–tan. *Leaves:* Evergreen, ~7 cm long, attractive, opposite, dark green above, bronze beneath when young; leathery, aromatic when crushed. *Flowers:* Showy, white. ~2.5 cm diameter, 4–5 petals, fragrant, borne singly in leaf axils, in spring, but also a few may occur during the summer. *Fruits:* Roundish, bright orange-yellow, ~2.5 cm diameter, with a thin skin.

The flesh is soft, juicy, aromatic, sub-acid–sweet and has a somewhat apricot-like taste. Fruit contains 1–4 large (~1.2 cm diameter), whitish seeds that are attached to a central cavity. Four–five green sepals, ~1.25 cm long, are left at the fruit's apex. *Yield/harvest:* The fruits form and mature within 4–6 weeks of the tree flowering. They produce a main crop in summer, and there may be a smaller crop in autumn. Seedling trees start to produce fruit ~6–9 years after planting; grafted trees can produce fruit after ~3–4 years. The pitomba is not as productive as some Myrtaceae. Care is needed when handling the fruit, as they easily bruise. *Roots:* The pitomba has a shallow root system and benefits from an organic mulch to reduce moisture loss, suppress weed growth and to add nutrients. Avoid mechanical cultivation.

Cultivation: Easy to grow, and needs relatively little maintenance to produce healthy, productive plants. *Location:* Is fairly salt tolerant, and can be planted in a maritime location. Grows best in full sun or semi-shade, but fruits ripen best in full sun. Trees are fairly wind tolerant. *Temperature:* Adapted to growing in warmer regions and prefers hot summers, though is relatively cold hardy and can tolerate temperatures as low as ~–3°C without significant damage. Younger trees are not as cold hardy and need extra protection if a frost is likely. *Soil/water:* Grows best in fertile, moisture-retentive, loamy soils, but trees will grow in a range of soils; however, their growth rate and yields may not be as good. They prefer somewhat acidic to mid-range pH values (pH 5–6.5) where they grow faster and are less susceptible to mineral deficiencies. If grown in alkaline soils, growth is slower and nutrient deficiency problems are likely, e.g. iron (which results in leaf chlorosis) or manganese, and the trees then need foliar chelates applied as micronutrients. Trees prefer regular moisture at all times because of their shallow root system, particularly during long dry spells. However, soils should be well drained, and trees can't tolerate waterlogging. Water and nutrients are particularly important through the spring–summer when the trees are flowering, and during fruit development. Give young trees applications of a balanced fertiliser (or similar) 2–3 times a year from early spring to autumn. Trees need less nutrients once they are established. *Pot culture:* Because of their slow growth and manageability, pitomba make good container plants with their blossom, evergreen leaves and attractive fruit. They can also be moved or given extra protection if grown in colder regions. Plant them in a light-coloured pot to avoid the roots overheating, and apply a thick, surface mulch to help retain moisture. They will need watering and feeding regularly. *Pruning:* Trees need very little attention, just the removal of damaged or diseased wood. They are sometimes pruned to form a hedge. Any pruning is best done after harvest, to avoid pruning off the season's fruit. *Propagation: Seed:* Plants can be easily grown from seed, but seedlings can take ~6–9 years before they start fruiting, and the progeny are variable. Seed germination rate is quite good, taking <4 weeks to germinate. Seeds are best collected from the summer crop and sown when fresh. They should be given warmth and protection during their first winter. Cuttings: Can be propagated by semi-ripe cuttings taken, with a heel, in summer from non-flowering or fruiting stems. Root plants in well-drained, warm compost. Grafting: Plants are often produced by veneer, cleft and side grafts, which give reliable progeny and the trees can fruit ~3–4 years later. *Pests and*

diseases: They are generally trouble free. The only serious pests are birds and fruit flies who both go after the fruit.

Cultivars: There are no named cultivars of pitomba. Individual trees vary in vigour and fruit quality, with some trees producing sweeter tastier fruit. It is best to select these trees for vegetative propagation, if possible.

Uses: *Food:* The fruits can be eaten fresh or used to make good-quality jellies, preserves, juice, or can be added to desserts, pies and sauces. They have a sweet and aromatic taste, not dissimilar to apricots. They also make a fairly good quality wine. *Nutrition:* Fruits contain good levels of vitamins C (40 mg/100 mg of flesh) and A. They also contain thiamine, riboflavin and niacin. **Warning:** The seeds should not be eaten as they can cause diarrhoea. *Other uses:* The leaves yield an aromatic essential oil containing many compounds, including citronella and geranyl. The leaves can be also used as a pot pourri, and the smell from the crushed leaves is said to repel flies. The bark contains ~25% tannin and is used to tan leather. *Ornamental:* The tree is sometimes planted for its ornamental value, for its flowers and bright orange fruit, either in a container or as a specimen. It can also be planted as a screening hedge. ◼

Eugenia uniflora, E. michelii, Stenocalyx michelii
Pitanga (Brazilian cherry, Surinam cherry)
MYRTACEAE
Similar species: Uvalha, *Eugenia uvalha*
Relatives: cherry of the Rio Grande, pitomba

The most widely known of the edible-fruited *Eugenia* species because of its great adaptability, pitanga is a native to several countries from northern South America down to southern Brazil and Uruguay. It is now grown in many warmer parts of the world, including India, southern Europe, eastern Asia and the southern USA. It is thought that Portuguese explorers originally took seeds from South America to India, and from there it was taken to other neighbouring countries and to Europe. It is a smallish tree, with a compact habit and is non-invasive. It fits well into smaller gardens and is ornamental, produces aromatic leaves, small white flowers and purplish, tasty fruit.

DESCRIPTION
A well-behaved, ornamental, evergreen tree that forms a compact, smaller tree or large shrub, 2–5 m tall. It has thin wiry branches.

Leaves: Evergreen, opposite, glossy, small (4–6 cm long), oval, with either blunt or lance-shaped tips. They are an attractive bronze colour when young, changing to deep green when mature; in colder winters they sometimes turn a reddish colour. Many leaf colours can occur at the same time, making this an attractive species. They are also resinous and wonderfully aromatic when crushed.

Flowers: Delicate, creamy-white, small, slightly fragrant, four-petalled, on long flower stalks, borne singly or in clusters of up to four flowers, from the leaf axils, occurring in spring, but sometimes also throughout summer in warmer areas. They are typically myrtle like and have numerous (~50), white decorative stamens topped by pale yellow anthers, which resemble a 'powder puff'.

Fruit: The fruits are globe shaped, ~2–4 cm diameter, shiny, thin-skinned, ribbed (~8 ribs) and occur singly or in small clusters on long stalks. They have a distinctive protuberance at their apex formed from the remains of the calyx. They look a little like a small red or yellow pepper with a nipple-like apex. Young fruits are green, turning to orange, to scarlet, to deep red–dark maroon when fully ripe. The fruits are very variable in quality between trees. The flesh from better fruits is orange-red, very juicy, succulent, aromatic with a mild acid–sweet taste; that of poorer fruit can have a bitter, resinous taste. It has one round or two semi-circular, central fairly large seeds that are loosely attached to the flesh. The fruit is borne singly or in clusters, on pendant, slender stems.

Yield/harvest: Trees start to produce fruits 2–3 years after planting, but seedlings may take 5–7 years or longer. A tree should yield ~2.5–4 kg of fruit a season, and sometimes more from unpruned trees. The fruits only take ~3–5 weeks to mature after pollination, and can be harvested in late spring, with additional crops during summer and into autumn in warmer locations with good soil and moisture conditions. They should only be harvested when fully ripe, when they have developed their full colour and are almost dropping from the tree. Unripe fruits are unpleasantly resinous.

Roots: It forms deep roots, which enable it to find water during dry periods, but the roots are not spreading and are non-invasive, so trees can be planted near houses or other structures. It does benefit from an organic mulch.

CULTIVATION
They are easy to grow, and need relatively little maintenance to produce healthy, productive trees.

Location: Trees grow best in full sun or light shade, and are fairly wind tolerant. They do not grow well in maritime conditions.

Temperature: They can be grown in warm-temperate, subtropical and tropical regions. However, this species is more cold tolerant than many other *Eugenia* species, and can tolerate temperatures as low as ~–6°C. Young trees are less cold tolerant and need extra protection when temperatures approach freezing.

Soil/water/nutrients: Trees will grow in almost any soil type: sand, clay, alkaline (although may suffer from iron deficiency: chlorosis), and can even tolerate waterlogging for short periods, but are intolerant of salt. Prefer a pH range from moderately acidic to neutral: pH 5–7.5. Fruit size and quality are largely determined by adequate nutrients and moisture during fruit development. Regular watering during fruit formation will give juicier, sweeter fruit. However, because of their deep roots, during other periods, they are relatively drought tolerant. Regular applications of a complete balanced fertiliser or organic supplement, particularly with extra magnesium, will promote fruiting. Once the tree has matured, fewer applications are needed, and a ratio with more nitrogen and potassium, plus additional magnesium, is recommended. Benefit from the addition of organic matter, such as leaf mould.

Pot culture: In colder temperate zones, it can be grown as a shrub in a pot for its attractive, aromatic leaves and bright fruits. It can then be given protection against the cold.

Pruning: Most productive if left unpruned. Any pruning should be done just after the fruits have been harvested to avoid removal of fruiting wood. However, this species is often severely pruned to form a hedge and should, even then, produce a few flowers and fruits. It can also be pruned to fit into a smaller garden and should produce some fruit.

Propagation: *Seed:* This is the usual method of propagation. They are best sown when fresh, as viability rapidly reduces. They take 21–28 days to germinate. Often seeds from fruits that have fallen will germinate around the tree, and these can be carefully transferred to pots to establish. Seedlings grow slowly to begin with, and although a few seedlings do produce fruits after only ~2 years, most trees take much longer (5–9 years). Trees from seedlings will be variable, as can fruit quality. *Cuttings:* Semi-ripe cuttings can be taken in summer and inserted in gritty, moist compost, with warmth, to root. *Layering:* This can be successful. *Grafting:* Sometimes done to obtain a desirable tree that has a tough rootstock with a good fruiting selection grafted onto it, although the rootstocks do often sucker. Veneer, cleft and side grafts can be used.

Pests and diseases: They have few serious pest or disease problems, other than the Caribbean fruit fly. The leaves are occasionally attacked by scale insects or caterpillars.

CULTIVARS
There are two main types: a common scarlet-fruited form, and a rarer dark maroon-fruited form, with the latter tending to be sweeter and less resinous.

uses

Food
Fully ripe fruits are often very tasty and can be eaten fresh or can be used in jellies, jams, salads, juices, pies, icecream, relish or sauces. The seeds should be removed. Chilling the fruit, with a little sugar or honey added, is said to remove any resinous taste. They can be substituted for strawberries. Brazilians ferment the juice into vinegar or wine, and sometimes prepare a distilled liquor.

Nutrition
Fruits contain very good levels of vitamins C (45 mg/100 mg of flesh) and vitamin A (~2600 IU). They also contain thiamine, riboflavin and niacin.

Medicinal
In Brazil, a tea made from the leaves is used to treat stomach problems, to eliminate internal parasites and as an astringent. **Warning:** The seeds should not be eaten as they can cause diarrhoea.

Other uses
The leaves yield a highly aromatic essential oil containing many compounds, including citronella and geranyl. The leaves can be also used as a pot pourri, and the smell from the crushed leaves is said to repel flies. The bark contains ~25% tannin and is used to tan leather.

Ornamental
Pitanga makes an attractive, ornamental tree suitable for smaller gardens, desirable for its aromatic leaves, delicate flowers and succulent fruit. It can be planted as a specimen tree or in a row to form a screening hedge.

SIMILAR SPECIES

Uvalha, *Eugenia uvalha* (meaning 'little grape'). This is a typical *Eugenia* species. It is a slow-growing, small, dense tree with narrow leaves and 'powder puff' creamy-white flowers. It needs a warm-temperate climate, and will then produce yellow, ~2.5-cm-diameter fruit, with a single small seed. The flesh is pleasant, juicy and slightly acid, but trees may take 10 years before they start to produce fruit. The tree is said to be slightly frost hardy. ■

Fagus spp.
Beech nut
FAGACEAE
American beech (*Fagus grandifolia*), European beech (*F. sylvatica*)

The common name for the beech tree may be derived from Teutonic dialects, and means either 'a book' or 'a beech', referring to the Runic tablets or early books that were made using this wood. *Fagus* is from a Greek word meaning 'to eat,' referring to the edible kernels. The word '*sylvatica*' translates as 'of forests'. They are a group of large, handsome trees that are widely grown through Britain and Europe, and their nuts have been used for food since prehistoric times. There are many *Fagus* species and cultivars; the two main species are described below.

GENERAL DESCRIPTION

Beautiful, grand, shade trees, with large, long, spreading or more vertical branches, which often form low down on the trunk and are then upswept. Trees can grow to 20–35 m tall, with a width of 12–18 m. Their foliage casts a dense shade beneath. They have long, tan-coloured, slender, pointed buds, which tend to lie in the same direction as the branches, and so give an overall, layered branching effect. The trunk is usually single, and has thin, unusually smooth bark, for the size of the tree. It is light–medium grey in colour and looks majestic in both winter and summer. Single trunks tend to lose their central-leader form and produce several upright powerful branches. Trees can live for >400 years, and have a slow–moderate growth rate. Once established, their dense shade and the compounds released from their leaf litter ensure that few other plants can live beneath the spread of their canopies.

Leaves: Deciduous, alternate, with toothed to nearly entire leaf margins, 5–10 cm long, usually medium–dark green (depending on position on the tree), shiny, but purple and variegated varieties exist. Young leaves are particularly attractive, and are thin, bright yellow-green, and are covered with a fine pubescence, which they lose as they mature. Fall colour is rust–golden–yellow–brown, or purple–brown for the purple-leaved varieties. Lower leaves and beech hedges often retain their leaves during winter.

Flowers: Monoecious. Borne in later spring, though partially obscured by the expanding leaves. *Pollination:* By wind. The male flowers consist of small, golden-brown tassels of stamens that tend to hang below the leaves. The female flowers are more erect, and consist of brown bracts, within which are 1–3 styles, and are less noticeable.

Fruit: Beech trees produce nuts. When female flowers are pollinated, they form egg-shaped green husks, surrounded by a spiny green-brown husk. The husk is 1.75–2.5 cm in diameter, and this partially opens when the kernels ripen in autumn. Within the husk are usually two triangular nuts (~1.5 cm long), though there may be 1–3.

Yield/harvest: Seedling trees do not start producing flowers and nuts for several years, though once they have started they then produce crops for many decades. Trees produce bumper crops of flowers and fruits once every few years, which are then sought after by people and wildlife alike. When nuts fall, they fall still within their husks, and need to be collected regularly as they soon deteriorate or are eaten by wildlife. They can be rolled underfoot to aid removal of the bur. In addition, the seedcoat also needs to be removed before eating the inner kernel. The nuts should be partly dried for storage to extend their life and quality.

Roots: Shallow roots, which become more prominent with age. Young trees benefit from an organic mulch to conserve moisture and add nutrients. Avoid mechanical cultivation.

CULTIVATION

Location: Can grow in full sun or semi-shade, and young trees are also tolerant of partial shade. Not tolerant of maritime exposure, and not very wind tolerant. Younger trees benefit from an organic mulch to suppress weed growth and conserve moisture.

Temperature: They like areas with cool summers, and cool but not very cold winters. They are frost tolerant, and grow best in medium-temperate climates.

Soil/water/nutrients: Trees need a deep, moist, well-drained, fertile soil, and do poorly in compacted soils with too much heat, drought or pollution. They grow best in slightly acidic soils, but are tolerant of neutral to alkaline

Food

Nuts are fiddly to remove from their shells and the kernels are fairly small, but roasting makes them easier to peel, after which they can be rubbed and sieved to remove any small hairs. After salting and drying, beech nuts can be eaten whole or ground into a flour and added to breads. The nuts have a good, sweet flavour. The kernel is more difficult to remove from American beech nuts. European beech nuts were used as a source of oil, especially in France, during the early 1800s, for cooking, as well as for oil lighting. It is said to be equivalent to olive oil in flavour. The nuts can be ground into a paste to extract the oil, which ages well if stored in dark, airtight jars somewhere cool. It can keep for up to 10 years, with oil more than 6 years of age considered to be the best, which is very unusual for oils as they usually do not keep well. Roasted beech nuts have been used as a substitute for coffee in Europe. The young leaf buds can be also eaten. At one time in Norway and Sweden, the sawdust from beechwood was boiled, baked and then mixed with flour and made into bread! **Warning:** As with other nuts, a few individuals have an unpleasant reaction to nuts, so try one or two first if you have not eaten them before.

Nutrition

The nuts contain ~20% protein, ~50% oil, of which 17–20% is a non-drying oil (similar to hazel), and ~20% carbohydrate.

Medicinal

Extracts from the kernels are stimulating and antiseptic, and have been used internally to expel phlegm in chronic bronchitis, or externally as a poultice on various skin diseases.

Other uses

The nuts are a very valuable food for wildlife. Beech wood is very hard and strong, although does not weather well. It has strong, even-grained wood that is used for furniture, flooring, carpenters' tools, panels, wooden bowls, turnery, parquet flooring.

Ornamental

A magnificent tree as a specimen and for shade, if you have the space. Can be planted to form a hedge, which can grow tall; they are useful because their leaves generally remain on the plant during winter. Especially attractive if one of the purple-leaved cultivars is used. Cultivars often have a weeping or columnar habit, or a cut-leaf character. Unpruned, these are large, beautiful trees.

pH soils. Trees are moderately drought tolerant once established. They are not tolerant of waterlogging. The deep roots are able to bring nutrients to the surface, and these species, more than many others, are able to circulate nutrients such as potassium through their leaf litter. Trees are not nutrient hungry, though young trees can benefit from occasional additions of a complete fertiliser until they are fully established.

Planting: Trees, particularly European beeches, are sensitive to being transplanted, and young trees benefit from regular moisture, mulching, etc. until established. Beeches form large trees, and should be spaced at ~12–14 m apart, though other faster-growing, shorter-lived species can be planted in between until the beech trees reach maturity.

Propagation: *Seed:* Germination is greater and quicker from larger nuts; however, almost the same results can be obtained by removing the seedcoat and planting the kernel. Stored seed can benefit from a period of warm stratification, followed by 2–3 months of cold treatment to break dormancy. Germination should occur in spring from autumn-sown seeds. *Grafting:* Cultivars are usually propagated by grafting onto seedling rootstocks by cleft-, whip- and side-whip-and-tongue grafts.

Pests and diseases: Have few disease or pest problems of significance.

SPECIES

American beech, *Fagus grandifolia*. Sharply and coarsely toothed leaves, 6–11 cm long, dark bluish-green above and light green below, with mature leaves being almost leathery in texture. It has small kernels. Tends to grow best on rich, well-drained soils and glacial soils. A further species, black beech, which is grown in Kentucky, has nuts that are black and about twice the size of the ordinary beech nuts. When these are oil- or dry-roasted they have a good flavour.

European beech, *Fagus sylvatica*. A native of Europe, Britain and the Middle East, its leaves have wavy margins, are minutely toothed, 5–10 cm long, glossy, dark green above and light green beneath. Branches tend to have an upright form. They have greater tolerance of soil compaction. Slow to establish, but then grow rapidly. ■

Feijoa sellowiana (syn. Acca sellowiana)
Feijoa (pineapple guava, guavasteen)
MYRTACEAE
Relatives: guavas, jaboticaba

The feijoa is the only representative of this genus. It is better known as *Feijoa sellowiana* than by its newer name, *Acca sellowiana*. A German explorer named Sellow 'discovered' this plant in 1819, hence its botanical name. It is a native of Brazil, Argentina, Paraguay and Uruguay, where it is common in the mountains as well as at the edges of forests. It is an attractive small tree with fluffy, bright red flowers and delicious fruit. Today's feijoa plant probably originates from a single collection of plants that were taken back to France with the early explorers; from there the plant material was spread around the world. The feijoa is probably more well known and liked in New Zealand than anywhere else. Three cultivars from Australia were originally introduced into New Zealand in about 1908. However, they remained little known for quite a while because of the variability in progeny produced from seedlings. Later on, selection for fruit quality and yield began, with vegetative propagation ensuring more predictable selected characteristics. They are now commonly grown in many areas of New Zealand, where the delicious fruits are widely enjoyed, with some fruits being exported to the USA, UK, Germany, Netherlands, France and Japan.

DESCRIPTION

A medium-vigorous tree, moderately compact; height 3–5 m, spread 2–5 m. The bark is pale grey and the branches are spreading, and are often white and finely pubescent when young. Can form a densely branched, twiggy tree if left to grow naturally, and may be single-stemmed, though are often multi-stemmed. Moderately long-lived.

Leaves: Evergreen, smooth, thick, leathery, opposite, short leaf stalks, bluntly elliptical, 2.5–6 cm long, 1.5–2.5 cm wide, soft olive green above, silvery beneath.

Flowers: Showy, fluffy red, ~2.5 cm across, borne singly or in small clusters. Typically Myrtaceae-like with many long, bright red stamens topped with yellow pollen. Each flower has 4–6 fleshy, small, white-tinged petals that are purple within. Flowers are borne in early summer. They are bisexual, so only need one plant to set fruit, though more than one plant can increase fruit-set and fruit quality. *Pollination:* Birds eating the petals may pollinate the flowers (particularly blackbirds), and bees may also aid pollination. If well pollinated, there should be 60–90% fruit-set, although hand pollination can give nearly 100% fruit-set.

Fruit: Irregular rounded–oval–pear-shaped, 5–9 cm long with a persistent calyx at their apex, therefore, these are classified as false berries. Skin is waxy, smooth to rough, dull blue-green to greyish-green and is not very edible. The fruit has a wonderful, distinctive aroma when it starts to mature and ripen. The flesh is juicy, succulent, granular with almost a pear-like consistency, yellowy or creamy-white. The flavour is sweet or sub-acid, distinctive and possibly suggestive of guava, or some say pineapple and strawberry. It contains ~20–40 small, edible, unnoticeable seeds. Fruit is borne on last season's growth. Fruits do not ripen until late autumn (or winter), and early winter frosts can be a danger.

Yield/harvest: Grafted trees produce ~6 kg of fruits when 3 years old, and ~18 kg of fruits on 5-year-old plants is common, with these yields increasing as the tree matures.

Yields can be good with a minimum of attention. Trees remain productive for at least 30–40 years, and can be rejuvenated by drastic pruning. Plants grown from seed can take 5 years or more before beginning to fruit; plants grown from grafts or cuttings should bear within 3 years. Fruits ripen 18–24 weeks after fruit-set. As the fruit matures, it changes colour subtly from green to greeny-yellow. Harvest fruit as they fall from the tree or, if still on the tree, just a light touch should dislodge them. If it does not, then it is best to leave them a little longer. Although they can be picked when still a little under-ripe and firm, and then allowed to ripen at room temperature, their depth and quality of flavour is not as good as that of tree-ripened fruits. Trees produce fruits over a period of weeks. *Storage*: Fruit can be stored in a fridge for 2–3 weeks. If left in the warmth, the fruit pulp rapidly turns brown and soft within a few days.

Roots: Has shallow roots, so trees benefit from a deep organic mulch to retain moisture and add nutrients. Avoid too much soil disturbance.

CULTIVATION
Feijoa trees are easy to grow and manage.

Location: Can be grown in full sun or part shade. Is wind tolerant, and can even be planted as a windbreak around more sensitive crops. Resistant to salty maritime conditions, though this can slow growth and reduce yields.

Temperature: They are quite cold hardy, though are best suited to warm temperate or subtropical climates. They can be grown in cooler temperate regions if they get extra protection during freezing temperatures. They can survive temperatures down to ~–10°C (hardier than tamarillos). Feijoas like cool winters and warm, long summers. In very hot, sunny areas, the fruit may split, deteriorate and their flavour may not be as good. Do need quite a long growing season for the fruits to ripen fully.

Chilling: Need >75 hours of chilling for good fruit

production. If there is less, this may increase the tree's susceptibility to frost damage in spring.

Soil/water/nutrients: Can grow in a wide variety of soils, though the best harvests come from trees grown in fertile, well-drained soils with a pH of 5.5–7.0. However, trees also grow surprisingly well in stony soils and also quite heavy clays. Although they can be quite drought resistant, regular moisture during fruit-set and fruit development ensures better quality, juicy fruits. Trees will tolerate heavy, wet soils, though not if they are waterlogged for extended periods. Fertiliser requirements are low, and trees need less nitrogen to avoid excessive vegetative growth. They are able to grow on relatively nutrient-poor soils. Potassium is probably the main nutrient needed (~10 g/m^2 per year). Trees also benefit from applications of compost and comfrey. Foliar applications of nutrients can be detrimental to trees. Mulching is beneficial for the shallow roots.

Pot culture: In colder regions, consider growing these trees in large containers. They are fairly slow growing, are very manageable and have evergreen, olive-like foliage, fluffy bright flowers and can produce fruits after only 3 years. With regular moisture and a good organic mulch they should do well, and can be given additional protection during very cold weather.

Planting: Space at ~1.5 m apart for a barrier hedge, or ~4–5 m apart for specimen trees.

Pruning: Fruit is borne on the tips of last year's growth and on short side stems. The bushier the plant, the sooner it will fruit. Pruning is not required to keep plants productive, but a light pruning after the fruits are harvested encourages new growth and increases yields the following year. Thinning of some of the many twiggy branches helps reduce disease, increases pollination and allows easier harvesting. Young, leggy plants can be trimmed to build a good framework and encourage the plant to start fruiting sooner. Older, established trees are better with a few larger branches removed each year; this encourages new canopy growth and flowering within the tree. Can also be pruned to form a hedge, and still continue to form flowers and fruits.

Propagation: *Seed:* Easy from seed, though progeny are variable. The tiny seeds can be more easily separated from the flesh by covering the pulp with warm water for 2–4 days and allowing it to partially ferment. The seeds can then be more easily removed from the pulp, then washed and dried before sowing. Seeds remain viable for a year or more if kept dry. Germination takes ~21 days. *Cuttings:* Semi-ripe cuttings (10–15 cm long), from side shoots, cut close to the base or with a heel of older wood, which is then trimmed off, in late summer. These should root within ~2 months with bottom heat and mist, or sooner if in moist sand in full sun. Hormone rooting powder can help. *Layering:* Ground-layering is successful and rooting occurs in ~6 months. Air-layering is also often successful, and these can fruit in their second year. *Grafting:* Whip-and-tongue-grafting, on their own rootstock, which should be the thickness of a pencil (~2 years old), gives a low percentage 'take', though grafted plants can bear in 2 years. Grafted plants also tend to sucker.

Pests and diseases: Remarkably pest and disease resistant. Occasional problems can be the guava moth, which burrows into fruits, also hard wax scale (*Ceroplastes sinensis*), with its associated sooty mould, greedy scale,

leaf-rolling caterpillars (*Tortrix* spp.), bagworm moth, bronze beetles and fruit flies, which can attack the ripe fruits.

CULTIVARS
'Andre': From Brazil. Fruit: medium–large, oblong–round, rough-surfaced, light green. Flesh: thick, few seeds, rich flavour, very aromatic. Self-fertile; bears heavily.

'Apollo': New Zealand cultivar. Large, oval fruit with smooth, thin, light green skin with blue-green surface bloom, subject to bruising and purpling. Very good flavour, good sugar–acid balance, excellent quality. Pulp well-developed, slightly gritty. Ripens mid to late-season. Tree upright and spreading, to ~2.5 m tall, vigorous and productive. Self-fertile, and will pollinate 'Gemini'.

'Besson': From Uruguay. Fruit: small–medium, oval, smooth,

uses

Food
Feijoas have pear–pineapple-tasting, aromatic, juicy flesh with a unique, but very good flavour. Fruits are delicious eaten fresh, or can be added to various desserts or salads, but can also be cooked in puddings, pies, etc, though do tend to go mushy when cooked. Fruits can also be preserved in syrup, crystallised or made into chutney, jam, jelly, conserves, relish or added to sauces. They make a tasty juice, and also make a refreshing, good-quality sparkling wine. Fruits oxidise and go brown once cut open, though this can be prevented by squeezing on lemon juice. The flower petals are spicy, sweet and tasty and, if picked without harming the stamens, their removal should not reduce fruit-set and formation. They can be added to salads.

Nutrition
Fruits have very good levels of vitamin C: ~50 mg/100 g of flesh, and high levels of iodine (1.6–4 mg/kg of fresh fruit). They also contain good levels of many other minerals: calcium, iron, manganese, magnesium, phosphates and potassium. They are also a good source of folic acid, with one fruit providing ~23% of an adult's daily needs, and lesser, but good amounts of B6, riboflavin, niacin and pantothenic acid. Have good levels of pectin.

Medicinal
The leaves, fruits (primarily seeds) and stems all have strong antibacterial properties, and the fruits have recently been shown to have powerful antioxidant properties.

Other uses
The wood is dense, hard and brittle.

Ornamental
The feijoa makes a reasonably attractive, evergreen specimen tree, and can be planted in smaller gardens to provide attractive flowers and abundant fruits. It can be planted to form a hedge, screen or windbreak, also espaliered, or trained as a small tree with one or more trunks. The flowers and fruits attract many birds.

reddish blush, thin-skinned. Flesh: medium-thick, smooth, juicy, numerous seeds, rich aromatic flavour.

'Gemini': New Zealand cultivar. Fruit: small–medium, irregular shape, with thin, smooth, dark green skin with a heavy bloom. Very good flavour and texture: sweet, with little acidity. Ripens in early autumn. Tree upright, spreading, to ~3 m tall. Moderately vigorous, high yielding, partially self-fertile, but cross pollination is recommended.

'Mammoth': New Zealand cultivar. Self-fertile, but can benefit from cross pollination. Fruits: large, oval, thick skin, somewhat wrinkled. Flesh: somewhat gritty, flavour very good. Tree: upright habit, to ~3 m, strong growing. Fruits mature earlier. Poor keeper.

'Unique': New Zealand cultivar. Self-fertile, productive. Smaller tree and good for small gardens, height ~2.5 m. Fruit: large, oval, smooth skinned, light green. Flesh: smooth, good flavour, early ripening. Vigorous, precocious; a regular, heavy bearer. Does well in colder areas. ■

Ficus carica

Fig

MORACEAE
Similar species: wild fig (*Ficus palmata*), giant Indian fig (*Ficus roxburghii*)
Relatives: rubber plant (*F. elastica*, *F. benjamina*), mulberry, breadfruit, jackfruit

The fig has been around for a long time; the *Ficus* species has been dated back to the beginning of the Cenozoic era (65 million years ago, following the last period of the dinosaurs). The fig is thought to be native, originally, to western Asia and was distributed by people throughout the Mediterranean area. Remnants of figs have been found in excavations of sites traced back to at least 5000 BC. The first known cultivation by humans has been dated back to ~3000 BC. Historically, Classical, Eastern and Biblical mythology are full of fig- and ficus-lore. The fig allegedly originated when and where a thunderbolt from Zeus struck the earth. The name 'fig' was used by the Ancient Greeks as slang for the female genitalia; to 'show [someone] the fig' was to make an obscene, disrespectful gesture. Buddha contemplated Buddhism while sitting beneath a fig tree. It was quite important to Adam and Eve in Eden. Mention of the fig occurs many times in the Bible, and symbolises peace, prosperity and fertility.

DESCRIPTION

Tropical, ornamental appearance. Height to ~16 m, but more usually to 3–10 m, spread: 8–15 m. The trunks of old trees sometimes form growths where branches have been shed. Its branches are twisting and wide spreading. The bark is smooth and grey. If injured, the tree exudes a white latex that can be irritating to human skin. It often grows as a multiple-stemmed tree, especially if subjected to frequent frost damage. It is a moderately fast, long-lived tree. There are thought to be >700 varieties of figs, and one of the reasons for its popularity as a fruit is its ability to be stored for extended periods.

Leaves: Deciduous, palmate, bright–deep green, single, alternate, deeply lobed into 3–7 lobes, up to 30 cm long, and large enough to cover up one's 'naughty' bits. Roughly hairy on the upper surface, often softly hairy beneath. They give a wonderful tropical effect.

Flowers: A very unusual plant in that the 'fruit' seems to form before the flowers and actually surrounds them. The flowers are tiny and are clustered within the green 'fruit', called a synconium, which is not actually a fruit. From outside, the synconium does not appear to contain any flowers. The true fruits are small drupelets that line the inner surface of the synconium, and form after the flowers. *Pollination:* There are four main types of fig, and only the common fig has flowers that are female but are also parthenocarpic, and can form fruits without pollination. In the other three types, a female fig wasp (*Blastophaga grossorum*) is needed for pollination. To get to the flowers, she has to pass through a small aperture in the synconium. There, she lays her eggs and, inadvertently, also pollinates the flowers; later the young wasps emerge out through the small 'eye'. The three types of fig that need pollination are the caprifig, which has male and female flowers, but is usually only grown as a male pollinator; the Smyrna fig, which needs cross pollination with caprifigs to develop normally, and the San Pedro fig, which is intermediate; its first crop does not need pollination (like the common fig), but its second crop does. This latter type can be useful in colder areas as it gives an earlier crop.

Fruit: Mature, ripe fruits are green/brown/purple with a fairly tough skin that is white within, and often splits when ripening to expose the pulp inside. Inside, are many small, edible seeds embedded within yellow/brown, soft flesh. The seeds are hollow, unless pollinated. Pollinated seeds give the characteristic nutty taste of dried figs. The first crop of the year of the common fig is known as the breba crop and ripens in spring–summer on fruit that formed in the previous autumn. They tend to be large and few in number. To encourage earlier development, remove the terminal bud of fruiting stems early in spring. Figs grown in regions with long summers often have a second crop: some cultivars are more likely to do so than others. The second crop is produced in late summer–autumn on new growth and is known as the main crop; it is often more prolific, and although the fruit are often smaller, they often taste better and sweeter than the breba crop. To enhance their development, new shoots can have their tips removed to leave 4–5 leaves in early summer (plants grown in containers generally do not need this). After harvesting the main crop, it is best to remove any late, not fully ripened fruit to help a good breba crop develop. Their removal also reduces the risk of fungal diseases infecting the fruit and stem.

Yield/harvest/storage: Figs begin to bear fruit after 3–5 years. Established fig trees should bear 180–360 fruits per year, to give 6–12 kg per tree (sometimes more). Trees remain productive for 15–20 years, after which, fruit production begins to decline, although trees can live much longer. The best figs come from fully tree-ripened fruits: figs picked when immature do not ripen properly off the tree. The harvesting season is fairly brief: ~3 weeks. Restricting the roots speeds up ripening, as does pruning to ensure the sun gets to the fruit. Folklore says to put a few drops of oil in the 'eye' of the synconium: this is supposed to 'seal' the fruit so that ethylene can build up inside. Harvest fruits gently to avoid bruising. Fresh figs do not keep well and can only be kept in a fridge for ~2–3 days. Many fig varieties are delicious when dried. They take 4–5 days to dry in the sun, and the longer and lower the heat, the better the taste. Dried figs can be stored for 6–8 months. Alternatively, if frozen whole, they can be kept for several months. The stalk may leak a latex fluid that can irritate the skin, so pickers may need to wear gloves.

Roots: The root systems can be wide, spreading, greedy and rather invasive, so do not plant too near houses, plumbing, etc. unless they are restricted in some way. They also form surface-feeding roots, so be careful with cultivation. Root restriction seems to increase fruit quality and the fruits ripen sooner. It also prevents them producing too much vegetative growth. Fine roots that spread out too far can be cut though without loss to the tree. Trees benefit from an organic mulch to retain moisture and add nutrients.

CULTIVATION

Location: Grow best and produce the best fruits in Mediterranean and dryer warm-temperate climates, and thrive where grapes do; however, with extra care, figs can grow in wetter, cooler areas. They do like full sun to ripen the fruit, although the trunk and branches are unusually sensitive to heat and sun damage, so these should be protected if particularly exposed. Can grow in coastal locations, but not too exposed. Trees become large, and can shade out anything growing beneath them.

Temperature: Mature, dormant trees can withstand temperatures down to –12°C, but plants in active growth may be damaged at –1°C, and the breba crop can be destroyed by spring frosts. However, plants killed to the ground will often resprout from their roots. Temperatures of >20°C ensure good sweet fruit, whereas fruit formation is stopped at temperatures of <16°C for a few days. 'Brown Turkey', 'Brunswick' and 'Celeste' cultivars are some of the best choices for colder areas. In cooler areas with <120 days between frosts, grow trees against a sun-facing wall to take advantage of the reflected heat, or grow figs as a multi-stemmed bush.

Chilling: Figs do need a short period of winter chill of 100–500 hours, so will not fruit or leaf well in tropical climates.

Soil/water/nutrients: Can be grown in a wide range of soils: light sand, rich loam, heavy clay or limestone, providing there is sufficient depth and drainage. A sandy soil, with lime, is good when the fruit are going to be dried. Soils should not be too acid: a pH of 6.0–7.8 is ideal. They are fairly tolerant of moderate salinity. Heavy clay soils can be good as they do not stimulate too much root growth. Figs can grow in fairly nutrient-poor soils, though sandy soil may attract nematode damage. Trees do not like waterlogged soils, particularly in winter. Too much rain during fruit development and ripening can cause the fruits to split and can decrease the number of breba figs that form. However, trees like adequate moisture, and a mulch can help retain moisture. In fact, figs can tolerate more moisture than many fruit species. If a tree is not getting enough water the leaves may turn yellow and drop, less fruit are formed, there is increased early fruit-drop and fruits may be dry. Drought stress also makes trees more susceptible to nematode damage. Fertiliser applications are usually only necessary for container-grown trees or if grown on low-nutrient sands. Too much fertiliser, especially nitrogen, produces lush growth at the expense of fruit production. As a general rule, fertilise fig trees if branches grew <30 cm the previous year. They like some lime and some potassium.

Pot culture: Figs are excellent for container growth; the restricted root growth makes them more manageable and also more fruitful. Their internodes (stem length between leaves) are shorter and this maximises fruit production for the size of the plant. The fruit also ripen sooner, and a restricted root system also means they do not produce too much vegetative growth. But they do need watering regularly. Replace most of the soil every 3 years, and keep the sides of the tub shaded to prevent overheating the roots. They can be espaliered in containers. Best to choose a slow-growing cultivar.

Planting: Because figs seem to produce better when their roots are constricted, plant them in holes that are constricted in some way, e.g. with rubble at the base. Will get less vegetative growth and more fruit. Space at 3–5 m apart, and train to a low, sprawling canopy. Young plants benefit from shading until they are well established. If you want to grow a full specimen tree, you will need to space plants at least 8 m apart. Never transplant or disturb a young tree while it is starting new growth in spring as this is likely to kill it.

Pruning: Figs can be severely pruned without ill effect down to about 3 m; unpruned, they can spread up to ~16 m. Figs can be pruned to an open centre, but trees are productive with or without heavy pruning, although allowing sunlight to reach the fruits will improve ripening. Pruning is more important during the initial years. Since the crop

Food

Figs can be eaten whole and raw, but are often peeled, so just the flesh is consumed. Processed figs are made into pies, pudding, cakes, jams, jellies and preserves. The whole fruits can be preserved in syrup or made into jam or marmalade, or added to various desserts, biscuits, cakes, pies, etc. They can be stewed with honey or stuffed with other fruits. They can be also used in savoury dishes such as pastas or with ham; they can be stuffed with a tasty creamy cheese and a dash of white wine. In Mediterranean countries, low-grade figs are converted into alcohol. An alcoholic extract from figs is used to flavour liqueurs and tobacco. For preserving, pick before they have fully ripened as the fruit will hold together better when cooked.

Nutrition

High in B vitamins. Figs are high in fibre: it has more dietary fibre per serving than any other common fruit. Most occurs as peptic fibre, which helps remove toxins from the system. They are high in sugar:~55%, and have the highest overall mineral content of all common fruits. They have very good levels of iron (1.2 mg/100 g flesh), calcium (144 mg/100 g flesh), phosphates (68 mg/100 g flesh), with the latter two minerals good for bone formation. They are also high in magnesium and manganese. In addition, they are high in polyphenols (1 g/100 g dried flesh: 1%), which are thought to reduce cancer risk. The seeds contain 30% oil, which contains the fatty acids oleic (19%), linoleic (33%), linolenic (33%), palmitic (5%). The oil can be used in culinary foods, but also as a lubricant. Low in vitamin C: 2 mg/100 g of flesh.

Medicinal

Extracts from figs have been shown to have some antibacterial activity and possible anti-tumour activity. The common fig has fairly high levels of a phytochemical called coumarin, which has been used to treat prostate and skin cancers. The figs are also well known for curing constipation. The latex from the stems has been applied to warts, skin ulcers and sores. In Latin America, a fruit juice is gargled to relieve a sore throat, and the fruits are used as a poultice on tumours and abnormal growths. A leaf tea has been used to treat diabetes and calcifications in the kidneys and liver. **Warning:** The latex from the unripe fruits and from the leaves and stems can be severely irritating to the skin, and may break down proteins within mucus membranes.

Other uses

In southern France, the leaves have been used as a source of perfume called 'fig-leaf absolute', a dark green, thick liquid with a woody–mossy odour, and is used to create woodland scents. The latex is collected from trees, dried and used to coagulate milk to make cheese and junket. It also contains a protein-digesting enzyme (ficin), which is used to tenderise meat, to render fat and to clarify beverages. The wood is weak and decays rapidly.

Ornamental

Can form a large, spreading attractive shade tree, eye-catching, and gives a restful feel to an area, but be aware of its invasive roots.

---

is borne on terminals of the previous year's wood, once the tree is established, avoid heavy winter pruning, which causes loss of the following year's crop. It is better to prune immediately after the main crop is harvested or, with late-ripening cultivars, summer-prune half the branches and prune the remainder the following summer. In colder areas, it is best to leave winter pruning until just before bud burst to reduce frost and rot damage. Some growers notch branches to induce lateral branching and increase yields. Keep 3–5 main scaffold branches on the tree and remove suckers. When pruning, cut branches back to a side shoot as the stumps are susceptible to rot infections. Figs can give good crops if they are fan-trained against a warm, sunny wall. These are pruned to stimulate plenty of young shoots, while allowing sunlight to reach the fruits and stems. In early spring, older or damaged wood is removed to leave an evenly spaced framework of branches and shoots. Pinch all new sideshoots back to 4–6 leaves during early summer to encourage new growth, which will then form next season's embryo breba crop.

Propagation: *Seed:* Can be raised from seed, even when extracted from commercial dried fruits. Remove any flesh from around the seeds before sowing in moist, warm compost. *Cuttings:* They grow well from cuttings. In spring, as the sap starts to rise, select 30-cm-long pieces of dormant wood that are less than 2.5 cm diameter, with 2-year-old wood at the base. Dip the base of the cutting in rooting hormone, seal the top cut from disease, and plant within 24 hours. Summer cuttings can also be done, but do best if they are defoliated and 'winterised' in a refrigerator for 2–3 weeks before inserting in compost. *Layering:* Ground- or air-layering can be done satisfactorily. *Grafting:* Figs are often grown on their own roots rather than a rootstock, though you can top-work trees by shield- or patch-budding, or cleft- or bark-grafting.

Pests and diseases: Rust on leaves can be problem, with copper sprays being the only main defence. Nematodes can cause root damage, particularly in sandy soils, form galls and stunt tree growth. You could plant trees in containers within a clay-based soil if you live in a sandy area. A heavy organic mulch should also deter them. Certain fruit beetles can enter the ripening fruits through their 'eye' and cause damage. These beetles also often breed in fallen citrus fruits, so clear these away near fig trees. Euryphid mites cause little damage but are carriers of mosaic virus. This virus can cause crop reduction, with symptoms of yellow spots on the leaves with light coloured veins. *Botrytis* can cause problems on terminal branches, but is usually self-controlling. Fig canker is a bacterium that enters through wounds or sunburnt areas, causing necrosis and loss of branches. A smut attacks fruits with larger open 'eyes'. Most ripe fruit losses are from *Fusarium* and *Aspergillus* rots, which are usually introduced by insects, and make the fruits burst open and produce a gooey exudate. Birds can cause a lot of damage to fruits; you may need to net the trees during fruit ripening.

CULTIVARS

The 'eye' of the fig is susceptible to water and pathogen entry, so it is desirable to have a closed or very small aperture. In addition, a long fruit stem allows the fruits to droop and prevents moisture entering through the eye and a green skin colour results in less bird damage. It can also be wise to pick a nematode-resistant rootstock in regions that have sandy soils. Many cultivars are available, and it is often best to pick one that grows well locally.

'Adriatic': Large, vigorous tree from central Italy. Fruit: small–medium, skin greenish. Flesh: strawberry coloured, distinctive flavour, very good quality. Light breba crop. Early into leaf so can be susceptible to late spring frosts. Pruning is beneficial.

'Black Mission' ('Beers Black', 'Franciscan', 'Mission'): From the Balearic Islands. Fruits are black-purple, elongated. Flesh: pinkish, fairly good taste. Easily dried. Brebas are prolific, fairly rich, followed by an early autumn crop. Tree is very large so plant at maximum spacing. Only prune young trees to establish them.

'Brown Turkey': Origin: Provence. Has early and late crops of good-sized, greenish-brown fruits with a basal purple blush. Few seeds. Flesh is pinkish–tan coloured, with a good, sweet flavour in warm summers. Can be pruned back hard. Light breba crop, large late summer crop. Well adapted to warm climates. Medium eye opening. Can be cold-damaged, though usually recovers well.

'Brunswick': Medium-sized fruits with purplish flesh; often have a hollow centre. Long season. Good quality. Does not need pollination. Fairly cold hardy.

'Celeste' ('Malta', 'Celestial'): One of the earliest figs, ready from mid summer onwards. Fruits are small (~2 cm long), violet-brown, covered in a heavy bloom, have a closed eye. Flesh is reddish-amber, is very sweet, almost seedless and is usually dried. A light or sometimes no breba crop. Small, productive, hardy. Does not require pollination. Main crop is heavy but of short duration, ripening in summer. Generally recovers from cold damage.

'Desert King' ('Charlie', 'King'): Fruit is large, skin is deep green, minutely spotted white; flesh is strawberry red, sweet, delicious fresh or dried. Tree is highly vigorous. Hardy; only crops once a year, in summer, but does not need pollination.

'Excel': Fruit is medium–large, yellowish-green skin. Flesh: light amber, very sweet, rich flavour, excellent all-purpose fig. Light breba crop. Tree vigorous.

'French Sugar': A small early crop, with a larger main crop. Ripe fruit are dark black-purple with purple stripes. Large fruits with light pink–amber flesh of good flavour.

'Purple Genoa' ('Black Genoa', 'Black Spanish'): Fruit: oblong, large; very dark purple with thick blue bloom. Flesh: yellowy, reddish at centre; juicy, sweet, rich flavour.

'Verte' ('Green Ischia'): Fruit: small, skin is greenish-yellow, flesh is rose-coloured. Excellent fresh or dried. Good breba crop. Small tree. Recommended for areas with shorter, cooler summers.

Above: *Ficus carica*, var. 'Brown Turkey'.

OTHER FIG SPECIES

Wild fig, *Ficus palmata*. A native of eastern Asia, from the Himalayan regions. A smaller tree, growing to ~9 m. It flowers through summer and fruits in autumn. It is similar to the common fig, *F. carica*, though the fruits are smaller and may need pollination by the fig wasp. Its cultivation, requirements and uses are similar to those of the common fig, but it may be somewhat less cold hardy and needs to be grown in warm, sheltered sites in colder areas. The fruits, ~2.5 cm wide, are said to be very sweet and tasty, and are often dried for later use. It has fairly good yields per tree.

Giant Indian fig, *Ficus roxburghii*. A native of eastern Asia, it is found growing in Burma, India and Malaysia. It does not need to be fertilised by the fig wasp. A medium-sized, handsome tree, ~10–15 m tall, it is characterised by deciduous, large, often heart-shaped leaves, and figs that are produced directly from the trunk and stems. The tree tends to form a short but stout trunk before developing several, smooth-barked main stems. It grows well in warm temperate to tropical climates. Its fruits are of reasonable quality and become very sweet, though lack any tanginess. They can be quite large, and turn purplish-red when ripe. Trees can give good yields in warmer regions. The figs have jelly-like, succulent flesh, though need to be fully ripe and remain hard and inedible until then. They sometimes do not ripen well in cooler climates. Trees grow best with regular moisture during their growing season, though can tolerate some drought once established. Trees are best planted in soils that are slightly acidic-neutral, are well drained and contain adequate organic matter. Can be grown in full sun or semi-shade. Its large leaves and cauliflorous fruits make this fig a good ornamental species and specimen tree. In India, the large leaves are sometimes used as plates during outside gatherings. ∎

Firmiana simplex
(*Sterculia simplex, Hibiscus simplex*)
Chinese parasol tree (Japanese varnish tree)
STERCULIACEAE
Relatives: cacao (chocolate), *Cola* spp.

A member of the chocolate bean and cola nut family, along with the flame tree and many other species that are mostly found in warmer climates. The Chinese parasol tree is native to eastern Asia and China, where it is a very popular ornamental specimen shade tree, with large leaves, pretty flowers and interestingly shaped pods of edible seeds. In China, the tree was often traditionally grown in the grounds of academic and artistic scholars.

DESCRIPTION

An unusual, attractive tree that grows to a height of ~15 m with a spread of ~10 m, and forms an upright- to oval-shaped crown. Naturally, it often forms a multi-stemmed tree, but can be pruned to a single stem. Its trunk and branches are thin, smooth, straight, and are coloured green with paler greenish-white stripes, but are easily damaged. The trunks of older trees turn grey-brown as they mature and often develop small shallow indentations. Buds are large, round and are covered in a reddish-brown fuzz. A quick growing, but short-lived tree, living only ~30 years, though this can be extended if it is grown in good soil and is pruned regularly to develop a good form.

Leaves: Deciduous, alternate, large, 15–30 cm long and wide, bright green, often shiny above and fuzzy beneath, 3–5 lobed (maple looking), with a long leaf stem. Has attractive yellow autumn colour.

Flowers: Large panicles (25–35 cm) of small, fragrant, lemon-yellow flowers, borne in upright, loose, open, terminal clusters in mid summer. Trees are monoecious and the flowers are bisexual, with trees being self-fertile, though more than one tree will probably give improved fruit-set. *Pollination:* By bees, butterflies and other insects, and also possibly by birds.

Fruit: Interesting green, turning greeny-brown when ripe. Papery pods, that split open into four petal-like sections (10–12.5 cm long), are often crinkly, irregularly oval in shape, and flattened. Inside are several rounded seeds, ~0.5 cm in diameter, that are a reddish-brown colour.

Harvest: The pods are harvested when ripe from late summer into autumn. The seed pods can be easily opened to access the edible seeds. Trees often have good yields.

Roots: Often grow close to the surface, especially in clay soil and especially near the trunk. Trees therefore need care with cultivation and benefit from an organic mulch to conserve moisture and provide additional nutrients.

CULTIVATION
Easy maintenance and under the right conditions can grow >2 m a year.

Location: Can grow in semi-shade or no shade, but needs protection from wind. It can be grown in sheltered maritime locations as it is quite tolerant of salty spray.

Temperature: Tender to strong frosts, but mature trees can survive down to ~–2°C. Some claim trees can survive snow. Give young trees extra protection. Best grown in warm temperate, subtropical or tropical climates.

Soil/water/nutrients: Grows best in well-drained loams though can grow in a wide range of soils, including sandy and clay soils, and can grow in fairly acidic or alkaline soils. Trees do need good drainage though, and their roots easily succumb to rot in wet soils. Likes regular moisture during hotter weather when young and becoming established, though can be somewhat drought tolerant once established. Is not very nutrient hungry, though benefits from an annual

uses

Food
The seed can be roasted, it has an oily texture and is fairly pleasant.

Medicinal
The seeds are said to reduce fevers, expel phlegm, act as an astringent, and can be used externally as a salve and to reduce swellings. A lotion made from the leaves has been used to treat carbuncles, haemorrhoids and sores.

Other uses
The ornamental pods can be used in flower arrangements. A fibre is obtained from the bark and is used to make cord and a coarse cloth. A hair wash can be made from the leaves and fibre. The wood is used to make furniture.

Ornamental
An excellent ornamental tree that gives a tropical appearance to the landscape and adds interest year round. Mature trees provide good shade, and hence their name.

addition of a balanced general fertiliser or similar at the beginning of the growing season.

Pot culture: Although fast growing, this tree can be pruned to grow in containers, and thus can be grown in colder regions and given extra protection during cold weather. Some gardeners even use this species as a bonsai and grow it indoors.

Planting: Space trees at 6–10 m apart. They are easy to transplant.

Pruning: Generally not needed, but for the best ornamental effect it should be grown with a single leader and pruned to develop a strong structure. Also prune out any narrow angled branches as these are more liable to break. Pruning to reduce damage to branches can prolong the life of the tree.

Propagation: *Seed:* Best sown when ripe and in warmth. Wash all pulp thoroughly from the seed. Stored seed, sown in spring, usually germinates within 2 months. Germination is good. Grow on for ~1 year before planting out.

Pests and diseases: Has few pest and disease problems. ∎

Flacourtia indica
Governor's plum (ramontchi, Madagascar plum, Batoko plum)
FLACOURTIACEAE

Other species: *Flacourtia sapida*, Coffee plum (*F. jangomas*)

Relatives: kei apple, dovyalis

A large shrub or small tree native to tropical Madagascar and South Asia. The fruits are popular locally and are often sold in markets. Although native to the tropics, it can withstand dry conditions and even a light frost. It has attractive evergreen, glossy leaves with many purple fruits.

DESCRIPTION
Very attractive plant. Bushy and spreading, height to ~15 m. Usually has sharp spines on the trunk and main branches, although some grafted varieties are thornless. The branches tend to arch and droop at their tips. Plants are fairly fast growing, often 1.5–2 m a year.

Leaves: Deep green, glossy, leathery, oblong–obovate, 2.5–5 cm long and are finely toothed. New growth is an attractive wine–bronze colour.

Flowers: White, small (~5 mm diameter), borne singly or in pairs from leaf axils. Generally produced during late spring or early summer. Mostly dioecious, so generally need more than one plant to get good fruit-set. A few cultivars are self-pollinating, and female trees planted on their own often bear some fruit, although these are often smaller. *Pollination:* By bees and insects.

Fruit: Round, 1.25–2.5 cm diameter, smooth, glossy, dark red-purple at maturity. Their flesh is deep orange–light brown, fleshy, acid–sweet, can be astringent if not fully ripe, slightly bitter. There are 4–10 small, flat, wrinkled seeds. Can produce lots of fruit. Similar in texture to a European plum, though is more accurately classified as a berry.

Yield/harvest/storage: Fruit takes 5–9 weeks to mature after fruit-set, and can be harvested from late summer. The fruits should be picked when fully coloured and ripe to achieve full sweetness; under-ripe fruits can be very astringent. The fruits of all these species keep well and can be easily dried for later use.

CULTIVATION
Location: Grows best in full sun, but will tolerate light shade. Can be grown in fairly sheltered maritime situations.

Temperature: Trees are suited to tropical, semi-tropical or warm temperate regions. They are not very cold hardy, though can tolerate temperatures down to ~–3°C without suffering much damage.

Soil/water: Is tolerant of a wide range of soil conditions, though grows best in deep, sandy soils, and likes moisture. Once established, they can be fairly drought tolerant.

Food
Many fruits are good eaten fresh when fully ripe, or can be used to make a high-quality jelly or jam. Some fruits can be sour, and may need to be cooked before eating. The flesh can turn brown in sunlight.

Medicinal
The pulverised bark, mixed with sesame oil, has been applied to rheumatic areas or can be used as a gargle. A root infusion is taken to treat pneumonia. The leaf juice has been given to reduce fevers, and to treat coughs, dysentery, diarrhoea and as a tonic. Recent research suggests that these species have leaves that have antibacterial properties.

Ornamental
Can be grown as an effective barrier hedge because of its spines. Plant a mix of female and male plants to increase fruit production. Can also be trained into a small tree.

uses

Pruning: Only needs a little pruning to keep it shapely.

Propagation: *Seeds:* Can be grown from seed, but you won't know the sex of the tree for several years. The seeds have a hard seedcoat, and germination is enhanced if the seed is scarified (scratched or cut) before sowing. *Cuttings:* Gives reliable progeny of known sex. Take cuttings from female trees or, ideally, from self-pollinating cultivars. Semi-ripe cuttings can be taken during summer, and inserted into well-drained, gritty compost. *Layering:* Air-layering can be practised successfully. *Suckers:* Occasional suckers can be dug up from around the plants, and established in pots before planting out.

Pests and diseases: Not many problems, though fruits may become infested with fruit flies.

OTHER SPECIES

Flacourtia sapida (syn. *F. remontchi, F. indica*). Grows naturally on low hillsides in India. The fruits are often eaten by locals.

Description: A tall, thorny, woody, spreading, deciduous tree or shrub. Height 4.5–7.5 m, has long thorns (4.5–5 cm) that can be often branched. The bark is light–dark brown. *Leaves:* Alternate, oblong, serrated, ~6 cm long, ~5 cm wide. They have a short leaf stalk, which, with the lower leaf surface, is downy. Young shoots are light red–bronze and attractive. *Flowers:* Dioecious. Male flowers are in clusters of 7–10. Individual male flowers are small (~0.4 cm in diameter), yellowish-green, with five sepals and many (100–150) stamens. Female flowers are small (~0.8 cm diameter), downy, green, with five sepals that form a cup shape around a central ovary with five pistils. *Fruit:* Almost spherical, 0.6–1.25 cm diameter, which turns red when fully mature. It has ~10 small seeds, ~0.2 cm long, embedded in the pulp. *Yield/harvest:* Full-grown trees in India can produce 7.5 kg of fruits in 4–5 pickings. Fruit are best picked when fully coloured and ripe.

Uses: *Food:* The fresh, ripe fruits are very sweet, tasty and good to eat. They can also be used in jams or dried and kept for long periods. *Nutrition:* 60% moisture. Very little acid, ~14% sugars. Has some pectin and fairly good levels of vitamin C (10.7 mg/100 g of flesh) and potassium. *Medicinal:* The fruits have been used to treat jaundice and an enlarged spleen. *Other uses:* The wood is hard and is used to make various agricultural implements.

Coffee plum (Chinese plum, Indian plum), *Flacourtia jangomas* (syn. *F. cataphracta*). A native of Asia, it forms a low-branched tropical tree growing to ~10–12 m tall. It grows best in warmer climates that are frost free, though can tolerate temperatures down to ~–3°C, but this is its lower limit. Grows best in full sun, in rich, well-drained soil. It has sharp spines on its trunk. *Leaves:* Long, pointed, thin and glossy. *Flowers:* Fragrant, dioecious. *Fruits:* Round, dark red–dark purple when ripe, with 6–12 small, hard seeds.

Uses: The flesh varies from acid to sweet, and can be eaten fresh or made into juice or marmalade. The fruits and leaves are used to treat diarrhoea. The dried leaves are used to treat bronchitis, and the roots are used to treat toothache. ∎

Flueggea virosa (syn. *Securinega virosa*)
Chinese water-berry (white-berry bush, witbessiebos, ragah, simple-leaf bushweed, snowberry, hepato)
EUPHORBIACEAE
Relatives: amla, manketti nut

A small tree that is native to many regions of Africa, being found from South Africa up to Zimbabwe. However, it has now naturalised in many diverse parts of the world including North America, Asia (especially Thailand, Indonesia) India, Australia, Madagascar, Japan, the Middle East and Polynesia. It can be found growing in grasslands as well as in deciduous forest, woodland margins, rocky outcrops, scrub, regenerating bush areas and even on termite mounds. Because of its adaptability, it has become a weed in some areas of the world, e.g. Florida. It is known by a wide range of different common names, depending on which country it is found growing in. Its small, white berries have been widely enjoyed by indigenous peoples, and its leaves have several interesting medicinal uses. This plant is now undergoing a revival of interest for its fruits and medicinal properties.

DESCRIPTION
Forms a multi-stemmed, bushy shrub or small tree, 2–4 m tall. Its branches are slender and supple. Lower branches often have a spine at their tips. Often has a weedy appearance.

Leaves: Evergreen or sometimes deciduous, elliptic–oval, ~5 cm long, ~3 cm wide, waxy and are dark green above, light greenish beneath. The apex is usually rounded. They have light-coloured veins.

Flowers: Abundant, small, inconspicuous, greenish-yellow in clusters from leaf axils. Mostly borne in spring. They are dioecious, so need more than one plant to set fruits. Male flowers tend to form in dense clusters, whereas female flowers are fewer and sparser. Male flowers also tend to be a little smaller, ~1.5 cm diameter (compared with 2 cm), are pleasantly fragrant and have numerous small stamens. *Pollination:* By bees and other insects.

Fruit: Small, ~0.4 cm diameter, rounded, waxy, ripening from green to white. They have an inner white, juicy flesh. The berries contain many, small (~0.2 cm long), yellowish-brown, edible seeds.

Yield/harvest/storage: Plants often have large crops of fruits. The fruits are best picked when fully ripe and are just turning soft. Fruits picked when under-ripe, or when over-ripe, do not have such good flavour, and leave a bitter aftertaste. The fruits only have a short harvesting period, and need to be promptly picked when ripe, as they soon drop and become spoilt. They ripen from summer till autumn, depending on location. They can only be stored for a short time, though can be dried for later use.

CULTIVATION

Location: Can grow on a range of sites from open grassland to woodlands, as well as on slopes with thin soils, and scrublands. Grows best in full sun. Is quite tolerant of salty conditions, and is moderately wind tolerant.

Temperature: Is usually found growing in tropical, semi-tropical and sometimes warmer temperate regions. It is frost sensitive.

Soil/water/nutrients: Grows best in well-drained loams, but also grows well in sandy, dry soils, and is quite drought tolerant once fully established. Does not tolerate waterlogging. Grows best in neutral to quite alkaline soils.

Planting: Space plants at 2–3 m apart, or at ~0.5 cm apart for a hedge.

Propagation: *Seed:* Fresh seed can be washed of pulp

Food
The fruits can be eaten fresh, including their seeds, and they are sweet, tasty and very juicy.

Medicinal
The leaves are used medicinally, both internally and externally. This plant is receiving increased interest for the ability of its leaves to treat malaria. The main active compound is bergenin, which also has an inhibitory effect on the growth of the parasite *Trypanosoma brucei* within the bloodstream. The leaves have been used traditionally to treat malaria, snake bites, diarrhoea, stomach disorders and pneumonia, and have been used as a poultice to treat itchiness and skin diseases.

Other uses
Its branches are used to make fish traps.

Ornamental
Although not a very attractive plant, it can grow in many locations, particularly difficult alkaline soils, and produces abundant crops of fruits as well. It is sometimes planted as a barrier hedge because of its spines on lower branches.

and sown in warm, moist, compost and should germinate well. Seedlings should be grown on in an alkaline-based compost. ■

Fortunella spp.
Kumquat (kinkan)
RUTACEAE
Fortunella crassifolia, F. hindsii, F. japonica, F. margarita
Hybrids: citrangequat, procimequat
Relatives: orange, lemon, lime

The kumquat was originally classified with citrus, and was then moved to its own genus, which was named after Robert Fortune, who introduced kumquats to Europe. They form attractive, evergreen shrubs or small trees, and are native to southern China: they were described in Chinese literature dating back to ~1200 AD. By the early 1700s, they were popularly grown and utilised for their ornamental qualities and for their edible fruits in Japan. However, they have only been grown in Europe and North America since the mid-19th century, originally, mainly as an ornamental garden species or as a pot plant for patios or greenhouses. They are now grown commercially in China and Japan, and in California and Florida, as well as other temperate and subtropical areas around the world, for both their ornamental qualities and their fruits. They can be grown at a much wider range of temperatures than most citrus: from ~36°C down to ~−10°C, being more cold tolerant, but also more heat tolerant than most citrus species. However, their appearance, physiology and their usage is similar to the citrus species. They are unusual in that their peel is edible and, in some species/cultivars, can be of better quality than the flesh.

DESCRIPTION

A slow-growing, compact, 2.5–4.5-m-tall shrub/small tree. The branches are light green, are thin and angled, with few if any thorns. All parts of the plant are aromatic.

Leaves: Citrus-like, evergreen, simple, alternate, lanceolate, 3–8.5 cm long, finely toothed from the apex to the middle, dark green and glossy above, lighter beneath, are aromatic when crushed. Have winged leaf stems.

Flowers: Sweetly fragrant, borne singly or in clusters (2–4), white, ~2.5–3.5 cm diameter. Flowers are monoecious and bisexual (i.e. usually both male and female). The flower has five small concave, pointed sepals that form a green calyx, and five white petals. There are numerous prominent stamens with bright yellow anthers. It has a superior ovary. Flowers are mostly borne from spring through summer. *Pollination:* The kumquat is pollinated by bees and other insects. They are self-fertile and have good fruit-set, so you only need a single tree to get fruit. In addition, depending on the species, many flowers are not pollinated, yet still go on to produce seedless fruits (parthenocarpy).

Fruit: Oval, oblong or round, 1.5–4 cm wide. The peel is golden-yellow to reddish-orange when fully ripe, with large, conspicuous oil glands; it is fleshy, thick, tightly clinging and edible, with the outer layer being spicy, and the inner layer is sweet. Pulp: scant, only a few segments (3–6), not very juicy, acid–sub-acid; few to no seeds; they are small, pointed, green-white. Fruits slowly ripen and are slow to change colour.

Yield/harvest/storage: Can produce very good crops of fruits, so much so that some thinning may be required to prevent biennial bearing and to even out yields. Are picked when fully ripe and have fully coloured, but are still firm. Because of their thick peel, they keep well and can be stored in a fridge for 2–3 weeks. Fruits ripen through late autumn–winter, and can be 'stored' on the tree for several weeks.

CULTIVATION

Are very easy to grow and need little maintenance. Cultivation needs are similar to that of citrus species.

Location: Grow best in full sun, but will grow in semi-shade, and will still produce fruits. Not very wind tolerant.

Temperature: Can grow in a much wider range of temperatures than many citrus species. They can grow in hot climates, up to ~36° C, but also down to ~–10°C without injury, which is considerably more cold hardy than citrus. However, kumquats grow best and produce larger, sweeter fruits with warm/hot growing seasons.

Chilling: Kumquats also vary from citrus in that they do need a period of winter chilling to initiate new shoots and flowers in spring, ~300–500 hours at ~6°C. If they don't get this, then few flowers are formed and growth is reduced.

Soil/water/nutrients: Kumquats grow best in well-drained, fertile loams, but can also grow in a range of soil types, including sandy soils or clay loams, although they do not grow as well. They dislike wet, poorly drained soils. They grow at a pH range of fairly acid to neutral (pH 5–6.5), and do not grow well in alkaline soils, where iron deficiency can cause chlorosis. Trees grow best with regular moisture, particularly when actively growing and producing fruit, though are more drought tolerant than citrus. A deeper, loose soil will promote a better root system and, with that, a greater ability to withstand drought. Nutritionally, trees need regular additions of a complete fertiliser containing, in particular, nitrogen, phosphorous, potassium, sulphur and calcium. Because they are evergreen and form fruit during the winter months, two or three applications of a citrus-type fertiliser throughout the year are beneficial.

Pot culture: Are an ideal pot plant, and can be grown indoors, if allowed enough natural light. They are small, easily managed, have attractive glossy foliage, pretty flowers and bright orange, edible fruits, all of which are scented. They grow better if regularly repotted, and are given regular moisture and nutrients. They are a popular pot plant in the USA: dwarf cultivars are usually selected.

Planting: Space plants at 2.5–3.5 m apart, or closer (~1.5 m) if planting as a hedge.

Propagation: *Seed:* Usually not grown from seed as they do not grow very well on their own roots. However, can sow seeds when fresh in well-drained compost. Grow on

Food
The fruits are often used decoratively on various dishes, or as a table decoration, and are often displayed in a cluster with several of their glossy, attractive leaves. The whole fruits of many cultivars can be eaten fresh, and have a mix of sweet, tangy, aromatic and spicy flavours. They can also be processed in many ways, and are best used when fully to almost over-ripe, when their flavours are fully developed. They can be preserved in sugar syrup, or they can be candied by soaking in hot water, with baking soda, overnight. The following day, they are halved and cooked briefly each day for 3 days in a heavy syrup, then dried and sugared. The fruits make an excellent marmalade. Or, fruits can be pickled by packing them in jars with water, vinegar and salt; the jars are then partially sealed for 4–5 days, the brine is then changed, and the jars are sealed and left to stand for 6–8 weeks. A kumquat sauce can be made by cooking chopped fruits with honey, orange juice, salt and butter. They can also be added to sweet and sour dishes. The Chinese are particularly fond of them.

Nutrition/medicinal
Have high levels of calcium and potassium, and good levels of vitamin C (~9–25 mg/100 g of flesh), with some vitamin A. They are not as nutritionally valuable as most citrus species. The leaves and twigs contain good levels of essential oils. The fruits have many of the health benefits of other citrus species (see orange uses) and its edible peel may also have many of the benefits of citrus peel, e.g. protection against skin cancer.

Ornamental
Ideal for smaller gardens or for growing in containers, with glossy attractive leaves, flowers and brightly coloured fruits that remain on the tree through winter. Plant near the house to appreciate their aroma.

seedlings for 2–3 years before planting out. *Cuttings:* Take semi-ripe cuttings in summer, and insert in well-drained compost to root. *Grafting:* This is the main method. In China and Japan they are grafted onto trifoliate orange (*Poncirus trifoliata*), probably the best rootstock for dwarfing trees. Sour orange and grapefruit are often used in warmer regions. Rough lemon is usually not used as it is too vigorous.

Pruning: Kumquats form a neat shape and need very little pruning, just the removal of any diseased or damaged wood. In general, because the tree is evergreen, much of its resources for flowering and fruiting are stored in the leaves; heavy pruning will remove these resources and can, consequently, reduce flowering and fruiting. However, they are often clipped for aesthetic reasons and can be pruned to form a neat hedge.

Pests and diseases: Can be susceptible to mealybugs and many of the other common citrus pests, such as citrus rust mites, several scale insects, whitefly, citrus blackfly, aphids and fruit flies. Possible diseases include greasy spot, the fungus *Diaporthe citri* affect stems, and various *Phytophthora* spp. can cause root rot. In addition, there are a number of viral diseases, which are often transmitted via grafting or pruning tools. However, kumquats are highly resistant to citrus canker.

THE SPECIES

Fortunella crassifolia, 'Meiwa' or 'Large Round Kumquat'. Tree: dwarfing, often thornless; leaves are very thick and rigid and partly folded lengthways, have many dark green oil glands. Fruit: rounded, ~3–4 cm diameter, very good quality and popular. The whole fruit can be eaten and enjoyed. Peel: orange-yellow, very thick, sweet–sub-acid. Flesh: ~7 segments, relatively sweet–sub-acid, often seedless. Often grown as an ornamental, and one cultivar in Japan has variegated fruits.

Fortunella hindsii, 'Hong Kong' (chin chü, shan chin kan, chin tou). A native of Hong Kong and neighbouring regions of China. Shrub: very thorny. Fruit: roundish,

1.5–2 cm diameter. Peel: orange–scarlet, thin. Flesh: 3–4 small segments, seeds are plump. The fruit are popularly picked from the wild in China. Elsewhere, they are usually grown as an ornamental pot plant.

Fortunella japonica (syn. Citrus maduremis), 'Marumi' or 'Round Kumquat'. Tree: to ~2.5–3 m tall, similar to 'Nagami', but is slightly thorny. Fruit: rounded, ~3–3.5 cm long. Peel: golden-yellow, smooth, large oil glands, thin, aromatic and spicy. Flesh: 4–7 segments, scant, acid, 1–3 seeds. Is tolerant of temperatures down to ~–5°C.

Fortunella margarita, 'Nagami'. Tree: ~4.5 m tall. Fruit: oblong; ~4–5 cm long. Peel: golden-yellow, smooth, large oil glands, thin, sweet and tasty. Flesh: 4–5 segments, with 2–5 seeds, somewhat acid. Can produce large crops of fruits. Tolerates temperatures down to –5 to –10°C.

HYBRIDS

Citrangequat. A hybrid between citrange and 'Nagami' kumquat, these are vigorous, erect small trees, growing to ~4 m, thorny or thornless, with mostly trifoliate leaves that are evergreen in warmer regions. It is highly cold-resistant (down to ~–15°C); needs some winter chilling, and has a deeper dormancy than most citrus, and so is good for areas with erratic spring weather. Fruits resemble the oval kumquat (~5 cm diameter), mostly very acid and relatively seedy. It is very juicy, and is valued for juice and marmalade. Fruit are best when fully ripe. Strongly resistant to citrus canker and very ornamental. The cultivars 'Snow Sweet' and 'Morton' are suitable for fresh eating. 'Sinton' is an oval kumquat and citrange hybrid that was first bred in Sinton, Texas. An attractive ornamental plant, with brightly coloured orange highly acidic fruit, its flesh is lemon-yellow with a few seeds. Fruits are harvested winter–spring.

Procimequat, *Citrus aurantifolia* x *Fortunella japonica* x *F. hindsii*. A cross between Eustic limequat and Hong Kong kumquat. A small, round fruit that grows in clusters on thorny branches with long, deep green leaves. The smooth, orange rind is soft and easy to peel. The flesh is dense and contains a few seeds. ∎

Fragaria x *Ananassa*
Strawberry
ROSACEAE

Similar species: alpine or woodland strawberry (*F. vesca*), musk strawberry (*F. moschata*), *Frageria grandiflora*

Relatives: blackberries, raspberries, *Potentilla* spp.

The strawberry plant is a cross between two species of American wild strawberry: a large-fruited species, *Fragaria chiloensis*, originally from Chile, and *F. virginiana*, originally from Virginia, USA. In the 17th century, a number of Chilean strawberry plants were dug up and shipped back to France by Amedée Frezier, a French army officer, who had been spying on the Spanish fortifications, as well as incidentally enjoying the wild strawberries he found growing in the area. Most died on the long journey back, but five plants did survive. These were then crossed with a North American variety, with the resulting progeny being large, juicy, tasty fruits, which, at that time, were called 'pineapple strawberries'. It is from these plants that all the common strawberries of today are descended. One of the main goals of modern, commercial, fruit production is the selection of firm, large fruits with long storage ability and, unfortunately, this has meant that many modern varieties of strawberries are large, but lack the intense taste of smaller, older varieties. For these reasons, and more, it is definitely a fruit that is much better when home grown, and can be grown in the smallest plot or even on a balcony.

DESCRIPTION

A short-lived (3–5 years), perennial, vigorous, stoloniferous herb, growing to ~10–20 cm height, 0.3–1 m spread.

Leaves: Trifoliate, on stalks which grow out from a central crown (a compacted stem, where many leaves are formed very close together); leaflets are oval–egg-shaped, deep green, with coarse serrations.

Flowers: White, 1–2 cm wide, bisexual, with ~30 stamens and ~300 pistils on a swollen, conical, yellowish receptacle. The first flowers to open are at the top and centre of the crown, and these produce the biggest fruits; flowers that open later produce smaller fruits. There are two main groups of strawberry cultivars, which are categorised according to the amount of light they need to induce flowering:

Short-day cultivars where flowers occur in spring. These plants are triggered to form flower buds in autumn as days get shorter, i.e. only 10 hours of daylight. They are usually planted in autumn and the flower buds remain dormant till the following spring. The fruits are then produced soon after: late spring–early summer. They only produce one crop a year, but if plants are healthy, they produce very good yields. Because they flower and fruit earlier, they are best grown in areas where there is a low risk of spring frosts.

Long-day and *everbearing strawberries*. These are of two types. (1) Those that need >12 hours of light a day before flower bud initiation. Therefore, these, produce fruits during summer and autumn; usually one crop in late spring and a further crop in early autumn. (2) Everbearers. These cultivars are insensitive to daylight length, so form flowers anytime as long as other factors, e.g. warmth, are optimum. However, because both these types produce fruits and runners at the same time, they also produce less of each compared with short-day cultivars. They also grow better in cooler temperatures: fruit production is poor during hot summers.

Pollination: By wind and insects. Strawberries are self-fertile. Bees are beneficial in transferring pollen in individual flowers.

Fruit: The true fruit of the strawberry is an achene, which is a small, dry seed loosely attached to the swollen ovary wall (receptacle). The flesh of the strawberry is, in fact, the ovary wall with many fruits/seeds on its surface. But, the greater the number of flowers that are pollinated and form seeds, the larger the ovary receptacle becomes. So good pollination, indirectly, leads to a larger 'fruit'. Areas of the receptacle where the flowers have not been pollinated do not swell (because no plant hormones have been produced to 'tell' the receptacle to expand in these areas), so leading to irregularly-shaped strawberries. Fruits form in spring (and sometimes autumn) depending on cultivar (see above). They can be produced within a few months of planting, and take from 3–6 weeks to mature after pollination, depending on temperature.

Yield/harvesting/storage: Depending on cultivar, can get ~200 g of strawberries per plant, particularly in the first year, but plants only produce for 3–5 years. Strawberries are ripe when fully red and are best picked with their calyx to prolong storage life. Unfortunately, they do not store well, and are very susceptible to fungal rots: maximum storage life is only 5–7 days at 1°C.

Roots: Are shallow, so plants need regular moisture, but not waterlogging. Shallow roots also mean that they are more susceptible to weed competition, and cultivation around the roots needs to be done carefully. Mulches are excellent for this plant.

CULTIVATION

Easy to grow, can be grown in pots, take up little space and fruit soon after planting. But often have problems with pests, diseases and everything else wanting to eat the fruits!

Location: Best planted in full sun.

Temperature: There are many cultivars, which have been developed to grow at a range of temperatures, but, in general, the following applies. *Flowers:* Short-day cultivars need short, cool days to form flowers. *Fruit:* Have better flavour when the days are sunny and the nights cool. Fruit grown in warm, humid weather have softer flesh and rot more easily. The best fruits develop at temperatures <22°C. Vegetative growth: In general, long, warm days are best for leaf and runner growth. *Frost:* Plants of many cultivars can be damaged or killed by winter temperatures below −10°C, so will need protection, particularly from late spring frosts.

Chilling: Strawberries need a short period of chilling to break dormancy (200–400 hours).

Soil/water/nutrients: Plants need moisture throughout the growing season, though less when fruiting. This can be provided by drip irrigation. Prefer a fertile soil and benefit from additional nutrients. Liquid seaweed, as well as micro-nutrients, applied round the roots every 2 weeks is appreci-ated and helps prevent many fungal diseases. Grow best in free-draining sandy to loamy soils at a pH range of 4.5–7: they grow well in fairly acid soils. Do not tolerate waterlog-ging, which increases the rate of disease, particularly root rots. Mulches, such as straw, coir, newspaper and pine needles, are excellent and retain moisture, reduce pests, diseases and weed growth. They may suffer deficiencies of all the major nutrients, though too much nitrogen encourages vegetative growth at the expense of fruit production.

Pot culture: Excellent for containers, as long as drainage and nutrient requirements are met. Ensure that good, fresh compost is used and that they receive regular moisture. Supplementary liquid feeding is beneficial. Plants grown in containers often come into fruit earlier than those in the ground. The choice of possible containers is vast: pots, hanging baskets, old shoes, barrels or planter boxes. Also, look out for tall, earthenware or ceramic strawberry planters with openings around the perimeter in which to place plants, resulting in a hanging garden of strawberries.

Planting: It is important to pick a cultivar suited to the climate, and plants are better grown on mounds (~15 cm high) to ensure good drainage, unless the soil is very free draining. They should be planted at ~20–35 cm apart, depending on cultivar size, in two staggered rows. Planting them too close increases the risk of disease, etc. When planting, ensure the crowns are not buried. Commercially, strawberry plants are often only grown as annuals; for the home garden one can simply replace plants as their yields decrease. Regular replacement also reduces disease. The time to plant will depend on cultivar. Short-day cultivars are best planted in autumn; everlasting and long-day cultivars can be planted in autumn or spring. In warmer areas, planting in winter should mean an early crop. In regions with colder winters, where the plants may be frost-damaged, it may be better to plant them out in spring. Mulching is very beneficial, but organic mulches can sometimes harbour slugs, etc. Alternatively, strawberries can be planted through black polythene, which also warms the soil quicker, though the polythene can 'burn' the fruit's surface. You may want to prune off all runners that develop during the first season so that all the energy is focused into fruit production. Strawberries are best not planted where Solanaceae species have been recently grown as these can harbour potential soil-borne diseases.

Propagation: *Runners:* Very easy and give reliable progeny. Runners form readily from the 'mother' plant during the summer months, particularly from short-day cultivars. Either allow the runner to naturally root around the mother plant and then snip off the connecting stem or, if growing through polythene, remove the plantlets and plant in a moist compost until they root. If runners are removed before the mother plant has flowered this can reduce the risk of viral and fungal disease.

Pests and diseases: Strawberries are very susceptible to many root diseases, such as *Fusarium* rot, *Phytophthora*, root weevils and *Verticillium* wilt. *Botrytis* or grey mould can be a real problem on fruit if the weather is damp as it ripens. Aphids can transmit viral diseases, so check for these. Leaf and plant hoppers can also transmit diseases. Leaf-roller caterpillars and mites can damage leaves. Other insect pests include the strawberry clipper and the tarnished plant bug. The fruits are particularly sought after by birds and also slugs. The removal of dead and old leaves reduces disease spread and the housing of pests. Replacing plants regularly and planting in new locations should also reduce pest build-up.

CULTIVARS

There are many cultivars available. The first buying decision is whether a short-day or an everlasting/long-day cultivar is required. Also, take into account the temperature range at your location and the fruit quality you seek: smaller, but tastier fruit vs. larger more watery fruits. Below are listed some examples of cultivars, but this is very limited and does not include many of the more interesting ones. Look out for local cultivars.

'Cambridge Favourite': Everbearing. Early variety. Good flavour, good autumn crop; can be grown in colder areas.
'Chandler': Medium-sized fruit, light red, firm flesh, good flavour. Good for containers and hanging baskets as well as garden culture.
'Earliglow': Summer bearing. Large, early, sweet, multi-purpose fruit. Plant is disease resistant, vigorous, productive.
'Fairfax': Summer bearing. An old-fashioned variety, lots of flavour.
'Ogallala': USA. Everbearing. Hardy, tangy wild-berry flavour, can grow in colder areas.
'Ozark Beauty': Everbearing. Hardy, very productive, popular in eastern USA.

Food
Delicious fresh, or as a dessert with a little sugar, balsamic vinegar and either cream, yoghurt or coconut cream. Good in preserves, juices, icecream, yoghurt dishes, tarts, as a coulis, or as a garnish on sweet and savoury dishes, etc. They can be cooked with other fruit, e.g. rhubarb, gooseberries, banana. A tea can be made from the leaves. Makes a good strawberry wine.

Nutrition/medicinal
Very high in vitamin C (55–90 mg vitamin C/100 g flesh), which is highest just after harvesting on a sunny day. Also good levels of manganese, potassium, some iron, vitamin A and calcium. Low in calories and high in fibre. Have fairly good levels of B6, folate and vitamin K. Are high in antioxidants and free-radical scavengers. They contain ellagic acid, which is being researched as an anti-cancer agent and also strengthens connective tissue; it may also inhibit the adsorption of HIV onto cells and also HIV-enzyme activity on DNA; helps blood clotting and reduces haemorrhages. They may also be effective in reducing the build-up of low-density lipoproteins: have been shown to have the 6th highest LDL inhibitory effect of all berries investigated. Are the third most effective in preventing oxidation in cells, and it is thought this may be due to their high anthocyanin content (which may actually increase with storage time). Strawberries are good for teeth and to treat mouth ulcers. The roots and leaves can be made into lotions and gargles. Tea made from the leaves was used by the indigenous tribes of America to cure diarrhoea.

Other uses
The flowers attract butterflies and bees. The plants seem to have an allelopathic (negative) effect on the growth of plants around them, including the germination of seeds and on nitrogen-fixing bacteria, so may not be good grown too near to leguminous crops.

uses

'Pajaro': From USA. Large fruit, firm textured, bright red colour, excellent flavour.

'Red Rich': Everbearing. Widely adaptable, somewhat tolerant of saline soils, productive.

'Sequoia': Summer bearing. Large, early-ripening good-quality fruits, popular with home gardeners.

'Shuksan': Summer bearing. Large fruit, excellent for freezing; plant tolerates wet soil better than most.

'Tioga': Summer bearing. Fruits early, but long season, good flavour, attractive, firm fruits.

'Tristar': Everbearing. Hardy, disease resistant, precocious. Fruit is medium-sized.

SIMILAR SPECIES

Alpine or woodland strawberry (fraise des bois), _Fragaria vesca, F. alpina_. Probably native to the alps in Europe, and was most likely the first strawberry to be cultivated. The alpine strawberry has lower yields than the common strawberry: there are fewer fruit and they are smaller, but are much tastier and are produced from early summer till late autumn. They are sometimes grown commercially for the luxury fruit market, and are also a popular ornamental plant in the UK and Europe. They grow very easily, and do not have as many pest and disease problems as the common strawberry. The flowers attract butterflies.

Cultivation: Can grow in full sun or part shade, often growing better in the latter. Forms a small, short-lived, 3–5-years, compact plant, sometimes without runners, less spreading than the common strawberry. Flowers are white; fruits can be cream or red. Can grow in part shade or full sun. Soil conditions same as for the common strawberry, though can also grow on heavier as well as more alkaline soils. Likes an organic-rich soil. Propagated easily by runners. Likes a mulch, particularly coniferous material.

Propagation: Plants only produce a few runners compared to common strawberry. Can be propagated by these (see above), but also can be grown from seed. Sow this in early spring in warmth. Can take ~4 weeks to germinate, and can be erratic. Slow growing at first, but then grow rapidly. Can also be propagated by dividing the crown.

Uses: As the common strawberry: are tastier, but smaller: ~1.5 cm diameter. Treat as a delicacy. Young leaves can be eaten in salads or cooked, or used as a tea substitute.

Fragaria grandiflora. A hybrid. The best cultivars have sweet, succulent ~3-cm-diameter fruit. Cultivation as for the common strawberry. Can be grown in semi-shade or full sun, though fruit production may be reduced. Is usually propagated from runners. Has delicious fruits, with uses as for common strawberries. Young leaves can be eaten raw.

Musk strawberry or hautbois, _Fragaria moschata_. A fast-growing, short-lived, small, spreading plant, native to central and eastern Europe and Scandinavia. Plants are less productive than commercial strawberries, but have tastier fruit. The flowers attract butterflies. Are semi-evergreen in warmer climates. Fruits are yellow or red, depending on cultivar. They can be grown in semi-shade or full sun. ∎

Fuchsia spp.
Fuchsia
ONAGRACEAE
Kotukutuku or tree fuchsia (_F. excorticata_), Peruvian berrybush (_F. corymbiflora_), _F. splendens_

Form a genus of ~100 species of plants that are native to the Southern Hemisphere. Fuchsias mostly occur in South America, with three species native to New Zealand. They are usually deciduous, but may keep their leaves year round in warmer climates. The species described here have attractive reddish stems and pinkish leaf veins. The fuchsias are known primarily, by most gardeners, for their attractive, bi-coloured, pendulous, waxy flowers that have long showy stamens. There are many ornamental, cultivated hybrids available, which vary from trailing to shrubby, to standard forms. Ornamentally, plants may be trained into standards, planted in hanging baskets, or can be grown up archways. Virtually all fuchsia species prefer to be grown in semi-shade and do not tolerate long, cold winters, although most species are moderately frost tolerant. A few fuchsia species also produce edible fruits, the size of which varies with species. In general, the more richly purple the fruit, the tastier they are. Some of the better fruiting species are described below.

GENERAL CULTIVATION
Pollination: By bees.

Soil/water: Plants prefer a fertile, organic-rich loam with regular moisture, and are not at all drought tolerant. They can grow in sandy and clay soils, but they must be well drained. Fuchsias prefer pH values of ~5.5–7.0. They benefit from additional leaf mould and bone meal, as well as additions of organic mulch to conserve moisture, add nutrients and help protect the roots from cold injury during winter.

Pot culture: Because these species are fairly frost tender, in cooler regions they can be easily grown in containers and then taken inside during cold winters. They grow best with organic-matter-rich compost, but need to be kept moist. They also need additional nutrients, particularly nitrogen and potassium, with the latter beneficial to flowering.

Propagation: *Seed:* Best sown when it is fresh, although it can be sown in spring, but germination may not be as good. Sow seeds on the surface of compost in the warmth: germination should take <6 weeks. Prick out seedlings and grow them on in pots until large enough to plant outside. *Cuttings:* Green, young internode cuttings (5–8 cm long) in spring. These should root easily and quickly. Grow on in pots for a year or so before planting out. Or semi-ripe internode cuttings can be taken in summer: this is also very quick and easy. *Suckers:* Plants have a tuberous root system, which produces suckers. These can be removed and potted up at any time during the growing season.

Pruning: Minimal, but pinching out the tips of main shoots in spring will encourage lateral branch formation, making it bushier and it will also form more flowers and fruits. Plants can be severely pruned back if they become too large or straggly, and some fuchsia species form good hedges. Remove any frost-damaged or diseased wood in spring.

Pests and diseases: Fairly resistant, with few problems. May succumb to root rot if grown in wet, cold soils.

FRUITING FUCHSIA SPECIES

Kotukutuku (tree fuchsia), *Fuchsia excorticata* (syn. *F. colensoi*).

A native of New Zealand, where it naturally grows in lowland woodland, particularly along streams and gullies. It is valued by the wildlife for its berries, and the Maori also used to eat them. Unfortunately, it is now less common due to deforestation, but particularly because of the introduced possum, who find the leaves very attractive to eat. However, it is making a slow comeback in the native bush and many people are also cultivating them.

Description: An attractive, medium-sized tree (~12 m tall) that is also the largest *Fuchsia* species. It has beautiful, orange-brown, peeling, papery bark, with yellow-brown, smooth bark beneath. Trunks can become substantial with age (~0.7–1 m in width), and take on a gnarled and twisted appearance. *Leaves:* Deciduous, dark green above, silvery-green beneath, thin (~8 cm long), oblong or lanceolate. *Flowers:* Green and purple when young (2–3 cm long), turning to red after they are pollinated. They are mostly borne in leaf axils, but can also occur directly on branches, and even on the trunk. They are one of the few flowers in the world to have distinctive bright blue pollen. They are borne from late winter–early summer. Flowers are either hermaphrodite or just female, but both types do not occur together on the same tree. The hermaphrodite flowers have blue pollen. It is, therefore, best to plant at least one of each flowering type. *Pollination:* By bees and insects. *Fruit:* Berries, shiny, maroon–purple-black, juicy and tasty, ~1 cm long, look like small plums, ripening in spring–late summer. Have several small seeds. Known as 'konini' to the New Zealand Maori.

Food

The berries are dark purple, juicy and have a sharp–sweet taste.

Medicinal

Very little research has been done on fuchsia's medicinal and nutritional properties, but in South America, the petals and juice from the berries have been used to treat skin ailments, small blisters and rashes.

uses

Cultivation: *Location:* Prefers semi-shade to full sun. Grows well in woodland conditions. Tolerates strong, but not salty winds. *Temperature:* Can survive brief frosts, and may be able to survive ~–10°C, but not long, cold winters. *Soil/water:* Needs regular watering during dry periods. Can grow in moist light or heavy soils, but not waterlogged. Prefers mid pH values. Very much benefits from an organic mulch, to retain moisture, protect roots from cold damage and add nutrients. *Propagation:* See notes above.

Uses: *Food:* The juicy fruits can be eaten fresh or can be added to sauces, pies, tarts, cakes, desserts, or can be dried. They have a sweet–sharp taste, and a unique flavour. The tree has sweet sap, which can be tapped, but it does not produce very much. *Other uses:* It has good-quality wood that is strong and durable, and has been used for ornamental work. The bright blue pollen was used by the Maori as a colouring for face decoration. *Ornamental:* An attractive tree for woodland margins and provides food (fruit, nectar, foliage) and a habitat for birds and insects. Will grow large under glass with a free root run.

Peruvian berrybush, *Fuchsia corymbiflora* (syn. *F. boliviana*).

Native from southern Peru to northern Argentina, high up in the Andes, this small tree or shrub has showy, scarlet flowers, followed by tasty, purple berries.

Description: Forms a small tree or bush, ~2–3 m height, 1–1.5 m spread, or a semi-climbing shrub which can be trained to a trellis. They have arching stems. *Leaves:* Large and hairy: ~8–15 cm long, ~10 cm width, oblong, opposite, deciduous, lanceolate, mid-green with pinkish veins. *Flower:* Very decorative, trumpet-shaped, ~8–12 cm long, crimson, borne in pendulous groups during spring–late summer. Flowers are hermaphroditic, so the plant may be self-fertile. *Fruit:* A delicious, small (~1.2 cm long, 1 cm wide), oval, purple berry. The fruits are cultivated and are sold locally in South American markets, where they are popular.

Cultivation: *Location:* They are best planted in full sun in cooler regions, but perhaps in semi-shade in hotter locations. They are not very wind tolerant. *Temperature:* They can survive some light frosts, but only of short duration. However, they are tenacious, and the roots and stems seem to survive in colder areas: younger stems may die back once the cold weather arrives, but then usually regrow when it gets warmer. Even if this new growth is hit by another cold period, stems will often still resprout again. *Pests and diseases:* Generally no problems.

Uses: *Food:* The juicy berries are delicious eaten fresh, and have a taste of ripe figs. Do not have the after-taste of some of the other fuchsia fruits.

Fuchsia splendens. A native of southern North America and Mexico. It forms a shrub ~2 m tall. *Fruit:* Berries are oval, ~4 cm long, ~1 cm wide. They are borne in late summer–early autumn.

Cultivation: *Location:* It can grow in heavy shade or in full sun, though the leaves become paler and somewhat bleached in full sun. *Temperature:* Tolerates short frosts, but

not long periods of cold. If plants are damaged by a frost, they have good powers of recuperation, and will resprout when warmer weather returns. Plants need protecting in colder areas, or need to be grown in a greenhouse. A deep mulch around the roots can help protect them from cold damage. *Soil/water/nutrients:* Prefers a fertile, well-drained loam, and a pH range of 5.5–7. Benefits from additional organic matter, and needs good drainage. *Propagation:* See main notes above. *Pests and diseases:* Generally have few problems, though are susceptible to whitefly.

Uses: *Food:* The juicy berries are delicious fresh, with an interesting lemony flavour and a peppery after-taste. They are recommended by many as one of the best fuchsia fruits. ∎

Garcinia livingstonei
Imbe
CLUSIACEAE (syn. Guttiferae)
Relatives: mangosteen

A native of eastern Africa, the imbe forms an interestingly-shaped tree and has numerous sweet–sub-acid, tasty bright orange fruits, which can be eaten fresh. It is only cultivated locally and is not widely known outside Africa, although deserves to be more widely grown as a garden fruit.

DESCRIPTION
A slow-growing shrub or small tree, reaching a height of ~3–6 m, and a spread of 2–5 m. The tree has a distinctive branching habit with most branches growing at right angles to the main stem, giving an attractive, interesting form. Is often multi-stemmed, each arching away from the main axis and producing several short, thick, side branches.

Leaves*:* Evergreen, oval, with rounded–pointed tips, tough, attractive, leathery, 10–15 cm long, 2.5–5 cm wide, and has a distinctive wide, central whitish midrib and veins.

Flowers: Greenish-yellow, in clusters from leaf axils along the branches, and are borne in late spring. They have a superior ovary. *Pollination:* By bees and insects. Trees are dioecious, so need more than one tree to set fruit. Isolated female trees sometimes produce a few fruit parthenocarpically (as do mangosteens), but they are usually rather small, so its better to have a male pollinator tree near by or, for smaller gardens, get a tree where a male branch has been grafted onto a female tree. The male flowers are showy and fragrant.

Fruit: A true berry, globose in shape, 2–3 cm in length, ~3–5 cm diameter, bright orange when fully ripe, and with a thin skin. They are borne in small clusters on older wood along the stems. Inside there is a thin layer of juicy–watery orange pulp surrounding 1–2 large seeds. The flesh has a sweet–sub-acid taste, somewhat like apricots. However, may also contain a sticky latex, which can be irritating. Fruits only take ~28 days to mature and ripen after fruit-set.

Yield/harvest/storage: Trees can give good yields. Seedling trees take 5–6 years to start producing fruits; grafted trees should start producing after ~3 years. Fruits are

harvested when fully coloured and ripe in mid–late summer. The fruits do not store well (only a few days), and are best eaten fresh or processed soon after harvesting.

CULTIVATION
Location: They have good salt tolerance and can be grown quite close to saline water. Trees are also quite wind tolerant, and so can be grown in fairly exposed maritime locations. Their leaves are quite tough. Trees are best grown in full sun, and will tolerate light shade, although heavy shade reduces fruit yields and quality.

Temperature: Trees are fairly cold hardy and mature trees can tolerate temperatures down to ~–4°C without serious damage. Can get some leaf damage at 0°C if the tree is not acclimatised. Young trees are more susceptible to freezing temperatures and need extra protection. Are more cold hardy than other members of this genus, such as mangosteen.

Soil/water/nutrients: Grow best in a fertile, well-drained soil, though can grow in sandy loams or fairly stony soils. They can grow in fairly acid to neutral soils of pH: 5.5–7; in alkaline soils, trees often develop micronutrient deficiency symptoms, such as iron chlorosis or zinc deficiency, which need remedying with applications of chelates. Established trees are quite drought tolerant, but moisture during fruit production gives better fruit development. Trees are reasonably nutrient hungry, and appreciate 2–3 annual applications of a balanced fertiliser, or the organic equivalent. Young trees can be given more frequent applications to speed up their slow growth.

Pot culture: Trees grow slowly and this makes them ideal for pot culture; in fact, many people grow imbe as a container plant in cooler regions, where they can then be taken inside or given extra protection during the winter months. They grow better with regular applications of a liquid feed. They make an interestingly shaped plant for a deck or patio, and should produce fruits.

Propagation: *Seed:* Easily from seed, but they are slow growing, and may be only ~30 cm tall after a year's growth. Wash pulp from the seed before planting, and sow when fresh, if possible. *Layering:* Air layering can be practised and is successful. *Grafting:* Superior cultivars can be grafted onto seedling rootstocks, which produce trees that fruit earlier, have more predictable fruiting qualities and the sex of the tree can be accurately predicted.

Pests and diseases: Few, although fruit flies can be a problem on ripening fruits in some areas.

CULTIVARS
Some cultivars have smaller seeds and tastier flesh, but these are not widely available. ■

Food
The fruit's flesh can be eaten fresh, or used in sauces, jelly, jam, milkshakes, icecream and added to various desserts. In Mozambique, the fruits are used to prepare a pleasant alcoholic drink.

Medicinal
Extracts from the leaves and flowers have antibiotic properties.

Ornamental
The trees are often grown ornamentally as landscaping specimens for their unusual shape.

Gaultheria spp.
Wintergreen, shallon, salal, snowberry, checkerberry
ERICACEAE
Creeping snowberry (*Gaultheria hispidula*), mountain checkberry (*G. ovatifolia*), wintergreen (*G. procumbens*), shallon (*G. shallon*), alpine wintergreen (*G. humifusa*)

Relatives: bilberry, blueberry, cranberry

As would be expected from members of the heather family, these plants are almost always found growing in colder regions in peaty, acid soils. In general, they are low, spreading plants that flower late in the season, and their fruits ripen in late autumn or winter. The *Gaultheria* are mostly native to northern America, but also China, northern India and Australasia. The species is not found in Europe, although it was introduced there in the 1700s as an ornamental. Several *Gaultheria* species are well known for their aromatic leaves, but also for their edible and tasty fruit, which although often grown in gardens are not cultivated commercially. The common names for these plants are numerous and often vary with different sources, so, if wishing to purchase a particular species, it is often better to refer to it by its Latin name.

GENERAL DESCRIPTION
All these species are very hardy, evergreen, low, creeping or spreading shrubs.

Leaves: Their low growth, with terminal tufts of small leaves, and their pungent, aromatic oils are all adaptations to cold, icy, windy weather. The leaves are often wonderfully aromatic, evergreen, small, oval and are usually dark green in colour. The leaves of many of these species can be easily damaged by sun scorch when they are wet or damp, so they are usually best sited in shady locations. Leaves that are scorched often die. Some species occur naturally as an understorey plant, other are pioneers of rock surfaces and mountain slopes.

Flowers: They have typical pretty, heather-like, urn-shaped flowers that are bee pollinated. The flowers may be single, but usually occur in groups to form small, graceful racemes. Because the warmth of spring is late where they naturally come from, most of these species flower later, i.e. late spring or summer, and the fruit do not ripen until autumn or even winter.

Fruit: Round berries, either red, black or white in colour, and ~1 cm in diameter. They have a sweet and unusual aromatic flavour, with some species having stronger tasting berries than others.

Roots: Most species have underground runners that often form suckers. They tend to be fairly shallowly rooted and benefit from an acidic organic mulch to retain moisture.

CULTIVATION
Location: They can be grown in shade or partial shade, as

uses

Food/medicinal

The berries are tasty and can be eaten fresh, though may be sour. They can also be added to jams or desserts, or can be dried. They are high in antioxidants.

Ornamental

Because of their small size they fit well into most gardens, and are excellent grown as a groundcover in shady locations, but they do prefer an acid soil.

long as there is air circulating within the area. (A few species can be grown in full sun.)

Temperature: Are tough, hardy species, native to harsh landscapes with cold temperatures. To get good fruit yields, plants will almost certainly require a long chilling period during winter. These species won't grow or fruit well in areas that have warm winters.

Soil/water/nutrients: Grow best in moist, acid, peaty soils, although can grow in soils up to ~pH 7, but won't grow in soils that are more alkaline. Do not like extended periods of waterlogging. Benefit from annual additions of a good mulch of acidic, organic matter, such as pine needles or peat. Growth can be improved by a modest application of a general fertiliser, but too much encourages excess leaf growth at the expense of fruiting.

Pot culture: These species could be grown in containers in regions where the soil is not suitable (e.g. not acidic enough) and the containers sited in a shaded location. These plants are easy to grow and control, but need regular moisture.

Propagation: *Seed:* Wash pulp from seeds and plant in a cool place in autumn. Stored seeds need a period of 2–3 months cold stratification before they will germinate. Seeds should be sown near the surface of a sandy compost in shade, in spring. Germination is usually good if kept warm (~20°C), and takes ~6 weeks. Do not over-water or may get damping-off. Grow on seedlings in pots with some protection for the first year or so. *Cuttings:* Semi-ripe cuttings, preferably with a heel, can be taken in summer and inserted in moist, gritty compost in a shady location. Can root in a month or so, but may not root till the following spring. Place them in a sandy medium, then move to a peaty soil once established. *Layering:* Stems can be pegged down in autumn: they take ~12 months to root. *Division:* Possible to divide plants in spring, but some species are slow to start active growth, e.g. shallon.

Pruning: Little if any needed; perhaps only to control spread if it is too great.

Pests and diseases: Generally trouble free.

SPECIES WITH EDIBLE FRUITS

There are many *Gaultheria* species with edible fruits and a few of these are listed below. The general description above applies to all these unless specifically mentioned.

Wintergreen (checkerberry, teaberry, partridge berry), *Gaultheria procumbens* (syn. *G. repens*). Forms a vigorous spreading plant ~0.2 m tall, with ~1+-m spread, in the right conditions. Native to eastern North America. The leaves are particularly aromatic and become tinged purple-bronze in late autumn–winter, with young spring leaves being red tinged, turning glossy, dark green in summer. White–pink flowers form in late summer and bright red fruits (~1 cm diameter) are produced in late autumn–early winter.

Cultivation: A very hardy species, tolerating temperatures to about –35°C. Unlike some *Gaultheria* species, once established it is reasonably drought tolerant. It can grow on poor acid soils. Can tolerate heavy shade, but will grow and fruit best in sunnier sites, though does not like hot summers. *Cultivar:* 'Dart's Red Giant' has particularly large berries.

Uses: *Food:* The berries may be best cooked, perhaps added to fruit pies or jam. They have a strong spicy 'antiseptic' flavour, which might not be to everyone's taste. They taste better after a frost, and the fruits can persist on the plant until spring if not eaten before by the wildlife. The very young leaves can be eaten fresh, though there are varying reports about their taste. The young leaves make a good-tasting tea, hence its name the 'teaberry'. *Other uses:* The well-know 'oil of wintergreen' can be distilled from this plant, and is used commercially to flavour various products, e.g. beer, confectionery, mouthwashes, etc. The oil contains very high levels of methyl salicylate (>95%), a similar compound to that in aspirins, and the oil, historically and also now commercially, is used externally to rub on aching joints and muscles, and to help with chest complaints. It has proven anti-inflammatory properties. It has been used to treat rheumatism, sciatica, muscle pain, neuralgia and catarrh. The leaves are picked at any time from spring to early autumn, and then dried for use in infusions or distilled to make oil. To improve the oil, the leaves should be soaked in warm water for ~12–24 hours before steam distillation. The oil can be used as an insect repellent. ***Warning:*** It is not advisable to ingest much, if any, of the oil. There are reports of it causing liver and kidney damage. In addition, because the oil is so powerful, some people may have a skin reaction. It is worth testing it first and, perhaps, diluting it with a blander oil before using it externally. *Ornamental:* A good groundcover plant for shady positions, though once established, its spread may need to be checked somewhat. Space plants at ~50 cm apart.

Alpine wintergreen, *Gaultheria humifusa*. A small *Gaultheria* species, height ~0.2 m, that is native to western North America. It flowers in late summer, and fruits in late autumn. A very hardy species. Can be grown in sunnier sites.

Uses: The fruits (~0.6 cm) can be eaten fresh or cooked, and are good in preserves. It has an aromatic, delicious taste with a wintergreen flavour. The leaves are more palatable than many *Gaultheria* species, and a few can be eaten fresh or can be lightly cooked. They also taste of wintergreen. A tea can be made from the leaves. *Ornamental:* Makes a good groundcover plant in sun or semi-shade.

Creeping snowberry, *Gaultheria hispidula*. A relatively fast-growing, delicate, creeping dwarf species that is native to northern North America and eastern Asia–Japan. It only grows to ~0.1-m height, spread ~1 m.

Description and cultivation: Can be grown in fairly wet soils. Young stems are covered in reddish hair and leaves are small (~0.4 cm long) and leathery, with small bristles beneath. The small (~0.2 cm), pink–white flowers usually occur singly on the plant in early summer. The white berries (~0.5–1 cm diameter) ripen in autumn, and can be eaten fresh or cooked, and are said to have a pleasantly acid and refreshing taste, with a delicate flavour and smell of wintergreen. They can be added to many desserts, pies, but also savoury dishes, and they make a delicious preserve. They are locally popular in regions where they naturally occur. The leaves can be eaten fresh, can be cooked, or can be made into a good-quality, tasty tea. It makes a good low-lying groundcover for shady, moister soils.

Miquel berry, *Gaultheria miquelima*. A native of Japan. It is evergreen, growing to 20–30 cm tall. Produces attractive white flowers in summer and its small white or pink berries ripen in autumn.

Mountain checkberry, *Gaultheria ovatifolia*. A small, sprawling plant, only ~0.2 m tall, but ~1 m spread. Does not like to be grown in open locations. Is very hardy, and seems to only grow well in colder regions. Flowers through the summer and the fruits (~0.6 cm) ripen in late autumn. Spicy and delicious, they can be eaten fresh or cooked. Makes a good groundcover plant in shady places.

Shallon (salal), *Gaultheria shallon*. A larger, vigorous species, height ~1.5–2 m, spread ~1.5–2 m, native to western North America, from southern Canada to California. Spreads by underground suckers. It has larger, evergreen, leathery leaves (~10 cm long, ~6 cm wide) and attractive, bristly red stems. Has pale pink–white flowers in early summer, and juicy, sour but tasty purple-black berries (~1 cm diameter) for a few weeks in late summer–autumn.

Cultivation: Very hardy, surviving temperatures down to ~–20°C. As well as growing on moist acid, humus, peaty soil, it can also grow on sandy soil. It prefers to grow in shade/semi-shade, though can grow in full sun. May be able to grow in drier locations and withstand some drought. *Propagation:* As for the general notes for *Gaultheria*, but, because it produces lots of suckers around the plant, it can also be propagated from these, which can be easily rooted in pots, and then grown on for a year or two before planting out.

Uses: *Food:* The fruits are good eaten fresh, and can also be used in preserves, added to a range of dishes (sweet and savoury), made into fruit drinks or dried for later use and used like raisins. A good-quality tea can be made from the leaves. *Other uses:* A purple dye can be obtained from the fruits. *Ornamental:* An easy-to-grow, popular ornamental *Gaultheria* species. Makes a good vigorous groundcover plant for shady locations, but can sometimes be invasive in smaller areas; however, it can be cut back to control its spread. Space young plants at ~1 m between plants. ■

Gaylussacia, *Vaccinium* and *Solanum* spp.
Huckleberries
ERICACEAE

Bear huckleberry (*Gaylussacia ursina*), black huckleberry (*G. baccata*), box huckleberry (*G. brachycera*), dangleberry or blue huckleberry (*G. frondosa*), dwarf huckleberry (*G. dumosa*)

Mountain huckleberry (*Vaccinium membranaceum*), cascade or blue huckleberry (*V. deliciosum*), hairy huckleberry (*V. hirsutum*), oval-leaved blueberry (*V. ovalifolium*), red huckleberry (*V. parvifolium*), dwarf red whortleberry (*V. scoparium*), evergreen huckleberry (*V. ovatum*)

SOLANACEAE

Garden huckleberry (*Solanum melanocerasum*), wonderberry (*Solanum* x *burbankii*)

Most people associate the name huckleberry with Mark Twain's character, Huckleberry Finn, and although the name is so familiar, not a lot of people have enjoyed its fruits. 'Huckleberry' is a corruption of 'hurtleberry', a name given to blueberries or bilberries. Huckleberries have become a general name for several species from two different genera, plus a couple from a separate family. There are more than 40 species of huckleberries within the USA and they are, in general, similar in appearance to blueberries, with their common names often interchanged. Several are members of the *Vaccinium* genus, along with blueberries, cranberries and bilberries, although huckleberries are in a different subfamily to these fruits, with the main difference being that their fruits are larger, are borne singly rather than in clusters, tend to have fewer (~10) but larger seeds, and their yields are often not as large. Other huckleberries are within the *Gaylussacia* genus, which includes shallon and the wintergreens. All huckleberry species are native to North America. The *Gaylussacia* species are only found in the east and southeast of North America, whereas western huckleberries belong to the *Vaccinium* genus. These fruits have been collected by the native peoples of North America for thousands of years, and later by European settlers. The fruits are of value to wildlife, and the flowers are a source of pollen and nectar for bees. Two very different huckleberry plants are included in this entry. Both members of the Solanaceae family, they are more closely related to tomatoes, Cape gooseberries and tamarillos.

GAYLUSSACIA SPECIES

Five main huckleberry species from the *Gaylussacia* genus are described below. They are all cold hardy. All grow best in moist, acid soils, and make good groundcover plants. They form a twiggy, densely-leaved, sprawling shrub, usually 0.5–1.5 m tall.

Leaves: Usually evergreen, dark green, small, oval–obovate, often thick, leathery and toothed, with numerous oil glands on their lower surface. Aromatic when crushed.

Flowers: Heather-like, urn-shaped, white or reddish, 0.5–1 cm diameter, five lobed, are borne late spring–early summer in racemes from the axils of lateral leaves. Each flower has 10 stamens and a single stigma. They have an inferior ovary. The flowers are bisexual, but may only be partially self-fertile, so you will get better fruit-set with more than one plant. *Pollination:* By bees. The flowers are popular for their nectar and pollen.

Fruits: Very dark blue, almost black drupes, when fully ripe, ~1 cm diameter, good quality and tasty, but are seedy, with a somewhat tougher skin. Their large hard seeds are one of the main reasons why they have not become more commercially popular. They have a shallow depression on their apex where the flower was attached. The fruits ripen in mid–late summer.

CULTIVATION

Often naturally found in moist woods or clearings. They can be grown in full sun, semi-shade or fairly dense shade. They are fairly cold hardy, tolerating frosts and temperatures down to ~–15°C, though not very cold winters.

uses

Food
The fruits can be eaten fresh or are also popularly used in pies, desserts, sauces, preserves, etc. They have a good flavour and are spicy and sweet. Are good eaten on their own when fresh, or added to other fruits, or they can be dried for later use.

Nutrition
The fruits have good levels of vitamin C.

Medicinal
An infusion of the leaves and bark has been used to treat dysentery and as a diuretic.

Ornamental
These shrubs can be used as larger groundcover plants in shady sites with acid soils.

Soil/water: They grow best on more acid soils and do not tolerate alkaline conditions. They grow well in moist, but well-drained sandy soils. Are moderately drought tolerant once established, though growth and fruit quality are better with regular moisture during the growing season. They are not tolerant of waterlogging. They are not very nutrient hungry, though do benefit from an annual addition of a complete acid-soil type fertiliser, with nitrogen as urea rather than as nitrate.

Propagation: *Seed:* Can be sown when fresh, and are over-wintered in cool conditions. Stored seed may need ~28 days of warm temperatures, followed by cold stratification for 2–3 months before sowing in peaty, well-drained compost in spring. *Cuttings:* Semi-ripe cuttings can be taken, with a heel, during summer and inserted in a sand and peat mix. *Division:* Plants can be divided in spring, and plantlets kept moist till established.

Pruning: Little needed, though can be cut hard back if they become straggly and plants then vigorously regrow.

Pests and diseases: Has few problems.

Bear huckleberry, *Gaylussacia ursina*. A native of southeastern North America, it forms a deciduous shrub growing to ~1.8 m. Flowers are borne in late spring–early summer and are bisexual, though may be partially self-infertile. The blackish fruits do not have very good flavour.

Black huckleberry, *Gaylussacia baccata*. A native of eastern USA, it forms a densely branched shrub ~1 m tall, ~1 m spread. Flowers are borne in early summer. It is probably the most popular huckleberry, and has good quality fruits. May be partially self-fertile.

Box huckleberry, *Gaylussacia brachycera*. A native of eastern North America, it forms a low, spreading, slow-growing shrub. A single plant of box huckleberry has been estimated to be 11,000 years old, surely the oldest organism alive on Earth, though the reliability of this estimation is unknown. It forms a dark green, densely-leaved shrub, ~0.5 m tall. It has pinkish, self-sterile flowers, so you need more than one plant to set fruits. It flowers in early summer and its fruits are light blue, ~1.2 cm diameter. The fruits are not highly regarded. Often does not set viable seed.

Dangleberry (blue huckleberry), *Gaylussacia frondosa*. This species grows along the North American coast. It forms a shrub 1–2 m tall. Has small, pinkish-green flowers. The fruits are large, purplish-blue, with a bloom. They are juicy, sweet, but spicy.

Dwarf huckleberry, *Gaylussacia dumosa*. A native of eastern North America, from Newfoundland down to Florida, this dwarf, suckering huckleberry is a low plant, ~0.3–0.5 m tall, with long clusters of white, bisexual, but probably only partially fertile flowers borne in early summer. Is best to plant more than one plant to get good fruit-set. Has good yields of small (~0.5 cm diameter) black, juicy, often tasty fruits. May be more tolerant of wetter soils than other *Gaylussacia* species.

VACCINIUM SPECIES

A genus that includes both fully cold hardy and tender plants that can be evergreen or deciduous. They are similar in many ways to *Gaylussacia*, being similar in appearance as far as the flowers and fruits are concerned. *Flowers:* Although flowers are bisexual, plants are not self-fertile, and need more than one plant to set fruits. They prefer an acid (pH 4.5–6), peaty moist soil to grow in. They can usually grow in full sun or semi-shade, though fruit better in full sun. They are usually not wind tolerant, and also do not like root disturbance, so are best not transplanted and should be planted out when they are still fairly small. They are fairly resistant to pests and diseases.

Propagation: Seed: Sow when fresh, if possible. Stored seed will benefit from a period of 2–3 months of cold stratification. Thoroughly wash all flesh from the seed before sowing shallowly in light shade, in a peat-sand compost. *Cuttings:* Semi-ripe cuttings can be taken, with a heel, in summer and inserted into gritty, acidic compost to root. But, rooting is slow and difficult. *Layering:* This can be done through the growing season. Layers take ~18 months to root. *Division:* Plants can be divided in spring or early autumn; this gives a good rate of success.

A few of the huckleberries are described below. It is likely that these fruits have similar health benefits as other members of this genus, and are high in antioxidants and vitamin C.

Cascade or blue huckleberry, *Vaccinium deliciosum*. A native of western North America, from northern California up to British Columbia. It forms a deciduous, small, ~0.5-m-tall shrub. It naturally grows at elevation in sub-alpine coniferous forests and alpine meadows. It may not grow very well in coastal locations or where temperatures fluctuate considerably, as this may make it more susceptible to cold damage. Its berries are bright blue when ripe and large, ~1 cm in diameter. Although rhizomatous, it is has a dense root system and transplants easily (unlike most other similar spp.). It will grow on wetter soils than many other huckleberries. As its name implies, the fruits are very flavourful and aromatic. Despite the size and quality of its fruits, it is not widely grown and, in the wild, is often ousted by other more dominant species. This species deserves to be more widely grown and recognised for its ease of cultivation and good-quality fruits.

Dwarf red whortleberry (small-leaved huckleberry, grouseberry, red alpine blueberry), *Vaccinium scoparium*. It is a native of western USA from California up to British Columbia, with smaller populations in the more central regions of North America. It forms a small, prostrate shrub, only growing ~10–40 cm tall. In the wild, it is found growing in alpine and sub-alpine meadows at high elevations. It is very cold hardy and can grow in regions with short summers. The plants form many rhizomatous roots, which produce shoots along their length to form a widely spreading plant. Fruits are bright red, small (~0.5 cm diameter), fairly acid, soft, tart, and have a fairly good flavour. Individual bushes, however, have low yields. They can be dried for later use, and are often used in jams and preserves.

Evergreen huckleberry (shot huckleberry, blackwinter huckleberry, California huckleberry), *Vaccinium ovatum*. A native of western North America, its fruits have been popular with the indigenous peoples because of their late harvest and ability to be dried. It is in a different subfamily (*Pyxothamnus*) to most *Vaccinium* huckleberries, but is very similar. It is grown commercially, to a limited extent, for its fruits, but also for its stems and leaves, which are popular in floral arrangements.

Description: It forms a vigorous evergreen shrub, 0.3–3 m tall, depending on soil, climate, etc. Its stems are often slightly hairy, and it has attractive, shiny, serrated, dark green, leathery leaves, 2–5 cm long. Leaves are larger and deeper green if grown in semi-shade. Young leaves are often reddish-bronze. The flowers are pink, urn-shaped, in clusters of 3–10. Its fruits are dark purple when ripe, ~0.7 cm diameter, are borne in small bunches, and ripen from autumn to early winter. They can then persist on plants for >4 weeks. Its roots are easily damaged during planting out or transplanting.

Cultivation: It is fairly cold hardy, tolerating temperatures of ~–15°C. It can grow in full sun, but also grows well in shade. It is drought tolerant once established. It is one of the few species within this genus that is happy growing in fairly exposed maritime locations. *Propagation:* As the general notes, but it can be difficult as germination rates can be poor and seedlings are slow growing. In addition, cuttings often do not root well. Plants from layers or division may give better results.

Uses: *Food:* The fruits are sub-acid, sweet and tasty, and become sweeter after frosts, though can be somewhat dry. Often used in preserves, pies, etc. The cultivar 'Thunderbird' produces good crops of fruits. *Medicinal:* A tea can be made from the leaves and dried fruit. The leaves have been used as an antiseptic, an astringent and a heart tonic. They are also said to help regulate blood-sugar levels and have been used to treat diabetes. *Ornamental:* Popular landscaping plant, with several ornamental cultivars.

Hairy huckleberry, *Vaccinium hirsutum*. A native of southeast North America, it forms a deciduous shrub. It is fairly cold hardy, tolerating temperatures down to ~–10°C. It flowers from late spring to early summer. The flowers are bisexual, are popular with bees and insects, but are not self-fertile, so need more than one plant to set fruits.

Uses: The fruits are small, ~0.6 cm diameter, and are generally fairly sweet and pleasant, though occasionally can be gritty without much taste.

Mountain huckleberry (black huckleberry, blue huckleberry, velvet-leaf huckleberry, thin-leaved huckleberry, globe huckleberry), *Vaccinium membranaceum* (syn. *V. globulare*). The mountain huckleberry is mostly native to the northwest states of the USA and into British Columbia, and is often found growing in thickets and woodland edges. It is the state fruit of Idaho. It is one of the more important huckleberries, and its fruits have long been used by the indigenous peoples. The berries were often dried, and were an important food during winters, and were also used as a trading commodity. It is now sometimes grown commercially for its fruits, more so than other huckleberries, and the fruits are also gathered from the wild. It forms a deciduous shrub, 0.3–1.5 m tall, depending on site conditions and climate. Its flowers are borne in spring, and can be susceptible to late spring frosts. Its roots are sparse, and it does not transplant well; they should not be disturbed when planting out. Plants benefit from an acidic, organic mulch, which helps retain moisture and adds nutrients.

Cultivation: It can grow in full sun or partial shade, though fruits better in full sun. It is a fully cold hardy plant, tolerating temperatures down to ~–40°C, and can grow in regions with a short growing season. It is happier growing at higher altitudes, where it can reliably acclimatise to cold. It is not wind tolerant. Shrubs grow best in acid (pH 4.5–6), well-drained soils that are rich in organic matter. Once established, they are very drought tolerant. Has few pest and disease problems. *Propagation:* As above.

Uses: *Food:* The fruits, ~0.5 cm diameter, ripen to dark purple or are sometimes dark red, occasionally white. They are very flavourful, sub-acid, but also sweet. They have good levels of vitamin C. *Medicinal:* The fruits can be used as an antiseptic, an astringent, a heart tonic and have been used to treat heart troubles, arthritis and rheumatism. *Ornamental:* It makes a good reclamation and groundcover plant.

Oval-leaved blueberry (Alaska blueberry, oval-leaved bilberry), *Vaccinium ovalifolium* (syn. *V. alaskaense*).
A native of western North America, from California to Alaska. These plants can also be found in Russia. They form vigorous, upright shrubs that can grow 0.6–2.5 m tall, depending on climate, soil, etc. They are very cold hardy and often grow at elevation. They have a compact root system, and can be transplanted easily (cf. with most other species). It has ~0.5-cm-diameter fruits that are an attractive blue colour when ripe. It readily hybridises with *V. deliciosum* and *V. membranaceum*, and then may produce plants with better fruit quality, but with the vigour and shape of this species.

Red huckleberry (red bilberry), *Vaccinium parvifolium*.
A native of western USA, from California up to British Columbia. It forms a vigorous shrub, ~3 m tall, depending on conditions. They are fully cold hardy and can grow at elevation. Can be grown in full sun or semi-shade. It makes a

good reclamation plant and will grow in many situations.

Uses: It has red, waxy fruits that are sour, but tasty. They are popularly used in jams and preserves, and were also popular with the indigenous peoples.

SOLANACEAE SPECIES

Below are listed another two plants that are also commonly called huckleberries, but are actually quite different, and are from a completely different family, the Solanaceae. The fruits of these particular species are good to eat, *but*, the plants and fruits do look similar to deadly or woody nightshades, both of which produce highly poisonous fruits. So, take extra care in the identification of these.

Garden huckleberry (sunberry), *Solanum melanocerasum* (syn. *S. nigrum guineense*). It forms a small shrub, growing 30–60 cm tall. They are very easy to grow and need very little maintenance. They can grow in a range of soils, though prefer a neutral pH, moist, loamy soil. They can be easily grown from seed and make a good annual plant as they produce fruits soon after germination (8–12 weeks). They flower in summer, and fruit in autumn. The plants are attractive to slugs and caterpillars. Their growth and cultivation is similar to that of tomatoes. They can be easily grown in pots. There are a number of cultivars. The fruits are small, dark blue, vary in flavour from sharp to sweet, and look similar to those of the nightshade species. The ripe fruits can be used in desserts, or cooked and used as a flavouring. The unripe (green) fruits are poisonous in the same way that green tomatoes are.

Wonderberry, *Solanum x burbankii*. An artificial cross between *Solanum villosum* and *S. guineense,* produced by Luther Burbank. It forms a small shrub, growing ~30–60 cm tall, and can begin fruiting when only ~10 cm tall. The plant is similar to garden huckleberry, but its fruits have a much better, sweeter flavour. It is very easy to grow, similar to tomato, but can grow in poorer soils, cooler temperatures, needs less regular watering and fruits sooner (in autumn). Can also be grown in full sun or semi-shade. Sow seeds early in spring, with warmth. Plants need little attention to flower and fruit. They flower in summer. They can be easily grown in pots. Fruits are small, ~1 cm diameter, dark purple and are similar in appearance to those of the nightshade species. The ripe fruits are usually cooked with sugar, and are often added to pies and desserts. The unripe (green) fruits are poisonous like those of unripe tomatoes. ■

Geoffroea decorticans
Chilean palo verde (chanar)
FABACEAE

A thorny shrub or small tree that is very tolerant of arid conditions and is found growing wild in central Argentina, Chile, Bolivia, Peru and Paraguay.

DESCRIPTION

A spreading, small tree or shrub that is armed with many sharp thorns, it can grow to 4–8 m in height. It has an open, irregular form and is often multi-stemmed. The bark is brown and smooth and tends to flake and peel off to form attractive patterns and display the green, young bark beneath. It is a fairly fast-growing tree.

Leaves: Pinnate, in 2–5 pairs of small leaflets, 1–4 cm long, with a larger terminal leaflet. The leaflets are leathery, sparse, grey-green, adapted to withstand dry conditions. The tree is semi-evergreen or deciduous, tending to lose its leaves in cold weather or during extended droughts.

Flowers: Small, orange–yellow, papery and are borne singly or in small clusters from leaf axils in early spring.

Fruit: Fleshy, oval pods, 2–3 cm long, which turn from green to browny-yellow as they ripen. An unusual legume in that it only produces a single seed inside the 'pod'.

Harvest: The pods are harvested when they have turned brown and are ripe in summer.

Roots: Plants tend to sucker and can form a thorny thicket if growing in good conditions. Form a symbiotic relationship with bacteria that fix nitrogen.

CULTIVATION

Needs very little maintenance.

Temperature: Can tolerate hot locations and grows best in full sun. It is also moderately cold tolerant, and can be grown in temperate regions where winter temperatures descend to ~–15°C.

Soil/water/nutrients: Once established, these trees are very drought tolerant, though grow and fruit better if given a good soaking every now and then. Can grow in poor-nutrient soils and need very little, if any, extra fertiliser.

Propagation: *Seeds:* Grows quite well from seed. *Suckers:* Any suckers can be easily dug up and establish readily. Similarly, root cuttings will also readily form stems. ■

Food
Both the seeds and pods can be eaten. They are fragrant and have a sweet, pleasant taste. An alcoholic drink is sometimes prepared from the seeds.

Medicinal
The oil from the seeds is of good quality, being similar to peanut oil in taste. It has very good levels of unsaturated oils, particularly oleic (~50%), and is being researched for its commercial potential. The seeds also contain 21% protein. The bark, leaves and flowers have been widely used traditionally to treat asthma, and extracts have been used to soften the skin.

Other uses
Its yellow wood is of good quality and is used to make furniture.

Ornamental
A good tree for arid soils and re-establishing areas. Makes a good barrier hedge.

uses

Gevuina avellana
Gevuina (Chilean hazel, Chile nut, avellana)
PROTEACEAE
Relatives: macadamia

The gevuina is native to Chile, where it naturally grows in temperate oceanic, cool, wet areas, with this species being the most cold hardy of the genus. Its nuts have been used by the native Mapuche people for hundreds or thousands of years, as a food for themselves as well as for their livestock. To them, the kernel is known as the 'avellana' and the plant as 'guevín'. Its kernels are roasted and sold in markets. It is not, however, grown commercially on a large scale. It is an attractive, ornamental plant with striking, evergreen foliage, and produces undervalued, tasty, high-quality nuts. The gevuina is presently being explored for its commercial possibilities within New Zealand. It was first introduced there in the 1950s, and efforts by Dr Stephan Halloy and the New Zealand Tree Crops Association have been, and still are, promoting research and development of this plant, although the tree does pose various cultivation problems. It is hoped that New Zealand will be the first country in the world to establish a market for this nut. They are now grown in the rolling hill country of the South Island, which have quite cold winters, but the summers are hot.

Food

The gevuina nut has a delicious, sweet taste and can be eaten raw or roasted. The nuts are rich in oils and can be processed into a gevuina paste like peanut butter. To roast the nuts, place kernels in a shallow pan in an oven at 120°C for ~6–7 minutes, then turn them and give them a further 7 minutes. Best to give less time rather than more, removing nuts if they start to brown. They can be dry roasted or can be sprinkled with olive oil. The nuts can also be added to any dish that uses nuts, but are best if their flavour can be clearly appreciated. Roasted nuts can be eaten as they are, or they can be salted, are excellent coated in dark chocolate, or can be honey roasted or roasted with chilli. Nuts can be stored in airtight jars in the cool and dark, or they can be frozen. The extracted oil is said to be similar to olive oil. The roasted kernels can be used as a coffee substitute.

Nutrition

They are high in monounsaturated fatty acids (~45%), which means they are great for people with elevated low-density-lipids. The kernels are highly nutritious. They also contain good levels of protein (~12%), vitamin E, phosphates, vitamin B1, sugars, albumins, calcium and iron. They contain less fats then macadamias, but may be considered superior to the macadamias in terms of oil type and their levels of antioxidants.

Other uses

The wood is light, strong, easily worked, elastic, not very durable. It is used for furniture, picture frames, oars, roof-shingles and for turnery. The leaves are popular in flower arrangements because of their shape and because they don't wilt. The oils from the nuts are used in cosmetic preparations; in particular, palmitoleic acid (~27% of the total oil) is easily absorbed by the skin and acts as a good, natural UV filter for sunscreen lotions.

Ornamental

It is an appealing, handsome ornamental plant with its attractive foliage, numerous panicles of creamy flowers and eye-catching red–black fruits. It also provides abundant nectar and pollen for bees.

DESCRIPTION

Attractive, rounded, medium-sized tree, 10–12 m tall, though can be considerably taller in its native habitat. It seems to grow best between 35–45° in latitude. In the right soil, these trees can initially be quite fast growing, and then their growth slows as they mature.

Leaves: Evergreen, attractive, dark glossy green, thick, very variable in shape, ranging from pinnate to bi-pinnate, with between 3–30 leaflets. The leaflets are opposite, oval, with a pointed or rounded tip and are coarsely serrated. The leaves seem to have poor stomatal control, and seem not to readily close under stress, such as a water deficit. Therefore, adequate water is important. This trait, along with it having a large superficial rooting system, are probably the main factors contributing to why many gevuina die after being transplanted.

Flowers: Attractive, creamy-white, slightly fragrant, numerous, clustered along panicles, ~15 cm long, are borne through summer, and into autumn in cooler areas. The individual flowers have a fluffy appearance as they consist mainly of numerous long stamens, with no true petals, but, instead, have four creamy-white sepals. The flowers are bisexual, having both male and female organs, and one tree will set fruit, though more than one tree results in cross pollination and seems to increase yield. *Pollination:* By bees and insects.

Fruit: Woody, rounded drupes (1.5–2.5 cm diameter) that change from green, to deep red and then to black as they mature, and are borne in clusters. It has a thin, easy-to-remove (much easier than macadamias), smooth shell. Smaller in size than a macadamia. The kernel is creamy-white with a crisp texture, and is not dissimilar to macadamia in taste. The nut takes a year to ripen, and so next year's flowers appear as last year's nuts are ripening.

Yield/harvest: About 3–5 kg a year, and possibly up to 15 kg. Seedlings do not start producing fruits until they are ~7 years old; trees from cuttings produce their first crop after 4 years, but take 7 years to start giving good harvests. The outer dark husk is removed, and the nuts are then gently dried in an oven or in hot sun until their moisture content is only ~2–5% (down from ~20%). If temperatures are too high, then nut quality is reduced. When dry, the shells can be removed without too much difficulty. The kernels will store well at room temperature without becoming rancid, as long as they have been sufficiently dried, or can be stored in airtight containers for longer.

Roots: Has many superficial roots that occur near the surface making this plant susceptible to drought, even though lower roots are in moist soil. It is also tricky (impossible) to transplant for this reason (as well as poor stomatal control), and trees often die. They also seem to form a symbiotic relationship with a fungus in the soil that the plants are dependant upon, and need to develop for the tree to grow well.

CULTIVATION

Location: Can grow in maritime areas, but not in too exposed locations. Grows best in full sun, though can be grown in semi-shade, but does not fruit as well.

Temperature: They like a cooler, temperate climate. Can tolerate temperatures down to ~–10°C, though younger plants need more protection and can be damaged at –6°C. Trees will acclimatise to cold, but do not like rapid drops in temperature, which can do more cold damage than the temperature itself. Young growth in spring, even on mature plants, can be frost-tender and so it is best to grow trees in a sheltered position away from early-morning sun. Does not like too much heat or drying winds, probably because of poor stomatal control and its shallow root system.

Soils/water/nutrients: Grows best in fertile, moist, but well-drained soils, though can tolerate some wetness around the roots. Trees can grow in stony or even clayey

---

soils. They seem to need somewhat acid soil conditions, with a pH range from 4.5–6.5 (not alkaline). Trees do need constant moisture, particularly till well established, and can even tolerate some waterlogging (they often naturally grow in marshy locations), though this tolerance varies with cultivar. Dry, hot weather dries out the soil and desiccates the leaves, causing stress, and can kill the trees. They benefit from additions of well-rotted organic matter, and a thick mulch will help retain valuable moisture, suppress weed growth and add nutrients.

Pot culture: Because of their relatively slow growth, these attractive trees can be grown in a large tub or container, and will produce nuts if well fed and watered.

Planting: When buying a plant, it is best to select one with a large root system and fewer leaves, rather than the other way around, to reduce the risk of water stress. Plant in autumn or early winter to reduce water stress, but you may need to provide frost protection until the plants are older. Plant in a cool, sheltered location. Space plants at 2–3 m apart.

Pruning: For fruiting, a vase system is better than a single-leader system. Because it tends to form a single leader, the tip may need to be removed to encourage laterals to form, and several scaffold branches should be selected around the tree to form a strong structure. These are then tipped to encourage the formation of further lateral branches, which produce the nuts. Exposing growing tips to light seems to encourage early fruiting, so remove older leaves that shade these areas.

Propagation: *Seed*: Best sown as soon as it is ripe, with heat. The seed often germinates well, but then sickens and dies, and this may be due to the plant needing the symbiotic fungal–root relationship. Adding some soil that has been carefully removed from around an established tree to the seed compost might improve success rates (as it does with macadamia). Grow on seedlings for a year or two before planting out. *Cuttings:* Take semi-ripe cuttings in summer and insert in gritty, well-drained compost. *Layering:* This method can be practised.

Pests and diseases: They are very subject to root rot caused by the soil fungus *Phytophthora*, mostly if the tree is stressed by other factors. This can kill them quickly. Broad mite and leaf-roller caterpillars can attack the leaves. ■

Ginkgo biloba

Ginkgo (maidenhair tree, pa kuo, yin hsing, kew tree, bai guo, silver apricot)

GINKGOACEAE

A genus of a single species. This is a fascinating, ancient tree that links the ferns and the angiosperms (flowering plants), and is often grouped in with conifers, although it is older and is, 'strictly', in a group of its own. It is, in fact, the world's oldest living tree: the species can be traced back over 250 million years and may have been food for dinosaurs during the Mesozoic Era. For this reason, Darwin referred to the ginkgo as a living fossil. The ginkgo was common and widespread in Asia, Europe and America, but disappeared from America about 7 million years ago, and from Europe about 3 million years ago. For many centuries, the ginkgo has been planted as a sacred tree in Chinese and Japanese Buddhist temple gardens, and in China, the fruits and leaves of ginkgo have been used for >5000 years to treat lung ailments and cardiovascular diseases. It is now also a popular ornamental tree in many temperate regions of the world, and has recently been re-discovered and researched for its wide-ranging medicinal properties.

DESCRIPTION

A very attractive, unusual, deciduous tree, reaching heights of 30–40 m, with a spread of ~8 m. The trunk diameter can occasionally become ~3–4 m wide. It is single-stemmed, straight, columnar and sparingly branched, with lower branches protruding almost at right angles, becoming more vertical as the tree gets taller. Young trees are pyramidal in shape, with regular, asymmetrical branches. The bark is brown–grey and rough, becoming fissured with age. Individual trees are long lived and can live for >1000 years, but are slow growing.

Leaves: Are leathery and smooth, and are borne in small clusters (~4) from short, knobbly shoots, or are sometimes borne singly from the tips of branches. Unique amongst plants, their venation pattern is open with many veins fanning outwards from leaf stalk, with no cross connections between the veins, unlike almost all other species. This gives them an attractive fan shape with a slightly irregular edge between the terminal veins. Leaves often form two distinct lobes, hence their name 'biloba'. One of its common Chinese names, pa kuo, means duck foot, for its resemblance in shape. They are bright, fresh green during the summer, turning a clear golden colour before dropping in autumn.

Flowers: Ginkgo trees are dioecious. They are unusual in that the flowers are formed on the same short stalks as the leaves. Male flowers are catkin-like, yellow-green in colour, and are borne in small clusters (~3–4) with the leaves, with both opening at the same time. Female flowers are simple, stalked, bi-lobed oval (no petals, sepals, etc.), in small groups (2–3). Flower buds need a long warm–hot summer to be formed. *Pollination:* By wind.

Fruit: The unusual female flowers ripen, once pollinated, into yellow–orange-coloured, plum-shaped pairs of fruits, each ~2.5 cm long. As they mature, the fruits turn brown and begin to emit a strong smell that many find unpleasant, which means that not many female trees are planted ornamentally. Inside the fruit is a large, single, brown seed.

Yield/harvest: Trees can take 20–30 years to start fruiting, which is a very long time to wait to find out if your seedlings are male or female. Grafted trees can fruit in 8 years, but, it still takes a long time to get any kernels. They are best planted in groups, with males planted surrounded by females, to enhance wind pollination. Once trees do start to produce fruits, they tend to produce many fruits one year

Food

The nuts have been reported to be toxic when eaten raw, so they need roasting. Probably best to not eat too many of them. However, the Japanese have long valued the nuts as a delicious food, and cook and serve them in various ways. They are known as 'ginnan'. They have a sweet taste a bit like chestnuts or pine nuts, or some say like Swiss cheese. The entire seed is usually steamed or roasted until the hard shell cracks open, then the kernel is removed and eaten as is, or can be used in pilaff, porridges, soups, vegetable dishes or mixed with rice, tofu, mushrooms and stir-fried vegetables.

Nutrition

Leaves contain several antioxidants, vitamins C and A, and flavonoids (ginkgolide, quercetin and kaempferol), ginkgolic acid, pro-anthocyanidins. Nuts contain ~60% starch and are low in fat at ~2.5%. They also contain tannin and resin.

Medicinal

In ancient Chinese and Japanese cultures, the nuts were used to prevent drunkenness and promote digestion. They have also been used as a vermifuge, to clear bronchial tubes and as a sedative. However, the leaves have the greatest medicinal properties. Many recent medical trials have researched ginkgo as a treatment for senility, for heart disease, for hardening of the arteries and for oxygen deprivation. The flavonoid compounds within the leaves act to specifically dilate micro-capillaries of the body, which has a widespread effect on the organs, especially the brain. This effectively increases blood circulation and increases oxygen levels to all parts of the body, but especially brain tissue. Ginkgo seems to increase the body's production of adenosine triphosphate, which boosts the brain's metabolism of glucose and, hence, increases electrical activity. Increased blood flow to the brain improves alertness, short-term memory, the ability to concentrate and may improve mood and counteract depression. Alzheimer's disease may be partially caused by the damaging effect of free radicals, which leads to fat being deposited in brain cells. Some research in Europe and the USA has shown that ginkgo can stabilise or, in some cases, improve mental functioning in Alzheimer's cases, but treatment appears to work best in the early stages of the disease. The flavonoids also act as powerful antioxidants, preventing platelet aggregation inside arterial walls, keeping them flexible and decreasing the formation of arteriosclerositic plaque. This ability to improve blood flow can help peripheral atherosclerotic disease (a condition that decreases blood flow to the extremities because of hardening of the arteries). These compounds are also used to treat eye ailments caused by poor blood flow (e.g. diabetes, cataracts), tinnitus, head injuries and other brain-related conditions. They counteract the effect of platelet-activating factor, which causes blood platelets to clot. By thinning the blood, ginkgo may protect against stroke, heart attack, angina attacks and pain caused by cholesterol build-up in leg blood vessels. Ginkgo has been shown to inhibit the chemical which causes asthma attacks by alleviating the swelling of bronchial linings. Its anti-inflammatory qualities can also be used to help shrink haemorrhoids, by swabbing the area with ginkgo tea three times daily. Taking a large dose of ginkgo tincture (see below) at the onset of a migraine will increase blood flow to the brain and may nip the migraine in the bud: 10 teaspoons of tincture are recommended. For those who suffer from migraines regularly, taking the standard dose can help prevent attacks. Ginkgo leaves are usually taken as a tincture. This can be made by placing 150 g of dried (400 g of fresh) leaves in a jar with 500 ml of vodka. Cover and store in a dark place for 4 weeks, shaking the jar daily. After 4 weeks, strain the mixture, and drink 1–3 teaspoons of tincture a day. For those wishing to avoid alcohol, a ginkgo tea can be made, though you need 2–3 cups per day to get the same effect. **Warning:** If already taking anticoagulant medications or taking aspirin to reduce the risk of heart disease, ginkgo should be taken with caution. Haemophiliacs should not take ginkgo because of its blood-thinning properties. In addition, it is best not to eat the nuts raw, as they have been known to cause sickness. Leaf extracts are considered relatively safe, though taking very large doses may lead to temporary diarrhoea, nausea and vomiting.

Other uses

Historically, the leaves were placed in books to repel bookworms. The wood is light and soft and also has insect-repelling properties.

Ornamental

Great for landscaping; these are beautiful trees with interestingly shaped leaves, and their ancient history makes them a special addition. Good yellow and golden late autumn colour. Older trees make beautiful specimen shade trees. Because of its tolerance to pollution and poor soil, its non-invasive habit and attractive leaves, the ginkgo is a wonderful tree for landscaping in towns.

but only meagre crops the next. Harvests can be evened out by thinning fruits in years when there are too many. The leaves are often used medicinally, and are picked in autumn as they start to turn yellow as flavonoid content is highest at this time. The nuts are also harvested in autumn. The flesh around the nuts needs to be washed off and gloves should be worn because the flesh contains anacardic acid, which can cause a severe rash in some people. Some people place the nuts in water or soil for the outer shells to ferment and fall off. It is the inner kernel that is eaten. The nuts can be partially dried and stored in a dark, airy place.

Roots: Deep. The roots form a fungal mycorrhizal association, which enables the tree to obtain nutrients, and phosphates in particular, more easily.

CULTIVATION
Easy maintenance.

Location: Likes a sunny spot. Tolerates relatively windy sites. Tolerates moderately exposed maritime locations and air pollution. Does not like competition from weeds, but be careful to avoid herbicide splash.

Temperature: It can adapt to a wide range of climates and is fairly hardy. It can be grown in temperate or subtropical regions. It tolerates frosts when dormant. Grows best in regions that have long, warm summers.

Soil/water/nutrients: Prefers a deep, well-drained lighter soil, but will grow in a wide range of soils, including clay. It will also grow at a wide range of pH values. Does not like waterlogged soils, though will adapt to clay soils that are fairly wet. Is relatively drought tolerant because of its deep roots. Trees respond to regular additions of nutrients, and will then grow and fruit better. Apply a regular balanced fertiliser twice a year, or mulch with well-rotted organic matter. The latter will also help suppress weed growth.

Planting: Space trees at ~8 m apart. If planting as an orchard, will need ~ one male tree for 19 female trees to ensure pollination. Need to encourage the male trees to grow tall to aid wind-borne pollination.

Propagation: *Seed:* Germinates readily in spring, or can sow when fresh in autumn. They are best sown fresh. Seedlings are grown on for 3–4 years in deep pots before planting out, but the sex of the seedling won't be known for 20–30 years! *Grafting:* This enables the sex of the tree to be known; however, these trees form a shape determined by where the graft material was taken, i.e. if a side branch was used as the graft material, the tree will always take this form of growth.

Pruning: Not a good idea. Any shoots or stems that are pruned will die back further.

Pests and diseases: Has a very high resistance to fungal, viral and bacterial disease, as well as insects and pollution.

CULTIVARS
Most have been selected for their ornamental properties. **'King of Dongting Mountain'** is from China, produces large seeds and starts producing harvests much sooner than most other cultivars, i.e. in 3–5 years, as long as it is grown in good soil. ∎

Gleditsia triacanthos
Honey locust
FABACEAE (syn. Leguminosae)
Relatives: carob, licorice, peanut, tamarind

The *Gleditsia* genus contains ~10 species of deciduous, attractive, temperate trees that are native to North America, Asia and Iran. The name *Gleditsia* is derived from the name of a German botanist, Gottlieb Gleditsch, and *triacanthos* is a Greek word meaning three-spines, and refers to its long thorns. Its common name refers to the sweet pulp within its pods. The honey locust is a native of the central states of the USA, and is popularly grown as an ornamental tree. It has also been introduced and is grown in many temperate countries, including the UK, Europe, India, New Zealand and South Africa. It is a medium-sized, leguminous tree, although it does not form a symbiotic relationship with nitrogen-fixing bacteria like most other species in this family. Apart from its ornamental appeal, it is often grown for fuel, animal food, shade and soil reclamation. However, it also produces fragrant flowers and pods that have a sweet, edible pulp surrounding their edible seeds. It is a very amenable and easy-to-grow tree, and is useful in areas with alkaline soils.

DESCRIPTION
A fast-growing, medium-sized tree, 6–12 m tall, spread 4–5 m (although some trees grow much larger), with a stout often short trunk (can be ~2 m wide in older specimens), sometimes dividing into several stems near the ground, with an open, spreading crown. Branches tend to be more horizontal than upright. Buds form along stems, but, unusually, not at the tips. The tree produces many stout

thorns on its lower branches and trunk, whereas flowers are formed higher up the tree. Thorns on the lower trunk can be particularly long (7–20 cm) and vicious, and may occur in branched clusters. As trees age, they produce fewer thorns on their upper branches, and so the tree creates a good defence system that prevents browsing at lower levels, as well as deterring creatures from climbing to feed on its flowers and pods. The bark on older branches and the trunk becomes narrowly ridged and fissured, whereas that on younger branches often peels into strips. The tree is strong and wind hardy. It is fairly long lived: >120 years.

Leaves: Very attractive, fern-like, pinnate, ~30 cm long, smooth. They are composed of 20–32 leaflets, which are sometimes simple or doubly pinnate, oval–oblong, rounded at their ends, yellowy green, ~1.5–3 cm long, margins are entire. Trees often have good, clear yellow autumn colour.

Flowers: Fragrant, racemes, 6–12 cm long, of numerous, not very noticeable, bell-shaped, greeny-yellow flowers, ~0.5 cm in diameter. These are borne in mid–late spring, after the leaves have opened. Most trees are monoecious, but other trees are dioecious, so although self fertilisation is likely, if the sex of the tree is not known, it is best to have more than one tree to ensure fruit-set. On monoecious trees, individual branches just bear the flowers of one sex. Female racemes tend to be smaller, 5–8 cm long, with fewer flowers, usually with 1–2 ovules (or sometimes more) and have vestigial, abortive stamens. *Pollination:* The nectar-rich flowers attract bees.

Fruit: A flat, smooth, shiny pod, ~30–70 cm long (sometimes much longer), 2.5–3.5 cm wide. When ripe it changes to a russet colour, becomes dry and twisted, and is compressed between the inner seeds. The pod does not dehisce (spring open when dry) like some leguminous species. Inside are many oval, dark brown seeds, ~1 cm long. The seeds are embedded within a sweet edible pulp. The pods ripen in autumn, and fall after maturing.

Yield/harvest/storage: One of the drawbacks with this species is the long time seedling trees take to start producing pods: usually 6–10 years. But, once they have started, they then produce good yields for 25–75 years, and sometimes for >100 years. Trees can produce huge numbers of these pods in some years, but also tend towards biennial production. Thin out pods, if feasible, soon after fruit-set in abundant years, or remove some of the flowering stems to even out yields. However, trees seem to produce some seeds every year, even in lean years. They are best harvested as they fall from the tree, as the tree's thorns can make picking the pods a painful process. They have a long harvesting season, often from autumn through winter.

Roots: Thick, fibrous, deep, wide-spreading, and much branched. The roots are not nitrogen fixing like most leguminous species. It seems that the nitrogen-fixing bacteria are unable to penetrate the roots and that the tree may excrete an antibacterial substance. They have a deep taproot system, which can penetrate to 3–6 m. Care needs to be taken when planting these trees that their taproot is not damaged.

CULTIVATION

An easy-to-grow hardy tree that needs little maintenance.

Location: Trees grow far better in full sun: shade slows growth considerably. Relatively wind hardy, and is fairly tolerant of salt, so can be grown in reasonably exposed maritime locations. They are fairly tolerant of air pollution.

Temperature: Can be grown in cooler and warm temperate climates, as well as semi-tropical temperatures. It is very cold hardy, and can tolerate temperatures down to ~–30°C if acclimatised and dormant. In warmer areas, trees retain their leaves for longer into the autumn and if there is a sudden drop in temperature, then these trees are more susceptible to frost damage. They like a warm, but not too hot summer, with temperatures in the mid 20s. If the temperatures become too high, trees can drop their leaves.

Soil/water/nutrients: Trees can grow in a wide range of soil types, though grow best in moist, fertile, deep, heavier soils. They seem to grow better in clays than sandy soils, and then form deeper roots, which is unusual. Trees do not grow well in shallow soils. Unusually for a tree with a long taproot, it is very tolerant of flooding, but not for extended periods. The tree is also drought-resistant and can be grown on dry slopes as long as the soil is fairly deep. Fairly tolerant of salty soils. They grow best in neutral to very alkaline soils, with a pH range of 6–8. They may be able to tolerate somewhat

Food
The seed pulp can be scooped out of the pods and eaten fresh. It is sweet and tastes of honey–molasses. It can also be added to desserts, etc., or used to make an alcoholic beverage. The pulp, when added to water, makes a sweet drink. The seeds, if eaten fresh, taste like uncooked peas. Young pods can be cooked and eaten as a vegetable, although older pods are very astringent. The seeds can be roasted and used as a coffee substitute.

Nutrition/medicinal
The seeds are rich in protein (~13%). The pulp contains ~40% carbohydrate and sugars. Historically, the pods have been used to treat catarrh, as a pain killer, as a narcotic and for indigestion. The bark was used for blood disorders, coughs and fevers.

Other uses
The flowers attract bees, and make a good honey. The seeds contain a gum, which can be substituted for acacia or tragacanth gums. The wood is dense, very heavy, very hard, resistant to shock and is durable outside. The sapwood is yellowish, while the heartwood is reddish-brown, and takes a high polish. Some use it for agricultural and general construction purposes, but it can also be used for finer woodwork.

Ornamental
Honey locusts are popular as ornamental shade trees (but they should be thornless), and are used for soil reclamation, as a windbreak and as a pioneer species. It coppices well, and quickly regenerates, though pod yields will be reduced. *Warning:* The thorns on some trees are particularly vicious and can injure people, livestock and can even puncture a tractor tyre.

more acidic soils, but it is best to add lime if in doubt. Also, strangely, although not able to fix nitrogen, they seem to grow better on poorer-nutrient soils that are low in nitrogen.

Planting: They form a fairly large tree and are best planted at a spacing of ~10 m (or more) apart. However, trees can be coppiced or pruned to be smaller if space is limited, and can then be planted nearer together.

Propagation: *Seed:* They grow easily from seed, but take longer to produce pods, have variable offspring and the sex of the tree won't be known for many years. Seeds are viable for a long period because of their hard impermeable seedcoat, which is designed to be eaten and pass intact through a digestive system. They can be stored in a cool, sealed container for several years. When sowing seed, the seedcoat needs to be scarified (with a file or similar, so that moisture and oxygen can enter), or soaked in dilute acid for 1–2 hours (after which all acid is thoroughly washed off), or soaked in hot water (~80°C) for a few hours, before sowing seeds in well-drained compost. Temperature requirements do not seem to be very important. Germination is good, ~85%, and takes ~21 days. Seedlings grow rapidly and can be planted out after a year. Grow seedlings in deep pots to enable them to establish a deep taproot. *Cuttings:* Softwood, semi-ripe and hardwood cuttings can all be taken from spring through to early winter, and should give good results. The good news is that if you take cuttings from a

thornless part of a tree, the plants produced also have no or very few thorns. Even though a tree may be monoecious, if a cutting is taken from a branch that has only female flowers, then it will produce a female tree. *Grafting:* Trees produced by this method fruit sooner and the sex of the tree can be predicted. Trees can be grafted or budded.

Pruning: None required except to remove any diseased or damaged wood.

Pests and diseases: Generally has few problems, though the leaves may be attacked by insects, which can stunt the tree during that season though seldom kill it. Examples of pests includes mites, leaf hoppers, leaf-rollers, caterpillars, bagworms and beetles. There are also some bark and wood borers and scale insects that can injure the bark. These attacks are more serious, and can allow the entry of fungal disease. Honey locust suffers from few diseases, unless already weakened.

CULTIVARS

Gleditsia triacanthus* var. *inermis has no thorns. Many of the ornamental cultivars, although selected to be more attractive, often do not produce many or any pods. The cultivar **'Sunburst'** is thornless and fast growing, with attractive bright yellow-green young leaves, which complement the older, darker green leaves, but bears no fruit. ■

Glycyrrhiza glabra
Licorice (liquorice)
FABACEAE (syn. Leguminaceae)
Relatives: carob, tamarind, honey locust

Licorice probably originates from eastern Asia, and has been grown there since early times. It is often grown for local use in China, the Middle East, Turkey, Pakistan, India, Russia, north Africa and the Mediterranean regions. Its roots and stolons were used by both the ancient Greeks and the Romans. Theophrastus recommended it for quenching thirst, and to relieve stomach ulcers and asthma. Apparently, Napoleon used to chew licorice so much so that it blackened his teeth. It is now grown commercially in Spain, France, Russia, Germany, England, the Middle East and Asia. In the early 16th century, licorice began to be cultivated in the monastery gardens at Pontefract, in England, and this became the centre of a well-known licorice confectionery industry.
It is a fully hardy, perennial, shrubby plant that is harvested every 3–4 years for its deep taproots and sweet-tasting stolons, which are, botanically, classified as underground stems. Licorice, therefore, is not really a fruit or a nut, but perhaps more correctly should be classified as a vegetable. The sweetness of licorice is derived from a compound called glycyrrhizin, which is reputed to be 50 times sweeter than refined sugar, and has many potentially important medical properties. Its genus name, *Glycyrrhiza,* aptly describes it, with 'glucos' being Greek for 'sweet' and 'riza' meaning 'root'. It is said that the sweetest licorice now comes form Italy and Spain. Although *G. glabra* is the main licorice species, other similar species are also grown for their edible roots, particularly in Russia and China. The Russian licorice is *G. echinata*, and Chinese licorice is *G. uralensis*.

DESCRIPTION
A very hardy, deciduous, perennial shrub that grows to 1–2 m in height. It dies back and becomes dormant during winter, after shedding its leaves. It is slow growing for the first couple of years, and then the shoots start forming luxuriant

growth, and the stolons start rapidly developing.

Leaves: Deciduous, graceful, pinnate, small and feathery (like *Acacia*), tending to droop at night or during drought, and perking up again at dawn.

Flowers: Attractive, lavender-blue-white or yellowish-white, pea-like, in spike-like racemes, in spring–early summer. *Pollination:* By bees and other insects.

Fruit: Small, flat, pea-like, smooth pods, 2–3 cm long, turning brown at maturity. They contain 1–7 very small, dark brown, kidney-shaped seeds. Ripen in late summer.

Root: The plant initially forms several (3–4) deep taproots, which grow downwards ~1 m, and there is also a network of finer roots near the surface. The roots are able to form a symbiotic relationship with bacteria, which can fix nitrogen. After a couple of years, when the plant's root system is fully established, it starts to produce horizontal runners or stolons (underground stems), which act as storage organs for sugars/starch for spring growth, and also enable the plant to vegetatively spread to new areas. These can grow outwards from the main plant for more that >2 m, and grow just under the soil's surface. In the spring, the plant produces new shoots from buds towards the ends of these stolons. When the plant has developed a good system of stolons, it can be harvested. The roots, when washed, are yellowish-brown externally, and are very flexible. Internally, the roots are juicy and light yellow in colour. They have a sweet, earthy fragrance.

Yield/harvest/preparation: Commercially, yields of 1–5 tonnes of stolons and taproots per hectare are achieved. Plants are ready to harvest in the autumn of the third or fourth year. Before that time, roots are not sufficiently sweet, and >4 years, they begin to become woody. The usual method is to first carefully remove soil from around the periphery of the plant to expose the stolons, before digging up the whole plant with its taproots. The stolons and taproots are then thoroughly washed, cut into lengths and sorted to remove any poor quality sections before gently drying them at ~30–40°C until they are fairly dry. The roots are then crushed or finely chopped, and then boiled in water. The resultant juice is then reduced to a thick consistency, which is then often rolled into ~2.5-cm-diameter sticks. Unfortunately, much licorice sold today is not pure licorice and contains other ingredients such as molasses, treacle and aniseed, and so it is an interesting project to produce your own real licorice.

CULTIVATION

An easy-to-grow plant that needs little maintenance, and could be easily squeezed into the edge of a border or vegetable patch, though does take 3–4 years to produce a crop.

Location: Plants grow best in full sun. They are not very wind tolerant. Once established, liquorice can be difficult to eradicate, as sections of stolon are often left in the soil and will readily regrow. Therefore, if space is at a premium, consider 'penning' the plant in with a brick or wooden barrier (or similar).

Temperature: They grow well in warm temperate and subtropical climates, and are said to do well wherever citrus can grown; they need warmth to develop fully sweetened roots and stolons. They can, however, also be grown in colder temperate regions, e.g. the UK, as long as they receive a warm–hot summer. In winter they die back, and can tolerate frosts and quite cold temperatures, although very cold weather can make the stems and roots woody.

Soil/water/nutrients: As with all root crops, they grow best in deep, loose, well-drained, sandy soil. They won't grow well in clay soils unless gypsum and compost are added to break up its structure. Alternatively, they can be planted on raised beds. They grow best in a neutral to slightly alkaline soil. They like some moisture during

Food

Licorice has a very sweet, distinctive taste, unlike almost anything else, though perhaps slightly hinting of aniseed or fennel. It is widely used in confectionery, and is popular with children and adults alike. It is also used in some desserts and alcoholic drinks (e.g. schnapps), and is sometimes added to tobacco as a flavouring. Unlike many sweets, licorice also has the advantage of being healthy. As well as forming sticks, the thick extract can also be moulded to form different shaped sweets: fun for kids. It is also often added to Chinese five-spice powder, and can be used to disguise the taste of unpleasant-tasting medicines.

Medicinal

It is widely used medicinally around the world, particularly in China, to treat many conditions, although its efficacy for many of those listed below is not fully proven. The main active compound is glycyrrhizin, which is ~4% of the root. Amongst its benefits are that it can inhibit gastric secretion, and has reduced the symptoms of gastric ulcers significantly. It is used to treat many inflammatory diseases, such as various skin disorders and rheumatic problems. It also stimulates the adrenal gland, which produces adrenaline, and so boosts energy levels. It contains glycosides, which are used to expel pulmonary phlegm, etc., and is often taken for coughs and colds. Recent research, in Germany, has found glycyrrhizin to be the most potent inhibitor they tested against SARS. Its antiviral benefits have also been used to treat HIV (though it is not fully proven or tested). It also contains a natural inteferon, which helps boost the immune system. It has a mild laxative effect and is good for digestive problems. Glycyrrhizin has also been shown, in Japan, to improve liver function in hepatitis C patients. It may also be a natural source of oestrogen, which could be of benefit for menstrual cramps and menopause, but not for uterine fibroids. It also seems to reduce the levels of low-density lipids ('bad' cholesterol) within the blood. The root extract can be simply eaten or a tea can be made from it. **Warning:** At moderate doses, licorice is completely safe and healthy to eat. However, there have been a few cases where large doses of highly concentrated licorice have proved to be dangerous. It can, apparently, at very high levels, induce the body to be hypersensitive to one of its own natural hormones, aldosterone, which can then result in dangerously lowered potassium levels, and may also cause tissue-water retention. Liquorice, in quantity, should be avoided by those with high blood pressure, obesity, heart problems or diabetes, and possibly by pregnant women also.

the growing season, but need very little during the winter months. They grow best in fairly fertile soils and well-rotted manure or similar can be mixed into the soil when planting. Their roots fix nitrogen, so less of this nutrient is required.

Planting: Space plants at ~40 cm apart in autumn or spring. Dig the soil deeply before planting to help give good root growth, and add some organic matter. The plants only grow slowly at first while establishing (to 30–50 cm in the first couple of years), but then start growing rapidly upwards and outwards, via stolons. Because of the plant's initial slow development, commercial growers often plant quick-growing crops between the rows of licorice during the first 2 years.

Pruning: The flower heads are usually removed to promote stronger stolon and root growth, as seed formation uses up a considerable amount of the plant's resources.

Propagation: *Seed:* The seed has a hard seedcoat that needs to be scarified before sowing: the seedcoat is scratched in some way, with a file or similar. Store seed in a sealed polythene bag over winter in a cold place (or the fridge) before sowing in spring. Purchased seed may benefit from a period of chilling before sowing (as well as stratification). Germination and early seedling growth can be slow, and root propagation is often preferred. *Cuttings:* Stolon cuttings will readily, quickly and successfully root and form new plants. Cuttings, ~20–30 cm long, with several healthy-looking buds are taken in summer or autumn. They are best planted vertically or at an angle in the soil. Keep them moist, but not too wet, until established.

Pests and diseases: Generally has very few problems, though wet soils may encourage root rots, etc. ■

Grewia asiatica (syn. *G. subinaequalis*)
Phalsa
TILIACEAE

The Tiliaceae family is also known as the linden or lime-tree family (not to be confused with the *Citrus* species) and has various deciduous representatives in temperate regions of the Northern Hemisphere, which are often known for their fragrant flowers. However, only one genus within the Tiliaceae family produces an edible fruit. The phalsa is indigenous to much of India and Southeast Asia. It is cultivated commercially for its fruit in the Punjab and around Bombay and also widely valued thoughout India for its many medicinal properties. At the beginning of the 20th century, it was introduced into the Far East, including the Philippines, where it is now naturalised in dry areas. It did not reach Western countries until much later in the century. These easy-to-grow, small trees produce tasty fruits. These are unlikely to be encountered for sale because of the protracted harvesting period needed, but are ideal for a small garden, where this is actually advantageous.

DESCRIPTION
Forms a large, gangly, straggly shrub or a small tree: ~4.5 m tall or more. It has long, slender, drooping branches, and the young stems are densely coated with hairs. The bark is rough and grey. There tend to be two forms of this species: taller plants that produce fruits that are acidic and not so good to eat, or shorter, more shrubby plants that produce fruits that are sweet and tasty.

Leaves: Alternate, deciduous, widely spaced, large (~15–20 cm long, ~10–15 cm wide), broadly heart-shaped or ovate, pointed at the apex, oblique at the base. They are coarsely toothed, with a light, whitish down on the underside, especially when young. The tree is slow to lose its leaves in autumn in warmer regions.

Flowers: Small (1–2 cm diameter), bright orange-yellow, borne in numerous dense clusters from the leaf axils, in late spring.

Fruit: Attractive round drupes, on ~2.5-cm stalks, produced in great numbers in open clusters; look just like cherries. Largest fruits are 1.25–1.6 cm wide. The skin turns from green to crimson to purplish-red, and finally very dark purple when mature, usually in summer. The skin is thin,

becomes soft and tender when ripe, and is covered with a thin, whitish bloom. The flesh is soft, fibrous, greenish-white, stained with mauve near the skin. As the fruit becomes over-ripe, this mauve colour spreads throughout the flesh and the skin begins to shrivel. They have a pleasant acid–sweet flavour that is somewhat grape-like. Larger fruits have two hemispherical, hard, buff-coloured seeds (~0.5 cm diameter); smaller fruits have a single spherical seed. Phalsa bears its fruit on the current season's growth.

Yield/harvest/storage: The average yield per plant is 7–10 kg of fruit in a season. Trees come into fruit fairly early, ~2–3 years. Fruit can be harvested when they have turned fully dark purple, but they tend to ripen unevenly within clusters. Therefore, it is not possible to harvest a whole cluster at once, and fruit need picking at regular intervals. A whole cluster can be harvested, but some of the fruits are then wasted. The fruits do not keep well once picked, and should be eaten when fresh, or processed soon after.

CULTIVATION
Phalsa is quite stress-tolerant and needs little maintenance once established.

Food
The fruits can be eaten fresh, made into a syrup, added to conserves or to other desserts. They are used extensively in the manufacture of soft drinks in India. The juice ferments readily and makes an interesting alcoholic drink.

Nutrition
The fruits contain good levels of calcium, potassium and vitamin A.

Medicinal
Astringent, somewhat under-ripe fruits have been eaten to aid stomach problems, to alleviate inflammation and to treat respiratory, cardiac and blood disorders, as well as fevers. A tea made from the bark may eliminate internal parasites, soothe inflammations, reduce fevers and treat blood disorders and diarrhoea. The leaves have been used as a poultice on skin eruptions and are known to have an antibiotic action. The root bark has been used to treat rheumatism, biliousness, and urinary and gynaecological troubles. In India, the roots or stem bark of phalsa are regularly used to treat gonorrhoea. According to Ayurvedic medicine, the ripe fruits are eaten as a tonic and an aphrodisiac, and also to treat various types of cancer, particularly leukaemia, and the flowers and leaves are used to treat diabetes.

Other uses
The bark is used as a soap substitute in Burma. Fibre extracted from the bark is used to make rope. The wood is yellow-white, fine-grained, strong and flexible. It is used for archers' bows, spear handles, shingles and poles. Stems can be used for garden poles and basket-making.

Location: Is fairly salt tolerant and is suitable for fairly sheltered maritime locations. Likes a sunny location, with only a little shade.

Temperature: Trees can tolerate light frosts, but not extended cold periods or hard frosts. They like warm–hot temperatures to give good quality, sweet, fully-ripened fruits.

Soil/water/nutrients: Trees produce the best fruit quality and yields in rich loams, but they can grow in most soil types: sand, clay or limestone. Although trees can be drought tolerant, they prefer regular moisture, particularly during fruit development. Trees benefit from nutrient applications, with extra phosphate increasing sugar content of the fruits. However, additional nitrogen can produce extra leaf growth and extra potassium can decrease fruit's sugar content and elevate its acidity.

Planting: Space young plants at 2.5–4.5 m apart.

Propagation: *Seed:* This is the usual means of propagation. Seeds can be sown when fresh, in warmth, and are reported to stay viable for years and still germinate in less than 21 days. *Cuttings:* Sometimes difficult to root. Take semi-ripe cuttings in spring or summer; treated with auxin hormone and given warmth, a reasonable success rate is possible. *Layering:* Stem-layering, by slightly scoring stems and pegging these down to the soil, is usually 50% successful, particularly if they are also dusted with rooting hormones. Air-layering can also be done, and this is reported to have 85% success.

Pruning: Moderate annual pruning to remove the ends of straggly branches encourages lateral branching. These produce more fruits and also give the tree more structural strength. Try to avoid drastic pruning.

Pests and diseases: Leaf-cutting caterpillars attack the leaves. In some areas, leaf spot can be a problem. Fruit flies are attracted to the fruits. ∎

Halleria lucida
Tree fuchsia (African honeysuckle, umbinza, notsung)
SCROPHULARIACEAE
Relatives: foxgloves, penstemons, snapdragons

There are not many tree species in the family Scrophulariaceae. Most members are herbaceous, and this tree is also one of the few members that has edible fruit. The tree fuchsia is not actually a 'true' fuchsia species. Its species name, *lucida*, means 'shining' and refers to its leaves. It is a native of semi-tropical/tropical Africa and naturally has sprawling growth in moist forest margins and wetter mountain slopes amongst rocks. It has been cultivated for its fruit in South Africa and Zimbabwe for many years, and is also burnt as a sacrifice to the sacred ancestors and to ward off evil spirits. In some regions this plant can become invasive.

DESCRIPTION

An attractive tree or large semi-climbing shrub that, when grown in a sheltered nutrient-rich location, can rapidly reach heights of >14 m, whereas in exposed locations with poorer soil, it may only grow slowly to reach ~2 m. Has grooved, pale grey-brown rough bark and is often multi-stemmed, with a spreading crown and arching branches. Is a pleasingly-shaped tree for the garden.

Leaves: Evergreen, attractive, oval, pointed, shiny bright green, smooth.

Flowers: Orange-red, tubular, nodding, nectar-rich flowers, ~2.5 cm long, produced in clusters. Bisexual, and are probably self-fertile. As well as being produced from the leaf axils, flowers are also produced cauliflorously, i.e. directly from the branches and trunk. This species makes an attractive and unusual sight, although the flowers are sometimes hidden amongst the leaves. *Pollination:* Its nectar attracts both birds and insects for a long period, from late winter to late summer.

Fruit: Berries are produced directly on the stems and trunk. The rounded, green berries (~1.5 cm in length) become juicy, very sweet and violet-black as they ripen from early spring onwards. Although sweet and flavourful, the fruit is more to some people's tastes than others', with some finding that they have a drying effect on the mouth. Seeds, very small, black, are found within the central pulpy flesh of the fruit.

Yield/harvest: Can get a first harvest in second year, but it takes a few years longer to produce optimum yields.

Pot culture: Although the tree fuchsia prefers tropical climates, it makes a good container plant and can be grown in colder climates if taken inside during winter. It can also be grown in a conservatory or cool greenhouse year-round.

CULTIVATION

It is a fairly resilient plant and is easy to grow: it can thrive under many different conditions.

Location: Prefers a sheltered site in sun (if not too extreme) or semi-shade.

Temperature: Is relatively frost hardy (down to a minimum of −7°C), but would probably not thrive in such conditions, and would definitely need protection when young.

Soil/water/nutrients: Prefers a well-drained yet moist, nutrient-rich loam. Prefers moisture year round, but can survive periods of drought.

Planting: Transplants easily. Space plants at 1–4 m apart, depending on climate. Incorporate organic matter in the soil during establishment.

Food
Fruits are extremely sweet and can be eaten fresh or can be added to a fruit salad to give it an exotic touch. They can also be added to other desserts, jams, etc.

Medicinal
The Zulu have used the dry leaves soaked in water for skin and ear complaints. This tree is considered to be a charm against evil: the twigs are burnt when offering sacrifices to the ancestral spirits.

Other uses
It has light-coloured yellowy wood that is hard, heavy and strong, and is well suited to carpentry.

Ornamental
This tree has an attractive drooping habit and interesting flowers and fruit, which are very good at attracting wild-life for their nectar and berries. It is ideal for small gardens, as long as kept under control, or can be planted in groups for larger gardens. It forms a shade tree by itself or can be planted in the shade as an under-storey tree. It can also be pruned to form an informal hedge. Needs to be planted with some care though, as it can become invasive, and is likely that the birds distribute its seeds.

Pruning: Mostly done to restrict its spread if it is becoming invasive and to encourage it to cover specific structures. Removal of excessive leaf growth and crossing stems will allow light and air to reach the fruits and flowers on the main stems, as well as making the attractive flowers more visible.

Propagation: *Seed:* Easy. Best sown in the warmer months as some heat helps germination. Germination takes ~6 weeks. *Cuttings:* Softwood, semi-ripe cuttings, with a heel if possible, can be taken from actively growing shoots in spring, or during summer and early autumn, respectively, and treated with a rooting hormone before being inserted in a moist, gritty compost, with some heat. Rooting should occur within 6 weeks. *Layering:* Is usually successful, and is often done in autumn. ■

Harpephyllum caffrum
Kaffir plum (wild plum)
ANACARDIACEAE
Relatives: cashew, sumach, ambarella, pistachio

An attractive smaller tree that is a native of southern Africa and is grown widely in this region and other parts of Africa as an ornamental garden tree. It also produces eye-catching red fruits.

Food
The fruits are sometimes eaten fresh, but they are tart and are more usually added to jelly, jams and preserves. They can also be added to pies, and other desserts, or made into a rosé wine.

Medicinal
A tincture from the bark is used externally to treat acne and eczema.

Other uses
The bark is also used for dyeing and gives a mauve–pink colour. Its wood is pale red in colour, but is not very durable, and is used in construction and for furniture.

Ornamental
An attractive smaller tree that is grown for its pleasing shape and its decorative red fruits. It is a popular tree in many countries, and is planted widely in California and in many cities in Africa. It also attracts many species of birds, butterflies and other creatures, particularly in its native homeland.

DESCRIPTION
A small–medium tree, 4–7 m tall, though some specimens in the wild can grow to ~15 m tall; upright or spreading form. It has an attractive, asymmetrical shape, and its branches tend to curve upwards. However, these are easily broken in heavy winds. It grows fairly slowly, and is fairly long lived. It usually has a single, straight stem, and this can become buttressed in more mature trees. The bark is smoothish and dark grey.

Leaves: Attractive, evergreen, glossy, alternate, and tend to cluster at the ends of stems. Leaves are pinnate, divided into 2–4 opposite pairs, and are somewhat drooping. The leaflets are sickle-shaped, and vary in length from 4–14 cm long. They have pointed apices, with rounded bases. Occasional leaves may be reddish. When young, they are covered with small, resinous hairs.

Flowers: Small, whitish-green, are borne in clusters at the ends of stems. Trees are dioecious, so need more than one tree to set fruits. They are similar, except that male flowers have 7–10 stamens, and these are not seen in the female flowers, which have a single stigma. Flowers are borne through summer. *Pollination:* By bees and insects, and perhaps butterflies.

Fruits: Technically, they are a fleshy drupe with a hard, inner endocarp, which contains the kernel. When ripe, the rounded fruits become different shades of cherry red, are aromatic and are ~2.5 cm in diameter. They are borne in clusters. They have a thin, waxy skin, and only a thin layer of flesh, within which is a large, hard stone. The flesh is sweet, but also sub-acid and tasty when ripe. The fruits ripen from late summer–autumn.

CULTIVATION
Location: Grows best in full sun. Is not tolerant of wind, and is best grown in sheltered locations.

Temperature: Is frost tender, and grows best in more subtropical climates.

Soil/water/nutrients: Likes a well-drained, loamy soil. Grows and fruits best with regular moisture during flowering and fruit-development stages.

Pot culture: Can be container grown, and taken inside or given extra protection in colder weather.

Planting: Space plants at ~3 m apart.

Propagation: *Seed:* Sow seed when it is fresh, if possible, with the pulp removed, in warm, moist compost at ~2 cm depth, and in the light. Stored seed should be soaked for ~24 hours in warm water before sowing. Germination rates are good, taking only 7–12 days. *Cuttings:* Semi-ripe cuttings can be taken in summer and inserted in gritty, well-drained compost to root. ∎

Helianthus annuus
Sunflower seeds
ASTERACEAE (Compositae)
Relatives: globe artichoke, Jerusalem artichoke

The sunflower is a fabulous messenger of summer, and it produces lots of tasty seeds that people and wildlife love. 'Helianthus' is derived from the Greek words 'helios', meaning 'sun', and 'anthos' meaning flower, so this plant was probably named because of the way its flowerhead turns to follow the direction of the sun through the sky. It is native to North America, from southern Canada to northern Mexico, and has been used by the indigenous Indians for many hundreds of years. They ground up the seeds for a flour and used the oil for cooking and as a hair product. The original 'wild' plants were multi-stemmed with several 'flower heads'. Selection and cultivation have led to many new cultivars, most of which have a single stem with one

large flowerhead. The sunflower is now a very popular, easy ornamental plant to grow, even in the smallest garden. Sunflowers are also grown commercially for their seeds and, in particular, for the oil they produce, which is one of the world's most popular vegetable oils. Strangely, although the plant was originally a native of North America, the Russians have been the major developers of oil-producing cultivars and are now the largest growers and producers of sunflower oil in the world, followed by Argentina, and thirdly the USA. Sunflowers are also grown for their kernels, which are commercially used in many products or prepared as snacks, but this is a much smaller market.

DESCRIPTION
An annual, with most modern cultivars just forming a single stem and flower that can reach heights of 1–3 m. Many cultivars produce large, extravagant blooms; other cultivars, though somewhat less showy, have been developed for their seed production. They only have a ~60-day life cycle.

Leaves: Mid-green, heart-shaped, largish, rough, coarse with some serrations.

Flowers: A single compound flower, ~30 cm across, consisting of many small individual flowers grown in a beautiful complex multi-spiral arrangement, surrounded on the perimeter by numerous sterile yellow flowers. The fertile flowers start out as green and change to brown–purple as the seeds ripens. *Pollination:* Are loved and sought after by bees.

Yield/harvest: Some cultivars produce more seeds than

uses

Food
The kernel can be eaten fresh or roasted and has a delicious nutty flavour, but is time-consuming to extract from its seedcoat. The kernels can be used in many ways, including being added to cereals, breads, savoury and sweet dishes, as a snack on their own, or can be sprouted to give fresh shoots that are tasty and nutritious. The kernels are delicious roasted in oil or also with tamari to make a snack. The roasted kernels can be used to make a tasty beverage. The seed can be ground and used to make a butter or a yoghurt; the latter, apparently, is best if the seed is germinated, blended with water and then left to ferment. The oil from the seeds has a high semi-drying quality and can be used in dressings or in many culinary dishes. It can be cooked to higher temperatures than olive oil without losing its taste or characteristics. The young flower buds can be steamed and served like globe artichokes, with sepals peeled off, dipped in yoghurt, garlic, butter, mayonnaise or similar, and then the fleshy base can be eaten. The leaf petioles can be boiled as greens and mixed with other foods.

Nutrition/medicinal
The seeds and oil are of very good nutritional value, and are a good source of protein. Seeds contain about five times as much vitamin E as uncooked olive oil. They also contain high levels of the B vitamins, particularly B6, folate and pantothenic acid, and vitamins A and D. They are very high in copper, phosphorus and manganese, and also have good levels of zinc and magnesium. It is widely used in many commercial preparations. They also contain good levels of dietary fibre. They are high in antioxidant, quercitin-type compounds, as well as containing more histidine than most, if not all, other plants. Histidine is an essential amino acid necessary for development, is needed indirectly by the immune system (involved in reducing histamine production), but is also said to prolong orgasm, and is used to treat arthritis and allergic disorders. The seeds contain active ingredients that can reduce fevers, act as a diuretic, relieve stomach ailments, remove phlegm and, in particular, are said to be successful in treating pulmonary problems. A tea made from the leaves also has astringent, diuretic, fever-reducing and expectorant properties. A tea made from the flowers has been used to treat lung ailments. It was used to treat malaria, when other medicines had failed. Some research is being conducted in the ability of the raw seeds to reduce tumours in cancer patients, possibly because of their high levels of vitamin E. Extracts can also be applied externally to treat bruises and wounds. The tasty oil, extracted from the seed, is high is in polyunsaturated oil (44–72% linoleic acid), though does contain ~10% saturated palmitic and stearic fatty acids, but no cholesterol. It is of good quality.

Other uses
The oil is also used in soaps, candles, varnishes, paint, as a lubricant and for lighting. A blotting paper is made from the seedcoat, and paper and cloth are made from the stalk. The pith from the stems is one of the lightest substances known (specific gravity of 0.028) and is used in many unusual products, e.g. making life-saving equipment, slides for microscopes. The dried stems also burn well and the ash is rich in potassium. A yellow dye is obtained from the flowers. Plants are sometimes just grown to make a green manure crop and trials to use them as a bio-fuel crop are being conducted.

Ornamental
A great short-term filler for borders with its large, cheerful, golden-yellow flowers. It is often effective planted in groups.

others; however, in general, yields are good for the size of the plant. The seeds can be collected in autumn once they and the seedhead have turned brown, and the outer sterile flowers have died back. The whole flowerhead can be cut off and hung upside down in a dry, warm, airy place. Once the receptacle is dry, the seeds can be easily scraped out. The shells can be lightly crushed to make them somewhat easier to remove, but there does not seem to be any really easy way to complete this task.

CULTIVATION

An easy-to-grow annual.

Location: Prefers a site in full sun, though can tolerate light shade, but does need a sheltered site, being intolerant of strong winds.

Temperature: Plants produce good crops in hot, dry summers, though some cultivars are being developed that will produce seeds in areas with cooler summers. Seeds from plants grown in cooler regions develop higher levels of polyunsaturated fatty oils. Frost will kill plants.

Soil/water/nutrition: Will grow in most soils, but prefers deep nutrient-rich loam. Sunflowers love lots of nutrients, so much so that their greediness can adversely affect the growth of other plants around them. In addition, the roots may secrete chemicals that also inhibit the growth of nearby plants, so this needs to be considered. It is advisable to change the location of where plants are grown from year to year. They prefer neutral pH or somewhat alkaline soils: lime may need to be added to acid soils. Once established, sunflowers are fairly drought tolerant. They do not tolerate waterlogging.

Planting: Seeds can be sown *in situ*, in spring, once it is warm, but there is a strong risk of them being eaten by mice, etc. It is safer and more reliable to germinate seedlings and grow them on till they have formed young plants. They can then be planted out at 30–45 cm apart. They are likely to need staking as they get taller.

Propagation: *Seed:* Easy and good rates of germination in 7–10 days. Germinate in seed trays and grow on as seedlings before planting out into their final site.

Pests and diseases: Young plants are very susceptible to slug damage. Plants can be attacked by powdery mildew.

CULTIVARS

There are a number of cultivars; some have been developed for their showy flowers, others for seed production. Amongst the seed cultivars there are two main types: one has smaller black seeds, and is grown mainly for the oil contained in the kernels, e.g. 'Peredovik', 'Progress' and 'Rostov'. The other has larger striped seeds, and is grown for its edible kernels, e.g. 'Grey Stripe', 'Hopi Black Dye', 'Mammoth Russian' and 'Sundak'. ■

Hibiscus sabdariffa var. *sabdariffa*
Roselle (red sorrel, Jamaica sorrel, Indian sorrel, Queensland jelly plant, jelly okra, lemon bush, Florida cranberry)
MALVACEAE

Other edible hibiscus species: Australian native sorrel (*H. heterophyllus*), hibiscus (rose of Sharon) (*H. syriacus*, *H. sinosyriacus*), Chinese hibiscus (*H. rosa-sinensis*)

The *Hibiscus* is a large genus of hardy and tender trees and shrubs. Many species have attractive flowers and are popular ornamentally. They are also valued for their edible flowers and leaves, for their medicinal uses, for their mucilaginous roots and for their fibre. The roselle species is rapidly gaining commercial interest for its many uses. It is native to and cultivated in India and the Far East. It is now also cultivated and has become naturalised in many other warmer parts of the world, including Africa, the West Indies, Australia and Central America. Its many uses have been known for hundreds of years: the leaves are tasty and edible, it has large, attractive flowers, which are harvested and the outer parts are used in a wide range of foods, a jute-like fibre is obtained from the stems and the plant also yields natural food colouring. In the late 19th century it was commercially grown in Queensland, and the calyxes were made into roselle jam that was exported to Europe. There are a number of roselle cultivars, some of which are primarily grown for jute production, whereas others have been selected for their flowers. The flowering variety *H. sabdariffa* var. *sabdariffa* is the main variety referred to here, and this variety is divided into a number of races: *bhagalpuriensi*, *intermedius*, *albus* and *ruber*. The race *ruber* is the main plant grown for its edible flowers, but the race *albus* is similar. The species *H. acetosella* is similar, but its calyxes are not as large or juicy.

DESCRIPTION

H. sabdariffa var. *sabdariffa* race *ruber* is a rapidly growing, erect, bushy, herbaceous shrub, ~3.0 m tall. It has smooth, red stems. It is usually grown as an annual.

Leaves: Alternate, 7–12 cm long, green with reddish veins. Leaves of young seedlings and upper leaves of older plants are simple; lower leaves on adult plants are deeply lobed (3–7 lobes), smooth and serrated. They vary in colour from dark green–red. Plants are virtually evergreen in warmer areas. In cooler regions, plants may lose their leaves for a period in winter.

Flowers and seeds: Ornamental, yellow–tan flowers that only live for a single day, but flower over a long period. They are borne singly from the leaf axils, large (~12 cm wide), have a dark red centre, and the flower turns pink as it withers at the end of the day. Borne in summer. The flower has an outer calyx surrounding the petals, which is usually a red colour and consists of five large sepals with a collar of 8–12 pointed bracts around the base. The calyx enlarges after the petals have withered and becomes fleshy, juicy, but crisp, 3–6 cm long. Within the calyx is a velvety seedpod, which is green at first, divided into five sections (1–2 cm long), with each section containing 3–4 kidney-shaped, light brown seeds (~0.4 cm long). The seedpod turns brown as it ripens and splits open when mature and dry. The calyx is harvested for use when the seedpod separates from the calyx, i.e. ~3–4 weeks after the flower has withered. The calyx, stems and leaves can be eaten and taste similar to cranberries. The flower needs shorter days to initiate flowering (i.e. 11 hours of light only), so they naturally either flower earlier or not until the beginning of autumn in temperate areas. (They flower throughout the summer in more equatorial latitudes.) *Pollination:* Hibiscus, in general, do not seem to be easily pollinated by birds or insects, so, for seed production, hand-pollination may help.

Yield/harvest: When grown in optimum conditions, a plant can produce 1–2 kg of calyxes (there is a report of 7.25 kg from Florida). The calyxes are harvested ~3–4 weeks after the flower has withered: flowers can bloom in spring, so plants are harvested in late spring–early summer. When ready, the large, reddish calyx surrounding the seedpods is picked while still fleshy, and before it becomes tough. The flower head snaps off more easily in the mornings than later in the day. Because picking the calyxes initiates the development of latent flower buds, the flowering season can be extended by a month or so. The fruits of roselle ripen progressively from lower down the stem upwards towards its apex. If the calyxes are not picked, the plant only produces a few flowers, the plant matures much faster and may die at the end of the season. The stems can also be harvested for fibre. Commercially, the stems are removed to just leave ~10 cm above soil level, and this can be repeated three times during a season before allowing the plant to produce flowers. The plant will need extra nutrients and care though if this regime is taken.

Roots: Has a deep, penetrating taproot, so plant carefully to avoid damage. Prefer its roots to be kept cool, but the plant top to be in the sun.

CULTIVATION

They are often grown as an annual.

Food

Virtually the whole plant can be eaten in one way or another. The calyxes can be eaten fresh or cooked. Their taste has been compared to cranberries, rhubarb, raspberry or plum (so quite a mix!). To prepare, cut around the tough base of the calyx below the bracts, remove it and then remove the seedpods. The fresh calyx can be used in salads (sweet and savoury), preserves, soups, juices, sweet-pie fillings, sauces (dessert and savoury), pickles, etc. It is rich in acid and pectin (~4%) and so makes good jam and jellies. It also makes a good red-coloured wine. Can be also cooked as a vegetable. The Jamaicans make a drink by mixing roselle, ginger and sugar in boiling water, leaving it to stand overnight, and then serving it the next day with ice and sometimes a dash of rum. It can also be added to herbal teas. Some cultivars have coloured juice that adds to their usage in dishes. The fruits can be roasted to make a coffee substitute. The leaves can be eaten raw or cooked: they have an acid, rhubarb-like taste. The juice from the boiled leaves and stems can be used in the same way as juice extracted from the calyxes. The oily seed can be roasted and ground for use in soups and sauces. Like many hibiscus species, the root is also edible, but this species has a fibrous, mucilaginous root that does not have much flavour.

Nutrition

The calyxes contain flavonoids, e.g. hibiscetine, and contain good levels of calcium for a fruit. The calyxes and leaves contain some vitamin C, iron, phosphorus, niacin and riboflavin. Fresh leaves contain 2% protein. The seed contains ~20% oil.

Medicinal

Extracts from roselle may lower blood pressure. It has a diuretic effect and helps to lower fevers. The calyxes have been used as an antispasmodic and seem to have good anti-parasitic and antibacterial properties. A tea made from the calyxes and leaves is said to be calming, to decrease blood viscosity, to stimulate intestinal peristalsis and to improve digestion and kidney function. The juice, with salt, pepper, asafoetida and molasses, is taken as a remedy for biliousness. They are eaten in Central America as a hangover cure. The mashed leaves help heal boils, ulcers and wounds.

Other uses

The stems are harvested for fibre. They are retted to remove the fibre and then washed and dried. The fibre length can be up to ~1.5 m and is used to make rough cloth, paper, twine, etc. Chickens love the seeds.

Ornamental

It goes without saying that these plants make good ornamental additions to a border or display because of their flowers. However, when planting in a border, ensure that they do not suffer too much competition from nearby plants.

Location: Best grown in full sun. They are surprisingly wind tolerant. They do not like competition from other species or weeds.

Temperature: Are susceptible to frost damage, but are fast growing and produce flowers soon after planting, so can be easily grown in many regions during a summer. They prefer annual temperatures of 12–28°C, with a long, hot summer. In colder regions, site them in the sunniest spot, or even under cover. The calyxes do not ripen properly if the summer is not warm enough.

Soil/water/nutrients: Prefers a well-drained, fertile, but moist loam, but will grow in other soil types. Will grow in soils with a wide pH range from 4.5–8.0, from fairly acid conditions to alkaline soils. They can tolerate temporary waterlogging and even stagnant water. Grow best with good irrigation. Plants given too much nitrogen will have excessive vegetative growth at the expense of flower/fruit production. However, additions of compost or manure are beneficial.

Planting: Seedlings can be planted at ~1 m apart. Best planted in late autumn in warmer areas, or early spring (possibly with protection) in cooler regions.

Pruning: Growing as a perennial, and pruning early, encourages branching and the development of more flowering shoots. Pruning can be fairly drastic; it removes old straggly growth and can 'renew' the plant.

Propagation: *Seed:* Easy from seed. Sow in early spring in warmth. They germinate in a few days. Raise seedlings in pots until ~10 cm tall before planting out. *Cuttings:* Fairly good results with cuttings, but the calyx yield can be less. Take half-ripe cuttings, with a heel if possible, in summer, and overwinter in a protected, warm location before planting out in spring once it is warm.

Pests and diseases: Their main foe is the root-knot nematode, therefore it is advisable to rotate the location where they are planted. Mealybugs can also be a problem. Also look out for scale insects and aphids. They can be attacked by several fungi and viruses.

CULTIVARS

'Archer' (syn. 'White Sorrel'): From Antigua. A tall, strong plant with green stems. Flower: yellow with deeper yellow eye and pale brown pollen. Calyx is greenish-white and smaller than some cultivars, but it usually produces more per plant than other cultivars. Plant is often grown for its use as a vegetable. The juice is almost colourless.

'Rico': Fairly low-growing, spreading, most leaves are simple. Flower: dark red eye, yellow pollen. Mature, rich red calyx is ~5 cm long; bracts are plump and horizontal. Very good yields. Calyx is used for juice and preserves.

'Victor': From USA. ~2 m tall, erect, strong. Flower: dark red eye, brown pollen. Calyx: slender, curves upwards. Juice and preserves of calyx and leaves are rich red.

OTHER EDIBLE SPECIES

The description of roselle applies to the species below unless noted otherwise.

Australian native sorrel, *Hibiscus heterophyllus*. A native of Australia, grows to a height of ~1.6 m. Has prickly stems. Flowers: beautiful, large, pale lemon, with red eyes. Cultivation is similar to roselle. The plant is not frost hardy. Propagation as roselle.

Uses: The calyx is eaten in the same way as roselle. It has a good, mild flavour. The leaves taste like sorrel and can be cooked like spinach. It does not seem to have the same medicinal properties as roselle. Produces a tough fibre. The root is edible, but very fibrous and mucilaginous.

Hibiscus (rose of Sharon), *Hibiscus syriacus* (syn. *Althaea frutox*). Attractive, ~3 m tall, ~2 m spread, hardy hibiscus species, native to East Asia, but now naturalised in southern Europe. Forms an erect, many branched shrub. Comes into leaf late in spring; these are often three-lobed. Trumpet-shaped flowers can be white/pink/red/purple, ~8 cm diameter, through summer–autumn; the seeds ripen in late autumn. Fairly frost hardy: can tolerate ~–15 to –20°C, but prefers warmer climates. The flowers only open in sunny weather. There are some variegated forms. *Propagation:* As for roselle. Can also easily self-seed *in situ*. It is also possible to take semi-ripe–ripe cuttings in early autumn; they should root well. Layering from mid summer–early autumn is possible.

Uses: *Food:* As for roselle. The calyxes have a mild taste and are a little mucilaginous. Are good in salads. Young leaves can be eaten fresh or cooked; they have a mild flavour, but can be somewhat tough. The seeds contain ~25% oil. Has an edible, but fibrous, mucilaginous root. *Medicinal:* The calyxes and leaves are said to help with eye and stomach problems, to act as a diuretic, and treat skin problems, possibly due to their antibacterial properties. The root bark is used to treat many conditions including diarrhoea, as a vermifuge and for period pains. *Other uses:* A low-quality fibre can be obtained from the stems. A hair shampoo can be made from the leaves and a blue dye from the flowers. *Ornamental:* Makes a good ornamental plant. Is sometimes planted as a hedge in southern Europe.

Hibiscus (rose of Sharon), *Hibiscus sinosyriacus*. This species is very similar to *H. syriacus*. Apart from the notes for *H. syriacus*, the following apply. The leaves do not appear till late spring, and are larger, as are the calyxes, than *H. syriacus*, but the plant is also a little less hardy, only tolerating temperatures down to ~–12°C. It also tends to flower later in the season and so may be at more risk for early autumn frosts. Younger plants benefit from winter protection in colder regions. There are a number of popular ornamental selections. See *H. syriacus* for uses.

Chinese hibiscus, *Hibiscus rosa-sinensis*. A medium-sized shrub, height ~2.5 m, spread ~2.5 m, and a native of southeastern Asia. The flowers are very important in Hindu devotional ceremonies, being sacred to the elephant god, Ganesh. Has red, showy, beautiful, typical hibiscus flowers from spring through summer, and into autumn in warmer areas. Is not hardy to hard frosts but can survive short dips below freezing and recover. Tends to lose its leaves in winter and become semi-dormant in cooler regions. Has dark green, coarsely toothed leaves. Produces numerous, ~13-cm-diameter, short-lived red flowers. (Selected cultivars can also have pink, yellow, white or salmon-coloured flowers.) Makes a good container plant, with its beautiful flowers, perhaps on a deck or patio where it could then be protected in colder weather. It does grow fairly fast, and could be grown as an annual if given an early start. Needs a good sunny location. Seems to benefit from fairly drastic pruning in early spring to renew the plant.

Uses: *Food:* The calyxes can be eaten fresh or cooked. They also produce a purple colouring, which can be used to dye other foods. (It has also been used as a mascara in China.) The young leaves can be used as a spinach substitute. The root is edible, but is very fibrous and mucilaginous. *Medicinal:* The plant has been used to check bleeding, to soothe irritated tissues and to relax spasms. The flowers have been used as an aphrodisiac and as a soothing, cooling skin cream. They are eaten to relieve

painful menstruation, cystitis, venereal diseases, fevers, chest infections and to promote hair growth. The leaves are said to ease pain, act as a laxative and to also soothe the skin, and may have similar antibacterial properties to roselle. The root is rich in mucilage and has been used to treat coughs. *Other uses:* Its fibre is used to make fabrics, cord, paper, etc. *Ornamental:* There are a number of ornamental selections. They make attractive, medium-sized shrubs in warmer areas. Can also be planted as an informal hedge in warmer regions. Because the flowers are so short lived, and if flowers are wanted for later in the day, in the morning simply pick flower buds that are about to open and place them carefully in a fridge; the cold will slow down their daily cycle so that they then are still open by evening. ∎

Hippophae rhamnoides
Sea buckthorn (sea berry, Siberian pineapple)
ELAEAGNACEAE

Similar species: Chinese buckthorn (*H. sinensis*), Tibetan sea buckthorn (*H. tibetana*), willow-leaved sea buckthorn (*H. salicifolia*)
Relatives: *Elaeagnus* species

Sea buckthorn is native to China, Mongolia, Russia and many areas of northern Europe. It has long been known for its juicy, orange-red berries. It is mentioned in the writings of ancient Greek scholars and its leaves and berries have been used for centuries in Europe and Asia. Their medicinal value has been known since at least the 8th century in Tibet. Recently, the berries have become of interest to many researchers around the world for their potential nutritional and medicinal benefits. It is considered to have significant economic potential. The Russians started investigating the biologically active substances found in the berries, leaves and bark in the 1940s, and factories were set up to develop products from the berries. These were then used by Russian cosmonauts as a cream for protection from cosmic radiation. Since 1982, >300,000 ha have been planted in China along with 150 processing factories producing ~200 products. The fruits of many cultivars, although somewhat sharp in taste, can be eaten fresh, though one probably wouldn't want to eat too many.

DESCRIPTION

Elegant, multi-branched, thorny shrub that can reach 2–4 m in height. They have stout branches that form a symmetrical, rounded head. Young branches are smooth, light brown/grey with needle-shaped thorns (2–5 cm) on 2–3-year-old wood. These make the fruits painful to pick, and efforts are under way to select varieties without thorns. The bark is brown or black. Shrub has moderate–vigorous growth rates of 30–45 cm/year. It does sucker freely though, so may not be suitable for smaller gardens.

Leaves: Deciduous, silvery grey-green on the upper surface, fine, slender, 4–6 cm long, alternate. Open in late spring.

Flowers: Small, inconspicuous, yellow-green, appear late in spring, but before the leaves. Dioecious. Male flower buds are smaller than those of the female. Flower buds are mostly formed on 2-year-old wood. The flowers are very frost resistant. *Pollination:* Wind-pollinated. Because plants are dioecious, plus being wind-pollinated, this species is best

planted in small groups to ensure good pollination and fruit-set. Site male plants within groves of females.

Fruit: Only female plants produce fruits, or drupes as they are more correctly termed. Mature berries are tasty, but sharp; juicy, oval, yellow or orange-red, 0.6–1.0 cm long, ~0.5 cm diameter. Have a central stone containing the kernel. They ripen at the end of summer–autumn, but can persist on branches all winter due to the absence of an abscission layer.

Harvesting/yield/storage: The fruits are ripe when bright orange, and are best harvested before they become over-ripe as they then develop a strong, musky smell with an unpleasant taste. Early autumn frosts can sweeten the fruits. However, harvesting can be time-consuming and painful, as the spines occur close to the fruits. Two-year-old plants may bear some fruits, but often take 3–4 years before commencing. Have relatively high yields of 3–5 kg per shrub and production is reliable. Fruits do not store well, and are best frozen if keeping for a longer period.

Roots: Has a very vigorous root system and can be planted on slopes to stabilise soil. The roots form a symbiotic relationship with bacteria that fix nitrogen, so is a good plant for poorer reclamation sites. Produces suckers freely, so do not plant in small areas.

CULTIVATION

Location: Likes an open sunny spot. Fruit yields are greatly influenced by exposure to sunlight: plants do not tolerate shade and won't fruit well in these locations. Grows well in coastal areas. Will tolerate strong winds. In its natural habitat, it often grows on riverbanks and coastal dunes.

Temperature: Very hardy: can withstand temperatures of ~–45°C!

Chilling: Will need some winter chilling to produce good yields and growth. Probably not suitable for cultivation in areas that have warmer winters.

Soil/water/nutrients: Can grow in a wide range of soil types, though grows best in deep, well-drained, sandy loams with lots of organic matter. In dry areas, water is needed for establishment. Can tolerate a very wide range of pH values (i.e. up to pH 8), although grows best at pH 5.5–7. Once established, it is very drought resistant, but some moisture will give better growth, particularly when the plants are flowering and fruiting. It can, however, also tolerate lots of wet weather, but not extended waterlogging. Young plants benefit from an organic mulch for the first 3–4 years, which will provide nutrients, help conserve moisture and reduce weed competition.

Plants are only moderately nutrient hungry, and benefit from an annual addition of fertiliser or an organic equivalent, particularly with extra phosphorus. However, the addition of extra nitrogen can inhibit nitrogen fixation by bacteria in the roots.

Planting: Space plants at ~3 m apart for a specimen plant and at ~1 m apart for a hedge. If possible plant hedges in a N–S direction to provide maximum light. Because plants are dioecious, a ratio of male to female plants of 1:6 is recommended.

Propagation: *Seed:* Grows easily from seed and there is a good germination rate. Clean seeds after collecting and sow outside when fresh in autumn, or can be sown in spring, but they then need a period of stratification in moist sand for ~3 months at 5°C to break dormancy. Unlike most species, the sex of sea buckthorn seedlings can be determined soon after germination, rather than having to wait until they first flower. In spring, the young male seedlings develop very prominent lateral buds, whereas females buds are clear and smooth. *Cuttings:* Plants grown from cuttings are predictable, their sex is known and they will fruit 1–2 years sooner than seedlings. Softwood or semi-ripe cuttings can be taken in late spring or summer, respectively, and should have all but the top few leaves removed. Dip cuttings in rooting hormone or willow soakings before planting in a gritty, moist, but well-drained compost. Take is variable. Hardwood cuttings, 15–20 cm long, can be taken in winter from the previous season's wood, but the rate of take can be poor. Cuttings can be stood in water for 7 days until roots form. Rooted cuttings are grown

uses

Food

The fruits can be added to sauces or other fruits, or used to make juice, jams, preserves, confectionery, a dressing, liqueurs and a wine. The fruit also freezes very well. A healthy tea can be made from the leaves, but they should only be picked from male plants, preferably in summer, so as not to disturb fruit-set on female plants. It can be used by itself and with other fruits to make a good-tasting, pleasantly aromatic juice. It is being increasingly used commercially for this purpose because of its health benefits.

Nutrition

The fruits are very nutritious and vitamin rich, and contain significant amounts of carbohydrates, proteins (~30%) and trace elements. The flesh is very high in organic acids, particularly malic acid, and is acidic (pH ~2.7). Berries have a high concentration of vitamin C, 100–400 mg/100 g fruit, which is higher than most other fruits. The seeds and flesh contain good levels of oil. Most of the oil is unsaturated (linoleic: 40%, linolenic acid: 30%, oleic acid: 15%). The oil contains fairly high levels of phytosterols, i.e. plant sterols, with structures related to cholesterol, and are capable of lowering cholesterol levels. The seeds and flesh also contain high levels of vitamin E (65–90 mg/100 g of seed; 200–480 mg/100 g berry). The seed oil and leaves have good levels of vitamins A and C, and the leaves also contain good levels of several B vitamins; flavonoids and phytosterols.

Medicinal

Recent research suggests that the fruits from this species are one of the most nutritious to be grown in temperate zones. Studies have reported that regular use can prevent cancer, and larger quantities have been shown to reverse the growth of cancerous tumours. The oil has been clinically tested in Russia and China, and is thought to be anti-inflammatory, antimicrobial, an analgesic and to promote regeneration of tissues. The expressed oil has been used externally to treat mucus glands within the mouth, rectum and vagina, but also radiation damage, burns, scalds, ulcers, chilblains and other skin damage. Expressed oil from the leaves and young stems is used to treat skin diseases and to prevent scarring. More than ten different drugs have been developed from sea buckthorn in Asia and Europe and are available in different forms.

Other uses

The oil from the seeds is used in cosmetics, such as facial cream. In Europe and Asia, the leaves and berries are used as an animal feed. In particular, it was a well-known tonic for horses: the leaves and young branches are added to fodder and induce rapid weight gain and a shiny coat. In fact, the generic name *Hippophae* means 'shining horse'.

Ornamental

An attractive large shrub that fixes nitrogen and is good in problem areas; an ideal plant to prevent soil erosion and to aid land reclamation.

on in pots until large enough to plant out. *Suckers:* Can be very easily transplanted, or plants divided, by removing suckers during the growing season. *Layering:* This is also very easy, in autumn, though can take several months to root.

Pruning: Some moderate pruning can increase yield and reduce any tendency to biennial bearing. Give an annual, general prune to remove old, crossing or straggly branches, which will also encourage the development of lateral fruiting shoots.

Pests and diseases: Affected by relatively few pests and diseases. Possible problems can be green aphid, rose leaf-roller, gypsy moth, gall tick, comma-shaped scale, fruit fly and caterpillars; also *Verticillium* wilt, *Fusarium* wilt, damping off, brown rot and scab. Birds and rats like the fruits.

CULTIVARS

'Indian summer': From Canada. Grows in many soils and even tolerates some salt. Has above-average drought tolerance and is fully hardy. Grows to 3–4 m. Won't tolerate waterlogging. Needs a frost-free period of at least 85–130 days.

'Leikora': From Germany. Large bush with large, ornamental orange berries. A female cultivar.

'Novostj Altaja': Sweeter fruits, but somewhat less nutritious than other cultivars. Fewer thorns than average; adapted to long, cold winters. A good cropper.

'Otradnaya': Early harvest. Good for harsh winters. Vigorous.

'Pollmix': Male cultivar, suitable as a pollinator for 'Leikora'.

'Prevoshodnaya': New Russian cultivar. Attractive ornamental. Fruits are of good quality.

'Sprite': Male selection. Grows to a height and spread of ~1.8 m. Leaves are silvery.

OTHER SPECIES

The species described below are similar to *H. rhamnoides* in many respects, and only differences between them are emphasised.

Chinese buckthorn, *Hippophae sinensis*. A medium-sized tree (~15 m tall) native to eastern Asia–western China. Fixes nitrogen. Flowers in spring; fruits ripen in autumn, and should be picked before they deteriorate. This species is similar to *H. rhamnoides*, but the fruits have even greater levels of vitamin C. Its cultivation methods, propagation, uses, etc, are as for *H. rhamnoides*.

Tibetan sea buckthorn, *Hippophae tibetana*. A medium-sized tree (~15 m tall) native to east Asia. Flowers in spring and fruits ripen in autumn. Hardy down to ~–10°C. Fixes nitrogen. Cultivation, propagation, uses, etc. as *H. rhamnoides*, except that fruits may be more acid, though are considerably larger. The fruits of this species, in particular, have been used to treat pulmonary diseases.

Willow-leaved sea buckthorn, *Hippophae salicifolia*. A fast-growing, medium-sized tree, height ~15 m, native to eastern Asia. Fruits ripen in early autumn, though their flavour becomes less sour if left to remain on the tree until after a frost. Very wind tolerant. Not as cold tolerant as sea buckthorn: can be damaged by temperatures below ~–10°C. Prefers moister soil. Fixes nitrogen. The fruits of this species, though sharp, are highly rated. Has nutritional and medicinal benefits similar to sea buckthorn. A good pioneer species. ■

Hovenia dulcis
Raisin tree (Japanese raisin tree, kenpo nashi, bei zhi qu)
RHAMNACEAE
Related genus: jujube, Darling plum

The 'fruit' of this tree is actually the flower stalk, which swells into a red-brown mass after flowering. The raisin tree is native to the moist areas and mountains of China, and the Chinese have known of its uses and cultivated this tree for centuries. Its cultivation also spread, long ago, to Japan, Korea and India, and it is still grown widely in these countries for its ornamental and edible uses. The plant was introduced to the West in about 1820. It forms a medium-sized, hardy tree that has attractive leaves and bears masses of cream-coloured flowers in spring, after which the many flower stalks swell and then drop from the tree once the seed has ripened. (The seeds are not edible.) When eaten, the stalks are sweet and taste somewhat of raisins. A good novelty tree that can be grown in a range of climates and is attractive ornamentally when grown as a specimen or in a group.

DESCRIPTION

A medium-sized, moderately fast-growing, spreading tree (~9–15 m tall, 5–8 m spread), with a rounded head and a single trunk. Branches are graceful; the lower ones tend to drop off to leave a high crown. It grows faster when younger.

The bark is grey, deeply furrowed, and sheds to reveal younger, brown bark beneath.

Leaves: Deciduous, alternate, shiny, large (~15 cm long), attractive, heart-shaped, dark green, sometimes drooping. Sometimes has yellow autumn colour.

Flowers: Fragrant, greenish-cream, small, but in large clusters that form numerous racemes (~8 cm long). The time of flowering is temperature dependent: in warmer regions they flower in late spring, but in cooler areas they may not

flower until late summer. They are bisexual and self-fertile. *Pollination:* The flowers are nectar rich and attract the bees.

Fruit: The edible 'raisins' are not a fruit, but are the short, swollen mature flower stalks. The actual dry seedpod is inedible and is not used. Once pollination has occurred, the flowers die back and the seedpod begins to develop, and so does the flower stalk. It swells to become fleshy, lumpy and changes colour to become reddish-brown. It can then be picked and eaten. The seedpod is round and small, and turns deep brown when ripe.

Yield/harvest: The stalks can either be picked from the tree, or they naturally drop. As they ripen their sugar level increases, as does their fruity taste. The stalks will be sweetest and can be harvested when the seeds have also ripened and have turned brown. Although the stalks are only small, there are many of them on a single tree. If the weather is cooler, and flowering is delayed until late summer, there might not be time for the pods to form, and so the stalks also do not swell and ripen sufficiently before colder weather arrives. It takes 7–10 years for trees to start fruiting if grown from seed, but only ~3 years if vegetatively grown.

CULTIVATION

Location: Are best grown in full sun in temperate regions, which will induce better flowering and ripening of stalks and seeds. However, they can also grow well in semi-shade, and in hot regions such sites are preferable. The trees are moderately wind hardy, but young plants will need shelter. They do not grow well in salty, maritime locations.

Temperature: They are very cold hardy trees and can withstand temperatures down to ~–30°C. However, late frosts can damage young spring growth and kill back the ends of branches, but they usually grow back during the spring and summer. They do not like intense heat; try planting them in cooler spots or in semi-shade in areas that have very hot summers.

Soil/water/nutrients: The raisin tree can tolerate a wide range of soil conditions, including sandy soils, but prefers a fertile, moisture-retentive loam. Can grow in moderately acid to moderately alkaline soils. Although it is somewhat tolerant of drought, the trees do much better with a regular supply of moisture. They are not particularly nutrient-hungry trees, though an application of a balanced fertiliser, or similar, in spring, is of benefit. Trees cannot tolerate waterlogging.

Pot culture: This tree can be grown for a few years in a large container.

Pruning: The tree tends to prune itself, dropping its lower branches as it grows taller.

Propagation: *Seed:* Tricky. The seeds have a hard seedcoat that needs scarifying before it will germinate: either scratch the surface or soak the seeds in a weak acid for a couple of hours to soften the outer layer. Wash the seed to remove any acid before sowing. Alternatively, the seed can be soaked in hot water for 3 days. Germinate in warm, humid conditions. They germinate better in light. Germination takes 7–30+ days. *Cuttings:* Semi-ripe cuttings, also root cuttings, can be taken in late summer.

Pests and diseases: Generally free of problems.

CULTIVARS

There are no known cultivars. ∎

Food
The swollen stalks are very tasty when just eaten fresh from the tree and can also be used in any dish that contains dried fruit, except that the 'raisin' stalks do not need to be dried. They can also be stored in a cool, dark place for up to 2 months, where the flavour is said to get even better. They taste like crunchy raisins with a somewhat acid apple-pear flavour. They can be added to cakes and desserts, or eaten as a snack with nuts. The Chinese prepare a sweet extract from the stalk and leaves that is added to candies. A wine vinegar can be also made from the stalks. The leaves may be edible when fresh, but quality seems to vary from tree to tree.

Medicinal
Recent research indicates that extracts from the raisin tree can lower blood-sugar levels, and may have future use as an effective anti-diabetic product. In China, historically, the stalks have been made into a drink called 'tree honey', which is said to relieve hangovers. Recent Korean research seems to confirm this and has shown that extracts from this plant have a protective effect on the liver and can reduce blood-alcohol concentration. It is also claimed to have 'anti-ageing' constituents.

Other uses
The wood has a good colour, is fine-grained and hard, and is used for building and fine furniture.

Ornamental
Makes a worthwhile shade tree and a good medium-sized specimen, or can be planted in groups. It has attractive leaves, lots of fragrant flowers and provides a good talking point with its edible flower stalks.

Humulus lupulus, H. japonicus
Hops (lupulin)
CANNABIDACEAE

Relatives: hemp (*Cannabis sativa*), stinging nettle (*Urtica dioica*)

It is likely that people have been using cannabis and the hop for at least 5000 years, and probably back to the mid Holocene. The hop plant is a perennial, twining vine that climbs trees and other structures in temperate regions, and is generally well behaved and not too invasive. It is native to Britain and other western European countries. Ale has been drunk for many hundreds of years in England and throughout Europe and was, and still is, made using fermented malt, which was then often flavoured with honey or with various bitter herbs. It was not until much later that hops were added to ale, with the hops' bitterness balancing out the sweetness of the malt. The name 'ale' still remains in common usage. The Romans added hops to their ale, and the Germans caught on soon after, although the English did not discover this usage of hops until the 16th century. Today, beer is, by far, the greatest usage for this plant; however, the young stems and leaves can

be eaten, and the flowers have long been valued medicinally for their sedative and muscle-relaxing properties. They are now cultivated in England, Germany, New Zealand, the USA, South America and Australia. It is the female fruit (strobile), shaped like a scaly cone, and containing resinous and bitter compounds, which gives beer its characteristic flavour. Nowadays, beer is widely available around the world, and there is revival in the development of breweries that produce speciality beers, which often use more hops in their brews, as well as various other ingredients. The English name 'hop' is derived from the Anglo-Saxon word 'hoppan', meaning to climb.

DESCRIPTION

Perennial root systems that produce annual stems which twist in a clockwise direction up supports to a height of ~6–8 m. The tendrils also form strong, hooked hairs, which strengthens their hold. Their ascent is rapid, and can be 10 cm a day with warmth and moisture, making them one of the fastest-growing plants. The stems are supple, yet tough. Once they have flowered and fruited, the stems die back and the plant becomes dormant during winter. Plants live, on average, for 12–20 years.

Leaves: Rough surfaced, sharply-toothed, mid-green, with 3–5 lobes, usually opposite, on long ~20–30-cm stalks. Smaller leaves are single lobed.

Flowers/fruits: The hop plant is dioecious, but only female plants are needed to produce 'cones'. Planting only females avoids seed production, which often gives better-quality, though often smaller, 'cones'. In many areas, only female hops are planted, with male plants being banned. However, cone quality is often improved if the flowers are fertilised (apart from the presence of the seeds), and so cultivars have been selected that are triploid (with an extra set of chromosomes), and male and female plants can then be planted together. The male pollen can fertilise the female, but the female flower does not set seed though receives the benefits of being fertilised. The pale green, female flowers are borne in clusters on lateral branches, and form a cone-like, papery structure, 2.5–10 cm long. The flowering heads contain many yellow glands, which contain a powder that gives hops much of their characteristic flavour and aroma. This powder rapidly deteriorates in quality with storage.

Flowers are borne in early summer; by ~28 days later they have developed into hop 'cones' and become larger and turn yellow-brown, while any male flowers wither away. The whole female flower is harvested for use. Hops can only be grown within a certain latitudinal band between 35–55° north or south. The plant will only grow if it receives at least 13 hours of light a day; if they receive less, then the plant's growth is very slow and the leaves are small. Conversely, flowering won't occur if the day is too long, i.e. if plants are grown too near to the Poles.

Yield/harvest: Plants start producing cones when about 3 years old. They have a wonderful, resinous, distinctive aroma when ripe. They are ripe when they become drier in texture and are lighter in weight. Also, when cut open, the lupulin sacs (containing the essential oils and bitter compounds) are a dark yellow colour and have developed their distinctive aroma. A light yellow colour indicates immaturity. The cones are usually harvested just before they are fully ripe, in late summer–early autumn, and are carefully dried at <65°C so that they dry evenly to ~15% moisture content. Overheating rapidly volatises the essential oils. Once dried, the hops can be stored in a dry, cool environment for a few months.

Roots: As plants mature, they form an extensive, far-reaching, woody root system. The roots may penetrate the soil to a depth of 5 m or more. They also develop shallow feeder roots, which are important during the growing season and should not be damaged by mechanical cultivation. A thick organic mulch will help conserve moisture and add nutrients. Plants also send out runners from the crown.

CULTIVATION

Location: Grows best in full sun, or a little shade. Is not tolerant of salty maritime conditions, and is not very wind tolerant. They need a structure to climb up. They can only be grown between 35–55° north or south.

Temperature: Is fully cold hardy when dormant, and can take long periods of low temperatures. Can survive ~–27°C. Grows best in a temperate climate, with a warm summer.

Chilling: Need winter chilling to initiate spring growth.

Soil/water/nutrients: They grow best in sandy, loose, well-drained soil that has lots of well-rotted organic matter or peat within it. They grow at a pH range from fairly acid to neutral: pH 5.5–7, and do not grow well in alkaline or saline soils. They like regular moisture during the growing season, particularly if there is a deep water table. They may tolerate some waterlogging, though not for extended periods. They also like regular applications of a well-balanced fertiliser during the spring and summer. In some hop yards, sheep are allowed to wander about and act as lawnmowers, stripping off the lower leaves, which are not needed.

Planting: Space plants at 2.5 m apart, near a structure they can grow up. Very little growth takes place during the first year. They need string or something with a roughish texture to grow up in their second or third year; wire tends to be too smooth. They can be planted near trees and do not seem to smother them or shade them out. Dig the soil deeply before planting and incorporate organic matter or peat. They are usually planted in spring.

Propagation: *Seed:* Hops are not usually grown by this method because many cultivars do not produce seed, or even if they do it is often not viable or reverts back to the wild hop. *Cuttings:* Often propagated by cutting sections off runners that arise near the crown of the plant. These can be taken during spring and summer. Each sections should have 2–3 healthy buds. These are then potted up with moisture to establish, and can be planted out the following year.

Pruning: Once fully established, and once the stems have grown ~40 cm, they can be assisted by encouraging them to twine clockwise around their support. Commercially, only 2–6 stems are allowed to grow from each plant to obtain maximum cone size, and other new shoots are removed throughout the season. More shoots produce more, but smaller cones. Shoot removal has other benefits, as they can be lightly cooked and then taste like tender asparagus. As the hop stems grow, the lower leaves are often removed to help prevent diseases such as downy mildew and spider mites. At the end of the season, all the stems may be cut down

Pests and diseases: The main insect problems are

uses

Food

The flower heads are used as a flavouring and preservative in beer. The young leaves and shoots can be lightly cooked and taste like asparagus. The fleshy runners can also be eaten.

Nutrition

Hops are rich in vitamins C and B. The flowers contain ~1% essential oils and 15–25% resinous bitter principles. They contain alpha acids (e.g. humulone, valerianic acid) and beta acids (e.g. lupulone, colupulone). The oil and bitter resins together are known as lupulin. They also contain tannins, flavonoids (rutin, quercetin and astragalin), phyto-oestrogens, asparagine and other compounds. The seeds contain gamma-linolenic acid, an essential fatty acid that has important functions within the human body and is rarely found in plants. The leaves contain rutin.

Medicinal

Recent studies have found that certain hop flavonoids can help prevent cancer, by inhibiting the enzyme cytochrome P450, which often activates the cancer process. Hops relax the central nervous system. The flowers act as a sedative, as a soporific, as a digestive tonic, as a hypnotic, an astringent, a diuretic, they reduce muscular contractions, dampen male desire (because of their phyto-oestrogens), but have also been used to treat premature ejaculation. Hops are often given for nervous tension, anxiety, indigestion and to increase appetite. They reduce muscular spasms within smooth muscle and can benefit nervous dyspepsia, irritable bowel syndrome, diverticulitis, Crohn's disease, palpitations, nervous or irritable coughs, and asthma. Very good for dissolving kidney stones. Humulone and lupulone have an anti-inflammatory action, and are antibacterial, particularly with Gram-positive bacteria, and are used to treat infections of the upper digestive tract, ulcers, skin eruptions and wounds. Unfortunately, Gram-negative bacteria are immune to the acids within hops as these acids are not able to enter the bacteria's membrane. Hops may also have some antifungal activity (e.g. *Candida albicans*). Hops may also have some activity against *Staphylococcus aureus*. They have been used to treat heavy or painful menstruation, and also to relieve some of the symptoms of menopause, with research being conducted in Belgium to further investigate its modes of action. It is also now accepted that beer (as well as red wine), in moderation, can reduce risk of heart attack. As a lotion, use ~14 g of dried flowers per 0.5 litre of water. Applied, it can act locally as an antiseptic. Placed in pillows, the volatile oils and valerianic acid help to overcome insomnia. **Warning:** Hops can act as a mild depressive and, therefore, should not be taken if depressed.

Other uses

The fibre from the stems can be used in cloth and paper, although, the fibres are difficult to separate and the stems need to be steeped in water throughout winter. The leaves and flower heads yield a good, brown dye.

Ornamental

They make attractive, non-invasive vines, and can be grown in smaller gardens up a pergola or similar. Good for summer shade, but allowing winter sun onto the deck; sitting beneath clusters of ripe yellowy-green hop flowers is pleasant. There are also some very attractive gold-leaved forms, which also produce flowers.

aphids, spider mites, wire worm, weevils and the two-spotted mite. The main diseases are powdery mildew, downy mildew, *Verticillium* wilt, *Phytophthora* root rot, with many of these being more common in high humidity. It helps to remove lower leaves during the summer, and older stems after harvesting the cones, to reduce over-wintering pests and diseases. Many European hop cultivars are more resistant to *Phytophthora* root-rot infections and, therefore, are often crossed with American cultivars to confer resistance. It is recommended to not plant hops where potatoes have been previously grown to reduce *Verticillium* infection. Hops are also susceptible to a number of viral diseases.

CULTIVARS

There are ~40 cultivars of hops, each with different hop characteristics. Hops are often classified into two types: bitter and aromatic. Examples of the former are 'Olympic', 'Nugget', 'Galena' and 'Chinook'; examples of aromatics are 'Cascade', 'Willamette', 'Mt Hood', 'Fuggle', 'Goldings', 'Tettnanger Spalt', 'Columbia' and 'Saaz', and the German cultivars 'Tettnanger', 'Hallertauer' and 'Hersbrucker'. Aromatic hops often mature before bitter hops, and often grow in cooler climates.

'Brewer's Gold' and **'Bullion':** From England. Bitter. Medium–late maturing. Both are vigorous, with good yields. Fairly resistant to downy mildew. High in essential oils with an alpha acid content of ~8%.

'Cascade': From England. Aromatic. Matures later than 'Fuggle'. Resistant to downy mildew, but susceptible to *Verticillium* wilt and some viruses. Has an oil content of 1–2%, an alpha acid content of 5–7% with a distinctive fragrance. Good yields.

'Eroica': From Oregon. Bitter. Late maturing. Alpha acid levels of 10–13%, with good yields. Fairly resistant to downy mildew and *Verticillium* spp.

'Fuggle': Has been grown commercially in England for >100 years. Aromatic. Is resistant to downy mildew, hop mosaic virus, but is susceptible to *Verticillium* wilt. Has ~1% essential oil content and an alpha acid content of 4–6%. It does make good-tasting traditional beer. Early maturing. Not very high yields. Commercially, growers often plant male plants with females to get larger cones.

'Galena': Derived from 'Brewer's Gold'. Bitter. Fairly resistant to downy mildew and *Verticillium* wilt. Susceptible to frost damage and can be difficult to establish. Alpha acid levels ~12%.

'Nugget': From Oregon. Bitter. Alpha acid ~12%, with ~2% essential oils. Good resistance to downy mildew, but is susceptible to *Verticillium* wilt.

'Olympic': From Oregon. Bitter. High in alpha acids. Many plants are males. Easily trained and frost tolerant, but is susceptible to many pests. Moderately resistant to downy mildew, though is susceptible to *Verticillium* wilt.

'Willamette': From Oregon. Aromatic. Derived from 'Fuggle'. Sometimes planted with male plants: pollinated cones are larger than unpollinated cones. Matures later than 'Fuggle'. Oil content 1%; alpha acid 6–7%. Resistant to downy mildew, but susceptible to some *Verticillium* spp.

OTHER SPECIES

Humulus japonicus. A species for warm-temperate areas. It originally comes from eastern Asia. It has large, 5–7-lobed leaves and climbs to ~6 m. There is a variegated cultivar called 'Variegatus'. ■

Hylocereus, *Selenicereus* and *Cereus* spp.
Pitaya (pitahaya, dragon fruit, thang loy, night-blooming cereus, moonflower, lady of the night, queen of the night)
CACTACEAE

Pitaya is a common name that applies to a number of warm-climate cacti fruits that occur on plants from several genera. The pitaya fruits occur on either climbing or columnar cacti species. The two main genera, *Selenicereus* and *Hylocereus*, are native to southwestern USA and Mexico, down to Peru and Argentina. Naturally, they are found growing from the branches of trees, sending down long roots for anchorage, and to obtain nutrients and water. Their use has been recorded in Aztec literature since at least the 13th century, and they are still cultivated in several Central American countries. The pitayas are an interesting group of cacti with potential for greater worldwide commercial production. They have stunningly eye-catching fruits that come in a range of vibrant colours and shapes, are edible, and have magnificent, fragrant flowers that open at night, hence their other common name 'night-blooming cereus'. They were once only seen in the finest restaurants and were used as an exotic addition to dishes, but are now becoming more widely seen and used. *Hylocereus* species have been commercially grown in the Americas and in Vietnam. They were imported into Vietnam by the French, and are locally regarded as a native species. Much of

the recent research and development of pitaya has occurred in Israel, Thailand, Taiwan, Malaysia and Australia. The fruits are best served chilled, and are almost always eaten fresh. However, their flesh tends to be somewhat bland, and there are ongoing breeding programmes to select for tastier fruit. At present, they are mainly produced for their colourful, exotic appearance.

DESCRIPTION

These species are cacti, and have green, fleshy, photosynthetic, segmented stems with no true leaves. The climbing genera also produce aerial roots that can reach down ~10 m or more, which enables the plant to anchor itself to rocks or trees and to 'send' roots down to the soils. Climbing cacti have tri-winged stems, with somewhat wavy edges, and are ~2.5–5 cm wide. Columnar cacti have indented fleshy stems that have between 5–8 wings. Each segment can grow quite long.

Leaves: These are reduced to spines, and occur in clusters of 1–5 spines (0.5 cm long), called areoles. These spine cluster are regularly spaced at ~4.5 cm apart along the edges of the stems. Compared to most other plants, these cacti have a different method of photosynthesis (Crassulacean). They can trap sunlight energy during the day, but do not open their stomata at this time, when it is hot and valuable water can be lost from their tissues. Instead, they open their stomata at night, which allows carbon dioxide to enter and to then biochemically react with the stored sunlight energy to make starch and sugars for growth. Thus, they lose much less water than most other plant species.

Flowers: As indicated by the name, the blooms appear for one night only, and then close soon after the day has started. They open from about 2 hours before dusk until about 3 hours after dawn. The small, light green flower buds emerge on the stem, and expand to ~25 cm after 16–17 days. The flowers then rapidly burst open at the end of a day. Flowers are pollinated in the evening and then, by ~2:00 a.m., they begin to wilt. The opening of blooms is affected by temperature and light intensity, with flowers opening later on cool or cloudy days. They are beautiful, very large (25–30 cm long, 30 cm wide), white, bell-shaped and wonderfully fragrant. Borne from late spring to late autumn in some species, they go on to produce a series of fruits during this long season. *Pollination:* In the wild, the flowers' scent attracts moths who pollinate them. For cultivated plants, hand pollination in the evening, with a soft, small brush, is necessary. Ants and bees do visit the flowers, but are not very effective at pollination. For the pitaya grower, because the flowers only last a single night, evening hand-pollination could be a regular practice for a few weeks. Some *Hylocereus* species are self-compatible, some are self-infertile, and cross pollination seems to be of benefit for both types, and can result in 100% fruit-set, so it is better to grow more than one plant. Flower buds form in response to day length, and plants can be induced to flower during the winter in warmer regions by interrupting their night period to give 4 hours of supplementary lighting between 10:00 p.m. and 2:00 a.m.

Fruit: The edible, vibrant mauve–deep red or yellow fruits are ~10–15 cm long, ~10 cm diameter, and are similar in appearance to those of the prickly pear (*Opuntia* spp.), but only contain very small seeds and, more importantly, unlike the prickly pear, the peel of pitaya fruits has no barbed hairs or spines, or it becomes spineless during ripening. The fruits form attractive, outer, symmetrical pointed scales (~0.25 cm long), which are peeled off when preparing the fruit. Fruits of the yellow pitaya do have spines (~1–2 cm long), but these abscise when the fruits ripen.

Yield/harvest/storage: Harvesting begins in late spring and can continue throughout summer, into late autumn. It takes only ~30–50 days from fruit-set to harvest, and individual fruits can weigh ~0.5 kg when fully ripe. The longer the fruits are left, the larger and sweeter they become. Plants can start producing fruit when they are just 2 years old, and will have reached full production by 5 years. Harvesting is much easier than for prickly pear. They are harvested when the fruits have fully changed colour and can be stored several days at room temperature, or for 20–30 days in a fridge.

Roots: The climbers have aerial roots, and would normally grow as epiphytes, germinating and growing in trees, and then sending roots down several metres to anchor them and obtain water and nutrients. The roots grow from the underside of the stems and become attached to the surface they are growing on. Until these roots are established, the plant is able to live on minimal moisture and nutrients. The roots are also able to find meagre water and nutrient supplies in branch crevices that they pass, which enables them to explore further. Roots and buds can form when the plants are just growing in sand. When commercially cultivated, plants are grown up trellises or frames, but can also be encouraged to grow up old tree stumps or wooden posts.

CULTIVATION

Location: Although these species are heat tolerant, they are best not grown in full sun in very hot regions. Semi-shade prevents the stems being bleached and burnt. Nets or blinds can be erected. In nature, these species grow in the shade supplied by the tree host. Strangely, these species also seem to be tolerant of sulphurous gases, so are a good choice if you live on the slope of a volcano or by a thermal area!

Temperature: Plants are heat resistant, but temperatures greater than ~38°C can seriously damage them, particularly if sited in full sun. Plants grow better in dry warm-temperate or semi-tropical climates, and late winter warmth encourages flower formation. They can also tolerate short periods of near freezing temperatures without much damage; columnar species seem to be more cold-tolerant than the climbers.

Soil/water/nutrients: They have amazingly hardy, tenacious roots and are able to absorb low levels of nutrients and water, but grow much better in semi-humid climates in rich, organic soils. They are drought resistant, and too much rain or moisture results in flower drop and fruit rot. Growth and yields are best if plants receive some moisture during their growing season, but only minimal watering is needed during winter or in early spring, during flower formation. Humidity increases the risk of fungal and bacterial disease is increased. Once fruits have started to form, then watering can be increased. In addition, plants will grow better if supplied with some nutrients during the growing season. Nutrients can be applied as a foliar spray, granular fertiliser or similar.

Pot culture: These species naturally lend themselves to being grown in containers and will grow best if given good compost. Climbing species (see below) need a structure to grow up against. If given regular moisture and nutrients, they will produce flowers and fruits. In colder areas, containers can be moved into glasshouses or conservatories.

Planting: Space climbing species at ~1–2 m apart, against posts or other upright structures. Columnar species do not need climbing structures.

Propagation: Seeds: This method is possible, but is not very worthwhile unless one is trying to create a hybrid. Seeds first need to be cleaned of pulp, rinsed and then excess moisture removed. For best germination, the seeds are left for ~28 days before sowing, preferably with some bottom heat. Plants take several years to grow from seed: for the first 1–3 years they only form a few fleshy stems; mature, fruiting stems are only formed later. *Cuttings:* These are much easier and quicker, and also have a high success rate. The gender and fruit quality of the progeny can also be accurately predicted. Sections, ~15 cm long, should be cut or broken from the plant; their broken or cut ends should then be allowed to callus over for about a week before they are planted in gritty, well-drained compost until they root.

Pests and diseases: They generally have very few problems. Most likely these will be birds, rats, etc. who seek out the fruit. If over-watered or grown in an environment that is very humid, bacterial rot of the stem (e.g. *Erwinia carotovora*, *Xanthomonas campestris*) or fungal attacks (e.g. *Dothiorella*, which causes brown spots on fruit) may occur.

THE SPECIES

There are many species that are commonly called pitaya; some of the main genera and species are listed below.

CLIMBING SPECIES

Hylocereus costaricensis. Has round fruits with a dark red skin colour and violet flesh. It has small scales. The variety 'Katom' has a yellow skin colour, with white flesh. The spines are easy to remove, and the fruit are oblong.

Hylocereus paolyrhi. Has a dark red skin colour, with violet-red flesh. It has large scales with dark green tips, and the fruits are oblong. The variety 'Ecuador' has a yellow skin colour, with white flesh. The spines are easy to remove, and the fruits are oblong.

Food
The fresh, thirst-quenching, juice-filled red or yellow fruits are frequently used as a garnish on various savoury and sweet dishes, and are added to icecream, juice, wine and fruit salads. The fruits have a pleasant, but somewhat insipid sweet–sour taste. Some judge the yellow fruits (*Selenicereus megalanthus*) to have more flavour, and the red fruits to be more musky. They can also be added to vegetable dishes, and are an ingredient of many types of drinks. The flowers can also be eaten.

Nutrition
The fruits have good levels of vitamin C and phosphates. They also have good levels of phytoalbumins (antioxidants). The fruits contain 13–19% sugars.

Medicinal
The fruits are used in Taiwan to help improve glucose control in non-insulin-dependent hyperglycaemic conditions. They are also used to reduce blood levels of triglycerides, total cholesterol and low-density lipids. The fresh flowers of *Selenicereus* species (and *S. grandiflorus* in particular) are used in the preparation of drugs that promote blood circulation. *Selenicereus megalanthus* contains the heart tonic captine. *Hylocereus undatus* fruits have been used to combat anaemia. The fruits have been used to improve eyesight and prevent hypertension.

Other uses
Left overnight in the room of someone who is unwell, they absorb the carbon dioxide and release oxygen to purify the air. The fruits are used in cosmetic preparations, and a perfume is extracted from the flowers.

Ornamental
These species are wonderful in containers, in glasshouses, in conservatories or grown outside in warmer regions, with their large, fragrant beautiful flowers and very attractive fruits. They are also very tolerant of neglect, though not of excess moisture. They are also often used as a rootstock for slower-growing ornamental cacti.

Hylocereus polyrhizus. Has a smaller fruit, with red skin, dark red flesh and small, black, edible seeds. The stems have more spines. This species can be grown in full sun.

Hylocereus undatus. A beautiful climbing cactus that has received worldwide recognition as an ornamental plant for its large, scented, night-blooming flowers. It produces red-skinned fruits, ~1 kg in weight, that have a light melon-like taste. The flesh is white and translucent, with tiny black, edible seeds. This species pollinates very well with

H. *polyrhizus*. The varieties 'Alice' and 'Alice Snow' are self-fertile. 'Alon' has fruit with a light red skin colour, with white flesh. It has large scales with light green tips. The fruits are oblong. This species, in particular, is affected by high temperatures and hot sun: shading is necessary.

Selenicereus megalanthus. Known as yellow pitaya, this is often confused with *H. triangularis* and *H. undatus*. Has yellow skin and sweet, white flesh with small, edible, black seeds. The flesh has a texture similar to kiwifruit, but is not as tart and is about 3–5 times larger. It has smaller fruit and higher levels of sugar than the *Hylocereus* spp. There is also a red variety, but the fruits are probably not as flavoursome, and it needs cross pollination.

COLUMNAR SPECIES
Columnar pitaya cacti include various species from *Stenocereus* (pitaya dulce), *Acanthocereus* and *Echinocereus* (Mexican strawberry).

Cereus spp. (Eden, koubo). Grow fairly rapidly and can produce many fruits. Seedlings start to produce fruits after 3–5 years, cutting-grown plants after only 2–3 years. The flowers are pollinated by bees, and the fruits are best eaten when fully ripe. Columnar plants are more heat tolerant than the climbing cacti; up to 45°C. They are also more tolerant of lower temperatures: they can survive ~–5°C. They are not tolerant of salt, or of high levels of calcium or potassium ions in the soil. They are drought tolerant, like all cacti.

Cereus peruvianus (apple cactus). Forms a columnar shape with many branches. The columnar five winged stems have spines, which can make harvesting difficult, but the fruits are spineless. The yellow–red fruits are medium sized. The flesh is white, aromatic and delicately sour–sweet in taste with very small, soft, edible, black seeds. This plant may also have further uses for the polysaccharides contained within its stems. It produces fruit early and has good yields. It is also a very attractive and drought-tolerant plant.

Cereus jamacaru. This is similar to *C. peruvianus*, but has stems with ~8 wings. ■

Inga edulis
Inga bean (icecream bean, pacay, guama)
FABACEAE (syn. Leguminosae) (Mimosoideae subfamily)
Relatives: carob, honey locust, licorice

The Mimosoideae, previously known as the Leguminosae, is an important group of plants, most of which develop a symbiotic relationship with nitrogen-fixing bacteria that form nodules on the plant's roots and provide it with nitrogen that they fix from the atmosphere. This family is often characterised by its distinctive pods, which usually contain several seeds. Many of these species are valued for their edible seeds, but a few are also valued for their pods' inner pulpy layer, surrounding the seeds, which is sweet and tasty, e.g. carob, tamarind and honey locust. The inga bean is similar in this respect and produces a pod that, when cracked open, contains a white, sugar-rich, tasty pulp, popular with children and adults alike. Its other common name, the icecream bean, gives an indication of its taste and usage.

The inga bean tree is a fast-growing semi-tropical–tropical tree, indigenous to South America, growing up to 15 m. It has been cultivated for thousands of years and the Incas carried its seeds up from the river valleys, where they naturally grow, to their mountain cities to cultivate. It forms a beautiful broad, spreading canopy, which is densely covered with leaves. Similar species are grown in the valleys and coastal areas of Peru and Ecuador. In these regions they are chosen for shade and street trees. They are also often grown as a quick-growing shade tree around coffee, tea or cocoa plantations. Inga pods have long been a favourite snack for many people in Central and South America, although the tree is still undervalued outside these regions. It is very easy to grow.

DESCRIPTION
A medium-sized, fast-growing, ornamental, tree, usually less than 15 m tall, although a few grow to ~40 m. It forms a densely-leaved, wide, almost flat, spreading canopy, and is valued as a specimen, shade tree. The young stems are angular in cross-section and are covered in brown fuzz. Trees are easy to establish, quick to grow and provide fruits for many years.

Leaves: Dark green, pinnate, ~25 cm long, reddish-bronze when young. Trees can be evergreen or deciduous depending on climate, losing their leaves during colder winters. The leaflets are large, simple, oval, in pairs (4–6), without a terminal leaf. The apical pair of leaflets is usually longer than the basal pair, being ~16 cm long. Between each leaflet there is a distinctive large nectary gland (2 to 3 mm), which is characteristic of this species. These sweet nectaries attract ants, which are thought to help protect the tree from other pests such as aphids. Seedlings have a characteristic grey-green sheen on their upper leaf surfaces.

Flowers: Fragrant, arranged in clusters forming spikes at the tips of stems or from leaf axils. Each flower consists of a short calyx tube, a greenish-yellow corolla tube with five fused petals (1–2.5 cm long), and numerous attractive, long (~4.5–7.5 cm), white stamens. *Pollination*: Their rich nectar attracts bees and other insects. Trees are monoecious and are self-fertile, so only need a single tree to set pods, although more than one tree will probably increase fruit-set.

Fruit: Pods take 8–12 weeks to mature after pollination, and they may be produced over a long period from late summer through to late autumn. In some regions (e.g. the Andes) there are two crops. The pods are brown, roughly hairy and become dry as they ripen. They have four ridges, running lengthways, and are either flat, and may be twisted, or are cylindrical. They have a distinctive appearance and vary in length, but can be more than 1 m long, though are usually 20–50 cm in length. The pods are constricted between the individual seeds. Inside, there is a white pulp that surrounds and cushions the seeds. These seeds are green, ~3 cm long, and can sometimes begin germinating whilst still in the pod, particularly if the weather is humid. Some cultivars produce seeds that are nucellar, and so produce seedlings that are genetically identical to the parent.

Yield/harvest/storage: Trees can produce many pods, and yields are generally reliable. Trees can start producing pods in 3 years. The pods are harvested when ripe and can be easily broken open to expose the pulp. They ripen over a long period, which gives a steady, but not excessive, supply of fruits. Pods do not store very well though, and need to be used within a few days.

CULTIVATION

An easy-to-grow, low-maintenance tree that can be grown in poorer soils.

Temperature: Trees are somewhat frost tender, but can be grown in warm temperate or semi-tropical climates: they can be grown in regions such as California and warmer areas of New Zealand. They can tolerate brief frosts, if acclimatised, but not for extended periods. They grow best with warm–hot summer temperatures, though not for too long at temperatures >30°C.

Location: Trees grow, flower and fruit best when grown in full sun, though will grow in semi-shade. They are fairly tolerant of salt, so can be grown in sheltered maritime locations. They are not very wind hardy.

Soil/water/nutrients: They can grow in a wide range of soil types, and grow well in loams and clay, even when the latter is compacted. They can also grow at a very wide range of pH values: pH 4.0–8.5. They can tolerate high levels of aluminium, which occurs in soils as acid as pH 4 and, unlike

Food
The inga bean has sweet and refreshing pulp that is usually eaten fresh, but can also be used to flavour various desserts. The pods are simply split open and their pulp is scooped out. In addition, the seed can be cooked and eaten as a vegetable, like peas or beans. In Mexico, the seeds are roasted and sold as a snack. An alcoholic drink is made in Colombia from the pulp, and is named 'cachiri' after a local street festival.

Nutrition/medicinal
Like other legumes, the seeds are a good source of protein, but they also contain trypsin- and chymotrypsin-inhibitors, which may inhibit enzymes that break down proteins within the digestive system. The roots, leaves and seeds are astringent and are used to treat diarrhoea, and as a lotion to treat arthritis and rheumatism.

Ornamental
The tree is valued as a shade tree, for its adaptability to differing soil conditions, for its ability to fix nitrogen and to stabilise soils. Crops grown in soil around or where inga trees have been planted are reported to give ~30% better yields.

uses

many legumes, the trees still form nitrogen-fixing nodules at acidic pH values. Very few leguminous species will grow in such acid conditions, or for that matter, in such alkaline soils. Trees also form symbiotic root mycorrhizal associations with fungi, where the fungi, with their large surface area, provide the tree with extra nutrients, especially phosphates, and in return receive sugars from the tree. This is particularly important in more acid soils, where phosphorus becomes unavailable. Trees are reported to be quite tolerant to waterlogging; however, nitrogen fixation and mycorrhizal associations may be impaired. They like regular moisture throughout the year, and can only tolerate short droughts.

Pruning: Minimal, just to remove diseased or damaged branches and to keep the tree to the shape and size required. Trees can also be coppiced, and will rapidly regrow.

Propagation: *Seed*: Mainly propagated by seed, which germinates very easily. Some seeds are nucellar, and so give predictable offspring that are clones of their parent. But, seeds do need to be sown when fresh as they lose their viability in 2–3 weeks. Wash any pulp thoroughly from the seed, and sow seeds <2 cm below the soil surface. Give the seed-trays warmth and shade. Germination rates are excellent: 95–100% within 2–3 days. Grow seedlings on in pots before planting out a few months later, or in the following spring in cooler regions. Initially, give young seedlings some shade, and then acclimatise them to full sun before planting out. *Cuttings*: Unfortunately, cuttings root poorly.

Pests and diseases: Seems to be resistant to most problems. ∎

Juglans spp.
Walnut
JUGLANDACEAE

English walnut (*Juglans regia*), black walnut (*J. nigra*), Andean walnut (*J. neotropica*), butternut (*J. cinerea*), Japanese walnut (*J. ailantifolia*), heartnut (*J. sieboldiana cordifolia, J. ailantifolia* var. *cordiformis*), Chinese walnut (*J. cathayensis*), California black walnut (*J. californica*), little walnut (*J. microcarpa*), Manchurian walnut (*J. mandschurica*), northern California walnut (*J. hindsii*)

Relatives: hickory nut

Some members of the walnut family can be traced back to the Cretaceous period when dinosaurs roamed the earth. The Juglandaceae family was one of the first angiosperms (flowering plants) to evolve. It is thought that walnuts originate from the Persian region although they are now found in the wild in many parts of the world, e.g. Middle East, China, Japan, India, and North and South America. The walnut is a general name for about 20 species of *Juglans* and most of these trees have been grown by people for their edible nuts. Walnuts have been used as a food source since at least Neolithic times, 8000 years ago. Remnants of roasted walnuts have been found in archaeological remains in France. They have also been found in caves in northern Iraq. The Afghanistan word for walnut is 'charmarghz', meaning 'four brains', because of its clear resemblance to a human brain. They are also known to have been cultivated since Babylonian times. They were popular with the Greeks, who also cultivated them, and the Romans dedicated the walnut tree to Jove, the chief of their gods, and used the walnut as a symbol. They also introduced the walnut tree into France and England. Nowadays, the USA and China are the main commercial producers of walnuts, supplying ~70% of the nuts sold worldwide.

GENERAL DESCRIPTION

Large, attractive, deciduous trees, with some species growing to >20 m in height. Often have wide, spreading branches.

Leaves: Deciduous, alternate, pinnate (20–45 cm long overall), consisting of 3–20 pointed, thick, oval leaflets (depending on species), often serrated, ranging in length from 4–20 cm long by 2–10 cm wide. When crushed, have an aromatic smell. Black-walnut leaves may be toxic to horses.

Flowers: Monoecious, but male pollen is often shed before the female flowers open, and this is often the reason for poor fruit-set. Therefore, to get good pollination more than one variety is needed so that there are some trees that produce male flowers later. Male catkins form in late spring, at the end of last year's shoot, are 5–10 cm long and produce lots of pollen. Small, green, female flowers form singly or in short spikes, usually in clusters of 2–3, at the tips of new shoots in late spring (and sometimes on 1-year-old lateral buds). They lack visible sepals and petals. *Pollination:* By wind, therefore pollinator trees should be planted so that the prevailing wind blows pollen towards the trees to be pollinated. Pollen can be carried ~70–100 m.

Fruit: May be classed as nuts or dry drupes, depending on how the fleshy husk is defined. The fruits, usually in groups of 2–3, have a yellow–green, fleshy, outer wall that covers the kernel and its shell until maturity. This dehisces to release a hard, furrowed shell that protects the edible kernel. Once removed, the brown inner kernel has the familiar convoluted, deeply folded appearance. The kernel is actually two primitive pre-cotyledons rather than an oily endosperm layer, with these primitive structures reflecting its ancient origins. The seed is sweet and very tasty, particularly when eaten fresh.

Yield/harvest/storage: Walnuts take 18–20 weeks to mature after flowering, and are harvested in autumn. Yields can vary depending on location, variety and other factors, but trees can produce good yields: ~100 kg per tree has been obtained in the US and Germany, and they can still produce crops when 75–100 years old! They tend to give greater yields than the closely related pecans. However, a grafted tree may need to be more than 5 years old before it starts to produce a crop and ungrafted trees may take 8 years before producing a good crop. Nuts are mature and can be picked 1–4 weeks before the outer husk dehisces, but once it has turned brown. Nuts in their shells can be stored for several months in the dry at room temperature or for several years if frozen. Pick the nuts in dry weather to reduce the risk of fungal disease.

Roots: Walnuts and, in particular, black walnuts, produce a chemical (juglone) within their roots that passes out into the soil and is toxic to other nearby plants and also inhibits the germination of seeds around them, including weed species. Generally, few plants will be found growing within the root area of walnuts unless the plants are shallow rooted and the soil is nutrient rich. They also have a deep taproot (~3–5 m when mature), which means that they can be difficult to transplant.

CULTIVATION

They make wonderful specimen trees and grow well in many temperate areas as long as soil conditions are favourable.

Location: Not suitable for maritime or exposed situations. Prefer a site in open sun in colder regions, but in semi-shade in warmer climates.

Temperature: Some species are more cold or warm tolerant than others, but, in general, too much sun can damage the nuts and trunk, although not enough warmth can result in poorly filled nuts. Trees can tolerate temperatures as low as –30°C, but late spring frosts can seriously damage flowers and young fruits.

Chilling: Most species need some winter chilling. The time varies depending on species from 400–1600 hours.

Soil/water/nutrients: Can grow in many different sites but prefers deep, well-drained alluvial soils. A slightly acidic to neutral pH of 6.0–7.5 is ideal, though will grow in moderately alkaline soils. Needs a deep soil because of its deep taproot, which also makes it very susceptible to waterlogging (24 hours of waterlogging can kill a tree), as well as quite drought tolerant. Does not grow well in clay soils. Prefers some moisture year-round for good yields. Mulching helps suppress weeds and retains moisture. Moderate additions of a balanced fertiliser, including N, P and K and micronutrients, benefits growth. They can be susceptible to boron deficiency, which produces twisted shoots and chlorotic leaves.

Planting: Choose a cultivar suitable for your area. For example, choosing a species or cultivar that needs a period of longer winter chill for a warmer region will result in poor leaf production and yield. Space trees at 9–16 m apart, depending on cultivar. Walnut trees like space. If they are planted closer they will need to be thinned later as they become larger. Usually benefit from staking for the first few years. Plant at least 7 m away from buildings because of invasive roots.

Propagation: *Seed:* Can be grown easily from seed. Seeds are either sown outside in a cold frame as they ripen, or stored seeds are best given a period of ~2–3 months of cold stratification before sowing in spring. Also, gently cracking open the outer shell and soaking the kernels for ~24 hours increases the rate of germination. *Grafting:* Common methods are whip-grafting, and ring- or patch-budding. This is commonly done in spring on vigorous 1-year-old seedling rootstocks. It is important to keep the grafted plants warm to encourage callus growth. *J. regia* is the most popular rootstock used worldwide, particularly in areas where blackline disease is a problem, though *J. nigra* rootstocks are often less susceptible to root rots. Hybridisation occurs easily between varieties.

Pruning: Many people do not prune walnuts at all, as they tend to bleed profusely, particularly in early spring. Any damaged or diseased branches are best removed in late spring or in late summer to avoid damaging the tree. Trees naturally form an open, spreading form. Commercially, trees

Food
The nuts are delicious fresh or added to various dishes. They are often used in stuffing, chocolates, cakes, biscuits and breads. The nut yields a delicate oil that can be used in both sweet and savoury dishes. The walnut tree can be tapped in spring in a similar way to maples, and the sap can be made into liquors, syrup and wine, though the tree needs 'rest' years to avoid it becoming over-stressed. Walnuts can also be pickled: the nuts should be picked and harvested while still green. They can be marinated for 3 days in brine, and then brought to the boil. This is repeated three times. The nuts are then drained, placed in a jar and covered with spiced vinegar, peppercorns, allspice, cloves and crushed ginger. Seal the jars and store in a cool place for several weeks. The green walnuts are made into a liqueur, nocino, in Italy.

Nutrition/medicinal
Walnuts are rich in protein (~15%) and oils (65%), which are mostly polyunsaturates (4–10% omega-3 fatty acid, 50–60% omega-6 fatty acid, with no cholesterol or trans fat). The kernel's very good levels of omega-3 fatty acids are thought to reduce the risk of cancer and other chronic diseases. Just a few walnuts (1.6 g for men, 1.1 g for women, according to the National Academy of Sciences) will provide enough omega-3 acids to meet the daily recommended intake. Walnuts also contain ~15% carbohydrate, are high in calcium, contain some iron and phosphates and are a reasonable source of thiamine, B6 and folate. Vitamin E content is good, but varies with location and variety, being between 25–35 mg/100 g of kernel. High levels of vitamin E protect the polyunsaturated fats in the nut from becoming oxidised (rancid).
Extracts of ellagic acid and juglone are being investigated for their use as a cancer therapy. Historically, because a walnut kernel resembles a human brain in shape, the nuts have been associated with a cure for mental problems. It is still used as a remedy for skin problems, such as acne and eczema, and the bark is used as a dentifrice in Pakistan.
Warning: Its pollen is a common allergen.

Other uses
The outer husk, when crushed, yields an oil that is used in soaps, paints, dyes and fine-art preparations, and a yellow dye that can be used to colour and protect wood. The crushed leaves can be used as an insect repellent. Walnut is well known for its dense, beautiful, fine-grained timber and is widely sought by furniture makers.

Ornamental
Makes a beautiful shade tree, but does need space.

are sometimes pruned when young to form a modified central leader system with whorls of four or five scaffold branches at intervals up the tree. Removal of scaffold tips encourages the formation of lateral branches, which can produce more nuts, but this needs to be balanced against not making the tree too densely branched.

Pests and diseases: Trees grown in small groups seldom encounter problems, but the following are possible problems that can occur: *Armillaria*, codling moth, walnut blight, European red mite, gall mites, leaf-rollers, nectria canker fungi, powdery mildew, two-spotted mite, root canker, walnut blight. Poor soil conditions also increase the risk of disease, e.g. bacterial diseases, which cause leaf and shoot die-back, poor fruit-set and decay of kernels. This can be particularly bad in English walnut. The risk of blight and rot is reduced in drier soils. Pruning can encourage the entry of fungal disease, which is exacerbated by frost damage. Adult grass-grub beetles can attack the flowers.

THE MAJOR SPECIES

Below are notes on the main walnut species. The above general description applies to these species unless specifically mentioned.

English walnut (Carpathian walnut, Persian walnut), *Juglans regia*. Originates from eastern Europe and the foothills of the Himalayas, but can now be found in the Americas, Europe and Asia. The Romans spread this species throughout southern Europe. This is the main walnut species grown commercially, and tends to be more cold hardy than other walnuts.

Description: A stately, handsome tree. Grows to >21 m tall with a spreading crown, and has smooth, light grey bark. Has a moderate growth rate. *Leaves:* Usually 5–7 leaflets, good autumn colour. Has non-serrated margins and prominent leaf veins. *Flowers:* 'Payne' is a recommended cultivar for overlapping pollination. *Fruit:* Its shells are easier to remove than those of black walnuts.

Cultivation: Relatively hardy, though this varies with cultivar. Needs a long, warm growing season to produce a good crop, though not too much heat or trees can suffer sunburn and the kernels can shrivel. *Temperature:* Prefers cold winters with mild, dry summers. Cold acclimation needs to be slow or trees can be severely injured or killed by sudden temperature changes in autumn. *Chilling:* Needs a relatively long chill period of 700–1500 hours, and won't produce well if it does not receive this. *Pests and diseases:* Too much moisture when the leaves first appear and during summer greatly increases the severity of bacterial walnut blight.

Cultivars: There is quite a lot of variation in taste, oil content, nut size and ease of cracking between the cultivars. Some nuts have a slight astringency.
'Chandler': Late-blooming, heavy bearing, high-quality kernel.
'Chico': Early into leaf and ripening, heavy bearer, excellent pollinator, but is susceptible to early frosts.
'Concord': From the USA. Medium-large tree, high-quality nuts.

'Franquette': From France. Late season, low yields, but very good quality nuts. Widespread commercial cultivar.
'Hansen': Smallish, disease-resistant tree. Thin-shelled nuts; widely adapted.
'Spurgeon': Late flowering, so good for regions with late spring frosts and rain. Good-quality nuts that ripen late.
'Waterloo': From USA. Late season. Medium-sized nuts of good quality.
'Wilson's Wonder': From UK. Popular cv, good yields, medium-sized nuts, good flavour. Thin shell. Vigorous tree.

Black Walnut, *Juglans nigra*. The black walnut is a popular tree for furniture-making and is found growing naturally throughout eastern USA.

Description: The tallest of the walnuts, growing to 45 m. Long lived, moderate growth, arching form, deeply ridged, dark grey bark. *Leaves:* Can be up to 60 cm long, with 15–20 leaflets. Late into leaf and bloom. *Fruit:* The nuts can be as good as English walnuts. Late harvest. Shells are hard and difficult to crack.

Cultivation: May tolerate wet soils better than English walnut. Can grow in a little shade, but prefers a sunny but sheltered location. *Temperature:* Late spring frosts can damage young leaves and blossom. Likes warm summer temperatures. *Pruning:* Optional.

Cultivars: 'Dublin's Glory': From New Zealand. Good, early yields, easy to harvest. Cold hardy, but early flowers can be susceptible to frosts. Stores well.
'Rex (152)': Developed in New Zealand. A smaller tree, medium–late flowering, more resistant to walnut blight than many cultivars. A small nut with a high percentage of polyunsaturated and monounsaturated fatty acids.

Uses: *Food:* Kernels are of good quality, but are only 12% of the nut weight and shells are difficult to crack. *J. nigra* is said to be more strongly flavoured than *J. regia*, and the nuts are used in cookies and as a meat substitute in many dishes. *Medicinal:* The bark, kernel and green husk have been used externally to treat many fungal and parasitic infections, and to help eliminate warts, eczema, herpes, psoriasis and skin parasites. These benefits are probably due to its high tannin and juglone content. The green husk has been found to contain iodine, which may aid in its antiseptic and healing properties. *Other uses:* Prized for its high-quality, fine cabinet wood. The ground shells are used for metal cleaning and polishing, oil-well drilling, and as an ingredient in paint, explosives, insecticides, plastics and make-up. Grown as an ornamental.

Andean walnut, *Juglans neotropica* (syn. *J. honoreii*). Native to the Andes and other regions of South America, it is now being grown commercially in many temperate–semi-tropical areas of the world and is prized for its nuts and good-quality, fine wood. It differs from most other walnuts in that it is virtually evergreen and has no chilling requirements.

Description: A large tree, growing to ~26 m. Can grow rapidly (~1.5 m/year) and often produces its first crops sooner than other walnut species (5–6 years). Tends to be grown more for its timber than its nuts, but this tree does have potential multi-use value in warmer temperate areas. *Leaves:* Almost evergreen, large, with a pungent smell. May lose its leaves in mid winter and then re-leaf in spring.

Flowers: In late spring. Does not need cross pollination for nut production. *Fruits:* Crops well and produces large, black, thick-shelled nuts. The kernels have a good flavour and can be used in desserts and pastries. The nuts are more difficult to extract from their husks than other walnuts, and the kernel is more difficult to remove from its shell. The nuts are ready for harvest in late autumn–winter in warmer areas.

Cultivation: Fast growing. Is relatively frost tender and its branches can be easily damaged by wind. No chilling requirements. More suited to warmer regions. *Temperature:* Can grow between –3° and 25°C. *Pests and diseases:* Seems to have few major problems.

Uses: In Ecuador, women prepare a famous sweetmeat, *nogada de Ibarra*, from sugar, milk and the kernels. A tea from the leaves has been used as a tonic. The wood is dark brown with blackish streaks, and can be milled in 30 years on good sites.

Butternut (white walnut), *Juglans cinerea*. The most cold-resistant species of the walnut family, withstanding at least –30°C. It is native to northeastern North America, but has problems with disease in the USA. Is susceptible to butternut fungus, which can kill trees. Slow growing, but starts to bear at a young age. Valued for its timber, which is lighter in colour than most other walnuts.

Description: Medium-sized tree, growing to ~15–18 m. Has ornamental white wood. Leaves are in groups of 11–17 and are somewhat sticky. Thick pointed shells, ~6 cm long. Small kernels, and they tend to break when the shell is cracked. Not very easy to propagate. Will pollinate the heartnut (see below).

Uses: Good-quality kernels with a high protein content (~23%) and 60% oils. Are used to make maple-butternut candy. In spring, the trees can be tapped like maples, and the sap used in a similar way. The buds, leaves and twigs are covered with a sticky coating, which, when boiled and reduced, makes a good light brown dye.

Japanese walnut (Siebold walnut), *J. ailantifolia*; Heartnut, *J. sieboldiana cordifolia*, *J. ailantifolia* var. *cordiformis*. Native to Japan, these species are smaller (10–15 m), but are wide spreading and make very ornamental shade trees. Fast growing, but a shorter life span (often ~30 years). Deciduous, large compound leaves. Prefer hot, humid summers. May be more cold hardy than English walnuts and are fairly wind tolerant. Produce good yearly crops of nuts (~2.5 cm diameter) with a pleasant, mild flavour. The nuts have a fairly high protein and oil content, which makes them less susceptible to turning rancid. Japanese walnut shells are easier to remove than those of the heartnut, which are heart shaped. Can grow on heavier soils and seem to be more resistant to fungal root-rot diseases and walnut blight. Timber is soft and dark brown, and is not as highly valued as other walnut timbers. The crushed shells have been used by the Japanese to poison fish. Can pollinate the butternut tree (see above).

OTHER SPECIES

California black walnut, *Juglans californica*. Large shrub or small tree. Drought resistant, not hardy.
Chinese walnut, *Juglans cathayensis*. ~21 m tall, very hardy, very thick shell.
Little walnut, *Juglans microcarpa*. Unusual small-fruited walnut, native to canyons of the southwest US.
Manchurian walnut, *Juglans mandschurica*. From China. 15–21 m tall. Very hardy walnut. Deeply pitted.
Northern California walnut, *Juglans hindsii*. 15–21 m tall. Thick shell. Fairly hardy. Often used as a rootstock for *J. regia*. ■

Kunzea pomifera
Muntries (native cranberry, munthari)
MYRTACEAE
Relatives: feijoa, jaboticaba, guava, rose apple

A native of the southern coast of Australia, this is often found in arid, hot areas, though is also quite cold hardy. It forms a dense, sprawling shrub that has many small, tasty fruits, which have recently become of increasing interest as a possible commercial fruit crop, although the Aborigines have valued and used the fruits for a long period. At present, there is some cultivation of this crop in Victoria and South Australia, although most fruits are still collected from the wild. In addition, it is being discovered as an ornamental and fruiting plant in New Zealand and elsewhere.

DESCRIPTION
The muntries are medium–fast-growing, prostrate or semi-upright, spreading, small, attractive shrubs, growing to ~0.3 m height, 1–2 m spread.

Leaves: Evergreen, small, yellowy-green, rounded, forming a dense canopy.

Flowers: Attractive, fluffy, white, typically Myrtaceae-like, with numerous attractive long stamens. They are borne

Food
The ripe fruits have a spicy-apple flavour, are crunchy and can be used like sultanas or apples, and added to a wide range of sweet and savoury dishes, or to relishes, pies, muffins, cakes, sauces, jams and conserves.

in clusters, in late spring and early summer, at the tips of stems. Too much moisture at this time can reduce flowering: plants flower better if watering is kept to a minimum during this period. Flowers are believed to be self-fertile, so theoretically only one plant is needed. However, yields and crop quality are likely to be improved if more than one plant is established. *Pollination:* They are popular with birds, bees and other insects.

Fruits: Rounded berries that are small, ~0.5–1.5 cm diameter, and green with a red-purplish tinge when ripe. They are borne in small clusters (3–9) on last season's wood. Their skin is relatively tough, though quite edible. The flesh is juicy and crunchy and contains several small, edible seeds.

Yield/harvest: Seedlings can start to fruit in 3–4 years; plants from cuttings can fruit in their second year. Yields increase annually to an optimum in about year 5. Can get 0.5–2.0 kg of fruits per plant. Fruits are best harvested when fully ripe, in late summer, although they may ripen earlier in hotter areas. Fruits often develop a white tinge when fully ripe. Fruits can be stored on the bush for 2–3 months after they ripen, though they do become somewhat less juicy and flavour can be compromised. After harvesting, the stems that bore the fruits then have a spurt of vegetative growth to form next season's fruiting wood.

CULTIVATION
Location: Plants grow best in full sun, and although they are found growing wild in fairly windy locations, they grow much better in protected sites, particularly if they are grown on a trellis system. Fruit-set is often reduced in exposed locations.

Temperature: It is fairly frost tolerant, though prefers warmer-temperate regions to grow in. It can grow in regions with hot summers. Young plants will need extra protection from cold.

Soil/water/nutrients: Can grow in a range of soil types, though prefers lighter, sandier soils. Can even grow on sand dunes. Does not grow well in clay. It prefers a neutral to somewhat alkaline pH range of 6–8. Is tolerant of arid climates and can tolerate drought once established, though does need periodic irrigation during fruit formation to produce better quality fruits and to prevent premature fruit drop (though less moisture during flowering). This species is very sensitive to waterlogging, and if there is any risk of this, establish plants on mounds. Generally, this species does not need much fertiliser; in fact, too much phosphate can be detrimental to growth and development. Young plants can benefit from regular applications of a general fertiliser (with less P) at the beginning of the growing and fruiting season, with fewer applications once the plants are fully mature.

Planting: Space plants at 1–2 m apart, and they can be grown up a trellis or post-and-wire system, similar to grapes, to make management and harvesting easier.

Pruning: For fruit production, remove stem tips during winter to encourage the production of more fruiting laterals the following year, as well as thickening and strengthening the main stems. However, bear in mind that flowers and fruits are borne on last season's wood, so removal of too much new growth in autumn will reduce yields the following year. If not pruned at all, the plant often becomes straggly and difficult to manage. If the branches become too dense and tangled, some of these should be removed to allow light and air to reach the flowers and ripening fruits. Remove any old or damaged wood.

Propagation: *Seeds:* Sow seed when fresh, with all pulp thoroughly removed. *Cuttings:* Semi-ripe cuttings, taken in autumn from new growth, can be inserted in well-drained gritty compost.

Pests and diseases: Plants seem to be susceptible to fungal root diseases if they are grown in wetter soils. ∎

Lapageria rosea
Chilean bellflower (copihue)
PHILESIACEAE (Liliaceae)

A genus of a single species, the Chilean bellflower is closely related to the lilies. It is the national flower of Chile, and is considered by many to be one of the most beautiful. It is widely grown there as an ornamental, but also for its tasty fruits. It has also been grown in the hot-houses of Europe since the last century. The genus was named after Napoleon's Empress Josephine, for her maiden name of de la Pagerie, in recognition of her keen interest in botany, which she greatly encouraged.

DESCRIPTION

It forms a slender, spreading shrub that can be free-standing, but can also form a vine 4–5 m tall. It naturally tends to climb more in shaded sites as a mechanism to reach the light in forests. The plant grows vertically at first, but then starts to grow more horizontally, with its stem tips circling in a clockwise direction as it seeks out a support to twist around. From there it sends out further shoots that twist their way upwards towards the sun.

Leaves: Evergreen, dark green, long, narrow, pointed, leathery, alternate, vary in size and thickness according to soil and exposure to sun and wind.

Flowers: Glorious, intense, deep red, fleshy, hanging, waxy bells that are ~10 cm long by 5 cm wide. Flowers can be borne for much of the year in warmer climates, and are borne on last season's growth. Appear singly in summer, but in autumn they often form clusters of 2–3, from the axils of upper leaves. The inner sections of the flower slowly develop a red colour, while the outer bracts retain some of their green colour. The red colouring is produced by a glucose substance in the sap, and a lack of this can result in white marks or even completely white flowers. The flowers can range in colour from bright crimson to carmine and pink, to pure white, or even bi-coloured with a marbled effect. The flower has three outer coloured sepals and three inner petals. If night temperatures are <15°C, the petals become firmer and more intensely coloured. *Pollination:* Mostly by birds, such as hummingbirds, which seek out the sweet nectar and pollinate the flowers at the same time. Although the flowers are bisexual, they are self-sterile, so you need at least two plants to set fruit. Plants may benefit from hand pollination in regions where there are few or no nectar-feeding birds, although bees and other insects will partially pollinate flowers.

Fruits: The pale yellow berries are ~6–8 cm long and oval in shape. Their flesh is sweet, juicy, pulpy and creamy-yellow, and contains numerous small, pale yellow, edible seeds. They are often called 'cucumbers' in South America, and have a good flavour. Fruits take 4–6 months to ripen after fruit-set.

Yield/harvest: Seedlings are ~4 years old before they start producing flowers and fruits, but can fruit in the first year from layered plants. Harvesting time varies as the flowers can be produced for much of the year, but the main harvest is in late autumn. They are picked when fully coloured and are slightly soft.

Roots: Has rhizomes that extend horizontally with nodes and small roots. The nodes produce thin aerial shoots that can extend some distance from the main plant. In ideal conditions, its spread may need to be controlled. Many of its roots are shallow and plants benefit from an organic mulch to reduce moisture loss and add nutrients. Deep mechanical cultivation is not advised. The roots like to be kept cool, shaded and moist. They dislike disturbance.

CULTIVATION

Location: Likes a sheltered site with not too much direct sun, although the tops of plants can be in direct sun. It can be grown in cool/warm shaded to semi-shaded sites. Shaded sites encourage more vine-like growth. Likes higher humidity.

Temperature: It is primarily a species for warm temperate

Food
The fruits are sweet and tender, have a good flavour, a bit like banana, and can be eaten fresh or can be added to desserts, juiced, etc. The roots are used as a substitute for sarsaparilla.

Medicinal
The fruits have been used to treat venereal diseases, gout and rheumatism. **Warning:** One report says the fruits may be slightly hallucinogenic.

or subtropical climates and does not grow well in colder regions. It may not be injured by a little frost, possibly down to –6°C, but needs additional protection if planted in colder areas.

Soil/water/nutrients: Grows best in fertile, moist, but well-drained soils, rich in organic-matter. Prefers more acid soils, with a pH below 5.5; does not grow well in limestone soils, nor with other root competition. Is not tolerant of waterlogging, though needs moisture during the growing season. Needs less water during colder months. Watering regularly with a weak solution of potassium-rich liquid fertiliser and occasional applications of blood-and-bone meal are beneficial.

Pot culture: Can be grown permanently in a container, but is better long term with room to spread. If grown in a container, a wire support needs to be erected for it to climb up.

Planting: Space vines at 45–60 cm apart. Can be planted to grow up fences or trees, or erect a wire structure before planting. They are often best planted against a sheltered wall. Incorporate some organic material when planting, but allow free drainage.

Propagation: Can be difficult to propagate. *Seed:* Germinates readily from seed, but growth is slow. All pulp should be thoroughly washed from the seed as it may contain germination inhibitors. Seeds can germinate better if first soaked in warm water for ~24 hours, and then briefly stratified in a fridge for a few days before sowing in a peaty, acid, but well-drained compost. Germination takes 1–3 months at ~16°C with constant moisture: you can seal pots in plastic bags. Seedlings grow slowly at first, and need less moisture during this stage as they are susceptible to damping-off and other fungal diseases. Lightly shade seedlings in summer. Grow on for 1–2 years before planting out. *Cuttings:* Are difficult and often take time to establish; they usually exhaust their carbohydrate reserves and die before establishment. *Suckers:* Aerial shoots removed from the rhizomes in spring and summer will root and establish well. *Layering:* Can be successful and is best done in early spring. Select shoots from the previous season's growth to peg down to the soil at ~15 cm from their tips. Longer shoots can be pegged in up to four places to produce several new plants. These may have rooted sufficiently by the following spring to be removed from the parent plant, though sometimes need 2 years to root well. They are then best potted up and grown on, in shade, for a further year. Do not allow young plants to become pot-bound. *Division:* Large clumps can be divided during the cooler part of the year.

Pruning: None is needed except to control their spread and remove any damaged or weak stems.

Pests and diseases: Generally have few problems

though young growth is vulnerable to attack from slugs and aphids, which can cause serious damage. Plants can be susceptible to root rots in wetter, colder soils.

CULTIVARS
Numerous cultivars have been selected for their ornamental characteristics, but are not described further here. ■

Lardizabala biternata
Zabala fruit (aquilbougil)
LARDIZABALACEAE
Relatives: akebia

Native to Chile and Peru, the species was taken to Europe in around 1850. It is also grown in Japan for its fruits and for its ornamental value. It is found growing naturally in lighter woodland and forms a fast-growing vine with pretty flowers that are borne in winter and interesting fruits.

DESCRIPTION
Attractive, interesting, fast-growing vine, reaching 3.5–6 m, or more in good conditions. Good for growing up trellises and walls.

Leaves: Evergreen, large, dark green, thick, oval, rough, glossy, wavy, pinnate, composed of 3–9 leaflets, arranged alternately, in twos or in threes.

Flowers: Flowers in late autumn or winter. Most plants are monoecious. It is likely, therefore, to be self-fertile, though more than one plant will probably increase fruit-set. Female flowers are solitary and grow from the leaf axils; male flowers form pendent racemes. The flowers are mildly scented and are a dark purple/rich brown in colour.

Fruit: Sausage-shaped, edible, sweet, 6–8 cm long, filled with pale pulp and black seeds. Needs a hot spring and summer to produce fruits.

Yield/harvest: Yields vary according to temperature, and other factors. The fruits should be picked when fully ripe.

CULTIVATION
Location: Can grow in semi-shade or moderately sunny locations, but does not do well in full sun. Is not tolerant of maritime conditions. Will grow better in a sheltered, protected location.

Temperature: Hardy down to ~–7°C, so can be grown in temperate regions if sited in a warm spot and given extra protection during cold weather. The winter flowers and young leaves in spring can be damaged by frosts. Needs protection from cold winds.

Soil/water/nutrients: Is not drought tolerant and prefers a moist, but well-drained sandy or loamy soil. Prefers a more acid soil, though can grow in neutral or somewhat alkaline soils. Is moderately nutrient hungry, and benefits from 1–2 annual additions of a complete fertiliser, preferably with nitrogen added as ammonia.

Pot culture: Could be grown in a container and taken into a conservatory or glasshouse over winter and then enjoyed for its flowers. It makes an interesting talking point and has year-round appeal. Plants should grow well with moist, nutrient-rich soil, and the pot can be sited in a semi-shaded area.

Pruning: Needs little or no pruning except to restrict its height and size for manageability. Removal of stem tips encourages the production of more fruiting laterals, but also makes the growth denser.

Propagation: *Seed:* Sow seeds in spring with moisture and warmth. Grow on seedlings in a warm location for their first year. Plant out in a protected location. *Cuttings:* A good percentage take can be obtained from 5–10-cm-long half-ripe stem cuttings taken, with a heel, in spring or autumn. Insert in gritty, moist compost to root.

Pests and diseases: No particular problems. ■

uses

Food
Fruit: sweet and pulpy, can be eaten fresh or cooked. Considered to be a delicacy in Chile where it is collected and sold in local markets, though others consider the fruits to have little flavour.

Other uses
A very ornamental plant and of particular interest because it flowers in winter and has interesting sausage-shaped dark purple fruits. Fibre can be obtained from the stems.

Ligustrum lucidum
(syn. *Fructus ligustri lucidi*)
Glossy privet fruit (Chinese privet, Nepal privet)
OLEACEAE
Relatives: olives

A group of ~45 evergreen or deciduous, hardy, flowering and fruiting shrubs or small trees that are often grown for their ornamental properties. Many privets are native to the Asian regions. Glossy privet is a native of China, Korea and Japan, and has been used in China for at least a thousand years for medicinal purposes, and is also regarded as a symbol of chastity. In these regions, it is often found growing wild along roadsides and river valleys. It is also widely grown as an ornamental plant, often as a hedge or a screen, in many temperate regions of the world. Indeed, it is becoming a weed in some areas (e.g. New Zealand and Florida) because birds distribute its seeds far and wide, and seedlings are able to grow in a wide range of environments. There is conflicting evidence about the toxicity of the fruits, while it is included within many medicines, in China and elsewhere, other reports say it may be mildly toxic if eaten in quantity. Yet another report said that it was toxic in small amounts, though this latter report referred particularly to *L. vulgare* (common privet). It is, therefore, advised to check the species carefully and to use these fruits with caution.

DESCRIPTION
It forms a large shrub or small tree, 3–6 m tall by 2–3 m spread, with many small branches. It often forms a bush if not pruned, or can be pruned to form a single-stemmed tree. It has a densely-leaved oval crown. The trunk has grey bark. It has fairly vigorous growth.

Leaves: Evergreen, oval, dark green, glossy above, ~7–12 cm long, with pointed tips that often point downwards. They are simple and opposite, with entire margins, and have short leaf stalks (1–2 cm long). They are thinner, softer and more pliable than those of *L. japonicum* (more commonly planted as hedging).

Flowers: Creamy-white, tubular, with four angled lobes at the end of the corolla. They have a strong, distinctive fragrance, are small (~0.6 cm diameter) and have yellow-tipped stamens. Borne in many, large pyramidal clusters (~25 cm long) from late spring through summer. The flowers are bisexual and self-fertile, so only need one plant to set fruit. *Pollination:* The flowers are a magnet for bees and insects.

Fruit: Elliptical or kidney-shaped, small, ~0.7 cm long, ~0.4 cm wide, turning purple-dark when fully ripe, are somewhat wrinkled and usually develop a powdery bloom. They are borne on the ends of stems in large clusters. They have a thin skin, with loose, soft purple pulp. There is a single yellow-brown, ridged seed that contains a single kernel, which is not eaten. The pulp has a sweet–bitter taste.

Yield/harvest: Although the fruits are small, plants can produce very good yields. These should be picked when fully coloured and ripe.

CULTIVATION
A very easy-to-grow, adaptable plant that will grow in many locations and will readily form a fruiting screen or hedge.

Location: Can be grown in full sun or semi-shade, though often does better in shadier locations in hotter regions.

uses

Food
The fruits can be eaten fresh, but are more usually dried for later medicinal usage. See warning below.

Medicinal
The fruit is antibacterial, antiseptic, anti-tumour, a cardiotonic, a diuretic and a tonic. The fruits contain several glucosides, including oleanolic acid, which is thought to increase coronary blood flow, relax vasoconstriction and lower levels of blood lipids. Modern research has shown that the plant increases white blood-cell count and has been used to prevent bone-marrow loss in cancer chemotherapy patients, and also has potential in the treatment of AIDS. Extracts of the plant show anti-tumour activity. Trials are being conducted on its ability to treat atherosclerosis. Good results have also been achieved when the fruit has been used to treat respiratory-tract infections, hypertension, Parkinson's disease and hepatitis. Historically, the fruit have been taken as a tonic for the liver and kidneys, and to promote visual acuity, to treat tinnitus and dizziness, and also for insomnia and for various cardiac problems, including heart palpitations. It is used to prevent premature greyness and premature ageing. **Warning:** The fruit may be mildly toxic if eaten in quantity, or one report says they are toxic even in small amounts.

Other uses
Is widely grown ornamentally as a hedge or screen, with its dense, evergreen leaves being very amenable to pruning. It can be grown as a pioneer species and to stabilise soil.

Is fairly tolerant of salt and wind, and makes an excellent screen or hedge, though not if exposed to very cold winds. It is tolerant of air pollution.

Temperature: A cold hardy plant, though not as hardy as some popular privet species, e.g. *L. japonicum*. It is reported to be hardy to ~–17°C. It can tolerate fairly hot summer temperatures.

Soil/water/nutrients: Is very adaptable to the types of soil it will grow in, and can grow in sandy or clay soils. Can grow at a range of pH values from somewhat acidic to chalky soils: pH 5–7.5. Prefers regular moisture, though can tolerate short periods of drought. It is not very tolerant of waterlogging. It is not a very nutrient-hungry plant, and only needs occasional additions of a complete, balanced fertiliser while plants are young and if they are growing in poorer soils.

Planting: Space plants at 2–3 m apart for specimens, but at 30–50 cm apart for a hedge. Incorporate some well-rotted organic matter into poorer quality soils.

Propagation: *Seed:* Can be very easily grown from seed. Sow seed in compost in spring. *Cuttings:* Semi-ripe cuttings can be taken in summer, with a heel, and inserted in gritty compost. These root well. Ripe cuttings (~20 cm long) can be taken during autumn and early winter, and rooted in a sand and peat mix, outside. These also root well, and should be ready to plant into their final position the following autumn or in 18 months time.

Pruning: Can be left to just grow naturally, and then forms more flowers and fruits. However, it can be pruned into many shapes, and is one of the species used for topiary. Can also be pruned to form a neat formal hedge. It will regrow from old wood if cut back hard.

Pests and diseases: Generally has few problems, though leafminers and thrips can damage foliage. Plants can also suffer from leaf spot, Texas root rot and be attacked by *Armillaria* honey fungus, with the two latter problems often resulting in death of the plant. ∎

Litchi chinensis (syn. *Nephelium litchi*)
Lychee (litchi)
SAPINDACEAE

Similar sprecies: Australian tamarinds (*Diploglottis* spp.)

Relatives: longan, rambutan

The lychee is the best-known edible fruit of the soapberry family, the Sapindaceae. It is a native of the lowlands of southern China, where it grows wild along rivers and near the coast. It has been used and valued for many years in China, and was recorded in the literature of 1059 AD, although was certainly widely appreciated before that time. Its cultivation has spread, over the years, to neighbouring regions of southeast Asia, to the warmer regions of New Zealand, to Queensland and New South Wales in Australia, and to the southern states of the USA. Its lack of popularity as a fruit in many parts of the world is surprising, considering its quality; although the fruits do not store well. It forms a handsome, medium-sized tree, with delicious, succulent fruits encased within an easy-to-peel rose-coloured skin.

DESCRIPTION
An attractive, dense, round-topped, symmetrical tree, 8–13 m tall, with 5–10 m spread, though is often smaller. The bark is smooth, grey, but it has a brittle trunk and limbs. It usually has a short bole, if not pruned, and many limbs begin within a metre of the ground; as a result, the canopy scoops downwards to almost touch the ground. The lychee can create a wonderful shade or specimen tree. It is slow growing, but is long lived: >90 years.

Leaves: Evergreen, 12–20 cm long. They consist of 2–6 pairs of compound leaflets. The leaflets are leathery, smooth, glossy, dark green above, grey-green beneath, lance shaped and 5–7.5 cm in length. New leaves are flushed an attractive bronze-pink colour, becoming shiny and bright green as they mature.

Flowers: Tiny, inconspicuous, without petals, yellowish-green, borne in terminal clusters, ~30 cm long. En masse, the blossom is eye-catching in spring, with cascades of flowers. *Pollination:* By bees and other insects. Pollination can be tricky. Although both male and female flowers occur on the same tree (monoecious), there are three flower types: two male types (i.e. M1 and M2) and one female type (~30% of the total). In general, M1 flowers open first, female flowers open second and M2 flowers (with more pollen than M1 flowers) open last. Many (~70%) flowers are male, and many of these do not produce very affective pollen, which may be why so many young fruits drop prematurely. Therefore, planting more than one tree increases fruit-set.

Fruits: Trees are very eye-catching when covered with clusters of rounded–heart-shaped, strawberry-red–rose–amber-coloured fruits hanging from the ends of branches against the bright green foliage. They are aromatic and are borne in loose, pendent clusters (2–30) from the leaf axils. Fruits are ~3–4 cm long, with thin, knobbly-textured, flexible, easily-peeled skin. Beneath, is juicy, succulent, translucent, white–pinkish, refreshing flesh, which usually separates readily from a central, inedible seed. The seed is usually oblong, ~2 cm long, hard, with a shiny, dark brown coat and is white internally. If pollination is faulty, then seeds may be shrunken and only partially developed. However, the fruits then have a greater proportion of flesh and are highly valued. Some fruits have a thin layer of juice just beneath the skin, others do not, with the latter being considered more desirable. Lychee trees can become alternate bearers, and need remedial pruning and/or fruit thinning to even out yields.

Yield/harvest/storage: Air-layered trees can fruit in 2–5 years after planting, but will not be at maximum production until they are 20–40 years old; seedling trees can take 7–12 years to start producing fruits. However, trees then continue to bear good crops for >100 years. It takes ~60 days from fruit-set until fruit maturity. Yields vary due to many factors, but, on average, a young tree can produce 500 fruits annually, and a 20-year-old tree 4000–5000 fruits (~100 kg or more). Huge crops of 680 kg have been reported from China, but large crops also mean that meagre crops may be produced for the following few years. Fruits should be fully ripe on the tree before harvesting in autumn. Fruits are best snipped off the tree with a short piece of stem still attached. If the stalk is removed, the fruits rapidly succumb to fungal infections. Harvesting is best done every 3–4 days (over a period of 3–4 weeks), but not when the fruits are wet. Fruits (with stalks) can be stored for ~14 days in a fridge, but only last ~3 days before beginning to deteriorate at room temperature. They can also be frozen or dried. Lychees dry naturally: as they get older they naturally dehydrate, and the skin becomes brown and brittle. The flesh turns very dark brown and shrivels to look like a raisin. The dried fruits can be then stored in airtight containers in the cool and dark for about a year. They retain their sweetness, but not all their tanginess.

Roots: Young trees often have weak roots, and trees develop better if grown in good, deep, well-drained soil with regular moisture until fully established. Trees tend to have fairly shallow roots, therefore mechanical cultivation is not advisable, and an organic mulch will help retain moisture and add nutrients.

CULTIVATION

Location: Grow best in full sun. Young trees are not wind tolerant, and grow best in sheltered areas. Hot, dry, strong winds can wreck blossom and split fruits. However, mature trees are much more tolerant of wind and have withstood typhoons (though not their flowers and fruits). They do not grow well in salty soils and are best not grown too near the coast.

Temperature: Warm, humid summers are best for flower and fruit development, with a cool winter with low rainfall. The trees become more hardy with age, and mature trees survive temperatures of ~–4°C, but not for extended periods. Young trees are much more susceptible to cold and can be killed by a light frost, but can also be killed by very high summer temperatures.

Chilling: Need a short period (100–200 hours) of chilling during winter (~4°C) to initiate flowering and fruiting in spring.

Soil/water/nutrients: Lychee trees grow best in deep, alluvial soils, but can grow in a wide range of soils from sandy soils to even heavy clay. They grow best at pH values between

5.5–7, and prefer more acidic to alkaline soils. In acidic soils, root growth is often better and they also form more symbiotic relationships with mycorrhizal fungi, which scavenge extra nutrients (particularly phosphates) for the plant, while the fungi receives sugars from the tree in return. The presence of organic matter, such as leaf litter, increases this relationship. There are also reports that trees can grow in alkaline soils, but may need additions of chelated iron to prevent chlorosis. Trees do best with regular moisture; they can tolerate brief periods of flooding, but not extended waterlogging. They are also moderately drought tolerant, though young trees need regular moisture until established. Too much moisture during flowering or fruit development can reduce fruit-set and split ripening fruits, although some moisture is needed to improve fruit quality and yields. Because young trees grow fairly slowly, their nutrient requirements are modest, perhaps just the addition of well-rotted manure or similar when planting. Too much nitrogen interferes with the uptake of other nutrients. Older trees need more nutrients and can be given fertiliser additions twice during their growing season.

Pot culture: Because of their frost sensitivity and slow growth, these trees are suited to growth in containers for a number of years in colder regions and, if kept warm during winter, and well watered and fed, they should flower and fruit. Some sources say that the roots can be pruned, which reduces the growth of the shoots.

Planting: Space plants at 8–12 m apart for a permanent orchard. Young trees need protection from cold, drought and wind.

Pruning: Prune young trees to establish a strong structure by encouraging a few strong scaffold branches, after which, these can be tipped to encourage the development of fruiting laterals. As the tree matures, all that's needed is the removal of crossing or damaged branches, although trees can be pruned more heavily to control size. Prune to encourage branches with wider angles as branches with narrow crotches tend to break easily.

Propagation: Seeds: Can be grown from seed, but the progeny are variable. Seed is best sown fresh as viability deteriorates rapidly (4–5 days); germination takes ~14 days. Young seedlings grow vigorously until ~20 cm in height, but then remain at about this height for ~2 years. During this time, root establishment is occurring, before continuing upwards shoot-growth. They are best established in well-drained, acidic compost. The main disadvantage is that seedling trees do not start bearing fruit until they are 5–12, or even 25 years old. *Cuttings:* Generally not very successful. *Layering:* Air-layering (marcotting) is the main method of propagation. It is very popular, particularly in China, where it has been practised for ~800 years. Branches that grow in direct sunlight, of any age, make better air-layers than branches that grow in the shaded regions of the tree. Air-layered trees can fruit in 2–5 years after planting. A disadvantage of air-layering is that trees often have weaker root systems. *Grafting:* Difficult. Wedge and bud grafts are possible, but seldom used.

Pests and diseases: Trees are generally trouble free, though leaf-curl can be a serious problem. Also, lychee webworm, mites, stinkbugs (can cause serious damage), scale and aphids can cause occasional problems. Birds like the fruit, as do other wildlife, and it may be necessary to cover the trees with netting while the fruits mature.

Food

A delicious, sweet, aromatic, succulent fresh fruit. Some fruits have a strong, fragrant taste which is not liked by all. They can also be dried or frozen. The skin and central stone are discarded. The flesh can be added to fruit salads and other fresh desserts, or can be stuffed with soft cheeses and served with pecans. The fruits can be layered with pistachio icecream and whipped cream for a dessert. They can be made into a wine, sauces or jams, or used as a topping on meats. They can also be spiced or pickled, or made into preserves. Dried, they can be used like raisins, and are popular eaten this way in China. The leaves can be dried and make a fragrant tea.

Nutrition/medicinal

Has good levels of vitamin C: 50–70 mg/100 g of flesh and also reasonable amounts of potassium. The lychee has been eaten to relieve coughs and is said to reduce tumours and enlarged glands. The Chinese use the seeds as an analgesic, but they are very astringent. In India and China the seeds are used to relieve neuralgic pains. In the USA, a cancer-screening programme has demonstrated that the roots have some anti-tumour activity.

Other uses

The seeds, because of their saponin content, can be used like soapberries as a hair shampoo. The flowers produce a very good-quality honey. The wood is used in China to make fine furniture.

Ornamental

Makes a beautiful larger, specimen tree with tiers of flowers and then red baubles of fruit. It is also an excellent shade tree.

CULTIVARS

'Brewster': A popular cultivar. Tree: large, vigorous, upright. Fruit: large, conical, red skin, with soft flesh, slightly acid, good flavour, with a largish seed. Mid season harvest. Resistant to *Anthracnose*. Good yields: 90–130 kg in a good year, but tends to only have one good crop every 3–4 years.
'Hak Ip': Chinese (meaning black leaf). Tree: densely-branched. Fruit: medium-red, sometimes greenish, thin, soft skin; flesh: white-pinkish, crisp and sweet. Has thin layer of fluid under the skin. Has good flavour. Resistant to *Anthracnose*.
'Mauritius': Chinese (Kwai Mi). Fruit: smaller, heart-shaped, rough red skin, tinged with green, often with a thin line running around the fruit. Seed is small. Flesh: very sweet, firm, fragrant, good flavour. Ripens early. Tends to have underdeveloped seeds with lots of flesh. Popular commercial cultivar. Bears very regularly, with good yields.

SIMILAR SPECIES

Australian tamarinds, *Diploglottis* species. The *Diploglottis* species are very closely related to lychees, though not to the 'true' tamarind, despite its common name. These species are native to Australia and are becoming increasingly valued and grown for their tart but tasty fruits.

Description: The trees are often large and majestic and have big (15–60 cm long), evergreen, pinnate leaves, consisting of even numbers of alternate, often hairy leaflets (8–12). Young leaves are particularly attractive, being often velvety and reddish-bronze in colour. *Flowers:* The flowers are borne in largish clusters and are coloured white, cream, brown or greenish. They are borne in autumn and the fruits form during winter. *Fruits:* Are similar in structure to lychees, and are borne at the ends of branches. The fruits consist of a browny-yellow or greenish, hairy capsule, often three-lobed, with each capsule containing a single round seed. The seed is surrounded by juicy, translucent, orange–red flesh. The fruits of most species ripen from spring to summer, and often tend to split open to expose the flesh beneath.

Cultivation: They can be grown in full sun or semi-shade. They are fairly frost sensitive, though some species can be grown in warm-temperate regions, or smaller species could possibly be grown in pots and taken inside during winter. They prefer slightly acidic to neutral soils that have good amounts of organic matter. Once established, they are fairly drought tolerant, though grow and fruit better with regular moisture. They can be grown quite easily from fresh seed. Remove any flesh and soak the seeds for ~12 hours before sowing in moist, warm compost.

Uses: The fruits can be eaten fresh or are, more usually, made into a refreshing drink or added to preserves, although honey or sugar is usually added. The trees are often grown as ornamental species in gardens or as street trees. The fruits are good at attracting birdlife.

Diploglottis diphyllostegia. A species suited to warmer climates. It forms a large tree, growing to ~30 m tall. It has tangy, orange-fleshed, edible fruits.

Giant-leaved tamarind, (*D. berniana*). A handsome, attractive, medium-sized tree, growing to ~7 m tall, ~4 m spread. Orange-fleshed, edible fruits.

Native tamarind, (*D. australis*). Forms a large, tall, upright tree, and can grow to ~30 m in its native habitat, though is often smaller in cultivation. Has large leaves that can be ~60 cm long. Clusters of yellow-orange fruits, each 1–2 cm wide, consisting of three lobes, containing large seeds, and with bright orange-red tangy, juicy flesh.

Native tamarind, (*D. cunninghamii*). A handsome, large tree. Fruits: clusters of reddish-brown hairy, fruits, with orange, juicy flesh surrounding a large brown seed. They ripen in summer and have a sharp, but pleasant taste.

Small-leaved tamarind, (*D. campbellii*). This species is now becoming rare in the wild. Makes a good shade tree. It forms a small–medium-sized tree. Has large, orange, juicy, highly recommended fruits. The fruits are usually three-lobed, with each lobe being ~4–6 cm in diameter. Each lobe contains a single seed.

Smith's tamarind, (*D. smithii*). Larger fruits with good-quality, red-orange juicy flesh. ■

Lonicera spp.
Honeysuckle
CAPRIFOLIACEAE

Blue honeysuckle (*Lonicera caerulea*), *L. angustifolia*, honeyberry (*L. kamchatika*), twinberry (*L. involucrata* var. *ledebourii*), wild honeysuckle (*L. japonica*), *Lonicera boczkarnikowae*

There are >200 species of *Lonicera*, most of which are native to the Northern Hemisphere and are either shrubs or vines. Many of these species are well-known and are popular as ornamental plants for their fragrant blossoms. Some *Lonicera* species, however, were valued in the past for their edible berries and for their medicinal properties, and the fruits were often harvested from the wild. The various uses of the fruits then declined, but have, more recently, been rediscovered. A few of these edible species follow the general description below. It should be noted that a few other *Lonicera* species are reported to have poisonous fruits (e.g. *L. caprifolium*), so care needs to be taken with their identification.

DESCRIPTION
The species with edible berries, in general, form sturdy, densely-leaved shrubs and tend not to be vines. They have a medium–strong growth rate.

Leaves: Bright green–dark green, oval–oblong, usually with pointed tips, simple, opposite, 6–10 cm long.

Flower: Long, thin and tubular, 1–3 cm long, with diverging lips. Often in pairs, which are sometimes fused, and these pairs are often grouped into small clusters, though may be solitary, from the leaf axils. The flowers have an inferior ovary. The flowers are often wonderfully and sweetly fragrant. They are often borne in early spring from last season's wood. Are usually dioecious, so need more than one plant to set fruit. Pollination is by bees, other insects, butterflies and hummingbirds.

Fruit: May be fused, like the flowers, and appear to be one fruit, but are divided into two segments. They are often translucent, waxy, and can be violet, turquoise or a rich red colour. Are usually globular, 0.5–2 cm in diameter, and have several, small oval, brown, edible seeds. Some species produce their fruits very early, i.e. by late spring. *Harvest:* Fruits should be picked when fully ripe and coloured. Plants should start producing fruits in their third year after planting.

Roots: Many roots grow near to the surface, i.e. within the top 50 cm of soil, with a few reaching deeper (~1 m). The roots can spread out as far as the crown of the plant. The roots are best if kept cool, either under stones or under a thick mulch, or are placed in the shade. Organic matter can help retain moisture.

CULTIVATION
Location: Grows best in full sun, or climbing species often grow better in semi-shade.

Temperature: Most of the species described here are fully frost hardy.

Soil/water/nutrients: They prefer a moist, well-drained soil. Prefer to grow in neutral pH soils. Like regular moisture during the growing season. They appreciate an annual

uses

Food
Can be eaten fresh, and are said to be good with cream and sugar, with a flavour resembling blueberries. The berries can also be dried, frozen, or processed for fruit salads, juices, desserts and jams.

Nutrition
They contain good levels of vitamin C, though this seems to vary from 30–170 mg/100 g of fruit, and also very good levels of flavonoids, reported to be 2800 mg/100 g of fruit: a huge 2.8% by weight. They also contain potassium, vitamin A (~0.25 mg/100 g of fruit) and various B vitamins (thiamine, riboflavin and folic acid). Most of their organic-acid content (~3%) is citric acid. They also contain some pectin and some amino acids (e.g. asparagine, glutamine, leucine, alanine).

Medicinal
The berries have been used medicinally for a long time to improve blood circulation, to reduce the risk of haemorrhage and to improve capillary structure. They have also been eaten to treat stomach and digestive problems, and used as a tonic. A decoction from leaves and flowers has been used as an antiseptic and as a diuretic. Externally, it has been used as a gargle for a sore throat and as an eyewash.

application of a balanced fertiliser (or blood and bone), but too much nutrients results in excess leaf growth at the expense of flower and fruit production.

Propagation: *Seed:* Slow to grow from seed. Sow fresh seed in well-drained compost, or stratify stored seed for

~2 months, and then soak for ~24 hours before sowing. *Cuttings:* Semi-ripe cuttings taken in summer and inserted into gritty compost root well. Grow on rooted cuttings for a further year before planting out. Hardwood cuttings can also be taken in autumn, and these should root well. *Layering:* Branches can be layered from mid summer–late autumn, and will readily root. They can be severed from the parent plant in the following year.

Pruning: May just need to tidy up any straggly growth, possibly remove crowded or any damaged wood. Tipping young shoots will result in the production of more flowering (and fruiting) laterals. Fruits are usually formed on last year's growth.

Pests and diseases: Are generally resistant to problems, but are susceptible to blister beetles. Also can have problems with red-spider mites, leaf spot, powdery mildew.

SOME EDIBLE HONEYSUCKLE SPECIES

Blue honeysuckle, *Lonicera caerulea* (syn. *L. caerulea* var. *edulis*, *L. villosa*). This species is native to Siberia, northern China and northern Japan. It is widely harvested and grown for its fruits in parts of China, northern Eurasia, Alaska and Newfoundland. Russian cultivars have been selected, and many natural varieties are known. In Russia, this berry was researched from the 1950s for its commercial potential. It is still a popular berry crop, but is now mostly grown on a small scale by gardeners. Later, the Japanese also selected cultivars of this species with better-quality fruits, and these are now very popular. It is now just being introduced into various regions of Europe and into the USA and Canada, where, as yet, it is little known. Most *L. caerulea* cultivars have tasty, sweet–sour fruits, but these do vary in quality, so it is worth trying the fruits from individual plants before propagating from them. Their very early ripening fruits make them a useful addition to the smaller garden, producing fresh fruits when little else is around.

Description: A long-lived shrub with thick branches, growing 1–2 m tall, often with a wider crown than its height (~2 m). It has brown–grey bark that peels into narrow strips. *Leaves:* Deciduous. New leaves often have a reddish-bronze tint. Can be smooth or covered with a fine velvet, and are sometimes finely serrated. Mature leaves are grey-green in colour. Often have good yellow autumn colour. *Flowers:* 1–2 cm long, pale yellow to greenish. Usually in twos, borne in very early spring. Dioecious, so need more than one plant to set fruits. *Pollination:* By bees and insects, though there may not be many around in late winter. Some hand pollination can increase fruit-set. Some fruits do set parthenocarpically, but these tend to be smaller and of poorer quality. *Fruit:* Dark blue, ripening very early in the season, usually long and oval, though sometimes more rounded in shape, ~1 cm long. They develop a whitish bloom when ripe. There are several, central, small, edible seeds. The flesh is very juicy. Fruit quality can vary: most fruits have a sweet–sub-acid, good aromatic flavour, though a few can be bitter, and still others can be somewhat tasteless. *Yield/harvest:* Plants can produce good yields regularly, and may produce a few fruits in their first year. A mature plant gives yields of ~6 kg. Fruits are best picked when fully ripe, which is by late spring–early summer: under-ripe fruits can be sour.

Cultivation: *Location:* Can grow in full sun in cooler regions or is best grown in partial shade in warmer areas. Plants are not very wind tolerant. *Temperature:* This species is extremely cold hardy, and can tolerate ~–40°C or colder, with its young leaves tolerating ~–15°C and even its very early flowers tolerating temperatures of ~–10°C without damage. In severe weather, it may be worth covering those plants in flower. *Chilling:* Only needs a short period of chilling and can come into leaf in late winter. Because of this, plants may grow OK in warmer regions. *Soil/water/nutrients:* Grows best in moist, organic-matter-rich, semi-acidic to neutral soils. Plants are not drought tolerant. Grows better with an application or two during the growing season of a complete fertiliser or an organic equivalent. Greatly benefits from an organic mulch, which helps conserve moisture and suppress weed growth. *Planting:* Space plants at ~1 m apart. Need to plant both male and female plants to get fruit-set. Their growth in the first year can largely determine the future productivity and vigour of the plant. Give young plants adequate moisture, some organic matter and shelter from very cold temperatures. *Propagation: Seed:* Are easily propagated from seed. These should have all pulp thoroughly removed. Unusually for a species from such cold climates, the seeds from this species do not need a period of cold stratification. Seeds can be just sown in moist, warm compost in summer to germinate. Rates are often very good. *Cuttings:* As fruit quality varies, select plants known to produce tasty fruits. Cuttings also give plants of known sex. Semi-ripe cuttings can be taken during summer, from non-fruiting stems, and these often root well. Hardwood cuttings can also be taken in late autumn–winter, but the success rate is not as high. *Pests and diseases:* Are generally free of pest and disease problems, though *Botrytis* can be a problem in more humid climates.

Uses: *Food:* The berries have a milder flavour than some honeysuckle fruits, and are often used in jams, preserves, etc. They also make a good-quality juice. In Japan, they are used in a wide range of food products and are a very popular, though expensive fruit. *Nutrition:* Have good levels of vitamin C: ~60 mg/100 g of flesh. Fruits are also very high in polyphenolics and contain high levels of anthocyanins and other antioxidants. *Medicinal:* They have extensive medicinal value, and have long been known to be beneficial in treating cardiovascular problems, and may lower blood pressure. They have also been used to treat digestive complaints, as a diuretic, for obesity and for liver disease.

Honeyberry, *Lonicera kamchatika*. A native of eastern Siberia. Has small, white, slightly fragrant flowers in spring. Dioecious. Fruit: blue, ~0.3–0.5 cm diameter, ripen early. They are aromatic, sweet–sour, tasty, but not very large yields. They store fairly well. Plants are easy to grow and are pest and disease resistant. Can be grown in full sun or semi-shade. Cold hardy to ~–40°C. Slow-growing shrub. Naturally grow in areas with poor soils and in exposed locations. The cultivar 'Berry Blue' grows to ~2.5 m height and has larger fruits; 'Blue Velvet' has attractive grey-green, velvety leaves, grows to 1–1.2 m tall and the same spread, but needs to be grown in shade.

***Lonicera angustifolia*.** A native of eastern Asia, it forms a shrub that grows to ~2.5 m tall. *Flowers:* Fragrant, in spring. *Fruits:* Ripen in summer. Small, ~0.5 cm diameter, dark blue-purple in colour, and are reported to be sweet and pleasant tasting. Prefer a location in full sun, with moist soil, and are more suited to warm temperate climates. They can tolerate some frost, but not prolonged. The fruits can be eaten fresh. Plants may produce a second crop in late summer. Has hard, close-grained wood.

Lonicera boczkarnikowae. Height ~2.5 m. A native of the Far East. Has fairly good quality fruits that store well.

Twinberry (inkberry), *Lonicera involucrata* var. *ledebourii*. A very adaptable plant that can grow in a wide range of soil, climatic and environmental conditions. A native of western America from the cold of Alaska down to Mexico, so has a wide tolerance to differing temperatures. Its young stems are yellowish. *Cultivation:* It is reported to grow in fairly acidic to quite alkaline soils: pH 4.5–7.5. Grows to a height of 1.5–3 m, spread 1–1.5 m. Is very cold hardy, tolerating temperatures down to ~–25°C, and is fairly wind hardy. Can grow in full sun or part shade, and tolerates wetter, or even temporarily flooded soils, and even brackish soil. Not very drought tolerant though. Can be grown in maritime locations. Tolerates air pollution. *Leaves:* Dark green, deciduous, colouring in autumn. *Flowers:* Orange-red, ~1.25 cm long, borne from early spring into summer, depending on location. Usually in fused pairs. *Fruit:* Attractive, very dark purple, quite sour, but edible, ~0.5–1 cm diameter each, but are usually in fused pairs so is ~2 cm in diameter. Are held within a large, showy, red bract. Ripen in late summer–autumn. Produces regularly and gives good yields. Often used in preserves, jams, etc. *Other uses:* A purple dye can be obtained from the fruits, or a grey dye if tin is used as the mordant. The berries can also be rubbed onto the scalp as a hair tonic, and are said to prevent greyness.

Wild honeysuckle (Japanese honeysuckle), *Lonicera japonica*. A native of eastern Asia. It is now grown in many areas of the world for its fragrant flowers and has become naturalised in some places, where it is sometimes considered to be a weed (e.g. New Zealand). A rampant, twining climber that can grow up trees to 6–9 m, spread ~5 m. It is fairly frost tolerant (down to ~–20°C). However, even if injured by cold, it usually grows back from its roots. It likes regular moisture, though can be drought tolerant. A tough plant and has virtually no pest and disease problems. *Leaves:* Evergreen, light green, finely downy. *Flowers:* Wonderfully fragrant and are borne from early summer–autumn, white–pale yellow, ~3 cm long, borne on the current season's growth. They, interestingly, open at dusk to be mostly pollinated by moths. You can eat the flowers; they have an aromatic and sweet flavour. *Fruits:* These only form after a hot summer. *Warning:* They should not be eaten, as they may be poisonous.

Uses: *Food:* The leaves contain saponins, so should not be eaten in quantity, but do have many uses. The leaves can be cooked and used as a vegetable, but only eaten in moderation (though cooking destroys most of the saponins). The flowers can be used as a vegetable, made into a syrup or added to desserts. *Medicinal:* This species, in particular, has many medicinal uses. The stems and flower buds have antibacterial, anti-inflammatory, antispasmodic qualities and are used as a blood cleanser, as a diuretic, for upper respiratory tract infections, for dysentery, to get rid of internal parasites and to reduce blood pressure. The stems are used internally to treat acute rheumatoid arthritis, mumps and hepatitis. The flowers are used to treat various infections and have been shown to lower blood cholesterol levels, and are antibacterial and antiviral. Externally, they can be applied as a wash to infectious skin rashes and sores. *Ornamental:* Good for screening unsightly structures and has fragrant flowers. Very little care once established. Plant at 1–2 m apart. ■

Lycium barbarum (syn. *Lycium halimifolium*, *L. chinense*)

Wolfberry, Chinese matrimony vine, box thorn, Duke of Argyll's tea tree, gou ji zi

SOLANACEAE

Relatives: tamarillo, Cape gooseberry, pepino

The name *Lycium* originates from Lycia, an ancient country in Asia Minor. It is generally thought that *L. chinense* and *L. barbarum* are the same species, though some consider them to be different. However, the name *L. barbarum* is the general name in usage. The wolfberry is a vine found from southeastern Europe to northwestern China, and the health-giving properties of its berries have been known in China since at least 1000–1400 AD. Research carried out by the Natural Science Institute of China along the Yellow River in Inner Mongolia found people who were mostly vegetarian and ate wolfberries daily, lived 20 to 40 years longer than other peoples in the region. They had a life expectancy of more than 100 years! They also seemed to have lower incidences of diseases such as arthritis, cancer and diabetes. As a result of findings such as these, the wolfberry has been declared a national treasure by the State Scientific and Technological Commission in China and they have undertaken numerous clinical studies over the last 20 years on the benefits of the wolfberry plant and its fruits.

DESCRIPTION

An attractive, moderately vigorous, perennial vine, growing to ~3 m, though often pruned to 1.5–2.0 m. It has a growth form similar to raspberry, with semi-climbing white stems which have spines at the nodes of older growth. Like raspberries, the wolfberry suckers freely and its spread may need managing. Grows fast, but is quite short lived: 7–10 years.

Leaves: Deciduous, narrow (~2–5 cm long, ~1 cm wide), entire, hairless, occurring singly in newer growth and in groups on older wood.

Flowers: Attractive, individual or small clusters of violet–pink flowers with a short-funnel form (~1 cm long), borne from spring–autumn. They are bisexual and are probably self-fertile, though fruit-set is probably better if planted in groups. *Pollination:* By bees.

uses

Food

The berries are often eaten when dried and have a sweet, cranberry–raisin-like taste with licorice overtones. Can be also used like other dried fruits in cereals, added to meat, vegetable or fish dishes, desserts, or in muffins and cakes. Can be soaked with wine and then stored to be enjoyed later. The fruits are added to boiled water to make wolfberry tea. The young leaves have a cress-like flavour and can be lightly cooked or used as salad greens, or made into tea. Note however, that the leaves wilt rapidly once harvested.

Nutrition/medicinal

The berries contain >15% protein, 21 trace minerals, 18 amino acids, 29 fatty acids and lots of vitamins B1, B2, B6, E, more vitamin C than oranges, and much more vitamin A than carrots. The wolfberry has been described as a 'nutrient-dense superfood in a class all its own'.

The main active component of the wolfberry fruit is a polysaccharide (LBP) that is thought to have significant anti-oxidant and immune-supporting properties. Many trials seem to indicate that wolfberries can increase the number and rate of cells connected with the immune system. The berry juice has been found to increase the number of immune cells within the spleen by 81%, to increase the lymphocyte-transformation rate within cancer patients as well as increase white blood-cell counts and strengthen immunoglobulin A levels (an index of immune function). It is hypothesised that, because immu-noglobulin A levels naturally decline with age, by increasing these levels, wolfberries act to ward off tissue degeneration. Studies have further shown that wolfberries can increase antioxidant levels by 40% and many Chinese medical studies have reported on the benefits of their use. They contain much higher levels of antioxidants than most other foods, including blueberries. The berries have been reported to increase hae-moglobin levels by 12%, and to reduce damaging lipid perox-ide levels by 65%, as well as improving both dark adaptation and acuity of eyesight. The berries have a high concentration of the amino acid, L-leucine, which is an essential amino acid that we cannot produce ourselves. It is claimed that the fruits can lower total and LDL cholesterol levels in blood while build-ing muscles, promoting fat decomposition and reducing blood sugar. An alcoholic extract of wolfberry fruits has been shown to inhibit tumour growth in mice by 50%. Some scientists believe that wolfberries may be a very good supplement to prevent various cancers because it exerts protection and anti-cancer effects at the same time.

The recommended dosage for the health benefits is thought to be just 10–15 g of dried fruits a day. Root extracts have also been shown to initiate recovery of leukocyte, erythrocyte and thrombocyte counts. In all, many studies have reported the far-reaching health benefits of this fruit. It is therefore probable that in the future the wolfberry will be grown and promoted worldwide to a much greater extent. **Warning:** There is a potential herbal–drug interaction between warfarin and *L. barbarum* and, thus, this combination should be avoided. It is also noted that, although there do not seem to be any records of toxicity for this species, some caution may be needed with the use of the leaves and possibly with the unripe fruits, as with many Solanaceae species.

Other uses

Wolfberry and its extracts are good for the hair and skin. Because the berries contain large amounts of 'phyto-proteins', it is thought that these might encourage skin protein metabolism and formation; plus, the high levels of antioxidants are also good for skin. Taurine in wolfberries may benefit hair growth.

Ornamental

Can be grown as an informal hedge, and in coastal areas. The extensive root system can help stabilise banks.

Fruit: Orange to dark red berries with thick, pulpy flesh. The best fruits are plump and sweet. When dried they are said to resemble cranberries. Contain an outer layer of firm flesh within which is a pulp layer containing 25–50 small, yellowish edible seeds. These become black if dried.

Yield/harvest/storage: Berries ripen from late summer to autumn, depending on the climate. They only take a few weeks to form after pollination. First crops are produced 2–3 years after planting and plants should be producing good yields and quality of fruits by 5 years. After picking, the basal calyxes can be removed and the fruit dried for later use. Allow warm, dry air to circulate around the fruits and then store in dry, cool containers.

Roots: Forms deep roots that can aid in soil stabilisation.

CULTIVATION

An easy plant to grow.

Location: Can grow in full sun or part shade. Can be grown in coastal locations, though does not tolerate strong winds.

Temperature: Is cold hardy, unlike most Solanaceae, tolerating temperatures down to ~–15°C; though is also reported to tolerate temperatures from as low as –27°C up to 39°C, but these reports may need treating with caution.

Soil/water/nutrients: Grows and produces best in rich, moist, loamy soils that are well drained. Prefers fairly acidic to neutral soils. Likes soils with moderate nutrient quality, and benefits from occasional additions of fertiliser or an organic equivalent, particularly with nitrogen added as ammonium, and calcium phosphate. Does not tolerate waterlogging, and does not grow well in heavy clay soils. Can grow in poorer soils, but yields are compromised.

Planting: Remove the main tip when planting to encourage bushiness. Space plants at ~1 m apart.

Propagation: *Seed:* Easy from seed. Best sown in early spring with warmth. Soak seeds in water overnight before sowing. Germination takes ~10 days and is usually good. Grow on seedlings with protection for the first year. Pinch out shoot tips to encourage bushy growth. *Cuttings:* Half-ripe cuttings can be taken during summer, with a heel if possible, and inserted in gritty, moist, warm compost to root. Hardwood cuttings can also be taken in autumn–late winter from the current season's growth. These are inserted in cold frames to establish. Should get a good percentage take by both methods. *Suckers:* Remove suckers in late winter and can be planted in a permanent location or established in pots before planting out. Easy. *Layering:* Long stems can be easily pegged down to root from their tips or from lightly scratched regions along their length. This family readily forms roots from stems.

Pruning: Best yields are obtained with regular and rigorous pruning every spring. This species is reported to be very tolerant of pruning and can even sprout from old wood. Prune to encourage ~3–6 fruiting laterals to develop each year.

Pests and diseases: Susceptible to aphids. ■

Lycium barbarum var. *goji*
Goji berry
SOLANACEAE

Relatives: wolfberry, Cape gooseberry, tamarillo

The goji berry is from Inner Mongolia and the Himalayas, and has been recently 'discovered' by the West. The berries are being included in many health preparations for their anti-ageing properties, which are due to their incredibly high levels of antioxidants. However, in their native habitat, goji berries have been used and valued by the Mongolians and Chinese for many thousands of years, and are said to be responsible for the longevity and health of many people in the region. They are also attributed with promoting a huge range of other health benefits. The goji berry is actually a variety of and very closely related to the wolfberry, but contains even greater levels of health benefits. It is a very versatile plant and is easy to grow, withstanding a wide range of conditions. One to include in even the smallest garden if possible.

DESCRIPTION

A sprawling, shrubby vine that lives for 5–8 years. Grows to 3–5 m, with some vine shoots extending further.

Leaves: Light grey-green, long, thin, tapering, 4–7 cm long.

Flowers: Like other members of this family, they are purple or very pale mauve (almost white), often with both colours on the same plant. Five-petalled with a prominent stigma, flowers from late spring through the summer. *Pollination:* By bees and other insects. Plants are self-fertile, so only need one plant to set fruit. Individual plants can also be hand pollinated to increase yields.

Fruits: Small red, shiny, oval berries, ~1 cm long. Many tiny, edible seeds in the centre.

Yield/harvest: Plants begin fruiting in their second year, and then yield increases annually until plants are ~5 years old, when it begins to decline. Fruits ripen from mid summer to late autumn, or until the first frosts. The fruits, like many

Food

The best fruits are sweet and juicy, with a taste that can be cranberry- or plum-like. Full sun to ripen the fruits should give the best flavour. The berries are often used in juices with other fruits. They can be added to jams, pies, desserts, cakes, curries, sauces, etc. in the same way as other dried fruits. They are often dried for later use. The dried fruits have a sweetish/tart taste a little like currants.

Nutrition/medicinal

They are very rich in vitamin C, possibly containing up to 5000 mg/100 g of fruit; an incredible 5%!). They are very high in vitamin A, which helps improve eye sight; they also contain good levels of vitamins B1, B2, B6 and E. About 18 amino acids naturally occur, resulting in a ~13% protein content, which is very high for a fruit. They are high in the mineral germanium (unusual in foods), which is being widely researched in many countries for its ability to reduce tumour growth and it may be effective in treating many types of cancer. The berries also have good levels of zinc, iron, copper, calcium, selenium and phosphorus, as well as some linolenic acid and betaine. They are also packed full of antioxidants, with probably the highest ORAC (oxygen radical absorbance capacity) value of any food, even greater than wolfberries! Because of their impressive nutritional content, these berries are claimed to prevent and cure a very wide range of ailments. They are said to prevent premature ageing, possibly partly by stimulating the secretion of human growth hormone (HGH). HGH stimulates the formation of muscle, increases cell division and growth, increases protein synthesis, but also preferentially stimulates fat breakdown to produce energy (rather than protein or carbohydrates), and increases blood sugar level. The berries are also said to help strengthen the immune system by increasing the production of white blood cells. They are said to enhance the production of platelets and red blood cells and to activate anti-inflammatory enzymes. Its antioxidant properties may also help reduce the development of and even help fight existing cancer. The berries are claimed to reduce 'bad' cholesterol and heart disease, and are said to inhibit lipid peroxidation. They have been taken in China as a mild tranquilliser to help insomnia and are said to improve liver and kidney function. They probably help weight loss (fat burning: see above) and have been used to treat sexual dysfunction as well as menopausal symptoms. They have been used to treat skin problems, including psoriasis. Possibly due to their betaine content, they are said to improve memory and recall faculties, as well as acting as a pick-me-up and promoting a feeling of cheerfulness and happiness. If only a few of these benefits are proven, this still seems to be a remarkable fruit. **Warning:** Diabetics may need to eat these with caution due to their possible blood-glucose-raising properties.

other Solanaceae, ripen and taste much better in full sun. Pick the fruit when red, but handle carefully as they easily blacken. In Mongolia, to avoid damage, the fruits are not touched by hand but are shaken from the vines when fully ripe. They can be picked when a little under-ripe and then left in sunlight to turn fully red.

Roots: Form a wide, very fibrous root system, so take care with mechanical cultivation once plants are established.

CULTIVATION

Much as for the wolfberry or Cape gooseberry. Needs little maintenance.

Location: Prefers a semi-protected spot that receives sun, though can be grown in semi-shade, but does not fruit as well. Plant against a fence or structure for it to sprawl or climb up.

Temperature: Grows best in temperate climates, and will grow through colder winters once it is dormant; can then withstand temperatures down to ~–30°C. Its natural habitat is mountainous regions, thus it can withstand fairly harsh environmental conditions and can tolerate summer heat up to ~35°C.

Soil/water/nutrients: Can grow in a wide range of soil types from sandy to quite heavy clays, but it grows best in well-drained, moderately nutrient-rich soil. Prefers more acidic rather than alkaline soils. Does not like waterlogging so plant on mounds or slopes if there is a risk of this. Once established, it can be surprisingly drought tolerant, though fruit quality may be reduced if extended dry periods occur during flowering to fruit formation.

Pot culture: Can be grown in containers as long as they receive adequate light. May need a structure to sprawl up. Feed during the summer season.

Planting: Plant out young plants in their final position against a fence or trellis, or with stakes. Place plants ~1 m apart.

Pruning: Mature plants tend to become straggly. Pruning reduces wind damage, reinvigorates the plant and makes it more compact and manageable. It can be pruned back quite severely and still resprout in spring. Best pruned after fruiting, in late autumn.

Propagation: *Seed:* Grows easily from seed, in the same way as Cape gooseberries, tomatoes, etc. Sow seeds just below the moist, warm, compost surface. Plant young plants outside once all risk of frost has passed. *Cuttings:* Young shoots can be removed in spring or summer and should root well if placed in moist, warm compost. *Layering:* Long, straggly young stems can be pegged down to the soil during spring and summer, and should readily form roots and new plantlets that can be separated and divided up.

Pests and diseases: Has few problems, though birds seek out the ripening fruits; netting at this time can reduce losses. ∎

Macadamia integrifolia x M. tetraphylla

Macadamia (Australian nut, Queensland nut)

PROTEACEAE

Similar species: red bopple nut (*Hicksbeachia pinnatifolia*)
Relatives: helicia nut, gevuina

Botanically, the Proteaceae family contains ~1000 species, and includes the well-known banksias and grevilleas. They are a very old family, dating back to Gondwana times. The many macadamia cultivars originate from two species of large, warm-temperate–subtropical Australian evergreen trees: the smooth-shelled macadamia (*M. integrifolia*) and the rough-shelled macadamia (*M. tetraphylla*). They are found growing naturally in rainforests, particularly along stream banks. In areas where the two species overlap, they often form natural hybrids, which have produced one of the best-tasting nuts in the world. The Aborigines, although being aware of the nuts, do not seem to have utilised them much as a food source, possibly because they confused them with the toxic *M. whelanii.* Initially, when grown elsewhere in the world, they were valued for their ornamental properties and the nuts were still not eaten as they were thought to be poisonous. In Brisbane, a botanist, Walter Hill, was interested in growing them and, because of their very hard shells, he believed that removal of this shell would aid germination. Consequently, he gave some of these nuts to an assistant to crack open, and to his horror found his assistant eating some of the kernels and proclaiming them delicious. Several days later, the assistant was still healthy and obviously not poisoned, and from then on the true value of these wonderful nuts became realised and their potential commercial value appreciated. Thus, one of the finest nuts in the world has only been known for a short period of time, and its development is still ongoing. Different hybrids between *M. tetraphylla* and *M. integrifolia* produce the sweet macadamia nut that is now grown commercially. Commercially, macadamia nut prices are high, partly because of the problems in extracting them from their notoriously hard shells. However, they are still in demand and many new plantings are being established around the world.

DESCRIPTION

Medium–tall (10–20 m high, 8–15 m wide), spreading, evergreen, attractive trees. The branches are hard, but brittle. The bark is rough but not furrowed, and is brown–dark red when cut. The trees are fairly slow growing, but are long lived: >200 years.

Leaves: Leaves are shiny, waxy and fairly thick. Those of *M. integrifolia* are 20–30 cm long, occur (usually) in whorls of threes, and are entire with few spines. New growth is pale green. Those of *M. tetraphylla* are spiny, often without a leaf stalk, usually in whorls of fours and can be 50 cm long. Its new growth is bronze-pink. Growth in mature trees of both species occurs in two main flushes, in spring and mid summer. Young trees may have four flushes of growth annually.

Flowers: Borne on long, fragrant racemes of many, small flowers (~1.25 cm diameter), from lateral buds. They have no true petals; instead, they have four creamy-white sepals. The racemes of *M. integrifolia* are 15–30 cm long; those of *M. tetraphylla* are ~30–40 cm long (flowers of these can also be pink). Flowers are usually borne in mid-winter from the leaf axils of the last two season's growth, but a few also develop on more recent flushes of growth. The time of flowering varies though, and it is not uncommon to have flowers, young nuts and mature nuts all on the tree at the same time. *Pollination:* By bees mostly; wind may also play a small part. The flowers are bisexual, and some trees are self-pollinating, but some cultivars are almost self-sterile, so this needs checking when choosing cultivars. If you have space, two different cultivars will ensure a better harvest. Cross pollination by hand can increase fruit-set and the quality of the nuts.

Fruit: The fruits are, botanically, a drupe. They are rounded and have an outer, thick, shiny green husk (forming the epicarp and mesocarp), which splits open as it matures. Inside, the nuts have a very hard seedcoat (the endocarp), which is smooth in those of *M. integrifolia*, or can be rough or smooth in those of *M. tetraphylla.* Inside, there is a single, creamy-white kernel, containing 70–80% oil. The quality of kernels from *M. tetraphylla* is more variable, and their appearance is less uniform. Hybrids of the two species produce nuts with characteristics of both.

Yield/harvest/storage: Trees produce between 10–30 nuts on each flower stalk, and yields from mature trees can be ~13–25 kg of nuts in shells per tree. Yields in Hawaii of 68 kg from a 10-year-old tree are claimed. Seedling trees take 8–10 years before producing fruits; grafted trees only take 2–6 years, and the yields then keep increasing for at least 20 years. If cared for, trees can produce nuts for 100–200

Food

The kernels are truly delicious, particularly when roasted. To roast the nuts, place kernels in a shallow pan in an oven at 120°C for ~6–7 minutes, then turn them and give them a further 7 minutes. Best to give less time rather than more, removing nuts if they start to tan. They can be dry roasted or can be sprinkled with olive oil. The nuts can be also added to any dish that uses nuts, but are best if their flavour can be clearly differentiated. Roasted nuts can be eaten as they are, or they can be salted, are excellent coated in dark chocolate, or can be honey-roasted or roasted with chilli or garlic. For a truly tasty, healthy appetiser, try avocado slices with macadamia nuts, sprinkled with a dash of olive oil and balsamic vinegar. Nuts can be stored in airtight jars in the cool and dark, or they can be frozen.

Nutrition

An excellent source of nutrients. Kernels contain 60–80% oils, of which ~82% is monounsaturated fatty acid (some of which is palmitoleic acid). Research has shown it to reduce overall cholesterol levels. Its palmitoleic acid (uncommon in other nuts) may increase fat metabolism, and so help to reduce the levels of stored body fat. Other oils are omega 3 (~2%), which is known to reduce the risk of heart disease and high blood pressure, and also ~3% omega-6 polyunsaturated oils. The kernels also contain flavonoids and vitamin E, both of which are potent antioxidants and help to protect against cancer and heart disease. They also contain vitamin A, thiamine, riboflavin, niacin and iron, and have ~4–6% sugar. Their protein content, ~9 g/100 g of kernel, is relatively low for a nut.

Medicinal

It has been found that people who eat nuts regularly (>5 times/week) have significantly lower rates of heart disease than those who eat nuts less than once a week and, also, that diets high in these fats (and with avocado) are at least as effective as low total-fat diets.

Other uses

The husks can be used in compost. The shells can be used as a mulch, for fuel, and for driveways and paths. The palmitoleic oil is highly beneficial to the skin: it moisturises, nourishes and conditions, does not irritate, penetrates the skin easily and can be safely used on babies. It is used in many cosmetic preparations, especially in Japan.

Ornamental

They make a great ornamental tree with exotic, evergreen leaves, long racemes of fragrant creamy or pink flowers, bronze-pinkish new leaves and long clusters of shiny, green fruits.

years. Nuts take 7–8 months to mature from fruit-set, and have a long harvesting period; depending on cultivar, this is from late summer through winter, although some nuts can mature almost year round. When mature, many cultivars have nuts that fall to the ground, and these are gathered periodically, although not if they are wet. A few cultivars have nuts that need to be picked, and the leaves are quite scratchy. Remove the husk very soon after harvesting to reduce any risk of *Aflotoxin* fungi developing (which is very toxic, and a risk with all nuts). If it is not possible to do this, then the husk needs to be thoroughly dried. Once the husk is removed, the nuts are gently dried in an oven or in hot sun until moisture content is only ~2–5% (down form ~20%). However, if it is too hot, nut quality is reduced. When dry, the shells can be removed, although they are still very hard! There are specialist macadamia nut crackers available for sale. *Storage:* Macadamias in their shells will store well at room temperature without becoming rancid, as long as they have been sufficiently dried. Kernels can be kept sealed in a bag or in the refrigerator.

Roots: The macadamia tree has proteoid roots, which consists of dense clusters of short lateral rootlets regularly spaced around a main central, deep taproot. These roots give increased surface area for maximum absorption of water and nutrients, and the more of these roots a tree has, the better the tree develops. Very fertile soils reduce the formation of these roots and, therefore, trees do not grow as well. Because the taproot is very sensitive to root disturbance, great care is needed when transplanting or moving trees. Roots of plants from the Proteaceae family also seem to release a growth-promoting substance, and if soil near to these roots is mixed with soil around seedlings, then the seedlings' growth is enhanced.

CULTIVATION

Location: They generally grow best in full sun, but in areas with very hot summers, are best given some shade. They do not grow well in exposed locations, and their brittle branches are liable to break in strong winds. They do not seem to tolerate salt very well, and are probably best not planted too near the coast.

Temperature: Trees grow best in warm temperate or semi-tropical climates. Mature trees can tolerate brief, short frosts, but young trees, young leaves, flowers and young fruit can be easily damaged at temperatures near 0°C. *M. integrifolia* grows better in warmer climates with more sunshine; *M. tetraphylla* is more tolerant of cooler climates and is more cold tolerant. In addition, if summer temperatures become too hot, this can reduce yields and direct sun can damage the trunk, particularly *M. tetraphylla*.

Chilling: They do not need any winter chilling, but a seasonal change in temperature may help to synchronise flowering.

Soil/water/nutrients: They grow best in a moist, deep, freely draining soil that is not too nutrient rich, and can grow in a range of soils: from sandy soils to heavy clay soils. Although fairly drought tolerant because of their deep taproots, they grow better with moisture throughout the year, particularly when the tree is young, but also during flowering and fruit-set in mature trees. They do not like waterlogged soils, and become highly susceptible to root rots. They do best at a pH range of 5.5–6.5, but can grow in more alkaline soils up to pH 7–8, though need to be checked for chlorosis caused by iron deficiency. They benefit from extra phosphates (but less potassium and nitrogen), particularly when young. Phosphate deficiency can show up as smaller leaves and leaf drop from the ends of branches. However, avoid applying too much fertiliser as this encourages excess leaf growth at the expense of nut production and also inhibits root growth, and, consequently, the tree's health. They are best given smaller applications more often, rather than a single large application. An organic mulch is beneficial to retain moisture and suppress weed growth, but avoid contact with the trunk.

Pot culture: Because of their relatively slow growth, these attractive trees can be grown in large tubs or containers, and will produce nuts if well fed and watered. Care is needed when handling the roots.

Planting: Space trees at ~6 m apart as they form fairly large trees; however, they are fairly slow growing and quicker-growing crops can be planted between them while they are developing. They grow best in a sheltered location. Planting more than one cultivar will increase cross pollination and yields. Beehives sited near the orchard can help.

Pruning: Trees are often pruned to a central leader, with scaffolds of branches allowed to grow at ~70-cm spacings up the main stem: this makes the tree much less prone to breakage. Once this shape is established, pruning is done to remove crossing or dense branches, or branches that compete with the central leader for dominance. If left to itself, the macadamia develops into a multi-stemmed, bushy tree that is difficult to harvest and is more prone to wind damage. When the tip of a stem is removed, all of the 3–4 leaf axils immediately below it (at the first cluster of leaves) will form shoots that grow upwards to form a multi-branched tree. However, if only one of these is allowed to develop, and the other 2–3 are pruned out, then, from beneath the pruned shoots, shorter, more horizontal branches will develop, and it is these that will flower and fruit. This process is repeated until a good framework is established. Pruning that is too severe drastically reduces yields.

Propagation: Seed: Can be grown easily from seed; germination is good and rapid, and seeds of *M. tetraphylla*, in particular, produce vigorous seedlings that are resistant to *Phytophthora* rots. However, seedlings take 8–12 years to bear fruits and the progeny are variable. Seed should be sown fresh as viability quickly diminishes. Because they have deep taproots and are very susceptible to transplanting, seedlings are best grown in deep, biodegradable pots. *Cuttings:* Can be tricky. Trees from cuttings may have shallower roots and not grow as well. *Layering:* Can be propagated by air-layering. *Grafting:* This is the most common method of propagation and is best done in spring or autumn. The best rootstock is *M. tetraphylla*. The usual method is by whip-and-tongue or a side graft, but the wood is hard. Top-working is also feasible, as is budding.

Pests and diseases: Possible problems include the red-shouldered beetle, the green vegetable bug (which can be serious and ruin a crop), leaf-roller bugs (however, the moth also helps with pollination) and guava moths. Rats avidly search out the nuts.

CULTIVARS

There are ~600 cultivars; just a few of these are listed below.

'Beaumont': An Australian hybrid. Widely available in nurseries. Tree: upright, ornamental, new leaves are reddish, flowers are attractive and bright pink. Nut: round, medium–large. Shell is medium-thick; kernel is of good quality with a high oil content. The nut does not drop when ripe. Yield: Good: ~25 kg of kernels in shells when 10 years old. Long harvest period. Good for home gardens. Trees are partially self-fertile, but crop better if planted in groups of more than one variety.

'Cate' (*M. tetraphylla*): Shell is of average thickness. Kernel: crunchy, good–very good flavour. Harvested in autumn. Tree is precocious, moderately hardy. Does not tend towards alternate bearing.

'Dorado' (*M. integrifolia*): From Hawaii. Tree: medium-tall, upright, attractive, begins to bear >5 years. Nuts: drop when ripe, cold resistant, medium-sized, ~2–2.5 cm diameter. Kernel: good flavour, oil content 75%. Very productive, yielding ~30 kg per year.

'Own Choice': Hawaiian variety. Has good-quality nuts. Ten-year-old trees produce ~22 kg. Nuts do not drop when ripe. A good pollinator for 'Beaumont', and is also mostly self-fertile. Hardy and vigorous. Good for small gardens as only need one tree.

'Vista': Californian hybrid. Tree: medium-sized, pyramidal, begins to bear after 3 years. Nuts: small–medium-sized, ~2–2.5 cm width. Excellent flavour, oil content ~75%. Shell very thin: can be cracked with an ordinary nutcracker. Nuts drop when mature. Flowers pink. Good for home gardens.

'Waimanalo' (*M. integrifolia*): From Hawaii. Tree: medium-sized, pyramidal, productive, begins to bear >5 years. Produces nuts in large clusters. Resistant to frost and disease. Nuts: large, occasionally with twin kernels, good flavour, oil content 75%. Shell relatively thick. Good yields. Grows well in cooler climates, particularly near the sea.

SIMILAR SPECIES

Red bopple nut (rosenut, rednut, monkey nut), *Hicksbeachia pinnatifolia*. A macadamia relative from the rainforests of Queensland and New South Wales. Attractive, interesting, slender tree, growing to 6–8 m. *Leaves:* Large, straight, palm-like, ~60 cm long. *Flowers:* Strongly scented, purplish, in long racemes. *Fruit:* Large, round, brilliant red–yellow husks, in long clusters, in winter. The outer husk may numb the mouth if bitten. Fruits are 3–5 cm long, 2–3 cm wide, containing a two-lobed, large black kernel. The kernel flavour is similar to macadamias, and can be used in the same ways. However, the species is often difficult to establish and the seedlings are often sickly, but once they have grown to >1 m they should survive. Seed should be sown as fresh as possible. Can be grown in coastal areas. Needs a fertile, well-drained soil. May not be as frost hardy as macadamias. ■

Mahonia aquifolium
(syn. *Berberis aquifolium*)
Oregon grape (dull Oregon grape, long-leaf mahonia, cascade barberry, agrecillo, mountain grape)
BERBERIDACEAE

Similar species: creeping Oregon grape (*Mahonia repens*), mahonia (*M. japonica*), Mexican barberry (*M. trifoliolata*), Oregon grape (*M. nervosa*), Texas mahonia (*M. swaseyi*)

Mahonia is a genus of about 70 hardy, evergreen shrubs that are often grown ornamentally for their leaves, for their golden racemes of early spring flowers, which are often scented, and for their toughness and minimum maintenance requirements. They also all produce purple or blue-black berries that in many species are somewhat sharp, but are edible and tasty, and can be used in pies or to make jam or jelly. They are closely related to the *Berberis* species, see p. 89. The Oregon grape is a native of northwestern USA, and is the state flower of Oregon. It is also a popular ornamental plant in Europe. It was introduced into England from North America in ~1820. Often plants grown under this name are actually hybrids of *M. repens* (see below) or *M. pinnata*. It is a very tough, versatile plant that needs minimum maintenance, and gives some ornamental interest year round. It also produces many purple berries that are quite edible, though this is not widely known. The plant was used by several native North American indigenous tribes to treat loss of appetite and debility.

DESCRIPTION
An evergreen, spreading shrub, ~1–2 m tall, 1.2–2 m spread. *Bark:* reddish-brown, scaly, rough. Inner bark of stems and rhizomes is bright yellow (due to berberine). Tends to sucker. Has a moderate growth rate. The plant lives for 3–10 years.

Leaves: Evergreen, glossy, leathery, stiff, dark green above, paler green beneath. They are pinnate, with 5–11 sharply toothed leaflets, each 5–7.5 cm long, they lack a distinct midrib: resemble large holly leaves. The leaves often turn reddish or purplish throughout late autumn and winter.

Flowers: Numerous, small, bright golden yellow, bell-shaped, fragrant, in dense erect clusters, 7.5–16 cm wide, borne from late winter–late spring, from leaf axils at the ends of stems. Flowers form on last season's wood. Monoecious and bisexual; therefore, the plants are probably self-fertile and only one plant is needed to set fruit; however, some growers report that more than one plant is needed for fruit-set. They readily cross fertilise with other *Mahonia* species.

Fruit: Dark purple-blue-black, tight clusters of berries (~0.5–1 cm diameter), with a whitish bloom when ripe, in late summer–autumn. It has slightly acidic, soft flesh, with many (3–9) small, edible seeds.

Yield/harvest: Pick fruit clusters when fully ripe and, if possible, after a first frost, when they are sweeter.

Roots: Has underground rhizomes that can spread and sucker. The rhizomes can be 2–8 cm wide, are odourless and have a bitter taste.

CULTIVATION
A very tough and easy-to-grow plant.

Location: It will grow in full sun or semi-shade, but also in dense shade under trees, although it may become somewhat straggly. Few species described in this book will grow in dense shade. It is not very wind tolerant, but is fairly tolerant of salty maritime locations.

Temperature: Very cold hardy down to ~–25°C.

Soil/water: It will grow in a wide range of soils, from heavy clays to sandy dry soils, although an organic mulch is beneficial in the latter. It can also grow in poorly drained soils, and does grow best with regular moisture. It prefers a pH range of 4.5–6.5, and so will grow in fairly acid soils. It won't grow well in limestone soils, unless peat or similar is combined with the soil. Only needs minimal additions of nutrients, unless the soil is poor.

Planting: Space plants at ~2 m apart for specimens, but at ~0.5 m apart for a hedge. Plants benefit from some organic matter mixed in with the soil when planting. Once planted, they may take a while to become established, but should then grow well.

Pruning: They need very little if any pruning, but can be pruned hard back into old wood if they become too large or straggly, and will readily resprout from older wood. However, this will probably remove next season's flower buds, and hence fruit. Prune either in late autumn or late winter. Plants produce many suckers, and these may need to be removed to prevent the formation of dense thickets.

Propagation: *Seed:* Wash the flesh from the seeds and sow fresh if possible, and allow to stratify over winter in a cool place. Stored, dry seeds need stratification in a fridge for ~4–6 weeks; they are then best soaked for 12–24 hours before sowing in well-drained compost. May take several weeks to germinate. Autumn-sown seed may germinate in ~6 weeks, or not until spring. Prick out seedlings and grow on in pots, with protection, for their first winter. *Cuttings:* Semi-ripe cuttings of non-flowering/fruiting shoots through summer. Can also take ripe cuttings in autumn. Remove most of the spiny leaves, and treat with a rooting hormone. Insert in well-drained compost, in shade, to root. Try to take cuttings from plants that have good-quality fruits. *Rhizomes:* Can be propagated by dividing the underground rhizomes and potting these up. *Suckers:* The suckers can be dug up in spring; best if established in pots before planting out.

Pests and diseases: Generally, they have few pest problems. May get occasional infestations of leaf spot, powdery mildew and rust. They are quite resistant to honey fungus.

SIMILAR SPECIES

Creeping Oregon grape, *Mahonia repens*. This is a similar species to *M. aquifolium* in its uses, propagation, etc, except that it, as its name suggests, is a low-lying (~0.3 m tall), creeping shrub that spreads by underground stems. It prefers drier soils, though can grow in clay. It is also not quite as cold hardy, only tolerating temperatures down to ~–15°C. It has blue-green bristly-toothed leaves, and dense clusters of deep yellow flowers in early–mid spring. The fruit are ~1 cm in diameter and are quite tasty.

Mahonia, *Mahonia japonica*. Originates from eastern Asia, especially China and Taiwan, and has probably been cultivated there for thousands of years. It forms a shrub ~2–2.5 m tall, spread 1.6–2 m, and flowers in early spring. It is very cold hardy, and can tolerate temperatures down to ~–20°C. It can grow in a wide range of soil types, like *M. aquifolium*, but does not like exposed locations. Its medicinal and food uses, and propagation are the same as for *M. aquifolium*. It has long (15–22 cm) racemes of lemon-yellow, scented flowers, from late winter till spring. The fruit are ~1 cm in diameter, and the shrub has good crops if grown in a sheltered location. The fruit are sharp, but pleasant tasting. They make a good ornamental plant with their early-blooming, fragrant flowers and ornamental leaves.

Mexican barberry (desert barberry), *Mahonia trifoliolata*. A native of southwestern USA and Mexico, this forms a ~2-m-tall shrub that produces clusters of yellow flowers in spring, which the bees love, and dark blue, sharp-tasting berries in autumn. It is less cold hardy then *M. aquifolium*, and is best treated as a warm-temperate plant: it thrives in hot, dry locations. It can grow in alkaline soils. It is used and propagated as *M. aquifolium*.

Oregon grape, *Mahonia nervosa*. Another Oregon grape, but this shrub only grows to ~0.6–0.8 m tall. Its cultivation, hardiness and other properties are similar to *M. aquifolium*. The flowers are small, bright yellow and are borne in long, upright racemes in spring. The fruits are acid, but tasty, and ~0.8 cm diameter. Good added to pies, jam; and the young leaves can be lightly simmered and eaten.

Texas mahonia, *Mahonia swaseyi*. Native to the southwestern states of the USA. It forms a ~1.7–2-m tall shrub with clusters of fragrant, yellow flowers in early spring, followed by large red-purple berries (~1.5 cm diameter) in autumn that have more flesh than most *Mahonia* species. It is being researched for its potential as a commercial berry

plant. The fruit are pleasantly acid, and can be used as *M. aquifolium*. The fruit can also be dried and eaten like raisins. Grows best in very sunny locations that have dry sandy soils, and it can grow in alkaline soils. It is very heat tolerant, but won't tolerate wet soils. It is not as cold hardy as *M. aquifolium*, only tolerating temperatures down to ~–8°C. Propagation and medicinal uses as *M. aquifolium*. ■

Food
The berries have a sub-acidic but pleasant-tasting soft flesh, often with a high seed-to-flesh ratio, though some plants have larger and juicier fruits. They can be eaten either fresh or cooked. They make an excellent jelly, and are good added to fruit desserts, sauces, porridge or muesli, or stewed, when they taste somewhat like blackcurrants. The berries also make a good wine. The fruit can also be dried and stored for later use. The flowers can be eaten fresh, and have been used to make a lemonade-like drink. The seeds can be ground and used as a coffee substitute.

Medicinal
Widely used in the USA as a medicinal herb. The roots of all *Mahonia* species contain a bright yellow substance called berberine, which has proven antibacterial and antifungal effects. (Apparently, eating liquorice at the same time, nullifies the effects of berberine.) They also contain oxycanthin. The roots are usually ingested, as external application is not very effective. The roots are used as a diuretic, a laxative and as a tonic. They improve digestion and are taken to treat syphilis and for liver disorders. They may also have anti-tumour activity. In particular, they have recently become popular and very successful in treating psoriasis. Their strong antioxidant compounds inhibit abnormal skin-cell growth. Roots can be harvested in late autumn or early spring and dried for later use. Just remove small parts of the rhizome, so the remainder of the rhizome/roots can regenerate. Recent research shows that, so far, it seems to be completely safe. The fruits are a gentle and safe laxative.

Other uses
The leaves are used by florists in displays. The berberine within the trunk and rhizomes can be used as a dye, and dark green, dark blue and purple dyes can be obtained from the fruits.

Ornamental
Makes a tough ornamental shrub for borders with its evergreen, glossy, attractive leaves, its abundant, bright clusters of flowers and its many dark purple berries. Because of its suckering habit, it makes a good, dense groundcover plant, but it is also a useful plant to fill shaded areas in shrubby borders. It can be grown as a hedge. It can also be grown as a useful reclamation plant, particularly in shaded areas. It is very low maintenance. A number of cultivars have been developed for their ornamental value.

Malpighia punicifolia
(syn. *M. emarginata, M. glabra*)
Acerola (Barbados cherry, West Indian cherry, cereza, cerisier, semeruco)
MALPIGHIACEAE
Relatives: nance

The acerola is probably native to Central America, and is now also found growing wild in the southern USA, Mexico, northern South America and the Caribbean. It has also been successfully introduced into many subtropical and tropical areas around the world, with some of the largest plantings in Brazil. In Puerto Rico, in about 1945, the fruits were found to contain large amounts of ascorbic acid (vitamin C) and, because of their attractiveness and superior eating quality, they soon became a common, local source of vitamin C. Local people eat them when they have colds or other infections. Trial commercial plantings were carried out in the USA several years ago, but have not taken off. However, this unfamiliar plant, with its marvellous properties, deserves to be more widely known and grown in gardens.

DESCRIPTION

A small, attractive tree, growing to ~6 m tall, ~6 m spread, but can be kept smaller. Its habit varies from spreading to more upright, but open. Can be single or multi-stemmed, or pruned to form a single trunk. Branches are covered in small, slender, brittle hairs that are easily broken, and can cause irritation. Trees can grow rapidly, 1–1.5 m per year, but are also relatively short lived: ~30 years.

Leaves: Young leaves are reddish-bronze, turning a glossy light or deep green as they mature. They vary in size from 2.5–7.5 cm long, and can be oval or lanceolate. The leaves, as well as the stems, have tiny hairs that can be irritating to the skin. Leaves can drop during extended periods of drought, though trees usually recover once they are watered.

Flowers: Attractive, tiny, five-petalled, pink, star-shaped, in umbels. Can be borne all year in warmer regions, though mostly occur in late spring and summer. Up to 90% of flowers can fall prematurely from the tree, but plant hormones can be sprayed to reduce this loss. Irrigation induces flowering. Flowers are mostly formed on last season's growth, or on older wood. *Pollination:* By bees. There is debate about the need for cross pollination. Some say that it is needed for certain cultivars, others report that fruit-set seems to occur even without obvious pollinators. Plants produce better yields, if planted in groups.

Fruit: A small berry, 2–3 cm in diameter, cherry-like, but often with three lobes. They are borne in the leaf axils, either singly or in clusters of 2–3, from mid summer; although in warmer areas some form year round, to give 3–5 main crops. When ripening, the fruit's thin skin changes from green to yellow, to a light or rich deep crimson at maturity. Skin is fully edible with the flesh, which softens as it matures. Fruits only take 24–42 days to mature after fruit-set, which is very rapid. The flesh is juicy and yellow-orange in colour. There are usually three winged, triangular seeds that should be discarded. The flesh of some fruits is quite

sharp; in others it can taste almost apple-like, and is quite sweet.

Yield/harvest/storage: Seedlings only take 3–4 years to start producing fruits; cuttings can start fruiting in their first year. Yields of 15–30 kg of fruit can be picked from an 8-year-old tree, and then productivity keeps increasing until the trees are 15–20 years old. It then tends to level off and begins to decline. Fruit are picked when ripe, fully coloured and soft; they need to be handled carefully to avoid bruising. Slightly under-ripe fruits can be picked when they are turning from yellow to red, and used in preserves. Fruits can quite rapidly become over-ripe, and lose their quality as well as their vitamin C content. Once picked, they can only be kept for a short time as they rapidly succumb to moulds, though they will last a few days in a refrigerator. Fruits can be processed, dried or frozen for storage.

Roots: Shallow and not spreading: trees can be toppled by wind. It is possible to upright them and they may recover. Avoid surface cultivation, and apply an organic mulch to conserve moisture and suppress weeds.

CULTIVATION

Location: Best grown in full sun. Will also grow in light shade, though fruiting may be reduced and plants tend to become spindly. Sensitive to wind; plant in a sheltered spot.

Temperature: Tropical–subtropical species, though can grow in some warm-temperate areas if protected. Fairly tender to cold, especially when young, and needs to be protected from temperatures below –1°C. Mature trees can withstand temperatures down to –2°C for short periods without damage.

Soil/water/nutrients: Grows best in well-drained loams, but can grow in marl, limestone, clay and other heavy soils as long as they drain well: waterlogging of roots will cause plant death. Neutral to alkaline soils of pH 6.5–7.5 are best; acerola cannot tolerate acid soils. Young trees need regular irrigation until well established; older trees only require watering during droughts. Although acerola is drought tolerant, watering induces flowering and further applications will reduce flower drop, improve fruit yield and extend the fruiting season. If subjected to an extended period of drought, trees may drop their leaves, although irrigation can result in new leaf and flower growth. Trees are fairly nutrient hungry and grow best with regular annual applications of lime, which increases productivity. Limestone can also reduce nematode attack. The addition of micronutrients, such as copper, zinc, boron, iron and manganese, can be beneficial. Foliar sprays are effective. However, over-fertilising can result in excessive vegetative growth at the expense of fruit production. Mulching is particularly beneficial in sandy soils where nematodes are a problem.

Pot culture: Can easily adapt to pot culture in a well-drained, non-acidic soil. Acerola can be kept to a smaller size and makes a good patio or deck plant. Potentially it can then be grown in cooler regions and taken inside or given extra protection during cold weather.

Planting: Space specimen trees at least 5 m apart. Plants for a border hedge can be as close as 60–120 cm. Mixed plantings with different varieties can produce a better crop.

Pruning: Plants can tolerate heavy pruning, but require time to recover, especially in cooler areas. Can be kept as a small bush (e.g. 1.5 m) and will produce well. Bushy varieties can be thinned to promote heavier yields. Pruning is usually done in early autumn, after the plants have finished fruiting. Pruning done later can result in cold damage and pruning in spring may reduce yields.

Propagation: *Seeds* Viability can be very low. Best to sow fresh seeds with all pulp thoroughly removed. *Cuttings:* This is the simplest method and, with the use of a standard rooting hormone, can give near 100% success. Semi-ripe cuttings, ~25 cm long, with 2–3 leaves attached, can be taken in summer and inserted in gritty, alkaline compost, preferably with mist, to root, which takes ~60 days. Grow on in pots for ~12 months before planting out. *Layering:* Air layering can be successful. This is best done in spring–summer when active growth is occurring; takes 6–8 weeks to root. *Grafting:* Can use side veneer or cleft grafts on young seedlings or on trees that produce inferior fruit.

Pests and diseases: Root nematodes are the biggest problem, particularly on sandy soils. These pests cause serious damage to young trees and reduce productivity of older trees. They weaken the plant, causing it to drop leaves and display symptoms of malnutrition. It is a difficult pest to eradicate, but is less problematic in alkaline, marl or clay soils. Acerola may also be attacked by aphids, whitefly, weevils, caterpillars and scale. Plant bugs may damage the fruit, affecting their flavour and reducing fruit size.

CULTIVARS

'B-17': A common variety. High in vitamin C, with a sub-acid–acid flavour.
'Dwarf': Low-growing, to ~60 cm tall. Grows well in a hanging basket. Can tolerate colder weather down to ~–6°C.
'Florida Sweet': Upright habit, large fruits, thick skin, apple-like semi-sweet flavour, high yield. Flesh very juicy.
'Manoa Sweet': Orange-red fruit, sweet. Tree upright, spreading, very productive. ∎

Food
The flesh is juicy, acid to sub-acid, nearly sweet, with a delicate flavour that is apple-like. The seeds are removed. The flesh is best eaten fresh, though can be used in jams, jellies, syrups and icecream. Can be frozen, but the fruit falls apart as it thaws. The pulp can be stewed with sugar, and then used as a topping on cakes, puddings or on other fruit. It can be added to other fruits for a juice. Cooking causes the flesh to turn from bright red to a brownish-red: it also destroys a lot of the vitamin C. The fruits ferment readily and make a good wine that is said to retain 60% of its ascorbic acid.

Nutrition
Acerola is one of the richest sources of natural vitamin C at 1650 mg/100 g of flesh; which is an incredible 1.6%, and can actually reach ~4500 mg per 100 g in partially ripe fruits, i.e. up to 4.5% of vitamin C compared with 0.05% in an orange. Sharper-tasting fruits also contain more vitamin C. Acerola is often grown commercially for its high vitamin C levels, although these levels rapidly decrease with storage. However, although cooking also destroys some, it does not destroy all of its activity. The fruits also contain amounts of magnesium, potassium and copper. Compared to oranges, acerola provides twice as much magnesium, pantothenic acid and potassium. The fruits also contain high levels of vitamin A (752–1000 IU), and have thiamine, riboflavin and niacin at concentrations comparable with other fruits.

Medicinal
Because vitamin C is a powerful antioxidant and a free-radical scavenger, acerola has many potential health benefits. Eaten fresh, the raw fruits are an excellent remedy for coughs and colds, and the juice may be gargled to relieve a sore throat. They are also used to treat liver ailments, diarrhoea and dysentery. **Warning:** There are minute stinging hairs on the new leaves and shoots. A recent study reported that acerola provokes a similar allergic reactivity to that of the well-known allergen, latex.

Other uses
This fruit's vitamin C content is also important in skin preparations, and has recently become popular in products that fight cellular ageing. Acerola also contains mineral salts that have been shown to help re-mineralise tired and stressed skin. The leaves, bark and fruit of acerola have active antifungal properties. The wood is very hard and heavy.

Ornamental
Acerola is an attractive shrub or tree that can be used for landscaping, as a specimen plant, and for hedges.

Malus spp. (*M. communis, M. domestica, M. pumila, M. sylvestrus*)
Apple, crabapple
ROSACEAE
Relatives: pear, quince, cherry, apricot, raspberry

Apples are classified as pome fruits, and are one of the main commercial fruits from the Rosaceae family. Pome fruit are derived from a flower with an inferior, compound ovary, whereas many members of the Rosaceae family have a single superior ovary, e.g. cherry, plum. The apple was originally given the Latin name, by Linnaeus, of *Pyrus malus*, the same genus as pears, but apples have since been moved to a separate *Malus* genus. Apples, pears and quinces all originate from the areas around eastern Turkey and northwards. They have been used as a food source since at least Neolithic times, and selected cultivars have spread throughout Europe over thousands of years. The domestic apple is a hybrid of many wild species. Because of their long history, apples are frequently mentioned in Greek, Roman and Norse mythologies, and are often portrayed as symbols of immortality, reincarnation and to bestow perpetual youth. They have been regarded as the food of the gods, and were often presented by deities as a reward to humans for heroic deeds. One's future spouse was revealed in a man's dreams if an apple was eaten on Halloween, hence, the origin of the bobbing-for-apples game. The first record of grafting apple cultivars is from Greece, in about 300 BC, and this was an important step in producing reliable, predictable trees and fruits. During the Middle Ages, peasants and monasteries produced many apple varieties, and in the 1500–1600s, wealthy people with large gardens selected numerous new varieties. Numerous other cultivars were developed by European settlers who moved to the New World; for example, 'Golden Delicious' arose as a chance seedling in 1900 in West Virginia and the 'Granny Smith' originated from a seedling in New South Wales, Australia in 1868.

DESCRIPTION

Trees vary, and there are many different cultivars, but, generally have rounded crowns, and can grow 7–12 m tall, with virtually the same spread. In cultivation, their height is usually kept to 2–5 m. They often have angular branches, with grey-brown coarse bark as they age. Older trees take on a gnarled appearance. Apple trees are moderately fast growing when young, but growth slows as they age. They can live for many years, at least a century, and some live for hundreds of years, with some specimens being of historical importance, e.g. in the UK the apple tree in which Charles II was supposed to have hidden, is still said to exist.

Leaves: Deciduous, elliptical, lightly serrated or smooth margins, dark green above, and mid grey-green beneath with a light grey pubescence. They are fairly thick and coarse.

Flowers: Typically Rosaceae, consisting of five white–pink simple petals that are oval and delicate. These surround numerous stamens in the centre, within which is the stigma and ovary containing five fused carpels or sections. The flowers are borne in clusters, either terminally on new shoots or on short spurs that occur on older wood. The central flower within a cluster generally produces the largest fruit. Trees blossom in later spring, after peaches, cherries and almonds. Late-spring flowering means they are less susceptible to late frosts. Fruiting spurs are short, lateral branches, which can produce flowers and fruits for 2–4 years. Crabapples tend to have pinker, showier flowers and more colourful fruits. *Pollination:* By bees and insects. Although the flowers

are bisexual, most cultivars will get a better fruit-set if there is some cross pollination; therefore, planting two or more varieties will ensure better yields. Flowers that are only partially pollinated, producing only 1–2 seeds, tend to prematurely drop. If short of garden space, it is possible to get trees that have two different varieties grafted onto the same tree.

Fruit: A pome; with seeds formed within an ovary situated within the fleshy receptacle tissue, with each segment producing one to a few seeds. The ovary position is inferior, and so a green calyx is left at the apex of the fruit. Because the best fruits are formed from fully fertilised flowers, and also to prevent over-stressing trees, apples are best thinned soon after fruit-set to leave one fruit per spur. This also reduces the risk of biennial bearing and evens out yields, as well as reducing the risk of disease spreading between tightly packed clusters. Apple colours range from green, yellow, orange to red, and their size is also variable between cultivars. Some cooking apples can weigh >0.5 kg, other apples are small, delicate, bright red and sweet. Apple flesh is generally white, and varies from soft to crisp. Apple varieties tend to be either predominantly spur- or tip-bearing, with spur-cultivars generally chosen for espaliered fruit-trees. Trees that produce fruits mostly on spurs tend to be more precocious and fruitful.

Yield/harvest/storage: On average, can get 35–60 kg per tree, and trees can bear in their second year after budding on dwarf rootstocks, or after 3–5 years after budding onto standard rootstocks. Apples take between 100–200 days to mature, depending on cultivar. They are best picked when ripe, and ripen poorly if picked too soon. When ripe, the pips cannot be heard rattling within the fruits, and pips have then turned brown. Apples are usually picked when fruits have developed full colour and size, though before they soften. Modern cultivars have been selected to be sweeter at an early stage of maturity. Apples, in general, store better than many fruits. They can be stored in a fridge for 6–8 weeks, and are often stored commercially in cold storage for periods of 6–12 months. Only undamaged fruit should be stored, and usually only those that are picked from the tree (apples that have fallen are usually damaged or bruised). Traditionally, each apple is wrapped in paper and then packed into boxes, which are kept cool and dark, but not in freezing temperatures. Individual wrapping means that any fruit that deteriorates and becomes infected with mould won't necessarily infect its neighbours. The smell of stored apples is wonderful.

CULTIVATION

More research has been done on apple varieties than on most other fruits and, consequently, more training systems, rootstocks and cultural techniques are available than for most other tree crops.

Location: Trees grow best with full sun. They can be moderately wind tolerant, though grow better in orchards with windbreaks. Not very tolerant of maritime exposure.

Temperature: Pome fruits are adapted to cooler, temperate areas; indeed, apples are the only fruit trees that can be grown in areas such as Russia, Scandinavia and the colder parts of Canada. They prefer areas that have a definite colder season and a warm, but not too hot summer. Fruit quality is best with warm days and cool nights, but with lots of sunshine. Trees can tolerate temperatures of –40°C when dormant, though flowers and fruitlets can be killed at ~–4°C, but this is not likely, due to their late blossoming time. In hotter areas, direct sun can burn the fruit's skin.

Chilling: Trees need a long period of ~1000–1600 hours of chilling each winter to produce flowers and come into leaf satisfactorily in spring.

Soil/water/nutrients: Apples grow best in deep, well-drained, loamy soils, though will grow in a variety of soil types, including sandy soils and clays. They grow best at a neutral pH of 6–7. If the soil is too acid, this can increase fruit disorders such as bitter pip; if the soil is too alkaline, then micronutrient deficiencies, such as iron chlorosis, often occur. Trees are only moderately nutrient hungry, and many people do not feed trees once they are established. However, moderate applications of nutrients, in spring, can increase growth and yields. Interestingly, green-apple cultivars, such as 'Granny Smith', seem to need more nitrogen than red-apple cultivars.

Planting: Space trees at 10–13 m apart; closer for smaller cultivars. Dwarf trees, either trained or as small bushes, are a better choice for small gardens.

Propagation: Seeds: Apple cultivars are not true to type when grown from seed, and so are not usually propagated by this method. If growing from seed, it is best sown after 1–2 months of cold stratification. Even then, germination is often slow, and seeds may not germinate for up to 12 months. *Cuttings:* Hardwood cutting can be taken in late autumn and inserted in a cold frame. *Grafting:* This is the usual method.

They are often T- or chip-budded onto a variety of rootstocks. Apples have more types of rootstocks than any other tree crop. The most commonly used rootstocks fall into three groups: the Malling series, the Malling-Merton series and apple seedlings, and their sizes range from the ultra-dwarf M.27 (0.6–2 m) to seedlings (6–7 m). Dwarfing rootstocks have been cultivated for hundreds of years. They were originally categorised by degree of dwarfing, and were given the roman numerals I–XXIV, which have now been changed and expanded to M.1–M.27. Apple seedlings are the most common and inexpensive rootstocks worldwide, but are more variable and are slower to start producing fruits.

Pruning: Commercially, trees are sometimes trained to a central-leader system, where one branch is allowed to grow vertically and form the main stem upon which fruiting branches are spaced at regular intervals of 0.3–2 m apart up a main stem. However, apple trees naturally tend to have a more open vase shape and are also often trained to form a modified leader with several strong scaffold branches and no main central leader. Basically, trees need to be pruned to allow light and air to penetrate into the crown, which gives good leaf and fruit production, as well as reducing the risk of fungal disease. Apples tend to form dense, crossed branches, which benefit from being thinned. After initially shaping, the only pruning necessary is the removal of these crossing branches, as well as the removal of too much twiggy growth, which can result in excess leaf growth at the expense of fruit production. Also remove any dead or damaged wood, and thin branches to retain an open centre. Also remove any suckers. Remember that trees produce apples on the same lateral spurs for several years. Pruning is often done in late winter, though some argue that silverleaf can then more readily infect trees through open cuts; therefore, summer pruning may be wiser.

Pests and diseases: Apples are commercially susceptible to a wide range of difficult-to-control fungal diseases, which can be minimised by not crowding trees together, open pruning of the crown, and disposal of fallen fruits, leaves, branches, etc. The home gardener is unlikely to experience many of the problems listed below; however, possible problems are apple-scab fungus, which affects leaves, flowers and fruit, although this is not usually too serious to the tree, and bitter-rot fungus, which only affects the fruit. More serious is fireblight, a bacterial disease that can spread rapidly in spring and can kill trees, though can be partly controlled by reducing nitrogen-fertiliser applications and, thus, lush new growth. Prune out any infected branches and burn them. Scale insects can infest branches, leaves and fruit. In addition, bronze beetle, capsid bug, codlin moth, European red mite, leaf-curling midge, mealybug, thrips, two-spotted mite, woolly aphid and various moth-roller species can attack trees. However, many of these diseases only superficially affect fruit appearance, etc. and are not too serious for the home gardener. More serious are nematodes, collar rot, *Armillaria*, black spot, target spot, glomerella, ripe spot, European canker, bitter pip and apple mosaic.

CULTIVARS

There are hundreds, if not thousands, of apple cultivars. In addition, the heirloom apple cultivars are also undergoing a revival of interest, with old, isolated apple trees being

Food

A fresh, crisp, sweet eating apple takes some beating. Apples can also be used in pies, desserts, jams, sauces, apple butter, etc. They make a good juice and a reasonable quality wine. They can be baked and stuffed with dried fruits. There are a multitude of recipes that include apples in both sweet and savoury ways, and they are often mixed with various fruits in desserts (e.g. dates, blackberries, bananas). Sour apples are used in cider and cooking. The fruits can be dried or frozen for later use. Apples produce ethylene, and if put with other fruit can help them to ripen. Apple petals can be eaten and have a slightly tart floral flavour.

Nutrition

Does an apple a day keep the doctor away? Most of the apple's nutrients are just under the skin, so don't peel it! They are a good source of potassium (160 mg/apple), folic acid and have good levels of vitamin C (22 mg/100 g of flesh) and vitamin A (340 IU). They are also high in fibre (as pectin: ~3.5 g) and calcium (9.5 mg/apple). Additionally, they contain trace amounts of B vitamins, particularly niacin. Apples also contain variable amounts of polyphenols, with the highest levels being in the peel of red apples (probably due to anthocyanins). These substances have many potential benefits, including helping to reduce the risk of carcinogenic tumours.

Medicinal

The bark and roots of most *Malus* species contain phloretin, which can act to suppress both Gram+/– bacteria. The bark from the crabapple tree (*M. diversifolia*) was used by North American Indians to treat diarrhoea (see Warning). The fibre (pectin) in apples (as distinct from the juice) has been shown to slow the release of sugars in blood and to also slightly drop blood-cholesterol levels. The fibre helps regulate normal bowel function and prevent diarrhoea and constipation; it seems to act as a mucillage and encourages the growth of beneficial bacteria in the digestive tract. Apples are a traditional remedy for joint pain and stiffness caused by rheumatism. Their high levels of malic and tartaric acids may also aid digestion. Green apples act as a liver and gallbladder cleanser and may aid in softening gallstones. Eating raw apples gives the gums a healthy massage and cleans the teeth. *Warning:* All Rosaceae species contain cyanogenic glycoside compounds, as amygdalin, within their seeds, leaves and bark. A little amygdalin actually induces a feeling of relaxation, but should only be consumed in moderation. Reportedly, a man who ate a cup of apple seeds died. In addition, apple juice has been implicated in chronic, non-specific diarrhoea in infants and young children. The high levels of fructose and sorbitol in apple juice may lead to poor absorption, and to diarrhoea in children.

propagated to keep these selections available. These older cultivars are often more disease resistant and also have vigorous growth. When choosing an apple-tree cultivar various considerations need to be made: the fruit taste required, e.g. a sour cooking apple or a small sweet, eating apple, etc., storability of the cultivar, the size of tree, its hardiness or tolerance to warmer climates, etc. There are centres that grow and specialise in apple cultivars, and an apple-tasting session is quite remarkable for the range of flavours and textures possible from just one fruit. Pollination of trees can be improved by planting a crabapple amongst newer cultivars. These ornamentals are able to pollinate most apple cultivars and are also often more attractive. A very few of the many apple cultivars available are listed below, and the gardener is encouraged to explore the many possible cultivars available in his/her locality.

'Braeburn': Late season. Developed from 'Granny Smith'. Fruit: greenish, faintly striped red; flesh: crisp, sweet, good flavour. Excellent cooked, needing little or no sugar. It is a spur-type tree, and is fairly precocious, though is prone to disease.

'Calville Blanc d'Hiver': Mid season. A very old European (pre-1600) variety. Medium–large fruit, pale green with light red spots if exposed to the sun. Aromatic, sweet, spicy, very good dessert quality, tender flesh and juicy. Has good levels of vitamin C. Good for stewing.

'Cox's Orange Pippin': Mid season. Fruit: medium-sized, deep yellow and streaked with red, delicious, crisp, tasty. I think it's one of the best, but is susceptible to many apple diseases. Has a flavour that is a good blend of sugar, acid and aromatics. It stores for 8–12 weeks, and is multi-purpose. Prefers colder winters, and needs some pruning. Spurs freely and bears well, but yields are much improved if there is a nearby pollinator.

'Ellisons Orange': Mid season. Fruit: medium-sized, golden yellow with crimson stripes. A cross between 'Cox's Orange Pippin' and 'Calville Blanc', and has Cox's good aromatic flavour. Picked early it is crisp, but if left for too long it becomes soft. Crops heavily and reliably, flowers over a long period, resists frost and is a good pollinator for other varieties. Resistant to scab, though is somewhat canker prone.

'Fortune' ('Laxton's Fortune'): Early–mid season. Cross of 'Cox's Orange Pippin' x 'Wealthy' in 1904. Fruit: sweet, aromatic, excellent flavour, crisp at first, becoming softer as it matures. Fruits mostly on spurs. Is remarkably resistant to disease.

'Freyburg': From New Zealand. A cross between 'Golden Delicious' and 'Cox's Orange Pippin'. Mid–late season. Fruit: small–medium-sized, light golden yellow, slightly russet. Interesting, rich flavour, some say is anise-like. The flesh is crisp, juicy, light yellow, sweet. Stores well.

'Fuji': Late season. Partly self-fruitful. Ripens very late, keeps for ~6 months. Fruit resists sunburn. Requires 100–400 chill hours: much less than most. Fruit: large, sweet, crisp, fine textured, complex flavour. Excellent eating.

'Granny Smith': Tart green apples, ripen very late and need a long growing season, but only needs 600–700 chill hours. Multi-use fruit. Flesh: hard, crisp, juicy, becoming sweet if tree-ripened. Can store for several months. Tree is very vigorous and crops heavily. Susceptible to black spot. Is a good pollinator. A tip bearer.

'James Grieve': Early–mid season. Fruit: medium–large, crimson over yellow. Flesh: yellowish, very juicy, soft, excellent flavour. Tree spurs freely and crops very heavily.

'Jonagold': Late season. Fruit: large, striped red over yellow, fine textured, juicy, sweet. Rated highly as a culinary apple. Best grown on dwarfing rootstocks, or it is too vigorous and spreading. Needs a pollinator: it is self-infertile as it is triploid. A multi-use apple. Stores ~3 months. Susceptible to mildew and scab.

'Northern Spy': Late season. Fruit: large, yellow with bright red splashes. Excellent flavour, slightly yellowish flesh, very crisp, juicy. Good culinary apple. Takes 3–4 years to start bearing on a dwarfing rootstock and longer on a standard rootstock. An old and popular New England variety. High in vitamin C. Stores for ~5 months. Not disease resistant.

'Rhode Island Greening': Mid season. Very old variety. Fruit: very large, firm, crisp, juicy, acid, yellowish-green, renowned as a cooking apple, but can be also eaten as a dessert apple if stored for a while or, in mild climates, if it is tree ripened. Is a triploid cultivar and, therefore, is self-infertile, and needs a pollinator. Tendency to biennial bearing.

'Roxbury Russet': Late season. Very old variety, pre-1700. Fruit: pale greenish-brown, tough skinned, russetted. Flesh: firm, crisp, slightly acidic, good for desserts and cooking. Stores very well.

'Sturmer Late Season': Fruit: medium-sized, yellowish-green, bronze blushed. Flesh: dense, crisp, only moderately juicy, sub-acid flavour. Particularly high in vitamin C, with ~3 times the level of red apples. Tree: not vigorous, compact, heavy spurring, requires little pruning.

CRABAPPLES

The term crabapple includes about 25 older-style apple species and varieties that have small (<5-cm width), very sour fruits which, although not eaten fresh, are popular in jam, jelly and chutney, or are mixed with sweeter fruits in pies. They are also reported to make a good wine. A couple of the best known are *M. sylvestrus* and *M. pumila*. They often have profuse, showy blossom that ranges in colour from white to pink, followed by large crops of showy, bright rosy red or orange fruits. The trees also often have good autumn colour. As a consequence, they are often grown more for their ornamental features than their fruits, and many ornamental varieties are available. The trees vary in shape, depending on species, from upright, to spreading, to drooping; they also vary considerably in height. Their cultivation is the same as for apple, but many crabapples tend to be somewhat tougher and can withstand a wider range of adverse conditions, including drought. Grow best in full sun. Birds love the fruit. Medicinally, the fruits are thought to have cleansing properties. ■

Mangifera indica
Mango
ANACARDIACEAE
Relatives: cashew, pistachio, marula, ambarella, poison ivy

The mango is the most economically important fruit in the Anacardiaceae family. It is a native of southern Asia. From there it was spread to eastern Asia, possibly by Buddhist monks in the 4th and 5th centuries BC, and to eastern Africa, possibly by the Persians in the 10th century AD. The selection of wild types has occurred for the last 4000–6000 years, and vegetative propagation has been practised for at least 400 years in India. Mangoes were only brought to England and Europe after the English occupied India in the 1800s. India is the world's largest producer of mangoes, and it has been estimated that there are >1000 varieties there, where the mango is often called the 'king of fruits'. The mango comes in two main types: one from India, and the other from southeastern Asia. The Indian types are intolerant of humidity, are subject to mildew and bear single embryonic fruits that have a strong red blush and a regular shape. Asian types tolerate excess moisture, resist mildew and form many nucellar (or polyembryonic), pale green, elongated, kidney-shaped fruits.

DESCRIPTION

Mango trees are often grown as majestic landscape specimens and shade trees. In warmer climates they are fast growing. They form a tall (10–30 m), broad, rounded, spreading canopy which may, with age, be as wide as it is tall, or may become more upright and oval. It has a sturdy trunk with grey-brown fissured bark. The tree is long lived, some specimens surviving to >300 years, and still fruiting.

Leaves: Shiny dark green above, paler beneath, contrasting with young pink–red–purple leaves at the ends of branches. Have a pale, conspicuous midrib, with many horizontal distinctive veins. Mature leaves are oblong with pointed tips, 10–30 cm long, 2–6 cm wide. Generally borne in clusters, spirally arranged on branches, separated by a length of naked stem bearing no buds. These gaps mark successive flushes of growth. Each flush of growth changes to a rich, dark green colour before the next flush of growth occurs. They are nearly evergreen, only losing their leaves in very cold weather.

Flowers: Abundant, fragrant, showy, white–pink/yellow, in panicles, borne at the ends of stems, beyond the shiny leaves, in spring. Flowers are a mix of bisexual and just male, with often more male than bisexual flowers. Therefore, although the tree can be self-fertile, planting more than one tree will increase fruit-set. Most flowers, being male, won't set fruit, so there are few fruits to the number of flowers. Fertilisation of flowers is reduced if night temperatures fall below ~12°C. Flowering is best in dry weather. Nucellar (see p. 15) mango types often do not need to be pollinated and will still form fruit. The flowers may form volatile oils (e.g. mangiferol, mangiferone), which some people find irritating to the respiratory system and eyes. *Pollination:* By various insects, butterflies, beetles, ants, but not much by bees. Some self pollination. Hand pollination can increase yields.

Fruit: A large drupe, often kidney-shaped with a long fruit stalk, borne on the outside of the tree's canopy. The thin, waxy, smooth skin ripens to a yellow–green colour, often with a red/orange blush. The skin contains oils that some people react to in a lesser, but similar way to poison ivy. The skin is inedible. The flesh is yellow-orange in colour and the best fruits are succulent, juicy pleasantly rich, sweet and very tasty; other fruits can have a turpentine-like taste and stringy flesh. The fruits have a large, difficult-to-remove, hard, elongated, ribbed central stone, which contains one or more large, starchy kernels. The kernels may just contain a single genetically-formed embryo, or can be polyembryonic, and may produce several seedlings from one seed. These latter seedlings are likely to be clones of the parent tree.

Yield/harvest/storage: Ripe fruits range in weight from 0.25–1 kg. At 10–20 years of age, a good annual crop of 200–300 fruits per tree is likely. Trees more than twice that age can produce double that amount. In Java, old trees have been known to bear 1000–1500 fruits in a season. There are reports of annual yields of 6500 fruits/tree, with a record of 29,000 fruits! Fruits take 120–160 days to ripen from fruit-set. Grafted trees take 3–5 years to start producing fruits; seedlings take 6–10 years. Trees less than 10 years old usually flower and fruit regularly every year; however, after this time, trees often become biennial bearing, although often not all the tree is affected at the same time. Fruit thinning and pruning can rectify this and balance out crop yields. Premature fruit drop is also common, as is the production of many small fruits. Despite the tree's numerous flowers, generally, there are only 2–3 mature fruits per panicle. Most fruits ripen in mid summer in tropical/semi-tropical climates, but may not mature until autumn in cooler climates. Trees produce fruits for ~4 weeks, but by choosing early- and late-ripening varieties, the season can be extended. They are best left to fully ripen on the tree, and harvested when fully coloured and becoming just soft to the touch (but not too soft). Fruits that are just under-ripe can be harvested and will ripen at ~22°C in a few days. *Storage:* They will suffer cold damage if stored in a fridge, but will keep for several days at room temperature. Washing the fruits after harvest removes any sap that may have leaked from the stem onto the fruit; if not removed, this sap damages the fruit's skin and makes it susceptible to rot.

Roots: Forms a long taproot, ~6 m deep, and needs great care when planting out or transplanting. They like regular moisture till established. They also have a dense, wide-spreading, shallow, feeder-root system that sends down anchor roots, which can also penetrate deeply. Although spreading, the roots are not destructive, and so can be planted near paths, etc.

CULTIVATION

Location: Grow best in full sun, and they grow well on slopes. Trees are not very tolerant of wind, and may need staking. Plant in a sheltered location, against a warm wall if possible.

Temperature: They basically require a frost-free climate. Although mature trees can withstand temperatures of –4°C for a few hours, this can injure leaves and small branches. Young trees are more susceptible and can be killed at ~–1°C. Flowers and small fruits can be killed if the temperature falls below 4°C for a few hours. They may be able to acclimatise somewhat to cold, but need warm, dry weather to set fruit. Often do best with distinct wet and dry seasons. However, they can grow and produce fruits in warm-temperate climates as long as they are cared for.

Soil/water/nutrients: Will grow in almost any well-drained soil, i.e. sand, loam or clay, but avoid heavy, wet soils. A pH between 5.5–7.5 is preferred. They are somewhat tolerant of alkalinity. They like a deep, moist soil to enable good root growth. Young trees benefit from fairly regular applications of nutrients. Initially, young trees need more nitrogen; as trees mature, phosphate and potassium become more important. Try to use a fertiliser that also supplies micronutrients, especially iron. Seaweed and organic fish fertilisers give good results. However, too much fertiliser can delay and reduce fruiting. They are fairly drought tolerant once established as their deep roots can usually reach down to the water table during dry seasons. However, additional moisture from flowering until fruit ripening can improve fruit quality. Very humid weather favours *Anthracnose* and poor fruit-set.

Pot culture: Because of their frost sensitivity, dwarf cultivars can be grown in containers or in a glasshouse in colder regions. They will grow best with warmth year round. In the greenhouse, give them full light and free air movement to reduce the risk of disease. Keep plants well watered when actively growing, but reduce moisture during winter.

Planting: Mangoes form large trees and need to be spaced at 8–15 m apart. Dig in well-rotted manure before planting. Young trees often need staking.

Pruning: Healthy trees require little pruning, although pruning to stimulate new growth reduces biennial bearing. Thinning young fruits in bumper years also reduces alternate bearing. When young, the trees can be pruned to ~3–5 main scaffold branches, but little pruning is needed after this. However, commercially, mature trees are often topped to control their size in summer after harvest. Because fruit are produced on the present season's growth they can be pruned in autumn, winter or early spring, though possible cold damage should be considered.

Propagation: *Seed:* Grows readily from seed, although that from supermarket fruit is of variable quality, depending on what treatments it has received. Germination rate and vigour of seedlings are best from seeds taken from fully ripened fruits, and when sown fresh. To speed up germination, gently prize open the stone without damaging the kernel. The kernel can then be placed sideways in well-drained compost, with about the top quarter protruding above soil level. Given warmth, it should germinate in 8–21 days. If the seed cannot be planted immediately, it can be 'stored' in moist sand/sawdust in a dark, cool place. Once germinated, seedlings are best established in deep, biodegradable pots to avoid damaging the taproot when planting out. However, some growers recommend removing the end of the taproot about a week before planting out so that lateral feeder-root growth is encouraged. Seedlings from Indian-type mangoes vary from their parents (they have a single genetically-mixed embryo). Seedlings from Asian-type mangoes are often polyembryonic, and because there has been little or no genetic mixing to create the embryo, they are clones of the parent plant. *Cuttings:* Rarely successful. *Grafting:* Mostly done with monoembryonic seedlings, which aren't true from seed. Mostly grafted by approach grafts, whip-and-tongue-grafting, chip-budding or topworking. The rootstock is usually a mango cultivar, e.g. 'Turpentine'.

Pests and diseases: *Anthracnose* on fruit and leaves is a serious problem for mango. Scale, mealybugs and mites are also common pests. Powdery mildew, especially in rainy weather or frequent fog, can be a problem, although a spray of powdered kelp at bud break can help control it. Sodium bicarbonate can also be used as a spray. Bacterial spot can affect the leaves and fruit. Various nutrient deficiencies may occur including manganese, zinc, boron, copper, magnesium and iron. Most of these are more likely in alkaline soils. Mango decline is a disease brought on by deficiencies of iron and manganese, and leads to a greater risk of fungal disease or attack by nematodes.

CULTIVARS

Many of the Indian types are more suited to cooler climates. There are many cultivars available; just a few of the hardier ones are listed below.

'Earlygold': From Florida. Tree: upright. Fruit: medium sized, ~0.5 kg, roundish, orange with red blush, no fibre, seed often abortive. Very early harvest. Resistant to *Anthracnose*. Good for coastal locations.

'Haden': Indian type. Tree: spreading. Fruit: large, ~1 kg, oval, yellow with a red blush, mild and sweet in flavour, little fibre. Early harvest. Susceptible to *Anthracnose* and alternate bearing. Could be grown in a greenhouse.

'Kensington Pride': From Queensland. Often from seed: it is polyembryonic. Tree: rounded, vigorous. Fruit: medium–large, almost round with a pink blush. Flavour: sweet. Fruit tends to drop when small. Mid season harvest.

'Keitt': Tree: small–medium, erect, open, very productive. Fruit: large, ~1 kg, oval, fibre only around the seed. Resists mildew. Skin: medium-thick, yellow with light red blush and a lavender bloom. Flesh: rich, sweet flavour, very good quality. Late harvest. Not for the coast.

'Pirie': From India, ancient. Tree: broad, spreading. Fruit: small, ~0.25 kg, almost round, yellow with red blush. Juicy, no fibre, rich flavour. Alternate bearing; blooms every 18 months. Early mid season harvest. For the greenhouse.

'Reliable': From California. Tree: broad, dense, slow

growing. Fruit: varies from 0.3–0.8 kg, oblong, yellow with a red blush. Regular bearing. Subject to *Anthracnose*. Long ripening season from autumn through winter.

'Villaseñor': From Los Angeles. Dwarfing, spreading. Fruit: medium sized, ~0.4 kg, oval, greenish-yellow with a pink blush, a mild flavour. Mid season harvest. ∎

uses

Food

Mangoes are delicious simply sliced and served with a squeeze of lime juice as an appetiser or a dessert. Mangoes can also be frozen (whole or sliced), though often go mushy. Mangoes can be peeled and sliced for a pie filling, used in jelly, marmalade, jam or sauces, or can be stewed, added to cakes, fruit salads, icecream, yoghurt and other desserts. The fruits can also be spiced and preserved in jars. Green mangoes make a wonderful chutney, often eaten with Indian curries; it can be also added to salsas, or can be salted, dried and used in chutney and pickles. The kernels can be astringent if not soaked first, or roasted or boiled. They can then be ground up and added to bread, etc. The oil from the kernel is white and solid, and is high in saturated fats. Some people cook and eat young mango leaves. The unripe fruits can be used to tenderise meat.

Nutrition

Has reasonable levels of vitamin C: 28 mg/100 g of flesh, and excellent levels of vitamin A (IU 4800), more than any other commercial fruit, including good levels of lutein and zeaxanthin (types of vitamin A). There is evidence that these compounds can help reduce the incidence of cataracts and macular degeneration. They also contain some B vitamins and have good levels of vitamin E (for a fleshy fruit).

Medicinal

The twigs, leaves and fruit skins are astringent, and are used to treat bronchitis, internal haemorrhage and toothache. The dried flowers (containing 15% tannin) are used to treat diarrhoea. The kernel is used as a vermifuge, and as an astringent in diarrhoea and haemorrhage. Extracts of unripe fruits, bark, stems and leaves have shown antibiotic activity. **Warning:** The sap from stems, leaves and the skin of unripe fruit contains various potential irritants, e.g. mangiferen, which is capable of blistering the skin in a similar way to poison ivy, often with a delayed reaction. Mango wood should not be burnt as its smoke is a high irritant.

Other uses

The bark contains ~18% tannin and has been used to tan hides. It also yields a yellow dye, or, with turmeric and lime, a bright rose-pink colouring. The wood is coarse-textured, medium–strong and hard, and is used in building construction, boats, agricultural tools, plywood.

Manilkara zapota
(syn. *M. achras, M. zapotilla*)
Sapodilla (chiku, nispero, chicozapote naseberry, sapota)
SAPOTACEAE
Relatives: canistel, lucmo, sapote

The sapodilla is considered by many to be one of the best tropical/semi-tropical fruits. It is borne on an attractive, large, slow-growing tree that has whorled leaves and is tolerant of a wide range of growing conditions. Native to southern Mexico and Central America, where it still grows wild in the forests, it has been cultivated since ancient times, and is still planted in gardens, particularly in Mexico. The Portuguese took plants from Central America to southern India, where it is now cultivated extensively. Some modern plantations in Central America have been established for fruit production, but most trees were planted for their gummy latex, called chicle, which was/is used in chewing gum. The chewiness of the dried latex was discovered by the Mayas many hundreds of years ago. It was not until the early 1900s that its use became commercialised in the USA and the first flavoured chewing gum was manufactured. By 1930, at the peak of its production, >6 million kg of chicle was being imported, from an estimated 100,000,000 trees, into the USA. It is tapped from the trees at 2–3-year intervals, like rubber. The name sapodilla is derived from the Spanish word 'zapotilla', meaning 'small fruit'.

DESCRIPTION

An elegant, very slow-growing, long-lived, wind-resistant, densely-leaved tree. The tree usually has a single trunk, a pyramidal shape when young, becoming mostly wide-spreading as it matures. It forms a thick, densely furrowed trunk. In warmer, wetter areas, the tree can grow to ~20 m tall in the open, and to 30 m tall when grown in groups; however, in cooler areas, the trees are considerably smaller. It has strong wind-resistant branches. Its bark is flaky and attractive as the tree gets older. The tree has thorns. It produces a white, gummy latex, which is harvested commercially.

Leaves: Ornamental, evergreen, light yellow-green, glossy, spirally clustered around the tips of forked stems. They are simple, oval, and pointed at both ends, 6–12 cm long, 2–4 cm wide. They form a dense canopy. The leaves have a pinkish tinge when young.

Flowers: Small (~1 cm diameter), with three, yellowy-brown, hairy outer sepals, white inner petals, bell-shaped, and borne from leaf axils on hairy brown stalks. Are bisexual. In warmer regions there can be several flushes of flowers a year. *Pollination:* Flowers may be self-infertile, so may need more than one tree. Insect pollinated: mostly by thrips, who actually live within the flowers, and move onto a new flower once food reserves have been depleted, inadvertently taking pollen with them. Pollination might be a problem in some locations, although bees will do some. Fruit-set is very variable, and many flowers do not develop into fruits.

Fruit: Yellowy-brown fuzz on the outside of the egg-shaped fruit (5–10 cm width), which externally looks like a rounded kiwifruit. As it ripens, it loses the brown fuzz to leave a thin, yellowy tan-coloured skin below. The fruit is hard and very astringent when immature, and exudes a sticky gum if cut at this time. When ripe, the flesh is smooth (in better fruits), or is somewhat grainy, similar to ripe pears, and is yellowish-brown in colour, often being greenish just below the skin. When ripe it is soft, juicy and fragrant, with a caramel, pear-like flavour. Sapodilla have a very high pulp to fruit ratio (~85%). Some fruits are seedless, but there are usually 3–12 oval, dark brown, shiny, flat, ~2-cm-long seeds that are held longitudinally in a whorl at the centre of the fruit. They should not be eaten, and are easy to remove. Fruit shape, size and quality varies considerably.

Yield/harvest/storage: Under ideal conditions, there can be two or more crops a year: The main crop is in late spring–summer and a second crop may occur in autumn. Seedling trees take ~6 years to start fruiting; grafted trees may begin to bear after 4 years (but can be longer); layered plants may produce fruit after only 3 years (see later). Yields increase annually for many years, and mature trees can give excellent crops. A 10-year-old tree may bear 45–180 kg of fruits a year. In India, it is reported that trees have produced 2500–3000 fruits a year when 30–35 years old. However, yield does vary with cultivar. Fruits take 20–40 weeks to mature from pollination to harvesting, depending an location, cultivar, etc. Fruits are best picked when fully ripe and the sugar level is highest, although it is not always easy to distinguish, when this is due to the lack of definitive skin-colour change. The loss of the fuzz can be a good indicator, or the fuzz can be easily rubbed off to reveal a yellow-brownish colour, rather than green. If the fruits exude any gum, then they are not ripe. Brown-skinned fruits that are still hard can be ripened at room temperature for a few days. Green fruits won't ripen satisfactorily. Conversely, fruits are best when not over-ripe or too soft. Mature fruits can last for about a week at room temperature, and maybe for longer in a fridge: they can be stored for ~6 weeks at ~1.5ºC.

Roots: Has shallow roots, with >80% of these occurring within the top 75 cm of soil, and their spread is only half the width of the canopy. Therefore, a deep, organic mulch will help conserve moisture, protect the roots, suppress weed growth and add nutrients.

CULTIVATION

A large tree suitable for warmer regions. Needs little maintenance and can produce an abundance of fruit.

Location: Likes a sunny, warm location. Is very tolerant of salt, and can be readily grown in maritime locations. They are extremely wind tolerant: can even survive hurricane-force winds (which is surprising, considering they have shallow roots).

Temperature: Prefers a frost-free location, although mature trees can withstand temperatures of ~–3°C for several hours. Young trees are much more tender and can be killed at –1°C unless they are protected. They do not fruit well in regions with colder nights.

Soil/water/nutrients: Can grow in a wide range of soil types (lighter clay, sand–gravel), including poor soils, though prefers a deep, organic soil with regular moisture. Once established, trees are quite drought tolerant, but can also tolerate periods of waterlogging, though do not grow well in these locations. Can also grow at a wide range of pH conditions, from fairly acid to almost pure limestone, where it does not seem to develop iron chlorosis, as do many plants. Can grow in surprisingly salty soils. In some areas of India, the trees are actually watered with brackish or saline water, which is said to reduce vegetative growth and promote fruiting. Trees benefit from applications of nutrients for at least the first few years, particularly containing extra potassium and some phosphate. Fertile soils with this balance of nutrients result in much better fruit quality and yield. Give applications 2–3 times a year during active growth.

Pot culture: Being a slow-growing species, it can be grown as a container plant for several years, though will at some point become to large to manage, unless a dwarf cultivar is chosen.

Propagation: *Seed:* Will remain viable for several years if kept dry. The best seeds are large, and these are usually obtained from large fruits. They germinate readily, but grow slowly; there is also great variation in quality and yield of fruits. *Cuttings:* Do not seem to take, probably because of the tree's gummy exudates. *Layering:* Air-layering seems to work well and air-layered trees may begin fruiting within 2–3 years of planting, although do take ~9 months to root. Select young branches and cover these for a period to eliminate light before air-layering. The application of rooting hormones to the wound can also help. *Grafting:* These seem to work well, and the sapodilla can be successfully grafted onto either itself, *Bassia latifolia*, *B. longifolia*, *Sideroxylon dulcificum* or *Mimusops hexandra* by cleft-, side- or whip-and-tongue-grafting, with the latter reported to be the most successful. Softwood grafts are reported to give a good success rate (~80% survival). Can also be shield-budded onto its own rootstock.

Planting: Space trees 9–13 m apart in deep, pre-fertilised soil.

Pruning: If young trees are straggly or have few lower branches, removing the tips of the taller branches will induce the formation of lateral branches. Branch-tip removal can be continued (in spring or summer) as the tree matures to encourage a more compact growth form. In addition, any damaged or diseased wood needs removing, and possibly the tree's height controlled. However, severe pruning can lead to crowding of branches and reduce the tree's life.

Pests and diseases: Are generally trouble free, though bats love the fruits in their native habitats.

Food

Can be eaten fresh, cooked or can be dried. Fruits need to be ripe: unripe fruit have high tannin levels and an inedible gummy exudate. The inner seeds should be removed. They are toxic when eaten in quantity and have a small hook that could catch in the throat. Fresh fruits can be simply cut lengthways and the flesh scooped out. It is at its best when slightly chilled. They can be also added to desserts, salads, sauces, etc. A dessert sauce can be made by mashing the flesh with orange juice, and then adding some whipped cream or yoghurt. If the fruits are cooked, the flesh changes colour to bright red. The fruits can be stewed (with e.g. ginger and lime juice), or even fried. Can be made into a jam, but the gummy latex on the surface while it is cooking needs to be removed. The dried fruits can be added to many sweet and savoury dishes, including curries.

Nutrition

Has good amounts of vitamin C: 15–35 mg/100 g of flesh, and some vitamin A (~150 IU). Also has good levels of iron, potassium, copper, and the B vitamins folate, pantothenic acid and B6. Has very good levels of dietary fibre. Flesh contains ~14% sugar. Immature fruit have high levels of tannins and are very astringent. **Warning:** The seeds contain 1% saponins and 1% sapotinin: eating >6 seeds may cause abdominal pain and vomiting.

Medicinal

Many of its medicinal uses are due to its tannin content: the young fruits are used to treat diarrhoea, a tea concocted from the older yellowy leaves, young fruits and flowers is drunk to treat coughs, colds and diarrhoea. An extract from the crushed seeds (see Warning above) has been used in Yucatan as a sedative and soporific, and a paste has been applied to stings and bites from venomous animals.

Other uses

A main commercial product of the sapodilla tree is its gummy latex, called chicle. It contains 15% rubber and 38% resin, and has, for many years, been the main ingredient in chewing gum. More recently, synthetic gums have replaced its use. Chicle is/was obtained by tapping the trees and then heating the latex until it thickens. It has no taste, and flavourings are added later. The wood is strong and durable: lintels and supporting beams in Mayan temples made from this wood are still intact within the ruins. It is used to make hard-wearing, strong items, including flooring, tool handles and for structural building. The good-quality red heartwood is used to make furniture, banisters and cabinetwork, but the sawdust can be irritating.

Ornamental

It makes a wonderful, elegant ornamental tree that is tolerant of a wide range of conditions, and produces lots of fruit. Also makes an excellent shade tree.

CULTIVARS

There are many local cultivars, and availability depends largely on where you live. Choosing local cultivars means they should be adapted to your specific conditions. There are some dwarf cultivars available, and these are a good option for smaller gardens or for growing in containers.

'Brown Sugar': A tall, bushy tree. Crops in 3–5 years. Has regular yields of ~125–200 kg/tree; fruits are round, 5–7 cm long, flesh is pale brown, good quality, slightly granular, fragrant, juicy, very sweet, keep well.

'Kalipatti': From India, where it's very popular. Trees are small, crop when young, high quality fruit with few seeds;

high yields (~160 kg/tree).

'Prolific': Grown in Florida. Fruit are roundish, 6–9 cm long, lose their brown fuzz when ripe. Flesh is pinkish-tan, mildly fragrant, good quality, smooth textured, sweet. Good yields (150–225 kg/tree) and first harvest is in 3–4 years. Fruits are easily bruised, so storage time can be short.

'Russell': Large, roundish fruit, ~8–10 cm diameter. Fruits have a brown fuzz with grey patches. Flesh: pinkish-tan, mildly fragrant, somewhat granular, sweet and rich. Slower to bear and less productive than some cultivars.

'Tikal': A new cultivar. Fruit: elliptical, pale brown skin, very good flavour, ripens early in the season. ■

Mespilus germanica
Medlar
ROSACEAE
Relatives: hawthorn, apple, pear, loquat

The medlar is a native of the Middle East and southeastern Europe. It has since become naturalised over much of Europe, including southern Britain. The medlar has been cultivated in Europe for millennia, particularly by the French, reaching a peak during the Middle Ages. It is often found growing in old gardens around Europe. It is an attractive tree, often grown as an ornamental specimen: for its shape, flowers, autumn colour and its edible fruits.

DESCRIPTION

A deciduous, spreading tree (4–6 m), height 7–8 m, with many crooked, often right-angled branches, giving it an untidy appearance. Sometimes spiny. Its bark is grey-brown, fissured into oblong sections. It is slow growing and long lived.

Leaves: Deciduous, dull green, oval, untoothed or finely toothed, large (5–13 cm long), often has yellow–russet autumn colour.

Flowers: Typically Rosaceae: attractive, white, sometimes pinkish, showy, saucer shaped, large (2.5–4 cm diameter), five-petalled, with red anthers. They are borne singly at the tips of shoots in late spring–early summer.

Fruit: A russet colour when ripe, resembling small apples, with a large, distinctive green, five-pointed calyx, which apples and pears do not have. They are classified as pomes. Fruits vary in size from 2.5–6.5 cm in diameter, and the skin is thin, but dry. The fruit contains firm whitish flesh and has a few central seeds.

Yield/harvest/storage: Trees start to produce fruit when very young. Grafted trees can produce fruit in their first year. Harvesting is in late autumn–early winter, when leaves begin to fall. They are a good late-season fruit, and the fruits can be left on the tree till the first frosts have sweetened them somewhat. Alternatively, they are picked when hard, but are too sour to eat at that stage. Instead, they are stored for ~3 weeks, and the flesh becomes soft, sweeter and edible, a process known as 'bletting'. The flesh is then brownish in colour and tastes like spicy stewed apples. They store well for a few weeks. But, if left too long, they succumb to fungal disease.

CULTIVATION

Location: Prefers a site in full sun. Is relatively wind tolerant.

Temperature: It is fully frost hardy, down to at least −15°C.

Chilling: Needs some winter chilling; probably as much as apples (~1000 hours <7°C).

Soil/water/nutrients: Grows best in fertile, moist, but

uses

Food
Can be eaten fresh if fully ripe, but is usually bletted; unripe fruit are very sour. The fruit are often cooked, and mixed with sugar, honey and cream. Makes good jams, conserves, chutneys, etc., and a wine can be made from them, although it lacks tannin.

Nutrition/medicinal
Only low levels of vitamin C: 0.3 mg vitamin C/100 g. Fruit and leaves have been used historically as a diuretic and as an astringent. The pulp of the fruit acts as a laxative. A tincture or a tea is made from the seeds and is taken by the Chinese to rejuvenate eyes and to improve eyesight. It is also used to treat glaucoma and cataracts. **Warning:** Like all Rosaceae species, the seeds contain cyanogenic compounds, which are toxic if eaten in quantity.

well-drained loam, but can grow in a variety of soil types. Does not like wet soils. May need additional nutrients in poorer soils, and benefit from a good organic mulch to help retain moisture, add nutrients and suppress weeds.

Planting: Young trees may need staking for the first few years.

Propagation: Seed: Best to sow seeds when fresh and let them over-winter outside in compost; even then they may take two winters to germinate. Stored seed needs a lengthy stratification, sometimes for >2 years. Offspring are unpredictable. Seedlings are grown on for 3–4 years before planting out. *Cuttings:* Take cuttings of ripe wood in late autumn, but expect only a poor take. *Layering:* Can be practised in autumn or spring. Takes ~18 months to root. *Grafting:* Is practised, and usually grafted onto quince, hawthorn or pear.

Pruning: Initially, when the tree is ~1 m tall, the tips of stems are removed to encourage a denser shape and more lateral fruiting branches to develop. After this, it needs little pruning, just to remove crossing, crowded branches, and any diseased or damaged wood.

Pests and diseases: Very few problems with pests and diseases, although check for aphids and caterpillars. A white fungus on new leaves may be apple mildew.

CULTIVARS
'Dutch': Large fruit, Spreading tree with crooked branches.
'Nottingham': Small, good-tasting fruit. Tidy tree.
'Royal': Small fruit, but crops well. Fairly spreading tree. ■

Mitchella repens
Mitchella (twinberry, partridge berry)
RUBIACEAE
Relatives: coffee

The *Mitchella* genus contains just two species, which are native to the acidic pine forests of North America, from Newfoundland down to the southern states of the USA. Named after the botanist Dr John Mitchell, who first 'discovered' it, the plant forms a low-lying, evergreen, very cold-hardy, spreading groundcover that also has edible berries. It was introduced into Britain in the mid 1750s, but did not become very popular.

DESCRIPTION
A low-lying, spreading, mat-forming, groundcover species that grows to only ~10 cm height.

Leaves: Evergreen. Small, 1–2 cm long, shiny, deep green, with a heart-shaped base and pointed tip. Often has attractive white veins.

Flowers: Pinkish-white (or purple), tubular-shaped, fragrant, and are borne in fused pairs from the present season's growth, in early summer. The flowers are bisexual but vary in structure from plant to plant. Some flowers have stamens longer than their stigma; other flowers are the other way round, so encouraging cross pollination between plants. Therefore, it is better to plant these species in groups. *Pollination:* By bees and other insects.

Fruit: The flowers become so fused that the fruit is fused as one, but has the remnants of two calyxes at the apex. The fruits are rounded, small, ~0.6 cm diameter, and ripen to a bright red. Has several to many small, edible seeds within the two segments. The flesh has a sub-acid, pleasant spicy taste.

Yield/harvest: Plants often only produce a few fruits. Fruits are best harvested when fully ripe. Can be 'stored' on the plant for some time after they are ripe, though are likely to be picked off by the wildlife.

Roots: Forms lots of rhizomatous roots that enable its spread into surrounding areas. Also has lots of fibrous roots near to the surface, so mechanical cultivation should be

minimal. The roots form mycorrhizal fungal associations which can obtain extra nutrients, particularly phosphates. An organic mulch helps this relationship, conserves moisture and suppresses weed growth.

Food
The ripe fruits can be eaten fresh or can be added to desserts, jams, etc., though yields are often small. Some fruits can be quite dry. A tea can be made from the leaves.

Medicinal
The leaves have been traditionally used to promote easy birth as well as relieving painful menstruation. But, the leaves should not be taken by women during early pregnancy, as can induce contraction of the uterus. The tea also has sedative, relaxing properties. A leaf decoction has also been used externally on rheumatism.

Ornamental
Popularly grown as a groundcover in colder areas. Also makes a good rockery plant.

uses

CULTIVATION

Location: Can grow in full sun or semi-shade, though fruits better in full sun. Tolerant of wind due to their small stature. Not very tolerant of maritime locations.

Temperature: Very cold hardy, tolerating temperatures down to ~–20°C. Probably won't grow well in warmer climates.

Soil/water/nutrients: Grows best in acidic, moist, but not waterlogged soils. Grows well in dryish, sandy soils, though cannot tolerate extended periods of drought. Appreciates a modest application of an acid-based fertiliser in spring, which includes urea and not nitrate as the nitrogen source. However, too much fertiliser can lead to excessive leaf growth at the expense of fruit production as well as inhibiting mycorrhizal relationships.

Planting: Space plants at ~30 cm apart. Plants can be tricky to establish, and benefit from having organic matter incorporated into the soil to encourage the formation of fungal–root symbiotic relationships.

Propagation: *Seed:* Fresh seed should be thoroughly washed of all pulp before being sown in compost and left to overwinter. Stored seed needs a period of ~3 months of cold stratification before sowing in spring. *Cuttings:* Semi-ripe cuttings can be taken during summer and inserted into gritty, acidic compost to root. *Suckers:* Suckers from rhizomes can be gently removed, in spring or autumn, with some root, and established in acidic compost before planting out. *Layering:* Layering of stem tips or regions of young stems can be done in spring, and should root well. ∎

Monstera deliciosa
Ceriman (Mexican breadfruit, monstera, Swiss-cheese plant, hurricane plant, fruit salad plant)
ARACEAE
Relatives: philodendron, arum lilies

A native of Mexico and Guatemala, the ceriman is found growing in subtropical–tropical forests. It is a popular ornamental that is often cultivated in shady wooded areas of many warm countries and is also often grown as a houseplant in temperate climates, especially in conservatories and greenhouses, though it does not usually flower in these environments. It was introduced as a pot plant into England in 1752. This easy-to-grow, ornamental plant has interesting flowers, which form edible fruits.

DESCRIPTION

A fast-growing, very large-leaved, attractive, stout vine that can spread for some distance over the ground and, if trained, can climb trees to a height of 9 m or more. The stems are cylindrical to horseshoe-shaped in cross-section, heavy, 6–7 cm thick, succulent, and are marked by attractive leaf scars. The stems also produce numerous long, tough aerial roots.

Leaves: Very distinctive, large (>90 cm in length, ~80 cm wide), exotic, leathery, deep dark green, oval, heart-shaped at the base, on stiff, erect leaf stalks, which can be ~1 m long. The leaves are deeply cut into ~20–30-cm strips around the margins and are also perforated on each side of the midrib with elliptic holes of various sizes. From one to several flowers develop from young leaf axils.

Flower/fruit: A cream-coloured spadix: a type of fleshy flower spike, which bears both male and female flowers that are partially contained within a waxy sheath. The flowers are borne in spring to summer. As the flowers mature, the spathe dies away and the spadix develops into a green compound fruit, 20–30 cm long, and 5–9 cm thick. It is covered with a thick, hard rind, made up of hexagonal plates or 'scales', which cover individual segments of creamy-coloured, soft, juicy, fragrant pulp. Between the segments there are thin, black spiky remnants of the flowers, which need to be careful-

ly removed before eating the flesh. Generally the fruits develop without seeds, but sometimes, pale green, hard seeds, the size of large peas, may occur in a few of the segments. The rind become a lighter yellow-green as the fruits mature, and often develops mauvish spots. The flesh is soft and pinkish. It is sometimes called the fruit salad plant because of its pineapple and banana odour and its spicy fruit-salad taste.

Yield/harvest: Suckers will fruit in 2–4 years; cuttings in 4–6 years, depending on location, soil type and attention given. Flowering and fruiting overlap because it takes 12–14 months from fruit-set until maturity. Therefore, there may be young spadix with unopened flowers, immature fruits and ripening fruits together on the same plant. The spadix ripens from early summer to autumn. To harvest the fruit, the spadix is cut from the plant with a short length of stem when the hexagonal sections have begun to become raised at their bases and begin to lift off. The spadix can then be kept at room temperature for about a week to fully ripen along its length. Wrapping the fruit during this time can increase ripening by retaining the ethylene gas produced around the fruit. The flesh should only be eaten from those areas where the scale segments are loose and can be easily removed. The central hard core is discarded. Once ripened, the fruit can be kept stored in a refrigerator for a week or so.

CULTIVATION

Out-of-doors or as a houseplant, the ceriman requires little maintenance.

Location: They grow best in semi-shade to heavily shaded locations. Does not like wind.

Temperature: Best grown in warmer temperate areas or subtropical climates; however, although it is frost sensitive (leaf damage can occur at 0°C and there can be serious damage at –1°C), it is often hardier than expected. Because plants are grown under other trees, this gives them additional protection in cold weather and they can be grown outside in warm temperate regions. They often survive cold weather better than other frost-sensitive species.

Soil/water/nutrients: It flourishes best in well-drained, rich loam though will grow vigorously in almost any soil, including limestone or even acid soils under pine trees. They grow best with regular moisture and a deep mulch, but do not like waterlogged conditions. Regular fertiliser or additions of organic matter can improve growth and fruiting.

Pot culture: In colder areas, the plant can be grown inside and is remarkably tolerant of these environments. It was a popular houseplant with the Victorians, who often lived in houses with little outside light as well as generous amounts of coal and wood smoke. However, dark shade induces smaller leaves, and they will grow better if set outside at least once a year in direct light. The leaves should be wiped free of dust at fairly frequent intervals, as well as being sprayed with water occasionally. Plants will tolerate considerable neglect, though frequent repotting into a peaty compost and regular feeds with a liquid fertiliser will encourage better growth. Plants should not be over-watered. Plants grown indoors are unlikely to fruit. They could also be grown on a shady balcony or deck. It is evergreen and highly ornamental.

Propagation: *Seeds:* Seedlings, upon germination, grow in the direction of the darkest area (not just away from light) until they encounter the base of a tree or bank to grow up. They will then begin to climb towards the light, which is generally upwards into the canopy of the tree upon which it is growing. *Cuttings:* Usually propagated by stem or tip cuttings, which should include a length of stem and one or two young leaves. These can be simply inserted in moist, warm compost. A new plant should then sprout from the leaf axil. Suckers or offshoots, with or without roots, can be separated from parent plants and can be transplanted successfully. Mulching is desirable as well as watering until new roots have become well established.

Pests and diseases: Generally have few problems outside. When grown indoors, the plants are subject to infestation by scale insects, mites and mealybugs. ■

Food
The fully ripe fruit is juicy and sweet, and tastes like pineapple without the acidity. The fruit is very tasty, and can be eaten fresh on its own, or it can be served as dessert with a little cream or added to fruit salads or icecream. They can be made into a preserve with water and sugar (or honey), with a little lime juice.

Medicinal
In Mexico, a leaf or root infusion is taken daily to relieve arthritis. **Warning:** Ensure that the small, black specks around the fruit sections are removed, or these can be irritating. Only eat the fully ripe fruits. Some children and adults have reported having diarrhoea or intestinal gas after consuming the flesh or other parts of the plant.

Other uses
The aerial roots have been used to make ropes in Peru; in Mexico, they are made into strong baskets.

Ornamental
Highly ornamental, an excellent choice for heavily shaded positions. Looks good with contrasting foliage plants.

Morus spp.
Mulberry
MORACEAE

White mulberry (*Morus alba*), black mulberry (*M. nigra*), red mulberry or American mulberry (*M. rubra*) and their hybrids

Related genera: Damarru (*Maclura conchinensis*)

Relatives: che, paper mulberry, breadfruit, fig

The white mulberry is native to eastern and central China, and became naturalised in Europe centuries ago. This tree was introduced into America, for silkworm culture ~200 years ago, and was naturalised and hybridised with the red mulberry, which is native to the eastern USA, from Massachusetts down to the Gulf coast. The black mulberry is native to

western Asia, and has been cultivated there for thousands of years. It has been grown for its fruits in Europe since before Roman times. The Greeks dedicated the mulberry to Minerva because it did not come into flower until late spring, thereby avoiding late frosts: hence the name 'morus', meaning delay. The leaves, particularly of the white mulberry, are the favourite food of the silkworm, and that tree has been grown for silk production in China for over 5000 years. Western cultivation of the mulberry was accelerated when some silkworms and mulberry seeds were smuggled out of China about 200 years ago, thus introducing silk production and the mulberry to the West. Meanwhile, the Celts invented the children's rhyme 'here we go round the mulberry bush', which apparently refers to the practice of dancing around a mulberry tree on mid summer's eve to ward off evil fairies and spirits. Apart from this use, mulberry trees also make handsome trees, with their stately form and spreading branches. Good specimen trees, producing many fruits, mulberries are very worthwhile and rewarding to grow.

DESCRIPTION

All three mulberry species are deciduous trees, and grow to varying sizes. White mulberries can grow to ~26 m and are the most variable in shape, being either pendulous or upright. In good, warm conditions, the red mulberry can reach 32 m in height. The black mulberry is the smallest of the three, sometimes only growing to ~10 m in height, and tends to form a bush if not trained when young. The species also vary greatly in their longevity: black mulberries have been known to bear fruit for at least 200 years, whereas red mulberry trees rarely live for more than 75 years. They are slow- to moderately fast-growing, attractive trees, which will bear fruits while still small and young.

Leaves: Deciduous, coming into leaf fairly late in spring, and losing its leaves fairly early in autumn. The leaves are rough and toothed. The white mulberry is named for the colour of its buds, rather than the colour of its fruit. They have thin, glossy, light green leaves, which can be unlobed or may have 2–5 lobes, with different leaf shapes occurring on the same tree. Leaves of the red mulberry are larger and thicker, blunt toothed and often lobed. They are rough on their upper surfaces and pubescent beneath. The smaller black mulberry leaves are similar to those of the red mulberry, but have sturdier twigs and fatter buds. Leaves are conspicuously veined. White mulberries generally come into leaf first in spring, almost 2 months before black mulberries. Leaf length varies from 8–23 cm depending on if they are growing on fruiting or non-fruiting shoots, respectively.

Flowers: Short, yellowy-green, pendulous catkins that hang from leaf axils of the current season's wood and also on spurs of older wood. Separate male and female catkins, with male catkins being more slender than female catkins. *Pollination:* Trees are usually monoecious, and are self-fertile, so only one tree is needed to get fruit-set, though, being wind-pollinated, more than one tree will increase fruit-set. Some cultivars set fruit without pollination (parthenocarpy). Trees produce lots of pollen, and asthma sufferers can be affected at this time of year.

Fruit: Botanically the fruit is composed of many small fruits that have become fused together, and each small fruit has been formed from an individual flower. This is similar to the raspberry fruit, but in raspberries, the drupes are derived from many embryos within a single flower, rather than from many flowers. The individual mulberry fruits each develop a succulent, juicy covering around the seed. Fruit colour can vary, and white mulberries, for example, can produce white, lavender or black fruits. The fruits from white mulberry are usually very sweet, but can lack the tangy flavour of fruits from black mulberries. Fruits from red mulberry trees are usually deep red–black and the best fruits are almost as good as those of black mulberry. Fruits from black mulberry trees are large and juicy, with a good sweet–sub-acid flavour that many consider makes them the best-flavoured species. They taste similar to raspberries or blackberries. Mulberries ripen over a long period, so need harvesting at regular intervals over a fairly long season. The trees usually produce abundant crops of fruits, though birds, wildlife (and children) find them very attractive.

Yield/harvest: Trees grown with a good water supply can produce 25–40 kg/tree. Some trees start producing fruits within 2 years of being planted, but it is usually ~4–7 years before large crops are obtained. White and red mulberry fruits (and hybrids) ripen quickly and are ready to harvest in late spring. The fruit of black mulberries ripen in summer to late summer. The fruits of white mulberries can be harvested by spreading a sheet beneath the tree and then shaking the limbs: many fruits can be harvested from a fairly small, young tree. Black mulberries are more difficult to gather, the berries tending to collapse as they are picked, like over-ripe blackberries. Can be a messy business, and also means the fruits do not keep long. If unwashed, berries should keep for several days in a fridge. Fruits can be picked before they are fully ripe and left to ripen in a warm location, although fruit quality is often not as good as that of tree-ripened fruit.

Roots: They have fairly deep roots, and need care when planting out that these are not damaged.

CULTIVATION

Location: All the mulberries like a sunny location, very little shade and enough space to spread themselves out. They are fairly tolerant of maritime locations, as long as they aren't too exposed. They are fairly wind tolerant, and are sometimes planted as windbreaks. The white, and to some extent the red mulberries, are quite tolerant of atmospheric pollution.

Temperature: The white mulberry is the most cold hardy of the three species, although this varies from one cultivar to another. Some can be damaged at ~–3°C, whereas others can tolerate ~–30°C. Red mulberries are usually hardy to sub-zero temperatures. The black mulberry is the least cold hardy of the three, although cold tolerance seems to depend on cultivar, and many can tolerate light frosts. The black mulberry does not grow well in either very cold or very warm, humid climates.

Chilling: Black mulberry needs ~400 hours of chilling.

Soil/water/nutrients: Mulberries grow best in warm, deep, well-drained loam. They do not grow well on shallow, gravelly soils. Because of their deep roots, trees also do not like extended periods of waterlogging, but their deep roots also mean they are fairly drought resistant (particularly the white mulberry). However, they do appreciate being watered during fruit formation or in dry spells, when fruit can prematurely drop. Although they can manage without compost, they do much better with a good supply of nutrients, particularly nitrogen.

Pot culture: They are slow- to moderately-fast growing trees, and make a good pot plant, for a few years at least. Makes a good containered tree for towns. It has attractive leaves, although is deciduous. Repot annually and give nutrients and regular moisture. Probably better to choose the smaller black mulberry or one of the dwarfing white mulberries.

Planting: Space trees at least 5 m apart, although the black mulberry can be planted closer together than the white or red mulberries.

Pruning: Trees are initially pruned to establish a few main, strong scaffold branches around the tree. Once these have established, only the removal of dead or overcrowded wood is needed. Removing the tips from laterals will encourage the formation of more fruiting spurs. Trees should only be lightly pruned, and only when dormant or in late summer. If heavily pruned, trees can bleed drastically from cuts, particularly in spring. Cuts of more than 5 cm in diameter generally do not heal, and should be avoided.

Propagation: *Seed:* Can be grown from seed, though trees can take 5–10 years to start bearing fruits. Seeds should be sown fresh if possible, although white mulberry seeds germinate better after stratifying for 1–3 months before planting. Germination usually takes ~14 days. *Cuttings:* Softwood cuttings in spring, semi-ripe cuttings in summer and hardwood cuttings in autumn, or root cuttings, are all possible methods. Take cuttings 25–30 cm long, with some older wood at the base, treat with rooting hormone and deeply insert into moist compost. They should root fairly rapidly, and form roots in ~6 weeks. Red mulberries root less easily. Black mulberries are also tricky because they tend to bleed a lot. *Layering:* This can be done in autumn. *Grafting:* Spring budding is the most common method for grafting mulberries, although other graft types are also often successful; however, there may be incompatibility between white and black mulberries. There is some evidence that grafted trees form a more extensive root system than trees grown from cuttings or seed.

Pests and diseases: These species are generally free of pests and diseases, although cankers and dieback can occur, as can occasional problems with mulberry-leaf spot or bacterial blight. The ripe fruits are very attractive to birds.

CULTIVARS

Most black mulberry varieties are similar in taste, and tend to be of better quality than white- or red-mulberry fruits. There are also some ornamental cultivars, but these tend not to produce many good-quality fruits.

'Black Persian' (*M. nigra*): Large black fruit, >2.5 cm long, ~2 cm wide. Juicy, with a rich, sub-acid flavour. Fairly drought resistant.

'Collier' (*M. alba* x *M. rubra*): Medium-sized, purplish-black fruit, ~2.5 cm long, ~1.5 cm diameter. Flavour sweet–slightly tart, very good quality, ripen over a long period. Tree: medium size, spreading, relatively hardy, very productive.

Food

The better fruits are both sweet and tart at the same time; lovely just eaten fresh or with other fruits in a fruit salad. Or, they can be used in ways that other berries are used, such as in pies, tarts, puddings, or can be sweetened and pureed as a sauce. They also make a good-quality jam. Slightly unripe fruits are best for making pies and tarts. Mulberries blend well with other fruits, especially pears and apples. They make an excellent summer pudding and go well with raspberries and blackberries. Can be made into a fool, also wine, and make excellent dried fruit, especially the black varieties. Mulberries can replace blackberries in many recipes. In addition, the leaves make a good-tasting, healthy tea.

Nutrition/medicinal

The ripe fruits of the black mulberry contain about 9% sugar with malic and citric acid. They have good levels of dietary fibre, and contain good amounts of potassium, magnesium and iron. Have good levels of vitamin C: ~50 mg/100 g of flesh. Also contains good levels of riboflavin and vitamin K, with some of the other B vitamins and vitamin E. One of its main healthy compounds is resveratrol (like grapes), which can inhibit tumour formation by reducing DNA damage, slow cell transformation from normal to cancerous, and slow tumour growth. It also has anti-inflammatory properties. It may form part of a future cancer drug, used particularly for colon and lung cancer. The leaves have been used medicinally by the Chinese since ancient times. These are best harvested in autumn. They contain many compounds, including quercetin-related flavonoids. The leaves seem to be able to inhibit the growth of several bacteria, including *Staphylococcus aureus*, and may be useful in treating diabetes as they contain compounds that suppress blood-sugar levels. The leaves may also help control blood pressure and reduce low-density-lipid levels. They seem to contain many compounds and several vitamins.

Other uses

It has rot-resistant wood, which is good for fenceposts, etc. The fruits make an excellent, long-lasting dye.

Ornamental

Makes a beautiful and, often large, stately, specimen tree, with spreading, shade-giving branches and soft, juicy, tasty fruits.

'Illinois Everbearing' (*M. alba* x *M. rubra*): Black, nearly seedless fruit, large and very long. Flavour good to very good, very sweet, considered by many to be the best. Matures over a long season. Tree vigorous and somewhat dwarfed, hardy and productive.

'Kaester' (*M. nigra*): Large black–deep purple, elongated fruit, ~3 cm long, ~1.5 cm diameter, are sweet, yet tangy. Good yields.

'Pakistan': From Pakistan. Very large ruby-red fruit, ~6–9 cm long, ~1.5 cm diameter. Firm flesh, sweet, yet tangy, excellent quality. Tree: spreading. Can grow in either mild or cooler winter areas.

'Tehama' ('Giant White'): Very large, white, plump fruit, ~6 cm in length, ~1.5 cm width. Very sweet, succulent, fruits. Attractive, large-leaved tree. Probably best in mild-winter areas.

'Wellington': Reddish-black, medium-sized fruit, ~3 cm long, ~1.5 cm diameter. Flesh soft, good flavour. Ripen over several weeks. Tree is a heavy producer.

RELATED GENERA

Damarru, *Maclura conchinensis*. An unusual plant from the Himalayan foothills. Wandering religious aesthetics in the Himalayas named the tree 'damarru' after its small yellow fruits, which resemble the tambors on Shiva's drum. The fruit is collected locally and eaten fresh. It can be grown as a beautiful vine or cut back to form a small free-standing shrub. Scrambles through the understorey. Drought resistant, it can grow in sun or shade, and is evergreen. New growth has small spines. Branches emerge from a short, 30-cm trunk and can stretch ~16 m, depending on available sunlight. Produces small sweet, round, velvety, yellow, peach/raspberry-flavoured fruits in the autumn, though not necessarily every year. ■

Musa spp.
Banana
MUSACEAE
Relatives: Abyssinian banana, *Strelitzia* (bird-of-paradise flower), traveller's palm

The Musaceae family are all monocots, and the *Musa* genera are related to the palms, grasses and orchids; this genus is, evolutionarily, fairly recent. There are ~300 *Musa* species, but only 20 species are commercially cultivated. The most common of these is a cross between *Musa acuminata* (a wild, edible banana) and *M. balbisiana* (a seedy, inedible species from south Asia that is used for its disease resistance, drought tolerance and hardiness). This cross has given further rise to the hybrid *Musa* x *paradisiaca* (syn. *Musa* x *sapientum*). The *Musa* species have been used by humans since before recorded history for a wide range of purposes including being a valuable food source, for building materials, medicinally and for clothing. The earliest mention of the domestication of the banana seems to be from ancient wall inscriptions found in Assyria, in southwestern Asia, which dates back almost 7000 years. Bananas were being cultivated 6000 years ago in the Indus Valley, and were also mentioned in Buddhist writings that date back to the 6th century BC. Although Alexander the Great encountered bananas in India, in ~300 BC, it is thought he did not bring them back to the West. Instead, they are believed to have only arrived in Europe by ~10th century AD. Early in the 16th century, Portuguese mariners took plants to western Africa and South America. Today, they are grown around the world in almost every tropical and subtropical area, and are the fourth largest fruit crop in the world, after the grape, citrus fruit and apple. The name banana is thought to be derived from an Arabic word 'banan', meaning finger, and refers to the small, finger-sized banana fruits that occurred at that time. They are wonderfully exotic plants, and give a terrific tropical feeling to a garden, plus providing numerous fruits.

DESCRIPTION
Fast-growing, fleshy, exotic-looking perennials that arise from underground rhizomes. They do not have a true stem, instead, the 'stem' is formed from fleshy, densely packed leaves, with older leaves on the outside and the youngest leaves pushing up through the centre of the plant. Eventually, a single, central, terminal inflorescence is formed that will later bear fruits. After flowering and fruiting, the stem then dies back, though the rhizome continues growing outwards to produce further stems. Because the stems are fleshy and have very little strengthening tissue, they are prone to breakage in exposed locations.

   Leaves: Large, oval, up to 3 m long, ~60 cm wide, and are held outwards by fleshy, deeply grooved leaf stalks. In warm, humid weather, leaves can unfurl at a rate of one per week. Leaves are usually an attractive mid-green colour, though some cultivars have leaves with maroon patches, others are green above and red-purple beneath, and still others have attractive red midribs running up through the centre of their leaves. Even when the wind shreds the leaves, the leaf veins are still able to function. About 30–40 leaves appear before the inflorescence.

Flowers: Exotic, unusual, borne from the tip of a stem that emerges from the centre of the plant and forms a large, purple, tapered bud that opens sequentially to expose white, nectar-rich, tubular flowers. These are arranged in whorled rows up the stalk, with each cluster covered by a thick, waxy, purple bract, which is deep red within. The bract lifts from the first rows (hands) in 3–10 days. Female flowers, with inferior ovaries, occupy the first 5–15 rows on the stalk (these are at the top when the flower bends over). The central flowers are often sexless, and male flowers are borne at the end of the flower stalk, which now dangles downwards because of its weight. Male flowers are shed after only 24 hours of opening (except for the cultivar 'Dwarf Cavendish', where they persist), which leaves the end of the flower stalk naked except for a large, purple, fleshy bud at the tip, which contains unopened male flowers. Interestingly, the flowers are negatively geotropic, which means that because the flower stalk is bending downwards, the flowers respond by turning upwards. *Pollination:* Most edible, cultivated bananas are sterile and infertile: the fruit is set without the female flowers needing to be pollinated. The unpollinated ovules can be seen as the brown specs in the centre of the fruit. Wild bananas in their native areas are probably pollinated by bats.

Fruit: The female ovaries, containing the unfertilised ovules, develop into the fruit. The fruit, botanically termed a berry, develops from the female flower that has an inferior (epigynous) ovary, hence the remnants of the calyx at the end of the banana with the 'ovary' below it. The whorls (or hands) of flowers, with each whorl having ~20 flowers, develop into the familiar bunch of bananas. There are 5–13 hands or bunches per spike, depending on species. Warmth and sun on the leaves and the green stem speed up fruit development. Initially, the fruit are green and then turn yellow (or red) at maturity, which is 90–120 days after flowering. Depending on the species, fruits range in size from 7.5–30 cm long and 2–5 cm wide. The flesh, depending on species, can be creamy-white, yellowy or almost pinkish. When unripe, the flesh can be hard and unsweet; as they ripen, the flesh usually becomes sweeter, softens and can become more mucilaginous or drier depending on cultivar and species. Some species, such as the plantains, are not sweet when ripe.

Yield/harvest/storage: An average spike of bananas, with about 10 hands, can weigh 35–50 kg. Time to fruit-bearing depends on the size of the propagated plant. A small plant with just a few roots can take ~3 years to first fruit in warm temperate climates, but can fruit in the first year when grown in the tropics. Plantains may take a little longer. When grown commercially, individual plants are replaced after ~4–5 years because yield from the rhizomes decreases; replacement can also help control disease. In the tropics, fruits ripen easily. In cooler regions, the fruit stalks sometimes form early enough in the summer for the fruits to ripen before winter arrives. However, fruit stalks are often not formed till late summer and then banana fruits have to over-winter before they can ripen, but the fruit is surprisingly hardy, and often survives cold

weather better than the leaves. The fleshy male end of the fruit stalk can be removed to encourage the development of the already-formed female bananas. Fruit can be harvested by cutting the stalk as the bananas become plump, but when they are still green. Parts of a stalk can be removed at a time. The fruit can be tree-ripened, but ensure that birds or other wildlife do not get there first. To ripen green fruit, place the fruits in a sack in a warm, dry place. Bananas naturally produce ethylene gas to aid ripening. By enclosing them in a bag, the ethylene gas produced circulates around the unripe fruits and stimulates these to ripen. The inclusion of a ripe banana speeds up this process further. After picking, bananas do not lose their nutritional benefits, as do many other fruits and vegetables, but ripe fruit can only be kept for a short time at room temperature; however, bananas can be dried for later uses. Most banana species are easily damaged by temperatures below ~12°C, and should not be refrigerated. Ideal ripening conditions are 17°C and 90% humidity.

Roots: Plants form rhizomes not far below the soil surface and these produce shallow, short roots. This makes plants susceptible to extended dry periods and unstable during strong winds. Avoid mechanical cultivation near to plants, and an organic mulch will help retain moisture and add nutrients. They also have photosynthesising stems, so be careful with the use of herbicides.

CULTIVATION

Location: They grow best in full sun in a sheltered location. Planting near buildings gives extra protection. Leaf damage caused by wind is common, but the leaf usually survives, although it becomes somewhat ragged.

Temperature: Bananas like it warm, and are best sited in sunny, sheltered spots in warm temperate regions. They will need moving inside or protecting in temperate areas, though some species are hardier than would be first thought. Virtually all growth stops at ~15°C, with those varieties with purplish or pinkish leaf areas tending to be more sensitive to cold. Frost can damage the leaves and the plants often look rather bedraggled after a long winter, but new stems usually appear in the spring. Plants can survive –2°C for short periods, but temperatures much below –4°C may kill the underground rhizomes. Wrapping the trunk and applying a thick mulch around the rhizomes can give some protection. The plant needs at least 10 months of frost-free conditions to produce a flower stalk. The more genes the plant has from the species *M. balbisiana*, the more cold hardy it is likely to be.

Soil/water/nutrients: Grows best in loamy, alluvial, well-drained soil, though can grow and fruit in poor rocky, sandy soils or even heavy clay, but not fine sand. Somewhat acid pH values are best, though a pH of <5.0 is almost too acid and lime may need to be added. Plants are not tolerant of saline conditions, although can be grown in sheltered sites near the coast. Bananas grow best with regular moisture during extended dry, hot periods because of the large transpirational area of their leaves and their shallow roots, particularly in sandy, light soils. Conversely, however, waterlogging can kill plants and causes root rot. Plants are moderately nutrient hungry, and benefit from fairly regular applications of nutrients during the growing season, particularly nitrogen and potassium. Young plants do not need as much.

Pot culture: If you live in a colder area, you might consider growing bananas in containers. Dwarf varieties could be a good choice. Give them deep containers with good, rich, moist compost. Plants will need feeding regularly and repotting as the new stems develop.

Planting: Spacing varies with variety, but ~2–4 m apart.

Pruning: There are various schools of thought about pruning. Commercially, all suckers are removed except for a single stem until after it has flowered, then one or two other suckers are allowed to develop. Choose healthy, vigorous, broad suckers: thinner suckers may not flower as well, if at all. These new suckers can start producing fruits 6–8 months after the main stem has been harvested. As an alternative, many people, particularly if only growing for home use, do not bother removing the suckers. Whichever method is used, it is helpful to cut down the fruiting stem once the bananas

Food

Many and varied uses. In many world economies, bananas are utilised almost as much as rice, wheat and maize. More than 70 million people in Africa rely on bananas as a staple crop. Apart from being eaten fresh, they can be prepared as baby foods, added to cakes, and are used in many desserts, added to curries and fish dishes. They can be dried, and a flour can be made from either bananas or plantains. If over-ripe or frost-damaged, they are delicious if lightly fried with a knob of butter, cinnamon and a dash of brandy. Or they can be dipped into a rich batter, deep fried and then sprinkled with sugar and lemon. Mashed bananas can be frozen for later use in desserts. In the Philippines, a banana ketchup is widely used. In India, they are added to confectionery, are made into a cool refreshing drink with yoghurt called 'lassi', and a sweet yoghurt cheese can be made with banana, pistachios and almonds, and spiced with cardamom. Banana split, served with icecream, and chocolate and strawberry sauce is a popular Western dessert, and Brazilians make a dessert with mashed bananas mixed with brown sugar, grated ginger, and cinnamon or cloves. This mixture is slowly cooked over a low heat until it thickens. When cool, it is moulded into a roll, then sliced and served cold. Plantains can be fried and then eaten like French fries. Ripe bananas are easy to ferment and make a good, sweet white wine. The terminal male flower bud can be boiled and eaten as a vegetable. Young leaves can be sliced and added to salads, they can be cooked in coconut milk, or they can be added to curries. Their flavour has been described as smoky, slightly cooling and delicately fragrant.

Nutrition

Fruits contain about 23% carbohydrate, 1% protein and 0.5% fat, with no cholesterol. They contain a high level of natural sugar (when fresh or dried). They are rich in fibre, which helps digestion and acts as a mucilage. They are a good source of the B vitamins, particularly B6, with one banana giving 40% of the RDA, but also have good levels of riboflavin and folic acid. They have good levels of vitamin C (~19.5 mg/100 g of flesh) and some vitamin A. They have excellent levels of potassium (higher than most other fruits and nuts), good levels of manganese and magnesium, some copper, as well as traces of other minerals. Plantains have higher levels of vitamin A.

Medicinal

Bananas provide a quick form of energy. Apparently two bananas provides enough energy for 90 minutes of strenuous exercise! The high levels of potassium within bananas help normalise the heartbeat, help send oxygen to the brain (which improves neurone activity) and help regulate the body's water balance. As a consequence, it is thought that eating bananas can help improve mental activity as well as reducing high blood pressure. Indeed, the US Food and Drug Administration has recently permitted the banana industry to make official claims for the fruit's ability to reduce the risk of high blood pressure and stroke. Recent research has reported that eating bananas as part of a regular diet can cut the risk of strokes by as much as 40%! Their good levels of fibre aid digestion, relieve constipation, reduce diarrhoea and can help soothe and heal intestinal ulcers and heartburn, and reduce morning sickness. They act as a natural antacid. They are a useful food for convalescence and, because they contain no gluten, they are of value in coeliac disease. A drink made from banana, honey and milk is a good hangover cure: the banana calms the stomach and builds up depleted blood sugar levels. They have exceptional levels of B6, more then most other food sources. B6 helps to regulate blood-glucose levels, fight infection and is needed for the synthesis of haeme (within haemoglobin). In addition, B6 regulates tryptophan, an amino acid that the body converts into serotonin, which has a calming effect, improves mood and gives a sense of well being. The inside of a banana's peel has antiseptic properties and can be wrapped directly around wounds or cuts in an emergency. When rubbed on mosquito bites, it may reduce swelling and irritation. The juice from the junction between the 'stem' and rhizome has been used to give relief from toothache, and is also being investigated in the USA for its ability to reduce the incidence of tumours.

Other uses

Ash from burned leaves and stems is used as salt. Fertilisers are made from dried, chopped banana stems and leaves. The stems yield a pulp that can be made into strong brown-paper products. There are dozens of construction and medicinal uses for banana leaves and other plant parts. The leaf fibre is strong and has many uses, including making tea bags, Japanese yen notes, ropes, string and thread. Banana leaves make good disposable biological plates. Starch extracted from banana and plantain stems can make a glue. Banana sap can be used as a dye.

Ornamental

A fabulous, exotic, tropical plant. It needs little maintenance, it takes up little room and can be grown near to buildings. It looks lovely near pools and ponds; it can be grown as a specimen plant in clusters for an exotic effect.

have been harvested: this tidies up the stand and allows light and air to reach the younger stems. The vegetation produced, as long as it is not diseased, can be used as mulch around the other banana stems.

Propagation: *Seed:* There are no viable seeds on bananas grown for their fruits. The ornamental Abyssinian bananas can be easily grown from seed. *Cuttings:* This is the main method of propagation. Portions of underground stem (the rhizome) can be carefully dug up, cut into lengths (>12 cm long) that include at least three healthy buds, which will go on to produce upright stems, and inserted into shallow, moist, warm compost to establish. The rhizome also produces short 'true' roots. When selecting rhizome material, choose a youngish stem, ~7–9 months old, but before it has flowered. The end of the rhizome near the upright stem will produce the most vigorous plants; older buds further back may not grow as well. Keep cuts clean to reduce the risk of disease. Some advise placing rhizome sections in the shade for 48 hours to partially callus over before planting. Alternatively, entire rhizomes, with a young, upright stem, can be carefully dug up during spring–summer, and grown on with regular moisture until established. Removal of outer leaves from the young stem reduces transpirational demand until roots have formed from the rhizome.

Pests and diseases: No major insect or fungal problems in most subtropical or warm temperate regions, though wildlife may seek out the ripening fruits. In the tropics, they suffer from Panama disease. Cold, wet weather can set the plants back and encourage root rot.

CULTIVARS

'Blue Java' (or 'Icecream'): Has a blue-green waxy bloom on the young fruits. Is named 'icecream' after its melting taste. Grows to a height of ~4 m. The leaves have a light pink mid-rib. Flower spikes are small, with 7–9 hands. Fruit: Pale yellow when mature, ~20 cm long; flesh: fragrant, sweet, white. Can be eaten raw or cooked. Susceptible to Panama disease.

'Ducasse' ('Pisang Awak'): Very vigorous and hardy. Height: ~5 m. Good cropper at ~35 kg of fruit per flower spike; produces small bananas with a light wax bloom. Time

to cropping: ~17 months. It sometimes produces fertile fruit, if it does then these contain hard, black seeds. Susceptible to Panama disease. Important variety in Thailand.

'Lady Finger' ('Pome', 'Pacha Naadan', 'Brazilian'): A good cultivar for cooler climates; it is also drought hardy and wind resistant. It has a good strong root system that gives the stem strength. Height: ~5 m. Fruit: small: ~12 cm long, light yellow when mature, thin skin, the flesh is of good quality. Good cropper, producing up to ~30 kg of fruit per flowering spike, although some of the fruits may be undeveloped. The flowering spike forms 10–14 hands, each with 12–20 fingers. Time to harvest: ~14–18 months.

'Misi Luki': More resistant to cold than many cultivars and is tolerant of poor soils. Height: 3–4 m. Fruit: sweet, medium-sized.

'Mons mari' (*M. acuminata*): More suited to semi-tropical regions. It is a quick-growing, dwarf Cavendish-type banana. Height: ~2.5 m. Large tasty bananas: ~18 cm long. Fairly good cropper.

'Japanese fibre banana' (*M. basjoo*): This is probably the world's cold-hardiest banana. It is hardy to –20°C and, with lots of rhizome protection, possibly even down to ~–30°C! It has even been grown in Canada. The fruit are not really edible and it is usually just grown for the fibre in the leaves.

'Mysore': Height: ~4.5 m tall. Vigorous. Somewhat tolerant of drought and poor soils. Produces tightly packed bunches; yields ~35 kg/flowering spike. Fruit: short, plump, bright yellow when ripe; flesh: pale yellow, a good sweet–sub-acid flavour. Is susceptible to Panama disease.

'Orinoco': Often grown in California as a landscape plant. Height: ~5 m, sturdy, particularly hardy. Time to harvest: 15–18 months. Can be a very good cropper. Fruit: ~15 cm long, good flavour, pinkish flesh. Although they can be eaten fresh, they are often better when cooked.

Plantains: There are many cultivars: some have pink, red or dark brown leaf sheaths, some also have coloured midribs or splotches on leaves or fruits. Plants are usually large, vigorous and resistant to Panama disease and Sigatoka. Fruit: usually large, angled and borne in few hands. Are mostly cooked and used in savoury dishes. ∎

Myrciaria cauliflora (syn. *Eugenia cauliflora*, *Plinia cauliflora*)
Jaboticaba (Brazilian grape tree)
MYRTACEAE
Relatives: jambolan, feijoa, guava, lillypilly, eucalyptus

A native of southern Brazil, but also found naturalised up to southern California, southern Florida and Hawaii. Are very popular native fruit trees in Brazil, where they have been cultivated for hundreds, if not thousands, of years. They are often grown in small commercial orchards, and the fruits are sold at local markets. Jaboticaba can grow in a range of climates from warm temperate to tropical, and makes a good decorative plant that has tasty fruits. Its main disadvantage is the long period it takes for trees to start producing fruits, particularly from seedlings, but grafted trees do reduce this wait somewhat.

DESCRIPTION

A slow-growing, bushy, small (3–5 m tall) tree. The trees form many densely packed, upright branches, making the crown dense, spreading, rounded and bush-like in form. Its bark is attractive, being multicoloured, mottled, creamy-tan, with pinkish or greenish highlights, and peels off in long thin strips. It makes an attractive specimen tree.

Leaves: Evergreen, fine-textured, simple, opposite, lanceolate to elliptic, fairly small, 2–10 cm long, ~1.25–2 cm wide. They are glossy dark green and have a leathery texture, with younger leaves tinted reddish-bronze. Their size, shape and texture can vary from one cultivar to another. They tend to shed more leaves in spring, just before the new flush of spring growth begins.

Flowers: Small, yellow-white, emerging from the trunks (cauliflorous), limbs and large branches in groups of four. The trunk can become covered in a profusion of these white flowers. Trees, although monoecious, seem to set more fruits when planted in groups rather than singly. Flowers are only open for a day or two and are mostly borne through the summer, though can flower at other times of year in warmer climates. *Pollination:* By bees and insects. Is poor if the weather is cool, humid and wet.

Fruits: Grape-like in appearance and texture, but with a thicker, tougher skin, which is dark purple when fully ripe. The true berries are ~2–3.5 cm in diameter, depending on variety. The juicy cream-coloured flesh has a pleasant, sub-acid grape-like flavour, though the skins can sometimes be more bitter. It contains 1–4 small seeds. The fruit look very attractive hanging in clusters (2–4 fruits) from the trunks and branches of the tree, which can produce large crops. Fruits only take 21–28 days to mature after fruit-set, and most ripen from autumn–early winter. There may be other smaller crops during the year in warmer climates: trees in Brazil can have 5–6 crops a year.

Yield/harvest/storage: Although the trees take a long time to start producing fruits, with seedlings taking 8–15 years, once they have commenced, they usually produce large and regular crops. However, grafted trees can start to produce fruits after 3–7 years. The fruits are picked when they have developed their full colour and have softened a little, similar to a ripe grape. They do not ripen if picked when still green. Once picked, the fruits can be kept for a few days to fully sweeten, but after this time will begin to ferment at room temperature and cannot be stored long. They are better eaten fresh or processed soon after harvesting.

Roots: Trees have mostly shallow roots that can dry out quickly. They are best given a deep organic mulch to retain moisture, suppress weed growth and to add nutrients. Avoid mechanical cultivation around the tree.

CULTIVATION

Location: Jaboticaba trees can grow in full sun or semi-shade. They are fairly wind tolerant, but do not like salty sea air. Small, young trees do best with some protection.

Temperature: Different plants vary in how much frost they can tolerate without being damaged. Plants, if acclimatised slowly to cold, should be able to tolerate temperatures down to ~–5°C without damage, but not for extended periods. Young trees can be damaged by temperatures of ~–1°C, and need extra protection. In areas where frost is a risk, they are best planted near a sun-facing wall or given some overhead protection. Potted plants can be moved to a frost-free area. They prefer a warm temperate to subtropical climate.

Soil/water/nutrients: They grow and fruit best in rich, deep soil with a pH of 5.5–6.5. They can, however, grow on a range of soil types, from heavy clay to sandy soils. They do not grow well in alkaline soils, although may do so if given regular applications of chelated micronutrients such as iron and manganese. The tree is not tolerant of salty soil. In their native areas, jaboticabas are often flooded by water, and they are fairly tolerant of wet or even waterlogged soils. They are not drought tolerant, and need regular moisture to initiate flowering, to produce good quality fruits and to grow well. One of the main causes of failure with this species is that their roots are shallow. Regular applications of nutrients (~3 times a year) can speed up their slow growth rate, but this needs to be balanced with the amount of warmth and moisture they receive.

Pot culture: The plant makes an excellent container specimen. It is very slow growing and so can be grown in containers for many years. It can then be easily checked for its moisture status, and given protection if frosts threaten. The trees have attractive, evergreen foliage and look good positioned amongst more flamboyant plants.

Planting: Space plants at ~4–6 m apart. Peat, compost or rotted manure can be mixed with the soil when planting. Growth is slow, and plants may take 3 years to reach ~0.5 m in height.

Pruning: Little or no pruning is usually necessary; simply to remove any diseased or damaged wood and to prevent too much crowding of branches. They can be pruned as a

Food

Mostly eaten fresh, and are juicy, tangy and sweet. Often only the flesh is eaten and the bitter skin discarded. Can also be used in jelly, jam, icecream and marmalade, with the addition of pectin, and the skins removed. They can also be made into a good-quality wine. The fruit can be frozen or dried for later use.

Medicinal

The skins contain quite high levels of tannins, and are used to treat asthma, diarrhoea and dysentery, and also as a gargle for tonsillitis. Large amounts of the skin should not be consumed over a long period of time.

Other uses

Its wood is hard, dense and strong.

Ornamental

They are ideal for smaller gardens, or can be readily inserted into larger planting schemes. Attractive foliage and bark while you are waiting for them to start producing flowers and fruits from their trunks and stems. Ideal for container or bonsai usage.

hedge, and still produce fruit because these are formed on the inner branches and trunk. Can be used for bonsai.

Propagation: *Seed:* Good, predictable but slow, from seed. Most seeds are nucellar and often polyembryonic (see p. 15), producing plants that are clones of the parent plant. Seed is best sown when fresh and all pulp has been removed. Seeds germinate in ~28 days. *Layering:* Air-layering can be practised and is generally successful. *Grafting:* Selected cultivars can be grown by inarching (approach grafting), or by veneer or side grafting. Budding is not easy because of the thin bark and hardness of the wood. Grafted plants will begin fruiting considerably sooner than seedlings, i.e. in 3–7 years compared to 8–15 years. Top-working is inadvisable because it is the trunk and inner branches that produce the fruit, and one would have to cut the tree right back to the ground in order to change its fruiting nature.

Pests and diseases: Generally not too many problems.

Rust may attack the fruits and flowers of some varieties during humid weather. A fruit-drilling moth can attack the fruits which, when ripe, are also a magnet for birds and other wildlife.

CULTIVARS
'Branca': Tree: medium size, heavy producer. Fruit: large, bright green, tasty, delicious. Recommended.
'Paulista': Tree: strong growing, highly productive, but only bears a single crop annually. Fruit: large, skin thick. Flesh is juicy, sub-acid–sweet, very good flavour. Ripens later in the season. Resistant to rust.
'Rajada': Tree: strong growing, highly productive. Fruit: very large, green-bronze, thin skin. Flavour is sweet and good. Mid season harvest.
'Sabará': Forms only nucellar seeds. A very popular tree in Brazil. Tree: medium sized, precocious, very productive. Fruit: small, thin-skinned, sweet. Early harvest, can bear four crops a year. Susceptible to rust. ∎

Myrciaria dubia
(syn. *Eugenia divaricata, E. grandiglandulosa, Marliera macedoi, Myrciaria caurenisis*)
Camu-camu
MYRTACEAE
Similar species: Rumberry (guava-berry), *Myrciaria floribunda* (syn. *M. protracta, Eugenia floribunda*)
Relatives: jaboticaba, guava, lillypilly

The camu-camu is a native of Brazil, and usually occurs naturally in swamps along rivers and lakes, often with the base of the trunk under water and, during the rainy season, the lower branches are also submerged for long periods. A useful plant that has fruit with very high levels of vitamin C. This has led to it being trialed as a commercial crop in South America where it is juiced or processed into vitamin C tablets. In addition, it seems to have many other properties and benefits, and its cultivation is being encourage as a commercial crop within South America. Although sour, the fruits are also a popular fruit in Peru, where they are made into drinks and added to icecream.

DESCRIPTION
A shrub or bushy tree, to ~3 m high, but usually smaller. Has small prickly hairs on the young branches and leaf petioles.
Leaves: Opposite, broad- or narrow-ovate, or elliptic, often lopsided; 4.5–10 cm long, 1.5–4.5 cm wide, pointed at the apex, rounded at the base and forming wing-like appendages.
Flowers: Fragrant, borne in small clusters of fours in or near the leaf axils. They have tiny, white petals and ~125 longer, fluffy, stamens (~0.8 cm long), with virtually no flower stalk. Flowers are bisexual, and only need one plant to set fruits, although more than one plant may increase yields and fruit quality. *Pollination:* By bees and other insects.
Fruit: A berry. They are nearly round, 1–2.5 cm diameter, yellow at first, becoming maroon to purple-black, and soft and juicy, but still acidic when ripe. The flesh contains three small seeds.
Yield/harvest: Plants take 4–5 years to start producing fruits. They then can have good yields: a single plant can

bear 400–500 fruits. On flooded land, a single plant can produce ~1000 fruits. Fruits are harvested when fully coloured and ripe, between summer and autumn. They are best eaten fresh as stored fruits can lose ~25% of their vitamin C content in less than a month (even if frozen).

CULTIVATION
Location: Can be grown in full sun or semi-shade. They are not very tolerant to wind exposure.
Temperature: Is a tropical or subtropical plant, but can survive brief temperatures of 0°C. It is not as hardy as jaboticaba.
Soil/water/nutrients: Prefers a deep, fertile loamy soil with a slightly acid to neutral pH. Grows best in a damp climate with water year-round. Is one of the few plants listed in this book that will stand flooding, and produces better yields of fruits if waterlogged. Reasonably nutrient hungry, and benefits from two annual additions of a balanced, complete fertiliser, or an organic equivalent. In drier sites,

uses

Food
Can be eaten fresh, but the pulp is fairly acidic. The fruits are commonly used in fresh juices, icecreams, sweets and sauces.

Nutrition
Half-ripe fruits have been found to contain an incredible 1950–2700 mg of ascorbic acid per 100 g of flesh (2–3% of the weight). Has >100 times the amount of vitamin C as an orange.

Medicinal
Its potential medicinal properties are awe-inspiring. Its main use is connected with its very high levels of vitamin C, and the fruits are used as an astringent, an antioxidant and as a nutritive tonic. It is also being researched for its powerful anti-depressant properties, possibly due to the vitamin C increasing serotonin in the brain. In addition, it seems to contain compounds that are able to effectively reduce *Herpes* infections. The fruits also contain beta-carotene, calcium, iron, leucine, niacin, phosphorus, protein, riboflavin, serine, thiamine and valine. In comparison to oranges, camu-camu provides ten times more iron, three times more niacin, twice as much riboflavin and 50% more phosphorus. It is also a significant source of potassium, providing 711 mg/kg of fruit. Alpha-pinene and d-limonene, compounds known as terpenes, predominate as the volatile compounds in this fruit. It is thought that it is best to eat the whole fruit (rather than as a vitamin supplement) to get the full benefit of its nutrition. Camu-camu has also been linked to possible treatments as an anti-mutagenic, antiviral and antioxidant, as well as for asthma, atherosclerosis, cataracts, colds, depression, oedema, gingivitis-peridontal disease, glaucoma, hepatitis, infertility, migraine-type headaches, osteoarthritis, as a painkiller and for Parkinson's disease. There are no reported contraindications or drug interactions.

Other uses
The juice from the fruits can be added to cosmetics or skin preparations and acts to soften and tone the skin.

it benefits from a deep organic mulch to help conserve moisture.

Pot culture: It can be grown in pots because of its smaller size, and could then be grown in cooler regions if it is taken inside or given additional protection during the winter. Needs a moisture-retentive soil and regular watering.

Propagation: *Seed:* Mostly propagated by seed. Wash all pulp from the seed and sow fresh if possible. Sow in well-drained, warm compost and germination should occur in 16–28 days. Seedlings may take 4–5 years to begin producing fruit, and there can be variability between progeny and fruit quality of seedlings.

SIMILAR SPECIES

Rumberry (guava-berry), *Myrciaria floribunda* (*M. protracta, Eugenia floribunda*) A tiny fruit, formerly in demand, and similar to camu-camu, the rumberry occurs wild over much of the West Indies and Central and South America. Throughout its natural range, when land is cleared for pastures, the tree is left standing for the sake of its fruits.

Description: An attractive shrub or slender tree reaching 10–15 m in height, with reddish-brown branches that are downy when young, with flaking bark. *Leaves:* Evergreen, opposite, ovate, elliptical, or lanceolate, 2.5–8 cm long, 1–3 cm wide, glossy, slightly leathery, minutely dotted with oil glands. *Flowers:* White, silky, with ~75 fluffy, long, white stamens. Flowers are borne in small clusters from leaf axils. Pollination is by bees: the flowers produce lots of nectar. *Fruit:* Round–oblate, 0.8–1.5 cm diameter; dark red and nearly black when ripe, or sometimes yellow-orange. They are highly aromatic and have a sub-acid–sweet, balsam-like flavour. They contain one roundish seed.

Cultivation: Grows well in warmer climates, generally needing subtropical conditions. Can be grown in sun, though prefers semi-shade. *Soil:* Can grow in dry or moist soils, or in alkaline soils.

Uses: *Food:* The fruits can be eaten fresh, or used in jam, desserts, sauces, etc. The fermented juice is rated as 'exquisite' (guava-berry liqueur), and is made from the fruits with pure grain alcohol, rum, raw sugar and spices. *Medicinal:* It may have similar properties to camu-camu. In folk medicine, the fruits have been used to treat liver complaints. ■

Nelumbo nucifera
Lotus (sacred lotus, lian, lin ngau, hasu, renkon, East Indian lotus, oriental lotus, lily of the Nile)
NELUMBONACEAE (sometimes, but incorrectly, grouped with the waterlilies, Nymphaeaceae)

There are about 100 lotus species and most are found in the semi-tropical or warm-temperate regions of Asia, Africa, Europe and North America. The best known of these is the sacred lotus (*N. nucifera*), which is native to southern

Asia. This beautiful flower has been held sacred for >5000 years. To Buddhists, the flower represents the perpetual cycle of reincarnation, with the flower closing at night, but then re-opening at dawn. Buddha is said to have been born in the heart of a lotus flower and he is often depicted sitting in a lotus flower or on its leaf. The lotus is likened to the ideal human heart: although the loutus grows in 'muck', it does not partake of it and, likewise, the human heart should stay independent of evil thoughts. The Hindus associate the flower with Brahma and the creation of the world. The Goddess of Wealth, Laxmi, is also named after the lotus flower. Vishnu holds a lotus flower in one of his four hands. The lotus motif was very widely used in the shrines, art and sculpture of the Jains. Ancient Greek Ionic architecture is derived from Assyrian and Phoenician designs that had the lotus as their basis. In Japan, it is also held as a symbol of purity and beauty. The sacred lotus is mainly native to southern Asia, but also grows in Iran, China, Japan and northeast Australia, with the latter country researching the commercial potential of its edible rhizomes. Apart from being revered for its ornamental beauty, all parts of the plant, including the rhizomes and seeds, have been used as a food for >3000 years in China. The name *nucifera* means 'to have a hard fruit', and refers to its ornamental, unusual seedhead.

DESCRIPTION

The lotus is a perennial, water-loving plant that forms thick rhizomes. Its roots readily grow when fully submerged in water; its aerial leaves and flowers on long stalks originate from buds on the rhizomes.

Leaves: Deciduous, with leaves dying back in the colder months. The plant's first leaves are flat and float on the water's surface. Later leaves are almost round, thicker, funnel- or inverted umbrella-shaped, have slightly wavy edges and can be large, 0.3–0.8 m diameter. These leaves stand 0.5–2 m above the water on long stalks. The leaves are coated with a fine velvety fuzz, which often carries glistening droplets of water on their surface. The leaves have their stomata on their upper surfaces (unlike most plants) and to allow oxygen to enter and travel down to the roots and rhizomes through specialist channels.

Flowers: Beautiful, fragrant, red, pink or white, large (15–25 cm diameter) and grow above the surface of the water on long flower stalks. They open in the early morning and then close again at night, to reopen at dawn; each flower can live for 2–5 days, until the petals finally darken before falling. The flowers appear one at a time on each plant. They have varying number of petals depending on cultivar: some are termed as single and have <25 petals, some are semi-double with 25–50 petals, and double flowers have >50 petals. Flowers are borne year-round in warmer climates, but in summer in cooler regions. *Pollination:* By bees and other insects.

Fruit: After blooming, the petals fall leaving a distinctive, ornamental receptacle consisting of a semi-spherical white cone, resembling the rose from a watering can. On the cone's surface are numerous symmetrical holes (15–20), within which are seated the individual seeds, each ~1.5 cm long. When ripe, the seeds become loose and rattle inside the receptacle.

Yield/harvest/storage: Plants produced from rhizomes produce a first crop of seed in the first year; seedlings produce their first seed crops either in their first or second year. The seeds ripen year round in warmer regions, but in autumn in cooler areas. To harvest, the seed receptacles are cut from the plant when turning brown, and are then partially dried, before being shaken to loosen the seeds. The seedheads need to picked just as they ripen; if left too long, the head droops to scatter its seeds into the water around

the plant. The outer, very bitter green seed covering needs to be removed, and the inner kernel can be then eaten raw or added to various dishes. The seeds, if dried, can be stored for extended periods in the cool and dark. The rhizome is usually harvested in late summer–autumn (though can be at other times as well), but it is probably best to let the plant fully establish for at least 2–3 years before harvesting any roots. Thereafter, plants can be divided every 3–4 years, with some material being replanted and the remainder harvested. Thoroughly wash and dry the root for food usage. Fresh rhizomes are best not stored in a fridge; instead, if kept at a cool room temperature, they will last for 2–3 weeks.

Roots: The lotus has thick, dense rhizomes that can grow when fully submerged. They are cream–buff-coloured, and are ~60–90 cm long. They are formed in sausage-like segments, with each segment being ~10–20 cm long, 4–8 cm wide. Internally, they are white, with many regularly-spaced longitudinal air passageways, which look like a spoked-wheel in cross-section. These air channels transport oxygen from the leaves to the roots. Short, thick roots emerge from the rhizomes, which anchor the plant and obtain nutrients.

CULTIVATION

Location: Grows best in a sunny location. Needs a protected, sheltered spot.

Temperature: During the growing season, the water temperature needs to be at least 18°C, but not more than ~26°C. Cooler temperatures cause the plant to go into dormancy, which can be difficult to break. In winter, in colder areas, plants can either be covered with an insulated covering, or the rhizomes can be lifted in autumn and stored in soil, but covered with water and kept cool (5–10°C) until spring. If plants are grown in deeper water, as long as the water does not actually freeze, then the plants should be OK.

Soil/water/nutrients: Plants grow much better in nutrient-rich soils. Well-rotted organic matter can be mixed with soil/clay when planting at the bottom of a pond or when placed in containers within the pond. They can grow at a wide range of pH values: 5.6–7.8 (up to quite alkaline), with an optimum of pH 6.5. During the growing season, plants also benefit from slow-dissolving fertilisers, such as bone meal, being sprinkled around their roots. Plants particularly benefit from more

Food

The seeds and roots are used in a wide range of both sweet and savoury dishes. The seeds have a pleasant nutty flavour. They can be eaten raw, roasted, boiled and can be added to many desserts, candies or cookies, or can be preserved in syrup, or popped like popcorn. They are also added to many meat and vegetable dishes in Asia. The dried seeds can be ground into a flour, which has an almond flavour. The rhizomes are even more popular to eat than the seeds. They look like a string of sausages and, when cut open, are full of air channels. They taste somewhat like artichokes and can be eaten raw, roasted, stir-fried, deep-fried, dried, pickled or ground up to make a flour. They can be added to desserts, as well as soups, salads, pickles and various savoury dishes. The Chinese value it as a delicacy. In Asia, the young leaves and flowers are also eaten in salads or are lightly cooked as vegetables. The stalks can be sliced and added to salads, and even the roots can be lightly cooked and eaten.

Nutrition

The seeds are high in vitamin C. They contain ~55% carbohydrate, 17% protein, 2.5% fat. The rhizomes have recently been shown to have good levels of antioxidants, which help to reduce cell damage and can help prevent diseases such as cancer and, possibly, neuro-degenerative conditions.

Medicinal

In China, the root is used as a baby food, and is given in cases of diarrhoea and dysentery. It is also said to increase mental acuteness. The seeds are used to treat fevers, nervous disorders, insomnia; to stop vomiting, to relieve indigestion, as a sedative, to stop diarrhoea or just as a tonic. The petals have been used to treat syphilis. The flower receptacle contains small amounts of the alkaloid nelumbine, which is effective in stopping bleeding. The leaves are used as a refrigerant, an astringent and as a diuretic.

Other uses

The leaves are used for serving or wrapping around other foods before they are cooked. Thread from the leaf stalks was used to make wicks for oil lamps in temples. Cloth was also made from it, and wearing the garment was believed to cure many ailments. All parts of the flower, seed and leaves have been used as a smoking mixture, and are said to have a relaxing, yet inebriating effect similar to that of mild cannabis.

Ornamental

The blooms are highly valued around the world, but particularly in Asia. In addition, the symmetrical, unusual seedheads are widely used in floral displays. The plants themselves, because of their large leaves, provide a habitat for many pond creatures.

nitrogen and potassium, but less phosphates. They appreciate good-quality fresh, not brackish, water.

Pot culture: Because of their sensitivity to winter cold, and their beauty, these plants make a fantastic addition to a deck or patio if grown in containers of water. Pots should be ~60 cm deep, and about the same diameter or wider if possible. A smaller volume of water warms up more rapidly in summer, giving better plant growth and more flowers; although, the water should not be allowed to get too warm in very sunny areas. Consider using a light-coloured container or erecting shade over plants in very hot weather. Plants can be planted directly in soil within the pot or can be grown in open-meshed pots, which can be then easily lifted out. Place ~25 cm of soil in a container or fill the open-meshed pot before planting the rhizome horizontally. Note, any organic matter needs to be well rotted down to avoid the water becoming anaerobic. Gradually raise the water level as the leaf stems grow taller. Container-grown plants can be easily protected in colder weather by covering the container, or by removal and storage of rhizomes over winter.

Planting: Space plants at ~70–150 cm apart. Plant rhizomes horizontally within the soil, with the top ~2.5 cm of rhizome above the soil surface. If feasible, gradually increase the depth of water as the leaves reach the water surface. Initially, just place ~10 cm of water above the rhizome, and gradually increase the depth to ~30–40 cm, but not deeper. If planting in an already established pond, the plant can be stood, within its container, on bricks or similar, which can be removed as the plant grows. If just growing for the flowers, the flower heads are best removed after the petals have dropped to conserve the plant's energy. *Warning:* If the climate and conditions are ideal, these plants can become invasive, and are best planted in wire-mesh pots to stop them taking over.

Propagation: *Seeds:* Plants can be grown from seed, but the seeds need pre-treatment before they will germinate. Because of their hard outer covering, seeds need to be scarified by carefully puncturing the coat with a knife or similar. The seeds can then be soaked for ~24 hours in warm (not hot) water to help remove germination inhibitors and to further soften the seedcoat. Sow seeds in very moist compost, or just warm water (changed daily), and these should germinate in 5–8 days. Seedlings produce variable offspring, and older seeds are often not viable. *Cuttings:* Pieces of rhizome, with 2–3 healthy buds, can be taken in spring–early summer and planted in very damp compost or shallow water, with warmth, to establish. Actively growing, rooted rhizomes can be then planted out (see planting notes). Flowers are borne earlier in the year if the rhizome was previously established at ~20°C before planting out. Plants can be divided every 3–4 years.

Pests and diseases: Few problems if kept healthy. Possible insect pests include aphids, water-lily beetle, caddis-fly larvae, cluster caterpillar. Diseases include leaf spot, powdery mildew, *Phytophthora* crown rot, lotus-streak virus, and the rhizome can be attacked by various *Fusarium* or *Pythium* spp.

CULTIVARS

There are many cultivars, with most selected for their flowers. 'Quandong' is the main commercial cultivar grown for rhizome production; the cultivars 'Singapore' and 'Brisbane' also produce good rhizomes, and the latter also has wonderful flowers. 'Vietnam-Red' is recommended for its flowers. ∎

Olea europaea
Olive
OLEACEAE

Other species: Madagascar olive, (*Noronhia emarginata*)

Relatives: lilac, privet, jasmine

The olive is a native of the Mediterranean region, as well as tropical and central Asia and various parts of Africa. Its use and cultivation have a very long history. The olive may have been cultivated in both Crete and Syria, independently, for its fruit and oil, with the latter being used as a food, but also for lamps. Archaeological evidence suggests that olives were being grown in Crete in 2500 BC. From Crete and Syria, olives were spread to Greece, Rome and other Mediterranean regions. Historically, the olive tree is associated with peace, mostly from the Book of Genesis (8:11) where the dove returns to Noah's ark with an olive leaf after God has made peace with Man and stopped the flood. The trees within the garden of Gethsemane were olives, which were being cultivated for their oil. The olive tree also signifies Christ's death and His Resurrection. It is now very widely cultivated in Greece, Italy and Spain, and each country, and its regions, like the grape, have their own unique cultivars. Some of these plantings (groves) are now hundreds of years old. Indeed, trees can be extremely long lived: up to 1000 years. Olive trees are now also commercially grown in many regions of the world, such as Australia, New Zealand, California and Israel. Olive trees are very easy to grow, are tough and are tolerant of many soil types, drought and salinity.

DESCRIPTION

An evergreen tree, growing to ~18 m in height, ~10 m spread, though is usually smaller. It usually forms a single trunk, though is sometimes multi-stemmed, and has an irregular crown of silvery-grey foliage. The branches often have a graceful, sweeping, shape. As it gets older, its branches become twisted and gnarled. Trees grow fairly fast when young and are given water and nutrients, but only grow very slowly as they get older or if neglected.

Leaves: Mid-green above, silvery grey-green beneath, evergreen, narrow (~5–9 cm long, ~2–3 cm wide), pointed, opposite, with smooth margins. They have a dense, leathery texture and sunken stomata to reduce water loss. They live for 2–3 years and usually fall in spring when new leaves are formed. Can also put on spurts of growth after rains at any time of year.

Flowers: Small, sweetly fragrant, inconspicuous, creamy, borne on long stems from the leaf axils of 1-year-old wood, in mid–late spring. Flowers are either bisexual (with both male and female structures) or are only male. Most trees are self pollinating, but do get better pollination if planted with other varieties. A few cultivars are incompatible with certain other cultivars, and this can be brought about by high temperatures. Although many flowers are formed, only a fraction of these actually set fruit. However, even then, there are often too many fruits, which may need thinning. *Pollination:* Mostly wind-pollinated: pollen can be carried 20–30 m. Bees may also contribute.

Fruit: A green, roundish–oval drupe, becoming purplish-black when fully ripe. A few varieties are green when ripe and a few turn a reddish-brown colour. Size, shape, oil-content and flavour vary considerably between cultivars. Some fruits are elongated with pointed ends.

Yield/harvest/storage: In ideal conditions, yields of 40 kg per tree are possible, but they are often considerably less. Trees from cuttings or grafts start producing fruit in 2–3 years, and reach full production after 8–11 years; they then remain productive for many decades. Seedling trees take 4–7 years to start fruiting. Trees tend towards biennial bearing, and excess fruits should be thinned in bumper years to even out yields, and this also results in larger, earlier ripening fruits of those that are left. Thin to ~3–6 fruits per 30 cm of stem: this should be done soon after fruit-set. Olives take 6–8 months to mature after fruit-set. However, table olives are usually picked earlier when still firm, but oil olives are left on the trees until ripe for their full oil content to develop. Pick olives carefully because they can bruise.

Roots: Relatively shallow rooted, so take care with cultivation. May be beneficial to spread roots when first planting. A mulch will suppress weed growth and help retain soil moisture. Usually shallow-rooted trees are susceptible to drought; the olive, therefore, must have many deeper roots as well to withstand adverse conditions in the way that it does.

CULTIVATION

Olive trees survive and fruit well, and grow in a wide range of soils and environments. They are easy to grow.

Location: Likes to be grown in full sun. Older trees are quite wind tolerant, though younger trees may need staking in exposed locations. Tolerant of salty, maritime locations, but not of lots of salt spray. It can grow in semi-arid or temperate regions.

Temperatures: Grows best in Mediterranean-type climates, with long, hot, dry summers and some winter cold: a long summer season is needed to ripen the fruit. They are generally fairly frost hardy, and can tolerate temperatures down to ~–12°C when fairly dormant, but not for long periods. Young leaves and blossom can be damaged by late frosts. A cold, wet spring can reduce the amount of blossoms by increasing the ratio of male-only flowers and, consequently, fruit-set. In warmer regions, leaves tend to keep growing year round.

Chilling: Olive cultivars vary in the amount of winter chilling they need. Some only need ~200 hours, others need >500 hours. Insufficient winter chilling can reduce the number of flowers and, therefore, fruit production. In tropical regions with warm winters, although the trees grow well, they produce very little, if any, fruit.

Soil/water/nutrients: Trees can grow in a variety of soils, from sandy or gravelly loams, to clay soils, and can often grow on soils too poor to support many other crops. They can also grow at a wide range of pH values: from fairly acid to very alkaline (pH 8.5), and are also tolerant of mildly saline soils. Young trees benefit from regular moisture till established and, when older, some moisture gives better fruit production. They grow best with more rain in winter, some moisture during flowering and fruit formation, and then less rain in late summer, which helps the fruit to mature. In general, the trees are fairly drought tolerant. They cannot tolerate high humidity, which induces disease and physiological disorders, or cold, wet soils. Olive trees are not very nutrient hungry, but an application of a complete fertiliser during flower and

fruit formation, or a foliar feed at fruit ripening, can improve fruit quality. Seaweed fertilisers are good and also provide trace elements. An application of nutrients every other year is usually all that's needed once trees are established. Too much nitrogen causes excess soft leaf growth, which makes the crown too large for its roots and, therefore, vulnerable to strong winds; it can also increase the risk of *Verticillium* wilt. Potassium and phosphate encourage flowering, and additional calcium can also be beneficial.

Pot culture: Olives grow well and look good when grown in containers. They are fairly slow growing and give an immediate Mediterranean feel to a patio or deck. They need little maintenance and tolerate quite a lot of neglect. They grow better in, but do not necessarily need, a large soil volume. Protect them from hard frosts.

Pruning: Pruning helps avoid biennial bearing and keeps them at a manageable height. It is best to prune out suckers and lower branches. Remove the tips of young long stems to encourage the formation of a vase-shaped tree, with 3–5 main scaffold branches (the tree has weak apical dominance). Try to keep the centre open, to allow light and air to enter. Because olives produce fruit on 1-year-old wood, the removal of some stem tips increases the number of fruiting laterals. Straggly or badly damaged trees can be severely pruned and should grow back from older wood. Olive trees can also be trained to espaliers.

uses

Food
The raw fruits contain an alkaloid which makes them bitter, and they need to be cured before eating (see below). A few varieties are sweet enough to be eaten after sun drying. The only difference between green and black olives is that green olives are less ripe. They are cured by being either oil-, water-, brine-, dry- or lye-cured. Green olives must be soaked in a lye solution before brining, whereas ripe black olives only need brining; they also contain more oil than green olives. The longer the olive ferments in its own brine, the less bitter and tastier it becomes. The fruits are tasty as a snack, with cheeses, biscuits, etc, and added to pizzas, pastas, cold meat and fish dishes, etc. Their oil has always been popular in Mediterranean regions, but worldwide has become much more popular over the last few years with the knowledge gained about the different qualities of oils and their health benefits. The oil can be simply just cold pressed, and is unheated or changed. The first pressing of this is the best quality, and is called 'extra virgin olive oil'. It has a low acidic level. The second cold pressing is 'virgin olive oil', and has a slightly higher acidic level. Normal olive oil is a mix of refined olive oil and a mix of virgin olive oils. 'Pomace' olive oil has been extracted with solvents and has been further refined, and its qualities are questionable. Indeed, there are questions about the levels of polycyclic aromatic hydrocarbons (PAHS) it contains. PAHS can be mutagenic and carcinogenic. Olive oils can be sampled like wines, with their quality and taste affected by their cultivar, but also the region and soil they were grown in. There can be 'good' and 'bad' olive years, as with wines. Some oils have a strong

spicy taste, others are mild and nutty. Olive oil needs to be sealed for storage and, although it is often kept for extended periods of time, it is best used during the first 6 months after pressing.

Medicinal
The oil, rich in oleic acid, is considered to be good for cardiovascular health. It is now well-known that the peoples of the Mediterranean, who have always consumed lots of oil or olives, suffer from far less heart disease than most other Europeans. Science has now determined that olive oil, as a monounsaturated fat, is rich in high density lipids (HDL; 'good' cholesterol). Virgin olive oil has recently been found to contain compounds that have a similar effect to non-steroid anti-inflammatories, such as ibuprofen. It is thought that its anti-inflammatory effects may be partly why it is associated with preventing many chronic diseases. The leaves have been used as an antiseptic, an astringent, as a tranquilliser and to treat fever. The oil aids digestion, is a mild laxative, soothes mucous membranes, and is used externally on burns, bruises, insect bites, sprains and itching. The oil, with alcohol, makes a good hair tonic, and with oil of rosemary, a good treatment for dandruff.

Other uses
The oil used to be burnt in lamps and used for lubrication.

Ornamental
A good choice for gardens in drier areas. They are non-invasive and easy to control, have evergreen, silver-green foliage, and require very little maintenance.

Above: Olea europaea.

Propagation: *Seed:* None of the cultivated varieties can be propagated by seed as seedlings from these revert to the original small-fruited wild variety. If you want to grow from seed, then the seedcoat needs softening or gently cracking to help germination. *Cuttings:* Hardwood cuttings are commonly taken from 2-year-old shoots in winter, treated with a rooting hormone and rooted in a cold frame. These should start fruiting in ~4 years. Semi-ripe cuttings can also be taken in spring or summer and rooted with mist. Small shoots that grow directly from the trunk can be removed, and these often rapidly root. *Grafting:* This method is sometimes used, often by feather grafting, but trees often produce lots of suckers. Top-working is also practised. *Rootstocks:* Most olives are grown on their own rootstocks, grown from cuttings.

Pests and diseases: Generally has fewer problems than most fruit spp. The main problems may be fungal diseases such as peacock spot and *Phytophthora*. Can also get problems with olive knot, branch dieback, monkey nose, thrips, scale, leafroller caterpillar and cicadas. Keeping plants healthy and the branching not too crowded can reduce the risk of many of these problems. Birds like eating ripe olives, and will rapidly clean a tree of its fruits.

CULTIVARS

There are >700 varieties of olives. See below for a list of a few, mostly table-olive, cultivars. Refer to specialist literature for further cultivars and oil-producing olives, and check out local cultivars in your area: some are of very good quality.

'Ascolano': A good table olive. Very large fruit. Skin colour is light, even when ripe, stone is small. Fruit is tender and bruises easily. Good flavour, and needs only moderate lye treatment for pickling. Tree is a heavy bearer, and is widely adaptable.

'Barnea': From Israel. Produces oil. Is prolific in growth and fruiting, but needs a pollinator, e.g. 'Manzanillo', 'Picual' or 'Picholene'. Has high vigour, but low tolerance to heavy frost and humidity. Has medium-sized pointed fruit with high percentage (15–20%) of good-quality oil. Fruits can also be pickled. Upright growth. Has high yields: ~45 kg of fruit per tree. Fruit detaches easily. Less tolerant of salty winds. Takes ~7 years to crop well.

'Hojiblanca': From Spain. A table olive. Tree is hardy and cold tolerant, used for both oil and table olives. Medium oil content, but is of good quality. Can grow in soils with a very high pH, i.e. >8. Is slow growing.

'Kadesh': From Israel. A high-quality table olive with a very low oil content. When pickled green, may only contain <3% oil. Has high flesh to stone ratio, with good taste and processing qualities. Crops well.

'Kalamata': From Greece. Excellent table olive, with high-quality fruits that are rich and fruity, and also produces good oil. Harvest when fully black and ripe. Crops moderate–heavy. Difficult to root from cuttings. Likes warmer sites. Fairly late ripening. Has large leaves.

'Manzanilla' (meaning 'little apple'): From Spain. The world's most popular table olive. Fairly small tree with a spreading canopy. Good yields of fruit early in the season. Can be pickled green or black. Fruit are large, rounded, lots of flesh. Skin is deep blue-black when mature. Excellent for oil and pickles. Tree has a vigorous, drooping habit; is a prolific bearer.

'Picual': From Spain. A table and oil olive. Very important commercial variety in Spain. Fast growing, early producing with a high oil content (~25%): it can start producing in 2–3 years. Tolerant of both wet and dry soils, and is fairly frost tolerant. Not suitable for humid regions. A large vigorous tree, susceptible to biennial bearing. Medium–large olives, late ripening. Susceptible to peacock spot.

'Sevillano': From Spain. A table olive with large fruits and large stone, but can also produce oil. Is somewhat cold tolerant, but is susceptible to alternate bearing. Fruits bruise easily and is slow growing. Ripens early. Likes a deep, rich, well-drained soil.

'Uovo di piccione' ('pigeon's egg'): From Italy. A table olive. Has very large fruit. Oil content low. Trees are slow growing, and do best in arid conditions. A good pollinator.

CURING OLIVES

There are several ways to cure olives. Detailed methods can be got from Maggie Blyth Klein's book, *Feast of the olives*, and the University of California Agricultural Sciences Publications, leaflet 21131. Two methods are briefly described here. *Brining:* Ripe black olives are soaked for ~3 weeks in salt solutions until they have lost their bitterness. They are then placed in a vinegar, lemon and herbal marinade to soak for a short while before eating. Or the olives can be soaked in water for 7–10 days, with the water changed daily. The olives are then heated in water to boiling point and the boiled water then thrown away, leaving the olives to cool. Repeat this three times, after which wine vinegar and salt are added before the whole is stored in clean jars for 2–4 months. Other ingredients/spices can also be added. Oil can be poured on the top of the jars to seal the contents from air. *Lye curing:* Green or near-ripe olives are soaked in a series of lye solutions to remove their bitterness, are then thoroughly washed with clean water, and finally transferred to a mild saline solution.

OTHER SPECIES

Madagascar olive, *Noronhia emarginata*. A handsome shrub (4–10 m tall, ~6 m width) from Madagascar, with light green, oval, thick leaves. Very salt tolerant and very tolerant of maritime, sandy locations. It has ~2.5-cm, round, purple fruits that have a small amount of sweetish flesh. They are frost susceptible. Prefers partial shade or full sun, and likes moisture. Has high wind tolerance, but medium drought tolerance. ∎

Oncoba spinosa
Oncoba (fried-egg tree, snuff-box tree)
FLACOURTIACEAE
Relatives: kei apple, Governor's plum

A native of southern Africa, from South Africa and Zimbabwe, and possibly regions around northern Africa, it is often found growing naturally along river courses. Unfortunately, it is now becoming less frequent in the wild, and has become a protected species in South Africa. It is spiny, hence its species name, but is a tough, small tree that produces large, fragrant, camellia-like flowers and many interesting, very hard-shelled fruits. Although the flesh within them is not very tasty, its ornamental value and ease of cultivation merit its inclusion here.

DESCRIPTION

Forms a spiny shrub or small tree, mostly multi-stemmed, growing to 2–6 m tall, with about the same spread. Its spines are 3–5 cm long, and occur along the stems from leaf axils. Plants seem to often become less spiny with age. It has a densely branched crown and grey, smooth bark. Young stems have distinctive lenticels. It grows at a medium rate, and can grow ~1 m a year under good conditions.

Leaves: Deciduous, waxy, simple, shiny, reddish-bronze when young, turning a rich green colour as they mature. Are oval and lanceolate at their tips, with a rounded base, 3–8 cm long. The margins are coarsely serrated.

Flowers: Attractive, sweetly fragrant, abundant, large (~5–8 cm diameter), and are borne solitarily from the leaf axils towards the ends of stems, through spring to early summer. Each flower only lives a day, but there are many flowers and these are borne over a long period. They are composed of many white rounded, delicate petals surrounding a centre consisting of a mass of long, decorative, yellow stamens. Its common name, the fried-egg tree, is derived from the appearance of these flowers, with their distinctive yellow centres surrounded by white. The flowers are bisexual and are self-fertile: only one plant is needed to set fruits. *Pollination:* Mostly be bees.

Fruits: Abundant, distinctive, rounded, with a somewhat pointed base and a very hard, outer shell, with remnants of the female pistil still at the apex. From green, it turns a mustard-yellow colour, before fully ripening to dark chestnut brown and falling from the plant. The hard casing is lightly marked into segments, usually seven. Inside, the pulp is yellowish and contains many small, brown, shiny seeds. The pulp is edible, but sour. It is popular with children in Africa, but is seldom eaten otherwise. However, its round, hollow, hard shells are often used (see Uses).

Yields/harvest: Even solitary trees seem to give good yields. Plants start producing fruits when only 3–4 years old. The fruits are best picked for eating when they are a mustard-yellow colour, in autumn. The pulp is then at its best. The fruits then turn a chestnut brown and the pulp also becomes brown and starts to ferment within the shell.

Roots: Forms deep roots that enable it to find water at depth; however, it also has some surface roots and benefits from an organic mulch.

CULTIVATION

A tough plant that needs little to no maintenance.

Location: Prefers a site in full sun, though can tolerate a little shade. It is moderately tolerant of salt, but not of strong winds, so could be grown in more protected maritime locations.

Temperature: Prefers subtropical or tropical climates, but can also be grown in warm-temperate regions, and will also fruit if given some protection from cold weather. Can tolerate brief frosts though, once acclimatised.

Soil/water/nutrients: Grows best in loamy, deep,

uses

Food
The flesh of the fruit is pumpkin-like in appearance, but is sour in taste, and is just about edible.

Medicinal
In Africa, the roots and leaves are used medicinally to treat diarrhoea and urinary problems.

Other uses
The hollowed-out hard shells are often used as containers, e.g. for snuff (hence, its other common name), or the fruits are dried whole, and the dried seeds left inside them to make a fun percussion instrument. Some paint the gourd-like shells for ornamentation. Its wood is tan-coloured, hard, but of small dimensions, so is used to make smaller objects. An oil can be extracted from the seeds, and this has been used in varnishes.

Ornamental
Can be grown as an ornamental plant with its fragrant flowers and interesting, numerous fruits, though its spines may mean that it is better planted as a barrier hedge rather than near thoroughfares.

but well drained soils, though can also grow in sandy soils. Grows best at more neutral pH soil values. Is drought tolerant once established, but does not tolerate waterlogging. Only moderately nutrient hungry, and only needs supplemental nutrients if grown in poorer soils.

Pot culture: Could be grown for a few years in a container and needs little maintenance, just some protection during cold weather. Its many fragrant flowers and interesting fruits, which it produces after only a few years, make it a possibility for a deck or conservatory in colder areas.

Planting: Space plants at ~4–6 m apart, as they can be quite spreading. Take care when planting that the deep roots

are not damaged.

Propagation: *Seed:* Mostly grown from seed, which germinates easily with good drainage, moisture and warmth. Seedlings are grown on in deep pots to encourage deep root growth. Growth can be slow, initially, while the plant establishes its roots, but the shoot then starts to grow more rapidly after a year or so. *Cuttings:* Semi-ripe cuttings taken during summer, inserted into gritty, moist compost, with warmth, may root.

Pruning: Minimal, just to reduce dense, crossing branches, or to remove any damaged or diseased wood.

Pests and diseases: Seems to suffer few problems. ∎

Opuntia spp.
Prickly pear (nopal, tuna, Indian fig, beaver tail, barberry pear, Indian pear, mission cactus)
CACTACEAE

Opuntia compressa, O. cymochila, O. dillenii (syn. *Cactus indicus*), *O. echinocarpa, O. erinacea, O. ficus-indica, O. humifusa, O. indica, O. lindheimeri, O. linguiformis, O. microdasys, O. mojavensis, O. phaeacantha, O. polycantha, O. triacantha, O. tunicata*
Relatives: pitaya

The *Opuntia* genus consists of ~250 species of succulents that vary in size from ~10 cm to ~5 m tall. They all have fleshy stems and leaves that are reduced to spines. Many of the smaller species are popular houseplants. They can be divided into two groups: those species that have round flattened stems (called pads or nopales), which are generally known as prickly pears; or those that have cylindrical stems, and are known as chollas. It is the former group that will be described here. Some of these species are difficult to tell apart, and there is often confusion over their Latin names as well as their common names. When choosing a prickly pear, if possible, select a plant that you know will grow well in your region, and that has good-tasting fruit. It is not known conclusively where the prickly pears originate from, but it is probably Mexico and the southwestern US states. The pads of these plants have been cultivated and eaten by indigenous populations since well before the Spanish arrived, and were a source of legends, magic and rituals. The Spanish took plants back to Spain, and from there they were taken to North Africa by the Moors. Prickly pear cacti are found in many dry areas of the world and in some instances have become a problem, e.g. in Australia, where it invaded 24 million hectares and needed the introduction of biological controls, cochineal mealybugs, a stem-boring moth and a red-spider mite, to stop its invasive spread. However, in gardens it is easy enough to control, though is very spiny. The prickly pear is now grown commercially in Mexico and parts of the USA, as well as in a few regions around the Mediterranean. It forms an interesting, ornamental, surprisingly cold-hardy succulent that has attractive eye-catching flowers, delicious fruit, edible stems and recently discovered important medicinal properties.

DESCRIPTION
Succulent, perennial cacti species with stems and branches that are jointed, green, and flattened into round–oval leaf shapes, called pads (or, botanically, phyloclades or cladophylls). Their height varies (0.1 m–5 m) depending on the species. Larger species can spread ~5+ m.

Leaves: Modified into clusters of sharp spines that are usually surrounded by short, barbed hairs called glochids: the largest spines are very stout, sharp and ~2 cm long. They form in clumps at regular intervals over the surface of the flattened pads. (*O. microdasys* is a spineless species, but still has barbed glochids.)

Flowers: Pretty, yellow (but can also be white, red, orange or purple), 5–8 cm diameter, many petals and stamens, bisexual and self-fertile. Flower buds are flushed pink. Has an inferior ovary containing numerous ovules (which will become seeds). Flowers are solitary and are borne along the rims of stems and upper parts of joints. The plant has a long flowering season from spring to late summer. *Pollination:* By hummingbirds, bees and other insects.

Fruits: Fleshy, inverted pear-shape, but concave at the apex, ~6–8 cm long, ~3–5 cm diameter, weight ~25 g. The fruits are covered with fine, hooked glochids. Inside, the flesh is vividly coloured, being often a rich red-purple, and has a juicy, mucilaginous texture. Has many (~125), small, flat, bean shaped seeds per fruit, which are edible. Fruits ripen from autumn through winter, and sometimes into spring, but can occur on the plant year round.

Yield/harvest: A mature plant yields ~2.5 kg of fruits a year. However, may have a few spines, and usually have numerous barbed glochids, so gloves are needed when harvesting. The spines are sharp and the smaller glochids enter the skin where the barb breaks off and remains embedded. To remove this, a plaster placed over the barb will cause it to rise to the surface of the skin where it can be rubbed off or pulled out. Once picked, fruits can be kept for several days at room temperature.

CULTIVATION

A very tough plant that is extremely drought tolerant, and needs minimum, if any, maintenance.

Location: Grows best in full sun, in warm, dry areas, but will also survive in cooler areas if given extra protection. Is quite salt tolerant and can be grown in maritime locations. Plants are fairly wind tolerant and can also grow in very hot areas; survives temperatures of ~50°C!

Temperature: Many prickly pear species can survive temperatures below freezing; some species will survive ~–30°C. The ends of 'branches' can be damaged by frost, but they seem to recover. If growing in colder areas, plant these against a sunny wall, or protect plants, e.g. with sacking, in cold weather. Cold-hardy prickly pears include: O. compressa (small, should survive –15°C), O. cymochila var. montana (medium size, golden spines, blue-green stems), O. echinocarpa (upright, white spines, yellow–red flowers), O. erinacea var. columbiana (Utah native), O. humifusa (small, wrinkled, large red and yellow flowers), O. indica (can survive ~–10°C), O. linguiformis, O. mojavensis (~1 m tall, yellow spines, hardy to 0°C), O. phaeacantha (~0.5–1 m tall, yellow/red blooms, very cold hardy), O. polycantha (smaller, yellow

uses

Food

For preparation of fruits and leaves, gloves are needed to remove spines and glochids. For the fruits, hold in a towel or similar and, with a small, sharp knife, slice down the length of the pear, cutting just through the skin; the skin can then be peeled off to leave the vividly-coloured flesh beneath. Gadgets are available that simplify the removal of the spines and glochids. The seeds can be eaten with the flesh. Fruits are mucilaginous, juicy, refreshing, cooling and sweet, like watermelon, but also pleasantly sub-acid. Plants with purple fruits are said to be the sweetest. The pulp and juice makes attractive and very good jams and jellies. A Mexican beverage is made using the fruit with rice, almonds and milk. The native American population fermented the juice to make an alcoholic drink that was ~18% alcohol. The fruits can also be dried for storage. The seeds can be roasted, ground and used as a thickener. The flesh from the pads (or nopales) is usually harvested between spring–autumn, with only the younger pads being selected. The spines are removed with a knife or similar, any coarse material is taken out, then after the flesh has been washed, it is usually sliced into sections. The pad flesh can be eaten lightly grilled or boiled; overcooking makes this somewhat sticky. When lightly boiled, they are said to be like mucilaginous green beans. The pad flesh can be also added to egg dishes, other vegetables or soups, or used as a tortilla filling. Grilled pads can be simply eaten fresh with a squeeze of lime and a dribble of olive oil. In Mexico they are also preserved in brine or made into marmalade for export. Once prepared, they can be stored in a fridge for up to 2 two weeks.

Nutrition

Fruit is 78.5% moisture, and is very low in fat. It has good levels of flavonoids (including quercetin) and reasonable levels of vitamin C (10–23 mg/100 g of pulp). The juice contains 6% sugars, most of which are reducing sugars. It contains some B vitamins, good levels of magnesium and some calcium (although this is largely unavailable), potassium and copper. It has good levels of fibre. Has 0.1% tannin and 0.3% pectin.

Medicinal

The *Opunita* genus are used medicinally to decrease blood-glucose levels, also reduce levels of low-density lipids within blood as well as increasing its hepatic turnover, thus reducing the levels of 'bad' cholesterol. Studies have also shown that *Opuntia* can control experimentally-induced diabetes, and this is being investigated further. It seems to prevent excess blood sugar from being converted into fats. The flavonoids may also act as an anti-inflammatory in gastric-ulcer prevention, and may ease hangover symptoms, such as nausea and a dry mouth. In particular, quercetin, but also other flavonoids, inhibit neuronal-cell injury and lipid peroxidation. The flesh of the stems, when mashed and applied as a poultice, cools the skin, reduces inflammation and is soothing to the eyes. The fruits are also said to cure biliousness, urinary complaints, piles, inflammation, anaemia and enlargement of the spleen. The flowers are astringent and are used to reduce bleeding and treat problems of the gastrointestinal tract, especially diarrhoea, colitis and irritable-bowel syndrome; they are also said to cure bronchitis and asthma. The ripe fruits, when eaten, dye the urine red. **Warning:** A recent study has found that when male rats were fed the stem it caused a very significant decrease in their fertility.

Other uses

The gum obtained from the stem can be mixed with oil to make candles. The juice from the fruits produces an attractive red-purple dye. The pulp from the pads is used in face and body lotions, hair gels and shampoo.

Ornamental

Although dangerous to weed around, they do make striking, unusual display plants, particularly if planted amongst other succulents or in pebble beds, and the fruits are tasty. They need very little maintenance and can grow in poor, dry soils. While unsuitable near paths, etc., they can make a very secure boundary hedge.

flowers, very hardy), *O. triacantha* (smaller).

Soil/water: Can grow on nutrient-poor soils, on sandy gravelly soils, limestone and igneous rock. Does not like wet or heavy soils; the soil must be well drained, but does do better with moderate additions of water in the growing season. However, the prickly pear is superbly adapted to live in dry places: it can rapidly absorb and store any rainfall, it is covered with a thick cuticle, the leaves are modified into spines and the stem acts as a water store. As a result of these features, it has a very much reduced surface-to-volume ratio, meaning there is much less surface area to lose water from. In addition, it carries out Crassulacean photosynthesis (see p. 20).

Pot culture: These plants can be easily grown in containers as long as the compost is gritty and free draining. Only water plants once the soil has become quite dry, and hardly ever during the winter months. They are happy growing in the same soil for several year without needing to be repotted. The spines of larger plants can be a liability if the containers are sited near paths, or if they need to be moved to larger containers. However, they are very low maintenance, can be easily controlled, have attractive flowers and fruits, and their form is very ornamental.

Propagation: *Seed:* Sow in spring in a gritty, free-draining compost, with heat. They take a considerable time to germinate. Once germinated, grow on seedlings in pots for 1–2 years before planting out. Young plants need extra protection during cold winters. *Cuttings:* Is easy to propagate by breaking off stem segments at any time of year. Allow the broken section to dry and callus over for 2–4 days (though will also root several weeks after being detached) before inserting in gritty compost to root. Do not over-water cuttings while they are establishing. They root quickly and easily. ■

Pachira aquatica
Malabar chestnut (Guiana chestnut, provision tree, money tree)
MALVACEAE (Bombacaceae)
Similar species: Saba nut (*Pachira glabra*)
Relatives: chupa-chupa, baobob, durian

The Malabar chestnut is an impressive, handsome, stout tree that forms buttressed roots when mature. It is a tropical native of southern Mexico to northern South America, and is often found growing along river courses and in swamps. It has large, fragrant, but nocturnal, flowers and produces exotic, large capsules of tasty seeds. Although a tropical tree, it can be grown outside in Florida, in parts of California and in other subtropical or almost warm-temperate regions.

DESCRIPTION
A showy, handsome, evergreen tree that can grow to >20 m in height, though often only grows to 5–10 m in cooler climates. Has a rounded, dense crown, and mature trees form a stout trunk with buttressed roots. Older bark is smooth and reddish-brown in colour; younger stems are greenish. It is very fast growing under the right conditions.

Leaves: Evergreen or semi-deciduous, with leaves often lost briefly during cooler weather. Leaves are waxy, bright green, alternate, compound, ~20–30 cm long, in groups of 3–9 palmate leaflets. May be pointed or have a rounded apex, have entire margins, and are shiny and attractive.

Flowers: Very decorative, very large (can be 15 cm long), with five creamy-yellow, slender, waxy petals surrounding many long, feathery, (7–12 cm), white stamens that are crimson-tipped; they only open in the evening, and have withered by morning. Flowers are bisexual and are self-fertile. *Pollination:* Flowers emit a strong, rich fragrance that attracts bats to pollinate them. It is possible moths also may do some pollination. In some areas, fruit-set is probably improved by hand pollination.

Fruit: Exotic, large, woody, capsules, up to 30 cm long, weighing up to 3 kg each, which change from green to brown when ripe. Contains five segments with many light brown chestnut-like seeds, ~1–1.5 cm long. The tough capsule, when ripe, can split to shed its seeds or can drop and remain intact and viable for a long period until the right environmental conditions are encountered. The seeds are surrounded by a creamy-coloured fluffy lining. The capsule is watertight and can be carried along in rivers for long distances to be deposited elsewhere.

Yield/harvest: Yields will depend on how successful pollination was and the location it is grown in. Yields can be high under the right conditions. The capsules may split into segments when ripe or can be cut open to release the numerous seeds. The seedcoat needs to be removed. If kept dry and cool, the kernels can be stored for several months.

CULTIVATION
Location: Grows best in full sun or can grow with a little shade. Not very tolerant of strong winds or of high salt levels.

Food
The kernels can be eaten fresh or are often roasted or fried. They usually have a tasty chestnut-like flavour, though their quality can vary. Kernels can also be dried, and ground into a flour for breads, muffins, etc. The young leaves can be eaten as a vegetable.

Nutrition/medicinal
The kernels contain ~15% protein and 40–50% oils.The rind from green fruits has been used to treat hepatitis.

Other uses
A yellow dye can be obtained from the bark.

Temperature: Basically a tropical plant, but can tolerate temperatures down to ~–2°C when established. Young trees need extra protection. Trees may drop their leaves during cold periods.

Soils/water/nutrients: Grows best in fertile, loamy, moist soils. Prefers a slightly acidic to neutral pH. Needs moisture throughout the year, though somewhat less during cooler weather. Is not drought tolerant, but can grow in wet soils, even those that are waterlogged for periods of time. It naturally often grows in swamps. Benefits from an organic mulch to retain moisture and add nutrients. Also, can be given 1–2 applications of a complete, balanced fertiliser, or the organic equivalent, while it is actively growing.

Pot culture: This exotic, interesting tree species could make a good pot plant, for a few years at least. If thus grown in cooler regions, it could be either taken inside or given extra protection during cold weather. It would also make a good plant for a conservatory or similar.

Pruning: Needs little if any pruning.

Propagation: Seed: Mostly grown from seed, which germinates well if removed from the woody husk. Sow in warm, moist compost. *Cuttings:* Semi-ripe cuttings taken during the growing season may root. The application of rooting hormone may help. Insert in gritty, moist compost in semi-shade to root. *Layering:* Air-layering may be possible.

Pests and diseases: Largely free from pests and diseases. Container specimens should be checked for the usual hot-house pests such as mealybugs.

SIMILAR SPECIES

Saba nut (French peanut, American chestnut), *Pachira glabra.* A native of Mexico and northern South America, this ornamental species also has large nocturnal flowers with green petals and numerous, long, white stamens. It has attractive palmate leaves and its trunk and stems are grey-green. It also produces a green, woody capsule that is smaller than that of *P. aquatica*, ~12 cm long. It contains 10–24 edible chestnut-like kernels that are either eaten fresh or are roasted or fried. They have a peanut-like taste. The seeds germinate very easily. Its cultivation requirements are similar to Malabar chestnut. ■

Palmae family
Palms with edible fruits
PALMAE (syn. Arecaceae)
Guadalupe palm (*Brahea edulis*), jelly palm (*Butia capitata*), Chilean wine palm (*Jubaea chilensis*), Quito palm (*Parajubaea cocoides*), queen palm (*Syagrus romanzoffianum*), California fan palm (*Washingtonia filifera*)

The palms are classified as monocots, as are grasses, lilies and banana but, unlike most monocots, they have a woody stem. Most palms are tropical or semi-tropical, with just a few able to grow in temperate regions. They are a very important genus in many locations and provide food, thatching, clothing, shade, soil stabilisation, fuel, medicines, oil and have many other uses. They are often amazingly tough, but are also usually very ornamental. There are an estimated ~2500 species of palms, and just a few of the hardier palms that have edible fruits are described below.

GENERAL DESCRIPTION
Botanically, palms are often grouped according to their stem (trunk) type: some just have a single stem, some are multiple-stemmed and some are classified as climbing palms. Those with only a single stem and, thus, only a single growing point, cannot survive if this is damaged, whereas multiple-stemmed palms have several growing points and are less vulnerable.

Leaves: In shade, many palm species form large, graceful, long and wide, arching leaves, whereas their length and width is often reduced somewhat when grown in full sun. They are typically known as fronds, and are usually formed concentrically around the top of the stem to form a crown. Some fronds can form beautiful fan shapes, others are long and wide, still others fishtail shaped. Other palm species have pinnate leaves that form an attractive feathery shape, e.g. the coconut, and this makes them more able to withstand wind than having a non-segmented frond. The palm, *Raphia regalis*, has pinnate leaves that can be 25 m long, which is probably the longest leaf in the world.

Flowers: Long clusters of white or yellow, bisexual flowers, borne on 1–3-m-long, drooping inflorescences that hang from the leaf axils. Only need a single tree to get fruit, but more than one tree will increase yields. *Pollination:* By wind and insects.

Fruit: Some palm species take just 3 years to start producing fruit, others take >40 years. Their fruits vary in shape and weight: some produce seeds that weigh only ~20 g, whereas another produces seeds that weigh ~20 kg (the largest seed in the world). Palm fruits usually have a thin skin (the exocarp), a layer of flesh beneath, which can be sweet and edible or may be fibrous (the mesocarp), within which is usually a single seed (though sometimes 2–3 seeds), covered by a fairly hard shell. The inner kernel of many species is edible and nutty in taste. Very few if any palm fruits are poisonous, but a few species contain calcium oxalate crystals, which makes them irritating to eat.

Roots: They form two main types of roots: deep roots, which are able to grow down far enough to tap the groundwater, even in dry, arid areas, and also many, dense, smaller surface roots that rapidly take up water and nutrients if it rains. In general, the roots of palm trees are fibrous and strong, and enable trees to survive where few other species can, and yet, are not widely spreading and so are not invasive, enabling trees to be planted close to buildings. They can also be moved, even when they are quite big, as long as they are left with a reasonably-large root ball, and will usually re-establish in a new location.

CULTIVATION

Most of the palms described here are very drought tolerant, can tolerate some frost and can grow in regions with cooler winters, although young trees will need protection from extremes until established. They are wind tolerant and can be grown in a wide range of soil types, plus, they make excellent ornamental trees.

Pot culture: Some of the smaller palm species can be grown in large pots, and this might be a solution in cooler regions, though they may not flower or fruit.

Propagation: *Seed:* Seeds are generally slow to germinate, and seedlings are slow to grow. If possible, they are best grown from fresh seed, although coconut is an exception to this. Stored seed germinates better if it is stored dry. Sow seeds in well-drained moist compost, with heat and shade. Germination can take 6–12 months. Once germinated, the seedlings should be grown-on in individual pots with well-drained, yet moist, organic soil, in shade. Young palms seem to grow slowly at first, but are actually putting their energies into establishing a good root system, before leaf growth. A widening base is a good sign that leaf growth should soon begin in earnest. Just before transplanting outside, plants should be slowly adapted to increasing sunlight. *Cuttings:* Unfortunately, very few palms

Food/nutrition
Some species have an edible, sweet and often date-like fleshy layer beneath the outer skin. Others have a tasty nutty kernel within the central seed. In some species, both of these can be eaten and enjoyed. Both the flesh and kernel can be eaten fresh or can be added to many dessert dishes, confectionery, etc. The flesh can be dried for later uses. The flesh of many palm fruits is high in dietary fibre, but also in sugars. They can also contain some vitamin B6, niacin and folate, as well as good levels of the minerals potassium, magnesium, copper and mangenese. The central kernel contains good levels of palm oil, which, like animal fats, unfortunately, contains a very high proportion of saturated fats. Therefore, people with raised cholesterol levels should moderate their intake of these oils and kernels. The oil does have good levels of vitamin E though and some vitamin K.

Ornamental
If you have the climate, then palms give a fantastic, tropical dimension to a landscape, either planted as a specimen or in groups. They also look stunning at night with front or up-lighting.

can be grown from cuttings because of their monocot form, i.e. they have only a single growing point at the top of each stem (and not several from leaf axils down the stem, as with dicots); even those with multiple-trunks and small side shoots are difficult to establish, if these are removed.

Pests and diseases: The palms, in general, have few if any major pest, disease or physiological problems.

THE SPECIES

Guadalupe palm, *Brahea edulis*. Guadalupe palms are native to Guadalupe Island, off the west coast of Mexico, but are now widely grown in many warm temperate areas of the world, including California and New Zealand.

Description: A medium-sized, slow-growing palm, ~9 m tall, with a crown of 30–50 leaves. *Trunk:* Smoothish with spirally arranged leaf scars. *Leaves:* Fan-shaped to form an attractive oval shape, stiff, folded, 1–2 m long, 0.8–1.2 m wide, dividing from about halfway way along into 70–80 segments that are deeply split at the tips. They sometimes have small teeth along the margins of leaf stalk. Leaves drop as they get older. *Flowers:* Large clusters of yellow, bisexual flowers, borne on 1.2–1.8-m-long inflorescences. *Fruit:* Plump, black, ~2.5 cm diameter, borne in long bunches from leaf axils. Are pleasant and sweet, and taste somewhat like dates. *Harvest:* The fruits are picked when fully black and have softened somewhat.

Cultivation: *Location:* Like a dry, sunny climate, but do not like it very hot or humid. Very wind and salt tolerant, and can be planted in exposed maritime locations. *Temperature:* Surprisingly cold hardy, and can tolerate temperatures down to ~−9°C, but not for extended periods. *Soil/water/nutrients:* The trees are widely adaptable to most soil conditions (except heavy clay), and are very drought tolerant, needing hardly any water once established. They also have very low nutrient requirements. *Pot culture:* They could be grown for several years in containers in cooler regions, and make an exotic, tough deck or patio plant, before they become too large. Need very little maintenance. *Pruning/Propagation:* The leaves usually self drop and so seldom need pruning. Germination of seed takes 2–4 months.

Uses: *Food:* They can be eaten fresh or made into jams and puddings. They can be stored for ~28 days in a fridge. *Ornamental:* Their slow growth, moderate size and attractive shape make them a good specimen tree.

Jelly palm (pindo palm, wine palm), *Butia capitata*. All *Butia* species are native to the grasslands, dry woodlands and savannahs of South America, and are still found there in the wild. It is probably the hardiest pinnate-leafed palm in cultivation, and is widely grown in many parts of the world, including northern California, up to British Columbia, southern UK and New Zealand. It makes a wonderful ornamental plant, with its beautiful blue-green, arching leaves, and it also has many uses and delicious fruits.

Description: Are slow-growing, smaller (~4–5 m tall) palms, with a crown of 40–50 leaves. *Trunk:* Thick, stout, with attractive, spirally arranged leaf scars. Trees can vary in height, trunk thickness, leaf colour, and fruit colour and taste. Trees live for ~20 years. *Leaves:* Beautiful 1.6–3 m long, pinnate, arching and curving back towards the stem: they vary in colour from blue-green to silvery-grey. Old leaf stalks often persist for many years. Leaves may have upward-pointing leaflets that form a pronounced V-shape. The leaf stalk is ~0.2 m–1.2 m long and has sharp spines along its margins. Leaflets are ~60–75 cm long, ~2.5 cm wide. *Flowers:* Numerous, small, creamy yellow–reddish, borne in 0.8–1.2-m-long drooping inflorescences, bearing both male and female flowers, at a ratio of 2:1, respectively, in late spring. *Fruit:* Unripe fruit are green, turning to bright yellow–orange when ripe. They are ~2.5 cm in diameter, round–oval, and are borne in long clusters from the leaf axils, often resting against the trunk. Each fruit contains a single, oval, large seed. The flesh is somewhat fibrous, but has a sweet–sub-acid flavour, reminiscent of apricot/banana. Trees produce many fruits in a season. *Harvest:* Fruit are picked when fully ripe and have lost all green coloration. Whole bunches can be harvested because they all tend to ripen at once. They can be kept for ~7 days in a fridge.

Cultivation: A beautiful, cold hardy and tough palm that is very easy to grow. *Location:* Grows best in full sun, though tolerates some shade, and the fronds then grow longer and wider. Trees are very wind-tolerant, and are fairly tolerant of maritime conditions. *Temperature:* It can tolerate temperatures down to at least ~−11°C when established, and does not grow well in very hot climates. *Soil/water/ nutrients:* Grows best in a sandy, well-drained soil, but can grow in many soil types and a fairly wide pH range, from fairly acidic to fairly alkaline. It is very drought tolerant, though can

also be grown in areas with high rainfall. Regular watering and moderate feeding will produce a faster-growing, more attractive palm. *Pot culture:* Their small size and slow growth make them good for growing in containers. They give a wonderful exotic look, and need very little maintenance. They can also be grown as an indoor plant providing there is adequate light. *Planting:* Needs enough space (3 x 3 m) to spread out and show off its beautiful foliage. *Pruning:* May only need to remove any untidy older lower leaves to show off the stem with its spirally arranged leaf scars. *Propagation. Seed:* Germination can take >6 months, but is faster after dry storage. However, look out for self-seedlings around mature trees, and these are easy to dig up and establish. This palm can hybridise with *Syagrus romanzoffiana* and with *Jubaea chilensis*. The resulting plants are very beautiful, but, unfortunately, are sterile.

Uses: *Food:* Their flesh is soft, sweet and tasty, with an apricot–banana flavour, though is somewhat fibrous. It can be eaten fresh and pureed, or they make a good-flavoured jelly or wine. In Uruguay, it is macerated in alcohol to make a popular liquor. The seed, when ground, can be roasted to make a beverage. *Ornamental:* A wonderful ornamental species, grown as a specimen or in groups. It has graceful, arching, tropical foliage, and looks great planted next to plants of contrasting shape, or near a patio or deck. It is also not too spreading and needs minimum maintenance; often planted in towns or in coastal areas.

Chilean wine palm (Chilean coconut, honey palm, coquito palm), *Jubaea chilensis* (syn. *J. spectabilis*). A warm temperate–semi-tropical palm that is native to the coastal valleys of Chile where it does not experience extremes of either heat or cold. This palm is now grown worldwide in Mediterranean-type climates and can be grown in areas such as California and the warmer areas of New Zealand. It is the most southerly representative of the palm family in South America. Unfortunately, in South America, because wine plams have been used for sap collection, which ultimately kills the tree, there are few species left in the wild; these are now protected by law in Chile.

Description: A slow-growing tree, ~10–12 m tall in ~100 years. Trunk, thick, ~1-m-diameter, dark grey, with attractive spirally-arranged diamond-shaped leaf scars. Has a crown of handsome pinnate leaves and makes a good specimen tree. *Leaves:* Stiff, spreading, 2–3 m long, consisting of pinnate leaflets. These are dull green above, grey beneath, ~60 cm long, ~3 cm width, tending to split at their ends. The trees tend to drop older leaves. *Flowers:* Long (~1 m) inflorescences of tiny purple flowers, in groups of three, consisting of a 2:1 male:female ratio of flower types, and are borne from the leaf axils in late spring. *Fruit:* Oval–round, rich yellow (when ripe), ~5-cm-diameter fruits, in long clusters. Their flesh is succulent and sweet. Each fruit contains a single, hard, smooth-shelled nut, ~3 cm diameter, which also has a pleasant, sweet, edible kernel, that tastes somewhat like coconut, but is a lot easier to crack. *Yield/ harvest/storage:* Unfortunately, it may be many years (>40, in some reports) before this tree starts to produce fruits. When it finally does, they are harvested as they ripen or fall to the ground in late summer–autumn. The fruits will keep for months if stored in a cool, dry place. To harvest the sap, the crown of leaves is cut off, after which the sap begins to flow. This can continue for several months, if a thin slice is regularly removed from the top of the tree, until the tree is exhausted and dies.

Cultivation: *Location:* They like a sunny or semi-shaded location, and do not grow well in hot, humid climates. They are wind tolerant, but only have a low salt tolerance, which makes them generally unsuitable for maritime locations. *Temperature:* They are fairly cold hardy, and can tolerate temperatures down to ~–7°C. *Soil/water/nutrients:* Can be grown in a wide range of soils and across a fairly wide pH range. They are very drought tolerant once established. Young trees benefit from an occasional addition of a complete fertiliser, although older trees generally grow fine without. *Pot culture:* Because of their slow growth, they can be grown for several years as a container plant, and need little maintenance; they make a good, tropical plant for a deck or patio setting. *Pruning/propagation:* Seldom needs any pruning as the tree usually drops older leaves. Seed is best sown fresh, and takes 6–12 months to germinate, and then may grow slowly for the first few years.

Uses: *Food:* The flesh tastes like coconut and the edible kernels are also nutty and good to eat, either fresh or prepared. They are often either eaten fresh or added to confectionery. The tree's sap is very sweet, and is used to make a drink, and in Chile, it is fermented to make a palm wine. Trees are reported to produce ~400 litres of sap before being killed. *Other uses:* The leaves are used for thatching, baskets, paper, etc.

Quito palm (cocumbe palm, mountain coconut), *Parajubaea cocoides*.

A graceful, elegant tree native to the Andes from the mountains of Ecuador to southern Colombia. It grows into a beautiful, graceful palm that is often planted in urban streets. It is a popular tree in northern South America for its nuts and ornamental qualities, but it is seldom grown much outside this region. However, a few trees are to be seen in northern California, northern New Zealand and in Sydney, Australia.

Description: Looks like a smaller coconut palm (~8 m tall) and has dainty leaves, a slender and sometimes curved trunk. It has a graceful, spreading crown of fronds, and is fairly fast growing, only taking 3–4 years to start fruiting. It is long lived. *Fruits:* It bears long clusters of 30–50 small fruits (~3–5 cm diameter) that look like very small coconuts, with three eyes and a hard, thick shell. They all ripen at about the same time, and then fall from the tree in autumn. The kernel is about the size of a macadamia nut and is good eaten fresh: it is sweet and has a good oil content.

Cultivation: *Location:* It can grow in areas with high rainfall, but is also fairly drought tolerant. It grows best in full sun. *Temperature:* It is fairly cold tolerant and can withstand temperatures below freezing, although temperatures much below –6°C may kill trees. However, it also seems to need cooler nights to grow well. *Soil/water/nutrients:* Trees can be grown in a wide range of soils and across a fairly wide pH range, from fairly acidic to fairly alkaline. They are drought tolerant once established. Young trees benefit from an annual addition of a complete fertiliser.

Uses: Although the fruit are small, the kernels are very tasty and can be used in similar ways to other nuts. It also

makes a beautiful ornamental species, and can be grown for a few years as a container plant.

Queen palm, *Syagrus romanzoffianum* (syn. *Arecastrum romanzoffianum*, *Cocos plumosa*).

The queen palm is a native of central South America, and is a popular ornamental plant in many subtropical and temperate regions of the world, including the warmer areas of New Zealand and California.

Description: A large palm: 8–13 m tall, 3–5 m spread. Usually forms a single, very straight, smooth trunk, often with bands of dark and light grey. It is fast growing. *Leaves:* Dense, glossy, soft, pinnate, graceful and arching, forming a whorled leaf arrangement up the stem. The fronds are 3–5 m long and grey-green in colour. They usually fall off the tree as they get older. The tree casts a lovely shade. *Flowers:* Cream–yellow, small, in long clusters, ornamental, in late spring. *Fruit:* Green, turning bright orange when ripe, ~2.5 cm long, oval, hanging in impressive ~1-m-long bunches. Succulent, date-like with sweet edible pulp. Can produce many fruits on a tree. Have a central seed, ~1.75 cm long, covered in fibres (like a small coconut) which are also edible and taste a bit like rich coconut. Ripen in autumn.

Cultivation: *Location:* Grow best in full sun, but can also grow in light shade. Is relatively frost hardy: established trees can survive ~–4°C. Damaged trees can recover, though this can take a couple of years. Does not like very exposed locations, and fronds can be damaged by strong winds; though can tolerate coastal salt. Relatively tolerant of urban environments. *Soil/water/nutrients:* Likes well-drained conditions and will withstand some drought, but prefers to be kept watered. Will grow in many soils, but prefers enriched sandy soils. Benefits from fertiliser, particularly nitrogen. In more alkaline soils, trees may suffer manganese deficiency and iron chlorosis, and may need to be given supplements with a general fertiliser about twice a year, in spring and summer. Manganese deficiency causes the leaves of the tree to look frayed and torn. *Pot culture:* Looks great in large pots and can also be grown indoors for periods of time. Low maintenance. *Planting/pruning:* Space plants at ~3–5 m apart. Prune only to remove dead fronds. *Propagation: Seed:* Better if it is fresh. Only takes ~28 days to germinate if warm, but 3–4 months if cooler. Self-seedlings often grow beneath trees and can be dug up and established. *Pests and diseases:* Susceptible to bud rot, which is difficult to detect because it occurs at the top of the tree. Try to buy healthy plants. When watering, try not to over-wet the trunk and leaves.

Uses: *Food:* The seed is covered with sweet, succulent edible pulp. **Warning:** Unripe seed may be toxic. *Ornamental:* Elegant, planted as a specimen, in an avenue or as a group. Great vertical effect for large gardens. Ideal for planting beside pools because it does not drop litter.

California fan palm (desert fan palm, petticoat palm), *Washingtonia filifera*.

Is a native of the deserts in California and southwest Arizona, and grows near streams and springs. It is a common ornamental plant in many parts of California, particularly those with Mediterranean-type climates.

Description: A larger, tough palm, ~16 m tall, with a large crown of 40–50 leaves. *Trunk:* Closely ringed, swollen at the base and is covered with many dead leaf stalks, if not pruned. Good trees ornamentally for avenues or as specimens. Not very good for container culture because of their relatively fast growth rate and large size. *Leaves:* Large, fan-shaped, round, greyish-green leaves are 1–1.2 m long, ~2 m wide, dividing about halfway into 50–70 pointed segments that bend and split at the tips, with threads in between. The leaves have a spreading form and have small spines extending along their margins. *Flowers:* Numerous, white–pinkish, on large, 3–5-m, arching, branched inflorescences that hang down from the leaf axils. *Fruit:* Small, brownish-black, with a thin, sweet pulp that tastes like sweet dates. Each fruit contains a single seed.

Cultivation: *Location:* Are wind-tolerant and do best in a sunny location. *Temperature:* Is fairly frost hardy and can tolerate temperatures down to ~–8°C. *Soil/water/nutrients:* Can grow in many soil types and fairly wide pH range. They are drought tolerant, but appreciate some moisture. In native stands they always grow near springs or other moist spots. Trees respond to occasional light fertiliser applications, particularly when young. Older trees seem to do fine without. *Pruning/propagation:* Remove older leaves, which do not readily fall off in this species. *Seed:* Germination takes 6–8 weeks. *Pests and diseases:* Major diseases include *Phytophthora* bud rot and diamond-scale fungus.

Uses: *Food:* The small fruits are harvested when ripe and can be eaten fresh or dried, or added to desserts and drinks. The seeds are also edible and have a reasonable nutty flavour. They were widely used by the indigenous American populations as a flour in bread or to make porridge. The young leaf bases can also be eaten raw or cooked. *Other uses:* A fibre from the leaves has been used to construct houses, rope and other similar items. ■

Pandanus spiralis
Pandanus (corkscrew pine, screw pine)
PANDANACEAE
Similar species: hala (*P. tectorius*)

The pandanus are not palms, though some people make this assumption; they are, in fact, more closely related to the lily family. Pandanus is a general name for about 600 species of evergreen, mostly tropical shrubs or small trees, whose flowers and fruit are usually only borne by fully mature plants. Many pandanus are grown for their ornamental, large, lance-shaped and often variegated leaves. Their other common name, corkscrew pine, is derived from their leaf arrangement as they spiral up the main stem, and for the corkscrew-shaped leaf scars left after they have fallen. Pandanus is a native and common on poorly-drained areas of northern Australia and tropical Asia. It can grow in a wide range of conditions, including swamps, floodplains and poorly drained woodland areas, and often forms dense clumps. It is one of the most useful plants in northern Australia and has been culturally, spiritually and practically used by many Aboriginal groups for, probably, many thousands of years. It has been used for its fruits and as a medicine as well as for its tough, strong fibre.

DESCRIPTION

It forms a distinctive, red-brown, occasionally single, though usually multi-stemmed, small tree, 3–7 m tall, 2–3 m spread. It tends to not have a central leader; instead, the stem regularly divides into two to form an attractive bifurcating shape. It often forms prop roots from high on the stem down to the ground when mature, and these, as well as propping it up in wind and wet soil, can obtain extra nutrients. It is fairly slow growing.

Leaves: Evergreen, long (~1–2.5 m long, ~6–8 cm wide), lance-shaped, with sharp tips and spiny leaf margins and midribs, thick, blue-green, waxy, tough, tightly arranged spirally around the main stem. They tend to become drooping as they get longer, and form an untidy tufted crown. They are renewed and lost throughout the year.

Flowers: Small, white, waxy. Trees are dioecious, so need more then one tree to get fruit. The male flowers occur in dense drooping racemes, are showier than female flowers and are pleasantly fragrant. The male flowers do not have petals or sepals, but instead have lance-shaped, white bracts. Female flowers occur in smaller rounded clusters. Both are borne at the branch tips in late spring–early summer. *Pollination:* They are bee and insect pollinated, and produce lots of nectar.

Fruit: Large, woody fruit, ~15 cm long by ~7 cm diameter, looks and is shaped like a pineapple, turns from greeny-brown to browny-red when ripe, and forms only on female trees. The fruits consist of many wedge-shaped woody segments, which have to be split open to extract the edible kernels. The nuts turn deep orange-red when ripe. They ripen from late summer–autumn.

Yield/harvest: Each fruit contains up to 15 seeds (or

kernels), and each fruiting head has up to 30 fruit. The fruits should only be harvested when fully ripe: they are very bitter when unripe. The kernels are tricky to release from the fruit; soaking can make it easier, but some physical force is often needed.

Roots: It has a dense, strong root system, and forms prop roots from the stem that reach down to the soil, and can almost push the plant out of the ground.

CULTIVATION

Can grow in a wide range of habitats, but needs a warm climate, or to be grown inside in colder weather. An easy-to-grow plant.

Location: Can be grown in full sun or semi-shade. Enjoys a humid climate. They are very tolerant of salty maritime locations, and are fairly wind tolerant.

Temperature: They are frost sensitive, and are seriously damaged by freezing temperatures. They grow best in semi-tropical–tropical climates.

Soil/water/nutrients: Can grow in a range of soil types, from sands to clays. They can also tolerate a wide pH range from fairly acid to fairly alkaline. They can tolerate waterlogging probably more than most other species described in this book, particularly when they are actively growing. However, they prefer a drier soil in winter. They can also be grown in drier areas, as long as they receive some moisture. They do not need a particularly fertile soil, but benefit from an application of a general fertiliser during the growing season.

Pot culture: Because of their growth form and frost sensitivity, these plants make a great container choice for a deck, patio or similar, and can be given protection or taken inside in colder weather. Keep the soil moist, but otherwise they need very little care.

Propagation: *Seed:* The kernels can be sown when fresh, and should germinate fairly well with warmth. The kernels germinate much better if they are removed from their woody segments, and are soaked for ~24 hours before sowing. *Suckers:* Mature plants produce basal suckers or offshoots, which can be easily removed in spring and will readily root in compost during the summer.

Pruning: None necessary.

Pests and diseases: Generally trouble free, but look out for red-spider mite and scale.

SIMILAR SPECIES

Hala, *Pandanus tectorius*. Originally a native of the Pacific Islands and northern Australia, this now grows in many other warmer climates. It is a tough adaptable plant and can grow in many locations. Its seeds have been used for thousands of years as a staple food on many Pacific islands, and other parts of the plant are used for their fibre and medicinal properties.

Description: It grows to 6–9 m tall, and mature plants often form prop roots from the main stem that help to keep it firm when growing in sand. It has a tall, stout trunk. It can become multi-stemmed and plants can then spread outwards to become as wide as they are tall. The branches emerge spirally from the spiny trunk and are borne almost

Food
The ripe nuts and other soft parts of the fruits should be either roasted or boiled, and not eaten raw. This removes any bitterness. The reported quality of their taste seems to vary from 'very pleasant' to 'not particularly tasty'. They should probably only be eaten in moderation. The fleshy bases of the leaves and young leaf tips can also be eaten, but also need to be briefly roasted.

Nutrition
The seed is high in oils and carbohydrates. The growing tip of the plant is also edible. The fleshy leaf and fruit bases contain carbohydrates.

Medicinal
Has been used as an analgesic. Extracts were used as a mouthwash for toothache and as a healing eyewash, and a poultice was used for joint and muscle pain, as well as for sores, boils, etc. **Warning:** If eaten raw, the kernels can cause diarrhoea and soreness of the mouth and throat.

Other uses
A green dye can be made from the fruit and leaves. New leaves can be soaked and stripped to make a leaf fibre, which is used for weaving bags, mats, etc. The leaves have also been used to make sails, paper, fish lures and for shelter. The Aborigines have also made jewellery from the seeds. The plant is also used to make their didgeridoo, a unique instrument with a wonderfully rich and resonant tone. It is made by removing a living section of the main trunk, immersing this in water for a period of time to soften the wood fibres, and then ramming the central pithy core out with a long stick until it is hollow. The outside of the trunk is then shaped and the inner hollow is singed with burning coals to shape and enlarge it.

Ornamental
It makes a striking, ornamental plant, either on its own or planted with other exotics. It can also be planted as a reclamation plant in poor wet soils.

horizontally. *Leaves:* Distinctive, narrow, long (~0.5–2 m long), lanceolate. Sharp spines often occur along the midribs and edges, although spineless forms are available. Older leaves fall to leave distinctive leaf scars. Leaves are grey-green, tough and fibrous. *Flowers:* Creamy-white, small, fragrant, waxy. Plants are dioecious. Female flowers are borne in rounded clusters. The male flowers are very fragrant and have large creamy-white bracts. They are borne in long, dense clusters, ~30 cm long. Both occur towards the tops of the plant and at the ends of stems. Both male and female plants can flower several times a year in warmer climates.

Although both male and female plants are needed to get good fruit-set, there are reports that plants can produce fruits parthenocarpically, without the need for fertilisation. *Pollination:* By wind and insects. *Fruit:* The female tree produces large, woody, rounded, pineapple-like fruits (~20 cm long). It is made up of 30–60 segments, 2.5–5 cm long, which consist of an outer woody end and a fleshy base. Each segment usually contains a single, but occasionally two or more, edible seeds. It can take 12 months from pollination to fruit maturity. *Yield/harvest:* Plants grown from cuttings take 4–6 years until they first produce flowers and fruits. Fruits turn from green to orange-red when ripe, and become wonderfully aromatic. They are best harvested when fully ripe.

Cultivation: *Location:* Grows well in full sun or part shade. It is very wind hardy as well as being very tolerant of coastal salt spray. *Temperature:* Prefers warmer climates, though can withstand temperatures down to freezing. *Soil/water/nutrients:* These plants can grow in pure sand and are very drought tolerant once established. They can grow in alkaline soils as well as salty soils. They need very little to no additional nutrients. *Pot culture:* Makes a good pot plant that needs minimum maintenance, and can be taken inside or given extra protection in colder areas. However, its spiny nature makes it inadvisable to site near to thoroughfares or where children are likely to play. *Propagation: Seed:* Seeds that can float are likely to be viable, those that sink probably are not. Remove kernels carefully from their segments. Can be grown from seed, and soaking the kernels for ~2 days before sowing can speed up germination. Sow kernels just beneath the surface of moist, well-drained, warm compost. Germination should take 6–8 weeks. *Cuttings:* Sections of stems, with most leaves removed, and particularly with some aerial roots, can be inserted into gritty, moist compost to root.

Uses. *Food:* The kernels, once removed from their segments, can be eaten fresh or cooked, though see the warning for Pandanus (page 311). The root tips can also be lightly cooked and eaten as a vegetable. *Medicinal:* The root tips are used medicinally as a tonic, a diuretic, a laxative and to treat skin infections and asthma; they may have an antibacterial action. The crushed leaves have been used internally to treat headaches, arthritis and stomach spasms, as well as being used externally to treat wounds. The seeds, when chewed, act as natural toothbrushes. *Other uses:* The fibrous leaves have been widely used as cord to make many articles such as hats, housing, baskets, mats, etc. *Ornamental:* An easy-to-grow popular ornamental plant. It is excellent at stabilising soil, even sandy, windswept dunes. It can be grown as an effective barrier hedge. ■

Passiflora spp.
Passion fruits
PASSIFLORACEAE

Passion fruit (*Passiflora edulis, P. edulis flavicarpa*), maypop (*P. incarnata*), sweet calabash (*P. maliformis*), banana passion fruit (*P. mollissima*), red banana passion fruit (*P. antioquiensis*), sweet granadilla (*P. ligularis*), giant granadilla (*P. quadrangularis*), water lemon passion fruit (*P. laurifolia*), incense (*P. incense*)

There are ~500 species of *Passiflora*, and they are all evergreen, vigorous climbers, and usually have exotic, interesting flowers. Most of the *Passiflora* species are native to South America, and about 50 of them have tasty fruits. In addition, the Spanish learnt of these plants' natural sedative properties from the indigenous South American populations in the mid 1500s, and introduced the vine into the warmer areas of Europe, where its leaves became popularly used as a calming herbal tea. In many European countries, and later in the USA and Canada, the passion-fruit vine has been used as a natural tranquilliser ever since. The vines have been introduced and are now grown in most tropical and subtropical parts of the world, and are of particular importance commercially in Australia, Hawaii, South Africa, New Zealand and Brazil. Australia is the largest single market for passion fruit and most is used in fruit juices. The origins of its name, the passion flower, are bizarre. The early South American missionaries thought the flowers symbolised the crucifixion, and that God placed the plant among the heathen (i.e. the native South American populations) as a teaching tool to help in their conversion. They believed that the flower's three male stamens represented the nails of the crucifixion and Christ's wounds, the filaments on the petals represented the crown of thorns, the petals and sepals stood for the Apostles and the tri-lobed leaves symbolised the Trinity.

GENERAL DESCRIPTION

A genus of climbing vines, with some being more invasive than others. They climb by tendrils, and naturally clamber up trees and shrubs. They form a woody stem as they mature. They are fairly short-lived perennials, and only live 5–7 years before becoming woody and unproductive.

Leaves: Mostly evergreen, some are semi-evergreen depending on climate. Are alternate, usually deeply three-lobed when mature, finely toothed, 7–20 cm long, glossy deep green above, paler and dull beneath, often with pointed tips.

Flowers: The flowers are usually borne singly from the leaf axils towards the ends of stems. Each flower is only open for a day, with many opening at dawn and then beginning to wilt by afternoon. The flower has an exotic appearance, with three large, green, leaf-like bracts, above which are five sepals and five petals, the colours of which vary with species. In the centre is a distinctive region of fine, stiff filaments. Within the centre are five stamens with large anthers, and a stalked, tri-branched ovary, which forms a prominent central structure. They are often fragrant. Flowering is initiated by a change to a longer day length; in the tropics and semi-tropics, where there is little variation in day length, they will flower for a much longer period. *Pollination:* The flowers are pollinated by bees and other insects, bats and hummingbirds. The flowers of many species are self-fertile, but cross pollination within and between species is common. Needs warm temperatures for the flowers to be fertile. The female stigma is often only receptive in the mornings, whereas pollen is often only produced by late morning. Therefore, hand pollination, done in the late morning, can significantly increase fruit-set, particularly in cooler regions.

Fruit: Are formed on the current season's wood. They vary in shape and colour between species, but are often rounded–egg-shaped and vary in size between 5–9 cm long. They have a tough, waxy, shiny, usually hard skin. Beneath the skin is a layer (~0.5 cm thick) of white pith, and in the central cavity are many (~250) small, dark brown seeds surrounded, in the common passion fruit, by membranous juicy sacks of fragrant, yellow–orange, delicious, tangy-sweet pulp. The seeds can be eaten with the juice.

Yield/harvest/storage: Vines grown from seed or cuttings often flower and produce fruit in the first year, but plants are fairly short lived: ~4–7 years. The fruits ripen from mid summer onwards, and take 60–80 days from fruit-set until maturity. They are ripe when the skin turns dark purple (or yellow) and fruits fall to the ground. The colour change can occur rapidly, and fruit are best harvested frequently. The fruits of most species store and keep well. For storage, spread the fruits on racks so they receive good air circulation. They easily last 2 weeks at ~10°C, and actually become sweeter as the skin begins to shrivel. Left too long though, and the inner juice dries up. Both the fruits and juice freeze well.

Roots: They have shallow, spreading roots and, therefore, benefit from a thick layer of organic mulch to retain moisture and suppress weed growth, but do not heap the mulch against the stem. Avoid cultivation near the roots.

CULTIVATION

Location: They can be sited in full sun or semi shade, although in sunny, hot climates they benefit from some shade. They are not wind hardy, and like protection from cold winds. Some species are vigorous and can be invasive: common passion fruits are not. Care is needed when siting the more vigorous species that they do not take over. They do not grow well in salty maritime locations.

Temperature: Plants can be grown in warm-temperate, subtropical or tropical climates. They are relatively frost tender, but frost-damaged plants will usually grow back from the base. Many species will withstand winter cold down to ~–12°C, and will flower in colder areas, but may not fruit if the summer is not long or hot enough. Plant against a sheltered wall or deck.

Soil/water/nutrients: Plants need a light, well-drained soil: waterlogging rapidly kills plants. Wet soil also makes the roots very susceptible to rots and cankers. If you have heavy soil then either establish plants on a mound or plant them in a container. They will grow best in a sandy, fertile loam with a pH of 5.5–7.0. Passion-fruit vines prefer a slightly acid soil, but the yellow passion vine will tolerate alkaline soils if adequate micronutrients are added. Vines need adequate moisture, particularly when young and when fruits are maturing. If allowed to dry out, the fruits are liable to drop and the skin can prematurely shrivel; however, if watered regularly, they should flower and fruit for a long period. Mulch to retain moisture, suppress weed growth and add nutrients. Passion-fruit vines need regular additions of nutrients. Apply a general, slow-release fertiliser at least twice a year between spring and late summer. However, too much nitrogen results in too much leaf growth at the expense of flowering and fruiting. Vines can develop deficiencies in potassium, calcium, zinc, magnesium and manganese (particularly in alkaline soils). It is important to keep the vines growing well: slow-growing nutrient-deficient plants, as well as not fruiting very well, are also more susceptible to disease.

Pot culture: In colder areas, or to control their spread, plants can be grown in containers against a sunny fence or wall, with their own support system, so that they can be moved inside in colder weather.

Planting: Space plants at 3–5 m apart. If tall when planting, the tops are best removed and the plants should be well watered to encourage root rather than shoot growth. Dig in plenty of organic matter and plant them in a sunny spot. Mulching with non-organic material, such as gravel or stones, will give good drainage and may help to protect and cool the roots. However, placing any mulch against the stem increases disease risk. Install any supporting structure before planting.

Pruning: Early pruning establishes a framework of leaders from which fruiting laterals can grow. Therefore, once the vine is established and it has attached itself to the support, the tips of the main leaders are pinched out. Try to prune to prevent the stems becoming tangled together. In regions with warm winters, vines can be pruned after harvest; however, in cooler areas vines should not be pruned until early spring to reduce the risk of frost damage. Annual pruning is recommended to remove tangled growth and to shorten vigorous stems to encourage the production of fruiting laterals. Although this can also remove some of the coming season's flowers and fruits, overall it will produce more vigorous fruiting growth. Fruits are formed on the current season's wood. Unless the vine is pruned, the fruit are produced further and further out, and the centre of the plant becomes a tangle of branches. Vines can be rejuvenated by cutting them back to ground level if they have become woody and straggly.

Propagation: *Seed:* Passion-fruit vines are usually grown from seed. Separate the seeds from the juice: if the juice is allowed to briefly (~48 hours) ferment in warmth, then the seeds are easier to remove. Wash the seeds and sow when fresh at ~1–1.5 cm depth, in well-drained compost. Germination takes ~10–20 days. Stored seeds take longer to germinate, and have a lower rate of germination. Soak stored seeds for ~12 hours before sowing, and germination may take several weeks. *Cuttings:* Take green cuttings in spring, or semi-ripe cuttings from non-fruiting stems in summer; they should start rooting in ~28 days (rooting hormone can increase take). Once established, grow on, with protection for the first winter in colder areas. Cuttings often produce more flowers and fruits in their first year than seedlings, but often form less vigorous plants. *Grafting:* This is a useful method to obtain hybrids and to reduce the risk of disease and pollination problems, and utilises resistant yellow passion-fruit rootstocks (e.g. *P. mollissima*). Either a cleft, whip or side-wedge graft are used. Probably best not to use the rootstock *P. caerulea* as this may have poisonous leaves, and this could be passed onto the shoot.

Pests and diseases: Purple passion-fruit vines can be attacked by nematodes; whereas yellow passion-fruit species are more nematode resistant. Nematodes are partially responsible for the short life of many vines. Root fungal rots, *Fusarium* cankers and bacterial grease spot can also be serious problems. Other more minor problems are the stink bug, leafhoppers, various mites, powdery mildew and *Anthracnose*. It is important that the soil is not wet and that the stem is not injured. Virus diseases affect many passion-fruit vines in Australia, and any vines whose leaves show mosaic or vein-clearing symptoms should be removed and destroyed. Snails can also be a problem.

MAIN EDIBLE SPECIES

Passion fruit, *Passiflora edulis, P. edulis flavicarpa.* This is the main commercial passion fruit, and it comes in two forms: the purple, *P. edulis*, and the yellow, *P. edulis flavicarpa*. The purple passion fruit is native from southern Brazil to northern Argentina; the yellow form is of unknown origin.

Description: Fairly vigorous: vines can grow 1.5–7 m per year once established, and need a strong support. Needs little maintenance. Has dark green, glossy leaves. The young stems and tendrils are tinged with red–purple, especially in the yellow form. *Flower:* Is 5–8 cm in diameter and has greenish-white sepals, white petals, a white and purple corona. The flower of the yellow passion fruit is more highly

uses

Food
The enticingly fragrant, tangy juice is excellent just scooped out and enjoyed fresh. It adds a new dimension to fruit salads, icecream, yoghurt, pie and cake fillings, juices or cocktails, somehow linking the flavour of banana with sharper tangy fruits such as citrus. Its flavour and nutrition are best when the juice is not cooked. The juice can be frozen and stored for up to a year.

Nutrition
Passion fruits have very good levels of vitamin C, e.g. the purple passion fruit has 30–130 mg/100 g of juice. Also have very good levels of vitamin A (700–1700 IU, and there are huge amounts in the yellow fruits: ~7000 IU). They are very high in potassium (the purple fruit in particular: 348 mg/100 g of fruit), with some phosphates, magnesium, iron and the B vitamins riboflavin, folate, niacin and B6. It has been found that picked fruit have higher vitamin C levels, sugar levels and acidity than fallen fruits. They also contain good levels of fibre. The seeds contain ~22% oil.

Medicinal
From historic to present times, the passion fruit (and its leaves) has been used widely as a natural sedative, as an antispasmodic and as a nerve tonic, particularly the species *P. incarnata*. It reduces spasms and acts as a painkiller by depressing the central nervous system: it helps to slow down the breakdown of neurotransmitters. The leaves and fruit are used to reduce anxiety, hyperactivity, hysteria, insomnia, irritability, muscle tension due to anxiety, narcotic-induced hangover, nervous headache, nervous tension, the anxiety of asthma, neuralgia, pain of shingles, painful menstruation, Parkinson's disease, restlessness, anxiety during menopause, gastrointestinal complaints of nervous origin and epilepsy. Most importantly, it does not have the side effects that many modern pharmaceutical drugs have. *Passiflora* is often found in many herbal-tea mixtures and medicines. It contains flavonoids and glycosides, plus several alkaloids (e.g. passiflorine). Individually, these compounds seem to actually have the opposite effect medicinally: it is only when they are combined that the plant has its sedative effects. In Madeira, the juice from the fruits is used to treat gastric cancer. It is also used as an infusion for eye strain and infections. The passion-fruit vines described here (but not *P. caerulea*, which is poisonous) are classified as safe by the FDA (Food and Drug Administration), and can be given to both children and infants. Both the leaves and fruit can be used. **Warning:** It probably should not be taken during pregnancy because of its possible stimulating effects on the muscles of the womb. A cyanogenic glycoside is found in the pulp of very young, unripe passion fruits, and these should not be eaten. In addition, the roots are said to be poisonous and should not be eaten. The leaves of *P. caerulea* are probably poisonous.

Ornamental
The vines are ideal for quickly covering structures, unsightly buildings, etc, and can be grown around a deck or trained to form an arbour or pergola. The vine also has exotic, attractive flowers and delicious fruit. But, some species are invasive, and may need tight control.

coloured. *Pollination:* Purple passion-fruit flowers are self-fertile, whereas those from yellow-fruited plants are bisexual, but are self-sterile, so need more than one plant of *P. edulis flavicarpa* to set fruits. *Fruit:* Egg shaped, 4–7.5 cm diameter, and is either dark purple or a light yellow colour when ripe. The pulp is yellow-orange and has an aromatic, musky, tangy flavour. The yellow fruits are often larger than the purple fruits, but the pulp of the purple is sweeter, is more aromatic, has a denser flavour and contains a higher proportion of juice (35–40%). There are many purple x yellow hybrids, with skin colour being variations of the two. The purple fruits mature in late summer; the yellow-fruited form flowers for longer and, so, fruits are produced from mid summer into winter. *Yield:* Get ~3.5–7 kg of fruit per plant, but this varies considerably with growing conditions.

Cultivation: The yellow-fruited form is more frost sensitive than the purple passion fruit. See general notes. Disease-wise, root rots are the main problem: grow vines in well-drained soil. See general notes for uses.

Cultivars: 'Australian Purple' ('Nelly Kelly'): Found in Australia and Hawaii. Has a mild, sweet flavour.
'Black Beauty': Vigorous vine, attractive mauve and white flowers. Dark purple fruit with juicy aromatic flavour.
'Common Purple': Thick skinned, with small seed cavity, but of good flavour and low acidity.
'Yee Selection': Yellow, round, very attractive, highly disease-resistant. Has a thick rind and low yield of juice, but it is of very good quality.
'Noel's Special': A recommended new cultivar. Has dark orange, richly flavoured juice. The vine is vigorous, begins to bear in one year, and is tolerant to brown spot.

OTHER SPECIES

Banana passion fruit (curuba), *Passiflora mollissima* (syn. *P. tomentosa* var. *mollissima*, *Tacsonia mollissima*, *P. mixta*). The name 'banana passion fruit' is given to either *P. mollissima* or *P. mixta*. They are similar and have long, oval-shaped, pale yellow fruit. Both species are very vigorous, and can be invasive when planted in some locations. The best fruit are sweet, juicy and delicious. They are native and are commonly found in the valleys of central South America. Their cultivation may have only begun shortly before the Spanish Conquest; however, today, it is commonly cultivated in South America and elsewhere, and the fruits are popular and are sold in local markets. It was grown in New Zealand for many years before its rampant nature resulted in it being classified as a banned plant.

Description: Vigorous, to 6–7 m. It has cylindrical stems that are densely coated with yellow hairs. *Leaves:* Medium sized, 7–10 cm long, downy above, greyish–yellow and velvety beneath. *Flowers:* Attractive, 5–7 cm diameter, grey-green sepals, often blushed red, with rose-coloured petals and a purple corona. *Fruit:* Egg-shaped, 5–12 cm long, with a thick, leathery skin, yellow-whitish or sometimes dark green in colour, with a fine down. The pulp is very aromatic, salmon-coloured, tangy, yet sweet and rich in flavour. Flowers in spring, but also sometimes in late summer, so it can have harvestable fruit throughout summer into late autumn.

Cultivation: It is probably more cold hardy than the common passion fruit and can tolerate short drops in temperature to –4ºC. It is native to the Andes and likes cooler, drier summers than most *Passiflora*. It can give good yields if the growing conditions are good and moisture is optimum, and will often produce 50–100 fruits. In Colombia, vines are said to produce ~300 fruits each. The first crop will be produced in 2 years. Pruning is usually minimal, and is generally only done for control purposes.

Uses: See general uses. The juice is considered by some to be the finest of all passion fruit juices; a wine is also made from it. In South America, the pulp is strained to remove the seeds, blended with milk and sugar, and served as a drink called 'sorbete de curuba'.

Giant granadilla, *Passiflora quadrangularis*. The giant of passion fruit vines. It can grow ~17 m in a single season, though does not seem to be too invasive. Its Latin name is derived from its quadrangular cross-sectioned stems. *Leaves:* Large, rounded–oval, 10–20 cm long. *Flowers:* Very large (~12–14 cm diameter), showy, has purple and white filaments against maroon-purple petals, fragrant, drooping (because of their weight) from the vine. *Pollination:* Is self-fertile and insect pollinated. Produces the best fruits in mild temperatures, and fewer fruit are set if it is too hot. Hand pollination can increase fruit-set. *Fruit:* Huge, for a passion fruit; can be 20–30 cm long, and is golden-green when ripe. They can fruit from summer into late autumn and, in good conditions, a single vine can produce up to 50–100 fruit. The fruits grow rapidly, but need regular moisture. They are rounded or oblong, with a thick, edible rind in addition to the small black seeds surrounded by pulp sacs.

Cultivation/uses: It will grow in many soil types, but not very alkaline or wet soils. They have few pest or disease problems. The pulp is purple, sweet/acid, pleasant, but not strongly flavoured. It can be cooked green like marrow, or ripened and eaten fresh. When fully ripe, is good mixed with other fruits in salads. The pulp, although somewhat bland, is cooling and refreshing.

Incense, *Passiflora incense*. A cross between maypop and *P. cincinnata*. The flowers are ~9–12 cm diameter, violet, fragrant. The pollen is sterile though, and won't fertilise other flowers. Not very vigorous. *Fruit:* Tasty, with a rose-like aroma. Hardy to ~–10°C.

Maypop, *Passiflora incarnata*. The maypop is a native of the southeastern USA. It has very tasty fruit and is the leading *Passiflora* species for its sedative properties. The juicy pulp has a tangy, apricot-like flavour.

Description: It forms a large, fast-growing, vigorous vine needing ~10–14 m of support. The vine will die back to the ground each winter if temperatures go below freezing. Established maypops produce many shoots. *Flowers:* Beautiful, large, scented, mostly white, ~3–5 cm diameter. *Pollination:* Is partly self-fertile, but cross pollination will increase yields, so it is best to establish more than one plant. *Fruit:* Yellow-green, egg-shaped, ~6 cm long.

Cultivation/uses: Can survive short frosts. Needs a well-drained soil. There is renewed interest in this species because of its sedative properties.

Red banana passion fruit (Colombian passion fruit), *Passiflora antioquiensis.* The red banana passion fruit is closely related to the banana passion fruits, except that it has very low vigour in comparison.

Description: Young leaves are narrow, whereas older, mature leaves are the familiar broader, tri-lobed shape. These latter need to have developed before the plant goes on to flower and fruit. *Flowers:* Very ornamental, large (~8–10 cm diameter) rose-pink–maroon, on pendulous stems. *Fruit:* Yellow, long (4–5 cm long), ovoid, somewhat pointed. The pulp has a very good, delicate flavour, is juicy, sweet, aromatic, pale yellow. The fruits take longer to form and mature than many *Passiflora* species, so they need a long, warm summer.

Cultivation/uses: Is more sensitive to cold than most other species. It can be grown in sun or some shade. Needs good drainage and plenty of organic matter. It looks good grown against a fence where the pendulous flowers are displayed. It can be grown as an indoor plant. *Pruning:* Prune this vine back in early spring to encourage new growth. *Uses:* See general uses.

Sweet calabash (hard-shell passion fruit), *Passiflora maliformis.* A native of northern South America and the West Indies. It is mostly cultivated and used locally.

Description: A vigorous vine, to 10 m tall. *Leaves:* May have a recurved point at their tips; light green, 6–15 cm long. *Flower:* Pretty, white and purple, fragrant, 5–6 cm diameter, with green sepals and greenish-white petals, dotted with red or purple. The corona is a mix of white, purple and blue. *Fruit:* Small (~3–5 cm diameter), apple-shaped and yellowish-brown when ripe. The skin can be very tough and difficult to open, and may be brittle or flexible. The orange-yellow juice is aromatic, musky and sweet, and contains many small black seeds. *Pests and diseases:* Noted for its resistance to pests and diseases compared with other *Passiflora* species.

Sweet granadilla, *Passiflora ligularis.* Sweet granadilla is a native and is commonly cultivated from western South America to central Mexico. It is a popular fruit in these regions, and is frequently sold in markets.

Description: Vigorous, woody at the base, tops the highest trees, can be invasive and smother the tree it is growing on. *Leaves:* Large (8–20 cm long), heart-shaped, pointed at the apex, conspicuously veined, medium-green above, pale green with a bloom beneath. *Flowers:* Late season: from summer–autumn. Very attractive, large (8–10 cm diameter), white and purple, fragrantly sweet and musky, often in pairs. Sepals are greenish-white; petals are pinkish-white; filaments are white horizontally, striped with purple-blue. In warmer areas, flowers may be borne in spring and early summer. *Fruit:* Large (6–7.5 cm long), sweet, orange-yellow with white specks when ripe. Skin is smooth, thin, hard and brittle. The pulp is white–yellow, translucent, very juicy, aromatic, good flavour, but perhaps not as tangy as some species. It sets fewer fruits than the common passion fruit, but can produce two crops a year. Does not keep well.

Cultivation/uses: Needs a strong structure to climb up. Can withstand a light frost, although probably not for extended periods at <1°C. It does not like very hot temperatures. Can grow in sun or semi-shade. *Pests and diseases:* It is resistant to root- and collar-rot and is, therefore, used as a rootstock for other passion-fruit species. *Uses:* See general notes.

Water lemon passion fruit (Jamaican honeysuckle, bell apple), *Passiflora laurifolia.* A vigorous vine, growing up to 15 m in warmer tropical areas. It has large shiny leaves, and very fragrant purple-filamented flowers. Smallish egg-shaped fruit, ~6 cm long, are deep yellow when ripe. The pulp is white, somewhat thin and watery, but sweet and aromatic. ■

Persea spp.
Avocado (alligator pear)
LAURACEAE
Relatives: laurels, camphor, cinnamon

This is one of the few edible fruit species within this genus. In ancient times, it is hypothesized that these fruits evolved to be eaten by now-extinct huge sloths, who actually consumed the whole fruits, including the stone. The latter passed through them intact and was deposited its own fertiliser source all ready for germination. Avocado trees are probably native to southern Mexico, though were being cultivated from the Rio Grande down to central Peru before the arrival of Europeans. Once 'discovered', this strange fruit was carried to many parts of the tropical, subtropical and warm-temperate regions of the world. They naturally grow into quite large trees, with handsome foliage, and have fruits with strangely textured, thick, oily flesh that does not taste like anything else, but is now widely popular and appreciated by many nations worldwide. In addition, the fruits have excellent health benefits, which have only recently become fully recognised. Although avocados are more commonly grown in the tropics and subtropics, with some winter protection from wind and frost, some cultivars can be and are successfully grown in warm temperate regions. There are three main types of avocados — Mexican, Guatemalan and West Indian, with each varying in fruit and leaf type, as well as tolerance to cold, etc.

DESCRIPTION

Trees are attractive and give an exotic effect. Their form is often erect, and they often grow to ~9 m tall, though can reach >18 m, with a trunk 30–60 cm diameter. Other trees may be shorter and have a more spreading crown, with branches beginning close to the ground. Avocados can grow for much of the year in warmer areas, though tend to just have 1–2 flushes of growth in cooler regions. The bark is dark grey-brown and, if injured, secretes a white substance.

Leaves: Mostly evergreen, though leaves may be shed during drought periods or in cold winters. Attractive, alternate, dark glossy green above, paler green beneath. Young leaves often have a reddish-bronze tinge. Are usually long and oval, with pointed tips, though can be more elliptic, varying in size from 7–40 cm long. Normally remain on the tree for 2–3 years. Leaves of West Indian cultivars are scentless, those of Guatemalan cultivars sometimes have an anise-like scent, whereas those of Mexican cultivars have a strong anise aroma when crushed. The leaves are high in oils and slow to compost.

Flowers: Small, yellowy-green, fragrant, with six petal-like lobes, nine stamens and a central, single-celled ovary. They are borne in early spring before the first seasonal growth, though a few can occur at other times. They occur in terminal panicles of 200–300 flowers, though each panicle only produces 1–3 fruits. Flowers are bisexual, containing both male and female parts, but these tend to be receptive at different times. In more tropical climates these periods often do not overlap, whereas in cooler areas receptivity overlaps more, so fertilisation is more likely. Trees also have one of two flowering types. Either the female stigma is receptive during the morning, then closes in the afternoon and doesn't open again till the following afternoon, when the male pollen from the same flower is shed, or the female is only receptive during the afternoon of the first day and the morning of the following day, with pollen from the same flower being shed in that morning. By planting both types of varieties, fruit-set can be improved because, although they produce lots of flowers, very few actually set fruit, and many of these often drop before maturing. Trees grown on their own may fail to produce many or any fruits due to poor fruit-set. Some recommend girdling the tree (see p. 36) to help retain fruit, particularly with 'Fuerte', but this can also damage and even kill trees. *Pollination:* By bees and hoverflies, and is best in warm weather: needs a minimum of ~15°C to set fruit.

Fruits: Avocados are classified as a single-seeded berry, with the inner seed consisting of an oily endosperm layer around a central ovule. The fruits are pear-shaped, oval or almost round, depending on cultivar. The skin varies in colour, but is usually dark green, and may be thin or thick and pebbled, depending on cultivar. Beneath the skin is a layer of oily, rich, pale green–cream-coloured flesh. It is a deeper green near the skin, becoming more yellowish nearer the single large, hard, inedible, ovoid seed. Mexican-type fruits are smaller (~0.25 kg) and have thin skins that turn glossy green–black when ripe. Guatemalan fruits are oval or pear-shaped, with fairly thick, pebbled, dark green fruits. West Indian fruits are the largest (~1 kg), almost round, with thick, shiny, green skin, though the oil content of their flesh is lower. Some cultivars are prone to biennial bearing (e.g. 'Hass'), and these benefit from being given more nutrients in the year prior to a large crop, and less nutrients in poor years to try and even out yields. Fruit thinning, soon after fruit-set, in bumper years may also reduce this problem.

Yield/harvest/storage: Seedlings take 4–10 years to start producing fruits; grafted trees should start producing in 2–5 years. Trees can then bear fruits for 50–100 years. Yields depend on cultivar, weather, etc., but vary between 20 and 100 kg. Avocados often take a long time to mature after fruit-set: >12 months, and even then they remain hard and inedible and never fully ripen when they are left on the tree because of a ripening inhibitor in the fruit stem. They need to be picked and kept at room temperature to ripen until they have a rich, creamy texture, or they can be placed in a bag with, e.g. bananas, which produce ethylene that aids ripening. Because fruits have to be picked to ripen, some cultivars, e.g. 'Fuerte' and 'Hass', can be left for several weeks 'to store' on the tree, and thus their season can be extended. Fruits are picked while hard, but are almost ripe, i.e. very under-ripe fruits do not develop a good flavour, but determining optimum harvest time can be tricky as any colour changes are subtle, although the fruit stem does tend to turn yellowish. Mexican fruits are quicker ripening, 6–8 months, but do not store very well; Guatemalan fruits take 12 or even 18 months to ripen, but can then be stored at ~12°C for up to 6 weeks. Any over-ripe or bruised fruits deteriorate rapidly, and the flesh becomes brown and poor tasting. In addition, the stone may become mouldy, which spreads to the flesh.

Roots: Avocados do have a taproot, but it is generally not very deep. Once established, the roots can be spreading and competitive, and can interfere with nearby plants or buildings. However, when young, their roots are notoriously susceptible to being moved or damaged, and take a considerable time to develop. Roots mostly lack the fine root hairs that most plants have to absorb water and nutrients. Instead, avocados seem to absorb through corky regions of cells at the tips of the roots and so any disturbance easily disrupts their intimate contact with the soil. Plants should be grown in long, deep, pots, which are biodegradable if possible, and planted with minimal root disturbance. Avoid mechanical cultivation around the roots to prevent damage. Trees benefit from a deep organic mulch to retain moisture, protect the roots from cold, and add nutrients as well as to suppress weeds, although this should not be stacked against the stem, particularly in grafted plants.

CULTIVATION

Location: Grows best in full sun, though can tolerate a little shade. Susceptible to wind damage, which breaks branches and reduces fruit-set and yields. It can also scar fruits, which leads to disease, bruising, etc. They can tolerate some salt, but need a sheltered spot in maritime locations as spray can burn the leaves. Some reports say they are very susceptible to too much chlorine. Once established, however, the avocado is a fairly tough tree.

Temperature: Avocados are warmer climate trees. West Indian trees can be seriously damaged at ~–1.2°C; Guatemalan trees are a little hardier, surviving short drops to ~–3°C, with Mexican trees being the hardiest and surviving –6°C. Established trees are much more cold hardy than young trees, which need extra protection. Frosts can damage early flowers, but trees sometimes re-flower later in the season, especially Mexican types.

Soil/water/nutrients: Avocados grow best in deep, fertile, well-drained loams, though can grow in a wide range of soils including clay, sand, lateritic soils or even limestone. However, they are very sensitive to poor drainage and waterlogging, and are best grown on well-drained slopes or on mounds if waterlogging is a risk. They are tolerant of somewhat acid or alkaline soils, though grow best at pH 6–7. Trees grow and produce better fruits if they receive regular moisture. West Indian cultivars prefer hotter, more humid climates, especially during flowering and fruit-setting, whereas Mexican cultivars can tolerate drier conditions. Young trees are fairly nutrient hungry and like rich, organic soils. Regular applications (~4 annually) of nutrients, particularly with added nitrogen, will give better growth. Mature trees need only one fertiliser addition in spring, during fruit-set, with a reduced nitrogen ratio. Too much nitrogen can result in excessive leaf growth at the expense of fruit production. In alkaline soils, trees can suffer from iron chlorosis, though this can be remedied with a chelated foliar spray of trace microelements, which contains iron. Boron and zinc deficiencies may also occur.

Planting: Space plants at least 6–7 m apart: branches can die back if they touch those of their neighbour. Trees benefit from an organic mulch, and from staking until established. Best sited in a protected, warm area.

Pot culture: There are a few dwarf cultivars available, which could be suitable for pot culture. To get fruit, if grown inside, you need to ensure that avocados get some cool nights, but also enough warmth during the day while flowering and setting fruit. Plant in good compost. They do not like hot roots, so ceramic pots may be preferable to plastic. Mulching the surface with bark or similar will help conserve moisture. Container plants should be occasionally leached to reduce salt build-up. Compost must be kept moist, but not too wet.

Pruning: If young trees just develop a single stem, the

uses

Food
The flesh is used in sandwiches and salads, halved and filled with all types of fillings including mayonnaise and seafood. With cream cheese and pineapple juice it can be blended as a creamy dressing for fruit salads. Mexican guacamole, a blend of the flesh with lemon or lime juice, onion, garlic, chilli or Tabasco sauce, and salt and pepper is a very popular dip. Because of its tannin content, the flesh becomes bitter if cooked. Diced avocado can be added to hot foods such as soup, stew, chilli, rice dishes or omelettes just before serving. It is delicious added to risotto-style dishes just before serving. In Brazil, the avocado is used more as a fruit and is mashed and added to sherbet, icecream or milkshakes. A New Zealand recipe for avocado icecream is a blend of avocado, lemon juice, orange juice, grated orange rind, milk, cream, sugar and salt, which is frozen, beaten until creamy, and frozen again. Some Oriental people in Hawaii also prefer the avocado sweetened with sugar and they combine it with fruits such as pineapple, orange, grapefruit, dates or banana. In Java, avocado flesh is thoroughly mixed with strong black coffee, sweetened and eaten as a dessert. Avocados are often eaten with soy sauce or grated horseradish in Japan.

Nutrition
Has a high oil content of 10–34%, depending on cultivar, which is largely monounsaturates. The only other fruit with a higher oil content is the olive. Recent clinical studies have shown that avocado oil can reduce blood cholesterol (~8%) and phospholipids, while not increasing body weight, while retaining high-density lipids ('good' cholesterol). Works better than a low-fat diet. A highly digestible food, recommended as a baby food and as a good, long-lasting energy source. The oil has excellent keeping quality, i.e. can be kept for >12 years. Avocado also has 2–4% protein, and the highest levels of potassium of most common fruits (~600 mg/100 g flesh: 1–1.5 times that of bananas). Also has good levels of iron, manganese, copper and magnesium. Avocados are high in dietary fibre. They are also high in antioxidants, supplying ~40% of the daily needs/100 g of flesh. Avocado oil is also rich in vitamins A (~600 IU in half a fruit) as well as E, plus good levels of the B vitamins, thiamine (more than most beef cuts) and riboflavin (B2), niacin (B3), pantothenic acid (B5) and pyridoxine (B6). They also have high levels of folate (half a fruit ~25–50% RDA). They contain good levels of vitamin C: 8–40 mg/100 g.

Medicinal
The seed, fruit skin and roots contain an antibiotic that prevents bacterial spoilage of food, and is the subject of two US patents. The skin has been used to expel parasites and to treat dysentery. The leaves are chewed as a remedy for pyorrhoea, and a leaf poultice can be applied to wounds, taken as a remedy for diarrhoea, sore throat, haemorrhage and for stomach disorders. The powdered seed is believed to cure dandruff. A piece of the seed or leaf placed over an aching tooth may help relieve pain. **Warning:** Unripe avocados are said to be toxic. Two resins derived from the fruit skins are toxic. Dopamine has been found in the leaves. The leaf oil contains methyl chavicol. Not all varieties are equally toxic. Ingestion of avocado leaves and/or bark has caused toxicity in cattle, horses, rabbits and goats, but, apparently, generally the animals recover. Avocado leaves in a pool have killed fish.

Other uses
The oil is included in hair dressing products, facial creams, hand lotions and fine soaps. It is said to filter out the tanning rays of the sun, is non-allergenic and is similar to lanolin in its penetrating and skin-softening action. The presence of the B vitamins is thought to help heal and restore skin. The seed yields a milky, almond-flavoured fluid that, because of its tannin content, turns red on exposure to air and makes an indelible dark red-blackish ink. The bark also yields a dye. The heartwood is pale red-brown, fine-grained, light, fairly brittle, not durable, but is easy to work and is used for turnery and carving. It takes a good polish. Honeybees love the flowers and produce a dark, thick honey.

tip can be removed to encourage a more bushy form. Most trees are usually never pruned: if branches become exposed to the sun they become susceptible to sunburn and die-back. Pruning is only necessary to shape young trees and remove diseased or damaged branches, though you can prune very vigorous stems to reduce tree height. Avocado fruits are self-thinning. Branches may need propping up to avoid breakage from the weight of fruits.

Propagation: *Seeds*: Rapidly lose their viability: ~28 days. Fresh seeds germinate in 4–6 weeks. Seeds germinate well if placed in warm, moist compost and are only partially buried. You can remove the brown seedcoat and cut a thin slice off the apex and base of the seed to aid germination. Plant by placing the wider, flatter base of the seed downwards. When roots and leaves are well formed, carefully plant seedlings in deep pots to establish before planting out. Avoid repotting to avoid root damage. Progeny from seedlings are variable. *Cuttings:* Generally difficult. *Layering:* Air-layering is successful with some cultivars, with Mexican-types rooting well. This is best done in spring and early summer. *Grafting:* Grafted or budded trees are more predictable in quality. Grafting is mainly done by whip, side- or cleft-grafting. Mexican-type rootstocks make the strongest growth, are hardier and are often used. Trees are sometimes top-worked.

Pests and diseases: Over-irrigation or heavy soils induce root rot, which is the most common cause of avocado failure, e.g. *Phytophthora*, which leads to yellowing of leaves, and can kill trees. 'Duke' is a resistant rootstock. A fungal canker, *Dothiorella*, may infect the internal tissues of trees and be serious as there is no treatment. Keep soil well drained. The addition of lime or gypsum encourages the formation of fungi that are antagonistic to rot fungi. *Verticillium* disease can cause branches to die back and forms brown-black streaking of inner wood. Leaf-roller, thrips, scale and aphids can occur. Leaf-rolling caterpillars can destroy branch terminals, and the six-spotted mite can cause leaf shedding. A virus called sun blotch can damage leaves and fruits: it is mostly spread through contaminated rootstocks or tools.

CULTIVARS

There are three main types: *Mexican* (Me): smaller fruits, large seeds. Fruits mature from summer–early autumn. There are very few 'pure' Mexican cultivars because of poorer fruit quality, and they are usually hybrids with the other types. Flesh has a high oil content: ~30%. *Guatemalan* (Gu): skin is usually hard, thick and is often gritty, has a small seed. Fruits mostly ripen from late autumn–spring, depending on the cultivar. They may be known as 'winter' or 'hardshell' avocados. Has up to 26% oil. Can be left to 'store' on the tree. *West Indies* (WI): skin is thin, smooth, leathery, pliable, has a large seed that is often loose within the centre. Fruit mature from summer–early autumn. Low oil content: ~12% oil. There are many hybrids between these three.

'Booth' (Gu x WI): There are several 'Booth' cultivars. Round–obovate, medium fruits. Skin smoothish, medium thick, brittle. Flesh has ~10% oil; seed medium–large. Late season. Good bearers. Fruits are of variable quality.

'Duke' (Me): Fruit: elongated, smallish. Skin: very thin. Flesh is excellent, ~18% oil, waxy green. Tree: large, symmetrical, wind and very cold-resistant, plus highly resistant to root rot, vigorous. Often used as a rootstock. Fruits ripen in autumn.

'Edranol' (Gu): Fruit: pear-shaped, medium size. Skin, slightly rough, thin. Flesh: good quality, nutty flavour, ~17% oil. Seed: small. Ripens in early summer. Is disease resistant.

'Fuerte' (Gu x Me): Fruit: large, pear-shaped, very high quality, ripens in early winter–spring. Skin: thin, with many small yellow dots, needs a pollinator, e.g. 'Hass'. Tree: smaller, spreading. Flesh: ~15% oil, small seed. Very productive, but can bear biennially. Cold tolerant to at least –3°C. Fruits susceptible to *Anthracnose*. Is not nutrient hungry.

'Hass' (Gu x Me): Fruit: medium size, very good flavour, ripens in spring and can 'store' on tree through summer. Skin: almost black when ripe, tough, leathery, pebbled, small seed. Precocious. Tree: large, upright. Popular cultivar. Oil ~19%. Hardy to ~–3°C. Can be pollinated by 'Fuerte'. Is fairly nutrient hungry.

'Hazzard' (Gu): Fruits: pear-shaped, medium size. Skin: rough, thin, flesh of good quality, 15–34% oil; seed small. Ripens in winter. Quite disease resistant. Tree: slow growing, only 4 m tall, precocious, regular bearing.

'Lula' (Gu x WI): Does not need cross pollination to set a good crop, fruits in autumn–winter. Large seed. Fruit: round, medium large, smooth skin, ~14% oil. Bears early and heavily; cold resistant to ~–2°C. Tree: dense, broad, prolific.

'Mexicola' (Me): Fruit: very small; skin: thin, purple-black; flesh: excellent flavour; seed: large. Bears early and regularly; very heat- and cold-resistant. Tree: tall, spreading, vigorous. Hardiest cultivar known, often used as a rootstock. Recovers rapidly from cold: defoliated at –7°C, trunk killed at ~–9°C.

'Reed' (Gu): Fruit: large, round, very high quality; skin: roughish, thick, pliable; flesh: faintly nutty flavour; seed: small–medium. Ripens late summer/autumn, but can 'store' on tree over winter. Precocious, and regular yields. Tree: erect, can be spaced more closely. Cold hardy to ~–3°C.

'Sharpless' (Gu): Fruit: slender, pear-shaped, large. Skin: slightly rough, dark purple, thick, granular; flesh: very good quality and flavour; seed small.

'Spinks' (Gu): Fruit: obovate, large; skin: rough, dark purple, thick, brittle; flesh: very good quality and flavour; seed: small. Tree: spreading. Oil ~16%. Cold hardy to ~–3°C.

'Taylor' (Gu x WI): Fruit: smallish, green, pear-shaped, high yields, ripen autumn–winter; skin: rough, has numerous small yellow dots, fairly thin; flesh: excellent quality and flavour, ~15% oil; seed: medium sized. Tree: cold hardy, very tall, slender.

OTHER SPECIES

Engkala (litsea), ***Litsea garciae.*** A native of Indonesia, which can grow in similar climates to the avocado. Can grow in warm temperate regions, with protection, or could be tried in a container in cooler climates. Likes lots of moisture. Forms an attractive, upright tree with large, oval, pointed, dark green leaves. Grows to ~10 m, and fruits in 4–6 years. Small fruits, ~2.5–4 cm wide, with pink–yellowish flesh has an excellent delicate, avocado-like flavour, but is sweeter and can be added to icecream and milkshakes. They can be also eaten in the same ways as avocado. Dipping the fruits in hot water may help them to fully ripen. The seeds contain fats that are used in the production of soaps and candles, and medicinally for skin burns. ∎

Phyllanthus emblica
(syn. *Emblica officinalis*)
Amla (myrobelan, kemloko, emblic, Indian gooseberry, aonla, dharty, ma-khaam pom)
EUPHORBIACEAE
Relatives: otaheite gooscberry, Chinese water berry

The amla is native to regions from Burma to Afghanistan, and it is now widely grown in many Asian countries such as India, Singapore and throughout Malaysia. In India, and to a lesser extent in Malaysia, the amla is important and is valued eaten fresh, as well as for its use in preserves, and it is used widely in folk medicine. Fruits from both wild and cultivated trees are gathered for their extremely high content of vitamin C. In Hindu mythology, the tree is worshipped as Mother Earth and is believed to nurture humankind because the fruits are so nourishing.

DESCRIPTION

A graceful, largish, ornamental tree that grows to ~18 m and, rarely, to 30 m. Its bark is fairly smooth, pale grey-brown and peels off in thin flakes. The branches tend to be brittle and break fairly easily. Trees are moderately fast growing in warmer areas, and are relatively long lived (~70 years).

Leaves: Although deciduous, shedding its branchlets as well as its leaves, the tree is seldom entirely bare and is, therefore, often described as an evergreen. The very small, oblong leaves, 1–2 cm long, ~0.3 cm wide, have a lemony scent when crushed, and are borne in clusters of ~100 on slender branchlets, 10–20 cm long. Young leaves in spring are reddish-bronze, turning green in 2–3 days.

Flowers: Small, inconspicuous, greenish-yellow, and are borne in compact clusters in the axils of the lower leaves in spring, although this varies with day length. In regions with less change in day length, i.e. more tropical, they may not flower until summer. Trees are usually monoecious. Some trees are dioecious, so is probably better to grow more than one tree to ensure fruit-set. Monoecious trees will also fruit better if planted with others. *Pollination:* By honeybees. Poor pollination can result in ~70% reduction of fruit-set; therefore, hand pollination is advisable.

Fruit: A round–oval drupe, 2.5–5 cm diameter, on very short stems, indented at their base, smooth, though can have 6–8 pale lines that run from the base to the apex, giving it a lobed appearance. Fruits ripen from light green to whitish or greeny-yellow, or occasionally orange-red when mature. Ripe fruits do not soften. The skin is thin and adheres to the crisp, juicy, translucent flesh. Within the centre of the flesh is a single stone, containing six small seeds. Even ripe fruits are astringent, acidic and some are bitter. Fruits take 7–8 months to ripen after fruit-set. Fruits are ready to harvest from late autumn–winter, and in areas without frost they can be 'stored' on the tree for a further 8–12 weeks.

Yield/harvest/storage: Yield varies considerably as many fruits can be lost prematurely. Yields also vary from tree to tree. Some trees can produce ~400 fruits per tree,

weighing ~10–25 kg. Seedling trees take a long time to start producing fruits: ~10 years. Grafted or budded trees start producing fruits in 5–7 years. However, trees then go on producing fruits for ~50 years. Fruits can be picked or shaken from the tree, and are best harvested when fully ripe, or they are very sour. Fruits are tolerant of handling and do not bruise easily. The fruits store fairly well, though are sometimes affected by mould as they age. Rinsing with very dilute borax or sodium chloride solutions is said to reduce this risk.

CULTIVATION

Location: Trees grow best in full sun. They can tolerate some salinity, but are not very wind tolerant.

Temperature: The amla is subtropical, though can tolerate light frosts. When established and acclimatised, it can tolerate more cold than similar semi-tropical species. However, in cooler regions, it is best planted in warm, sheltered locations, and given extra protection during cold weather. Wild specimens of this species are, apparently, very resistant to frost; unfortunately, most selected cultivars have lost this hardiness.

Soil/water/nutrients: The amla is noted for being able to grow in soil too poor for many other fruit crops. Trees do grow best in deep soils, but can grow in soil types ranging from sandy to clay. They can also grow in soils that range from slightly acidic to slightly alkaline: pH 5–7.5. At higher pH, nutrient deficiencies such as iron chlorosis can occur and need remedying with foliar applications of chelated micronutrients. They can grow in both dry and humid climates, and are quite drought tolerant once established, though will grow and fruit better with regular moisture during the growing season. Are not tolerant of waterlogging. Trees are not very nutrient hungry, though benefit from 1–2 annual additions of a balanced, complete fertiliser that contains extra nitrogen. These are best applied at fruit-set and a few months later. Older trees also grow better with additional potassium and phosphates.

Planting: Space trees at 9–12 m apart. They are best planted in soils that have had some organic matter added. Keep soil around young trees moist until they are established.

Pruning: Trees should be pruned to reduce the risk of their brittle branches breaking. Remove branches with tight crotch angles and also shorten branches that become long and are in danger of breaking under the weight of fruits. Remove any crossing or damaged branches.

Propagation: *Seeds* Should be taken from fully ripened fruits. The seeds are removed from the stone by gentle drying or cutting it carefully open. Seeds planted still within their stone will take much longer to germinate and germination is poorer. The seeds can be floated on water, and those that sink are viable. Germination is then very good and takes only 7–10 days. Seedlings grow fairly rapidly and easily. *Cuttings:* Can take root cuttings from surface rhizomatous roots, and these should establish well. *Grafting:* The Forkert or patch techniques give 85–100% success.

Chip-budding, using rootstock seedlings ~18 months old, is easier, but slightly less successful (60–80%). This is usually done in summer. Trees can also be top-worked.

Pests and diseases: Has few serious diseases, although fungi may be a problem in damper areas.

CULTIVARS

'Banarsi': From India. Fruit: medium–large, in six segments that are paired. Skin: thin; flesh: slightly fibrous, medium juicy, moderately astringent. Earliest in season. Tree: semi-spreading, light yields, tends to biennial bearing unless interplanted.

'Chakaiya': From India. Fruit: flattened at base and apex; 6–8 segments, medium sized. Flesh: fibrous. Tree: spreading, prolific. Has good yields.

'Francis': From India. Fruit: round–oval, bulged at apex; 6 segments, large. Has good crops, but fruit tend to often drop prematurely. ■

Food

Very refreshing, though sharp and acidic, ripe fruits can be eaten fresh, but only in small quantities. However, if water is drunk after eating the fruits, their taste becomes sweeter. They are very refreshing and make a good cordial. The fruits can be mixed with other sweeter fruits in fresh desserts or added to tarts, pickles, jams, relishes, etc. They are often used as a seasoning in foods in the same way as lemons or tamarinds. Their juice is used to flavour vinegar. They are high in pectin, making them ideal for jam and chutneys. In India, a sauce is made from the dried flesh, which is cooked in water, then mixed with caraway seeds, salt and yoghurt.

Nutrition

Very high levels of vitamin C; second highest level of all fruits. Has ~625 mg/100 g. Its ascorbic acid is also very stable as it is protected by tannins or anthocyanins, which retard its oxidation. Extracted juice will retain its vitamin C levels for at least a week, and only 30% is lost when heated to 65°C; but it loses most if it is boiled or, strangely, if it is refrigerated: it can then lose 40% in 7 days.

Medicinal

Phyllemblin (ethyl gallate) can be isolated from the dried fruits, and this acts as a mild central-nervous-system depressant and can reduce spasms. Recent trials have shown that extracts from the plant can lower low-density lipids and other potential cardiac-damaging compounds. They have been shown to reduce serum cholesterol levels and to have a significant anti-atherogenic effect. Additionally, the fruits have a more pronounced anti-mutagenic action than if vitamin C is taken alone, with the sum being greater than its parts. It is often used for problems with digestion such as irritable bowel syndrome. The fermented juice is prescribed for jaundice, indigestion, to remove phlegm, to treat anaemia, some cardiac problems and to overcome

the retention of urine. The fruit is considered a diuretic and laxative. The juice and infusions of the seeds have also been used as an eyewash, particularly for inflamed eyes. The seeds contain proteolytic and lipolytic enzymes, phosphatides and a small amount of essential oil, as well as ~16% oil: they are used to treat asthma, bronchitis, diabetes and fevers. The leaves have been used internally to treat indigestion, diarrhoea, but also as a mouthwash. The milky sap of the tree is applied to sores, and the plant as a whole is considered to have antiseptic, antibacterial and antifungal properties. It has been shown to be effective against, e.g. *Helicobacter pylori*, now thought to be a major cause of stomach ulcers. The flowers have been used as a refrigerant and a laxative. **Warning:** The leaves, bark and the seeds have quite a high tannin content, which in smaller amounts is beneficial, though in larger, regular dosages can act as an anti-nutrient, by precipitating proteins, and as a carcinogen.

Other uses

This oil is one of the world's oldest, natural hair conditioners and is renown for rejuvenating hair that is dull and damaged. The oil, derived from the kernels, is used as a hair-restorer and shampoo in India and the USA. In India, the kernels are soaked in coconut oil for several days to extract the oil-soluble vitamins from the fruit. The fruit and leaves yield a yellow-brown fabric dye, ink or hair dye. When sulphate of iron is added as a mordant, the colour becomes black. The tannin-rich bark and leaves are used to tan leather. Its wood is hard, flexible, red, but is subject to warping and splitting; it is used to make smaller items of furniture, implements, etc. The wood chips can be added to water to clarify it.

Ornamental

An attractive, specimen tree for its leaves and when laden with fruits.

uses

Physalis ixocarpa, P. aequata (syn. P. philadelphica)

Tomatillo (Mexican husk tomato)

SOLANACEAE

Similar species: Husk tomato (*P. pruinosa*)

Relatives: Cape gooseberry, tamarillo, naranjilla

The tomatillo is native to South America and its fruit were popular in Aztec and Mayan times. It is still often seen in local markets and grows wild around Mexico and Guatemala. Although it fruits well where the Cape gooseberry can be grown (to which it is similar), it has not achieved the same popularity, but there is potential for this plant to become more widely grown and used. Limited commercial cultivation occurs in South Africa, California and Queensland. As its name suggests, its fruits are similar to small tomatoes. The name tomato is derived from the Nahuatl word 'tomatl', which broadly means a round fruit that has juicy flesh containing many small seeds.

DESCRIPTION

The shrub is similar to tomatoes in growth and shape. It forms a sprawling, semi-annual, herbaceous plant (1–1.5 m tall), but its branches and leaves are smooth, not hairy. It germinates rapidly, and then flowers and fruits within a few weeks, but usually only lives a few months.

Leaves: Ovate, ~6 cm long, ~3 cm wide, with pointed tips and is wedge-shaped at the base, sometimes with wavy margins.

Flowers: Borne singly from leaf nodes, often from the main stem, along with a single leaf and two lateral branches. Plants can start flowering when they are only ~5 weeks old. Has a yellow, five-petalled flower (1–2 cm long) with dark brown markings near its centre. They are borne from mid–late summer. There are many tomatillo cultivars; some of these need long days before they initiate flowers, others need shorter days. Therefore, it is best to source seed locally or to select long-day cultivars for cooler regions (and viceversa). *Pollination:* A problem plant to pollinate. Unlike most Solanaceae species, it is very self-infertile, so definitely needs more than one plant for pollination. However, it will easily cross pollinate with nearby cultivars or other *Physalis* species. Pollination is by insects.

Fruit: As with other *Physalis* species, the fruit is enclosed in a distinctive, papery, pale yellow husk (the enlarged calyx). However, in contrast to the Cape gooseberry, the husk stops expanding before the berry has finished growing and so the husk has often split open by the time the fruit is ripe. The 'true' berries are round, largish (~3 cm diameter) and are green or purplish in colour. Inside, the pale yellow flesh varies from being crisp and juicy to soft, and can be sweet, sub-acid or apple-like in flavour, but has, in general, a good taste. In the fruit's centre is a pulp containing many small, edible seeds. The largest fruit are produced from the first lower flowers on the main branches. Fruits produced on lateral branches are considerably smaller. It may only take the plant ~6–16 weeks from germination to start producing the first fruits: they then produce fruits for ~6 weeks.

Yield/harvest/storage: The fruits ripen from late summer to autumn, and lots of sun and warmth speeds up and improves fruit quality. A single plant can produce 60–200 fruits in a season. An indication of their ripeness is when the husk splits open rather than a change to the skin's colour, which can vary from yellowish-green to purple. It is advisable to harvest the fruits frequently. In Mexico, the fruits are often picked when still a little unripe and are used in a range of savoury dishes. Like the tomato, the fruit can be picked before it is fully ripe and allowed to ripen in the sun. Fruits that are picked when over-ripe have less flavour. The fruits can be kept for several weeks, or even months, if stored within their husks and arranged loosely in a cool, dry place.

CULTIVATION

The cultivation of tomatillos is easy and is similar to tomatoes. They can produce a lot of fruits per plant.

Location: They like a sheltered, sunny site.

Temperature: In colder areas, as with tomatoes, they should be grown as an annual and given shelter and extra warmth, if possible. A temperature greater than 16°C is desirable.

Soil/water/nutrients: Grows well in any soil that tomatoes would grow in, so appreciates a fairly nutrient-rich soil with a pH of neutral to slightly acid. Although they prefer a moist soil, they cannot tolerate wet soils. Additional nutrients, as organic matter or as fertiliser, increases crop yields, in particular extra nitrogen and phosphates. Liquid tomato feeds could be used. Organic mulches can add nutrients and retain soil moisture.

Planting: Space plants at ~40 cm apart. They tend to sprawl, so may need some staking to keep them under control and help reduce fruit damage. Water regularly, fertilise, and keep well-mulched for best results.

Propagation: *Seed:* Usually grown from seed. Has good rates of germination and germinates in 7–10 days, even if seeds have been stored. Sow, with warmth, in spring. Grow on seedlings until late spring before planting out. Plants grown from seeds do vary, as does the quality and size of the fruits produced. *Cuttings:* Because it tends to cross pollinate with similar species, there are many forms of tomatillos. It may be worth taking cuttings from plants that produce good fruits and endeavouring to keep these going through the winter. Can be also easily grown from stem cuttings, which naturally form adventitious roots. Plants naturally form plantlets after the stems touch the ground and root.

Pruning: Larger, better-quality fruits can be obtained by pinching out some of the flowers on lateral branches as this encourages flowers nearer the main stem to develop preferentially. Removing some older leaves and some bushy sub-lateral stems enables more light to reach developing fruits within the canopy, as well as reducing the leaf:fruit ratio.

Pests and diseases: Subject to similar pests and diseases as other members of the Solanaceae family. Many diseases of the Solanaceae family remain in the soil for several years, so it is advisable to rotate their planting location around the garden. Viruses can reduce tomatillo yields by ~35%.

CULTIVARS

'Mayan Husk Tomato': From the USA. Semi-prostrate, vigorous, starts branching at ~15 cm. Fruits: round, yellow, with pale yellow, firm flesh and a mild-acid flavour.

'Pineapple Tomatillo': Plants are short, spreading, only ~80 days to crop. Fruits: sweet, tangy.

'Purple Tomatillo': Plants are vigorous, productive; fruit in ~80 days. Fruit: small, purple, sweet–tart flavour.

'Toma Verde Tomatillo': Plants are semi-climbing, easy to grow and prolific; fruits in ~80 days. Fruit: ~3 cm wide, green, sweet–tart. Recommended for salsa.

SIMILAR SPECIES

Husk tomato (strawberry tomato, ground cherry, bladder cherry, aklekengi), *Physalis pruinosa*. Another husk-covered fruit from the Solanaceae family. It is a native of South America and is similar to, but smaller than, tomatillo.

Description: Grows to ~30 cm tall. *Leaves:* Oval–heart-shaped, fuzzy. *Flowers:* Buff-yellow–white, with five brown spots inside. Are bisexual and self-fertile, so only need one plant to set fruits, though more than one plant can give

Food
Tomatillos are often eaten after being cooked, but can be eaten fresh. Are used in savoury and sweet dishes: can be stewed, fried, baked, cooked with chopped meat, made into soup, marmalade and a dessert sauce. Good in salads and curries, and are popular in salsa in Mexico, with chillies, as a dressing on tacos or enchiladas.

Nutrition
High in vitamin C and nicotinic acid, also good levels of vitamin A and potassium.

better fruit-set. Pollinated by insects. *Fruit:* Greenish-yellow (some cultivars have bright orange-scarlet fruits), ~1.5–2 cm in diameter, produced inside a papery husk. When ripe, the husk turns brown and the fruit drops from the plant. Seeds are small and edible. If left in the husk, it can keep for several weeks. Fruits mature from mid–late summer.

Cultivation: Growth and general culture are similar to tomatillo. Best planted in a sunny location, or with a little shade. Grow easily and well. Plants are usually grown as an annual, like tomatoes, but can be grown as a perennial in warmer areas. Sensitive to frost damage. *Soil:* Likes a fertile, well-drained soil that remains moist during the summer. Can grow in sandy–clay loamy soils, with a pH of slightly acid to neutral. *Planting:* Space plants at 60–90 cm apart. *Propagation:* Seeds can be sown in early spring, in warmth, starting them indoors in cooler regions. Plant out seedlings after all risk of frost has passed. *Pests and diseases:* Have few insect or disease problems. *Cultivars:* Both upright and trailing cultivars are available.

Uses: The husk is removed, and the whole fruit eaten. Fruits have a delicious, distinctive, sub-acid–sweet flavour, and can be eaten fresh or used in the same ways as fresh tomatoes, or in desserts. Can be added to jam, conserves, pies, sauces or cakes. ∎

Physalis peruviana (syn. *P. edulis*)
Cape gooseberry (golden berry, husk cherry, Peruvian ground cherry, poha)
SOLANACEAE
Strawberry tomato (*Physalis pruinosa*), Chinese lantern (*P. alkengi*)

Relatives: tomatilla, naranjilla, potato, tamarillo

A member of the *Physalis* genus, which all have a distinctive papery husk that encloses the fruit, the Cape gooseberry is native to South America and was known to the Incas. It is found growing wild in the foothills of the Andes and the highlands of Peru and Chile. Early in the 19th century, seeds

were taken to South Africa and to the Cape of Good Hope. From there it was taken to Australia, where it acquired the name of Cape gooseberry, despite it not being native to the Cape or being related to gooseberry. Although not widely cultivated, the plants deserve to be grown more frequently, both for their ease of cultivation and adaptability (being much easier to grow than tomatoes), but above all, for their relatively unknown, tangy, delicious, plentiful fruits.

DESCRIPTION
A smallish, shrubby perennial, not dissimilar in appearance to a tomato plant, though the foliage is more grey-green. Grows to a height of 0.8–2.0 m. The side branches can grow wider than the plant is tall, causing it to sprawl. The purplish branches are ribbed and covered with fine greyish hairs.

Leaves: Velvety, heart-shaped, nearly opposite, pointed, randomly-toothed, 6–15 cm long by 4–10 cm wide.

Flowers: Delicate yellow, bell-shaped, with dark purple-brown spots in the throat, ~2 cm wide, from the leaf axils.

uses

Food
The ripe, fresh fruits have an individual, tangy, delicious flavour and can be added to salads, desserts and cooked dishes, or can be used to decorate cheesecakes and cakes. It has been recommended to add Cape gooseberries to cooked apples or ginger to make a distinctive dessert. They can be stewed with honey. Chilled, the fruits provide a crisp, tart-sweet addition to many dishes. They can also be used in sauces and with meats and seafood, where they add a tasty uplifting flavour. The fruits can also be dipped in chocolate or other glazes, and make a good addition to jams and preserves. The fruits can be dried into tasty 'raisins'. The husk is discarded.

Nutrition
An excellent source of provitamin A (3000 IU of carotene/100 g) and vitamin C, as well as some of the vitamin B complex (thiamine, niacin and vitamin B2). Part of the vitamin A occurs as lutein and zeaxanthin, which can help reduce the incidence of cataracts and macular degeneration. It has very high protein and phosphorus contents for a fruit. It is rich in iron and contains flavonoids. The pulp contains a lot of pectin and pectinase, which means it is ideal for jams and preserves.

Medicinal
In Colombia, a leaf decoction has been used as a diuretic and as an anti-asthmatic. In South Africa, the heated leaves are applied as a poultice to inflammations. **Warning:** Unripe fruits can be poisonous, in the same way green tomatoes are.

Ornamental
Useful as a border plant, where the soft grey-green foliage can be used to offset other species. It can be used as a groundcover plant to protect land from erosion.

Tend to hang downwards below the leaves. Produced all summer to late autumn, or until the first frosts. Initially surrounded by a purplish-green, hairy calyx. Fruit buds are produced after 8–10 stem internodes are formed. *Pollination:* Self-fertile and easily pollinated by bees, insects and wind. In addition, you can gently shake the flowers to improve pollen distribution.

Fruit: Has an interesting appearance: after flowering, the calyx expands to form an ochre-coloured papery husk that encloses the round, yellow fruit. The fruit is a berry, and has smooth, waxy, orange-yellow skin when ripe. It is similar to a tomato, but has a slightly thicker skin. The pulp is juicy and contains many very tiny, yellowish, edible seeds. In warmer climates, the plant often flowers and fruits all year.

Yield/harvest: Fruits take 70–80 days to mature after flowering. A single plant may yield as many as 300 fruits a year, though often less. Plants can be kept productive for as long as 4 years by cutting back after each harvest, but these plants may become more susceptible to pests and diseases. The time of harvesting will depend on when it was planted: if it was planted in autumn, it should be ready to harvest the following late summer/autumn. Fruit can be ripened like tomatoes and they change from greenish-yellow to golden-yellow. This is often just visible through the husk. The husk also becomes an attractive straw-tan colour when they are ripe. Eaten before this, they are sour and may be somewhat toxic, as are green tomatoes. Harvest when the husks are dry to reduce fungal deterioration. Fruits often fall from the plant when ripe, or are only held very loosely. The fruit can be stored for several months if kept in a dry container.

CULTIVATION
Versatile and easy to grow, the Cape gooseberry is an undervalued crop.

Location: Likes a sunny spot, sheltered from strong winds. Grows well against sunny walls and trellises. Moderately tolerant of salt spray.

Temperature: Plants can be frost tender and killed at temperatures below –2°C. Because of this, it is often grown in colder areas as an annual, like the tomato. In warmer regions, it can fruit for several years. As with tomatoes, early seedlings planted out in spring, or even in autumn in warmer areas, will give a longer fruiting and growing season. They are good plants for greenhouse culture.

Soil/water/nutrients: Can grow on a range of well-drained soils, particularly poor sandy or gravelly loams. They will also grow in heavy clay, as long as it's well drained. On soils that are more fertile, there is a tendency for too much vegetative, straggly growth at the expense of fruit production, plus the fruit may not fully mature. Will grow at a wide range of pH conditions: pH 4.5–8.2. They like moist soil during spring and summer and when producing fruit, but too much moisture can encourage fungal disease, may reduce fruit-set and can split ripening fruit. Plants are quite tolerant of drought and survive better than many species, even continuing to flower and fruit, though fruit size is reduced. In very dry periods, plants may become dormant. Seems to thrive on neglect, unlike the tomato. Frequent additions of fertiliser often only result in increased plant growth at the expense of fruit production: in most situations they do not need any fertiliser. Applications of 1% KCl solution at, before and just after blooming may enhance fruit quality.

Pot culture: Great as a pot plant, though tends to be somewhat straggly.

Planting: Space at 0.5–1.5 m apart. Too much summer heat is sometimes not good for fruit development; therefore, planting in early spring, or even the autumn before, will result in earlier fruit-set.

Pruning: Very little pruning is needed. Pinching back growing shoots will encourage plants to be more compact and shorter. If growing for more than 1 year, prune back hard in spring to encourage new growth for fruiting. Plants may need staking if they become straggly.

Propagation: Seed: Usually grown from seed. Seed is small and can be mixed with fine sand or compost to aid sowing. High humidity helps germination. Seeds germinate well. *Cuttings:* Can also take cuttings from 1-year-old stems treated with a rooting hormone. Plants grown this way flower and yield well, but are less vigorous than seedlings.

Pests and diseases: Generally tend to have few problems, though in wetter soils plants can suffer various root rots and viral diseases. Powdery mildew can also occur.

Insect pests include cut worm, stem borer, leaf borer, fruit moth, flea beetle, striped cucumber beetle, white fly and aphids. Stored fruit can be affected by fungal disease.

CULTIVARS

'Giallo Grosso': Fruits: large, tasty; can be eaten fresh or used in dishes. Can live several years in milder areas.

'Giant': Fruits: large orange, ~2.5 cm diameter, delicious, tangy. Vigorous, spreading plants, ~1–1.7 m tall. Needs a long growing season.

'Giant Poha Berry': Fruits: ~2.5 cm in diameter. Leaves: fuzzy, green-grey, different from other *Physalis*. Plant is variable in size: 0.3–2.2 m tall.

'Golden Berry': Rich golden fruit, ~2.5 cm in diameter, some reaching 5 cm. Pulp is full of flavour and sweet. Its juice is said to be similar in colour and intensity of flavour to orange juice. Dried fruits are of good quality. May be fairly resistant to light frosts. In cooler climates, takes 12–18 months to begin bearing well. Said to be superior to other types.

SIMILAR SPECIES

Strawberry tomato, *Physalis pruinosa*. Similar to Cape gooseberry, but is said to be sweeter and more fragrant. Grown easily from seed, see p. 323 for further details.

Chinese lantern, *Physalis alkengi*. Similar to Cape gooseberry and requiring the same cultivation methods, but berries are red. ■

Pinus pinea and other *Pinus* spp.
Pinenuts (pinyon, umbrella nut)
PINACEAE

The *Pinus* genus is comprised of ~100 species that vary from small, spreading shrubs to very tall trees, but they all have characteristic pine needles (leaves) and cones; they are also often very tough and can live in poor soils. There are ~20 species of *Pinus* that produce kernels large enough to be edible, but only a few of these are cultivated for these seeds. The stone pine (*P. pinea*), from Europe, and the Korean pine (*P. koraiensis*), from China, are two of the main species cultivated. The stone pine (*P. pinea*) is native to the northern coastline of the Mediterranean regions, and grows from Portugal–Spain in the west, to Lebanon in the east. It has been used for many purposes as well as for its seeds, and is an important species in Italy, Spain and Portugal, with Italy producing most of the world's supply of pinenuts. The Korean pine (*P. koraiensis*) used to form large forests that spread across Europe, from Russia through Siberia and across to China, and Korea. Sadly, most of these forests have been now felled, and the pinenuts produced today represent only a tiny fraction of their former spread and popularity. Another important pinenut species is Siberian pine (*P. sibirica*), which is very cold tolerant, and produces moderate yields. Russian monks used to plant *P. sibirica* in their monasteries as sacred trees and distributed seeds to pilgrims for planting elsewhere. Others pinenut species include *P. albicaulis*, *P. armandii*, *P. ayacahuite*, *P. cembra*, *P. cembroides*, *P. coulteri*, *P. edulis*, *P. flexilis*, *P. gerardiana*, *P. jeffreyi*, *P. lambertiana*, *P. monophylla*, *P. quadrifolia*, *P. sabiniana*, *P. sabirica*, *P. torreyana*.

The cones of stone pines have probably been harvested for their edible seeds for at least half a million years, and trees have been cultivated specifically for these for at least 6000 years or longer: remains have been found in fire pits in Nevada that date back ~6000 years. In prehistoric times, the seeds were widely traded. Remains of pinenuts have been found in the ruins of Pompeii. The Romans and Greeks both believed that the seeds had aphrodisiac powers, and recommended eating them with honey and almonds at bedtime for the best results! A Roman celebrity who loved good food, and whose recipes (such as walnut-stuffed dormouse) were used up until the Middle Ages, recommends a mixture of pinenuts, cooked onions, white mustard and pepper to increase sexual potency.

DESCRIPTION

The stone pine is a large–medium-sized (10–20 m tall), fairly slow-growing attractive tree. They often form multi-stemmed spreading crowns that have an arching, upside-down-umbrella shape, with branch tips that are upswept. They form a straight trunk, with furrowed, red–brown–orange bark, in long plates. The young shoots have red-brown, scaly buds. Some pine species can live for several thousand years, with bristlecone pines probably being the oldest trees known. A specimen, named 'Methuselah' lives in California, and is estimated to be an incredible 4767 years old! However, most pine species have more modest life spans of a mere ~150 years.

Leaves: Evergreen, stiff, paired needles, 10–20 cm long, bright–light green, often twisted, with a 1–1.5-cm sheath. The needles remain on the tree for 2–4 years. Young leaves have a bluish-grey bloom, are much shorter and have a different appearance to older needles, and can remain on seedlings for several years, particularly if a young tree is damaged.

Flowers: The flowers of conifers are not classified as true flowers, and are more correctly called stobili. There are separate male and female 'flowers' on the same tree (monoecious). They are wind-pollinated. Male stobili form at the ends of new growth, are oval in shape and orange-brown when shedding pollen in early summer. The female stobili forms in clusters on the stem, below the male stobili. Because the fertilised cone takes 3 years to mature, younger cones and shoots then form beyond the fertilised cone, to leave a conveyor-belt effect of cones at differing stages of maturity along the pine branches. *Pollination:* The trees are wind-pollinated and are often self-fertile, though pollination is much better when planted in groups. They readily cross hybridise between species.

Fruit: The cones of stone pines are more chunky and rounder than some pinecone species, and have flattened bases. They are symmetrical and fairly large, 8–14 cm long, 5–10 cm diameter when closed. They are green when young, ripening to a shiny, smooth, brown, with grey tips to the rounded scales, in spring at 3 years after pollination (which is a year older than most other pine species). The scales are multi-spirally arranged up the cone, and are stiffer and harder than some pinecone secies. The wonderful patterning of the scales, both clockwise and anticlockwise, follows the intriguing Fibonacci sequence. Each scale is in two parts: a basal, infertile scale that forms within the first year, and a larger, fertile seed that forms in the second year. The seeds are larger than those of many pine species (1.5–2 cm long), pale brown and covered with a fine, dark brown fuzz, with a loosely attached yellowish wing. The cones may open while on the tree, alternatively they may drop and not open to release their seeds for up to 12 months later. The first to be shed are the infertile basal scales, followed by the large seeds. In the wild, birds disperse the seeds.

Yield/harvest/storage: Trees take ~5–6 years to start producing cones if grown in fertile conditions, but can take 10+ years to first produce a crop on poorer soils. Trees do not reach full yield potential until ~40 years old. Each stone-pine cone contains ~50–100 seeds, which comprises ~20% of the weight of the cone. A mature tree should yield 5–15 kg of kernels. Trees tend to produce bumper crops every 3–4 years. Cones are harvested when they are a rich red-brown colour, and this usually occurs in autumn. They may open on the tree, and may need harvesting before they drop or are eaten by the wildlife. A pole with a hook is useful. Cones are then gently dried in the sun, if possible, and artificially if not, to allow any closed cones to open and their seeds to be released. The kernels are covered by a thin seedcoat, which can be simply removed by sifting. For storage, they are best left in their shells and placed in a ventilated, cool, shaded place, and can then be stored for a year or more because of their low moisture content and low levels of rancid oils. Alternatively, they can be frozen.

Roots: Trees have a strong taproot, and are able to penetrate hard soil; this also enables them to be fairly drought tolerant and obtain ground water at depth. See notes on mycorrhizal fungi below.

CULTIVATION

They are tough, easy-to-grow trees and can grow in a range of environmental conditions.

Location: Trees can be very wind tolerant, and can tolerate salt: are excellent for exposed maritime locations. Once established, trees do not like disturbance. They prefer to grow in full sun.

Temperature: They grow best with hot, dry summers and cool, wet winters. They can grow in temperate, warm-temperate or Mediterranean-type climates. They can tolerate winter temperatures down to ~−22°C.

Soil/water: Pine trees will grow in almost any soil, including sand and clay, but not very alkaline soils. They prefer a pH range from ~4.5–7. They prefer well-drained soils, but can grow in wet soils, although root growth is usually reduced, and it may make the tree susceptible to disease and toppling over. Trees are drought tolerant. Although not hungry for nutrients, fertile soils will give better growth, and trees benefit from an organic mulch. Growth of pine seedlings is greatly enhanced by adding soil and decomposing leaf-litter obtained from around mature pine trees. This contains mycorrhizal fungi, which form a symbiotic relationship with the roots of the pine seedling and provide it with additional nutrients, particularly phosphates. In return, the fungi receive sugars from the tree.

Planting: Space plants at ~8 m apart for nut production, or ~5 m apart for a shelterbelt. Because they have a deep taproot, care needs to be taken when planting and transplanting seedlings.

Propagation: *Seed:* Easily propagated from seed (*P. pinea* has a ~70% germination rate), but seed is best sown when fresh, in well-drained gritty compost at a temperature of ~18°C. A short stratification (~4 weeks) can increase germination in some species. Higher temperatures (>25°C) can inhibit seedling establishment. Seedlings should not be over-watered. Carefully plant seedlings in deep, biodegradable pots to establish. *Cuttings:* Very difficult by this method. Cuttings have to be taken from trees <10 years old. Take short shoots, with their bases, from smaller branches. Removing buds from chosen shoots several weeks before taking the cutting, can help. They take a while to root. *Grafting:* Is unusual to graft conifers; however, there are some trials in Italy to do this using a cleft graft in mid summer.

Pruning: Just to remove lower branches, after trees are >3 years old, to allow access for maintenance, harvesting, grazing, etc. Pine trees cannot really be pruned as they do not resprout from a cut branch like angiosperms ('true' flowering species). It is usually better to remove the whole branch if branching is too dense around the trunk. This practice opens up the tree, allows easier harvesting and encourages phloem to fully circulate around the tree. However, pine trees should not have too much foliage removed at any one time.

Pests and diseases: Trees generally have very few problems. Look out for adelgids, which eat the stems and leaves, and leave a white, woolly exudate; also check for caterpillars and sawfly. In addition, trees can succumb to fungal disease if grown in very wet soil or have other environmental stresses. Rusts can also occur (see notes on barberry).

OTHER PINENUT SPECIES

Below are brief descriptions of a few of the other many pinenut species.

Chilgoza pine (Noosa pine), *Pinus gerardiana*. A potentially good seed species. Is naturally found in northwest Himalayas from Afghanistan to Tibet, on dry stony ground. Grows to 15–25 m, often dividing near the ground into several branches. Bark is thin and shedding. Needles are 5–10 cm long. Cones are 15–20 cm long, kernels are ~2.5 cm long. A tree can bear ~25 cones, with each cone producing 50–100 seeds. The nuts have a delicate flavour.

Food
The kernels taste their best if very lightly roasted (they can be easily over-roasted) before eating, as this removes any slight 'turpentine' taste they may have; they can also be smoked. Pinenuts have a subtle, delicious flavour. They are either eaten fresh, or can be added to numerous foods: breakfast cereals, breads, confectionery, stews, meat and vegetable dishes, curries, pastas, to make a nut butter, as a garnish on fish, stuffing, soups, sauces, in salads, pesto, coated in chocolate, etc. The oil can be extracted and is of a fine, good quality, particularly when extracted by cold pressing. The inner bark can be removed from many *Pinus* species, cut into strips and lightly boiled: it has a sweet taste.

Nutrition/medicinal
Kernels contain 12–30% protein, are rich in oil (40–60%, of which most is monounsaturated fats) and are a very good source of thiamine (B1). They contain 12–20% carbohydrate and also good levels of lecithins. Recent research in New Zealand at the University of Canterbury has identified *P. radiata* bark to contain high levels of antioxidants, the level of which seems to be largely dependent on the environment it grows in. Extracts are used to treat and prevent retinopathy (a loss of vision due to blocking of fine capillaries at the back of the eye, sometimes related to diabetes), chronic venous insufficiency and several inflammatory conditions, such as asthma, eczema and some types of arthritis. Pinenut oil contains pinolenic acid, a polyunsaturated fatty acid, which is marketed in the USA to stimulate cell proliferation, prevent hypertension, decrease blood lipid and blood sugar, and to inhibit allergic reactions. Turpentine, obtained from the resin of pine trees, is an antiseptic, diuretic, increases blood flow and eliminates internal parasites. It is a valuable remedy used internally in the treatment of kidney and bladder complaints, and externally as a rub and steam bath in the treatment of rheumatic problems and skin complaints. It is beneficial to the respiratory system, being used to treat complaints such as coughs, colds, influenza and TB.

Other uses
The resin, oleoresin, obtained by tapping pine trees, has been used to make glue, for waterproofing and for dressing wounds. However, tapping seems to reduce the cone yield, even when discontinued. The wood, although not usually of high quality, is used for many construction and coarser timber projects. The oil is used in cosmetics, as a massage oil and as a wood finish. The washings from the leaves contain turpene, a compound that inhibits the germination of seeds, so it can work as a good weed inhibitor, but, also inhibits the germination of other seeds if added to potting composts.

Ornamental
Stone pines make good specimen trees. They can be grown as a shelter belt and for erosion control, and are of benefit in poorer, dry soils, particularly in coastal locations. Do not prune off lower branches for this usage.

Colorado pinyon (single-leaf pinyon), *Pinus monophylla*. Native to western North America. Height to ~10 m. Is slow growing and long lived (>400 years). Cones take 2 years to mature. Produces good pinenuts, but are lower in oils and proteins, and higher in carbohydrates, than most other pinenuts.

Coulter's pine (big cone pine), *Pinus coulteri*. From California. Height ~13 m. Has needles in groups of three. Somewhat cold hardy. Produces huge cones: ~30 cm long, 15 cm diameter, orange-brown in colour, can weigh up to 2 kg each, with ~200 seeds. Can take 2 years to ripen, but have slow growth, taking 12+ years before they first start producing cones. The seed has a lower oil content than *P. pinea*.

Digger pine, *Pinus sabiniana*. Native to California. Height 15–25 m. Fairly fast growing, but also fairly short lived. Only moderately cold tolerant, down to ~–7°C. Often forks near the base with a sparse crown. Wiry, pale grey-green needles 17–32 cm long. Produces large cones (15–25 cm long), can remain 7 years on the tree after the nuts have fallen. Kernels ~2 cm long, but are tasty, particularly after roasting. Seed has a lower oil content than *P. pinea*. Prefers hot, dry summers. Was popular with indigenous peoples. Poor-quality timber.

Korean nut pine (cedar pine), *Pinus koraiensis*. Very hardy, fast growing. Native to eastern Asia and China. Height 30–50 m, becoming spreading with age. Cones are 7.5–15 cm long, with leathery cone scales. Kernels are ~1.3 cm long, often persistent in the cone and are of good quality. Many are exported from China. Trees have good-quality, rot-resistant timber.

Mexican nut pine, *Pinus cembroides*. Provides seeds to the US market. Difficult tree to cultivate. Grows slowly to ~10 m, likes an arid environment, hates competition. Needs wind protection, especially when young. Grows in warmer areas: does not like temperatures below ~–5°C. Was widely used by the indigenous peoples, who ground the kernels to make a paste. Kernels may have greater protein levels than other pine species. May take 20 years to crop significantly, and may only produce a main crop every 3–4 years.

Siberian pine, *Pinus sibirica*. Height >30 m. Very cold hardy. Its pinenut oil has many medicinal uses including being used to decrease blood pressure, boost the immune system, and is used externally to treat a range of skin problems. Trees produce good-quality, rot-resistant timber.

Soledad pine, *Pinus torreyana*. Native to California. Grows very fast to ~8 m, but has poor-quality nuts and timber. The cones shed their kernels while still on the tree.

Sugar pine (big pine), *Pinus lambertiana*. Large pine, to ~70 m, so an obvious problem with harvesting! Has a tall, clear trunk to the unequal-length lateral branches that give it a ragged appearance. Native to Oregon. Cones can be ~60 cm long. Kernels can be ~1.25 cm long. Gets its name from the sweet resin it produces when injured.

Swiss stone pine (arolla pine), *Pinus cembra*. Common pinenut in Europe. There are 2000-year-old trees in Russia that still produce small kernels. Very hardy and attractive, ~16 m tall, and slow growing. The kernels remain within the cones when they drop: if sown fresh they have good germination. Trees take many years before producing cones.

Two-leaved pinenut (Rocky Mountain pinyon), *Pinus edulis*. Short, slow-growing, but long lived (~400 years) mountain species, native to southwest USA. Very cold hardy: down to ~–35°C. Height to ~15 m. Delicious nut, high in fat, and contains vitamins A and D. Poor timber. Takes ~25 years to produce first cones. Cones open on the tree, so need to be picked before they fall. ■

Pistacia vera
Pistachio (pistache, green almond)
ANACARDIACEAE
Similar species: Chinese pistache (*P. chinensis*), *P. lentiscus*
Relatives: cashew, mango, ambarella, sumac, poison ivy

The pistachio is a small tree native to the Middle East. There were forests of pistachio trees on the hills and mountains from Lebanon to northern Iraq and Iran and the nuts are still collected by local tribespeople in Iran and Afghanistan. The trees are suited to these dry, hot climates and need a long, hot summer for the fruit to mature, yet also have a high chilling requirement, as evolution on mountain slopes might dictate. The nuts were used as long ago as 7000 BC. The pistachio was introduced into Italy from Syria early in the 1st century AD. Subsequently, its cultivation spread to other Mediterranean countries. After the war in Iran in 1979, most of the world's pistachio crop disappeared for a time until other commercial orchards were developed. Other major pistachio-producing areas are Turkey and, to a lesser extent, Lebanon, Syria, India, Spain, Cyprus, Greece, Italy, Pakistan, Israel, California and Australia. It is a very long-lived tree. Trees of 700 years old have been recorded, and they can also produce fruits throughout much of this time.

DESCRIPTION

It is a very slow-growing, broad, bushy, small–medium-sized (height ~8–10 m, spread ~8–10 m) tree, with a single- or multi-stemmed form. When young, pistachios have strong apical dominance, and tend to form long, gangly branches. Trees tend to do most of their growing early in the season.

Leaves: Attractive, deciduous, leathery, pinnate, 3–9 leaflets (5–10 cm long), broadly oval with entire margins, blunt leaf tips. Often has good yellow-golden autumn colour.

Flowers: Borne before the leaves. Numerous, large flower buds form in leaf axils of 1-year-old wood. Trees are dioecious, so need a minimum of one of each sex to set fruit (or a branch from a male tree can be grafted onto a female tree). Male trees are usually taller than female trees. When they open in early summer, the flowers are small, brownish-green and without petals, and are grouped together in racemes. The stigmas of female plants develop a red tinge when receptive (~4 days). The male anthers have bright yellow pollen. Unfortunately, the male flowers often open at a different time to the female flowers, so you need to select a male cultivar that will produce pollen during the short time the female flowers are receptive. *Pollination:* Fruit-set can be very poor: only ~10%. It is wind-pollinated. Pollinators (males) are often planted at about a 10:1 ratio, with a male tree within a group of female trees. Because the apical flowers open first, these are usually pollinated first, and these then release substances that inhibit flowers further down the stem from setting fruit. As a consequence, although there are numerous flowers on a female tree, only those at or near the stem tips will bear fruit.

Fruit: The pistachio is technically a drupe. It forms an oval–globose, single-seeded fruit, ~1–2 cm long, ~1.25 cm diameter. It has a fleshy, green mesocarp, within which is a hard, tan-coloured endocarp (shell). This often dehisces along its length when ripe to expose a pale–rich green kernel, with a delicious flavour. Generally, it is thought that the deeper the shade of green of the kernel, the better its flavour. The drupes are borne in clusters like grapes, from the ends of branches. Pistachio trees tend towards biennial bearing, producing a large crop one year, and very little or none the following year. During years with heavy crops of fruits, the following year's flower buds tend to prematurely drop off during the summer, making it impossible for the tree to produce a crop the following year. Therefore, thinning of fruits needs to be done early in the season of bumper years.

Yield/harvest/storage: Trees begin fruiting when they are 5–8 years old, but can take 15–20 years before they are fully bearing; however, trees then go on to produce fruits for at least another 40–60 years. The average yield is 5 kg of kernels/tree, with adult trees producing ~16 kg of hulled nuts a year (only ~30% of the hulled nut's weight is kernel). The trees also tend to form blanks: fruits without kernels, which is usually caused by embryo abortion, with some cultivars, e.g. 'Kerman', producing many blanks, ~20% of fruits. At harvest, these can be easily identified because they float. It takes ~8–10 weeks from pollination to form a full-sized nut, and then a further 4–6 weeks to ripen. Ripeness is determined by the shell sometimes splitting open, and the kernel will also become loose within its shell. Nuts can be fairly easily shaken from a tree onto a cloth spread beneath. Once harvested, the hulls are

best removed within 24 hours to reduce staining of the shell, but, more importantly, to reduce the risk of fungal aflotoxin development within the fleshy hulls. Shells can be encouraged to open (if they are not already) by briefly soaking them in water and then drying them in the sun. Although the kernels are best when fully ripe, if they are left too long on the tree they are more susceptible to being attacked by pests. The kernels store better if they are partially dried and placed in sealed bags; they can then last for 4–6 weeks in a fridge or for several months if frozen. If roasting the kernels, it is better to do this just before use, as roasted nuts tend to absorb moisture.

Roots: Trees have a deep taproot, which makes them susceptible to root rot in wetter areas, and to being transplanted, but does help make them drought hardy.

CULTIVATION

Location: Trees are best planted in full sun. They are quite wind tolerant.

Temperature: This Mediterranean plant needs both hot summers with low rainfall and a cold winter to get enough chilling time. Trees can tolerate temperatures down to ~–18°C, although late spring frosts can result in a greater number of blanks. In the wild, they grow in desert and semi-arid conditions, tolerating high temperatures (~40°C).

Chilling: Trees need ~600–1500 hours of winter temperatures below ~6°C.

Soil/water/nutrients: Trees do best on soils that are deep, well drained, but also that retain moisture, with a pH of 7–7.8. But, they can survive in a wide range of pH conditions and soil types: e.g. stony, calcareous, highly alkaline, slightly acid, saline soils, and are more tolerant of these conditions than most other commercial trees. This makes them valuable for reclamation and conservation purposes. Pistachios are probably more tolerant of alkaline and saline soil than most tree crops. They cannot tolerate wet or damp climates, mostly due to disease susceptibility. Wind and rain during pollination can reduce fruit-set. They are very drought hardy, and do not grow well in humid climates, though some moisture during the growing season is of benefit. Although this tree can grow and survive in poor soils, it does benefit from modest applications of nutrients, which increase growth and yields, but do not need much and only infrequently because of their slow growth. Fertiliser applications, with ratios of more nitrogen than phosphate or potassium, are beneficial. Zinc, magnesium and boron deficiencies sometimes occur. Adequate boron is needed for flower set and fruit development.

Food

Most pistachios are consumed as in-shell snacks. The tasty kernels can be used in confectionery, icecream, candies, desserts, dressings, casseroles and other dishes. They are, however, usually simply enjoyed as a snack, and are eaten raw or roasted. Sprinkled with salt and then roast for 20 minutes at ~140°C.

Nutrition

The kernels contain ~55% oils, but the quality and amount varies between species. Turkish and Iranian pistachios contain ~10% saturated fats, ~60% monounsaturated oils and ~25% polyunsaturated oils of the total fats present: most of the nut's oil is not saturated. They are high in protein (~20%), thiamine and have ~20% carbohydrate/fibre. They are a good source of calcium (131 mg/per 100 g serving), magnesium, vitamin A, vitamin C (30 mg/100 g kernels, which is unusual as most nuts have none or very little), and have good levels of potassium and phosphates. They also contain phytosterols. They contain no cholesterol.

Medicinal

The kernels have been used to treat sclerosis of the liver, abdominal ailments, abscesses, bruises and sores, chest ailments and circulation problems. Leaves have been used to enhance fertility in Lebanon, and the Arabs consider the nuts to be an aphrodisiac. The mastic obtained from some pistachio species is used to prevent dental disease, is made into chewing gum and is used as a blood-clotting agent.

Other uses

The hulls can be composted and used in the garden. In India, the husks are used as a dye or for tanning. The wood is of good quality and is good for carving, making cooking utensils and for furniture making.

Ornamental

Is a very drought tolerant, hardy species suitable for Mediterranean-type climates and can be planted to form a windbreak, or as a specimen tree for yellow autumn colour. Because of their ability to grow in poor saline soils the trees can be planted for reclamation and conservation purposes.

Planting: Plant trees in groups with one male per ~10 female trees. Space young trees 6–10 m apart. Because the trees grow so slowly, a faster-growing crop can be planted between them while they are establishing. Young trees tend to spread and become gangly, and may initially need staking. When planting, handle trees carefully to avoid damaging the deep taproot or any leaf buds, which are easily broken.

Pruning: It is important to prune young trees for the first 5 years to get a good, strong structure. Trees are pruned to form ~3–4 main scaffold branches that spread out around a single trunk. Because the main central leader of the tree has strong apical dominance when young, its tip needs to be removed to encourage lateral branching. The scaffold branches are selected and other competing side shoots are removed for the first ~3 years. After development of the scaffold branches, the tips of these are also removed to encourage development of secondary lateral branches. If this branching is not encouraged, then trees form long, gangly branches, fruits only set at the ends of stems, which weighs them down, and the centre of the tree is left with no lateral branches and no fruit. It is important to prune when trees are young because, as the trees matures, they form fewer vegetative buds near their stem tips, and so the removal of tips no longer has the effect of stimulating lateral branching. Instead, the tipped branches die back to their point of origin. After this initial training, little pruning is needed except to remove interfering branches and any damaged or diseased wood. Heavy pruning reduces yields.

Propagation: *Seed:* Best sown while fresh. Scarification (scoring or scratching) of seed shells speeds up and increases germination, or the seed can be soaked to remove the seedcoat (which contains germination inhibitors). Germination takes ~14–21 days at 20°C. Transplant seedlings into deep, biodegradable pots to establish. *Grafting:* The pistachio is usually propagated by T- or chip-budding or grafted onto seedling stocks of *Verticillium*-resistant *P. integerrima*, *P. atlantica* (susceptible to temperatures <–7°C), *P. terebinthus* (can tolerate below –10°C) and slower-growing, more cold sensitive *P. chinensis*. These rootstock species have good vigour and are more disease and pest resistant than most pistachio cultivars. But, grafting onto pistachios is not easy.

Pests and diseases: A number of fungi attack the pistachio, e.g. *Verticillium* wilt, which can do serious damage. Pistachios are now often grafted onto *Verticillium*-resistant *P. integerrima* rootstocks. Trees can also be attacked by the honey fungus *Armillaria mellea*. Insect pests include aphids and several species of leaf-eating bugs. The nuts are also sought by squirrels and some birds.

CULTIVARS

'Kerman': From California. Female trees are usually planted. Shells split well and are easily opened. Good-sized kernels. High quality, good yields. Does produce many blanks though. Tree is vigorous, upright–spreading. Blooms late, produces heavily, but biennially. Named after the major pistachio region of Iran.

'Peters': Male tree often planted as a pollinator. Its blossom coincides with early flowering cultivars, as well as with later-blooming 'Kerman'. Has a tendency to be gangly and somewhat weak.

SIMILAR SPECIES

Pistacia lentiscus. From the eastern Mediterranean. Its stems are tapped for a gum mastic (one of the oldest known resins), which is used in many products including medicines, perfumes, dental adhesives and high-grade varnishes. It is extensively cultivated on the Greek island of Chios. ∎

Pleiogynium timorense
(syn. *P. solandri, P. cerasiferum, P. papuanum*)
Burdekin plum (lumba, woigiek, injo wato, tulip plum)
ANACARDIACEAE
Relatives: mango, cashew, pistachio

A handsome medium–large tree that is native to Australia and Papua New Guinea, and is often found growing in woodland areas and along watercourses. The fruits have been popular with the Aborigines for thousands of years, and were also popular with the early settlers in Australia, who mostly used them in jams and jellies. The usage of the fruits then fell out of vogue, but is now undergoing a revival in interest.

DESCRIPTION
A medium–large, substantial, shapely tree, growing to ~20 m tall in good conditions. In poorer soils, with little moisture, it is often much smaller, and environmental effects can vary its shape considerably. Its bark is dark grey and is often furrowed and peeling. Seedlings are often slow growing, but then young trees start growing more rapidly.

Leaves: Evergreen, though may become deciduous in colder areas. The leaves are pinnate and consist of oval, often shiny, alternate leaflets, occurring in 2–5 pairs, with a terminal leaflet. They are a rich deep green colour and are sometimes covered with fine hair. Young leaves often have a reddish-bronze colour.

Flowers: In panicles, from leaf axils. They are greeny-yellow and insignificant. Trees are monoecious. The pale yellow, small flowers are borne in spring and form elongated clusters that hang from the leaf axils; male flower clusters are larger than those of the female. *Pollination:* By bees and insects. Trees are self-fertile, though yields may be increased if you have the space to grow more than one tree.

Fruit: Dark purple when ripe, 3–4 cm diameter, with a rounded–globose shape. The flesh is thin, and has a pleasant though sub-acid flavour. Flesh colour varies from tree to tree, with those with reddish-purple flesh being more tangy and sub-acidic, whereas those with paler greenish-white flesh are less tart, but are also less tasty. Crosses between these two colours of flesh give fruits that have the best quality. They have a woody, rounded, large, ribbed seed that fills most of the fruit's centre.

Yield/harvest/storage: Seedling trees take 7–10 years to start producing fruits, though trees then often produce large crops. Fruits ripen from autumn, through winter, into spring, depending on location. Fruits need to be harvested as late as possible, and are usually gathered once they have fallen. Because fruits never fully ripen on the tree, and to develop their best flavour, they need to be softened for several days in paper bags in the dark. The Aborigines used to bury the fruits underground for several days before eating them. Unripe fruits, if eaten, have an unpleasant drying, astringent taste.

CULTIVATION
Location: Can grow in full sun or semi-shade. Are fairly tolerant of salty conditions.

Temperature: Grows best in tropical and subtropical climates, though can tolerate temperatures towards freezing, and is grown as far south as Sydney. Some reports say they can tolerate considerable frost.

Soil/water/nutrients: Grows best in well-drained, organic, loam or sandy soils. Good growth and fruit production can be induced with regular moisture, although mature trees are quite drought tolerant. Is not very nutrient hungry, and only needs occasional additions of a complete fertiliser, although does benefit from additional potassium.

Planting: If growing as a specimen tree, space trees at least 10 m apart.

Propagation: *Seed:* Mostly grown from seed, though the hard seedcoat benefits from scarification by being scratched before being soaked in warm water for ~24 hours. They are then sown in moist, warm compost. Germination can take a while and the number of seeds that germinate can vary. *Cuttings:* Semi-ripe cuttings taken during the summer and inserted in moist, warm compost can root. *Grafting:* This may be possible, and would produce plants with reliable fruiting qualities, as well as reducing the time until fruits are produced. ∎

uses

Food
The better fruits can be eaten fresh (after ripening), and are tasty. However, they are more usually made into jams and jellies. The seeds are discarded. They can also be used to make a sauce to accompany meat or game dishes, and also make a reasonable quality wine.

Nutrition
Fruits contain some vitamin C, several minerals and are high in fibre, though nutritional content varies considerably between trees.

Other uses
The wood from fallen trees is sought after and is popular with woodturners. It has a yellow-brown colour, and is strong and dense. It is very durable, and was used for flooring, building ships and for decking.

Ornamental
Makes a handsome specimen and shade tree, and attracts many wildlife species. The flowers attract bees.

Podocarpus totara
Totara
PODOCARPACEAE
Relatives: Illawarra plum

The *Podocarpus* genus contains about 70 species, which are found mostly in the Southern Hemisphere in New Zealand, South America and Australia. They are classified as conifers, though do not have typical pine-like cones, rather, their fruits consist of a seed that extends beyond a fleshy, brightly coloured receptacle and, for this reason, they are sometimes known as plum pines. The totara is a massive, stately, handsome tree that is only native to New Zealand. Its appearance is somewhat similar to yew, but it is larger and its fruits are definitely not poisonous. It is the juicy fleshy, receptacle of these fruits that is eaten. These have been enjoyed by the Maori for thousands of years and are still sought after by children and adults, as well as by the native birds.

DESCRIPTION
A fairly slow-growing, large coniferous tree, growing to ~30 m. Mature solitary trees are magnificent. As specimen trees, the crown becomes fairly spreading and oval or pyramidal in shape. Trees growing in the bush are more upright. The branches on old trees tend to become sparse. Mature trees can develop trunks up to 2 m wide, and their bark is reddish-brown in colour and becomes distinctly thick and stringy, tending to peel off in long strips. Trees are very long lived, with some trees growing to >1000 years old. (The oldest tree in New Zealand is ~1800 years old.)

Leaves: Evergreen, and have the appearance of yew leaves. They are small, 1.5–3 cm long, narrow (~0.3 cm wide), with a sharp tip. Young leaves are a brighter green, turning olive green as they mature. The leaf veins are indistinct. They are borne more or less opposite, but lie at a variety of angles around the stem rather than in a flat plane.

Flowers: Trees are dioecious, so need both male and female trees to set fruits. The male flowers are cone-like strobili, ~1.5–2 cm long, light yellow-green in colour and consist of many scales. These are borne singly or in small clusters (of 2–5) from the leaf axils of last season's growth. Female flowers are similar, but are borne on short stalks, have much fewer scales and occur singly or in pairs at the base of the new season's leaves. *Pollination:* The male cones produce wind-borne pollen in late spring–early summer.

Fruit: Eye-catching, unusual, consisting of a plump, oval, shiny, fleshy receptacle that becomes bright red when ripe and is ~0.6 cm long. From this extends a single, oval but pointed, light yellowy-green seed. The fruits ripen during autumn.

Yield/harvest: Yields vary from being quite poor to good. Trees almost certainly take many years before they start producing fruits. Pick the receptacles of the fruits when they are bright red and juicy, but before the birds find them. Some will also drop once ripe and can be gathered that way.

Roots: Forms a large, spreading and deep root system, so is best not to plant trees too near buildings, roads, etc.

CULTIVATION
A fully hardy, tough, adaptable tree, needing little to no maintenance.

Location: They can be grown in full sun or semi-shade. They are wind tolerant and are also tolerant of maritime conditions.

Temperature: Once established and acclimatised, it is cold hardy, and grows from the sub-alpine regions of southern New Zealand to the semi-tropical climates in the north. It can tolerate temperatures down to ~–10°C or lower, once acclimatised. However, some reports question its cold hardiness, and this may depend on location, soil, length of winter, etc.

Soil/water/nutrients: Can grow in a wide range of soil types from quite sandy soils to heavy clays. They generally prefer somewhat acidic to neutral pH conditions, though may tolerate some alkalinity. Once established, they are quite drought hardy, but grow better with regular moisture.

uses

Food
The fleshy receptacle is juicy, tangy and tasty, although under-ripe fruits have a somewhat turpentine-like flavour, as do the seeds which are usually discarded. The receptacles are best eaten fresh, as a snack.
Warning: Eaten in excess they may cause constipation.

Other uses
It has very good quality wood that has been used by Maori to make canoes. It is strong, red, straight grained and resists decay, though tends to be brittle. Has many modern uses including fenceposts, flooring, construction, furniture.

Ornamental
Makes a handsome, specimen, shade tree or can be grown as a hedge or screen. Its fruits attract many types of birds, and it is a valuable wildlife tree in New Zealand.

Trees cannot tolerate extended periods of waterlogging. They are not fussy about nutrients and can grow in poor soils, although the occasional addition of organic matter or a sprinkling of a complete fertiliser will be appreciated.

Pot culture: Because of their slow growth, they can be grown in a container for many years before being planted in their final site. Trees are fairly tough and hardy, though appreciate regular moisture and some fertiliser from time to time.

Planting: Seedlings are often very slow growing to begin with, and need protection and regular weed removal while they are establishing to avoid being swamped out by competing vegetation. Plant trees 10–20 m apart for specimen trees (or further, if you have the space); alternatively, they can be planted ~1–2 m apart to form a screen or hedge.

Propagation: *Seed:* This is the main and best method of propagation. Seed is best sown fresh, with all pulp removed. Insert just below the surface in moist, but well-drained compost. Stored seed may take longer to germinate and benefits from being soaked in warm water for ~24 hours before sowing, to soften the seedcoat. Seedlings are grown on for a year or more before planting out. *Cuttings:* Semi-ripe cuttings can be taken in summer and inserted into gritty, moist compost to root. However, the rate of take is often poor.

Pruning: Trees need little to no pruning. However, they are very tolerant of pruning and can be trimmed back to form a hedge or screen.

Pests and diseases: Few problems apart from wildlife seeking out the fruits. ∎

Pouteria australis
(syn. *Planchonella australis*)
Black apple (black plum)
SAPOTACEAE
Relatives: miracle fruit, lucumo

A native of NSW and Queensland, where it is often found growing in rainforests. The Aborigines have used the large, juicy fruits for many hundreds, if not thousands, of years. Is now undergoing a revival of interest in Australia, for its fruits, and is becoming more available at nurseries and garden centres.

DESCRIPTION
A tall tree, growing to 20–30 m under good conditions, but is often smaller in cultivation. Has a fluted trunk, with a milky sap. Grows slowly but steadily.

Leaves: Attractive, dark green, smooth, shiny, leathery, simple, alternate, entire, with a milky sap.

Flowers: Small, insignificant. Are bisexual, and are probably self-fertile, so may only need one plant to set fruits. *Pollination:* By bees and insects.

Fruit: Classified botanically as a berry, despite its common names. It is purple-black when fully ripe, and looks like a large plum, ~4–6 cm long, weighing ~50 g. The flesh, when ripe, is purple, soft and quite sweet. It contains 3–5 flattish, shiny brown seeds. Fruits ripen from late spring into summer.

Yield/harvest: Trees take at least 10 years to start fruiting, but fruit production from mature trees can be good, producing several hundred fruits per season. However, trees tend towards irregular bearing, producing large crops in some years, and meagre crops in others. If this is due to overproduction in some years (and not other environmental factors), fruits can be thinned in bumper years to even out yields.

CULTIVATION
Location: Can grow in semi-shade or in full sun. Is tolerant of maritime spray and is relatively wind hardy.

Temperature: Prefers a subtropical or tropical climate,

Food
The fruits have been variously described as 'one of the most delicious of all bush foods [in Australia]', to also being 'not particularly tasty'. It is likely that fruit quality varies from tree to tree, although further selection by growers should overcome this. The fruits are usually used in jams and desserts. It is becoming a popular bush fruit in Australia and is sometimes served in restaurants.

Other uses
The wood is hard, attractive and is good for making cabinets, etc.

Ornamental
Makes an attractive, tropical-looking plant with its large dark green leaves and purple fruits. Good as a smaller specimen tree or planted within borders with plants that have contrasting coloured and shaped foliage.

uses

though could be grown in warm temperate regions in a sheltered, warm site.

Soil/water/nutrients: It grows best in moist, deep, fertile loams, though can grow in heavy clays, or also in light sandy soils. It benefits from organic matter mixed in with the soil. It can grow at a range of pH values from ~5–7.5. Trees grow better and produce better crops with regular moisture, but can be somewhat drought tolerant once established. Trees grow slowly at first, and growth can be increased by watering frequently and giving applications of a general, complete fertiliser.

Pot culture: The black apple is a good species for container cultivation. It grows slowly, and can even be raised indoors when small. It can be grown for several years as a container plant before it becomes too large. It can also be taken inside or given extra protection in cooler areas in winter.

Propagation: *Seed:* Soak fresh seeds in water overnight to soften the seedcoat and remove germination inhibitors. Sow in moist, warm compost: seeds take 21–35 days to germinate. *Cuttings:* Semi-ripe cuttings can be taken during summer and inserted in gritty, moist, warm compost to root. *Grafting:* Because trees take so long to start producing fruit,

it is ideal for grafting, and fruits should then be produced after 3–4 years.

Pests and diseases: Generally, has few problems, though scale can be an issue. In addition, the fruits can attract various wildlife.

SIMILAR SPECIES

Pouteria, *Pouteria sericea*. Native to Queensland and the Northern Territory. A bush or small tree, to ~7 m high, though often smaller in cultivation. It likes warmer climates and is more frost sensitive than black apple. It grows well in maritime locations, and is very tolerant of salt spray. Its leaves have a rusty fuzz on their under-surface. The fruits are dark purple, ~3 cm long, and the yield from trees varies from area to area. The fruit are very sweet and tasty, and can be borne almost all year round. The timber is often used to make woomeras (spear throwers) and axe handles. Can be propagated from seed, and cuttings can be tried using young stems from trees that are known to give good yields of tasty fruits. ■

Pouteria obovata (syn. *P. lucuma, P. insignis*)
Lucuma (lucmo, lucma, cinnamon apple)
SAPOTACEAE
Relatives: sapote, miracle fruit, sapodilla

Lucuma is a member of the Sapotaceae family, which contains mostly tropical plants. Most are native to various tropical regions of the world. However, the lucuma is one of the few species of this family that be grown in cooler semi-tropical or warm temperate regions, and is grown in areas such as northern California and northern New Zealand. The lucuma is native to the Andean mountains of Chile, Peru, Bolivia and Ecuador, and its fruits and wood have been used by the local peoples since ancient times. Archaeologists have found it frequently depicted on ceramics at ancient burial sites in coastal Peru. However, it has not been cultivated much elsewhere in the world outside South America, although its use has recently increased commercially in, e.g. China and the UK, where it is added to icecream. Trials for its commercial cultivation are underway in Queensland, Australia and in northern New Zealand. The lucuma is an attractive, medium-sized tree that has greeny-brown, heart-shaped fruits with yellow, dry flesh, which has an unusual sweet smell and taste, somewhat like maple syrup/butterscotch.

DESCRIPTION

A handsome tree, 8–15 m in tall, with a dense, rounded crown. Younger stems are covered with fine, velvety hairs; if broken they exude a copious, bitter, white latex.

Leaves: Evergreen, clustered at the tips of small branches, oval–elliptic in shape, blunt at the apex, pointed at the base. They are fairly large, 12.5–25 cm long, thin or slightly leathery, and are dark green on their upper surface, but pale or sometimes with fine brown velvet beneath.

Flowers: Abundant, borne singly or in small clusters (2–3) from the leaf axils. They blossom throughout much of the

year in warmer regions, though mostly in spring–summer in cooler regions. They are tubular, ~1.25 cm diameter, with 5–7 fused, yellowish-green petals, with hairy sepals. You need more than one plant to get fruit-set. *Pollination:* By bees and other insects. Also benefit from hand pollination between trees to increase fruit yields.

Fruit: Fairly large, elegantly shaped and are distinctly heart-shaped lengthways. They are 7.5–10 cm long, with a pointed (or sometimes depressed) apex. The skin is thin, delicate and variable in colour when ripe, but can be brown-green, bronze or mostly green. Inside, the flesh is firm, dry and varies from light yellow–mustard-yellow in colour. Over-ripe fruit become very soft. It is very sweet, and can taste like maple syrup/ butterscotch. In the centre are usually ~2 (but can be 1–5) rounded–flattened oval, dark brown, shiny seeds, with a small whitish region where the seed is attached to the fruit (hilum), on one of its sides. The seeds are easy to remove. A few fruits are formed parthenocarpically, without pollination, and have no seeds. Trees sometimes tend towards biennial bearing, and fruit thinning, just after fruit-set, can even out yields.

Yield/harvest: Fruit vary in size, but can be quite large, weighing up to 1 kg, and a single, healthy tree can produce ~500 fruits during a year. Fruit should only be harvested when fully coloured and ripe, and just beginning to soften. Unripe fruits are inedible and contain a bitter white latex. They ripen throughout the year in warmer regions, but in late summer– autumn in cooler areas. Fruit often drop and can be harvested as they fall. If not quite ripe, they can be kept for a few days at room temperature. The indigenous Peruvians bury them in dry hay or leaves, or similar materials, until they become soft.

Roots: Has deep roots, and needs care when planting out or transplanting. Is susceptible to waterlogging.

CULTIVATION

Location: Grows well in full sun (if not too fierce) or in semi-shade. Is not very wind tolerant. Is fairly tolerant of salt and can be grown in more sheltered maritime locations.

Temperature: This species prefers a subtropical/warm climate. It is not suited to very hot climates, or to areas with very cold winters. It can tolerate light frosts once established, but may be seriously damaged by temperatures much below ~–5°C. It needs a similar climate to that of the lemon. Young trees need protection from frost for the first few years.

Soil/water/nutrients: Grows best in deep alluvial soils that are high in organic matter, though is also naturally adapted to growing in sandy and rocky sites, but it does need well-drained soils. It is fairly drought hardy, but won't tolerate waterlogged soils or extended humid weather. It can grow at a pH range of 6–7.5, and grows fairly well in calcareous soils, though chlorosis, due to iron deficiency, is possible, and will need correcting with applications of iron chelates, as well as other micronutrients.

Propagation: *Seed:* This is the usual method, and germination is quite good. It is best sown when fresh and the

Food
The fruits are very popular locally in parts of South America, and are sold at local markets. The fruit can be eaten fresh, though are very dry and only a small amount is usually eaten in this way. The fruit has a strange aftertaste that is not to everyones liking, although others rate them highly. They have a strange, dry, flesh and its flavour has been likened to maple syrup or butterscotch, with macadamia overtones: it is very sweet. It is often added to icecream, or can be added to juice or milk-shakes. It can also be used as a pie filling and in other desserts, or made into chutney, preserves, etc. The fruits have a high starch content, and are very filling to eat. They can be easily dried and can be stored in this way for several years. Because the fruits contain so much carbohydrate they can be ground up (when dried) and used as a flour. Fresh (undried) pulp can be frozen and stored for long periods.

Nutrition
Lucuma has a surprisingly low water content for a fruit, 60–70%, but is a very good source of carbohydrate and calories. It also contains good levels of vitamin A and C, riboflavin and niacin (B3). It is a good source of iron and carotene.

Other uses
The wood is pale, dense and durable, and is used for construction. Apparently, chickens love the fruit and it promotes their growth and gives their eggs bright yellow yolks.

pulp must be thoroughly washed from the seed. Sow in well-drained gritty compost. Seedlings are best planted in deep, biodegradable pots because of their deep taproots. *Grafting*: Trees can be grafted onto their own rootstocks or those of other *Pouteria* species. ∎

Prosopis glandulosa, P. juliflora, P. pubescens, P. velutina
Mesquite (prosopis, creosote bush)
FABACEAE (Leguminosae)
Similar species: *Prosopis alba, P. chilensis*
Relatives: mimosa, carob, honey locust, tamarind

The *Prosopis* genus consists of ~45 species that are native to the warmer areas of the Americas, Australia, northern Africa and eastern Asia. Most occur in semi-arid, temperate regions. The seedpods of several species of *Prosopis* are edible

and are used as a food source. The mesquite species have spread and hybridised, which has resulted in a number of species that are all known by the common name of mesquite (see above). Sometimes considered weeds in Australia and the USA, these are tough plants with many uses, producing edible pods, which contain many medicinal properties. They are able to grow in very dry regions where few other crops can survive, and are still able to produce many pods. They can adapt to a wide range of environmental conditions, even surviving on brackish water.

DESCRIPTION

Mesquite is a slow-growing, deciduous shrub or small tree, ~5–7 m tall. Although mesquite can be confused with mimosa, a related species, they can be told apart by mimosa having more than 10 stamens per flower, whereas mesquite has 10 stamens, and mesquite spines are straight, whereas those of mimosa are curved. Mesquite branches are numerous and angular. The main trunk is often short and the bark is grey–brown, smooth when young, becoming furrowed with age. The branches bear spines: single and paired. In *P. pubescens*, the spines occur on the leaf stems; those of *P. glandulosa* occur at branch nodes.

Leaves: Deciduous, feathery, pinnate and compound; leaflets are long and narrow, oppositely arranged. Those of *P. pubescens* are often smaller than those of *P. glandulosa*. Those of *P. velutina* have grey hairs.

Flowers: Small, yellow, numerous, delicately fragrant, and are borne on a cylindrical spike, in spring–summer. Each flower has a five-petalled fused corolla and ten long stamens that extend beyond the petals. *Pollination:* They produce a lot of nectar and are popular with bees and other insects. Although both male and female structures occur in the same flower, the flowers are self-incompatible, with female flowers becoming receptive before the male pollen has been released. Therefore, it is better to grow more than one plant to ensure pollination and subsequent pod production.

Fruit: Mesquites produce flattened, leathery pods that are somewhat constricted between seeds. They do not spring open at maturity to release their seeds like those of many other leguminous species. The pods are ~10–25 cm long, ~1-2.5 cm wide, and can be very curved, almost ring shaped. Inside are several, small, bean-shaped, flattened seeds (or beans), which are separated by a spongy, edible pulp. In *P. glandulosa*, the pod is dull green; in *P. velutina*, the pod is brown and that of *P. pubescens* is coiled and yellow-brown.

Yield/harvest: Trees can yield prolific numbers of pods, particularly in dry years, i.e. a mature tree can produce ~1,000,000 seeds, or 40 kg of pods, per year. The seeds are mature when the pods have become partly dried, usually in late summer or autumn. (Green pods are harvested in early summer.) The pods can be picked from the tree or harvested from the ground once they have dropped, but need to be gathered before wildlife gets to them. The pods are then gently dried, preferably in the sun, or in an oven at ~30°C for 18 hours. Once dry, the pods can be easily crushed and the seeds removed. Plants start to produce seed after ~3 years.

Roots: Plants have long taproots, which reach down to water depth in the ground: they can grow downwards as much as 25 m. Also have a network of fine, surface roots that are able to soak up any surface moisture. The roots also form an association with nitrogen-fixing bacteria.

CULTIVATION

A tree for dry, hot areas, particularly with problem salty soils. It is a great tree for colonising, and is tough and hardy, though can become invasive.

Location: They are tolerant of salty soils and brackish water and can be grown in maritime or arid environments. They grow best in full sun.

Temperature: They are moderately frost tolerant, surviving temperatures down to ~–4°C, or even to –12°C. They are able to grow in very hot environments.

Soil: They can grow in a range of soil types such as sand, gravel, clay, limestone, and even compacted clays and hardpans. They grow best at soil pH values between 6–8, so can grow in alkaline conditions. They only require minimal rainfall, and can withstand extended periods of drought. They can even tolerate seasonal flooding. Their symbiotic relationship with nitrogen-fixing bacteria also helps them to grow in nutrient-poor soils as well.

Planting: Avoid handling or damaging the long taproots; also avoid moving plants once they are established. Space plants at ~3–4 m apart, but wider apart if the soil is poor and dry.

Propagation: *Seed:* This is the main method of propagation. In the wild, livestock often eat the pods, but are unable to digest the seeds; however, their passage through the gut is enough to germinate them, sometimes even before they pass out the other end. If the seeds are not eaten, they can lie dormant in the soil for up to 10, or even up to 40 years, but will then readily germinate if placed in manure. Seeds can be somewhat difficult to cleanly remove from the gummy pulp. Gently drying the pod makes the seed easier to separate, but do not overheat. The seeds also have a hard seedcoat that needs to be scarified (with a sharp file or similar), or softened by soaking seeds in weak acid or bleach for ~2 hours (and then thoroughly rinsed) before sowing at ~2.5–5-cm depth in moist compost. Germination takes from 14–28 days at ~30°C. Grow on seedlings in deep, biodegradable pots until they are ~30–45 cm tall, before planting out. Initially, the seedling's root growth can be ~10 times greater than that of its shoot. *Cuttings:* This method is possible, but is rarely done. Either stem or root cuttings can be used, but cuttings are fussy about light intensity and air temperatures, and often do not do very well.

P

uses

Food

The pods have a strong chocolate-cinnamon aroma, and the ripe pods and beans can be ground up and used as a flour in breads, muffins, cakes and cookies, or can be fermented to make an alcoholic beverage. The green pods can be boiled in water to make a syrup or molasses. A tea or broth can also be made from the pods. The gum around the seeds can be used to make a candy. A jelly is made from the pods, and a pleasant honey is produced from the flowers. Gum can be collected from the stems, and this is used medicinally.

Nutrition/medicinal

The pods contain 70% carbohydrates (of which 35% is sugar), 13% protein, 20% fibre and 3% fat. The mesquite species contain numerous important active ingredients. They contain a compound known to act as an antidepressant, quercetin, which has analgesic, antiallergenic, antibacterial, anti-inflammatory and antiviral activities, and a further compound that has hepato-protective activity. There are high levels of tannins within the bark, root and wood, which have antibacterial, anti-diarrhoeic and antiviral activities. These properties have been long known and utilised by the native American Indians. The branches, stems and inner yellow bark have been used as a purgative. The bark has also been used to treat bladder infections, measles and fever. The pods are used to make an eyewash; a paste from the beans is used to treat sunburn. The gum exuded from the trunk is used as an eyewash, for sores, wounds, burns, chapped fingers, sunburn, stomach ailments, diarrhoea, to settle digestion, for throat and chest infections, fever reduction, painful gums, haemorrhoids and as a purgative. The leaves are also used as an antiseptic eyewash, for intestinal problems, diarrhoea, headaches, painful gums and bladder infections. The flowers are used as a tonic to purify the blood and for skin diseases. *Warning:* Eating the seeds has been known to cause indigestion, and the pollen from its flowers can cause hay fever. The gum can cause irritation in some individuals.

Other uses

It has hard, durable red-brown heartwood that is often used for construction, tools and furniture; it is also used to smoke foods. The bark has been used to make cloth, baskets and rope. The gum is used to make face paint, dye, pottery paint and is used as a glue for mending pottery.

Ornamental

These are thorny plants and should not be planted next to paths, etc. Because of their amazing tolerance to many poor soil conditions and heat and their nitrogen-fixing ability, they are an excellent plant to use in dry, difficult soils or when a coloniser species is needed, though care should be taken that they do not become invasive.

SIMILAR SPECIES

Prosopis alba, P. chilensis. These species are native to the semi-arid regions of northwest Argentina and northern Chile. They are medium-sized, fast-growing, thorny trees (~12 m tall). Both species can grow in saline soils.

Description: *Flowers:* Numerous, greenish–yellow, in racemes. *Pods:* Beige–cream, are high in sugar (~35%) and contain 10% protein.

Uses: *Food:* The pods are often dried, ground up and used as flour; they taste somewhat like carob. A good honey is produced form the flowers. *Other uses:* The red-brown, hardwood is valued for furniture, doors and parquet floors, and has very little shrinkage. *Ornamental:* They are often grown as ornamental shade trees or thorny windbreaks in Argentina, Arizona and California. They are also planted for their medicinal gum and for apiculture. Good trees to plant in poor soils and as a coloniser species. ■

Prunus armeniaca
Apricot (golden apple)
ROSACEAE
Relatives: almond, plum, cherry, peach

Very few apricot cultivars are grown throughout the world, unlike most other commercial *Prunus* species, and almost all are derived from *P. armeniaca*. The apricot is native to northeastern China, near the Russian border, and not Armenia as its name suggests. From there, apricots were taken to central Asia. Cultivation in China dates back ~4000 years, and movement to Armenia and then to Europe was slow. The Romans introduced apricots to

Europe in 70–60 BC, through Greece and Italy. The apricot may have been the 'forbidden fruit' of the Garden of Eden, as the apple isn't adapted to grow in the arid, drier hotter climates of Biblical lands, and so whenever 'apple' occurs in the Bible, it may mean apricot. The Romans gave it the botanical name it bears today because Armenia was a renowned source of the fruit. They also called it 'malum praecocum', meaning 'early-ripening apple', with 'praecocum' meaning 'precocious', which eventually changed, via the Moors, into the English 'apricot'. Apricots arrived in England during the reign of Henry VII or Henry VIII, and were taken from there to California in the 18th century.

DESCRIPTION

Small–medium-sized trees, 3–9 m tall, 5–8 m spread, with some dwarf cultivars that are <3.5 m. Trees have a spreading, dense canopy. In cultivation, they are usually pruned to <3.5 m. The branches become gnarled with age and can break relatively easily. They have a lifespan of ~40–60 years, though fruiting becomes reduced after 10–20 years.

Leaves: Deciduous, broadly oval, with a pointed tip and tapering base, glossy, mid-green, shallowly toothed. New leaves can be reddish-bronze, turning green as they mature.

Flowers: Extremely early bloomer, the apricot has pretty, delicate blossom in early spring, although it is not as showy as some peach cultivars. Typically Rosaceae-like, ~2.5 cm in diameter, white to pinkish, saucer-shaped flowers are borne in clusters from leaf axils of 1-year-old wood or on short spurs from older wood, with spurs producing flowers and fruits for 2–3 years. Have five, simple, oval petals and many central stamens. *Pollination:* Many cultivars are self-fertile and do not require a pollinator. However, a pollinating tree can increase fruit yields.

Fruit: A drupe, about 3–4 cm wide that ripens to yellow-orange, and has a characteristic fine, felty pale yellow fuzz. Some cultivars develop a reddish-brown flush when ripe. The fruits are formed in small clusters. Their flesh is yellowish and contains a central, gnarled, hard stone, within which is the kernel, which is the equivalent of the almond nut, and these are generally not eaten (see warning below). Trees tend towards biennial bearing, and some fruits are best thinned in bumper years to even out yields and prevent meagre-fruiting years. Apricots picked from the tree, fresh and ripe, are usually sweet and tasty, and often have more character than commercially produced fruits.

Yield/harvest/storage: Yields of 15–35 kg per tree are possible, and these mostly ripen in early–mid summer. Trees can bear in 2–4 years. Fruits are best picked when fully coloured and just becoming soft. If picked when under-ripe, their flavour is not as good. Apricots tend to ripen all at once and then drop to the ground quickly after ripening, so trees need to be checked frequently around this time. They need handling carefully to avoid bruising. Apricots, once picked, last ~2–4 weeks at 0°C.

Roots: Forms quite a lot of surface roots, so avoid mechanical cultivation. An organic mulch helps conserve moisture and suppress weed growth.

CULTIVATION

Location: Does not like cold winds, and grows best in a sheltered location. Grows best in full sun, and needs sun for good fruit colour and ripening. Relatively tolerant of salt spray.

Temperature: Because they flower so early in spring, the blossoms are often damaged by frosts. Grows best in warmer temperate climates, though, with protection, can be enticed to grow in colder temperate regions. Most cultivars are not very tolerant of hard frosts and long, cold winters, though can survive brief exposures to frosts. Conversely, they do not grow well in very hot climates, or in regions with high humidity. Apricots can be cultivated in colder regions if they are hybridised with a cold hardy species, such as *P. sibirica*, and can then, reportedly, survive ~–40°C!

Chilling: Apricots need some winter chilling, usually 400–1000 hours, depending on cultivar. Insufficient chilling can result in flower buds not opening or dropping prematurely.

Soil/water/nutrients: Need fairly well-drained soil, unless they are grafted onto a plum rootstock. Grow best in deep, fertile, well-drained soils. However, apricots are moderately tolerant of high soil pH and salinity. If the soil is too acid, root growth and tree health can be affected by aluminium and manganese toxicity; conversely, if too alkaline, then manganese deficiency may occur. They grow better in drier regions: high humidity encourages brown rot. However, regular moisture during the growing season gives better tree growth and fruit quality. Trees need moderate applications of fertilisers. Too much nutrients results in increased leaf growth at the expense of fruit yield and quality. Trees do well with 1–2 applications of a general fertiliser, with micronutrients, at the beginning and midway through the growing season. Applications of bonemeal are beneficial.

Planting: Space plants at 7–8 m between trees. They are best planted against a sunny wall in colder regions. Plant carefully to avoid damaging the roots, and avoid transplanting once established.

Pruning: Trees are best trained to a vase shape, with a fairly open centre. Trees also often grow quite tall, and branches may need to be trimmed to keep the fruits within reach. Trees can be pruned fairly heavily, if required, as they often bear too many fruits and are too vigorous. In general, most new growth and crossing or tangled branches are removed annually, which also exposes the inner fruiting spurs to more sunlight. Because trees are relatively short-lived, pruning is important as it stimulates new, vigorous fruiting growth. Prune in autumn or late winter while the trees are dormant. Fruits can form on spurs of wood up to 4 years old, as well as directly on last season's growth. Because many fruits are borne on short spurs, they don't need such drastic yearly pruning as peaches or nectarines. Fruits may need thinning in bumper years. Trees are often fan-trained to grow against walls.

Propagation: *Seed:* Not usually grown from seed, though can be. It is best to remove the outer stone, if possible, to

Food

Ripe apricots can be eaten fresh, though are usually cooked and added to many desserts, jams, chutney, icecream, yoghurt, made into sauce, or are used as a garnish or an accompaniment to various savoury meat or poultry dishes. The fruits dry well and are popular in breakfast cereals, trail mixes, etc. Drying concentrates all their nutrient values several-fold. The kernels are sometimes eaten and are said to be sweet and taste like almonds, and have been used as a substitute for these nuts, though see the warning below. The seeds are eaten in China and the Mediterranean regions.

Nutrition

The fruits are very high in vitamin A (i.e. carotene, 1 apricot contains ~900 IU, or ~3000 IU/100 g of flesh), making them almost the highest source of vitamin A of all common commercial fruits. Canned apricots contain about half these levels of vitamin A. Fruits are also high in potassium. Have fairly good amounts of vitamin C: 15 mg/100 g of flesh. They contain reasonable levels of several B vitamins as well as potassium and some antioxidants. They also have good levels of dietary fibre. The oil from the seeds contains ~70% monounsaturated and polyunsaturated fats, and good levels of vitamin E.

Medicinal

The drug laetrile is derived from the seeds, and is used as a controversial therapy for cancer. There are some reports of tumour regression and pain reduction, and it is still used in therapy in Mexico. It is thought to work by breaking down to release cyanic compounds, but only when in contact with ß-glucuronidase, an enzyme that is common in tumour cells; therefore, these compounds are released preferentially at tumour sites. Apricot seeds have been used to treat tumours for ~2000 years, and apricot oil was still used to treat tumours and ulcers in England in the 1600s. Apricot seeds contain the highest amounts of these cyanogenic compounds. *Warning:* Cyanogenic glycosides, found in the seeds, bark and leaves, are dangerously toxic if eaten in excess.

Ornamental

Trees are planted as ornamental specimens or in small groups, mostly for their early spring blossoms. There are several ornamental cultivars, though fruit quality in these cultivars is reduced.

Above: Prunus armeniaca blossom.

increase germination rate and reduce germination time. The kernels may also need 1–2 months of cold stratification before sowing in moist, warm compost. Germination can still then be slow, and take >12 months. *Cuttings:* Semi-ripe cuttings, with a heel, can be taken from spring through summer, though rooting rate is poor. Dusting them with rooting hormone may improve the rate. *Grafting:* This method is the most popular. Grafting is best carried out in spring. T- or chip-budding onto a variety of seedling rootstocks is done in summer, with apricot seedlings being the most popular rootstock worldwide.

Pests and diseases: Like all stone fruits, apricots are subject to silverleaf fungal disease, brown rot and peach scab of fruit. Other problems can be red-spider mite, larvae of light brown apple moths and scale insects. If grown in drier climates, apricots have much fewer problems with

fungal disease than peaches or cherries. They shouldn't be planted where *Verticillium* wilt has been a problem: this is a serious disease and can kill the tree. It shows up as brown-black wood and yellowing of leaves as the branch dies. Remove any infected wood and destroy. Can also get apricot scab on leaves and fruit, and bacterial gummosis. Birds can be a problem.

CULTIVARS

'Blenheim' ('Royal'): Fruit: medium–large, sweet–sub-acid, firm flesh. Highly productive trees. Moderately cold hardy.
'Golden Amber': Fruit: large, fine textured, yellow flesh, firm, excellent flavour. Late-season fruits that ripen over an extended period. Trees are upright, vigorous, highly productive.
'Jordanne': Fruit: large, golden-orange, very good flavour, but needs a pollinator.
'Puget Gold': Adapted to cool summers and mild winters. A semi-dwarf cultivar. Blooms late, ripens in mid summer.

SIMILAR SPECIES

Black apricot, *Prunus dasycarpa*. A lesser-known similar species that is often grown in the Middle East. It forms a taller tree than common apricot, and is much cold hardier. The trees have large flowers, but the fruits are smaller and are a dark brown almost black colour. The flesh is soft, sub-acid–sweet and juicy, but is said to not be of equal quality to the common apricot. Propagation is good from seed, and the progeny do not vary much from the parent plant. ■

Prunus spp.
Cherry
ROSACEAE

Sweet cherry (*Prunus avium*), sour cherry (*P. cerasus*), bush cherry (*P. humilis*), Cambridge cherry (*P. pseudocerasus*), dwarf American cherry (*P. pumilla*), greyleaf cherry (*P. canescens*), holly-leaved cherry (*P. ilicifolia*), Japanese bird cherry (*P. grayana*), Korean cherry (*P. japonica*), Mongolian cherry (*P. fruiticosa*), Nanking cherry (*P. tomentosa*), rum cherry (*P. serotina*), western sand cherry (*P. besseyi*)

Cherries are hardy deciduous species that have a single stone in their centre. Most modern cherries originate from two wild forms, *Prunus avium*, the sweet cherry, and *P. cerasus*, the sour cherry, e.g. morellos. Both species are probably originally natives of Asia, but are now found growing wild in many countries. The former, as their name suggests, are delicious fresh, whereas sour cherries are often added to various cooked desserts. As well as being tasty, they are very nutritious. Cherries are known to have been cultivated by the Greeks and Romans 2000 years ago, and there are now many cultivars. There also many other wild cherry species, some of which are listed below.

GENERAL DESCRIPTION

The sweet cherry is usually grown as a single-stemmed standard tree, whereas the sour cherry can be grown as a multi-stemmed larger shrub or small tree. They have attractive often rusty-brown or grey, smooth bark that is covered by many, wide distinctive lenticels. Sweet cherries form larger trees, often 9–14 m tall, whereas sour cherries are often shrubby and 4–6 m tall. There are no dwarfing cultivars of sweet cherries, so they tend to be more suited to larger gardens. Sour cherries, in particular, tend to form many suckers, particularly if the roots are damaged, and can form a thicket. Cherries live for ~80 years and have a moderate growth rate.

Leaves: Deciduous, long, oval, with pointed tips and serrated edges. Usually deep green in colour, often glossy, smooth, thin, 8–14 cm long. Often have good red/yellow/orange autumn colour.

Flowers: Typical Rosaceae flowers, consisting of simple five-petalled, pretty, delicate white or pink flowers, in small clusters from leaf axils or on short spurs. They have numerous stamens and a central ovary. Many sour cherry cultivars are self-fertile, so only need one tree to set fruits, whereas sweet cherries are not self-fertile, and need more than one tree to set fruits. The flowers are borne in spring, often before the leaves emerge, and many cultivars are grown ornamentally for their delicate, pretty, spring blossom.

Fruits: A round, shiny, dark or lighter red drupe, though some are more yellow. Juicy, succulent flesh surrounding a central hard stone, within which is a single kernel.

Yield/harvest/storage: Seedling trees can take 6–10 years to start producing fruits (some species produce sooner). Sweet cherries are best harvested with their stems, which improves their storage life and helps prevent injury to the easily bruised fruits. Sour cherries can be picked without their stems. They are best picked when fully ripe, as they do not ripen well if picked when still hard. Cherries ripen in late summer–early autumn. Cherries do not store for very long, though can be kept for a few days in a fridge, or can be processed for longer keeping.

Roots: Cherry trees are mostly shallow-rooted so avoid deep cultivation. They also benefit from an organic mulch to retain moisture and supply additional moisture. Injury to the roots initiates suckering.

CULTIVATION

Location: Trees like to be grown in full sun, though some species tolerate light shade. They are not very tolerant of maritime conditions or of exposed locations.

Temperature: They are fairly cold hardy, tolerating cold frosts when fully dormant, but because many species come into blossom early in spring they can be susceptible to late frosts and are best not planted in frost pockets. They grow best in temperate regions.

Chilling: Need some winter chilling, 700–1400 hours, depending on species, and if they don't receive an adequate amount then flowering and leaf formation are poor. Therefore, most species do not perform well in subtropical climates.

Soil/water/nutrients: Cherries grow best in more neutral pH soils, though also do well in mildly alkaline soils. If the soil is too acid, trees are susceptible to aluminium and manganese toxicity. Conversely, alkaline soils can cause manganese and iron deficiencies. Young trees need much less nitrogen than older trees. In general, give applications of a balanced, complete fertiliser that includes potassium and phosphates in particular. Sweet cherries need better quality, deeper, more nutrient-rich soils to grow well. Trees need less moisture while dormant, but need a regular supply during spring and summer to ensure good fruit quality, though too much rain just before harvest can cause the fruit to split. Trees are not at all tolerant of waterlogging. They greatly benefit from a deep organic mulch to conserve moisture and suppress weed growth. Additions of well-rotted manure improve fruit quality and yields.

Pot culture: Cherry trees can be grown in pots, and can give good harvests. Use a large pot with good soil and limit the size of the tree with pruning. You will get beautiful spring blossom as well as fruit.

Planting: Space sweet cherry trees at ~6–10 m apart, and sour cherries at ~4–6 m apart. Incorporate organic matter with the soil when planting.

Propagation: *Seed:* Many are hybrids and do not come true from seed. Seeds are best sown fresh, though germinate better with 2–3 months of cold stratification before sowing in spring. Germination can take 18 months. Grow on seedlings for a year or so before planting out. *Cuttings:* Semi-ripe cuttings, with a heel, can be taken in summer and inserted into gritty, moist compost to root. *Suckers:* These can be dug up, with some root if possible, and potted up to establish. However, on grafted trees, these will produce plants with parentage of the vigorous rootstock rather than the grafted cultivar. *Layering:* Can be practised in spring. *Grafting:* Most trees are produced by grafting or by budding. Most are grafted onto wild cherry rootstocks.

Pruning: Cherries are usually pruned to form a single-stemmed standard tree. After initial shaping of trees, the only pruning necessary is the removal of excess twiggy growth. They do tend to form an open centre, but it is advisable to encourage a central-leader habit when the tree is young, changing to a modified-leader or open-centre system as it matures. Sweet cherries form fruits on 1-year-old wood and also short spurs of 2–4-year-old wood. Sour cherries tend to produce most fruits on last season's growth, and less on fruiting spurs. This needs to be considered when pruning. Do not prune in the wet or entry of bacterial disease and silverleaf can be increased. More horizontal branches will produce more fruit. Trees are usually pruned in early autumn.

Pests and diseases: Cherries have their fair share of problems. Bacterial canker can be a big problem and can kill trees. It multiplies within the vasculature of the tree, damages new buds and leaves, and exudes as a gummy liquid through lesions on the bark. Infection may be reduced by keeping the soil moist, even after the fruits are harvested. Many cherries are propagated onto resistant rootstocks such as Malling F12/1. Honey fungus can be a risk in some areas, as can silverleaf, which is also serious. Shot hole of the leaves, caused by a fungus, can also occur. In addition, some birds, e.g. finches, eat the flower buds and can do considerable damage; many birds love the ripening cherries. If possible, fruit needs protection with netting.

MAIN SPECIES

Sweet cherry, *Prunus avium.*
Description: Large trees, with a spread of ~10 m. Attractive rust-brown bark with distinctive, wide lenticels. *Flowers:* Prolific, white, blooming later in spring. Not self-fertile, though there are quite a few cultivars that can act as cross pollinators and a few that are universal pollinators. *Fruit:* Fruit matures in late summer. *Yield/harvest:* Can get 20–50 kg per tree.

Food
Despite the problems of growing sweet cherries, they are worth the effort for their delicious fruits. They are often expensive to buy fresh because of the time they take to harvest and their short shelf-life. Many sour cherries can also be eaten fresh, but are more usually added to various desserts, pies, conserves and sauces. Cherries also complement many savoury dishes, such as an accompaniment for duck, fish or meat. They are used to make delicious liqueurs, and can be made into wine or juiced. An edible gum can be obtained from the bark.

Nutrition/medicinal
Both fresh sweet and sour cherries have ~10 mg of vitamin C/100 g of flesh. They are high in antioxidants, being 7th in the list of common fruits. Twenty cherries provide 25 mg of anthocyanins. Anthocyanins protect artery walls from plaque build-up and heart disease. However, anthocyanins levels deteriorate during cherry processing and freezing, so fruits are best eaten fresh to get their full benefits. They are very high in vitamin A, particularly sour cherries at 1000 IU/100 g of fruit: ~10 times more than sweet cherries. Light-coloured varieties probably have less vitamin A and anthocyanins than dark-skinned varieties. A recent survey of cherry growers shows that they have a lower incidence of cancer and heart conditions than the general public, with growers eating, on average, ~3 kg of sour cherries per year. Cherries are also very effective at reducing the build-up of LDL (low-density lipoprotein). Cherries also contain perilyl alcohol, which has been shown to switch tumour cells to a less malignant form. Clinical studies indicate that it can shrink pancreatic tumours, as well as help prevent tumours of the breast, lung, liver and skin. The gum from the trunk has been used to treat coughs. **Warning:** Like all Rosaceae, the seeds, leaves and bark contain cyanic-based compounds that can be toxic if eaten in quantity, though one is unlikely to eat many cherry stones by mistake! In small amounts, these compounds are said to stimulate respiration, improve digestion and give a sense of well-being.

Other uses
A green dye can be obtained from the leaves and fruits. The wood is attractive, hard and is often used for furniture and ornamental objects.

Ornamental
Many cherries have been selected for their bountiful spring blossom, their ornamental shape and attractive bark. Fruiting cultivars, although not as attractive, also produce profuse blossom. Trees attract a wide range of wildlife.

Cultivation: See general notes. Trees don't like competition from weeds, but are also susceptible to herbicides so it is best to mow, mulch or manually remove weeds. *Pests and diseases:* See general notes above. Birds are particularly a problem. The sweet cherries can also suffer from leaf spot, brown rot of fruit and slugs.

Cultivars: 'Angela': Highly-rated flavour, very prolific, ripens in mid summer. Likes cool summers and mild winters.
'Emperor Francis': Light-coloured fruit, reliable, productive. Likes cool summers and mild winters.
'Kristin': Black fruit, ripens in mid summer; the hardiest sweet cherry.
'Lapins': Self-fruitful, will pollinate all other sweet cherries.
'Royal Ann': Large yellow fruit, highly rated fresh, but prone to crack in heavy rain. Dislikes severe heat.
'Stella': Self-fruitful, will pollinate all other sweet cherries. May be adapted to warmer areas better than most cultivars. Flowers well in warmer areas.

Sour cherry, *Prunus cerasus.* Widely cultivated in Europe and North America. In Europe, morello-type sour cherries are mostly grown, which are dark red, with a rich, dark red juice. In North America, more amorelle types are grown, which have clear juice, white flesh and a bright red skin. Amorelle cherries are less acidic than the morellos, but are still sour, and are not generally eaten fresh.

Description: Forms a rounded tree, much smaller in size than the sweet cherry. Has attractive rust-brown bark. *Flowers:* Most cultivars flower later than sweet cherries (~10–14 days later) and ripen early. Are borne mainly on 1-year-old wood. They are usually self-fertile. *Fruit:* Trees are more precocious than sweet cherries and can start fruiting in their second season. Yields of 20–50 kg/tree are possible. Fruits are picked when fully ripe and should be processed within 24 hours to prevent browning and loss of flavour. The fruits can be picked without their stalks.

Cultivation: Are hardier than sweet cherries. Can be grown where sweet cherries grow, but also in areas with milder summers and colder winters and in less fertile soils. Will grow in semi-shade. They are less susceptible to fruit splitting and rot after rain. They are very cold hardy, tolerating temperatures down to ~–20°C. *Chilling:* Need 700–1200 chill hours. *Soil:* Tolerate wet soil better than sweet cherries. Prefers a sandy soil. *Pests and diseases:* Birds are less attracted to sour cherries, particularly morellos. Sour cherries are less susceptible to bacteria and brown rot, but are susceptible to silverleaf.

Cultivars: 'English Morello': Late ripening, tolerates heat better than average, grows to ~3 m. Fruit is milder than average.
'Montmorency': An amorelle. Fruits ripen in early summer. Yields of ~20 kg/tree. Will pollinate most sweet cherries. Grows to ~5 m. Fruits are yellowish-red with clear juice.
'Northstar': A dwarfing species. Productive, ~3 m height; needs ~1000 chill hours; resists leaf spot and other fungi. The fruit is deep red.
'Richmorency': An amorelle. Matures in early summer.
'Schattenmorelle': An amorelle. Fruits mature in early summer. Yields are ~20 kg/tree.

Uses: *Food:* The fruits are sour, and can be eaten fresh, but are usually cooked in pies, desserts, cakes, confectionery, jams and used for drinks. The fruits can also be dried. Oil obtained from the seed can be used in salads, etc. *Medicinal:* Regular consumption of sour cherries can reduce the pain associated with inflammation, arthritis and gout. The production of the hormone prostaglandin is responsible for joint pain, and the production of this hormone is directly related to two enzymes. It is thought that sour cherries contain compounds that inhibit these enzymes. *Other uses:* An oil from the seed is used in cosmetics. The gum from the trunk can be used as an adhesive.

OTHER SPECIES

The general notes above also apply to these species unless specifically stated.

Bush cherry, *Prunus humilis.* A native of eastern Asia. Cultivated in China for its fruits, it forms a small shrub, ~1.5 m tall, is fairly cold hardy and grows best in full sun. The fruits, ~1.2 cm in diameter, are sour, but tasty. They may act as a diuretic and lower blood pressure.

Cambridge cherry, *Prunus pseudocerasus.* A native of eastern Asia and China, where it is sometimes cultivated for its fruits. Forms a shrub or small tree, ~3.5 m tall. It is moderately cold hardy. It flowers early in spring and fruits in early summer. The fruits are fairly large, ~1.5 cm in diameter, and are sweet. In China, the flowers buds are salted and used as a tea.

Dwarf American cherry, *Prunus pumilla.* One of the main North American cherries. It is native to eastern North America and can grow in dry sandy soils. Very cold hardy (down to ~–35°C), though grows best in full sun. Does not grow well in humid areas, where it becomes vulnerable to fungal disease. It forms a small shrub, only ~0.5 m tall. Fruits ripen in early autumn. They are ~1 cm in diameter and are usually sweet and tasty, though a few may be sour. They can be eaten fresh, added to desserts or dried for later use. A good shrub for areas with short growing seasons. Often used as a rootstock for sour cherry.

Greyleaf cherry, *Prunus canescens.* A native of eastern Asia and western China, it forms a shrub ~3 m tall. It is moderately cold hardy and can grow on fairly alkaline soils. Has good yields of fruit, ~1 cm diameter and with a pleasant flavour. Often used as a rootstock for other cherries.

Holly-leaved cherry, *Prunus ilicifolia.* A native of California, it forms a shrub or small tree, to ~4 m tall. It is not very cold hardy, and is best grown in warmer areas. Trees are fairly fast growing, but can live for >100 years. They grow best in partial shade. Trees do not flower till mid summer, and fruits do not ripen till early winter. In some years it produces many fruits, which are sour, but tasty. They can be mixed with lemon to make a sauce.

Japanese bird cherry, *Prunus grayana.* A native of eastern Asia and Japan, it forms a tree, ~8 m tall. It is moderately cold hardy, and grows best in full sun. In Japan, the small cherries and flower buds are salted, and have a pungent taste.

Korean cherry, *Prunus japonica*. A native of eastern Asia and Korea, where it is sometimes cultivated for its fruits, and forms a shrub ~1.5 m tall. They are fairly cold hardy to at least ~–15°C. Fruits are ~1.5 cm in diameter and have a sour but good taste. They are often used in pies. They are very ornamental plants, but are susceptible to die-back.

Maraschino cherry, *Prunus cerasus marasca*. A subspecies. A native of southeastern Europe and western Asia, it forms a tree ~7 m tall. It is a vigorous, very cold-hardy species, tolerating temperatures down to ~–20°C. Famous for its use in a liquor. The fruits are pleasantly acid, and can be eaten fresh.

Mongolian cherry, *Prunus fruiticosa*. Despite its name, this is probably a native of Europe, and forms a small, suckering shrub, ~1 m tall. Fruits are ~1.5 cm diameter and sour. They are usually made into preserves or dried for later use. It is fully cold hardy, and should tolerate temperatures down to ~–45°C. Can grow in fairly alkaline soils.

Nanking cherry, *Prunus tomentosa*. A native of northeastern China, where it is sometimes cultivated for its fruits. It forms a very spreading, smaller tree or shrub, 1.2–2.5 m tall, ~2–3 m spread. It is fast growing. *Flowers:* Early, white, in clusters of 2–4, are frost resistant and are borne on least season's growth. Needs cross pollination. *Fruit:* Bright red, small, with a large stone. Ripen in mid summer. Can get yields of 5–17 kg tree, but fruits do not store well. Is more cold hardy than most cherries, especially the cultivar 'Northern Limit'. *Soil:* Does not like wet or alkaline soils. Grows best on rich, well-drained soil. Can be grown in full sun, and tolerates hot summers. *Propagation:* By seed, cuttings, grafts. Plants grown from cuttings do not develop a taproot and, therefore, are drought intolerant, otherwise the plant tolerates drought. *Pests and diseases:* Minimal. Damp conditions increase the risk of leaf-spot. Fruits, ~1.2 cm diameter, are sub-acid–sweet. Unripe fruit are sour and can be pickled or are boiled in honey or used in pies. Can be grown as an ornamental, or can be pruned as a hedge. Also see general uses for sweet cherries.

Rum cherry, *Prunus serotina*. A native of many regions of North America, from Canada down to Arizona and Florida, it is fully cold hardy, but can also tolerate heat. It forms a fast-growing, large tree to ~18 m tall. Prefers to grow in moist, fertile soils in protected locations. Cultivated for its timber in central Europe. Its fruits ripen in autumn, and trees tend to have a bumper crop every ~4 years, though usually has fairly good crops. The fruits need to be fully ripe when eaten or they are sour–bitter. When ripe, the fruits, ~1 cm diameter, are usually pleasant and tasty, and are often used as a flavouring. They do not start fruiting well until ~10 years old, but can then continue fruiting for ~100 years. An extract from the bark of this species is used commercially in drinks, confectionery, etc. The wood is light, strong, shock-resistant, seasons well and is popular for making furniture, cabinets, panelling, etc.

Western sand cherry, *Prunus besseyi*. A native of central North America, it forms a small, cold-hardy shrub, to ~1.2 m tall. It has small black, sour fruits, which are sweetish when fully ripe. Fruits can be dried. Is extremely cold hardy, tolerating temperatures down to ~–50°C. There are selected strains with superior fruits, e.g. 'Black Beauty' and 'Hansens'. Sometimes used as a rootstock for plums. ∎

Prunus dulcis (syn. *Amygdalus communis*)
Almond
ROSACEAE
Relatives: rose, cherry, peach, plum

The almond is native to the eastern areas around the Mediterranean, from Turkey to northern Greece and North Africa. It has been cultivated for a long time: it was known to have been grown in China in the 10th century BC and in Greece in the 5th century BC. In Greece, almonds were rated for their ability to prevent intoxication. Plutarch cites a prolific wine drinker as saying: 'Five or six, being taken, fasting, do keepe a man from being drunke.' In Egypt, almonds were added to breads that were served to the pharaohs. In Anatolia, ca. 6500 BC, almonds, with apples and pistachios, were popular crops. In the Bible, almonds were said to symbolise hope and in Roman times, almonds were thrown over newly married couples to represent happiness, good fortune, good health and children. From these regions the almond was taken to western Europe. In the UK, it is mainly grown for its early spring blossom. It is now distributed worldwide and there are extensive commercial orchards in California, where about half a million trees produce ~70% of the world's supply. Almonds are also still grown extensively in countries around the Mediterranean.

DESCRIPTION

A medium-sized tree, 6–10 m tall. It has a fairly upright shape when young, which becomes spreading with age. Unlike the peach, it is a relatively long-lived tree (>70 years).

Leaves: Deciduous, lance-shaped, finely toothed, ~8 cm long by 4–5 cm wide.

Flowers: One of the first trees to come into flower in spring; blossom is white or pink, and is a welcome sight after a long winter. However, the very early blossom can be easily damaged by spring frosts and only some of it will actually set fruit. *Pollination:* Mostly by bees and insects; however, because of the almond's early flowering season, bees are often not around. Most varieties are not self-pollinating and generally more than one variety is needed for good pollination: they are best planted in a group. There are a few self-fertile cultivars, and peaches can also pollinate almonds (and viceversa), so one could plant peaches mixed with almonds.

Fruit: The nuts are classified as drupes. Some fruits are produced on 1-year-old wood, but also some on spurs 2 to 3 years old. The spurs grow slowly (~2.5–5 cm/year) from short lateral branches. The fruits look like small, green, furry peaches, where the equivalent of the pulp from the peach (the mesocarp) here consists of a hard coat. Inside, the almond kernel is enclosed in a hard shell. There are two main forms of almonds: bitter or sweet. Bitter almonds used to be grown widely, but now, with selection, sweet almonds are preferred for their sweeter nuts and because they don't possess poisons in the skin as do bitter almonds (see below).

Yield/harvest/storage: Can obtain 4.5–10 kg per tree after 10 years (equivalent to 2–3 kg of kernels), but irrigation and good management can increase this. It takes 3–4 years for trees to start producing fruits, and maximal cropping occurs in 6–7 years. Trees can then fruit for another 50 or more years. Fruits are harvested as the seedcoat turns brown, from late summer to autumn, and once the fruits in the centre of the tree have opened. These are the last to ripen, and so the tree can then be harvested in one go. Fruits can be knocked off the tree. After harvesting, the outer hard, green husk layer should be removed, and the kernels within their stones can be stored in the dry. In some varieties, the shell around the kernel is very hard and difficult to remove. For this reason, varieties have been selected with either 'soft' or 'paper' shells. Those with soft shells can be easily opened with a nut cracker, whereas paper-shelled almonds can be opened by hand, but, because of their softness, they may be more susceptible to insect and bird damage. Kernels can be stored for long periods if kept dry, or even for years if frozen.

Roots: It is a deep-rooted tree. Plant young trees with care so as not to damage the taproot.

uses

Food

The nuts can be sweet and tasty, avoid the bitter varieties if possible. Roast by covering them with a light vegetable oil and place in a pan in an oven at ~150°C for ~10 min or until they begin to change colour. Don't over-roast. They can then be tossed in a little salt. Almonds can also be blanched, chopped or sweetened. They can be eaten as a snack, or added to desserts, cakes, confectionery, vegetable and fish dishes, or stir fries. They can be covered in chocolate. In Indian cooking, they are often fried together with various spices and then mixed with yoghurt to make a tasty sauce, or are added to curries. In northern Europe, almonds are well known for being the main ingredient in marzipan. It is made by kneading ground almonds, sugar and essences. Almond oil is used as a flavouring in cakes and cosmetics. Gum, exuded from the tree, is used as a substitute for tragacanth.

Nutrition/medicinal

The kernels are an excellent food and are very nutritious. They contain ~50% oil: of this ~80% is oleic acid (a monounsaturated fat), 15–20% is polyunsaturated omega-6 fat. It also contains a little omega-3 oil, and has a small percentage of saturated fats. It has a similar composition to olive oil. Recent US studies suggest that the oil may help prevent heart disease by lowering low-density lipid ('bad' cholesterol) levels when consumed in the place of saturated fat. It has also been shown to be a more potent cholesterol-reducing agent than olive oil. Because of their oil content, together with ~20% good levels of dietary fibre and carbohydrate, almonds are digested slowly and sustain and normalise blood-sugar levels. They are rich in many minerals, including calcium (260 mg/100 g of kernel), magnesium (296 mg/100 g of kernel), manganese, phosphorus, potassium and copper. Almonds have high levels of protein; approximately 20%. Almonds also have a very high content of vitamin E, giving them high antioxidant properties. The kernels are also a good source of the B vitamins, particularly riboflavin, but also thiamine and niacin (3.5 mg/100 g of kernel), with some folate. A possible negative is that some find the nuts somewhat difficult to digest, so almonds need to be chewed well. The oil is used to treat inflammatory problems, and aches and pains. It is also used in sedative medicines and health preparations. **Warning:** As with all nuts, great care needs to be taken by those with allergies. In addition, bitter almonds contain cyanogenic glycosides (as amygdalin 3–5%) in the kernels, bark and leaves, as do other members of the Rosaceae family. If eaten in large quantities, bitter almonds can cause convulsions and death: 50–70 kernels can cause death in adults, 7–10 in children. They also contain prussic acid. However, these poisons are very volatile and are broken down at higher temperatures; so cooked dishes containing bitter almonds are not dangerous. Also, because of hundreds of years of selection and cultivation, sweet almonds are very low in amygdalin and so are not toxic.

Other uses

The crushed kernel makes an excellent face scrub and emollient. The hulls can be finely ground and used as a buffering and polishing agent for metal objects and used in filters. Hulls have also been burnt in California to generate electricity.

Ornamental

Grown in many areas for their wonderful early spring blossom.

CULTIVATION

Location: Likes an open, sunny, but relatively sheltered position. This is particularly important during pollination. Relatively tolerant of salt.

Temperature: Mediterranean to temperate climates. Can tolerate quite cold winters, but flowers and young leaves are susceptible to spring frosts. In areas with longer winters, it may be wiser to choose late-flowering varieties. Frost damage to flower buds occurs at –2 to –4°C; young nuts can be damaged at 0.5°C. Prefers hot, dry summers and is susceptible to high humidity.

Chilling: Does need 300–500 hours of winter chilling, but this is short compared to most other temperate species, which means that it comes into flower earlier.

Soil/water/nutrients: Will grow in any well-drained soil at a wide range of pH values: 5.3–8.3, but does best at ~pH 7.3. Ideally, the tree prefers deep, fertile, well-drained soil. It will grow in sandy loams, but these soils can be deficient in nutrients. It can also grow in surprisingly heavy soils as long as the drainage is good. Does not like waterlogging. Too much rain in spring can reduce pollination and encourage fungal disease. Because of its deep roots, the trees are fairly drought tolerant. Regular additions of nutrients can improve growth and crop yield. Additions of nitrogen, in particular, can increase growth and improve yield. Potassium, zinc, copper and boron deficiencies can occur.

Planting: Space trees at 7.5 m apart in poorer, drier soil, but plant them closer, at 4–5 m apart, if conditions are more favourable. It is recommended to plant at least one pollinating cultivar for every 2–4 fruiting trees.

Propagation: *Seeds:* Almonds can be raised from seed, but usually need a period of 2–3 months of cold stratification to germinate. Kernels will also germinate much better if removed from their shells. Grow on seedlings in deep pots to encourage the growth of well-formed taproots. Seedlings can often be planted out after ~1 year. *Grafting:* mostly by T- or chip-budding, with bitter almond, almond or peach seedlings used as rootstocks. Because peach trees have shorter life spans, if grown on peach rootstocks, almonds can lose vigour after 15 years. Other possible rootstocks are Marianna plum and apricot.

Pruning: Usually trained to an open centre or a modified central leader. Fruiting on spurs more than 4–6 years old will decline, so it is best to prune out older wood to encourage new fruiting spurs. Not all blossom will set fruit, so it is usually not necessary to thin the flowers to prevent biennial bearing.

Pests and diseases: There are a number of potential problems, though small plantings are less likely to be affected. Trees are susceptible to many fungal diseases in humid conditions. Rainfall during fruit development and before harvest can cause fungal and bacterial diseases. Possible fungal problems are brown rot, leaf-curl, leaf rust, stone fruit blast. Silver leaf can be a problem and, although it cannot be controlled, summer pruning may reduce the risk. Crown gall can be a problem on sandy soils: trees grown on peach rootstocks are less susceptible. Insect problems include green peach aphid, leaf-roller caterpillar, coddling moth and San Jose scale. Mites can cause leaf damage. Wildlife often seek out the nuts.

CULTIVARS

'All-in-one': Small tree. Kernels are large and plump and have a tasty, sweet flavour. Not very suitable for humid areas as disease can shrivel the kernel.

'Butte': Semi-soft shelled. Small, plump nuts. Good cropper. Late flowering and late harvest, but tree starts bearing before many other cultivars.

'Carmel': Soft-shelled. Large, plump nuts. Tree has a rounded shape. Comes into bearing early. Flowers in mid season, but late harvest.

'Davey': Soft-shelled. Late flowering. Tree is upright and vigorous, making it more difficult to harvest.

'Kapareil': From California. Paper-shelled, but nut tends to open on tree. Late flowering, late harvest. Vigorous, medium spreading.

'Nonpareil': Paper-shelled. Mid-season flowering. Good, high-quality kernels. Growth is vigorous, tree is medium-spreading. More frost resistant than many varieties, but susceptible to bacterial canker and tends to biennial bearing, especially in dry soils.

'Peerless': Hard-shelled. Early flowering, therefore best not grown in colder regions. Early harvest. Large shell, fairly good kernel quality. Nuts drop easily. Medium-sized trees.

'Thompson': Soft- or paper-shelled. Trees start bearing early. Good cropper. Is medium-sized and upright. Late flowering, mid-season harvest. ■

Prunus insititia, P. domestica insititia, P. spinosa
Damson (bullies, bolas) and bullace; greengage; sloe (or blackthorn)
ROSACEAE (Prunoideae subfamily)
Relatives: plum, cherry, peach

These stone-fruit species have been cultivated for many hundreds of years throughout most of Europe. They are closely related to both European plums and Japanese plums, with the species described here being the ancestors of modern-day plums. They have been less selected, and their fruits are often overlooked in modern times. Their fruits are small, oval, and coloured-purple for damsons and sloes, yellow-green for greengage and bullace. They usually have a heavy bloom and are used primarily for jams, jellies and preserves, although greengages are valued for their fresh-fruit qualities. These hardy, tougher older plum species can grow in a range of climatic and environmental situations. They are more adaptable than many fruit trees and can often tolerate poor, heavier soils, and even some waterlogging. Below is a general description of these species.

DESCRIPTION

Small- to medium-sized trees, with grey bark.

Leaves: Oval or elliptic with either pointed or blunt tips, usually a dark grey-green colour.

Flowers: Typical Rosaceae flowers, white, slightly scented. Abundant clusters consisting of 2–3 flowers, or can be solitary. *Pollination:* Mostly by bees, but also by other insects. These species although partially self-fertile, do benefit from being planted in groups for cross pollination.

Roots: Tend to have many shallow roots, and these produce suckers if damaged. Do not cultivate deeply around trees and remove weed competition. Trees benefit from an organic mulch.

CULTIVATION

These plum ancestors are very easy to grow and more tolerant of soil conditions and temperatures than other stone fruits. Need very little maintenance.

Location: They can grow in a sunny or semi-shaded location.

Temperature: They are quite hardy and can survive winter frosts. Early spring frosts can damage the blossom of sloe.

Soil/water/nutrients: They do best on deep, well-drained loams, but can also grow in a range of poorer soils, including those with poor drainage (except greengage). They can grow in heavier, clay-based or even compacted soils. They grow best within a pH range of 5.5–6.5. Trees benefit from moist soil during fruit formation, which results in plumper, juicier fruit. Trees are fairly drought tolerant. Need very little extra nutrition, though do benefit from applications of organic mulch.

Planting: Space young trees at 3–5 m apart.

Pruning: Pruning is minimal with these species. They are normally just allowed to grow, and any pruning is to control shape, or to remove any damaged or diseased wood. They produce fruit at the base of shoots formed the previous year and on short spurs along older stems. You can remove some older side shoots in winter to make way for young shoots, as well as shortening the length of long main branches.

Propagation: *Seed:* Trees are occasionally grown as seedlings, but they are quite variable. Seed can either be sown fresh in cold frames and over-wintered or, if stored, will need 2–3 months of cold stratification, and are then sown early in spring. Seed can take 18 months to germinate. Prick out seedlings and grow on in pots for another year or so. *Cuttings:* Take semi-ripe cuttings, with a heel, in summer and insert in gritty, well-drained, moist compost. *Layering:* This can be done in spring.

Pests and diseases: They are hardy and healthy trees compared with other stone fruits, and seldom suffer from serious disease or pest attacks. The most serious risk is probably silverleaf, which can kill trees, but it is possible to vaccinate trees with a biological-control agent when they are young. The other main problem is likely to be birds, etc., after the fruits.

MAIN SPECIES

Damson (bullies, bolas) and bullace, *Prunus insititia*. Natives of the UK, southeast Europe and northern and central Asia. They commonly grow in woodland margins, in hedges and there are still some surviving older orchards. Although often grouped with the European plum, of which they are likely to be an ancestor, they are a separate species. They are probably the oldest cultivated plums, are mentioned in ancient Mesopotamian records and probably grew in Babylon's Hanging Gardens. The name for damson is probably derived from 'plum of Damascus'. The damson and bullace are very similar, and both have the same species name. The discussion below refers to both plants. Some damson trees produce huge amounts of fruit, and bullace can be even more productive in both temperate and warm-temperate areas. However, this varies from tree to tree, so it is probably a good idea to vegetatively propagate from a tree known to be productive. They also seem to vary in how much winter chilling they require, and this may be why there is the variation in yield. These trees can grow in a wide range of conditions and are very easy to cultivate.

Description: A tall shrub/small tree: ~5 m tall. Appearance is similar to sloe (*Prunus spinosa*), but they do not have such vicious thorns, and have straight, not crooked branches, with only a few terminating in spines. In addition, the bark

Food

The fruits of these species are often sour until they are fully ripe, and are often used in cooked dishes rather than eaten fresh. *Warning:* Like all the Rosaceae family, the seeds contain cyanogenic glucosides, which are toxic if eaten in quantity, which is unlikely to occur with stone fruits, but the bark and leaves also contain this compound. In small amounts, this poisonous compound stimulates respiration, improves digestion and gives a sense of well-being.

is brown, not black like that of sloe. Younger branches are downy. *Leaves:* It has larger leaves than sloe, and these are alternate, downy beneath and are finely toothed. *Flowers:* White, like those of many Rosaceae, ~1.5–2 cm in diameter, with broad petals. They are borne in loose clusters, and open just after the leaves have begun to unfold. The flowers are later than those of many plum species, so are less susceptible to frost damage. *Fruit:* Small to medium size, ~2.5–3.5 cm long. Those of damson are oval; those of bullace are more rounded. They hang in small groups and have a distinctive bluish bloom. Damson becomes very dark purple when ripe, and somewhat soft. Their flesh is greeny-yellow and juicy. Bullace fruit and flesh becomes yellow-green when ripe. There is a single, oval stone in the centre, ~1.5 cm long. They can be sour when under-ripe, and are best left till fully ripe before harvesting. They have more flavour than many plum species, and can be juicy and delicious.

Cultivation: These species grow well in temperate and warm-temperate regions, in a variety of soils, though prefer more acidic to alkaline. They can be grown in fairly heavy soils and in wetter, colder areas than European plums. Fairly wind tolerant and very disease resistant.

Cultivars: 'Mirabelle': A particularly famous wild variety. The fruit are small, round, yellow, with yellow-red dots. The flesh is firm, yellow and has a sweet, mild flavour. Valued in the Alsace region of France as a fresh fruit, it is used in pastries and also made into Quetsch brandy. A very productive, spreading tree. It is a good pollinator for other varieties. It only fruits for a short period each year.
'Royal bullace': Fruit is large, ~3 cm diameter, yellowish-green when ripe, mottled red and has a thin, grey bloom. Flesh is green, separates from the stone, has a tangy but sweet flavour. Ripens in late autumn.
'White bullace': Fruit is small (1.5–2 cm long), round, pale yellow, mottled red. Flesh is firm, juicy, sub-acid, becoming sweeter when fully ripe at the end of autumn.
'Essex bullace': Fruit is ~2.5 cm long, yellowish when fully ripe. Flesh, juicy, fairly sweet, ripens at the end of autumn.

Uses: Fully ripe fruits can be eaten and enjoyed fresh. Because some fruit can be fairly acid, they are very good for making jams and pies, or can be stewed with sugar. They have high pectin levels, and make excellent, rich, thick jam, and can be added to sauces, etc. They also make a good traditional wine and are used to flavour damson gin.

Greengage, *Prunus domestica insititia.* Greengage is

probably a native of western Asia. There are various forms of greengage: some are vigorous, others are not. The tree produces tasty, juicy fruits that are thought by many to be of superior quality to plums, but generally they tend to be undervalued and overlooked. The tree is named after Thomas Gage, who introduced it into England in ~1725.

Description: Forms a smallish tree, ~4 m tall. *Flowers:* White. Some cultivars are self-fertile, although there is better fruit-set if more than one tree is planted. *Fruit:* Ripen in late summer–autumn. Small- to medium-sized, rounded, yellowish-green when ripe. Flesh is greenish-yellow, translucent, smooth, sweet, juicy. Has good yields, but tends to produce biennially.

Cultivation: Greengages grow and fruit best in dry,

Greengage, *Prunus domestica insititia.*

sunny summers. They are best planted against a sunny wall. However, they also need a fairly long period of winter chilling, >600–800 hours, and so do not fruit well, if at all, in regions that have warm winters. They are not as hardy as European plums. Susceptible to silverleaf. *Pruning:* In general, established trees only need minimal pruning, i.e. once every 2–3 years. The fruits are often produced on spurs, and the same spurs can produce fruit for several years (from 2–5 years). The fruit buds are produced during the spring–summer on the current season's growth. The trees are usually then pruned to an open-centre shape, to form spreading branches that allow light and air to freely circulate. After the initial cut back, several strong shoots around the tree are selected as the main 'scaffold' branches. Initially, for the first year, other competing shoots or vigorous laterals should be removed so that the scaffold stems preferentially develop. Once the scaffold branches are established, the tree only needs a light prune to remove stem tips to encourage the growth of laterals. Too much pruning results in excess stem and leaf growth at the expense of flower and fruit production. Pruning is best done in late autumn. Greengages can tend towards biennial bearing. To even out the harvest, some of the young fruits should be removed in bumper years. Thinning the number of fruits also reduces disease risk and gives, overall, a better-quality crop.

Cultivars: It is best to choose a local cultivar that suits the climatic conditions as there is considerable variability between plants.
'Coe's Golden Drop': Early blossom. Fruit is large, oval, yellow skinned. Flesh, yellow, firm and sweet, good flavour when tree ripened. Good for drying. Small yields and needs a pollinator, e.g. 'Greengage'. Bears fairly well in warm temperate areas.
'Gross Grune Reneklode' (syn. 'Greengage'): Mid season. Small round greenish-yellow prune plum. Used a lot as a pollinator for other greengages and plums.
'Reine Claude de Bavay': Late season. Superb dessert quality.
'Bavay's Greengage': One of the best greengages. Fruits well in warm areas. Juicy, sweet, tasty flesh. Productive and highly recommended.

Uses: The fruit are enjoyed fresh, but can also be used in pies, jams or can be stewed, etc.

Sloe or blackthorn, *Prunus spinosa*. A native of UK and Europe, this is one of the first trees to bloom in springtime, producing masses of small, white flowers long before any leaf buds have burst, and they brighten up hedgerows in what can otherwise be a very dull time of year. They then produce large numbers of dark purple fruits (technically known as drupes) in autumn. Sloes are very dry and bitter until they are fully ripe and have caught the first frosts of winter. Late autumn–early winter is a good time to collect them, if the birds have not done so already.

Description: A tall, dense, slow to medium-growing shrub or small tree, ~4 m tall. Appearance is similar to damson, but it has many more thorns (~1.5 cm long), forms a denser structure, and it has angled branches, which often terminate in a spine. Its bark is black. *Leaves:* Deciduous, smaller than those of damson, grey-green in colour, alternate. *Flowers:* Masses of small, white flowers in spring, before the leaves open. Many flowers are clustered together. *Fruit:* Smaller

than damson, ~2–2.5 cm long, oval. Ripen to dark purple, though never really soften in late autumn. They stand erect on stalks on branches. They are best left on the bush as long as possible before picking.

Cultivation: They will grow in a wide range of soil types and locations. Can grow in full sun or semi-shade, in light woodland or open scrubland. May even get better crops on poorer soils. They need little to no maintenance, just an occasional trim to keep them under control. Space plants at 3–4 m apart.

Uses: *Food:* The fruit are not usually eaten fresh as they are too dry and sour, but they can be added, with other ingredients, to jam, jellies, pies. One of their best-known uses is to make sloe gin. The berries are pricked and left standing in gin for several weeks for the juices to infuse the liquor; it has a delicious, unique flavour. *Ornamental:* They make a useful barrier hedge because of their spines and their dense growth. ■

Prunus pensylvanica
Pincherry (fire cherry, bird cherry, pigeon cherry)
ROSACEAE
Similar species: chokeberry (*Prunus virginiana*)
Relatives: aronia, cherries, plum, peach, almond

This is another Rosaceae species with edible fruits. It does not have the tastiest, largest fruit, but it is a tough plant, and may be suitable for areas with poor soils or to grow as a pioneer species. Native to a wide variety of climates and situations, from the northeastern USA, to western and eastern Canada, and from Newfoundland down to Georgia, the pincherry has been eaten by indigenous populations for many hundreds of years. It forms a smallish tree, with attractive bark, white blossom and small, scarlet, edible fruit; it also often develops good leaf colour in autumn.

DESCRIPTION
A shrub or small tree, ~1–5 m tall (but can be up to 10 m). Trunk is straight, with a rounded crown. The branches form lower on the trunk when it is grown in full sun. Bark: dark reddish-brown, with large, orange, horizontal lenticels, with the outer bark tending to peel off in horizontal strips. Inner bark is green, pungent and very bitter. Buds are red-brown and clustered at the branch tips. Fast growing but short lived.

Leaves: Deciduous, alternate, lanceolate, bright shiny green, 3–11 cm in length, with finely serrated edges. Autumn colour is bright red-orange.

Flowers: Small (~0.6–1 cm diameter), pretty, white, with five rounded petals, in clusters of 5–7, borne from spring–mid summer, depending on location. The flowers are bisexual, but trees do need cross pollination for good fruit production. Ideally, a group of 2–3 cultivars will give the best fruit-set (although the cultivars need to all have the same parents). *Pollination:* Bees are attracted to the flowers and do most of the pollination.

Fruit: Small (~0.5–0.8 cm diameter), scarlet, rounded,

thin flesh, edible, but sour, with a largish stone in the centre. Produced from mid summer–autumn, depending on location.

Yield/harvest: Yields can be good: 14–22 kg per tree are possible. Yields vary between trees, and trees tend towards alternate bearing, sometimes only producing a bumper crop every second or third year. Will need fruit thinning on bumper years to even out yields. The first fruits are formed after 2–4 years of age, though good yields may not occur till >10 years old. Maximum production occurs when trees are between 15–25 years old. Fruit are harvested when fully coloured, and this is usually during mid to late summer.

Roots: Deep, with wide-spreading laterals. Once the tree is ~1 m tall, it will also form lots of shallow (i.e. ~0.3–0.6 m deep) lateral, feeder roots. Take care with mechanical cultivation. An organic mulch will help suppress weeds, retain moisture and add nutrients.

CULTIVATION
Location: They grow best in open sunny locations or semi-

shade. They do not like dense shade or competition from plants that are too close.

Temperature: Extremely frost and cold tolerant, can survive temperatures of –35°C. Will probably need a fairly long winter-chilling period to fruit well. Can also grow with summer heat: grows OK at temperatures of 30°C.

Soil/water/nutrients: Prefers fertile, moist soil, but will grow in all types, including heavy, moist soils, fairly dry soils and very stony soils: it is a good pioneer species. Grows best at pH 6–7.5. It can grow on limestone soils, but may suffer from iron deficiency (chlorosis) in very alkaline soils.

Planting: Space trees at 3–4 m apart. It transplants with difficulty.

Propagation: *Seed:* This is the main method used (and tissue culture, which is not described further here), but seedlings are highly variable. Clean the pulp off the seeds before storing or sowing. If not planted outside when fresh, spring-sown seeds will need stratification to break dormancy: 60 days of alternating warmer temperatures of 20–30°C and then 90 days of temperatures between 3–5°C. Germination rate can be good if the seeds are soaked for 24 hours in a weak bleach/acid solution, then thoroughly rinsed, and given a few days of varying temperature changes before sowing. Germination may be best under partial shade. It can take a long time to germinate. Strangely, germination may be better in older seed, possibly because seedcoat germination inhibitors lose their potency over time. It is estimated that some buried seeds retain their viability for 50–150 years! *Cuttings:* Semi-ripe cuttings in spring–summer from non-fruiting stems, but there is only a poor rooting rate. Root cuttings (~10 cm in length) will grow easily in good, moist compost. Cuttings give reliable progeny from selected trees, and trees will come into fruit sooner. *Layering:* This may be possible in spring. *Grafting:* Pincherries are often commercially used as a rootstock for sour cherries.

Pruning: After initial shaping of trees to an open-centre, only minimal pruning is necessary to remove excess twiggy growth. Fruits are often produced on spurs, and individual spurs continue to produce fruits for a number of years, so it's important not to prune these out. Prune to encourage horizontal branching, which will produce more fruit. To avoid alternate bearing, it may be necessary to thin the fruit and to carry out most pruning in bumper years. Do not prune in wet weather as this increases the risk of bacterial and fungal disease, e.g. silverleaf.

Pests and diseases: Many diseases can attack pincherry, particularly cherry-leaf spot (*Coccomyces hiemalis*), which is recognized by purplish–brown shot holes in leaves and can lead to premature leaf fall. Other leaf spots on pincherry are *Cercospora circumscissa*, *Coryneum carpophyllum*, and three species of *Phyllosticta*. Additional pincherry diseases are powdery mildew, rust and leaf-curler. May also get black knot and *Fomes pomaceus*. Insects include ugly-nest caterpillar, eastern tent caterpillar, cherry-leaf beetle, Bruce spanworm, fall canker worm and a web-spinning sawfly. Birds like the berries.

CULTIVARS

Look out for local selections that suit the area and, if possible, because of variations in fruit yield, pick good fruiting individuals to propagate from.

Food
The fruits are too sour to be eaten fresh, but make an excellent jelly, and can be added to juices, sauces, syrup and make a reasonable quality wine. For syrup, boil down the berries in a small amount of water, strain and add sugar to taste. **Warning:** Although the flesh of the fruit is safe to eat, the leaves, seeds and bark contain cyanogenic compounds (as amygdalin), as do other *Prunus* species, which is poisonous to livestock and humans.

Other uses
The attractive outer bark is used for baskets and similar items. It is watertight and resists decay.

Ornamental
A tough tree that can grow in many soil types, including dry and wet conditions. It makes a good pioneer species. It grows well in areas that have had a recent fire.

SIMILAR SPECIES

Chokeberry, *Prunus virginiana*. The chokeberry is a native of North America and is found from Canada down to California, often growing on sunny slopes or the edges of woodland. It is related, though not closely, to aronia (see p. 78), which is also known as black chokeberry. *P. virginiana* is more similar to pincherry.

Description: Chokeberry is a fully cold-hardy, fast-growing, but short-lived, somewhat straggly shrub, ~1–4 m tall. It has smooth, reddish-brown bark, without the prominent horizontal lenticels that are characteristic of pincherry. It tends to form thickets. The leaves are bright green above, duller beneath, 5–10 cm long, oval and tapering at both ends with finely serrated edges. The flowers are white with five rounded petals, borne in long clusters at branch tips. The fruits are borne in early autumn and are shiny, dark red–purple juicy, but are often sour (though some cultivars have sweeter fruits). Yields are usually good, and should give ~14 kg per plant. Plants start to flower at 3–4 years of age, and then have ~40 years of fruit production.

Cultivation: Is best grown in full sun, does not tolerate shade. Tolerates most soil types, though is not tolerant of waterlogging. *Propagation:* As above.

Uses: They are often used to make good-quality pies, jellies, jams, syrups and wine, and the fruits are sweeter when dried. The fruits have been used to stimulate appetite and to treat diarrhoea. The roots and bark have been used as a blood tonic, a sedative and an appetite stimulant, but see the Warning above. The inner bark has been used externally to treat wounds. Often grown as an ornamental or for erosion control. ■

Prunus persica
Peach and nectarine
ROSACEAE (Prunoideae subfamily)
Relatives: almond, plum, cherry

Peaches originate from and have been cultivated in China for thousands of years. They were taken to Persia (Iraq) along the silk-trading routes. The Chinese believe peaches impart sincerity, a long life, and were also seen as a symbol of female genitalia. The ancient Egyptians offered the peach to the God of Tranquillity. The name *persica* is derived from Persia, which is where Europeans first saw them. The Greeks and, especially, the Romans spread the peach throughout Europe and England, starting in 300–400 BC. King Louis XIV of France developed the fruit's qualities significantly. In New Zealand, in 1814, they were already found growing and established around maraes and coastal areas when the first UK passenger ships turned up, meaning that the very first Europeans to arrive must have left peach stones to cultivate. This has resulted in many different varieties of peaches existing in New Zealand, including many smaller golden peaches known as 'Maori peaches'. There are thousands of peach cultivars worldwide and, when selecting a peach variety for the garden, it is worth considering a local variety because, although possibly smaller in size, they are often tastier and are frequently less susceptible to local pest and disease problems. No single peach or nectarine cultivar is dominant worldwide, or even nationwide. Peaches can be either freestone, which have luscious, melting flesh, and is the main peach type sold fresh; or clingstone, which are firmer and are used for canning. Basically, nectarines are peaches without fuzz, and only a single gene is responsible for this.

DESCRIPTION

A small tree with a spreading canopy, ~2–3.5 m tall in cultivation. They are fast growing. Peaches tend to be hardier than nectarines. Dwarf cultivars can be easier to maintain than full-sized trees, and have about a third of the yield. Trees are short-lived, sometimes only living ~4 years, often only 8–10 years, although healthy trees can live 12–18 years.

Leaves: Tapered, long, acute tips, folded slightly along the midrib, deep green, slightly serrated, ~9–14 cm long. Sometimes have good, yellow autumn colour.

Flowers: Showy, white–pink–deep red–purplish, ~2.5 cm diameter. Petals can be large and showy, or small and curved, depending on the cultivar. Many cultivars have been selected for their ornamental spring blossom and have double flowers. Flowers are borne on short stalks, from lateral buds on 1-year-old wood, and usually occur singly or in pairs. They blossom in early spring and so are susceptible to late spring frosts, particularly nectarines. *Pollination:* Most cultivars are self-fertile, and can be normally grown without a pollinator. They are pollinated by bees and insects.

Fruit: A drupe: a single seed inside a superior ovary (or endocarp), surrounded by juicy flesh (or mesocarp) and a thin outer skin (or exocarp). The endocarp protects the kernel from being eaten along with the flesh.

Yield/harvest/storage: Trees begin to bear fruit early, from 2–3 years after planting. They soon begin to produce good crops, so much so that they tend to become biennial bearing, and fruit thinning is then advisable, i.e. thinning out any tight clusters of very young fruits. A tree can produce >30 kg of fruit. Pick peaches when ripe: if fruit are picked when unripe, they never develop their full sweetness, juiciness or flavour. Harvest fruits when they are just beginning to soften; colour change is not always reliable because cultivars vary in skin colour, e.g. the skin of white-fleshed peaches never turns a true 'peach' colour. Fruits take 3–5 months to mature after pollination, which is slightly quicker than almonds. They ripen in mid–late summer. Handle fruit gently as they bruise easily. Several harvests are needed throughout the season to pick fruit at their best stage of ripeness. *Storage:* Peaches do not last long at room temperature, or even in the fridge (~<14 days), before they become oversoft or succumb to fungal disease.

Roots: Peach trees have many roots near the soil surface and these are susceptible to drying out and also being damaged by mechanical cultivation. A deep, organic mulch is beneficial; it also suppresses weed growth.

CULTIVATION

Peaches can be a problem as the trees succumb to many pests and diseases; they are short lived and the early blossom is susceptible to late frosts. Having said that, it is wonderful to be able to pick and enjoy your own fresh, succulent, juicy fruits.

Location: Peaches grow best and for longer in a sunny, sheltered location, though will also grow in semi-shade. Cool, wet climates increase the risk of disease and reduce fruit quality. They are not very wind tolerant.

Temperature: Trees grow best with a hot, dry summer. Some cultivars, when dormant in winter, are very cold hardy and can tolerate temperatures down to –30°C; however, spring blossom can be killed at only ~–2°C. This risk can be lessened by avoiding planting trees in frost pockets. They grow best in warm-temperate or Mediterranean-type climates, though can be (and are) grown in colder regions with winter protection.

Chilling: Peach trees need some winter chilling (600–1000 hours at <7°C), though less than apple or pear, with dwarf cultivars needing less than other peach trees. If trees do not receive enough chill time they are likely to have poor leaf growth, and diminished fruit yields and quality.

Soil/water/nutrients: Peaches need well-drained soil, and waterlogging can rapidly kill them. They grow best in deep (~1.5 m deep) loam at a pH range of 6–7, though can grow in sandy or even clay soils, as long as they are well drained. Peach trees are moderately drought tolerant, though fruit quality and yield are improved with regular moisture during fruit formation. In soils that are more alkaline, nutrient deficiencies of iron, zinc and manganese are likely. Peaches and nectarines are fairly nutrient hungry, particularly for nitrogen, and 2–3 applications of an organic or regular fertiliser a year will improve growth and fruit production (unless your soil is naturally fertile). Their fertiliser needs, apart from N, P and K, are particularly for magnesium, and zinc.

Planting: Avoid areas that may be frost pockets. Space trees at 6–8 m apart. As most peach cultivars are self-fertile, they can be planted singly or in groups. Young trees grow poorly with weed competition. A deep, organic mulch can reduce this problem, and will also help retain moisture and supply nutrients.

Propagation: *Seed:* Peach trees can be successfully and easily grown from seed, even seed obtained from purchased fruit, although there will be variation in the progeny. Seedling trees are often tougher, grow better, live considerably longer and are less likely to become diseased than grafted or budded trees. They also often have tastier fruit, particularly if you pick a cultivar that grows well in your area, and they start fruiting within a couple of years, which is unusual for most seedling-grown fruits. Sow seed, if possible, when fresh. Cracking the hard outer seedcoat (without damaging the kernel) or soaking the stone for a day or so before sowing in moist, but well-drained compost, will speed up germination. If the seed is obtained or collected in autumn, it can be stored in a refrigerator (but not the freezer) in a plastic bag till early spring. *Grafting:* Trees are often T- or chip-budded. The most common rootstocks used are peach seedlings, which need a dry soil to grow in; almond seedlings, which tolerate more alkaline soils; or plums, which gives a smaller tree that is more tolerant of wet soils.

Pruning: Most peach trees form fruit on the previous season's growth. The main style of pruning used is the open centre, which allows air and light to enter the crown of the tree. Trees can be pruned in late winter when dormant, but when most of the cold weather has passed. It is not advisable to prune in autumn (see Pest and disease notes below). Initially, about four, strong lateral branches, spaced evenly around the tree, are selected as the main scaffold branches. Prune out other lateral branches and allow the scaffold branches to become strong and established. In the second year, the tips of the scaffold branches are removed to encourage lateral fruiting branches to develop. Trees also tend to form vertical, tall branches, and reducing the length of these keeps the fruit within reach! Peach trees need annual pruning to maintain an open centre, and to encourage the formation of fruiting laterals. Try not to remove the coming season's flower buds: flower buds are plump; leaf buds are flatter. Also prune out any diseased or damaged wood. Peach trees are short lived, but also come into fruit when young, and so the emphasis is on stimulating new, vigorous growth, but not so much that the tree produces too much fruit and tends towards biennial bearing. Peaches can also be pruned to form a fan shape and can be grown against a sunny wall. Peach and nectarine trees are unusual in that the practice of girdling their scaffold branches does not seem to harm them, indeed, if done with care, it can result in larger, increased and earlier harvests of fruit. (See Introduction, p. 36 for details.)

Food
Beautiful, juicy and sweet when fresh. They can also be added to preserves, many desserts, chutney, flans, a topping for cakes, icecream, yoghurt, added to liquor, or can be dried for later use. The flowers can be eaten fresh or cooked, and can be added to salads or used as a garnish.

Nutrition
Fruits contain a little vitamin C: ~7–12 mg/100 g of flesh, but are high in vitamin A (~550 IU), including lutein and zeaxanthin, which can help reduce the incidence of cataracts and macular degeneration. They are a good source of potassium and also contain some niacin, copper, magnesium, phosphorus, as well as some vitamin E and K. They contain good levels of fibre, but also sugar.

Medicinal
A compound called phloretin is found in the bark and roots, which has antibiotic activity, acting against both Gram+ and Gram– bacteria. The leaves, stones and bark have been used for various medical purposes, but care needs to be exercised because of their cyanogenic compounds. The stones, in particular, have high levels of these compounds and, in small amounts, it has been used, often controversially, to treat cancers. It has, however, been used in China for this purpose for at least ~2000 years. The leaves and bark have also been used as a sedative, a diuretic, to eliminate internal parasites, as an astringent, to expel phlegm, to sooth inflammation and to treat chest complaints. ***Warning:*** Like all members of the *Prunus* genus, the leaves, flowers and, especially, the seeds and bark contain cyanogenic glycosides, which are toxic or lethal in large doses. Strangely, in small amounts, this poison is reported to stimulate respiration, improve digestion and give a sense of well-being.

Other uses
A green dye can be obtained from the leaves and fruit. The oil from the seed (~50%) can be used as a substitute for almond oil in cosmetic preparations. A gum obtained from the stem can be used as an adhesive.

Ornamental
There are many ornamental cultivars, which have been selected for their abundant, pretty, white-pink blossom and their yellow autumn colours.

Pests and diseases: Peaches are prone to many problems including leaf-curl (often occurs in wetter areas, and can be controlled by a copper spray), peach rust (yellow-brown spots on leaves), brown rot (of the fruit), powdery mildew, brown spot (can seriously damage flowers, leaves and fruit), silver-leaf (serious fungal disease that spreads throughout the tree and can kill it), bacterial blast, white peach scale, stink bugs, scab, aphids, tent caterpillars, galls and borers. However, the healthier the tree, and the less humid the climate, the fewer problems the tree is likely to have. However, the fruits still need protecting from rats, birds, possums, etc. In addition, peach trees sometimes suffer sudden death when they are still young. It is usually characterised by browning and death of the cambium and phloem vasculature of the tree. A variety of factors may contribute to this. It is hypothesised that pruning in autumn seems to increase auxin (a plant 'hormone') production within the plant, which, in turn, decreases the dormancy level of the tree and makes it more sensitive to late-winter temperature fluctuations. A late-winter warm period, followed by a cold spell can then often fatally damage the tree. In addition, attacks by nematodes also seem to initiate an increase in auxin levels, leading to the same physiological problems.

CULTIVARS

There are many hundreds, if not thousands, of peach and nectarine cultivars. Probably the best advice is to grow trees from seed obtained from a neighbourhood tree that is known to be healthy and has tasty fruits. The white-fleshed peaches, in particular, although not as attractive in skin colouring, often have much tastier fruits. ∎

Prunus spp.
Plum and prune
ROSACEAE (Prunoideae subfamily)

European plum and prune (*Prunus domestica*), Japanese plum (*P. salicina*)

Other species: apricot plum (*P. simonii*), pissard plum (*P. cerasifera*), plumcots umeboshi (*P. mume*)

Plums have been cultivated for many hundreds of years in many temperate regions of the world. They are native to the Middle East, China, northern America and throughout most of Europe. The Romans first introduced the fruit into northern Europe. Plums are, taxonomically, a very diverse group of fruits, consisting of many species and cultivars. Most have been cultivated and originate from crosses between wild plum species. They have a greater number of rootstocks than any other stone fruit, and the fruits come in a wonderful range of sizes, colours and shapes. Some have also been selected for their blossom and coloured leaves. Cultivars have also been selected to grow in a wide range of climatic and environmental situations. World production is now mainly in China, but there are also many cultivated in Russia, Eastern Europe, Italy, USA, France, Germany, Spain, UK, Australia, New Zealand and many other countries. Plums are very adaptable compared to many other fruit species and can often tolerate poor, heavier soils, and even some waterlogging. The plums are classified into a number of groups: the European plums, *Prunus domestica*; the Japanese plums, *P. salicina* and hybrids; the damsons, sloe and greengages, *P. insititia*, *P. spinosa* (see p. 345), which are wilder, older cultivars; and the plum cherries, which are natives of North America (see p. 357). Plums have also been crossed with other fruit species, e.g. apricot, to create hybrids such as 'Plumcot' (50% plum/50% apricot), 'Aprium' (75% apricot/25% plum) and 'Pluot' (75% plum/25% apricot).

GENERAL DESCRIPTION

Plum species form small to medium-sized trees, with a more erect shape than peach.

Leaves: Oval or elliptic with either pointed or blunt tips, usually a mid-green colour, with short petioles.

Flowers: A typical Rosaceae flower, but smaller than peach, white, and has longer flower stalks. Slightly scented. Occur in numerous clusters of 2–3 flowers, or can be solitary, on short spurs of 2-year-old wood (European plums) or in the axils of 1-year-old wood (Japanese plums). Japanese plums, in particular, produce blossom very early in spring.
Pollination: Mostly by bees, but also by other insects. Most European species are self-fertile, though do benefit from cross pollination; most Japanese species are self-fertile and do not usually cross pollinate with each other. Japanese and European plums cannot cross pollinate each other because they have different numbers of chromosomes.

Fruit: A smooth drupe, with a thin, edible skin. Oval-shaped or round in European cultivars; rounder or heart-shaped in Japanese cultivars. Fruit size varies with the cultivar, but Japanese cultivars are often larger. The fruits come in a beautiful range of skin colours, depending on cultivar, ranging from lemony-yellow, gold, pinkish, deep red to dark purple. The fruits often have a bloom. They are fleshy, juicy, yellow–orange–rich red, depending on cultivar, and are sweet, often tangy, and refreshing. There is a single stone in the centre, ~2 cm long. Fruits form on short spurs or from leaf axils of 1-year-old wood.

Yield/harvest/storage: Plums take 10–24 weeks to mature after pollination, although Japanese cultivars tend to mature more quickly, ~12 weeks. European plum trees are older when they first begin fruiting, usually in 3–5 years, compared with 2 years for Japanese plums. Plums mature from summer through to autumn, depending on cultivar. They are best picked when ripe. Although they can ripen in cold storage if picked when hard, their flavour does not seem as sweet or rich as when they are tree-ripened. Ripeness is best determined by skin colour and softness of the fruit. Plums picked to produce prunes are harvested when the fruits are fully ripe. The fruits can bruise easily, so need to be handled carefully. Once ripe, they can be kept for ~14–21 days in a fridge. Ripe fruits are susceptible to mould, and are best eaten fresh or processed soon after picking.

Roots: Tend to have many shallow roots, and these produce suckers if damaged. Trees benefit from an organic mulch. Do not cultivate deeply around trees but also try to minimise weed competition.

CULTIVATION

Plums are easier to grow and more tolerant of soil conditions and temperatures than other stone fruit. The rootstock species has a significant effect on how they grow in different soils and their resistance to disease. Plums grown on plum rootstocks will have a toughness and tolerance to wetter soils; those grown on peach rootstocks, in contrast, are likely to be more susceptible to disease, waterlogging and may not live as long. (See notes below on the specific rootstock species to judge how the grafted trees may grow.)

Location: They prefer a sunny, fairly sheltered location.

Temperature: They have a similar cold hardiness to apples and pears, and are hardier than peaches. European plums are generally cold hardier than Japanese cultivars. They can be grown in regions that have regular frosts. Japanese plums tend to bloom in early spring, and so late frosts can kill the blossom.

Chilling: Japanese plums need only 500–800 hours of winter chill (i.e. at <4°C); European plums need >1000 hours.

Soils/water/nutrients: Plums do best on fertile, deep, well-drained loams, but can also grow in a range of poorer soils, including those with poor drainage (this is unusual for most fruit species). They can grow in heavier, clay-based or even compacted soils. They grow best within a pH range of 5.5–6.5. If trees are grown in soils that are too acid, root growth is reduced and trees can suffer toxicity from the high levels of aluminium and manganese. Conversely, in soils that are too alkaline, trees may suffer manganese deficiency or iron chlorosis. Trees benefit from moist soil during fruit formation, which results in plumper, juicier fruit, but also need minimal water around harvesting time to reduce the risk of fungal disease. Trees are moderately drought tolerant. Plums grown for prunes and Japanese plums, in particular, do better in regions with lower humidity. Trees benefit from moderate additions of balanced nutrients at the beginning of the growing season and, as trees get older, they prefer a greater proportion of nitrogen and phosphate. Applications of organic mulch are beneficial.

Planting: Space young trees at 3–5 m apart.

Pruning: In general, Japanese plum trees have more vigorous growth and need more frequent pruning than European plums, which may only need pruning every 2–3 years. The fruits are often produced on spurs, and these can produce fruits for several years (from 2–5 years). The fruit buds are produced during the spring–summer on the current season's growth. When planting, cut back the trees to ~60 cm to allow the tree to put its energies into root production. Plums are then usually pruned to an open-centre shape, to form spreading branches that allow light and air to freely circulate. After this, several strong shoots around the tree are selected as the main scaffold branches. To allow the scaffold branches to preferentially develop, other competing shoots or vigorous lateral are removed for the first year or so. Once the scaffold branches are established, the tree only needs the tips of scaffold branches removed to encourage the growth of laterals. Too much pruning results in excess stem and leaf growth at the expense of flower and fruit production. However, Japanese plums need pruning more often than European plums, and this is best done in late autumn. Trees can be pruned to a fan shape, and tied against a warm sunny wall or a fence. Plums tend to produce a heavy crop one year, and very little the next. To even out the harvest, some young fruits can be thinned in bumper years. This practice also reduces disease risk and gives an overall, better-quality crop.

Propagation: Seed: Trees are occasionally grown as seedlings, but are quite variable. Seed can be sown fresh in a cold frame and over-wintered or, if stored, needs 2–3 months of cold stratification before being sown in warm moist compost in early spring. Seeds can take ~18 months to germinate. Prick out seedlings and grow on in pots for another year or two. Cuttings: Take semi-ripe cuttings, with a heel, in summer. Layering: This can be done in spring. Grafting: This is the main propagation method, where various cultivars are grafted onto hardy rootstocks. Plums are commonly T- or chip-budded onto a variety of rootstocks, which include plum, apricot, peach and almond. The plum species most used in Europe are *P. domestica* and *P. insititia*. In the USA, *P. cerasifera* is commonly used as a rootstock.

Pests and diseases: They are relatively hardy and healthy trees compared with other stone fruits, but can be affected by disease, with the severity often being dependent on how wet and humid it is. Possible pests are mites, aphids, scales, caterpillars and slugs; possible diseases include brown rot, blossom blight, prune rust, shothole, bladder plum and bacterial gummosis. The most serious risk is probably silverleaf, which can kill trees, but it is possible to vaccinate trees with a biological-control agent when they are young. The other main problem is likely to be birds, etc.

EUROPEAN SPECIES

European plum and prune, *Prunus domestica*. These were originally native to areas around the Caspian Sea, and are a natural hybrid between *P. cerasifera* (Pissard or cherry plum) and *P. spinosa* (sloe). It is thought that they may have only hybridised within the last 2000 years. They are often smaller than Japanese varieties, and usually have soft–firm yellow flesh and a juicy, aromatic taste. They are eaten fresh, but can be also cooked in desserts or dried. They range in skin colour from green–yellow–purple. This species includes the sweet prune plums, small yellow prunes and Lombard-type prunes (e.g. Victoria plums). The prune plums tend to be very sweet and are picked when fully ripe.

Description: Small–medium-sized trees, height: 8–15 m, spread: 5–8 m. They are moderately long lived, ~50 years. *Flowers:* Late blooming, numerous cluster of white–pink flowers. *Pollination:* Many European plums do need a pollinator tree planted with them to get good fruit-set, e.g. 'Bluefree' and 'Stanley' are common pollinators for European plums. Others are self-fertile, e.g. 'Burgundy' (USA), 'Kelsey' (USA), 'Nubiana' (USA), 'Simka' (USA), 'Methley' (USA), 'Reine Claude', 'French' and 'Sugar' prune types. *Fruit:* The taste colour and size varies with cultivar, but are usually juicy, sweet, often with yellow flesh. *Yield:* A tree can produce ~5–16 kg of fruit per season. Trees bear fruit in 3–5 years.

Cultivation: Trees are tolerant of wet soils and, in general, grow better in temperate rather than warm-temperate areas. They need a longer winter chill (>1000 hours) than Japanese plums. *Propagation, pruning, pests and diseases, etc.* As the general notes.

Cultivars: 'Cacak best': Mid season. Large blue-black prune plum. Used to make the potent Slivovitz plum brandy. Recommended.

'Hauszwetsche': From Germany. Late season. Fruit:

attractive, small, blue-black prune plum; is self-fertile. Good for baking and making schnapps.

'Italian' (syn. 'Fellenburg'): Well-known in western USA. Fruit: large, dark blue with a heavy bloom, sweet, plentiful. Bears extremely heavily, but can drop a lot of fruits in summer. Flesh: yellowish, but turns dark when cooked. Self-fertile. Ripens in late summer. Good for prunes. Tree is disease resistant. Needs ~800 chill hours.

'Macverna': Big, vigorous tree, recommended. Very little disease. Fruit: red with pink flesh. Delicious. Freezes well. May tend to biennial bearing

'Mirabelle': French. Is self-sterile, so needs a pollinator. Grows well in maritime climates. Is used in brandy and in Belgian beer. A spreading tree. Fruits are yellow, speckled red. Recommended for all uses.

'Stanley': Very popular in USA and Europe. Late season. Fruit: large, purplish-blue, freestone. Flesh: greenish-yellow, juicy, sweet, but somewhat bland. Is self-fertile, and is also a useful pollinator. The tree is large and spreading, and starts to fruit when young. It crops heavily, but the fruit is very susceptible to brown rot, also to splitting after rain.

'Victoria': Popular in the UK. Named after Queen Victoria. It is sweet and tasty and can be eaten fresh, but is also used in preserves, etc. Ripens mid summer.

ASIAN SPECIES

Japanese plum, *Prunus salicina*. Although called Japanese plums, they originate from China where they have been cultivated for thousands of years. It is an important tree historically, and the plum blossom is said to be sensitive to the beauty of lute music, and flutters in the breeze. Lao-tse was born beneath a plum tree. It was taken to Japan 200–400 years ago, and from there it has spread around the world. These plums are usually larger, rounder and firmer than European plums and are primarily grown for eating fresh, though they can be preserved. Vary in colour from yellow–red–purple, and have either yellow or dark red flesh. They are important commercially because they ripen before European plums. Trees have rougher bark, more persistent spurs and more numerous flowers than European types. They are also more precocious and vigorous than European plums.

Description: A fast-growing tree, height 8–12 m, spread 5–8 m. Has arching branches and lives ~50 years. Has broad, oval leaves. *Flowers:* Many clusters of attractive white–pink flowers. Blooms very early in spring, so do not plant in areas susceptible to spring frosts; this makes them more suited to warm-temperate areas. They often tend to set too many fruits, and these need thinning. *Fruit:* Tend to be juicier than European plums. Usually have large, round fruits. A tree produces ~5–17 kg of fruit. Most are self-fertile, although pollinators are often planted in commercial orchards. Trees take 2–4 years to start producing fruit.

Cultivation: Do not tolerate poorer, heavy soils as well as European plums. They need less chilling than European plums (500–800 hours). They grow more rapidly than European plums, and need pruning and their fruit thinning more often (see general notes above). Brown rot can be a problem for Japanese plums, particularly in humid maritime regions.

Cultivars: 'Black Doris': Late season. Fruit: medium to large, very dark purple, freestone, with dark red, delicious, tasty flesh. Good for bottling (and jam) because of its

uses

Food
Wonderful just eaten fresh, but they can also be cooked in a wide range of desserts, bottled, made into jams, chutneys, etc. or dried. They also make a reasonable wine. The petals have a mild flavour and a sweet fragrance.

Nutrition
In studies, plums and prunes have been shown to have excellent levels of antioxidants, being amongst the top five commercial fruits in being effective in preventing oxidation in cells, and most of this activity is from the fleshy part of the fruit. Prunes have exceptionally high levels, higher than all other commercial fruits. Plums are a good source of vitamin A (~590 IU), copper, manganese, potassium and fibre. They also have moderate levels of vitamin C (15 mg vitamin C/100 g of flesh), and some vitamin K. Plums also contain some riboflavin, and are low in fat.

Medicinal
Their high antioxidant levels help to boost the immune system, reduce inflammation, help fight cancers, reduce cardiac problems as well as strokes, and has many other benefits. Plums, particularly prunes, also stimulate bowel movement. It is the skin that contains the compounds that have most of this effect, so removing the skin removes most of its benefits. **Warning:** Like all the Rosaceae family, the seeds contain cyanogenic glucosides, which are toxic if eaten in quantity, which is unlikely to occur with stone fruits, but the bark and leaves also contain this compound.

firmness and deep colour. Is a vigorous, upright tree. A favourite. Stores well. Pollinator is 'Duff's Early Jewel'.
'Hollywood': Highly ornamental variety: Leaves are purple-red, as are the fruits, which ripen in mid summer.
'Santa Rosa': Very popular, partly self-fertile. Early season. Fruit: medium large, purplish-red, yellow flesh, firm, sweet, juicy. Tree is hardy, upright and vigorous, and highly productive. Pollinators could be 'Duff's Early Jewel' and 'Omega'. Good for bottling and cooking.
'Satsuma' (syn. 'Blood Plum'): Mid season. Fruit: large, deep red skin and flesh, juicy, very good flavour. Good for jam and desserts. Tree is upright. 'Methley', 'Santa Rosa' and 'Beauty' are its possible pollinators. Needs 300–500 chilling hours.
'Shiro': Excellent all-rounder. Good for eating fresh, bottling, freezing, cooking. Very heavy cropper. Small tree. Very hardy.

OTHER SPECIES

Apricot plum, *Prunus simonii*. A native of eastern Asia and northern China. A smaller tree: height ~6 m. It flowers in early spring. Has large fruits: ~6 cm diameter.

Cultivation: It is somewhat cold hardy, but cannot tolerate late spring frosts. Can grow in more alkaline soils than most of the species described above. *Propagation, pests and diseases, etc.:* see general notes above.

Uses: The fruit can be eaten fresh or cooked. It is aromatic, tasty and fleshy, though quality varies from tree to tree, with some trees having more bitter fruit.

Pissard plum (cherry plum), *Prunus cerasifera* (syn. *P. domestica myrobalan*). A native, probably of western Asia. A small, moderate–fast-growing, upright tree: height ~8 m. It has a rounded crown. It is not very long lived, and starts to decline after ~15 years. The purple-leaved variety, *P. cerasifera* 'Atropurpurea' has young ruby-red leaves that turn reddish-purple in summer, and then, finally, to greenish-bronze in autumn. *Flowers:* Abundant, attractive, small, white–pink, usually borne before the leaves, in early spring.

Fruit: Often numerous, ~2.5–5 cm diameter, purple, fleshy, thin skin, edible and ripen in autumn. Tends to produce many more fruits some years than others.

Cultivation: Prefers warmer climates. Trees grow best in sunny locations, and the leaf colours of ornamental varieties are then more vibrant. Not as tolerant of compacted clays as the species described above. Grows well in alkaline soils. *Propagation, pests and diseases:* as the general notes above. Is susceptible to canker and leaf spot. Needs little to no pruning.

Uses: *Food:* The fruits can be eaten fresh or used in pies, tarts, jams, etc. They have a nice sweet flavour. *Other uses:* The plant is one of the five ingredients in the Bach flower 'Rescue remedy' and is used for 'desperation', 'dread' and 'fear'. A green dye can be obtained from the leaves and fruit. It is often used as a rootstock to give the tree a semi-dwarfing habit. *Ornamental:* The variety *P. cerasifera* 'Atropurpurea' is very popular because of its wonderful leaf colour, as well as its prolific blossom and edible fruits. Looks good as a specimen tree. Can be propagated by cuttings.

Plumcots. A cross between an apricot and plum (*P. armeniaca* x *P. domestica*). It has ~75% plum genes and ~25% apricot genes. Fruits have smooth skin like a plum and are usually self-fertile. Trees start blooming from early spring, and have attractive, larger white flowers. The crosses are trademarked. 'Aprium' is a cross that consists of ~75% apricot genes and ~25% plum genes, and these fruits are covered in a very fine fuzz, as are apricots. These hybrids have a sweet, good flavour. There are a number of cultivars available.

Umeboshi, *Prunus mume*. Has >300 named varieties. It forms a ~6-m tree, and has fragrant, beautiful flowers. A Japanese favourite, the brine-pickled fruit of *P. mume* is an acquired taste. It is pickled for about 2 weeks and then the leaves from a Japanese herb, *Perilla frutescens* var. *crispa*, are added, followed by 4 further weeks of pickling; the plums are then dried. The pickle is often eaten with miso and rice. It is thought to act as a bactericide, to aid digestion and combat fatigue. A dye is also made from the bark and fruit. ■

Prunus spp.
Plum cherry
ROSACEAE (Prunoideae subfamily)

American plum (*Prunus americana*), beach plum (*P. maritima*), Canadian plum (*P. nigra*), chickasaw plum (*P. angustifolia*), hog plum (*P. hortulana*), Mexican plum (*P. mexicana*), Pacific plum (*P. subcordata*), wildgoose plum (*P. munsoniana*)

The *Prunus* stone fruits have been cultivated for many hundreds of years in many temperate regions of the world. They are native to the Middle East, China, northern America and throughout most of Europe. They are, taxonomically, a very diverse group, consisting of many species and cultivars.

The *Prunus* plums are classified into several groups: the European plums, *Prunus domestica*; the Japanese plums, *P. salicina*; the damsons, sloe and greengages, *P. insititia*, *P. spinosa*; and the plum cherries. The plum cherries are natives of North America and often have tasty, but somewhat smaller fruit. These species are sometimes collected from the wild and eaten, but are also cultivated on a small scale for their fruit and ornamental appeal. They are also valuable as a cross with Japanese plum hybrids. Some of the species described here have been selected for their ornamental leaves and blossom as well as for their fruits.

GENERAL DESCRIPTION

Plum cherries form small to medium-sized trees, with branches that tend to be more erect. They have brown, rough bark.

Leaves: Oval or elliptic with either pointed or blunt tips, usually a mid-green colour, with short petioles. Small teeth on margins.

Flowers: Typical Rosaceae flower, white, slightly scented. Occur in numerous clusters of 2–3 flowers, or can be solitary, on short spurs of 2-year-old wood or from the axils of 1-year-old wood. *Pollination:* Mostly by bees, but also by other insects. Some species are self-fertile, though do benefit from cross pollination.

Fruit: A smooth drupe, with a thin edible skin. Oval-shaped or round. Fruit size varies with species. Fruit colour depends on cultivar, but ranges from yellow–purple. They often have a bloom. When ripe, they are fleshy, sweet–acid and refreshing. There is a single stone in the centre, ~1.5–2 cm long.

Yield/harvest/storage: Fruits take 10–24 weeks to mature after pollination. Trees are usually ~3–5 years old when they first begin fruiting. *Harvest:* Most of the fruits described here are harvested in autumn. They are best picked when ripe. Ripeness is best determined by skin colour and softness of fruit. In particular, fruit picked for drying should be fully ripe when harvested. The fruits can bruise easily, so need to be handled carefully. *Storage:* Once ripe, they can be kept for ~14–21 days in a fridge. Ripe

fruits are susceptible to mould, and are best eaten fresh or processed soon after picking.

Roots: Many of the species described below have large, extensive root systems, which enable them to grow in dry, poor soils. Most other plum species have shallow roots. Many of the species described below also readily form suckers from their roots. Trees benefit from an organic mulch. Do not cultivate deeply around trees.

CULTIVATION

They are easier to grow and more tolerant of soil conditions and temperatures than other stone fruits.

Location: They prefer a sunny, fairly sheltered location.

Temperature: They have a similar cold hardiness to apple and pear. Most can be grown in regions that have regular frosts.

Soils/water/nutrients: These plums do best on deep, well-drained loams, but can also grow in a range of poorer soils. They grow best within a pH range of 6.0–7.5. If trees are grown in soils that are too acid, root growth is reduced. They can grow in more alkaline soils; however, if the soil is too alkaline iron deficiencies can occur, which leads to leaf chlorosis, and will need to be remedied with a foliar feed or similar. Trees benefit from some moisture during fruit formation, which results in plumper, juicier fruit, but they need minimal water around harvesting time to reduce the risk of fungal disease. These species are moderately–very drought tolerant. Trees benefit from moderate additions of balanced nutrients at the beginning of the growing season, and as they get older they prefer more nitrogen. Applications of organic mulch are beneficial.

Planting: Space young trees at 3–5 m apart.

Pruning: In general, these plum species only need pruning every 2–3 years. Fruits are often produced on spurs, and the same spurs can produce fruits for several years (from 2–5 years). The fruit buds are produced during the spring–summer on the current season's growth. Prune young trees to several strong shoots to form the main scaffold branches. The tree is grown with an open centre, to allow light and air to freely circulate. To allow the scaffold branches to preferentially develop, other competing shoots or vigorous laterals are removed for the first year or so. Once the scaffold branches are established, the tree only needs the tips of scaffold branches removed to encourage the growth of laterals. Too much pruning results in excess stem and leaf growth at the expense of flower and fruit production. Pruning is best done in late autumn.

Propagation: *Seed:* Trees are occasionally grown as seedlings, but they tend to be variable. Seed can either be

Food

The fruits can be eaten fresh, though can be somewhat sharp. They can also be stewed, made into jams or chutneys, added to sauces, etc.

Nutrition

Probably has the same high antioxidant and vitamin A content as modern plums. **Warning:** Like all the Rosaceae family, the seeds contain cyanogenic glucosides, which are toxic if eaten in quantity, which is unlikely to occur with stone fruits.

Other uses

A green dye can be obtained from the leaves and fruit. The wood is heavy and dense, but is not used extensively because of its limited dimensions.

sown fresh in cold frames and over-wintered or, if stored, it needs 2–3 months of cold stratification, and can then be sown in early spring. Seeds can take 18 months to germinate. Prick out seedlings and grow on in pots for another year or so. *Cuttings:* Take semi-ripe cuttings, with a heel, from spring and through summer. *Layering:* This can be done in spring.

Pests and diseases: They are hardy and healthy trees compared with modern plum varieties, and are seldom affected by major problems. Fungal diseases can be a problem if the trees are grown in humid, wet environments. The insects, plum curculio (*Conotrachelus nenuphar*) and Japanese beetle, can attack these species. Plums may also be attacked by plum-pockets disease, which leaves hollow fruits. The other main problem is likely to be birds, etc. who seek out the ripening fruits.

THE SPECIES

American plum, *Prunus americana*. A native of North America, from New York to Florida, and extending west as far as the Rocky Mountains. The indigenous peoples of the USA have used the fruits for many hundreds of years, and they were dried for winter use. There is limited commercial cultivation in various areas of the USA, and there are several local varieties.

Description: Forms a small, fast-growing, often multi-stemmed tree, ~8 m tall, which is quite short lived. The tree has some spines and red-brown, fairly brittle branches and sharply pointed leaves, 7–10 cm long. The flowers, ~2.5 cm across, are fragrant and are borne in early spring. Fruits are ~2.5 cm in diameter and have a thickish skin: they ripen in autumn to a red-purple (sometimes yellow-brown) colour. The roots sucker more than most other plum species, and can be a nuisance. The trees can form thickets. They have wide-spreading roots.

Cultivation: They are not very wind hardy, and are best planted in fairly sheltered locations. Are best grown in full sun or semi-shade; fruits ripen best in full sun. Fruits need a hot summer to get good fruit quality. Trees are very cold hardy, and can tolerate temperatures as low as –50°C when dormant. *Soil/water/nutrients:* Likes a rich fertile soil. See other general notes above. *Propagation:* See general notes. It is more difficult to propagate from cuttings, but can be easily grown from suckers. These are best dug up during the growing season and established in pots before planting out. This species is often used as a rootstock for other plum species in the USA.

Uses: *Food:* The fruit can be eaten fresh, but is often cooked and used in pies, preserves, etc., or can be dried for later uses. These plum cherries are succulent, juicy, acid–sweet, and can be very pleasant. *Medicinal:* A tea made from the inner bark is used to treat mouth ulcers. *Ornamental:* They have a wide-spreading root system, which makes them a good species for soil stabilisation. It is valued by the local wildlife.

Beach plum, *Prunus maritima*. The beach plum is a shrub that is native to the coastal areas of the eastern USA, from Newfoundland to North Carolina. Plants are tough and survive drought, low nutrient levels, high winds, high salt levels and being sand blasted. It is grown commercially on a small scale in the eastern USA, and the fruits are sometimes sold locally in markets. Recently, it has been investigated in the USA as a tree that, as well as producing fruits, also has a low environmental impact and will stabilise the soil within which it grows, even sand. This plant is also being explored for its commercial possibilities in Australia.

Description: A smaller tree (~1.5–4 m tall, spread ~1.5–4 m) with glossy green leaves (~6 cm long) and red-brown bark with numerous lenticels. It has attractive, white, spring flowers (~1.25 cm diameter) that are borne singly. The fruits are ~1.5–2.5 cm in diameter and were used by the indigenous peoples and early settlers of the USA as a tasty food supplement, and were also dried for winter use. Unlike many plum species, the roots of this species are large and extend over a wide area, trees also form many suckers and can form thickets.

Cultivation: A very adaptable, tough plant, only needing a minimum of maintenance. *Location:* Prefers a location in full sun. It is very salt tolerant, and is ideal for maritime locations. Indeed, it seems as though the fruit do not ripen as well when grown inland. *Temperature:* Is tolerant of a wide range of temperatures, from warm and humid to hard winter frosts. *Soil/water/nutrients:* Can be grown in poor-quality, low-nutrient soils, and will even grow in sand. It will also grow on fairly alkaline soils, though if the soil is very alkaline, iron chlorosis can develop, which will need to be remedied with a foliar feed or similar. This species is drought resistant. Although it is very hardy, like most plants, it will grow and fruit better with regular moisture and reasonable soil quality. It also benefits from the addition of an organic mulch. *Propagation:* See notes above. Additionally, because fruit quality varies from plant to plant, it is best to vegetatively propagate from known good-fruiting individuals. It can be easily propagated from suckers taken during the growing season and then established in pots.

Cultivars: 'Eastham': Fruit large, good flavour; is a heavy cropper.
'Hancock': Fruits ripen early, and are sweet and juicy.
'Squibnocket': Good-quality fruits. Rugged plant for stabilising dunes.

Uses: *Food:* The fruits can be eaten fresh or used in pies, preserves, etc., or can be dried for later use. They do vary in quality from location to location. The best fruits are juicy, sub-acid–sweet. *Ornamental:* Makes an excellent land-reclamation plant. Is very tough, needs a minimum of maintenance and produces edible fruit.

Canadian plum, *Prunus nigra*. The Canadian plum is a native of eastern North America. It is locally cultivated for its fruit, and there a few named varieties. It is closely related to *P. americana*.

Description: Forms a medium-sized, slow-growing tree, ~8 m tall, spread ~5 m. It has long thorns and numerous lenticels, also a suckering root system. *Flowers:* Attractive, white, very fragrant, borne in spring, ~2 cm diameter. *Fruit:* Smallish (~3 cm diameter), red when ripe. They have a thick skin and a large stone; they ripen in autumn. They are sweeter if harvested after the first frosts. Has a suckering root system.

Cultivation: See general notes. It grows best when planted in full sun or semi-shade, though will fruit best in full sun. It is fully cold hardy. *Propagation:* See general notes. Can also be propagated by suckers taken during the growing season, and then potted up to establish.

Uses: *Food:* The fruit is fairly acid and, although they can be eaten fresh when fully ripe, they are more usually used in pies, preserves, etc., or are dried for later use.

Chickasaw plum, *Prunus angustifolia*. A native of North America, this plant is also grown locally for its edible fruits. There are some named varieties.

Description: Small (~4 m tall, ~4 m spread), moderately fast-growing, but short-lived tree with short stems and a rounded crown. It can be multi-stemmed, and may need pruning if a single trunk is required. Has shiny, dark green leaves, many, thin thorny branches and numerous lenticels on its reddish-brown stems. The leaves are small: ~2.5–5 cm long. *Flowers:* Attractive, white, abundant, small (~1 cm diameter), fragrant, borne in spring before the leaves. *Fruit:* Small (~1.25–2.25 cm diameter), fleshy, tasty, juicy and popular with wildlife. Fruits ripen from bright yellow to red in early summer. Tree has an extensive root system and is a useful plant for reclamation and for fairly exposed locations. It also produces many suckers, which can form a thicket and may need to be controlled.

Cultivation: Easy to grow and has no special cultural requirements. It grows best in full sun or semi-shade, though fruits ripen best in full sun. Although it is fully frost hardy, it prefers warm or hot summers. It is quite wind hardy. *Soil:* It tolerates drought, sandy or clay soil. Unlike the other species described here, this plum prefers more acidic soils and does not grow well in alkaline soils. Also see general notes. *Propagation:* See general notes. It can be easily propagated from suckers, which can be taken during the growing season and then established in pots before planting out.

Uses: *Food:* The fruits are either eaten fresh or are used to make a delicious jelly. The best fruits are sweet and juicy, and are good eaten when fresh. They can also be used in pies, preserves, etc. *Ornamental:* This species is sometimes used for shelterbelt planting, and for soil stabilisation. It is sometimes planted as a street tree.

Hog plum, *Prunus hortulana*. A native of the southern and central states of the USA, it forms a tree ~8 m tall. It has been cultivated for many years and is now cultivated locally for its edible fruit. There are a few named cultivars.

Description: Bark is dark red-brown. Leaves are dark green, ~7–9 cm long. Flowers in clusters of 2–4, white, ~1.25 cm diameter, borne in late spring. Fruits have a thin skin, are often smallish (~1.5–2.8 cm), rounded and are red or yellow when ripe. They contain one large seed and ripen in autumn.

Cultivation: *Location/temperature:* Can grow in full sun or semi-shade, though fruits ripen better in sunny locations. It not as hardy as some plum species. Does need a hot summer to produce good fruit crops, and is probably not suited to colder temperate regions. *Soil/water/nutrients:* See general notes. *Propagation:* See general notes. Additionally, because fruit quality varies from plant to plant, it is best to vegetatively propagate from known good-fruiting individuals.

Uses: *Food:* The fruits can be eaten fresh or used in pies, preserves etc. The fruits can be fairly tasty, though quality varies from tree to tree.

Mexican plum, *Prunus mexicana*. Mexican plum is an attractive North American native tree that is sometimes grown in gardens for its ornamental value, as well as for its fruit. It is closely related to *P. americana*.

Description: It forms a spreading, fairly slow-growing, medium-sized tree, ~7–10 m tall, ~8 m spread. It usually forms a single trunk. The bark is dark grey and furrowed. Leaves are yellowy-green, shiny, but fuzzy beneath. It has thorny branches. Sometimes has good orange autumn leaf colour. *Flowers:* Abundant, pretty, white, fragrant, and are borne in late spring. *Fruit:* Are ~3 cm diameter and have a single large stone. Has purple-red, juicy acid–sweet fruits, ~2.5–6 cm diameter.

Cultivation: See general notes. It can grow in full sun or semi shade, though fruits best in full sun. Established trees can be fairly drought resistant. *Propagation:* See general notes. Additionally, because fruit quality varies from plant to plant, it is best to vegetatively propagate from known good-fruiting individuals. The tree has been used as a rootstock for cultivated plums in North America.

Uses: *Food:* The fruits can be eaten fresh or cooked. The flesh of ripe fruits is juicy, but varies in quality from tree to tree. It is not grown commercially for its fruit. *Ornamental:* This tree is sometimes planted as an ornamental specimen tree for its plentiful blossom, its fruit and its autumn colour. It can also be planted in groups or as an under-storey tree.

Pacific plum, *Prunus subcordata*. A native of southwest North America, from Oregon to California. It is cultivated locally for its edible fruit, and there are a few named varieties.

Description: It forms a smallish tree, ~7 m tall. The flowers are borne in spring. Fruits are ~3 cm diameter, and have a very good flavour. Has a single, large seed. Ripens in autumn.

Cultivation: See general notes. Grows and fruits best in full sun. *Propagation:* See general notes

Uses: *Food:* The fruits can be eaten fresh or used in pies, preserves, etc. They have a pleasant acid–sweet taste. The best fruits have a distinctive flavour and are good in a range of desserts, sauces, etc. It is considered by many to be one of the best-flavoured wild fruits of Pacific North America.

Wildgoose plum (wild plum), *Prunus munsoniana*. A native of central North America, it forms a fast-growing medium-sized tree, ~8 m tall. It has been cultivated for many hundreds of years and is now cultivated locally for its edible fruit. There are some named cultivars.

Description: Bark is red-brown at first, turning grey on older wood. Leaves are 6–10 cm long, shiny green above, slightly hairy beneath. *Flowers:* White (~1.5 cm diameter), borne in clusters of 2–4 early spring before the leaves. *Fruit:* ~1.8 cm diameter, and have thin bright red skins when they ripen in late summer. The tree can start to produce fruit when ~3 years old, but is only short-lived.

Cultivation: It is fairly cold hardy. See general notes. It has been hybridised with other species to produce new fruiting cultivars.

Uses: The fruit is good eaten fresh or can be cooked. Has juicy aromatic flesh that is suitable for desserts, pies, preserves, etc. or can be dried for later use. ∎

Prunus salicifolia
Capulin cherry (tropic cherry)
ROSACEAE
Relatives: cherries, plum, chokecherry, almond, peach, apricot, apple

The capulin cherry is a native of, and commonly found throughout, southern North America into Mexico, where it is grown for its fruits. It has been cultivated since early times and is also extensively naturalised in Central America and over much of western South America. The fruit has been an important food, not only for the indigenous Indians, but was also popular with the invading Spaniards. Today it is cultivated in the Andes more than in its northern homeland and the fruits are abundantly available in Andean markets. It is also grown to a limited extent in New Zealand, California and Florida. It does best in regions with warm temperate or subtropical climates, unlike its more common cherry relatives, which need more winter chill.

DESCRIPTION
An erect tree, somewhat umbrella-shaped, with a short, stout trunk and rough, greyish bark with distinctive lenticels. It is very fast growing, reaching ~3 m height in 12–18 months. It can eventually reach ~8 m.

Leaves: It is semi-deciduous, only shedding its leaves in colder regions. The leaves are alternate, aromatic, large, ~6–18 cm long, slender with serrated edges. They are deep glossy green above and pale greyish-green beneath. New leaves are often tinged pinkish-bronze.

Flowers: Abundant, pretty, dangling racemes of white, five-petalled, fragrant flowers in early spring with one or more leaves at the base. They are borne from leaf axils or on short spurs. Individual flowers are ~2 cm diameter with a conspicuous tuft of yellow stamens. Flowers are bisexual and self-fertile, though more than one tree can improve fruit-set and quality. *Pollination:* By bees mostly.

Fruit: Attractive bunches of 15–20 light red–deep purple-red drupes, 1–2 cm diameter. They have a thin, tender skin, which may occasionally be slightly bitter. Many fruits can fall before maturity, particularly in dry weather. Depending on climate and variety, they ripen from early- to mid summer. The flesh is pale green, firm, juicy, sweet, yet sub-acid and tasty, and is similar to wild cherries or some say like plums in taste. There is a single largish stone with a bitter kernel that shouldn't be eaten. They ripen before most other major cherries.

Yield/harvest: For a cherry tree, they are very early to start producing, and can produce fruits when only 3 years old. Also, if grown with good soil, warmth and moisture, trees can set a second crop in autumn. For reasons unknown, trees with pale grey bark seem to produce larger fruits than those with darker bark. Fruits can be picked without their stems. They are best picked when fully coloured and have just started to soften, as they do not ripen well if picked when still hard. Fruits do not bruise very easily and store fairly well: they can be kept in a refrigerator for >4 weeks.

CULTIVATION
Not recommended for containers because of their size and growth rate.

Location: Best grown in full sun. Trees do not like windy situations or too much salt.

Temperature: They are adapted to warm temperate and subtropical climates. However, they are also surprisingly frost tolerant; some reports say they can tolerate temperatures colder than –20°C, though will probably benefit from some cold acclimatisation. Frosts can damage smaller branches.

Chilling: One of the few cherry species that does not need a long period of winter chill to form flowers the following spring, so can be grown in warmer regions than most cherry species.

Soil/water/nutrients: They are adaptable to soil type and will grow in any reasonably fertile soil. They can thrive in poor soil, even clays, but prefer dry, sandy soils with a pH of 5.5–6.5 They cannot tolerate waterlogging. Trees are somewhat drought tolerant once established, though grow better and produce better fruit with regular watering, particularly during the spring–summer period. They respond well to light applications of nitrogen when the blossoms first appear, otherwise, in reasonably good soils, the trees only need an annual mulch of compost.

Planting: Space trees at 6–8 m apart. Stake young trees as they grow rapidly and will need protection from strong winds.

Propagation: *Seed:* Easily propagated from seed, but fruit quality is variable. Seeds are best sown fresh, though germinate better with a short period of cold stratification before sowing in spring. Germination can take 18 months. Grow on seedlings for a year or so before planting out. *Cuttings:* Semi-ripe cuttings, with a heel, can be taken in summer and inserted into gritty, moist compost to root. Hardwood cuttings can also be made. *Grafting:* Seedling plants are often used as rootstocks for desired cultivars, using tip, wedge or cleft grafts.

Pruning: Trees need very little pruning to remain productive, just to keep their fruits within reach for harvest. However, they can cope with radical pruning and can be grown as a fruiting hedge. They are usually pruned to form a vase shape, with an open centre, which they tend naturally to form anyway. After initial shaping of trees, the only pruning necessary is the removal of excess twiggy growth. Trees are usually pruned in early autumn.

Food

Fruits can be eaten fresh or used in desserts, or can be preserved whole or made into jam. In Mexico they are used to fill tamales. The flesh can be mixed with milk and served with vanilla and cinnamon as a dessert. They can be fermented to make an alcoholic drink. The juice can be mixed with cornmeal to make a cake.

Nutrition

Relatively high levels of vitamin C: ~10 mg/100 g of flesh. They are also high in anthocyanins, which may protect artery walls from damage. Fruits are best eaten fresh to get their full benefits. They are high in vitamin A. Recent research on cherry growers has shown that they have a lower incidence of cancer and heart conditions than the general public, with growers eating, on average, ~3 kg of sour cherries per year. They are also effective at reducing the build-up of LDL (low-density lipoprotein), a contributor to heart disease, stroke and arteriosclerosis. Cherries also contain perilyl alcohol, which has been shown to switch tumour cells to a less malignant form. The gum from the trunk has been used to treat coughs. They also have good levels of phosphorus.

Medicinal

A syrup made from the fruits is taken to alleviate respiratory troubles. The leaves can be used to treat diarrhoea, dysentery, colic, neuralgia and as an antispasmodic, and are applied in poultices to relieve inflammation. The pounded bark has been used as an eyewash. *Warning:* Like all Rosaceae, the seeds, leaves and bark contain cyanic-based compounds that can be toxic if eaten in quantity, though one is unlikely to eat many cherry stones by mistake!

Other uses

The seeds contain 35% of a yellow, semi-drying oil that is used in soaps and paints. The flowers are much visited by honeybees. The heartwood is reddish-brown, fine-grained, very hard, strong, durable and is used for furniture, panelling, cabinets, turnery, etc.

Ornamental

Good for planting to prevent erosion, and can be interplanted with field crops. Also makes an attractive garden tree with pretty blossom, almost evergreen leaves and abundant fruits.

Pests and diseases: Relatively free of many of the problems that beset other cherries and stonefruit trees. However, bacterial gummosis can be an occasional problem, and some varieties are prone to die-back for unknown reasons. Pests may include mites, pear slugs and scale. Birds are attracted to the fruit, but they seem to be less of a problem on Capulin cherries than on regular cherries.

CULTIVARS

'Ecuadorian': Very large, round fruits, 2.5–3.25 cm diameter. Light green, sweetish flesh, good quality, free of astringency when ripe. It forms a drooping tree and has very good yields.
'Fausto': Large fruit, 2–2.5 cm diameter. Flesh is green, rich, sweet flavour. Ripens late. Tree: upright, but drooping. Has reliable, abundant yields.
'Harriet': A dwarfing tree. Fruit: large, flattened, ~2 cm diameter, purple-black when ripe. Flesh is green, slightly sub-acid, good flavour, small seeds. Poorish yields.
'Huachi Grande': Fruit: large, round, ~2.5 cm diameter, mild-flavoured and not tangy, good yields. Ripens early–mid season. Fruits have more flavour with hot summers. Tree: large crops, can over-produce.
'Lomeli': Fruit: large, roundish, 2.5–3 cm diameter. Flesh is fairly astringent, good flavour, small seed. Has very good yields, can produce >100 kg of fruit. Does well in cool coastal locations.
'Werner': Fruit: small, very good flavour, low yields. Tree: very fast growing: ~5 m/year. ∎

Psidium cattleianum
(syn. *P. littorale*, *P. chinense*)

Cattleya guava (strawberry guava, red cherry guava, purple guava, yellow cherry guava, Chinese guava, Calcutta guava, giant Puerto Rican cattleya)

MYRTACEAE

Relatives: tropical guava (*Psidium guajava*), Brazilian guava (*P. guineense*), jaboticaba, camu-camu, eucalyptus

This species was named after William Cattley, an English horticulturist who encouraged its cultivation in England in the early 1800s. It also has a wide range of common names that it is known by. Cattleya guavas make excellent small trees for landscaping, but can also be easily grown and will fruit when planted in large containers, or can be grown as an ornamental hedge and should still fruit. In a few regions it has become naturalised and has been classified as a weed, e.g. Norfolk Island. There are two main forms of cattleya, a yellow-fruited form and a red-fruited form. The yellow-fruited guava (*Psidium cattleianum* var. *lucidum*) has large round yellow fruit with sweet, delicious aromatic flesh, but is generally not very tangy. The red cattleya (*P. littorale* var. *longipes*), has delicious, tangy flesh and is a smaller tree than the yellow type. It is more suited to smaller gardens, and will still produce fruits if trimmed to fit into a small space. Both cattleya guavas are good plants for a home garden because of their ornamental properties, the great range of soil pH conditions they can grow in, their non-invasive root systems, their fruit production for many years, even if pruned, and their attractive foliage and flowers.

DESCRIPTION

Small trees with almost horizontal branches that spread out from the main stem, close to the ground. Mature trees have attractive reddish-brown peeling bark. They sometimes produce suckers from roots near the base of the trunk. Their growth can be moderately vigorous in good soil with plenty of warmth and moisture. The yellow-fruited species is larger, growing to ~12 m (and has larger leaves), compared to the red-fruited cattleyas, which range in size from 2–4 m tall.

Leaves: Glossy, deep green, evergreen, attractive, ~3–12 cm long, 1.5–6 cm wide, depending on species. New growth is reddish-bronze.

Flowers: Fragrant, attractive, 1.5–6 cm wide, depending on species, white with many fluffy, powder-puff-like, prominent stamens, ~2 cm long. Flowers are borne singly or in small clusters (of ~3) from the leaf axils of the present season's growth in spring. The have an inferior ovary. *Pollination:* By bees and other insects, and possibly by nectar-feeding birds. Trees are monoecious and the flowers are bisexual. They are self-fertile, so only need one tree to set fruit, though more than one tree can increase fruit-set.

Fruits: Taking the form of false berries, they are round–oval, and have a distinctive protruding 4- to 5-sepalled calyx at their apex. The fruits of red species are smaller, ~2.5 cm long, are sweet, but tangy. They turn deep red-purple and drop when fully ripe. Red-skinned species have pinkish-white flesh. Yellow-skinned fruits are larger and have pale yellow, sweet flesh. In both types, the flesh is aromatic, thin, ~0.5 cm thick, and surrounds a juicy, pulpy centre that is filled with hard, flattened, small (0.25 cm long), edible seeds. These guavas often tend to be fairly seedy, though there are some nearly seedless cultivars. The fruits are sharply tangy, but tasty and spicy.

Yield/harvest/storage: These guavas are very productive and trees can produce good yields once established. Seedling plants take quite a long time to start producing fruit: 7–8 years. Both types fruit from summer through to late autumn, depending on climate, with fruits becoming slightly soft and fully coloured when fully ripe. There can be a smaller second crop in mid winter in warmer regions. Once picked, the ripe fruits cannot be stored for long and quickly deteriorate after 3–4 days at room temperature. Keep picked fruits in a cool place till eaten or processed.

Roots: Trees form many shallow roots, which benefit from an organic mulch to retain moisture and provide nutrients. Avoid mechanical cultivation. Exudates from their roots tend to inhibit the growth of weeds around their root system.

The red-fruited types also form deep taproots, which makes them more drought tolerant, but also more susceptible to flooding. The plant's roots form a mycorrhizal fungal relationship, which enables them to obtain extra nutrients, such as phosphates, and, in return, the fungi receive sugars from the tree. In general, the red types form less spreading roots then the yellow types, and the former can be planted near buildings, etc.

CULTIVATION

Location: Trees are best grown in full sun, though can grow with a little shade. They have good salt tolerance. Their branches are strong, making them tolerant to high winds. They can be planted in exposed maritime locations.

Temperature: Is somewhat more cold hardy than the tropical guava, with these species being the hardiest of the guava family. They can tolerate freezing temperatures down to ~–5.5°C without damage, and even lower temperatures for brief periods with minimal damage. Young trees are less cold tolerant and need extra protection. Have a climatic range similar to orange trees. The yellow form is somewhat more cold tender than the red-fruited guava. Trees do not like very hot summer temperatures.

Food
The fruits are usually eaten fresh, but can also be used in jellies, jams, icecream, sauces, cakes, tarts, drinks, chutney, etc. They have a tangy yet sweetish flavour that some compare to strawberries. They do not have the musky flavour of tropical guavas.

Nutrition
Good levels of vitamin C, 37 mg/100 g of flesh, though not quite as high as those of tropical guava. The fruits also contain some niacin, iron, calcium and phosphorus. They also contain good levels of fibre.

Ornamental
The red type is more suited to small gardens and forms a tidy, upright, small tree. The yellow types can be grown as a specimen tree in larger gardens. The tree is often used in landscaping, and the red type, in particular, can be trimmed to form a hedge.

Soil/water/nutrients: The cattleya guava can grow in poorer soils than many other fruit trees. Like the tropical guava, the cattleya guava can grow in soils with a very wide pH range, from very acid to moderately alkaline: pH 3.5–7.5. Drought tolerance is high in the red-fruited species, with the yellow-fruited types being more tolerant to short periods of flooding. Trees produce better-quality fruits if given regular moisture during fruit formation. Although they can grow in poor soils, these trees grow and fruit better with additions of a complete, balanced fertiliser 2–3 times a year when trees are young, with applications still continuing as the tree matures, but of lesser amounts. In particular, they benefit from the addition of calcium and magnesium, as well as the micronutrients. If fruiting heavily, they may benefit from additional nitrogen.

Pot culture: The red species is ideal for container growth. It makes a very attractive small tree with its glossy leaves, attractive flowers and aromatic fruit. It does not need much maintenance, but if given regular moisture and nutrients, it should produce fruits.

Planting: Space red-fruited species at 2–4 m apart, and yellow-fruited species spaced at >4 m apart.

Pruning: Prune trees in late autumn or early spring. Flowers and fruits are produced on the present season's growth so do not prune once spring growth has commenced. Young trees may need some training to establish a few main, strong scaffold branches. They can be trained to a vase shape. Once this has been established, older trees need very little pruning. If too many fruits are formed in some years, these can be thinned to even out yields for the following year(s). Guavas can be pruned or trained to form a large bush to allow easier harvesting, or into a small tree with a single trunk.

Propagation: *Seed:* Often propagated by this method, although progeny from red-type guavas are variable in growth, fruit quality, etc. Yellow-fruited guavas produce mostly nucellar seeds, which produce seedlings that are clones of the parent. However, any non-nucellar seeds will produce variable seedlings. Those seeds that germinate first are more likely to be of nucellar origin. Wash seeds free of any pulp before sowing in well-drained compost with warmth. *Cuttings:* Semi-ripe cuttings can be taken during summer and inserted into gritty compost. Cuttings from any runners can also be taken, choosing sections that have 2–4 healthy buds. Plant just below the soil surface and keep moist. *Layering:* Root layering can be successful and this is best done during the growing season. *Grafting:* Budding and grafting are not usually practised because of the thinness of the bark.

Pests and diseases: Very few problems. Can get fruit flies going for the fruit, as do birds and animals. ∎

Psidium guajava
(syn. *P. pomiferum, P. pyriferum*)
Tropical guava
MYRTACEAE

Similar species: Brazilian guava, *Psidium guineense*
Relatives: Cattleya guava, rumberry, eucalyptus

The tropical guava probably originates from an area extending from Mexico, through Central America into South America. Tropical guavas have been valued in South America for thousands of years, and their seeds have been found at Peruvian archaeological sites. Europeans took the seeds from South America to Africa, Asia, India and the Pacific, and this species is now grown in many warm temperate, subtropical and tropical areas of the world. In some tropical areas, it has become wild and forms thickets in pastures, roadsides and wasteland, and is sometimes classified as a weed in these regions. However, it behaves itself in temperate climates, and will grow well in a very wide range of soil types and conditions. It is more cold hardy than its name suggests, is easy to grow, has attractive foliage, fluffy white flowers over a long period and produces abundant sweet, juicy fruits.

DESCRIPTION

Small trees, to 3–8 m tall, with spreading, almost horizontal branches that form from the main stem close to the ground. Young twigs are four-sided and downy. Mature trees have attractive bark, which is smooth, thin, papery, mottled, green or reddish brown, and peels off in thin flakes to reveal the young light greenish layer beneath. They sometimes produce suckers from roots near the base of the trunk. Their growth can be quite vigorous in good soil with plenty of warmth and moisture.

Leaves: Evergreen, large, dull mid-green, coarse, opposite, with prominent veins. The stiff, leathery leaves are slightly downy beneath and are oval or elliptic in shape, 6–14 cm long. They have a short leaf stalk. Crushed leaves are pleasantly aromatic. Leaves turn an attractive maroon colour in cooler weather.

Flowers: Attractive, faintly fragrant, soft, fluffy white, produced from late spring–through summer over a long season, and for most of the year in warmer regions. Borne singly or in clusters from the leaf axils of the present season's growth, are ~2.5 cm diameter, with 4 or 5 white petals. These petals soon fall to leave the numerous (~250), fluffy, white stamens, which are tipped with yellow pollen. They have an inferior ovary. Each bloom lasts about 24 hours. Flowers are monoecious and bisexual, so trees are self-fertile and only need one plant to set fruits, though more then one tree encourages cross pollination. *Pollination:* By bees and other insects, and possibly nectar-feeding birds.

Fruit: They range in shape from round–oval–pear-shaped, and from 5–9 cm long, weigh from ~50–300 g, and are borne on the present season's growth. They have a small, green calyx left at their apex, and so are classified as false berries. Their skin colour is usually yellow. Their flesh can be variously coloured from white–yellow–rose–red. There is an outer firm flesh layer, with a central region filled with small, soft seeds and juicy pulp. The latter contains harder seeds and less juice in inferior fruits. Fruits may have a thin skin with many seeds, or can be thick skinned with only a few seeds: cultivars differ widely in flavour and seediness. Most trees are self-fruitful. When ripe, the fruit have a distinctive, pleasant aroma which tends to be stronger in hotter climates. When unripe, the fruits are green, hard, very astringent and have a gummy latex. Fruits soften as they ripen and the flesh becomes creamy and succulent in warmer regions, though the quality of the fruit can sometimes be disappointing in cooler regions. It is possible to eat the rind of some cultivars.

Yield/harvest/storage: Trees grow rapidly and can fruit in 2–4 years from seed. They live 30–40 years, but yields decline after the ~15th year. A healthy tree in good soil should produce ~3–50 kg of fruit per year. Can get very good yields from young trees. Fruits take 3–6 months to mature, soften, turn fully yellow and develop a rich aroma. They are harvested from late summer into winter depending on climate. Are best picked when fully ripe. Can get two crops a year in the tropics: a heavier crop with smaller fruits in autumn, and a smaller crop but with larger fruits in early spring. The skins bruise fairly easily, so need to be harvested carefully. Under-ripe fruits will ripen somewhat if picked early and left at room temperature or placed in a polythene bag with ripe ethylene-producing fruits, e.g. banana or apple. Mature green fruits can be stored for 2–5 weeks in a fridge; ripe fruits can only be stored for a few days before they start to decompose.

Roots: Trees form many shallow roots, which benefit from an organic mulch to retain moisture and provide nutrients. Avoid mechanical cultivation. Exudates from their roots tend to inhibit the growth of weeds around the root system. They also form deep taproots, except for trees grown from cuttings or air layers. The plants benefit from a mycorrhizal fungal relationship with the roots, which enables the plant to obtain extra nutrients, such as phosphates, and, in return, the fungi receive sugars from the tree. Trees are planted in South America for their ability to improve soil structure, and well as for their fruits and medicinal properties.

CULTIVATION

They are tougher and easier to grow than would be first thought and, once established, need little maintenance, surviving considerable neglect. Despite their common name, 'tropical', they are in fact tougher than many semi-tropicals or warm temperate species, depending on the cultivar chosen.

Temperature: The tropical guava is best adapted to warmer climates, and can tolerate hot summer temperatures. It can grow in both humid and dry climates, but tends to produce better fruit in areas with definite winter and summer seasons. They can survive a few degrees of frost and usually recover from brief frost of ~-3°C, but may suffer some leaf damage. Young trees, in particular, need extra protection from freezing temperatures. Older trees have been killed to the ground, but usually send up new shoots from their base, which go on to produce fruit. Planting them against a sunny wall or on sunny slopes gives them extra warmth and protection in cooler regions.

Location: They grow best in full sun. They are not very wind tolerant if grown from cuttings or have been air-layered, and the whole tree can topple over; other trees are more tolerant. Are fairly salt tolerant, so could be grown in sheltered maritime locations.

Soil/water/nutrients: Trees grow best in a fertile, moist deep loams, but will also grow in many other soil types, including heavy clay, marl, sand–gravel soils or on limestone. They tolerate an extremely wide pH range of 4.5–8.5, which is wider than many other fruiting species. They are also somewhat salt-resistant. They grow best with good drainage, but can survive wet or even waterlogged soils, although they struggle somewhat. In general, they prefer regular moisture during spring–summer to flower, and to retain and mature a good crop, although the surface soil should be allowed to dry out between watering sessions. Young trees are quite nutrient hungry and benefit from regular applications of a balanced, complete fertiliser, with liquid sprays of micronutrients that include copper, manganese, iron and zinc, during the growing season. If producing heavily, extra nitrogen can be beneficial, particularly in spring. Mature trees do not need as many applications.

Pot culture: Tropical guavas make good container plants because of their smaller size, and can be taken in or given extra protection in colder regions. They have evergreen foliage, which develops colourful tints during the colder months, pretty, white fluffy flowers and many, delicious fruits.

Planting: If possible, allow 5–8 m between trees, with wider distances in areas where trees grow vigorously. To enhance fruit flavour, site the trees where warm autumn temperatures are likely.

Pruning: Shaping the tree and removal of suckers or damaged stems is often all that is needed, though trimming off the ends of the main stems will encourage new lateral growth, which will produce more fruit. The other possibility is that trees become too top heavy and dense, produce too much fruit, and their branches are liable to be damaged; trees may need thinning to prevent this. Trees can be pruned to a vase shape with 4–5 main scaffold branches. Encourage branches with wide angles, which allow light to penetrate and fruit to form better. Because fruits are borne on new growth, pruning does not interfere with next year's crop. It can be trimmed to form an informal hedge or screen. Trees can be rejuvenated by drastic pruning.

Propagation: Seed: Trees can be propagated from seed, but the progeny are variable. Its seed remains viable for many months. Once sown, it often germinates in 2–3 weeks, but can take ~8 weeks. *Cuttings:* Take semi-ripe cuttings through summer, dip in a rooting hormone and insert in well-drained,

Food

Better fruits are delicious eaten fresh, with firm, sweet–sub-acid outer flesh and juicy sweet inner pulp with soft, small edible seeds. They can also be used in various desserts or salads. Some people cook the fruits, and they may be stewed, though this will destroy their vitamin C content. Fruit can be added to icecream, sauces, jam, cakes, drinks, chutney, etc. In South America, a thick guava paste and a guava cheese are made, as is guava jelly.

Nutrition

Vitamin C content is a very high 200–400 mg/100 g of fresh fruit, being greatest in just-ripened fruits, and then declining with age. Most vitamin C is in the skin, but also in the outer firm flesh. They also have good levels of vitamin A, some niacin and potassium, and also contain ellagic acid. They have 7–10% sugar. They also contain good levels of fibre. The seeds contain ~14% of an aromatic oil.

Medicinal

The fruits have been recently shown to have remarkable antioxidant properties. The ellagic acid has been found to help prevent tumours. The fruit may also reduce triglyceride levels in the blood (a risk indicator for heart disease) and reduce hypertension, while increasing the level of high density lipoproteins ('good' cholesterol). The fruit enhance the absorption of dietary iron better than other fruits. The roots, bark, leaves and immature fruits, because of their tannin and astringency, are often used to treat gastroenteritis, diarrhoea and dysentery. Crushed leaves are applied to wounds, ulcers, skin diseases and rheumatic areas, and leaves are chewed to relieve toothache. A leaf decoction is taken to treat pulmonary disorders, and is gargled to relieve oral inflammations. The leaves contain quercetin, which has been recently shown to inhibit the spasmolytic effect of the gut and prevent diarrhoea. The leaves have also been shown to reduce coughing spasms and contain flavonoids that react against *Staphylococcus aureus* and other microbes. They may also help with menstrual pain and heavy periods.

Other uses

The wood is yellow–reddish, fine-grained, compact, fairly strong and is used in carpentry and turnery. The leaves (~10%) and bark (~30%) are rich in tannin and are used to tan hides and to make a black fabric dye.

Ornamental

Makes a good specimen tree with its evergreen foliage, flowers and aromatic fruits. They are planted as a regeneration species in some areas because of their ability to improve soil structure.

gritty compost. Root cuttings can also be taken and covered with 5–10 cm of moist soil. *Layering:* Can also be air-layered, but trees from cuttings or air-layers do not form a good taproot, and are apt to blow down in the first 2 or 3 years. *Grafting:* Approach grafting gives ~90% success. Budding is also practised, with the Forkert method proving to give the best results (~90%); shield- and patch-budding are also used. A problem with this method is that many water sprouts and suckers are often produced by the rootstock because a vigorous seedling rootstock is usually used.

Pests and diseases: Generally have few problems, but *Anthracnose* can be a problem in humid areas. Other problems are scale, root-rot nematodes, thrips, guava whitefly, guava moth. Caribbean and Mediterranean fruit flies can be a big problem, and tropical guava acts as a host for these species. In addition, can get mealybugs, scale and common white flies. Wilt, associated with *Fusarium* and *Macrophomina* spp., can slowly kill young trees, and is often caused by under-nourishment.

CULTIVARS

There are many different cultivars around the world, some of which have been more developed for canning and have a thicker skin and harder seeds. Some of the better cultivars have yellow skin and pink flesh.

'Detwiler': Fruit: medium–large, roundish. Skin: greenish-yellow, moderately thick. Flesh: yellowish–pinkish, medium firm, relatively sweet, pleasant flavour. Quality very good. A very heavy bearer.

'Hong Kong Pink': From Hawaii. Fruit: medium–large, roundish. Flesh: pinkish-red, very thick, smooth-textured, sub-acid–sweet, very pleasant, few seeds. Tree spreading, high yielding.

'Lucknow 42': Fruit: medium size, roundish. Flesh: creamy-white, soft, sweet, pleasant, very few seeds, good quality, keeps well. Tree bears heavily.

'Mexican Cream': From Mexico. Skin: yellow. Flesh: creamy-white, soft, thick, very sweet, fine-textured, good eating. Medium pear-shaped–roundish fruits. Fairly soft seeds. Tree upright.

'Philippine': Yellow skin, white, soft flesh, sweet. Medium–large fruit.

'Red Indian': Fruit: aromatic, medium–large, roundish–globose, yellow skin. Flesh: medium thick, red, sweet flavour; numerous small seeds. Good eaten fresh. Fairly productive.

'Ruby': Oval with green skin. Flesh: pink, soft, thick, aromatic, sweet, relatively few seeds. Medium-sized fruit. Good eaten fresh; fairly productive.

'Sweet White Indonesian': Fruit: large, roundish. Skin: pale yellow. Flesh: thick, white, melting, sweet, delicious, seed softer and edible. Vigorous, fast growing tree, can bear several times a year.

SIMILAR SPECIES

Brazilian guava (guisaro, Guinea guava), *Psidium guineense.* A similar species that is also native to South America. It prefers to grow in warm temperate climates, though can withstand brief exposure to temperatures of ~2°C. It prefers to grow in loamy or sandy soils, and does not grow well in clay or waterlogged soils. It is relatively drought tolerant once established. Propagation as for tropical guava. It forms a small, shrub or small tree, rarely growing to 3 m tall. It has small, grey-green leaves, and grows best in full sun. The white, attractive flowers are borne singly or in small clusters. They have numerous long, fluffy stamens, as is typical of this family. Shrubs can start producing fruits in ~2 years. However, they benefit from cross pollination and produce best fruits if planted in small groups.

Uses: The round or pear-shaped fruits, which can be yellowish or red, are small (1.5 cm diameter), but are often sweet and are said to have a pineapple or strawberry flavour. However, some fruits are reported to be quite sour, particularly those from yellow-fruiting cultivars. The flesh is fairly firm, even when ripe, and contains several small seeds. Sweeter fruits can be eaten fresh, or they are often used in jams, desserts, etc. Medicinally, the bark, which is high in tannin, has been used to treat diarrhoea, and urinary diseases. The leaves have been used to treat colds and bronchitis. The bark contains a lot of tannin and has been used to tan hides, etc. The wood is strong, though of small proportions. ∎

Punica granatum

Pomegranate (granada, grenade)

PUNICACEAE

The Punicaceae family is small, and has just two species; one is endemic to the Middle East and India, and the other is confined to the island of Socotra in the Arabian Sea. The family is similar in many ways to that of the Rosaceae, but the fruit and flower structures are different. The pomegranate is found in many regions of the world because of its long association with humans, who have distributed it far and wide. It has been cultivated for thousands of years and is now naturalised around Mediterranean and northern African regions. The Chinese have also known about and cultivated the pomegranate for more than 2000 years. It has been widely recorded by many civilisations throughout history, and only the fig is mentioned as much in mythical and Biblical writings. The fruit was recorded in Egyptian mythology and art; it was praised in the Old Testament and in the Babylonian Talmud and was also known to have been carried by desert caravans across Africa. It has been cultivated in the Far East for many hundreds of years. In ancient Greece, the fruits were associated with fertility due to its multitude of delicious seeds. Its name pomegranate is derived from 'pomum', a Latin word meaning 'fruit', and from 'granum', the Latin term for seed, hence a 'seedy fruit', which it certainly is.

DESCRIPTION

A smallish, attractive tree, ~4–7 m tall, ~5 m spread, although there are also various small, bushy cultivars. Has a neat, rounded crown and a somewhat exotic appearance. The branches are stiff, angular and are often spiny, with spines being 5–8 cm long. The bark is red-brown, becoming grey as the tree ages. Although long-lived (>200 years), it is slow growing and its vigour can decrease after only ~20 years. It needs hot summers to produce the best fruits. It does sucker wildly.

Leaves: Usually deciduous, but in warmer, more humid areas the leaves may remain on the tree year-round. They are glossy, opposite or in whorls of five or six, lanceolate, 3–10 cm long, leathery, mid green.

Flowers: Showy, long-lasting, scarlet, crinkled, waxy, bell-shaped flowers (>3 cm), borne terminally on wood in clusters of 1–5 flowers from spring, through summer, and even into late autumn in warmer areas. There are numerous stamens. The ovary is inferior, so seeds form within the receptacle, which is the pomegranate fruit. They are bisexual, self-fertile and only need one tree to set good crops of fruits, although cross pollination improves fruit quality and quantity. Some cultivars have variegated red/white flowers. The thick, tubular, red calyx persists on the fruit and has 5–8 pointed sepals. *Pollination:* By insects or hummingbirds.

Fruit: Pink–red–deep red, ~5–10 cm diameter, irregular rounded shape, and classified as a pome. The leathery rind has a prominent red calyx. Under the rind lies a thin white layer of endocarp. The interior of the fruit is separated into membranous white-walled compartments, with many seeds in each compartment, each surrounded by very juicy sacs of pink–ruby-red juice, which is sweet–acid, and the single, angular seed can be soft or hard and they make up ~50% of the weight of the fruit. Although trees will grow and produce fruits in temperate areas, they produce more, better quality fruits when grown in hot, sunny Mediterranean-type climates.

Yield/harvest/storage: It takes 5–7 months for fruits to mature after pollination. Young trees can begin to bear fruits as soon as the second year after planting out, but it usually takes 3–4 years. Once mature, a tree produces ~15–30 kg/tree. Younger trees (2–5 years old) can undergo severe fruit drop, and this may be caused by over-watering or over-fertilisation. Mature trees do not seem to suffer fruit drop in this way. Fruit ripen in late autumn–winter. They can be harvested when they have developed a full red colour and have a metallic sound when tapped. They should

Food

Fruits can be consumed fresh by cutting in half and then removing and eating the clusters of juice sacs. The fruits are often used for their juice, which, in the best varieties, is a sweet–tart mix. The sacs can be removed and squeezed to obtain the juice. Another method is to warm the fruit slightly, roll it gently between the hands, then cut a hole in base and suck out the juice. The juice can be added to jellies, sorbets, cold or hot sauces, made into a sweet and sour sauce, added to chutney, or used to flavour cakes, desserts, etc. Pomegranate syrup is sold commercially as grenadine, and is the 'sunrise' in tequila sunrise. The juice can also be made into a wine. The sacs are attractive as a garnish. In India, the wild fruits are often dried to make 'anardana'. The juice sacs are exposed to the sun till quite dry and are then sold as a spice. The rind is bitter and is usually not eaten. The seeds can also sometimes be bitter.

Nutrition/medicinal

Contain reasonable levels of vitamin C: ~10 mg/100 g of flesh, and good levels of B6, pantothenic acid, vitamin K, potassium and copper. Contains ellagic acid, which is protective against cancer and strengthens connective tissue. The fruits have very good levels of flavonoids within them, i.e. 2–3 times that of red wine and green tea. In addition, in the UK, they are being researched for the production of a compound that kills viruses, which is hoped could be an antiviral agent against HIV. In India, a preliminary study has found that the seeds have potent antimicrobial properties against a number of bacteria. The fruit are also being researched for their cancer-fighting properties, including breast cancer. Another study in Israel found that the juice was able to slow down cholesterol oxidation by almost 50%, and to reduce the retention of low density lipids. In a separate study, it was found that if the juice was taken daily, it prevented the thickening of arteries. Recent research has also found that pomegranates seem to be able to block the enzymes that contribute to osteoarthritis. The fruits also may contain phyto-oestrogens, which may aid the symptoms of menopause. Historically, the ripe fruits have been eaten as a tonic, laxative and to clean the blood. They are also used to treat a sore throat, sore eyes and chest troubles. In Mexico, a decoction of the flowers is gargled to relieve oral and throat inflammations. The bark (~28%), root, fruit rind (~25%) and leaves (~10%) all contain high amounts of tannins, so should probably not be consumed in large amounts. They have been used as a hypotensive, an antispasmodic and to eliminate internal parasites.

Other uses

The leaves, seeds, roots and bark have been used to tan leather and as a dye for textiles. The dried rind yields a fast yellow dye, which is used for cloth and as a hair dye. A black ink can be made by steeping the leaves in vinegar. In Japan, an insecticide is derived from the bark. The pale yellow wood is very hard and has been used in woodcrafts.

Ornamental

The pomegranate makes a good-sized, specimen tree for smaller gardens, with attractive leaves, pretty flowers and edible, refreshing fruit. It is more suited to regions that have hot summers, where the fruits are of better quality. A dwarf form is popular in Japanese bonsai.

not be picked until fully ripe as they won't ripen properly afterwards. Conversely, if left too long on the tree, the fruits tend to split, particularly in wet weather. Fruits formed in later summer often do not get time to fully mature before cold weather begins. Fruits have a long storage life and, if kept cool and shaded, they can be stored for ~7 months without spoiling; indeed, the fruits actually improve, become juicier and develop more flavour during storage. Because of its long storage time, it was viable to use the fruit on extended journeys by desert caravans.

CULTIVATION

An easy-to-grow tree that has attractive leaves, flowers and fruit. Needs little maintenance, but will do best in hotter regions.

Location: Is fairly salt tolerant, so can be grown in maritime areas. Regions with hot, dry summers and cool winters are ideal. They prefer to grow in full sun, but can also be grown in semi-shade.

Temperature: The warmer the climate, the sweeter and tastier the fruit. In cool-summer areas 'Eversweet' could be a good choice. Trees can be severely injured by temperatures below ~−10°C, but are more cold hardy than citrus species. When dormant, it can survive cold winters, but late spring frosts can kill flower buds.

Chilling: Needs only a minimum of winter chilling (i.e. temperatures <~5°C) for it to come into leaf and bloom in spring, ~100–200 hours, and some reports say it needs even less, if any.

Soil/water/nutrient: Trees grow best in deep, fairly heavy, moist soils with a pH range of 5.5–7.0. However, they will grow on most soils, including calcareous or acidic loams, rocky or gravelly soils, fairly saline soils, sandy soils and even heavy clay, though they may not produce good yields on sandy soil. Although trees can grow in fairly acid or fairly alkaline soils, they may not thrive. They are fairly drought tolerant, but prefer a moist but well-drained soil. They do not do well in humid climates, which affect fruit formation. Young trees should be regularly irrigated during their growing season until established and benefit from applications of fertiliser, with extra nitrogen. Once established, trees need little or no extra nutrients, though appreciate a good organic mulch around their roots.

Pot culture: The pomegranate makes a worthwhile

container plant. It looks good, with its attractive leaves, flowers and fruits, though it is thorny. It can tolerate dry, warm conditions. There are dwarfing cultivars. It will often keep its leaves year round. It can also be moved or given protection in cold winters.

Planting: Space plants at 5–6 m apart. Initially, the stems of young trees are cut back to allow root establishment.

Pruning: They need little pruning. Young trees may be pruned to allow four or five scaffold branches to develop evenly around the main stem. Remove any suckers. Because fruits are formed at the tips of new stems, a branching shape encourages more fruits to form. Therefore, for the first 3 years, branches should have their tips removed to encourage lateral branches and a rounded shape to develop. After the third year, only suckers and damaged branches need to be pruned out, as well as light pruning after fruiting to encourage new growth. Trees may also be pruned to an espalier shape.

Propagation: *Seed:* Can be grown from seed, but the progeny are variable. Wash pulp from the seeds and sow in warm, moist compost. Prick out seedlings and grow on for a year or more before planting out. Give young plants extra protection from cold weather. *Cuttings:* Can take semi-ripe cuttings, with a heel, during summer and insert in gritty, moist compost to root. Alternatively, take hardwood cuttings in winter, 25–50 cm long. These root better if treated with rooting hormones before being inserted in fairly dry compost. Insert most of the length of these cuttings in soil, with only 1–2 buds above the soil surface, and leave for ~1 year until they root. These can bear fruit after ~3 years. *Layering:* Air-layering can be done successfully.

Pests and diseases: Trees are generally free of most pests and diseases. Minor problems are leaf and fruit spot, white flies, thrips, mealybugs and scale insects. The pomegranate butterfly can do a lot of damage to fruit, and can seriously damage a crop. Fruits may need protecting from borers, birds and other wildlife. Twig dieback may be caused by either *Pleuroplaconema* or *Ceuthospora phyllosticta*. Excessive rain during harvesting may induce soft rot.

CULTIVARS

Note that double-flowered cultivars are attractive, but don't set fruit.

'Cloud': Medium-sized fruit, a green-red colour. Juice sweet and white.

'Dholka': Large, yellow-red fruit with patches of purple at the base, or all over greenish-white. Has a thick rind. Flesh: purplish-white, sweet; hard seeds. Plant is evergreen and non-suckering.

'Fleshman': Large, roundish fruit, ~7 cm diameter, pink outside and in. Very sweet flavour, very good quality. Seeds: relatively soft.

'Nana': A Japanese dwarfing cultivar, growing to only ~1 m. More cold hardy. Has narrower leaves. Fruits are ~5 cm long, and has good yields. Makes a good container cultivar.

'Paper Shell': Round, medium–large fruits, pale yellow, blushed with pink; very thin rind, fleshy, reddish or pink, sweet, very juicy pulp, soft seeds. Bears heavily.

'Sweet': Fruit is light in colour, slightly greenish with red blush when ripe. Pink juice, flavour much sweeter than other cultivars. Trees are highly ornamental, bear at an early age, productive.

'Utah Sweet': Very sweet, good-quality fruit. Pink skin and pulp. Seeds are soft. Attractive pinkish-orange flowers.

'Wonderful': Large, deep purple-red fruits. Rind medium thick, tough. Flesh: deep crimson, juicy, delicious vinous flavour. Seeds not very hard. Better for juicing rather than eating out of hand. Plant is vigorous and productive. ■

Pyrus spp.
Pear
ROSACEAE

European pear (*Pyrus communis*), Asian pear (syn. Japanese pear, Oriental pear) (*P. pyrifolia* syn. *P. serotina*), Ussurian pear (*P. ussuriensis*)
Relatives: apple, quince, loquat, medlar

Apples, pears and quince all originate from areas around Asia Minor, and may all have had the same parental species, which is probably now extinct. The genus *Pyrus* is composed of about 22 species, which are native to Asia, Europe and northern Africa. The pear has been cultivated for many thousands of years: the Asian pear has been grown in China for at least 3000 years, and the European pear has been selected and improved since at least 1000 BC. The Greeks cultivated pears, as mentioned in the Odyssey, in 800 BC. European pears are possibly an original cross between sloe and cherry plum, or *P. caucasia* and *P. nivalis* (snow pear), and the Asian pears are often hybrids between *P. ussuriensis*, *P. pyrifolia* and *P. bretschneideri*. A lesser known, but cultivated pear, is the Ussurian pear (*P. ussuriensis*), from China.

Food

The fruits are usually enjoyed fresh. European pears are satisfyingly juicy, sweet and refreshing when fully ripe. Pears are also used in many desserts, pies, jams, chutneys, sauces, as a garnish in many savoury dishes and they make a reasonable fruit wine. They can also be dried and are added to trail mixes and cereals. In Europe, a Perry cider is made from *P. nivalis*, the snow pear. The Asian pear is eaten when crisp and is almost apple-like; it usually does not develop the sweetness or flavour of European pears.

Nutrition

They contain reasonable amounts of polyphenolics, vitamin A and folate. They also contain good levels of fibre.

Medicinal

Pears have an antibiotic-like substance (phloretin) in their bark. *Warning:* Pear juice, like apple juice, has been implicated as a cause of chronic, non-specific diarrhoea in infants and children. This may be caused by its very high levels of fructose and sorbitol, relative to glucose, compared with other foods. In addition, pears, like all Rosaceae species, contain cyanogenic glucosides in their seeds, which can be toxic if eaten in large quantities.

GENERAL DESCRIPTION

Small–medium sized, upright trees, to 10 m tall, often 3–5 m in cultivation. They have a rounded crown. They can be quite long lived: >200 years, but fruit yields become reduced as they get older. Fissured brown-grey bark. Older trees take on a gnarled appearance.

Leaves: Deciduous, oval with rounded tips, mid green: 5–10 cm long. Some cultivars have good autumn colour.

Flowers: Has clusters (5–7) of white, slightly fragrant, pretty flowers, borne terminally on short, lateral spurs, which arise from 2–5-year-old wood. They flower about 3 weeks before apples, so can be more susceptible to late frosts, but less so than earlier-flowering stone fruits. The ovary position is inferior, with five ovarian segments embedded within the receptacle tissue. The segments usually contain two seeds, attached from the centre of the fruit. *Pollination:* Most European and Asian pear cultivars need cross pollination, except for 'Bartlett', 'Orient', 'Baldwin', 'Kieffer' and 'Spalding'. They are pollinated by bees, but, unfortunately, the flowers have a low nectar content and so the bees are not very attracted to them: siting hives nearby can help pollination.

Fruit: Pear-shaped! A pome, like the apple, with the edible flesh being the swollen receptacle tissue. Most fruits form on 2–4-year-old spurs. Sometimes spurs can be older and still produce fruit, but these become of poor quality and are best thinned. Fruit thinning is only necessary if there are very large crops; this is more likely on Asian than European pears, where the latter tend to drop excess fruit naturally. Pears contain grit cells in their flesh, particularly if tree-ripened, and skin russeting is common.

Yield/harvest/storage: Trees can begin to bear fruit in the second year after budding onto dwarf rootstocks, and 3–5 years after budding trees onto normal rootstocks. Unpruned trees may be 6–7 years old before fruiting.

Roots: They do have some deeper roots, but the majority are more shallow, so take care with mechanical cultivation, and an organic mulch will help conserve moisture and suppress weed growth.

CULTIVATION

Much research has been done on pear varieties and, as a consequence, there are more training systems, rootstocks and cultivars than for most other tree crops.

Location: Site trees in a sunny, sheltered spot. They are not very tolerant of maritime conditions, or of wind.

Temperature: Pears need a fairly warm summer to fully ripen fruits. Although adapted to cooler temperate areas, they can also grow in warmer, more humid areas than apples. When dormant, trees can tolerate temperatures as low as ~–30°C, but flowers and fruits can be killed at ~–1°C in spring.

Chilling: Pears need a fairly long chilling period of ~900–1000 hours.

Soil/water/nutrients: Pear trees can grow in a variety of soil types, and can tolerate poor drainage and heavy clay soils better than most fruit trees, but are not as productive under these conditions. They grow best in a deep, fertile, sandy loam with good drainage, and at a pH range of 6–7. If the soil is too acid it can increase fruit disorders. If it is too alkaline, then trees may become deficient in iron, boron and manganese. Boron deficiency can cause wilting, flower drop and poorly formed fruits. Pears benefit from at least one annual addition of a balanced fertiliser, with additional trace elements, particularly manganese, boron and copper. Too much fertiliser can make trees susceptible to fire blight.

Planting: Space trees at ~4 m apart. Do not fertilise trees when planting. Add an organic mulch.

Pruning: Trees tend to naturally grow tall, vertical shoots, which, if unpruned, result in the tree taking several extra years to produce fruit, harvesting becomes more difficult and yields can be poorer. Pear trees are usually trained to a modified central leader system, or to a central leader form, but are then taller. They are best pruned to form a tree with 4–5 scaffold branches around the main stem. Other smaller stems are removed for the first 2–3 years, and the scaffold branches are encouraged to develop a strong structure. In addition, because pear branches are so upright, and because more fruits are produced on horizontal branches, scaffold branches can be secured to encourage them to grow more horizontally. Once established, the tips of scaffold branches can be removed to encourage the formation of lateral fruiting branches. Pear trees usually produce fruits on spurs, short stubby laterals attached to the main branches, and these produce fruits for 2–4 years (or longer). If there are too many fruits, there is a risk of biennial bearing, and some fruiting spurs can be removed. Once established, a light annual pruning to remove dead or damaged wood and encourage a spreading form is better than irregular heavy pruning. If pruning out diseased wood, particularly if affected by fireblight, cut well below the infected area, burn any diseased wood and sterilise pruners with alcohol or dilute bleach after each cut, to avoid spreading infection.

Propagation: *Seed:* There is a lot of variation between seedling-grown trees, and pears are usually grafted. If growing from seed, it is best sown in a cool frame to over-winter or can be stratified and stored in a fridge until spring. Seeds should germinate in early spring, and seedlings should be grown on until large enough to plant outside. *Grafting:* Pears are sometimes grafted onto pear seedling rootstocks, but these tend to sucker badly. European pears are often grafted onto quince, which keeps the tree smaller (~3 m tall) and, although quince also suckers, they are easier to control than pear rootstocks. In addition, quince rootstocks begin fruiting earlier; however, the trees are not as tolerant of alkaline or wet soils, and are more susceptible to fireblight. If there are no other pear trees locally, more than one tree needs to planted, and one of them needs to be a pollinating cultivar, or trees can be purchased that have a pollinating branch grafted onto them, which is particularly useful in smaller gardens.

Pests and diseases: Pears are susceptible to a wide range of difficult-to-control blights. Most pear cultivars can develop fireblight, particularly with high humidity and a wet spring (see pruning notes). Cold, wet springs encourage bacterial canker (*Pseudomonas* spp.). If trees are planted too deeply they may develop crown rot (*Phytophthora* spp.). Codling moth can also be a problem, but thinning fruit can reduce this. Other problems include powdery mildew, stink bugs and plant bugs. Two-spot spider mites can be a serious problem, especially if the trees are water stressed.

THE SPECIES

Asian pear (nashi, sand pear; apple pear), *Pyrus pyrifolia.* The Asian pear is a native of central and southern China, and probably was one of the first domesticated wild fruits. Chinese gold prospectors introduced the pear into the American Wild West. This is a large group of cultivars and fruits are usually crisp in texture. When mature, they can be stored for several months if kept in a fridge. This makes them very appealing commercially as they can be shipped long distances: they store much better than European pears. They are sometimes called apple-pears because of their crisp and juicy texture, compared to the soft-fleshed European cultivars. All Asian pears are selections from crosses with a wild pear. They have been grown commercially in Asia for centuries: today ~500,000 tonnes are grown a year in Japan. Nashi is Japanese for 'pear'. *P. pyrifolia* is the Japanese variety, and is the most common of Asian pears; *P. ussuriensis* is a Chinese species that is very cold hardy, is probably a parent of the Asian pear and is often used as its rootstock.

Description: *Flowers:* Flowers are borne in early spring, so there is a risk of late frost damaging the blossom. *Pollination:* Some Asian pears are partially self-fertile, but have better crops if two or more cultivars are planted together. Cross pollinated fruit tend to be larger and more uniform in size than non-cross pollinated fruit. Early-blooming cultivars 'Ya Li', 'Tsu Li' and 'Seuri' are compatible and can be planted together. *Fruit:* Similar to the European pear, but its shape is usually more rounded. The skin is yellow or brown, and is often heavily russeted. Has a crisp and granular texture, low acidity, and a somewhat bland or watery-sweet taste. Fruit often need heavy thinning to obtain good size, to prevent biennial bearing and to avoid limb breakage. Once the fruits are set, 1–2 fruits are cut from each spur. Commercially, 4–5-year-old trees are thinned to 100–200 fruit per tree; 8–10-year-old trees are thinned to 200–400 fruit per tree. *Yield/harvesting/storage:* Give yields of 35–55 kg per tree. Trees start producing fruit in 2–4 years (earlier than European cultivars). Fruit are best left to fully ripen on the tree, and until they have fully changed colour to russet-brown or yellow, depending on cultivar. Asian pears are best stored in a fridge; russeted varieties tend to keep longer and ripen later, and some cultivars can be stored for ~3 months. At room temperature, the fruits begin to deteriorate after 14–21 days.

Cultivation: *Temperature:* Most Asian pears are not as cold hardy as European pears. *Chilling:* Most varieties need ~600 hours of chilling. *Soil:* They can tolerate moderately wet soils. *Propagation/pruning:* All Asian pear cultivars will grow on the rootstocks of *Pyrus betulaefolia* (is vigorous, has large fruit and tolerates wet soils), *P. calleryana* (not very cold hardy), *P. serotina* (very cold hardy), *P. ussuriensis* (very cold hardy) and *P. communis*. They can be pruned to either a central leader or an open centre. Branches may need training to be more horizontal. Pruning should encourage limbs with wide-angled branches.

Cultivars: Because Asian pears have usually finished flowering before European pears have started, cross pollination is difficult. Need a late-blooming Asian cultivar and an early-blooming European cultivar to get cross pollination between these types. There are hundreds of cultivars of Asian pear, but they tend to come in three main types: (1) fruits are rounded with green–yellow skin; (2) fruits are rounded with a russeted skin; or (3) fruits are pear-shaped with a green or russet skin.

'Hosui': Tree: vigorous, medium–large, spreading–drooping branches. May need more winter chill than some cultivars. Flowers: abundant. Fruit: medium–large, russet, with prominent lenticels, mid season. Have a good flavour and are sweet and juicy, except in cool summers, when they can be more acidic. Fruit will store for months in a fridge. Not very self-fertile, but sets well with 'Shinseiki' and 'Shinsui'. A popular cultivar, but can be very susceptible to fireblight. 'Kosui': Fruit: small, early, bronze-russet, medium-sized, crisp, very sweet, very juicy and tender fleshed, maintains its quality in many growing conditions. Matures in mid summer. Abundant fruit. Can be cross pollinated by, and will pollinate, 'Hosui' and 'Shinseiki'. Tree: not too vigorous. Tends to have brittle branches, so needs a sheltered site. Is fairly susceptible to disease, especially in humid climates. Leaves sensitive to two-spot spider mite and many sprays. 'Ya Li': A popular Chinese cultivar. Tree: very hardy, very productive, vigorous on all rootstocks. Early flowering. Fruit: pear-shaped, yellow-green, bruises easily, is sweet and mild. Matures mid–late summer. Needs cross pollination. Stores well. Has good, deep red autumn leaf colour. Needs 200–550 hours of chilling. Uses: The fruit is very crisp and is good in salads. Only has low vitamin C levels: 4 mg/100 g of flesh.

European pear, *Pyrus communis*. These pears have been enjoyed across Europe for many thousands of years, but it is the French who have particularly developed, used and enjoyed these fruits, and they include them in many dishes.

Description: The tree is strongly upright and is fairly slow growing. *Flowers:* abundant, white, borne in spring, before apples, but after Asian pears. Usually need to plant a pollinating cultivar to get good fruit-set. *Fruit/harvest:* Harvested in autumn (after Asian pears). Trees can take 5–8 years before bearing fruit. Best to pick European pears when still firm and a little under-ripe. If they are then kept at room temperature, the fruits ripen more quickly and develop a better flavour than if left to fully ripen on the tree. They do not develop such a gritty texture as tree-ripened fruit. Harvest when there is some colour change from dark to light green, the seeds have become dark, but the fruits are still firm. These are best eaten when the flesh has softened, but is not over-ripe.

Cultivation: Most cultivars need 600–1000 hours of chilling. They prefer drier, warm, inland locations. They can tolerate moderately wet soils. *Pruning:* Usually pruned to an open centre or a central leader (see notes above), or can be pruned into a cordon or an espalier. *Propagation:* Pears are often grown in Europe on quince stocks, but quince is highly susceptible to fireblight and is cold tender. The pear rootstocks, *P. communis* and *P. calleryana*, can be used to gain extreme blight and nematode resistance.

Cultivars: There are many cultivars of European pears. 'Buerre Bosc': Vigorous, productive tree. Fruit: rough skinned, russeted brown, a classic pear, with a long and often curved neck. Flesh: very sweet, very good flavour, juicy, creamy when fully ripe (gritty when not). Stays firm when cooked. Ripens well off the tree, and stores reasonably well. Harvested in autumn. Pollinator: 'William's Bon Chretien'. 'Conference': Fruit: medium large, long and thin, green russeted. Flesh: sweet, juicy, melting, rich and aromatic, has a slight pinkish tinge when ripe. Is partly self-fertile and is a reliable, profuse cropper. A classic French pear. Good storage. Blooms early, will cross pollinate with most Asian pears. 'Doyenne du Comice': Tree: upright, vigorous, tends toward biennial bearing. Fruit: large, yellowish-green, with a pinkish blush, thickish skin. Considered by some to be the best

flavoured pear: has very fine, smooth flesh, and is very sweet and very juicy. If not grown well, the fruit can be grainy and somewhat astringent. For best results, they should be refrigerated before they are taken out to ripen. Harvested in autumn. Pollinators are, for example, 'Beurre Bosc' or 'William's Bon Chretien'.
'Seckle' (syn. 'Honey pear'): Fruit: reddish-brown, crisp fleshed, very sweet yet spicy, juicy, perfumed, very distinctive flavour, ripening mid season. It can be fully ripened on the tree without deteriorating. Stores poorly. Tree: vigorous, hardy, very productive, reliable. Is somewhat self-fertile. Resists fireblight.
'William's Bon Chretien' (syn. 'Bartlett'): Tree: vigorous, upright, reliably productive. Fruit: large, yellowish, classic pear shape, late flowering, but early fruiting (early autumn). Flesh: smooth, moderately juicy, sweet. Ripeness can be hard to determine: can be too soft or too crisp: best ripened off the tree. Good for bottling and cooking. Its pollinators include 'Beurre Bosc', 'Winter Nelis', 'Doyenne du Comice' and 'Conference'. Stores poorly.

Uses: Fruits have poor levels of vitamin C: 4 mg/100 g flesh. *Food:* see general notes. Go well with apples in desserts.

Ussurian pear, *Pyrus ussuriensis*. A native of China, this is a medium-sized tree: height ~8–13 m, spread ~8–13 m. Dense, rounded, attractive form, moderately fast growing. *Leaves:* glossy green, turning to yellow–purple in autumn. Has masses of very attractive pink–white early spring blossom (2.5-cm-diameter flowers) before the leaves open. *Fruit:* greenish-yellow when mature, small (~2.5–3.5 cm diameter). They vary in quality. Better fruit, although small, have quite a pleasant flavour, but are rather dry; other fruits can be of poor quality. Trees need cross pollination.

Cultivation/uses: Fairly tolerant of wet soil. Likes a sunny location. Is tolerant of atmospheric pollution and is fairly drought tolerant. It is mostly now grown for its attractive form, its stunning spring blossom and autumn colours, rather than for its fruit. It is also used as a rootstock because of its cold hardiness; it can survive ~–15°C. There are a few named cultivars that have been selected mostly for their ornamental features. ∎

Quararibea cordata (syn. *Matisia cordata*)
Chupa-chupa (South American sapote, zapote)
MALVACEAE (Bombacaceae)

This tree grows wild in the lowland rainforests of Peru, Ecuador and adjacent areas of Brazil, but is little known outside its natural area. It is a shame that it is not more widely grown in warmer climates because it makes an interesting tree for larger gardens, with attractive evergreen leaves, strangely shaped flowers during winter and large, good yields of brown fruits that are borne directly on the main stems. It is not related to other sapotes, and the name 'chupa-chupa' is derived from a local word describing the way the flesh needs to be eaten from the often fibrous seeds.

DESCRIPTION

An attractive, fast-growing, erect, large tree, 40–45 m high in the wild, though often only ~10 m in cultivation. It is sometimes buttressed, has stiff branches that tend to grow in whorls up a main stem, and produces a gummy yellow latex when wounded. Grows well in protected areas.

Leaves: Evergreen in warmer areas, tending to be semi-deciduous elsewhere. Has attractive, dark green, coarse, large, usually heart-shaped leaves, which can be 15–40 cm long, 15–30 cm wide. They have clear veination, are alternate, have long leaf stalks, and are clustered in rosettes near the ends of the stems.

Flowers: Strangely shaped, abundant, yellowish-white or pinkish, ~2.5 cm wide, five petals, with five showy, long, hairy stamens with a prominent central ovary. They are borne singly or in small clusters directly from lesser branches and directly from the trunk (cauliflorous) during winter. Flowers are bisexual and some trees are fairly self-fertile, though more than one tree will increase fruit yield and quality. Has a superior ovary. *Pollination:* By hummingbirds, bees and wasps. In the afternoon, some trees become self-fertile.

Fruit: The fruit have an interesting appearance and are large (10–14 cm long, ~8 cm wide), greeny-brown, round, fuzzy, with a distinctive, nipple-shaped apex. They have a 2–5-lobed, persistent, leathery calyx at the base. The skin is thick, leathery and covered with a fine, brown fuzz. The outer flesh is an apricot colour, the inner flesh is a deeper orange-yellow, and is soft, fibrous, juicy, sweet, with a good flavour. In the centre are 2–5 largish seeds, ~4 cm long, ~2.5 cm wide, from which long fibres extend through the flesh, similar to mango fruits. Fruits are borne directly from the main stems.

Yield/harvest: Seedling trees take ~5–6 years to start producing fruits, which can weigh up to 800 g each. A good crop in South America is reported to be >3,000 fruits! One should probably expect more modest yields elsewhere. The fruits do not naturally drop, and will remain on the tree until they become over-ripe. Their stem needs to be cut with a knife to remove them, which makes them difficult to harvest on larger trees. When they ripen in late summer–autumn, the fruits become lighter yellow-brown around the calyx. They will ripen further once picked if kept in the warmth.

CULTIVATION

Can be grown with avocados. This works well because both species have the same soil requirements and chupa-chupa provides shade for the avocados.

Location: They grow best in full sun. Trees are not very wind tolerant, though can be grown in fairly sheltered maritime locations.

uses

Food
The fruits are highly valued in several areas of South America and are often sold locally in markets. They are usually eaten fresh, though some fruits can be fairly fibrous, and others can lack flavour. The flesh has a flavour that is a mix of apricot and mango. The fruits can be added to desserts, sauces, chutney, etc, or made into juice.

Nutrition
The flesh is full of fibre. The fruits are also quite high in phosphates and have ~10 mg of vitamin C/100 g of flesh.

Ornamental
Makes a good specimen tree for larger landscape gardens in warmer areas, with attractive leaves, flowers and fruits.

Temperature: A tropical to subtropical species that is susceptible to temperatures much below freezing, though are grown in warm-temperate regions, with care. Young trees need protection from winter cold.

Soil/water/nutrients: Grow best in fertile, damp, deep soils, but can also tolerate drier soils and can grow in fairly alkaline conditions, where additional organic matter and a deep mulch is helpful. They cannot tolerate waterlogging, and prefer well-drained conditions, though like plenty of moisture. Benefit from regular additions of fertiliser or an organic equivalent.

Planting: Space plants at least 8–10 m apart.

Propagation: *Seed:* Almost always propagated by seed. Remove all pulp before sowing in well-drained, moist compost with warmth. *Grafting:* Occasionally by side-whip-and-tongue grafting, which gives good results. Budding is not feasible.

Pruning: Not usually pruned except for removal of diseased or damaged wood.

Pests and diseases: Fruits are very prone to attack by fruit flies. ■

Quercus spp.
Acorn
FAGACEAE

Relatives: chestnut (*Castanea* spp.), beech (*Fagus* spp.)

Oaks are a genus of about 500 species of trees and shrubs that are found across the Northern Hemisphere, from America to China. Acorns have been a traditional food source for many human societies since at least 5000 BC. The oak has been revered and worshipped far back into pre-history. Religious idols were carved from oak wood and

witches often danced beneath the boughs of a great oak tree. Some old beliefs were that a piece of oak wood, when carried, protected its bearer from all harm, that planting an acorn in the dark of the moon ensures you will receive money in the near future, or that carrying an acorn around with you increases fertility and strengthens sexual potency. Acorns are still an important food source in many parts of the world, including Korea and Morocco. Deciduous oaks may be divided into two types: white oaks and red oaks. There are also several evergreen oak species. *White oaks:* Bark: softer, grey, scaly; rarely furrowed. The acorns mature in their first season. Roots develop from the seed in autumn. Has thick scales on its crown, a smooth shell and white meat. The leaves have deep scallops, but the tips are rounded or have no lobes. The acorns are sweeter than those of red oaks and contain less tannin. The chestnut oak is included within this group. *Red and black oaks:* Bark: harder, dark grey, furrowed, rarely scaly. Roots develop from seeds in spring. Leaves are deeply scalloped with very pointed tips. Acorns have yellow meat and a downy lining, are very bitter and need two growing seasons to mature. The following is a general description of the oak species.

DESCRIPTION

Height varies from ~6 m to magnificent, huge specimens up to 35 m tall. They have a distinctive irregular form with very little symmetry. They develop a broad, often spreading crown with heavy branches and often have a massive trunk. Buds are always irregularly clustered on twigs. Can live for many hundreds of years. Are often fairly slow growing.

Leaves: *Deciduous species:* 2.5–8 cm long, 2–6 cm wide, irregular rounded lobes. Open later in spring, emerging with a reddish tint which turns a fresh, light yellow-green and then becomes a dark, bluey-green when mature. There is a second flush of growth in late summer. The leaves are slightly aromatic. Many species have attractive autumn colour. Bark is dark grey, with older bark quite furrowed. *Evergreen species:* 2.5–8 cm long, 2–6 cm wide. Elliptical–oblong, with a short point at the apex, and rounded at base. Margins are often turned under and often have spiny teeth (especially on young twigs). Leaves are thick and leathery, shiny green above, dull, yellowish, with a fine down beneath, and often become grey in the second year. *Bark:* light grey, nearly smooth or sometimes scaly.

Flowers: Monoecious. Appear before, or at the same time as the leaves open. Both male and female flowers occur close together on the same shoot, which is formed on the present season's wood. Male flowers form slender, drooping, short-lived catkins that are solitary or in small clusters. Female flowers are inconspicuous, solitary or in small clusters and have small green scales around their base, which later form the acorn cup. *Pollination:* By wind. Some species produce abundant pollen.

Fruits: A nut, more commonly known as an acorn: a light brown oval seed, sitting within a grey-green, woody, usually rough-surfaced cup, which is formed before the nut, and is sometimes left on the tree after the fruit has ripened and dropped. The nut's shiny, hard coat has a small dimple on its apex, and contains a single kernel.

Yield/harvest/storage: Individual, mature trees have been known to produce 900 kg per tree in a single growing season, although this is exceptional; however, yields are often good. Some species can take 20–30 years before they start producing acorns. Trees then produce very good yields, once about every 2–4 years. Acorns can be gathered as they fall from the tree. They will have changed from green to a tan-brown colour. The cups of mature acorns become loose and the acorn is easily removed when it is ripe. Nuts need

collecting before other wildlife get to them. In their shell, acorns will store for some time, but must be kept dry.

Roots: Most oaks have a deeply penetrating taproot, therefore seedlings must be raised in deep bags and care taken to prevent root damage when planting out. Roots are sensitive to any subsequent root disturbance, so avoid transplanting. The roots of large specimens also spread widely, and can lift pavements or disturb foundations.

CULTIVATION

Very easy to grow and need little to no maintenance.

Location: Grow well in full sun, though younger trees can tolerate a little shade. Are quite wind hardy, and are often planted as isolated individuals in a landscape. Most oaks are not very tolerant of maritime conditions, apart from several of the evergreen species.

Temperature: Most deciduous species are fully cold hardy and become dormant through the coldest months. They also come into leaf and flower in late spring, after the danger of late frosts has passed. They grow best in warmer summers. The evergreen species are usually acclimatised to warmer areas, and can tolerate more heat, but not such severe winters.

Soil/water/nutrients: Like a deep rich loam, but will grow on most types, including sand or clay, as long as the soil is deep enough for the roots to develop and retains adequate moisture. Oaks generally grow best in somewhat acid to neutral soils, though many will also grow in fairly alkaline soils. Young trees benefit from regular moisture during the summer until fully established. Trees need few nutrients once established, and mature oaks are rarely fertilised.

Planting: Space trees at several metres apart, depending on the final size of the tree. Add some organic matter to the soil when planting. Younger trees benefit from an organic mulch to retain moisture and suppress weed growth.

Pruning: Need no pruning, unless branches are crossing or damaged. Because flowers and fruits are formed on the present season's growth, any pruning necessary is best done in autumn after harvest or in early spring.

Propagation: *Seeds:* Float acorns in water; those that sink should be viable. Acorns can be sown fresh in autumn, planted in soil at ~2.5 cm depth, and left to over-winter, or they can be stored in cool, moist conditions at 1–2°C until spring. Seeds from white oaks can germinate straight away in autumn, but survive much better if kept cool throughout the winter. Red oak acorns exhibit seed dormancy and generally do not germinate until the following spring. Seedlings are best planted in deep pots to allow their taproots to develop well. Keep seedlings moist, but well drained.

Pests and diseases: Generally not affected by many problems. White oaks are less susceptible to wilt and mildew than red or black oaks. Caterpillars can eat leaves, and galls can be formed by gall wasps, though neither are usually serious. Neglected trees can be attacked by bracket fungi; other fungal problems are canker, dieback and honey fungus, with several of these being serious. Powdery mildew on leaves can also occur.

EDIBLE ACORN SPECIES

Quercus acutissima. Native of eastern Asia. Height: ~5 m. Quite cold hardy. Reliable producer, but very bitter acorns, ~2.5 cm long. Starts producing in ~6 years. Often grows with *Pinus* spp.

***Quercus aegilops*, manna oak.** From Mediterranean regions and the Near East. Acorns used to make flour for bread in Iran and Iraq. Acorns are eaten raw or cooked.

***Quercus agrifolia*, coast live oak.** Native of California. Height ~15 m. Acorns, ~3 cm long, can be eaten fresh or roasted; they are ground for baking.

***Quercus alba*, white oak.** Native of eastern North America. Height ~20 m. Cultivated for its edible seed, though takes ~30 years to start cropping. Acorns are sweeter, and can be dried, boiled or roasted, also used as a coffee substitute. Good to eat. Boil to remove tannin. Seed ripens in 1 year.

***Quercus aucheri*, boz-pirnel oak.** Native of the Mediterranean. Grows to ~5 m. Evergreen. Moderately shade tolerant. Very good quality acorns, ~2 cm long; sweet and with low tannin, needing little or no leaching. Take 2 years to ripen. Said to taste like sunflower seeds and popcorn.

***Quercus bicolor*, swamp white oak.** Native to eastern North America. Height ~25 m. Prefers warmer summers. Takes 25–30 years to start producing. Acorns, 2–3 cm long, fairly sweet, but variable, best left ~2 weeks before eating. Take 1 year to ripen. Good timber. Likes moist conditions. Tree is hardy and easy to transplant. Dull autumn colour.

Quercus castanaefolia. Similar to *Q. cerris* (Turkey oak), but bigger, bitter acorns. Prolific producer.

***Quercus cerris*, Turkey oak.** Ornamental. Great producer of ~2.5-cm-long, bitter, acorns. Ripen in second year. Matures late. Takes 5–8 years to crop. Produces a resin, called manna in Iran, which is used as a sweetener in foods.

Quercus cornea. From China. Acorns are ground into a paste and made into a flour.

***Quercus douglasii*, blue oak.** Native to California. Height ~12 m. Likes a warmer summer, and is not very cold hardy.

Acorns: ~3 cm long, were a traditional native food. Sweeter and lower in tannin than most other varieties.

***Quercus emoryi*, emory or blackjack oak, bellota.** Native to southwestern USA and northern Mexico. Slow growing. Height ~12 m. Evergreen. Needs a warmer summer, not very cold hardy. Variable yields, with some meagre years. Acorn quality is sweetish; was used as a native food, can be eaten fresh or roasted, ground into meal.

***Quercus frainetto*, Hungarian oak.** Native to eastern Europe, Balkans. Height ~30 m. Cold-hardy species. Acorns ~3 cm long, ripen in first year. They are usually roasted, sometimes used as a coffee substitute.

***Quercus gambelli*, shin oak.** Native to western North America. Height only ~4–5 m. Is very cold hardy. Acorns ~2 cm long, small, sometimes quite sweet. Small tree or shrub, drought tolerant and productive in a good year.

Quercus glabra. Native to Japan. Eaten locally.

***Quercus grisea*, grey oak.** Native to southwestern USA and northern Mexico. Was a staple native food. Likes warmer summers; not very cold hardy. Sweetish acorns.

***Quercus ilex*, holm oak.** Native to Mediterranean regions. Evergreen. Height ~25 m. Will grow in limestone. Tolerant of maritime exposure and many soil types. Moderately cold hardy. Slow growing. Recommended as best European acorn by some. Can be eaten dry or roasted: are as good as chestnuts. High yield in alternate years. Fairly large acorns, ~3 cm long, only a little bitterness. Late maturing. Good oil producer. Nut quality varies from tree to tree.

***Quercus ithaburensis macrolepis*, valonia oak.** Native of southeastern Europe and western Asia. Height 5 m. Moderately cold hardy; likes a warmer summer. Acorns, large, ~4 cm long, sweetish, low tannin, take 2 years to ripen.

***Quercus libani*, Lebanon oak.** Native to the Near East. Height ~8 m. Moderately cold hardy. Acorns ripen in second year. Often roasted.

***Quercus lobata*, valley oak (Californian white oak).** Native to California. Height, tall, to ~35 m. Somewhat cold hard; prefers warmer summers. Slow growing. Acorns ripen in first year. Large, sweet, 2.5–5 cm long, low in tannin, needs little or no leaching, often roasted, traditional food.

***Quercus lyrata* x *virginiana*, Compton's oak.** Native of central and southeastern USA. Height ~30 m. Is cold hardy. Likes warm summers. Acorns very good, tasty and crunchy with little bitterness, ~2.5 cm long, low tannin. Seed ripens in first year, though trees take 25–30 year to start producing.

***Quercus macrocarpa*, bur oak.** A native of eastern North America. Height ~15–22 m. Grows over a wide range of climates. Acorns large, ~5 cm, sometimes sweet, lower tannin than most, raw or roasted, ripen in first year. Takes ~30 years to start producing, but then gives crops for

Food

All acorns contain some tannin, which needs to be leached out prior to eating. Leaching white-oak acorns takes ~1 hour, red-oak acorns take ~24 hours. Place acorns in a bucket of water; only those that sink should be used. Remove the outer shell and the brown skin covering the nut as these are high in tannin. Boil the acorns for 10–15 minutes to soften the shell. Then soak the kernels in cold water for several hours, or boil the water and then drain, repeating this several times till all bitterness has gone and the water is clear. The acorns can then be ground if required, and dried for storage. Treated acorns can also be used whole, or can be deep fried or mixed into soups. Finely chopped acorns can be added to bread and muffins, or other dishes where chopped nuts would be used. Ground acorns can be mixed with other flours. Leached, roasted and ground acorns make a reasonable coffee substitute. Acorn oil is used for cooking in parts of North Africa. Acorns keep well. They have been used as feed for livestock, particularly pigs and ducks.

Nutrition/medicinal

Acorns contain vitamin C and are high in magnesium, calcium and phosphorus. They contain 5.2% protein (lower than most nuts), 43% fat and 45% carbohydrates. Unfortunately, acorns also contain high tannin levels, so do need to be leached. The oak tree has long been important medicinally. Because of their high tannin content, parts have been used as an anti-inflammatory, antiviral, antimicrobial, antiseptic, astringent, decongestant, to stop bleeding and as a tonic. The bark is the main part used—for treating diarrhoea, dysentery, fevers, haemorrhage, etc. Externally, it is used to bathe wounds, for skin eruptions, sweaty feet, as an antiseptic vaginal douche and as a mouthwash for infections. It is used in Bach flower remedies to treat 'Despondency', 'Despair, but never ceasing effort'. Acorns are used by Asians medically, ground up and boiled with water to make a paste/jelly. This is then taken for stomach problems and to purify the blood. **Warning:** If not properly leached, the high tannin levels, if consumed regularly and in large quantities, can act as a carcinogen and prevent proteins from being digested. In lesser doses, tannins can cause stomach pain, constipation, diarrhoea and excessive thirst and urination.

Other uses

Several species of oaks have been used as a source of natural dyes because of their high tannin contents, particularly *Quercus alba*, *Q. rubra* and *Q. muehlenbergii*. They produce a range of colours, depending on the mordant used. A tan to medium-brown colour is produced with chrome, dark brown with iron, and golden brown with chrome and tin. Acorns are important as food for wildlife. Some oak species are known to be a home for literally hundreds of different creatures. A mulch of the leaves can repel slugs, grubs, etc., though fresh leaves may inhibit the growth of young plants. Many species produce excellent timber for furniture, construction, boat building. It is hard, tough, durable and stains well.

200–300 years! Tree is slow growing, drought resistant, air-pollution tolerant, can survive hot summers. Various crosses with this are also available. *Q. m.* x *alba* (bebo oak). Variable sweetness, but generally good. Reliable producer. *Q. m.* x *bicolour* (Schuettes oak). Excellent productivity. Fairly sweet. Most palatable. *Q. m.* x *gambelli* (bur gambel oak). Very productive. Medium-large acorn, sweeter than Schuettes. *Q. m.* x *robur* (bur English oak). Extremely productive. Large acorns, astringent. Good timber.

Quercus macrolepis, camata, camatina or valonia oak. Native to Balkans, Aegean. Can be boiled or eaten fresh.

Quercus michanxii, swamp chestnut oak. Native of southeastern USA. Height ~20–25 m. Acorn generally very sweet, ~2.5 cm long. Likes moist conditions and a warm summer; is moderately cold tolerant.

Quercus muehlenbergii, sweet oak (yellow chestnut oak). Native to eastern North America. Likes dry alkaline soils, but will grow 18–24 m on moist soil. Fully cold hardy, though likes warm summers. Fairly fast growing. Acorns ripen in first year, sweet, good eating, some say one of the finest, only 1.25 cm long. High oil content.

Quercus oblongifolia, Mexican blue oak. A native of southwestern USA and northern Mexico. A shrub, to ~8 m. Prefers warmer summers; not very cold hardy. Acorns ripen in first year, year round, very sweet, low tannin, ~2 cm long.

Quercus petraea, sessile oak. A native of Britain and northern Europe. Height to ~40 m. Fully cold hardy. Acorns bitter, roasted for coffee, etc. Used medicinally. Important timber species with good quality wood.

Quercus persica. Used in southern Europe and the Middle East in bread. Used in Norway and France. A sweet acorn.

Quercus prinus, chestnut oak. Native to eastern USA. Height ~20 m. Slow growing, though can live ~400 years. Acorns ~3 cm long, sweet (some say bitter), used in traditional food, eaten raw or roasted, ground into flour. Tree likes dry sites and can be grown on rough, steep land. Also tolerant of drought and cold. Yields are variable.

Quercus prinoides, chinquapin oak. High yields, good quality nut.

Quercus stellata, post oak. Native to east-central USA. Height: ~20 m. Is cold hardy, drought resistant and slow growing. Acorns ripen in first year, ~2.5 cm long, sweet, low tannin, traditional food, eaten raw or roasted, ground into flour. Takes ~25 years to start fruiting. Good quality timber.

Quercus suber, cork oak. Native of western Mediterranean area. Evergreen. Height ~15–20 m. Cork is thick and can be peeled off without killing the tree: has many uses. Cork is harvested at ~15-year intervals. Acorns only just edible. Pigs live in the orchards and eat the acorns in Spain and Portugal.

Quercus variabilis, Chinese cork oak. Native to eastern Asia. Ornamental. Can be coppiced. Cold hardy. Reliable producer. Acorns, small–medium size, very bitter, but nutritious, ripen in second year. Starts producing in year 6.

Quercus virginiana, live oak. A native of southeastern USA. Evergreen. Semi cold hardy. Height ~30 m. Good in coastal locations. Acorn ~2 cm long, traditional food, sweet, eaten raw or roasted, ground into flour for baking, yields a sweet cooking oil, said to be similar to olive oil, low in tannin. Nut is dark brown to black. Has good yields.

SIMILAR SPECIES

Lithocarpus spp. The acorns of several species of *Lithocarpus* are locally important food sources in Asia. The acorns of *L. edulis*, a species indigenous to Japan, are sweet and edible. *Lithocarpus corneus* is an evergreen species, native from southern China to Vietnam, its edible nuts are often sold in local markets. A medium-sized tree, growing to ~15 m tall, it is cold hardy in most temperate climates. Grows best in deep fertile, moist, well-drained soils. Trees can flower year round in warmer regions, though mostly in spring. Fruits mature mainly in autumn, and are formed on last year's growth. The nuts have thick white shells and sweet kernels, though the kernels from some trees can be somewhat bitter. The trees and kernels can be propagated, grown and used in similar ways to acorns.

Pasania cornea. An evergreen tree from China that is closely related to the oak. The thick-shelled nuts have a flattish appearance. Kernels are white with a sweet good flavour, popular in China. ◼

Reynosia septentrionalis
Darling plum (red ironwood)
RHAMNACEAE
Relatives: jujube, raisin tree

A native of the coast of Florida, the Darling plum is a very tough plant surviving salt and dry conditions, and will grow where many other plants won't. Forms an attractive, very easy-to-manage tree that has olive-sized, sweet fruits in summer. Although called a plum, it is not related to these domesticated fruits.

DESCRIPTION
A shrub or small tree, slow growing, but wide spreading, to ~7 m height or more, and can be ~7 m spread, but easily maintained at 2–3 m height. It has reddish bark, and tough, strong wood.

Leaves: Leathery, evergreen, new growth is in shades of bronze-red.

Flowers: Tiny, yellow, without petals, inconspicuous, borne in spring.

Fruit: Dark purple–black, olive-sized (~2 cm long) drupe, with a pointed tip and single, oval stone, ~1 cm long. Fruit ripen soon after fruit-set, in summer.

CULTIVATION
Will grow in arid locations where little else survives.

Location: Is best grown in full sun. Has high salt and drought tolerance. Is also tolerant of wind.

Temperature: Grows best in warmer temperate or subtropical climates. Is frost sensitive.

Soil/water/nutrients: Grows best in sandy, well-drained soils. Is very drought tolerant, but does not tolerate waterlogging. Is not very nutrient hungry and needs little if any additional nutrients, unless grown in very poor soil.

Pot culture: Fine for containers, particularly in hot areas; can be given protection or moved inside in colder regions.

uses

Food
Fruits are very sweet and edible, and are said to taste similar to pears. Can be eaten fresh or added to desserts, jam, pies, etc. Can also be dried for later use.

Other uses
Wood is close-grained, very hard; used for cabinetwork.

Ornamental
Makes a good screening or windbreak plant, but does not tolerate lots of pruning. Can be planted in dry, poor soils as a reclamation plant. Good for infilling in landscaping.

Propagation: *Seed:* Sow seeds when fresh, with all pulp removed. Soaking in warm water for a few hours before sowing can speed up and increase germination.

Pruning: Little if any required, just to control its size or to remove any damaged wood.

Pests and diseases: Very few if any problems reported. ◼

Rheum spp.
Rhubarb (pieplant)
POLYGONACEAE
Relatives: sorrel, dock, buckwheat

The *Rheum* species originate from northern and eastern Asia, and Siberia. It is usually only the stem that is eaten and, indeed, much of the rest of the plant is poisonous. The plant has been cultivated for a long time: records of its use in China date back to at least 2700 BC. It was then used more for its medicinal properties rather than for its edible stems. The roots were used as a laxative, to reduce fever and cleanse the body. It was not until the 18th century that the edible stems were harvested. It became popular in Victorian England because it could be 'forced' to grow out of season and produce stems when little else was around. Several species have been used over the years, but the modern rhubarb is a hybrid, possibly between *R. rhaponticum* and *R. palmatum*. There are several different cultivars of rhubarb now grown worldwide. It is grown commercially on a small scale in the northwest of the USA. The rhubarb plant also makes an exotic, interesting ornamental plant for a border with its huge, lush, extravagant leaves and its red stalks.

DESCRIPTION

A herbaceous perennial that re-emerges each year in the spring and is productive for >5 years. It can grow to ~1.2 m tall in a season in an organic-rich soil. The rhizome clump becomes larger and spreads with time.

Leaves: Large, up to ~1 m in diameter, deciduous, thin, shallowly lobed, bases are heart-shaped. If the leaves are forced and remain in the dark as they form, they remain yellow.

Stems: Over the years, varieties have been selected for their redness of stem and a thin skin. The stems are long and have a channel that runs up the inner side. The leaves and stem are 'designed' to funnel moisture down to the crown. The stems can be forced to grow in the dark: a bucket or similar can be placed over the rhizomes to get an early spring crop. This traps some warmth and initiates growth earlier than normal. Forced stems develop a pinker colour than ordinary rhubarb, which is naturally a darker red and tend to have a more delicate flavour and texture. It is best to not pick all the stems from a plant, and allow the plant to rest every other year.

Yield/harvest/storage: Most varieties can be cropped from the second year: it is best to let the plant develop and grow naturally in the first year. Harvest in spring–early summer (unless forced), by pulling the stems while they are still tender and not fibrous. Harvest just a few stems in the second year, but more can be pulled in the third year. However, it is advised to only harvest a third of the plant's stems each season to avoid over-stressing. The stems should not be broken as this can introduce disease. The poisonous leaf blades should be discarded or kept to use as an insecticide (see below). Stems can be kept for ~3 weeks if placed in a polythene bag in the fridge. Rhubarb freezes and bottles well.

Flowers: The flowers do not grow from leaf axils, but directly from the rhizome. They form tall leafy panicles (~2.5 cm tall) of cream-coloured flowers that can be very ornamental, but see the notes on 'Pruning'.

Roots: Forms fairly shallow, thick, woody rhizomes. Keep cultivation shallow and remove weed competition. The crowns are very susceptible to rot in wetter soils so either plant on raised beds or in a well-drained soil.

CULTIVATION

Rhubarb is very hardy and easy to grow, and also makes an unusual, exotic garden plant.

Location: Can grow in semi-shade or sun: does not like it too hot.

Temperature: Unless they are forced, the plants are very tolerant of frost and cold. If they are forced, then plants do need protection from freezing temperatures. They do not grow well in high temperatures: rhubarb leaves wilt very quickly on hot days, and if temperatures go much above 30°C stem and leaf growth are suppressed until temperatures drop.

Chilling: Needs winter temperatures of <4°C to stimulate the stems and leaves to grow in spring.

Soil/water/nutrients: Will grow in most soil types, including heavy soil, but does best with an organic-rich soil. Likes a moist, but not waterlogged soil. Rhubarb plants like nutrients: better growth will be achieved if some nutrients are applied each spring, particularly nitrogen, so use either a high-ratio N fertiliser or add well-rotted manure or similar. Plants also like an organic mulch, unless the soil is wet, but do not cover the crown of the plant. Rhubarb is tolerant of fairly acid soil (~pH 5), but grows best in more neutral soils (pH 6.0–6.8).

Planting: Plant with the crown buds of the plant ~5 cm below the soil surface in spring. Mix organic matter into the soil before planting. Space plants at ~1–1.3 m apart. Planting in a raised bed protects the crown from fungal rot diseases.

Propagation: *Seed:* Grows well from seed, but plants can be variable and often produce lots of flower stalks. *Rhizomes:* Older plants are often divided after 4–5 years to

Food

To prepare the stems, simply cut them into sections; they do not need to be peeled. Because it is so acidic, cook rhubarb in pans made of e.g. stainless steel, enamel (or similar). Cooking in aluminium or iron will discolour the pan and the rhubarb. The sour stems are usually stewed with sugar, to make desserts, such as rhubarb crumble, and they make a delicious rhubarb fool. The true rhubarb-lover can eat the younger stems raw, dipped in sugar. Cooked rhubarb goes well with ginger or strawberries. The French sometimes make it into a sauce to accompany fish. The stems make a good wine. The early-season unopened flowers are cooked as a delicacy in Asia, and are still cultivated for this purpose.

Nutrition

Reasonable levels of vitamin C (~10 mg/100 g of stem), potassium and manganese, with good levels of fibre in the stems. High in vitamin K. But the stem is very acidic (pH 3.1). It also has a high calcium content, but this is bound by oxalic acid and so is not easily absorbed by the body.

Medicinal

Rhubarb seems to stimulate the liver: it is said to stimulate secretions from the liver, which convey the bile salts, and assists the intestine in regulating the absorption of fats. It is used as a laxative, and to treat gastro-intestinal haemorrhage, menstrual disorders, conjunctivitis and superficial sores and ulcers. *Warning:* The leaves are poisonous as they contain high levels of oxalic acid. Although it has been calculated that a person would need to eat ~5 kg of leaves in a sitting to cause death, and this would be difficult to do, lesser amounts can cause serious illness. The leaves should not be fed to livestock. Too much oxalic acid in the diet can result in kidney or bladder stones. The stems also contain a little oxalic acid and need to be eaten in moderation by those with digestion problems.

Other uses

The juice is excellent for cleaning tarnished metals, such as copper, and to clean burnt saucepans. The oxalic acid reduces iron compounds, and is used in metal polishes, stain removers and writing inks. When it absorbs oxygen, it is used as a bleaching agent, in detergents and as a mordant in dyeing processes. The root has been used as a hair bleach, but needs to be used with caution. Small amounts of root are mashed in water and the juice is just poured through the hair. The stems produce fibre that has been used to make paper. The leaves can be boiled or chopped up to extract the juice, and this can be used as an organic insecticide in the garden. The leaves make a good garden compost.

Ornamental

Makes an attractive herbaceous plant with its red stems, long flower stalks and large ornamental leaves.

---

produce new plants, known as 'crowns' (though plants can produce stems for >15 years without division, but yields become reduced). Divide plants when dormant in either autumn or early spring: each rhizome section should have at least one strong bud. Allow these to establish for a year or two before harvesting any stems. Progeny will be predictable by this method.

Pruning: Remove developing flower stalks during spring and summer (unless growing them for ornamental purposes) because, if allowed to develop, they reduce the vigour of stem and leaf growth: the plant 'thinks' it has finished its job for the season.

Pests and diseases: There is a rhubarb beetle that can bore into the stalks, crowns and roots. It also attacks wild dock, so make sure there are no dock weeds in the vicinity. Root rot of the crown is common in wet soils. ∎

Rhodomyrtus tomentosa
Ceylon hill gooseberry (downy rose myrtle, hill guava)
MYRTACEAE
Relatives: feijoa, guava, cherry of Rio Grande, eucalyptus

An ornamental, flowering and fruiting shrub, originally native to tropical Asia, but now grown in many tropical, temperate and warm temperate regions of the world for its attractive appearance and sometimes for its fruits. In some areas, this species has become invasive and is at risk of displacing native flora and fauna, e.g. Florida and Hawaii, and its usage is now discouraged, although it used to be widely grown in these areas for its fruits, which were gathered and sold commercially and made into jams and jellies.

Food/medicinal

The fruit are delicious fresh or can be used in jams, jelly, desserts, sauces, juice, salads and pies. Are similar in taste to blueberries/raspberries, but have a thicker, richer juice. Extracts from the leaves have recently been shown to contain active compounds that are effective against *Escherichia coli* and *Staphylococcus aureus*.

Ornamental

A very attractive smaller plant that is a popular ornamental for its flowers. It is often grown as a decorative, fruiting hedge. Birds and other wildlife love the berries and carry the seeds far and wide, which is the main reason it has become a problem species, though if you are able to get to the fruit before the wildlife this should minimise this problem. It is also, apparently, fire-adapted, and can vigorously resprout after a fire.

DESCRIPTION

A densely twiggy shrub, growing to ~1.5–2 m tall, but occasionally to ~3 m tall. It tends to form thickets where it's planted, though this seems to be from seedlings rather than from runners. Older branches are yellowish, and become fissured with loose bark. Young branches are covered with short, soft hairs. It is a fast-growing plant.

Leaves: Evergreen, opposite, simple, entire, elliptic–oval, to 5–8 cm long, either with a rounded or a sharp tip. Are glossy green above and softly hairy and grey beneath, though are sometimes yellowish. They have three main leaf veins from the leaf base, and a wide leafstalk.

Flowers: Very pretty, abundant, flowers, ~2–2.5 cm across, occurring singly or in small clusters (2–3) from leaf axils, throughout spring. The five petals are whitish outside, but are a delightful deep rose-pink or mauve inside. There are also five hairy sepals and many pink stamens. *Pollination:* By bees and other insects. Flowers are bisexual, and only need one plant to set fruit, though more than one may increase fruit-set.

Fruit: Round–oblong, small, grape-size (~1.5 cm), greenish turning to dark bluey-purple when ripe. It has a persistent calyx on its apex, ~1 cm wide. Looks similar to blueberry but is more oblong. Inside the flesh is divided into 3–4 cells, filled with juicy, sweet, aromatic pulp, with a double row of small, disc-shaped seeds in each section.

Yield/harvest: Shrubs produce fairly good yields once established. Pick fruit when fully coloured, ripe and have developed their full sweetness. Seedlings start producing fruits at 2–4 years.

Roots: Has fairly shallow roots, and benefits from an organic mulch to conserve moisture and add nutrients. Avoid deep mechanical cultivation.

CULTIVATION

Location: Grows best in full sun or semi shade. It is not very tolerant of maritime salty spray.

Temperature: This species is fairly frost hardy and can fruit in temperate climates. It can tolerate temperatures of ~–5°C without damage, though not for prolonged periods. Not suited to long cold winters.

Soil/water/nutrients: It can grow in a range of soil types, but prefers more acidic pH conditions: ~4.5–6. It does not tolerate very saline soils. Likes regular moisture, particularly when young, and can be grown in fairly wet soils. It naturally comes from wet forests and boggy margins. It is not drought tolerant.

Pot culture: Makes an ideal container plant because of its smaller size, and it can be taken inside or given extra protection in cold winters. Its attractive flowers look good on a deck or patio.

Pruning: Generally needs little attention, just to thin out competing branches and to allow light and air to penetrate into the centre of the plant. Can be pruned to form a hedge.

Propagation: *Seed:* Usually propagated by seed. Best sown when fresh. Thoroughly wash off all flesh before sowing in shade in moist acidic compost. It has a hard seedcoat, designed to pass intact through a digestive system, and so scarification to penetrate the seedcoat, or briefly soaking in acid (then thoroughly washing) should hasten germination. It then should germinate readily, with a high success rate. *Cuttings:* Semi-ripe cuttings can be taken during summer and inserted into gritty compost. ∎

Rhus spp.
Sumach (sumac)
ANACARDIACEAE

Flameleaf sumach (*R. copallina*), fragrant sumach (*R. aromatica*), skunkbush sumach (*R. trilobata*), smooth sumach (*R. glabra*), stag's horn sumach (*R. typhina, R. hirta*), smoke tree or Venetian sumach, (*Cotinus coggyria*, formerly *Rhus cotinus*), lemonade drupe (*R. integrifolia*)

Relatives: cashew, mango, pistachio, poison ivy

All of the Anacardiaceae family have some level of toxicity, but this varies from very high to very low. Some, such as pistachio, have low toxicity, whereas cashew fruits contain a very caustic oil. The sumachs are within the *Rhus* genus, which consists of ~250 species of hardy deciduous shrubs and small trees. Some *Rhus* species are poisonous, and should not be eaten, touched or handled. This genus includes species such as poison ivy, poison oak, poison sumac, though these are sometimes listed in the *Toxicodendron* genus. In contrast, the sumachs listed have very low toxicity, and only a few individuals may find them a skin irritant. You can identify the poisonous species from sumachs: if it has flowers that form at the ends of shoots and the fruits are red and covered by crimson hairs, then the species is not poisonous; if it has flowers that form in the internodes, and produces smooth white or pale cream-coloured fruits, then the plant is likely to be poisonous. The non-poisonous sumachs are popular ornamental trees and shrubs, have an elegant shape, and usually have dazzling red/yellow leaves in autumn. They originate from the Mediterranean, Africa and Middle East, where there are no poisonous species of *Rhus*. The word sumach is derived from the Arabic word 'summaq'.

DESCRIPTION

The notes below apply to the sumachs described in this section, and not to all sumach species. Sumachs are shrubs or small trees. Young stems are usually covered with a fine hair and are often red in colour; older wood may be grey or reddish. When cut, they exude a resinous substance.

Leaves: Pale–mid green, pinnate, elliptical, slightly serrated, deciduous, brilliant autumn colour.

Flowers: In panicles, with a citrus fragrance, greenish-white, their size varying with species, produced in spring to early summer. They are often dioecious (so need more than one plant to produce drupes); this also means that male plants do not produce fruits. A few plants can be bisexual.

Fruits: Are small drupes, in conical bunches, smallish, crimson, covered with crimson-brown hairs. They ripen from autumn–early winter. Easy to harvest. They contain a hard central stone.

Roots: Often have an extensive root system, which is useful in areas of soil erosion.

CULTIVATION

Location: Sumachs prefer a sunny, sheltered location. Their branches are brittle and are easily damaged by strong winds. Only moderately tolerant of salt.

Temperature: The species listed here are all very hardy and can tolerate temperatures down to ~–25°C.

Soil/water/nutrients: Prefers a well-drained, organic soil, but will tolerate surprisingly poor soils. However, they grow and fruit much better with one or two applications of a general, complete fertiliser annually. Grows best in loamy soils, though can grow in quite heavy clay soils as long as not waterlogged for an extended period. Prefers neutral to alkaline soils (pH 6–7.5). Mature plants are fairly drought tolerant.

Propagation: *Seed:* Best sown when fresh. Both fresh and stored seed will germinate better after soaking in warm water for 24 hours to remove germination inhibitors. *Cuttings:* Take half-ripe stem cuttings in summer and place in a sandy soil, with some warmth and, ideally, with mist. Once rooted, pot these up in compost and grow on in a protected area for the first year. Root cuttings can be taken in winter and planted vertically in pots to root. There is a good percentage take. *Suckers:* These can be removed in late summer and autumn, and are easily rooted in pots. Plants transplant easily. *Layering:* This can be practised using long, healthy stems. Usually done in autumn.

Pruning: Many sumachs sucker freely (see above) and these should be removed to retain the original shape of the tree and to prevent it losing growth potential. Trees need very little

Food

The fruits have a sour, but fruity, musky taste. The fruits of a few species can be eaten fresh, but are usually prepared in some way. Can be used in dressings and to flavour savoury meat and rice dishes, and kebabs, or can be mixed with cornmeal or oats, etc. or used in confectionery and cereals. Their use is popular throughout the Middle East. The Arabs dry and grind up the drupes to form a red–purple powder that is used as a spice, often where lemon might be used; it is said to taste a little like tamarind. It may be mixed with other herbs and spices, e.g. thyme, sesame, marjoram, cumin, or black pepper. The powder can be stored if kept in a dark, airtight container. The juice extracted from sumach is popular in salad dressings and marinades and, when powdered, is used in stews and casseroles. A mixture of yoghurt and sumach is often served with kebabs and, mixed with thyme, is used to flavour 'labni', a cream cheese made from yoghurt. For a refreshing drink, harvest the drupe clusters, rub them gently and then soak them for ~15 minutes in cold water. After straining, add a little honey to the pink water, chill, and enjoy.

Nutrition

Berries have good levels of vitamin C. The whole plant contains high levels of tannins. Organic acids give them their tart taste.

Medicinal

Sumachs are said to have fever-fighting and diuretic properties. The plants have been used for digestion and bowel problems.

Other uses

Leaves and bark are rich in tannin (~25%) and can be used as a brown dye or as a mordant. Oil from the seeds has been used in candles.

Ornamental

Are elegant, smaller trees that have scented blossom, attractive drupes and vivid autumn colour.

pruning except for the removal of diseased or damaged branches. If removing parts of branches, take care as partially pruned branches often die back to the main stem. Some species can be cut back to ground level and will regrow.

Pests and diseases: Generally, few problems. Resistant to honey fungus; watch for *Verticillium* wilt, coral-spot fungus.

FRUITING SPECIES

Below are some of the better fruiting sumachs and, unless stated, the above general notes apply. None are poisonous.

Flameleaf sumach (dwarf sumach), *Rhus copallina*. An ornamental shrub, native to eastern North America. Its size varies according to the location it is grown in, but ranges between 1–7 m tall. It is fairly fast growing, but relatively short lived. **Cultivation:** Prefers moist soils and can grow in sun or shade. **Uses:** *Food:* Fruits are small (~0.4 cm), but tasty and easy to harvest. *Other uses:* A black dye can be obtained from the fruits. The timber is light, soft and coarse grained. Copal resin, which is a main ingredient in one of the finest varnishes, is obtained from this tree.

Fragrant sumach (lemon sumach), *Rhus aromatica*. A shrub, native to eastern and central North America. **Description:** A variable, low, suckering fast-growing shrub, growing to ~1.5–3 m height, ~1.5–3 m spread. The leaves are fragrant and occur in threes. They look a little like those of poison ivy, but the fruits are completely different. Has small, greenish-yellow flowers in early spring. The round, dark ruby-coloured drupes (~0.5 cm across) are harvested in autumn. **Uses:** The fruits can be eaten for the treatment of stomach aches, toothaches and gripe. The leaves and root bark have been used as an astringent and a diuretic, and have been used in the treatment of colds, stomach aches, and bleeding. It should not be used if inflammation is present.

Skunkbush sumach (three-leaf sumach, squawbush sumach), *Rhus trilobata*. A fast-growing shrub that is native to western North America, growing to ~ 2.0 m tall, ~3 m spread. Leaves with three leaflets, pungent when crushed. Has small creamy-coloured flowers in late spring. The round fruits are orange-red (~0.5 cm round) and occur from mid summer to autumn. Some people may be allergic to the fruit. Very drought tolerant. **Uses:** A yellow dye can be obtained from the twigs. The branches can be stripped of their bark and split lengthwise and used to make baskets.

Smooth sumach, *Rhus glabra*. A very ornamental, fast-growing shrub with larger leaves. Is found throughout the USA and southern Canada. Grows to ~3–5 m tall, ~3 m spread, but does not live long if kept to a single stem. Coppicing the tree in early spring encourages numerous stems and prolongs its life significantly. Each leaf consists of 20–30 leaflets. Has outstanding autumn colour. Hairless stems. Small, green-white flowers in early summer. Produces small (~0.3 cm), round, dark red, hairy drupes that ripen from late summer to autumn, but can persist into winter. It is similar to, and can hybridise with, *R. typhina*. **Cultivation:** Can tolerate growing in poor, dry sandy soils and is very hardy. Likes full sun. **Uses:**

The fruits, though small, can be easily harvested. *Medicinal:* A tea made from the root bark is said to be an astringent, a tonic and, in particular, a good antiseptic. It is used to treat diarrhoea, fevers, general debility, sore mouths, uterine prolapse. The drupes are said to be a diuretic. *Other uses:* A black dye can be obtained from the fruit and an orange-yellow dye from the root. *Rhus glabra* has a particularly extensive root system, and is more wind tolerant than many other sumachs, so can be planted as a screen or as a pioneer species to stabilise soil. Its timber is soft, light and brittle. It is a good bee plant.

Stag's horn sumach, *Rhus typhina* (syn. *R. hirta*). A fast-growing, small tree (~6 m tall, ~6 m spread) native to eastern North America, though common in garden in Europe. Has distinctive velvety young branches and flower stalks. Large (~20 cm) panicles of small greenish-white flowers in early summer. Fruits from early summer to early autumn. Leaves consist of 10–30 leaflets, which turn fiery-red in autumn. Round, dark red drupes (~0.3 cm) in autumn, which can persist on the tree into winter. Although single trees are fairly short lived, it can be coppiced in early spring to extend its life. This species suckers very freely and its tenacious spread can become a problem in smaller gardens. Closely related to and hybridises with *R. glabra*. **Cultivation:** Can grow in poorer soils and is drought resistant. More wind hardy than many sumachs. Can be grown in full sun or semi-shade. **Uses:** *Food:* Drupes are usually cooked because they are sour. They can then be sweetened or mixed with other fruits. Fruits are small, but easily harvested. *Medicinal:* A tea made from the bark has astringent, tonic and antiseptic properties. A tea made from the leaves has been used to treat asthma and diarrhoea, and the drupes have been used to treat a sore throat. *Other uses:* A black ink can be made by boiling the leaves and fruit. The plant has an extensive root system and so can be planted as a windbreak and to prevent soil erosion. The timber is soft, light and brittle.

Smoke tree (Venetian sumach), *Cotinus coggyria* (was *Rhus cotinus*). A small, slow-growing, spreading tree, native to Europe and Asia (height 3–5 m tall, 3–5 m spread). Likes full sun. Grows in most soils, even poor, rocky soils. Is hardy and drought resistant, though prefers better soils with moisture. Will grow in acid to alkaline soils, and tolerate some salt. Has oval light green leaves (some cultivars have purple/mauve foliage). In early summer, has yellow flowers and attractive, terminal feathery, wispy, sterile flowers that have long 'hairs', in white, brown and pink, which give it its attractive 'smokey' appearance. These remain on the tree till autumn or sometimes later. Often has good yellow-orange autumn colour. Has dark red drupes covered with fine purplish hair that ripen in late summer–autumn, but can persist into winter. Best not to prune this tree. **Uses:** An essential oil is made from its stems by steam distillation and according to a perfumery text, this has an aroma that is 'resinous-balsamic with a green and galbanum note'. This oil is used in perfumes and cosmetics, and as a flavouring in the food, wine and tobacco industries. A popular and attractive ornamental tree.

Lemonade drupe, *Rhus integrifolia*. An evergreen shrub or small tree, 1–3 m tall, with thick and leathery leaves, can also be grown as a hedge. Likes a warm to hot dry climate. ■

Ribes spp.
Currants
GROSSULARIACEAE (syn. Saxifragaceae)

Black currant (*Ribes nigrum*), red and white currants (*R. sativum*, *R. rubrum*, *R. petraeum*, *R. vulgare*), alpine currant (*R. alpinum*), clove black currant (*R. odoratum*), buffalo currant (*R. aureum*), jostaberry (*R. nidigrolaria*), *Ribes valdivianum*, Worcesterberry (*R. americanum*), rock red currant (*R. petraeum*), American black currant (*R. divaricatum*), currant gooseberry (*R. hirtellum*), flowering currant (*R. oxyacanthoides*)

Relatives: gooseberry, mock orange (*Philadelphus* spp.), saxifrage, hydrangea

The name 'currant' may be derived from a corruption of 'Corinth', the Greek city that shipped small raisins called 'currants' (which were actually dried grapes) throughout Europe. The genus *Ribes* is native to the colder regions of the Northern Hemisphere, and its species are found in northern Europe, northern Asia and North America. Currants have been utilised by indigenous populations for many thousands of years. In Europe, their cultivation has been practised since at least the 1500s. These small, tasty fruits are full of healthy nutrients and are also very flavoursome. However, mostly because of their small size and the costs involved in harvesting them, they are seldom available for purchase when fresh. These species generally form smallish shrubs and could be easily squeezed into a smaller garden, where they would produce fruits for many years. Currants come in three main colours: red, pink and white, and these are predominantly derived from the European species *R. rubrum*, *R. petraeum* and *R. sativum*, respectively.

GENERAL DESCRIPTION

The shrubs consist of a multi-stemmed clump of canes that grow ~1–1.5 m tall and the same distance wide. Each year, renewal canes grow from the base of the plant, and these then fruit for ~3 years. They can also be trained to form a standard. These species are generally fast growing, particularly in spring. Plants can live ~15–30 years, with black currants being less long-lived than red currants or gooseberries.

Leaves: Deciduous, alternate, single, lobed, maple-like. Black-currant leaves are pale green; red-currant leaves are deep blue-green.

Flowers: Clusters of ~20 flowers, which form a delicate, drooping strig (or raceme), on a 12–15-cm-long stem. Flowers are green or yellow on red-currant bushes, and pink on black currants. They are borne in spring, towards the base of 1-year-old stems and on spurs of older stems. Most currants are self-fertile, but a few cultivars, particularly black currants, are partially self-sterile, so set more fruits with cross pollination. The degree of self-fertility is influenced by climate. *Pollination:* By hoverflies, bees and other insects.

Fruit: Currants that are red, white and pink are translucent; black currants are matte, very dark purple. The flowers' ovaries are inferior, so currants are classified as false berries. They contain 3–12 tiny, edible seeds. Many berries can form on a single strig. Black currants usually ripen from the top down, which encourages birds to eat them over a period as they ripen. Modern red-currant varieties have been selected so that their fruits ripen at the same time on a strig, so can be harvested in one picking. To increase fruit size and number, the flowers can be thinned by removing some of the strigs while they are flowering.

Yield/harvest: Seedlings and plants from cuttings can start to bear fruits when 2–3 years old. Yield varies depending on growing conditions and cultivar, but can be 1.5–5 kg from a single bush. Depending on cultivar, fruits ripen from 70–100 days after fruit-set, usually in about mid summer. Few fruits are lost before they fully ripen. If eating fruits fresh, pick when absolutely fully ripe; you can leave them ~3 weeks after they have coloured on the bush. Fruits to be stored should be picked when dry. To avoid damaging the fruits, pick whole strigs by cutting the stem.

Roots: Are superficial, only extend outwards 20–40 cm, and are fine and easily damaged by cultivation. Plants greatly benefit from an organic mulch to reduce moisture loss and weed competition, also to add nutrients.

CULTIVATION

Location: Currants grow best in areas with cool humid summers and winters that are cold enough to get sufficient winter chilling. They are even grown into northern Sweden. Plants like the morning sun, but prefer afternoon shade to protect them from sunburn and overheating. Not many fruit plants are happy in partial shade; they can be grown in the shade of fruit trees or on the south side of buildings. The leaves are easily burned by bright sunlight and plants quickly wilt if the soil or air temperature goes above 30°C. Need some sun though to get good fruit production. Cannot tolerate too much salty air as this damages the leaves.

Temperature: Very cold hardy, surviving very cold periods. Plants only need 120–140 frost-free days to mature fruit and complete their vegetative period.

Chilling: Needs a longish chilling period of 800–1600

uses

Food
Currants are tart, often sharp, but sweeten when fully ripe, and are then very juicy and flavoursome. They can be eaten fresh, but are frequently added to various desserts, often with other fruits, where they contribute their individual flavours and rich colours. Currants make good jellies and jams, and are high in pectin. They are also good in pies, sauces and cheesecakes. Currants have also been used for wine, and are said, by some, to be similar in flavour to Graves or Rhine wines. Black currants are a traditional source of juice and of the French liqueur, cassis, as well as a brandy called 'Noir de Bourgogne'.

Nutrition
Black currants have almost the highest vitamin C content of all temperate fruits at 155–215 mg/100 g of flesh (340% of RDA). Red currants and gooseberries have 73–95% of the daily allowance: 58–80 mg of vitamin C/100 g of flesh. Currants also contain excellent levels of flavonoids, 140–1200 mg/100 g of flesh, both proanthocyanidins and anthocyanins, which have many health benefits (see p. 44). Fruits are also high in potassium, iron, calcium and manganese. Red currants contain good levels of dietary fibre (~20%).
Warning: The leaves of some *Ribes* species (e.g. red currants) may contain cyanide-like compounds and should not be eaten in quantity; however, the fruits are quite safe to eat.

Other uses
A yellow dye can be obtained from many currant species' roots and a black dye from their fruits.

Ornamental
There are various ornamental *Ribes* species.

hours. The number of flowers and fruit-set are reduced if there is a lack of winter chill.

Soil/water/nutrients: They will grow in various soil types, but prefer heavier soils, rich in clay. A thick organic mulch is beneficial and helps to keep the soil cool in summer. Sandy soils dry out too fast. Because they are shallow rooted, deep soils are not necessary. They grow best at a neutral pH of 6–6.5. Plants do not tolerate alkaline or salty soils. They grow best with regular moisture as they have shallow roots, but also cannot tolerate waterlogging. Moisture is particularly important during fruit development. After harvesting, watering can be reduced until spring. Plants stressed

during the growing season are susceptible to mildew and have reduced leaf size and number, as well as poor-quality fruits. Currants only need moderate applications of fertiliser; usually one dose annually at the beginning of spring. Too much nitrogen makes the plants susceptible to disease. Plants benefit from extra potassium; deficiency shows up as a marginal scorching of the leaves. However, do not add potassium as potassium chloride because currants are sensitive to the chloride ions.

Pot culture: Are an interesting possibility for container culture. Only form a smallish plant and could be grown in a pot if short of garden space.

Planting: Best to plant currants in autumn because they begin growth early in spring. Train up fences or wires for easy fruit harvesting. Space plants at ~1 m apart for a hedge, or ~2 m apart for individuals. Remove all weeds, and mulch or use bark or black plastic to suppress weeds. Plant them deep enough to encourage shoot growth below the soil surface. Prune off shoots to ~20–30 cm to encourage root establishment.

Pruning: Can be grown as free-standing bushes, as a hedge or as a small tree. Black currants fruit mostly on 1-year-old wood, so these canes should be encouraged, with older weaker canes being removed. Conversely, red currants fruit mostly on spurs of 2–3-year-old shoots, so more of a balance between younger and older canes is maintained. For red currants, in the winter of the plant's first season remove all but 2–3 stems at ground level. Similarly, during the following winter, remove all but 2–3 stems that grew during that season. The bush will now have equal numbers of 1- and 2-year-old stems. Continue this for the third year, but in the fourth winter start removing any stems more than 3 years old. Also shorten any long straggly stems. Do not prune after spring growth has commenced.

Propagation: *Seeds:* Should germinate if stratified for 3–4 months at ~2–4°C. Seedlings are prolific and do not vary much from parent. *Cuttings:* Easily propagated by cuttings of semi-ripe wood in autumn. Insert cuttings to leave just two buds above the soil surface. Hardwood cuttings can also be taken (~30 cm long) in late winter; dip the base in rooting hormone and pot in ordinary soil. Cuttings will quickly root, and are best kept in part shade for the first year. Seeds can remain viable for >15 years. *Grafting:* Can be grafted, but no advantage is gained. The usual rootstock used for a tree form is *R. aureum*.

Pests and diseases: Are susceptible to various pests. Gall mite can attack the new buds during summer, and can do serious damage. Plants need to be dug up and destroyed. Another serious pest is the clear-winged borer who lays eggs on stems in late spring. The larvae then bore into the stems and kill them. If not controlled, they can kill the whole plant. In addition, black currants may be attacked by reversion virus, which can weaken and kill plants. Spread by common and gall mites, it is endemic in Europe and, unfortunately, there is no cure. Aphids and spider mites can distort leaves. *Ribes* species are also a host for white-pine blister rust, which causes few problems for currants, but is lethal to five-needle pines; therefore, currants may be banned in countries where these pines are extensively grown. Can also be attacked by two-spotted mites, and leaf and bud eelworm. *Botrytis* and *Anthracnose* can cause leaf rot and loss of young growth, particularly of stems lying close to the soil. Gooseberry mildew can infect currants, especially in humid areas. Currant roots are susceptible to both *Armillaria* and *Phytophthora*.

RIBES SPECIES

Black currant, *Ribes nigrum*. The European black currant is native to northwest Asia and northern Europe, where it is particularly popular. Black currants have a characteristic aroma and are very tasty and juicy.

Description: Leafs out very early in spring, and grows to ~2 m tall. *Leaves:* Large, soft green; when crushed they have a strong currant fragrance. *Flowers:* Yellow-green. Generally self-fertile, though growing more than one plant can increase fruit-set. *Fruit:* Borne on last season's shoots and on short laterals formed from them. Ripen in mid summer. Bear heavily in suitable climates, producing ~4.5 kg on a healthy bush. Pick the strigs when they are fully black. *Roots:* Surface rooting, so needs care with cultivation and regular moisture.

Cultivation: Grows best in cool, moist locations. They are early into flower and leaf, so can be damaged by late spring frosts. Need 800–1500 chill hours, and may not flower or leaf without sufficient winter chill. Do not like maritime conditions. *Soil/water:* Grow best in moist, yet well-drained, fertile soil with lots of organic matter. Can grow on wetter soils than most other berries. Do best at pH 5.4–7.0, and are more tolerant of acid soils. *Pruning:* Aim for a vase-shaped bush with well-spaced branches that allow light and air to enter. Fruit forms on last year's wood, so prune to renew this and remove old unfruiting wood. Aim to have ~8–10 shoots per bush. Can renew the plant every third year by cutting off all shoots to ground level.

Cultivars: 'Ben Sarek': From Scotland. Is disease and frost resistant, high-yielding, tasty. Plant is smaller than average: ~1.2 tall.
'Blacksmith': From UK. Hardy, very vigorous, much branched. Productive, strigs long, good flavour.
'Goliath': Large, mild and sweet flavoured fruit, but thin skinned. Bush is erect. Long harvesting period.
'Noir de Bourgogne': From Dijon, France. An old cultivar, traditionally used for cassis. Bush is spreading, low, open, fairly productive, but slow to begin producing. Strigs are short, but have many berries of very good flavour.
'Brodtorp': Very hardy bush. Fruits ripen early and are good dried.

Red and white currants (*R. sativum, R. rubrum, R. petraeum, R. vulgare*). The red currant was first cultivated in Scandinavia, appearing in London markets at the end of the 16th century. Red currants often have good yields: ~4.5 kg per bush. Unlike black currants, they can be pruned into cordons (but only yield ~0.5–1 kg), espaliers or fans.

Description: Plants are 1–3 m tall, 0.3–2 m spread. The flowers have an attractive lacy appearance, but are borne early so can be hit by late frosts. Fruits are small, bright red, shiny, translucent. They ripen before black currants and can stay on the bush longer.

Cultivation: Need 800–1500 chill hours. Do not like

maritime locations. Have brittle shoots so are susceptible to wind damage. Generally need less nutrients than black currants, but do benefit from additional potash. Are hardy to ~–20°C. *Pests and diseases:* See general notes. *Pruning:* Easy to prune. Fruits form on older wood, which needs to be borne in mind when pruning. Reduce main stems to encourage lateral branching and prune to leave 8–10 main branches. Prune to remove younger shoots to encourage lateral fruiting branches to develop on older wood. After 4 years, the older wood can be removed. Pruning in summer encourages the plant to route its photosynthetic products into developing fruit and lateral buds.

Uses: Red currants are mainly used for juice, jellies and purees. They are are more tart than white currants. The fruit will store well if picked dry.

Cultivars: 'Fay': An old cultivar forming a large spreading bush that has brittle wood and early blossom. Fruits are early ripening, dark red, sweet, flavourful.
'Gloire des Sablons' (*R. vulgare*): A common pink currant of ancient French origin. Skin is colourless, flesh is pink. Bush upright, not branching, productive. Berries are quite large, but few on strig.
'London's Market': A tough cultivar, withstanding disease and heat. Bush is upright and productive; the fruit are red and tart.
'Red Lake': Bush is vigorous, much branching, tolerates some dryness, cold hardy. Resists mildew. Early into leaf and flower, though has a long flowering and fruiting season. Fruits: dark red, productive, late-ripening.
'White Dutch': Old European cultivar. Bush is sprawling, with small, flavourful, white, less acidic fruits.
'White Imperial' (*R. rubrum*): Bush spreading, not upright. Fruits are small, round, white berries with lowest acidity of currants, excellent flavour. Small ornamental plant, very productive.
'Wilder' (*R. vulgare*): Bush is spreading. Largest of red currants. Very productive. Pale red berries. Ripen late, hold long on bush.

OTHER CURRANT SPECIES

Alpine currant, *Ribes alpinum*. A medium-sized currant bush, growing to ~1.2 m, with a spread of ~ 1 m, and native to the UK. Flowering is somewhat later in spring, and fruits ripen in autumn. A few cultivars have been selected for their ornamental value. Flowers are fragrant, but male and female flowers occur on separate plants, so you need more than one plant to set fruit. If planting as a group, one male for every five female plants will result in good fruit-set and yields. Fruits are ~0.5 cm diameter and are red when fully ripe.

Cultivation: Can be grown as other currants, but will also grow in poorer soils, or in fairly alkaline soils. Can be grown in full sun or semi-shade. Fully cold hardy to ~–25°C.

Uses: Fruits can be eaten fresh or cooked. They are quite sweet and sometimes lack the tangy flavour of other currants.

American black currant, *Ribes divaricatum*. A larger shrub, to ~2.5 m, and a native of western North America. Hardy to at least –20°C. Grows and fruits best in full sun (performs poorly in shade). Fruits are small, blue-black, yellow, or orange. It is sometimes cultivated for its fruits. Can harbour white-pine blister rust, but is resistant to mildew.

Uses: Fruits are sweet–sub-acid, tasty, are more gooseberry-like, and also have a strong resinous flavour. Can be eaten fresh or added to jam, sauces, desserts, etc.

Buffalo currant (golden currant), *Ribes aureum*. Native to midwest USA, these are very hardy, productive bushes. In some ways, is more similar to gooseberry. Forms a wide, tall bush (~2.2 m tall) with weeping branches that eventually touch the ground. *Leaves:* Small, felty, grey-green, many-lobed. *Flowers:* Abundant, showy, yellow, fragrant, in spring. *Fruit:* Abundant, large (for a currant), shiny, varying in colour from red, gold, brown, purple when ripe. Ripe fruits can last up to 2 months on the bush. Is a very ornamental plant, and there are a few selected cultivars.

Cultivation: Is adaptable to a range of climates, and is cold hardy down to at least ~–20°C. Tolerates a range of soils, even alkaline. Does not require much winter chill. Is quite wind tolerant. Can grow in full sun or shade, though fruit may be better in full sun. *Propagation:* Often spreads by underground rhizomes, and can be readily propagated by removing suckers or taking cuttings from these. *Pruning:* Needs no pruning; stems tend to fizzle out, shedding dormant buds after the first year. It can harbour white-pine blister rust.

Uses: Berries can be eaten fresh or cooked; flavour resembles gooseberry when cooked. The leaves can make a tea or are used as a flavouring. A very ornamental plant.

Clove black currant, *Ribes odoratum*. A native of eastern North America. A very fragrant, shrubby plant, ~2.5 m tall, 0.5–2 m spread. *Leaves:* Open very early in spring. Have some autumn colour. *Flowers:* Yellow. *Fruits:* Turn black before they are fully ripe, so can be tested for ripeness by their ease of removal from a strig. Fruits ripen from mid summer through to autumn. They are ~1 cm in diameter and are usually sweet and tasty. Bushes take 2–4 years to start producing fruits. Have reasonable yields. Tends to sucker.

Cultivation: Prefers part shade and clayey soil. Needs 800–1500 chill hours. Hardy to at least ~–25°C, but also likes hot summers. *Pruning:* Fruits are borne on 1- and 2-year-old wood, so prune as black currants. Resists powdery mildew better than most currants. It can harbour white-pine blister rust. *Cultivars:* 'Crandall': (USA). Good fruit quality. Bush rather weak, weeping, fruit hidden inside leaves.

Uses: Can be eaten fresh or used in preserves, desserts, etc. The leaves can be used to make a tea and as a flavouring. Fruits are high in pectin. Is a good ornamental plant, can be planted as a hedge and is popular with wildlife.

Currant gooseberry, *Ribes hirtellum*. A native of northern North America, from Newfoundland down to Virginia. Forms a smaller shrub, to ~1 m tall. It is early flowering. *Fruits:* ~1 cm diameter, smooth-skinned and are purple-black when ripe. Plants are cold hardy, surviving to at least –20°C. Grows best in a sunnier position. This species is quite disease resistant and has been used as a cross in other hybrids. Can harbour white-pine blister rust.

Uses: Fruits are not usually eaten fresh (because of their tartness), but are often used in pies, preserves, etc. They can be easily dried for later use.

Flowering currant (American mountain gooseberry), *Ribes oxyacanthoides*. A native of northern North America. Is fully cold hardy below –25°C. It forms a medium-sized shrub, to ~1.5 m tall. It can grow in full sun or shade, though fruits are of better quality when grown in sun.

Uses: Fruits are small, black, with a pungent sweetness and a strong, pleasant resinous flavour. They are often used in jams, preserves, sauces, etc.

Jostaberry, *Ribes nidigrolaria*. A hybrid between black currant and the American gooseberry (*R. hirtellum*), produced in Germany, 1930–1950s. The shrubby bush is ~1.5–3 m tall, spread: 0.3–2 m. No thorns. Growth is vigorous. Tends not to branch much. Lateral buds tend to shed, leaving straight branches. Needs an organic-rich soil to grow well. *Leaves:* Glossy, larger than gooseberry, lobed, scentless, resists mildew. *Flowers:* Pretty, but small. *Fruit:* Purple or brownish-red, ~1.5 cm long, borne in small clusters. Fruit ripens in mid summer–autumn. It survives full sunlight, but requires a lot of winter chilling. Most fruits form on 2- or 3-year-old wood. Can be espaliered. Fruits can be eaten fresh, but are mostly used in preserves. Freeze well.

***Ribes valdivianum* (syn. *R. glandulosum*).** Native of Chile; popular in South America, but is not cultivated much outside this region. A deciduous, fairly hardy shrub, probably can tolerate temperatures down to ~–15°C, though early spring flowers can be damaged by frosts. Can grow in full sun or shade, though fruit quality is better in full sun. *Height:* ~3.5 m. *Flowers:* Self-fertile. *Cultivation and propagation:* As for black currant above, though it prefers to be grown in warmer regions. Produces suckers. Has tasty fruit. The main benefit of this species is that it has a very high total phenolic content of ~1800 mg gallic acid/100 g fruit): lots and lots of antioxidants! Can harbour white-pine blister rust, so should not be grown near pine trees. Can also be propagated by hardwood cuttings from the current season's growth, in winter. Plant in a cold frame to root in spring–summer.

Rock red currant, *Ribes petraeum*. A native of the mountainous regions of central and western Europe. It forms a medium-sized shrub, to ~1.5 m. It is fairly cold hardy, down to ~–20°C. Many currants have this species as a parent.

Uses: The fruits tend to be seedy and very tart, and are usually cooked and added to pies, sauces, jam, etc.

Worcesterberry, *Ribes americanum*. A native of eastern North America, from Canada down to Virginia. Medium-sized, fairly vigorous shrub to ~1.6 m. Flowers in spring, fruits ripen in autumn. May be a cross between gooseberries and black currants: fruits are smaller than gooseberries, but larger than black currants. They ripen to a purple-black colour. Their flavour seems to vary from insipid to very tasty. A very cold hardy plant, to at least –20°C. Can grow in sun or shade, though may have better fruits in the former. Can harbour white-pine blister rust. Propagated from cuttings.

Uses: As for black currants above. A tea made from the roots has been used to treat kidney ailments. ∎

Ribes spp.

Gooseberry

GROSSULARIACEAE (syn. Saxifragaceae)

American gooseberry (*Ribes hirtellum, R. cynobasti*), European gooseberry (*R. grossularia, R. uva-crispa*)

Relatives: currants

The genus *Ribes* is native to the high latitudes of the Northern Hemisphere, and contains many species. Europe, Asia and North America all have native species. The European gooseberry is the main type used in cookery and desserts, and has been cultivated for many hundreds of years. However, it is not as popular as it was, possibly because of its thorny stems. The Normans probably brought the gooseberry to England, and then gooseberry production began in Europe in ~1700. Nowadays, gooseberries are mostly derived from two species: the European gooseberry (*Ribes grossularia*) and the American gooseberry (*R. hirtellum*), native to northeastern USA and southern Canada. The European cultivars are usually pure species, whereas virtually all American cultivars have European genes included within them. The term 'gooseberry' could be derived from the German 'jansbeere', meaning 'John's berry', because it ripened during the feast of St John, or from the French word for currant, 'groseille', or because it was commonly eaten in a sauce that accompanied goose. In the 18th century, horticultural clubs in northern England held annual shows that awarded prizes for the largest gooseberry, with these clubs continuing until the beginning of the 20th century, or later, and the record for the heaviest gooseberry was set in 1852, with a gooseberry that weighed in at nearly 50 g, half the weight of a medium-sized apple. (Apologies in advance for not recording weights that may have superseded this!) The methods needed to achieve these results were kept secret, but the main principle was to strip bushes of all the fruits, before they were ripe, except for a very few chosen fruits. The variety was important, but of more importance were abundant supplies of water and manure, plus whatever secret ingredients might be added. Unfortunately, the American gooseberry, although more productive, is smaller, and does not have the same zingy character. Growers in colder climates, looking for a gooseberry substitute, could consider jostaberry or buffalo currant (*Ribes aureum*).

DESCRIPTION

A prickly fellow. Low–medium-sized bushes, 1–1.2 m tall, ~1–2 m spread, with thorny, erect thin stems. They form a thorn at each axil and the American gooseberry may form additional thorns. Unfortunately, there are few varieties that have fewer thorns: a species that wants to protect its fruits at all costs. Gooseberry bushes are moderately–fast growing under good conditions, and can live for ~15–30 years.

Leaves: Deciduous, small, rough, thin, alternate, 3–5 lobed with rounded tips and finely to coarsely toothed margins. Come into leaf early in spring. American types can be finely pubescent. Leaf size and number are reduced with heat or light stress; they are easily burned by intense sunlight.

Flowers: Inconspicuous, in small racemes (strigs) of 1–4 flowers, green with pinkish petals that open early in spring. Borne laterally on 1-year-old wood and on short spurs of older wood. Flowers have inferior ovaries (the calyx is left at the apex of the fruit). *Pollinators:* Flowers are self-fertile and are pollinated by wind, bees and insects, but their self-fertility is influenced by climate. Although self-fertile, the cultivation of groups of plants, particularly in difficult areas, will result in better fruit-set.

Fruit: The fruit, a false berry, takes 6–9 weeks to mature after fruit-set. The plant forms renewal fruiting stems (or canes) either from the crown or from beneath the soil, and these stems fruit for ~3 years, so a sequence of these stems needs to be developed, with older, non-fruiting stems removed.

Fruits are borne singly or in clusters (1–4) and are green–grey to green–yellow, with shades of red–pink–purple developing as they mature. European gooseberries are oval, ~2 cm long (unless grown by an avid gooseberry club); American gooseberries are smaller (~1.2 cm), round, also becoming pink to wine-red at maturity. Skin colour is most intense in full sunlight. Most fruits form on the previous season's growth, with a few occurring on older spurs and wood.

Yield/harvest: A typical yield from a mature plant is ~4 kg. Plants first fruit in ~5 years from seed, or in 2–3 years from cuttings. Fruits are harvested in late summer, and they often drop when fully ripe. Yields can be less in warmer areas because of a lack of winter chill.

Roots: Have shallow, fibrous, wide-spreading roots that like lots of organic material. Roots are easily damaged by deep cultivation. Benefit from a deep organic mulch that retains moisture and adds nutrients.

CULTIVATION

Relatively easy to grow, but is prickly.

Location: Do not like to be grown in full sun and prefer partial shade: can be grown on the shady side of structures. They prefer cool, moist conditions, so generally do not do well in warmer climates. American gooseberries are more sun tolerant. Although they produce more fruits in full sun, their leaves are easily sunburnt and can drop prematurely. It is best

Food

The best fruits are delicious eaten fresh, and have a sub-acid, sweet, very juicy taste. Others may be too sour and sharp, and need to be included in sauces, jams, jellies, puddings, pies, gooseberry fool (cream folded into ripe, sweetened stewed fruit – delicious), or added to preserves and pickles, or made into 'British champagne'. Fruits with a red blush are usually sweeter than the green varieties. The fruits can be cooked with other sweeter fruit and/or with honey. They are excellent added to sweet-and-sour sauces or used as flavour enhancers (in the same way as lemon), or added to stuffing that accompanies meat or chicken. The French have always valued gooseberries and use them in sauces that accompany fish, particularly oily fish, where the sharpness of the fruit balances the oil. The leaves provide a slightly bitter, but pleasant taste in salads.

Nutrition

Fruits have good levels of vitamin C: ~46 mg/100 g of flesh, and fairly good levels of vitamins A and B6, and are high in fibre, potassium, copper and manganese.

Ornamental

Can be grown as a defensive hedge because of their thorns. The leaves often have good yellow autumn colour.

not to crowd plants too closely: they like good air circulation. However, too much exposure to wind is likely to break branches. They do not grow well in exposed maritime locations.

Chilling: Without 800–1500 hours of chilling, plants come into leaf poorly and yields are reduced. Therefore, gooseberries do poorly in warmer areas; however, some cultivars need less chilling than others.

Temperature: Are very frost hardy, tolerating at least −10°C when dormant. Do not like hot summer temperatures >28°C: they are a cool-temperate species.

Soil/water/nutrients: Grow better in acid or poorer soils than most small fruits. They tolerate a wide range of soils, except those that are waterlogged or alkaline. In hotter summer regions, bushes may grow better and produce more fruits when grown in heavier soils, which retain more moisture and stay cooler. A thick mulch of organic material helps keep the soil cooler. Sandy soils are less suitable. They like regular moisture to grow well and produce good-quality fruits. They are not drought tolerant, and often grow poorly, after recovering from drought. They are moderately nutrient hungry and like regular additions of a balanced fertiliser, and of potassium and magnesium (e.g. dolomitic limestone) in particular, during their growing season. A shortage of potassium shows up as early leaf drop and scorched leaf margins. Alternatively, plants relish 1–2 annual additions of well-rotted manure during their growing season. Too much nitrogen can encourage lush growth, which encourages

mildew diseases, as well as poor flowering and fruiting.

Planting: Space plants at ~1–1.5 m apart, in rows ~3.0 m apart. Because of their thorns, do not plant near thoroughfares.

Pruning: Can be grown as bushes, as a small tree (~2 m) or as cordons, if short of space, but the latter need more care. Often grown as hedges, but the branches can form a prickly mass. In general, prune the bush over the first couple of years to form an open framework. Often best to remove the lower hanging branches. Shorten all shoots by about a third, remove weak, diseased and old (>4–5-year-old) shoots. In late summer, prune all laterals back to about five leaves, but do not prune the main leaders. Instead, in winter, cut these leaders back to half, to an inward-pointing bud or lateral, which helps overcome the gooseberries' tendency to droop. Fruits form mostly on spurs on 2–3-year-old shoots, so some 1-year-old canes can be removed (without affecting yields too much), to leave a balance between 1- and 2-, and 3-year-old shoots.

Propagation: *Seeds:* Sow seeds when fresh. They benefit from cold, moist stratification, at just above freezing, for 3–4 months, before sowing. *Cuttings:* Generally easily propagated from 1-year-old hardwood cuttings that have at least 3–5 healthy buds. Or cuttings can be taken in autumn, before the leaves have dropped, from the current season's growth, with lower buds removed, and then inserted into well-drained soil. This method is particularly effective for American gooseberries. These cuttings can be more successful if their bases are dipped in rooting hormone. Grow on cuttings in part shade for the first year. Often, American cultivars are easier to root than European cultivars. *Layering:* Often a surer method for European gooseberries. Either the tips or areas of lightly injured stems should form roots. Ensure the stems are adequately buried. American gooseberries have weeping stems that will root wherever they touch the ground to the point of becoming invasive. *Grafting:* Can be grafted by the whip-and-tongue method during the growing season. These plants should form single stems to 30–45 cm height. Grafted plants often suffer less from powdery mildew, are less susceptible to frost damage and can have higher yields.

Pests and diseases: Possible problems are gooseberry fruitworm (pulp-eating, web-spinning borers) and currant worm (foliage strippers). Aphids may attack young leaves, distorting them. Spider mites can be a problem in summer. The clear-winged borer lays its eggs on stems in spring and can kill plants. *Botrytis* and *Anthracnose* can cause rots of leaves and loss of young growth. Gooseberry mildew is a common problem, affecting both European and American types, as well as grey mould. It is worst in humid areas and in drought-stressed plants. Keep plants well watered and not water stressed, but not over-watered. Roots are susceptible to both oak root fungus (*Armillaria mellea*) and *Phytophthora*. Birds can be problem: it is advisable to net the fruits as they ripen.

CULTIVARS

There are several thousand named cultivars.

'Glenndale' (*R. missouriense* x *R. grossularia*): American gooseberry. Vigorous, dark red–purple berries, better adapted to warmer areas than most. Tall, bushy, generally rooting at tips. Prolific production. Tolerates bright sun.

'**Hinnonmakis**': Hybrid from Finland, somewhat resistant to mildew. Fruit ripens mid season with a smooth, yellow skin. Fruit size is variable, excellent flavour, very hardy.

'**Invicta**': American gooseberry. Vigorous growth, resistant to mildew. Fruit: green when ripe, covered in pale hairs. Excellent flavour; fruits are ideal for processing. Matures early to mid summer.

'**Oregon**': American gooseberry. Bush tall, weeping. Stems bristly, spiny. Rarely roots at tips. Begins growth very early.

Prolific. Fruits small, bland, sweet, greenish-yellow on maturity.

'**Poorman**': An American–European cross, often recommended for home gardens. Very hardy, vigorous, and nearly thornless, with red berries, which are sweet when fully ripe.

'**Silvia**': Very shade tolerant, very hardy, grows through Canada. Fruit: green, with a red blush.

'**Winham's Industry**': Old English variety. Leafs out much later than average. Slow growing. Fair production of round, red-yellow berries, many small violet-red bristles. Flavour good. ∎

Ricinodendron rautanenii (syn. *Schinziophyton rautanenii*)

Manketti nut (mongongo, umgongo, feather-weight tree)

EUPHORBIACEAE

Similar species: *Ricinodendron heudelotii* var. *africanum*

Relatives: amla, Chinese waterberry

The manketti is a fairly undervalued and unexplored species outside Africa, though is found and cultivated in South Africa, Namibia, Angola, Botswana, Zambia, Zimbabwe and Mozambique. Locally, has been widely used by the indigenous peoples such as the Bantu, Kung San and the Bushman, for many hundreds to thousands of years. It is still an important part of many peoples' diets, with its kernels being full of good-quality oils, proteins and sugars. The fruit's flesh can also be dried and used as a food source that can be stored for many months. In addition, this tough tree is tolerant to a wide range of environmental situations and needs little to no maintenance. It can grow in dry, arid climates, and trials were at one time undertaken to grow this plant commercially in Australia and Israel.

DESCRIPTION

The manketti-nut tree forms a medium–large-sized tree, to ~15 m tall. It has a straight main stem and a broad, spreading crown. Branches tend to be short and twisted. Its stout trunk can help store water for dry periods.

Leaves: Deciduous, pinnate, in groups of 5–7 elliptical to oval leaflets (~15 cm long) that are borne on long leaf stalks, ~15 cm long. Mature leaves are dark green, and the leaves and stalks are often covered with fine hair. Trees tend to lose their leaves in winter or during extended dry periods, but can then readily recover.

Flowers: Small, whitish-yellow, ~3 cm long and are borne in loose clusters. Trees are dioecious, so need both a male and female tree to set fruits. Flowers are borne mostly from spring to mid summer. *Pollination:* By bees and other insects.

Fruits: A drupe, the fruit is plum-shaped, ~3.5 cm long, ~2.5 cm wide. Young fruits are green and somewhat finely hairy. The skin is fairly tough and thick, and is usually discarded. However, the flesh beneath, although thin (only ~20% of the fruit), is sweet, aromatic and is of good flavour when fully ripe and has turned from green to brown. It then has a date-like flavour. In the centre is a large, hard, irregularly furrowed stone, within which is a single (or occasionally two) kernel(s). Apparently, the stone is so hard and resistant to damage it can survive passing through the gut of an elephant intact, and is then able to germinate in what is considered by many to be the best-quality manure in the world. The creamy-coloured inner kernel is ~1.5 cm long.

Yield/harvest/storage: A long wait until the first fruits are produced: can be ~25 years, but trees then start to give very good yields, with a female tree producing ~900 fruits a year, given sufficient moisture. Through autumn until early winter, fruits tend to fall even before they are fully ripe, and need to be gathered at intervals before they spoil or are eaten by wildlife. The fruits are initially yellowish, but turn reddish-brown when left to fully ripen and soften for a few days at room temperature; the flesh then develops its finest flavour. Very ripe fruits can still be enjoyed. The fruits store well. They can be easily dried and, if kept cool at a low humidity, they can be stored for several months.

Roots: Forms extensive, deep roots and should be transplanted with care, if at all. Only forms a few surface roots.

CULTIVATION

Are tough trees that need little/no maintenance once established.

Location: Trees grow best in full sun, though can also grow in light shade. They are moderately wind tolerant, though cannot tolerate saline soils.

Temperature: Can grow in hot climates, tolerating temperatures up to ~40°C. They are also quite cold tolerant, surviving drops in temperature down to ~–6°C, and also seem to tolerate rapid changes in temperature.

Soil/water/nutrients: Grows best in well-drained, sandy soils; able to grow in almost pure sand. Trees, once established, can tolerate extended periods of drought.

uses

Food

The fruit flesh is the part that is eaten, with the tough skin usually being discarded. In South Africa, the flesh is often boiled, which sweetens it and this is then often used in a sweet porridge that is said to taste like stewed apples. The inner kernel is also of good quality, though has to be extracted from the hard stone. The kernel is highly nutritious. The oily kernel is good eaten fresh or roasted with a little salt. Roasted kernels are said to taste like cashews. It is reported that, if roasted for longer, they taste like fine old cheese.

Nutrition

The kernels contain ~55% fat, of which ~42% is polyunsaturated fats (mostly linoleic acid), ~17% is saturated fats (palmitic and stearic) and ~18% is monounsaturated fats (oleic). They also contain sugars and ~25% protein, as well as good amounts of calcium (193 mg/100 g), magnesium (527 mg/100 g), and some thiamine, riboflavin and nicotinic acid. They also contain very good levels of vitamin E (~560 mg, mostly as alpha-tocopherol). Because of this high vitamin E content, the oil is very stable, stores well and does not easily go rancid. The oil is high in phytosterols.

Other uses

The oils from the kernels are valued in skin preparations to rejuvenate and soften skin, and to protect it from harsh environmental conditions. Its wood is very lightweight and can be easily worked, hence its common English name.

Ornamental

The trees can be planted to stabilise poor soils and will grow in arid areas where few other species can survive.

However, they cannot tolerate waterlogged soils. They grow best in somewhat acidic to neutral soils and do not seem to grow well in alkaline soils, being susceptible to iron chlorosis. Trees are not nutrient hungry and require little or no fertiliser applications.

Planting: Plant seedlings at 7–10 m apart for specimen trees.

Propagation: *Seed:* If possible, it is probably best to use fresh seed. Unless you have a convenient elephant nearby to soften the seed as it passes through its gut, you may have to resort to either removing the hard outer covering to expose the kernel, or to scarifying and scratching or puncturing the outer covering to allow the exchange of moisture and gases. A soak in weak acid may also help, though ensure stones are washed thoroughly afterwards, before sowing them in warm, moist compost. In Africa, the seed is sometimes briefly roasted to make the outer shell easier to crack, though avoid overheating the kernel as this will kill it. Germination can then be erratic and can occur over a long time period. Seedlings, because they tend to form deep taproots, are best planted in deep pots. Plant out seedlings carefully to avoid any root damage.

SIMILAR SPECIES

***Ricinodendron heudelotii* var. *africanum*.** Native to tropical Africa, from Guinea down to Angola and Uganda, this is a fast-growing tree, reaching 20–30 m tall. Like the manketti, it is dioecious. Each fruit contains 2–3 kernels, which are said to be smoother, plumper and have as good a taste as manketti nuts, though the trees may not be as cold hardy. ∎

Rosa rugosa (*R. eglanteria*)
Rosehips (rugosa rose, saltspray rose, beach tornado)
ROSACEAE

Other hip-bearing species: apple rose (*R. pomifera*), dog rose (*R. canina*), *Rosa moyesii*

Relatives: apple, cherry, peach, raspberry

Roses are grown around the world in temperate and even some semi-tropical regions. They have been cultivated for thousands of years. The Romans were known to cultivate them for their fragrance and used them widely; the petals were strewn on floors, in baths and beneath chariot wheels. They were an important part of many occasions such as weddings, banquets and civil ceremonies. It was customary to hang a rose over the dinner table to show that all confidences spoken during the meal would remain secret; today, the plaster work in the centre of a ceiling is still known as a 'rose'. Roses have been widely praised and written about for their scent and beauty, including by Shakespeare. Today, many cultivated roses are hybrids that have been selected for their flowering attributes. The wilder, older roses are still grown and appreciated though, and are often used as rootstocks in propagation. They usually have simpler flowers and may not be as showy, but often have wonderful scents, are more resistant to pests and diseases and often have large, edible hips. One of the better known of these is *Rosa rugosa*. It has beautiful flowers with a delightful fragrance, and it will grow where many other hybrid roses will not. It was originally a native of northern China, Korea and Japan, and was brought to the West in the 1800s. Its name *rugosa* is derived from 'rugose', meaning wrinkled, and refers to its distinctive wrinkled leaves.

DESCRIPTION

A tough, fairly fast-growing rose that is often used as a rootstock for many ornamental hybrid roses. It grows to 1–3 m height, 0.3–2 m spread. Has prickly, hairy stems and a sprawling form.

Leaves: Deciduous, deep green, pinnate arrangement of 5–9 oval leaflets, glossy above, downy beneath. The leaves are distinctively wrinkled. This is formed by the indented veins, which occur within the raised leaf tissue. There may be a few short thorns on the lower surface of the leaves. Some cultivars have good yellow/orange/red autumn colour.

Flowers: Often solitary, deep pink (some cultivars are other colours, e.g. white, magenta-purple), 5–9 cm width, with a heavy scent. They have a cluster of bright yellow stamens, and an inferior ovary. There are single-, half-double- or double-flowered cultivars. They flower from early summer onwards, and sometimes into autumn until the first frosts. *Pollination:* Their scent attracts bumblebees and other insects. They are self-fertile.

Fruits: The hip is usually orange-red, but some cultivars have colours from yellow to brown. They ripen from early autumn onwards. The hip or ovary has a tough outer waxy coating that surrounds the red–orange juice and seeds within. The seeds look like small, wiry hairs (achenes). These achenes act like small hooks if eaten, and need to be carefully removed by passing through a fine mesh. *Rosa rugosa* bears one of the largest rose fruits: ~2.5 cm diameter. Some cultivars with double flowers may not produce fruits.

Harvest: Need to wear gloves. Pick when the hip is fully coloured and swollen.

Roots: Roses have fairly deep extensive root systems. It is fairly safe to carry out surface cultivation. They relish an annual addition of well-rotted organic matter.

CULTIVATION

Fully hardy, tough, easy-to-grow species.

Location: Will grow in salty conditions, shade or full sun. Fairly wind tolerant.

Temperature: It is one of the hardiest species of roses: it can tolerate temperatures down to –50°C without damage. Can be grown in warmer climates, but may grow better if planted in a cooler, semi-shaded area of the garden.

Soil/water/nutrients: Can grow in poor soil, as long as it is fairly well-drained. Can even grow well in sand or clay. Ideally it likes a slightly acidic soil: ~pH 5.5–6.0, but can grow in soils outside this range. Prefers a moist soil, but is quite drought tolerant. Benefits from the addition of organic matter such as well-rotted manure, spent mushroom compost or garden compost: this improves growth as well as flowering and fruit production. A mulch reduces weed growth and retains moisture. An annual addition, in spring, of sulphate of potash can increase growth and health of the plants.

Planting: Space plants ~2 m apart if planting ornamentally, or at 30–50 cm apart for a hedge. Plant in late autumn or early spring. Some staking and support may be needed for the more straggly species, particularly in more exposed locations. Garlic planted nearby may help protect the plant from disease and insect attacks.

Propagation: *Seed:* The best results are obtained from sowing ripe, but green seed (i.e. when it has developed, but before the hip has dried) immediately. It may germinate by late winter, but can take up to 18 months. Stored seed is more difficult and needs treating before it will germinate. It needs to be scarified: either by scratching the seedcoat or by soaking it briefly in weak acid, before sowing in damp compost at ~28–32°C for 2–3 weeks. After this, the seeds need ~4 months of cold stratification at ~3°C, by which time they may start to germinate, but it can take considerably longer. Grow on seedlings in pots for the first year or so. *Cuttings:* Cuttings usually take well. Plant softwood cuttings in early summer. Remove all lower leaves. Rooting powder may help. Hardwood cuttings, 20–25 cm long, are taken during winter. Insert these in soil, outside, with only the top 2.5 cm of stem above ground level. They may take a year to establish, but there is usually a good success rate. *Suckers:* Can remove vigorous suckers at most times of the year, with some root if possible. Plant deeply in compost till fully rooted and actively growing. Removal of the stem tip may reduce stress until the roots have formed. *Layering:* Is possible, but can take 12 months. *Budding:* This method is popular for modern rose propagation.

Pruning: *R. rugosa* suckers freely, but is fairly easy to control. May need longer stems cutting back occasionally to tidy it up. Prune to an outward bud to encourage the stems to grow outwards and allow light to reach the centre of the plant. Remove old dead wood. These roses can be severely cut back if they become too unmanageable

Food

You can eat the rosehips raw or cooked (see Warning below). The flesh can be made into juice or rosehip jam, jelly, desserts, etc. It has a sweet and pleasant taste, though it takes patience to prepare a reasonable quantity of fruit. *R. rugosa* has large hips and does have relatively thick flesh. A popular, pleasant tea can be made from the fruit. The flowers can be eaten fresh or cooked, or can be dried. Use young, dry flowers before they have fully opened. Discard the tougher lower edge of the petal and any sepals, seeds, etc. They can be used in jellies and preserves. They are used as a delicate flavouring in foods and drinks, make a wonderful, delicate wine, and have been used to make liquors in France. Rose water (made from distilled petals) was widely used as a soothing lotion for the skin and as an eyewash. Mrs Grieves (see bibliography) even has a recipe for rose-petal sandwiches. Young shoots can be cooked and used as a potherb. A tea can be also made from the leaves.

Nutrition

The fruit is very rich in vitamin C, containing up to 2.75% dry weight (1150–2500 mg vitamin C/100 g), though remember that heat destroys vitamin C. Hips also have good levels of vitamin A, flavonoids, malic and citric acid, and are a fairly good source of essential fatty acids, which is fairly unusual for a fruit. The red petals contain the glucoside quercetin. The seed is a good source of vitamin E; it can be ground and mixed with flour or added to other foods.

Medicinal

The *Rosa* species are being investigated for their properties to halt or reverse the growth of cancers. The leaves are used to treat fevers and as a mild laxative. The flowers are made into a tea to treat spleen and liver disorders, to promote blood circulation, to increase appetite and to improve digestion. The root is used to treat coughs. The essential oil from roses is highly antiseptic. *R. gallica* is the main species listed as having medicinal properties, but most old roses should also have these properties. However, the petals need to be a deep red colour to have these active properties. **Warning:** The achenes within the hips should be removed by passing the juice through a fine sieve or filter paper; they cause irritation to the mouth and digestive tract if ingested.

Other uses

Many perfumes are made from rose oil, and the petals and rosehips are often used in potpourris. The Navajo made a tan-coloured dye from the leaves and twigs (with alum).

Ornamental

A plant with beautiful, scented blooms, this rose is easy to grow. It looks lovely in older-style cottage or wild gardens. Can be planted as a specimen or as a hedge, but it loses its leaves in winter. Its fragrance makes it good to plant near the house.

or straggly; they grow back vigorously and produce many new shoots. Flowers may form on new or older wood, so it is best to prune these types of roses once the hips have been harvested, but preferably before hard frosts. Pruning in spring might result in the removal of some of the coming season's flower buds. However, if severe frosts are likely, it is safer to prune in spring to avoid frost damaging the plant.

   Pests and diseases: *R. rugosa* has few if any problems compared to many modern roses. Possible ones are powdery mildew, cankers, rusts, blackspot, fireblight, crown gall, honey fungus, aphids, beetles, borers, leafhoppers, scales, mites, slugs and more.

CULTIVARS

Many cultivars are available. *R. rugosa* hybridises freely with other members of the genus.
'Frau Dagmar Hastrupp': Compact shape. Flowers: beautiful, very fragrant, silver-pink, yellow stamens. Hips: has good yields, yellow–orange colour. Very good disease resistance.
'Hansa': Somewhat straggly growth, ~2 m tall. Leaves: blackspot-resistant, yellow–orange autumn colour. Flowers: lilac-pink, semi-double blooms, very fragrant. Hips: has good yields.
'Scabrosa': Large flowers and hips.

OTHER SPECIES

The description of *R. rugosa* applies to the species below unless noted otherwise.

Apple rose, *Rosa pomifera*. The name '*pomifera*' means fruit. It grows to ~2 m height, ~2 m spread. *Leaves:* Grey-green, resin scented. *Flowers:* solitary, pale pink, ~7 cm diameter. *Hips:* large, round, dark red and covered with short bristly hairs; they ripen from early autumn. This rose is often grown ornamentally for its eye-catching hips.

Dog rose, *Rosa canina*. A very popular rose as a rootstock for many modern roses. It is naturalised in Britain. It is very tough, hardy and disease resistant. Height 2–3 m, spread 1.2–2 m. *Flowers:* smallish (~4–5 cm), solitary, white–pale pink, from early summer. Not strongly scented. *Hips:* red, egg-shaped, shiny, ~2.5 cm long. The flowers, leaves and hips have been used for many hundreds of years.

***Rosa moyessi*.** A native of western China, it forms a larger handsome plant, ~4 m tall, ~3 m spread. Dark green leaves. Fewer prickles than some species. *Flowers:* pink to rich red, ~5–7 cm diameter, produced from early summer. *Hips:* attractive, large, flask-shaped, ~5–7 cm long, in autumn. ■

Rubus spp.
Blackberry (Pacific dewberry)
ROSACEAE

Rubus ulmifolius, R. ursinus, R. villosus, R. macrocarpus, R. discolor, R. vitifolius, R. cuneifolius, R. arcticus, R. alleghleniensis, R. laciniatus, R. pentalobus

All the *Rubus* fruits, although commonly called berries, are actually botanically classified as aggregates of drupelets. Within this group, raspberry drupelets can be pulled free from its receptacle, whereas blackberry drupelets come with the receptacle still attached, and this is somewhat crunchy. The fruits consist of many ovaries within a single flower. *Rubus* is one of the most diverse genus of angiosperms, consisting of 12 subgenera, some with hundreds of species. Their geographic distribution ranges from the Arctic Circle to the tropics, and they occur on every continent except Antarctica. Three of these subgenera contain edible fruiting plants, and the subgenera containing blackberries is well known and appreciated by many. Blackberries are native to Asia, Europe, North and South America, and have often escaped cultivation and become naturalised. Blackberry plants have been used in Europe for >2000 years for their tasty fruits, medicinally and as thorny barrier hedges. Blackberry remains have been found in Ireland, Denmark and England, and show that blackberries were important in the diets of the Vikings. Blackberry-leaf tea was included in the ancient Roman dispensary. Blackberry plants have an erect or a trailing form, and modern cultivars are often selected to be thornless. A few of the many species and hybrids of blackberries are described below, though the blackberry x raspberry hybrids, loganberry and boysenberry are described under 'raspberry' (see p. 398).

DESCRIPTION

Plants are prostrate to erect, generally sharply thorny, and produce renewal shoots from the ground (called canes). They are classed as perennials because their roots are long-lived. Individual canes grow vegetatively for the first year and also form flower buds in late summer; the following year, the canes fruit and then die back. The plants often have numerous recurved thorns on their stems as well as a few on their leaves. Wild blackberries can be invasive, spreading, trailing and painfully thorny, and can rapidly over-run shrubby waste ground, often smothering out other species, although the wildlife love them as a safe place to nest and feed. The cultivated blackberry has been selected to usually have semi-erect canes that can be easily managed and trained. Their flowers are often attractive and large, and many cultivars are more or less thornless, but the fruit, although larger than wild blackberries, often lack the sweetness and depth of flavour of wild types.

Leaves: Compound, in 3–5 leaflets, with the middle being the largest. They are somewhat rough, often with prickles on midribs, and are thin, mid green, with doubly serrated, irregular margins.

Flower: Small (1–1.5 cm), white–pinkish, five petalled, typically Rosaceae, with numerous central stamens. They are borne terminally in clusters of 10–20 flowers, forming in the first year and flowering in the second. Often those flowers in the centre of the cluster open first. Each flower receptacle contains 40–80 ovaries, each of which may form a drupelet. *Pollination:* Are popular with bees as they produce lots of nectar. They may also be partly wind-pollinated. To obtain a large, well-formed fruit, most of the ovaries need to be effectively pollinated. The flowers are bisexual, and many commercial cultivars are self-fertile, so need only one plant to set fruits. However, most trailing berries are self-sterile, and need more than one plant to get fruit-set.

Fruit: An aggregate of drupelets, derived from many ovaries from a single flower. The fruit is picked with its crunchy receptacle. Each drupelet contains a small, edible seed. Fruits develop in a short time, taking 40–60 days to ripen after fruit-set. Blackberries with thorns are said to be sweeter than thornless cultivars.

Yield/harvest: Yields can be fairly good from established plants, which start producing fruits in their second year and go on producing for >10 years before beginning to lose vigour. Fruits can be harvested from late summer until early winter, depending on cultivar and conditions. They are picked when fully coloured, a rich dark purple and have softened. Under-ripe red fruits are hard and sour. Need to be picked several times during a season, which often lasts 3–6 weeks. They are easily squashed, and need to be handled gently. They also do not store well, lasting only 2–3 days at 0°C.

Roots: Very shallow, so need to avoid mechanical cultivation, but weed control is important to maintain good growth and yields. Studies have shown that a plastic mulch is the most effective in controlling weeds, followed by pine bark, though an organic mulch will also provide some nutrients.

CULTIVATION

They are reasonably easy to grow.

Food

Blackberries can be simply eaten fresh or mixed with other fresh fruits. They can be added to many desserts to give a sharpness and distinct flavour. Go well with apples in pies, crumbles, etc. The fruits are also excellent in jams, jellies, fruit sauces, icecream, yoghurt and for many other uses. They freeze well for later use. The honey derived from blackberry flowers is light in colour and has a good flavour. The young leaves and shoots of many of these species are a tasty vegetable when lightly cooked.

Nutrition

Reasonable vitamin C levels of 30 mg/100 g of fresh fruit. The fruits also have good levels of folic acid, and are very rich in antioxidants (e.g. ellagic acid, anthocyanins, flavonols): rated fourth highest in fruits and vegetables, but second in actually preventing oxidation of cells. They may also reduce the build-up of low-density lipoproteins ('bad' cholesterol), a contributor to heart disease, stroke and atherosclerosis. Fruits also contain phyto-oestrogens, fibre and salicylic acid. They have good levels of manganese, potassium, magnesium and copper and contain vitamins A and E and good levels of fibre.

Medicinal

The fruits were used in Europe to treat infections of the mouth and eyes until the 16th century. The salicylic acid found in blackberries probably has the same protective value against heart disease and strokes as aspirin. Ellagic acid is known to act as an antioxidant and a flavour enhancer, and is found at 5–6 times higher levels in blackberries and raspberries than other fruits. In the human body, ellagic acid appears to impede cancer by blocking various hormone reactions and metabolic pathways. Their high anthocyanin content, which gives blackberries their deep purple to black colour, is linked to improving vision and circulation, preventing cancer, controlling diabetes and even retarding ageing by preserving memory and motor skills. Its flavonols, e.g. quercetin and catechins, are both antioxidants and anti-carcinogens. In addition, quercetin helps to treat allergy symptoms as it reduces the release of histamines. Their high fibre levels can improve digestive function, lower LDL cholesterol levels and reduce risks from some cancers. The leaves are high in tannin, and have been used widely for years to treat diarrhoea, gout and upset stomachs. For ~2000 years, they have been chewed for bleeding gums. A strong infusion of the leaves may reduce blood-sugar levels. The leaves are applied as a poultice for burns and scalds. The bark and rhizome contain tannin (~20%), gallic acid and saponins (e.g. villosin). Bear in mind that too much tannin is toxic. Gallic acid, a benzoic-acid derivative, can be used as an astringent and to reduce haemorrhages. Also used in wine and whiskey production.

Other uses

A mauve dye can be obtained from the fruits.

Ornamental

Wild blackberries offer good cover and food for wildlife, make a good barrier for stock and a hedge around gardens.

Location: Can be grown in full sun or can tolerate partial shade. Not very wind hardy or salt tolerant.

Temperature: Most plants are fully cold hardy, except for a few cultivars adapted to warmer regions. Frost is usually not a problem to any blossom. Blackberries are less cold hardy than raspberries, but they can withstand more heat. In addition, thorny blackberries are more cold hardy than thornless cultivars, surviving temperatures down to ~–20°C, compared to ~–17°C.

Chilling: Blackberries need 200–800 hours of chilling, depending on cultivar. They are more suited to temperate climates, and may not receive sufficient chilling in warm temperate regions unless specific cultivars are chosen.

Soil/water/nutrients: Are surface rooting, so prefer a moist yet well-drained, fertile soil. Sandy or loamy soils with pH 5.0–7.0 are ideal. Likely to suffer mineral deficiencies on alkaline soils. Cannot tolerate wet, heavy soils, but otherwise can grow on soils too poor for other crops. Although fairly drought tolerant, plant growth and fruit quality are better if soils are kept moist during the spring and summer. They like nutrients, but too much results in excessive leaf growth over fruit production. Nitrogen requirement is fairly low. Apply a general fertiliser with micronutrients in spring and late summer.

Propagation: *Seed:* Can be grown from seed, but the seed has a hard seedcoat and germination can be slow. Most species need warm stratification of 20–30°C for 3 months, followed by cold stratification of 2–5°C for a further 3 months, with warmer cultivars needing less of each. Soaking seeds in weak sulphuric acid, and then thoroughly washing them, can increase germination rate. Seed is sown in spring, ~0.5 cm below the soil surface. *Cuttings:* Root cuttings are the fastest and easiest method to propagate erect blackberries. Roots are dug up in early spring, cut into sections with several buds, ~10–15 cm long, and planted ~6 cm deep in soil in pots or outside in early spring. Although there may be numerous buds on the roots, not all of these develop into canes. Trailing blackberries do not produce root suckers in the same way, and are more often propagated by stem cuttings, or tip layering. Leafy stem cuttings can be taken in summer from brambles and trailing species, and inserted in moist, gritty compost. *Suckering:* Basically the same as root cuttings, except the adventitious buds have sprouted, and these are detached from the parent plant with some root, transplanted and kept watered till established. *Layering.* An easy method for trailing species. Simply bury shoot tips of vigorous new stems in late summer. These readily form roots and can be separated from the parent plant by the following spring.

Planting: Blackberries are often planted in rows, and erect cultivars are spaced at 2–4 m apart, depending on cultivar. Trailing blackberries are spaced closer together at 1–1.8 m apart. Planting is best in winter, and the canes are cut back to ~15 cm to allow the roots to establish. If possible, try to gently spread the roots. Allow space around and between plants to reduce the risk of fungal infections and allow light and air to reach flowers and fruits.

Pruning: The first year's growth is vegetative, and semi-erect plants are tipped at ~1.5–2 m height, with ~1 m width, to encourage the formation of fruiting lateral branches and keep plants manageable. Trailing types are usually tied or twisted around wires on a trellis, usually 2–3 wires spaced 50 cm apart, and are tipped at 1–1.5 m. Second-year canes flower and fruit, and are then removed after fruiting or in winter. Tips of stems are removed to prevent excessive drooping and thus avoid fruits being formed near to ground level. Allow 4–6 canes to develop per plant; a greater number may result in too many smaller fruits being produced. Thus, there will be 4–6 2-year-old fruiting canes and 4–6 vegetative 1-year-old canes per plant.

Pests and diseases: In wet and humid areas, plants can be attacked by fungal diseases. Leaf-spot fungi can occur on leaves as dark red spots with a whitish centre and can weaken plants. *Anthracnose* appears as greyish areas with a purplish-brown margin on both canes and fruit stems, causing some leaf deformation, browning and withering of berries. Remove any badly infected canes. Erect varieties have greater disease resistance. Blackberries can be vulnerable to bacterial and viral diseases. Several kinds of insects including thrips, spider mites, caterpillars, stink bugs and beetles may attack blackberries, as can bramble bud moth and raspberry bud moth larvae. In addition, birds love the fruits, so plants may need temporarily netting.

CULTIVARS

'Apache': Erect, thornless with large, black, juicy fruits.
'Arapaho': Erect, thornless. Fruit: medium-sized, good quality, ripens early. Is moderately vigorous.
'Ashton Cross': Mid season, heavy cropping, very good flavour, but thorny.
'Chickasaw': Erect, thorny bush with high yields. Berries: long, cylindrical, firm, sweet.
'Choctaw': Erect, thorny, high yielding. Fruit: medium-sized, sweet, good flavour. Early ripening.
'Kiowa': Erect, thorny. Fruit: large, firm, sweet, flavourful.
'Loch Ness': From UK. Early–mid season, heavy cropping, semi-erect habit, thornless. Fruits: good flavour. For cooler climates.
'Navaho': Erect, thornless. Fruit: small–medium, fairly sweet, good flavour. Late, prolonged ripening period.
'Oklawaha': Is semi-evergreen or evergreen, trailing so needs trellising. Moderate in size and vigour.
'Waldo': From the UK. Very early, crops. Fruit: very good flavour, not too vigorous, but is thorny.

HYBRIDS

Auroraberry: Looks like a blackberry, a large, firm black shiny fruit. Flavour is very good; aromatic, with a clean taste and no bitterness. It can be acidic if it isn't fully ripe. Ripens early, at the beginning of summer. A weaker bramble, which is an advantage in all areas except wet and humid locations where brambles are subject to disease. Will need to be tied onto wires. Has thorns.

King's Ace berry: A blackberry x raspberry hybrid. A moderately vigorous plant to ~2 m tall. Self-fertile. The fruits are sweet and juicy; often used in desserts, jams, etc.

Lowberry: A blackberry x dewberry hybrid. Is semi-evergreen in warmer areas. Has stout trailing stems up to 6 m long. Is self-infertile, and needs a pollinator species. The fruits are large, dark purple and sweet. Excellent eaten fresh.

Marionberry: A bramble cross between a *R. ursinus* (American blackberry) and the olallie berry from Oregon. Bright black, medium–large-sized, soft, aromatic fruit. Needs more than one plant to set fruits. Has a better flavour than boysenberries, with smaller seeds and is probably a bit hardier. Very vigorous plant and very thorny, relatively disease resistant. Needs a wire or fence to grow on.

Olallie berry: A bramble cross between a black loganberry and a youngberry. Berries are black, long, narrow, firm and sweet, somewhat like wild blackberry when fully ripe. Plants are highly productive, vigorous and thorny.

Tayberry Aurora: Blackberry x raspberry cross, selected in Scotland. Longer, larger, dark red; less downy and brighter in appearance than loganberry. Recommended; very good flavour. Early season. Canes: long, thorny, moderately vigorous.

Veitchberry: A blackberry x raspberry hybrid. A vigorous, upright plant that grows like blackberry. The fruits ripen before blackberries, are very large and are a deep maroon colour when ripe. Their taste is a cross of blackberry and raspberry.

SIMILAR SPECIES

Alegheniensis blackberry, *Rubus allegheniensis*. A native of eastern North America, from Nova Scotia down to North Carolina. It is often cultivated for its fruits and is the parent of many cultivars. It is fully cold hardy, tolerating temperatures of at least ~–20°C. This plant can be grown in full sun or semi-shade, though prefers a drier site. It forms a shrub up to 3 m tall. It flowers in summer, and fruits ripen in autumn. The fruits are fairly large, ~3 cm long, and are tasty and pleasant, and somewhat spicy. They can be eaten fresh, added to preserves, pies, etc., or can be dried for later use.

Arctic blackberry, *Rubus arcticus*. A native of northern North America, northern Europe and northern Asia. It forms a sprawling shrub, only ~0.2 m tall, but with a spread ~1 m. It is exceedingly cold hardy. It prefers some moisture during the growing season, and unlike most *Rubus* species, can grow on fairly alkaline soils. It prefers to grow in full sun. Not suitable for cultivation in warmer areas. It flowers in summer, and fruits ripen by late summer. It has a short growing season. The fruits are very sweet, juicy and tasty, with a pineapple-like aroma. They are good either eaten fresh or added to preserves, pies, cakes, etc. Plants only give poor yields in warmer areas, such as Britain! The flowers can be eaten fresh, and are sweet and delicious. The leaves can be used as a tea substitute.

Giant Colombian blackberry, *Rubus macrocarpus*.
Native to Colombia. Its canes, leaves and flowers resemble those of blackberries, while its light red fruits resemble raspberries in appearance and loganberries in taste. Fruits are huge: up to 5 cm long, 2.5 cm wide. Attempts, so far, to grow this species outside its natural region have failed.

Himalayan giant blackberry, *Rubus discolor* (syn. *R. procerus*). A small, multi-stemmed tree, growing to ~10 m. It is native to central Europe, and is sometimes cultivated for its fruits. It flowers in mid–late summer, and fruits do not ripen till late autumn. It is cold hardy and can tolerate temperatures down to ~–15°C. Can be grown in full sun or semi-shade. Although a blackberry, its stems (canes) often live and fruit for longer than 2 years. The fruits are large and have a rich, good flavour. They can be eaten fresh or used in preserves, pies, etc. They can also be dried for later use.

Orangeberry (Creeping Taiwan bramble), *Rubus pentalobus* (syn. *R. calycinoides*). A native of Taiwan, this is a fast-growing, evergreen groundcover plant that can grow in many sites where other *Rubus* species won't. It is hardy and grows 15–25 cm tall, with a ~0.5–2 m spread, bearing prickly shoots which readily root into the ground as they grow. *Leaves:* Attractive, dark green above, grey beneath, 3–5 lobed, heart-shaped, turn purple–reddish during winter. *Flowers:* White, during early summer. *Fruit:* Orange, ~2 cm long, ripen in summer, are ripest when soft and the calyx has turned back to expose the fruit. When ripe they have a tangy orange flavour.

    Cultivation: Grows in full sun–semi-shade, though best fruit may be produced in sunnier sites. Fairly frost hardy. A tough plant. Usually does not need extra nutrients. It is fairly drought tolerant (unusual for a *Rubus*), but does not like wet soil. Will grow in sandy or clay soils. *Pot culture:* Can be grown in containers and can fruit well. Looks good trailing down the sides of a pot. *Pruning:* Just needs trimming to control spread.

    Uses: Tasty fruit that give a bright rich orange colour to fruit salads and other dishes. *Ornamental:* Makes a good evergreen, groundcover plant for small or larger gardens. Looks good in rockeries or grown on the top of walls. Can be planted to stabilise banks and suppress weeds.

Oregon cut-leaf blackberry, *Rubus laciniatus*. An American species that is sometimes cultivated for its good-quality fruits. A fast-growing, deciduous shrub, growing to 2.5 m. Cold hardy to ~–20°C. Plants can be grown in full sun or semi-shade. Grows best in moist soil and is not very tolerant of drought or waterlogging. Unlike other blackberries, the canes of this species can be allowed to grow ~3.5 m long to get better crops of fruits. *Flowers:* Borne in summer; fruits ripen soon after in late summer–autumn. Flowers are bisexual and may be self-fertile, though many fruits are formed by nucellar fertilisation. The seeds produced are genetic copies of the parents, and only one plant is needed to set fruits. Fruits are medium-sized, ~2 cm diameter, and are sweet and juicy with a very good flavour, enjoyable eaten fresh or cooked. Plants produce good yields. A high-yielding cultivar with good-quality fruits is 'Oregon cut-leaf thornless', which has no prickles.

Pacific blackberry, *Rubus vitifolius*. A very sprawling shrub, only ~0.2 m tall. It is a native of western USA. It is fairly cold hardy. A parent of the loganberry. Its fruits can be eaten fresh or cooked, and are sweet and pleasant. They can be dried for later use.

Sand blackberry, *Rubus cuneifolius*. A native of eastern USA, it forms a sprawling shrub to ~0.5 m high. It is fairly cold hardy, to ~–10°C. Once established, plants are quite drought tolerant. It can grow in full sun or semi-shade. It flowers in summer and fruits from late summer–early autumn. It is self-fertile and produces many fruits by nucellar propagation, where the seeds are clones of the parent. The fruits range in size from 1–2 cm in diameter; they are rather dry, but are tasty and have a good flavour. ■

Rubus chamaemorus
Cloudberry (bakeapple, molte)
ROSACEAE

The cloudberry is a wild *Rubus* species native to the colder areas of the Northern Hemisphere, and is found in Scandinavia, Canada, Russia, northern USA and Scotland. It is a small herbaceous bramble common to sphagnum peat bogs, and is frequently surrounded by forest. The fruit has a strong musky flavour, quite distinct from that of other bramble crops, and is highly prized as a dessert fruit in Scandinavia. It is a common plant in northern Norway, and has become a new potential crop there. Current research, mostly in Norway, is aimed at breeding higher yielding female plants and the development of hermaphrodite cultivars.

DESCRIPTION

A low, small, creeping, herbaceous perennial shrub with few to no prickles. It grows from young buds on the spreading rhizomes, which grow about 10 cm below the soil surface and outwards for some distance beyond the plant. Vegetative/flowering shoots are erect, ~7–25 cm high, and are unbranched and hairless. Plant growth is slow.

Leaves: Annual shoots have leaves with 1–4 lobes, are roundish, ~5 cm long and ~7 cm wide. They are somewhat leathery and are on long leaf stalks. Their margins have blunt teeth. Glandular hairs occur mainly on the leaf's underside and on the leaf stalks. Young leaves are bright green, whereas mature leaves are darker green.

Flowers: A single white flower, which is either male or female, though are similar in appearance, 2–3 cm diameter, with 5(+) hairy petals. Flowers are borne at the ends of the present season's growth. Male flowers open earlier and secrete abundant nectar, whereas female flowers produce only small amounts. In male flowers, when the petals drop, the calyx persists and spreads out flat, whereas, in female flowers, the calyx surrounds the young aggregate fruit. Flowers are borne in early–mid summer. *Pollination:* By bees and other insects, though wind may also contribute. Plants are dioecious, so need more then one plant to set fruit.

Fruits: Although commonly called a berry it is botanically classified as an aggregate of drupelets. It resembles a large, deep orange raspberry, consisting of 5–25 drupelets, each containing a smooth, tiny seed, with the number of drupelets dependent on temperature and humidity during pollination and fertilisation: stable, warm conditions increase fruit-set. When unripe, they are pinky-red, changing to orange at maturity. In warmer areas, they ripen in mid summer; in colder regions fruits ripen in late summer.

Yield/harvest: Plants may only produce ~20–50 kg of fruits/ha, but they can be grown in boggy areas where little else will grow. Plants also take ~7 years before they start to produce flowers and fruits.

Roots: They have an extensive, branched rhizome system. Most roots occur within the 15–20-cm soil horizon, so are shallow. Needs care with mechanical cultivation and a peaty-sandy mulch will help retain moisture and add nutrients. Because the plants grow from buds off the rhizomes, an individual plant can cover an area of several square metres. Fungal mycorrhizal associations do not seem to occur.

CULTIVATION

Ideal for colder acid soils, and needs little maintenance.

Location: Very wind tolerant. Can be grown as a pioneer plant in peaty soils and areas that have been disturbed. Can grow in partial shade or sun, though yields are better in shade. Individuals have long shoots and larger leaves in shady sites, but short shoots and smaller leaves in open areas.

Temperature: Can be grown in extremely cold locations: is found as far north as the sub-Arctic.

Chilling: Need at least 600–800 hours of winter chilling.

Soil/water/nutrients: Plants grow best in acid, peaty, poor-nutrient soils. Likes peat bogs of 0.5–1-m depth, with pH values of 3.5–4.5 (very acidic), and ground water not far below the surface. It is fully tolerant of cold, waterlogged soils, but not of drought because of its shallow roots. Extra

Food

They are delicious, with a sweet, tangy aromatic taste, and are picked for many uses. The fruit has a distinctive musky flavour that some say is apple-like. They can be eaten fresh or cooked, with added sugar and cream. Can be used in desserts, syrups, jam, juices, sauces, cakes and they make a fine liqueur and wine. They have a wonderful colour when added to other fruits. They can be frozen.

Nutrition/medicinal

The fruit contains good levels of vitamin C: 60–150 mg/100 g of flesh. They retain this well if they are frozen or are preserved immediately after picking. Also rich in benzoic acid and, therefore, can be easily stored for several weeks or longer under normal refrigeration. They are also a source of micro- and many macronutrients: iron, copper, manganese, zinc, magnesium, potassium, calcium and phosphates. The essential oil extracted from the fruit contains 80 components. The oil isolated from seeds (~12.5%) is mostly linoleic. Cloudberries also have good levels of flavonoids and phenolic acids, including high levels of ellagic acid at ~160 mg/100 g of dry fruits. Ellagic acid is a potential anti-tumour, anti-carcinogenic, hepato-protective substance that also has antimicrobial properties. Berries also contain phyto-oestrogens and rubixanthin, which is used as a natural food colouring. Because of its vitamin C content and its ability to be stored for long periods, this berry has been used as an important remedy for scurvy among hunters in the Arctic. It is are likely to have similar properties to blackberry (see p. 391).

Other uses

Ellagic acid inhibits insect growth and deters insects from feeding on certain plants, so the mashed-up fruits could be used as an insecticide.

phosphates, additional to a complete fertiliser, can increase yields considerably when applied at the commencement of the growing season. Will prefer its nitrogen source as ammonium rather than nitrate.

Pot culture: These plants are small and need minimum maintenance. They may be suitable for cultivation in pots in areas that do not have acidic soils or regular moisture.

Planting: Space plants at ~0.5–1 m apart for a groundcover.

Propagation: *Seed:* Are best sown fresh and allowed to chill during winter. Stored seeds need 6–8 months of cold stratification before they will germinate. In addition, thorough removal of any flesh and some scarification (scratching, scoring) of the seedcoat can speed up and increase germination. Seeds can also be briefly soaked in a weak acid or bleach to partially soften the hard seedcoat, though need to be thoroughly washed before sowing. Germination rates are often <50%. In addition, unfortunately, many seedlings (~75%) are males. *Cuttings:* More difficult to propagate than other bramble species. Large clumps need to be dug up when taking root cuttings. Rhizome cuttings (15–20 cm long) are most successful when taken in spring–summer. Pot these up in a peat and sand mix, and keep moist till fully established.

Pruning: They have typical cane growth, and form new stems each year that flower and fruit in their second year, and then die back. Because this plant has a trailing form it can be trained or tied onto wires to make management and harvesting easier. Once old stems have fruited they should be removed. Long, young, trailing stems can also be shortened in their first year to encourage shorter fruiting laterals, but should not be pruned in their second year or potential flowers and fruits can be removed. Allow 5–7 main, young stems to mature each year, removing other weaker new shoots.

Pests and diseases: Generally few problems, though can be infected with *Botrytis*. The fruits may need protecting from birds.

CULTIVARS

There is a blackberry x cloudberry cross that is much more vigorous than the cloudberry. Has also been crossed with raspberry, but all the offspring are sterile. ∎

Rubus spp.
Dewberry
Rosaceae

Canadian dewberry syn. American dewberry (*Rubus canadensis*), dewberry (*R. pubescens*), northern dewberry (*R. flagellaris*), Pacific dewberry (*R. ursinus*), phenomenal berry (hybrid cross), southern dewberry (*R. trivialis*), young berry (hybrid cross)
Similar species: raspberry, blackberry

All the *Rubus* fruits are classified as aggregates of drupelets. However, dewberry receptacles are soft, and are removed with their fruit, compared to raspberry drupelets which when pulled free, leave the receptacle on the plant, and blackberry drupelets which come with the receptacle, but the receptacle is hard. Dewberries form erect, but more usually sprawling, stems each year; these fruit in their second year and then die back. The roots are perennial though, and plants can live for ~15 years. They usually have some thorns, but this varies with species, and are usually not as thorny as blackberries. In the wild, the stems sprawl outwards for some distance from the plants, and will readily root at nodes where they touch the soil. In the shade, the stems tend to grow longer and are fewer in number; in full sun, plants are often multi-stemmed. They are often covered with a fine powdery bloom.

DESCRIPTION

Leaves: Compound, 3–5 leaflets, with the middle leaf being the largest. Leaves are coarse, somewhat rough, margins are serrate, and they have a pleasant smell when crushed. They are often lighter grey-green beneath. Leaves on 2-year-old canes become darker and thicker before dying off.

Flower: Small (~1–1.5 cm), white–pale pink, borne terminally in small groups or singly on the current season's growth. They are formed in late summer, but do not open till the following spring. They have numerous stamens, and the receptacle consists of many embryos, which can all develop into drupelets, although it has fewer embryos than blackberries. *Pollination:* Flowers produce a lot of nectar, which attracts bees and other insects. Although the plants are self-fertile, they can be planted in groups, and this may improve fruit-set and fruit quality. Damp weather reduces pollination.

Fruit: Numerous drupelets, or flesh-covered seeds, clustered around a soft receptacle, which remains with the fruits when they are harvested. Fruit are usually a very dark wine-red–purple colour, often becoming almost black when fully ripe; they are more like blackberries than raspberries but often have a whitish powdery bloom as they ripen. They are usually a reasonable size: ~1.5–2.5 cm long. Fruits only take 4–6 weeks to form after pollination.

Yield/harvest: New plants take ~2–3 years to give good yields. Yields vary considerably with species. They are tricky to harvest once ripe, as they become soft and thus easily squashed. Once harvested, they only last for a short time: 2–3 days in a refrigerator. The fruits can be easily crushed and damaged, and are best placed in shallow baskets. Fruits can be dried or frozen for storage.

Roots: They tend to form many surface roots, which makes them susceptible to dry soil, weed competition and mechanical cultivation, though a few species are quite tolerant of drier soils. An organic mulch helps retain moisture and add nutrients.

CULTIVATION

Dewberries are ideal for smaller gardens. There are a range

of species described here that suit a variety of climates, although most prefer more temperate conditions.

Location: They like a sunny site in cooler climates, but in warmer areas they will need some shade. They can generally fruit in sun or shade. They are not wind tolerant.

Soil/water/nutrients: Plants grow best in slightly acidic soils that are rich in humus and have good potassium levels. Loamy soils with pH 5–7.0 are ideal. They like moist, but well-drained soil. Most species are not drought resistant and need supplementary watering in dry weather, particularly during fruit development. Although they benefit from fertile soil, do not add too much nitrogen as this can result in too much leaf growth at the expense of fruiting. Apply fertiliser at the beginning of the growing season.

Planting: Can either be done in late autumn or early spring. They tend to naturally sprawl form a groundcover; however, for fruiting, they are more easily managed if tied onto wires as they grow. Establish plants in a prepared area that is weed free and has supporting wires already erected. At planting, remove tops of plant stems to encourage root establishment rather than shoot growth. Remove any flowers that form on new plants to allow the plant's energy to go into establishment. Plant in well-drained soil to reduce the risk of root rots, and it is better to plant in soil that has not recently had Solanaceae species growing in it.

Propagation: Seed: Usually not grown from seed, although some of the species described below produce nucellar seeds. If grown from seed, this needs ~1 month of stratification at ~3°C before sowing and is best sown in early spring. Grow on seedlings in pots for ~1 year, till they are large enough to plant out. *Cuttings:* Semi-ripe cuttings can be also taken from young canes in summer. They will root better in a humid atmosphere. *Layering:* Once the first-year canes have become long, in mid summer, then the stems can be pegged down to the soil and lightly buried, where they will readily root. By later in the season, or by the following spring, these stems should have rooted and can be carefully removed from the parent plant. *Division:* This can be done in early spring or just before leaf-fall in autumn by digging up established plants and separating the root runners into smaller plants. These should be watered regularly until established.

Pruning: Once established, pruning becomes an overlapping cycle of maintenance. The new canes are tied onto wires during the first year, and the tips of vigorous species can be removed for manageability. Just allow ~5–7 new canes to develop each year from each plant, pruning out the surplus. Too many canes per plant reduces the overall quality of fruits. The 2-year-old fruiting canes will flower and fruit and are then pruned out. Pruning and removal of old canes reduces the risk of disease and makes management easier. Each year there will be some young canes and some fruiting canes.

Pests and diseases: Dewberries are less susceptible to pests and diseases than raspberries, though check for aphids, stink bugs and beetles, and for fungal diseases such as blight, honey fungus, grey mould, silver leaf, *Anthracnose*, leaf spot as well as the bacterial disease, crown gall. For many of the above, not growing plants in soils that are too wet and allowing space between plants should minimise the risk of these problems. Birds and other wildlife are attracted

Fruits are rounded, large and juicy, somewhat sour, but popular in many areas of the USA and Canada. Many find dewberries to have more flavour and interest than commercial blackberries. The fruits are usually good eaten fresh, but they are also popularly used in jam, jellies, juice, as well as making a good wine. They may have similar health benefits to raspberries (see p. 401).

to the fruits, and it may be necessary to temporarily enclose the plants in netting while the fruit ripen.

SOME DEWBERRY SPECIES

American dewberry, *Rubus canadensis*. A native of northeast North America, from Newfoundland down to North Carolina, the American dewberry is a deciduous shrub, growing to ~2.5 m. It does not flower until mid summer. It is self-fertile and also produces nucellar seeds. These are embryos that have formed without any genetic exchange and, thus, the progeny are clones of their parent, resulting in plants with very predictable qualities.

Cultivation: Is less cold hardy than many *Rubus* species and is more suited to warm temperate regions. This species only tolerates light frosts. Can be grown in full sun or semi-shade. Soil and water requirements as above. *Pruning:* It forms canes that grow in the first year, fruit in the second, and then die back. See general notes above. *Propagation:* As general notes above.

Uses: The fruits are fairly large (~2.5 cm long), sweet and richly flavoured, and are recommended by many as one of the best blackberry-type fruits. The fruit can be eaten fresh or can be added to pies, juice, jam, sauces, fruit salads, etc., or they can be dried for later use. The young leaves and shoots can be added to salads or can be lightly cooked as a vegetable. A tea can be made from the fresh or dried leaves. *Medicinal:* The fruit and leaves can be eaten to ease diarrhoea, vomiting and general stomach problems. *Other uses:* A purple-blue dye can be obtained from the fruits. The fruits attract birds and wildlife.

Dewberry, *Rubus pubescens*. Native to North America. A small scrambling deciduous plant, with many small prickles. Its stems will root as they touch the ground, its leaflets come in threes, and it has white, ~2.5-cm-wide flowers in spring. Its small fruits ripen to almost black in mid summer, though are often not very numerous. It naturally grows in woodland margins.

Cultivation: It prefers a little light shade, and can grow in both moist or drier soils. Cold hardy and can tolerate frosts.

Uses: The fruits are sweet and full of flavour.

Northern dewberry, *Rubus flagellaris*. A small scrambling, spreading, deciduous plant from North America, growing to ~20–40 cm in height, spreading to ~2 m. Its leaflets occur in threes and fives, and are often prickly, as are its green or reddish stems. Its flowers are ~2.5 cm wide and are borne in late spring–early summer. The flowers are self-fertile and produce nucellar seeds. They produce plants that are clones of their parent, making aspects such as fruit quality reliable. The fruits, ~1–2 cm long, are almost black when ripe, and are borne in mid–late summer. It is sometimes cultivated on a small scale for its fruits.

Cultivation: It is very cold hardy, and can tolerate quite heavy frosts. Can be grown in full sun or semi-shade. Soil and water requirements as above.

Uses: The fruits have a sweet, rich, tasty flavour, and are eaten fresh or are often used in jams, jellies, etc., or they can be dried for later use. The young leaves and shoots can be added to salads or can be lightly cooked as a vegetable. A tea can be made from the fresh or dried leaves. *Other uses:* A purple-blue dye can be obtained from the fruit.

Pacific dewberry, *Rubus ursinus*. A native of south-western North America, from California to Oregon. This deciduous, sprawling species is the parent of many hybrid cultivated forms, including loganberry and boysenberry. It has slender, trailing stems that can grow to ~6 m in length in shady areas, and tends to be multi-stemmed when growing in full sun. The leaves are usually three lobed. Flowers are bisexual and self-fertile. The fruits are ~2.5 cm long and are dark purple when ripe. It is quite a vigorous plant, and may not be suited to smaller gardens.

Cultivation: Is fairly cold hardy, and does not grow well in areas with warm winters and hot summers. Can be grown in full sun or semi-shade. Soil and water requirements as above. *Pruning:* It forms canes that grow in the first year, fruit in the second, and then die back. See general notes above. *Propagation:* As general notes above.

Uses: The fruits are fairly large and are usually sweet and pleasant when ripe. Some may lack depth of flavour. The fruit can be eaten fresh or can be added to pies, juice, jam, sauces, fruit salads, etc., or they can be dried for later use. The young leaves and shoots can be added to salads or can be lightly cooked as a vegetable. A tea can be made from the fresh or dried leaves. *Medicinal:* The fruit and leaves can be eaten to ease diarrhoea, vomiting and general stomach problems. The bark of the root is an astringent and has been used to treat diarrhoea and dysentery, and as a wash for skin wounds or infections. *Other uses:* A purple-blue dye can be obtained from the fruit.

Phenomenal berry (a dewberry x raspberry hybrid). Similar to loganberry in growth and fruit taste, though may be somewhat hardier. Good for jam and desserts.

Southern dewberry (southern blackberry), *Rubus trivialis*. A native of southeast North America, from Florida to Texas, often found growing wild as well as being cultivated on a small scale for its fruits. A smaller deciduous shrub, growing to 0.5–1 m in height, it has a sprawling form, with its stems rooting at nodes where they touch the ground. Its stems are covered in many small prickles, so it can be tricky to harvest. Leaves consist of 3–5 leaflets, and are often spiny. Flowers are self-fertile, solitary and open in early spring. It fruits ripen early in the season, usually by early summer. Several fruiting cultivars have been selected in the USA.

Cultivation: Can grow in drier, sandier soils than many *Rubus* species. It is fairly cold hardy and can tolerate frosts, though not very cold winters. It can be grown in full sun or semi-shade. *Pruning:* It forms canes that grow in the first year, fruit in the second, and then die back. See general notes above. *Propagation:* As general notes above.

Uses: The fruits are fairly large (~2–3 cm long), almost black, juicy, sweet and have a good flavour. Can be eaten fresh or added to pies, juice, jam, sauces, fruit salads, etc., or they can be dried for later use. *Medicinal:* The fruit and leaves can be eaten to ease diarrhoea, vomiting and general stomach problems. The bark of the root is an astringent and has been used to treat diarrhoea, rheumatism and as a tonic, and as a wash for piles. *Other uses:* A purple-blue dye can be obtained from the fruit.

Young berry (a phenomenal berry x dewberry hybrid). This hybrid cross forms a semi-scrambling deciduous plant, with moderately vigorous growth. It is not very cold hardy and is more suited to warmer regions. It has few thorns. Fruit are very dark red when ripe, shiny, with a sweet and mild taste. Are better if picked when a little under-ripe as they are then more tasty and tangy. Fruits ripen in early–mid summer. ■

Rubus idaeus
Raspberry (red raspberry)
ROSACEAE

Similar species and hybrids: boysenberry, laxtonberry, loganberry, Arctic raspberry (*R. arcticus, R. stellatus*), bush lawyer (*R. moorei*), Ceylon raspberry (*R. niveus*), cloudberry (*R. chamaemorus*), golden evergreen raspberry (*R. ellipticus*), Mora de Castilla (*R. glaucus*), native or Atherton raspberry (*R. fraxinifolius*), Nepalese raspberry (*R. nepalensis*), *Rubus flagelliflorus*, salmonberry (*R. spectabilis*), whitebark raspberry (*R. leucodermis*), wild raspberry (*R. crataegifolius*)

Relatives: thimbleberry, wineberry, dewberry, blackberry

Rubus is a genus within the large Rosaceae family that contains many fruiting species. Raspberries have superior ovaries, with the flower and fruit formed above the sepals and petals. Each flower contains many individual ovules around a receptacle. When pollinated, each ovule goes on to form a drupelet with a single seed. The fusion of these many drupelets creates the juicy, aggregate fruit. The fruit can be pulled free from the receptacle. They are not actually berries, as their common name suggests. The main raspberry species, *Rubus idaeus*, is a native of southeastern Europe and Asia Minor, and has been cultivated from the warmer Mediterranean regions to as far north as Iceland and the UK. It is known to have been cultivated in Greece some 2000 years ago, and was then called an 'Ida berry', after Mt Ida, where it may have been first 'discovered', hence its Latin name *idaeus*. From there raspberries were spread, probably by the Romans, to most of Europe and Britain. The Romans were cultivating them by the 4th century, and seeds have been discovered at Roman forts in Britain. The British popularised and selected improved cultivars of raspberries throughout the Middle Ages. Modern raspberries are often a cross between *R. idaeus* and other raspberry species. The canes, though needing a fair amount of attention, do grow easily; it is more a question of keeping them in check and disease free. Raspberry fruits have a succulent, rich taste, and a fruity, heavenly aroma. Their flavour and quality is hard to beat.

DESCRIPTION

Raspberry plants form several erect or sprawling stems each year. At the same time the 2-year-old canes die back. They usually have some thorns, but are not nearly as prickly as blackberries. The roots are perennial, though the canes usually only live 2 years. There are two main groups of raspberries: summer fruiting and autumn fruiting. Summer-fruiting raspberries tend to grow and fruit better in cooler temperate zones, and usually only produce fruits on 2-year-old canes. They grow vegetatively for a year, to reach 1.5–2 m height, during which they form flower buds in late summer. These bloom the following spring and fruit in summer, before the cane dies back. Autumn-fruiting cultivars often grow better in warmer-temperate regions and produce their first harvest on canes from the present season, as well as a smaller crop the following spring. The plants of both types can live for ~15 years.

Leaves: Compound, 3–5 leaflets, with the middle leaf being the largest. Leaves are coarse, somewhat rough, margins serrated, and have a pleasant smell when crushed. Leaves on 2-year-old canes become darker and thicker before dying off.

Flower: Small (~1–1.5 cm), white–pale pink, borne terminally in small clusters. They have numerous stamens. They are formed in late summer in summer-fruiting species (but do not open till the following spring), or in spring for the autumn-fruiting raspberries (primocanes). The receptacle consists of 60–80 embryos, which can all develop into drupelets. *Pollination:* Flowers produce a lot of nectar, which attracts bees and other insects. Although the plants are self-fertile, they are usually planted in groups, and this may improve pollination. Wind may also aid pollination, whereas damp weather tends to reduce it.

Fruit: Numerous drupelets, or flesh-covered seeds, clustered around a receptacle, which is left behind when the fruit is picked, to leave the fruit with a hollow centre. Fruits are usually a rich red colour, though there are cultivars with yellow, black or light red fruits. Fruit size is ~2 cm long. Different cultivars have been selected to fruit at different times of the year from spring until autumn. Summer-fruiting raspberries fruit after strawberries, in mid summer. Autumn-fruiting raspberries fruit in autumn and again the following spring. Fruits only take 30–35 days to form after pollination.

Yield/harvest/storage: New plants take ~2–3 years to give good yields. Can expect ~1 kg of fruit per bush by year 3. One of the time-consuming aspects of raspberries is the slowness of harvesting, and they also need picking several times during the fruiting season, often at 2–3-day intervals. Once picked, they only last for a short time: 2–3 days in the fridge. They can also be easily crushed and damaged; for this reason, they are best placed in shallow baskets.

Roots: Raspberries form many surface roots, which makes them very susceptible to dry soil, weed competition and mechanical cultivation. The roots are so close to the surface that they can be damaged and even killed by direct fertiliser applications. A good mulch can solve these problems.

CULTIVATION

They are ideal for smaller gardens and, although they take some maintenance, the 'fruits' of your labour are rewarding. They are usually grown in cooler climates, although a few cultivars, mostly black fruited, have been developed for warmer regions.

Location: They like a sunny site in cooler climates, but in warmer areas they prefer some shade. They will fruit in sun or shade. Are not wind tolerant nor very salt tolerant.

Temperature: Tend to need cooler summers than blackberries. Are very frost tolerant, becoming dormant in winter, and can withstand long, cold periods.

Chilling: Red raspberries need some winter chill. They need more chilling hours than blackberries, i.e. 800–1600 hours.

Soil/water/nutrients: Plants grow best in slightly acidic soils that are rich in humus and have good potassium levels. Loamy soils with pH 4.5–7.0 are ideal. They like a moist but well-drained soil. Plants grow better with an application of organic compost in spring, which helps suppress weed growth and retains moisture. They are not drought resistant and need supplementary watering in dry weather, particularly when fruit are developing. Although they grow well in a fertile soil, do not add too much extra nitrogen as this results in too much leaf growth at the expense of fruiting. A plastic-sheet mulch is reported to give greater fruit yields compared to mulches of mushroom compost, pine needles or no mulch, as well as giving very good weed control. Fertiliser applications are best done in spring, possibly mixing it with compost to reduce the risk of damaging the roots.

Planting: Can either be done in late autumn or early spring. Raspberries need support when growing, so plant into a prepared area that is weed free and has supporting wires already erected. Erect posts at intervals with 2–3 strands of wire between them up to a height ~1.7 m. They can also be grown against a wall. Dig in some organic matter. New plants should have their tops removed to just leave 20–30 cm length of cane. This enables the plant to put resources into root establishment rather than shoot growth. Try to gently spread the roots out when planting at ~30–40 cm apart within rows, with ~2–3 m between the rows. As the canes grow during the season, they will need tying onto the wire trellis. Remove any flowers that form on newly planted raspberries to allow their energy to go into establishment. Trailing canes will root wherever they touch the soil, and make the rows difficult to navigate. Plant in well-drained soil to reduce the risk of root rots, and it is better to plant in soil that has not had Solanaceae species recently grown in it.

Propagation: Seed: Usually not grown from seed. However, if planning to do so, seeds need 1–2 months of stratification at ~3°C before sowing in moist, well-drained compost, in early spring. Grow on seedlings in pots for ~1 year until large enough to plant out. *Cuttings:* Root cuttings are a common method of propagation for raspberries, and are similar to suckers. Choose only disease-free plants to take cuttings from. Take cuttings during late summer– autumn and insert in moist, warm compost to establish. Black and purple cultivars do not produce adventitious buds on their roots, so cannot be propagated by this method: they are usually tip-layered. Semi-ripe cuttings can be also taken from young canes in summer. These root better in a humid atmosphere. *Suckers:* Red raspberries produce a profusion of suckers, often at some distance from the main plant. These can be dug up, with some rooted underground stem if possible, in late autumn–winter, and inserted in pots to establish. Remove the tops of taller suckers. *Layering:* Once the first-year canes have become tall, in late summer, then the tips of canes can be buried in soil where they will readily root. By the following spring these tips should have rooted, and can be carefully cut off from the parent plant, and either planted directly out in another location or grown on for a year.

Pruning: Once established, pruning takes on an overlapping cycle of maintenance. For summer-fruiting cultivars, the young canes, for manageability and harvesting, are pruned to a height of ~1.2–2 m tall, except for some sprawling species. These new canes are also tied onto wire supports and, generally, ~5–7 canes are allowed to develop each year from each plant, pruning out the surplus. Too many canes per plant reduces the overall quality and yield of fruits. It is also beneficial to prevent suckers from spreading out too widely as they make harvesting and maintenance more difficult; therefore, select vigorous canes growing near the parent plant for fruit production. The 2-year-old fruiting canes do not need pruning or tying in; they are simply harvested for their fruits and then pruned out. Pruning and removal of old canes also reduces the risk of disease. Each year there will be some young canes and some fruiting canes. For primocanes (or autumn-fruiting cultivars), the canes are secured to the trellis as they grow, and then there are a variety of pruning methods one can use. The tips can be removed from some of the canes once they are ~1.6–2 m tall, with this practice encouraging the formation of fruiting lateral branches. These canes are then usually pruned out after fruiting in autumn. The remaining canes then produce fruits the following spring, after which these are also pruned out. Another method is the removal of cane tips after the autumn harvest from all canes, and then these same canes produce a smaller spring crop. Commercially, the autumn-fruiting cultivars are completely cut down to the ground at the end of each year, so there is no spring crop: benefits of reducing pest and disease damage outweigh the loss in crop yield.

Pests and diseases: Raspberries are susceptible to a number of problems, including strawberry weevil, aphids, raspberry-bud moth, cane spot, which can be serious and kill the plant (forms round spots on the canes), spur blight, honey fungus, grey mould, silver leaf, cane borer, thrips, gall midges, stink bugs and beetles. They can also suffer from many fungal diseases, including *Verticillium*, *Anthracnose* (causes small purplish scars on canes; the disease can kill canes), leaf spot (occurs as dark red spots on leaves), orange rust (forms an orange mass of spores on the underside of leaves in spring) and a bacterial disease, crown gall (look like reddish–brown potatoes at the base of the canes; it spreads by entering through damaged tissue). For many of the above, good hygiene around the plants will help (e.g. washing tools after handling infected plants, etc.), not growing plants in wet soils and not overcrowding them. Another pest problem is the fierce competition with wildlife for the fruits: it may be necessary to temporarily enclose the area in netting while the fruits ripen.

CULTIVARS

'Allen': Large, attractive, black, sweet and firm fruits; makes good jam. Ripens mid season over a short period. Vigorous, productive.

'Amber': Productive. Fruits are yellow with lots of flavour.

'Amethyst': Fruit: black and trailing, somewhat acid, but plant is very vigorous and reliable. Early ripening. Does well in warmer regions.

'Black Hawk': Vigorous, hardy, does not sucker. Fruit: large, black, ~2 cm diameter, firm, sweet–sub-acid. Ripens mid season. Good quality when fresh, frozen or processed. Good yields.

'Cumberland': Fruit: black and trailing. Popular cultivar. Is vigorous, productive, but not disease-resistant. Fruit is excellent.

'Fairview': A long mid season harvest. Large berries with excellent flavour. Good for home gardens.

'Fallgold': Everbearing, early ripening, excellent fresh, large yellow fruit.

'Haut': Medium-sized black fruit, sweet, firm, excellent quality, ripens over a longer period. A vigorous, high-yielding plant. Is disease-resistant.

'Indian Summer': Red, large fruits, are everbearing, good eaten fresh or cooked.

'Jewel': Large, black, attractive fruits, firm, flavourful, high quality. Ripens in mid season. Vigorous, productive, winter hardy, fairly disease resistant.

'John Robertson': Fruit: large, black, medium firm, juicy, very good quality. Productive and very hardy: grows in Canada.

'Lowden': Very large black fruit, juicy, sweet flesh, excellent flavour. Ripens late. Forms an upright, fairly vigorous, productive, very winter-hardy plant.

'Munger': Important cultivar worldwide. Fruit: black, trailing, rich in ellagic acid.

'Plum Farmer': Fruit: large, black, firm, high quality, short season. Very hardy and drought resistant.

'Sumner': Excellent for all uses, red fruits, early ripening, tolerates heavy soil.

SIMILAR SPECIES AND HYBRIDS

There are many raspberry species similar to *R. idaeus*, as well as many hybrid crosses. Some of these are listed below.

Hybrids

Boysenberry: A cross between raspberry and blackberry. Popular with a trailing habit (like blackberries), but fruits more similar to raspberries, though larger and more purple in colour. The cultivar 'Boysen' is grown commercially in the USA and New Zealand. Cultivation as for raspberry. *Pruning:* Tie-in young trailing canes to a trellis system; they fruit in their second year. Cut off cane tips if they become too long, to encourage the formation of fruiting laterals. Prune out canes after their harvest, in the second year. Often fruit early.

Laxtonberry: A raspberry x loganberry cross. Grows to ~2–3 m, more similar to a loganberry than raspberry. Is only partially self-fertile and fruits better if planted near a raspberry or loganberry plant. The fruit is loganberry-like.

Loganberry: Another cross between raspberry and blackberry. This also has a trailing habit. The fruits have a similar colour and appearance to raspberry, but the receptacle remains within the fruit when it is picked (like blackberry). Their taste is a cross between raspberry and blackberry. Juicy large drupelets. The fruits are also good for drying and making juice. Prune as for boysenberry.

Similar species

Arctic raspberry, *Rubus arcticus*, *R. stellatus* and their hybrids. These are natives of northern Europe and are locally important for their fruits and their cold hardiness. They flower in late spring–early summer, and fruit a month or so later. Their berries are strongly aromatic and full of flavour. Unfortunately, like other *Rubus* spp., they do not keep well, and need to be eaten fresh or processed into juice, preserves and liqueurs. They form a low-lying, sprawling plant and prefer a sunny spot, though only grow and fruit well in colder regions. Often the cultivars are self-sterile, so need more than one cultivar, and to be planted in groups. They are popular and widely grown in Scandinavia. The leaves can be used as a tea substitute.

Bush lawyer, *Rubus moorei*. Native of eastern Australia, it forms a deciduous plant, growing to ~3 m tall. Fruits (~2.5 cm long) are eaten fresh or cooked (pies, preserves, etc.). Have a delicious, tangy flavour but also a lot of hard seeds.

Food
Fruits are wonderful just eaten fresh with a sprinkle of brown sugar, and cream or yoghurt. They can be added to pies, desserts, fruit salads, sauces (for sweet and savoury dishes), made into great jam and a good wine. Raspberry vinegar can be made from the fruit, by adding sugar and white wine, and is, at present, experiencing a renewal in popularity. The young leaves and shoots of many *Rubus* species can be picked, peeled and eaten raw or lightly cooked like asparagus.

Nutrition/medicinal
Fruit contains reasonable quantities of vitamin C (25–30 mg vitamin C/100 g). They probably also have the highest content of ellagic acid of any fruit: this has proven anti-carcinogen and anti-mutagenic properties, and strengthens connective tissue. It has been clinically proven to cause the death of some cancer cells. Ellagic acid from raspberries is readily absorbed by the body. It retains its potency after heating, freezing and processing. These antioxidant properties particularly apply to black raspberries. They also have the second highest ability to inhibit the formation of low density lipids. In addition, raspberries may also help reduce the risk of heart attacks and strokes due to a natural form of aspirin (salicylic acid) they contain. They may also help reduce blood-sugar levels and, therefore, could be useful in the management of diabetes. They are high in fibre, and contain pectin, citric and malic acids, and mineral salts. Raspberries have been used to treat fevers and sore throats. A tea made from their leaves has been used by pregnant women for many hundreds of years; it is thought to reduce miscarriage, ease childbirth and improve lactation. It has also been used to reduce diarrhoea in children.

Other uses
The fruits yield a strong-coloured dye. They contain a fragrant volatile oil, ionone, which is also the fragrant molecule found in violets.

May tolerate light frosts, but prefers warmer locations. Some forms have hairy stems, others are hairless.

Ceylon raspberry (Mysore raspberry), *Rubus niveus*. A native of eastern Asia. Forms a deciduous, only moderately hardy plant, height ~4 m. Has flexible stems that are downy when young, becoming purple later. Has sharp, hooked thorns. Grows better in warmer regions; is fairly frost sensitive. *Uses:* Fruits are 1.25–2 cm in diameter, juicy and sweet, with a rich black-raspberry flavour. Good eaten fresh or are excellent in pies, tarts, jams and jelly. Fresh fruits can be frozen for future use Very good quality fruit, but can only be stored for ~24 hours. A plant yields ~0.6 kg of fruits/season. A purple-blue dye can be obtained from the fruits.

Cloudberry, *Rubus chamaemorus*. An extremely cold hardy perennial, ~0.3 m height, 1 m spread. Flowers during summer; fruits ripen from mid–late summer. Flowers are dioecious, so need more than one plant to set fruits. Cultivation as for raspberries, but can also grow in very acid soils; dislikes alkaline soils. Grows best in full sun; dislikes shade. Is not drought tolerant, but can be grown in wet and waterlogged soils. *Uses:* Fruits can be eaten fresh or can be stewed, or added to pies, jams, desserts, etc. Are sour, but delicious, with a taste somewhat like baked cooking-apples. Are rich in vitamin C. The leaves can be used to make a tea.

Golden evergreen raspberry, *Rubus ellipticus*. A native of India; still found growing wild in the hills there. Very popular locally and the fruits are often sold at markets. Now grown in Florida as both a fruit and as an ornamental plant. Plants vary in shape, fruit quality and yields. Select vigorous plants to propagate from, particularly those with good fruit yields.

Description: Has mostly erect, prickly canes that live ~ 2 years (one year of growth, the second year they fruit). Can grow to ~2–4 m. Has 6–7 canes per plant. *Leaves:* Evergreen, compound, trifoliate, irregularly toothed. *Flowers:* White, five petals, bisexual, ~1 cm in diameter, in clusters of 30–40 flowers. *Fruits:* Yellow skin and flesh, easily picked. Have a quality, sweet–sub-acid taste, similar to raspberries. Has many very small seeds. Can get ~0.7 kg of fruits/plant. Plants at lower elevations may be more productive than those at higher elevations. Fresh fruits only keep for ~24 hours.

Cultivation and uses: As for raspberry, though will grow in much warmer climates. They like moist soil. The fruits are good eaten fresh or make a good jam. Low in vitamin C: 4.5 mg/100 ml of flesh. May not have the nutritional benefits of dark-coloured raspberries. The plant can be grown as an ornamental hedge or can be trained to cover fences.

Mora de Castilla, *Rubus glaucus*. A common plant in the Andean region of South America. The fruits are locally popular and are sold in markets. A vigorous plant with hooked prickles on their stems. Grows better in warmer regions. Prefers to grow in fertile, moisture-retentive, deep soils, but can be grown in heavy clays or sandy soils. Does not tolerate dry soils. Large fruits (~3 cm long), dark red–black in colour. Are very juicy and have a good, rich, but tart flavour and aroma, and rich, red juice. Seeds are small and hard. In warmer areas, the plant can fruit for most of the year and give good yields. Fruits store poorly and need to be eaten fresh or used in juices, jams or preserves. They are sometimes processed in South America to make a soda drink.

Native or Atherton raspberry, *Rubus fraxinifolius*. A native of eastern Australia this grows well in warmer climates, though grows better with regular rainfall. Is not too fussy about soil type or care, and readily forms a thicket of canes that grow to ~0.7–1 m tall, though are fairly thorny. Will grow in semi-shade. Has attractive light green leaves: canes are similar in appearance to common raspberry plants. Produces many tasty, juicy fruits. The fruits are bright orangey-red, rounded and ~1.5–2 cm long.

Nepalese raspberry, *Rubus nepalensis*. A native of eastern Asia. It forms a fairly frost-sensitive, evergreen, small plant to ~0.2 m tall, ~1 m spread which can be trained up structures. Sends out ground-hugging stems and suckers. A fairly tough species, and can tolerate some competition with other species. Can tolerate light frosts and can be grown in many areas of the UK. Prefers to be grown in semi-shade in hot regions. Does not tolerate salt. Flowers in early summer. The plant is self-fertile. Fruits ripen in late summer–autumn, are ~1–1.5 cm long and have a good, sub-acid flavour. Cultivation and propagation as for raspberry. They do need moisture. *Uses:* Can be eaten fresh or cooked. Have a good though sour flavour. Yields are often good. Plant is ornamental and makes an effective, useful groundcover in warmer areas, though in colder regions it may lose some of its leaves in winter. A purple-blue dye can be obtained from the fruits. Can be propagated by division almost year-round.

Rubus flagelliflorus. A native of eastern Asia. A somewhat hardy, evergreen, scrambling climber (has hooked prickles), growing to ~1.8 m. Will not tolerate heavy frosts. Flowers all summer. Cultivation and propagation as for raspberry. Easy to grow, but likes a shady location. Pruning is best done in spring, just to remove old and dead wood. Plants produce numerous new shoots from the base each year; these usually flower and fruit in their second year. *Uses:* The fruits (~1.2 cm diameter) can be eaten fresh or added to juices, pies, etc. A purple-blue dye can be obtained from the fruits.

Salmonberry, *Rubus spectabilis*. A native of North America, from California to Alaska. A deciduous plant, ~1.8 m tall. Is fully hardy to ~−25°C. Produces biennial stems: grow one year, fruit the next. Flowers in spring; fruits ripen in summer. Cultivation, uses and propagation as for raspberry. It is a very attractive plant, but can be invasive. The fruits are very juicy, have a good flavour and range in colour from yellow–orange–red, ~2 cm long. Seems to fruit and taste better in warmer regions, as can be somewhat bitter in cooler regions. A tea can be made from the leaves. The root is used as a painkiller, an astringent, a disinfectant and to ease stomach problems. The bark has been ground up or made into pastes and has been widely used on burns, sores, wounds, toothache and to generally ease pain.

Whitebark raspberry, *Rubus leucodermis*. A native of northwestern USA. A deciduous, hardy plant, height ~2.5 m. Suitable for temperate gardens. Flowers in early summer; fruits ripen during summer. Has biennial stems: grow the first year; fruit in the second year before dying back. Cultivation, uses and propagation as raspberry. Does not grow well in windy, exposed locations. *Uses:* The black fruits can be eaten fresh or added to pies, jams, etc., or can be dried. Have a good flavour, but are soft and easily spoil. Good levels of vitamin C. This species is cultivated for its fruits in northern USA. The leaves make a good-tasting tea, high in vitamin C. The young shoots and leaves can be eaten. *Medicinal:* The whole plant acts as an astringent. The roots and leaves are used to treat diarrhoea and upset stomachs. A poultice made from the stems has been used to treat cuts and wounds. A purple-blue dye is obtained from the fruit.

Wild raspberry, *Rubus crataegifolius*. A native of eastern Asia. It forms a hardy, deciduous plant, height ~2.5 m. Easy to grow. Has biennial stems: grow in the first year; fruit and die back in the second. Flowers in early summer; fruits ripen in late summer. Cultivation and propagation as for raspberry. Sometimes cultivated for its fruit. *Uses:* The fruits can be eaten fresh or used in pies, juices, etc. Has large, tasty, transparent fruits that taste like raspberries. A purple-blue

dye is obtained from the fruit. *Medicinal:* Recent studies in Korea have reported that extracts from the roots could inhibit the growth of cancer cells. They also have anti-inflammatory properties. Has potential for being further developed commercially. *Cultivar:* 'Jingu Jengal': From Korea, gives high yields. Very large fruit, up to 2 g in weight. ∎

Rubus parviflorus
Thimbleberry
ROSACEAE
Similar species: *R. odoratus*, *R. occidentalis*
Relatives: raspberry, blackberry, huckleberry

Within the *Rubus* genus, there is a great deal of overlap of common names, and thimbleberries are sometimes grouped with raspberries, which are very similar. They are called thimbleberries because of their distinctively shaped fruits. They are natives of the USA and, unlike raspberries, have perennial stems. They make attractive ornamental plants and provide tasty fruits. All *Rubus* fruits are classified as aggregates of drupelets and consist of many pollinated ovaries from a single flower, which are formed around a receptacle. In thimbleberries, the fruits can be pulled free from their receptacle, leaving a hollow centre. The native Indians used thimbleberries extensively, treating the leaves as a vegetable and a tea-making ingredient. The berries were included in many food dishes as well as being dried for winter use.

DESCRIPTION
Rubus parviflorus is a native of northwestern USA, from California to Alaska, and is often found growing in dense clumps in open forests and on forest margins. A very hardy, rapidly-growing, erect, deciduous shrub, height ~1.5–2 m, with perennial cane-like stems that are hairy when young, but have no prickles. Has brown–grey shedding bark.

Leaves: Alternate, deciduous, large (~10–18 cm wide), simple, usually five-lobed and maple-like; green above, pale beneath, with fine velvety hair on both sides. They form a fairly dense shade. Good autumn colour of bright orange–deep red.

Flowers: Attractive, white or sometimes pink, 3–5 cm wide, crumpled appearance, occurring singly or in clusters of 2–7, which are borne terminally on the current season's growth. They have numerous stamens. They open in early summer. *Pollination:* Flowers produce a lot of nectar, which attracts bees and other insects. Wind may also aid pollination; damp weather tends to reduce it.

Fruit: Thimble shaped, consisting of a dense aggregate of pink, turning red when ripe, fuzzy, drupelets, 1.5–2 cm wide. The fruits are soft when they ripen in summer, and easily fall apart when picked or handled. They can ripen very fast, within a few hours on a sunny day. Fruits take 30–40 days to ripen after pollination.

Harvesting/storage: Need to be picked several times during the fruiting season and, once picked, only last for a short time: 2–3 days in a fridge. Can be easily crushed and damaged, therefore they are best placed in shallow baskets.

Roots: Form many surface roots, which makes them susceptible to dry soil, weed competition and mechanical

cultivation. The roots are so close to the surface that fertilisers can burn and even kill them. A good mulch can solve these problems. They form some rhizomatous roots, which can be used for propagation.

CULTIVATION
An easy-to-grow species that has ornamental value as well as providing tasty fruits.

Location: Prefers a humid, moist location, in semi-shade. In colder regions it can be grown in sunnier locations. Some sun gives a better fruit harvest. Its natural range is often on forest margins.

Temperature: It does grow naturally in a wide range of climates, from the hot climate of California, where many plants are frost sensitive, to Alaska. They can, therefore, tolerate extremes of temperatures.

Soil/water/nutrients: Plants grow best in slightly acidic soils that are rich in humus. Loamy soils with pH 4.5–6.0 are ideal. They like a moist but well-drained soil. They will also grow in clay-type soils and quite sandy soils. Plants benefit from an annual addition of organic compost in spring to help suppress weed growth and retain moisture. They are not drought resistant and need supplementary watering in dry weather, particularly during fruit development. Although they benefit from fertile soil, do not add too much nitrogen, which results in excessive leaf growth at the expense of fruiting. Fertiliser applications should be done in spring, and possibly mixed with compost to reduce the risk of root damage. They particularly benefit from extra potassium.

Planting: Space plants at ~2 m apart. Can either be planted in late autumn or early spring. They may need support

Food
The fruits (~2 cm diameter) have a sweet, pleasant taste, particularly in warmer, wetter regions. They are good for making jellies, jams and preserves, but do have a lot of hard seeds. They can also be dried. The young shoots and leaves can be eaten either fresh or lightly cooked like asparagus.

Nutrition/medicinal
The fruits and leaves are rich in vitamin C. They may have health benefits similar to raspberries (see p. 401). The leaves are used to treat stomach and digestion problems, diarrhoea, anaemia, as a blood tonic and to stop vomiting. They have been used to help reduce heavy menstrual periods. They are used as a poultice on wounds, burns and swellings, and to treat pimples and blackheads. The roots have been eaten to increase appetite, and are also an astringent and are used for stomach disorders, diarrhoea and dysentery.

Other uses
A purple-blue dye can be obtained from the fruits.

Ornamental
Makes a good ornamental shrub with attractive blossom, wide, velvety leaves and bright red fruits. They can make a good screening plant, though are not very wind tolerant. A good plant for attracting wildlife, e.g. butterflies and birds. Can be planted as a pioneer species in moist regions.

from wires or a fence. Dig in some organic matter. Remove any flowers that form in the first year to allow their efforts to go into root and shoot establishment. Plant in well-drained soil to reduce the risk of root rot, and preferably in soil that has not had Solanaceae species recently grown in it.

Pruning: These canes are perennial and do not die back like those of raspberry or blackberry after they have finished fruiting in the second year. However, the removal of some older wood encourages the growth of younger canes. Trimming longer trailing stems also encourages the growth of fruiting laterals.

Propagation: *Seed:* Can be grown from seed, though may not be easy. Separate the seed from the pulp before sowing. If the seed is stored, it will need ~1–3 months of stratification at ~3°C before sowing in early spring. Grow on seedlings in pots for ~1 year, till large enough to plant out. *Cuttings:* Rhizome cuttings can be a good method. Choose disease-free plants from which to carefully dig up and cut rhizomes into sections during winter: root these in a cold frame. Semi-ripe cuttings can be also taken from young canes in summer, or hardwood cuttings during winter. *Suckers:* Some of these species produce suckers. These can be dug up, with some rooted underground stem if possible, in late autumn–winter,

and planted in pots to establish. Remove the tops of taller suckers to encourage preferential root development. *Division:* Can be readily divided in autumn or early spring; though in colder regions it may be best to be done in spring, and establish plantlets in pots or a sheltered site until established. *Layering:* Long, young stem tips can be bent to touch the soil, and then buried, where they will readily root. By the following spring, these tips should have rooted and can be carefully removed from the parent plant, and either planted in their final location or grown on for a further year.

Pests and diseases: Although much less susceptible, they may suffer from the same problems as raspberries, which include weevils, aphids, cane spot, spur blight, honey fungus, grey mould, silver leaf, thrips, gall midges, stink bugs and beetles, as well as the fungal diseases *Verticillium*, *Anthracnose*, leaf spot and possibly the bacterial disease crown gall. Another problem is the fierce competition with wildlife for the fruit: it may be necessary to temporarily enclose the area in netting while the fruits ripen.

SIMILAR SPECIES

Thimbleberry or flowering raspberry, *Rubus odoratus*. A native of northeastern North America, from Tennessee to Quebec, it forms an attractive shrub with fragrant flowers and edible red fruits.

Description: It forms a fairly fast-growing, hardy, deciduous, suckering plant, height ~1.5–2.5 m, spread 1.5–2.5 m. It has perennial stems, without prickles. The stems have glandular hairs that emit a powerful resinous scent, somewhat like cedarwood, when crushed. Has peeling bark. *Leaves:* Deciduous, large and soft, pinnate, usually with five lobes, bright green. *Flowers:* Large. (~3–5 cm diameter), white–pink–purple, fragrant, bowl-shaped, from early–late summer. Are borne singly or in small clusters of 2–7, towards the ends of the current season's growth. Have numerous stamens. *Pollination:* Produce a lot of nectar, which attracts bees and other insects. Wind may also aid pollination; damp weather can reduce it. *Fruit:* Scarlet–orange, somewhat sticky. Ripen from mid summer to autumn. Similar in appearance and taste to raspberries.

Cultivation: Similar to *R. parviflorus* (see notes above). Likes to grow in partial shade. Fully frost hardy, tolerating temperatures down to ~–30°C. Likes a moist soil; not drought tolerant. Benefits from an annual addition of a fertiliser or an organic supplement, particularly with extra potassium. *Planting/Pruning/Propagation and Pests and diseases:* As for *R. parviflorus* above.

Uses: *Food:* Fruit are fairly dry and somewhat acid, and are usually cooked or dried, or used in pies, jams, preserves, etc. Fruits better in regions with warmer summers. Makes a delicious, good-quality wine. *Nutrition/medicinal:* May have health benefits similar to raspberries (see p. 401). The root and leaves are astringent and are used to treat dysentery and diarrhoea. The berries have been used as a diuretic. The plant is presently being researched for the use of its tannins as an anti-cancer agent. A liquid obtained from roots and stems, when peeled and boiled, can stop vomiting. *Other uses:* A purple-blue dye can be obtained from the fruits. *Ornamental:* Is ornamental and can be grown as a tall groundcover plant in large areas. It is a good plant for attracting wildlife.

Thimbleberry or black raspberry, *Rubus occidentalis*.
A hardy native of central and eastern USA. It naturally grows
to ~1.5–2.5 m tall, and tends to have a sprawling habit.
The canes are often reddish in colour, have a white bloom
and hooked prickles. Flowers are white, and are borne
in early summer. Fruits are dark purple-black, and ripen
in late summer. Unlike the other thimbleberries, its stems
live for 2 years, growing one year, then fruiting and dying
back the next. See pruning notes for raspberry. There are
several cultivars. The cultivation, propagation and uses are
very similar to those of raspberry. Fruits are tasty, ~1.5 cm
diameter, with uses as for *R. parviflorus* above. ∎

Rubus phoenicolasius
Wineberry (Japanese wineberry)
ROSACEAE
Relatives: raspberry, thimbleberry, blackberry

All the *Rubus* fruits are classified as aggregates of drupelets; however,
wineberry drupelets can be pulled free from the receptacle, whereas blackberry
drupelets come with the receptacle still attached. The 'fruit' consist of many
ovaries from a single flower, each ovary forming an individual seed within a
juicy drupelet, with the many drupelets aggregating to form the 'fruit'. The
wineberry is a native of eastern Asia: Japan, Korea and China, though is now
grown as an ornamental, for its fruit and as breeding stock in many temperate
areas of the world. It was introduced into the UK and the USA in the late 1800s. Although it has red fruit, it has a recessive
gene for yellow fruit. This has been selected and has produced cultivars, often crossed with, for example, the common
red raspberry, which produce hybrids with yellow fruit. This species has also been used to detect plant viruses that often
occur in other *Rubus* species. It forms a tall, upright, attractive red-stemmed shrub that produces tasty fruits. However,
because of its vigorous growth, it has become an invasive species in some areas of the USA where it has escaped from
gardens or cultivation.

DESCRIPTION
Wineberry has fast-growing, upright, graceful, arching, prickly
biennial stems (canes), up to ~2–3 m tall, with individual plants
spreading ~3 m. The name *phoenicolasius* means 'purple
hairs' and refers to the reddish hairs on the plant's long stems,
which give them their ornamental, attractive colour. Wineberry
is an attractive plant year-round. It has a similar growth cycle
to raspberry and can be trained and pruned in a similar way.

Leaves: Attractive, pinnate, consisting of three roundish
leaflets (5–10 cm long), which are silvery and woolly beneath,
and have purplish veins on their upper surface. They have
toothed margins.

Flowers: Small, pinkish-white, with small reddish hairs, in
spring–early summer. *Pollination:* Flowers produce nectar,
which attracts bees and other insects. Although the plants
are self-fertile, they can be planted in groups to improve
pollination. Wind may also aid pollination; damp weather
tends to reduce it.

Fruit: Numerous drupelets, or flesh-covered seeds,
clustered around a large receptacle, which is left behind
when the fruit is picked, to leave the fruit with a hollow
centre. The shiny fruits are yellow at first, turning scarlet as
they ripen (~2 cm long); they are juicy and taste similar to
raspberries, but perhaps a little more sour. They ripen in
mid–late summer. They are enclosed within a calyx until they
ripen, when the calyx peels back to expose the fruit.

Yield/harvest/storage: Fruits only take 30–35 days to
form after pollination. There have good yields, but, once
picked, only last for a short time (2–3 days) in a fridge. They
are also easily crushed and damaged so are best placed in
shallow baskets.

Roots: Wineberries form many surface roots, which make
plants very susceptible to dry soil and mechanical cultivation.
A good organic mulch can overcome these problems.

CULTIVATION
Location: Can grown in sun or semi-shade. May be best to
contain its spread as it can become invasive and take over
areas. Plants do not like windy, exposed locations.

Temperature: Is fairly frost hardy and can tolerate
temperatures down to ~−15°C.

Soil/water/nutrients: Plants grow best in slightly acidic
soils that are rich in humus and have good potassium levels.
Loamy soils with pH 4.5–6.5 are ideal. They like a moist, but
well-drained soil. Plants grow well with additions of organic
compost applied in spring, which help suppress weed
growth and retain moisture. They are not drought resistant
and need supplementary watering in dry weather, particularly
when developing fruits. Although they benefit from fertile soil,
too much nitrogen can result in excess leaf growth at the
expense of fruiting.

Planting: Space plants at ~1–2 m apart. As the stems are
tall and arching they benefit from tying onto a frame, trellis or
similar. This also prevents them from rooting where the tips
touch the ground and, therefore, makes them less invasive.

Pruning: Once established, pruning takes on an

overlapping cycle of maintenance. The canes live for 2 years: in the first year, the cane grows and forms flower buds in early autumn; in the second year, the cane fruits

uses

Food

The fruits are juicier, but perhaps not as sweet as raspberries, but they do have lots of flavour. The seeds are hard, so it is best to strain puréed berries. They freeze well. Can be just eaten fresh, with a sprinkle of brown sugar and cream or yoghurt, or can be added to pies, desserts, fruit salads, sauces (for sweet and savoury dishes), or made into wonderful jam. Also make a good wine.

Nutrition

They may have health benefits similar to raspberries (see p. 401). Contain good quantities of vitamin C, and probably a high content of ellagic acid (similar to raspberries): a phenolic compound that is a proven anti-carcinogen and anti-mutagen, and strengthens connective tissue. Ellagic acid also retains its potency after heating, freezing and processing. They are high in fibre, and contain pectin, citric and malic acids, and mineral salts.

Ornamental

Although an attractive, vigorous plant, with year-round interest from its striking red stems, as well as its tasty fruits, care needs to be taken when choosing a site because it can form dense thickets that are invasive and difficult to control. It is a weed problem in some areas of the USA, and has become a problem in the wild by often replacing native species where it occurs. It grows in a variety of habitats, including fields, the edges of wetlands, woods and prairies.

and then dies back. In the first year, therefore, the canes, for manageability and harvesting, can be pruned to a height of ~1.2–2 m tall, and tied into supports. Generally, ~5–7 canes are allowed to develop annually from a plant. Too many canes per plant reduces overall quality and yield of fruits. Because this is a potentially invasive species, do not allow stems to self-root away from the main plant or for suckers to spread out too far. In the second year, the fruiting canes are simply left to flower and fruit, after which they naturally die back and are usually pruned out to keep the plant tidy and manageable. Remove prunings to reduce the risk of disease.

Propagation: *Seeds:* Will grow easily from seed. Seeds are washed free of pulp and are either sown in autumn and over-wintered in a cool place, or stored seeds germinate better if given 1–2 months of cold stratification at ~3°C before sowing in moist, well-drained compost, in early spring. Grow on seedlings in pots for ~1 year until large enough to plant out. *Cuttings:* Forms root buds that grow up to form new plants. Root cuttings can be taken in autumn or early spring, with at least one healthy bud; the root cuttings are potted up, and then allowed to establish before being planting out. Choose only disease-free plants to take cuttings from. Semi-ripe cuttings can be also taken from young canes in summer. These root better in a humid atmosphere. *Suckers:* The plant suckers readily, and these can be removed in early summer and will root easily. *Layering:* Stems can be easily layered by burying the stem tips in late summer/autumn around the parent plant. These should have rooted by the following spring/summer and can be removed from the parent plant.

Pests and diseases: Wineberries, although more resistant, may be susceptible to the same pests and diseases as raspberries, such as weevils, aphids; cane spot, spur blight, honey fungus, grey mould, silver leaf, thrips, gall midges, stink bugs and beetles, also the fungal diseases *Verticillium*, *Anthracnose* and leaf spot, and the bacterial disease, crown gall. Another problem is the fierce competition with wildlife for the fruit: it may be necessary to temporarily enclose the area in netting while the fruits ripen. ■

Saccharum officinarum
Sugar cane (noble cane)
POACEAE (Graminaea)

Sugar cane is a member of the grass family and is believed to be native to southern Asia. It is now grown in many parts of the tropics and subtropics worldwide. However, it can be grown as far as north as 36° (Spain) and as far south as 35° (northern New Zealand). Sugar cane was probably first cultivated >2000 years ago. Alexander the Great recorded sugar cultivation as early as 327 BC. In the Caribbean, it was introduced by Christopher Columbus in the late 15th century, but it was not until the 18th century that sugar-cane cultivation began in the USA. It is also an important crop in Queensland, Australia, the Caribbean, Cuba, the USA, Brazil, many parts of Africa, India and Thailand. The plant is a fast-growing tall grass with many stems (or canes). The sugar is derived from thick sap that fills the centre of the hollow canes. Sugar cane provides ~50% of the world's sugar, with sugar beet providing the remainder.

DESCRIPTION

It can grow 3–8 m tall and the stems (canes) are 2.5–7 cm in diameter, tending to be smaller in colder regions. The plant forms many hard, but juicy stems, with short lower internodes, where the leaf sheaths overlap those above. As the plant ages, these lower leaves often drop off.

Leaves: The plant forms clumps of canes, to which are attached long, graceful, lanceolate leaves (~4–6 cm wide), with a thick midrib. Stem colour varies between whitish, yellow, green, purple, red or violet.

Flowers: Has panicles (20–50 cm long) of numerous, feathery spikelets of inconspicuous flowers (~0.4 cm long), with silky hairs that are two to three times longer than the spikelet.

Yield/harvest: The time to harvest the canes varies with climate and cultivar, but is ~12–20 months after planting the rhizome. The canes become tough and turn pale yellow when ready for cutting. They are cut as close to the ground as possible because the base of the stem contains the most sugar. The rhizomatous plant will continue to crop for ~3–5 years, and sometimes >8 years. Young stems are covered with small prickles and should be handled carefully. Before crushing the cane, remove the leaves and cut the cane into shorter lengths. When grown on a small scale it can be harvested by squeezing out the sugar juice by passing the stem through a mangle or an old-style printing press, but does need something that can apply significant pressure. Spraying the cane with water helps dissolve additional juice. Extra sugar juice can be also extracted if the stem is passed through the crusher about three times with each crush set to increasingly finer settings. The resulting sugarcane liquid is green-grey in colour and can be somewhat acidic. Commercially, a milk of lime is added to the raw juice, then it is heated and left for precipitated material to separate out, which leaves a clear sugar juice. White cane sugar is made by adding other chemicals at this time. The resulting juice is then reduced to a thick syrup, and further boiled until the sugar crystallises out of the liquid. These are raw sugar crystals, which, commercially, are usually refined further.

CULTIVATION

If the soil and warmth are adequate, it is easy to grow a few clumps of sugar cane.

Location: Prefers a well-drained, sunny site. Will grow in relatively exposed locations.

Temperature: Grows best in a hot, humid climate that alternates with dry periods, though can grow in both moist and dry climates from warm-temperate through to tropical. Grows best at temperatures between 16–30°C, though can grow in cooler and hotter temperatures. Canes can be damaged by temperatures of ~–5°C, but this depends on the frequency and length of frost, as well as the cultivar. Prefers warm night temperatures because that is when stem elongation occurs, so although the plant still grows, sugar yields may be poor if nights are cool.

Soil/water: Likes a well-drained and very fertile soil, but can grow on a wide range of soils types: volcanic, alluvial, many tropical soils and even clay. Can grow at a wide pH range: 4.5–8.5, i.e. from fairly acidic to alkaline soils, although additions of lime are thought to increase the sugar content of canes. Regular additions of organic matter or fertiliser will substantially increase growth and yield. Can be grown in the same area for several years without problems. Sugar cane likes a good water supply, particularly when actively growing and can even tolerate occasional waterlogging. Weed control is very important, as competition can significantly reduce yield.

Propagation: Stem cuttings: This is the usual method. Sugar-cane sections can be planted vertically or horizontally

Food

Sugar is a carbohydrate that occurs naturally in every fruit and vegetable. It is the major product of photosynthesis. Carbohydrates provide energy, yet contain no fat. Although conflicting, there does seem to be growing evidence that diets high in sugar can cause disease, particularly diabetes (see glycaemic index on p. 40). However, sugar does have a place in our diets: it acts as a preservative in preserves and canning, it adds sweetness to many sour and bitter foods, and is necessary for brewing and fermentation. Like many foods, eaten in moderation, and in combination with other types of foods, it is probably fine, and can provide our bodies with a quick burst of energy. In its raw state the cane can be simply chewed, or it can be crushed and the liquid enjoyed as a drink or added to other food preparations.

Nutrition/medicinal

From sugar cane, ~13–20% of the sap is sucrose, and 1 m of cane can produce a glass of juice. Sugar is reported to be an antiseptic, a bactericide, a cardiotonic, a diuretic, a laxative, and to relieve irritation and aid digestive problems. It is a folk remedy for numerous complaints, many connected with chest infections and wounds on the body. *Warning:* Sugar in the diet has been proven to increase the rate of tooth decay. The plant contains hydrocyanic acid, which is known to cause damage to fetuses (and is known to cause somatic mutations in plants). Too much sugar in the diet may cause diabetes and other health problems.

Other uses

The leaves make a good compost. Commercially, the plants produce huge amounts of biomass, apart from the sugar obtained, and there is research into the different uses for this material, including biofuels (for example, in Queensland, Australia), which can be used to generate electricity, make paper and be used as fuel for cars. The quality of its biofuel is quite high. The stems can be made into pens, mats, screens and baskets.

Ornamental

It can be grown as a shelter-belt in situations that are not too exposed, and makes an attractive, exotic-looking plant. It is relatively easy to control.

in the ground and will root and sprout from the internodes. Select sections of cane that have healthy buds and, if planting vertically, bury as much stem (at least) as is left above ground. This is best done in spring, and then the cane sections should be kept moist. Shorter or longer sections of cane can be used: whole canes can be laid in trenches. Space plants at ~0.5–1 m apart. *Division:* Plants can also be divided and sections planted with the tops of the shoots removed until the roots have developed.

Pests and diseases: Small plantings are unlikely to suffer problems, but commercially, sugarcane is susceptible to a number of viruses and can also be attacked by a number of fungi and nematodes. It is best to select healthy, disease-free vegetative material for propagation.

CULTIVARS
There are many commercial cultivars, but the wild cane from Asia (*S. spontaneum*) is used as the basis for other hybrids. ∎

Sambucus spp.
Elderberry
CAPRIFOLIACEAE

Common or European elderberry (*Sambucus nigra*), American elderberry (*S. canadensis*), blue elderberry (*S. caerula*), Mexican elder (*S. mexicana*), red elderberry (*S. pubens*, *S. racemosa*)

Relatives: honeysuckle

This genus consists of ~40 species of hardy deciduous shrubs and small trees, usually with pinnate leaves, panicles of numerous small flowers and many small berries. The name *Sambucus* may be derived from the Latin (as used by Pliny) for the name of an instrument, the 'sambuke'.

Common or European elderberry, *Sambucus nigra*
The main elderberry species is *Sambucus nigra*, which is native and common within Europe and the UK and is found growing wild along hedgerows, edges of woodlands and on waste ground. Elderberry fruits and flowers have been used for many thousands of years, with the fruits traditionally made into juice, preserves and wines, and the whole plant is important medicinally. There is an old saying that 'he who cultivates elderberry will die in his own bed'! The fruits were used in Neolithic times, and then later in Ancient Greece. The Romans introduced the plant into Britain and elsewhere. Traditionally it was revered for its magical powers, but was also unfairly associated with sorrow and death, as it was believed that it was the tree that Christ was crucified from, which is highly unlikely. In contrast, the Russians and English believed the trees drove away evil spirits. In Denmark it was regarded as having magical properties and that if one stood beneath an elder tree on mid-summer's eve, one would see the King of Fairyland ride by. It was not often (and still isn't) cultivated widely in Europe as it is so commonly found in the wild. *S. nigra* can be grown as a shrub, or can be trained into a small tree; it is easy to grow and needs little maintenance. *S canadensis*, the American elderberry, originates from northern America, and looks similar to *S. nigra* (see below). *S. caerulea*, the blue elderberry, and *S. mexicana,* are similar species, with the latter originating from warmer climates. They have bright blue fruits. There is also a red-fruiting elderberry (see below).

DESCRIPTION
A large, vigorous, multi-stemmed shrub, which can be trained to form a small tree to 6 m (or taller), spread 1–2 m. Stems often hollow or contain a soft pith, which can be easily pushed out. Younger stems have distinctive warty lenticels, whereas older wood matures to form corky, fissured reddish-yellowy bark. It is a fast-growing tree.

Leaves: Deciduous, long, pinnate, medium green, 5–15 cm long, similar to walnut leaves. Leaflets number 5–11, in opposite pairs with a terminal leaflet. They are oval, tapering at the base with a tipped apex, and the margins are lightly toothed. The leaves and stem have a strong smell when crushed that some find unpleasant. One of the first to come into leaf in spring. Can have good yellow autumn colour.

Flowers: Distinctive, strongly musky–sweet scented, large, flat-topped, creamy clusters (10–16 cm wide) of many small flowers, which often cover the shrub in late spring–early summer. Each flower consists of five sepals, five petals and five stamens, with a central ovary. The flowers are bisexual, and plants are self-fertile, although more than one plant can increase fruit-set and yield. *Pollination:* Mostly by flies and other insects.

Fruit: Trees are covered by numerous flat, wide clusters of many, small (~0.3–0.5 cm diameter), dark purple to black, juicy berries. The skin is edible, and moderately thick for the size of the fruit. The fruits are filled with a very dark, purple, juicy pulp, which is sweet and tasty when ripe. They have 3–5 small, hard, black seeds in the middle that are edible.

Yield/harvest: Trees can produce good yields of fruits. Fruits take 60–90 days to mature after fruit-set, and are harvested in late summer–early autumn. Pick by cutting off the clusters. Remove the berries using the tines of a fork to dislodge them. The fruits do not keep for long and need to be eaten or processed within a day or two.

Roots: Elderberries form fast-growing, shallow, fibrous root systems that benefit from an organic mulch to retain moisture and add nutrients. Avoid deep cultivation in their vicinity.

CULTIVATION

Cultivation is easy and trees need minimal maintenance.

Location: Grows in sun or light shade. Can tolerate moderate wind and some air pollution. Not very suited to salty conditions.

Soil/water/nutrients: Elderberries grow best in sandy loam soils, but will tolerate a wide range of conditions, even some poor drainage, though not extended periods of waterlogging. They grow better in moist soils, and like an organic mulch or the addition of well-rotted manure. Can tolerate a wide pH range of soils, even alkaline soils. Benefit from 1–2 additions a year of a balanced complete fertiliser.

Planting: Space plants at 2–5 m apart; they can be planted close together to form a screen or an informal hedge. Do not plant trees >20 m apart if cross fertilisation is required.

Propagation: *Seed:* Either sow seed when it is fresh in a cool seedbed, or sow in spring, although the seed germinates better after a period (60–90 days) of cold stratification before sowing. In addition, it has a hard seedcoat that may benefit from being soaked in warm water for several hours or scarified (scratching or scoring) before sowing. Seeds should be sown just below the soil surface. Germination can be erratic, with some seeds germinating in a few weeks, whereas others may take 12 months or more. Seeds stay viable for many years if dried and stored at 5°C. Grow on seedlings for a year or two before planting out. *Cuttings:* Semi-ripe cuttings, with a heel, taken in summer should root well. Hardwood cuttings taken in autumn (25–30 cm long), with three double buds should also root. Plant the latter so that only the top pair are above the soil surface. Cuttings may root better if dusted with rooting powder. Given warmth and moisture, cuttings can root in 14–21 days. *Suckers.* Trees often produce suckers and these can be removed during the growing season and established in pots before planting out.

Pruning: Prune to prevent the shrub becoming invasive. Cut back plants severely and they will regrow; some cut plants right back to the ground in some years. Fruit is produced on the current season's wood. Once established, new stems can grow >2 m in a single season. Cutting down older stems in autumn produces lots of vigorous new stems in spring. Plants are sometimes pruned to five or six 1-year-old shoots, and only one or two 2-year-old stems are left. Trees can be left multi-stemmed or can be pruned to form a single-stemmed tree.

Pests and diseases: Pests and diseases are rarely a problem, though plants can get occasional attacks by aphids.

CULTIVARS

There are several attractive ornamental cultivars, e.g. with golden-coloured leaves. A subspecies, *S. nigra fructo-lutea*, has yellow fruits. There is also a recently introduced English cultivar, 'Gerda' that has very striking purple-black leaves, large panicles (~25 cm diameter) of pink flowers, with a lemon fragrance, and dark purple, tasty berries.

OTHER SPECIES

American elderberry, *Sambucus canadensis* (syn. *S. simpsonii*). A small, fast-growing, multi-stemmed tree to ~3 m tall (spread 2–3 m) that is native to the USA. Of similar

Food

The berries and flowers of the black-fruited *S. nigra* have been used for hundreds of years as a food, have been used in various drinks and for various medicinal purposes. Elderberry wine is an old favourite and is easy to make. The flowers can also be used to make a splendid, refreshing, fizzy cordial for hot summer days. They also make a bubbly, tasty white wine. Fruit can be also used in pies, sauces and jelly. The flowers have an appealing mild floral flavour and are often used in pancakes, or dipped in batter and fried. Can combine the fruit with rhubarb in cooking and can cook the flowers with gooseberries.

Nutrition/medicinal

Have good levels of vitamins A (~870 IU), C (50 mg/100 mg of flesh), B6, iron and potassium, and are a very good source of dietary fibre (40% of the fruit is fibre). Also contains some thiamine, riboflavin and niacin. The fruits contain a wide range of amino acids and good levels of many flavonoids, including quercetin and rutin. The berries and flowers have been long known to cure colds, fevers and flu. Recently, the fruit have been shown to inhibit the replication of several human influenza viruses. A trial in Israel showed that >90% of people who ate elderberries, and who had contracted flu rapidly, found relief from the fever and other flu symptoms several days sooner than people just taking a placebo. It was remarked that elderberries had successfully treated influenza A and B, and that no standard medication was able to do this. The fruits and flowers have also been used to treat headaches, rheumatism and urinary infections. The flowers also have anti-inflammatory properties. A tea made from the leaves and young shoots has been used as a diuretic (but see warning below). The flowers and fruits of this species are quite safe to eat. **Warning:** Fruits from related species that are red, or unripe fruits, leaves and other parts of the plant may be dangerously purgative and should not be ingested. There are also contradictory reports that fruits from the American species, if cooked, are then quite safe to eat. The fruits of the European species are perfectly safe.

Other uses

The wood is light, fine and white, and is used to make delicate instruments.

Ornamental

Trees can be planted to form windbreaks and screens. They are useful in areas that need soil stabilisation. Lots of wildlife are attracted to the flowers and berries.

appearance to *S. nigra*, it can grow vigorously and can tend to sucker. It is fully cold hardy and moderately drought tolerant. It has panicles of flowers (15–20 cm wide) that are more dome-shaped than those of *S. nigra*, and are borne in late spring–early summer, after *S. nigra*. They have many purple-black fruits in autumn. The fruits are probably quite safe to eat fresh, but because of contradictory reports, it may be safer to cook them before use.

Blue elderberry (tapiro), *Sambucus caerula* (syn. *S. cerulea*, *S. coerulea*). Plants are similar in appearance to *S. nigra*, but have bright blue fruits. This species is very similar to *S. mexicana*, and they are often described as a single species, though *S. caerula* is more cold hardy. It is native to the warmer temperate regions of northwest North America, though tolerates temperatures down to ~−10°C. It is a self-fertile tree. It is much more drought tolerant than *S. nigra* or *S. canadensis*. It can be grown in full sun or partial shade. Trees can grow in many soil types, including clay, and can tolerate some waterlogging. It has panicles of creamy-white flowers. The berries are usually cooked and added to pies, jelly, etc., and are said to have a fairly good flavour. They can also be used to make wine.

Mexican elder, *Sambucus mexicana*. A small tree, very similar to *S. caerula*, but grows in warmer regions and is not as cold hardy. It is drought hardy once established. It has bright blue berries that are edible, though may be better cooked beforehand, and are often used in pies, to make wine, etc.

Red elderberries (scarlet elderberries), *Sambucus pubens*, *S. racemosa*. Similar to the species described above and are very ornamental, with bright red berries in autumn. *S. pubens* is a native of North America and *S. racemosa* is a native of eastern Europe and western Asia. The red fruits from these species are reported to be toxic and should not be eaten, although some reports say they are edible after being cooked. ■

Santalum acuminatum
Quandong (desert quandong, Australian native peach, sweet quandong, goorti, katanga, burn-burn, mangata)
SANTALACEAE
Similar species: Quandong, bush plum, wild plum (*S. lanceolatum*), Australian sandalwood (*S. spicatum*)
Relatives: sandalwood

The *Santalum* genus contains the aromatic sandalwood tree. Members of this genus are root parasites: their roots attach to the roots of other species and tap into their phloem vessels to 'steal' the host's sugars, water and nutrients. Often, members of this species, such as sandalwood, kill their host over the long term. However, it seems as though quandong is more lenient with its host and the latter struggles through. Because of their parasitic habits, quandongs seem to be difficult to propagate; they do not grow at all from cuttings, and with difficulty from seed. They are best established in cultivation with host plants such as various grass species. Quandongs are native to the drier parts of Australia, and fossilised quandongs have been discovered in the coal seams of Victoria, Australia. These seams have been dated to ~40 million years ago, when Australia was still linked to the Antarctic continent. The Aborigines used, and still do use, the red, tart fruits of the quandong and they gave it its name. After the early settlers learnt of its use as a food, they would take their families out for a quandong picnic, when the fruit was in season. The ripe fruit would be gathered, peeled and then used to make jams, chutneys and quandong pies. It was a valuable fruit during droughts and when times were hard. More recently, with a revival in interest in Australian bush-food, the quandong is being rediscovered and small-scale cultivation is rapidly developing, with the fruit being used in an increasing number of exciting food products. Its ability to grow in arid, salty soils is being explored in Australia so that it can be cultivated where few other commercial plants are possible. Its species name, *Santalum*, is derived from the Greek 'santalon' and the Arabic 'sandal' for the aromatic scent of its wood. Quandong should not be confused with the bitter quandong (*S. murrayanum*). Several species are commonly called quandong within Australia, and these range from large buttressed trees to smaller shrubs.

DESCRIPTION
Desert quandong is a small shapely tree or shrub, ~3–6 m tall, spread 2–3 m. It forms an erect plant with a dense, leathery crown of leaves. The bark is light brown and slightly furrowed. It is a partial root parasite.

   Leaves: Evergreen, paired, narrow, thick, leathery, lance-shaped with a curved point, olive-green, 4–15 cm long, 4–12 mm wide, opposite, on a short stalk. Older leaves have prominent veins. There are two main flushes of leaf growth, in spring and late summer.

Flowers: Small (0.2–0.4 cm), green-white, fragrant, in late summer–autumn, but also throughout the year in warmer areas. They are borne in clusters on short, pyramid-shaped panicles, on 1-year-old wood. Each flower has four segments, which remain attached to the ripe fruit. *Pollination:* Mostly by bees, wasps and other insects, but self-incompatibility is a problem, and it is best to plant more than one plant to encourage pollination and fruit production.

Fruit: Greenish-yellow fruits that ripen to orange to pink–maroon from late winter into spring, and are available when there are few other fresh fruits. They are round, shiny, waxy and ~2.5 cm in diameter. There is not much flesh around the seed, but it is firm and has a tart, apricot-peach flavour. The flesh is white or pale brown when ripe. They have a single, large, knobbly, rounded, hard, tan-coloured, central seed, 1–3 cm in diameter. The seedcoat is hard and difficult to remove, but the kernel inside is often tasty, and can be eaten fresh or roasted, though some seeds are bitter.

Harvest/yield: Trees take 4–5 years to produce fruits after pollination. It takes ~4–6 months for fruits to mature, usually in late winter–early spring. If the plants receive too much moisture as they ripen, the fruit skins tend to split. Fruits can be gathered just after they have dropped from the trees and when the seed can be heard rattling inside. Fruit yields vary, but a 10-year-old tree can produce 2.2–4.5 kg of fruits. Some 15-year-old trees, growing in optimum conditions, have produced 15 kg of fruits in a season. Fresh fruits do not have a long storage life, and are usually processed quickly if picked for drying or freezing.

Roots: Has long, spreading roots that grow outwards to find those of another tree, which it then parasitises. It penetrates the host's roots to take its moisture and nutrients. It will readily parasitise a wide variety of plants. It is, therefore, probably best not to grow quandong too near other plants you value! However, sacrificial plants can be planted, e.g. an invasive grass such as kikuyu, for it to live off. It seems to do best with a host plant that has surface roots, tends to store water or is nutrient hungry, e.g. acacias and casuarinas. It also has a long taproot, so take great care not to damage or handle the roots.

CULTIVATION

Once established, these are tough plants, and have evolved to survive in harsh environments. Given a reasonable soil, moisture and nutrients they can grow very well: growth rates of ~1 m a year have been recorded.

Location: In its native environment the quandong grows well in arid and semi-arid areas, and can fruit without extra water. It grows best in areas with hot, dry summers and cool, wetter winters. It likes an open, sunny position, though does grow in light woodland. It can tolerate soils with high salinity levels, so could be grown in maritime locations.

Temperature: It is relatively frost resistant, though can be injured by heavy frost. It can grow surprisingly well in a wide range of temperatures, from very hot (~40°C) to quite cool, and tolerates temperatures down to near freezing.

Soil/water/nutrients: It is very drought tolerant and grows readily in dry, stony or sandy soils. It will get some of its water needs through its host's roots. It does not grow well in wet soils, and becomes susceptible to root disease.

However, it does not mind brackish water. It also seems to not mind the soil type it grows in (sand or gravel), probably because it is able to get virtually all its water and nutrients from its host. However, if quandongs are regularly watered and given reasonable soil they will grow and fruit very well. When carrying out weed control, remember that many herbicides can be translocated from the weeds around the plant to any root connections with quandong. Other methods are probably safer, although even physical weeding can cause breakages of links with the host plant and reduce the

Food
Fruits can be eaten fresh, but are somewhat acid. They are more usually dried or processed. They have a tart apricot/guava/peach/rhubarb flavour, some say even like a good red wine. The best fruits are a rich red colour, with white or cream flesh. Aborigines dried them and stored them in the hollows of trees for many years. The fruits can be easily dried or frozen for 8+ years. They can then be soaked with sugar and reconstituted without any loss of flavour. They are often stewed with sugar, water and orange juice, then left overnight and served with icecream or used in pies or tarts. The fruits are also made into a delicious jam with ginger, into dipping sauces, or added to pies, liqueurs, chutney, confectionery and jellies. They have been combined with peaches, figs, bananas or fresh ginger in both sweet and savoury dishes, giving a unique fruity flavour to many recipes. They are also pickled, used as a glaze, made into a syrup or coated in chocolate. The kernels from most desert quandong trees are delicious when dry roasted and have a good almond flavour, but each one has to be removed from its hard seedcoat. These kernels can be used in dishes where other nuts would be used. **Warning:** The seeds from similar species can be bitter, and contain methyl benzoate.

Nutrition
The flesh is rich in vitamin C (~six times that of oranges) and has high levels of potassium. The kernels contain ~60% oil and 25% protein.

Medicinal
The leaves have been used internally as a purgative, or as an ointment for sores and boils. The roots were dried, ground and used to treat rheumatism. The crushed kernels have been used to treat skin problems.

Other uses
The wood of the quandong, not surprisingly, gives off an aromatic scent when burnt. Its heartwood is hard, close-grained and pinkish; it is excellent for cabinet-making and polishes up beautifully.

Ornamental
Is a tough, attractive ornamental species, especially for dry, hot gardens.

quandong's growth. They can grow in slightly acidic to quite alkaline soils, though iron chlorosis can occur in very alkaline soil, which can be remedied by applying foliar chelated micronutrients. Plants can tolerate very-poor nutrient soils, although occasional applications of a balanced, complete fertiliser will increase growth and fruit yields.

Planting: Space plants at 3–4 m apart in spring. Quandongs can be difficult to establish, but the main reason for this seems to be root disturbance. Minimise any disturbance of the long taproot and grow seedlings in deep biodegradable pots. Do not transplant plants once they are established. When planting out, the quandong and the host should both be planted at the same time, e.g. kikuyu grass, lucerne or other prostrate plants. And, depending on the host, these might need pruning or cutting back so they do not out-compete the quandong till it is established. (Do not choose host plants that grow too vigorously.) Although quandongs are adapted to growth in arid and semi-arid conditions, young plants should be kept moist until they are established (~12 months).

Pruning: Just need minimal pruning to establish the tree's shape. It can be pruned to form a single stem. Also prune out branches with narrow angles between them, which are liable to break, and remove closely crossing branches. Once the tree is established, pruning need only consist of tidying up and the removal of dead or diseased wood.

Propagation: *Seed:* This is the usual method, but the hard seedcoat needs to be pre-treated before sowing. It is best to use seeds that have been cross fertilised rather than seeds collected from isolated trees. It is recommended to sow seed when it is more than 1 year old. Scarification is usually practised: lightly score the hard seedcoat with a file or similar, or seeds can be soaked in a weak acid or bleach for 2 hours. (Rinse any residue from the seeds before sowing.) Seeds are then placed in damp sand and kept at ~18°C, in the dark, until germination takes place in 3–8 weeks. Germination can be erratic, though the addition of gibberelin to the germinating seeds may help. Seeds often succumb to mould. Pot up seedlings in deep pots (to avoid having to repot them as they grow larger) for ~12 months with a host plant, or seedlings can be placed directly with an established host plant, although there is then a greater risk of the latter taking over. Trials have been conducted to grow quandongs without a host, but they do not seem to grow well. Seedling trees are variable and take several years before they start to yield fruits. *Cuttings:* They will not grow from cuttings. *Grafting:* This is the only way to vegetatively grow this species and, therefore, to be able to predict the progeny. In addition, trees start to fruit sooner than seedling-grown trees. Cleft-grafting is a popular method. They can be grafted to a sandalwood rootstock and may grow faster on these than on a quandong rootstock.

Pests and diseases: The quandong moth in Australia is the crop's most significant pest, and damages the flowers. Other minor pests are caterpillars, a leaf hopper, scale insects and mites. Fungal diseases can kill trees, such as *Phytophthora* and *Pythium*, and these occur particularly in wet soils. Snails, rabbits, etc. may attack young plants.

CULTIVARS

'Frahn's Paringa Gem': From South Australia. Is a compact, vigorous tree, and is non-suckering. Fruit: rich, cherry-red, pale flesh. A high flesh-to-stone ratio, with a good quandong flavour. Resistant to quandong moth and skin splitting. High yields, precocious.

'Powell's No.1': From South Australia. The tree is vigorous, healthy, with a pendulous habit. Fruit: deep red, round, medium–large, fine-textured flesh, good flavour. Resists skin splitting and the seeds are easy to remove.

SIMILAR SPECIES

Quandong (sandalwood, bush plum, wild plum), *Santalum lanceolatum*. A species native to northern Australia, it forms a bush, ~3 m tall, which grows in arid, sandy areas as well as grasslands. Its leaves are suited to hot, dry areas and are euclayptus-like in shape, colour and drooping habit. The fruits, 1–1.5 cm diameter, are green, changing to red and then to a dark purple-black when ripe. The flesh is a rich, dark red, and surrounds a large central stone. The fruits can be eaten fresh, and have a sweet–sub-acid flavour.

Australian sandalwood, *Santalum spicatum*. The outer flesh of the fruit is too thin to be eaten, but the kernel shell is thinner than that of quandong, and the seed is larger and is reported to have a good taste and flavour. The timber of this tree is used in Australia. ■

Schisandra chinensis (syn. *S. japonica*, *Kadsura chinensis*)

Schisandra (magnolia vine, wu wei zi)

SCHISANDRACEAE

Similar species: Schisandra (*Schisandra grandiflora rubiflora* syn. *S. rubiflora*)

Schisandra is a member of the Schisandraceae family and is a native of northeastern China and the former Soviet Union. It is grown and highly valued in these areas, mainly for its medicinal properties. Its Chinese name is wu wei zi, which means 'five-taste fruit', derived from its mix of sour, sweet, bitter, warm and salty tastes. In China, it is cultivated for its fruits, but these are also often harvested from the wild. It forms an attractive vine, with fragrant flowers and edible red berries. It is also grown as an ornamental plant in many gardens throughout the world.

DESCRIPTION

A non-invasive, attractive, woody, twining vine that winds its way clockwise around branches. It can grow to ~8 m.

Leaves: Deciduous, long, dark green, elliptic–egg-shaped, leathery, with a lemony scent. It has red stems.

Flowers: Fragrant, small, numerous, white–pale pink, in drooping clusters of 2–3 bowl-shaped flowers formed from leaf axils. Thick, waxy petals. Flowers in late spring. *Pollination:* Plant is usually dioecious, so more than one plant is needed to get fruit-set.

Fruit: Has bright, attractive, small red–orange berries (~7 cm diameter) that grow in grape-like clusters (~10 cm long). They ripen in autumn and can persist on the vine into winter. They have an acid–sweet, pleasantly aromatic taste.

Harvest: Pick the berries when they are fully orange–red. They ripen over a period of several weeks, so need to be picked several times during the season. Vines start producing fruits ~3 years after planting.

Roots: As with many climbers, they grow better if their roots are kept cool and in the shade.

CULTIVATION

These are hardy, easy-to-grow, non-invasive vines. Their growth needs are similar to those of grapes.

Location: Plant in sun or semi-shade in cooler regions against a protected wall or trellis. In warmer areas, they grow better in semi- or deeper shade. Are not wind tolerant, or very tolerant of salty conditions.

Temperature: Hardy and can tolerate frosts: survives temperatures down to ~–15°C.

Soil and water: Vines grow best on fertile, well-drained, but moisture-retentive soils. However, they can grow on a range of soils. Prefer a soil pH of somewhat acid to neutral: not too alkaline. Add humus to more alkaline soils before planting. Annual additions of organic mulch will benefit growth and help retain soil moisture. You will need to water plants during dry periods in the summer; they are not drought tolerant.

Planting: Space plants ~0.75–1 m apart and allow them to grow up a fence, trellis, arbour, etc. They can be planted with the same wire system as grapes. Tie plants onto their

Food
The fruits can be eaten fresh, and have a sweet-sour flavour. Or can be used in desserts, jams, preserves, sauces, etc., or can be dried for later use. The Chinese eat them fresh, or mix them with vinegar or honey, steam them, and then dry them in the sun for later use. Dried thus, they are later sweetened and added to desserts, sauces, juices and preserves. The dried fruits are said to be very sustaining, and are eaten by the Chinese on long journeys. The young leaves can be lightly cooked and used as a vegetable.

Nutrition
Fruits have good levels of vitamin C. They also contain vitamin E, magnesium and potassium. The seeds contain various compounds, including lignans, which make up ~20% by weight of the seed (and includes a compound called schizandrin); these are thought to be responsible for its medicinal actions.

Medicinal
Extracts from schisandra are used in many medical products. The plant is very well known in China, and also Russia, and has been used for many hundreds of years to treat many complaints, e.g. asthma, many respiratory ailments, rheumatism, diarrhoea, insomnia, impotence and kidney problems. In China, it is one of the fifty fundamental herbs. It is said to increase male stamina and increase the female's excitability. Hunters and athletes have used schisandra to increase endurance and combat fatigue under physical stress and to give clarity. It is said to help both short- and long-term memory and, in China, is known as a 'smart herb'. It is said to help the body handle stress, and to increase zest for life. It is sometimes taken with ginseng. The lignans seem to have a protective effect on the liver and improve its function and stimulate liver-cell regrowth. It has been used in China to successfully treat hepatitis, with no side effects. It is thought to act by activating the enzymes in liver cells that produce glutathione, which is an important antioxidant. The seeds are used in the treatment of cancer. **Warning:** Although studies have found schisandra to be relatively non-toxic, large doses have very occasionally resulted in an upset stomach, hives, appetite suppression, a rash or heartburn.

Other uses
A mucilaginous product obtained from the fruits and stems is used to size paper and in hair dressing. The dried wood has a lovely fragrance.

Ornamental
It is a hardy, easy-to-manage, attractive and useful ornamental vine to cover trellises, posts, etc.

uses

supporting structure until growth is established.

Propagation: *Seed:* Germination rate and number varies. Seeds are best sown fresh, in autumn, in a cold frame. If seed is stored over winter, soak it in warm water for ~12 hours before sowing in a warm, moist compost in spring. *Cuttings:* Fairly successful. Take ripe or semi-ripe cuttings, with a heel, in summer and insert into a gritty sand/compost mix, preferably with some bottom heat. Pot up cuttings that have rooted and grow them on with protection for the first year or two. *Layering:* Is possible in autumn from stems near the ground. Takes ~12 months to root.

Pruning: Any pruning should be done in late winter or early spring. The type and amount of pruning will depend on what structure they are being grown on and what effect/ result is required. For ornamental growth, limited pruning is required, just to remove straggly and damaged stems, and to encourage new growth to cover structures, etc. For fruit production, excess stem and leaf growth should be reduced by pruning to encourage development of fruiting laterals.

Pests and diseases: Generally, there are few problems, except for aphids.

CULTIVAR
'Eastern Prince': Has pink flowers and red fruits.

SIMILAR SPECIES

Schisandra grandiflora rubiflora (syn. S. rubiflora). Also commonly know as schisandra, this is a smaller plant than *S. chinensis*, growing to only ~5 m. A moderately fast-growing vine with attractive scarlet flowers (~2.5 cm diameter) in spring, and red fruits in autumn. A little less hardy than *S. chinensis*: tolerating temperatures down to ~−12°C. It may not have the same medicinal properties as *S. chinensis*. It is a popular ornamental species. ■

Sclerocarya caffra (syn. *S. birrea*)
Marula
ANACARDIACEAE
Relatives: mango, cashew, pistachio, ambarella, poison ivy

The 60 genera of Anacardiaceae consist of ~600 species of trees and shrubs that are mostly native to tropical and warm-temperate regions of Europe, eastern Asia, Africa and the Americas. Many species are cultivated commercially for their timber, lacquer, oil, wax and dyes, and also for their edible fruits or nuts. Archaeological remains indicate that the marula fruits were known and enjoyed by peoples in Africa as long ago as 10,000 BC. The marula is a medium to large, deciduous tree that produces vivid red flowers, and is highly valued for its tasty fruits and kernels, with the latter becoming increasingly used as an ingredient in alcoholic drinks. The tree occurs naturally and is also cultivated in eastern and southern Africa, often in moister regions. It has been introduced into other regions of the world, including Australia. The genus name *Sclerocarya* is derived from the Greek words 'skleros' and 'karyon', meaning 'hard' and 'nut', respectively, and refers to the hard stone of the fruit.

DESCRIPTION
A medium to large tree, usually 9–12 m tall, but in optimum locations it can reach 18 m tall, with a dense, spreading crown. It has a single, short (~4 m), stout (up to ~1.2 m width) trunk. The bark is grey and often peels off in flat, round disks, to expose younger, pale yellow bark beneath. Trees are fairly fast growing, reaching ~3 m in 8 years, with adequate moisture and temperatures.

Leaves: Deciduous, alternate, ~20 cm long from the ends of branches. They are pinnate and consist of ~11 (but can be 5–23) elliptical leaflets, which are dark grey-green above, paler and bluish-green beneath, often changing to pale yellow in autumn. In cooler regions, trees lose all their leaves in autumn but, in warmer regions, they may only lose half of their leaves annually.

Flower: Flowers are borne in unbranched sprays, each strand being 5–8 cm long. Trees are usually dioecious, although are occasionally monoecious. So, will need more than one tree to be sure of setting good crops of fruit. Male flowers are borne in clusters of threes from leaf axils of new leaves, and are dark red when young, turning pink–white when open. Female flowers are borne below new leaves on long flower stalks, on the current season's growth. Initially, they have four, deep red petals, which change to purple, and then white after opening. They have numerous infertile stamens and a long, shiny ovary. Flowering takes place in the dry season, in southern Africa, in spring. The flowers live for ~8–10 days, and can be produced over a period of 3 months.

Fruit: Female trees bear clusters of ~3 plum-sized fruits at the ends of twigs, on new growth. Fruits are round–oval drupes, often wider than they are long, diameter ~3–4 cm. When ripe, the thick, soft, leathery peel becomes a rich yellow colour. The flesh is translucent, white, juicy and highly aromatic. It is delicious, sweet–sour and refreshing, although very over-ripe fruits have a turpentine-like aroma. The flesh clings tightly to a central, 2–3-cm-long, hard stone, surrounded by fibrous flesh that is difficult to remove. The stone is divided into 1–4 cavities or sections, with each section containing a single, edible kernel. The kernel is covered by a hard lid that remains attached until germination.

Yield/harvest: Reasonable yields of ~30 kg per tree can be obtained, although some reports claim yields of ~500 kg per tree, or 70,000 fruits on a single tree! An average fruit weighs 28 g, but some can be considerably heavier. Trees can start to bear fruits in their fourth year. Fruits take 3–4 months to ripen, and mature at the beginning of the rainy season, which, in Africa, is from mid summer till early autumn. However, the fruits drop before they are fully ripe, and are still green in colour with firm flesh. To fully ripen, fruits need to be placed in a polythene bag with other ripe fruits, e.g. bananas, for ethylene production, which hastens the ripening process. They should be kept moderately warm during this time until they are completely yellow. Fruits left to ripen in cool conditions are less sweet and juicy. Ripe fruits are best eaten fresh or preserved; they do not store well and quickly ferment. They should be stored in a cool place, but not in a fridge, as they can suffer cold damage at 4°C.

Roots: Has a thick, relatively short taproot (~2.5 m long) and surface lateral roots that grow in the top 60 cm of soil, but can extend outwards as far as 30 m. It forms a symbiotic mycorrhizal association between fungi and its finer roots, which enables it to obtain extra nutrients, particularly phosphates. Because of its taproot, transplanting should be done carefully to avoid damage. Also, mechanical cultivation should be limited to avoid damaging surface roots. A mulch will help retain moisture and add nutrients.

CULTIVATION
Grows best in warm temperate or semi-tropical regions. They naturally grow on hillsides, lightly wooded grassland or on arid lands.

Location: Grows best in a sunny location. It is highly salt tolerant, and is excellent for maritime locations. It is quite wind tolerant. Best not planted too close to buildings, etc. due to its spreading root system.

Temperature: Are not very frost hardy, and can be seriously damaged at temperatures less than ~–7°C, but seem to tolerate short-term cold temperatures or light frosts. Frost-damaged trees often resume growth in spring, but may become multi-stemmed if branches have been killed back; they also tend to form new sprouts from the base of the trunk. It is possible that hardening the trees before winter, by withholding irrigation, may increase their tolerance to cold. Grows best in regions with relatively warm winters and hot summers.

Soils/water/nutrients: Prefers well-drained sandy soils and loams, although will grow in clays. The tree is very drought resistant, and is not tolerant of any waterlogging. It is not very nutrient hungry, though would benefit from some additional nutrients on very poor soils.

Propagation: Seed: This is the usual method. Seed can be sown fresh. However, the seed is hard and benefits from scarification with a file, or similar, or soaking for a couple of

Food
The fruit is aromatic, and the flesh has a flavour similar to lychee–apple–guava–pineapple. The fruits are eaten fresh, or used in juices, jams and jellies. They may be dried for later use. The flesh is used to brew beer, and a spirit is also distilled from it. A rapid alcoholic drink is made by removing the stone, and adding 50% volume of water to the pulp. After 24 hours it is strained and ready to drink, though by 4 days it has deteriorated too far. The delicious 'Amarula Cream' is made from the sweetened, fermented, distilled flesh. This tree is now grown commercially for the production of various alcoholic drinks. The kernels within the central stone can be eaten; they have a delicate nutty taste, and are either eaten fresh or the oil is used in cooking or dressings.

Nutrition/medicinal
The fruits are high in vitamin C: ~65 mg/100 g of flesh. The flesh also contains useful amounts of magnesium, potassium and phosphates, as well as citric and malic acids and fruit sugars. The seeds are nutritious and contain ~60% oil, which is of good quality, is non-drying and is mostly unsaturated. The kernels are also high in protein (~30%) and contain iodine. The bark, which has high levels of tannins (~20%), has been used to treat circulatory and digestive problems, as well as fevers, inflammation, diarrhoea, and has been used as an analgesic and an antiseptic.

Other uses
The wood is soft and, unfortunately, can warp when dried, though is used for utensils and carving. The kernel oil has been used in lamps. The oil is also used in soap, skin moisturisers, sun screen, medicines, to treat insect bites and as an insecticide. The gum secreted from the stems and trunk can be used to make an ink by dissolving it in water and then adding soot.

Ornamental
The flowers are a nectar source for bees. The tree makes a good ornamental, specimen, shade tree.

hours in weak acid or bleach (and then thoroughly rinsing the seeds). There is some evidence that stored seed germinates quicker. Seeds can take up to 9 months to germinate, but germination rates can then be good: 70–85%. *Cuttings:* Long cuttings, ~2 m in length, are planted at a depth of ~1 m, in summer. Root cuttings can be taken in summer, and these easily develop new shoots.

Pruning: Trees can be coppiced in warmer regions in autumn, and regenerate rapidly, but you will lose many potential fruiting branches.

Pests and diseases: Generally few disease or pest problems. ∎

Shepherdia argentea
Buffalo berry
ELAEAGNACEAE

Similar species: soapberry (*S. canadensis*)

Relatives: autumn olive, sea buckthorn, oleaster

Although the buffalo berry is from the Elaeagnaceae family it is not an *Elaeagnus* species. It is a native of the Great Plains of the USA and across Western Canada, but is also found growing in areas down to the heat of New Mexico. Its name is thought to be derived from the indigenous Indian practice of using the fruits in a sauce that was eaten with buffalo meat; alternatively, they may have been named after bisons, who ate the plants and used them for shelter along the watercourses of the plains. It has been, and still is occasionally cultivated for its edible fruit, and the fruits have been commercially made into jams and jellies. Its popularity is undergoing a revival.

DESCRIPTION

An ornamental, silvery shrub or small tree, growing at a medium rate to 2–6 m tall, ~4 m spread. Branches tend to grow at right angles. It has silvery, smooth younger stems, which turn grey-brown as they mature, and become rougher and darker with age. The bark sometimes shreds into long strips. Many sharp spines occur on older and younger wood.

uses

Food
Fruits can be eaten fresh or cooked, or can be dried and used like currants. Fruits vary in quality from plant to plant, but are generally tangy, tart but pleasant in flavour, and become sweeter after a frost. Yellow fruits are usually sweeter. They are reported to make an excellent jelly. They can be used in juices, desserts (fresh and cooked), preserves, etc.

Nutrition/medicinal
The fruits are very high in vitamin C, with 100–150 mg/100 g of flesh. They are also high in pectin. They have been used to treat stomach ailments and as a laxative. **Warning:** The fruits contain low concentrations of saponins. Although toxic, saponins are poorly absorbed by the body and so tend to pass through without causing harm. They are also broken down by thorough cooking.

Other uses
A red dye can be obtained from the fruits.

Ornamental
It is quite an ornamental shrub and its ability to fix nitrogen and to survive on nutrient-poor soils means that it is good for reclamation purposes. It can be grown as a hedge, a windbreak and for wildlife plantings. It is also good for maritime, salty locations, and its thorns make it a good stock fence or barrier screen.

Tends to form suckers from its spreading roots.

Leaves: Deciduous, opposite, with entire margins, oblong, 2–5 cm long, 0.5–2 cm wide, stalked. Both sides of the leaf are silvery, and leaves have rounded apices. Buffalo berry can be distinguished from soapberry (*S. canadensis*), to which it looks similar, because it lacks rust-coloured spots on the underside of its leaves.

Flowers: Small, yellow-brown or scarlet, ~0.5 cm diameter, without petals, are borne in small dense clusters in early spring, 1–2 weeks before the leaves. Plants are dioecious, so need both male and female plants to set seed and fruits. The male flowers are about twice the size of female flowers, and average three flowers per cluster, whereas female plants average six flowers per cluster. *Pollination:* By bees and insects.

Fruit: Classified as berries. Vary in colour, size and quality from one plant to another. Generally, they are reddish-orange, ~1 cm long, though yellow-fruited specimens are often considered to have better quality fruits. They are borne singly or in small clusters over a long season from mid summer well into winter. They contain a single seed, which is discarded.

Yield/harvest: Plants can give good yields, but are painful to harvest because of their sharp spines. Fruits also adhere strongly to the branches. Female seedling plants produce their first fruits after 4–6 years, and can then continue to produce well for many years. Plants that are vegetatively propagated will produce fruits sooner. Fruits are best picked when fully coloured and ripe, or they can be very sour and astringent; ideally, they are best picked after a frost(s) when they are at their sweetest.

Roots: They have both deep taproots that can obtain water from depth and shallow roots that can rapidly take up any moisture and nutrients near the soil surface. Plants form a symbiotic relationship with nitrogen-fixing bacteria, which enables buffalo berries to grow in poor-nutrient soils. Avoid damaging the deeper roots when planting.

CULTIVATION
A tough, very adaptable plant that needs minimum maintenance.

Location: Plants grow best in full sun, or possibly a little shade. Can tolerate exposed and salty, maritime sites.

Temperature: Extremely winter hardy, tolerating temperatures down to below ~−25°C. In addition, its flowers, which it produces early in the year, are frost tolerant. It also tolerates summer heat.

Soil/water/nutrients: Can grow on a range of soil types, from sand to clay soils. Likes well-drained, but moist soil. It is fairly drought tolerant once established, but grows and produces better quality fruits with some moisture during the growing season. It is even reported to tolerate short-term waterlogging. Plants can grow in nutritionally poor soil, and at a wide range of pH values, including alkaline soils. Does not need additional fertiliser unless grown on very poor soils, and then it is best to use a fertiliser with a lower ratio of nitrogen.

Planting: Space plants at 3–4 m apart. Plant carefully to avoid any root damage; plants do not like to be moved once established. For fruit production, need to establish male and female plants at a ratio of 1 male:5–6 females.

Propagation: Seed: Is best sown fresh and should not be allowed to dry out. It is best sown immediately in a cold frame. Stored seed needs 2–3 months of cold stratification in moist sand. Germination takes ~21–28 days, and seedlings are then pricked out, once large enough, and grown on individually until the following summer or for a further year if not large enough. Won't know the sex of seedlings though till they first flower, and progeny and fruit quality are variable. *Cuttings*: Can take semi-ripe cuttings in summer, dip these in rooting hormone and insert in damp, gritty compost, with warmth and mist (if possible). Some of these should root. Hardwood cuttings can also be taken in autumn and can be inserted in soil outside to root by the following summer. *Layering*: Long, young shoots can be lightly cut and pegged down and lightly buried in the soil in autumn. They should have rooted by the following autumn. *Suckers:* Suckers that form around the plant can be carefully removed, with some

root if possible, and planted in moist compost to establish. The tops of the suckers can be removed to reduce moisture usage while the roots are establishing. Unfortunately, male plants are reported to produce more suckers than females.

Pruning: Very little or none. Possibly just to tidy up any straggly growth or to thin out any dense growth.

Pests and diseases: Generally trouble free, including being resistant to honey fungus.

CULTIVARS
'Sakakaweja': The fruits have a good flavour and are larger.
'Xanthocarpa': Has yellow fruits.

SIMILAR SPECIES

Soapberry, *Shepherdia canadensis*. A native of the prairies of Canada, Alaska, northern USA down to New Mexico, the soapberry is similar in appearance to the buffalo berry, but grows only ~2.5 m tall, and the leaves have reddish spots on their undersides. It flowers in spring, and fruits ripen in autumn. The fruits are usually red or yellow and are ~0.5 cm diameter.

Cultivation: Unlike the buffalo berry, this species is happier in light shade; otherwise, it can be grown in similar soil and environmental conditions to the buffalo berry. Is fully cold hardy.

Cultivars: 'Xanthocarpa' has yellow fruits and 'Rubra' has red ones.

Uses: The fruits are usually tart and tasty, but become sweeter after a frost. They are not as highly rated as those of the buffalo berry. They can be dried and used as currants. The fruits also contain saponins, possible more so than buffalo berries: see warning above. *Other uses:* When macerated, the fruits produce a foamy soapy substance that can be used as such. The foam is also sweet and has been added to icecream! ∎

Smilacina racemosa
False spikenard
LILIACEAE
Similar species: star-flowered lily of the valley (*S. stellata*)

The genus of ~25 *Smilacina* species are hardy, shrubby perennials that naturally grow in damp woodlands. Of these, the false spikenard is one of the few that, apart from its ornamental value, also has edible fruit. It is native to North America and can grow in wide-ranging climates that stretch from British Columbia–Nova Scotia down to Georgia and Missouri. It is usually encountered as a popular ornamental herbaceous plant in temperate climates, and is grown for its graceful shape and arching flower clusters. However, it also produces edible, tasty fruits, and is worth growing in herbaceous borders for its many attributes.

DESCRIPTION
A perennial, herbaceous shrub, growing to ~1 m tall, with a spread of ~0.6 m. It forms many stems, which arise annually

from the perennial rhizomes, then die back in autumn after fruiting.

Leaves: The stems are triangular in cross-section, erect

Food

The fruit can be eaten fresh, or can be cooked or made into jellies and molasses. They have a delicious bitter-sweet flavour, like bitter molasses. They may be better cooked as some report that the raw fruits can have a laxative effect if eaten in large quantities, whereas cooked fruits do not. The young leaves can be eaten in salads or can be lightly cooked as a vegetable, and taste somewhat like asparagus. The roots can be soaked in alkaline water (to get rid of any disagreeable taste) and then cooked like potatoes, or they can be pickled.

Nutrition

The fruits contain good levels of vitamin C.

Medicinal

This species is often used medicinally to treat coughs and colds, and is effective in reducing congestion and mucus within the respiratory system. A tea made from the roots has been also used to regulate menstrual disorders, although half a cup of leaf-tea drunk each day, for 7 days, is said to prevent conception. The root has also been used to treat wounds.

Ornamental

A good plant for herbaceous borders, or as a groundcover plant, particularly in shady, damp locations.

and carry attractive, alternate, glossy leaves, which bear several longitudinal distinctive veins. They are light green, long, and lanceolate in shape.

Flowers: Has long, arching flower stems in late spring–early summer, upon which are borne terminal sprays of densely arranged, creamy-white, fragrant flowers. The individual flowers are small (<0.5 cm diameter), delicate, 3–6-petalled, with central yellow stamens. The flowering panicles are ~10 cm long.

Fruit: Small (~0.8 cm diameter) berries, in clusters, which turn translucent and bright red when ripe, in autumn. The berries contain 3–4 small, edible seeds.

Yield/harvest: Fruits are harvested in late autumn when fully coloured and ripe. The fruits keep well, particularly if stored in a refrigerator. The roots, from mature plants, can also be harvested in late autumn and dried for later use.

Roots: Fairly shallow rooting, so avoid deep mechanical cultivation. Plants also form rhizomatous roots that enable vegetative spread to new areas. These rhizomes become dormant in winter. The distinctive scars left by older stems that have grown from the rhizomes account for this plant's other common name, 'Our lady's seal'.

CULTIVATION

An easy plant to grow.

Temperature: Grows best in temperate climates and is fully frost hardy, tolerating temperatures down to ~–20°C. It dies back in autumn, leaving its rhizomes at, or just below, soil level.

Location: These species prefer shady locations to full sun, and flower and fruit better in shade. Are not tolerant of strong winds or of exposed maritime conditions.

Soil/water/nutrients: Plants grow best in deep, fertile, humus-rich, moisture-retentive soils typical of woodlands, with lots of leaf litter. They prefer a fairly acid to neutral pH, and are not tolerant of alkaline soils. Plants need moisture throughout the growing season and are not tolerant of drought. They are fairly tolerant of waterlogging.

Planting: Plant the rhizomes during winter–early spring and keep moist. Space rhizomes at ~30–50 cm apart. As with many rhizomatous species from wetter areas, the plants take a few years to become fully established, and should not be disturbed during this period. Avoid mechanical cultivation around plants. However, once established, these plants can begin to spread and may need controlling within smaller gardens.

Pruning: Apart from a tidy-up of old stems after fruiting at the end of the season, pruning is not necessary.

Propagation: *Seed*: Best sown when fresh, and left to overwinter in damp, cool conditions. Germination can be slow: it can take ~18 months. Soaking seed in warm water before planting may help speed up germination, as can other treatments that soften or penetrate the seedcoat (e.g. scarification by scratching or cutting). Stored seeds take even longer to germinate (>2 years). Only separate seedlings once they are quite established, and then grow these on for a further year in shade, with moisture, warmth and nutrients. *Division*: Being rhizomatous, once established, plants can have sections of rhizome removed in spring or early autumn, and these can be placed in pots to establish roots.

Pests and diseases: Generally few, if any, problems.

SIMILAR SPECIES

Notes for *S. racemosa* (above) apply to this species unless stated otherwise.

Star-flowered lily of the valley (starry Solomon's plume), *Smilacina stellata*. A native of North America, from British Columbia down to California, and from Newfoundland down to Virginia, this is a similar, but smaller, herbaceous species, which can grow in many different climates. It forms a rhizomatous plant that sends up annual shoots. Its leaves are ~0.6 m in length, and the plant can spread >1 m. Flowers are produced in late spring–early summer; fruit ripen in autumn.

Cultivation: As above. Plants fruit best when grown in shade. This species is hardy down to ~–25°C. *Propagation:* As above, though may be able to grow in somewhat drier soils.

Uses: The fruits can be eaten fresh or cooked. They are reported to have a good sweet to sub-acid flavour. They may also act as a laxative (see *S. racemosa* above), if eaten in quantity or if not cooked. The young shoots and leaves can be lightly cooked and taste asparagus-like. The roots can also be eaten (see notes above). *Nutrition:* A good source of vitamin C. *Medicinal:* As above. *Ornamental:* Can be planted as a groundcover in shady, moist areas. ∎

Solanum muricatum
Pepino dulce (melon pear, melon shrub)
SOLANACEAE
Relatives: naranjilla, cocona, tamarillo, Cape gooseberry

The pepino dulce is a member of the Solanaceae family, along with many well-known fruits and vegetables. In Spanish, pepino dulce means 'sweet cucumber', which it does taste and look like. It is a native of the temperate mountainous regions of western South America, although it does not seem to occur there any more in the wild. It grows well in temperate and warm-temperate climates, similar to the tomato. In Japan, they are thought of as a specialist fruit, and are sometimes offered as a gift: they may be individually wrapped, boxed and tied with ribbons. There are recent improved cultivars now available, and the cultivation and popularity of this little-known fruit is likely to become more widespread. At present, the fruits are grown on a small scale, commercially, in New Zealand, Chile and Western Australia, and many people grow this small, easy-to-cultivate plant in a border.

DESCRIPTION
A small, herbaceous shrub, with a woody base and fibrous roots. Growth can be sprawling or erect: plants can be ~1 m tall, ~1–2 m spread, but are often smaller. It has a similar growth form to that of a tomato vine, but a denser, more compact shape. It often needs staking or supporting to prevent the fruit from lying on the ground. The pepino dulce grows quickly and can flower and set fruit 4–6 months after planting.

Leaves: Mid green, with short, sparse, bristly small hairs. It looks similar to a potato plant, but the leaves may take many forms: simple and entire, lobed or divided into leaflets.

Flowers: The flowers are smallish (~2 cm diameter) and have five bluey-mauve fused petals that form the corolla, with whitish margins. They have a similar appearance to other Solanaceae species, particularly potato flowers. There is a green, basal calyx that persists on the fruit. The stamens have yellow pollen, and are shorter than the corolla and stigma. Flowers are borne during spring, through summer and often into late autumn. However, the flowers do not set fruits until night temperatures reach >17°C, so autumn flowers may not set fruits. *Pollination:* Can be parthenocarpic, which means they do not need pollination to set fruit, and the fruits are seedless. However, self-pollination or cross pollination greatly increases fruiting. Pollination is by bees and insects. As the stigma is longer than the anthers, this probably prevents self-pollination, and pollination is more likely between plants. Hand pollination can also be carried out.

Fruit: The fruits are usually egg-shaped–rounded, but may also be pear or heart-shaped. Some fruits have many small seeds, other fruits only have a few. The skin is usually smooth, and the fruits measure ~6–10 cm long, with a few being >15 cm long. Their skin colour varies from pale creamy-green, with or without purple stripes, to solid green or green with purple stripes, to completely purple. The flesh is greenish–white or yellowish-orange. The best fruits are juicy, fairly sweet and refreshing, and taste like a cross between cucumber, pear and cantaloupe melon. Some fruits may have a somewhat unpleasant aftertaste. Fruits take 30–80 days to mature after pollination.

Yield/harvest/storage: If grown in good soils, they can have good yields throughout summer and into late autumn. Fruits are best harvested when quite ripe, and have fully developed their colouring. Fruits can be picked when still somewhat under-ripe and stood on a warm windowsill to fully ripen, but may not develop such good flavour and sweetness as vine-ripened fruits. Fully ripe fruits have a delicate flavour, but are delicious. Over-ripe fruits tend to lose their flavour. Handle fruit carefully as they bruise fairly easily. Cool, wet weather during harvesting can result in skin cracking and fungal infections. *Storage:* Harvested fruit can be kept in a fridge for ~3–4 weeks.

Roots: They have fairly spreading, but shallow roots. They grow better with regular moisture and benefit from a mulch to conserve moisture, help suppress weed growth and add nutrients. Avoid deep mechanical cultivation.

CULTIVATION
Its cultivation is similar to that of tomato or eggplant, but needs less regular maintenance. It can be grown as an annual in colder regions, but plants will live for several years in warmer areas.

Location: They can grow in full sun or semi-shade. They prefer a sheltered location and are not very wind tolerant. In cooler regions, they are best grown where one would grow tomatoes, and like a warm sunny wall to grow against.

Temperature: Plants are not very cold hardy. They will survive brief frosts, but it knocks them back and they often lose most of their leaves. If cold weather is likely, plants can be temporarily covered. In dry regions, irrigation is beneficial. Plants grow best at a temperature range of 18–24°C, and can tolerate brief periods of temperatures >30°C as long as

uses

Food

Pepino dulce fruits are good eaten fresh, with the flesh scooped out of the skin. They are thirst quenching and juicy, with a pear–cantaloupe flavour, but are not over-sweet. In South America, they are often prepared more as a vegetable than a fruit. Although some fruits can have numerous seeds, like tomatoes, they are soft, tiny and unnoticeable. The skin is often not eaten as it can be somewhat tough and bitter. The fruits can be used in fruit salads, juice, in desserts, or added as a garnish to savoury dishes such as fish, pastas, cold meats. The fruits can also be frozen or dried.

Nutrition

Fruits contain good levels of vitamin C (35 mg/100 g of flesh). They also have fairly good levels of vitamin A and iodine.

they have adequate moisture. However, fruit production may decline with high temperatures, particularly if both day and night temperatures are high.

Soil/water/nutrients: Plants grow best in fertile (but not too fertile), free-draining loam, with a pH range of 6.5–7.5. Alkaline soils are likely to cause iron (chlorosis) and manganese deficiency. They are not as tolerant of salinity as the tomato. They need regular moisture, and although established plants can survive dry periods, their growth, fruit-set and fruit quality are reduced. They cannot tolerate wet soils or waterlogging. Plants like a fairly nutrient-rich soil and like some good garden compost or well-rotted manure mixed in with the soil, but if the plants are given too much fertiliser there can be problems with fruit-set and fruit quality. Too much nitrogen, in particular, results in too much leafy growth and reduced flowering and fruit formation, plus an increase in pest problems. Fertilise with low-nitrogen-based fertiliser in early spring, and again in mid summer.

Pot culture: They are ideal plants for pot culture in cooler regions because of their size and they can also be moved to a frost-secure area if needed. They could be grown on patios,

like tomatoes, and they should flower and fruit heavily.

Planting: Space plants at ~60–80 cm apart. Plant in early spring after the last frosts. Some plants have a fairly upright growth and are self-supporting; others tend to sprawl and need to be staked to keep the fruit off the soil. They can be grown against a trellis.

Propagation: *Seed:* They can be grown from seed, but are usually propagated vegetatively. Grow seedlings as one would tomatoes, with warmth and moisture, and plant seedlings out once all risk of frost has passed. The progeny will be variable. *Cuttings:* Take ~15-cm-long cuttings in mid–late summer. Treatment with a rooting hormone can increase rooting and development. Place in well-drained, but moist compost, with warmth. Or, pieces of stem, with a heel, can be placed horizontally within compost, with just a few leaves left above the soil surface. These usually root quickly along the stem length, and have a high success rate. Rooted cuttings can be planted out in spring, and should start flowering soon after. The fruits then have time to grow and ripen during the summer. Like tomatoes, an early start to the season makes a considerable difference to when the fruits can first be harvested.

Pruning: Pruning is not needed unless the plant is being trained to a trellis or has become straggly. Removal of larger, older leaves allows the sun to reach the fruit more easily, hastens ripening and improves fruit quality. Plants can be cut back after harvesting, although they do not need to be, and will regrow in spring.

Pests and diseases: Pepino dulce seems to be quite resistant to problems, though may be affected by many of the diseases and pests that afflict tomatoes and other Solanaceae species. These include fungal diseases such *Alternaria* spp. and *Phytophthora* spp., and also bacterial spot and *Anthracnose*. They can also be attacked by spider mite, cut worm, hornworm, fruit flies, leafminer and flea beetle. Plants grown under cover may be also attacked by white flies and aphids. It is best to establish plants in soils that have not had other Solanaceae species recently grown in them.

CULTIVARS

'Miski Prolific': From California. Fruit: creamy-white, slightly pinky, with some purple striping. Flesh: pinky-peach, rich, sweet, aromatic, with no soapiness. Seeds: few or none. Matures early. Strong-growing plant; bears well without pollination.

'New Yorker': From Chile. Medium–large, oval fruit, apex pointed. Skin: smooth, golden yellow when mature, striped with deep purple. Flesh: firm, juicy, yellow-orange, sweet. Seeds: few. Keeps for several weeks. Upright growth habit. Sets fruit well without cross pollination.

'Rio Bamba': From Ecuador. Has a vine-like growth habit, and makes an excellent climber or can be grown in a hanging basket. Dark green leaves with reddish-purple veins, purple stems. Flowers darker than normal: makes an excellent display. Very good flavoured fruit.

'Toma': From Chile. Medium-sized, oval fruit, ~8–10 cm long, ~7 cm diameter, pointed apex. Skin cream-coloured when ripe, and striped dark purple. Flesh: firm, white-cream colour, very juicy, sweet, refreshing. Seeds usually present. Keeping quality excellent. ■

Solanum quitoense (syn. *S. angulatum*)
Naranjilla
SOLANACEAE
Relatives: Cape gooseberry, tamarillos, pepino

The naranjilla is believed to be indigenous to and is most abundant in Peru, Ecuador and southern Colombia. The first records of its cultivation date back to the mid 1600s in Ecuador and Colombia. The Spanish name 'naranjilla' means 'little orange' because of its round, bright orange fruits. It is an eye-catching, interesting member of the Solanaceae family, and is often grown as an ornamental plant for its arresting large, fuzzy green leaves with bright purple veins. In Ecuador, they are locally grown for their fruits, which are widely sold in local markets. Because little breeding work has been done on naranjilla, the plants grown today probably differ little from those cultivated hundreds of years ago. As yet, it is not widely known, ornamentally or for its fruit, but has considerable development potential.

DESCRIPTION
Extremely attractive, bushy–spreading, perennial, short-lived (3–5 years), herbaceous shrub, height 1.5–3.5 m, with thick, coarsely hairy stems that become somewhat woody with age. They often have spines in the wild, but cultivated plants have few or no spines. The species *S. quitoense* is normally spineless; another similar species, *S. septentrionale*, often does have spines, but is hardier.

Leaves: Large (up to 45 cm long, ~25 cm wide), very attractive, roughly hairy/woolly. They are shallowly lobed and are somewhat wavy. There may be occasional spines on the leaf stalk, midrib and lateral veins: both above and beneath. Young leaves, young stems and petioles are coated with bright purple hairs. The mature leaves are a dark, acid-green colour and have distinctive purple veins on their upper surface, and mauve veins beneath.

Flowers: Borne in small clusters (4–10) from leaf axils, slightly fragrant, ~3 cm diameter, typically Solanaceae-like in shape, with five petals, white on the upper surface, mauve and finely hairy beneath, with five prominent yellow stamens. The unopened buds are similarly covered with fine purple hairs. Seedlings should flower 4–6 months after planting. *Pollination:* The plants are monoecious and the flowers are bisexual (perfect), so only one plant is needed for pollination, though more than one plant may increase fruit-set.

Fruit: A true berry. Rounded, ~4–6 cm diameter, thickish green skin, turning bright orange when ripe. The skin is covered in a dense brown fuzz that needs to be rubbed off before eating. The fruits have a basal five-pointed green calyx. The fruit flesh is bright lime green in colour and, internally, resembles a tomato. It consists of four compartments, separated by membranous partitions, which are filled with translucent, juicy flesh. The flesh is sharp and tangy when fully ripe, and has been likened to pineapple–lemon. There are numerous, small, flat, straw-coloured, edible seeds.

Yield/harvest/storage: A healthy plant can bear 50–150 fruits a year. Plants produce their first fruits when 8–12 months old, and then for ~3 years. Grafted plants can fruit even sooner: flowering at 3–4 months, and producing mature fruits by 6 months. It fruits more or less continually in warmer regions, but mainly during spring–early summer in more temperate climates. (This may be due to temperature or may be because flowers need longer periods of daylight to initiate flowering.) When the plants reach 4 years of age, productivity declines and they begin to die. Fruits can be harvested when they are fully orange in colour, and the calyx naturally separates from the fruit. However, fully ripe naranjillas do not store well and, if not eaten fresh, they soon start to deteriorate and ferment. If fruits are picked when still greeny-orange, they can be kept at room temperature to fully ripen for a week or more, or for 1–2 months at ~8°C, with a relative humidity of ~75%.

CULTIVATION
Given a semi-tropical climate, adequate moisture and good soil, the naranjilla will grow quickly and fruit well. However, in cooler regions it can be temperamental; seems to be growing well one day, and then just loses its leaves the next. The more you can spoil and protect these plants, the better the results.

Temperature: Frosts and freezing temperatures can seriously damage these plants, although, because of their smaller size, it is easy to pop some frost protection over them. Temperatures <10°C reduce the plant's growth: it grows best at 15–25°C. But, it also does not like it too hot, and starts to seriously wilt and struggle at temperatures >30°C. It also won't set fruit in areas that have elevated night temperatures.

Location: Prefers a semi-shaded location, rather than full sun, which burns the large leaves. They also look much better in semi-shade, particularly in a spot where they just receive early-morning sun. They are not tolerant of wind, or of salty maritime locations, although they can be grown near the coast if placed in a sheltered spot.

Soil/water/nutrients: The naranjilla grows best in rich, organic soil, although will also grow in poor, stony ground or in limestone soils. It grows at a wide pH range from ~5.5–7.5. Plants must have good drainage: short

Food

It can be simply eaten fresh, although it is too sharp for some. When fully ripe, it has an aromatic, tangy flavour. The skin is generally too tough and bitter to be eaten. It is most popularly used to make an excellent, refreshing green-coloured juice that is chilled, sweetened and shaken until frothy. It can also be used in many other ways, including as a garnish for savoury dishes, added to fruit salads, cheesecake, icecream, yoghurt or pies, or made into sauces, preserves or chutneys. The juice also makes a reasonable wine. The shells can be stuffed with a mixture of banana, naranjilla fruit and other ingredients, and then baked: tangy and delicious. The fresh juice can be frozen for later use.

Nutrition

Has fairly good levels of vitamins A and C. May contain a pepsin-like enzyme, which digests protein. **Warning:** People with very sensitive skin may find the hairs on the plant and fruits irritating, and may need to wear gloves when harvesting.

Ornamental

Makes a stunning, eye-catching plant for sheltered, shaded spots, and is ideal for container growth or as a main feature in a shaded bed, perhaps with shingle or dark coloured bark around it, to set off its striking large, colourful leaves and round golden-orange fruits.

Plants can survive in poor-nutrient soils, but growth and fruit yields are decreased.

Pot culture: In temperate regions, this ornamental plant can be grown in containers, and its striking foliage can be admired year round as long as it is taken inside in colder weather. If given some warmth year round, it should also produce fruit.

Planting: Space plants at 1.5–2 m apart. It is beneficial to dig in extra organic compost to the soil when planting. Plants may need some staking as they get larger; their stems are fairly brittle and they often have a semi-sprawling, top-heavy habit.

Propagation: *Seed:* Often propagated from seed. Germination is quick and easy. But there will be variation in the progeny. Seeds germinate better if they are thoroughly cleaned of pulp. Seedlings are grown in the same way as tomato seedlings, and can be planted out in 2–3 months. It is a good idea to save some seeds each year in case the plant is killed during colder winter months. *Cuttings:* Can take semi-ripe cuttings or stem sections, and these root well if placed in moist, well-drained compost in the shade. Often older wood will root better than younger. *Layering:* Can be air-layered. *Grafting:* This can be successful, and is often done by cleft, or saddle, side or whip grafts. It is often done onto rootstocks of other Solanaceae species to give the naranjilla more resistance to adverse soil conditions, temperature, etc. However, all Solanaceae species have poisonous leaves and roots, and some have poisonous fruits (e.g. deadly nightshade), so be careful when selecting a rootstock that a toxin won't be transferred to the naranjilla fruits!

Pruning: Just to reduce straggly growth and take out older, woody branches.

Pests and diseases: Naranjilla are susceptible to root rots and, therefore, must be planted in well-drained soil with good fertility. They are also susceptible to root-knot nematode damage, and this can be avoided by not growing them in very sandy soils. *S. hirtum* is resistant to root-knot nematodes, and can be crossed with naranjilla, but resistant varieties are not yet widely available.

CULTIVARS

There are very few named cultivars commercially available. ∎

periods of waterlogging can rapidly kill them. However, they also need moisture year round, and need to be watered during dry periods. A good, deep, organic mulch can help conserve moisture and provide nutrients. The naranjilla is a heavy feeder, and if it is growing rapidly it needs regular applications of a complete fertiliser or an organic equivalent.

Solanum sessiliflorum

Cocona

SOLANACEAE

Relatives: naranjilla, tomato, Cape gooseberry

Another fruit from the ubiquitous Solanaceae family, the cocona is similar to, but not as well known as, the naranjilla. It is common in South America where it is only known as a cultivated plant, and has not been found in the wild. The fruits are enjoyed by the indigenous population and are sold throughout Latin America. In Colombia and Brazil, the cocona is grown commercially on a small scale, and in Peru it is used in the production of fruit juices.

DESCRIPTION

A much-branched, herbaceous shrub, ~2 m high, with a downy stem and densely white-hairy shoots. New shoots have rust-coloured hair on their underside. It is similar in appearance to naranjilla, but is shorter, has little or no purple coloration of veins, and has greenish-white flowers. It is a fast-growing, short-lived plant.

Leaves: Large, ~45 cm long, ~40 cm wide, ovate, being curved at the base of the leaf, with scalloped margins. Its upper surface is finely downy, and it has prominent veins beneath.

Flowers: Five pale greenish-yellow petals, five yellow stamens and a dark green, five-pointed calyx. They are ~2.5 cm diameter, and are borne in clusters of two or more from leaf axils. Plants begin flowering when ~6 months old. Flowers are bisexual. *Pollination:* Bees are popular visitors to the flowers and natural crosses are common. However, cocona are self-fertile, and only need one plant to set fruit, though will get better yields with more than one plant.

Fruit: Borne singly or in compact clusters on short stalks. The berries are capped with a persistent green calyx. Fruits are oblong–round with a bluntly rounded apex. They are 2.5–10 cm long, and 2–6 cm wide. Their skin is thin, tough and has a prickly fuzzy coating until fully ripe, which is not as tenacious as that of naranjilla. Once ripe, the skin becomes smooth and turns golden-yellow-orange, burnt-orange-red, or deep purple-red. Beneath the skin is a thin (0.5–1 cm-wide) layer of firm, creamy-white flesh, which has an aroma and taste similar to tomatoes. In the centre is a yellow, juicy pulp containing many, very small, oval, whitish, edible seeds. The fruit pulp has a pleasant, tangy, lime-like flavour. Fruits mature ~8 weeks after fruit-set.

Yield/harvest/storage: An average annual yield is 5–25 kg per plant, and in good fertile soil a plant can produce up to ~140 fruits. Plants start producing fruits in their first year. The fresh fruit keeps well for 5–10 days at normal room temperatures.

CULTIVATION

Location: Likes a site in full sun. Is not very wind tolerant, but is relatively tolerant of salt.

Temperature: Prefers a semi-tropical or warm-temperate climate and can be killed by frosts. Like many of these species, including tomatoes, it can be grown as an annual in cooler regions.

Soil/water/nutrients: It is adaptable to the type of soil it can grow in, tolerating sand, clay and even limestone soils, but it does need good drainage and cannot tolerate cold, wet soils. Regular moisture will give more vigorous growth and the best-quality fruits. They grow best in more fertile soils and benefit from regular applications of a balanced fertiliser, similar to the types used to feed tomatoes. The addition of extra phosphate can be beneficial in some soils, as can the addition of urea and chlorate of potassium.

Planting: Seedlings are planted out when about 3–4 months old and are spaced at 1.5–2.5 m apart, depending on the fertility of the soil. Flowering commences 2–3 months after planting, and then continues for several months. Establish plants in well-prepared, fertile soil in full sun.

Propagation: *Seeds:* Each fruit contains 800–2000

Food

The fruits are often used for juice, with its aroma and taste being less pronounced than naranjilla. The peeled, ripe fruits can be also eaten fresh. The fruit can be added to fruit salads, or it can be cooked with fish and added to meat stews. Sweetened, it can be used in sauces and pies. Makes good jam, marmalade, paste and jelly, and is sometimes pickled or candied. In Brazil, the leaves are cooked and eaten as a vegetable.

Nutrition

The fruit has a high level (~0.8%) of vitamin C and good levels of carotene, niacin, iron as well as some vitamin A. The fruits may also contain fairly high levels of tannin, so should not be eaten in excess over a long period of time.

Other uses

The fruits are used by the native Indians of Peru to rid the head of lice.

seeds, and many of these will germinate. They often spring up voluntarily from seeds left in the soil from fallen fruits from the year before. To prepare seeds, thoroughly wash off any pulp, or you can leave seeds to ferment for a couple of days in warmth, and then any pulp is more easily removed. The seeds are sown at 0.5–1 cm depth, and ~25–50% should germinate in 2–5 weeks. *Cuttings:* Cuttings can be taken from laterals or older stems, and these should readily root along their length. This method is used if selecting for particularly good fruiting characteristics of a plant. *Layering:* Can be successfully propagated by air layers and layering, as this family readily forms roots from any wounds on stems or if the stems contact the soil.

Pests and diseases: Coconas do not have as many problems as naranjilla, though are susceptible to root-knot nematodes. Avoid soils where this has been a problem in the past, and avoid soils that contain a high proportion of sand. Seek out plants with some nematode resistance. Other problems are mealybugs, cutworms and leaf-eating insects.

CULTIVARS

In Peru, there are several main types of coconas, which are classified according to their fruit characteristics: small and purple-red, medium and yellow, round and yellow or pear-shaped. ∎

Sorbus spp.
Rowans, mountain ashes, service trees and whitebeams
ROSACEAE

American mountain ash (common whitebeam) (*Sorbus americana, S. decora*), European mountain ash (*S. aucuparia*), service tree (*S. domestica*), whitebeam (*S. aria*), wild service tree (*S. torminalis*)

Relatives: apple, juneberry, plums, pear, elderberry

The *Sorbus* genus consists of ~100 species of hardy, deciduous trees and shrubs found in Asia, Europe and North America. They are known by many common names, and often these common names are used for more than one species. They tend to fall into two groups, the rowans with pinnate leaves and the whitebeams with non-pinnate leaves. The species are hardy and are usually tolerant of a variety of adverse environmental conditions. Historically, the rowans, and in particular *S. aucuparia*, were used to impart healing energy, and psychic and supernatural powers. The tree is said to be a protection against enchantment; crosses of rowan were placed over doorways of houses or in pens of livestock. Planting a rowan near the house is said to protect it from lightning and other evil influences. Staffs of rowan were carried on ships to prevent storms. The rowan tree also played a central role in Druid ceremonies. The *Sorbus* species described below have edible fruits and are used for a variety of purposes.

GENERAL DESCRIPTION

The species described here are small–medium-sized trees.

Leaves: Deciduous. Rowans have pinnate, toothed, dark green leaves, in odd numbers. Whitebeam and the wild service tree have silvery leaves that are, respectively, elliptic and maple-shaped. Many *Sorbus* species have good autumn colour, but this seems to vary with location.

Flowers: Creamy-white, five-petalled, small, numerous and usually borne in flattened clusters, produced in late spring–early summer.

Fruit: Vary in colour with species. Produced in late summer or autumn. The berries consist of 2–5 cells, with each cell containing 1–2 small, brown seeds. Seeds are mostly dispersed by birds. Trees grown from seed may not produce fruits for up to ~15 years, but should then start to produce good, regular yields.

Harvest: Fruits can be picked when slightly immature, but then need after-ripening. Frost improves their sweetness.

CULTIVATION

Location: Can be grown in sun or semi-shade, though they fruit better in sunny positions. Are resistant to wind. Most species are tolerant of air pollution.

Temperature: All the species described here are fully frost hardy.

Chilling: These species probably benefit from some winter chilling to come into leaf and fruit well; therefore may not be suitable for regions that have warmer winters.

Soil: Can grow in a range of soil types. Prefer good drainage, but most species like moist soil, growing poorly in dry soils.

Propagation: *Seed:* Wash the flesh from harvested fruits and sow seeds when fresh in a cold frame. If the seed has been stored, germination is better if given ~14 days of warmth, then 14–16 weeks of cold stratification. Prick out seedlings next spring–summer and grow on in pots for the first 2–3 years. Germinated seeds grow very slowly to begin with while they develop their root systems. If seeds are sown late or are not sufficiently preconditioned, or conditions are too warm, germination can be delayed until the second or even third year. *Cuttings:* Softwood or semi-ripe cuttings in late spring–summer. *Grafting:* Can be done in winter.

Pruning: None needed, except to keep the trees to size.

Pests and diseases: May suffer from the same problems as other Rosaceae species: apple canker, fireblight, honey fungus, rust, silverleaf.

EDIBLE *SORBUS* SPECIES

The above general description applies to the *Sorbus* species below unless stated otherwise.

American mountain ashes, *Sorbus americana* (common whitebeam) and *S. decora*. These are native to the USA and Canada, and are found in cool, mountain valleys. They are very hardy, slow growing, but also fairly short lived. They grow to ~4–6 m tall, ~3–5 m spread. Have sticky, winter leaf buds. (Those of *S. aucuparia* are not sticky.) Young branches are hairless, while those of *S. aucuparia* are hairy. These characteristics readily separate the two species. *Leaves:* Pinnate, with an odd number (11–17) of leaflets, 4–10 cm long, light green. Often good golden–red autumn colour. *Flowers:* White–cream, a little smaller (~0.6 cm width) than those of *S. aucuparia*, borne in late spring in flattened clusters (~10–12 cm wide), from mid spring to mid summer. *Fruit:* Bright red, ripen in late autumn. Fruits are often sourer than those of *S. aucuparia*; though frosts may sweeten the fruits somewhat. The fruit of *S. decora* is said to be tastier than that of *S. americana*, which is sharper. *Cultivation:* Tolerates air pollution. Can tolerate some waterlogging. *Chilling:* Probably needs ~750(+) hours of chilling at <7°C. *Cultivars:* 'Edulis' has better-quality fruits. 'Rabina' and 'Shipova' are other cultivars.

European mountain ash, *Sorbus aucuparia*. A native of Europe and western Asia. Forms a round-headed tree, height: ~6–12 m, spread 3–4 m. Its winter buds are white, woolly and not sticky like those of *S. americana*, and young branches are pubescent. The branches have an upright form. *Bark:* Soft, spongy, yellow–grey on the surface, with many thin, light brown layers beneath. *Leaves:* Has smaller leaflets than those of *S. americana* (~5 cm long) (13–15 leaflets). Sometimes has good yellow-red colour in autumn, particularly in colder areas. *Flowers:* White–cream, ~0.8 cm diameter, in flattened clusters 10–15 cm across, in spring. *Fruit:* Striking, profuse, orange, maturing to red in late summer. Better quality and less sour than those of *S. americana*. The birds love the berries. Trees may not live as long when planted in alkaline soils. *Uses:* Fruits contain parascorbic acid, which can act against Gram+ bacteria and protozoa. They are a popular ornamental species in Britain, in gardens and in urban areas.

Service tree, *Sorbus domestica*. Native to southern Europe, north Africa and the Near East, this tree used to be popular for its fruit in Britain and southern Europe. It has attractive orange-brown bark that becomes fissured. The tree forms a slow-growing (to ~14 m) domed shape, with spreading branches. Buds exude a resin. Leaves are pinnate (13–21 leaflets). Creamy flowers (~1.5 cm diameter each) in flattened clusters are borne in late spring. Fruits are brownish-red, larger (~2–3 cm diameter) and tend to be sour, but are edible when over-ripe, bletted or after they have been exposed to frost. The fruits can also be dried and used like prunes. There are two main forms: *S. domestica pomifera*, with apple-shaped fruits (which ripen from early autumn) and *S. domestica pyriformis*, with pear-shaped fruits (which ripen later in autumn). Grows better in drier soils in a sunny spot. Has good-quality timber.

Whitebeam, *Sorbus aria*. A native of Britain. Can grow larger than most other *Sorbus* species listed here: height ~5–12 m, spread ~3–9 m. Tree has a domed shape with upswept branches. Leaves are not pinnate, but elliptic in shape (~8 cm long). They are finely hairy and silvery-grey when young, turning dull yellow-green above as they age (but the underside remains silvery). In older trees, leaves form a dense shade. Sometimes have good orange–gold autumn colour. Flowers in summer, flattened clusters (10–15 cm wide). Fruit are brownish-red, speckled (~1–1.2 cm diameter); they ripen in autumn. *Cultivation and uses:* Can grow in a range of soils, from acid to alkaline. Often naturally grows in chalk soils. Can grow in heavier clay soils. Is very salt tolerant and is a good tree for maritime locations. Very tolerant of pollution. Can be planted as a windbreak and also makes a good pioneer species. Can be coppiced. Good-quality wood. A popular garden plant in Britain.

Wild service tree, *Sorbus torminalis*. Native to Britain. Its fruits used to be gathered and were even sold in local markets; they are now seldom explored or used. A larger *Sorbus* species, height ~18 m, though is often smaller. Older trees become spreading. Trees have smooth, grey bark that tends to crack in mature trees. Trees are self-fertile. Leaves are not pinnate, but are larger (~10 cm long, ~8 cm wide) and somewhat maple shaped. Alternate. Have dark red–purple autumn colour. Flowers are creamy-white, ~1 cm in diameter, form loose bunches in late spring. *Fruit:* Apple-like in form, ~1–1.5 cm diameter, brown speckled, ripen in autumn. The flesh is soft and sweet. They are rich in vitamin C. Trees can be grown in clay soil and on soils with a wide range of pH, but not too acid. Trees can be coppiced. ∎

Food

The berries have a high tannin content and should be as ripe as possible before eating. They can be sun-dried for 15–20 days to improve their sweetness. The fruits are best left until after the first frosts. They can be eaten raw if bletted: this involves storing the fruit until it is almost, but not quite, going rotten. At this stage, the fruit is said to have a delicious taste. The fruits have good levels of pectin and, when ripe, make good jams and jellies. A popular jelly is made to accompany cold game or wild fowl. It makes good ketchup. A good-quality cider can be made from the fruits; in northern Europe, a strong spirit is fermented from them; and they also make a fairly good-quality wine, particularly if the fruits are fully ripened.

Nutrition/medicinal

The berries are rich in vitamin C. They also have high levels of tannins when under-ripe, contain tartaric acid before they are fully ripe, and citric and malic acids when fully ripe. The taste of malic acid is used as a flavouring and in wine. A decoction of the bark has been used to treat diarrhoea. The ripe berries can be used as a gargle for sore throats and inflamed tonsils. The berries have been eaten to improve eye problems, including glaucoma. **Warning:** As with all the Rosaceae family, the seeds contain toxic cyanogenic compounds, so it is probably best to either remove seeds or not to eat too many.

Other uses

Most parts of the trees have a high tannin content, particularly the bark, and it has been used for tanning and dyeing. The wood is fine grained, very hard and dense: it is good for furniture, etc.

Ornamental

Many of the *Sorbus* species are popular ornamental plants. They are easy-to-manage, small–medium-sized trees that have attractive leaves, often with good autumn colour, and eye-catching red–orange autumn berries. They are hardy and can be grown in a range of situations. The trees are usually many-branched and many species have attractive, smooth, grey bark. The birds love the fruit.

Spondias dulcis (syn. *S. cytherea*)

Ambarella (vi, otaheite apple, golden apple, makok-farang, hog plum)

ANACARDIACEAE

Relatives: mombin, mango, cashew, sumach

A very attractive tree, the ambarella is native to Melanesia, through Polynesia, and has been introduced into tropical areas of both the Old and New World. It is common in Malaysian gardens and is fairly frequently found in India and Sri Lanka. Due to a demand for its fruits in Australia, there is a growing number of small commercial orchards being set up in both New South Wales and Queensland. The trees are quite hardy and establish very quickly.

uses

Food

Fruits can be eaten fresh, cooked or pickled. Ripe but still firm fruits are crisp, juicy, sub-acid, with a somewhat pineapple-like fragrance and flavour. More ripened, softer fruits become more fibrous, and their flavour becomes musky. It is best enjoyed before it becomes too soft. The fruits are usually peeled. The flesh can be diced and eaten on its own, or can be added to other fresh fruits. Is good with a little honey on top, with a drizzle of cream and rum. Makes a delicious juice. Some stew the flesh with a little water and sugar to make a rich-flavoured, fruity sauce. If further reduced with the addition of cinnamon, or similar, it makes a good preserve. Unripe fruits can be used to make jelly, pickles, relishes, savoury sauces, or added to soups and stews. The flesh can also be dried. Young leaves are sometimes eaten fresh or are lightly steamed and eaten as a vegetable with salted fish and rice. They are sometimes cooked with meat to tenderise it.

Nutrition/medicinal

A fairly good source of vitamin C: 40–70 mg/100 g of flesh. It is also a good source of iron. Unripe fruits contain 9.76% of pectin (excellent for jams, chutney, etc.), and also supply valuable dietary fibre. Also a very good source of vitamin A: 1382 IU. The fruits have been used to treat heart ailments and urinary troubles, and have been used on wounds, sores and burns, and for digestion.

Other uses

The wood is light brown, buoyant, but not very durable.

Ornamental

A handsome specimen tree for larger areas, with a tropical appearance and eye-catching fruits. The flowers attract bees.

DESCRIPTION

A highly ornamental, rapidly growing tree, 12–18 m tall. It usually has a single, solid trunk with an upright crown that has a rigid and symmetrical appearance, giving it a stately effect. It has graceful branches, but these can be somewhat brittle. The bark is nearly smooth, light grey-brown. When injured, the tree exudes a mucilaginous gum.

Leaves: Deciduous, handsome, pinnate, 20–60 cm in length. They are composed of 9–25 glossy, elliptical or obovate leaflets, 6–10 cm long, which are toothed toward their apices, and tend to roll inwards. They have a resinous aroma when crushed. At the end of summer, the leaves turn yellow before falling, but the silhouette of the tree is still attractive for the short time that it remains bare.

Flowers: Small, fragrant, but inconspicuous, whitish, borne in large terminal panicles. The clusters consist of mixed male, female and bisexual flowers, and trees are self-fertile. Flowers are borne on last season's growth, and sometimes older wood. *Pollination:* By bees and insects.

Fruit: Has interesting fruits (drupes). They dangle on long stalks, in large bunches of more than ten fruits. The fruits are oval or sometimes knobbly in shape, 6–9 cm long, 2.5–4 cm wide, with a thin but tough skin, often golden-yellow to russet-red coloured when ripe. A number of green fruits may fall before fully ripening. The flesh of ripe fruits is firm, orange-yellow, and contains a single, large, five-celled stone, similar to the mango, but has spiny protuberances which can be painful if bitten into. The flesh has a taste somewhat like pineapple or apple. When over-ripe, the fruits become fibrous. Poorer quality fruits may have a turpentine-like flavour. The woody inner stone contains 1–5 flat seeds. Fruits take 6–8 months to mature after flowering.

Yield/harvest: Fruits vary in size, but in warmer regions they can be large and weigh ~0.5 kg each. Seedling trees start producing fruits after 3–5 years, whereas vegetatively-grown plants start to produce fruits after 2–3 years. Fruits are generally harvested when ripe. They have then become fully coloured and the flesh has just begun to soften, but must be picked before they become too soft. Fruits can be harvested when they are still green and firm, and can ripen if kept at room temperature, but these do not achieve the richness and tanginess of flavour that tree-ripened fruits have.

CULTIVATION

Location: Trees are best grown in full sun for good fruit production, but will produce some fruit in light shade. Young trees like some light shade. Can tolerate some salt spray. Mature trees have somewhat brittle branches, which can be damaged by strong winds; therefore, sheltered locations are preferred.

Temperature: Thrives in humid, subtropical areas, where it can grow ~2 m in a single season. The tree is slightly less cold hardy than mango, and basically requires a frost-free climate, although mature trees can withstand temperatures below freezing for a few hours. Trees are cold sensitive when small and need extra protection. Flowers and small fruits can be killed if the temperature falls below 4°C for a few hours. They need warm, dry weather to set fruit. Often do best in areas with distinct wet and dry seasons.

Soil/water/nutrients: Ambarella trees grow best in a deep, fertile loam, but are very versatile and can grow in many soil types, from limestone to acid sands, so long as they are well drained. Trees can suffer from nutritional disorders, such as iron chlorosis, if the soil is too alkaline. Mature trees are quite tolerant of drought and do not usually require supplemental irrigation, though trees grow and fruit better with some moisture during the growing season. Young trees need regular moisture until established. Plants are not nutrient hungry and can be grown in moderately fertile soils without the addition of nutrients. In poor, infertile soils, a complete, balanced fertiliser can be applied 1–2 times annually during the growing season, particularly to younger trees.

Pot culture: Suit container planting, for a few years at least, until they become too large. A possible way to cultivate them in cooler regions, where they can be taken inside or given extra protection in winters.

Planting: Form large trees and need to be spaced 8–15 m apart. Dig in well-rotted manure before planting. Young trees often need staking.

Pruning: Trees need little pruning, and form a good shape naturally. Pruning can reduce their natural beauty. Maintenance pruning can be done to remove dead or damaged wood. Branches that are cut back past the previous season's growth will not bear fruit for at least a year.

Propagation: *Seeds:* Easily propagated by seeds, which germinate in ~28 days. Best to use fresh seeds, extracted carefully from the stone. *Cuttings:* Semi-ripe and hardwood cuttings can be taken through summer into autumn. Insert in moist, well-drained compost to root. These should root well. Large, older wood cuttings are reported to root well and can be grown to form a live fence or hedge. *Layering:* Can be air-layered successfully. *Grafting:* Grafting or shield budding on *Spondias* rootstocks is possible; however, seedling trees are more vigorous than budded or grafted trees.

Pests and diseases: Has no particular pest or disease problems. ■

Staphylea spp.
Bladdernut
SAPINDACEAE
European bladdernut (*Staphylea pinnata*), American bladdernut (*S. trifolia*)
Relatives: lychee, longan

There are ~10 species in the *Staphylea* genus and these are native to southeastern Europe, North America and western Asia, from temperate-climate areas. The species are all cold hardy, deciduous and have pretty flowers in spring. The bladdernut is often grown ornamentally for its flowers and interestingly shaped fruits, and some species have edible tasty seeds.

DESCRIPTION
The European bladdernut is a popular ornamental shrub in Germany and other regions of Europe. A deciduous, upright shrub, growing to ~4.5 m, with the same spread. Has grey bark with a distinctive net-like pattern. It is often naturally multi-stemmed.

Leaves: Deciduous, opposite, pinnate with an odd number of leaflets (3–7). Leaflets are ovate–oblong, 5–12 cm long, 2–5.5 cm wide, thin, toothed, light green above, paler grey-green beneath, with fine hair around the base of the midrib.

Flowers: Long, white, often tinged pinkish-red, drooping, bell-shaped, borne in panicles, in spring. They are small, ~1 cm diameter. Plants tend to flower best in years that follow hot summers. Flowers are bisexual, and are fairly self-fertile so only need one plant to set fruits, though more than one plant may increase fruit-set. *Pollination:* By flies.

Fruit: Produce interesting triangular-shaped fruits with three pointed segments, which some consider look like a bladder. Length 3–4.5 cm, width ~2 cm. They have a thin, papery, puffy husk that is light green when ripe. Each segment contains ~3 small, smooth, hard, shiny, chestnut-brown seeds. Fruits ripen in autumn, but can then remain on the bushes during winter.

CULTIVATION
Location: Can grow in full sun or semi-shade. Is moderately wind tolerant.

Food

The kernels are sweet and have a nutty pistachio-like taste. They can be eaten fresh or roasted.

Nutrition

Contain a sweet oil that can be used for culinary purposes.

Ornamental

A popular ornamental plant, with spring flowers and interestingly shaped fruits.

Temperature: Very cold hardy tolerating temperatures down to ~–20°C.

Soil/water/nutrients: Tolerant of a wide range of soils, as long as they are not too dry, though prefers a rich loamy soil. Grows best in neutral to slightly acid soils, but also tolerates some alkalinity. Is not tolerant of waterlogging. Is moderately nutrient hungry, and benefits from one or two annual additions of a complete, balanced fertiliser.

Propagation: *Seed*: Can be very slow to germinate, ~12–18 months or more, and it is best sown as soon as it is ripe. Stored seed should be sown as early in the year as possible after receiving 2–3 months of cold stratification. *Cuttings*: Semi-ripe cuttings, 5–8 cm long, with a heel, can be taken in summer and inserted in moist, gritty compost to root. There is a fairly good percentage take. *Suckers:* Plants may produce suckers; these can be removed in the dormant season and planted out. *Layering:* This can be done during summer, but needs ~15 months to root, though often a good percentage take is possible by this method.

Pests and diseases: Generally has few problems, and is resistant to honey fungus.

SIMILAR SPECIES

American bladdernut, *Staphylea trifolia.* The American bladdernut is a native of eastern North America, from Quebec south to the Mississippi. It is a shrub with a medium growth rate, ~3–5 m tall. Its leaves are arranged in threes. It has similar cultivation, propagation, etc. to the European bladdernut. Its seeds are also pistachio-like in flavour, and can be roasted. The bark has been ground and infused to make a soothing face wash. ∎

Sterculia quadrifida
Peanut tree (monkeynut tree)
STERCULIACEAE
Relatives: Chinese parasol tree

The peanut tree is an attractive native of the coastal regions of northern and eastern Australia. The Aborigines have used this tree for many hundreds, if not thousands, of years for its bark and leaves, and its nuts have been either eaten raw or roasted.

Food

The seeds have a delicious nutty flavour and taste very similar to peanuts. The outer skin of the kernel is best removed before eating. Can be eaten raw or roasted. The taproots of young plants are also edible. Leaves may be used to flavour cooking.

Medicinal

The taproot has several medicinal uses. The crushed leaves have been used as a poultice by the Aborigines to treat insect stings, open wounds and sores, and to control heavy bleeding. A bark infusion is used to treat eye disorders.

DESCRIPTION

Attractive, bushy, medium-sized tree; height ~12–15 m, spread ~4 m, often smaller in cooler regions. Grows in a variety of habitats in Australia. It has attractive bark.

Leaves: Often briefly deciduous in cooler regions or when placed under environmental stress. Attractive, 10–20 cm long, shiny, bright–dark green, heart-shaped, simple, alternate in pseudo-whorls, on 5–12-cm-long petioles.

Flowers: Forms racemes of inconspicuous, small (~1 cm long), creamy-yellow, somewhat hairy, lemon-scented, bell-shaped flowers, from early–mid summer. Flowers are often produced on the tree during its leafless stage.

Fruit: Leathery, boat-shaped, ~8 cm long, red-orange, eye-catching pods, containing edible seeds, are often produced in large numbers. Mature from late spring to summer: the pod splits open when ripe. The attractive, crimson interior contains 4–8 shiny, black, peanut-sized seeds. Inside the seed, the kernel is creamy-white and can be eaten fresh. In warmer areas, they can be produced for much of the year.

Yield/harvest: Often get abundant yields. Pick the pods when they are fully coloured and ripe, but before the seeds are dispersed.

Roots: Forms a taproot, so care is needed that this is not damaged when planting. Forms a symbiotic mycorrhizal association with fungi in the soil, which enables it to obtain extra nutrients, particularly phosphates.

CULTIVATION
Location/temperature: Grows best in full sun, but can also grow in semi-shade. Likes Mediterranean, warm-temperate or subtropical locations. Makes a good coastal plant. This tree is frost tender.

Soil/water: Grows best in loamy, medium-textured soil, though can also grow in dry, sandy soils. Is drought tolerant. Requires good drainage and does not like waterlogging.

Other uses
The fibrous inner bark of the tree is used to make string, rope, fishing nets and fishing line. *Ornamental:* It is a handsome, ornamental tree, and makes a good specimen with its glossy foliage and interesting, brightly coloured pods. A good shade tree, or a suitable shrub for a rockery. The seeds attract the native birds.

Pot culture: This plant could be grown in a container, for a few years at least, and could be taken inside or given extra protection in cooler regions. Needs minimum care and attention.

Propagation: Fresh seeds germinate easily and quickly, sometimes within 3 days. Best sown when fresh. ■

Stevia rebaudiana
Stevia (kaa he-he)
ASTERACEAE

A short-lived perennial that is a native of Paraguay and is now found in several other South American countries. It is the only member of the Asteraceae family to have sweetness properties. This plant has been used by the indigenous populations for many hundreds of years as a sweetener in mate tea and in many foods as well as also being eaten on its own. Although the plant is not particularly attractive, its leaves, when chewed, have an amazingly sweet, liquorice-type flavour because it contains the chemicals stevioside and steviol. When the Spanish arrived in South America, they soon learnt of its amazing taste and the knowledge of this plant, which many say is superior to sugar in its sweetness, spread to many other South American countries. Despite this, it was not produced commercially until early in the 20th century. The first small stevia crops were harvested, and knowledge of its existence became more widespread. Unlike cane sugar, which needs considerable processing (see p. 406), stevia leaves only need to be dried and crushed before use. Since those times, the use of stevia has been promoted as a safe sweetener for diabetic use as well as having many other benefits. The first crops of stevia were taken to the USA in ~1920, and it was recommended as a new crop with great potential. However, there are reports that the big sugar companies were not thrilled at the idea of commercial stevia production. More recently, in Japan, because artificial sweeteners were banned or strictly regulated in their country, the Japanese have 'discovered' stevia, and its use has become widespread. By 1988, it represented ~40% of the market share of sweetener products consumed. It is used in Japan in many foods, including desserts, icecream, confectionery, soft drinks, etc. Apart from in South America, it is now grown and used in a number of other countries, e.g. China, Malaysia, Thailand and South Korea. In the USA, stevia can only be sold as a 'dietary supplement' and, although it can be found in some health-store products, is not officially allowed to be called a 'sweetener'. It is also not legal to sell stevia in the EU because of EC directives. This plant has aroused much debate, which is still not resolved, and for those interested in growing it, I suggest searching the internet for more detailed information.

DESCRIPTION
A sprawling, short-lived perennial herb (height ~70 cm, spread ~50 cm), often grown as an annual.

Leaves: Smallish, elliptic, parallel veins, yellow-green, lightly toothed, in pairs at 90° intervals up the stem.

Harvest: The leaves should be harvested as late in the

year as possible, with cooler temperatures and shorter days increasing their sweetness. This should be done before the first frosts, unless the plants can be protected. Because the plant is usually grown as an annual, the leaves can be simply stripped off the stems, along with the stem tips. The leaves are gently dried for a fairly short period, e.g. 12 hours: long,

Food

The leaves are extremely sweet and, when refined, can be 150–300 times sweeter than sugar. Home-cultivated stevia is not as sweet, but is still ~15 times sweeter than sugar. Its taste is sweeter if the leaves are dried, rather than eaten fresh. An extract can be made by adding 1 part warm water to 0.25 parts of crushed stevia leaves; leave to stand for ~24 hours. This extract can then be refrigerated and added to various dishes. When cooking with stevia, be careful not to add too much and over-sweeten dishes. Could be added to fruit salads, cream/yoghurt-based dishes, or used with honey or maple syrup. However, stevia does not have all the benefits of sugar: it cannot be dissolved or melted in dishes, it cannot be caramelised, or easily added to cakes, or used with yeast.

Nutrition/medicinal

Stevia, compared with sugar, has much fewer calories and, more importantly, because the sweetness passes through the digestive system without being chemically absorbed, stevia can be used as a sweetener without the medical risks of sugar, i.e. with diabetes. As yet, there do not seem to be any definite reports of adverse effects from the moderate use of stevia, although see the Warning below. Stevia does not adversely affect blood-sugar levels and does not contribute to dental caries. Its use has been suggested for diabetes, obesity, hypertension, high blood pressure, carbohydrate cravings. It also increases glucose tolerance in patients with hypoglycaemia, and reduces indigestion, skin diseases and yeast infections. In addition, some research has shown that stevioside and steviol are able to stimulate insulin secretion, and so may also help treat type-2 diabetes mellitus, as well as help prevent it. It has also been reported to have antibacterial, antiviral and anti-yeast activity. As well as not contributing to tooth decay, some research has shown that stevia leaf extracts actually prevent dental caries by inhibiting plaque-forming bacteria. **Warning:** Although many Japanese studies have not found any adverse effects from stevia consumption, the Food Standards Agency, UK, warn that the extract has the potential to produce adverse effects in the male reproductive system that could affect fertility and that a metabolite produced by the human gut microflora, steviol, is genotoxic (i.e. damages DNA)'. (See also http://www.food.gov.uk/multimedia/pdfs/stevioside.pdf). In addition, at very high intakes, stevia may cause hypoglycaemia; therefore, diabetics should monitor their blood-sugar levels as medications may need adjusting. It may also lower blood pressure, therefore persons with low blood pressure should avoid ingesting large amounts of stevia. It may also reduce heart rate, so those with bradycardia or on medications that decrease heart rate should also be wary.

hot drying reduces leaf quality. Allow plenty of air to circulate. Leaves can then be finely crushed and stored in a dark, air-tight container for several months. They are very sweet with a somewhat liquorice flavour.

Flowers: Tiny, white–light mauve, in small clusters of 2–6 that form loose panicles in spring/early summer. They may be self-sterile. Are insect pollinated

Fruit: Has small, mostly infertile seeds. These are found singly within a small (~0.4 cm long), dry seedcoat that is covered by numerous hairy bristles. The seeds tend to be black or tan, with the latter probably being infertile.

Roots: Has an extensive root system. Has some shallower roots, so care is needed with cultivation and an organic mulch will help conserve moisture and add nutrients.

CULTIVATION

Location: Prefers semi-shade in hotter regions, though likes a hot summer with day length being more important than light intensity, i.e. warm-temperate latitudes with long days produce the best leaves, whereas shorter days initiate next year's flower-bud formation. Does best in non-exposed locations.

Temperature: Can be grown in a wide range of climates, from semi-tropical to cold-temperate regions. However, plants need protecting from frosts, particularly when young, and are usually grown as annuals in colder areas. Can survive winter in climates suitable for citrus species, but will only live for a few years. If trying to overwinter a plant, it is best to not harvest whole stems, and to retain some basal leaf growth. They can be grown indoors in colder areas, but need supplementary lighting that provides ~15 hours of light a day. Plants that survive winter can give better yields in their second year, though leaf quality usually deteriorates by the third year, and plants then need replacing.

Soil/nutrients: Does best in a rich, loamy soil, and a good organic mulch conserves moisture and adds nutrients. However, can survive in poor, sandy soils. Stevia can tolerate a wide range of pH, and often naturally grows in somewhat acid soils. Does like a moist soil, particularly when actively growing, but not waterlogging. Fertilisers should have less nitrogen compared to the other major nutrients: too much nitrogen results in growth that is lush, but lacks sweetness.

Pot culture: Can be grown easily in containers, and greatly benefits from an organic mulch. Easily controlled and takes up little space.

Planting: Space at ~0.5 m apart, with more space between rows. Plant in semi-shade in hotter regions.

Propagation: *Seed:* Difficult. Germination is poor because many seeds are infertile, and any progeny vary considerably. Studies have shown that black seeds are more viable. The lack of fertile seed may be a reason for its limited popularity. *Cuttings:* Cuttings taken in spring from over-wintered plants can be successful. Alternatively, cuttings can be taken in autumn, but these root reluctantly, though treatment with rooting hormone or willow soakings can improve rates. Remove most leaves from cuttings before inserting in a sandy compost, in the warm and light, and they should root within a few weeks.

Pests and diseases: Very few problems. Has been hypothesised that, although not toxic, stevia plants have some insect-repelling properties. ∎

Synsepalum dulcificum
Miracle fruit (miracle berry)
SAPOTACEAE

The miracle fruit is a native of tropical west Africa. It is so named because of its fruit's remarkable natural sweetener properties, which have been known of and used in Africa for many hundreds of years. If one eats a sour fruit, e.g. a lemon, straight after having eaten some miracle fruit, no acidity from the lemon is experienced, and this sweetening effect can remain for a couple of hours. These properties are just beginning to become more widely utilised elsewhere in the world. Although it is native to tropical regions, this species can be grown in both subtropical and warm temperate regions (with care), and will also produce fruits. Plants are suitable for container culture and so could be grown in cooler regions.

DESCRIPTION
It forms a slow-growing, evergreen bush or tree, growing to ~5–6 m in height in its native habitat, but rarely to 1.6–1.8 m elsewhere.

Leaves: Deep green, elongated and arranged in a spiral around the main stem. Can vary in size and be smooth or hairy.

Flowers: Small, ~0.75 cm in diameter, white, produced in flushes through many months of the year.

Fruit: Small, orange-scarlet, oblong, ~2–3 cm long. They contain a white or yellowish, fleshy pulp and a large, single seed. Although the flesh itself is not particularly sweet, when a single fruit is eaten slowly, followed by a sharp-tasting fruit, such as lime or lemon, a 'miraculous' effect occurs. The aroma and flavour of the citrus remains, but the sharpness almost completely disappears. This effect can remain from 30 minutes up to 2–3 hours. It occurs because of a 'double protein' within the miracle berry; once this is cleaved during digestion, then the sweetness effect is lost. If the seeds are chewed with the flesh, then this also nullifies the 'miracle' effect.

Yield/harvest: Only takes 3–4 weeks from fruit-set till fruit maturity. Fruits are produced throughout the year, and hundreds of berries can be harvested from a single plant. Plants start to fruit when ~4 years old.

CULTIVATION
Easy to grow.

Temperature: They originate from hot, wet tropical lowlands, but will tolerate temperatures down to freezing for brief periods, if acclimatised. Established plants can survive a light frost (down to ~–3°C) without too much damage, but it is best avoided if possible as plants grow better and produce more fruits in warmer climates.

Location: They grow best in semi-shade. They are not very wind tolerant, and like a sheltered location. They prefer high humidity to dry climates.

Soils/water: Plants grow best in a moist, fertile loam. They need an acid pH of 4.5–5.8. If the soil is more alkaline, then peat (or similar) or pine needles, for example, can be added to the soil when planting. The soil should be well-drained, but they do need enough moisture year round: this is important for the plant's growth and survival. However, continually waterlogged plants will succumb to root rot. Plants grow best with good nutrient levels and appreciate applications of a general water-soluble fertiliser when actively growing.

Pot culture: Unless cultivated in a warm-temperate or semi-tropical climate, these plants, because of their frost sensitivity, are ideal for growing in containers, where they can be given winter protection in a glasshouse or conservatory. They are smallish plants, and make a good conversation topic on a patio or deck. If grown indoors in winter, provide the plant with as much light as possible; in the summer, they can be sited in a warm, sheltered, but lightly shaded spot. Allow the roots of the plant to fill the container before transplanting into a larger size. When grown indoors, because plants need moisture, in winter, as well as at other times, a clear plastic bag around the leaves helps to maintain humidity, as does standing pots on pebbles within a tray filled with water to just below the base of the pot. Regular spraying of the leaves with water also helps.

Pruning: There is no need to prune this plant, except to tidy up any straggly growth or remove any damaged wood.

Propagation: *Seed:* Best sown when fresh as its viability decreases quickly. Wash the seeds and sow just below soil level. Stored seed should be kept in sealed containers and not allowed to dry out, and should be sown as soon as possible. Sow seeds in well-drained compost, and keep moist until they germinate in 8–10 weeks. They grow

Food
Berries should be eaten fresh; they go well with blueberries. If stored, even in a fridge, they tend to lose their effect. They are being investigated as a possible source of a natural sweetener.

uses

slowly for the first year, often being only 5–8 cm tall after 12 months, and are only 40–50 cm after 3–4 years; they then start to grow more rapidly. *Cuttings:* Can be rooted from cuttings under mist, but they take a long time to root and seem to grow even slower than seedlings.

Pests and diseases: Generally not affected by insects or diseases. If grown indoors, watch out for mealybugs, spider mites and other similiar plant pests.

CULTIVARS
'**Hirsutus':** Has hairy leaves. Fruits are oval, red, larger than those of most other types. ■

Syzygium jambos (syn. *Eugenia jambos, Jambosa jambos*)
Rose apple (plum rose, Malabar plum, pomarrosa)
MYRTACEAE
Similar species: water berry (*Syzygium cordatum*)
Relatives: blue lillypilly, Java plum, guava, jaboticaba, jambolan

The rose apple, despite its name, does not resemble an apple. It is native of southeastern Asia and is now cultivated and naturalised in many parts of India, the Pacific Islands, southern USA, and from Mexico down to Peru, including the West Indies. It is a small or medium-sized, decorative, evergreen tree with large, scented flowers and pale yellow, edible fruits. Although it grows best in the semi-tropics and tropics, it can also be grown in regions such as northern California and northern New Zealand, and can tolerate some frost.

DESCRIPTION
A small–medium height (~5 m tall, ~5 m spread), slow-growing, decorative, evergreen tree. It has low, wide-spreading branches that are often wider than its height. The branches are strong, yet flexible. Has pale brown bark.

Leaves: Glossy, abundant, leathery, shiny, elliptical, long and thin (~15–20 cm long, ~5 cm width), tapering to a point, and are scented when crushed. New leaves are dark red-bronze in colour, turning dark green as they mature. Forms a dense crown.

Flowers: Large, showy, white–pale cream, sweetly scented, ~5–8 cm width, with many long (~2.5 cm), white stamens, giving a fluffy, attractive appearance. Are borne on new wood in terminal clusters of 4–5 flowers any time from late winter–summer (varying with climate). The last season's fruit may still be on the tree as the next season's flowers open. Flowers are bisexual and are self-fertile. *Pollination:* Bees and other insects love the nectar-rich flowers.

Fruit: Ripen to a pale yellow colour, often with a slightly pink tinge. They are guava-like in appearance, 3–5 cm long, round–egg shaped with a distinctive, prominent apex and remnants of the calyx. It is classed as a 'false' berry. They have smooth, thin skin. The flesh is firm, crisp, juicy, pale yellow, fragrant, with a sweet taste. Fruits have a hollow centre, which contains 1–4 round, brown, seeds that are easy to remove. (These should be discarded as they are probably poisonous.) Fruits take 3–4 months to form and ripen.

Yield/harvest: It has poor yields for the size of the tree; a mature tree growing in optimum conditions may only yield ~2 kg of fruits a year. Trees grown from seedlings may take >4 years to produce fruit; trees grown vegetatively should produce fruits in 3–4 years. Fruits need to picked carefully because they easily bruise. Can only be stored for a short period, and are best eaten fresh or need to be preserved.

CULTIVATION
Can be grown as much for its ornamental attributes as for its fruit. It is more suited to warmer regions. Once established, it needs little maintenance.

Location: Grows best in warm, sunny locations. The tree is fairly wind resistant and is moderately tolerant of salt, so can be grown in relatively exposed maritime locations. Will eventually form a wide, spreading tree, so needs space.

Temperature: Can withstand temperatures down to ~−3°C, but not for prolonged periods. It will grow in colder areas, but may not bear fruit. Can grow and fruit in warm-temperate locations such as northern New Zealand and northern California. Plant trees in sunny, protected sites in colder regions. Younger trees need additional protection from frost.

Soil/water/nutrients: Trees can grow in a wide range of soil types, although a deep, moist, but well-drained loam is best. Can be grown in sand, stony soils or limestone. Will grow at a pH range from somewhat acid to fairly alkaline: pH 5.5–7.5. However, on more alkaline soils, deficiency symptoms, such as iron chlorosis, may occur and the addition of chelated micronutrients may be necessary. Does not tolerate waterlogging. Will grow in drier soils, but does not like extended periods of drought. Needs less moisture when the weather is colder. Seems to grow fairly well in poorer soils and is not nutrient hungry. However, it benefits from an occasional organic mulch.

Pot culture: This tree could be grown in a container for

The fruits of the rose apple.

a number of years, so enabling it to be given protection in colder regions. It is slow growing, is attractive and may also produce fruit if the conditions are right.

Pruning: Generally not needed. It can also be grown as a large, dense hedge, in which case hand pruning would be needed to avoid damaging the appearance of the long, attractive leaves.

Propagation: *Seed:* This is the main method used. The seeds have no dormancy and germinate well. They lose viability quickly, so are best sown when fresh. The seeds are unusual in that they have 3–4 embryos (instead of the usual single embryo), and so produce more than one shoot. However, the progeny do vary, as does fruit quality. Some trees produce poor-quality, dry fruit. *Cuttings:* Semi-ripe cuttings in summer are fairly successful. Progeny are then predictable. Select known good-fruiting trees to take cuttings from. *Layering:* Long stems can be ordinarily layered in late autumn, and will take several months to form roots. Additionally, air-layering can be practised and is reported to be successful.

Planting: If growing as a specimen tree, allow plenty of space between trees: they spread widely. Young trees benefit from cold protection and also some shade.

Pests and diseases: Has few serious diseases or insect problems. Can get occasional aphid attacks. Root rots can be a problem, e.g. *Fusarium*.

CULTIVARS
There are no known cultivars.

SIMILAR SPECIES

Water berry (syn. umdoni), *Syzygium cordatum*. A native of central and southern Africa, it forms a medium-sized tree, 8–15 m tall. It grows best in moist soil of slightly acidic to neutral pH. Is relatively tolerant of cold once established, and could be grown with care in warm-temperate climates. Has evergreen, thick, shiny, rounded, bright green leaves with a heart-shaped base. Has abundant, white, fluffy flowers with distinctive long stamens characteristic of this family. These produce abundant nectar and are borne mostly in spring. Its fruits are oval, ripening to dark purple. They contain a single green seed. Fruits ripen soon after fruit-set, from late spring. They have a crisp and crunchy texture that is often sweet

Food
The fruit are sometimes eaten fresh. They have a guava-like sweet taste and a rose-like scent, though some plants produce fruits with little taste. More usually, they are stewed with honey, or used in syrup, jellies and jams, often with lemon and other fruits, and seem to retain their distinctive rose-water flavour when cooked. A more unusual dish can be prepared by stuffing their hollow cavity with a rice/nut/chicken/meat mixture, covering the fruit with a tomato-and-garlic sauce, and then baking for ~20 minutes. In Jamaica, the sliced fruits are stewed in a very syrupy sugar with cinnamon. A sweet-smelling type of rose-water can be made from the fruits. The flowers can be candied, and the bees make a good honey from the nectar.

Nutrition
Reasonable levels of vitamin C: ~22 mg/100 g of flesh, and of vitamin A (340 IU). Also contains some niacin, potassium and calcium.

Medicinal
In India, the fruits are used as a tonic for the brain and liver. They also act as a diuretic. A tea made from the flowers may reduce fever. The seeds, bark and leaves have been used medicinally, but this may not be advisable. **Warning:** The seeds, roots and leaves may be poisonous. They contain hydrocyanic acid and also an alkaloid, jambosine.

Other uses
A yellow, essential oil can be distilled from the leaves and contains pinene and limonene, which is used in the perfume industry. The flexible branches have been used to make baskets. The bark has been used for tanning and yields a brown dye. The heartwood is dark red–brown, fibrous, close-grained, heavy, strong and has been used to make furniture, parts of boats, construction beams, frames for musical instruments and for turnery. It is not durable in the ground.

Ornamental
Makes an attractive specimen tree, with scented flowers and attractive leaves. It is also planted as a shade tree in warmer areas.

and quite good, though some fruits are of poorer quality. The fruits are usually just eaten fresh, though can be added to desserts, or used to make an alcoholic drink. Parts of the plant are high in tannins and have been used medicinally to treat diarrhoea, and stomach or respiratory problems. The bark has also been used as a fish poison. Its flowers and fruits attract a wide range of insects and birds. It is usually propagated from seed. Its timber is reddish, fine grained, durable and of good quality. ■

Syzygium spp.
(syn. *Eugenia, Acmena, Waterhousea*)
Lillypilly (Australian brush cherry)
MYRTACEAE

Some edible species: Australian brush cherry (*S. paniculatum*), riberry (*S. luehmanii*), blue lillypilly (*S. oleosum*), brush cherry (*S. australe*), powderpuff lillypilly (*S. wilsonii*), river cherry (*S. tierneyanum*), Francis' water gum (*S. francisii*), Coolamon (*S. mooreii*), native apple (*S. eucalyptoides*), blue lillypilly (*S. coolminianum*), lady apple (*S. suborbiculare*), *Syzygium cormiflorum*
Relatives: rose apple, cloves

Most species of *Syzygium* occur in southeastern Asia, with others occurring in India, southern China, Africa, Hawaii, Australia and New Zealand. Australia has ~60 indigenous species known as lillypillies, all of which seem to be edible. The lillypillies used to be known under the *Eugenia* genus (or also *Acmena* or *Waterhousea*), and are sometimes still listed under these names. Also, their common names are often interchanged, and lillypilly sometimes refers to a group of plants or sometimes a specific species. Here, the main edible lillypilly species are described. They range in size from being a small bush to a large tree, and are valued for their ornamental qualities. They form handsome plants and have become very popular throughout Australia, and are often used for hedges, as ornamentals and container subjects. The fruits are becoming more popular and familiar as the interest in Australian bush-food has evolved. They are an important genus in the Australian bush and are a food source for both blossom-feeding and fruit-eating animals and birds.

DESCRIPTION

Often multi-stemmed large shrubs or smaller trees, though some species form large trees. The species described here have attractive, red, smoothly flaking bark. Most have a spreading canopy.

Leaves: Evergreen, glossy, bright–dark green, oval, with rounded or pointed tips, opposite. They are usually small, ~1.5–2.5 cm long. The young leaves are bronze-red in colour.

Flowers: Abundant masses of, usually, white–cream (sometimes pink–maroon), powder-puff-like flowers, which are borne from late spring–summer. They are borne in clusters at the ends of branches from leaf axils. They have many, long central stamens, giving them a fluffy appearance. The flowers have an inferior ovary. *Pollination:* The flowers produce lots of nectar that attracts birds; they are also visited by butterflies.

Fruit: Trees produce clusters of small, attractively-coloured, tasty berries in autumn, which are also valued by the wildlife. They range in colour from white–pink–maroon–purple, are round–oval–pear-shaped, ~1–2.5 cm in long, and are waxy, smooth. Many species are indented at their apex and have a large central seed. Fruits are juicy, but also often crunchy, frequently sour, but pleasant. Some species have fruits that can be eaten fresh, but they are more often used in jams, conserves, etc.

Yield/harvest: Some species produce very good yields of 60–80 kg per tree. Fruits are best harvested when fully ripe, fully coloured, just becoming soft and are as sweet as possible.

Roots: Mostly forms surface roots, which prefer regular moisture and an organic mulch, though plants can tolerate quite a lot of disturbance around them (unlike many shallow-rooted species).

CULTIVATION

Generally, they are easy to grow, and need little maintenance if they are given fertile, moist soil and not too much cold.

Location: Grow best in full sun, but can also grow in semi-shade; are best grown with some shade in very hot regions. Many species are fairly wind tolerant and can be grown as a windbreak. They are not salt tolerant and are not suitable for exposed maritime locations.

Temperature: Many do not tolerate freezing temperatures, and are best grown in containers in colder regions. A few species will tolerate brief frosts, but not extended cold periods. They grow best with warm–hot summers, and cool (~5°C) but not very cold winters.

Soil/water/nutrients: Plants grow best with a moist soil during spring and summer, but less water during winter. They are not very drought tolerant, and will drop their leaves if the soil becomes too dry. They grow best in humid regions, but do not like waterlogged conditions. Growth is best in slightly acid to neutral soils: they are tolerant of alkaline soils. Lillypillies are fairly nutrient hungry and grow best with regular applications of an acid-type general fertiliser, mainly in summer. The use of blood-and-bone or slow-release fertiliser is recommended. Plants benefit from a good organic mulch, which helps retain moisture, adds nutrients and suppresses weed growth.

Pot culture: They grow well in containers and can be taken inside if frost threatens or grown indoors year-round if given enough light. Plant in a fertile, acid compost and mulch the soil surface. Choose smaller species. They appreciate regular repotting. If the roots are becoming too large they can be pruned hard back to keep the plant smaller.

Pruning: Best done in autumn or early spring. It naturally forms a bushy plant and, in general, needs little attention.

Diseased or damaged branches should be removed. Plants are mostly pruned for ornamental shape. Can be cut back hard, as they are often vigorous growers. Frequently pruned to form a hedge, though this may remove some of the fruiting laterals. Respond well to both root and branch pruning and make very good bonsai plants.

Propagation: *Seed:* Sow fresh seeds in autumn. Wash seeds thoroughly of pulp, and they usually then germinate well. *Cuttings:* Take semi-ripe cuttings in summer and insert in gritty, well-drained compost in the warmth and with mist. *Layering:* Air-layering can be successful.

Pests and diseases: Generally not a lot of problems, but can get scale, mealybugs, Caribbean fruit fly, aphids, red-spider mite. Sooty mould can also be a problem.

SOME EDIBLE SPECIES

Australian brush cherry (magenta cherry), *Syzygium paniculatum* (syn. *Eugenia myrtifolia*). A native of Queensland and New South Wales, it forms a smaller, attractive tree or large shrub, to ~6–8 m. Has very small, glossy, green leaves which, when grown in full sun, develop a red tint. Has flaky attractive bark. *Flowers:* White, in summer. *Fruit:* Fragrant, fleshy, white–maroon–purple, round–egg-shaped, 1.5–2.5 cm diameter. They have a large central seed.

Cultivation: Needs a warmer winter temperature, but is reported to be able to withstand several degrees of frost. An easy-to-grow plant in most temperate and subtropical climates, and can grow in most soil types (not alkaline).

Uses: *Food:* Most fruits have a pleasant, crisp flesh that is sour, but aromatic. If the fruits are too sour, their flavour is usually improved by cooking. The berries are eaten to quench thirst and are made into jams and jellies. *Other uses:* A popular garden ornamental and bonsai plant because of its extremely small leaves. It is also grows very well in containers. Is often grown as a hedge in California and Florida.

Riberry (small-leafed lillypilly, cherry alder), *Syzygium luehmanii*. Native to the rainforests of Queensland and New South Wales, this is one of the few lillypillies in commercial production in Australia. It was one of the first native fruits to be appreciated by Europeans, and Joseph Banks recorded that Captain Cook first tasted this lillypilly in 1770.

Description: It is a very attractive, dense-leaved, often quite erect, smaller tree, ~6 m tall, though trees in the wild can grow to ~30 m tall and can form buttressed trunks. Has young leaves that range in colour from purple–red. Mature leaves are lanceolate, very glossy green, ~6 cm long. The branches often droop down to the ground. *Flowers:* Creamy-white, and are borne in spring and summer. *Fruit:* Has masses of red egg-shaped fruits (~1–1.25 cm long) that are juicy, sub-acidic with a clove/cinnamon-like flavour: Mature trees can yield up to 80 kg. There are some seedless varieties. They can only tolerate light frosts. Produces fruit in 3–5 years.

Uses: *Food:* They are a very popular ingredient in bush-food dishes in Australia. They are also used in jams, icecreams, tarts, marmalade, sauces for meats or fish, and in cakes. *Ornamental:* It is a very attractive and popular ornamental species in Australia, as well as being sought for its fruits.

Blue lillypilly, *Syzygium oleosum* (syn. *Eugenia coolmaniana*). Native to Queensland and New South Wales, it forms a shrub/small tree to 3–7 m tall, sometimes taller in the wild. *Leaves:* Shiny, deep green, elliptical, ~10 cm long. Have numerous oil glands, which give off a distinctive smell when crushed. *Flowers:* Have reddish buds, opening into white, fluffy, showy flowers. *Fruit:* Bluey-purple, ~2.5 cm diameter, juicy, crunchy, of good quality, used for jam, etc. Trees start to bear after 2 years. May be moderately frost tolerant.

Brush cherry, *Syzygium australe*. Native to the rainforests of Queensland and New South Wales, it forms a medium–large tree, up to ~20 m in an ideal habitat, though is more often ~10 m. It is fairly cold hardy, and can tolerate some frost. Has attractive red-bronze new leaves. Older leaves are elliptical, ~2.5–8 cm long. Four wings at the nodes of young stems help to identify this species. The flowers are white with numerous white fluffy stamens. *Fruits:* Red–purple, oval, ~2–3 cm long, have a crisp, refreshing texture, with a large seed. A prolific bearer.

Uses: *Food:* Fruits are often used in jams, or are eaten fresh. *Ornamental:* Attractive tree, often grown as a screen or for shade. Has been grown as a bonsai species.

Powderpuff lillypilly, *Syzygium wilsonii*. Native to Queensland and New South Wales (as far south as Sydney), it forms a shrub or small tree, 2–6 m tall, often with a weeping habit. *Leaves:* Narrowly oval, with young leaves tinged red–bronze. *Flowers:* Large, crimson-coloured, fluffy, ~10 cm diameter, borne in spring and early summer. *Fruits:* White, oval. This lillypilly is fairly cold hardy, and is easy to grow in most temperate and subtropical climates. It will grow in sunny

Food
The fruits vary a lot in taste from species to species, but all have a high pectin content, which makes them ideal for jams and other preserves.

Nutrition/medicinal
The fruits have good levels of vitamin C and various minerals. Their pectin makes them good for digestion. The trees have been used as a local anaesthetic to treat syphilis.

Other uses
Many of the species are valued for their hard timber. They are also considered fairly fire retardant in Australia, and are often used as garden plants in fire-prone areas.

Ornamental
Their shape and form makes them excellent specimen plants with their attractive bark and eye-catching young leaves, which vary in colour from pink–red–rust, turning to glossy dark green as they mature. They also have abundant, attractive fluffy flowers and strikingly-coloured edible fruits. They are used for screening, as a windbreak and to attract wildlife.

uses

locations, but is also happy in semi-shade. *Ornamental:* It is a very attractive, ornamental species for both its flowers and leaves, and makes a good specimen or container plant. *S. wilsonii* var. *crytophlebium* has more erect growth. If acclimatised, it is probably more hardy than most lillypillies.

River cherry, *Syzygium tierneyanum*. Native to Queensland and New South Wales, it forms a fast-growing, dense, spreading shrub/small tree, with glossy, dark green leaves. Has red–bronze new leaves. Not as cold hardy as some. *Flowers:* Abundant, cream-coloured, in summer. *Fruit:* Clusters of pinkish-red berries, not often eaten fresh because of their sour taste; but made into jam, conserves, etc. *Ornamental:* Can be planted as a windbreak, or if the lower branches are pruned off it makes a good shade tree.

Francis' water gum (giant water gum), *Syzygium francisii*. Native to southeast Queensland and northeast NSW, it forms a larger lillypilly tree, up to 15 m tall, with an attractive very spreading canopy (~15 m), though can be ~30 m tall in the wild. It has small, glossy, dark green, lanceolate leaves, with new leaves being bright pink–red. Can be pruned to keep it small and dense. *Flowers:* Small, white, fluffy. *Fruit:* Abundant, ~1.5 cm diameter, oval, red–mauve–purple. Can be grown in full sun and can tolerate light frosts.

Coolamon, *Syzygium mooreii*. Native to Queensland and NSW; 25–30 m in height. The species is endangered and may be difficult to get hold of. Has long (~22 cm), thick, glossy, dark green, elliptical leaves and fluffy, cerise-coloured flowers borne on older wood. The edible fruits are large (~6 cm diameter) and ripen to a greeny-white colour.

Native apple, *Syzygium eucalyptoides*. A native of northern Australia, this species can tolerate dry, sandy, gravelly conditions. Its leaves are long, lanceolate and eucalyptus-like, and have a drooping form reminiscent of many eucalyptus species, and hence its species name. It forms a shrubby tree, reaching ~5 m tall. Its flowers are white, with numerous fluffy stamens, and are borne during spring–summer. The fruits are rounded, small (~2 cm diameter), and turn pinkish when ripe. They have crisp, dry flesh that is tart but tasty. The tannins within the leaves and bark were used as a medicine to treat skin problems and fever.

Blue lillypilly, *Syzygium coolminianum*. Native to the rainforests of northern NSW and Queensland. Can be grown from warm temperate–tropical regions. It is not frost tolerant. Flowers are white and showy. Fruits are rounded, purple-blue, not too sour, and can be eaten fresh.

Lady apple (red bush apple), *Syzygium suborbiculare*. Native to northern Australia and needs a more tropical climate to grow well. They have long been used by the Aborigines as a food source, but also for medicinal purposes. Often found in tropical woodland. Grows to ~12 m. Has leathery, roundish leaves. Flowers are white with many fluffy stamens, and are borne during summer. The fruits are oval, in tight clusters. They turn from grey-green to a rosy tint when ripe. The flesh is crisp. The fruits are best harvested when fully ripe, and can be eaten fresh, though are still fairly tart. The seeds are best discarded. The leaves, bark and seeds are high in tannin, and have been used as a poultice on wounds to stop bleeding, and were ingested to treat diarrhoea. ∎

Tamarindus indica
Tamarind
FABACEAE (Leguminosae) (subgroup Caesalpiniaceae)
Relatives: carob, honey locust, licorice

An attractive tree, probably native to tropical east Africa. It was taken to southeastern Asia and is now grown in many semi-tropical and tropical regions of the world, including Australia and southern USA. Its fruits have been used for many hundreds of years: it is mentioned in Indian scriptures written ~800 BC and in Buddhist writings from 650 AD. It is a popular garden and street tree in many areas of the world, e.g. India and Asia, and has delicate, attractive leaves, pretty flowers and ornamental seed pods, which are sweet and contain tasty pulp that is used widely as a flavouring but also medicinally.

DESCRIPTION
A large tree, 12–20 m tall, strong, slow growing, and can live >150 years. Has a short trunk, with twisting spreading branches that form a light, rounded, open canopy. The bark is rough-textured.

Leaves: Finely-textured, feathery, pinnate, consisting of many small, bright green leaflets, ~1.25 cm long, evergreen, arranged in groups of 10–15 pairs. They have the familiar shape and organisation of many Fabaceae. The leaflets close at night and in cold, wet weather, and may drop during cold winters or in very dry seasons. The tree casts a light shade. There are no spines.

Flowers: Small racemes of five-petalled fragrant flowers, forming unequal lobes, ~2-cm across, pale yellow, with fine red veins, in early summer. Only the upper three flowers of the cluster develop. Flowers are bisexual and self-fertile. *Pollination:* By bees.

Fruit/harvest/yield: Long (8–25 cm), ornamental, velvety, green pods that turn rich brownish-red when ripe. There is a long period between pollination and fruit harvest of about 9 months, so pods ripen from the following late spring to summer. Dry weather at this time improves pod quality. The pods become indented between the inner seeds, are very brittle when ripe and can be easily removed. Inside, a sticky, tangy, sweet–sour rich brown pulp surrounds 6–10 seeds embedded longitudinally within. It is the pulp that is mainly used.

Yield/harvest/storage: Grafted trees take 3–4 years to start producing fruits; seedlings take 6–8 years to begin. Trees can give good yields, though seem to vary: some report 10–100 kg per tree, others have reported 800 kg/tree, though the former is probably more likely. The pods should be fully dark brown when harvested or the pulp may be acidic and fibrous. Pods tend to drop when ripe. The pulp can be readily compressed and stored for long periods.

Roots: Large, deep and extensive, though not usually invasive. Although a member of the legume family, the tamarind does not seem to have a symbiotic relationship with nitrogen-fixing bacteria.

CULTIVATION

Once established, tamarinds are very easy trees to grow, needing minimum attention.

Location: They have high wind tolerance and can tolerate salt spray, so are excellent as specimen trees in maritime locations. Prefer a location in full sun.

Temperature: Although often found in hotter climates, mature trees can tolerate fairly cold conditions down to ~–3°C or lower, though some reports say that it is more frost sensitive than this. They can be grown successfully in many warm-temperate–subtropical regions, and could be grown in colder regions with added protection and suitable positioning. Young trees need additional protection from winter cold.

Soil/water/nutrients: Prefers a deep loam with a pH of ~5.5, but can adapt to most soil types, including coarse stony soil, and a pH range of 4.5–8.5. Trees grow best in moist, well-drained soil, though, when mature, can tolerate drought as well as brief flooding, but not for extended periods. Are only moderately nutrient hungry, benefiting from 1–2 applications of a general fertiliser annually if grown in poorer soils.

Pruning: Only need minimal pruning, possibly to form 4–5 main scaffold branches around the central leader when young, with the tip of the central stem removed once a suitable height is attained. Older trees just need damaged or diseased wood removed.

Propagation: *Seed:* Good germination from ripe or stored seed in ~7–14 days, particularly if the seed is soaked for a few hours first. Seedlings grow easily, but after a few months they will have formed a long taproot, so plant in deeper pots and avoid replanting too often to prevent root damage. Seedlings need some shade. Vegetative propagation methods give more reliable progeny and a shorter time until pod production. *Cuttings:* Can take semi-ripe cuttings during summer and insert in moist, warm, gritty compost, in semi-shade, to root. *Layering:* Trees can be air-layered

successfully. *Grafting:* Can be whip-and-tongue-grafted or shield-budded.

Pests and diseases: No major problems, although ripe fruits, if left on the tree, can become infected by moulds, etc. ∎

uses

Food
Is widely used in Asian and Indian cuisine in sauces and chutneys. The seed pulp, when extracted, has a sweet–sour molasses-like flavour. It can be eaten fresh but is more usually added to dishes, and is also made into a flavoursome drink that is said to be similar to lemonade. It is called *refresco de tamarindo* in Latin America, *tamarinade* in Jamaica, and is also a popular drink in the Middle East. It is also an ingredient of Worcestershire sauce. The pulp can be compressed and stored for later use. It is then soaked and the juice drained from the pulp and added to savoury dishes. The pod can also be eaten when ripe and sweet; however, when under-ripe, it is sour and is then used to season meat and fish dishes. The seeds are also used and are generally boiled or fried. The flowers and young leaves can be eaten, and may be added to curries and chutneys.

Nutrition/medicinal
Ripe pulp contains high levels of fruit acid (~20%): citric, malic, oxalic and tartaric; sugars (~35%): fructose, glucose and sucrose, as well as pectin. It has good levels of several minerals, including calcium, potassium, phosphorus and iron, and several B vitamins, i.e. thiamine, in particular, but also riboflavin and niacin. Has good levels of dietary fibre and reasonable levels of protein. It has low levels of vitamin C (~4 mg/100 g of flesh). The tree as a whole has been proven to cure many medical problems. The ripe tamarind fruit have proven medical value to reduce fever, relieve wind and cure intestinal ailments, and are used as an ingredient in cardiac and blood-sugar-reducing medicines. The pulp is also used as an astringent on skin infections, to soothe sore throats, as a mild laxative, to cure biliousness, for bile disorders, and to alleviate sunstroke and alcoholic intoxication. The leaves and flowers, either dried or boiled, are used externally for swollen joints, sprains and boils, for conjunctivitis, as an antiseptic, as a vermifuge, and to treat dysentery, jaundice, erysipelas and haemorrhoids.

Other uses
The seeds contain an oil (10–15%) that is used in varnishes, textile finishing and paints. The leaves yield a yellow dye. The wood is hard and dense, but is difficult to work, although is used in some furniture manufacture.

Ornamental
It is frequently grown as an ornamental in gardens and along streets because of its light delicate shade, attractive shape and many uses. It is also an attractive tree to birds, bees and butterflies. Many peoples around the world consider the tree to be sacred.

Telfairia pedata

Oyster nut (telfairia nuts, fluted pumpkin, kweme, Zanzibar oil vine, krobonko)

CUCURBITACEAE

Similar species: *Telfairia occidentalis*

Relatives: melon, pumpkin

Oyster nuts are native to eastern and mid Africa. The nuts, which are actually seeds, are obtained from a gourd from the pumpkin family. They are borne on large, perennial vines that either scramble along the ground or up trees. With the right growing conditions, this vine can be invasive and may need controlling in warmer climates. The flesh is generally not eaten, but does make an excellent marmalade. However, its very large, round, flat seeds are flavoursome and have a nutty taste similar to Brazil nuts or almonds when roasted. In Kenya they are highly prized, to the extent that pregnant women are said to divorce their husbands if they do not provide them with nuts for nutrition and to help lactation! Oyster nuts are just beginning to be marketed in other countries.

uses

Food

The husk is discarded because of its bitter taste; however, the kernels have an excellent flavour, with a high oil content. They taste sweet and creamy, with a taste that is said to be like hazelnuts, Brazil nuts, almonds or cashews. They can be roasted, boiled or eaten fresh, or ground up and added to soups, etc. They can be used in the same ways as other nuts, i.e. in desserts, as a snack, in confectionery, added to cookies or to savoury dishes. They are also good coated in chocolate. The kernels are sometimes ground to a paste, then wrapped in a banana leaf and cooked with fish. In Africa, they are used to make cakes, soups and added to many types of dishes. The oil is sometimes extracted from the seeds and used for cooking. The flesh can also be used. Recent trials have found that it makes a very good marmalade that is indistinguishable, both in consistency and taste, from orange marmalade, and does not seem to go mouldy in storage. The shoots from the female plants can be cooked and eaten.

Nutrition

The seeds are high in protein (~25%), carbohydrate and minerals, and contain ~60% fat/oils. The flesh contains good levels of potassium, iron, phosphate, sodium, manganese, as well as pectin. It is also surprisingly acidic (pH ~3). The leaves contain vitamins A, C and E.

Other uses

The oil from the seeds can be used in cosmetics and soaps.

DESCRIPTION

The edible seed from a gourd produced by a large, perennial, fast-growing, vigorous vine that scrambles across the ground or up trees, and can easily grow to 15–35+ m spread under the right conditions. The trees they grow up can be eventually smothered and crushed by the weight of the vine. A single plant, as it gets older, can cover a large area, so it does need careful control. The main stem can be 7–10 cm wide. It can live for 15–20 years.

Leaves: Large, ~15–20 cm width, rough and hairy, particularly beneath. Stems are also coarse, rough and somewhat prickly.

Flowers: Plants are ~18–24 months old before they flower, which is considerably longer than pumpkin, but this vine then goes on to produce fruits for many years. Develops large, papery, white and purple, trumpet-shaped flowers. Male and female flowers are on separate plants, so at least one plant of each sex is needed to ensure pollination. It is best to plant at least three vines to ensure good fruit-set. *Pollination:* By bees and other insects. Hand pollination can increase fruit-set.

Fruit: The female plants produce large, elongated, torpedo-shaped, distinctly furrowed or fluted gourds, 30–60 cm long, 20–30 cm wide, weighing 10–20 kg. Botanically, they are classified as berries! They have a tough yellowish skin, within which is a rich yellow-coloured, fibrous flesh containing many seeds in a central cavity. The seeds are large (~3 cm diameter, ~1 cm thick), flat, circular, pale yellow and look like an oyster. They have a greenish fibrous shell around the edible kernel. The larger the gourd, the larger the seeds inside. Because the fruit are so heavy and the vine so spreading, the tree or structure the vine grows up can often be broken or damaged, so its best to choose a rugged or unsightly wall or building to grow them up.

Yield/harvest: Plants take ~2 years to start producing gourds, and then can produce for a further 15–20 years, often producing two crops a year in warmer locations. They then have excellent yields: each gourd can weigh ~15 kg, and can measure ~60 cm long by 20 cm wide. There are usually 10–30 gourds per vine and each gourd contains ~75–150 large oyster-shaped nuts. The gourds take 4–5 months to mature after fruit-set. As they ripen, the gourds become softer and split to expose the seeds. The flavour is greatly improved if the gourd is left to fully ripen on the vine. To harvest the kernel, its somewhat fibrous, bitter skin needs to be removed, and this can be tricky. One method is to cut round the edge of the seedcoat to release the kernel; another method is to hold the nut on its edge and give it a few sharp taps to crack the seedcoat: the kernel is then easy to extract. Once harvested, if kept cool, dry and in a sealed container, they can be stored for several weeks or longer, with one report claiming that if stored within their husks oyster nuts could be kept for 8 years.

Roots: Thick, fleshy and extend deeply. Some can be spreading and are near the surface. Take care with mechanical cultivation. Plants benefit from an organic mulch to retain moisture.

CULTIVATION

It is a tough plant and, once established, if it does not take over, it will produce fruits for many years. Easy care.

Location: Grows best in a sunny location, but is not tolerant of cold winds, so plant in a warm, sheltered site.

Temperature: It is not frost tolerant, and will need protection in colder regions, particularly when young.

Soil/water: Grows on a wide range of soils. It is very drought tolerant, but will grow better with regular moisture, particularly during flowering and while the fruits are developing. Likes a nutrient-rich soil, and benefits from regular additions of either well-rotted manure (or similar) or a balanced fertiliser.

Planting: Plant in a sheltered, warm location, perhaps where there is an unsightly fence or building you want to cover. It will benefit from an organic mulch to retain moisture and provide nutrients.

Pruning: Because of the size and spread of these vines, they are often cut back or some stems removed to keep them manageable.

Propagation: *Seed:* Best to sow the seeds when fresh. Viability is greatest from seeds taken from fully naturally ripened gourds. Seeds have a good germination rate: they germinate in 7–21 days. If over-wintered, the seeds benefit from being soaked before sowing in warmth in spring. Soaking can help to soften the outer seedcoat and also washes away germination inhibitors in the shell. *Layering:* Burial of stem tips or sections of the stems readily provides new plants. This method also gives predictable plants of known sex.

SIMILAR SPECIES

Telfairia occidentalis. A dioecious, perennial from West Africa. It is a drought-tolerant plant that scrambles up trees and over structures. The gourds are fluted and large, up to 13 kg, with edible seeds that are similar to those of oyster nut. Contain ~30% protein, and can be boiled and then eaten or ground up into a powder for soup. The shoots from the female plants can be also cooked and eaten. ■

Terminalia catappa
Sea almond (Indian/tropical almond, ketapang, false kamani, lingtak)
COMBRETACEAE
Relatives: kakadu plum

The *Terminalia* genus contains many trees that are found in Australia and southeastern Asia. A medium-sized, ornamental tree, originally a native of India, it now grows on rocky and sandy coasts of the Indo-Pacific oceans. The sea almond is a decorative tree with distinctive horizontal bifurcating branches, large leaves and edible kernels. It often drops its leaves twice a year, each time giving a glorious colourful display, and then goes on to produce new leaves along with flowers and fruits, so producing two harvests a year. It is a very common tree in gardens and streets throughout India and Malaysia, where it is cultivated and grows wild, and is often grown in coastal locations. Several other closely related *Terminalia* species, particularly *T. arjuna*, have recently been found to contain numerous powerful compounds (including many polyphenols) that seem to be effective in treating heart disease as well as being antibacterial and possible anti-mutagenic, and it is possible that this species may share some of those properties.

DESCRIPTION

A medium-sized, fast-growing tree, height ~12–20 m tall (sometimes taller in ideal conditions), and a spread of ~12 m. It has a characteristic pagoda shape because of its distinctive whorled horizontal branches that form at intervals up the main trunk. These whorls become more flattened as the tree grows, so that a vase shape is formed in older trees. The branches tend to have a bifurcating form, repeatedly dividing each season, with the newer stems carrying the leaves. Tends to form multiple trunks. The wood is not very strong, and branches may break off at a crotch or elsewhere along their length. The bark is grey, fissured and flaky.

Leaves: Deciduous, large (~30 cm long, ~15 cm wide), glossy, dark green, egg-shaped with the base of the leaf narrower. The leaves also form in whorls, and are found only at the ends of branches. Good leaf colour as the leaves fall, of mostly rich golds and reds: such colour is unusual in trees that grow in the semi-tropics or tropics. Trees only lose their leaves for a short time and are soon replaced by new growth. This often occurs twice a year: in autumn and again in spring. They first drop their leaves when 3–4 years old.

uses

Food
The flesh of these fruits is edible and sweet when the fruits are young, though becomes bitter later. The inner kernels taste like almonds, and can be used in similar ways. They are enjoyable eaten fresh; removing the hard endocarp can be frustrating though. The kernels contain high quantities of a good-tasting oil, which can be used in dressings or in cooking.

Nutrition/medicinal
The whole plant is reported to have many medicinal properties. Different parts of the tree are high in tannic acid. The leaves, bark and fruits have been used to treat rheumatic aches, skin disease, dysentery and colic. The fruits and bark have been used to treat coughs and asthma. The leaves have been used to eliminate intestinal parasites, to treat eye problems, wounds and skin diseases, and have antioxidant properties. Modern research has identified active principles that could be used to treat high blood pressure. The kernel may have aphrodisiac properties. An extract from the leaves has shown potential to treat sickle-cell disorders, and also possibly help prevent cancer. The oil from the kernels has been used externally to treat scabies and swellings.

Other uses
Its heartwood is dark, reddish-brown and is hard, dense and strong. It is often used to make heavy-duty items, such as posts. Tannin and a black dye can be extracted from the bark, leaves and fruit. The plant is used in tropical fish aquariums to reduce bacterial and fungal diseases.

Ornamental
An adaptable tree, planted for its unusual shape, attractive coloured leaves and its fruits. It makes a good shade tree, and is grown as an ornamental urban specimen in many warmer areas of the world, though is not very tidy as it is either dropping leaves, flower stalks or fruits.

Flowers: Small, greenish-white, star-shaped, inconspicuous, formed on 15-cm-long, slender spikes, which occur on upper leaf axils in spring. The trees are monoecious, with flowers towards the stem tips being female and those below male. Sometimes the whole flower spike has only male flowers. They have a pungent odour that some find unpleasant. The flowers are borne at the same time as the new leaves open. This may be once or twice a year. *Pollination:* Bees avidly seek out the nectar-rich flowers.

Fruits: Many, almond-shaped, flattened drupes, ~6 cm long, greeny-yellow, turning brown–purple when ripe, in autumn. They have an outer yellowish smooth skin covering a thin layer of white sweetish flesh. Beneath this is an inner fibrous, corky layer surrounding the stone. This allows the fruits to be dispersed by water. The stone consists of a hard, rough endocarp, inside which is an inner, green, nutty kernel. The fruits mature rapidly after fruit-set, and tend to fall when ripe.

Yield/harvest: Trees produce many fruits. They ripen in late summer, but persist on the tree into winter, if not eaten before by the wildlife, particularly bats. There is often a second crop if the tree sheds its leaves twice during the year. When harvesting, the endocarp can be hard to remove.

CULTIVATION
A tree for warmer locations, but is easy to grow once established.

Location: Grows best in full sun. Is fairly wind tolerant. Is very salt tolerant; can be grown in maritime locations, even on sandy beaches.

Temperature: Does need protection from freezing temperatures, though may be more frost tolerant than once thought.

Soil/water/nutrients: Can be grown in a wide range of soils: clay and loam, but particularly in sand. Can grow at a wide range of pH from fairly acidic to fairly alkaline. Likes a well-drained soil, and grows best with good levels of moisture, though can be very drought tolerant once established. It naturally often grows in similar areas to mangroves, though it grows in sand rather then fine sediment. Growth is best in fertile soils, and trees grow and fruit best when given a good organic mulch and regular nutrients, though will grow in poorer soils.

Pot culture: Because of the frost sensitivity of this species, some might like to try growing it in a container where it can be given protection during colder weather. Can be grown in containers for several years.

Propagation: *Seeds:* This is the main method of propagation. Germination is best when seed is sown fresh, and scratching the hard seedcoat increases germination as does soaking the seed for a short time in weak acid. Germination is ~25%.

Pruning: Because of the tree's spreading nature, drooping branches may need pruning. It can be grown as a multi-stemmed tree, or pruned to form a single trunk. Judicious pruning will develop a strong structure.

Pests and diseases: Generally trouble free. There may be occasional problems with thrips or leafspot. ■

Terminalia ferdinandiana
Kakadu plum (billy-goat plum, salty plum, murunga)
COMBRETACEAE

Other species: damson (*Terminalia sercocarpa*)

Relatives: sea almond

The *Terminalia* genus has been used extensively as a food, for traditional medicine and for timber in many parts of the world, usually by indigenous peoples. The Kakadu plum is a native of northwestern Australia. It is named after a beautiful region within the Northern Territory, and has been used by the Aborigines for its fruits for thousands of years. It naturally grows in grasslands in these regions. Recently, there has been increased interest in the bush-foods of Australia and this is one of the more widely valued species. The fruits, at present, are often sourced from the wild, but some plantations have been recently established.

DESCRIPTION

A medium-sized tree, to ~8 m tall, ~4 m spread, forming a slender, elegant or spindly crown. It grows in semi-tropical and tropical regions. Its bark is rough, creamy-grey, finely marked and is somewhat flaking.

Leaves: Deciduous, spirally arranged around the stems, are fairly sparse and tend to be crowded towards the ends of branches. They are light green, very large and oval in shape, ~25 cm long by ~15 cm wide, and turn yellow before they fall in autumn.

Flowers: Small, insignificant, creamy-white, fragrant, and are borne an spikes from leaf axils towards the ends of branches, mostly in spring and early summer.

Fruit: Produces many, yellow-green or purple, almond-sized fruits (~2–3 cm long), oval–tear-shaped, with a distinctive protuberance at their apex, and consist of a single, large, hard, woody seed covered by a layer of flesh. The flesh is edible and is incredibly high in vitamin C. It is very tasty, and is said to taste like gooseberry, although the fruits are best eaten when fully ripe: unripe fruits can be somewhat bitter. Some fruits have a salty taste, hence one of its common names. They ripen from autumn into winter, in northern Australia.

Yield/harvest: Smaller, more compact trees, with a larger canopy, yield more fruit when grown under good conditions. Fruit are best harvested when fully ripe.

CULTIVATION

Location: Plants can grow in full sun or in semi-shade. They do not tolerate weed competition or crowding very well, and fruit yields are then significantly reduced. Are not very wind tolerant.

Temperature: A hardy tree, but does need a warmer, more tropical climate, and is probably not at all frost tolerant. Can tolerate very high temperatures and humid climates. Are fairly tolerant of salts, and could be grown in sheltered maritime locations.

Soil/water/nutrients: Grow best in deep loam, though also grow well in sandy soils. Grow best in somewhat acid to slightly alkaline soils. They are fairly drought tolerant once established, but cannot tolerate waterlogging. Are not very nutrient hungry, and only require modest applications of additional nutrients in poorer soils.

Pot culture: It may be worth trying to grow these trees in pots in cooler regions, and then they can be taken inside or easily given protection during winter. It should be able to

uses

Food
The Aborigines ate the flesh raw as well as adding it to various foods. However, it does tend to have a drying effect in the mouth, and so is usually cooked, although some people enjoy the fruits fresh when fully ripe. Both the skin and flesh can be eaten, or can be dried or frozen for later use. The seeds are difficult to remove from the flesh. At present, the fruits are mainly used to make a very tasty, highly recommended jam, and for sauces; they are popular in specialist Australian restaurants, airlines and hotels. However, they should be only heated mini-mally to retain their full vitamin C value. They are also like-ly to be included, commercially, within juices, icecream, cosmetics, as a flavouring and in pharmaceuticals, within the near future. When cooked, the flesh turns a lovely golden colour and has a wonderful, rich, sweet flavour.

Nutrition
Has amazing levels of vitamin C, reported to be higher than any other plant, and >120 times higher than orange. Varies from 3000–5000 mg/100 g of flesh (3.5–5% of the flesh).

Medicinal
The gum from the bark has been used to treat sores, boils, backache and ringworm.

Other uses
The fruits are rapidly becoming more sought after for their use in cosmetics, such as body- and hair-care products, because of their high vitamin C level, which is believed to have anti-ageing properties. The Aboriginal peoples pounded the fruit and used it as an antiseptic and a soothing balm for aching limbs and feet.

grow for many years within a pot before becoming too large.

Propagation: *Seed:* Can be grown from seed. The use of fresh seed is best, but all seeds can be slow to germinate. Scarification of the seed with a file or knife, so that air and moisture can reach the kernel, can improve germination rate and time. *Cuttings:* This is probably the best method. *Layering:* Air-layering may not be very successful.

Pruning: Trees need minimal pruning, simply to remove any damaged or diseased wood. Removing stem tips will promote more branching of lateral fruiting branches.

SIMILAR SPECIES

Damson, *Terminalia sercocarpa*. A handsome, spreading tree from northern Australia, which produces pink–purple, hairy-skinned fruits in summer. Has a delicious, edible kernel with an almond flavour. ■

Cephalotaxus fortunei.

Torreya nucifera
Torreya (Japanese torreya, Japanese nutmeg, kaya, plum yew)
TAXACEAE (Cephalotaxaceae)
Similar species: Chinese nutmeg (*Torreya grandis*), Japanese plum yew (*Cephalotaxus harringtonii*), Chinese plum yew (*C. fortunei*)
Relatives: yew

The *Torreya* genus is an ancient one, and consists of six species, which are native to quite different parts of the world, suggesting its distribution was much more widespread in the past. Three species are native to China, one is found in Japan and Korea, another in California, and one in Florida. They are classified as conifers, though do not have typical pine cones. Rather, their kernels are surrounded by a fleshy aril, which is attractive to birds and aids in the kernels' dispersal. The Japanese torreya, as its name suggests, is native to central and southern Japan, and is also found in eastern Asia. It is a long-lived, attractive, evergreen coniferous tree that produces tasty kernels within its fleshy receptacle. The kernels are valued as a tasty snack in Japan and China.

DESCRIPTION

A large tree, growing to ~13–25 m height, 8–10 m spread, but is often smaller, particularly in temperate areas where it can be more shrubby. It is a coniferous species and looks like a yew tree. It is often multi-stemmed with long graceful, spreading, whorled, irregular, strong branches that sometimes dip downwards. The tree has a natural conical–ovoid shape. Younger stems are orange-brown, changing to brown-grey as they age. It is very slow growing, and the tree can live hundreds of years.

Leaves: Glossy, evergreen, simple, hard, shiny, needle-shaped with a shiny tip, bright green, small (~2 cm long, 0.25 cm wide), flattened, with no veination; these occur spirally arranged, but spreading horizontally along the twig. Have a very pungent juniper- or sage-like smell when crushed. The dense canopy of leaves forms medium to dense shade beneath the tree.

Flowers: Does not have 'true' flowers because it is a conifer, instead it forms insignificant male and female cone-like flowers. In this species, male and female flowers occur on different trees (dioecious), so need to plant at least one male and a female tree to get fruits. The female flowers are often in pairs, at the base of the current year's growth, and the whitish-green male flowers occur towards the stem tip. *Pollination:* Is by wind.

Fruit: As with many conifers, the process of seed formation and subsequent ripening can take several years.

Pollinated 'flowers' have formed fruits by the following season (which is then on older wood), but need at least a further 2 years of growth and ripening before maturity. The fruits are small, green, olive-shaped, tinged with mauve, ~2–3 cm long. They have a fleshy outer covering (aril), within which is an edible almond-sized kernel that has irregular folds. The kernel is very oily. The tree can give very good yields. The kernels mature in autumn.

Roots: It does have some surface roots, but these are not invasive or a problem to buildings, etc.

CULTIVATION

An easily cultivated, but slow-growing specimen tree.

Temperature: Quite cold hardy: can tolerate periods of frost and cold, though possibly not very cold, severe winters.

Location: Can be grown in fairly dense shade or in part sun. Grows best in sites that are protected from cold, winter winds. Likes humid, hot summers.

Soil/water/nutrients: Trees can be grown in a range of soil types: clay (well drained), loam or sand, but prefer neutral to acid soils, though will tolerate a little alkalinity. Grows best in well-drained soils, though prefers regular moisture during the growing season. Once established, is moderately drought tolerant. Not tolerant of waterlogging. Trees are not nutrient hungry and only need minimal additions of fertiliser in poorer soils and perhaps while trees are young.

Propagation: *Seed:* Best germination occurs from fresh

seeds, sown in autumn, in a cool place. Stored seeds can be sown in spring, but may take 12 months to germinate. These benefit from a period of cold stratification before sowing in moist, but well-drained compost, but can take 12–18 months to germinate. Grow on seedlings with some protection for at least the first year. Unfortunately, the sex of the seedlings will not be known for several years. *Cuttings:* Semi-ripe cuttings can be taken through summer into autumn, with a heel if possible, but the take is not very good, and root formation very slow. However, the sex of the tree will be known. *Layering:* May be possible to layer drooping stems.

Pruning: May need a little pruning to develop a good shape or to remove damaged or dead wood; however, its branches are strong.

Pests and diseases: Usually not affected by pests or diseases; scale insects cause occasional problems.

CULTIVAR

'Shibunashigaya': Considered to be the best for kernel production.

SIMILAR SPECIES

Chinese nutmeg, *Torreya grandis*. Native to China. A large tree (to ~40 m). Not very hardy. Has edible nuts and is used medicinally.

Japanese plum yew, *Cephalotaxus harringtonii* and Chinese plum yew, *C. fortunei*. These are similar species that form slow-growing, densely-leaved trees and produce good crops of seeds regularly. They are natives of eastern Asia and grow to heights of ~5–6 m to form small, shrubby trees. They are very shade tolerant, which is unusual for most nut-producing trees, and although they can be planted in sunny sites, they do not grow very well. Are quite cold hardy, tolerating cold winters and freezing temperatures. They grow best in slightly acidic to fairly alkaline soils, and prefer well-drained soils and a sheltered location. They are often grown from seed, which germinates better after cold stratification during winter, though germination can still be slow (>18

Food
The kernels are a very popular dessert nut in Japan and China. They can be eaten fresh or cooked, and are said to have an agreeable, pleasant, though slightly resinous taste. An oil can be extracted from the kernels, which can be used in cooking.

Medicinal
The kernels are used as a mild laxative and for digestive remedies, including the relief of flatulence, and to relieve pain. The kernels are also said to help eliminate intestinal worms, etc. Lignan, from the bark of torreya, has shown significant neuroprotective activity against glutamate-induced toxicity in rat cortical cells.
Warning: Ensure that *Torreya* species are not confused with *Taxus* species, which include the yew. Most parts of yew trees are poisonous, except for the fleshy aril.

Ornamental
An attractive, dense, specimen tree, or it can be pruned to form a screening hedge. Because the foliage is dense, not many species will grow well beneath it. The fruit are attractive to birds.

months). Semi-ripe cuttings are also possible. The trees can be monoecious or dioecious, so usually need more than one tree to set fruits. Occasionally, dioecious female trees can set fruits without fertilisation; in addition, trees can also sometimes change sex. They flower in spring. The kernel is fairly large, ~3 cm long by ~1 cm wide, and is found within a fleshy aril. Needs to be fully ripe when eaten, otherwise is very bitter, with an unpleasant turpentine flavour. However, when fully ripe, in late autumn–early winter, it is sweet and can be eaten fresh or roasted or added to various dishes. Makes a good hedging plant, though not in exposed locations. ∎

uses

Ugni molinae (syn. *Myrtus ugni*)
Chilean guava (ugni, Chilean cranberry, murta, murtilla, strawberry myrtle, tazziberry)
MYRTACEAE
Similar species: myrtle berry, *Myrtus communis*
Relatives: tropical guava, lillypilly, camu-camu, feijoa

The Chilean guava was very popular in the 1800s in England, and was a favourite with Queen Victoria, but has only recently begun to regain popularity as a fruiting and ornamental plant. In Chile, it is cultivated for its fruits, which are sold locally, but are also exported to Japan. It can be readily grown in colder areas and makes a good plant in shrubby borders. Its small fruits are very tasty. It is sometimes grown instead of cranberry because of the cold and acid conditions needed by the latter. Once established, it is easy to grow and needs little maintenance. It is a very undervalued plant, given its ease of cultivation and the good quality of its fruits.

DESCRIPTION

An attractive, compact shrub, ~1.5–2.5 m tall with sweeping branches. It can become densely branched. It is fairly slow growing.

Leaves: Small, ~1–1.5 cm long, round–oval, evergreen, glossy, dark green. The leaves have pointed tips, a distinctive central indented midrib, are often slightly curved and are fragrant when crushed. New growth is tinged red.

Flowers: Numerous, delicate, cup-shaped, white–pink-tinged flowers are borne in small clusters in summer. Makes an attractive, pretty ornamental. *Pollination:* Mostly by bees. The flowers are bisexual and self-fertile, so only need one plant to set fruit.

Fruit: Abundant, small, tasty, sweet yet tangy, resinous fruit with a wonderful rich strawberry-like aroma. It is easy to be tempted to eat many of them. They are roundish, ~1.5 cm in diameter, purplish to deep rose colour when ripe. They have a thin skin and juicy flesh with small, edible seeds. Recommended.

Yield/harvest: Flowers and fruits well even when the plants are young; can start fruiting after 2–3 years. Plants give good crops of fruits, particularly if watered and fed well, and you can get ~1 kg of fruit from a 3-year old bush, with yields increasing by a kg a year for several years. Fruits ripen from late summer to early autumn. Easily harvested.

CULTIVATION

Easy to grow and needs little maintenance.

Location: Unlike many other fruiting plants, it grows and fruits well in partial shade. Can be also grown in full sun in cooler areas. They are fairly tolerant of salty maritime air, and are moderately wind tolerant, though grow better in sheltered sites.

Temperature: They are quite cold hardy, tolerating temperatures down to −10°C. Ideal for temperate and subtropical climates, though not in areas that have long, cold winters.

Soil/water/nutrients: Grows best in a fertile, well-drained loamy soil, though can grow in many other soil types including sandy soils and clays. They are fairly drought tolerant once established and do not like waterlogging. They respond to applications of a balanced, complete fertiliser once or twice during the growing season.

Pot culture: Because of their slow growth and smaller size, Chilean guava can be easily grown in a container and their small evergreen leaves are attractive year round; they are also fragrant and have abundant blossom. In colder regions, they can be taken inside during very cold weather. Ideal for a shadier location.

Propagation: *Seed:* Grows well from seed, but germination is better if sown when fresh. Seeds can be soaked in warm water for ~24 hours to soften the seedcoat and remove any germination inhibitors before sowing just below the surface of well-drained warm compost. Prick out seedlings and grow on in individual pots for a year or so before planting out. *Cuttings:* Semi-ripe cuttings can be taken, with a heel, in summer and inserted in moist, gritty compost. These should root fairly well, with a high percentage take possible, and can be planted out the following year. Hardwood cuttings, with a heel, can be taken from the current season's growth in early winter. Insert these in gritty compost in a shaded, frost-free location over winter. These should also root well. *Layering:* Stems can be pegged onto the soil in autumn and should have rooted by the following summer.

Pruning: Prune after fruiting to maintain a compact bushy shape. Tends to become straggly if left unpruned. With patience, it can be trained up a stake and trimmed to form a standard. It can also be trimmed to form a hedge.

Pests and diseases: Are generally pest and disease free, though birds may seek out the fruits.

SIMILAR SPECIES

Myrtle berry, *Myrtus communis*. Probably native to western Asia, though is now found naturalised in various parts of southern Europe, this well-known ornamental species has been cultivated and used throughout history. This is the myrtle that is commonly referred to in many texts for its fragrant leaves, which were often incorporated into wedding bouquets because of its association with love and peace.

Description: Forms a moderately fast-growing, densely leaved, attractive, fragrant shrub or small tree, growing to ~5 m tall. *Leaves:* Narrow, small, dark green, glossy, fragrant, and rich in essential oils that have been used since ancient times. *Flowers:* Abundant, ~2 cm diameter, saucer-shaped, white, sweetly fragrant. Have numerous, attractive, long, central stamens. Borne from mid spring until summer. Pollination is by insects. *Fruit:* Small, oblong, ~1 cm diameter, becoming blue-black when ripe in late autumn.

Cultivation: *Location:* Grows best in full sun and is fairly wind hardy. Can also tolerate moderate maritime conditions. *Temperature:* Is fairly frost hardy, down to ~−12°C, though cannot tolerate very cold, long winters. Prefers a warm-temperate climate. Grow against a protected, sunny wall in colder regions. Can also be grown as a screen hedge. *Soil/water/nutrients:* Grows best in acidic to neutral soils. Does not tolerate alkalinity. Can tolerate some drought once established. Will grow in stony, poor soils, though grows

uses

Food

The fruits are very tasty and are good eaten fresh or can be added to other fruits in desserts. They can also be added to juice, sauce, jam, yoghurt, icecream or can be dried and used as other dried fruits. The leaves can be used as a tea substitute and, if you can be bothered, its tiny seeds can be roasted and used as a coffee substitute.

Ornamental

A good ornamental that can grow in shade, has lovely flowers, and fruits with a wonderful aroma. It is non-invasive so can be planted next to patios or windows to enjoy the fragrance. Tolerant of trimming, it can be grown as a small hedge and easily clipped to form a low formal style.

better with moderate applications of a balanced fertiliser. *Pot culture:* Can be grown as a pot plant for several years, at least. Give plants an organic-rich mulch and regular moisture. Plants can then be given extra protection during cold weather. *Propagation:* From fresh seed sown in summer or stored seed that has been soaked before sowing. Cuttings can be taken in summer, with a heel, and give a good take. Hardwood cuttings can also be taken in autumn. *Pruning:* Generally none needed, just to tidy up straggly growth. Also can be pruned to form a hedge or screen, though there may be some loss in fruit production. *Pests and diseases:* Few problems.

Uses: *Food:* The fruits are juicy and have a musky, interesting flavour. Can be eaten fresh or are often used in sauces, jams, desserts, pies, etc. Also used to make a liquor, as well as a flavouring in the Middle East. Are said to

be an aphrodisiac. The fruits can also be dried. *Other uses:* Young leaves are used as a flavouring in various dishes, and the essential oil obtained from various parts of the plant is used as a food flavouring, also in cosmetics, skin-care products, etc. Has dense hard wood, though is of small proportions. *Medicinal:* The aromatic leaves contain myrtol, which is quickly absorbed by the body and has antibiotic properties. It has been used to treat urinary and vaginal infections, as well as bronchial disorders, including coughs. In India it is used to treat cerebral disorders, i.e. epilepsy. Externally, it is used to treat acne, rheumatism, mouth infections and haemorrhoids. The fruits have been used to treat heart problems, diarrhoea and ulcers. *Ornamental:* A very attractive plant with evergreen, fragrant leaves, pretty, scented flowers, plus edible fruits. It can be pruned to form a hedge or screen. ■

Vaccinium spp.
Bilberry (dwarf huckleberry, whortleberry, whinberry, huckleberry, blaeberry)
ERICACEAE

Bilberry (*Vaccinium myrtillus*), dwarf bilberry (*V. caespitosum*) kamchatka bilberry (*V. praestans*), red bilberry (*V. parvifolium*), bog bilberry (*V. ulignosum*)

Relatives: cranberry, blueberry, huckleberry

The name 'bilberry', sometimes called 'bulberry', may be derived from the Danish word 'bollebar', meaning 'dark berry'. Its other wonderful common names are mostly derived from Britain. They are closely related to many other *Vaccinium* species, including blueberries, huckleberries and cranberries, with the differences between these categories often overlapping or merging. Often the same species can be known by several common names. Herein, the main bilberry species are described, though the reader is encouraged to look up its relatives for other suggestions. Bilberries grow abundantly in mountainous districts, including North America, northern Europe, northern Asia and Greenland. In some areas it is the dominant type of vegetation, e.g. the taiga communities of Russia. They have been eaten and enjoyed for many hundreds, if not thousands, of years, and have been a valued winter food source when the berries are dried. In addition, the fruits have been used for medicinal purposes since at least the Middle Ages. Saint Hildegard of Bingen, ~1120, recommended the plant for inducing menstruation. In the 16th century, German herbalists recommended the berries for treatment of bladder stones, liver disorders and for coughs and lung ailments. Many of these medicinal purposes have now been shown to have proven biochemical validity, and the health benefits of these fruits are impressive.

Bilberry, *Vaccinium myrtillus*
This is the main bilberry species, and is the one most commonly cultivated and referred to. Several other bilberry species are also described below. The common bilberry is native to Britain, northern Europe, North America and northern Asia, where it often grows on the edges of moist coniferous woods, often at higher elevations. They are popular with local populations for their tasty fruits, and are often picked from the wild and may be dried for winter use. They are also cultivated commercially and are popular in gardens. In addition, the bilberry has long been known to have medicinal properties, and is full of antioxidants.

DESCRIPTION
A small, branched shrub, 15–50 cm tall, 15–30 cm spread, with wiry angular branches. Tends to freely sucker when growing well.
Leaves: Deciduous, leathery, similar to those of myrtle, hence its species name. They are at first rosy, turn yellowish-

green, then purple, red and gold in autumn, and are very ornamental.
Flowers: Greeny-white, often flushed pink, translucent, urn-shaped, ~0.5 cm long, waxy, and are borne singly from leaf axils from late spring–early summer. Bisexual, having both male and female organs, but are only partly self-

fertile, so more than one plant increases fruit-set and yield. *Pollination:* By bees, flies, moths and butterflies.

Fruit: Has blue-purple-black berries when ripe, 0.5–1 cm diameter, which are covered with a delicate whitish-grey bloom. They are usually formed singly from leaf axils and ripen from late summer–autumn. They are rounded, with a flat apex, and contain juicy, succulent sour, dark blue-black pulp, which contains many, very tiny, edible seeds.

Roots: Dislikes root disturbance; plants are best grown in pots until planted out in their permanent positions. They have rhizomatous roots, and many surface roots with few root hairs, so mechanical cultivation should be minimised. Adding soil from around an established plant, leaf mould or humus can be beneficial. An organic mulch will help retain moisture and provide additional nutrients.

CULTIVATION

Location: Can grow in semi-shade, though fruit better in a sunny position. Very tolerant of strong winds and exposure, but cannot tolerate maritime exposure. Plants quickly regenerate if they are burnt and also tolerate some grazing.

Temperature: They are extremely cold hardy, tolerating long, cold winters.

Soil/water/nutrients: Prefer a well-drained, moist sandy or loamy soil that is rich in peat or with added organic matter. Can grow below pine and fir woods, or under azaleas and rhododendrons. Can grow in very acid soil: pH 4.5–6. Plants soon become chlorotic in alkaline soils. They only need moderate additions of nutrients, and an annual application of an all-purpose fertiliser, with micronutrients, with nitrogen added as urea rather than as nitrate.

Propagation: *Seed:* Sow when fresh in late winter, in a cold frame, in a lime-free compost, only just covering the seed. Stored seed might need 2–3 months of cold stratification. Seedlings are pricked out and grown-on in individual pots in acidic compost for at least their first winter. *Cuttings:* Semi-ripe cuttings are taken, with a heel, in late summer and inserted in gritty, acidic compost to root. This can be slow and difficult. Can take cuttings of mature wood in late autumn. *Layering:* Healthy stems can be layered from spring–early autumn; they take ~18 months to root. *Division:* Can be propagated by digging up suckers in spring or early

Food
Fruits can be stewed with a little sugar and lemon peel, and included in pies or tarts. The fruits have a rich, sub-acid taste and are juicy. They make an excellent preserve or jelly, or can be added to many fresh or cooked desserts, as well as added to sauces, icecream, yoghurt. As a jelly, it often accompanies meat and poultry dishes. In France, tcha-tcha is made from fresh bilberries, crushed with sugar, and then spread on buttered bread. They are delicious on pancakes. In the USA they are used in chicken salads, with pears, also added to a dressing made with yoghurt, black pepper, bilberry juice, a little honey or oil, and balsamic vinegar.

Nutrition
Low in vitamin C: 1 mg/100 g, but are very high in antioxidants, mostly anthocyanidin flavonoids (25–36%). Because flavonoids work so well with vitamin C, consider mixing these fruits with e.g. kiwifruits, and then add some fibre-rich banana for a truly healthy dish.

Medicinal
Recent studies have confirmed that the fruit's antioxidant activities inhibit the aggregation of blood platelets (thereby reducing a tendency for clotting), produce a slight relaxation of vascular smooth muscles and reduce chronic inflammatory diseases. The fruits inhibit enzymes, such as elastase, which cause degradation of collagen; thus, the fruits lead to a reduction in inflammatory conditions such as atherosclerosis, pulmonary emphysema and rheumatoid arthritis. The flavonoids are particularly effective in strengthening capillaries, connective tissues and blood vessels. They are essential for the proper absorption and use of vitamin C and, with vitamin C, they help prevent progressive loss of sight. Weak capillaries, common in ageing, are associated with poor blood circulation to connective tissues, and have

been related to inflammatory conditions such as arthritis, and other diseases such as arteriosclerosis, hypertension, varicose veins, liver disorders and peptic ulcers, and bilberries have been shown to improve many of these problems. In Europe, preparations are now used to enhance poor micro-circulation, including eye conditions such as night-blindness and diabetic retinopathy. Compounds within bilberries seem to increase the regeneration rate of rhodopsin, a purple pigment essential for helping the rods in the eye adapt to light and dark, and has been proven to significantly improve night vision. In addition, trials in Italy have shown that 76% of patients with myopia (short or near-sightedness) had a marked improvement in retinal sensibility after eating bilberry fruits daily for 15 days, along with vitamin A. Studies have shown that leaves contain glucoquinine, which has a proven weak anti-diabetic activity and can lower blood sugar levels. The leaves also contain quinic acid, which German research has shown to be a potential treatment for rheumatism and gout. The fruits are astringent, and have been used to treat diarrhoea and dysentery. A tea made from the leaves and root-bark has been locally applied to ulcers in the mouth and throat; they also have diuretic properties. The fruit is also helpful for urinary complaints. **Warning:** The leaves have a fairly high tannin content and, therefore, it is advised to not consume too many leaves at one time.

Other uses
A green dye can be obtained from the leaves and fruits, which is used to colour fabrics. A blue or black dye can be obtained from the fruits.

Ornamental
Makes an excellent groundcover plant in acidic conditions. Excellent for stabilising acidic slopes. The fruits are popular with wildlife such as birds and insects.

autumn, and establishing them in moist compost before planting out.

Pests and diseases: Generally have very few problems, and plants within this genus are resistant to honey fungus. The berries are a favourite food of birds and other wildlife.

OTHER BILBERRY SPECIES

The information above applies to the species below, unless specifically mentioned.

Dwarf bilberry (dwarf blueberry, dwarf huckleberry, dwarf whortleberry), *Vaccinium caespitosum*. Dwarf bilberry is native of Canada and western North America down as far as Mexico. It is still commonly found on dry and wet acidic soils, often in elevated sites. It is a very adaptable plant, growing in many different conditions and temperatures. It forms a small, sprawling shrub, growing from ~8–50 cm tall. Its fruits, ~0.5 cm diameter, are bright blue when ripe, and have an excellent flavour. They have been, and still are, extensively harvested by local populations, though are seldom grown commercially because of the size of the fruit, but do make a compact, ornamental groundcover plant, which has delicious fruits, and would fit into most gardens. It could also be grown in a container with acid soil.

Kamchatka bilberry, *Vaccinium praestans*. A native of northern North America and northeastern Asia, it is often found growing in bogs and swampy woods, as well as in elevated sites and on slopes. It forms a very slow-growing, sprawling, small, deciduous shrub, growing only to ~15 cm tall, with a spread of ~30 cm. It flowers in early summer,

and is self-fertile. The fruits are ~1.2 cm in diameter, and are dark purple-blue when ripe. They are cold hardy, tolerating temperatures below ~–20°C. As with other *Vaccinium* species, they need a moist, peaty, acid soil, and can grow in very acidic conditions. Can be grown in full sun or semi-shade, though not with all-day sun in warmer areas. *Uses* The fruits can be eaten fresh or added to various desserts (see 'Uses' above). They are sweet, aromatic, almost strawberry-like, and delicious. *Ornamental:* A good groundcover plant for cool moist shady areas.

Red bilberry, *Vaccinium parvifolium*. A native of western North America, from Alaska to California, tolerating a wide range of temperatures, and often found growing near the coast, frequently in shade. It forms a spreading shrub, growing to ~3 m tall. It flowers in early summer, and fruits ripen in autumn. Its dark purple fruits, ~1.2 cm in diameter, are fairly acid, but tasty, and are often used in preserves and various desserts, often mixed with other fruits. The fruits can be dried for later use.

Bog bilberry (bilberry, tundra bilberry, alpine bilberry, ground hurts), *Vaccinium ulignosum*. A native of the colder regions of North America, Asia, Europe and Greenland. These small, rhizomatous shrubs grow from ~2.5 cm–0.8 m tall, depending on location, exposure, etc., and can grow in dry or wet soils, often at considerable elevations. They are ideal for sites with wet, cold, acidic soils. They are extremely cold hardy and take on a ground-hugging form in more exposed locations. The fruits are an eye-catching bright blue in colour when ripe, ~0.5 cm in diameter, and have a good to very good flavour. They are often picked from the wild for home and commercial use. The fruits are rich in anthocyanins. ∎

Vaccinium spp.
Blueberry
ERICACEAE (Cyanococcus)

Highbush blueberry (*Vaccinium corymbosum*), rabbit-eye blueberry (*V. ashei*), lowbush blueberry (*V. angustifolium*), southern highbush (*V. corymbosum x V. darrowi* or *V. ashei*), half-high highbush (*V. corymbosum x V. angustifolium*), Mortiño (*V. floribundum*)

Relatives: rhododendrons, camellias, heather, heath (*Erica*)

Many species of *Vaccinium* are grown commercially for their fruits. Some of the best-known fruits of this genus are the blueberries, and three commercially important blueberry species are recognised, highbush, lowbush and rabbit-eye, as well as two main hybrids, southern highbush and half-high highbush. The blueberry is a North American plant, and the fruits have been collected by the native peoples for thousands of years, and later by European settlers. They incorporated the berries into their diets, eating them fresh off the bush and adding them to soups, stews and many other foods. They were also dried for use during the long, cold winters. However, their cultivation only began seriously in the 20th century. About 73,000 ha are now under cultivation worldwide, with 90% of this in the USA and Canada. These delicious, health-giving fruits are now, deservedly, becoming more popular, and the small size of the plant and the many regions within which these different species can grow makes this plant a useful inclusion for smaller gardens.

DESCRIPTION

Erect or spreading, rhizomatous shrubs that have many stems. Most grow 1.5–3 m tall, and species vary in vigour, but are generally slow growing. Unfortunately, their branches can break easily. The shrubs start fruiting early and can then live ~80 years.

Leaves: Evergreen or deciduous, oval, small, 2.5–4 cm long, pointed tips, often with bronze new growth, changing to a deep green at maturity. Leaves often develop attractive shades of rust, orange and scarlet in autumn and winter. Leaves are waxy, non-serrated and smooth.

Flowers: White–cream or pinkish, in clusters of 7–10, borne in short racemes (2.5–5 cm wide) towards the ends of 1-year-old wood. The flowers are an inverted urn-shape, and are borne on very short flower stalks. The flower buds are larger and more conical than the vegetative buds.
Pollination: Mostly by bumble bees, who pollinate flowers more effectively than honey bees. Apparently, this is because the frequency of wing flaps of bumble bees causes anthers to dehisce and release pollen, whereas those of honey bees have a different wing-beat speed and fail to stimulate pollen release as effectively. Adequate pollination can sometimes be a problem. Species vary in their ability to be self-fertile.

Fruit: False berries that are formed from an inferior ovary. They are borne in clusters of 5–10. The rounded berries turn from green to pink, and then gradually to a dusky blue colour when fully ripe, which is from early–late summer. They often develop their best flavour several days after they have turned blue, and can be then left on the bush for some time to gain their full flavour and sweetness.

Yield/harvest/storage: With good pollination, can get 1–2.5 kg (and sometimes up to 5 kg) berries/plant after 3–4 years. A healthy bush can produce fruits for 50 years or more. Fruits are picked when fully ripe, and are a full, dusky blue colour. Fruits take 60–90 days to mature after fruit-set. Ripe berries can remain on bushes for several days to weeks for sugars to accumulate. Because fruits mature over a period of weeks, bushes need to be picked several times. High rainfall or humidity during harvest can adversely affect fruit quality. After picking, blueberries do not store well, and only have a shelf-life of ~14 days at 0°C.

Roots: Plants are shallow-rooted and not spreading, so care is needed with mechanical cultivation and to reduce competition with weeds around young plants. Plants need water and nutrients placed near to the plant canopy to ensure that they reach the roots. The root systems are very fibrous, but have few root hairs, which results in the plants being much more susceptible to water fluctuations. They very much benefit from a deep, organic, acidic mulch to conserve moisture, supply nutrients and suppress weed growth. The roots are also adversely affected by extremes of temperatures, and mulching can reduce this problem as well.

CULTIVATION

Are relatively low maintenance once established. It is important to choose the right species for your area, with chilling requirement being one of the main factors to consider. They will generally grow well where acid-loving plants such as rhododendrons and azaleas are happy.

Location: Blueberries like some shade in very hot areas; otherwise they like full sun.

Temperature: Highbush and rabbit-eye plants are hardy; only killed at –30 to –40°C; flower buds are killed at ~–20 to –30°C when dormant, but because they flower early, it may be wise to give blossoms some protection if expecting very heavy frosts. Lowbush cultivars can be even more cold hardy.

uses

Food

The fruits can be eaten fresh, and are tart but tasty. They can also be mixed with other fruits to make delicious fruit salads, or they can be added to other fresh or cooked desserts, used in muffins, cakes, icecream, sauce, yoghurt, preserves, chutneys. They can accompany savoury as well as sweet dishes. They can also be made into a juice or a good-quality wine.

Nutrition/medicinal

The fruits have reasonable levels of vitamin C: 14 mg/100 g of flesh. They contain good levels of vitamins A, E and several B vitamins, as well as manganese. They are also high in dietary fibre. Their main health benefit though is their very high levels of antioxidants (135–280 mg/100 g flesh). They are ranked third in quantity overall in the common fruit and vegetables, though are first in their actual antioxidant effectiveness. This is mostly due to their very high levels of anthocyanins, which have extensive antioxidant and anti-inflammatory properties, and these develop more, the longer fruits are left on the bush to ripen. Therefore, if you grow your own, you can pick fruits at the last moment for optimum benefits. Most of the antioxidant activity is within the juicy flesh. The berries are very effective at lowering and reducing low density lipids ('bad' cholesterol), which contribute to heart disease, stroke and atherosclerosis. Recent studies have shown that blueberries can improve, and also actually reverse, some of the effects of ageing, particularly loss of balance and co-ordination, a 'normal' feature of advancing age. Studies have shown that a cup of blueberries a day enables people to be 5–6% better at motor-skill tests than a control group, and women have also reported improved mood feelings. In addition, another compound has been identified in the fruits that promotes urinary-tract health and reduces the risk of infection. It appears to work by preventing bacteria from adhering to cells that line the walls of the urinary tract. In Sweden, blueberries have been used to treat childhood diarrhoea. This benefit is attributed to anthocyanosides, naturally found in blueberries, which are believed to be 'lethal' to *E. coli*. Fruits contain ellagic acid and folic acid (which may guard against cervical cancer, and is essential during pregnancy).

Ornamental

A useful ornamental for acidic areas, for their flowers, autumn colour and to attract the birds! Makes a good plant for shrub borders.

Chilling: All blueberries need a fairly long period of winter chill, except for a very few selected cultivars. Highbush need 800–1100 hours of chill; rabbit-eyes need 350–800 hours; southern highbush need 400 hours. If plants receive insufficient winter chill, they do not flower and leaf properly.

Soil/water/nutrients: Can grow on a wide range of soil types from sandy or silty soil, volcanic soils, to highly peaty soils. However, soil with lots of clay is not usually very suitable, unless abundant gypsum, organic matter and sand are added. They like a pH of 4.5–5.2, which is fairly acid, with a high organic matter content (20–50%), which retains moisture, buffers pH and releases nutrients. Areas near pine trees can provide a good soil type for blueberries, or you can add rhododendron/azalea compost to the soil. If the pH is alkaline, then iron chlorosis often occurs, where iron becomes unavailable for plant uptake. The pH can then be reduced by adding peat or ammonium sulphate. Plants also form symbiotic mycorrhizal fungal relationships, which help the plant's roots to absorb nutrients, particularly phosphate, as well as other minerals, and the fungi receive sugars from the plant. If a good fungal relationship is developed, plants need little extra phosphates (or other nutrients); in fact, additional phosphate can result in iron chlorosis because it tends to form insoluble compounds with iron, and thus makes it unavailable to the plant. Plants need moist, but not waterlogged, soils. In wetter soils, plants can be established on a slightly raised bed, to ensure good drainage. Plants need regular moisture for fruit development and for the surface roots. Young plants are particularly sensitive to drought stress. Blueberries only need a little additional nutrients in their first few years, depending on soil type, though the use of organic mulches is always beneficial. Because they are adapted to acid soils, they need nitrogen as urea rather than nitrate. Small additions of potassium, as KSO_3, in late summer, can enhance bud set for the following year, as well as improve autumn colour. The most common deficiencies are of nitrogen and iron, particularly in more alkaline soils.

Pot culture: The slow growth of this plant makes it ideal for container culture, with its attractive, small, evergreen leaves and round, blue fruits. It also means that plants can be given an acidic soil, and as long as a good supply of acidic organic matter and regular moisture are given, then they should fruit well.

Planting: Space plants at 0.6–1 m apart for a hedge, ~2 m apart for individual bushes. They can be grown as an inter-crop plant with deep-rooted trees. Plant height is best kept at ~2 m for ease of harvesting. The plants need to form a good root system to crop well in future years, so it is beneficial to pinch out the flowers in the first season to divert energy to the roots. This is especially important with some southern highbush cultivars that flower heavily as young plants. Weed control is very important during young plant establishment.

Pruning: Plants require pruning each year to ensure good-quality berries: too much growth results in small berries. Pruning stimulates the development of new stems, which are more productive. Flower buds are formed on the outer parts of the present season's growth in late summer as the stems mature. Thus, fruits are borne on last season's wood, with vigorous wood bearing the largest fruit. Remove any dead or diseased wood, weak growth and old twiggy branches. After 4–5 years, a few of the oldest branches can be removed each year to encourage vigorous new growth, and this results in no stems being more than 3–4 years old. Pruning to shape may be done at any time, but heavy pruning is best done during winter dormancy. Severe pruning produces fewer but larger berries and more new wood.

Propagation: *Seed:* Not usually propagated by this method. Wash all pulp from the seeds and sow, if possible, when fresh, just below the surface of damp, acidic compost. Stored seed will germinate better with 2–3 months of cold stratification. Seedlings are best grown in light shade, and pricked out and then grown-on individually until large enough to plant out. *Cuttings:* Green or semi-ripe cuttings can be taken from spring through summer, inserted in gritty, moist, yet well-drained, acidic peat-sand compost, in a shady location. Can take a while to root. Can also take hardwood cuttings, of the present season's growth, in early winter, store these in a fridge, then insert in compost in spring. Hardwood cuttings tend to form more upright plants. *Layering:* Can be done on long, young healthy stems from spring–early autumn. They may take ~18 months to root. *Suckers:* Easily divided in spring or early autumn. Plant in moist, acidic compost to establish. *Tissue culture:* Is practised commercially.

Pests and diseases: Blueberries get few pest and disease problems. Possible problems are stem-blight and *Phytophthora* root rot, with the latter particularly occurring in wet, cold soils; also *Botrytis* and *Anthracnose* can affect fruits. If there are fungal problems, removal of old mulch can reduce any over-wintering fungal spores. Plants may also succumb to several viruses. Fruits are attractive to many birds, and may need netting over the bushes while fruits are ripening.

BLUEBERRY SPECIES

Highbush blueberry, *Vaccinium corymbosum*. The main blueberry produced worldwide. It has a high chill requirement so is only grown in cooler areas. It is a native of sunny, acidic, swampy areas of eastern North America.

Description: An erect, shrub, to ~2–4 m. *Leaves:* Deciduous, small, 2.5–4 cm long, ovate or elliptic. New leaves often have a bronze tinge, turning dark glossy green in summer, followed by autumn hues ranging from burgundy to yellow. *Flowers:* Are self-fertile, but get better fruit-set and larger fruit when cross pollinated. *Fruit:* Bushes produce fruits in 2–4 years. Blue-black, large, of good quality. Only a short time from fruit-set till ripening: 45–75 days. Can be stored for ~28 days. Average yield is ~6 kg. Fruits are good eaten fresh, though they also retain their flavour when cooked.

Cultivars: 'Berkley': Fruits: in mid season, very large berries of fairly good quality. Bush: open, spreading, very productive. Has relatively high chill needs.
'Burlington': Late harvest. Vigorous, heavy cropper, small berries.
'Herbert': Late season. Smaller bush, heavy cropper, very large fruit of very good flavour.
'Paru': Developed in New Zealand. Early to mid season. Bush: upright, moderately vigorous. Can have two crops. Yield: 3–5 kg per bush. Large, firm light blue fruits, excellent flavour.
'Reka' (meaning bright, big and blue in Maori): Developed in New Zealand. Very early season. Bush: upright, vigorous, can grow in mineral soils. Fruits: large, firm, yields of up to

12 kg per bush, moderate size, dark blue, excellent flavour. May need to thin fruit buds as plants tend to over-crop.

Rabbit-eye blueberry, _Vaccinium ashei_. Native to river bottoms and swampy, acid soils of southeastern USA. Similar to highbush in habit, but lower chilling requirement (earlier bloom) and longer period from flowering to maturity (90 days).

Description: Are evergreen, with small leaves. Fruits have a somewhat thicker skin with larger seeds. Tends to ripen later than highbush, and fruits are best left for ~7 days after ripening to develop full sweetness. Shrub: erect, tall, 10 m, though 1–3 m in cultivation. Tolerates less acid soil. Bushes are mostly not self-fertile, so require a pollinator. Fruits are blue-black, of good quality.

Cultivars: 'Delite': Mid season. Very vigorous, growing to >2 m, high yields, very good flavour.
'Rahi' (Maori, meaning abundance and large): Developed in New Zealand. Late season. Bush: upright, non-suckering, vigorous. Fruits: medium–large, light blue, good flavour. Can crop in second season after planting. Good yield and storage.
'Walker': Mid season. Often, good sweet fruits.
'Woodard': Mid–late season. Bush: medium-size, adapted to warmer areas. Fruit: large, light blue, good flavour.

Lowbush blueberry, _Vaccinium angustifolium_. Grown commercially, a low-growing (<1 m, usually ~20 cm, can spread ~2 m), trailing, rhizomatous shrub. Forms lots of rhizomes, ~5 cm under the soil surface, which produce upright shoots along their length, concentrated at tips. Also forms a taproot. Leaves, deciduous, smaller than highbush or rabbit-eye (1.25 cm long), with mildly serrate margins. Highly self-infertile and must have a pollinator to set fruit. Fruit ripens 70–90 days. Fruits are small, black to bright blue in colour, not of best quality, though can be stored for 3 months.

Southern highbush, _Vaccinium corymbosum_ x _V. darrowi_ or _V. ashei_. Similar in many ways to highbush, but only need minimum chilling: 250–500 hours. Fruits ripen very early. Good for warmer areas. They are mostly to completely self-infertile and need a pollinator.

Half-high highbush, _Vaccinium corymbosum_ x _V. angustifolium_. Bushes are short, 0.5–1 m, very cold hardy, and similar to highbush in fruit characteristics. Adapted to extreme winters and snow loads.

Mortiño, _Vaccinium floribundum_. Grows well in northern South America, and is sold in markets in Ecuador. A blueberry for warmer climates. Easy to grow. Shrubs are 1–4 m tall, though can form a tree, growing up to 12 m high, with reddish, flaking bark. Berries are black, roundish, ~1 cm diameter, sweet, juicy, in clusters of 10–15. The skin is somewhat tough. Fruits are used in preserves, pastries, frozen desserts and wine. ■

Vaccinium macrocarpon (syn. _Oxycoccus macrocarpos_)
Cranberry
ERICACEAE

Relatives: blueberries, heather (_Calluna_), heath (_Erica_), rhododendrons

Cranberry is one of the most economically important _Vaccinium_ species in the world. It is native to North America and southern Canada, and the acid bogs where it grows have been harvested by native Indians for thousands of years and by English colonists since the 1600s. Early travellers, especially hunters and trappers, ate and dried these autumn fruits to last them through the long, cold winters. As well as being tasty, fruits were valued for their ability to prevent scurvy and were also used as a diuretic. Cranberries are now grown commercially in many northern states of the USA, Canada and Chile. Today's plants have been selected to have increased yields, provide winter protection and for ease of harvest. This is one of the few fruit species described in this book that prefers to grow in waterlogged locations, is very cold hardy and can grow in very acidic soils. Commercially, bogs are actually created and managed to cultivate cranberries, and are designed to enable water control during the year and provide freeze protection in colder winter areas.

DESCRIPTION
A low-growing, trailing, woody vine with a perennial habit. The plant forms a thick mat of runners over the soil surface, with each runner being 0.3–2 m long. It also has upright stems that grow ~1.2 m tall, and sprout from buds on the runners in the second year. These upright stems then flower and fruit the following year. The upright stems grow 5–20 cm a year, with the base sagging as the upright elongates; hence, only the top 12–20 cm remains in a vertical position.

Leaves: Evergreen, small, dense, ~2 cm long. During the growing season, the oval leaves are dark green and glossy, but turn reddish-brown during winter.

Flowers: Point downwards from fairly long, stiff flower stalks, and give the appearance of a crane's head, hence its original name 'craneberry', which has continued as a misspelling of cranberry. Flowers are ~1 cm long, and have an ovary that contains ~50 ovules, though few of these develop. Flowers take ~16 months between flowering and harvesting the fruit. Terminal buds are initiated in the year before the crop and are triggered by changing day length. The buds continue to develop throughout the rest of the summer and autumn, with tiny floral buds formed within the terminal bud. As the weather becomes colder, the flower buds become dormant until the following spring, they then need enough winter chilling to initiate spring flowering and leaf burst. The attractive pink flowers open ~4 weeks after the leaves in spring. *Pollination:* By bees and other insects. Plants are mostly self-fertile, though cross fertilisation with other plants increases fruit-set and quality. Seedless fruits develop occasionally (parthenocarpy), but most fruit have some seeds.

Fruit: The name *macrocarpon* means 'large fruit'. The fruit is derived from an inferior ovary, and is therefore classified as a 'false berry', as it is formed from some receptacle tissue. The fruits (1–2 cm diameter) have a waxy bloom when mature and are a dark wine-red colour. Most are formed on the upright stems, with a few occurring at the ends of runners. Irrigation is particularly important during fruit formation. Fruits do not naturally fall from the plant when ripe, and can remain attached through winter.

Yield/harvest/storage: Fruit mature in 60–120 days after fruit-set, depending on cultivar and weather, and can be harvested from early to late autumn. Fruits are usually picked when fully ripe, though early frosts can further sweeten them. Plants take ~5 years to come into full bearing, but can then crop well for 60–100 years. Fruits can be stored for 5 months because of their waxy surface. Early colonists stored them in barrels of fresh icy water; frozen dry they will keep for a year.

Roots: They have a shallow root system that is very fibrous, but devoid of root hairs. This makes them very sensitive to fluctuations in soil moisture. They dislike root disturbance; they are best grown in pots until planted out in their permanent positions. They also benefit from a deep peaty, organic mulch to conserve moisture and to add nutrients.

CULTIVATION

Low maintenance, apart from weeding around the plant and pruning back to encourage strong, dense growth.

Location: Likes full sun or light shade, though fruits better in full sun. Needs shelter from strong winds.

Temperatures: Cold hardiness is excellent; spring buds and leaves can tolerate temperature of –20, or even –40°C. Can also tolerate fairly hot summer temperatures.

Chilling: Is unknown, but is probably fairly long due to natural distribution and relatively late commencement of growth in spring.

Soil/water/nutrients: Cranberries thrive in a soil pH of 3.2–4.5: extremely acid, and are similar to blueberries in this respect (see p. 447). They do not like alkalinity, and easily become chlorotic. Naturally, cranberries grow in soil that consists of alternate layers of sand and organic matter, so it is good to mimic this situation and add sand and organic matter every 2–5 years to encourage upright-stem production and maintain productivity. These soils require no mechanical tilling. Cranberries are unusual in being able to

Food
The berries tend to be fairly acid and are usually added to pies and other desserts, or they can be stewed, dried, made into preserves or a sauce to accompany turkey. Because cooking largely destroys their vitamin C content, they could be added to other sweeter fruits and eaten fresh in this way.

Nutrition
Good levels of vitamin C: 40 mg/100 g of flesh, fairly good levels of vitamins E and K, and some vitamin B6, potassium, magnesium and copper.

Medicinal
Recently, cranberries have been found to contain anthocyanidin flavonoids. These flavonoids are particularly effective in strengthening capillaries and, with vitamin C, help prevent progressive loss of sight. They also help in the proper absorption and use of vitamin C, and assist in maintaining intercellular collagen, which forms much of the connective tissue throughout the body. They are well known for their ability to prevent and relieve urinary problems, e.g. cystitis. This may be partly due to the high levels of benzoic acid present, which is thought to acidify the urine and reduce infection. In addition, the proanthocyanidins are thought to prevent *Escherichia coli* bacteria from adhering to cells on the urinary tract wall, which is a critical step in the development of infection; the bacteria are simply flushed out with the urine. Cranberry (and the related *V. oxycoccus*) may also be able to lower blood-sugar levels and lower low-density lipid levels ('bad cholesterol'). Native Americans used the cranberry as a poultice on wounds and infections.

Other uses
A dye can be made from the fruits.

Ornamental
Has good autumn colour. Can be grown as a groundcover if planted ~1 m apart each way. The plants spread rapidly when they are thriving. Excellent for problem gardens with acidic, wet soil.

tolerate wet and flooded soils. However, during the active growing season (spring–autumn), good drainage is needed for proper root growth and function. During winter, growers often protect cranberries by flooding them with water that often freezes over. They sometimes also apply sand to the ice as it thaws, which filters down to the plants, encourages new growth and may also aid pest control. This species grows better in nutrient-poor soils: nutrient-rich soils result in too much leaf growth at the expense of flower and fruit production.

Pot culture: Cranberries form slow-growing, easy-to-manage, small plants that can be easily grown in containers if your garden soil or environment is not sufficiently acidic or damp.

Planting: Space plants at 0.6–1.2 m apart in a peaty, sandy soil. Keep young plants moist. Runners should cover the surface by the end of the season of planting, and uprights are formed in the second year.

Pruning: Fruit is borne on the previous year's growth. Plants just need selective pruning to reduce straggling stems and tangled growth. If fruiting is poor, stem tips can be removed to encourage the production of more fruiting laterals.

Propagation: *Seed:* Sow shallowly, when fresh, in a peat and sand mix. Stored seed may need ~3 months cold stratification. Grow on seedlings in individual pots in a semi-shaded, protected location for at least the first winter. *Cuttings:* Semi-ripe or green cuttings taken in spring, of shoots ~15 cm long, are inserted into a moist sand–peat mix. Or half-ripe cuttings can be taken during autumn, ~7 cm long, with a heel, and inserted in a cold frame, though this latter method is problematic. *Layering:* Plants can be layered, but they take ~18 months to root. *Suckers:* Division of suckers in spring or early autumn is easy.

Pests and diseases: Have very few problems and are also resistant to honey fungus.

CULTIVARS

'Bergman': A strong-growing plant that fruits mid season. Fruit: medium red when ripe with a good flavour. Attractive groundcover plant with strong purple autumn leaf colour.

'Early Black': Small fruit, ripening early, has firm flesh, good for keeping. Turns almost black when fully ripe, but colours well in storage if picked green. Plant is more upright than other species.

'McFarlin': Fruits are large, dark red, juicy, tender and of good flavour. They ripen mid season and are variable in keeping quality.

'Smack': Large, good flavoured fruit, make excellent jellies, jams and pies.

'Wilcox': Medium-sized fruit, deep red when ripe, ripens very early and stores fairly well. Plant is vigorous, very productive, somewhat resistant to false blossom virus. ∎

Vaccinium vitis-idaea
Lingonberry (cowberry, partridge berry, moss cranberry, mountain cranberry, red whortle berry, alpine cranberry)
ERICACEAE
Relatives: cranberry, bilberry, blueberry

The lingonberry is a creeping, evergreen, dwarf shrub from northern European and north American colder temperate regions up to sub-Arctic areas. These tough little plants produce small, cranberry-like fruits, and are common in many colder regions of northern Europe (from Scandinavia down to northern Italy and the Caucasus), across northern Siberia, and the colder areas of Japan, northern China and Korea. There are two varieties of lingonberry: *V. vitis-idaea* var. *minus*, from North America, but also found in northern Europe, and *V. vitis-idaea* var. *vitis-idaea*, found in Europe and northern Asia. They are similar, although the *minus* variety is often shorter. They are often harvested from the wild, and can be found growing in a remarkably wide range of environments, including temperate forests, exposed and windswept sites, bare rocky headlands, scree, high moorlands, sea cliffs, swamps, sand dunes, arctic locations, and mountain summits. At the southern edge of their range, they often grow around peat bogs, but in the north they grow on both wet and dry sites. The fruits have been an important food source for the Slave, Athabaska, Cree and Inuit peoples for thousands of years and, apart from being eaten fresh, they were also dried, or boiled and mixed with oil, for use during the long winters. The leaves and berries were also valued for their medicinal properties. The fruits are now often locally picked and utilised, but are also commercially marketed in Newfoundland, and northern Europe, particularly Scandinavia, Russia and Germany.

DESCRIPTION
Low, dense, creeping, evergreen, mat-forming shrub, often 10–20 cm tall, but if given the right conditions, can be 30–50 cm tall, with 0.3–2 m spread. In very harsh environments, its growth is more limited and stunted. Its stems are semi-woody, and bear numerous very thin shoots, ~2-mm in diameter. Plants are, generally, slow growing.

Leaves: Evergreen, alternate, glossy, elliptical, dark green on the upper surface, light green beneath, small, ~0.5–1 cm long, and usually bronze-red when new. They often turn purplish in autumn, and can persist on the bush for up to 3 years.

Flowers: Pink–white, bell-shaped, singly or in clusters, on the tips of 1-year-old wood. Few flowers are produced until plants are 5–10 years old. The flower has an inferior ovary. Flowering lasts 9–28 days, depending on conditions. If growing in reasonable soil and with warmer temperatures, plants can bloom successfully twice in a year, with the second bloom occurring in mid summer, as the first fruits are ripening. However, frost can damage the spring flowers, so, in colder regions, only the second bloom produces fruit. European cultivars usually flower twice, whereas the North American *minus* cultivar often only flowers once per season, unless grown in warmer regions. *Pollination:* By bumblebees and bee flies. Plants are self-fertile, but cross pollination improves fruit quality.

Fruit: The inferior ovary produces a 'false' berry. It is rounded, a rich wine-red colour when ripe and ~1 cm in diameter. Inside, the berry is divided into four sections and contains many (3–15) tiny seeds, which are usually dispersed by birds. The flesh is sharp–acidic. Plants often produce good crops of fruits.

Yield/harvest/storage: Trees grown from seed can take 5–10 years to start producing fruits, though, in good conditions and for some cultivars, it can be sooner. Yields can be good from plants grown in sheltered locations with no late spring frosts, a peaty soil and adequate moisture. European cultivars give better yields than the North American varieties. In harsh, exposed environments, plants may not flower. Fruit takes ~85 days to mature after fruit-set. Harvesting is done when the fruits are fully ripe to get full sweetness. If possible, they should be left till after the first frosts for the fruits to become sweeter. Fruits can be left on the bush through winter. Refrigerated (unwashed), immediately after picking, the fruits can keep for ~3 weeks.

Roots: Plants form a shallow but wide-spreading network of rhizomes and runners. The regularly bifurcating branched rhizomes have many fine roots that form a fibrous, shallow network. Plants may also form a main taproot, but most roots occur in the top 5–30 cm of soil. Most of the plant's biomass (~80%) is underground. The roots and rhizomes have two main periods of active growth: in early spring and in early autumn.

CULTIVATION

Temperature: Strangely, this plant is not that cold tolerant, even though it grows in such harsh environments, and can be killed by freezing temperatures if not covered by a layer of protective snow. Cold-acclimatised plants can survive temperatures down to ~–12°C, but unacclimatised plants can be killed by temperatures of only ~–3°C. Temperatures of –1.5°C can kill 50% of flowers, and temperatures of –3.5°C can kill 50% of new buds and unripe fruit. In colder areas, it is advisable to cover plants with straw/pine needles, etc., if snow is unlikely in freezing weather.

Location: Plants are best grown in full sun, and then produce more flowers and better-quality fruits. They can also grow in semi-shade, but may not produce flowers. They are fully wind hardy. Although they will grow in maritime locations, their growth is reduced and they may not flower or fruit well.

Soil/water/nutrients: Lingonberries grow best in moist, acidic, sandy soils that have some organic matter added, with a pH of 4.5–6. Peat moss or pine needles can be mixed in with the soil or used as a mulch. They grow well beneath conifers, unlike most most species. (Perhaps plant these with some pinenut trees for company.) They do not grow well in soils that are at all alkaline or are high in salts. They do not like extended waterlogging and prefer good drainage. They are fairly drought tolerant once established, but young plants need moisture till fully established. Plants only need a single application of an acid-based fertiliser, with urea rather than nitrate as the nitrogen source. Too much fertiliser results in too much soft leaf growth, and also reduces fruit yields. Yields are best in peat soils.

Pot culture: Because of their small size, they can be easily grown in pots and given a good peaty soil, which is particularly useful if you live in an area with alkaline soils.

Planting: Space plants at ~1 m apart, in spring or autumn. They grow well in groups, and often get larger fruits and heavier yields. They dislike competition from weeds, particularly when young. Dig in peat and/or pine needles when planting, and mulch with straw or pine needles to protect the plant in cold weather, retain moisture and suppress weed growth. Mulches may also increase plant growth, yield and fruit size. Young plants do not need additional fertilisers. As a groundcover, space plants at 30–60 cm apart.

Propagation: *Seed:* Readily grown from seed, following a period of several weeks of cold stratification. Fresh seed, after ~3–6 weeks of cold treatment at ~–3°C, should give good germination in 2–8 weeks. *Cuttings:* Can take stem or rhizome cuttings in spring–early summer; insert these in peaty, but gritty compost, with warmth and mist if possible. Cuttings can also be taken in spring and autumn, and dipped in rooting hormone. Cuttings take 2–10 weeks to root. Rhizomes can be simply cut into sections that include a few healthy buds, and partially inserted in peaty soil to

uses

Food
The berries can be eaten fresh or added to other fresh fruits. They can also be added to various desserts, preserves, sauces and used in similar ways to blueberries.

Nutrition
Have very good levels of vitamin C, and good levels of calcium and magnesium in summer berries.

Medicinal
They have been widely used medicinally. The leaves were taken to treat bladder problems, gout and rheumatism. Medicinal fruit jellies were used to treat sore throats and colds. The berries and leaves are high in antioxidants and may lower cholesterol levels and fight kidney and bladder infections. Arbutin, obtained from the leaves and stems, is used by pharmaceutical companies in drugs that treat bladder and intestinal disorders, as well as urinary tract infections.

Ornamental
Makes an excellent groundcover plant in colder areas and can put up with many adverse conditions. It is evergreen, and should also produce fruits if the conditions are right.

root. Trailing or creeping stems will also root at their nodes. Cuttings from stems, although they root well, may not form as good a root and rhizome system as plants grown from rhizome cuttings or from seed. The crown can also be split in spring, and plantlets potted up to establish roots and leaves before planting out. *Tissue culture:* Is also practised.

CULTIVARS

'Erntekrone': Dark green leaves and large fruits.
'Erntesegen': Vigorous. Fruit: large, flavourful, and milder than average.

'Koralle': Award-winning Dutch selection, and is the main commercial cultivar. Plant: ornamental, upright, ~30 cm tall, vigorous, but slow-spreading. Fruit: <1 cm diameter, brilliant red, tart, flavourful. Is extremely productive in good, acidic soils. Starts bearing early.
'Red Pearl': A Dutch cultivar. Fruit: large, dark red, early-ripening, mild-flavoured, excellent quality. Plant resists *Phytophthora* root rot. Not as productive as 'Koralle', but is more adaptable to different soil types. A good pollinator for 'Koralle'. ■

Viburnum spp.
Viburnum berries (drupes)
CAPRIFOLIACEAE

Edible species: American cranberry (*V. trilobum*), guelderberry (*V. opulus*), hobbledrupe (*V. lantanoides*), moosedrupe (*V. edule*), nannydrupe (*V. lentago*), stagdrupe (*V. prunifolium*), *V. grandiflorum*, withe rod (*V. cassinoides*)

A large genus of both deciduous and evergreen long-lived shrubs and small trees, viburnums are native to northern temperate locations from the USA, across Europe to eastern Asia. Most are fully frost hardy. A lot have wonderfully imaginative common names! Many species are very popular garden ornamentals in temperate regions. Some species flower during winter and are sought after for their richly fragrant blooms. Others have lots of showy flowers in spring; still others are grown for their attractive berry-like drupes that, in many species, are sweet and tasty, being somewhat like currants or dates in flavour. Listed below are some species with these attributes.

GENERAL DESCRIPTION

Leaves: Generally pointed, elliptical, deeply veined, and many deciduous species have good autumn colour.

Flowers: Are borne in flat clusters, and are tubular with five, often creamy-white-pinky waxy petals. Many species are fragrant. The species either flower in late winter or in spring. Flowers are bisexual, but are self-sterile. *Pollination:* By bees and other insects, but there are problems. Often there are not many pollinating insects around when the flowers open. In addition, because they are self-infertile, more than one plant is needed to set fruits. Even then, pollination is often poor, and hand pollination is needed to get good yields.

Fruits: Drupes with a fairly large, central stone, these often only have a thin layer of edible flesh. Range in colour from dark red, to dark blue, to dark purple when ripe. The skin can be fairly tough and is often discarded. Fruits ripen in autumn or early winter.

Yield/harvest: Can take several years before plants start producing good crops. Fruits should be picked when fully ripe; under-ripe fruits are sour and hard. For many species, a frost further sweetens the fruits and improves their flavour.

CULTIVATION

Viburnum species are easy to grow.

Location: Best sited in relatively protected locations as they do not like cold winds. Grow best in full sun, though can tolerate partial shade. Not tolerant of high salt levels.

Temperature: All are cold hardy, and many are tolerant of long, cold winters. Probably not well-suited to warmer climates, and need a period of winter cold to grow well.

Soil/water/nutrients: Although most species can grow on a range of soil types, they prefer good loamy, moist, neutral to acid soil. Most species do not grow well in dry soils. Can tolerate fairly cold, wet soils, though not extended periods of waterlogging. These species are only moderately nutrient hungry, though an annual application of a balanced, complete fertiliser in spring is beneficial.

Propagation: *Seed:* The best germination is obtained from sowing seeds that are almost fully ripe, but are still greenish. Even then, germination can take several months, and up to 18 months for older seed. Stored seeds need ~8 weeks of moisture and warmth, followed by ~12 weeks of cold stratification; they then often take many months to germinate. Once germinated, grow on seedlings with protection for the first year or more. *Cuttings:* Soft-wood cuttings can be taken in late spring, semi-ripe cuttings in mid–late summer. Insert these in moist, warm, gritty compost. Give rooted cuttings protection for at least the first winter, and longer if not enough growth has occurred. Hardwood cuttings can be taken from many *Viburnum* species during winter, and these are inserted in a cold frame to root. Give protection, but not too much heat, till spring. *Layering:* Good results from layering vigorous stems of many *Viburnum* species. Use material from the current season's growth in summer. Takes ~15 months for new plants to establish.

Pruning: Plants generally just need a tidy-up to remove damaged or older wood. Prune after fruiting. The removal of dense crossing branches ensures that light and air can enter the canopy.

Pests and diseases: Few major problems, though aphid or whitefly attacks may occur. If a plant is physically or frost damaged then there can be a greater risk of fungal disease entering. Try to prune to limit frost damage. Fungus can also cause leaf spot.

EDIBLE SPECIES

Below are a few *Viburnum* species with better-tasting fruits.

American cranberry, *Viburnum trilobum*. A large bush or small tree, native to northern North America, growing to ~3 m. It is closely related to *V. opulus* (see moosedrupe below). Large amounts of *V. trilobum* fruit have been known to cause nausea in some people; others claim it has very low toxicity unless eaten in large quantities and uncooked. However, many consider the fruits to be very tasty and make a good substitute for cranberries. They are rich in vitamin C. The fruits (~0.8 cm long) are sweeter and taste better after a frost and make good jam.

Cultivation: Can be grown on heavier clay soils, but is not as hardy as some *Viburnum* species. Birds love the drupes.

Guelderberry (guelder rose), *Viburnum opulus*. A well-known ornamental species in Britain and Europe, where it is also a native. Forms a multi-stemmed shrub, with grey bark. It has good autumn colour. Needs little attention, growing on most soil types, including chalk. Needs minimal pruning. Propagated from seed or cuttings. Has white flowers, in flat clusters, in late spring, with larger, showy but sterile flowers around the edge of the cluster that attract pollinators to the central receptive blossom. Has bright red, roundish berries in autumn. Some have a good sub-acid, cranberry-like taste. They are popularly used in preserves, jam, desserts and to make a wine. **Warning:** If eaten in large numbers the raw fruits can cause nausea in some people, though if they are cooked they do not have this effect.

Hobbledrupe, *Viburnum lantanoides*. A shrub, native to eastern North America, growing to ~3 m high. Is a very hardy plant, tolerating temperatures down to ~–30°C. It flowers in late spring/summer. Sweet, tasty drupes that ripen in autumn, and are sweeter after a frost. Has a large central stone. Grows best on moist, more acid, sheltered sites. Does not like competition from other species or alkaline soil. Plants can be easily layered.

Nannydrupe (sheep drupe, wild raisin), *Viburnum lentago*. An attractive bush, native to northern North America, height ~3 m. Flowers late spring/summer. Sweet-tasting, juicy drupes that ripen in autumn, though are variable in size, being ~1.5 cm long. Has a thicker skin than many *Viburnum* fruits. The plant is extremely hardy, surviving temperatures down to ~–30°C, and is tolerant of wetter soils. An easy-to-grow plant.

Uses: The fruits can be eaten fresh or cooked, or can be dried. The fruits are often sweeter after a frost, but may also be somewhat dry. *Medicinal:* The drupes have been used as an antispasmodic. *Ornamental:* The plant can be pruned to form a hedge. The drupes are attractive to birds.

Moosedrupe, *Viburnum edule*. A bush, native to East Asia and eastern North America, growing to ~2.5 m. It flowers in early summer, and produces sweet, tangy drupes (~0.8 cm long) in mid–late autumn, and these are better if harvested before a frost. Plants can grow well in heavy clay soils, with a slightly acidic pH.

Uses: The drupes can be eaten fresh or cooked, or can be dried for winter use. The skins are often removed first. It is highly valued for jam. The flowers can be used in fritters. **Warning:** This species is closely related to *V. opulus* (guelder rose), whose raw fruits can cause nausea in some people. There are no reports of sickness from eating the fruits of *V. edule*; care just needs to be taken in identification. *V. edule* has no sterile flowers in the inflorescence and produces more and larger fruits than *V. opulus*.

Stagdrupe (stagbush, black haw, sloe), *Viburnum prunifolium*. Native to the southeast of USA, this is a small tree, height ~4–7 m, spread 5 m, producing white flowers in summer, with drupes ripening in late autumn. The black fruits are sweet and tasty, though are drier than those of many species. Are variable in size (~1.5 cm long) and somewhat variable in quality. Unlike many other *Viburnum* species, the stagdrupe can grow on poor soils and in drier locations. It is also very cold hardy, down to –40°C.

Uses: *Food:* Because the fruits vary in quality, they are often used in cooking rather than eaten fresh. The fruits become sweeter after a frost. *Medicinal:* This species, in particular, has been researched for its medicinal properties. The bark of the root and stems contains a coumarin-type chemical that can cause constrictions of various body tissues and has, therefore, been used to induce abortions. It also acts as an antispasmodic, a painkiller and a sedative, as the bark also contains a compound similar to that found in aspirin. A tea can be drunk to ease painful menstruation. The bark should be harvested either in autumn before the leaves

Food
Ripe fruits can be sweet and tasty, and somewhat date-like, but do not have much flesh. They can be eaten fresh or added to jam, desserts, etc.

Nutrition
The fruits usually contain good levels of vitamin C.

change colour, or in the spring before the leaves open. It can be dried for later use. ***Warning:*** The roots and stems should not be taken during pregnancy. *Ornamental:* This species can be pruned to form an informal hedge.

Viburnum grandiflorum. A native of eastern Asia and China, this very hardy species makes a beautiful ornamental plant, ~3 m height, ~2 m spread. Clusters of drooping creamy-pink flowers, ~5 cm long, bloom from mid winter to early spring and have a wonderful scent. A great plant to grow in colder areas for it produces flowers when little else is growing. Plant near to the house or a path to appreciate its scent. The flowers can survive down to –10°C. The black drupes are ~2 cm long and have sweet, tasty flesh, which

can also be dried. There is a large central stone.

Cultivation: As for the general description above, but is also more sensitive to cold, windy sites. Grows and flowers best against a sheltered wall.

Withe rod, *Viburnum cassinoides*. Native to eastern North America. Forms a shrub ~2.5 m tall. Flowers in early summer and fruits in late autumn. Produces smallish, black drupes (~1 cm long) with sweet, tasty flesh, though they do have a large stone in the centre. An ornamental variety is 'Nanum', which has a dwarf habit and rich autumn leaf colours.

Uses: The drupes can be eaten fresh or cooked and are a good source of fresh fruits in late autumn/winter. The leaves can be made into a pleasant-tasting tea. ∎

Vitis spp.
Grapes
VITACEAE

European or wine grape (*Vitis vinifera*), American bunch grape (*V. labrusca* syn. *V. labruscana*)

The grape has been cultivated for a very long time. Egyptians were making wine at least 6000 years ago, and dried raisins have been enjoyed for even longer. Seeds have been found in Bronze-age dwellings in south-central Europe and have been dated at 3500–1000 BC. Egyptian hieroglyphics detail the culture of grapes in 2440 BC. The Phoenicians carried grape varieties to Greece, Rome and southern France before 600 BC, and Romans spread the grape throughout Europe. The Greek and Roman wine gods were named Dionysus and Bacchus, respectively. The drunken state was believed to result from possession by the gods, allowing one to see into the future, and wine has been symbolic of the blood of life in several religions. The vine was introduced into France by a Tuscan and the Romans introduced it to England. By the end of the Renaissance, all of Europe was drinking wine. Europeans had established vineyards in Chile by 1540, and Francis Drake writes of seizing a boatload of Chilean wine in 1578. The vine was established in California by Spaniards at the beginning of the 18th century. Only in the 18th century was the art of bottling sufficiently advanced to allow wine to age gracefully rather than turning to vinegar, and vintages were established. Grapes can be found growing around the world in temperate to Mediterranean-type climates. The genus contains >80 plants that are both evergreen and deciduous. There are two main commercial subgenera of *Vitis*: *Euvitis* and *Muscadinia*. The latter includes the muscadine grapes and is described on p. 460, with other less usual *Vitis* species. *Euvitis* are classified as 'true grapes' or 'bunch grapes', and consist of long clusters of fruits (berries) that remain on their stalks at maturity, and have forked tendrils. Within the *Euvitis* group are two main species: the Old World or European grape and American bunch grapes. The European grape (*V. vinifera*) accounts for >90% of world production and probably originated from the Middle East. The American bunch grape (*V. labrusca*), because it is resistant to Phylloxera, is mostly used as a resistant rootstock for European grapes. It is also used to make grape juice, jam, preserves and some wine. The American species, *V. labrusca*, can be found growing wild in the eastern USA. It was first seen by Viking explorers, before Columbus's voyages, who named the maritime provinces of Canada as 'Vinland', meaning 'grape land', due to the abundance of wild grapes growing in its forests. Early settlers to the northeast then domesticated this species.

DESCRIPTION

These *Vitis* species form a woody vine, with a height of 1.2–3.5 m, and a spread of 2–5 m. The plants can live for more than 70 years and can still be productive. Stems with

diameters of >60 cm have been known. They are moderately fast growing.

Leaves: Deciduous, opposite, at nodes, can be large (20–25 cm width), sometimes deeply lobed, as in many

V. vinifera cultivars, or rounded with entire or serrate margins. Has forked tendrils for climbing. Some varieties have bright autumn colour.

Flower: Small (~0.2 cm), in drooping panicles on current season's growth. Bunch grapes may have 100+ flowers per panicle, whereas muscadine grapes have only 10–30 flowers per cluster. Flowers and shoots are borne on 1-year-old wood. *Pollination*: Have bisexual flowers and are self-fruitful. All grapes need pollination to set fruit: even seedless cultivars such as 'Thompson Seedless' need pollination, but their embryos are aborted shortly after fruit-set, so they have no seeds. This process is called stenospermocarpy.

Fruit: Grapes are classified as a true berry. Colours of skin (and flesh) range from pale green to deep purple-black. The flesh is juicy and succulent. Fruits have 2–4 oval, pointed, tan-coloured seeds. Lots of sun on the fruit encourages sweetness and ripening, and removal of leaves around the fruit enhances this. About 6–8 leaves per bunch are left for development.

Yield/harvest/storage: Bears fruits after 2–4 years. The number of days from bloom to maturity is least for *V. labrusca*, more for French–American hybrids and longer for European grapes. The yield of wine grapes is usually ~4–5 kg per plant, which makes a gallon of wine: table grapes produce greater yields. Bunch grapes are normally green, red or reddish-black when ripe, depending on the cultivar, and are harvested in mid–late summer. The stems also turn a straw colour when fruits are mature. Grapes should only be picked when ripe, as they won't ripen and sweeten properly if picked too early. Grapes for raisins need to be fully to almost over-ripe as they then begin to lose moisture and become sweeter; however, they do need to be harvested before the rains begin. For wine, the time of grape harvesting is a balance between sugar content (brix) and pH, with pH being more difficult to adjust later than sugar. Wines less acidic than pH 3.2 are considered to be unstable. Table grapes are best left on the vines till quite ripe. Raisin grapes are picked and placed between drying papers in single layers or in small clusters. They are turned regularly every 7–10 days while they gently dry to 13–15% moisture content, i.e. when juice can no longer be squeezed from them when pressed. Once dry, they can be stored for long periods at room temperature. Grapes can also be frozen for storage. At room temperature, fresh grapes, if kept cool, can be kept for 2–6 weeks, depending on species.

Roots: Has some surface roots, so avoid deep mechanical cultivation. They also form deep taproots that can grow down ~5 m. Mulches can help to control weeds and conserve moisture.

CULTIVATION

Do need a fair amount of attention to get good crops.

Location: Best grown in full sun with good air circulation to reduce fungal disease and reduce frost risk, and also need some protection from strong winds. Train them over a trellis, pergolas or around a patio or veranda. Training increases yield. Can tolerate some salt, so can be grown near the coast in sheltered locations.

Temperature: Bunch grape buds can be damaged by temperatures lower than ~–20°C; and branches can be injured or killed below –22°C. Labrusca grapes can tolerate lower temperatures. However, late frosts can kill young buds

in some areas. Cool climates result in lower sugar and higher acid flavours in the fruit, whereas higher temperature results in high sugar and low acids. Generally, hotter temperatures are needed for red wine cultivars, and cooler temperatures for white wine cultivars. They prefer a long growing season.

Chilling: Highly variable amongst grape species; some grapes can be grown in the tropics and need little or no chilling. Labrusca generally needs high chilling: 1000–1400 hours; European grapes only need 100–500 hours.

Soil/water/nutrients: Grapes grow best in deep, well-drained, light-textured soils, although nutrient deficiencies may be more common in these soils. However, they can grow in a wide range of soils, including poor soils. In fact, rich, fertile soil produces poor wine-making grapes because vigour and yield need to be controlled. They grow best in soils with a pH range 5.8–6.8, with a minimum pH of 5.5. Traditionally, they are best grown on poor, limestone-based slopes, although they can also grow in clays. Rootstocks allow adaptation to various soil situations. Mulching will help prevent moisture loss and control weed growth. American grapes like a humid, temperate climate; European grapes prefer a drier climate, particularly during fruit ripening, and too much moisture results in poor-quality fruit and increased disease susceptibility. Extra water is only beneficial for table and raisin grapes, where high yields are desired. For all grape types, it is beneficial to deeply water plants prior to bud burst, if the winter has been dry. Plants are not too affected by salinity or waterlogging, but within reason! Grapes are not nutrient hungry and only need an application of a balanced, complete fertiliser once early in the growing season, while the vines are young. Keep fertiliser away from the stem and water-in well. Additional nitrogen results in excessive vegetative growth and causes other nutrient problems. Older plants need little, if any, additional nutrients. The main deficiencies are likely to be nitrogen (yellowish, small young leaves), potassium (yellow/bronze leaf margins or blue-black flecks on the upper leaf), magnesium (yellowing of margins of older leaves) and boron. May get aluminium and manganese toxicities (black stripes along the leaf stalks, the leaf can become rolled and often falls) on wet, acid soils, and of boron on light, alkaline soils. The difference between boron excess and deficiency is narrow, so care is needed when adding boron in fertiliser. Weed control maximises the benefits of fertilisers and irrigation.

Planting: Grapes can be trellised and grown in rows, with ~3–5 m between rows and 1–2.5 m between vines within a row. In arid regions, they can be grown more widely apart to give a larger water-catchment area. Prepare the trellis-wire system (or support) before planting. A trellis can be constructed by putting up a single wire ~1.25–2 m high, or two wires, which give more productive plants, but can cause more disease problems. Prepare the planting hole with compost and a slow-release fertiliser. Where feasible, the rows should be set in a north–south direction so that both sides of the vines receive some sunlight during the day. Protect young plants from rabbits, wind and weed competition. Keep the plant moist, but do not fertilise for the first year.

Pruning: Pruning is important for grapes more than most other fruiting species. If not pruned and trained, they produce irregular, poor crops of fruits. Prune annually, from late winter through to early spring, before the leaves emerge. Depending on the severity of winter temperatures, pruning in early spring in colder regions reduces possible cold damage. Grapes produce fruit on lateral growth from 1-year-old stems, and are pruned to limit the number of new laterals and the number of fruit clusters per lateral. It is best to thin young fruits to direct more of the plant's strength into producing fewer, better fruits. The more buds left on a vine, the higher will be the yield in that year, but, in future, the size of bunch, quality of fruit and vigour will decrease. Pruning often causes bleeding from the cuts, which usually stops once the leaves have appeared, and does not seem to adversely affect the health of the plant.

Training: In the first winter after planting, select the longest, strongest stem to become the main stem and remove all others. During the second spring, allow one terminal and two lateral buds to form shoots (a cordon). Better-quality grapes are obtained if each cane is limited to only one cluster or no fruit production for the first 2–3 years. After 4 years of bearing, half the grape clusters can be left to mature. Tie young vines onto wires as they develop. There are more training systems for grapes than for all other fruit crops combined. Overall, these pruning methods are designed to allow more buds to develop on fruit-producing table-grape varieties, and for fewer buds on wine-producing grapes.

Grapes are often trained to have two main scaffold shoots growing off from a central stem to wires spaced at different heights, or just a single pair of scaffold branches from one wire (a cordon). Laterals from these then develop to produce the fruiting laterals. The number of fruiting laterals allowed to

uses

Food

Grapes are wonderful fresh. They can be added to sauces, salads and desserts, and make a tasty juice. They are good with cheeses. Grappa, a powerful alcoholic drink (100% proof), is distilled from the fermented skins, seeds and stems which are left over from pressing the juice, and is often taken as an after-dinner drink in Italy. The young leaves are tasty after blanching and can be stuffed with rice, vegetables, bacon, etc. They are commonly used in many Middle Eastern and Mediterranean dishes.

Wine making (enology)

The pH of wine-making grapes should be about 3.2. Wine is basically made by crushing the grapes and extracting the juice (must: juice + skins + seeds ± stems for red; juice only for white). The pH is then assessed, and sugar is added if needed. Commercially, sulphur dioxide is then added as a preservative. The must is then either partially fermented with the skins to produce red wine, with lesser contact for a rosé, or with no skin contact for a white wine. Higher fermentation temperatures are used for red wine (24–28°C) compared to white (14–18°C). After a period of time, the wine is then filtered and placed in oak barrels (or similar) in a cool environment. Red wine is usually aged for between 1–10 years, whereas white wine usually only needs <1 year. The wine can then be bottled.

Nutrition

Low levels of vitamin C: 4–11 mg/100 g of flesh, but fairly high levels of vitamin A, B1, B2 and potassium. In red wine, two main types of polyphenols occur, a non-flavonoid type (caffeic acid), which is found within the flesh, and flavonoid types, which include flavonols (also called pycnogenols or proanthocyanadins), and are found mostly in the seed, and anthocyanins, found within the skin. White wine only contains non-flavonoid polyphenols as it has no contact with skins or seeds. The flavonoids are very potent free-radical scavengers and have a strong antioxidative effect.

Medicinal

In times past, people used to tap the grape vines in spring, and the sap was drunk for its medicinal properties, which are the same as for its leaves and fruits. The sap was also used to treat eye infections. Red grapes contain good quantities of resveratrol, an anti-carcinogenic compound, discovered in 1996. It can inhibit tumour formation by stopping DNA damage, slowing/halting cancerous cell transformation, and can also slow tumour growth. It also has anti-inflammatory properties and may be very useful for colon-cancer prevention. It is still experimental, but may be a useful cancer drug in the future. It is thought to work by neutralising a toxic compound, piceatannol, which only occurs in cancer cells. Resveratrol is, naturally, a phytoalexin, i.e. a compound formed by plants to defend itself against fungal attacks. Grape seed extract, because of its flavonols, greatly enhances the activity of vitamin C within the body, and acts as a powerful free-radical scavenger and antioxidant. It has ~50 times more antioxidant activity than vitamins A and E, or selenium, and ~20 times greater activity than vitamin C. It helps to promote tissue elasticity, heal injuries, reduce swelling and oedema, restore collagen and improve peripheral circulation, prevent bruising, strengthen weak blood vessels, protect against atherosclerosis and inhibits the enzymes that lead to histamine formation. It is rapidly absorbed and distributed throughout the body within minutes. Removes and prevents lipofuscin formation in the brain and heart, conferring anti-ageing benefits. Increases elasticity and flexibility of muscles, tendons and ligaments, and acts as smooth muscle relaxant in blood vessels. Both flavonoids and non-flavonoids reduce the levels of low density lipoproteins ('bad' cholesterol). Grapes also contain ellagic acid, tannic acid and gallic acid as well as the flavonoid, quercetin, which seem to protect against cancer and strengthen connective tissues. In addition, grapes also contain good levels of lutein and zeaxanthin (types of vitamin A), which are proven to help reduce the incidence of cataracts and macular degeneration. *Warning:* Despite their wonderful health benefits, it is also worth bearing in mind that grape seeds and skins contain tannins, which can be carcinogenic if taken in excess.

Ornamental

The vines can create great summer shade over a pergola, balcony or deck, and then conveniently lose their leaves during winter to allow the winter sun to enter. Grapes have attractive leaves and give a truly Mediterranean effect in the garden.

develop depends on cultivar and usage, with less vigorous species needing more buds, and more vigorous ones needing fewer buds. After a period of years, these main scaffold branches are often renewed by other laterals that are allowed to develop from the main stem.

Apart from allowing scaffold branches to develop (off which fruiting laterals develop) there is a commercial pruning system, often called the Guyot, which just allows the main single trunk to remain permanently, and the horizontal arms are renewed annually. The latter, also called spur pruning, leaves only stubs with 2–6 buds on each of the two renewal canes. This is used on very vigorous cultivars or on wine cultivars where high quality fruits rather than high quantities of grapes are required, with only a few fruiting laterals branches allowed to develop. Other laterals are either removed or are pruned back to 2–3 buds to form next year's fruiting laterals. Cultivars that are less vigorous are pruned to leave 9–16 buds on last year's canes. These stems are then removed after they have fruited.

Grapes can also be pruned into a fan system or can be trained to cover an arbour.

Propagation: Seed: Usually not propagated by seed, though they do germinate quite easily. However, progeny do vary. Seeds are best sown in a cool place when fresh, with all pulp washed from them. Stored seed benefits from being soaked in warm water for ~24 hours before a period of 6–8 weeks of cold stratification. Germination usually takes place in spring, though can take longer. Grow on seedlings in pots until of a reasonable size. *Cuttings:* Are easy and fine as long as they are disease (especially *Phylloxera*) free. If there is little risk of disease, then grapes can be grown from cuttings. Hardwood cuttings (~30 cm long) are taken in winter from younger, green wood, with two or more buds. Wrap the cutting in damp paper and polythene and leave in the fridge at ~4°C until planting in spring, or take cuttings just before bud burst and plant these in a pot with just two buds above the soil surface. The bottom cut should be made just below a bud and the top cut ~2.5 cm above a bud. Short stem cuttings can have a thin, narrow strip of the bark, ~3 cm long, removed from the base of the stem. This encourages the formation of roots. Root cuttings in a cool, shady location; they should take ~6 weeks to start rooting. *Layering:* Sometimes difficult, but can be tried during the growing season. *Grafting:* The most common method is bench and cleft grafting; T-budding is also used. The use of rootstocks is important for imparting disease resistance. From the 1860s, the aphid Phylloxera (*Dactylosphaera vitifolii*), also known as grape-root louse, caused huge devastation; it was accidentally introduced into French vineyards from North America. By the end of the 19th century, it had killed two-thirds of *V. vinifera* vines within Europe. Resistance to this pest was only obtained by using a rootstock from North American *V. labrusca* vines, which have developed a resistance to this disease. Most rootstocks used today are hybrids of American rootstocks.

Pests and diseases: European grapes are extremely susceptible to Phylloxera, which forms galls on the roots and eventually kills the plant, so best to choose plants grown on American vines. The European grapes are more susceptible to fungal disease and cold, particularly 'Thompson Seedless' and 'Cabernet Sauvignon'. The main fungal problems are powdery and downy mildew. Reduce the risk by pruning to form an open canopy and space plants with room around them. Also, limit the application of nitrogen as too much encourages fungal growth by producing lush, thin leaves. Black spot may also occur. In warmer, more humid areas, the muscadine grapes can be a good option. Lacewing, a wasp that nests in blackberries, feeds on leaf-hoppers that feed on grape leaves, so plant some blackberries in your vineyard. Mites can be a problem, as can mealybugs. Birds love to eat grapes.

CULTIVARS
Wine grapes
'Cabernet Franc': Makes a fairly good-quality red wine. Very cold-hardy vine. Black fruit, ripens earlier.

'Cabernet Sauvignon': Red wine grapes. One of the most cold-hardy cultivars and is fairly disease resistant. Black fruit is late ripening, but does OK in areas with shorter summers, though performs better in warmer regions.

'Chardonnay': Is cold hardy, but is not quite as hardy as 'White Riesling'. Good wine quality. Early and reliable white fruit. Moderately vigorous. Susceptible to *Botrytis* rot. Need to remove some leaves and train vertically to reduce risk.

'Gewürztraminer': Red fruit, but makes a white aromatic, spicy wine. Less cold hardy than many *V. vinifera* cultivars. Plants are vigorous and large, and leaves often shade the fruit, leading to uneven ripening. Needs a long summer season. Good resistance to *Botrytis* rot.

'Limberger': A black grape grown in northern Europe. Good cold hardiness and resistance to *Botrytis*. Good yields. Wine is highly rated; has a deep red colour and is rich in tannins.

'Merlot': Red wine. Needs a long, warm summer for black fruit to ripen well. Fairly vigorous and forms a fairly dense canopy, which makes it more susceptible to *Botrytis* rot.

'Pinot Blanc': A white-fruited type. Important in Germany, Alsace and the Loire Valley. Has more resistance to *Botrytis*. Cold hardy.

'Pinot Gris': A light red grape. Not as cold hardy as 'Pinot Blanc', but more cold hardy than reds. Fairly resistant to *Botrytis*. Makes a fuller-bodied white wine. Best where summers are long and not too hot.

'Pinot Noir': Produces very good-quality red wines. Early ripening compared to other red cultivars. Is fairly cold hardy. Black fruits are thin skinned and susceptible to *Botrytis*.

'Sauvignon Blanc': A vigorous vine; needs a long warm–hot summer. Is fairly cold hardy. White fruits are very susceptible to *Botrytis*, and its dense growth increases the risk.

'Syrah' (syn. 'Shiraz'): Black fruits. Vigorous, cold hardy, disease resistant; small fruit.

'White Riesling': Very cold hardy. Makes excellent quality white wines. Susceptible to *Botrytis*: so need to remove some leaves and train vertically to reduce this risk. Late harvest.

Table seedless grapes
'Thompson Seedless', the major raisin cultivar, is a popular sweet seedless grape.
American x European species include **'Baco Noir'**, **'Catawba'**, **'Cayuga'** (white), **'Syval Blanc'** (resists mildew), **'De Chaunac'**, **'Seibel 9110'**.
'Schuyler', *Vitus* hybrid, is a very sweet black table grape with a slight currant flavour. Disease resistant. Good rich red autumn colour, even in mild climates.

American cultivars
V. labrusca vines have fruit with soft pulp that pops out of the skin, are cold hardy, do not need such hot summers and are more disease resistant. Types include:
'Albany Surprise': Mid season, popular. Heavy crops of medium-sized bunches of large, mild flavoured black berries with a juicy texture. Hardy variety.

'Candice Seedless': Moderate–heavy crops, medium red, fleshy, thin-skinned, spicy, tasty grapes, good eaten fresh. Fruits mid season. Fairly cold hardy. Disease resistant. Good seedless variety.
'Concord': The best known of the American varieties. Named after where it was first developed. A dark purple fruit, often used for wine, sometimes for table grapes. Popularly made into a jelly for sandwiches in the USA.
'Diamond': Good yields. Large greeny-yellow, juicy fruits. Strong pineapple flavour. Hardy. Fruits mid season.
'Glenora': Ornamental, good autumn colour, early–mid season ripening. Fruit, blue, spicy, seedless.
'Niagara': Popular green-yellow cultivar. Cold tolerant, does not need as much heat in summer. Regular heavy crops of medium–strong aromatic, white, juicy, pulpy, tasty fruits in medium–large bunches. Very hardy and vigorous, less troubled by birds. Fruits early–mid season. Resistant to fungal disease, so can be grown in wetter regions.
'Himrod': A white seedless grape for the table. Highly-rated, sweet flavour.
'Venus': A seedless grape, excellent fresh. Ripens early. ■

Vitis rotundifolia
Muscadine (scuppernong)
VITACEAE

Similar species: Californian grape (*V. californica*), grape (*V. lanata*), riverbank grape (*V. riparia*), Spanish grape (*V. berlandieri*), sugar grape (*V. rupestris*), summer grape (*V. aestivalis*), sweet mountain grape (*V. monticola*), sweet winter grape (*V. cinerea*)

Relatives: European and American grapes

The *Vitis* genus contains >80 plants that are both evergreen and deciduous. There are two main commercial subgenera of *Vitis*, the *Euvitis* and the *Muscadinia*. The *Euvitis* includes the wine and many table grapes and is described on p. 456. *Muscadinia*, or muscadine grapes, are smaller, thicker skinned and the berries detach easily as they mature; they also have unforked tendrils. It is a shame that these grapes are not more widely grown and appreciated as they have many of the characteristics of *Euvitis* grapes, and some consider them to have tastier fruits. In addition, they can be grown in warmer climates and are also much more disease resistant. One of the main species is the muscadine or scuppernong, *V. rotundifolia*, which has aromatic, fruity grapes that can be eaten fresh and make a flavoursome juice.

The muscadines are native to southeastern USA, and the fruits have been cultivated by indigenous peoples for more than 400 years. This species has been enjoyed and appreciated by southerners, but has received little attention elsewhere. Under good conditions, the vines can reach a great age and size. One example was a scuppernong, found to be ~200 years or more old, with a trunk ~60 cm thick; its sprawling vines covered an area of about half an acre!

DESCRIPTION
Very vigorous, deciduous vines, which can grow 20–30 m up trees in the wild. They have hard, smooth, non-shedding bark, prominent warty lenticels and unbranched tendrils. Vines can live for a very long time, i.e. centuries, and can attain great girth and spread of stems. The vine is capable of 10–20 m of growth per year. Without support, it often grows into a shrubby plant, only ~1 m in height, though stems grow outwards a long way in search of a support. If growing in shade, the vine often sends down aerial roots that may or may not reach the ground. The shoots are short-jointed, angled with fine hair. The vine's leaves, flowers and fruits ripen late in the season.

Leaves: Glossy on both sides, becoming firm and dull at maturity, 5–12 cm long. Are dark green above, greeny-yellow beneath, heart-shaped–roundish, not lobed. Margins have wide, irregular teeth.

Flowers: Dioecious, small, greenish, borne in short, dense panicles. Some self-fertile cultivars have been developed with almost-bisexual flowers, which can also serve as a pollen source for female plants. For best results, one bisexual-flowered vine to every 3–5 vines is needed to get good fruit-set. Male plants are not usually planted because a self-fertile variety will produce fruits as well as being a pollinator. Flowers have a superior ovary. *Pollination:* By bees and insects. Grapes are not parthenocarpic and all fruits need pollinating: even seedless fruits have embryos that have aborted shortly after fruit-set.

Fruit: Classified as true berries. Borne in small, loose clusters of 5–30 grapes: fewer than wine grapes, the fruits are smaller (~1.5–2 cm diameter) and have tougher skins. They come in colours of red, yellow, bronze, blue, purple and black. Some varieties may contain up to five seeds; other varieties are seedless. Sugar content varies from 15–25%, and some older cultivars have a more musky flavour than modern cultivars.

Yield: A mature vine can yield ~10 kg of fruit. The fruits take longer to ripen than European or American grapes. They are harvested when fully ripe and coloured, in mid–late autumn. Fruits tend to ripen unevenly, and also drop when ripe, so need to be regularly harvested. The grapes keep well for ~3 weeks, particularly if refrigerated, or can be gently dried with good aeration. They are usually dried to 15% moisture content, i.e. when juice can no longer be squeezed from them when pressed. Once dry, they can be stored for long periods at room temperature.

Roots: Have shallow feeder roots, mostly within the top 30 cm, so mechanical cultivation should be avoided. An organic mulch retains moisture and adds nutrients.

CULTIVATION

Easier to cultivate and less maintenance than European grapes, but needs a warmer, more humid climate to do well.

Location: Likes full sun, heat and good air circulation.

Temperature: Adapted to warm, humid conditions, but it is more susceptible to frost, although is generally not injured until temperatures fall below −12°C. (Vines may be killed below ~−16°C.) Does need summer heat as well as a long growing season, or the fruit tend to be small and not as sweet.

Chilling: Muscadines need 500–1000 hours of chilling.

Soil/water/nutrients: Grow well on a wide range of soils, but best results are from well-drained sandy loams, with a pH of 5.5–6.5. Do not tolerate waterlogging, though prefer a humid, temperate climate. They grow best with regular moisture and do not tolerate drought very well. Young plants benefit from watering through dry summers for the first 2–4 years. They are somewhat more nutrient hungry than the European grapes, and benefit from 1–2 additions of a balanced fertiliser (or similar) a year, particularly with extra nitrogen.

Planting: Can be trellised and grown in rows, with ~3–5 m between rows and 1–2.5 m between vines within a row, or planted in a small group to grow up a pergola or similar. Prepare the trellis-wire system (or support) before planting. A trellis can be constructed by spanning two wires at ~1.25- and 2-m heights. Prepare the planting hole with compost and a slow-release fertiliser. Where feasible, the rows should be set in a north–south direction so that both sides of the vines receive some sunlight during the day. Protect young plants from rabbits, wind and weed competition. Keep the plants moist.

Pruning: This species bleeds a lot when pruned, so is best pruned in late winter, when dormant. It is important to encourage the formation of new fruiting wood, but also to prevent vines from becoming a dense mass of unfruiting branches. A system with a permanent trunk and 2–3 permanent arms is commonly used. Remove tendrils and all branches not needed for spurs and fruiting arms. Prune out all stems that are <0.5 cm in diameter, leaving 2–3 buds per spur, depending on the vigour of the branch. Use a cordon system (see p. 459) with short (7.5 cm) spurs for all muscadines; space spurs ~15 cm apart on the permanent arms. Often the basal buds on stems of muscadines produce little if any fruit, so these laterals can be removed once they have fruited.

Propagation: *Seed:* Can be easily raised from seed. Sow seed when it is fresh, if possible, but it is best if given ~6 weeks of cold stratification to improve germination rates. Clean off any pulp before sowing. Germination should then take place in spring, but may take 12 months or longer. *Cuttings:* Can take mature cuttings (15–30 cm long) from last season's growth in late autumn. Can also take 5-cm-long stem sections, with at least one bud. A thin, narrow strip of bark (~3 cm long) can be removed from the base of the stem to encourage callusing and root formation. These cuttings are taken during summer, and should be given warmth, moisture and protection. *Layering:* Can be practised at any time, but is often done in summer. Stems of the current season's growth are bent to soil level and covered with earth, with the tips left uncovered. By autumn, the stems should have developed roots and can be severed from the parent. *Grafting:* Seedling plants can be grafted onto desirable cultivars, with bench grafting being the usual method. The muscadine rootstock is not suitable for American and European grapes because of incompatibility problems.

Pests and diseases: Have much fewer problems with disease than American or European grapes, in fact they are almost disease resistant. They are essentially immune to Phylloxera, nematodes, black spot and Pierce's disease. Birds can be a problem though, and watch out for the grape-berry moth, grape curculio, grape-root borer and Japanese beetles.

CULTIVARS

'Black Beauty': Female variety. Large fruit, ~2.5–3 cm diameter, skin black. Clusters are large. Quality very good. Sugar content 25%. Ripens mid–late season. Vine very vigorous. One of the best black muscadines.

'Cowart': Fruit very large, skin black. One of the largest self-fertile cultivars. Quality is very good. Sugar content 20%. Early–mid season ripening. Vine vigorous, productive. Good disease resistance. Large clusters of fruits. Makes a good wine.

'Darlene': Female variety. Large fruit, ~2.5–3 cm diameter, skin bronze. Excellent taste. Sugar content 25%.

'Dixieland': Fruit large, skin bronze. One of the largest self-fertile cultivars. Flavour excellent. Sugar content 20%. Ripens mid season. Vine vigorous and productive.

'Hunt': Female variety. Black grape, medium–large fruits, with large, early-ripening clusters. Excellent quality. Recommended. Excellent for wine, juice, jelly, preserves.

'Magnolia': Self-fertile variety. Large fruit, skin white, smooth, attractive. Quality excellent. Sugar content 15%. Clusters medium to large. Ripens in mid–late season.

Excellent for wine. Vine vigorous and very productive.
'Noble': Self-fertile variety. Medium-sized fruit, skin black. Quality good. Sugar content 18%. Ripens early–mid season. Vine has medium vigour, very productive. Good disease resistance, except for powdery mildew. Clusters large. Excellent for red wine.

Food
The fruits are very tasty eaten fresh, or added to jellies, jams, juice, sauces, and various desserts or made into an excellent dessert wine. The fruit has a distinctive musky or fruity aroma. The fruit are also tasty eaten dried and can be used as other dried fruits. The young leaves and tendrils can be lightly cooked and eaten as a vegetable. Food can be wrapped within the leaves, which impart an almost asparagus-like flavour. The sap, which bleeds freely from cuts, makes a pleasant, sweet drink.

Nutrition/medicinal
High in Vitamin C and contains potassium, vitamin B and trace minerals. Muscadines can be made into wine, which contains the same types of polyphenols as wine grapes: both non-flavonoids and flavonoids. Muscadines contain good quantities of resveratrol, an anti-carcinogenic compound, which can inhibit tumour formation by stopping DNA damage, slowing/halting cell transformation from normal to cancerous, and slowing tumour growth. It also has anti-inflammatory properties and may be very useful for colon-cancer prevention. The flavonols within the fruit's seeds greatly enhance the activity of vitamin C within the body, and act as a powerful free-radical scavenger and antioxidant. It helps to promote tissue elasticity, heal injuries, reduce swelling and oedema, restores collagen and improves peripheral circulation, prevents bruising, strengthens weak blood vessels, protects against atherosclerosis and inhibits the enzymes that lead to histamine formation. It is rapidly absorbed and distributed throughout the body within minutes. Removes and prevents lipofuscin formation in the brain and heart, conferring anti-ageing benefits. Increases elasticity and flexibility of muscles, tendons and ligaments, and acts as smooth muscle relaxant in blood vessels. Both flavonoids and non-flavonoids reduce the levels of low density lipoproteins ('bad' cholesterol). Muscadines also contain ellagic acid, tannic acid, gallic acid and quercetin. **Warning:** Despite its wonderful health benefits, it is worth noting that the seeds and skins contain tannins, which can be carcinogenic if taken in excess for prolonged periods.

Ornamental
These vines are particularly attractive and make great summer shade for a pergola or fence. They have attractive leaves, giving a traditional Mediterranean effect, but because they are deciduous they do not cast shade in winter.

'Scuppernong': Female variety. Medium–large fruit, skin bronze, medium–thin. Flesh sweet with excellent, distinctive flavour. Clusters medium. Sugar content ~18%. Quality excellent. Ripens early. Vines vigorous, production good. An old variety, but still one of the best.
'Sugargate': Female variety. Very large fruit, skin black. Excellent flavour. Large clusters. Sugar content 20%. Ripens earliest of all cultivars. Vines: very vigorous, production good. Recommended.
'Sweet Jenny': Female variety. Numerous very large fruit, ~2.5–3.5 cm diameter, skin bronze. Clusters large. Quality very good. Sugar content ~25%. Ripens early–mid season. Vine vigorous, very productive. Disease resistant.

OTHER *VITIS* SPECIES

Californian grape, *Vitis californica*. Attractive vine that is native to California, growing to a height of 5–10 m. Good for covering structures; fairly rapid growth. Has clusters of small, yellow–purple grapes, but are not highly rated. Bees love the flowers. Will grow in coastal areas. Likes regular moisture, and may tolerate seasonal flooding; also may be fairly tolerant to drought. Can be grown in full sun or part shade, and in more alkaline soils. Fairly cold hardy. Good autumn colour: brilliant burgundy red with orange highlights.

Grape, *Vitis lanata* (syn. *V. cordifolia*, *V. henneana*, *V. rugosa*, *Cissus vitiginea*). A native of the foothills of the Himalayas. Forms a large, woody, deciduous climber, with long, forked tendrils. Can grow to ~25 m. *Leaves:* Simple, ~13 cm long, back of leaf has orange hairs. *Flowers:* bisexual, green. *Fruit:* ~1 cm in diameter, purple, ~60 berries per cluster. *Yield:* An average vine yields up to 18 kg of fruit. Very few problems with pests or disease. Grows OK in humid areas, but is not very cold hardy. *Uses:* Fruits are sweet, and also sub-acid: tasty, though slightly sharper than cultivated grapes. Overall fruit quality is good.

Riverbank grape, *Vitis riparia*. Native to much of the northern USA, a vigorous climbing vine which can grow up to ~15 m. Has large stems, and tendrils are slender, intermittent. Is quite cold hardy. *Leaves:* Medium–large, thin, 3–5-lobed, sharply serrated teeth, light green in colour. *Flowers:* Fragrant. *Fruit:* Clusters: medium–small black berries with a heavy blue bloom. Small seeds. Fruit is very variable in flavour and time of ripening. Can be sharply acid. When thoroughly ripe or over-ripe, they are favoured by many. The flesh separates readily from the seed. Early bloomers, but late ripeners.
   Cultivation: Can withstand temperatures lower than –40°C. Can be moderately drought resistant. More able to grow in alkaline soils than many *Vitis* species. Very resistant to Phylloxera and somewhat resistant to rot and mildew, though is susceptible to the leaf-hopper. *Propagation:* Grows readily from cuttings and makes a good stock for grafting.
   Uses: The fruit is best for wine when left on the vine until over-ripe and even slightly shrivelled.

Spanish grape, *Vitis berlandieri*. A native of the southern states of the USA, a moderately vigorous vine, to ~10 m. *Fruit:* Large clusters of small fruits.

Cultivation: Prefers partial shade, but can grow in full sun. Likes a warm, sunny position for the fruit to ripen. Semi hardy. Does not like clays soils. *Pruning:* In winter, when dormant, or they bleed profusely.

Uses: *Food:* Fruits can be eaten fresh or can be dried for winter use. Have a rich, pleasant flavour, though sometimes slightly bitter. Are best when fully ripe. Young leaves, when wrapped around other foods and then baked, impart a pleasant flavour. Young tendrils can be eaten fresh or cooked. *Other uses:* Can be used as a rootstock. A yellow dye is obtained from the fresh or dried leaves.

Sugar grape, *Vitis rupestris*. Native to southeastern USA. Small, many branched shrub or vine, usually 2–2.5 m or less, ascending or prostrate, sometimes trailing. Will grow in gravel, sand and dry areas with poor soils. Not a very long-lived grape. *Leaves:* Small, thick, heart-shaped. Young leaves are often folded and lighter beneath. *Fruit:* Small (0.6–1.2 cm diameter), in clusters of 12–24 berries. Fruits are globular, purple-black. Vary from sweet to sour, tasty. Wine made from the grape is highly esteemed. Skin thin. Seeds small. Fruit ripen in late summer–early autumn. The young leaves and tendrils can be eaten as a vegetable.

Cultivation: Has deep roots, which make it fairly drought resistant. Resistant to Phylloxera. *Grafting:* Bench-grafts well, but is less successful in field grafts. Used in France as a rootstock.

Summer grape, *Vitis aestivalis*. A native of southeastern USA, this is a vigorous vine, growing to ~20 m and very frost hardy. Often grown for its tasty berries (~0.8 cm diameter), in large clusters, which are sweetest after a frost. They are used in a wide variety of ways, and can also be dried. The leaves can be lightly cooked and eaten, or food can be wrapped within them. The watery sap from the stem makes a sweet, pleasant drink. The vine is Phylloxera resistant, and is sometimes used as a rootstock.

Sweet mountain grape, *Vitis monticola*. Native to North America, forming a slender climber, height ~10–15 m. Leaves turn from pale red to bright green as they mature, and always appear healthy. Small (~1.2 cm diameter), dark purple grapes in clusters of 15–50, somewhat tart-sweet and not very juicy (though other reports say they are). The young leaves and tendrils can be eaten as a vegetable. Can grow on poor, calcareous soils. Full sun or partial sun. Hardy to –8°C and below. Has been used as a rootstock for planting in dry climates and very alkaline soils.

Sweet winter grape, *Vitis cinerea*. A native of central and eastern USA, a moderately vigorous vine which is somewhat cold hardy. Has sweet tasty, small fruits (~0.5 cm diameter), in fairly large bunches. Can be eaten fresh, used in various desserts, or dried. The young leaves and tendrils can be used as a vegetable. The sap makes a tasty drink. ■

Yucca filamentosa (syn. *Y. concava, Y. flaccida, Y. smalliana*)

Yucca, Adam's needle, Spanish dagger, Eve's darning needle

AGAVACEAE

Similar species: banana yucca (*Y. baccata*)

The *Yucca* genus contains ~40 species of hardy and tender, strikingly handsome plants that are mostly native to the arid regions of North America. They form a distinctive rosette of stiff leaves, which are usually sharply pointed, and may form a short woody trunk, which can branch and become tree-like. The genus name *Yucca* is derived from the Arawak name for tapioca (*Manihot esculenta*), a plant with which it was mistaken. Confusingly, many yucca species are known as Adam's needle, and many species are very similar. The species *Y. flaccida, Y. smalliana* and *Y. concava* are sometimes listed as separate species, but are also often all grouped as *Y. filamentosa* (as here). *Yucca filamentosa* is native to the southeastern states of the USA, and naturally grows in dry, sandy, rocky soils. It was used by several native American tribes medicinally, as a food source, for its fibre and a soap was obtained from its roots. It has now become naturalised elsewhere in the USA and also in southern Europe. It forms a surprisingly cold hardy, tough plant that has a dramatic, handsome shape, with a tall stem of numerous fragrant flowers, which, if pollinated, go on to produce tasty, date-like fruits. Similar species with edible fruits are *Y. glauca* and *Y. whipplei*.

DESCRIPTION

A hardy, evergreen shrub, growing ~1–2 m tall, ~1–1.5 m spread. Has a slow to medium growth rate. It forms a central rosette of leaves, which lives for ~4 years before flowering, and then dies back. However, many young rosettes develop around it and continue growing after the main rosette has died. In addition, new plants can develop from rhizomes that have grown some distance from the parent plant. Although individual rosettes are only short lived, the plant as a whole can live for many years.

Leaves: Evergreen, strap-like, tough, grey-green, with pointed tips, ~0.6–1 m long, ~2.5–4 cm wide, often arching. They grow from a basal region, and form a spiral, rosette form, with new leaves growing from the centre. The leaf's margins have long curly threads hanging from them, which peel off as it grows.

Flowers: Dramatic and showy, consisting of 30–50 flowers, divided into small, drooping clusters arranged up a tall stem (~1.5–3.5 m tall) that grows out from the centre of a rosette. The stem becomes taller in warmer climates. Individual flowers are white–cream, ~5–7 cm long, bell-shaped and are borne from mid–late summer. They are fragrant, particularly at night, to attract pollinating moths. The rosette dies after flowering and fruiting (monocarpic: a single flowering period before dying), but produces many lateral buds that form new rosettes. The flowers are bisexual and have both male and female floral structures. *Pollination:* In its native habitat, the flowers are only pollinated by the yucca moth, so to produce fruits elsewhere, the flowers need to be hand pollinated. This can be done with a small, soft brush.

Fruit: Purplish-green, oblong, ~5–7 cm long, ~2.5–3.5 cm wide, with a rough, irregular surface, though can be ridged lengthways into six segments. Has a dry, hard, brown covering. Inside its flesh contains 120–150 small black seeds. The flesh of this yucca is fleshy and edible, but that of some species is dry.

Yield/harvest: Fruits are harvested in autumn. Plants take ~4 years to produce a flower stem, and then the rosette dies, so you do not get large, regular yields, but the roots readily form new rosettes nearby, which go on to flower in the future. If you get serious about the fruits, then a hedge of yuccas could be an answer.

Roots: It forms both deep and shallow roots, which can become dense and far reaching. They also have large, thick rhizomes, which grow from rosette to rosette, but also spread to new regions of soil to form new clumps. They act as storage organs for moisture and nutrients until new clumps have become established. They do not really need a mulch as they are drought tolerant and do not need additional nutrients. They are even quite tolerant of weed competition.

CULTIVATION

This species is very tough and hardy, and needs virtually no maintenance.

Location: Grows best in a sunny location, and is tolerant of direct, hot sun, though will tolerate light shade. Is wind tolerant, and is also tolerant of salty maritime exposure.

Temperature: Is cold hardy, and can tolerate temperatures down to ~–15°C. Can be grown in temperate areas, but cannot tolerate extremely cold winters.

Soil/water/nutrients: Grows best in well-drained soil; is not tolerant of cold, wet soils. Can grow in a wide range of soil types, including nutrient-poor, sandy or stony soils. Grows best at mid range pH values: it does not grow well in peaty or chalky soils. Naturally grows in dry, arid areas and

Food

The fruits can be used as a date substitute, and can be eaten fresh or dried for later use. The flowers are edible and vary in quality; some are delicious and taste somewhat like artichoke, others are bitter. The flowering stem can be cooked and used like asparagus. The root tubers are also edible, but see the warning below.

Nutrition

The fruits contain vitamins A, B and C, as well as some calcium, copper, manganese, potassium and phosphorus.

Medicinal

The roots contain a high proportion of saponins and have historically been, and still are, used either as a poultice or taken internally to treat sores, skin diseases, rheumatism and arthritis. The saponins are believed to indirectly inhibit the normal formation of cartilage. Yuccas also contain antibacterial and antifungal properties that are believed to cleanse the colon and help keep the kidneys and liver free of toxins. The fresh flowers are currently being investigated for their possible anti-tumour activity. The plant was used as a sedative to induce sleep. **Warning:** Saponins can be toxic, but are poorly absorbed during digestion and their properties are also nullified during prolonged cooking.

Other uses

The fibre from the leaves is extremely strong and is used to make twine, ropes, cloth, mats, paper, etc. To obtain the fibre, the leaves are cut in summer, scraped to remove the outer cuticle and then soaked in water for ~24 hours. The fibres are then heated with lye for ~2 hours, and then beaten for ~4 hours. They make a cream-coloured paper, or the fibres can be used as paint brushes. A good soap/shampoo/detergent can be obtained by boiling the roots, which is also good for dandruff and hair loss. The saponins are approved for use as a foaming agent in such products as root beer.

Ornamental

Gives a wonderfully exotic, subtropical appearance to a garden. Excellent in rock gardens and looks terrific planted amongst pebbles with succulents, grasses, cacti and palms, giving a visually exciting variety of textures and forms. They also make an interesting barrier hedge. Are best not planted too close to paths or near where children play because of their sharp, spiny leaf tips. Yucca plants are also attractive to wildlife, with pollen-rich flowers that entice moths, butterflies, bees and hummingbirds.

is very drought tolerant. Is not nutrient hungry, and does not usually need additional nutrients.

Pot culture: They are ideal for growing in containers because of their minimal maintenance requirements and drought tolerance. They do not need regular repotting, and make a very striking display on a deck or patio. They can also be moved inside in very cold regions, but do have sharp, spiny leaves.

Planting: Space plants 1–2 m apart, depending on their usage or effect required. Water plants during dry periods in the first year or until the roots are established.

Propagation: *Seed:* Can be sown in autumn or spring. Germination can be speeded up if they are soaked for ~24 hours before sowing in warmth, although can take 1–12 months to germinate. Protect young plants from cold for the first few years. *Cuttings:* Root cuttings can be taken in early spring by removing sections of rhizome that have healthy, plump buds. Plant in well-drained, gritty soil to establish. *Suckers:* The removal of young rosettes is an easy and quick method. Dig up young rosettes and plant them in well-drained compost, in light shade, and they should soon develop roots. Removal of rosettes stimulates the remaining roots to produce further rosettes to take their place.

Pruning: Minimal to none. Perhaps just to tidy the plant up and remove any dead leaves or old flower stems.

Pests and diseases: Very few problems. May get leaf spot or blight if plants are grown in wet soils.

CULTIVARS

There are a number of cultivars, which have been usually selected for their ornamental attributes. There are several variegated forms.

SIMILAR SPECIES

Banana yucca, Spanish bayonet, Spanish dagger, Yucca baccata (syn. Y. circinata), vars. baccata, brevifolia, vespertina. The banana yucca is a native of the arid regions of southwestern North America and Mexico. It is a tough, drought-resistant, hardy species that has been valued and used by the native indigenous populations for hundreds of years for many different uses, but mostly for their large, edible fruits.

Description: A long-lived succulent, 1–2 m tall, 2–3 m spread. In older plants, their spread can be much wider and they can form a plant with >60 rosettes. Forms individual rosettes of spiky leaves that are topped by an attractive flower. As the plant ages, it sometimes forms a short, stem (~1 m tall). *Leaves:* The terms 'dagger' and bayonet' are apt descriptions for the tough, strap-shaped, sharply pointed leaves (50–75 cm long). The cross-section of the leaf is concave in shape. They are bluish- to grey-green, succulent, evergreen, and are thick and rough, with small wiry fibres along their margins. The rosettes form progressively outwards around the centre of the plant. The inner rosette dies off after flowering, but side rosettes usually develop before this dies, and these then grow on to flower in a few years' time. *Flowers:* A single flower spike grows from the centre of each rosette (~0.6–1 m tall) a few years after its formation. It forms a spray of beautiful, eye-catching, waxy, creamy-white, bell-shaped flowers (7–8 cm long), in

spring or early summer. It flowers best in hot, dry summers. *Pollination:* In its natural environment, it is only pollinated by a specific species of moth, which is not found in most other locations. Therefore, in most areas, the flowers need to be hand pollinated: this is quite easy with a small, soft brush. *Fruit:* Several, oval, fleshy, large (15–20 cm long, 5–8 cm wide), dark purple, banana-shaped fruits on each flower spike. Seeds are thick and black, 0.6–1 cm wide, almost triangular in shape. The fruits are best eaten when fully ripe: under-ripe fruit can be very bitter.

Cultivation: Easy to grow. Are very tough, drought-resistant plants once established, though somewhat hazardous to garden around. *Location:* Grows best in full sun, but can grow in some shade. Can withstand maritime conditions. *Temperature:* Can withstand very hot temperatures, and surprisingly cold temperatures; some specimens can survive frosts and snow. Some reports claim this species can survive severe frosts, but these seem to vary. *Soil/water/nutrients:* Can be grown in most soils, including poor, rocky soils, but prefers a sandy loam. Plants may develop to be hardier if grown on poorer soils. They can be grown on very dry, sandy slopes. Does not tolerate too much water or any waterlogging. Rain during fruit ripening helps the fruit to swell and become juicier. *Pot culture:* Grows well in a container, which can then be moved inside in very cold winters, though consideration needs to be given to its sharp, spiny leaves. Needs very little maintenance. *Pruning:* None needed. Can remove the old flower stalk to tidy the plant. *Propagation: Seed:* Sow in spring, after soaking for ~24 hours in warm water. Can get good germination if kept warm (~20°C), but length of time to germination varies considerably from 1–12 months. Prick out seedlings and grow on in pots for the first year or so. May need some winter protection for the first few years, and longer if hard frosts are expected. *Cuttings:* Small semi-rooted rosettes can be removed in spring/early summer and are easily established in moist compost. It also forms underground suckers that can be removed and readily established as new plantlets.

Uses: *Food:* Fruits are usually eaten fresh, but can also be steamed or sautéed. They are fleshy, sweet and flavoursome; however, they also act as a laxative, so it may be wiser to not eat too many at one time! The flower buds and stalks can also be cooked, but some reports say they have a soapy taste, and that older flowers are much sweeter and better tasting. The root is sometimes sold locally in parts of the USA and Mexico today. These can be soaked in sugar and then fried. The seed can be roasted, ground and used as a flour. *Medicinal/other uses:* The roots are rich in saponins and can be used as a soap substitute, and makes a good hair wash. Because of its saponins, the root has been used as a stimulant in the past, but care needs to be taken because saponins can be toxic unless cooked for a long period. Fibre obtained from the leaves can be used to make rope, baskets, etc. *Ornamental:* An interesting addition to the garden with its striking foliage and lovely, tall, flower stalks. A hedge planted of this would keep most intruders away, but the spines are also a hazard when gardening. In their natural habitat, the fruit are a popular food for many animals. ■

Zizyphus jujuba (syn. *Z. mauritiana*)

Jujube (Indian jujube, Chinese red date, tsao, sour date)
RHAMNACEAE

Similar species: Lotus date plum (*Zizyphus lotus*)
Relatives: raisin tree, Darling plum

A medium-sized, warmer-climate tree, probably originating from China, or perhaps India, the jujube has been widely cultivated in China for more than 4000 years where more than 400 cultivars have been selected. Jujube seedlings were introduced into Europe at the beginning of the Christian era, and were spread throughout the southern countries of the Mediterranean. They are now grown in many temperate and semi-tropical regions of the world for their ornamental properties, and also for their tasty fruits. The plants are grown, commercially, to some extent in northern Africa, southern Europe, the Middle East and the southwest USA. In China they are a very common and well loved fruit, and are rated as popularly as the apple is in the West. The fruits are mostly dried and are widely sold as a tasty food item, but also for their health benefits. They are also widely grown and sold in Korea, Vietnam and India. The trees are valued in Asia because of their ease of culture and adaptability; they suffer very few pest and disease problems, will grow on poorer soils and in wide range of climates, and produce abundant regular crops of tasty fruits, as well as being ornamental. As yet, they are not widely grown in other regions of the world, but have considerable potential.

DESCRIPTION

A small–medium-sized, fairly spreading tree, 8–10 m tall, with spines, in pairs, from the leaf axils, which are either short and hooked, or long and straight (there are some spineless cultivars). It has a somewhat gnarled, angled trunk and branches, with often an open, almost drooping form, although some trees are more upright. Trees are often multi-stemmed if not pruned. The wood is very hard and strong. Trees do tend to sucker from their roots around the tree, and these often have spines, which can be a nuisance. It is a fairly fast-growing tree, and should be 5–12 m tall, 3–10 m spread, after 30 years of growth.

Leaves: Oval, simple, dark green and shiny on their upper surface, very pale green–white beneath. They have attractive veination that runs longitudinally up the leaf. Deciduous, 2.5–6.5 cm long, with finely serrated leaf margins. Leaves are borne on short stems. Trees have golden-yellow autumn colour, although only in some years.

Flowers: Yellow–white, fragrant, small (~0.75 cm diameter), five-petalled, borne in clusters from the base of leaf axils, for several weeks between late spring–summer. This means that flowers are usually safe from being damaged by late frosts. Form on the present season's growth. *Pollination:* By bees, insects and ants. The trees are self-fertile, but individual flowers are only receptive to pollen for about a day. Although only one tree is needed to set fruit, more than one tree will increase fruit yield.

Fruits: Plum shaped, ~2.5–3.5 cm diameter, fleshy, ripening in autumn–winter, often once the leaves have fallen. The drupe has a thin, edible skin that surrounds whitish flesh, which has a sweet, agreeable flavour, though the fruit's low acidity means they are not markedly flavoursome. They have a single hard, rough stone, which contains two brown seeds. Fruits are picked when ripe as under-ripe fruits do not ripen once picked. Ripe fruits are dark red–dark orange-brown and the flesh is still crisp; 3–5 days later, the fruit begins to soften, its skin wrinkles and its taste becomes musky. They can be eaten fresh, when they are still crisp, or when they have become wrinkled, although people often prefer eating them in the interval between. Fruits can be harvested over a period of several weeks. They can be left to dry on the tree in drier climates, and the dried fruits are some-what like dates, though not quite as sweet.

Yield/harvest: Trees are very precocious, and can produce some fruit in their second year from seed or grafting, though may take longer. They are reliable producers of heavy fruit crops, and can produce ~40–60 kg of fruit per year in long, warm summers. Young trees can produce as many as 5000 to 10,000 small fruits a year in India, with some grafted trees reported to be able to produce ~30,000 fruits. Yields are considerably reduced if the summer is cool. Ripe fruits will keep for ~7 days at room temperature, and for 2–3 weeks in a fridge; they can also be dried or candied.

Roots: Jujube form a deep taproot, so care is needed when planting out. They are good trees for stabilising soils and preventing erosion.

CULTIVATION

Easy to grow, and need a minimum of maintenance, but only produce abundant fruits if grown with enough heat and a fertile soil.

Location: Grow best and produce the best fruits in full sun, but can be grown in partial shade, although not heavy shade. Can be grown in maritime locations. Is fairly wind tolerant.

Temperature: The jujube can withstand a wide range of temperatures, although is best suited to warm temperate–subtropical (or tropical) climates. Tolerates very hot summer temperatures and fruits well. When dormant in winter, trees in China are reported to be able to tolerate temperatures down to –20°C, but this may be exceptional or only with certain cultivars. Usually, they tolerate some frost, but not for long or not too cold. It is likely that gradual cold acclimatisation increases their tolerance to cold. If damaged by cold temperatures, trees usually recover. They can grow in both drier and humid climates, though the latter can result in increased disease.

Chilling: Plants only need a small amount of winter chill to enable flower and leaf formation.

Soils/water/nutrients: Jujube trees tolerate many soil types, but prefer a sandy, well-drained soil and do less well in heavy, poorly drained soils, although some reports say that trees can tolerate some waterlogging. Fertile soils will increase yields. They can grow in slightly acid to fairly alkaline soils, pH 5.5–7, and can tolerate salinity. Trees are quite drought tolerant, though regular watering is important during fruit development: water-stress can cause immature fruit drop. Trees only need moderate additions of nutrients, possibly 1–2 applications of a balanced fertiliser a year when the tree is young; however, commercially-grown trees are often fed intensively and the trees are then claimed to produce much greater yields. They benefit from additions of well-rotted manure.

Planting: Space plants at 5–7 m apart. Dig the soil deeply to encourage good, deep, taproot growth.

Pruning: Unpruned trees often produce as well as pruned trees. If you are going to prune, it is recommended to do this in winter when the tree is dormant. Prune to remove diseased or damaged wood and to keep the fruits in reach. Can be pruned to form a single trunk. Trees can be pruned when young to encourage a few strong branches, which can be tipped later to encourage the formation of fruiting laterals. May need to remove suckers.

Propagation: Seed: Trees are often grown from seed, which can be viable for ~30 months, but the progeny are variable. Seed that is self-fertilised is reported to have poor viability: cross-fertilised seed is better. Use seed only from fully ripened fruits. Wash all pulp thoroughly from the seed. If floated on ~20% salt solution, those that sink are more likely to be viable. To speed up germination, the stones are cracked and the kernels removed. These should germinate in ~7 days. Seeds left within the stone germinate in 21–28 days. Plants seedlings in deep biodegradable pots to avoid damaging the taproot when planting out. *Cuttings:* Hardwood cuttings may root, but results are variable, and 2-year-old wood may give better results. *Layering:* Air-layers should root if dusted with rooting hormone (and boron). *Grafting:* This is commonly practised commercially, and cultivars are grafted onto wild-type jujubes by shield- or T-budding. Grafted plants tend to be less thorny than seedlings, but the wild rootstock often suckers badly. Trees are also top-worked.

Pests and diseases: The jujube has few serious diseases or pests, although the virus witches broom is a problem in China and Korea. Occasional problems can be fruit flies, various caterpillars and mites. Powdery mildew can be a problem in humid areas. Other possible diseases include sooty mould, leafspot and occasional leaf rust.

CULTIVARS

'Chico': Fruit: apple-shaped, excellent taste either fresh or dried, late maturing.

'GA 866': Has very sweet, elongated fruits.

'Li': A very popular cultivar. Tree: upright, many branched, ~4.5 m tall. Fruits: abundant, round, 3–5 cm diameter, sweet. Matures early (late summer) and can be picked when yellow-green: is good for areas with a short growing season. Self-fertile.

'Lang': A popular cultivar. Tree: upright, very few spines, >5 m tall. Fruit: oval–pear-shaped, ~5 cm long, has thicker skin. Less sweet than 'Li', usually eaten dried, needs to be fully ripe when harvested. Very few thorns.

'Sherwood': Tree: narrow, weeping, attractive. Fruits: 2.5–4 cm diameter, later ripening, store well.

'Shui Men': Fruit: good quality, fresh or dried. Ripen in mid season.

SIMILAR SPECIES

Lotus date plum (dom tree), *Zizyphus lotus*. Native to Greece. Similar to jujube, but the fruits are a little smaller and less sweet. ■

Food
The fruits contain ~20% sugars, but have little acidity (4–5%), which makes them not very tangy. They taste somewhat like sweet apple or date. They can be used like dates or other dried fruits, and are eaten as a snack or added to various desserts, or preserves. They can be made into a sweet sauce to go with pancakes, etc.

Nutrition
Good levels of vitamin C: ~70 mg/100 g of fresh flesh, and potassium. They also contain some malic and oxalic acid, as well as the antioxidant quercetin. The leaves contain saponin.

Medicinal
The fruit has been used medicinally for thousands of years by many cultures. It is mostly the seeds that contain the active ingredients. They are frequently used for coughs, colds, etc. They contain a compound called betulinic acid, which may be effective in reducing the growth of cancer cells. The fruits and seeds are used to treat diabetes (type II), to treat biliousness, for wound healing and for their proven sedative properties, possibly due to the flavonoid, spinosin. The kernels are used to treat insomnia and have been recently shown to regulate the heartbeat. An infusion of the flowers has been used as an eye lotion. The leaves are used as a poultice, and are also taken for liver troubles, asthma and fever, though should be used with care because of their saponin content. The astringent bark is taken to halt diarrhoea and dysentery, and for gingivitis. The roots have been used to treat fevers, though they may be toxic in larger amounts.

Other uses
The leaves' saponin content means that they can be used as a soap, etc.

Ornamental
Often planted as an ornamental in Asia, as well as for its abundant fruits, jujube has an attractive shape and can be grown in many situations. It can be grown as a bonsai.

PLANTS FOR DIFFERING CONDITIONS AND USES

Below are suggestions of species that can be grown in adverse conditions, have particular health benefits or are have value ornamentally. Most species described within the book are good at attracting wildlife as the majority have nectar-rich flowers and produce tasty fruits or nuts that attract a wide range of species, so these haven't been listed here.

LOCATION (most species are suitable for sunny locations)

Semi-shade

Akebia, apple berry, black apple, carissa, ceriman, Chilean bellflower, Chilean guava, chinquapin, cloudberry, coffee, *Cordia* spp., Cornelian cherry etc., crowberry, currants, dewberry, false spikenard, fuchsia, gevuina, glossy privet, gooseberry, hazel, huckleberry, inga bean, jaboticaba, kakadu plum, kumquat, midgen, miracle fruit, naranjilla, Oregon grape, passion fruits, pitaya, raisin tree, rhubarb, rose apple, sea grape, soapberry, thimbleberries, torreya, tree fuchsia, wineberries, wintergreen spp.

Windy sites

Beach plum, bilberry, black apple, bunya-bunya, cherry of the Rio Grande, cattleya guava, cloudberry, crowberry, hawthorn, honey locust, hottentot fig, lingonberry, longan, mayhaw, medlar, mitchella, monkey-puzzle tree, mulberry, myrtle berry, palms (many), paper mulberry, pine nut, pitanga, pitomba, prickly pear, roselle, rowan, sapodilla, screw pine, sea buckthorn, sea grape, sugar cane, tamarind, totara, whitebeam, yucca spp.

Maritime

Australian desert lime, beach plum, black apple, buffalo berry, burdekin plum, carissa, carob, cashew, cattleya guava, Chilean guava, Chinese parasol tree, Chinese waterberry, cider gum, cocona, cordia, crowberry, Darling plum, *Elaeagnus* spp., feijoa, gevuina, goji berry, honey locust, hottentot fig, imbe, inga bean, jujube, kakadu plum, karanda, kei apple, lemon, lingaro, loquat, manketti nut, marula, mesquite, monkey-puzzle tree, mulberry, olives, oleaster, Oregon grape, palms, pandanus, peanut tree, phalsa, pine nut, pitomba, pomegranate, pouteria, prickly pear, quandong, rose apple, roses, sapodilla, screw pine, sea almond, sea buckthorn, sea grape, strawberry tree, sugarberry, tamarind, totara, whitebeam, wolfberry, yucca spp.

TEMPERATURE

Fully cold hardy

Akebia, American persimmon, apples, Arctic beauty kiwi, aronia, asimoya, Australian desert lime, barberry, Berberis, bilberry, birch, blackberry, bladdernut, blueberry, blue honeysuckle, buffalo berry, *Chaenomeles* sp., che, cherry (many spp.), cloudberry, Cornelian cherry, cranberry, crowberry, currants, damson, date plum, *Elaeagnus* spp. (many), false spikenard, glossy privet, gooseberry, greengage, hardy kiwi, hawthorn, honey locust, honeysuckle, hop, huckleberry, kumquat, licorice, lingonberry, mayhaw, medlar, mitchella, monkey-puzzle tree, oak, Oregon grape, pear, pecan, pincherry, pine nut, pistachio, plums, plum cherries, quince, raisin tree, raspberry, rhubarb, roses, rowan, salmonberry, saskatoon, schisandra, sea buckthorn, sloe, silver vine, soapberry, strawberry tree, sugar maple, sugarberry, sumachs, thimbleberries, trifoliate orange, *Viburnum* spp., walnuts, whitebeam, wineberries, wintergreen spp., wolfberry

Tolerate heat

Acerola, ambarella, amla, atemoya, Australian desert lime, avocado, babaco, bael fruit, banana yucca, black apple, buffalo berry, burdekin plum, calamondin, camu camu, carambola, carissa, cashew, Ceylon hill gooseberry, cherimoya, Chilean bellflower, Chilean palo verde, Chinese parasol tree, Chinese waterberry, chupa chupa, cocona, coffee, cordia, Darling plum, Davidson's plum, fig, Governor's plum, honeysuckle, hottentot fig, imbe, jackfruit, jujube, kaffir plum, kakadu plum, karanda, kei apple, malabar chestnut, mango, manketti nut, marula, melons, mesquite, miracle fruit, oncoba, oyster nut, palms, pandanus, papaya, paper mulberry, peanut, pincherry, pineapple, pistachio, pitaya, pomegranate, prickly pear, pumpkin seeds, quandong, sapodilla, screw pine, sea almond, sea grape, soapberry, sugar cane, sunflower, tamarind, thimbleberries, tropical apricot, tropical guava, watermelon, yucca spp.

SOIL

Acid pH

Aronia, bilberry, blueberry, Cape gooseberry, cashew, ceriman, chestnut, chickasaw plum, Chilean bellflower, cattleya guava, cloudberry, cranberry, crowberry, *Elaeagnus* spp., huckleberry, inga bean, lingonberry, manzanita, mitchella, miracle berry, Oregon grape, peanut, pineapple, pine nut, raspberry, roselle, saskatoon, strawberry, sugar cane, sugar maple, sugarberry, tamarind, tea, thimbleberries, tropical guava, wineberries, wintergreen spp.

Alkaline pH

Acerola, American persimmon, bael fruit, Cape gooseberry, carissa, cashew, cherimoya, Chinese waterberry, cordia, *Elaeagnus* spp., grape, honey locust, hottentot fig, inga bean, lucuma, mesquite, muntries, naranjilla, olives, paper mulberry, peanut, pecan, pistachio, pitanga, quandong, rose apple, roselle, sapodilla, sea almond, sea buckthorn, sea grape, strawberry tree, sugar cane, sugarberry, tamarind, Texas persimmon, tropical guava

Dry soils

Apple berry, Australian desert lime, bael fruit, banana yucca, beach plum, carissa, carob, cashew, chickasaw plum, Chilean palo verde, Chinese waterberry, cider gum, *Cordia* spp., Darling plum, honey locust, hottentot fig, jujube, karanda, kei apple, manketti nut, marula, mayhaw, mesquite, mulberry, olives, oncoba, oyster nut, palms, paper mulberry, peanut tree, peanut, pine nut, pineapple, pistachio, pitanga, pitaya, pomegranate, prickly pear, quandong, roses, sapodilla, screw pine, sea almond, sea buckthorn, sea grape, strawberry tree, tamarind, totara, watermelon, yucca spp.

Wet soils

Barberry, black sapote, camu-camu, cider gum, cloudberry, cranberry, damson, false spikenard, hawthorn, honey locust, lotus, malabar chestnut, mayhaw, mesquite, pandanus, prickly pear, roselle, screw pine, sea grape, sloe, sugarberry, sugar cane, sugar maple, tigernut, wintergreen spp.

Poor-nutrient soils

Amla, Australian desert lime, bael fruit, banana yucca, barberry, birch, buffalo berry, Cape gooseberry, carissa, carob, cashew, Chilean palo verde, chinquapin, cider gum, Cornelian cherry, cranberry, damson, Darling plum, *Elaeagnus* spp., feijoa, goji berry, grape, greengage, honey locust, hottentot fig, inga bean, kei apple, manketti nut, marula, mesquite, olives, oncoba, pincherry, pine nut, pistachio, prickly pear, quandong, roses, screw pine, sea grape, sloe, strawberry tree, sugarberry, sumachs, Texas persimmon, totara

Reclamation species

American persimmon, birch, buffalo berry, carob, cashew, Chilean palo verde, chinquapin, cloud berry, Darling plum, *Elaeagnus* spp., glossy privet, inga bean, manketti nut, mesquite, peanut, pincherry, pine nut, pistachio, sea buckthorn, sea grape, shagbark hickory, smooth sumach, soapberry, stag's horn sumach, tropical guava

Air pollution

American persimmon, *Chaenomeles* spp., elderberry, ginkgo, glossy privet, hawthorn, honey locust, mayhaw, paper mulberry, pitaya, sea grape, strawberry tree, sugarberry, Texas persimmon

POT CULTURE — Plants suitable for growth in containers

Acerola, ambarella, apple-berry, asimoya, atemoya, babaco, banana, barberry, *Berberis*, bilberry, black apple, black sapote, bunya-bunya, calamondin, camu-camu, Cape gooseberry, carambola, carissa, cattleya guava, ceriman, cherry of the Rio Grande, Chinese parasol tree, coffee, cloudberry, *Cordia* spp., cranberry, Darling plum, Davidson's plum, feijoa, fig, fuchsia, gevuina, goji berry, grapefruit, hibiscus spp., hottentot fig, imbe, jaboticaba, kaffir plum, kakadu plum, kiwifruit, kumquat, lemon, lillypilly, lingonberry, loquat, lotus, lychee, macadamia, malabar chestnut, mango, midgen, myrtle berry, olives, oncoba, orangeberry, palms, papaya, pawpaw, peanut, peanut tree, pepino, pineapple, pitanga, pitaya, pitomba, pomegranate, prickly pear, strawberry, tree fuchsia, tropical guava, wolfberry, yucca

HEALTH BENEFITS

Low glycaemic index

Almond, avocado, banana, cashew, hazelnut, gevuina, macadamia, manketti nut, peanut, pecan, pine nut, pumpkin seeds, walnut

High in vitamin A

Acerola, ambarella, apricot, asimoya, Cape gooseberry, capulin cherry, carambola, *Elaeagnus* spp., elderberry, goji berry, grapefruit, jackfruit, loquat, lucuma, mango, melon, papaya, passion fruits, peach, persimmon, pitanga, plum, tropical guava, tangerine, wolfberry

High vitamin C

Acerola, ambarella, amla, buffalo berry, calamondin, camu-camu, Cape gooseberry, carambola, carissa, cattleya guava, cashew apple, casimiroa, cloudberry, cocona, Cornelian cherry, cranberry, crowberry, currants, elderberry, feijoa, gooseberry, grapefruit, honeysuckle, huckleberries, jujube, kakadu plum, kei apple, ketembilla, kiwifruit, lemons, longan, lychee, marula, melon, mulberry, muscadine, orange, papaya, passion fruits, pitanga, pitomba, quandong, rose apple, rose hips, rowan, schisandra, sea buckthorn, strawberry, tamarillo, tangerine, thimbleberries, tomatillo, tropical apricot, tropical guava, *Viburnum* spp., wampee, wineberries

High vitamin E

Almond, *Elaeagnus* spp., gevuina, hazelnut, kiwifruit, macadamia, mango, manketti nut, palms, pecan, sea buckthorn, sunflower seeds, walnut

High in polyphenols

Amla, aronia, bilberry, blackberry, blueberry, calamondin, capulin cherry, cherry, *Citrus* spp., cloudberry, coffee, cranberry, crowberry, currants, *Elaeagnus* spp., elderberry, fig, ginkgo, grapes, grapefruit, hawthorns, honeysuckle, huckleberries, kiwifruit, lemons, lingonberry, macadamias, mayhaws, mesquite, mulberry, muscadine, olives, orange, Oregon grape, peanut, pineapple, pistachio, plum, plum cherries, pomegranate, prickly pear, prune, raspberry, saskatoons, sea almond, sea buckthorn, strawberry, sunflower seeds, tea, tropical guavas, walnuts, wineberries, wolfberry

High in polyunsaturates

Almond, avocado, cashew, gevuina, hazelnuts, macadamia, malabar chestnut, manketti nut, marula kernels, olives, pecan, pine nut, pistachio, pumpkin seeds, sea buckthorn, sunflower seeds, walnut

High in minerals

Almond, apple, banana, cloudberry, feijoa, fig, hazelnuts, kiwifruit, melons, palms, papaya, passion fruits, peanut, pistachio, pumpkin seeds, tamarind

High in fibre

Amla, apple, banana, blackberry, blueberry, buffalo berry, Cape gooseberry, cattleya guava, chupa chupa, currants, feijoa, fig, kiwifruit, palms, papaya, peach, peanut, pistachio, quince, raspberry, sapodilla, saskatoons, strawberry, sunflower seeds, tamarind, tropical guava

High in protein

Almond, beech, carob, cashew, *Elaeagnus* spp., hazelnut, gevuina, goji berry, inga bean, macadamia, malabar chestnut, manketti nut, marula kernels, mesquite, oyster nut, peanut, pine nut, pistachio, pumpkin seeds, sea buckthorn, sunflower seeds, walnut, wolfberry

Cosmetic/shampoo etc.

Acerola, almond, amla, asimoya, avocado, bael fruit, banana yucca, bergamot, calamondin, cashew, chestnut, Chinese hibiscus, Chinese parasol tree, cordia, gevuina, hibiscus, kakadu plum, lemons, limes, macadamia, manketti nut, myrtle, native sorrel, olives, oyster nut, papaya, pitaya, prickly pear, sea buckthorn, sour orange, tea, twinberry, wampee, wolfberry, yucca

HEDGING SPECIES

Acerola, ambarella, barberry, beech, *Berberis*, buffalo berry, carissa, cattleya guava, Ceylon hill gooseberry, *Chaenomeles* spp., Chilean guava, Chilean palo verde, Chinese hibiscus, Chinese waterberry, Cornelian cherry, currant, *Elaeagnus* spp., elderberry, fuchsia, glossy privet, gooseberry, hawthorn, hazelnut, hibiscus spp., jujube, kei apple, kumquat, lillypilly, midgen, myrtle berry, pitomba, pitanga, prickly pear, roses, screw pine, sea buckthorn, sea grape, tea, torreya, totara, tree fuchsia, *Viburnum* spp., yucca

GROUNDCOVER

Arctic blackberry, bilberry, Cape gooseberry, ceriman, cloudberry, creeping dogwood, cranberry, crowberry, false spikenard, hottentot fig, huckleberry, lingonberry, manzanita, Nepalese raspberry, orangeberry, wintergreen spp.

WINDBREAKS

Chestnut, Darling plum, feijoa, glossy privet, hawthorn, lillypilly, myrtle berry, pine nut, pistachio, sea buckthorn, sea grape, smooth sumach, totara

VINES

Akebia, apple-berry, ceriman, Chilean bellflower, grape, honeysuckle, hops, karanda, kiwifruits, muntries, oyster nut, passion fruits, pitaya (some), porcelain berry, schisandra, tree fuchsia, zabala

GOOD AUTUMN COLOUR

Aronia spp., asimoya, beech, bilberry, birch, California grape, cherry, chestnut, Chinese parasol tree, Chinese quince, elderberry, ginkgo, gooseberry, jujube, kakadu plum, mayhaw, medlar, oak, pear, persimmons, pincherry, pistachio, quince, rose hips, rowans, saskatoon, sea almond, sugar maple, sugarberry, sumachs, thimbleberry, wampee, whitebeams

SHOWY FLOWERS

Akebia, almond, banana, *Berberis*, capulin cherry, cattleya guava, ceriman, Ceylon hill gooseberry, Chilean bellflower, Chinese parasol tree, Cornelian cherry, elderberry, false spikenard, gevuina, hottentot fig, licorice, lillypilly, lotus, macadamia, malabar chestnut, mango, manzanita spp., muntries, oncoba, Oregon grape, passion fruits, peach flowers, pineapple, pitanga, pitaya, pitomba, plums (many), pomegranate, prickly pear, quince, rhubarb, rose apple, roses, roselle, saskatoon, strawberry tree, sunflower, tigernut, tree fuchsia, tropical guava, *Viburnum* spp., yucca

Abscisic acid: A plant 'hormone' responsible for abscission of leaves in autumn and helps retain winter dormancy.

Aggregate of drupes: Many individual, fertilised ovules within a single flower that become fused together, e.g. raspberry.

Air-layering: A method of propagation. Regions of stems are wounded and encouraged to form roots. The rooted stem can then be later removed to form a new plant.

Alternate bearing: The tendency of many fruiting species to produce large crops one year, but only meagre crops in the next year(s). Often remedied by thinning.

Angiosperms: True flowering plants that produce a range of flower types and seeds that are enclosed within a fruit of some sort. Includes both dicots and monocots.

Anther: The tip of the male structure that produces and releases pollen grains.

Antioxidant: A compound that can react with destructive free radicals (charged oxygen molecules) and reactive metal cations to render them harmless before they are able to affect DNA.

Apical dominance: The tendency of a plant to form a main single stem, and to inhibit, biochemically, the growth of lateral branches. Apical dominance varies considerably between species.

Aril: A fleshy covering of some seeds (e.g. totara), which has a fruit-like structure. Some conifers form these instead of the typical cone. A single seed becomes surrounded by a fleshy, oval, cup-like structure, which is often edible and becomes brightly coloured as it ripens to attract birds.

Auxin: A plant 'hormone' responsible for apical dominance, but is also used as a rooting hormone.

Berry: Contains seeds surrounded by a fleshy pericarp.

Biennial bearing: The tendency of many fruiting species to produce large crops one year, but only meagre crops the year(s) after. Often remedied by thinning.

Bisexual: Having both viable male and female structures within the same flower. The terms 'perfect' or 'hermaphrodite' are also often used.

Bletted: Some very astringent fruits are best if bletted. The fruits are left to ripen until they are very soft and are almost rotting to bring out their full sweetness and flavour.

Budding: A form of grafting whereby buds are bound to the cambium of another plant so that they become fused as one.

C4 photosynthesis: A photosynthetic mechanism used by many monocot species that enables them to use carbon dioxide more efficiently, which leads, indirectly, to reduced moisture loss.

Calyx: The remnants of sepals from the flowers that are often seen at the base or apex of fruits.

Cambium: Actively dividing tissue that produces xylem and phloem in stems and roots. Forms a layer (usually) in dicots and is scattered in monocots and conifers.

Carpel: A female structure, often containing a single ovule, or many carpels can be formed together and become fused. They are then often referred to as an ovary.

Cauliflorous: The production of flowers and fruits directly from the main stem and branches, e.g. jackfruit, Davidson's plum.

Central leader: The main, dominant stem of the plant. Pruning can be done to encourage the formation of a single strong stem or leader and reduce the number of competing branches.

Chlorophyll: Green pigments found within leaves (and sometimes stems) that are able trap the sun's energy in a process called photosynthesis.

Chloroplasts: Structures that hold the photosynthetic pigment, chlorophyll.

Compound fruit: Many individual flowers produce small fruits that become fused together to form a large 'fruit', e.g. pineapple.

Crassulacean metabolism: A photosynthetic mechanism used by many xerophytic species to conserve moisture, while still being able to photosynthesise.

Cross pollinated: Pollination between separate plants, which is crucial for dioecious species, but also often improves fruit-set and quality of bisexual and monoecious species.

Cultivar: A subgroup of a species. Is often used interchangeably with the term variety. Cultivars may be formed naturally or can be selected for advantageous qualities. Cultivars can be crossed genetically with each other within a species.

Cv.: Abbreviation for cultivar.

Cytokinin: A plant 'hormone' responsible for cell division. It is sometimes used to initiate flowering.

Dicotyledons (or dicots): Having two cotyledons, or first leaves. Are mostly broadleaved species with net-like veining. Flower parts are in multiples of 4's and 5's.

Dioecious: Having female and male flowers on different trees, so a female and male plant are needed to ensure pollination.

Drupelets: Small drupes. Many individual, fertilised ovules within a single flower that become fused together to form an aggregate of drupes, e.g. raspberry.

Endocarp: The outer layer of the pericarp. It may be hard or often forms a skin in fleshy fruits.

Endosperm: A layer of storage tissue that forms around the seeds of some species and provides nutrients to the developing seedling.

Endospermic: Where the endosperm is not all used up and the seed is oily.

Epicarp: The inner layer of the pericarp. Often a hard layer that protects the inner kernel, e.g. shell of almond or macadamia, but not always, i.e. berries.

Ethylene: A gas, produced by many ripe fruits, which speeds up ripening of under-ripe fruits in their vicinity.

Family: A taxonomic group that contains genus and species as subgroups.

Fibrous roots: Usually formed near the surface, these roots have a large

surface area to absorb moisture and nutrients.

Filament: The stalk of the male structure, below the anther.

Gamete: Sex cells, either female (egg) or male (sperm), which contain half the number of genes of the parent. These fuse with that of its opposite sex upon fertilisation.

Genetic variation: Variation in offspring due to the exchange of genetic information either from different plants or on the same plant, if pollination has occurred.

Genus: A subgroup of a family, containing a varying number of species. All members have particular floral characteristics in common.

Giberellin: A plant 'hormone' responsible for many reactions, including plant height. It can also be used to break seed dormancy.

Girdling: Cutting partially around, or constricting, a stem to increase the subsequent fruit quality of that branch, e.g. peach. This technique is not without its risks to the tree.

Grafting: Propagation by binding the cambium of two stems together so that they become fused as one.

Gymnosperms: Primitive plants, formed before the advent of pericarp production. Plants are woody, perennial and usually evergreen. Their kernels are usually contained within cones (e.g. pines) or arils (e.g. bunya-bunya). Needles are usually needle-, scale- or fern-like.

HDL (high-density lipid): Found in the blood, associated with cholesterol. Often termed 'good' cholesterol as it can decrease the risk of heart disease.

Heavy metals: These elements (e.g. arsenic, lead, cadmium) can become toxic in industrial soils or in mine waste, and also become much more soluble and may reach toxic levels in ordinary soils if they become waterlogged for extensive periods.

IAA (indole acetic acid): Another term for auxin, a plant hormone.

Inarching: A form of grafting whereby two plants are grown side by side before the rootstock and scion are severed.

Inferior ovary: Where the ovary is formed below the sepals, petals and other structures. Fruits formed from these have an apical calyx (sepal remains).

Involucre: The leafy or scaly structure, often fused, which forms around the base of many true nut species, e.g. acorn, hazelnut.

IU: International Units: another measure of nutrient content (like mg or g). IU is usually used when the nutrient occurs at very low concentrations.

Kernel: The mature embryo: the seed.

Lateral branch: A branch that grows off a main branch. Once a stem tip is removed, this occurs readily in the region below the cut.

Layering: The partial burial of stem tips or lightly injured sections of stem to encourage rooting. Once rooted, these sections can be removed to form new plants.

LDL (low-density lipid): Found in the blood, associated with cholesterol. Often termed 'bad' cholesterol as it can increase the risk of heart disease.

Marcotting: Another term for air-layering.

Mesocarp: The middle layer of the pericarp. Can be hard and fibrous, e.g. almond, or fleshy, e.g. peach.

Micronutrients: A nutrient needed by plants, but only in a small amount. There is often a fine line between deficiency and toxicity, and applications should be done with care.

Modified leader: A pruning method whereby the main leader is removed and a few branches are selected to take its place.

Monocotyledons (or monocots): Having only one cotyledon, or first leaf. Mostly grasses, palms, lilies, bromeliads. In general, have narrow leaves with parallel veins, flower parts in multiples of 3's.

Monoecious: Having both female and male flowers on the same tree, although not necessarily bisexual.

Mycorrhizal association: A symbiotic relationship between fungal species and the roots of plants that enables plants to obtain extra nutrients, while the fungi obtains sugars from the plant.

Non-endospermic: Seeds where the endosperm is not developed; these tend to be non-oily. Often, future storage for the seedling is within cotyledons, within the seed, e.g. leguminous species, walnuts.

Nucellar embryony: Pollination occurs, but there is no exchange of genetic information. Instead, the embryo is formed from tissue surrounding the ovule (not within), and the progeny produced are clones of the parent.

Nut: The kernel is held within a hardened pericarp.

Obovate: Basically, an egg-shaped leaf, but being slightly wider near the apex.

ORAC value (oxygen-radical absorption capacity): A measure of the antioxidant value of foods, with high values being better.

Ovary: A female structure, usually containing several ovules. Consists of several carpels that have become fused together, often with the intervening walls broken down to form a vessel.

Ovule: Female structures that, if fertilised, go on to form an embryo and then a kernel.

Parasitic association: A relationship between organisms whereby only one of the organisms gains an advantage. In some instances it can lead to death of the host, but parasitism is often partial to avoid killing the host, e.g. quandong.

Parthenocarpy: The formation of fruits, e.g. banana, many citrus spp., without pollination. Fruits develop, but are seedless.

Pericarp: A layer around the kernel of most fruits and nuts. It is sometimes clearly divided into three layers: the endocarp, mesocarp and epicarp. Variations in its form determine many of the structural features of fruits or nuts.

pH: A logarithmic scale of the concentration of hydrogen ions. Acid soils (<pH 6) have more free hydrogen ions; alkaline soils (>pH 7) have fewer.

Phloem: Conducting tissue within the stems and roots that transports sugars from the leaves, and carries sap upwards in spring.

Photosynthesis: The trapping of the sun's energy at specific wavelengths, which can then be used to bind carbon dioxide and water to make sugars.

Pip fruit: Another term for a pome fruit.

Pollen grain: The male sex cells (sperm) that are released from the anthers.

Polyphenolic: A very large group of compounds, many of which are related to tannins, which often give fruits and flowers their bright colours, as well as contributing to autumn leaf colour. They occur throughout the plant and have a myriad of, as yet, largely unknown properties, though many are proving to be very efficacious medicinally.

Pome fruit: Fruits formed with an inferior ovary. The receptacle then develops to form the fleshy part of the fruit, e.g. apple.

Receptacle: The structure around which the ovules or the ovary are formed.

Root hairs: Fine, cellular projections from the main roots, particularly formed near root tips. They can squeeze in between soil particles to absorb water and nutrients much more efficiently than the main corky roots.

Rooting hormone: Plant 'hormones', prepared usually as a fine powder, in which cuttings can be dipped to enhance rooting.

Rootstock: Often a hardy seedling species upon which a selected scion is to be grafted. The rootstock is sometimes the same species as the scion and often reduces the time the grafted plant takes to begin producing fruits.

Scaffold: Branches that are selected to become the main, strongest branches of the tree, from which fruiting laterals are encouraged.

Scarification: The scratching or cutting of hard seedcoats to enable the entry of water and gases to speed up germination.

Scion: A section of stem from a plant with desired qualities that is to be grafted onto a rootstock.

Self-fertile: Able to fertilise itself, i.e. a bisexual of monoecious species often does not need a further species for pollination (though there are also many examples of self-infertility within these groups).

Self-infertility: Practised by a number of monoecious and bisexual plants to prevent self-fertilisation by, e.g. mechanical or timing mechanisms, ensuring that cross fertilisation is necessary and variability of offspring is assured.

Sp. or spp.: Abbreviations for one species and several species, respectively.

Species: A subgroup of a genus. All members within a species can cross fertilise each other. Members of different species, usually, cannot.

Spur: Short, stubby, lateral branches that grow from the branches of several fruiting species, e.g. apples, peaches, and produce fruits for 2–4 years.

Stamen: Inclusive term for the anther and filament, the male structures that produce pollen.

Stigma: The outer, often sticky surface, of the female structure, on which pollen grains land and then grow downwards.

Stomata: Pores through which carbon dioxide enters the leaf, and from which oxygen, as a waste product, and water are released. They are situated mostly on the under-surface of dicot and conifer leaves, but tend to be on both sides of monocot leaves.

Stone fruit: Another term for drupe. The pericarp has a hard epicarp, a fleshy mesocarp and a protective skin (endocarp).

Stratification: Usually applied to cold stratification. A period of cold given to seeds (usually from temperate regions) to reduce the time and increase the rate of germination. It makes the plant 'think' it has been through a winter, which initiates biochemical changes within the seed.

Style: The tube down which the pollen grain(s) grows to reach the ovule below.

Superior ovary: Where the ovary is formed above the sepals, petals and other structures. Fruits formed from these have a basal calyx (sepal remains).

Symbiotic relationship: A relationship between two organisms where both gain some benefit, e.g. nitrogen-fixing bacteria.

Taproots: One or more deep, main roots from which a few lateral roots branch off. They are able access water and nutrients at depth, but are susceptible to damage during transplanting, etc.

Testa: The seedcoat. This is sometimes reduced to a very thin covering in drupes, etc., but is more substantial in seeds, and gives the kernel protection.

Thinning: Removal of some fruits, just after fruit-set, from plants in years when they tend to overproduce, to balance out yields.

Variety: A subgroup of a species. Is often used interchangeably with the term cultivar. Varieties may be formed naturally or can be selected for advantageous qualities. Varieties can be cross pollinated within a species.

Winter chilling: A period of cold, of temperatures of 4–8°C, which many temperate species need to effectively come into flower and leaf in spring.

Xerophyte: Plants that are able to grow in very dry, arid climates with minimal rainfall.

Xylem: Water- and nutrient-conducting tissue within plants.

BIBLIOGRAPHY

General references

Barwick, M. *Tropical and subtropical trees: A worldwide encyclopaedic guide.* Thames and Hudson, 2004.

Bell, P. & Woodcock, C. *The diversity of green plants.* Edward Arnold, London, 1983.

Bidwell, R.G.S. *Plant physiology.* Collier/Macmillan, New York, 1979.

Bown, D. *Encyclopaedia of herbs and their uses.* Dorling Kindersley, London, 1995.

Brimble, L.J.F. *Intermediate botany.* Macmillan Press, London.

Bryan, J. & Castle, C. *Edible ornamental garden plants.* Pitman Publishing, 1976.

California Rare Fruit Growers have a wonderful, fact-filled Internet site at http://www.crfg.org/pubs/frtfacts.html. Information on many unusual (as well as the more usual) fruits and nuts can be accessed here, and is regularly updated.

Center for New Crops and Plant Products, Purdue University, West Lafayette, IN, USA, have an Internet site with lots of information on possible new crops, as well as many links to other sites. They can be found at http://www.hort.purdue.edu/newcrop/default.html.

Chiej, R. *Encyclopaedia of medicinal plants.* Macdonald, 1984.

www.davesgarden.com has lots of information on a wide range of plants and gardening topics that has been gathered from many people.

http://www.desert-tropicals.com is a useful and interesting site that describes many plant species from warmer climates, plus lots of other information on a variety of gardening and science topics.

Donahue, R.L., Shickluna, J.C. & Robertson L.S. *Soils: an introduction to soils and plant growth.* Prentice-Hall, New Jersey, 1971.

Duke, J.A. Handbook of energy crops. Unpublished, but text can be accessed through the Centre for New Crops and Plant Products. Purdue University (www.hort.purdue.edu/). 1983. Contains a wide range of plants with particular emphasis on their health benefits.

Environmental Horticulture Department, Florida Cooperative Extension Service have a website at http://www.ces.ncsu.edu/ that contains a lot of information about horticulture and agriculture for the south-eastern states of the US.

Facciola, S. *Cornucopia: a source book of edible plants.* Kampong Publications, California, 1990.

Finn, C. "Temperate berry crops". In: Janick J. (ed.), *Perspectives on new crops and new uses.* ASHS Press, Virginia, USA, 1999. Describes various species.

Furlong, M. & Pill, V.B. *Wild edible fruits and berries.* Healdsburg: Naturegraph Publishers, 1974.

Hedrick, U.P. *Sturtevant's edible plants of the world.* Dover Publications, 1972.

Hedrick, U.P. *The Small Fruits of New York.* A wonderful selection of older style smaller fruits are described in this book published in 1925. It can be accessed through http://www.ars-grin.gov/cor/sfny.html.

Hernándo Bermejo, J.E. & León, J. (eds), *Neglected crops: 1492 from a different perspective.* Plant Production and Protection Series No. 26. FAO, Rome, Italy, 1994. Various chapters.

Huxley, A. *Royal Horticultural dictionary of gardening.* Macmillan Press, 1992.

Janick, J. (ed.) *Perspectives on new crops and new uses.* ASHS Press, Virginia, USA, 1999. Various chapters.

Janick, J. (ed.) *Progress in new crops.* ASHS Press, Virginia, USA, 1996. Various chapters.

Janick, J. & Simon, J.E. (eds), *New crops.* Wiley, New York, 1993. Various chapters.

Janick, J. & Whipkey, A. (eds), *Trends in new crops and new uses.* ASHS Press, Virginia, USA, 2002. Various chapters.

Kavasch, B. *Native harvests.* Vintage Books, 1979.

Kunkel, G. *Plants for human consumption.* Koeltz Scientific Books, 1984.

Lamberts, M. & Crane, J.H. "Tropical fruits". In: Janick, J. & Simon. J.E. (eds) *Advances in new crops.* Timber Press, Portland, Oregon, USA, 1990. Various chapters.

Launert, E. *Edible and medicinal plants.* Hamlyn, 1981.

Lehninger, A.L. *Principles of biochemistry.* Worth Publishers, New York.

Lukasiewicz, J. "Nuts with commercial potential for America's heartland". *New Crops News*: 4(1). 1994.

Mark Reiger's Fruit Crops site, University of Georgia, has lots of useful, information at http://www.uga.edu/fruit/.

McCain, R. "Goldenberry, passionfruit, and white sapote: potential fruits for cool subtropical areas". In: Janick, J. & Simon, J.E. (eds) *New crops.* Wiley, New York, 1993.

Menninger, E.A. *Edible nuts of the world.* Horticultural Books, Florida, 1977.

Mills, S.Y. *The dictionary of modern herbalism.* Thorsons, 1985.

Mizrahi, Y., Nerd, A. & Sitrit, Y. "New fruits for arid climates". In: Janick, J. & Whipkey, A. (eds) *Trends in new crops and new uses.* ASHS Press, Virginia, USA, 2002.

Morton, J.F. *Fruits of warm climates.* An excellent book, packed with detailed information about many fruit and nut species found in semitropical and tropical regions: highly recommended. It also has a huge bibliography. Published by Julia F. Morton and distributed by Creative Resource Systems, Inc., Box 890, Winterville, NC 28590, USA.

Natural Food Hub (www.naturalhub.com) have lots of information on many unusual foods, e.g. the manketti nut, plus more.

North Carolina State University website (http://www.ces.ncsu.edu/) contains several interesting fact sheets on many gardening topics.

Nutrition Data, found at http://www.nutritiondata.com/facts-001-02s01kd.html, gives the nutritional contents of many foods, including many of the more common fruits and nuts.

http://www.Nutritionfocus.com has lots of information about health issues, as well as being a jumping-off point for other links.

Ohio State University website (http://ohioline.osu.edu/lines/bulls.html) has many fact sheets and bulletins on a wide range of horticultural and agricultural topics.

PFAF (Plants for a Future): A very informative Internet site that describes a large number of unusual, edible plants. It can be accessed at: www.pfaf.org or http://www.ibiblio.org/pfaf/D_search.html. It also has a very useful database where plants can be easily accessed by usage or attribute. Recommended.

Phillips, R. & Rix, M. *Shrubs.* Pan Books, 1989.

Raintree nutrition at www.raintree.com for lots of ethnobotany information, particularly on tropical plants.

Reader's Digest *Encyclopaedia of garden plants and flowers.* Reader's Digest Association Ltd., London.

Reader's Digest *The gardening year.* R. Hay (Consultant Editor). Reader's Digest Association Ltd., London.

Rosengarten. F. Jr. *The book of edible nuts.* Walker & Co., USA, 1984.

Royal Horticultural Society *Gardener's encyclopaedia of plants and flowers.* C. Brickell (Ed. in Chief). Dorling Kindersley, London, 1991.

Russell, E.W. *Soil conditions and plant growth.* Longman, London, 1973.

Schauenberg, P. & Paris, F. *Guide to medical plants.* Lutterworth Press, London, 1977.

Simmons, A.E. *Growing unusual fruit.* David and Charles, 1972.

Simon, J.E., Chadwick, A.F. & Craker, L.E. *Herbs: an indexed bibliography. 1971-1980. The scientific literature on selected herbs, and aromatic and medicinal plants of the temperate zone.* Archon Books. Hamden, Connecticut, USA, 1984.

Stuart, G.A. *Chinese materia medica*. Southern Materials Centre, Taipei, 1987.

Tanaka, T. *Tanaka's encyclopaedia of edible plants of the world*. Keigaku Publishing, 1976.

Taylor, J. *The milder garden*. Dent, 1990.

Tous, J. & Ferguson, L. "Mediterranean fruits". In: Janick, J. (ed.) *Progress in new crops*. ASHS Press, Virginia, USA, 1996.

Triska, Dr. *Hamlyn encyclopaedia of plants*. Hamlyn, 1975.

Uphof. J.C.T. *Dictionary of economic plants*. Weinheim, 1960.

Usher. G. *A dictionary of plants used by man*. Constable, 1974.

References by common name or country

Akebia: More information about akebias can be found at Paghat's garden page at http://paghat.com/akebiafruit.html

Amla: Parmar, C. "Amla and its wild Himalayan strain". New Crop Fact Sheet. Centre for New Crops and Plant Products. Purdue University, 2000.

Asimoya: Callaway, M.B. Pawpaw (*Asimina triloba*): a 'tropical' fruit for temperate climates. In: Janick, J. & Simon, J.E. (eds), *New crops*. Wiley, New York, 1993.
Layne, D.R. "Pawpaw". New Crop Fact Sheet. Centre for New Crops and Plant Products. Purdue University.

Australia: Australian plants online is a useful website written by a non-profit organisation dedicated to the growing, conservation, promotion and appreciation of Australian native plants. http://farrer.riv.csu.edu.au
Birmingham, E. Byron Bay Native Produce have lots of information on the finger lime at www.fingerlimes.com.
Elliot, W.R. & Jones, D.L. *Encyclopaedia of Australian plants suitable for cultivation*. Lothian Publishing Co., Sydney, 1982.
Hiddins, L. *Explore wild Australia with the Bush Tucker Man*. Explore Australia Publishing Pty Ltd, Australia, 2003.
Isaac, J. *Bush food* (with a chapter about kakadu plums). Lansdown Publishing, Sydney, 1997.
Lassak, E. & McCarthy, T. *Australian medicinal plants*. Mandarin Australia Publishers, Melbourne, 1990.
Low, T. *Wild food plants of Australia*. Angus and Robertson, Sydney, 1995.
Smith, K. *Grow your own bushfoods*. Reed New Holland Publishers, Sydney, 1999.
Wrigley, J.W. & Fagg, M. *Australian native plants: propagation, cultivation and use in landscaping*. (5th ed.) Reed New Holland, Sydney, 2003.

Bael fruit: Misra, K.K. "Bael". New Crop Fact Sheet. Centre for New Crops and Plant Products, Purdue University.

Banana: All about this fruit can be found at www.banana.com.

Blueberries: Muggleston, S. *Outstanding new blueberry cultivars*. Hort Research, Mt Albert, Auckland, NZ.

Bunya bunya: The Society for Growing Australian Plants has put together a good site for more detailed information about bunya bunyas at http://www.sgapqld.org.au/bushtucker8.html

Burdekin plum: *SGAP Townsville Newsletter*, Queensland, Australia, August 1997, has lots of information about growing and cultivation of the burdekin plum. This information has also been published in *The Native Gardener*.

Canada/USA: Alaska Geographic Editors *Alaska wild berry guide and cookbook*. Alaska Northwest Books, 1983.
Coffey, T. *The history and folklore of North American wild flowers*. Houghton & Mifflin, 2000.
Craighead, J. et al. *A field guide to Rocky Mountain Wildflowers*. Riverside Press, 1963.
Elias, T. & Dykeman, P. *A field guide to North American edible wild plants*. Van Nostrand Reinhold, 1982.
Elias, T. *The complete trees of N. America. Field guide and natural history*. Van Nostrand Reinhold, 1980.
Ferguson, L. & Arpaia, M. "New subtropical tree crops in California". In: Janick, J. & Simon, J.E. (eds) *Advances in new crops*. Timber Press, Portland, Oregon, USA, 1990.
Foster, S. & Duke, J.A. *A field guide to medicinal plants of Eastern and Central-north America*. Houghton Mifflin, 1990.
Harrington, H.D. *Edible native plants of the Rocky Mountains*. Univ. of New Mexico Press, 1967.
Lauriault, J. *Identification guide to the trees of Canada*. Fitzhenry and Whiteside, Ontario, 1989.
Saunders, C.F. *Edible and useful wild plants of the United States and Canada*. Dover Publications, New York, 1976.
Schofield, J.J. *Discovering wild plants – Alaska, Western Canada and the Northwest*. Alaska Northwest Books, Anchorage, 1993.
Sweet, M. *Common edible and useful plants of the West*. Healdsburg: Naturegraph Publishers, 1976.
Turner, N.J. & Szczawinski, A. *Edible wild fruits and nuts of Canada*. National Museum of Natural Science, Canada, 1978.
Viereck, E. *Alaska's wilderness medicines: healthful plants of the Far North*. Edmonds: Alaska Northwest Publishing Co., 1998.

Vines, R.A. *Trees of central Texas*. University of Texas Press, 1987.
Vines, R.A. *Trees of north Texas*. University of Texas Press, 1982.

Chestnuts: New Zealand Chestnut Council at http://www.nzcc.org.nz/factsheet.html
Detailed fact sheets on chestnuts can be found at http://www.caes.state.ct.us/FactSheetFiles/IndexHeadingFiles/FSnut.htm written by the Connecticut Agricultural Society.

Chilean bellflower: Information on this plant can be found at http://members.aol.com/_ht_a/lapageria/myhomepage/garden.html.

China: Duke, J.A. & Ayensu, E.S. *Medicinal plants of China*. Reference Publications, 1985.

Chinquapin: Payne, J.A. et al. "Chinquapin: potential new crop for the south". In: Janick, J. & Simon, J.E. (eds) *New crops*. Wiley, New York, 1993.

Citrus: Purdue University website has lots of detailed information on citrus species: http://www.hort.purdue.edu/newcrop/tropical/lecture_32/lec_32.html

Cloudberry: Thiem, B. "Cloudberry: *Rubus chamaemorus* L.: a boreal plant rich in biologically active metabolites: a review". *Biological Letters* 40(1): 3–13, 2003.

Cocona and naranjilla: Heiser, C.B. "The naranjilla (*Solanum quitoense*), the cocona (*Solanum sessiliflorum*) and their hybrids". In: Gustafson, J.P. et al. (eds), *Gene conservation and exploitation*. Plenum Press, New York, 1993.

Cranberry: The American cranberry site contains lots of information. http://www.library.wisc.edu/guides/agnic/cranberry/cranhome.html

Elderberry: Zakay-Rones Z. et al. "Inhibition of several strains of influenza virus *in vitro* and reduction of symptoms by an elderberry extract (*Sambucus nigra* L.) during an outbreak of influenza B in Panama". *Journal of Alternative and Complementary Medicine*. 1(4):361–369, 1995.

Europe/UK: Bean, W. *Trees and shrubs hardy in Great Britain*. Murray, 1981.
Edlin, H.L. *The tree key*. Frederick Warne Ltd., London, 1978.
Flora Europaea (various authors) (6 volumes): Cambridge University Press, 1964.
Komarov, V.L. *Flora of the USSR* (25 volumes; translated). Israel Program for Scientific Translation, 1968.

Mitchell, A.F. *Conifers in the British Isles*. Her Majesties Stationery Office, 1972.

Mitchell, A.F. *Field guide to the trees of Britain and Northern Europe*. Collins, London, 1974.

Polunin, O. *Flowers of Europe – a field guide*. Oxford University Press, 1969.

Ginkgo: Sierpina, V.S. et al. *Ginkgo biloba*: *American Family Physician* 68(5), 2003. A detailed review on the health benefits of ginkgo.

Tyler, V.E. "Herbs affecting the central nervous system". In: Janick, J. (ed.), *Perspectives on new crops and new uses*. ASHS Press, Virginia, USA, 1999.

Honeysuckle: Thompson, Prof. M. (Oregon University): Blue honeysuckle (*Lonicera caerulea* L.): a potential new berry crop. Paper delivered at the *Ninth Australasian Conference on Tree and Nut Crops*, Perth, Australia, April 2001.

India: Chopra, R.N. et al. *Glossary of Indian medicinal plants*. Council of Scientific and Industrial Research, New Delhi, 1986.

Kiwifruit: Finn, C. "Temperate berry crops". In: Janick J. (ed.), *Perspectives on new crops and new uses*. ASHS Press, Virginia, USA, 1999.

Licorice: see the site http://www.licorice.org/ for all about this plant and its uses.

Simon, J.E., Chadwick, A.F. & Craker, L.E. *Herbs: an indexed bibliography. 1971-1980. The scientific literature on selected herbs, and aromatic and medicinal plants of the temperate zone*. Archon Books, Connecticut, USA. 1984.

Maple syrup: *North American maple syrup producers manual*, Bulletin 856, Ohio State University Extension and the North American Maple Syrup Council. Detailed information about all aspects of maple-sap production.

Mayhaw: More information can be obtained from www.lsuagcenter.com/Communications/pdfs_bak/pub2484mayhaw.pdf

Payne, J.A. & Krewer, G.W. "Mayhaw: a new fruit crop for the south". In: Janick, J. & Simon, J.E. (eds), *Advances in new crops*. Timber Press, Portland, Oregon, USA, 1990.

New Zealand: Crowe, A. *A field guide to the native edible plants of New Zealand*. Collins, 1981.

Ferguson, A.R. "New temperate fruits: *Actinidia chinensis* and *Actinidia deliciosa*". In: J. Janick (ed.), *Perspectives on new crops and new uses*. ASHS Press, Virginia, USA. 1999. pp. 342–347.

Hewett, E.W. "New horticultural crops in New Zealand". In: Janick J. & Simon J.E. (eds), *New crops*. Wiley, New York, 1993.

NZTCA (New Zealand Tree Crops Association) supply a regular journal devoted to various research aspects of tree crops that can be grown in New Zealand.

Salmon, J.T. *The Reed field guide to New Zealand native trees*. Reed, 1986.

Williams, D. *Home fruit growing in New Zealand*. Government Printing Office, Wellington.

Olives: Blyth Klein, M. *Feast of the olives*. Chronicle Books, 1994; and University of California Agricultural Sciences Publications leaflet 21131 (information on curing).

Palms: The FAO Forestry Department website has lots of information about palms at http://www.fao.org/documents/show_cdr.asp?url_file=/docrep/X0451E/X0451e03.htm

Pawpaw: Callaway, M.B. "Pawpaw (*Asimina triloba*): A 'tropical' fruit for temperate climates". in: Janick, J. & Simon, J.E. (eds), *New crops*. Wiley, New York, 1993; pp. 505–515.

Peanut: Putnam, D.H. et al. "Peanuts". *Alternative field crops manual*. Univ. of Wisconsin, 1991.

Pest control: A detailed website about various pests and diseases, it is general, but is geared towards problems in the UK: http://www.which.net/gardeningwhich/advice/pests/factsheets/

Phalsa: Yadav, A.K. "Phalsa: a potential new small fruit for Georgia". In: Janick, J. (ed.), *Perspectives on new crops and new uses*. ASHS Press, Virginia, USA, 1999.

Pitaya: Mizrahi, Y. & Nerd, A. "Climbing and columnar cacti: new arid land fruit crops". In: Janick, J.(ed.), *Perspectives on new crops and new uses*. ASHS Press, Virginia, USA, 1999.

Prickly pear: Mondragon-Jacobo, C. & Perez-Gonzalez, S. "Native cultivars of cactus pear in México". In: Janick, J. (ed.), *Progress in new crops*. ASHS Press, Virginia, USA, 1996.

Pumpkin: Lira Saade, R. et al. In: Hernándo Bermejo, J.E. & León, J. (eds), *Neglected crops : 1492 from a different perspective*. Plant Production and Protection Series No. 26. FAO, Rome, Italy, 1994.

Loy, J.B. "Hull-less seeded pumpkins: a new edible snackseed crop". In: Janick, J. & Simon, J.E. (eds), *Advances in new crops*. Timber Press, Portland, Oregon, USA, 1990.

Quandong: comprehensive text about quandong cultivation, marketing, etc. has been written by the Department of Primary Industries and Resources at http://www.pir.sa.gov.au/pages/

agriculture/agfactsheets/vegetation/quandong.pdf. Also see an excellent page on its propagation at Australian plants online at http://farrer.csu.edu.au/ASGAP/APOL7/sep97-2.html.

Rhubarb: http://www.rhubarbinfo.com/

Sapodilla: Mickelbart, M.V. "Sapodilla: a potential crop for subtropical climates". In: Janick, J. (ed.), *Progress in new crops*. ASHS Press, Virginia, USA, 1996.

Saskatoon: Mazza, G. & Davidson, C.G. "Saskatoon berry: a fruit crop for the prairies". In: Janick, J. & Simon, J.E. (eds), *New crops*. Wiley, New York, 1993.

Sea buckthorn: Li, T.S.C. "Sea buckthorn: new crop opportunity". In: Janick, J. (ed.), *Perspectives on new crops and new uses*. ASHS Press, Virginia, USA, 1999.

South Africa: Palgrave, K.C. *Trees of Southern Africa*. Struik Publishers, Cape Town, 1983.

South African Biodiversity Institute has an interesting website (http://www.plantzafrica.com/) that describes many South African plants, as well as information on their medicinal uses.

Venter, F. & Venter, J. *Making the most of indigenous trees*. Briza Publications, Pretoria, 1996.

South America: Advisory Panel on Technology and Innovation, the Board on Science and Technology for International Development, and National Research Council. *Lost Crops of the Incas: Little-known plants of the Andes with promise for worldwide cultivation*. National Academy Press, Washington, DC, 1989.

Campbell, R.J. "South American fruits deserving further attention". In: Janick, J. (ed.), *Progress in new crops*. ASHS Publishers, Virginia, USA.

Sánchez Veg, I. "Andean fruits". In: Hernándo Bermejo, J.E. & León, J. (eds), *Neglected crops: 1492 from a different perspective*. Plant Production and Protection Series No. 26. FAO, Rome, Italy. 1994.

Stevia: http://www.stevia.net

Sugar maple: Magness, J.R. et al. *Food and feed crops of the United States. Interregional Research Project IR-4*, Bulletin 828, New Jersey Agricultural Experimental Station, 1971.

UK: see Europe/UK.

USA: see Canada/USA.

Wintergreen: Sievers, A.F. *The herb hunters guide*. Misc. Publ. No. 77. USDA, Washington DC, 1930.

Photo credits